TOTAL BASEBALL 1990 UPDATE

EDITED BY
John Thorn and Pete Palmer

A BASEBALL INK BOOK

WARNER BOOKS

A Warner Communications Company

To the memory of
A. Bartlett Giamatti—
classmate, mentor, friend

 A Warner Communications Company

Printed in the United States of America
First printing: March 1990
10 9 8 7 6 5 4 3 2 1
ISSN: 1047-8914

Contents

Acknowledgments

Our appreciations for this volume are much the same as those printed in its forebear, and so we take this occasion to restate our thanks to those who made *Total Baseball* a success and—to echo the words of The Great Prophet, Yogi Berra— made this book necessary. Many of the people named below who helped to produce *The 1990 Total Baseball Update* also did yeoman service on the big book.

David Reuther extended his role as project manager. Marc Cheshire carried over his design for *Total Baseball* to this volume. Peter Bird, president of Gendell Graphics, supervised the composition and kept composed as things (inevitably) went haywire in the last weeks. Rick Horgan returned as our editor, and the entire Warner Books team, led by president Larry Kirshbaum, provided much-appreciated encouragement and support.

A new member of the Baseball Ink staff, managing editor Richard Puff, made vital contributions to the *Update* and coordinated the efforts of its many players. Also contributing to the book's production was Gypsy da Silva, a Baseball Inkette of books past. Bill Deane provided an update to the Hall of Fame balloting, a subject whose history he had covered in *Total Baseball*. And Bob Carroll, another contributor to the earlier volume, this time wrote the fine essay "Baseball 1989," which is the central prose feature of the *Update*.

Baseball 1989:
A Scandalous, Tragic, Exciting Season

The year in baseball, 1989, presented fans with everything they could have dreamed of, and a good deal that exceeded their worst nightmares. Yes, there were four crackling pennant races; players and teams that performed heroic and even record-setting deeds; far-reaching judicial decisions that affirmed baseball's unique station in our society; new television contracts that heralded significant changes in America's baseball-viewing habits. All the same, to baseball fans 1989 was marked as The Year of the Pete Rose Scandal. Until it became The Year of the Commissioner's Death. And until it became The Year of the Earthquake.

Even though the California calamity and Bart Giamatti's untimely demise put into perspective the personal disaster that befell Charlie Hustle, the Rose Scandal dominated the sports news for a longer period and, from baseball's admittedly parochial viewpoint, will have a longer-lasting effect on the game itself. Never before have newspapers, radio talk shows, television news programs, and the "man on the street" devoted so much time and talk to a single baseball topic. And, when it had seemingly ended after five gut-wrenching months, the fates provided an additional tragic coda.

In the long run, the Rose Scandal revealed no universal truths except the old one about the frailty of Man. For a while it threatened to break new ground regarding the Commissioner's right to govern baseball, but that was short-circuited before it could be tested. *The Sporting News* referred to the climactic day of August 24 as the "Darkest Day in Baseball." Maybe so, maybe not. But there can be no doubt that the contest between Pete Rose and the Commissioner of Baseball was the story of the year.

Preliminary Scandals

The year began with the public being titillated by a more mundane scandal. Boston Red Sox third baseman Wade Boggs, the American League's leading hitter in five of the past seven seasons, was being sued by Margo Adams, an attractive young woman who alleged she had been Boggs' "wife" on the road for four years. She demanded that Boggs compensate her for income she had lost while on her travels with him. He had promised to marry her, she said.

Boggs admitted the four-year affair but denied he and Adams ever had any understanding about marriage. He even confessed to being "addicted to sex," having been turned on to the very possibility of such an affliction by airwave healer Geraldo Rivera. At one point he and his real wife, who stuck

by him, were interviewed by Barbara Walters on nationwide TV. Boggs promised to do penance by having his best year ever at bat.

Meanwhile, Margo sold her story to *Penthouse*, the magazine that positions nudes and exposés cheek by jowl in its belief that "nothing is more naked than the truth." Bob Guccione's bastion of the First Amendment even took out a full-page ad in *The Sporting News* under the banner "WADE BOGGS' WORST ERROR?"

Not only was the Boggs family subjected to ridicule and heartache, Margo threatened to "tell all" about the sexual hijinks of other Red Sox players as well as to broadcast the deliciously malicious comments made by Boggs and others about teammates and opponents. The *Penthouse* article was to be the appetizer; the trial promised the full menu.

Numerous experts predicted the Red Sox would never survive Adams' revelations. They expected Boggs to be traded—if any team would have him—before the season was very old.

By the time the denouement rolled around, much of the public was too caught up in *la vie en Rose* to care about a third baseman's sexual peccadilloes or off-hand comments. For the record, everyone lost. Margo lost her case, the Red Sox lost the pennant, and Boggs lost his batting championship. However, he did remain with the team throughout the season and collect 200 or more hits for the seventh consecutive season.

Almost lost between the lurid Boggs Scandal and the tragic Rose Scandal was the admission by longtime Dodger and Padre first baseman Steve Garvey that he had fathered a couple of children out of wedlock. In another year, the story might have been big news, considering Garvey's carefully nurtured squeaky-clean image. In 1989, it was only the stuff of footnotes: seen in San Diego were bumper stickers reading "Steve Garvey is not *my* Padre."

First Sight of the Iceberg's Tip

The initial public sign of what would become the Rose Case came during spring training and raised few eyebrows. On February 20 Pete Rose, baseball's all-time hit leader and current manager of the Cincinnati Reds, was called to New York to meet with Commissioner of Baseball Peter Ueberroth and then National League President A. Bartlett Giamatti, who was scheduled to replace Ueberroth on April 1. Rose was known to be a heavy gambler, but he would not say afterward whether his gambling was discussed. Word soon leaked out that it was. However, the focus of the meeting was apparently on a rumor that Rose and a partner were involved in a $265,660.20 "Pik Six" payoff at Turfway Park, across the Ohio River from Cincinnati. The question seemed to be about possible tax irregularities.

A few rumors concerning Rose's gambling activities continued to make the rounds during the next month. Then, on March 20, the news exploded across front pages. The Commissioner's Office released a statement that it was investigating "serious allegations" concerning Rose. John M. Dowd, a Washington attorney, had been hired as special counsel by baseball to investigate the charges. The allegations, which included betting on baseball games, sent reporters scurrying to baseball's rules. What they found was *21-d: any player or club official who bets on a game not involving his team is suspended for one year. Anyone who bets on a game involving his own team is suspended for life.*

In the pantheon of America's baseball heroes, no living man held a higher position than Rose. He had been a leader and one of the leading lights of Cincinnati's "Big Red Machine" during the championship years of the 1970s; *The Sporting News* had voted him the Player of the Decade. Later, he had helped bring Philadelphia a World Championship. We had watched and rooted for (or against) him in his unsuccessful pursuit of Joe DiMaggio's consecutive-game hitting streak in 1978. In 1985, he had broken Ty Cobb's seemingly insurmountable record for career basehits. No one in baseball history had played more games or gone to bat as many times.

But Pete's hold on America's heart was more than statistical. Even fans who didn't like him—who considered him crude and ego-possessed—admired him. For more than twenty years Rose had been the embodiment of all-out, hell-for-leather, no-holds-barred baseball. He was Everyman, winning not by talent but by trying harder. His nickname, "Charlie Hustle," was far better known to the non-fan than the real names of many players with million-dollar contracts.

By contrast, A. Bartlett Giamatti was an unknown factor to most fans, many of whom knew little more than that he had once been president of Yale. His academic background struck many as effete and unsuited to the job of administering baseball. His pudgy figure and smooth language signified anything but athleticism—most particularly not Rose's brand of gung-ho brawn. To some who knew him only through TV "bites," Giamatti seemed better cast in the part of a diabolical villain in a James Bond movie than as the protector of baseball's integrity. They remembered that as National League President, Giamatti had suspended Rose for thirty days in April 1988 after Pete shoved umpire Dave Pallone. Now, only a year later, it was easy for Rose diehards to suspect the incoming Commissioner of attempting to establish his own authority by humbling baseball's leading icon.

More Charges

The March 27 issue of *Sports Illustrated* alleged that Ron Peters—the owner of a restaurant-bar in Franklin, Ohio, who had been arrested for cocaine trafficking—was Rose's principal bookmaker. Furthermore, *SI* stated that authorities had recovered from Peters betting slips in Rose's handwriting. An affidavit used by IRS agents to search Peters' home and business suggested that a person codenamed "G-1" and iden-

tified by some sources as Rose bet on baseball games through another person named Janszen. According to the affidavit, bets made by "G-1" early in May 1987 "averaged $2,000 per game on four to eight games per day, approximately four days per week." Paul Janszen, a bodybuilder serving a six-month sentence for evading taxes from sales of steroids, told *SI* that Rose had signaled bets to the stands from the dugout.

Rose called Janszen's charges "ridiculous," and denied Peters was his "principal" bookmaker. However, he didn't deny placing bets with Peters and was evasive about baseball betting. "My best comment is no comment," he said. He soft-pedaled reports that to raise money he had been selling off prized memorabilia of his career.

Rose continued to stonewall into April, as the baseball season opened and more charges surfaced. Tommy Gioiosa, indicted by a federal grand jury for income tax evasion and conspiracy to distribute cocaine, claimed to have run bets for Rose in 1986 when he lived in Rose's home. "I don't know where Tommy is," said Rose; "I don't know what he is doing now." Meanwhile, Janszen was reported to have told baseball investigators that Rose did indeed bet on baseball, though he was unable to furnish proof. Rose reportedly owed Janszen $50,000 in gambling debts.

Rose and the Reds seemed to be holding up well in face of the media blitz. "Have I had trouble keeping my mind on baseball? No, haven't had any trouble for forty-eight years," Pete said.

Despite massive media coverage and constant talk-show chatter, no one seemed certain just what, if anything, Rose might have been guilty of. Betting with bookies? Evading taxes? Betting on baseball? Betting on—or worse, against—the Reds? "Well, maybe I am guilty of one thing," Pete said, "of being a bad picker of friends."

Most comments in the media took a wait-and-see attitude, pointing out that all the charges had been leveled by either convicted felons or men under indictment. Several columnists castigated new Commissioner Giamatti for revealing the ongoing investigation before it had been resolved, thereby leaving Rose and the Reds "twisting slowly in the wind." The attitude of most Cincinnati fans was typified by a local restaurant owner who said, "Pete Rose is no altar boy, but he'd never do anything sacrilegious. He'd never break the sanctuary of baseball. I'd go before a firing squad and say he didn't bet on baseball."

At one point, Reds relief pitcher John Franco was accused of carrying betting information to Rose during games. He strongly denied ever relaying any information on baseball bets, but admitted passing on football scores to Pete.

The Hearing Never Heard

On May 9, John Dowd's report on his investigation was submitted to Commissioner Giamatti, who set a hearing date of May 25. Meanwhile Rose and his chief counsel, Reuven Katz, were given copies of Dowd's 225-page report and seven volumes of exhibits. According to Giamatti, about forty witnesses including Rose had been interviewed during the ten-week investigation.

Rose's lawyers asked for and received a one-month extension of the hearing date to allow them to study Dowd's report and prepare a response.

On June 19 Rose went to court seeking a temporary restraining order postponing his hearing with Giamatti. It was Rose's contention that the Commissioner had already found him guilty. He cited an April 18 letter from Giamatti to a U.S. District Judge urging leniency in the sentencing of Ron Peters because of his cooperation in providing evidence against Rose. Six days later Hamilton County Common Pleas Judge Norbert A. Nadel decided that Giamatti had indeed prejudged Rose. The letter, he said, served as a "smoking gun." Nadel ruled that Rose could neither be disciplined by baseball nor fired by the Reds for two weeks. On July 6 he would consider a motion to make the injunction permanent.

In effect, Rose's suit upped the ante. No longer was the issue simply the baseball fate of one the game's major stars; at stake was baseball's right to govern itself through its Commissioner. Baseball quickly moved to have Rose's suit heard in federal court rather than the presumably friendly state court.

Although a hastily scrawled sign at the Reds game that night proclaimed: "PETE 1, BART 0, THANKS NORB," Rose may have lost more in public favor than he gained in breathing time. For the first time, details of John Dowd's investigative report were revealed. None of them helped Rose. In two days of testimony, Dowd listed telephone records, taped conversations, and checks signed by Rose. Betting slips taken from Rose's home by Paul Janszen, he said, had Rose's fingerprints and, according to a handwriting expert employed by baseball, three of them contained writing verified as Rose's. On the matter of credibility, Dowd said, of the nine witnesses who had supplied information about Rose's betting on baseball, only two were in jail. His report cited 228 bets Rose had made on baseball games; 52 of them involved the Reds.

Meanwhile Ron Peters appeared on ABC's *Nightline* and called Rose "just a sick gambler" who bet as much as $20,000 a day on baseball games between 1984 and 1987. Specifically, Peters charged Rose had bet $2,000 that the Reds would defeat the Padres on April 10, 1987. (The Reds won the game, 6–3.)

After having hedged for two months, Rose for the first time publicly denied gambling on baseball.

Was Pete an Immortal?

Nearly everyone had an opinion as to what Rose, the Reds, and the Commissioner should do. The scandal crowded other baseball news off the front sports page, but most of it was a swirl of opinion and speculation.

Much of the Rose talk centered on whether he should or could be elected to the Baseball Hall of Fame if he was found guilty of betting on games. He will become eligible in 1992. Opinion among sports writers ranged from "No, if . . ." to "Yes, regardless." Rose himself had no doubts: "I'm a Hall-of-Famer," he said, citing his stats.

Many references were made to the "Black Sox" Scandal of seventy years earlier, when eight members of the Chicago White Sox were barred from baseball for life by baseball's first Commissioner, Judge Kenesaw Mountain Landis, for fixing the 1919 World Series. Such discussions were fueled by the popularity of the recent movie *Eight Men Out*, which dealt sympathetically with the Sox players' conspiracy with gamblers. Commentators pointed out that Landis ruled against the players even though they had been found not guilty in a Chicago court when much of the evidence mysteriously disappeared. An eerie resemblance could be found between Joe Jackson, the most famous of the Black Sox, and Rose. Although Jackson holds baseball's second highest lifetime batting average, he's never been elected to the Hall of Fame; could the same fate await baseball's leading hitmaker? Rose's defenders denied any similarity between the two. Jackson had thrown games. No one was suggesting that Rose had ever tried to lose.

Ironically, the Reds were scheduled to play the Boston Red Sox in the annual Hall of Fame exhibition game in Cooperstown on July 24, the day after the induction of four greats, including former teammate Johnny Bench. Rose absented himself, with the permission of Marge Schott, Cincinnati's president and chief executive officer. "It was something I had to do," Pete said. "I didn't want to detract from the inductees. I've been around this media circus for four months now and there's no sense in taking this circus to Cooperstown. Cooperstown is for legends."

Rose in the Rose Garden

Pete's legend was crumbling. His accusers were interviewed over and over on national television, honing their charges, while Rose turned down interviews and the chance to speak out strongly on his own behalf. More than one analogy was drawn with President Jimmy Carter's unsuccessful "Rose Garden Strategy" during the Iran Hostage Crisis. Carter had let the Iranians monopolize television time. Rose seemed to be handing the stage to his accusers. His supporters defended the strategy, explaining that Pete's shoot-from-the-hip verbal style and volatile personality could make him look worse. Yet even they were confused by his promise that one day "I'll sing my song," while doing everything in his power to avoid a hearing. Rose's credibility nosedived.

His team had also tumbled in the standings. From July 16 to July 26, Cincinnati lost ten games in a row. A crushing spate of injuries made the most credible explanation for the Reds' slump—their starting lineup looked like the Nashville farm team—but the day-to-day storm surrounding their manager must have been a factor.

Notwithstanding, several critics suggested that the scandal was actually preserving Rose's job. If there had been no allegations, they reasoned, there would have been no injunction against firing him.

All eyes focused on July 31, when the ruling would be made as to whether Rose's lawsuit charging the Commissioner with bias would be heard by the state or federal courts. Rose's lawyers wanted the final decision to rest with Norbert A. Nadel, the Cincinnati judge who had granted the injunction in Pete's favor in June. Baseball's attorneys wanted the case tried in the federal courts, where the Commissioner's powers had been upheld in previous cases.

Curiously, much of the public seemed to be more upset that Rose might be lying about betting on games than that he might have actually made the bets. Many fans, of course, bet on baseball themselves. So long as Pete's wagers had been for his team to win, they could see no harm. (More astute observers noted that the pressure to win a single game on which he had placed a wager might, for example, cause him to utilize his bullpen in a way that might undermine the Reds' chances in future contests.) As Rose himself said, while admitting to using illegal bookies as a "convenience": "If I'm not mistaken, there's a lot of money bet through bookmaking."

The other side of the coin, as critics hastened to explain, was that any baseball person heavily in debt to bookies could possibly be pressured to fix games. Moreover, the very pattern of bets provided other gamblers with "inside information." If, for example, Rose bet on his own team four days in a row and then did not bet on the fifth, he was in effect telling the bookies that he expected his team to lose that fifth game.

The End in Sight

On the last day of July, the Rose Scandal moved into its semifinal phase. In Cincinnati, U.S. District Judge John Holschuh ruled that Pete's lawsuit against the Commissioner should be heard in federal court. It was a major loss for Pete. No one doubted that he would lose in federal court and that Giamatti would eventually rule on his participation in betting on baseball. And Giamatti's decision seemed a foregone conclusion.

On August 11 Judge Holschuh made another ruling that seemed likely only to delay the inevitable. He decreed that baseball must forgo any hearing until the 6th U.S. Circuit Court of Appeals ruled on a motion by Rose's lawyers to have Holschuh's decision set aside.

The day before Judge Holschuh handed over Rose's suit to the federal court, Pete gave one sign that the constant pressure was beginning to affect him. He banished baseball writer Hal McCoy of the *Dayton Daily News* from his office for writing a column suggesting that, for the good of the team, Pete should resign or take a leave of absence as Reds' manager during the duration of the dispute.

On August 16 Pete was caught in still another twist. The *Boston Globe* reported that a legally wiretapped conversation indicated that Rose had called Massachusetts bookmaker Joseph Cambra to place a $6,000 bet on a pro football game in 1984. The transcript seemed to show that Pete had placed bets regularly with Cambra—yet in his interview with John Dowd, Rose had insisted he didn't know Cambra was a bookie.

On August 17, a three-judge panel of the 6th U.S. Circuit Court of Appeals refused to intervene: strike three for Rose in his efforts to take the case back to Judge Nadel. Judge Holschuh was scheduled to hear Pete's suit against Giamatti on August 28. Experts predicted that soon after, Giamatti would be sitting in judgment on Rose.

Resolution

The end came with sudden finality. On August 24 Commissioner Giamatti suspended Pete Rose from baseball for life.

At a press conference in New York, Giamatti announced that an "agreement" had been reached with Rose and his lawyers. After five months of headlines and court battles, the scandal was resolved in what at first appeared to be a compromise. However, when reporters heard the terms of the five-page, 862-word agreement, they found nearly total victory for baseball.

• Rose was barred for life.

• He agreed not to challenge the Commissioner's authority in court.

• And, although the text said the settlement "is not an admission or a denial of guilt by Peter Edward Rose," Pete

also "acknowledges that the Commissioner has a factual basis to impose the [lifetime] penalty imposed herein."

Reporters recognized that, since a lifetime suspension was mandated for betting on one's own team, Rose's admission of a "factual basis" could well be construed as a confession of guilt.

At Giamatti's press conference, the Commissioner was unequivocal about Rose's betting on Reds games. "In the absence of a hearing—because Mr. Rose refused a hearing—and in the absence of evidence to the contrary, yes, I've concluded that he bet on baseball." When asked if that included Reds games, the Commissioner said, "Yes." Giamatti showed no sign of triumph. His demeanor was suitable to a physician announcing the death of a loved one to a grieving family. "The banishment for life of Pete Rose is the sad end of a sorry episode," he said. "There have not been such grave allegations since the time of Landis."

At an equally grim press conference held an hour later in Cincinnati, an ashen-faced Rose continued to insist that he had not bet on Reds games. He took some solace in the fact that the agreement stipulated he could apply for reinstatement after one year. "I've never looked forward to a birthday like I'm looking forward to my new daughter's first birthday," he said, "'cause two days after that I can apply for reinstatement. My life is baseball. I hope to get back into baseball as soon as I can." But those aware of baseball's rules noted that Giamatti had not granted Rose a special right of appeal. Under baseball's rule 15(b), anyone suspended for life can appeal for reinstatement to the Commissioner after one year. Though he must hear the appeal, the Commissioner does not have to grant relief.

To those who speculated that Rose had caved in because of a possible "side agreement" that the suspension would be lifted after one year, Giamatti said, "There is no understanding or deal or sidebar or wink or whisper that is not reflected in the document. There is absolutely no deal for reinstatement. That is exactly what we did not agree to."

Although any speculation about an end to the banishment was premature, the Commissioner said, "The burden to show a redirected, reconfigured, rehabilitated life is entirely Pete Rose's. I will say that steps toward rehabilitation ought to be taken in a direction that has not been the direction hitherto taken." He was referring to the widely held belief that Rose was a compulsive gambler more in need of treatment than punishment. But in Cincinnati Pete said, "I don't think I have a gambling problem at all. Consequently, I won't seek any help at all."

Some Rose-watchers were amused and others were outraged to learn that immediately after signing the agreement on August 23, Pete flew to Minneapolis to hawk baseball memorabilia on a TV call-in shopping show. The lifetime ban allows him to continue selling his mementos but bars him from product endorsement. "Who wants his endorsement now?" asked one wag. "Vegas?"

Requiescat in Pace

Only eight days after announcing Rose's punishment, Commissioner A. Bartlett Giamatti was dead. He was 51.

The man who had gradually won the confidence of baseball fans during the long summer suffered a massive heart attack on September 1 at his summer home in Edgartown, Massachusetts. Speculation was immediate that the ordeal of the Rose Case was responsible, but realists cited Giamatti's chain smoking and sedentary lifestyle as more likely culprits. He had been elected to a five-year term as Commissioner; he served five months.

Deputy Commissioner Francis T. (Fay) Vincent, Jr., whom Giamatti had brought into baseball after he had served as chairman and chief executive officer of Columbia Pictures Industries, was immediately named interim Commissioner. "This is a terrifically tragic day for me," Vincent said. "I lost a great friend, I lost a partner, and it's difficult to talk about the future. I will be happy to serve."

On September 13 at a meeting in Milwaukee, the club owners unanimously elected Vincent baseball's eighth Commissioner. His first official act was to dedicate the 1989 World Series to the memory of Bart Giamatti. When the Series turned out to be a San Francisco–Oakland, across-the-bay meeting, those looking for a Twilight Zone connection noted that the two cities were connected by the Bay Area Rapid Transit or—as it is better known there—BART.

It is unlikely the baseball world will need dedications—or weird coincidences—to remember Giamatti. He was eulogized as baseball's "Renaissance Man," equally at ease in the groves of academe, the fields of play, and the halls of business. In his short term in office, he came to signify the best in baseball, a man who understood the deep feelings Americans have for their national game and the game's unique power of connecting us with our past, individually and collectively. Regardless of history's final assessment of his accomplishments and particularly of his handling of the Rose Situation, Bart Giamatti certainly left an indelible mark.

In 1977, he wrote a loving essay about baseball. One sentence about the game, with a few changes, might be used to describe his five months as Commissioner: "(It) begins in the spring, when everything else begins again, and it blossoms in the summer, filling the afternoons and evenings, and then as soon as the chill rains come, it stops and leaves you to face the fall alone."

As the first sentence of the paragraph in which those words appear says, "It breaks your heart."

The Game of the Once-in-a-While: A New Deal in TV-Ball

In 1989 baseball laid the groundwork and prepared itself for an exciting and extremely lucrative new era of television in the 1990s. TV contracts, beginning with a landmark deal with CBS in December 1988 and continuing through an unprecedented cable contract signed in January 1989, spelled Big Money for the owners. Whether fans were likely to come out ahead or behind in the new scheme of things was a subject of hot debate throughout the season.

The contract with CBS ended NBC's forty-two-year association with baseball, continuous since 1966 when *The Game of the Week* became a Saturday afternoon fixture for most fans. Despite its longevity, the program's ratings had declined in the past few years, raising questions of cost-efficiency. As recently as two years ago, Baseball Commissioner Peter Ueberroth predicted a falloff in TV revenue when the next contract was signed. In 1983 each team received $2 million from TV. Over the next six seasons that increased to an average of $7 million per team. But, warned Ueberroth, the gravy train was about to chug to a stop and back onto a siding. Ueberroth's train prediction turned out to be about as accurate as an Amtrak ETA. Instead of paying less, over the next four seasons CBS will bombard baseball with $1.1 billion! Each team will receive nearly $10 million per season.

CBS later dropped $50 million more in the kitty for radio rights.

Replacing NBC's TV-announcer pairings of Vin Scully and Tom Seaver, backed up by Bob Costas and Tony Kubek, will be Brent Musberger and Tim McCarver for CBS.

Perhaps the most surprising aspect of the TV contract was that CBS agreed to pay more for less. Fewer games. Whereas NBC's *Game of the Week* had been just that, with twenty-six Saturday afternoon games on display, CBS planned to broadcast only twelve regular season games. Also gone were ABC's occasional prime time broadcasts.

The reduction made sense from baseball's viewpoint. Had Ueberroth insisted that a new contract be for a full weekly schedule of twenty-six games, he would have cut ABC and CBS out of the bidding. ABC is already committed to broadcasting golf in the summer and college football in the fall. CBS has previously signed contracts for college football, the golf Masters, and the tennis U.S. Open. By inviting all three major networks to the bidding, Ueberroth, who was scheduled to leave his Commissioner's chair in a little over three months, gave the owners a bonanza of a farewell present.

Whether CBS will come out ahead was debated on both sides. The short view was that the network would never retrieve its money—reportedly $200–$300 million more than NBC offered. Of course, it was argued, CBS had the money after receiving $4 billion from the sale of its recording, book, and other divisions. Still, "if ya got it, flaunt it" didn't seem like a sound business decision.

Most observers felt CBS hoped to use the World Series—the real plum in the contract—as a springboard to higher ratings, much as NBC did with the Los Angeles Olympics in 1984. It was reported that CBS had planned to bid nearly $500 million for the 1992 Summer Olympics until it was outbid by ABC. For twice the money they would have paid for seventeen days of Olympics, they received four years of baseball, with an absolute minimum of 16 World Series broadcasts. Currently third in ratings among the big three networks, CBS can use the World Series not only for its own audience, but also to promote the network's new shows for four Octobers, just when most of them are making their bows (or bow-wows). Furthermore, the Series was bound to disrupt the other networks' new-season scheduling.

Viewed as a long-term investment, CBS's gamble made sense.

The losers, according to most commentators in the print media, were going to be the fans. *The Sporting News* headlined Jack Craig's "Sportview" column of January 2, "TV DEAL: VICTORY FOR OWNERS, DEFEAT FOR FANS." Craig brushed aside observations that the fourteen Saturday afternoons no longer used for Game of the Week telecasts would open a window for more local baseball broadcasts. It made no difference that fans almost universally preferred watching their "own" team play over watching two teams of strangers, despite the melodious tones of Vin Scully. "The loss of coverage on NBC every Saturday . . . is a blow to baseball fans living outside of the major league markets," Craig wrote, citing an estimate that this encompassed 50 percent of the nation.

He quoted Curt Smith, author of *Voices of the Game*, who said bluntly, "It is a rape, the most catastrophic in broadcasting since the first radio broadcast."

Had most print critics been big-league-club owners, they would presumably have turned down the billion-dollar deal for the sake of that small percentage of fans in the hinterlands who never attended games in person but would now be allowed to watch fourteen fewer contests for free. Was there something in the Bill of Rights about free baseball for Montana?

By September new Commissioner Fay Vincent was saying that the CBS coverage might be increased to fifteen to sixteen games a season.

The Game of the Almost-Every-Night

On January 5, any complaints about a lack of baseball on TV received a kick in the slats. For $400 million, ESPN will broadcast 175 regular-season games on cable during the 1990 season. When added to CBS's largess, the newest windfall will double every team's seasonal TV-take.

ESPN announced a plan that was truly breathtaking to baseball junkies: single games on Sunday and Wednesday nights, doubleheaders on Tuesday and Friday evenings, plus opening day, holiday, and spring training games. Moreover, ESPN said, they would be able to switch from their feature game to another game if something extraordinary was happening. "If someone is pitching a no-hitter or there's a long hitting streak, for instance," crowed Ueberroth, "we could switch to that game so that everyone could see it."

The effect on local broadcasts and superstations (such as Ted Turner's TBS with its extensive Atlanta Braves telecasts) will be "limited," according to Bryan Burns, baseball's senior vice president for broadcasting. The superstations won't be allowed to telecast on Wednesday nights because team broadcasts will be limited to cable. Sunday night will also be virtually exclusive to ESPN because only one or two games will be on the major league schedule.

"For the first time in baseball history," Ueberroth promised, "the whole baseball season will be presented to fans who want to follow it on television. We will present all teams and all divisions in both major leagues, and that's an incredible thing for baseball."

The USA network, which cablecast games on a limited basis in 1979 and 1983, made "an aggressive bid," according to its president, but was limited to a 130-game schedule by prior contract commitments.

The nay-sayers quickly pointed out that ESPN is available to only about 50.1 million American homes. Coupled with the CBS deal, 1990 would be feast or famine for baseball fans.

The Name of the Game Is Money

Somewhat overlooked in the huffing and puffing about how many free and ESPN games Americans would or would not see in 1990 was another deal that may ultimately have more bearing on the quality of baseball seen in the next decade. In New York, owner George Steinbrenner announced a twelve-year, $500 million contract with a local cable station to cablecast Yankee games.

Milwaukee Brewers President Allan (Bud) Selig called

Steinbrenner's coup "one of the most significant events in the history of sports." His point was that the Brewers, who could hope for $3 million a year from their local broadcasting rights, will find it difficult—perhaps impossible—to compete with the Yankees in signing free agents.

"He can buy whatever he wants—and a few things he doesn't want," wrote columnist Bob Verdi of Steinbrenner.

Alarmists also suggested a trend toward "studio baseball," in which attendance was secondary or even extraneous to TV money. Visiting teams, of course, get no slice of that melon.

Baseball on the Labor Front

Contracts or even talk of a 1990 season may be premature, many critics caution. They predict a work stoppage—perhaps a long one. No apparent progress was made toward signing a new agreement between the Players Association and the owners' Player Relations Committee before the old agreement ran out with the 1989 season.

One scenario predicts a lockout by the owners, beginning with opening day. The idea would be to force the players to negotiate with little money in their pockets, rather than let the players strike later in the season after they've built up their savings. While the Player Relations Committee denied a planned lockout, specific lockout language was written into many players' contracts. Among other odd happenings: the Texas Rangers declined to exercise their option to renew pitcher Charlie Hough's contract for $900,000, then signed him a few days later for $1 million. The reason: for another $100,000, Hough agreed to a contract clause that he would not be paid in case of a work stoppage, be it identified as a strike or a lockout.

Both sides often seemed less intent on avoiding a disruption of play than in avoiding the public's wrath when the disruption came. At issue were the usual conflicts over free agency, arbitration, and salary ceilings.

The lush TV contracts signed during the 1988-89 winter put dollars in the owners' pockets but made their complaints about player salaries sound slightly hollow. The complaints became positively cavernous when, in his State of Baseball Address, outgoing Commissioner Ueberroth stated that none of the twenty-six major league teams had lost money in 1988. Major league baseball, he said, would make an industry profit of $100 million in '89.

Labor wanted its share.

On the other hand, at the monetary levels being discussed, the term "labor" seemed stretched. In mid-July *The Sporting News* counted twenty-two players who had signed contracts averaging $2 million a year or more in the last two years. It was difficult for the man in the bleachers to equate Orel Hershiser (three-year, $7.9 million) with Norma Rae.

According to *USA Today*'s fifth annual team-by-team salary survey:

TEAM	TEAM PAYROLL
Baltimore Orioles	$10,944,500
Boston Red Sox	19,032,390
California Angels	14,947,830
Chicago White Sox	9,058,909
Cleveland Indians	10,064,500
Detroit Tigers	14,147,760
Kansas City Royals	17,026,050

Milwaukee Brewers	11,741,500
Minnesota Twins	14,253,000
New York Yankees	18,394,485
Oakland Athletics	17,643,000
Seattle Mariners	8,662,499
Texas Rangers	10,759,280
Toronto Blue Jays	15,911,666
Atlanta Braves	9,035,334
Chicago Cubs	11,932,000
Cincinnati Reds	12,132,000
Houston Astros	16,688,000
Los Angeles Dodgers	20,492,506
Montreal Expos	14,960,389
New York Mets	21,410,878
Philadelphia Phillies	8,527,000
Pittsburgh Pirates	12,438,000
St. Louis Cardinals	16,037,333
San Diego Padres	13,894,000
San Francisco Giants	16,619,667

The average major league salary was $513,730.

That figure, however, did not include the penalty club owners would pay in "Collusion I"—$10,528,086.71. The penalty decision for Collusion I, the first of three grievances filed by the Players Association charging owners with a conspiracy against free agents in 1985, had been awaited since arbitrator Thomas Roberts ruled in favor of the players in 1987. On August 31, Roberts announced his $10.5 million decision.

Even more worrisome to clubowners, arbitrator George Nicolau ruled for the players in "Collusion II" (1986 free agents) and that penalty is expected to be even greater. A decision in "Collusion III" (1987 free agents) had not yet been announced when the 1989 season ended, but there was no doubt which way the wind was blowing.

Adding more than a dollop of confusion to the mix was the prospect that 1990 may see a third league in competition with the American and National (not counting the winter's sideshow of the Senior League, an over-35 circuit born of the same delusions that provided Walter Mittys for the fantasy camps). Reportedly the brainchild of two lawyers with major league connections, the new major league would ideally begin operation in eight cities. Players would be culled from major league free agents, recently released players, and youngsters signed out of college and high school. Ten to twenty "name" players is the goal for the first season.

Many baseball people discounted the new-league talk, terming it a bargaining ploy thought up by agents and the Players Association to toughen their stance in the upcoming agreement negotiations. Commissioner Bart Giamatti referred to the project as the "union league," but he might have checked his history. The original union league (actually known as the Union Association) was a one-year failure in 1884; the Players League, to which this proposal bears more of a resemblance, played its only season in 1890—exactly 100 years ago.

Milestones

Baseball passed a milestone in February 1989 when the National League owners unanimously named Bill White as their president to succeed Bart Giamatti, newly installed as Commissioner. White's election marked the highest baseball executive position achieved thus far by a black man. Although

news of the vote received nearly universal approval, it was noted that to advance this far had taken baseball 42 years since Jackie Robinson first put on a Dodger uniform (number 42) and 113 years since the founding of the National League.

For the first time in baseball's history, the presidents of both leagues are former players. Dr. Bobby Brown, the American League President, was a Yankees third baseman after World War II. White, a former all-star first baseman with the Giants, Cardinals, and Phillies, had been a broadcaster with the New York Yankees for eighteen years.

When asked why he had accepted a job that would mean a $100,000 pay cut and a far more taxing schedule, White joked, "The motivation comes from working eighteen years with Phil Rizzuto." In a more serious vein, he said the opportunity to become baseball's first black president played no part in his decision. "You just do the job whether you're red, yellow, purple or whatever."

Another baseball first was achieved by the Griffeys—father and son. Although there have been more than a hundred father-son combinations in baseball history, never before had both been in major league lineups during the same season. Ken, Sr., in his seventeenth big league season, hit .263 in 106 games for the Reds; 19-year-old Ken, Jr., hit .264 (with 16 home runs) in 127 games with the Mariners.

Amazing Nolan Ryan placed a couple of milestones in the record books that may stay forever. On the night of August 22 at Arlington Stadium, he struck out Oakland's Rickey Henderson in the fifth inning for the 5,000th "K" of his career. Ryan—at 42 the majors' oldest pitcher—sat down Henderson with a fastball clocked at 96 mph.

A little over a month later, Ryan became the oldest pitcher—by eleven years!—to strike out 300 batters in a season. The previous oldest had been Houston's Mike Scott at age 31 in 1986. The last American Leaguer to compile 300 strikeouts was—who else?—Nolan Ryan in 1977. Ryan's record performance came in his final 1989 start—a 2–0 three-hitter over the Angels at Anaheim Stadium for his 16th win of the season, 289th of his career, and 57th career shutout. He fanned 13 Angels, his 199th ten-or-more-whiff performance, to finish the season with 301 (exactly 100 more than the number garnered by the National League strikeout leader, Jose DeLeon of the Cardinals). Appropriately, the stadium sound system blared out "Forever Young" in his honor.

Hail . . .

Several players enhanced their records in 1989.

Tony Gwynn of the Padres won his third straight National League batting championship (and fourth in the last six years) with a .336 mark. Gwynn had to go 3-for-4 in each of the Padres' last two games—both against San Francisco—to edge out the Giants' Will Clark, who ended at .333. The Padres' outfielder is the first NL player since Stan Musial (1950–52) to win three straight batting titles.

After challenging for several seasons, Minnesota's Kirby Puckett took his first American League batting championship by going 2-for-5 at Seattle while Oakland's Carney Lansford, the 1981 champ, went hitless in three tries against Kansas City. Puckett closed at .339, Lansford at .336. Puckett also led both leagues in total hits with 215, becoming the first righthanded batter to do it in two consecutive years.

San Francisco's Kevin Mitchell was the majors' top power

hitter, leading both leagues in home runs (47), RBIs (125), total bases (345), and slugging percentage (.635). Toronto's Fred McGriff led the American League in homers with 36, but Ruben Sierra had the top AL RBI total with 119, and led in total bases (344) and slugging (.543).

Cal Ripken, Jr., again played in every Orioles game, extending to 1,250 his consecutive-game streak, the third longest of all time behind Lou Gehrig's 2,130 and Everett Scott's 1,307. The Baltimore shortstop, who made only eight errors all season, put together one forty-seven-game span of 237 chances without a miscue.

The Cubs' Ryne Sandberg broke Manny Trillo's mark for consecutive errorless games in a single season by a second baseman when he played in his ninetieth straight on the final day of the regular season. Next year, he'll need one more spotless game to tie Joe Morgan's major league record.

Vince Coleman of the Cardinals eclipsed Davey Lopes's record of 38 consecutive stolen bases without being caught. He was successful on his first 44 attempts in 1989 to bring his streak to 50. Montreal catcher Nelson Santovenia finally gunned him down on July 28.

Robin Yount of Milwaukee cracked out 195 basehits to lift his career total to 2,602. Kansas City's George Brett also moved past 2,500 to 2,528. Teammate Bill Buckner increased his career hits to 2,707—the top total for an active player—but played only part time for the Royals.

Darrell Evans, used sparingly by Atlanta, moved past Duke Snider in all-time home runs, upping his total by 11 to 414.

Besides Nolan Ryan, two other veteran pitchers defied nature by registering outstanding years. Righthander Rick Reuschel, the National League's oldest hurler at 40, helped lead San Francisco to a pennant. The Giants' "Big Daddy" won the 200th game of his career early in the season and went on to post a 17–8 record to lift him to 211 career wins.

When Bert Blyleven struggled to a 10–17, 5.43 ERA mark with Minnesota in 1988, the Twins figured the 38-year-old curveballer was near the end of a great career and let him go to the Angels for three minor leaguers. He turned back the clock in California with a remarkable comeback, going 17–5 with a 2.73 ERA. (With a little more support, he would have won 20; in 11 no-decision starts, his ERA was 2.56.) His 5 shutouts moved him to eighth place in career whitewashings with 60.

Kansas City's Bret Saberhagen led all major league pitchers in wins with his 23–6 mark and was also top man in winning percentage (.793), ERA (2.16), innings pitched (262⅓), and complete games (12). Oakland's Dave Stewart won 20 games (21–9) for the third straight year, the only pitcher to string together three straight 20-win seasons in the 1980s. Mike Scott of the Astros was the NL's win leader and only 20-game winner (20–10). Bullpen laurels were taken by Mark Davis of San Diego, who with 44 saves came within one of the NL record and two of the major league record. The Rangers' Jeff Russell topped the AL with 38.

... And Farewell

Time finally ran out for lefthander Tommy John in his record-tying twenty-sixth major league season. The bionic-armed ancient one was the Yankees' opening day pitcher, winning 4–2, but struggled after that to a 2–7 mark. On Memorial Day, New York gave him his release. John, who entered the majors in 1963 and laid out the 1975 season while his pitching arm was rebuilt with a ligament transplant, won 20 or more games three times after the operation and finished with a career record of 288–231.

Future Hall of Fame third baseman Mike Schmidt also announced his retirement on May 29. With his comments interrupted by heaving sobs, the Phillies' three-time MVP told reporters that his skills had deteriorated to the point where he couldn't perform up to his personal standards. At the time, Schmidt was hitting only .203. He leaves behind a potent slugging record that includes 548 career homers and 1,595 RBIs.

Buddy Bell also retired after a career that earned him 2,514 hits and far fewer plaudits than his overall play merited.

Perhaps the most tragic story of the summer was not Pete Rose's but that of former pitcher Donnie Moore. An outstanding reliever with the California Angels, Moore set a club record with 31 saves in 1985. But in the 1986 playoffs, while trying to save a win that would have put the Angels in the World Series, he was the victim of Dave Henderson's ninth-inning, two-out, two-strike, two-run homer. California eventually lost that game and the next two, as Boston took the pennant. Moore never recovered emotionally from that incident. He drifted into the minors and was released by the Omaha Royals in June 1989. On July 18, he shot and seriously wounded his wife, then turned the gun on himself. He was 35.

It Ain't Over, Etc.

The season saw two come-from-behind rallies that fans will be talking about for years.

When Pittsburgh jumped off to a 10–0 lead in the first inning at Philadelphia's Veterans Stadium on June 8, Pirates broadcaster Jim Rooker joked, "If we lose this game, I'll walk home." Then, to Rooker's chagrin, the Phillies used two homers each by Von Hayes and Steve Jeltz to rally for a 15–11 victory. True to his word, Rooker walked the 337 miles back to Pittsburgh—waiting until the season was over, of course. "Rook's Unintentional Walk," as his trek was termed, began at Veterans Stadium on October 5, ended on October 17 at Three Rivers Stadium, and was expected to raise $100,000 for Pittsburgh's Children's Hospital and (former Pirate broadcaster) Bob Prince's Charities. Before beginning, Rooker cracked, "I'll still be walking to my car. It'll just take me two and a half weeks to get there."

The Cubs pulled off a come-from-way-backer in August that made believers out of many who were waiting for them to crumble. They trailed Houston 9–0 after six innings at Wrigley Field, but tied the game in the ninth and won in the tenth.

The Dodgers were the long-game champs, losing a twenty-two-inning, seven-hour and fourteen-minute marathon at the Astrodome. Third baseman Jeff Hamilton, the Los Angeles emergency reliever, took the loss. The next day, the Dodgers and Astros played thirteen innings, and over the four-day period Los Angeles put in fifty-three innings on the field—the equivalent of nearly six games. Later in the season, the Dodgers won a twenty-two-inning, 1–0 thriller at Olympic Stadium. Veteran catcher Rick Dempsey was the Dodgers' hero at Montreal. In the bottom of the twenty-first inning, he snuffed out an Expo threat by picking Tim Raines off first. He homered to give L.A. the lead in the twenty-second and then ended the game by cutting down a Montreal steal attempt at second.

Coming Back Strong

On an individual basis, Blyleven had the most spectacular comeback season in the American League, but Oakland's Dave Parker, Baltimore's Mickey Tettleton, and Seattle's Jeffrey Leonard all had solid slugging records to re-establish themselves.

In the National League, two heartwarming stories dominated comeback news.

Lonnie Smith was released by Kansas City after the 1987 season. Smith had been a .300 hitter with the Phillies and Cardinals, but his career was tainted by drug problems. Atlanta offered him a minor league contract and eventually he played 43 games with the Braves in 1988, batting only .237. But in 1989, he came all the way back. At age 33, he batted .315 with career highs of 21 homers and 79 RBIs, plus the league's top mark in batting average with men in scoring position. The Braves finished last in the NL West, but Manager Russ Nixon said, "I'd hate to imagine being without him."

Giants lefthander Dave Dravecky wasn't expected to pitch at all this season; he was happy to be alive. In October 1988 surgeons removed a cancerous tumor from his pitching arm. Amazingly, he took the mound for San Francisco on August 10 at Candlestick Park and stopped San Diego, 4–3, having allowed only one hit through his first seven innings of work. Five days later, he took a shutout into the sixth inning at Montreal, but his comeback ended when he collapsed on the field. He had suffered a stress fracture of the humerus, the large bone between the elbow and shoulder. Doctors explained that a freezing process used in the surgery had left the bone susceptible to such a fracture. Even though Dravecky's arm was again broken during the Giants' victory celebration after the League Championship Series, doctors predict a full recovery. Anyway, his comeback was already complete.

Hall of Fame

Four new members were added to Baseball's Hall of Fame in 1989. The Baseball Writers Association of America named Cincinnati's great catcher Johnny Bench and longtime Red Sox slugger Carl Yastrzemski to the Hall in January. In March, the Veterans Committee tagged Red Schoendienst, an outstanding second baseman who flourished in the 1950s, and former National League umpire Al Barlick.

Harry Caray, the voice of the Chicago Cubs, was named the winner of the Ford C. Frick Award for outstanding contributions as a broadcaster. The J. G. Taylor Spink Award for outstanding sports reporting went to Bob Hunter of the Los Angeles *Examiner* and *Daily News* and the late Ray Kelly of the *Philadelphia Bulletin*.

Sadly, between the naming of Bench and Yastrzemski and their induction, the Hall lost four of its members to death: Bill Terry, the National League's last .400 hitter; former Yankees pitcher Lefty Gomez; longtime umpire Jocko Conlan; and Judy Johnson, a great third baseman from the Negro Leagues.

The American League East

Rated as baseball's strongest division only a couple of years ago, the American East has fallen on hard times. More than one critic has tagged it "the American League *Least*." But what the division may have lacked in dynastic power was more than offset in 1989 by the majors' most dynamic pennant race. The astonishing turnaround of the Baltimore Orioles from laughing stock to blue-chip stock made for baseball's most popular underdog story all season. Countless allusions were made to the 1969 Miracle Mets, appropriately celebrating their twentieth anniversary. Even though the Orioles' miracle didn't quite come off, the Birds hung in—amid constant predictions of their imminent fold—until the next-to-last day of the season. It was an exciting and impressive show. The turnaround from a record of 54–107 in 1988 to 87–75 earned Manager of the Year honors for Frank Robinson.

Detroit's Tigers, on the other hand, were far more depressing than impressive. After winning the division title in 1987 and almost repeating in '88, the Tabbies stumbled out of the gate, staggered through the summer, and reached October thoroughly stomped on by just about everyone.

On May 19 Manager Sparky Anderson was sent home suffering from physical exhaustion. In his absence, with coach Dick Tracewski as interim manager, the Tigers won 9 of 17. When Sparky returned after seventeen days, the team welcomed him back by losing 25 of its next 35 games. Later Anderson, desperate to find a silver lining, said, "This team takes its whippings without a complaint." Practice makes perfect.

On their way to 103 losses, only one shy of the team record, the 1989 Tigers were a model of consistency: last in team batting average (.242), slugging (.351) and ERA (4.53). They were bad at Tiger Stadium (38–43) and awful on the road (21–60).

The Tigers suffered from too much age, too many injuries, an unproductive farm system, and ineffective trades. They had hoped that this would be the year in which they replaced a successful but aging team with a solid mixture of youth and veterans. Instead, the young players proved themselves unready and the veterans were either unwell or, worse, just old. Shortstop Alan Trammell, one of the most valuable Tigers of recent seasons, was hurt all year and batted only .243 with 43 RBIs. Outfielders Fred Lynn and Chet Lemon were at .241 and .237, respectively. Catcher Matt Nokes, a promising slugger only two seasons ago, spent time on the DL with a knee injury, came back, hurt his arm, and couldn't throw for the final month. Second baseman Lou Whittaker was the surprising power leader with 28 home runs (no one else reached a dozen) and 85 RBIs.

Expected to be one of the team's strengths, the veteran pitching turned out to be one of its weaknesses. Lefty Frank Tanana, by his own reckoning, had a "great" year. His 3.58 ERA was his best in four seasons, but he struggled to only a 10–14 mark. Righthander Doyle Alexander went 6–18, with one stretch of 0–8. Jack Morris, until this season the American League's most consistent winner of the decade, was consistently thrashed and finished 6–14. The top winner was Mike Henneman, whose 11 victories came in relief. Guillermo Hernandez was in charge of the bullpen when he wasn't nursing a sore arm; he led the team with 15 saves, but his 5.74 ERA was suited more to an arsonist than a fireman.

Anderson faces a massive rebuilding job. He received a two-year contract extension in September, so he'll probably be around to try.

In late August Sparky told reporters he was going to try to forget the '89 season completely. "I'm going to say a ball hit me in the head in spring training and I didn't remember a thing after that." A few days later during warm-ups, Sparky was hit in the head by a ball.

It was that kind of year in Detroit.

Across Lake Erie in Cleveland, things were much better—for a while. The Indians were a mere 1½ games out of first place on August 4, and some optimistic Ohioans were actually predicting an end to the Tribe's thirty-five-year pennant drought, while they fitted skipper Doc Edwards for Manager of the Year honors.

Then the Indians went into a dive worthy of a 9.6 at the Olympics. On September 12, with Cleveland in hot pursuit of the Tigers' last-place slot, Edwards was fired. John Hart, previously a special assignments scout, was named Cleveland's eighteenth manager since a pennant last flew over Municipal Stadium.

What happened? Edwards never had much of an attack to work with. Joe Carter put up big numbers (35 homers, 105 RBIs), but was still labeled "unproductive" by some Tribe-watchers. Second baseman Jerry Browne, picked up in the trade that sent Julio Franco to Texas, hit a creditable .299, but his stats paled alongside those of Franco. Third baseman Brook Jacoby continued to suffer from the power outage that has dogged him since 1987. Outfielder Cory Snyder struggled with a back problem all year, as his batting average dropped to .214 and his home runs to 18. The team was dead last in the league in scoring runs.

Cleveland had pitching, and for more than half a season that carried them. But ace Greg Swindell went on the DL in July and Tom Candiotti, Bud Black, John Farrell, and bullpenner Doug Jones couldn't pick up the slack despite yeoman efforts.

For 1990, Cleveland must face a Catch-22 trade situation. Should they weaken the pitching in hope of improving the moribund offense? Or should they deal Carter, their only proven run-producer, to take on a new load of potential? Huge and drafty Municipal Stadium is often called "The Mistake on the Lake," but for thirty-five years, most of the mistakes have been made in the Indians' front office.

Someday Yankee historians will have to differentiate the Steinbrenner Years with Roman numerals like Super Bowls—Bronx Zoo XVIII and so on. How else will they tell them apart? In 1989, the manager was fired, Don Mattingly was terrific, the pitching was awful, the traffic between Yankee Stadium and the Columbus farm club produced its own gridlock, a player got into trouble with the law, and the Yankees finished down in the standings. Nothing new.

If discussion of the pinstripers were limited to the right side of the infield, it was a good year. First baseman Mattingly had an ordinary (for him) season—.303, 23 home runs, 113 RBIs. Second baseman Steve Sax, swept into Steinbrennerville on a tidal wave of free agent money, actually looked to be worth most of it—.315 with 205 hits.

There were a few other hopeful signs. Young Roberto Kelly showed flashes of becoming a star in center field, and Jesse Barfield, acquired in a May trade from Toronto, hit 23 into the stands, suggesting that the bat that led the league in homers in 1986 might be capable of resuscitation.

But what can you say about a pitching staff where the "ace" is journeyman Andy Hawkins? Well, you might mention that it finished thirteenth in the league in ERA at 4.50—which was .30 better than Hawkins' mark. Or you could point out that fourteen different hurlers started games during the season, but only Hawkins started more than twenty.

Of course, stability is not highly valued on a team that stamps all players' effects "Property of New York and/or Columbus." The most interesting call-up/send-back was "Neon" Deion Sanders, a first-round Atlanta Falcons draft choice taking a flyer at baseball to fill his empty summer hours. In 14 well-publicized games, Sanders hit 2 home runs, stole 1 base, batted .234, and talked Hall of Fame.

One legitimate Hall of Fame candidate of the future was missing from the Zoo all season. Dave Winfield underwent back surgery in the spring and will not play again until 1990.

Not likely to be in pinstripes next year is outfielder Luis Polonia, the young outfielder acquired in a trade that improved Oakland by Rickey Henderson. Although Polonia hit .300 on the nose, he was also arrested and convicted in Milwaukee on a charge of statutory rape.

The umpty-umpth rendition of "So Long, It's Been Good to Know You" was sung to a Yankees manager when, to the surprise of absolutely no one, Dallas Green was canned on August 18. The move had been expected since Green was hired in November 1988. Between them, Green and owner George Steinbrenner have enough strong will to levitate Yankee Stadium, and, despite Steinbrenner's insistence that he wouldn't interfere in Green's decisions, rumblings were heard in spring training. By August the two were airing criticisms of each other in the press. In the seventeenth managerial change since Steinbrenner took over in 1973, Bucky Dent, another Columbus call-up, became the newest holder of this forever interim job.

Eleven days later, Syd Thrift, the Yankees' senior vice president since March, resigned or was forced out.

The Milwaukee Brewers' season was more sane and sensible, but only slightly more successful. After closing to within a half game of the lead on August 21, the Brew Crew went 1–6 on a trip to Baltimore and Toronto to plummet from the race. They finished a middle-of-the-pack 81–81.

Center fielder Robin Yount was his typically excellent self, with 21 homers and 103 RBIs to go with a .318 batting average. Paul Molitor had a fine .315 year. But the attack lacked consistency after its one-two punch. Outfielder Rob Deer slugged 26 homers but limped home with a .210 batting mark. First baseman Greg Brock and outfielder Glenn Braggs were only intermittently productive.

Shortstop Gary Sheffield, all but conceded Rookie of the Year status in preseason, couldn't get untracked, was sent to the minors for a while, and then fractured a bone in his foot. Second baseman Jim Gantner crashed in August, the victim of a rolling block while making a double-play pivot.

Injuries also laid low the team's stopper, lefty Teddy Higuera. One of the league's best when healthy, Higuera battled a sore ankle and sore arm to a so-so 9–6 mark. Chris Bosio became the main starter and did well—15–10, with a 2.95 ERA—but the starting pitching was thin all season. Great bullpen work by Dan Plesac (33 saves) and Chuck Crim (9–7 with 7 saves) kept the staff from unraveling.

The Red Sox and their bedroom exploits were baseball's snigger champs, but the team finished third in the AL East at 83–79. How much the Boggs-Adams revelations hurt them is a matter for speculation. Like a splinter in the thumb, it couldn't help. Neither could the sniping some players did at manager Joe Morgan, or the skipper's angry charge of "babyness" leveled at some of his troops.

Verifiably injurious were the injuries that limited Ellis Burks (.303, 12 homers) to 97 games and cut into Mike Greenwell's power stats (.308, 14 home runs, 95 RBIs). Former MVP Jim Rice (.234, 3 home runs) was a forgotten man most of the season and was not offered a contract for 1990.

Staff ace Roger Clemens was adequate at 17–11, but despite his 230 strikeouts, he was seldom the overpowering "Rocket" of yore. Curveballer Mike Boddicker managed a 15–11 mark. Greatly missed most of the time was a healthy Oil Can Boyd, who appeared in only 10 games. And gone all the time but definitely not forgotten was Bruce Hurst, who took his free-agent left arm to San Diego.

Reliable Dwight Evans (.285, 20 homers, 100 RBIs) and Nick Esasky (.277, 30, 108), the former Reds first baseman acquired over the winter, made up for a lot of poor pitching, but the "Morgan Magic" of 1988 did not return to Fenway Park.

The magic had moved to Baltimore.

In 1988 the Orioles led off the season with a record twenty-one straight losses and crawled to a 54–107 record, so manager Frank Robinson's statement that the club's future was "very bright" and that it "is going to be competitive in a very short time" had all the credibility of one of those tabloids on sale at the supermarket checkout. Moreover, general manager Rollie Hemond made seventeen deals in seventeen months, bringing in mostly players no one ever heard of but sending out such established names as Terry Kennedy, Mike Boddicker, and Eddie Murray. The smart money said the Birds might get out of the cellar in 1990—or 2000.

Instead, the Orioles roared out of the gate and held first place for ninety-eight days. Toronto finally passed them on September 1, but the Birds hung tough. By the season's last three games, they needed to win two out of three at Toronto to tie the Blue Jays. They captured only one—just missing becoming the first team ever to bound from last to first in a single season. It wasn't the brass ring, but it was close enough, amazing enough, and thrilling enough to deserve a whole box of cigars.

Despite rumors to the contrary, they didn't do it with mirrors. The defense was the speediest and most reliable in the AL. No weekly highlight film was complete without at least one spectacular catch by a Baltimore outfielder.

The offense, while considerably less spectacular, used speed where it lacked power and seemed always to find a hero for the moment. Mainstay Cal Ripken (.257, 21, 93) has had bigger years, but he glued the attack together. Catcher Mickey Tettleton surprised with 26 home runs. Second baseman Tim Hulett, called up in a pinch, astonished with timely hitting. Phil Bradley, Joe Orsulak, and Randy Milligan had their moments. And Craig Worthington was one of the top rookies in baseball.

The no-name pitching staff—which included a former slow-pitch softball all-star and a 29-year-old rookie discovered in a mobile home outside Baltimore—kept coming through. The top starters were underpowering Jeff Ballard (18-8) and rookie Bob Milacki (14–12). Rookie reliever Gregg Olson (1.69, 27 saves) was voted team MVP and AL Rookie of the Year.

Somehow Robinson convinced this crew that they could

win. Then they went out and convinced everyone else. Certainly Baltimore fans believed. They set a club attendance record with 2,534,875 while spouting the team's slogan: "Why not?"

Why not indeed?

The Toronto Blue Jays had the reason; it was only a question of whether they had the will. Typecast as Goliath to Baltimore's David, the Jays each year would flex their muscles and threaten to become the AL's dominant team. The closest they had come to a pennant, however, was losing the 1985 LCS after leading three games to one.

They began 1989 as if they just wanted to get this summer's unpleasantness over as quickly as possible. When the count went to 12–24 and 10 games out, manager Jimy Williams was fired. His replacement—after the Yankees refused Toronto permission to negotiate with Lou Piniella—was hitting coach Cito Gaston, who would just as soon have kept coaching instead of managing. Given the Blue Jays' history, who could blame him?

The opening of the Toronto Sky Dome on June 5, baseball's newest and most high-tech ballpark, provided a perfect setting for the team to change its reputation, but that wasn't as easy as retracting the roof. Milwaukee won the first game played there, 5–3. The dome became an attraction in itself and helped the Jays to a record attendance—3,375,573. Club officials are hoping for 4 million in 1990.

Under Gaston's relaxed leadership, Toronto climbed back into the race. First baseman Fred McGriff (.269, 36, 92) went on a home run tear, and George Bell (.297, 18, 104) returned to his 1987 MVP pace. Third baseman Kelly Gruber (.290, 18, 73) was another key bat. Shortstop Tony Fernandez (.257, 11, 64) wasn't up to his usual standard at the plate, but was brilliant in the field, committing only 6 errors all season.

Mookie Wilson was an important acquisition from the Mets. The Mookster batted .298 in 54 games and provided a needed spark and a burst of speed.

Aside from Dave Stieb (17–8 and a couple of near-no-hitters) the starting pitching was shaky. Jimmy Key (13–14) fought off injuries to pitch well down the stretch, but Mike Flanagan (8–10) and Todd Stottlemyre (7–7) were only occasionally effective. However, the bullpen duo of Tom Henke (former resident of Jimy Williams' doghouse) and Duane Ward combined for 35 saves.

The Jays moved into first place in September, but the division championship came down to the final three-game series with the Orioles at the Sky Dome—a perfect opportunity for Toronto to fold in the clutch once again. On Friday, September 29, Baltimore led 1–0 into the eighth, but the Jays tied it and then won in the eleventh on Lloyd Moseby's single. The next day Moseby's sacrifice was the key to a three-run eighth-inning rally that gave the Blue Jays a 4–3 win and the title.

Something besides the ballpark had changed in Toronto.

American League West

The 1989 AL Western Division race that many predicted would be a cakewalk for the returning champion Oakland Athletics turned into a first-rate competition. The A's made it harder for themselves with injuries, but Kansas City and California were stronger than expected. All three won more games than Eastern champ Toronto. The Texas Rangers and

Minnesota Twins were never pushovers either.

Western Division clubs were 314–273 against the Eastern counterparts, for a winning percentage of .534; Toronto finished first in the East only a little higher at .549.

Nothing demonstrated the West's dominance over the East so much as the final pitching stats. The first three teams in earned run average were Oakland, California, and Kansas City. The Athletics and Angels tied for the most shutouts, and the Royals tied Cleveland for the next slot. The four winningest pitchers were from the West, as were five of the top seven men in strikeouts. Ultimately, Oakland won in a pitching-rich division because the Athletics had even more of that commodity than their competition.

One team not rich in established pitchers was the Chicago White Sox. Melido Perez (11–14) led the staff in wins but had a 5.01 ERA. Eric King (9–10) was the most reliable starter. Fortunately most of the starters figure to have their best years ahead of them. Perhaps they'll learn how to finish what they start: Pale Hose starters set a new AL record with a mere 9 complete games. Part of that, however, was due to having one of baseball's best closers in the bullpen in Bobby Thigpen. He tied his own team record with 34 saves, an impressive number in itself but doubly so for a team that won only 69 games.

The team batting average of .271 was misleading. The Sox could get on base, but a power outage left them considerably less adept at getting home. Their 94 homers made them the only AL team under the century mark. Ivan Calderon was the club leader in homers and RBIs, with 14 and 87, respectively.

If nothing else, the Sox can take credit for deciding the *Eastern* race—they split twelve games with the Orioles but lost eleven to the Blue Jays.

There *are* a few bright spots: manager Jeff Torborg, who brought a positive outlook in his first year; slick-fielding shortstop Ozzie Guillen (the *other* "Wizard of Oz"); Calderon; Thigpen; and the crop of young starters. Nevertheless, a lot more will be needed to get out of last place in the standings. Or, more important, last place in American League attendance. Maybe the new stadium opening in 1992 will help.

Generally speaking, the Seattle Mariners' Kingdome is the ballpark most disliked by opponents. One can understand pitchers' anathema, but even many rival hitters find fault with its cozy confines. On the other hand, *playing* the Mariners has always been an oasis for the rest of the American League. Last year was the thirteenth consecutive losing season for Seattle. That's bad enough, but in case you don't know, the team has been in existence for exactly the same number of years. The *Sub*mariners hope to get their heads above water in 1990.

New owners Jeff Smulyan and Michael Browning and general manager Woody Woodward vow things are going to change. They think they've got a handle on what went wrong before. "Too many times in the past, this organization had a disappointing season and decided to revamp." From now on, Woodward promises, no more wholesale changes.

They have a few blocks to build on. Ken Griffey, Jr., looks like a future star. Rookie Greg Briley (.266, 13, 52) may be another. Jeff Leonard made a nice comeback to hit 24 homers and bat in 93 runs. He may have another couple of good years left in this fountain of youth for hitters. In Alvin Davis (.305, 21, 95) they have a solid first baseman. Second baseman Harold Reynolds (.300, 9, 43) gives them half an infield, at least offensively.

Something must be done about the gloves. Davis had 10 errors last season, Reynolds 17, shortstop Omar Vizquel 18, and third baseman Jim Presley 18 in only 117 games. There's talk of hiring an infield coach; they might do better with a barrel of glue.

Mike Schooler set a club record with 33 saves. Right-hander Scott Bankhead (14–6, 3.34) was named Mariners' MVP and the rest of the staff has its share of potential. Of course, Seattle has a history of developing good pitchers who then go into the big, wide world and pitch great—for someone else. Remember Mark Langston? Remember Mike Moore?

Speaking of young pitchers, Twins fans hated the deal in which Minnesota gave up Cy Young Award winner Frank Viola for five Mets second-line and minor-league pitchers. Viola was pitching more like Curt Young than Cy Young before the August deal, but none of the kid pitchers set the Metrodome on fire either. Rick Aguilera, the only former Met anyone in Minnesota had ever heard of, pitched fairly well but has a history of arm trouble. David West, Kevin Tapani, and Tim Drummond all threw regularly in September with so-so results. Still, if only two of the new kids develop into solid starters, the Twins will be ahead down the road.

Shane Rawley, last year's big new mound hope, bombed at 5–12 with a 5.21 ERA and won't be asked back. Except for potential, the Twins' pitching—major league style—was mostly Allan Anderson (17–10, 3.80) and Roy Smith (10–6, 3.92). Stopper Jeff Reardon saved 31 games despite a great big 4.07 ERA.

As usual, the Twins didn't lack for hitters, although injuries slowed down Kent Hrbek (.272, 25, 84) and Gary Gaetti (.251, 19, 75). Another power hitter wouldn't hurt, especially in the friendly Metrodome. Minnesota hit only 117 homers all season. Considering the Dome's dimensions, you would think they could do that on a long weekend. Dan Gladden had a good .295 year, and Brian Harper was a pleasant surprise. After years as a fringe player, he was given a shot as the regular catcher and responded by hitting .325.

Batting champ Kirby Puckett saw his home runs drop to 9 and his RBIs to 85. But, with 215 basehits, he still ranks as one of the four best players in the league. Add in a couple of pitchers and Minnesota can challenge for the division title in 1990. They already have the bats.

Nolan Ryan drew so much national attention with his 5,000 strikeouts, 16–10 record, and so forth, that many people outside of Texas never noticed that the Rangers have been corralling quite a herd of good ballplayers.

For instance, Ruben Sierra was just about as good as anybody in the league. In what looks to have been his breakthrough year, he led the AL in slugging percentage and hit .306, with 29 home runs and a league-leading 119 RBIs. Julio Franco (.316, 13, 92) had his best season ever. Harold Baines (.309, 16, 72), one of baseball's most reliable hitters in his years with the White Sox, was picked up by the Rangers in a midseason deal; Baines gives manager Bobby Valentine a third strong bat. Stopper Jeff Russell led the league with 38 saves.

The Rangers still have too many "but" players. As in: Pete Incaviglia slugged 21 homers *but* struck out 136 times; center fielder Cecil Espy stole 45 bases *but* was caught 20 times; first baseman Rafael Palmeiro tore up the league for the first two months *but* hit only .235 over the last 110 games.

No buts about the starting pitching, though. The Rangers need a lot more. How long can 43-year-old Ryan or 42-year-old Charlie Hough (10–13) pretend they're still in their 20s?

Will rookie Kevin Brown (12–9) come back from the rotator injury that sidelined him at the end of the season? And can Bobby Witt (12–13, 5.14) ever be the consistent winner his stuff says he should be?

The Rangers finished on the plus side at 83–79 in '89, *but* after an early flurry they weren't in the race.

The California Angels surprised the division by winning 91 games. The Angels combined quality pitching, tight defense, and a home-run lineup to win sixteen more games in 1989 than in '88. They held first place for most of July and only a tail-off in September dropped them to third, a game behind Kansas City. Manager Doug Rader earned a lot of support for Manager of the Year.

Perhaps Rader's most important decision—certainly his most controversial—was to install rookie Jim Abbott in the starting rotation. Abbott, a 1988 Olympics pitcher, was born without a right hand, and his tug-at-your-heart story was an early sports page staple. But many doubted he was ready for the majors, not having spent a day in a minor league uniform, and some even whispered he was being used as a publicity stunt to take the focus off what was expected to be a lackluster season in Anaheim. Abbott, however, proved an unusually levelheaded young man. He matured as a pitcher as the season wore on and finished a creditable 12–12, 3.92.

Abbott's presence helped make up for a poor year by Mike Witt (9–15, 4.54). Blyleven's remarkable comeback season was even more to the point. His 17 wins left him with 271 career victories, within hailing distance of 300. Kirk McCaskill (15–10, 2.93) and Chuck Finley (16–9, 2.57) were two more quality starters, and Bryan Harvey saved 25 out of the bullpen. The pitching improvement over 1988 was dramatic, as the team ERA dropped more than a run a game, from 4.32 to 3.28.

A better defense was also part of the Halos' revival. They gathered 92 games without a bobble and had only 96 errors all season. Both are new team records.

California led the league in home runs with 145, even though no Angel challenged for the individual title. Chili Davis (.271, 22, 90) was named team MVP. Wally Joyner (.282, 16, 79), Brian Downing (.283, 14, 59), and Johnny Ray (.289, 5, 62) were productive even if all three have had better years. Catcher Lance Parrish (.238, 17, 50), acquired from the Phillies to replace ageless Bob Boone, was a bit disappointing, as was Devon White (.245, 12, 56, with 44 stolen bases).

Kansas City meandered through the season, and a late run for the top succeeded only in moving them into second place. Still, the Royals' 92 wins were the third highest total in the majors and the third highest in the team's history.

Much of the onus for placing instead of winning went on the hitters. Despite a talented lineup, the team was shut out 18 times. Many blamed strikeouts in the meat of the order for the occasional run famines. Bo Jackson (.256, 32, 105), awesome at times, was awful at others. Bo knew a league-leading 172 strikeouts. Danny Tartabull (.265, 18, 62), number two on the club in power, was also number two in K's with 123.

All-time Royals George Brett (.282, 12, 80), Frank White (.256, 2, 36), and Willie Wilson (.253, 3, 43) didn't play up to their usual level, in part because of injuries. Pleasant surprises included catcher Bob Boone (.272, 1, 43), who sets a new "most games caught" record every time he squats behind the plate, and outfielder Jim Eisenreich (.293, 9, 59), whose career seemed over only two years ago because of a nervous

disorder. Third baseman Kevin Seitzer (.281, 4, 48) was solid, and Kurt Stillwell (.261, 7, 54) has finally ended the Royals' longtime shortstop problem.

The bullpen also looked to be in good shape for the first time since Dan Quisenberry stopped getting people out. Steve Farr was okay with 18 saves, but Jeff Montgomery, who also saved 18, came on late to nail down the stopper's role.

Bret Saberhagen, who seems to be at his best in odd-numbered years, led the pitching staff—and, for that matter, all of baseball. He had ample help from starters Mark Gubicza (15–11, 3.04) and rookie Tom Gordon (17–9, 3.64). The youngster, of course, was nicknamed "Flash"—a Gordon not called "Flash" is as hard to find as a Rhodes not called "Dusty"—and there were the inevitable "flash in the pan" comments when he struggled late in the year after building up a head of steam toward 20 wins.

Life lays little booby traps for the cocksure. Around New Year's Day 1989 the Oakland Athletics looked like the surest bet in baseball. Even coming off their shocking World Series loss to the Dodgers, the A's were widely regarded as the best team in either league. They had more of everything, including the AL's 1988 Most Valuable Player, Rookie of the Year, and Fireman of the Year. Three aces over a full house.

So MVP and 40–40 man Jose Canseco broke a bone in his wrist and missed half the season. Shortstop and top rookie Walt Weiss tore up a knee and also missed half the season. Pitcher and top fireman Dennis Eckersley went on the sideline for over a month. And suddenly A's fans discovered their chicken count to be premature. The team that had walked over the opposition in '88 had every excuse to trip in '89.

Instead, the Athletics sucked it up and scratched, scrambled, and scrapped their way through. Third baseman Carney Lansford (.336, 2, 52) had one of his best years, finishing second in the league batting race. DH Dave Parker (.264, 22, 91) had a fine comeback season. Catcher Terry Steinbach (.274, 12, 57) and center fielder Dave Henderson (.250, 15, 80) were solid. First baseman Mark McGwire (.231, 33, 95) unlimbered his home run bat after a slow start.

Help arrived in June. Oakland sent outfielder Luis Polonia and some expendable middle relief pitching to the Yankees for premier leadoff man Rickey Henderson. Henderson (.274, 12, 57 for the entire season following a slow start with New York) proceeded to reach base in 63 of his first 67 games with the A's, while setting a personal high with 126 walks and, as usual, leading the AL in steals with 77.

Weiss was still limping at season's end, but Canseco showed no lasting effects of his injury. He returned to the lineup for 65 games and had 17 homers and 57 RBIs.

For all the firepower, New York's Don Mattingly probably got it right when he said, "Take their pitching away and they ain't no better than anybody else. They have some outstanding players. Canseco is extraordinary. Rickey and Carney are great. But, really, it's their pitching that sets them apart from the rest of us." Oakland had four starters with at least 17 wins: Dave Stewart (21–9), Mike Moore (19–11), Storm Davis (19–7), and Bob Welch (17–8). Stewart became the only pitcher of the decade to win 20 or more three straight seasons and was on track to his first Cy Young Award until K.C.'s Saberhagen got hot.

The bullpen was extra deep. Setup men Rick Honeycutt, Todd Burns, and Gene Nelson became lifesavers when Eckersley was hurt, combining for 23 saves. And when The Eck returned, he was still the best closer in baseball. He finished

4–0, with a 1.56 ERA and 33 saves in only 51 appearances.

Problems or not, Oakland's 99 wins were the most in the majors, and their road record of 45–36 tied them with the NL's Cubs as most unwelcome visitors.

The ALCS was a set piece—sort of like Bambi versus Godzilla with Toronto cast as Bambi. Rickey Henderson ran roughshod over the Blue Jays, as the Athletics won in five games. The victory made them the first team to win back-to-back pennants since the Yankees and Dodgers of 1977–78.

Any bets for 1990?

National League East

As late as September, some experts were still calling the Mets "the team to beat" and predicting the inevitable, historical, late-season slump of the Cubs. They were half right. The Mets *were* the team to beat. They proved it by *getting* beat. The Cubs, however, must have been reading a different history book.

Watching the Mets stumble was an enjoyable spectacle for baseball fans of the Midwest. The Mets have not been middle America's favorite team for the past few seasons. Part of it is the usual anti-New York feelings you can find on any street west of the Adirondacks. Part of it is envy of the Mets' recent success. And part of it is a heartfelt belief among midwestern baseball fans that the Mets are "arrogant." Aside from their taking curtain calls after even the most meaningless Shea Stadium home runs, the Mets' lack of an endearing humility is hard to document and even harder to differentiate from the pride of players on other teams. But in baseball as in most things, perception is all.

In Pittsburgh, an upcoming series with the Mets was promoted with the slogan "One more reason to hate New York."

The flip side: the Cubs Eastern Division crown was a satisfying ending for almost every fan (if their own team couldn't win). Chicago, after all, doesn't *seem* that much bigger than St. Louis or Pittsburgh or even Muncie. And the Cubbies have been inoffensively inept for oh so many years (1984 was a forgivable aberration). Best of all, Cub players come across as just-plain-folks—when described by the king of blue collardom, Harry Caray. Pitching in Chicago, Mitch "Wild Thing" Williams is lovably eccentric; in a Mets uniform, he would be just "another New York weirdo."

Both the Cubs and Mets are available on cable TV nationwide. Fans tune in to WGN if the Cubs are winning. Or to WWOR if the Mets are losing.

Speaking of losing, there's always Philadelphia. The Phillies under rookie manager Nick Leyva had half of an average team—the half that batted. The remainder, which was supposed to pitch and field, seldom did either on a major league level.

But the phutile Phillies are a team in transition, with major changes having taken place in 1989. Bullpen ace and former Cy Young winner Steve Bedrosian was packed off to San Francisco for some younger arms. Former three-time MVP Mike Schmidt retired to make way for a younger bat. Juan Samuel, one of the few remaining marquee names, was swapped to New York for a desperately needed center fielder and, in the absence of Bedrosian, relief pitcher. And finally, disappointing Chris James was traded to the Padres for unhappy and disappointing John Kruk. Meanwhile, several homegrown youngsters were force-fed into the lineup.

The upshot was that the Phils were a better team at the end of the season than at the start. Not good enough to get out of last place, mind you, but better.

Kruk (.300, 8, 44) lost weight but improved his disposition—he was once benched by the Padres for uttering profanities (!)—and regained his batting eye. Roger McDowell wasn't the closer he had been a few years ago for the Mets (nor the stopper Bedrosian had been), but he saved 25 for the season and made the Mets wistful for his services. Combined with Jeff Parrett (who at 12–6 tied for the team lead in wins), McDowell gave the Phils a bullpen. Lenny Dykstra (.237, 7, 32) was a disappointment at bat, but he was a far better center fielder in Philadelphia than Samuel was in New York. Of the young bats, first baseman Ricky Jordan (.285, 12, 75) and third baseman Charley Hayes (.257, 8, 43) showed the most promise. Sooner or later, they even may learn to field.

Von Hayes (who, after a torrid start, tailed to a line of .259, 26, 78) and shortstop Dicky Thon (.271, 15, 60) give Leyva a couple of solid veterans to build around.

The starting pitching, except for some good work by Ken Howell (12–12, 3.44), was horrendous. The team ERA of 4.04 was dead last in the NL by almost a third of a run.

Pittsburgh tied the Mets for the title of "Biggest 1989 Disappointment." After finishing second in '88, the Pirates swooned to the bottom at the start of the season and stayed there. Only the presence of the Phillies kept them out of last place.

What happened? The Pirates' party line is "injuries," but that's just another way of saying the team wasn't very deep in talent to start with. Every team had injuries, but when Pittsburgh had 'em, they couldn't cope.

Examples: Bullpen ace Jim Gott went out for the season after two-thirds of an inning. Setup man Jeff Robinson was moved up to closer and crashed. Pittsburgh went through the first two months of the season trying to find someone—anyone—who could hold a lead. By the time Bill Landrum (1.67, 26 saves) nailed down the job, the whole pitching staff was out of sync. Losing starter Brian Fisher for all but 17 innings left a hole in the rotation that was never filled. Still, Doug Drabek (14–12, 2.80) and John Smiley (12–8, 2.81) could have had a dozen more wins between them with help from the bullpen.

Center fielder Andy Van Slyke (.237, 9, 53) was waylaid by a rib-cage injury and knee problem, cutting his hitting contributions in half. Catcher Mike LaValliere (.316, 2, 23) missed the first half of the year while enemy baserunners ran wild. First baseman Sid Bream's absence was most felt on defense as throw after throw sailed unhindered past the cabinet of first sackers who tried to replace him.

But even Bream couldn't have caught all of the 35 errors by third baseman Bobby Bonilla (.281, 24, 86), or the 18 by second baseman Jose Lind (.232, 2, 48), or the 19 in 71 games by shortstop Rey Quinones (.209, 3, 29).

Quinones, acquired for three players from Seattle, was supposed to solve the Pirates' longtime shortstop woes. Instead, he was such a disaster at bat, in the field, and in the clubhouse that Pittsburgh released him halfway through the summer. Jay Bell, a flop with Cleveland, won the Buccos' job simply by playing with enthusiasm.

Montreal gave it a good go for a while, but just when people were saying there could be an all-Canada World Series (if Toronto could catch Baltimore), the Expos went south like the geese, losing 22 of their last 32. After being in first place for forty-one consecutive days through the late summer, Montreal finished 81–81. At the end of the debacle, manager Buck Rodgers was still in place, but four of his coaches were axed. "After the way we finished, it is apparent we have to make changes," general manager Dave Dombrowski announced ominously. "There is nobody in the untouchable category."

Highly touchable were the Expos' expected big hitters, who got the lion's share of the blame. The final stats for Tim Raines (.286, 9, 60), Tim Wallach (.277, 13, 77), Hubie Brooks (.268, 14, 70), and Andres Gallarraga (.257, 23, 85) weren't *awful*. A bit below par for each. But, taken as a group, they spelled death to Montreal pennant hopes.

Traditionally, the Expos have been weak up the middle, where traditional wisdom says a contender needs strength. They got a little better in 1989. Nelson Santovenia (.250, 5, 31) is a catcher with a major league arm, and shortstop Spike Owen (.233, 6, 41) is no all-star but won't embarrass them. Second base and center field still need upgrading. Rodgers' "bullpen by committee" wasn't as effective as in the past, although closer Tim Burke (9–3, 2.55, 28 saves) had a good year.

Montreal's strength was in its starting pitching. Dennis Martinez (16–7, 3.18) had his best season. Mark Langston (12–9, 2.39), acquired for a mere arm and leg from Seattle, was being called the league's best lefthander by some. Bryn Smith (10–11, 2.84), Kevin Gross (10–11, 4.38), and Pascual Perez (9–13, 3.31) rounded out a reliable fivesome.

The bad news is that Smith, Perez, and Langston all are 1990 free agents. Langston is, at this writing, almost surely lost. He's already turned down Montreal's offer of three years for $9 million, presumably waiting for a bid from OPEC.

Three million fans (plus another 82,000) were drawn into Busch Stadium to watch the Cardinals, and they usually got their money's worth. Whitey Herzog's starting pitching was so thin it should have been checked for anorexia, and Cardinal home runs were rarer than icebergs in August, but St. Louis used speed and defense to finish a respectable third.

First baseman Pedro Guerrero (.311, 17, 117) had a remarkable year as perhaps the league's most valuable batsman, considering his surroundings. Right fielder Tom Brunansky (.239, 20, 85) was the only other Redbird likely to reach the seats without a tailwind, but too often he didn't reach anything, including first base.

As usual, second baseman Jose Oquendo (.291, 1, 48), shortstop Ozzie Smith (.273, 2, 50), and third baseman Terry Pendleton (.264, 13, 74) provided soft singles and stone-wall defense. Milt Thompson (.290, 4, 68) was also useful, what with Willie McGee (.236, 3, 17) injured all year. McGee may not be back. Nor may catcher Tony Pena (.259, 4, 37), despite having his best all-around season since coming to St. Louis. Young Todd Zeile, who joined the club late, is expected to provide a better bat.

Left fielder Vince Coleman (.254, 2, 28) is a base-stealer *par excellence*. He swiped 65 to lead the league again. Unfortunately, his .316 on-base percentage brings up that old saw about the base you *can't* steal, and his 28 ribbies in 563 at bats is a truly awful number for a left fielder. His defense is nothing to write home about either.

Although Joe Magrane (18–9, 2.91) and Jose DeLeon (16–12, 3.05, and a league-leading 201 strikeouts) ably filled two of Whitey's starting slots, the rest was up for grabs once Danny Cox and Greg Mathews were sidelined for the year. The experience given Scott Terry (8–10, 3.57) and Ken Hill

(7–15, 3.80) may pay off in 1990, especially if Cox and Mathews are whole. The bullpen was strong with Todd Worrell, Ken Dayley, and retreaded Dan Quisenberry combining for 38 saves, but Worrell's September arm miseries gave cause for concern in the coming year.

A funny thing happened to the Mets on the way to the pennant. They finished second.

It certainly wasn't from lack of starting pitchers. The Mets started the season with five established starters in place, at least one more than anyone else could boast. Then, when Montreal picked up Langston, New York went out and got Frank Viola, 1988 AL Cy Young winner. Viola (5–5, 3.38) arrived in time to pick up the slack when ace Dwight Gooden (9–4, 2.89) went on the shelf with a sore arm. Meanwhile, David Cone (14–8, 3.52), Bob Ojeda (13–11, 3.47), Ron Darling (14–14, 3.52) and Sid Fernandez (14–5, 2.83) kept on truckin'.

Yet the Mets had pitching problems, particularly after sending their middle relievers to Minnesota for Viola and Roger McDowell to Philadelphia. Stopper Randy Myers (24 saves) was just okay, but that was better than the rest of the bullpen. New York lost a a staggering twenty games after taking a lead into the seventh inning.

Had it not been for Howard Johnson, the Mets might have dropped from the hunt by the All Star break. Johnson (.287, 36, 101) had his best season offensively. Defensively, he struggled from time to time, perhaps because of manager Davey Johnson's insistence on stationing him at shortstop whenever the others Mets' bats faltered. The Mets *have* a shortstop, their best in a long, long time. His name is Kevin Elster, but because he fields better than he hits (.231, 10, 55), Johnson regards his glove as a luxury rather than a necessity.

The rest of the hitters ranged from disappointing (Kevin McReynolds, .272, 22, 85), through poor (Daryl Strawberry, .225, 29, 77), to disastrous (Keith Hernandez, .233, 4, 19, and Gary Carter, .183, 2, 15). Hernandez and Carter, Met co-captains, were released after the season.

Other best-laid plans of mice and Mets that went astray included "sure" Rookie of the Year Gregg Jefferies (.258, 12, 56), who finished strong but started miserably. More than anything, he boxed plays at second base as ploddingly as George Foreman stalks an opponent. Meanwhile a real second baseman, Juan Samuel (.235, 11, 48) was acquired from the Phils to play center field. He was dreadful. The resulting criticism didn't help his hitting either, which didn't approach what was expected. By the end of the year, he was begging to get out of New York.

The Mets have all the parts to win in 1990 if they ever learn that the parts aren't interchangeable.

As if the Cubs needed another legend, there was a new one in 1989. That "everybody" picked them to finish last. Not so! Most of the "body's" who had heard of Philadelphia picked the Cubbies to finish *fifth*.

Certainly they didn't stand a chance for the division title. They had shaky starting pitching and no bullpen at all. The hitting was only fair even when the wind blew out at Wrigley. Their manager, an oversized gerbil named Don Zimmer, had been in baseball for more than forty years without convincing anyone he was a genius. And general manager Jim Frey had traded away one of the team's best hitters, Rafael Palmeiro, for a relief pitcher who needed a map to find home plate.

And when they got off to a surprisingly good start, the Cubs were bushwhacked by so many outfield injuries that they had to fill their pasture with minor leaguers. Then later, Damon Berryhill—on his way to being one of the league's best catchers—was lost for the last third of the season with a rotator cuff injury.

So—how did they finish on top of all those supposedly better teams?

The kid outfielders included Jerome Walton (.293, 5, 46) and Dwight Smith (.324, 9, 52), one-two for Rookie of the Year honors. Berryhill's replacements Joe Giraldi (.248, 1, 14) and Rick Wrona (.283, 2, 14) played better than anyone had a right to expect.

The starting pitching shored up with a reliable Greg Maddux (19–12, 2.95), a suddenly mature Mike Bielecki (18–7, 3.14) and still able Rick Sutcliffe (16–11, 3.66) and Scott Sanderson (11–9, 3.94). The bullpen got great work from Les Lancaster (4–2, 1.36), and good work from Jeff Pico (3–1, 3.77) and former Atlantan Paul Assenmacher (3–4, 3.99), but the revelation was lefty Mitch "Wild Thing" Williams. Hopelessly wild as a Ranger, he found the plate regularly enough to register 36 saves.

Andre Dawson (.252, 21, 77) and Vance Law (.235, 7, 42), stalwarts in the past, slumped badly, but Mark Grace (.314, 13, 79) and Ryne Sandberg (.290, 30, 76) made up for it. Sandberg, in fact, deserved consideration for his second MVP. How many other 30-homer men set fielding records?

But if you're looking for the biggest day-to-day improvement over the 1988 Cubs, try shortstop Shawon Dunston (.278, 9, 60). He always had great talent; you just couldn't depend on him using all of it. Great one day, less than adequate the next. In 1989 he was a complete player for a complete season. Give an assist to Manager Zim, who cajoled, criticized, and cheered Shawon into being the player he should be.

Zimmer also deserves credit for bringing along his other young players, keeping his veterans motivated, and juggling a thin pitching staff. "Genius" still seems a bit highfalutin, but it's hard to find a better managerial performance in 1989.

So the Boys of Zimmer won, and their NLCS loss to the Giants hardly tarnished a wonderful season.

When Chicago won the division in 1984, Jim Frey was manager and Zimmer was his third base coach. In the interim, they were fired and rehired at better jobs. Sooner or later, good things come to those who deserve them. Ask any Cubs fan.

National League West

After Pete Rose (admittedly, a long way after), the biggest story in the National League's Western Division was the emergence of San Francisco's Kevin Mitchell as the Slugger of the Year. Mitchell had been dangerous with a bat in his hands for a couple of seasons, but in 1989 he reached the heights: newspaper charts comparing his progress toward Roger Maris' home run record. When he cooled off in the season's second half, they stopped running the charts, but he had built up such a head of steam, he still finished with a .291 batting average, 47 homers, and 125 RBIs.

About the time Mitchell descended to human proportions, Will Clark, the San Fran first baseman, came to the fore. The biggest argument was whether Mitchell was helped most by having Clark hit in front of him, or Clark was helped more by having Mitchell behind him. By season's end, the most serious debate was over which Giant deserved the MVP Award—Mitchell or Clark—but no one doubted that together they made the NL's best one-two punch.

Meanwhile, the Atlanta Braves must be getting downright punchy from finishing last. Once more they won the fewest games of any NL team—63. It's become a ritual, one that most of America can marvel at thanks to Ted Turner's TBS Superstation. If Ted decides to colorize the Braves, he should make their faces red.

The Braves were the only team in baseball to draw fewer than a million—984,930. Sometimes it was so quiet at the stadium you could hear a batting average drop.

Except for Lonnie Smith, Atlanta didn't have much to frighten opposing pitchers. Former MVP Dale Murphy has reached the point where he's just another National League hitter—.228, 20, 84. It was his second consecutive season under .230. Second baseman Jeff Treadway (.277, 8, 40), shortstop Andres Thomas (.213, 13, 57) and third baseman Jeff Blauser (.270, 12, 46) were the rest of the "attack." The catchers—all three of 'em—hit a collective .180 with 34 RBIs.

And you couldn't chalk these marks up to glovemen who were providing sterling defense. The Thomas-Blauser left side of the infield had 50 errors between them.

All the same, take out your microscope and you'll find a silver lining. The Braves actually won nine more games than in the previous year and avoided losing 100. That's progress. And first baseman Gerald Perry will be back whole in 1990 after missing more than half of '89. But the one thing you can hang your hat on is that the young pitchers will get better. John Smoltz (12–11, 2.94), Tom Glavine (14–8, 3.68), Derek Lilliquist (8–10, 3.97), and Pete Smith (5–14, 4.75) make one of the best young rotations in baseball. They finally got some help out of the bullpen late in the year, when lefty Mike Stanton saved 7 in 20 appearances.

Just how much the Pete Rose to-do hurt the Reds is anybody's guess. Cincinnati, favored by many in preseason to win the West, staggered home fifth with only 75 wins, and all that focus on Pete's travails didn't help. Considering the Reds' hospital list, however, the team couldn't have finished much higher.

All Star center fielder Eric Davis (.281, 34, 101) missed time with various leg hurts—something that is almost a given with Davis. When his contract is up next year—or maybe by the time you read this—he'll be out of Riverfront Stadium playing on a home field with God's own grass.

The other Cincy big guns, Paul O'Neill (.276, 15, 74), shortstop Terry Larkin (.342, 4, 36), and third baseman Chris Sabo (.260, 6, 29), were out from a third to a half of the season. Ace Danny Jackson (6–11, 5.60) was operated on twice and wasn't much use in between. Righthander Jose Rijo (7–6, 2.84) got off to a strong start and then he was kayoed for the year. Lesser players had lesser hurts, but it added up. There have been wars with fewer wounded than the Reds' roster.

Some of the rare healthy players were disappointing. Reds' fans kept comparing Nick Esasky's Red Sox stats with those of the first baseman he was traded away for, Todd Benzinger (.245, 17, 76). Closer John Franco got 32 saves but blew several leads and then was surprised when Cincinnati fans booed him. (*Dear John: So it goes.*) Rick Mahler (9–13, 3.83) was finally jerked out of the starting rotation. Tim Leary (8–14, 3.52) stayed in it but couldn't buy a win. Tom Browning (15–12, 3.39) won six straight in August and was named Pitcher of the Month, then lost every start in September and was named mud.

The Reds' most interesting stat: rookie Rolando Roomes had 100 strikeouts in only 315 at bats.

Dodgers Manager Tommy Lasorda went on a well-publicized diet and lost thirty or forty pounds. Writers had a field day relating his weight loss to the Angelenos' dwindling chances in the NL West. The 1989 World Champions plunged to fourth in the division, 77–83. Tommy didn't get dumber as he got thinner; not even Einstein could have found a theory to get the punchless Dodgers back in the race. They were dead last in the majors in scoring runs—30 behind Atlanta.

Inevitably, some of the blame fell on free agents Eddie Murray and Willie Randolph. That was unfair. Murray (.247, 20, 88) wasn't up to the standards he had set in Baltimore, but he was the only power threat Los Angeles could muster most days. Randolph (.282, 2, 36) didn't hit in '89 as well as Steve Sax, the free agent he swapped places with, but Willie never was as good with a bat as Sax. He continued to be better with a glove and his offense wasn't bad. Not by Dodgers' standards.

Everyone else was awful at bat. In the title year, Kirk Gibson, Mike Marshall, and John Shelby drove in 222 runs; in 1989 they knocked home 82. Former MVP Gibson (.213, 9, 28), playing on wheels that Goodyear would condemn, hobbled into only 91 games and was disabled by July 23. Marshall (.260, 11, 42) missed more than 50 games for the third time in four years. He has a bad back. Shelby (.183, 1, 12) had no excuse—he simply had a bad bat.

Cincy's Kal Daniels was brought in on July 18 to provide some punch. He hurt a knee (requiring his fifth operation) and was out for good after August 1.

Through it all, Dodger pitching was as good as ever. Fernando Valenzuela (10–13, 3.43) made a strong comeback, and Tim Belcher (15–12, 2.82) was excellent. Orel Hershiser, everybody's favorite cover boy in '89, was almost as effective as in his Cy Young days, sporting an ERA of 2.31, but finished 15–15. L.A. was shut out in six of his starts; in his last 62 innings, the Dodgers scored 6 runs (that's no typo).

Most up-front quote: "You can't judge your pitching against the Dodgers because those poor guys can't hit." (Whitey Herzog)

With Hershiser getting no support, Houston's Mike Scott took the "best NL starter" title. Scott (20–10, 3.10) was the league's only 20-game winner and was a major factor in the Astros' two-thirds-of-the-season challenge for first. The Houston pennant drive was fitting; they had about two-thirds of a championship team.

Besides Scott, rookie manager Art Howe could call on Jim Deshaies (15–10, 2.91) and, late in the season, young Mark Portugal (7–1, 2.75) for starters. Alas! he could only dream of having Nolan Ryan. The Astros let the strikeout king go as a free agent after 1988, confident he would be replaced by younger, less costly free agents Jim Clancy and Rick Rhoden. Jim and Rick flopped for a combined 9–20.

Also belly-up was second baseman Bill Doran's bat. Always a great gloveman and, to midseason, a dangerous hitter, Doran had an astronomical slump after the All Star Game, powder-puffing a paltry .131 in the season's second half.

Shortstop Rafael Ramirez had some key late-inning hits but a mere .246 over all. He made his usual 30 errors. Death,

taxes, and the hole in Rafael's glove.

Glenn Davis (.269, 34, 89) is one of baseball's best run producers when he has someone to drive in. And two rookies came on strong, catcher Craig Biggio (.257, 13, 60)—a so-so thrower but otherwise okay behind the plate—and third baseman Ken Caminiti (.255, 10, 72), a hard-nosed type.

Outfielder Eric Anthony hit only .180 in a brief, 25-game look-in, but some people are already penciling him in as 1990 Rookie of the Year. How quickly we forget Gregg Jefferies and Gary Sheffield!

San Diego's Jack McKeon—"Trader Jack"—went all out to make the Padres pennant contenders. He brought in slugger Jack Clark and lefty Bruce Hurst as free agents for something over 10 million of Joan Kroc's dollars. Do you know how many Big Macs that's going to take? (She does, and that may be part of the reason she's put the Pads up for sale.) After the season began, he swapped disenchanted John Kruk and Randy Ready to Philadelphia for disappointing Chris James, and pried (it wasn't really that hard) Calvin Schiraldi out of Chicago. The newcomers did about as well as could be hoped for, but San Diego still finished second.

Small wonder. In what is becoming a Mission tradition, the Padres treated the season as if it started in August. They dillied and dallied their way to 60–63 and 10 games back before waking up to go 29–10 the rest of the way. For 1990 McKeon will have to convince his players that the games before the All Star break count in the standings, too.

Other than an inability to understand the relationship of the calender to the schedule, the Pads are in pretty good shape. In right field they have the best contact hitter in the National League, Tony Gwynn (.336, 4, 62). Left fielder James (.243, 13, 65) improved a lot as soon as he left Philly. Clark (.242, 26, 94) is an authentic home run threat when he isn't striking out (145 K's last year) or drawing walks (an eye-popping 132). Third baseman Bip Roberts (.301, 3, 25) scored 81 runs but might be better batting second than leading off.

For whatever reason, second baseman Roberto Alomar (.295, 7, 56) forgot how to field for a while. He got over it eventually but finished with 28 errors, eight more than shortstop Gary Templeton (.255, 6, 40). You don't see many teams winning with their second sacker the big error man.

McKeon needs a center fielder. It's dollars to doughnuts that one of two catchers, regular Benito Santiago (.236, 16, 62) or minor league star Sandy Alomar (Roberto's brother), will go for someone to play center, particularly if the guy can lead off.

Hurst (15–11, 2.69) was fine, and retread Ed Whitson (16–11, 2.66) turned out to be the ace, but rookie righthander Andy Benes (6–3, 3.51) was the top starter going down the stretch. The rest of the starters were ordinary, but closer Mark Davis (4–3, 1.85) was sensational. His 44 saves made him only the seventh pitcher ever to top 40. In games or in the whole season, the Padres were at their best at the end.

Because they held first place from mid-June and because they had so much punch in the Mitchell-Clark duo, you might think San Francisco's trip to the title was a waltz. The beat was right—one, two, three, *slide*—because the Giants never knew where their fourth starter was coming from. Once Kelly Downs went down with arm miseries in May, the Giants' rotation never jelled. They could lead off with the ERA leader, ex-reliever Scott Garrelts (14–5, 2.28), who became effective after he stopped trying to throw every pitch at Mach

1. They could follow with 40-year-old Rick Reuschel (17–8, 2.94) whose fastball will bend most cobwebs. And they could trot out Don Robinson (12–11, 3.43), who was always willing and often able. But the next starter was whatever number came up in the pool—if he wasn't already in the hospital. Manager Roger Craig kept looking all season for a fourth pitcher who could do five innings until he could bring on the bullpen—Craig Lefferts, Mike LaCoss, or Steve Bedrosian.

He never found him, but Craig's brigade finished third in league ERA even though they were last in strikeouts. Only Garrelts (119) and Reuschel (111) topped the century mark.

For all the kudos due Mitchell-Clark, they got a lot of help from the first and second spots in the batting order. Center fielder Brett Butler (.283, 4, 36) scored 100 runs; second baseman Robby Thompson (.241, 13, 50) scored 91. And, just when they needed a power surge, third baseman Matt Williams came up from the minors to pop 18 homers and bat in 50 runs in just over 200 at bats.

On the other hand, the bottom part of the batting order was kind of puny. And Craig's search for a right fielder who could hit and/or field was as fruitful as his hunt for a fourth starter.

The Giants were like the little girl with the curl. But if part of their lineup and part of their pitching staff was horrid, the other part was very, very, *very* good.

League of Dreams

Easily the most exciting new development in baseball for the dyed (gray) in the wool (shawl) baseballer came on November 1 in Florida when the Senior Professional Baseball Association opened its first season. Loosely inspired by the success of the Men's Senior Golf Tour, the SPBA was developed as a 35-or-older (catchers can be as "young" as 32) baseball league. Despite a potbelly full of Geritol jokes, it promised serious baseball by players just past their major league prime—a curtain call for former fan favorites.

The idea for the league came to Jim Morley, a Denver real estate man (but *once* a minor league outfielder) while he sat on the beach in Australia. He reasoned that there were scads of overage former major leaguers who had not gotten baseball out of their systems and who would jump (although not as high as they once could) at the chance to play competitively again. He knew there would be jokes about every day being an Old-timers' Game, but that was exactly what he *didn't* want—none of this huff-and-puff-through-three-innings-of-laughs stuff. Morley wanted real baseball—not on a major league level, admittedly, but certainly on the plane of a high minor league. What was lost in eroded skills could be made up in nostalgia, he figured, if the baseball itself was worth seeing. He contacted the Major League Players Association and the Baseball Alumni Team, and received advice and encouragement.

Morley sent out postcard queries to 1250 former players, focusing on those who had entered the majors between 1969 and 1977. Eventually he got back over 700 letters of interest. Hope springs eternal . . .

Because the league's season would be played during the winter and rental on indoor stadiums was out of the question, the SPBA was by necessity confined to the South. Florida was ideal—not only for climate and a growing population, but also for the availability of cozy spring training ballparks that would let fans sit practically next to their heroes of yesteryear.

For league commissioner Morley enlisted Curt Flood, the former Cardinals' outfielder whose suit against major league baseball in the 1970s was instrumental in destroying the once sacrosanct reserve clause. The commish—a hero to many players today as well as one to any fan around in the 1960s—helped give the SPBA legitimacy. Flood admitted he was tempted to try a comeback himself at 51. "The top of my body wants to play, but my wheels aren't up to it."

Finding backers for his proposed eight-team league was the next step for Morley. Franchises were pegged at about $850,000. However, Morley and Flood were not simply looking for the biggest bucks or the biggest risk-takers. From the start, they insisted that their owners be "hands-on" types who would work to involve their communities in the new enterprises. A per-player salary cap of no more than $15,000 per month ($7,000 was the average) helped convince potential team owners that the proposition was fiscally viable. Additionally, the $550,000 limit that a team could spend on salaries helped assure a competition based on baseball "smarts" rather than heavy spending. Eventually, teams were established in eight Florida cities: the Bradenton Explorers, Gold Coast Suns (in Pompano Beach), Ft. Myers Sun Sox, St. Lucie Legends, Orlando Juice, St. Petersburg Pelicans, West Palm Beach Tropics, and Winter Haven Super Sox. Morley himself owned the St. Petersburg franchise.

The SPBA later signed a modest cable television contract with the Prime Sports Network for Friday night and Sunday morning telecasts. The season of 72 games was scheduled from November to January 31. Estimates were that teams would have to average about 2,000 attendance per game to break even.

In August and September of 1989, while the "junior" major league competition was boiling down to the Cubs, Giants, Blue Jays, and A's, SPBA general managers lent a Rotisserie League aura to their new toy by divvying up the ripe talent through a draft and trades. Perhaps the most bizarre trade in baseball history saw Luis Tiant swapped for a load of teddy bears (plus the rights to Ralph Garr).

Such successful former major league managers as Dick Williams and Earl Weaver came aboard. Among the "names" in the league were Ferguson Jenkins, Amos Otis, Bill Madlock, Steve Kemp, and Hal McRae.

Why did they risk embarrassment (and coronaries) to play a game supposedly designed for kids?

Health. Bill "Spaceman" Lee, who later became the first SPBA manager to be fired when his team limped off to a 1–6 start, insisted, "We're saving lives and lowering insurance premiums. There are guys here who would have been dead in ten years, and we're adding fifteen years to their lives." Bernie Carbo points out, "I was up to 228 and my blood pressure was way too high. When I heard about this league I got down to 196 and now my blood pressure is 120 over 82."

Hope. A few, like 35-year-old slugger Steve Kemp, still harbor dreams of returning to the majors.

But the most important reason these "Boys of Winter" joined the SPBA was expressed by Graig Nettles: "Hell, if I can stay in baseball, I may never have to grow up."

And isn't that what loving baseball is all about? In this scandalous, tragic, exciting season, the fading fields of summer turn, as they do year after year, to the green fields of the mind, where we are forever young.

Team and League Abbreviations

The National League is abbreviated in this book as N or NL, while the American League is termed A or AL. The team abbreviations are:

Abbrev	Team	Abbrev	Team
ATL N	Atlanta	BAL A	Baltimore
CHI N	Chicago	BOS A	Boston
CIN N	Cincinnati	CAL A	California
HOU N	Houston	CHI A	Chicago
LA N	Los Angeles	CLE A	Cleveland
MON N	Montreal	DET A	Detroit
NY N	New York	KC A	Kansas City
PHI N	Philadelphia	MIL A	Milwaukee
PIT N	Pittsburgh	MIN A	Minnesota
STL N	St. Louis	NY A	New York
SD N	San Diego	OAK A	Oakland
SF N	San Francisco	SEA A	Seattle
		TEX A	Texas
		TOR A	Toronto

Symbols

*   Indicates playing manager; for vital statistics, consult the player or pitcher register

▲   Tied for first place, involved in league or division playoff

●   Tied for position in standings

◆   League Championship Series win

★   World Series win

National League Championship Series

The Giants' Will Clark earned the NL Championship Series MVP. He didn't have the speed dimension of his AL counterpart, Rickey Henderson. Actually "Will the Thrill," no dash man to start with, limped through the series on a bad wheel. No stolen bases for him. All Clark did was hit. And hit. And hit. He finished with a .650 batting average, a 1.200 slugging average, 2 homers, 8 RBIs, and 8 runs scored. The Cubs' Mark Grace ran a close second with .647 and 8 RBIs, but he didn't have the supporting cast Clark did.

In Game One at Wrigley Field, Clark's first series homer helped put the Giants in front 4–3 in the fourth when Will came up with the bases loaded and two out. Don Zimmer elected to let struggling starter Greg Maddux pitch to Clark. Boom! Grand slam. Scott Garrelts took it from there. *San Francisco 11, Chicago 3.*

The Giants hit four homers in the second game, two by Kevin Mitchell, but the Cubs used lesser hits to jump all over Rick Reuschel for six first inning runs. Chicago starter Mike Bielecki didn't last five innings, so the win went to Les Lancaster in relief. *Chicago 9, San Francisco 5.*

The series moved to Candlestick. Chicago scored two in the first, but the Giants scored three. The Cubs were back in front, 4–3, in the seventh when Zim brought in Lancaster with a 1–0 count on Robby Thompson and Brett Butler on base. Many wondered why he didn't call in Wild Thing Williams, especially after Thompson homered. *San Francisco 5, Chicago 4.*

Clark had three hits in Game Four, scored twice and had a takeout slide that broke up a double play and created a run. But the hero of the day was third baseman Matt Williams. In the fifth, with the score tied, he battled Cubs reliever Steve Wilson through eleven pitches and then smacked the next one into the stands for a game-winning two-run homer. *San Francisco 6, Chicago 4.*

Reuschel and Bielecki locked up in a pitcher's duel for the final game. The Cubs got a run in the third, but the Giants evened it up in the seventh as Bielecki began to slip. Mike got two out in the eighth before he crashed and walked three in a row. Zimmer called in the left-handed Williams to face the left-handed Clark in the confrontation of the series. The count was 1–2 when Clark wrapped up his MVP award with a two-run single to center. The Cubs battled back in the ninth. After the first two men

San Francisco Giants (West), 4
Chicago Cubs (East), 1

SF (W)

PLAYER/POS	AVG	G	AB	R	H	2B	3B	HR	RB	BB	SO	SB
Bill Bathe, ph	.000	2	1	0	0	0	0	0	0	0	1	0
Steve Bedrosian, p	.000	4	0	0	0	0	0	0	0	0	0	0
Jeff Brantley, p	.000	3	0	0	0	0	0	0	0	1	0	0
Brett Butler, of	.211	5	19	6	4	0	0	0	0	3	3	0
Will Clark, 1b	.650	5	20	8	13	3	1	2	8	2	2	0
Kelly Downs, p	.000	2	3	0	0	0	0	0	0	0	1	0
Scott Garrelts, p	.000	2	4	0	0	0	0	0	0	1	1	0
Atlee Hammaker, p	.000	1	0	0	0	0	0	0	0	0	0	0
Terry Kennedy, c	.188	5	16	0	3	1	0	0	0	1	4	0
Mike LaCoss, p	.000	1	1	0	0	0	0	0	0	0	0	0
Craig Lefferts, p	.000	2	0	0	0	0	0	0	0	0	0	0
Greg Litton, 3b	1.000	1	1	0	1	0	0	0	0	0	0	0
Candy Maldonado, of	.000	3	3	1	0	0	0	0	0	1	2	0
Kirt Manwaring, c	.000	3	2	0	0	0	0	0	0	0	0	0
Kevin Mitchell, of	.353	5	17	5	6	0	0	2	7	3	3	0
Donell Nixon, of-2	.000	3	3	0	0	0	0	0	0	0	1	1
Ken Oberkfell, 3b-1	.000	3	4	0	0	0	0	0	0	0	0	0
Rick Reuschel, p	.000	2	2	0	0	0	0	0	0	0	0	0
Ernie Riles, ph	.000	1	1	0	0	0	0	0	0	0	0	0
Don Robinson, p	.000	1	0	0	0	0	0	0	0	0	0	0
Pat Sheridan, of	.154	5	13	1	2	0	1	0	0	0	4	0
Robby Thompson, 2b	.278	5	18	5	5	0	0	2	3	3	2	0
Jose Uribe, ss	.235	5	17	2	4	1	0	0	1	1	5	1
Matt Williams, 3b-5,ss-1	.300	5	20	2	6	1	0	2	9	0	2	0
TOTAL	.267		165	30	44	6	2	8	29	17	29	2

PITCHER	W	L	ERA	G	GS	CG	SV	SHO	IP	H	ER	BB	SO
Steve Bedrosian	0	0	2.70	4	0	0	3	0	3.1	4	1	2	2
Jeff Brantley	0	0	0.00	3	0	0	0	0	5.0	1	0	2	3
Kelly Downs	1	0	3.12	2	0	0	0	0	8.2	8	3	6	6
Scott Garrelts	1	0	5.40	2	2	0	0	0	11.2	16	7	2	8
Atlee Hammaker	0	0	0.00	1	0	0	0	0	1.0	1	0	0	0
Mike LaCoss	0	0	9.00	1	1	0	0	0	3.0	7	3	0	2
Craig Lefferts	0	0	9.00	2	0	0	0	0	1.0	1	1	2	1
Rick Reuschel	1	1	5.19	2	2	0	0	0	8.2	12	5	2	5
Don Robinson	1	0	0.00	1	0	0	0	0	1.2	3	0	0	0
TOTAL	4	1	4.09	18	5	9	3	0	44.0	53	20	16	27

CHI (E)

PLAYER/POS	AVG	G	AB	R	H	2B	3B	HR	RB	BB	SO	SB
Paul Assenmacher, p	.000	2	0	0	0	0	0	0	0	0	0	0
Mike Bielecki, p	.200	2	5	0	1	0	0	0	2	0	2	0
Andre Dawson, of	.105	5	19	0	2	1	0	0	3	2	6	0
Shawon Dunston, ss	.316	5	19	2	6	0	0	0	0	1	1	0
Joe Girardi, c	.100	4	10	1	1	0	0	0	0	1	2	0
Mark Grace, 1b	.647	5	17	3	11	3	1	1	8	4	1	1
Paul Kilgus, p	.000	1	0	0	0	0	0	0	0	0	0	0
Lester Lancaster, p	.000	3	1	0	0	0	0	0	0	0	1	0
Vance Law, 3b-1	.000	2	3	0	0	0	0	0	0	0	3	0
Greg Maddux, p-2	.000	3	3	1	0	0	0	0	0	0	0	0
Lloyd McClendon, c-2,of-1	.667	3	3	0	2	0	0	0	0	1	0	0
Domingo Ramos, ph	.000	1	1	0	0	0	0	0	0	0	0	0
Luis Salazar, 3b	.368	5	19	2	7	0	1	1	2	0	0	0
Ryne Sandberg, 2b	.400	5	20	6	8	3	1	1	4	3	4	0
Scott Sanderson, p	.000	1	0	0	0	0	0	0	0	0	0	0
Dwight Smith, of	.200	4	15	2	3	1	0	0	0	2	2	1
Rick Sutcliffe, p	.500	1	2	0	1	1	0	0	0	0	0	0
Jerome Walton, of	.364	5	22	4	8	0	0	0	0	2	2	0
Mitch Webster, of-2	.333	3	3	0	1	0	0	0	0	0	0	0
Curtis Wilkerson, 3b-1	.500	2	2	1	1	0	0	0	0	0	0	0
Mitch Williams, p	.000	2	0	0	0	0	0	0	0	0	0	0
Steve Wilson, p	.000	2	0	0	0	0	0	0	0	0	0	0
Rick Wrona, c	.000	2	5	0	0	0	0	0	0	0	3	0
Marvell Wynne, of-2	.167	4	6	0	1	0	0	0	0	0	0	0
TOTAL	.303		175	22	53	9	3	3	21	16	27	3

PITCHER	W	L	ERA	G	GS	CG	SV	SHO	IP	H	ER	BB	SO
P. Assenmacher	0	0	13.50	2	0	0	0	0	0.2	3	1	0	0
Mike Bielecki	0	1	3.65	2	2	0	0	0	12.1	7	5	6	11
Paul Kilgus	0	0	0.00	1	0	0	0	0	3.0	4	0	1	1
Lester Lancaster	1	1	6.00	3	0	0	0	0	6.0	6	4	1	3
Greg Maddux	0	1	13.50	2	2	0	0	0	7.1	13	11	4	5
Scott Sanderson	0	0	0.00	1	0	0	0	0	2.0	2	0	0	1
Rick Sutcliffe	0	1	4.50	1	1	0	0	0	6.0	5	3	4	2
Mitch Williams	0	0	0.00	2	0	0	0	0	1.0	1	0	0	2
Steve Wilson	0	0	4.91	2	0	0	0	0	3.2	3	2	1	4
TOTAL	1	4	5.57	16	5	0	0	0	42.0	44	26	17	29

went out meekly, they tallied a run and placed two men on before Steve Bedrosian induced Ryne Sandberg to ground out. *San Francisco 3, Chicago 2.*

San Francisco's victory set up the first all-Bay Area World Series.

GAME 1 AT CHI OCT 4

SF	301	400	030	11	13	0
CHI	201	000	000	3	10	1

Pitchers: GARRELTS, Brantley (8), Hammaker (9) vs MADDUX, Kilgus (5), Wilson (8)
Home Runs: Grace-CHI, Clark-SF (2), Sandberg-CHI, Mitchell-SF
Attendance: 39,195

GAME 2 AT CHI OCT 5

SF	000	200	021	5	10	0
CHI	600	003	00X	9	11	0

Pitchers: REUSCHEL, Downs (1), Lefferts (6), Brantley (7), Bedrosian (8) vs Bielecki, Assenmacher (5), LANCASTER (6)
Home Runs: Mitchell-SF, Williams-SF, Thompson-SF
Attendance: 39,195

GAME 3 AT SF OCT 7

CHI	200	100	100	4	10	0
SF	300	000	20X	5	8	3

Pitchers: Sutcliffe, Assenmacher (7), LANCASTER (7) vs LaCoss, Brantley (4), ROBINSON (7), Lefferts (8), Bedrosian (9)
Home Runs: Thompson-SF
Attendance: 62,065

GAME 4 AT SF OCT 8

CHI	110	020	000	4	12	1
SF	102	120	00X	6	9	1

Pitchers: Maddux, WILSON (4), Sanderson (6), Williams (8) vs Garrelts, DOWNS (5), Bedrosian (9)
Home Runs: Salazar-CHI, Williams-SF
Attendance: 62,078

GAME 5 AT SF OCT 9

CHI	001	000	001	2	10	1
SF	000	000	12X	3	4	1

Pitchers: BIELECKI, Williams (8), Lancaster (8) vs REUSCHEL, Bedrosian (9)
Attendance: 62,084

American League Championship Series

The American League season-ender turned out to be a special edition of The Rickey Henderson Show. He won the ALCS Most Valuable Player Award hands down, as the Athletics bested the Blue Jays in four out of five. While the Oakland left fielder left no doubt who was the star of the show, there were still plenty of meaty roles available to the supporting players.

The Athletics' 20-game winner Dave Stewart was a little rocky early in the opener at Oakland. He trailed 3–2 after five and a half. Then Henderson turned the game around—while being put out! His slide into Toronto second baseman Nelson Liriano broke up a double play and caused a wild throw that allowed two runs to score, putting the A's out front. Once in the lead, Stewart pitched two more shutout innings and then handed over to Dennis Eckersley for the *coup de grace. Oakland 7, Toronto 3.*

The next day, Henderson had two hits, reached base four times, stole four bases, and scored twice. Mike Moore had a three-hitter through seven. Reliever Rick Honeycutt showed the Jays a little light at the end of the tunnel, but The Eck came in to slam the door. *Oakland 6, Toronto 3.*

The LCS moved to Toronto and the Blue Jays won their only game, as Jimmy Key (with help from Jim Acker and Tom Henke) bested Storm Davis. Tony Fernandez had a pair of doubles for the Jays and scored the go-ahead run in a four-run fourth. Henderson stole two more bases and his speed led to two of Oakland's three runs. *Toronto 7, Oakland 3.*

Rickey stole no bases in Game Four, eschewing speed for power. He drove in four runs on two homers. Jose Canseco hit a monster into the fourth row of the fifth tier of the Sky Dome, a five dollar cab ride. Oakland needed them all. Bob Welch pitched into the sixth inning but was only so-so. Honeycutt was ineffective for the third straight time as Toronto closed to within a run in the eighth. Then Eckersley came in to put a stop to that nonsense. *Oakland 6, Toronto 5.*

He was back to speed in the finale. His steal of second set up a first-inning run. In the third, he tripled home the second A's run. Dave Stewart was in control until the ninth, when he needed the estimable Mr. Eckersley. *Oakland 4, Toronto 3.*

Stewart won two of the five games, and The Eck saved three.

Oakland Athletics (West), 4; Toronto Blue Jays (East), 1

OAK (W)

PLAYER/POS	AVG	G	AB	R	H	2B	3B	HR	RB	BB	SO	SB
Lance Blankenship, 2b	.000	1	0	0	0	0	0	0	0	0	0	0
Jose Canseco, of	.294	5	17	1	5	0	0	1	3	3	7	0
Storm Davis, p	.000	1	0	0	0	0	0	0	0	0	0	0
Dennis Eckersley, p	.000	4	0	0	0	0	0	0	0	0	0	0
Mike Gallego, 2b-2,ss-2	.273	4	11	3	3	1	0	0	1	0	2	0
Ron Hassey, c	.167	2	6	0	1	0	0	0	1	1	2	0
Dave Henderson, of	.263	5	19	4	5	3	0	1	1	2	5	0
Rickey Henderson, of	.400	5	15	8	6	1	1	2	5	7	0	8
Rick Honeycutt, p	.000	3	0	0	0	0	0	0	0	0	0	0
Stan Javier, of	.000	1	2	0	0	0	0	0	0	0	1	0
Carney Lansford, 3b	.455	3	11	2	5	0	0	0	4	2	1	2
Mark McGwire, 1b	.389	5	18	3	7	1	0	1	3	1	4	0
Mike Moore, p	.000	1	0	0	0	0	0	0	0	0	0	0
Gene Nelson, p	.000	1	0	0	0	0	0	0	0	0	0	0
Dave Parker, dh	.188	4	16	2	3	0	0	2	3	0	0	0
Ken Phelps, ph	1.000	1	1	0	1	1	0	0	0	0	0	0
Tony Phillips, 2b-3,3b-3	.167	5	18	1	3	1	0	0	1	2	4	2
Terry Steinbach, c-3,dh-1	.200	4	15	0	3	0	0	0	1	1	5	0
Dave Stewart, p	.000	2	0	0	0	0	0	0	0	0	0	0
Walt Weiss, ss	.111	4	9	2	1	1	0	0	0	1	1	1
Bob Welch, p	.000	1	0	0	0	0	0	0	0	0	0	0
Matt Young, p	.000	1	0	0	0	0	0	0	0	0	0	0
TOTAL	.272		158	26	43	9	1	7	23	20	32	13

PITCHER	W	L	ERA	G	GS	CG	SV	SHO	IP	H	ER	BB	SO
Storm Davis	0	1	7.11	1	1	0	0	0	6.1	5	5	2	3
Dennis Eckersley	0	0	1.59	4	0	0	3	0	5.2	4	1	0	2
Rick Honeycutt	0	0	32.40	3	0	0	0	0	1.2	6	6	5	1
Mike Moore	1	0	0.00	1	1	0	0	0	7.0	3	0	2	3
Gene Nelson	0	0	0.00	1	0	0	0	0	1.1	1	0	0	2
Dave Stewart	2	0	2.81	2	2	0	0	0	16.0	13	5	3	9
Bob Welch	1	0	3.18	1	1	0	0	0	5.2	8	2	1	4
Matt Young	0	0	0.00	1	0	0	0	0	0.1	0	0	2	0
TOTAL	4	1	3.89	14	5	0	3	0	44.0	40	19	15	24

TOR (E)

PLAYER/POS	AVG	G	AB	R	H	2B	3B	HR	RB	BB	SO	SB
Jim Acker, p	.000	5	0	0	0	0	0	0	0	0	0	0
George Bell, dh-3,of-2	.200	5	20	2	4	0	0	1	2	0	3	0
Pat Borders, c	1.000	1	1	0	1	0	0	0	1	0	0	0
John Cerutti, p	.000	2	0	0	0	0	0	0	0	0	0	0
Junior Felix, of	.273	3	11	3	3	1	0	0	3	0	2	0
Tony Fernandez, ss	.350	5	20	6	7	3	0	0	1	1	2	5
Mike Flanagan, p	.000	1	0	0	0	0	0	0	0	0	0	0
Kelly Gruber, 3b	.294	5	17	2	5	1	0	0	1	3	2	1
Tom Henke, p	.000	3	0	0	0	0	0	0	0	0	0	0
Jimmy Key, p	.000	1	0	0	0	0	0	0	0	0	0	0
Manny Lee, 2b	.250	2	8	2	2	0	0	0	0	0	1	0
Nelson Liriano, 2b	.429	3	7	1	3	0	0	0	1	2	0	3
Lee Mazzilli, dh-2	.000	3	8	0	0	0	0	0	0	0	2	0
Fred McGriff, 1b	.143	5	21	1	3	0	0	0	3	0	4	0
Lloyd Moseby, of	.313	5	16	4	5	0	0	1	2	5	2	1
Rance Mulliniks, ph	.000	1	1	0	0	0	0	0	0	0	1	0
Dave Stieb, p	.000	2	0	0	0	0	0	0	0	0	0	0
Todd Stottlemyre, p	.000	1	0	0	0	0	0	0	0	0	0	0
Duane Ward, p	.000	2	0	0	0	0	0	0	0	0	0	0
David Wells, p	.000	1	0	0	0	0	0	0	0	0	0	0
Ernie Whitt, c	.125	5	16	1	2	0	0	1	3	2	3	0
Mookie Wilson, of	.263	5	19	2	5	0	0	0	2	2	2	1
TOTAL	.242		165	21	40	5	0	3	19	15	24	11

PITCHER	W	L	ERA	G	GS	CG	SV	SHO	IP	H	ER	BB	SO
Jim Acker	0	0	1.42	5	0	0	0	0	6.1	4	1	1	4
John Cerutti	0	0	0.00	2	0	0	0	0	2.2	0	0	3	1
Mike Flanagan	0	1	10.38	1	1	0	0	0	4.1	7	5	1	3
Tom Henke	0	0	0.00	3	0	0	0	0	2.2	0	0	0	3
Jimmy Key	1	0	4.50	1	1	0	0	0	6.0	7	3	2	2
Dave Stieb	0	2	6.35	2	2	0	0	0	11.1	12	8	6	10
Todd Stottlemyre	0	1	7.20	1	1	0	0	0	5.0	7	4	2	3
Duane Ward	0	0	7.36	2	0	0	0	0	3.2	6	3	5	5
David Wells	0	0	0.00	1	0	0	0	0	1.0	0	0	2	1
TOTAL	1	4	5.02	18	5	0	0	0	43.0	43	24	20	32

Dave Parker had a pair of homers, and Carney Lansford hit .455. They all took a back seat to Henderson, who set a postseason record with 8 stolen bases. He also scored 8 runs and drove in 5, batted .400, had an on base percentage of .609, and a slugging percentage of 1.000!

Oh, he made one error. So much for perfection.

GAME 1 AT OAK OCT 3

| TOR | 020 100 000 | 3 5 1 |
| **OAK** | 010 013 02X | 7 11 0 |

Pitchers: STIEB, Acker (6), Ward (8) vs STEWART, Eckersley (9)
Home Runs: D.Henderson-OAK, Whitt-TOR, McGwire-OAK
Attendance: 49,435

GAME 2 AT OAK OCT 4

| TOR | 001 000 020 | 3 5 1 |
| **OAK** | 000 203 10X | 6 9 1 |

Pitchers: STOTTLEMYRE, Acker (6), Wells (6), Henke (7), Cerutti (8) vs MOORE, Honeycutt (8), Eckersley (8)
Home Runs: Parker-OAK
Attendance: 49,444

GAME 3 AT TOR OCT 6

| OAK | 101 100 000 | 3 8 1 |
| **TOR** | 000 400 30X | 7 8 0 |

Pitchers: DAVIS, Honeycutt (7), Nelson (7), M.Young (8) vs KEY, Acker (7), Henke (9)
Home Runs: Parker-OAK
Attendance: 50,268

GAME 4 AT TOR OCT 7

| **OAK** | 003 020 100 | 6 11 1 |
| TOR | 000 101 120 | 5 13 0 |

Pitchers: WELCH, Honeycutt (6), Eckersley (8) vs FLANAGAN, Ward (5), Cerutti (8), Acker (9)
Home Runs: R.Henderson-OAK (2), Canseco-OAK
Attendance: 50,076

GAME 5 AT TOR OCT 8

| **OAK** | 101 000 200 | 4 4 0 |
| TOR | 000 000 012 | 3 9 0 |

Pitchers: STEWART, Eckersley (9) vs STIEB, Acker (7), Henke (9)
Home Runs: Moseby-TOR, Bell-TOR
Attendance: 50,024

The Longest Short World Series

The 1989 World Series will go down in history as one of baseball's most famous, but not because of anything the players did on the field. The 7.0 earthquake that struck just before the scheduled start of Game Three rendered the world championship of baseball insignificant next to the greater questions of life and death. The Giants-Athletics series that had been touted as a celebration of the San Francisco Bay area became instead a symbol—first of a community's reordering of priorities in time of disaster, then of controversy over whether games should continue in the face of crisis, and finally of hope that life can and will return to normal.

Except for the earthquake, the Series itself was one of the least memorable in drama, tension, or competitive balance. The Athletics sweep was complete, utter, consummate, and absolute. The Giants were not only unable to win a game, they never at any time *led* in a game.

Perhaps the 1989 World Series was decided in October 1988, when the favored Athletics lost to the Dodgers. Embarrassed by their loss to a manifestly less talented team, the A's determined to go all the way in '89. They survived several serious injuries to win their division, roared through the LCS, and entered the World Series on a mission.

The Giants, on the other hand, played as though they were simply happy to be there.

But for those who disdain psychological rationalizations, a simpler explanation is available. The Oakland club had better fielding and hitting, and far better pitching. In retrospect, only an Act of God could have stopped the Athletics, yet, ironically, even the tragic earthquake worked in their favor.

The Series opened at the Oakland Coliseum before 49,385 on Saturday evening, October 16, with the NL's ERA leader Scott Garrelts pitching for the Giants and the A's countering with 21-game winner Dave Stewart. Oakland took control in the second inning, sending eight men to the plate and scoring three runs. To all intents and purposes, the game was over. Dave Parker and Walt Weiss hit later solo homers, but the additions were merely cosmetic. Stewart, pitching probably his best game of the season, scattered five hits and one walk to shut out San Francisco. Only in the ninth, when Will Clark and Kevin

Oakland Athletics (NL), 4; San Francisco Giants (AL), 0

OAK (A)

PLAYER/POS	AVG	G	AB	R	H	2B	3B	HR	RB	BB	SO	SB
Lance Blankenship, 2b	.500	1	2	1	1	0	0	0	0	0	0	0
Todd Burns, p	.000	2	0	0	0	0	0	0	0	0	0	0
Jose Canseco, of	.357	4	14	5	5	0	0	1	3	4	3	1
Dennis Eckersley, p	.000	2	0	0	0	0	0	0	0	0	0	0
Mike Gallego, 2b-1,3b-1	.000	2	1	0	0	0	0	0	0	0	0	0
Dave Henderson, of	.308	4	13	6	4	2	0	2	4	4	3	0
Rickey Henderson, of	.474	4	19	4	9	1	2	1	3	2	2	3
Rick Honeycutt, p	.000	3	0	0	0	0	0	0	0	0	0	0
Stan Javier, of	.000	1	0	0	0	0	0	0	0	0	0	0
Carney Lansford, 3b	.438	4	16	5	7	1	0	1	4	3	1	0
Mark McGwire, 1b	.294	4	17	0	5	1	0	0	1	1	3	0
Mike Moore, p	.333	2	3	1	1	1	0	0	2	0	1	0
Gene Nelson, p	.000	2	0	0	0	0	0	0	0	0	0	0
Dave Parker, dh-2	.222	3	9	2	2	1	0	1	2	0	2	0
Ken Phelps, ph	.000	1	1	0	0	0	0	0	0	0	0	0
Tony Phillips, 2b-3,3b-2,of-1	.235	4	17	2	4	1	0	1	3	0	3	0
Terry Steinbach, c	.250	4	16	3	4	0	1	1	7	2	1	0
Dave Stewart, p	.000	2	3	0	0	0	0	0	0	0	1	0
Walt Weiss, ss	.133	4	15	3	2	0	0	1	1	2	2	0
TOTAL	.301		146	32	44	8	3	9	30	18	22	4

PITCHER	W	L	ERA	G	GS	CG	SV	SHO	IP	H	ER	BB	SO
Todd Burns	0	0	0.00	2	0	0	0	0	1.2	1	0	1	0
Dennis Eckersley	0	0	0.00	2	0	0	1	0	1.2	0	0	0	0
Rick Honeycutt	0	0	6.75	3	0	0	0	0	2.2	4	2	0	2
Mike Moore	2	0	2.08	2	2	0	0	0	13.0	9	3	3	10
Gene Nelson	0	0	54.00	2	0	0	0	0	1.0	4	6	2	1
Dave Stewart	2	0	1.69	2	2	1	0	1	16.0	10	3	2	14
TOTAL	4	0	3.50	13	4	1	1	1	36.0	28	14	8	27

SF (N)

PLAYER/POS	AVG	G	AB	R	H	2B	3B	HR	RB	BB	SO	SB
Bill Bathe, ph	.500	2	2	1	1	0	0	1	3	0	0	0
Steve Bedrosian, p	.000	2	0	0	0	0	0	0	0	0	0	0
Jeff Brantley, p	.000	3	0	0	0	0	0	0	0	0	0	0
Brett Butler, of	.286	4	14	1	4	1	0	0	1	2	1	2
Will Clark, 1b	.250	4	16	2	4	1	0	0	0	1	3	0
Kelly Downs, p	.000	3	0	0	0	0	0	0	0	0	0	0
Scott Garrelts, p	.000	2	1	0	0	0	0	0	0	0	1	0
Atlee Hammaker, p	.000	2	0	0	0	0	0	0	0	0	0	0
Terry Kennedy, c	.167	4	12	1	2	0	0	0	2	1	3	0
Mike LaCoss, p	.000	2	1	0	0	0	0	0	0	0	0	0
Craig Lefferts, p	.000	3	0	0	0	0	0	0	0	0	0	0
Greg Litton, 2b-2,3b-1	.500	2	6	1	3	1	0	1	3	0	0	0
Candy Maldonado, of-3	.091	4	11	1	1	0	1	0	0	0	4	0
Kirt Manwaring, c	1.000	1	1	1	1	1	0	0	0	0	0	0
Kevin Mitchell, of	.294	4	17	2	5	0	0	1	2	0	3	0
Donell Nixon, of	.200	2	5	1	1	0	0	0	0	1	1	0
Ken Oberkfell, 3b	.333	4	6	1	2	0	0	0	0	3	0	0
Rick Reuschel, p	.000	1	0	0	0	0	0	0	0	0	0	0
Ernie Riles, dh-2	.000	3	8	0	0	0	0	0	0	0	1	0
Don Robinson, p	.000	1	0	0	0	0	0	0	0	0	0	0
Pat Sheridan, of	.000	1	2	0	0	0	0	0	0	0	0	0
Robby Thompson, 2b	.091	4	11	0	1	0	0	0	2	0	4	0
Jose Uribe, ss	.200	3	5	1	1	0	0	0	0	0	0	0
Matt Williams, ss-4,ss-3	.125	4	16	1	2	0	0	1	1	0	6	0
TOTAL	.209		134	14	28	4	1	4	14	8	27	2

PITCHER	W	L	ERA	G	GS	CG	SV	SHO	IP	H	ER	BB	SO
Steve Bedrosian	0	0	0.00	2	0	0	0	0	2.2	0	0	2	2
Jeff Brantley	0	0	4.15	3	0	0	0	0	4.1	5	2	3	1
Kelly Downs	0	0	7.71	3	0	0	0	0	4.2	3	4	2	4
Scott Garrelts	0	2	9.82	2	2	0	0	0	7.1	13	8	1	8
Atlee Hammaker	0	0	15.43	2	0	0	0	0	2.1	8	4	0	2
Mike LaCoss	0	0	6.23	2	0	0	0	0	4.1	4	3	3	2
Craig Lefferts	0	0	3.38	3	0	0	0	0	2.2	2	1	2	1
Rick Reuschel	0	1	11.25	1	1	0	0	0	4.0	5	5	4	2
Don Robinson	0	1	21.60	1	1	0	0	0	1.2	4	4	1	0
TOTAL	0	4	8.21	19	4	0	0	0	34.0	44	31	18	22

Mitchell led off with singles, were the Giants a threat to score. Oakland manager Tony LaRussa bypassed his bullpen and stuck with Stewart, who struck out Matt Williams and Ernest Riles and then induced Candy Maldonado to ground out to third. *Oakland 5, San Francisco 0.*

The next night, three more people showed up at the Coliseum, but none of them brought the Giants new bats. Mike Moore was nearly as dazzling for the A's as Stewart had been, granting four hits and two walks over seven innings. The Athletics got off to a first-inning lead when Rickey Henderson walked, stole second, and scored on Carney Lansford's double. Giants' starter Rick Reuschel escaped without further damage, and in the top of the third, San Francisco scratched out a tying run on Clark's sacrifice fly. The 1–1 score was the Giant's high point of the Series, but it lasted only to the bottom of the fourth. Reuschel walked Jose Canseco, who scored on Parker's

GAME 1 AT OAK OCT 14

SF	000	000	000	0	5	1
OAK	031	100	00X	5	11	1

Pitchers: GARRELTS, Hammaker (5), Brantley (6), LaCoss (8) vs STEWART
Home Runs: Parker-OAK, Weiss-OAK
Attendance: 49,385

GAME 2 AT OAK OCT 15

SF	001	000	000	1	4	0
OAK	100	400	00X	5	7	0

Pitchers: REUSCHEL, Downs (5), Lefferts (7), Bedrosian (8) vs MOORE, Honeycutt (8), Eckersley (9)
Home Runs: Steinbach-OAK
Attendance: 49,388

GAME 3 AT SF OCT 27

OAK	200	241	040	13	14	0
SF	010	200	004	7	10	3

Pitchers: STEWART, Honeycutt (8), Nelson (9), Burns (9) vs GARRELTS, Downs (4), Brantley (5), Hammaker (8), Lefferts (9)
Home Runs: Williams-SF, D.Henderson-OAK (2), Phillips-OAK, Canseco-OAK, Lansford-OAK, Bathe-SF
Attendance: 62,038

GAME 4 AT SF OCT 28

OAK	130	031	010	9	12	0
SF	000	002	400	6	9	0

Pitchers: MOORE, Nelson (7), Honeycutt (7), Burns (7), Eckersley (9) vs ROBINSON, LaCoss (2), Brantley (6), Downs (6), Lefferts (8), Bedrosian (8)
Home Runs: R.Henderson-OAK, Mitchell-SF, Litton-SF
Attendance: 62,032

double to right. Dave Henderson walked, and after Mark McGwire struck out, Terry Steinbach clobbered Reuschel's belt-high delivery into the left field seats. Moore cruised through three more innings, then turned it over to Rick Honeycutt and Dennis Eckersley to mop up. *Oakland 5, San Francisco 1.*

On Tuesday, Game Three was only eleven minutes away when the earthquake struck at 5:04 P.M. Candlestick Park suffered slight damage, but the oft-criticized Giants' home stood fast. The crowd of more than 60,000 filed out, many still in a holiday mood until they learned the extent of the damage.

New Commissioner Fay Vincent, faced with the first major decision of his term, kept baseball in perspective. After conferring with Bay Area officials, he announced that the Series would go on, but only after enough time had elapsed to allow the area's recovery to begin and for any necessary repairs to be made to Candlestick.

A few writers criticized Vincent, insisting that the loss of life and property demanded cancellation of the Series. Significantly, most of the critics were from the east, with no interest in a far-west playoff. A newspaper poll in the Bay Area found that 80 percent of the respondees favored resumption of the games. The fact that football games were played, bars were opened, and even the stage version of *Les Miserables* opened during the interim—all to large crowds—undercut those who lobbied for cancellation. They were left to grumble that it was too late to play baseball and the weather would be terrible.

The weather was perfect when the World Series resumed at Candlestick Park on Friday, October 27, after a delay of ten days. The Bay Area was announcing to the world that it was on its way back. Unfortunately, the same couldn't be said for the Giants. Stewart, making his second start, wasn't up to his Game One performance, but he didn't need to be. The Athletics trashed Garrelts and four other Giants'

pitchers for 14 hits and 13 runs. Dave Henderson cracked a pair of homers and a double for the A's to drive in four runs. Canseco, Lansford, and Tony Phillips also homered for Oakland. San Francisco closed to 4–3 with a pair of runs in the bottom of the fourth, but the Athletics quieted the 62,038 mostly Giants fans with four more runs in the top of the fifth. Stewart had a ten-run lead by the time he turned the game over to the bullpen in the eighth. A four-run rally by San Francisco in the ninth gave the Giants a momentary lift, but the reality was that the A's were poised for a sweep. *Oakland 13, San Francisco 7.*

To make matters worse, Reuschel, who'd been slightly injured in warmups before Game Three, was unable to go in Game Four, forcing Giants' manager Roger Craig to start Don Robinson, coming off a leg injury. Meanwhile, the Athletics had a well-rested Mike Moore, the winner of Game Two.

Robinson lasted an inning and two-thirds. The A's Rickey Henderson led off the game with a home run. Then in the second, Oakland scored three in an inning highlighted by Moore's two-run double, the first World Series hit by an American League pitcher in ten years. The A's stretched their lead to 8–0 before Moore weakened. Two Giants runs in the sixth and four off the relief corps in the seventh had some of the 61,032 fans imagining one of the greatest rallies in Series history. The Giants brought the tying run to the plate but then fell short. The A's tacked on another run in the eighth, but Clark quelled the rally by snatching Phillips' foul fly on a diving catch into the first base seats (and Commissioner Vincent's lap).

Three runs down, the Giants dug in for a last-ditch turnaround. It was not to be. Todd Burns set down San Francisco without incident in the eighth. Eckersley came on in the ninth and got Donnell Nixon and Jose Uribe. Brett Butler cracked one past a diving McGwire but Phillips got to it on the outfield grass

and threw to The Eck. The Athletics were World Champions—*Oakland 9, San Francisco 6.*

Each Athletic took home $159,620.76 for his Series share; the Giants received $119,407.90 per player.

The biggest loser was ABC, as the combination of a one-market Series, the earthquake, and the A's complete dominance saddled the network with the lowest ratings since televising of the Fall Classic began.

Oakland heroes included Steinbach with 7 RBIs; Lansford and Rickey Henderson, who both batted over .400; Dave Henderson with a pair of homers; Phillips, who fielded brilliantly; and Moore, with two winning starts. But Dave Stewart was named the Series Most Valuable Player. A few suggested it was a consolation prize for his being turned aside on three straight Cy Young Award ballots. Such quibbles overlooked the fact that he not only got his team off to a flying start with his Game One shutout but also jump-started his team in Game Three after the delay.

GAME 60
Anaheim Stadium,
Anaheim, California
July 11, 1989
AL, 5–3

NL	200	000	010	3	9	1
AL	212	000	00X	5	12	0

PITCHERS: Reuschel, SMOLTZ (2), Sutcliffe (3), Burke (4), M.Davis (6), Howell (7), Williams (8) VS Stewart, RYAN (2), Gubicza (4), Moore (5), Swindell (6), Russell (7), Plesac (8), Jones (8)
HOME RUNS: Jackson-A, Boggs-A
ATTENDANCE: 64,036

Bo knows the All Star Game.

Bo Jackson, the football star turned outfielder, provided an awesome display of power and speed in leading the American League to a 5–3 win over the National League at Anaheim in the sixtieth All Star Game. After years of losses to the NL, the victory was the AL's third in the last four games and the first back-to-back wins for the junior circuit since 1957–58.

But the game started as another National League walkover. The 64,036 fans were hardly in their seats when the Nationals jumped into the lead. Oakland's Dave Stewart, the AL starter, was lucky to escape with only two runs charged to him after being roughed up for three hits and two walks in the top of the first. Jackson ended the onslaught with a fine running catch of Pedro Guerrero's liner with two men in scoring position.

In the bottom of the first, Jackson changed the momentum with one swing of his bat. AL manager Tony LaRussa, on a suggestion by coach Dave Duncan, had chosen to bat Jackson leadoff in hope that either his speed or his power could get something started. Seldom has an idea worked so well. Bo smashed Rick Reuschel's pitch high and deep to center for a 448-foot home run. Moments later, Wade Boggs smacked another homer, and the game was tied.

Nolan Ryan, back in the American League after nine years in the National, closed down his old league in the second and third innings. When Bo's forceout knocked in Ruben Sierra with the go-ahead run in the bottom of the second, the 42-year-old Ryan became the oldest pitcher ever to get an All Star victory.

After the American League added two more runs off Rick Sutcliffe in the third inning to move to a commanding 5–2 lead, the pitchers took over. Only one run was scored over the last six innings—a cosmetic NL marker in the eighth—as ten pitchers held baseball's greatest hitters to eight hits. Cleveland's Doug Jones, who pitched the last inning and a third, received credit for a save.

Jackson, the game's Most Valuable Player, added a single and a stolen base to his night's work before he was replaced late by Boston's Mike Greenwell, but his statistics were secondary to his impact. His combination of speed and power left the fans in awe. Even his seventh-inning strikeout on three Mark Davis pitches gave them a thrill.

Awards and Honors

Rookie of the Year

National League	1st	2nd	3rd	Total
J. Walton, CHI	22	2	0	116
D. Smith, CHI	2	19	1	68
G. Jeffries, NY	0	1	15	18
D. Lilliquist,ATL	0	1	3	6
A. Benes, SD	0	0	3	3
C. Hayes, PHI	0	1	0	3
G. Harris, SD	0	0	2	2

American League	1st	2nd	3rd	Total
G. Olson, BLT	26	2	0	136
T. Gordon, KC	1	19	5	67
K. Griffey, SEA	1	2	10	21
C. Worthington, BAL	0	4	4	16
J. Abbott, CAL	0	1	7	10
K. Brown, TEX	0	0	2	2

Cy Young

National League	1st	2nd	3rd	Total
M. Davis, SD	19	4	0	107
M. Scott, HOU	4	14	3	65
G. Maddux, CH	0	3	8	17
O. Hershiser, LA	1	0	2	7
J. Magrane, STL	0	1	4	7
T. Belcher, LA	0	1	1	4
S. Garrelts, SF	0	0	4	4
R. Reuschel, SF	0	1	0	3
M. Bielecki, CHI	0	0	1	1
M. Williams, CH	0	0	1	1

American League	1st	2nd	3rd	Total
B. Saberhagen, KC	27	1	0	138
D. Stewart, OAK	1	24	3	80
M. Moore, OAK	0	2	4	10
B. Blyleven, CAL	0	0	9	9
N. Ryan, TEX	0	0	5	5
J. Ballard, BAL	0	1	0	3
D. Eckersley, OAK	0	0	3	3
G. Olson, BAL	0	0	3	3
J. Russell, TEX	0	0	1	1

Most Valuable Player

National League	1st	2nd	3rd	4th	5th	6th	7th	8th	9th	10th	Total
K. Mitchell, SF	20	2	2	0	0	0	0	0	0	0	314
W. Clark, SF	3	15	6	0	0	0	0	0	0	0	225
P. Guerrero, STL	1	4	10	6	3	0	0	0	0	0	190
R. Sandberg, CHI	0	1	4	9	6	2	1	1	0	0	157
H. Johnson, NY	0	2	2	6	8	5	1	0	0	0	153
M. Davis, SD	0	0	0	1	4	5	1	3	3	1	76
G. Davis, HOU	0	0	0	0	0	5	6	2	4	1	64
T. Gwynn, SD	0	0	0	0	1	4	5	3	0	2	57
E. Davis, CIN	0	0	0	0	0	0	5	3	7	1	44
M. Williams, CHI	0	0	0	2	0	2	1	2	2	3	41
L. Smith, ATL	0	0	0	0	1	1	0	2	3	11	34
J. Clark, SD	0	0	0	0	1	0	0	2	1	2	16
J. Walton, CHI	0	0	0	0	0	0	2	1	1	1	14
M. Grace, CHI	0	0	0	0	0	0	2	0	0	1	9
M. Scott, HOU	0	0	0	0	0	0	0	1	1	1	6
B. Bonilla, PIT	0	0	0	0	0	0	0	1	1	0	5
B. Butler, SF	0	0	0	0	0	0	0	1	0	0	3
T. Raines, MON	0	0	0	0	0	0	0	1	0	0	3
M. Thompson, STL	0	0	0	0	0	0	0	1	0	0	3
S. Garrelts, SF	0	0	0	0	0	0	0	0	1	0	2

American League	1st	2nd	3rd	4th	5th	6th	7th	8th	9th	10th	Total
R. Yount, MIL	8	6	5	4	1	1	2	1	0	0	256
R. Sierra, TEX	6	5	4	7	1	0	0	2	1	1	228
C. Ripken, BAL	6	3	3	7	1	4	0	2	0	0	216
G. Bell, TOR	4	1	4	9	2	2	1	0	1	1	205
D. Eckersley, OAK	3	0	1	2	6	1	0	3	1	0	116
F. McGriff. TOR	0	1	0	1	2	6	4	3	5	3	96
K. Puckett, MIN	0	0	3	3	0	2	5	1	3	0	84
B. Saberhagen, KC	0	3	1	1	4	1	0	2	2	1	82
R. Henderson, OAK	0	0	0	1	2	3	8	0	0	1	67
B. Jackson, KC	0	0	0	2	2	2	4	2	1	0	46
D. Parker, OAK	0	0	1	2	3	0	1	0	1	1	44
G. Olson, BAL	0	0	0	0	0	3	1	3	1	5	35
B. Blyleven, CAL	0	0	0	2	1	0	2	3	3	3	32
D. Stewart, OAK	0	0	1	1	1	1	0	0	1	2	30
D. Mattingly, NY	0	0	2	0	0	0	0	1	2	2	25
J. Carter, CLE	0	0	0	1	0	0	3	0	2	0	23
C. Lansford, OAK	1	0	0	0	0	0	0	1	1	1	20
N. Esasky, BOS	0	0	0	0	0	1	0	3	1	3	19
T. Fernandez, TOR	0	1	0	0	0	0	0	0	0	0	9
M. Moore, OAK	0	0	0	0	1	0	0	0	0	0	6
W. Boggs, BOS	0	0	0	0	0	0	0	0	1	1	3
S. Sax, NY	0	0	0	0	0	0	0	1	0	0	3
A. Davis, SEA	0	0	0	0	0	0	0	1	0	0	2
N. Ryan, TEX	0	0	0	0	0	0	0	1	0	0	2
C. Davis, CAL	0	0	0	0	0	0	0	0	1	1	1
M. McGwire, OAK	0	0	0	0	0	0	0	0	0	1	1
M. Wilson, TOR	0	0	0	0	0	0	0	0	1	1	1

1989 Gold Glove Award

National League
1B: Andres Galarraga, Montreal
2B: Ryne Sandberg, Chicago
SS: Ozzie Smith, St. Louis
3B: Terry Pendleton, St. Louis
C: Benito Santiago, San Diego
OF: Andy Van Slyke, Pittsburgh
OF: Eric Davis, Cincinnati
OF: Tony Gwynn, San Diego
P: Ron Darling, New York

American League
1B: Don Mattingly, New York
2B: Harold Reynolds, Seattle
SS: Tony Fernandez, Toronto
3B: Gary Gaetti, Minnesota
C: Bob Boone, Kansas City
OF: Devon White, California
OF: Gary Pettis, Detroit
OF: Kirby Puckett, Minnesota
P: Bret Saberhagen, Kansas City

1989 Hall of Fame Elections

by Bill Deane

To nobody's surprise, former Reds' catcher Johnny Bench and Red Sox outfielder–first baseman Carl Yastrzemski were both elected to the Baseball Hall of Fame in their first tries in 1989, coinciding with the Hall's fiftieth anniversary celebrations. With a record 447 members of the Baseball Writers' Association (BBWAA) voting, Bench was named on 431 ballots, Yaz on 423—the two highest raw totals ever.

Making it to the Hall on one's first try is no longer the rare honor it once was. By now there have been twenty-four rookies elected, including the five original inductees. Nobody made it on his first ballot in the period 1937–61, but nineteen have done so in the past twenty-six elections, including eleven in the past eleven years. The 1990 elections, not yet announced as this book went to press, are likely to have added two more names to this "exclusive list."

What *was* impressive about the 1989 Hall of Fame ballot was the percentage of the vote commanded by Bench (96.4) and Yaz (94.6). Bench's showing ranks third all-time, behind Ty Cobb's (98.2) and Hank Aaron's (97.8), while Yaz stands seventh, behind those three, plus Babe Ruth (95.1), Honus Wagner (95.1), and Willie Mays (94.7).

Other rookies on the ballot in 1989 included Gaylord Perry who, with 304 votes, finished third, 32 votes short of the 75 percent required for induction; Ferguson Jenkins (234 votes), Jim Kaat (87), Bert Campaneris (14), Bobby Murcer (3), Don Money (1), and Gene Tenace (1). The latter four, not having received even 5 percent of the vote, will by the voting rules be dropped from further consideration—as will the eleven newcomers who failed to receive a single vote: Jim Barr, Terry Crowley, Joe Ferguson, Woodie Fryman, Cesar Geronimo, Dave Goltz, Jon Matlack, Rudy May, Bake McBride, Bill Robinson, and Richie Zisk. Frivolous votes seem to be on the decline.

The presence on the ballot of Perry, Jenkins, and Kaat, who combined for 881 pitching victories, severely diminished the support of three other hurlers, who totaled a comparatively modest 660 wins. Jim Bunning, who missed election by just four votes in 1988, dropped down to 63 percent, and his

future prospects look slim. Luis Tiant (named on 31 percent of the 1988 ballots) and Mickey Lolich (26 percent), dropped dramatically to 11 percent apiece.

The eighteen-member Hall of Fame Committee on Baseball Veterans made two mildly surprising choices for enshrinement, selecting former second baseman Red Schoendienst and umpire Al Barlick. The four new inductees brought the total membership of the Hall to 204.

Baseball writers Bob Hunter and the late Ray Kelly were honored with the J. G. Taylor Spink Award, while announcer Harry Caray was given the Ford C. Frick Award. Regardless of what you read and hear elsewhere, recipients of these awards are *not* members of the Baseball Hall of Fame.

Following is the complete roll of vote-getters in the BBWAA election, listed both alphabetically and numerically:

ALPHABETICAL		NUMERICAL	
Dick Allen	35	Johnny Bench	431
Johnny Bench	431	Carl Yastrzemski	423
Bobby Bonds	29	Gaylord Perry	304
Ken Boyer	62	Jim Bunning	283
Jim Bunning	283	Ferguson Jenkins	234
Bert Campaneris	14	Orlando Cepeda	176
Orlando Cepeda	176	Tony Oliva	135
Elroy Face	47	Bill Mazeroski	134
Curt Flood	27	Harvey Kuenn	115
Ferguson Jenkins	234	Maury Wills	95
Jim Kaat	87	Jim Kaat	87
Harvey Kuenn	115	Ron Santo	75
Mickey Lolich	47	Ken Boyer	62
Sparky Lyle	25	Minnie Minoso	59
Bill Mazeroski	134	Elroy Face	47
Minnie Minoso	59	Mickey Lolich	47
Don Money	1	Luis Tiant	47
Manny Mota	9	Joe Torre	40
Thurman Munson	31	Dick Allen	35
Bobby Murcer	3	Vada Pinson	33
Tony Oliva	135	Thurman Munson	31
Gaylord Perry	304	Bobby Bonds	29
Vada Pinson	33	Curt Flood	27
Ron Santo	75	Sparky Lyle	25
Gene Tenace	1	Bert Campaneris	14
Luis Tiant	47	Wilbur Wood	14
Joe Torre	40	Manny Mota	9
Maury Wills	95	Bobby Murcer	3
Wilbur Wood	14	Don Money	1
Carl Yastrzemski	423	Gene Tenace	1

The Annual Record and Player Register

The Player Register contains the most important career batting, baserunning, and fielding statistics of every man who played a major league game in 1989, excepting those who were primarily pitchers. The players are listed alphabetically by surname and, when more than one player bears the name, alphabetically by *given* name, not by "use name." Each page of the Player Register is topped at the corner by a finding aid: in capital letters, the surname of, first, the player whose entry heads up the page and, second, the player whose entry concludes it. Another finding aid is the use of boldface numerals to indicate a league-leading total in those categories in which a player is truly attempting to excel (no boldface is given to the "leaders" in batter strikeouts, times caught stealing, at bats, or games played).

The record for a man who played in more than one season is given in a line for each season, plus a career total line. If he played for more than one team in a given year, his totals for each team are stated on separate lines. And if the teams for which he played in his "traded year" are in the same league, then his full record is stated in both separate and combined fashion.

For a key to the team and league abbreviations used in the Player Register, flip back to page 19 of this volume.

Looking at the biographical line for any player, we see first his use name in full capitals, then his given name and nickname (and any other name he may have used or been born with, such as the matronymic of a Latin American player). His date and place of birth follow "b." Then come his manner of batting and throwing, abbreviated in the usual manner. Next is the player's debut date in the major leagues.

The explanations for the statistical column heads follow; for more detail or technical information about formulas and calculations, see the final page of this book or the Glossary in *Total Baseball*.

YEAR	Year of play (When a space in the column is blank, this indicates that the man has played for two or more clubs in the last year stated in the column; if those clubs were in the same league, then the man will also have a combined total line, beginning with the abbreviation "Yr" placed in the TM/L column.)
TM/L	Team and League
Yr	See comments for YEAR
G	Games
AB	At bats
R	Runs
H	Hits
2B	Doubles
3B	Triples
HR	Home Runs
RBI	Runs Batted In
BB	Bases on Balls
SO	Strikeouts
AVG	Batting Average
OBP	On-Base Percentage
SLG	Slugging Average
PRO	Production (On Base-Percentage plus Slugging Average)
/A	Normalized to league average and park-adjusted (A mark of 100 is a league-average performance. Pitcher batting is removed from all league batting statistics before normalization.)
BR	Batting Runs (Linear Weights measure of runs contributed *beyond* what a league-average batter or team might have contributed, defined as zero)
PF	Park Factor (A measure of run scoring at the batter's home park in a given year or, in the Totals line, of all his various home parks; above 100 signifies a park or aggregate of parks favorable to hitters, below 100 signifies a park or aggregate of parks unfavorable to hitters. Park Factors for batters and pitchers are calculated differently and vary somewhat.)
CHI	Clutch Hitting Index (Actual RBIs over expected RBIs, adjusted for league average and position in batting order; see final page of this book for precise formula.)

RC	Runs Created (Bill James's formulation for run contribution from a variety of batting and baserunning events; the formula for players active in 1989 is stated on the final page of this book.)
TA	Total Average; a formulation of offensive contributions from batting and baserunning events derived by Tom Boswell, with modifications based on the work of Barry Codell. See final page for formula.
SB	Stolen Bases
CS	Caught Stealing
SBR	Stolen Base Runs (A Linear Weights measure of runs contributed *beyond* what a league-average base stealer might have gained, defined as zero and calculated on the basis of a 66.7 percent success rate.)
FR	Fielding Runs (A Linear Weights measure of runs saved *beyond* what a league-average player at that position might have saved, defined as zero; this stat is calculated to take account of the particular demands of the different positions; see final page for formulas.)
POS	Positions played; this is a ranking from left to right by frequency of the positions played in the field or at designated hitter. An asterisk to the left of the position indicates that in a given year the man played 100 or more games there. When a slash separates positions, the man played those positions listed to the left of the slash in 10 or more games, and the positions to the right of the slash in fewer than 10 games; in the absence of a slash, he played all positions listed in 10 or more games.
TPR	Total Player Rating; the sum of a player's Adjusted Batting Runs, Fielding Runs, and Stolen Base Runs, minus his positional adjustment, all divided by the Runs per Win factor for that year.

The Annual Record for 1989 on the following two pages contained the team standings and records in batting, baserunning, fielding, and pitching. For additional useful information about team performance, consult the Home/Road section. Also offered were the top five players in each of forty-eight categories, based on the customary criteria of 502 plate appearances for batters or 162 innings for pitchers. Below you will find brief explanations of the stats offered uniquely in this section.

SBA	Stolen Base Average; stolen bases divided by attempts
FA	Fielding Average; also known as Fielding Percentage
E	Errors
DP	Double Play
FW	Fielding Wins;
PW	Pitching Wins;
BW	Batting Wins;
SBW	Stolen Base Wins (In each case, that category of linear weights runs divided by the number of runs required to create an additional win beyond average, or a winning percentage of .500.)
DIF	Differential (The difference between the team's actual won-lost record and that predicted by the total of its Pitching Wins, Batting Wins, Fielding Wins, and Stolen Base Wins.)

Other stats carried on an individual basis in the Annual Record portion of *Total Baseball* but not in the Registers are:

Starter Runs: Identical to Pitching Runs but confined to starting pitchers, defined as those who average more than three innings per appearance. *Relief Runs:* Identical to Pitching Runs but confined to relief pitchers, defined as those who average less than three innings per appearance.

Relief Ranking: Adjusted Relief Runs, weighted for the greater value of a bullpen "closer" who limits his opponents' scoring in the late innings; see final page for the formula.

Total Baseball Ranking: The "MVP" of statistics, this ranks pitchers and position players by their total runs contributed in all their endeavors, revealing the most valuable performers in a given year.

Total: The lifetime record is shown alongside the notation "Total x," where *x* stands for the number of years played.

TEAM	G	W	L	PCT	GB	R	OR	AB	H	2B	3B	HR	BB	SO	AVG	OBP	SLG	PRO	/A	BR	/A	PF	CHI	RC	TA	SB	CS	SBA	SBR
EAST																													
CHI	162	93	69	.574		**702**	623	5513	**1438**	235	45	124	472	921	**.261**	.322	.387	**.709**	99	**54**	0	108	101	685	.652	136	57	70	7
NY	162	87	75	.537	6	683	595	5489	1351	**280**	21	**147**	504	934	.246	.313	.385	.698	108	30	52	97	102	676	**.657**	158	53	**75**	**16**
STL	164	86	76	.531	7	632	608	5492	1418	263	47	73	507	**848**	.258	**.323**	.363	.686	101	16	12	101	97	652	.630	155	54	74	14
MON	162	81	81	.500	12	632	630	5482	1353	267	30	100	**572**	958	.247	.322	.361	.683	98	13	-1	102	96	645	.636	**160**	70	70	6
PIT	164	74	88	.457	19	637	680	5539	1354	263	**53**	95	563	914	.241	.314	.359	.673	104	-12	27	94	100	629	.622	155	69	69	5
PHI	163	67	95	.414	26	629	735	5447	1324	215	36	123	558	926	.243	.316	.364	.680	99	1	-4	101	99	634	.623	106	50	68	2
WEST																													
SF	162	92	70	.568		699	600	5469	1365	241	52	141	508	1071	.250	.318	**.390**	.708	**111**	50	**67**	97	102	683	.653	87	54	62	-5
SD	162	89	73	.549	3	642	626	5422	1360	215	32	120	552	1013	.251	.321	.369	.690	102	22	17	101	98	644	.635	136	67	67	1
HOU	162	86	76	.531	6	647	669	5516	1316	239	28	97	530	860	.239	.308	.345	.653	89	-49	-63	102	**109**	606	.599	144	62	70	6
LA	160	77	83	.481	14	554	**536**	5465	1313	241	17	89	507	885	.240	.308	.339	.647	98	-60	-14	93	96	576	.574	81	54	60	-7
CIN	162	75	87	.463	17	632	691	5520	1362	243	28	128	493	1028	.247	.312	.370	.682	96	1	-18	103	99	639	.623	128	71	64	-3
ATL	161	63	97	.394	28	584	680	5463	1281	201	22	128	485	996	.234	.300	.350	.650	94	-63	-77	102	103	575	.578	83	54	61	-7
TOT	973					7673		65817	16215	2903	411	1365	6251	11354	.246	.315	.365	.680								1529	715	68	30

TEAM	CG	SHO	SV	IP	H	H/G	HR	BB	BB/G	SO	SO/G	ERA	/A	OAVG	OOBP	PR	/A	PF	CPI	FA	E	DP	FW	PW	BW	SBW	DIF
EAST																											
CHI	18	10	**55**	1460.3	1369	8.4	106	532	3.3	918	5.7	3.43	110	.249	.319	11	**53**	107	104	.980	124	130	.6	**5.7**	.0	.5	5.3
NY	24	12	38	1454.3	**1260**	**7.8**	115	532	3.3	**1108**	**6.9**	3.29	101	**.231**	**.303**	32	6	95	95	.976	144	110	-.6	.6	5.6	**1.4**	-1.1
STL	18	18	43	1461.0	1330	8.2	**84**	482	3.0	844	5.2	3.36	104	.243	.308	21	23	100	95	**.982**	**112**	134	1.4	2.5	1.3	1.2	-1.3
MON	20	13	35	1468.3	1344	8.2	120	519	3.2	1059	6.5	3.48	103	.245	.313	3	15	102	101	.979	136	126	-.1	1.6	-.1	.4	-1.8
PIT	20	9	40	1487.7	1394	8.4	121	539	3.3	827	5.0	3.64	91	.247	.317	-24	-56	94	98	.975	160	130	-1.4	-6.0	2.9	.3	-2.8
PHI	10	10	33	1433.3	1408	8.8	127	613	3.8	899	5.6	4.04	88	.258	.336	-87	-74	102	101	.979	133	136	.1	-7.9	-.4	-.0	-5.7
WEST																											
SF	12	16	47	1457.0	1320	8.2	120	471	**2.9**	802	5.0	3.30	101	.243	.306	30	7	96	102	**.982**	114	135	1.2	.7	**7.2**	-.8	2.7
SD	21	11	52	1457.3	1359	8.4	133	481	3.0	933	5.8	3.38	104	.248	.312	18	21	101	106	.976	154	147	-1.1	2.2	1.8	-.2	5.2
HOU	19	12	38	1479.3	1379	8.4	105	551	3.4	965	5.9	3.64	98	.247	.317	-24	-9	103	96	.977	142	121	-.4	-1.0	-6.7	-.4	12.8
LA	**25**	**19**	36	1463.3	1278	7.9	95	504	3.1	1052	6.5	**2.95**	110	.237	.306	89	47	93	**107**	.981	118	**153**	.8	5.0	-1.5	-1.0	-6.3
CIN	16	9	37	1464.3	1404	8.6	125	559	3.4	981	6.0	3.73	97	.253	.324	-38	-16	104	102	.980	121	108	.8	-1.7	-1.9	-.6	-2.5
ATL	15	8	33	1447.7	1370	8.5	114	**468**	**2.9**	966	6.0	3.70	98	.250	.309	-32	-12	104	94	.976	152	124	-1.1	-1.3	-8.2	-1.0	-5.4
TOT	218	147	487	17534.0		8.3			3.2		5.8	3.49		.246	.315					.978	1610	1554					

Runs		Hits		Doubles		Triples		Home Runs		Total Bases	
Sandberg-Chi	104	Gwynn-SD	203	Wallach-Mon	42	Thompson-SF	11	Mitchell-SF	47	Mitchell-SF	345
Johnson-NY	104	Clark-SF	196	Guerrero-StL	42	Bonilla-Pit	10	Johnson-NY	36	Clark-SF	321
Clark-SF	104	R.Alomar-SD	184	Johnson-NY	41	VanSlyke-Pit	9	Davis-Hou	34	Johnson-NY	319
Mitchell-SF	100	Guerrero-StL	177	Clark-SF	38	Coleman-StL	9	Davis-Cin	34	Bonilla-Pit	302
Butler-SF	100	Sandberg-Chi	176	Bonilla-Pit	37	Clark-SF	9	Sandberg-Chi	30	Sandberg-Chi	301

Runs Batted In		Runs Produced		Bases On Balls		Batting Average		On Base Percentage		Slugging Average	
Mitchell-SF	125	Clark-SF	192	Clark-SD	132	Gwynn-SD	.336	L.Smith-Atl	.420	Mitchell-SF	.635
Guerrero-StL	117	Mitchell-SF	178	V.Hayes-Phi	101	Clark-SF	.333	Clark-SD	.413	Johnson-NY	.559
Clark-SF	111	Johnson-NY	169	Raines-Mon	93	L.Smith-Atl	.315	Clark-SF	.412	Clark-SF	.546
Johnson-NY	101	Guerrero-StL	160	Bonds-Pit	93	Grace-Chi	.314	Grace-Chi	.407	Davis-Cin	.541
Davis-Cin	101	Bonilla-Pit	158			Guerrero-StL	.311	Guerrero-StL	.398	L.Smith-Atl	.533

Production		Adjusted Production		Batter Runs		Adjusted Batter Runs		Clutch Hitting Index		Runs Created	
Mitchell-SF	1.027	Mitchell-SF	194	Mitchell-SF	62.1	Mitchell-SF	64.0	Guerrero-StL	154	Clark-SF	136
Clark-SF	.958	Clark-SF	177	Clark-SF	55.6	Clark-SF	57.6	Clark-SD	140	Mitchell-SF	136
L.Smith-Atl	.953	Johnson-NY	169	L.Smith-Atl	47.0	Johnson-NY	48.1	Murphy-Atl	134	Johnson-NY	127
Johnson-NY	.932	L.Smith-Atl	167	Johnson-NY	45.7	L.Smith-Atl	45.6	Hatcher-Hou-Pit	131	L.Smith-Atl	113
Davis-Cin	.916	Davis-Cin	154	Guerrero-StL	38.3	Guerrero-StL	37.9	Doran-Hou	127	Guerrero-StL	109

Total Average		Stolen Bases		Stolen Base Average		Stolen Base Runs		Fielding Runs		Total Player Rating	
Mitchell-SF	1.109	Coleman-StL	65	Doran-Hou	88.0	Coleman-StL	13.5	Pendleton-StL	27.6	Mitchell-SF	6.3
L.Smith-Atl	1.057	Samuel-Phi-NY	42	Biggio-Hou	87.5	Johnson-NY	7.5	Oquendo-StL	20.6	L.Smith-Atl	5.0
Johnson-NY	1.045	R.Alomar-SD	42	Coleman-StL	86.7	Raines-Mon	6.9	Foley-Mon	19.5	Clark-SF	4.8
Clark-SF	1.017	Raines-Mon	41	D.Martinez-Mon	85.2	Samuel-Phi-NY	5.4	Young-Hou	19.1	Bonilla-Pit	4.1
Clark-SD	.975	Johnson-NY	41	Johnson-NY	83.7	Doran-Hou	4.8	Dykstra-NY-Phi	16.2	Bonds-Pit	3.9

Wins		Win Percentage		Games		Complete Games		Shutouts		Saves	
Scott-Hou	20	Bielecki-Chi	.720	Williams-Chi	76	Hurst-SD	10	Belcher-LA	8	Davis-SD	44
Maddux-Chi	19	J.Martinez-Mon	.696	Dibble-Cin	74	Belcher-LA	10	Drabek-Pit	5	Williams-Chi	36
Magrane-StL	18	Reuschel-SF	.680	Parrett-Phi	72	Scott-Hou	9	Langston-Mon	4	Franco-Cin	32
Bielecki-Chi	18	Scott-Hou	.667	Dayley-StL	71	Magrane-StL	9	Hershiser-LA	4	Howell-LA	28
Reuschel-SF	17	Magrane-StL	.667	Agosto-Hou	71	Browning-Cin	9	Glavine-Atl	4	Burke-Mon	28

Innings Pitched		Fewest Hits/Game		Fewest BB/Game		Strikeouts		Strikeouts/Game		Wins Above Team	
Hershiser-LA	257	DeLeon-StL	6.36	Robinson-SF	1.69	DeLeon-StL	201	Langston-Mon	8.90	Scott-Hou	5.0
Browning-Cin	250	Fernandez-NY	6.45	Lilliquist-Atl	1.84	Belcher-LA	200	Fernandez-NY	8.14	J.Martinez-Mon	4.9
Hurst-SD	245	Howell-Phi	6.84	J.Martinez-Mon	1.90	Fernandez-NY	198	Belcher-LA	7.83	Glavine-Atl	4.8
DeLeon-StL	245	Smoltz-Atl	6.92	Whitson-SD	1.90	Cone-NY	190	Cone-NY	7.77	Bielecki-Chi	4.8
Drabek-Pit	244	Garrelts-SF	6.95	Glavine-Atl	1.94	Hurst-SD	179	DeLeon-StL	7.38	DiPino-StL	4.5

Earned Run Average		Adjusted ERA		Opponents' Batting Avg.		Opponents' On Base Pct.		Starter Runs		Adjusted Starter Runs	
Garrelts-SF	2.28	Langston-Mon	149	DeLeon-StL	.197	Garrelts-SF	.260	Hershiser-LA	33.8	Hershiser-LA	26.4
Hershiser-LA	2.31	Garrelts-SF	147	Fernandez-NY	.198	Scott-Hou	.268	Garrelts-SF	25.9	Langston-Mon	23.2
Langston-Mon	2.39	Hershiser-LA	140	Smoltz-Atl	.212	DeLeon-StL	.269	Hurst-SD	22.1	Garrelts-SF	22.9
Whitson-SD	2.66	Whitson-SD	132	Garrelts-SF	.212	Fernandez-NY	.272	Langston-Mon	21.7	Hurst-SD	22.6
Hurst-SD	2.68	Hurst-SD	131	Scott-Hou	.212	Smiley-Pit	.276	Whitson-SD	21.2	Whitson-SD	21.6

Clutch Pitching Index		Relief Runs		Adjusted Relief Runs		Relief Ranking		Total Pitcher Index		Total Baseball Ranking	
Langston-Mon	135	Andersen-Hou	19.2	Andersen-Hou	20.1	Davis-SD	30.1	Hershiser-LA	3.8	Mitchell-SF	6.3
Hershiser-LA	124	Lancaster-Chi	17.3	Lancaster-Chi	19.4	McDowell-NY -Phi	27.4	Maddux-Chi	3.1	L.Smith-Atl	5.0
Lilliquist-Atl	117	Davis-SD	17.1	Davis-SD	17.3	Howell-LA	24.9	Langston-Mon	2.6	Clark-SF	4.8
Maddux-Chi	115	Howell-LA	17.1	Dibble-Cin	16.9	Dibble-Cin	23.8	Garrelts-SF	2.5	Bonilla-Pit	4.1
Drabek-Pit	112	Landrum-Pit	16.5	Darwin-Hou	16.6	Darwin-Hou	20.5	Hurst-SD	2.5	Bonds-Pit	3.9

TEAM	G	W	L	PCT	GB	R	OR	AB	H	2B	3B	HR	BB	SO	AVG	OBP	SLG	PRO	/A	BR	/A	PF	CHI	RC	TA	SB	CS	SBA	SBR
EAST																													
TOR	162	89	73	.549		731	651	5581	1449	265	40	142	521	923	.260	.326	.398	.724	**109**	18	60	94	102	724	.676	144	58	71	8
BAL	162	87	75	.537	2	708	686	5440	1369	238	33	129	593	957	.252	.329	.379	.708	100	-5	4	99	102	678	.657	118	55	68	2
BOS	162	83	79	.512	6	**774**	735	5666	**1571**	**326**	30	108	**643**	755	**.277**	**.355**	**.403**	**.758**	108	**106**	**73**	105	93	**802**	**.702**	56	35	62	-3
MIL	162	81	81	.500	8	707	679	5473	1415	235	32	126	455	791	.259	.321	.382	.703	100	-21	3	97	**106**	677	.653	**165**	62	73	12
NY	161	74	87	.460	14.5	698	792	5458	1470	229	23	130	502	831	.269	.334	.391	.725	99	26	-2	104	98	709	.670	137	60	70	5
CLE	162	73	89	.451	16	604	654	5463	1340	221	26	127	499	934	.245	.312	.365	.677	86	-71	-95	104	98	622	.608	74	51	59	-7
DET	162	59	103	.364	30	617	816	5432	1315	198	24	116	585	899	.242	.320	.351	.671	91	-73	-53	97	100	616	.612	103	50	67	1
WEST																													
OAK	162	99	63	.611		712	**576**	5416	1414	220	25	127	562	855	.261	.334	.381	.715	97	12	-11	103	101	687	.668	157	55	74	14
KC	162	92	70	.568	7	690	635	5475	1428	227	41	101	554	897	.261	.332	.373	.705	102	-8	21	96	101	682	.655	154	51	**75**	**16**
CAL	162	91	71	.562	8	669	578	5545	1422	208	37	**145**	429	1011	.256	.313	.386	.699	97	-37	-26	99	103	663	.628	89	40	69	3
TEX	162	83	79	.512	16	695	714	5458	1433	260	**46**	122	503	989	.263	.329	.394	.723	100	18	1	102	98	694	.660	101	49	67	1
MIN	162	80	82	.494	19	740	738	5581	1542	278	35	117	478	**743**	.276	.338	.402	.740	101	53	7	107	98	751	.680	111	53	68	2
SEA	162	73	89	.451	26	694	728	5512	1417	237	29	134	489	838	.257	.323	.384	.707	94	-15	-37	103	102	679	.641	81	55	60	-8
CHI	161	69	92	.429	29.5	693	750	5504	1493	262	36	94	464	873	.271	.331	.383	.714	108	4	53	93	100	696	.646	97	52	65	-1
TOT	1133					9732		77004	20078	3404	457	1718	7277	12296	.261	.328	.384	.712								1587	726	69	41

TEAM	CG	SHO	SV	IP	H	H/G	HR	BB	BB/G	SO	SO/G	ERA	/A	OAVG	OOBP	PR	/A	PF	CPI	FA	E	DP	FW	PW	BW	SBW	DIF
EAST																											
TOR	12	12	38	1467.0	1408	8.6	99	478	2.9	849	5.2	3.58	101	.255	.317	48	5	93	99	.980	127	164	-.1	.5	6.1	.5	1.0
BAL	16	7	44	1448.3	1518	9.4	134	**486**	3.0	676	4.2	4.00	96	.271	.333	-19	-28	99	104	**.986**	**87**	163	**2.3**	-2.9	.4	-.0	6.2
BOS	14	9	42	1460.3	1448	8.9	131	548	3.4	1054	6.5	4.01	101	.260	.330	-19	6	104	99	.980	127	162	-.1	.6	**7.4**	-.6	-5.3
MIL	16	8	45	1432.3	1463	9.2	129	457	2.9	812	5.1	3.80	98	.264	.324	13	-9	96	102	.975	155	164	-1.8	-.9	.3	.9	1.5
NY	15	9	44	1414.7	1550	9.9	150	521	3.3	787	5.0	4.50	91	.280	.347	-97	-65	105	102	.980	122	**183**	.1	-6.6	-.2	.2	-.0
CLE	23	13	38	1453.0	1423	8.8	107	**452**	**2.8**	844	5.2	3.65	111	.256	.315	37	64	104	96	.981	118	126	.4	6.5	-9.7	-1.0	-4.3
DET	24	4	26	1427.3	1514	9.5	150	652	4.1	831	5.2	4.53	85	.274	.353	-103	-108	99	103	.979	130	153	-.3	-11.0	-5.4	-.2	-5.1
WEST																											
OAK	17	**20**	**57**	1448.3	1287	**8.0**	103	510	3.2	930	5.8	**3.09**	**128**	**.238**	**.307**	**127**	**140**	102	103	.979	129	159	-.2	**14.3**	-1.1	1.1	4.0
KC	27	13	38	1451.7	1415	8.8	**86**	455	**2.8**	978	6.1	3.55	104	.256	.316	54	23	95	97	.982	114	139	.7	2.3	2.1	**1.3**	4.5
CAL	**32**	**20**	38	1454.3	1384	8.6	113	465	2.9	897	5.6	3.28	116	.253	.314	97	82	98	**107**	.985	96	173	1.7	8.3	-2.6	.0	2.5
TEX	26	7	44	1434.3	**1279**	**8.0**	119	654	4.1	**1112**	**7.0**	3.91	102	**.238**	.327	-4	11	103	92	.978	136	137	-.6	1.1	.1	-.2	1.6
MIN	19	8	38	1429.3	1495	9.4	139	500	3.1	851	5.4	4.28	96	.269	.334	-63	-23	106	97	.982	107	141	1.1	-2.3	.7	-.0	-.4
SEA	15	10	44	1438.0	1422	8.9	114	560	3.5	897	5.6	4.00	100	.259	.331	-18	3	104	98	.977	143	168	-1.1	.3	-3.8	-1.1	-2.4
CHI	9	5	46	1422.0	1472	9.3	144	539	3.4	778	4.9	4.23	86	.268	.339	-54	-94	93	101	.975	151	176	-1.6	-9.6	5.4	-.4	-5.3
TOT	265	145	582	20181.0		9.0			3.2		5.5	3.88		.261	.328					.980	1742	2208					

Runs
R.Henderson-NY-Oak 113
Boggs-Bos 113
Yount-Mil 101
Sierra-Tex 101
McGriff-Tor 98

Hits
Puckett-Min 215
Sax-NY 205
Boggs-Bos 205
Yount-Mil 195

Doubles
Boggs-Bos 51
Puckett-Min 45
Reed-Bos 42
Bell-Tor 41
Yount-Mil 38

Triples
Sierra-Tex 14
White-Cal 13
Bradley-Bal 10

Home Runs
McGriff-Tor 36
Carter-Cle 35
McGwire-Oak 33
Jackson-KC 32
Esasky-Bos 30

Total Bases
Sierra-Tex 344
Yount-Mil 314
Carter-Cle 303
Mattingly-NY 301
Puckett-Min 295

Runs Batted In
Sierra-Tex 119
Mattingly-NY 113
Esasky-Bos 108
Jackson-KC 105
Carter-Cle 105

Runs Produced
Sierra-Tex 191
Yount-Mil 183
Bell-Tor 174
Mattingly-NY 169
Greenwell-Bos 168

Bases On Balls
R.Henderson-NY-Oak 126
McGriff-Tor 119
Boggs-Bos 107
Seitzer-KC 102
Davis-Sea 101

Batting Average
Puckett-Min 339
Lansford-Oak 336
Boggs-Bos 330
Yount-Mil 318
Franco-Tex 316

On Base Percentage
Boggs-Bos 434
Davis-Sea 428
R.Henderson-NY-Oak .413
McGriff-Tor 402
Evans-Bos 402

Slugging Average
Sierra-Tex 543
McGriff-Tor 525
Yount-Mil 511
Esasky-Bos 500
Davis-Sea 496

Production
McGriff-Tor 927
Davis-Sea 924
Yount-Mil 898
Sierra-Tex 895
Boggs-Bos 883

Adjusted Production
McGriff-Tor 169
Yount-Mil 156
Davis-Sea 155
Baines-Chi-Tex 148
Sierra-Tex 145

Batter Runs
McGriff-Tor 46.8
Boggs-Bos 46.6
Davis-Sea 44.2
Yount-Mil 41.2
Sierra-Tex 37.4

Adjusted Batter Runs
McGriff-Tor 51.4
Yount-Mil 43.9
Boggs-Bos 42.9
Davis-Sea 42.0
Sierra-Tex 35.5

Clutch Hitting Index
Brett-KC 141
Evans-Bos 132
Greenwell-Bos 131
Parker-Oak 131
Franco-Tex 130

Runs Created
Yount-Mil 125
Boggs-Bos 122
Sierra-Tex 122
McGriff-Tor 121
R.Henderson-NY-Oak 110

Total Average
R.Henderson-NY-O 1.017
McGriff-Tor 995
Davis-Sea 978
Yount-Mil 933
Boggs-Bos 896

Stolen Bases
R.Henderson-NY-Oak 77
Espy-Tex 45
White-Cal 44
Sax-NY 43
Pettis-Det 43

Stolen Base Average
Thurman-KC 100.0
Franco-Tex 87.5
Yount-Mil 86.4
Finley-Bal 85.0
R.Henderson-NY-Oak 84.6

Stolen Base Runs
R.Henderson-NY-Oak 14.7
Thurman-KC 4.8
Felder-Mil 4.8
Franco-Tex 4.5

Fielding Runs
Reynolds-Sea 26.2
Fernandez-Tor 22.1
Espinoza-NY 21.1
Howell-Cal 19.9
White-KC 17.9

Total Player Rating
Yount-Mil 4.5
R.Henderson-NY-Oak 4.3
Molitor-Mil 4.0
McGriff-Tor 4.0
Boggs-Bos 4.0

Wins
Saberhagen-KC 23
Stewart-Oak 21
Moore-Oak 19
Davis-Oak 19
Ballard-Bal 18

Win Percentage
Saberhagen-KC 793
Blyleven-Cal 773
Davis-Oak 731
Stewart-Oak 700
Ballard-Bal 692

Games
Crim-Mil 76
Murphy-Bos 74
Rogers-Tex 73
Russell-Tex 71
Guetterman-NY 70

Complete Games
Saberhagen-KC 12
Morris-Det 10
Finley-Cal 9

Shutouts
Blyleven-Cal 5
Saberhagen-KC 4
McCaskill-Cal 4

Saves
Russell-Tex 38
Thigpen-Chi 34
Schooler-Sea 33
Plesac-Mil 33
Eckersley-Oak 33

Innings Pitched
Saberhagen-KC 262
Stewart-Oak 258
Gubicza-KC 255
Clemens-Bos 253
Milacki-Bal 243

Fewest Hits/Game
Ryan-Tex 6.10
Gordon-KC 6.74
Stieb-Tor 7.13
Moore-Oak 7.18
Saberhagen-KC 7.18

Fewest BB/Game
Key-Tor 1.13
Saberhagen-KC 1.48
Blyleven-Cal 1.64
Bosio-Mil 1.84
Witt-Cal 1.96

Strikeouts
Ryan-Tex 301
Clemens-Bos 230
Saberhagen-KC 193
Gubicza-KC 173
Bosio-Mil 173

Strikeouts/Game
Ryan-Tex 11.33
Gordon-KC 8.45
Clemens-Bos 8.18
Witt-Tex 7.70
Viola-Min 7.06

Wins Above Team
Saberhagen-KC 8.3
Blyleven-Cal 5.7
Ballard-Bal 4.9
Bankhead-Sea 4.9
Henneman-Det 4.5

Earned Run Average
Saberhagen-KC 2.16
Finley-Cal 2.57
Moore-Oak 2.60
Blyleven-Cal 2.73
McCaskill-Cal 2.93

Adjusted ERA
Saberhagen-KC 171
Moore-Oak 152
Finley-Cal 148
Blyleven-Cal 139
Welch-Oak 132

Opponents' Batting Avg.
Ryan-Tex 187
Gordon-KC 210
Saberhagen-KC 217
Stieb-Tor 219
Moore-Oak 219

Opponents' On Base Pct.
Saberhagen-KC 252
Ryan-Tex 276
Moore-Oak 288
Blyleven-Cal 289
Bosio-Mil 291

Starter Runs
Saberhagen-KC 50.0
Moore-Oak 34.4
Blyleven-Cal 31.0
Finley-Cal 29.3
Bosio-Mil 24.4

Adjusted Starter Runs
Saberhagen-KC 44.5
Moore-Oak 36.5
Blyleven-Cal 28.5
Finley-Cal 27.2
Clemens-Bos 25.7

Clutch Pitching Index
Cerutti-Tor 130
Finley-Cal 124
Ballard-Bal 123
McCaskill-Cal 116
Davis-Oak 113

Relief Runs
Montgomery-KC . . . 25.7
Olson-Bal 20.7
Henke-Tor 19.4
Lamp-Bos 19.3
Burns-Oak 17.4

Adjusted Relief Runs
Montgomery-KC . . . 23.7
Lamp-Bos 21.4
Olson-Bal 20.1
Guetterman-NY 18.7
Burns-Oak 18.2

Relief Ranking
Jones-Cle 42.8
Russell-Tex 39.2
Montgomery-KC . . . 33.7
Eckersley-Oak 29.5
Olson-Bal 29.3

Total Pitcher Index
Saberhagen-KC 4.9
Moore-Oak 4.2
Blyleven-Cal 3.2
Candiotti-Cle 2.7
Clemens-Bos 2.7

Total Baseball Ranking
Saberhagen-KC 4.9
Yount-Mil 4.5
R.Henderson-NY-Oak 4.3
Moore-Oak 4.2
Molitor-Mil 4.0

YEAR	TM/L	G	AB	R	H	2B	3B	HR	RBI	BB	SO	AVG	OBP	SLG	PRO	/A	BR	/A	PF	CHI	RC	TA	SB	CS	SBR	FR	POS	TPR
■ SHAWN ABNER	Abner, Shawn Wesley b: 6/17/66, Hamilton, Ohio BR/TR, 6'1", 190 lbs. Deb: 9/08/87																											
1987	SD-N	16	47	5	13	3	1	2	7	2	8	.277	.306	.511	.817	116	1	1	97	93	8	.794	1	0	0	1	O	0.1
1988	SD-N	37	83	6	15	3	0	2	5	4	19	.181	.227	.289	.516	49	-6	-6	97	67	5	.414	0	1	-1	-3	O	-1.0
1989	SD-N	57	102	13	18	4	0	2	14	5	20	.176	.215	.275	.489	39	-8	-8	101	166	6	.400	1	0	0	-8	O	-1.7
Total	3	110	232	24	46	10	1	6	26	11	47	.198	.238	.328	.565	58	-14	-13	99	115	19	.476	2	1	0	-10	O	-2.6
■ JIM ADDUCI	Adduci, James David b: 8/9/59, Chicago, Ill. BL/TR, 6'5", 200 lbs. Deb: 9/12/83																											
1983	StL-N	10	20	0	1	0	0	0	0	1	6	.050	.095	.050	.145	-60	-4	-4	98	0	0	.105	0	0	0	-0	/1O	-0.4
1986	Mil-A	3	11	2	1	1	0	0	0	1	2	.091	.167	.182	.348	-5	-2	-2	102	0	0	.300	0	0	0	-0	/1	-0.1
1988	Mil-A	44	94	8	25	6	1	1	15	0	15	.266	.266	.383	.649	77	-3	-3	103	153	9	.507	0	1	-1	-4	OD/1	-0.8
1989	Phi-N	13	19	1	7	1	0	0	0	0	4	.368	.368	.421	.789	124	1	1	101	0	3	.667	0	0	0	-1	/1O	0.0
Total	4	70	144	11	34	8	1	1	15	2	27	.236	.247	.326	.573	58	-8	-9	102	98	12	.438	0	1	-1	-5	/O1D	-1.3
■ LUIS AGUAYO	Aguayo, Luis (Muriel) b: 3/13/59, Vega Baja, P.R. BR/TR, 5'9", 173 lbs. Deb: 4/19/80																											
1980	Phi-N	20	47	7	13	1	2	1	8	2	3	.277	.306	.447	.753	100	0	-0	107	132	6	.686	1	1	-0	2	2/S	0.3
1981	Phi-N	45	84	11	18	4	0	1	7	6	15	.214	.283	.298	.580	58	-4	-5	112	98	8	.515	1	0	0	0	2S/3	0.0
1982	Phi-N	50	56	11	15	1	2	3	7	5	7	.268	.339	.518	.857	146	2	3	94	72	9	.837	1	1	-0	1	2S/3	0.5
1983	Phi-N	2	4	1	1	0	0	0	0	1	2	.250	.400	.250	.650	83	-0	-0	101	0	1	.667	0	0	0	-0	/S	0.0
1984	Phi-N	58	72	15	20	4	0	3	11	8	16	.278	.350	.458	.808	123	2	2	102	103	12	.774	0	0	0	-1	32S	0.3
1985	Phi-N	91	165	27	46	7	3	6	21	22	26	.279	.383	.467	.850	134	9	8	102	88	29	.841	1	0	0	-2	S2/3	1.1
1986	Phi-N	62	133	17	28	6	1	4	13	8	26	.211	.271	.361	.632	70	-5	-6	104	86	13	.550	1	1	-0	-1	2S/3	-0.5
1987	Phi-N	94	209	25	43	9	1	12	21	15	56	.206	.275	.431	.706	80	-6	-7	104	66	24	.643	0	0	0	-2	S/23	0.0
1988	Phi-N	49	97	9	24	3	0	3	5	13	17	.247	.336	.371	.707	102	1	0	101	44	13	.680	2	0	1	-1	S3/2	0.2
	NY-A	50	140	12	35	4	0	3	8	7	33	.250	.291	.343	.633	80	-5	-4	96	56	13	.505	0	2	-1	1	32/S	-0.2
1989	Cle-A	47	97	7	17	4	1	1	8	7	19	.175	.245	.268	.513	43	-7	-8	104	107	6	.417	0	0	0	-3	3S2/D	-0.8
Total	10	568	1104	142	260	43	10	37	109	94	220	.236	.307	.393	.700	91	-13	-16	103	80	133	.634	7	5	-1	-7	S2/3D	0.9
■ MIKE ALDRETE	Aldrete, Michael Peter b: 1/29/61, Carmel, Cal. BL/TL, 5'11", 180 lbs. Deb: 5/28/86																											
1986	SF-N	84	216	27	54	18	3	2	25	33	34	.250	.355	.389	.743	109	2	3	96	111	31	.714	1	3	-2	-2	1O	-0.2
1987	SF-N	126	357	50	116	18	2	9	51	43	50	.325	.398	.462	.860	132	15	17	96	106	68	.866	6	0	2	-1	O1	1.3
1988	SF-N	139	389	44	104	15	0	3	50	56	65	.267	.360	.329	.689	105	2	4	94	146	47	.633	6	5	-1	-4	*O1	-0.4
1989	Mon-N	76	136	12	30	8	1	1	12	19	30	.221	.321	.316	.637	81	-3	-3	102	105	14	.566	1	3	-2	-4	O1	-1.0
Total	4	425	1098	133	304	59	6	15	138	151	179	.277	.366	.383	.748	112	16	22	96	121	159	.710	14	11	-2	-11	O/1	-0.3
■ ANDY ALLANSON	Allanson, Andrew Neal b: 12/22/61, Richmond, Va. BR/TR, 6'5", 220 lbs. Deb: 4/07/86																											
1986	Cle-A	101	293	30	66	7	3	1	29	14	36	.225	.263	.280	.543	50	-21	-20	98	136	22	.455	10	1	2	6	C	-0.5
1987	Cle-A	50	154	17	41	6	0	3	16	9	30	.266	.307	.364	.670	76	-5	-5	103	98	17	.569	1	1	-0	2	C	0.0
1988	Cle-A	133	434	44	114	11	0	5	50	25	63	.263	.307	.323	.630	75	-13	-14	102	128	42	.516	5	9	-4	15	*C	0.2
1989	Cle-A	111	323	30	75	9	1	3	17	23	47	.232	.291	.294	.586	63	-15	-16	104	64	27	.486	4	4	-1	-9	*C	-2.1
Total	4	395	1204	121	296	33	4	12	112	71	176	.246	.292	.310	.602	66	-53	-55	101	109	109	.499	20	15	-3	14	C	-2.4
■ BEAU ALLRED	Allred, Dale Le Beau b: 6/4/65, Mesa, Ariz. BL/TL, 6', 190 lbs. Deb: 9/07/89																											
1989	Cle-A	13	23	0	6	3	0	0	1	2	10	.261	.320	.391	.711	96	-0	-0	104	43	3	.647	0	0	0	1	/OD	0.1
■ ROBERTO ALOMAR	Alomar, Roberto (Velazquez) b: 2/5/68, Ponce, P.R. BB/TR, 6', 184 lbs. Deb: 4/22/88																											
1988	SD-N	143	545	84	145	24	6	9	41	47	83	.266	.328	.382	.709	106	2	4	97	74	68	.670	24	6	4	13	*2	2.6
1989	SD-N	158	623	82	184	27	1	7	56	53	76	.295	.352	.376	.727	107	7	7	101	78	85	.708	42	17	2	5	*2	1.6
Total	2	301	1168	166	329	51	7	16	97	100	159	.282	.340	.378	.719	107	9	10	99	76	153	.690	66	23	6	18	2	4.2
■ SANDY ALOMAR	Alomar, Santos (Velazquez) Jr. b: 6/18/66, Salinas, P.R. BR/TR, 6'5", 200 lbs. Deb: 9/30/88																											
1988	SD-N	1	1	0	0	0	0	0	0	0	1	.000	.000	.000	.000	-99	-0	-0	97	0	0	.000	0	0	0	0	H	0.0
1989	SD-N	7	19	1	4	1	0	1	6	3	3	.211	.318	.421	.739	109	0	0	101	220	2	.688	0	0	0	1	/C	0.1
Total	2	8	20	1	4	1	0	1	6	3	4	.200	.304	.400	.704	99	-0	-0	101	210	2	.647	0	0	0	1	/C	0.1
■ BRADY ANDERSON	Anderson, Brady Kevin b: 1/8/64, Silver Spring, Md. BL/TL, 6'1", 170 lbs. Deb: 4/04/88																											
1988	Bos-A	41	148	14	34	5	3	0	12	15	35	.230	.317	.304	.621	69	-5	-6	109	108	16	.576	4	2	0	3	O	-0.3
	Bal-A	53	177	17	35	8	1	1	9	8	40	.198	.232	.271	.504	43	-14	-13	95	70	11	.422	6	4	-1	9	O	-0.5
	Yr	94	325	31	69	13	4	1	21	23	75	.212	.273	.286	.559	56	-19	-19	101	88	27	.491	10	6	-1	11		-0.8
1989	Bal-A	94	266	44	55	12	2	4	16	43	45	.207	.324	.312	.636	81	-6	-6	99	65	31	.662	16	4	2	2	O/D	-0.2
Total	2	188	591	75	124	25	6	5	37	66	120	.210	.297	.298	.594	67	-25	-25	100	77	57	.568	26	10	2	13	O/D	-1.0
■ DAVE ANDERSON	Anderson, David Carter b: 8/1/60, Louisville, Ky. BR/TR, 6'2", 185 lbs. Deb: 5/08/83																											
1983	LA-N	61	115	12	19	4	2	1	2	12	15	.165	.244	.261	.505	40	-9	-9	100	24	8	.480	6	3	0	2	S/3	-0.3
1984	LA-N	121	374	51	94	16	2	3	34	45	55	.251	.335	.329	.664	84	-5	-7	104	101	44	.631	15	5	2	15	*S3	2.2
1985	LA-N	77	221	24	44	6	0	4	18	35	42	.199	.311	.281	.592	72	-9	-7	93	97	21	.557	5	4	-1	8	3S/2	0.2
1986	LA-N	92	216	31	53	9	0	1	15	22	39	.245	.315	.301	.616	75	-8	-7	94	88	20	.526	5	1	1	1	3S/2	-0.1
1987	LA-N	108	265	32	62	12	3	1	13	24	43	.234	.300	.313	.613	68	-14	-11	92	60	26	.557	9	5	-0	2	S3/2	-0.1
1988	LA-N	116	285	31	71	10	2	2	20	32	45	.249	.327	.319	.646	81	-4	-6	106	82	30	.569	4	2	0	6	S23	0.6
1989	LA-N	87	140	15	32	2	0	1	14	17	26	.229	.312	.264	.576	72	-6	-4	93	141	13	.514	2	0	1	-1	S3/2	-0.2
Total	7	662	1616	196	375	59	9	13	116	187	265	.232	.314	.304	.617	74	-56	-52	98	87	161	.562	46	20	2	33	S3/2	2.3
■ KENT ANDERSON	Anderson, Kent McKay b: 8/12/63, Florence, S.C. BR/TR, 6'1", 180 lbs. Deb: 4/15/89																											
1989	Cal-A	86	223	27	51	6	1	0	17	17	42	.229	.286	.265	.551	57	-13	-12	99	112	17	.438	1	2	-1	2	S/23OD	-0.5
■ ERIC ANTHONY	Anthony, Eric Todd b: 11/8/67, San Diego, Cal. BL/TL, 6'2", 195 lbs. Deb: 7/29/89																											
1989	Hou-N	25	61	7	11	2	0	4	7	9	16	.180	.286	.410	.696	95	-0	-1	102	76	7	.667	0	0	0	-1	O	-0.1
■ TONY ARMAS	Armas, Antonio Rafael (Machado) b: 7/2/53, Anzoatequi, Venez. BR/TR, 5'11", 182 lbs. Deb: 9/06/76																											
1976	Pit-N	4	6	0	2	0	0	0	1	0	2	.333	.333	.333	.667	89	-0	-0	100	193	1	.500	0	0	0	-0	/O	0.0
1977	Oak-A	118	363	26	87	8	2	13	53	20	99	.240	.279	.380	.660	82	-12	-10	95	119	37	.556	1	2	-1	2	*O/S	-1.1
1978	Oak-A	91	239	17	51	6	1	2	13	10	62	.213	.251	.272	.523	47	-17	-17	101	72	16	.400	1	2	-1	-4	*O/D	-2.5
1979	Oak-A	80	278	29	69	9	3	11	34	16	67	.248	.292	.421	.712	101	-5	-1	89	89	33	.628	1	0	0	8	O	0.4
1980	Oak-A	158	628	87	175	18	8	35	109	29	128	.279	.313	.500	.813	126	13	17	95	108	89	.732	5	3	-0	12	*O	2.6
1981	Oak-A	109	440	51	115	24	3	**22**	76	19	115	.261	.295	.480	.775	125	9	11	96	114	61	.714	5	1	1	6	*O	1.6
1982	Oak-A	138	536	58	125	19	2	28	89	33	128	.233	.279	.433	.712	97	-8	-5	95	119	61	.628	2	2	-1	9	*O/D	0.0
1983	Bos-A	145	574	77	125	23	2	36	107	29	131	.218	.258	.453	.711	90	-10	-11	101	120	55	.605	0	1	-1	1	*OD	-1.1
1984	Bos-A	157	639	107	171	29	5	**43**	**123**	32	156	.268	.304	.531	.834	114	18	10	110	111	97	.771	1	3	-2	-6	*OD	0.0
1985	Bos-A	103	385	50	102	17	5	23	64	18	90	.265	.301	.514	.816	116	8	6	102	97	54	.734	0	0	0	1	OD	0.7
1986	Bos-A	121	425	40	112	21	4	11	58	24	77	.264	.306	.409	.715	94	-4	-4	100	112	49	.610	0	3	-2	1	*O/D	-0.8
1987	Cal-A	28	81	8	16	3	1	3	9	1	11	.198	.207	.370	.578	50	-6	-6	99	92	5	.471	1	0	0	-5	O	-1.0
1988	Cal-A	120	368	42	100	20	2	13	49	22	87	.272	.313	.443	.756	116	3	6	94	96	46	.655	1	3	-2	-6	*O/D	-0.3
1989	Cal-A	60	202	22	52	7	1	11	30	7	48	.257	.282	.465	.748	109	1	1	99	92	26	.664	0	0	0	1	O/1D	0.1
Total	14	1432	5164	614	1302	204	39	251	815	260	1201	.252	.290	.453	.742	103	-11	-2	99	107	629	.652	18	20	-7	21	*O/D1S	-1.4
■ LARRY ARNDT	Arndt, Larry Wayne b: 2/25/63, Fremont, Ohio BR/TR, 6'1", 195 lbs. Deb: 6/06/89																											
1989	Oak-A	2	6	1	1	0	0	0	0	0	1	.167	.167	.167	.333	-6	-1	-1	103	0	0	.200	0	0	0	0	/13	0.0
■ ALAN ASHBY	Ashby, Alan Dean b: 7/8/51, Long Beach, Cal. BB/TR, 6'2", 185 lbs. Deb: 7/03/73																											
1973	Cle-A	11	29	4	5	1	0	1	3	2	11	.172	.226	.310	.536	51	-2	-2	97	98	2	.458	0	0	0	0	C	0.0
1974	Cle-A	10	7	1	1	0	0	0	0	1	2	.143	.250	.143	.393	15	-1	-1	101	0	0	.333	0	0	0	0	/C	0.0
1975	Cle-A	90	254	32	57	10	1	5	32	30	42	.224	.309	.331	.639	81	-6	-6	100	124	26	.565	3	2	-0	0	C/13D	-0.3

YEAR	TM/L	G	AB	R	H	2B	3B	HR	RBI	BB	SO	AVG	OBP	SLG	PRO	/A	BR	/A	PF	CHI	RC	TA	SB	CS	SBR	FR	POS	TPR
1976	Cle-A	89	247	26	59	5	1	4	32	27	49	.239	.314	.316	.630	85	-4	-4	100	137	24	.536	0	2	-1	2	C/13	0.0
1977	Tor-A	124	396	25	83	16	3	2	29	50	51	.210	.301	.280	.582	58	-21	-23	103	98	34	.495	0	2	-1	14	*C	-0.6
1978	Tor-A	81	264	27	69	15	0	9	29	28	32	.261	.334	.420	.755	111	4	4	100	83	35	.684	1	1	-0	6	C	1.1
1979	Hou-N	108	336	25	68	15	2	2	35	26	70	.202	.264	.277	.541	53	-24	-20	90	140	24	.438	0	0	0	-9	*C	-2.7
1980	Hou-N	116	352	30	90	19	2	3	48	35	40	.256	.323	.347	.670	89	-6	-5	98	145	38	.575	0	0	0	-12	*C	-1.5
1981	Hou-N	83	255	20	69	13	0	4	33	35	33	.271	.359	.369	.727	121	3	7	88	122	34	.665	0	2	-1	2	C	1.0
1982	Hou-N	100	339	40	87	14	2	12	49	27	53	.257	.313	.416	.729	103	0	1	99	111	44	.660	2	0	1	-1	C	0.1
1983	Hou-N	87	275	31	63	18	1	8	34	31	38	.229	.307	.389	.696	102	-4	-0	90	103	31	.616	0	0	0	-5	C	-0.2
1984	Hou-N	66	191	16	50	7	0	4	27	20	22	.262	.335	.361	.696	103	-1	1	93	131	24	.621	0	0	0	-1	C	0.2
1985	Hou-N	65	189	20	53	8	0	8	25	24	27	.280	.364	.450	.814	132	7	8	96	91	29	.759	0	0	0	0	C	1.0
1986	Hou-N	120	315	24	81	15	0	7	38	39	56	.257	.339	.371	.710	93	-1	-2	103	110	40	.651	1	0	0	-18	*C	-1.8
1987	Hou-N	125	386	53	111	16	0	14	63	50	52	.288	.371	.438	.809	122	8	12	93	119	61	.759	0	1	-1	-14	*C	0.6
1988	Hou-N	73	227	19	54	10	0	7	33	29	36	.238	.324	.374	.699	107	0	2	93	124	28	.640	0	0	0	-6	C	0.0
1989	Hou-N	22	61	4	10	1	1	0	3	7	8	.164	.261	.213	.474	36	-5	-5	102	93	4	.396	0	0	0	1	C	-0.2
Total	17	1370	4123	397	1010	183	13	90	513	461	622	.245	.323	.361	.684	93	-53	-35	96	116	478	.606	7	10	-4	-41	*C/13D	-3.3
YEAR	TM/L	G	AB	R	H	2B	3B	HR	RBI	BB	SO	AVG	OBP	SLG	PRO	/A	BR	/A	PF	CHI	RC	TA	SB	CS	SBR	FR	POS	TPR

■ **WALLY BACKMAN** Backman, Walter Wayne b: 9/22/59, Hillsboro, Ore. BB/TR, 5'9", 160 lbs. Deb: 9/02/80

YEAR	TM/L	G	AB	R	H	2B	3B	HR	RBI	BB	SO	AVG	OBP	SLG	PRO	/A	BR	/A	PF	CHI	RC	TA	SB	CS	SBR	FR	POS	TPR
1980	NY-N	27	93	12	30	1	1	0	9	11	14	.323	.400	.355	.755	117	2	3	96	110	13	.681	2	3	-1	-2	2/S	0.2
1981	NY-N	26	36	5	10	2	0	0	0	4	7	.278	.350	.333	.683	94	-0	-0	101	0	5	.654	1	0	0	1	2/3	0.1
1982	NY-N	96	261	37	71	13	2	3	22	49	47	.272	.387	.372	.759	115	7	7	99	81	39	.759	8	7	-2	-1	2/3OS	0.9
1983	NY-N	26	42	6	7	0	1	0	3	2	8	.167	.205	.214	.419	16	-5	-5	99	132	2	.297	0	0	0	1	2/3	-0.3
1984	NY-N	128	436	68	122	19	2	1	26	56	63	.280	.362	.339	.701	98	1	1	100	69	57	.702	32	9	4	-3	*2/S	0.6
1985	NY-N	145	520	77	142	24	5	1	38	36	72	.273	.321	.344	.666	89	-10	-8	97	85	61	.626	30	12	2	-10	*2/S	-1.6
1986	NY-N	124	387	67	124	18	2	1	27	36	32	.320	.378	.385	.763	116	7	9	96	71	59	.725	13	7	-0	-13	*2	-0.2
1987	NY-N	94	300	43	75	6	1	1	23	25	43	.250	.308	.287	.594	60	-17	-17	99	103	28	.524	11	3	2	-8	2	-2.0
1988	NY-N	99	294	44	89	12	0	0	17	41	49	.303	.390	.344	.733	124	7	10	90	67	42	.704	9	5	-0	-0	2	1.3
1989	Min-A	87	299	33	69	9	2	1	26	32	45	.231	.307	.284	.592	64	-12	-15	107	117	28	.506	1	1	-0	-20	2/D	-3.4
Total	10	852	2668	392	739	104	16	8	191	292	380	.277	.349	.337	.686	94	-20	-14	98	84	334	.644	107	47	4	-56	2/S30D	-4.4

■ **HAROLD BAINES** Baines, Harold Douglass b: 3/15/59, Easton, Md. BL/TL, 6'2", 175 lbs. Deb: 4/10/80

YEAR	TM/L	G	AB	R	H	2B	3B	HR	RBI	BB	SO	AVG	OBP	SLG	PRO	/A	BR	/A	PF	CHI	RC	TA	SB	CS	SBR	FR	POS	TPR
1980	Chi-A	141	491	55	125	23	6	13	49	19	65	.255	.284	.405	.689	90	-11	-9	97	82	50	.574	2	4	-2	-14	*O/D	-2.7
1981	Chi-A	82	280	42	80	11	7	10	41	12	41	.286	.320	.482	.802	129	9	9	100	97	41	.745	6	2	1	-5	O/D	0.3
1982	Chi-A	161	608	89	165	29	8	25	105	49	95	.271	.326	.469	.794	118	11	13	97	119	91	.751	10	3	1	-2	*O	0.7
1983	Chi-A	156	596	76	167	33	2	20	99	49	85	.280	.336	.443	.779	109	9	7	103	127	85	.715	7	5	-1	-1	*O	0.3
1984	Chi-A	147	569	72	173	28	10	29	94	54	75	.304	.364	**.541**	.906	133	35	27	111	101	109	.885	1	2	-1	-1	*O	2.1
1985	Chi-A	160	640	86	198	29	3	22	113	42	89	.309	.353	.467	.820	122	19	19	100	118	98	.736	1	1	-0	-18	*O/D	-0.1
1986	Chi-A	145	570	72	169	29	2	21	88	38	89	.296	.343	.465	.808	117	14	13	101	103	87	.738	2	1	0	8	*O/D	1.7
1987	Chi-A	132	505	59	148	26	4	20	93	46	82	.293	.353	.479	.832	110	13	7	109	130	84	.783	0	0	0	-1	*D/O	0.5
1988	Chi-A	158	599	55	166	39	1	13	81	67	109	.277	.351	.411	.762	116	11	13	97	120	83	.692	0	0	0	-1	*D/O	1.2
1989	Chi-A	96	333	55	107	20	1	13	56	60	52	.321	.426	.505	.931	174	29	33	93	111	72	.962	0	1	-1	-1	DO	3.0
	Tex-A	50	172	18	49	9	0	3	16	13	27	.285	.335	.390	.725	101	1	0	102	82	21	.620	0	2	-1	-0	D/O	0.0
	Yr	146	505	73	156	29	1	16	72	73	79	.309	.397	.465	.863	148	30	33	96	102	93	.842	0	3	-2	-1		3.0
Total	10	1428	5363	679	1547	276	44	189	835	449	809	.288	.345	.462	.807	119	139	131	101	111	823	.745	29	21	-4	-35	*OD	7.0

■ **DOUG BAKER** Baker, Douglas Lee b: 4/3/61, Fullerton, Cal. BB/TR, 5'9", 165 lbs. Deb: 7/02/84

YEAR	TM/L	G	AB	R	H	2B	3B	HR	RBI	BB	SO	AVG	OBP	SLG	PRO	/A	BR	/A	PF	CHI	RC	TA	SB	CS	SBR	FR	POS	TPR
1984	Det-A	43	108	15	20	4	1	0	12	7	22	.185	.241	.241	.482	35	-10	-9	96	184	7	.416	3	0	1	-1	S/2D	-0.5
1985	Det-A	15	27	4	5	1	0	0	1	0	9	.185	.185	.222	.407	10	-3	-3	106	66	1	.273	0	0	0	-1	S/2	-0.2
1986	Det-A	13	24	1	3	1	0	0	0	2	7	.125	.192	.167	.359	-1	-3	-3	95	0	1	.286	0	0	0	0	S/2D	-0.1
1987	Det-A	8	1	0	0	0	0	0	0	0	1	.000	.000	.000	.000	-99	-0	-0	97	0	0	.000	0	0	0	0	/S23	0.0
1988	Min-A	11	7	1	0	0	0	0	0	0	5	.000	.000	.000	.000	-94	-2	-2	106	0	0	.000	0	0	0	-0	/S23	-0.1
1989	Min-A	43	78	17	23	5	1	0	9	9	18	.295	.382	.385	.767	109	2	1	107	117	13	.745	0	0	0	-4	2S	0.0
Total	6	133	245	38	51	11	2	0	22	18	62	.208	.271	.269	.540	50	-16	-16	101	126	22	.462	3	0	1	-5	/S23D	-0.9

■ **STEVE BALBONI** Balboni, Stephen Charles b: 1/16/57, Brockton, Mass. BR/TR, 6'3", 225 lbs. Deb: 4/22/81

YEAR	TM/L	G	AB	R	H	2B	3B	HR	RBI	BB	SO	AVG	OBP	SLG	PRO	/A	BR	/A	PF	CHI	RC	TA	SB	CS	SBR	FR	POS	TPR
1981	NY-A	4	7	2	2	1	1	0	2	1	4	.286	.375	.714	1.089	207	1	1	100	157	2	1.200	0	0	0	0	/1D	0.1
1982	NY-A	33	107	8	20	2	1	2	4	6	34	.187	.230	.280	.510	41	-9	-9	96	44	7	.409	0	0	0	-2	1/D	-1.0
1983	NY-A	32	86	8	20	2	0	5	17	8	23	.233	.298	.430	.728	99	-1	-0	99	128	11	.662	0	0	0	-1	1/D	-0.1
1984	KC-A	126	438	58	107	23	2	28	77	45	139	.244	.320	.498	.818	123	12	12	99	104	69	.785	0	0	0	-4	*1/D	0.0
1985	KC-A	160	600	74	146	28	2	36	88	52	166	.243	.309	.477	.786	109	7	6	102	94	86	.733	1	1	-0	-8	*1	-1.2
1986	KC-A	138	512	54	117	25	1	29	88	43	146	.229	.290	.451	.741	99	-2	-2	100	112	67	.682	0	0	0	-4	*1	-1.5
1987	KC-A	121	386	44	80	11	1	24	60	34	97	.207	.275	.427	.702	80	-10	-13	104	101	43	.634	0	0	0	-0	1D	-1.7
1988	KC-A	21	63	2	9	2	0	2	5	1	20	.143	.156	.270	.426	16	-7	-7	103	86	3	.333	0	0	0	-1	1/D	-0.8
	Sea-A	97	350	44	88	15	1	21	61	23	67	.251	.299	.480	.779	106	5	2	108	107	48	.708	0	1	-1	-1	D1	-0.2
	Yr	118	413	46	97	17	1	23	66	24	87	.235	.279	.448	.726	94	-2	-5	107	104	49	.646	0	1	-1	-2		-1.0
1989	NY-A	110	300	33	71	12	2	17	59	25	67	.237	.302	.460	.762	107	3	2	104	121	39	.695	0	0	0	-1	D1	0.0
Total	9	842	2849	327	660	121	11	164	461	238	763	.232	.295	.455	.749	100	-1	-9	102	103	375	.688	1	2	-1	-22	1D	-6.4

■ **CHRIS BANDO** Bando, Christopher Michael b: 2/4/56, Cleveland, Ohio BB/TR, 6', 195 lbs. Deb: 8/13/81

YEAR	TM/L	G	AB	R	H	2B	3B	HR	RBI	BB	SO	AVG	OBP	SLG	PRO	/A	BR	/A	PF	CHI	RC	TA	SB	CS	SBR	FR	POS	TPR
1981	Cle-A	21	47	3	10	3	0	0	6	2	2	.213	.245	.277	.521	54	-3	-3	93	181	3	.395	0	0	0	-0	C/D	-0.1
1982	Cle-A	66	184	13	39	6	1	3	16	24	30	.212	.303	.304	.607	67	-8	-8	100	98	17	.530	0	0	0	-6	C/3	-1.0
1983	Cle-A	48	121	15	31	3	0	4	15	15	19	.256	.338	.380	.718	92	-0	-1	105	101	15	.635	0	1	-1	-2	C	0.0
1984	Cle-A	75	220	38	64	11	0	12	41	33	35	.291	.383	.505	.888	135	13	12	106	111	41	.873	1	2	-1	2	C/13D	1.6
1985	Cle-A	73	173	11	24	4	1	0	13	22	21	.139	.236	.173	.409	15	-20	-19	94	172	7	.333	0	1	-1	5	C	-1.0
1986	Cle-A	92	254	28	68	9	0	2	26	22	49	.268	.329	.327	.655	82	-6	-6	98	116	27	.544	0	1	-1	5	C	0.3
1987	Cle-A	89	211	20	46	9	0	5	16	12	28	.218	.260	.332	.592	55	-13	-14	103	75	17	.480	0	0	0	2	C	-0.4
1988	Cle-A	32	72	6	9	1	0	1	8	8	12	.125	.222	.181	.403	14	-8	-8	102	199	3	.328	0	0	0	3	C	-0.4
	Det-A	1	0	0	0	0	0	0	0	0	0	—	—	—	—	—	0	0	94		—	—	0	0	0	0	/C	0.0
	Yr	33	72	6	9	1	0	1	8	8	12	.125	.222	.181	.403	14	-8	-8	101	199	3	.328	0	0	0	3		-0.4
1989	Oak-A	1	2	0	1	0	0	0	1	0	1	.500	.500	.500	1.000	177	0	0	103	389	1	1.000	0	0	0	0	/C	0.0
Total	9	498	1284	134	292	46	2	27	142	138	197	.227	.303	.329	.633	73	-46	-47	101	120	134	.542	1	5	-3	9	C/3D1	-1.0

■ **JESSE BARFIELD** Barfield, Jesse Lee b: 10/29/59, Joliet, Ill. BR/TR, 6'4", 215 lbs. Deb: 9/03/81

YEAR	TM/L	G	AB	R	H	2B	3B	HR	RBI	BB	SO	AVG	OBP	SLG	PRO	/A	BR	/A	PF	CHI	RC	TA	SB	CS	SBR	FR	POS	TPR
1981	Tor-A	25	95	7	22	3	2	2	9	4	19	.232	.270	.368	.638	74	-2	-4	111	91	8	.550	4	3	-1	4	O	0.0
1982	Tor-A	139	394	54	97	13	2	18	58	42	79	.246	.323	.426	.750	96	2	-3	109	104	54	.695	1	4	-2	-9	*O/D	-1.7
1983	Tor-A	128	388	58	98	13	3	27	68	22	110	.253	.300	.510	.810	109	7	3	108	95	55	.746	2	5	-2	-0	*O/D	0.0
1984	Tor-A	110	320	51	91	14	1	14	49	35	81	.284	.359	.466	.824	124	11	11	102	102	55	.822	8	2	1	4	O/D	1.4
1985	Tor-A	155	539	94	156	34	9	27	84	66	143	.289	.371	.536	.907	143	33	32	101	92	106	.941	22	8	2	18	*O	4.9
1986	Tor-A	158	589	107	170	35	2	**40**	108	69	146	.289	.371	.559	.929	143	40	36	105	102	122	.950	8	8	-2	22	*O	**4.9**
1987	Tor-A	159	590	89	155	25	3	28	84	58	141	.263	.332	.458	.789	106	6	5	101	97	87	.737	3	5	-2	1	*O	0.0
1988	Tor-A	136	468	62	114	21	5	18	56	41	108	.244	.306	.425	.731	103	0	1	100	90	60	.676	7	3	0	15	*O/D	1.3
1989	Tor-A	21	80	8	16	4	0	5	11	5	28	.200	.256	.438	.693	98	-1	-1	94	87	9	.621	0	2	-1	2	O	0.0
	NY-A	129	441	71	106	19	1	18	56	82	122	.240	.362	.410	.772	112	12	10	104	98	70	.780	5	3	-0	12	*O	2.0
	Yr	150	521	79	122	23	1	23	67	87	150	.234	.347	.415	.762	111	11	9	103	97	78	.755	5	5	-2	14		2.0
Total	9	1160	3904	601	1025	181	28	197	583	424	977	.263	.339	.475	.814	117	108	90	103	97	624	.789	60	43	-8	71	*O/D	12.8

■ **SKEETER BARNES** Barnes, William Henry b: 3/3/57, Cincinnati, Ohio BR/TR, 5'11", 175 lbs. Deb: 9/06/83

YEAR	TM/L	G	AB	R	H	2B	3B	HR	RBI	BB	SO	AVG	OBP	SLG	PRO	/A	BR	/A	PF	CHI	RC	TA	SB	CS	SBR	FR	POS	TPR
1983	Cin-N	15	34	5	7	0	0	1	4	7	3	.206	.372	.294	.666	84	-0	-0	103	122	4	.724	2	2	-1	-1	/13	-0.1

YEAR	TM/L	G	AB	R	H	2B	3B	HR	RBI	BB	SO	AVG	OBP	SLG	PRO	/A	BR	/A	PF	CHI	RC	TA	SB	CS	SBR	FR	POS	TPR
1984	Cin-N	32	42	5	5	0	0	1	3	4	6	.119	.196	.190	.386	8	-5	-5	106	107	2	.316	0	0	0	-1	3/O	-0.6
1985	Mon-N	19	26	0	4	1	0	0	0	0	2	.154	.154	.192	.346	-4	-4	-3	94	0	0	.208	0	1	-1	1	/3O1	-0.3
1987	StL-N	4	4	1	1	0	0	1	3	0	0	.250	.250	1.000	1.250	215	1	1	99	171	1	1.333	0	0	0	0	/3	0.1
1989	Cin-N	5	3	1	0	0	0	0	0	0	0	.000	.000	.000	.000	-97	-1	-1	103	0	0	.000	0	1	-1	0	H	0.0
Total	5	75	109	12	17	1	0	3	10	11	11	.156	.246	.248	.494	37	-9	-9	102	89	7	.429	2	4	-2	-1	/31O	-0.9
■ **MARTY BARRETT** Barrett, Martin Glenn b: 6/23/58, Arcadia, Cal. BR/TR, 5'10", 175 lbs. Deb: 9/06/82																												
1982	Bos-A	8	18	0	1	0	0	0	0	0	1	.056	.056	.056	.111	-63	-4	-4	110	0	0	.056	0	0	0	-0	/2	-0.3
1983	Bos-A	33	44	7	10	1	1	0	2	3	1	.227	.277	.295	.572	57	-3	-3	101	60	4	.457	0	0	0	-3	2/D	-0.4
1984	Bos-A	139	475	56	144	23	3	3	45	42	25	.303	.361	.383	.744	96	5	-1	110	94	66	.671	5	3	-0	-2	*2	0.2
1985	Bos-A	156	534	59	142	26	0	5	56	56	50	.266	.338	.343	.681	85	-8	-10	102	112	62	.603	7	5	-1	15	*2	1.0
1986	Bos-A	158	625	94	179	39	4	4	60	65	31	.286	.355	.381	.735	102	3	3	100	92	87	.685	15	7	0	-1	*2	1.0
1987	Bos-A	137	559	72	164	23	0	3	43	51	38	.293	.354	.351	.704	90	-7	-7	99	74	74	.645	15	2	3	**35**	*2	3.9
1988	Bos-A	150	612	83	173	28	1	1	65	40	35	.283	.334	.337	.670	81	-9	-16	109	109	69	.568	7	3	0	5	*2	0.0
1989	Bos-A	86	336	31	86	18	0	1	27	32	12	.256	.324	.318	.643	78	-7	-9	105	101	35	.551	4	1	1	9	2/D	0.2
Total	8	867	3203	402	899	158	9	17	298	289	193	.281	.343	.352	.694	88	-31	-47	104	96	397	.617	53	21	3	60	2/D	5.6
■ **TOM BARRETT** Barrett, Thomas Loren b: 4/2/60, San Fernando, Cal. BB/TR, 5'9", 157 lbs. Deb: 7/02/88																												
1988	Phi-N	36	54	5	11	1	0	0	3	7	8	.204	.306	.222	.529	53	-3	-3	101	100	4	.455	0	0	0	-1	2	-0.3
1989	Phi-N	14	27	3	6	0	0	0	1	1	7	.222	.250	.222	.472	36	-2	-2	101	67	2	.333	0	0	0	1	/2	-0.1
Total	2	50	81	8	17	1	0	0	4	8	15	.210	.289	.222	.511	48	-5	-5	101	90	6	.415	0	0	0	-1	/2	-0.4
■ **KEVIN BASS** Bass, Kevin Charles b: 5/12/59, Menlo Park, Cal. BB/TR, 6', 183 lbs. Deb: 4/09/82																												
1982	Mil-A	18	9	4	0	0	0	0	0	1	1	.000	.100	.000	.100	-74	-2	-2	94	0	0	.111	0	0	0	-5	O/D	-0.7
	Hou-N	12	24	2	1	0	0	0	1	0	8	.042	.042	.042	.083	-77	-6	-6	99	392	0	.042	0	0	0	-1	/O	-0.6
1983	Hou-N	88	195	25	46	7	3	2	18	6	27	.236	.259	.333	.592	70	-10	-8	90	100	16	.477	2	2	-1	-8	O	-1.7
1984	Hou-N	121	331	33	86	17	5	2	29	6	57	.260	.279	.360	.639	85	-10	-8	93	91	32	.528	5	5	-2	0	O	-1.2
1985	Hou-N	150	539	72	145	27	5	16	68	31	63	.269	.316	.427	.743	110	3	5	96	99	71	.694	19	8	1	1	*O	0.3
1986	Hou-N	157	591	83	184	33	5	20	79	38	72	.311	.359	.486	.845	127	23	21	103	96	97	.811	22	13	-1	0	*O	1.8
1987	Hou-N	157	592	83	168	31	5	19	85	53	77	.284	.347	.449	.796	117	7	13	93	111	90	.770	21	8	2	7	*O	1.4
1988	Hou-N	157	541	57	138	27	2	14	72	42	65	.255	.316	.390	.706	109	0	5	93	116	66	.682	31	6	6	-3	*O	0.4
1989	Hou-N	87	313	42	94	19	4	5	44	29	44	.300	.362	.435	.796	124	11	10	102	120	51	.787	11	4	1	6	O	1.6
Total	8	947	3135	401	862	161	29	78	396	206	414	.275	.325	.419	.744	109	16	30	96	107	424	.696	111	46	6	-2	O/D	1.3
■ **BILLY BATES** Bates, William Derrick b: 12/7/63, Houston, Tex. BB/TR, 5'7", 155 lbs. Deb: 8/17/89																												
1989	Mil-A	7	14	3	3	0	0	0	0	0	1	.214	.214	.214	.429	22	-1	-1	97	0	0	.385	2	0	1	1	/2	0.0
■ **BILL BATHE** Bathe, William David b: 10/14/60, Downey, Cal. BR/TR, 6'2", 200 lbs. Deb: 4/12/86																												
1986	Oak-A	39	103	9	19	3	0	5	11	2	20	.184	.208	.359	.567	55	-7	-6	94	84	7	.465	0	0	0	-4	C	-0.7
1989	SF-N	30	32	3	9	1	0	0	6	0	7	.281	.281	.313	.594	72	-1	-1	97	242	3	.435	0	0	0	-0	/C	0.0
Total	2	69	135	12	28	4	0	5	17	2	27	.207	.225	.348	.573	59	-9	-8	94	121	10	.459	0	0	0	-4	/C	-0.7
■ **KEVIN BATISTE** Batiste, Kevin Wade b: 10/21/66, Galveston, Tex. BB/TR, 6'2", 175 lbs. Deb: 6/13/89																												
1989	Tor-A	6	8	1	2	0	0	0	0	0	5	.250	.250	.250	.500	44	-1	-1	94	0	1	.333	0	0	0	-1	/O	-0.1
■ **BILL BEAN** Bean, William Daro b: 5/11/64, Santa Ana, Cal. BL/TL, 6' ", 185 lbs. Deb: 4/25/87																												
1987	Det-A	26	66	6	17	2	0	0	4	5	11	.258	.310	.288	.598	63	-4	-3	97	84	6	.490	1	1	-0	1	O	-0.2
1988	Det-A	10	11	2	2	0	1	0	0	0	2	.182	.182	.364	.545	52	-1	-1	94	0	1	.444	0	0	0	-1	/O1D	-0.1
1989	Det-A	9	11	0	0	0.	0	0	0	2	3	.000	.214	.000	.214	-36	-2	-2	97	0	0	.273	0	0	0	-2	/O1	-0.3
	LA-N	51	71	7	14	4	0	0	3	4	10	.197	.250	.254	.504	48	-5	-5	93	67	4	.390	0	2	-1	-8	O	-1.5
Total	3	96	159	15	33	6	1	0	7	11	26	.208	.267	.258	.525	49	-11	-10	95	64	11	.423	1	3	-2	-10	/O1D	-2.1
■ **BILLY BEANE** Beane, William Lamar b: 3/29/62, Orlando, Fla. BR/TR, 6'4", 195 lbs. Deb: 9/13/84																												
1984	NY-N	5	10	0	1	0	0	0	0	0	2	.100	.100	.100	.200	-44	-2	-2	100	0	0	.100	0	1	-1	-2	/O	-0.4
1985	NY-N	8	8	0	2	1	0	0	1	0	3	.250	.250	.375	.625	75	-0	-0	97	133	1	.500	0	0	0	-1	/O	0.0
1986	Min-A	80	183	20	39	6	0	3	15	11	54	.213	.258	.295	.553	47	-12	-14	108	95	12	.438	2	3	-1	-6	O/D	-2.2
1987	Min-A	12	15	1	4	2	0	0	1	0	6	.267	.267	.400	.667	78	-1	-0	96	66	2	.545	0	0	0	-1	/O	-0.1
1988	Det-A	6	6	1	1	0	0	0	1	0	2	.167	.167	.167	.333	-7	-1	-1	94	398	0	.200	0	0	0	-2	/O	-0.2
1989	Oak-A	37	79	8	19	5	0	0	11	0	13	.241	.241	.304	.544	51	-5	-5	103	178	5	.429	3	1	0	-2	O/1C3D	-0.7
Total	6	148	301	30	66	14	0	3	29	11	80	.219	.247	.296	.542	46	-21	-23	106	118	20	.423	5	5	-2	-13	O/D13C	-3.6
■ **BUDDY BELL** Bell, David Gus b: 8/27/51, Pittsburgh, Pa. BR/TR, 6'1", 180 lbs. Deb: 4/15/72																												
1972	Cle-A	132	466	49	119	21	1	9	36	34	29	.255	.310	.363	.673	93	-1	-4	107	78	52	.589	5	6	-2	0	*O/3	-1.0
1973	Cle-A	156	631	86	169	23	7	14	59	49	47	.268	.327	.393	.720	105	1	3	97	77	76	.633	7	15	-7	24	*3/O	1.8
1974	Cle-A	116	423	51	111	15	1	7	46	35	29	.262	.323	.352	.675	94	-3	-3	101	113	46	.571	1	3	-2	-0	*3/D	-0.3
1975	Cle-A	153	553	66	150	20	4	10	59	51	72	.271	.334	.376	.710	101	0	0	100	97	69	.635	6	5	-1	-5	*3	-0.2
1976	Cle-A	159	604	75	170	26	2	7	60	44	49	.281	.332	.366	.698	105	3	3	100	101	71	.595	3	8	-4	6	*3/1	0.6
1977	Cle-A	129	479	64	140	23	4	11	64	45	63	.292	.354	.426	.780	114	8	9	98	113	68	.695	1	8	-5	7	*3O	0.9
1978	Cle-A	142	556	71	157	27	8	6	62	39	43	.282	.329	.392	.721	109	1	6	93	110	65	.606	1	3	-2	25	*3/D	2.8
1979	Tex-A	162	670	89	200	42	3	18	101	30	45	.299	.331	.451	.782	109	6	6	100	105	95	.694	5	4	-1	17	*3S	2.8
1980	Tex-A	129	490	76	161	24	4	17	83	40	39	.329	.379	.498	.877	138	25	25	100	112	88	.829	3	1	0	15	*3/S	3.9
1981	Tex-A	97	360	44	106	16	1	10	64	42	30	.294	.373	.428	.801	143	15	19	91	144	58	.768	3	3	-1	**27**	3/S	4.6
1982	Tex-A	148	537	62	159	27	2	13	67	70	50	.296	.379	.426	.806	130	17	22	93	106	87	.775	5	4	-1	**37**	*3/S	5.5
1983	Tex-A	156	618	75	171	35	3	14	66	50	48	.277	.335	.411	.746	103	3	2	101	84	78	.653	3	5	-2	17	*3	1.7
1984	Tex-A	148	553	88	174	36	5	11	83	63	54	.315	.388	.458	.845	133	26	26	100	123	95	.800	2	1	0	21	*3	4.8
1985	Tex-A	84	313	33	74	13	3	4	32	33	21	.236	.311	.335	.647	71	-10	-13	108	115	31	.557	3	2	-0	10	3	-0.5
	Cin-N	67	247	28	54	15	2	6	36	34	27	.219	.313	.368	.682	86	-3	-5	105	139	27	.613	0	1	-1	-6	3	-1.1
1986	Cin-N	155	568	89	158	29	3	20	75	73	49	.278	.365	.445	.811	117	18	15	104	101	91	.771	2	8	-4	0	*3/2	0.8
1987	Cin-N	143	522	74	148	19	2	17	70	71	39	.284	.370	.425	.796	106	9	7	104	108	84	.766	4	1	1	-17	*3	-1.0
1988	Cin-N	21	54	3	10	0	0	0	3	7	3	.185	.279	.185	.464	34	-4	-5	105	120	3	.370	0	0	0	1	3/1	-0.3
	Hou-N	74	269	24	68	10	1	7	37	19	29	.253	.302	.375	.678	100	-3	-1	93	124	29	.576	1	1	-0	-1	3/1	-0.2
	Yr	95	323	27	78	10	1	7	40	26	32	.241	.298	.344	.642	87	-7	-6	96	124	32	.539	1	1	-0	1		-0.5
1989	Tex-A	34	82	4	15	4	0	0	3	7	10	.183	.247	.232	.479	35	-7	-7	102	61	4	.366	0	0	0	1	D/31	-0.6
Total	18	2405	8995	1151	2514	425	56	201	1106	836	776	.279	.343	.406	.750	109	102	106	100	105	1218	.672	55	79	-31	180	*3O/SD12	25.0
■ **JAY BELL** Bell, Jay Stuart b: 12/11/65, Eglin A.F.B., Fla. BR/TR, 6'1", 180 lbs. Deb: 9/29/86																												
1986	Cle-A	5	14	3	5	2	0	1	4	2	3	.357	.438	.714	1.152	213	2	2	98	123	5	1.333	0	0	0	0	/2D	0.2
1987	Cle-A	38	125	14	27	9	1	2	13	8	31	.216	.269	.352	.621	62	-7	-7	103	104	13	.561	2	0	1	-7	S	-1.0
1988	Cle-A	73	211	23	46	5	1	2	21	21	53	.218	.292	.280	.571	60	-11	-11	102	128	18	.500	4	2	0	-11	S/D	-1.9
1989	Pit-N	78	271	33	70	13	3	2	27	19	47	.258	.309	.351	.660	94	-4	-2	94	110	28	.563	5	3	-0	-10	S	-0.8
Total	4	194	621	73	148	29	5	7	65	50	134	.238	.298	.335	.633	78	-19	-18	98	115	64	.555	11	5	0	-28	S/D2	-3.5
■ **GEORGE BELL** Bell, Jorge (Mathey) b: 10/21/59, San Pedro De Macoris, D.R. BR/TR, 6'1", 190 lbs. Deb: 4/09/81																												
1981	Tor-A	60	163	19	38	2	1	5	12	5	27	.233	.256	.350	.606	66	-6	-8	111	65	14	.508	3	2	-0	0	O/D	-0.9
1983	Tor-A	39	112	5	30	5	4	2	17	4	17	.268	.305	.438	.743	94	-0	-1	108	121	13	.644	1	1	-0	-3	O/D	-0.4
1984	Tor-A	159	606	85	177	39	4	26	87	24	86	.292	.328	.498	.826	123	18	17	102	93	95	.775	11	2	2	-2	*O/3D	1.2
1985	Tor-A	157	607	87	167	28	6	28	95	43	90	.275	.331	.479	.811	118	14	13	101	106	97	.800	21	6	3	1	*O/3	1.4
1986	Tor-A	159	641	101	198	38	6	31	108	41	62	.309	.352	.532	.884	131	31	27	105	105	113	.839	7	8	-3	0	*OD/3	1.9
1987	Tor-A	156	610	111	188	32	4	47	**134**	39	75	.308	.357	.605	.962	148	41	40	101	111	125	.955	5	1	1	-4	*O/23D	3.1
1988	Tor-A	156	614	78	165	27	5	24	97	34	66	.269	.308	.446	.754	109	5	5	100	118	78	.663	4	2	0	-12	*O/D	-0.9

YEAR	TM/L	G	AB	R	H	2B	3B	HR	RBI	BB	SO	AVG	OBP	SLG	PRO	/A	BR	/A	PF	CHI	RC	TA	SB	CS	SBR	FR	POS	TPR
1989	Tor-A	153	613	88	182	41	2	18	104	33	60	.297	.337	.458	.795	130	16	20	94	128	89	.712	4	3	-1	-10	*OD	0.8
Total	8	1039	3966	574	1145	212	32	181	654	223	483	.289	.332	.495	.827	123	118	113	101	109	626	.773	56	25	2	-30	O/D32	6.2
■ JUAN BELL	Bell, Juan (Mathey) b: 3/29/68, San Pedro De Macoris, D.R. BR/TR, 5'11", 172 lbs. Deb: 9/06/89																											
1989	Bal-A	8	4	2	0	0	0	0	0	0	1	.000	.000	.000	.000	-99	-1	-1	99	0	0	.250	1	0	0	0	/2SD	0.0
■ JOEY BELLE	Belle, Albert Jojuan b: 8/25/66, Shreveport, La. BR/TR, 6'1", 190 lbs. Deb: 7/15/89																											
1989	Cle-A	62	218	22	49	8	4	7	37	12	55	.225	.272	.394	.666	83	-5	-6	104	137	22	.583	2	2	-1	0	OD	-0.6
■ RAFAEL BELLIARD	Belliard, Rafael Leonidas (Matia b: 10/24/61, Pueblo Nuevo, D.R. BR/TR, 5'9", 139 lbs. Deb: 9/06/82																											
1982	Pit-N	9	2	3	1	0	0	0	0	0	0	.500	.500	.500	1.000	164	0	0	110	0	1	2.000	1	0	0	0	/S	0.1
1983	Pit-N	4	1	1	0	0	0	0	0	0	1	.000	.000	.000	.000	-97	-0	-0	103	0	0	.000	0	0	0	0	/S	0.0
1984	Pit-N	20	22	3	5	0	0	0	0	0	1	.227	.227	.227	.455	30	-2	-2	94	0	1	.500	4	1	1	0	S/2	0.0
1985	Pit-N	17	20	1	4	0	0	0	1	0	5	.200	.200	.200	.400	12	-2	-2	103	100	1	.250	0	0	0	1	S	0.0
1986	Pit-N	117	309	33	72	5	2	0	31	26	54	.233	.299	.262	.561	56	-18	-18	100	153	26	.494	12	2	2	5	S2	0.0
1987	Pit-N	81	203	26	42	4	3	1	15	20	25	.207	.288	.271	.559	47	-15	-16	104	103	17	.500	5	1	1	-3	S/2	-0.9
1988	Pit-N	122	286	28	61	0	4	0	11	26	47	.213	.288	.241	.529	55	-16	-16	98	64	21	.449	7	1	2	-9	*S/2	-1.5
1989	Pit-N	67	154	10	33	4	0	0	8	8	22	.214	.253	.240	.493	45	-12	-10	94	87	10	.403	5	2	0	-5	S2/3	-1.3
Total	8	437	997	105	218	13	9	1	66	80	155	.219	.283	.253	.536	51	-65	-64	99	102	76	.465	34	7	6	-10	S/23	-3.6
■ BRUCE BENEDICT	Benedict, Bruce Edwin b: 8/18/55, Birmingham, Ala. BR/TR, 6'1", 175 lbs. Deb: 8/18/78																											
1978	Atl-N	22	52	3	13	2	0	0	1	6	6	.250	.328	.288	.616	66	-2	-2	112	26	5	.538	0	0	0	1	C	0.0
1979	Atl-N	76	204	14	46	11	0	0	15	33	18	.225	.333	.279	.613	63	-8	-10	109	104	20	.552	1	3	-2	-3	C	-1.3
1980	Atl-N	120	359	18	91	14	1	2	34	28	36	.253	.309	.315	.624	74	-12	-12	101	113	34	.514	3	3	-1	0	*C	-1.1
1981	Atl-N	90	295	26	78	12	1	5	35	33	21	.264	.344	.363	.707	101	1	1	100	115	37	.637	1	1	-0	11	C	1.4
1982	Atl-N	118	386	34	95	11	1	3	44	37	40	.246	.317	.303	.620	69	-12	-16	107	137	37	.528	4	4	-1	-1	*C	-1.7
1983	Atl-N	134	423	43	126	13	1	2	43	61	24	.298	.388	.348	.735	100	6	3	106	111	57	.673	1	3	-2	4	*C	1.0
1984	Atl-N	95	300	26	67	8	1	4	25	34	25	.223	.304	.297	.601	63	-12	-15	110	97	27	.512	1	2	-1	8	C	-0.4
1985	Atl-N	70	208	12	42	6	0	0	20	22	12	.202	.281	.231	.512	42	-15	-16	106	166	13	.406	0	1	-1	3	C	-1.1
1986	Atl-N	64	160	11	36	10	1	0	13	15	10	.225	.299	.300	.599	64	-7	-8	102	108	13	.496	1	0	0	6	C	0.0
1987	Atl-N	37	95	4	14	1	0	1	5	17	15	.147	.277	.189	.466	24	-10	-11	108	95	6	.417	0	1	-1	5	C	-0.3
1988	Atl-N	90	236	11	57	7	0	0	19	19	26	.242	.298	.271	.569	62	-10	-12	104	119	20	.454	0	2	-1	-1	C	-0.9
1989	Atl-N	66	160	12	31	3	0	1	6	23	18	.194	.299	.231	.530	52	-9	-9	102	60	13	.469	0	0	0	-1	C	-0.6
Total	12	982	2878	214	696	98	6	18	260	328	251	.242	.322	.299	.621	71	-90	-108	105	113	282	.532	12	20	-8	32	C	-5.0
■ MIKE BENJAMIN	Benjamin, Michael Paul b: 11/22/65, Euclid, Ohio BR/TR, 6'3", 195 lbs. Deb: 7/07/89																											
1989	SF-N	14	6	6	1	0	0	0	0	0	1	.167	.167	.167	.333	-5	-1	-1	97	0	0	.200	0	0	0	0	/S	0.0
■ TODD BENZINGER	Benzinger, Todd Eric b: 2/11/63, Dayton, Ky. BB/TR, 6'1", 185 lbs. Deb: 6/21/87																											
1987	Bos-A	73	223	36	62	11	1	8	43	22	41	.278	.348	.444	.792	110	3	3	99	139	34	.753	5	4	-1	9	O/1	0.9
1988	Bos-A	120	405	47	103	28	1	13	70	22	80	.254	.294	.425	.719	91	-2	-7	109	132	48	.629	2	3	-1	-5	1O/D	-1.8
1989	Cin-N	161	628	79	154	28	3	17	76	44	120	.245	.297	.381	.677	90	-8	-10	103	112	70	.593	3	7	-3	-14	*1	-4.2
Total	3	354	1256	162	319	67	5	38	189	88	241	.254	.305	.406	.711	94	-7	-13	104	123	152	.633	10	14	-5	-10	1O/D	-5.1
■ DAVE BERGMAN	Bergman, David Bruce b: 6/6/53, Evanston, Ill. BL/TL, 6'1.5", 185 lbs. Deb: 8/26/75																											
1975	NY-A	7	17	0	0	0	0	0	0	2	4	.000	.105	.000	.105	-69	-4	-4	99	0	0	.118	0	0	0	0	/O	-0.3
1977	NY-A	5	4	1	1	0	0	0	1	0	0	.250	.250	.250	.500	37	-0	-0	99	396	0	.333	0	0	0	-1	/O1	0.0
1978	Hou-N	104	186	15	43	5	1	0	12	39	32	.231	.364	.269	.633	84	-3	-2	95	95	20	.615	2	0	1	-1	1O	-0.5
1979	Hou-N	13	15	4	6	0	0	1	2	0	3	.400	.400	.600	1.000	187	1	1	90	66	4	1.000	0	0	0	0	/1	0.1
1980	Hou-N	90	78	12	20	6	1	0	3	10	10	.256	.341	.359	.700	98	-0	-0	98	42	10	.661	1	0	0	-1	1/O	-0.3
1981	Hou-N	6	6	1	1	0	0	1	1	0	0	.167	.167	.667	.833	145	0	0	88	56	1	.800	0	0	0	0	/1	0.0
	SF-N	63	145	16	37	9	0	3	13	19	18	.255	.341	.379	.721	99	1	0	105	80	19	.679	2	0	1	-1	1O	-0.1
	Yr	69	151	17	38	9	0	4	14	19	18	.252	.335	.391	.726	102	1	0	104	78	20	.684	2	0	1	-1		-0.1
1982	SF-N	100	121	22	33	3	1	4	14	18	11	.273	.367	.413	.780	126	3	4	94	89	20	.798	3	0	1	1	1/O	0.3
1983	SF-N	90	140	16	40	4	1	6	24	24	21	.286	.394	.457	.851	134	7	7	101	116	25	.858	2	1	0	-0	1/O	0.5
1984	Det-A	120	271	42	74	8	5	7	44	33	40	.273	.358	.417	.775	118	6	7	96	131	41	.741	3	4	-2	7	*1/O	0.5
1985	Det-A	69	140	8	25	2	0	3	7	14	15	.179	.253	.257	.510	38	-12	-13	106	62	9	.413	0	0	0	3	1/OD	-1.1
1986	Det-A	65	130	14	30	6	1	1	9	21	16	.231	.338	.315	.653	84	-3	-2	95	81	15	.602	0	0	0	2	1/OD	-0.2
1987	Det-A	91	172	25	47	7	3	6	22	30	23	.273	.384	.453	.838	126	6	7	97	91	32	.858	0	1	-1	1	1/OD	0.0
1988	Det-A	116	289	37	85	14	0	5	35	38	34	.294	.376	.394	.771	123	7	10	94	108	43	.714	0	2	-1	-1	1DO/3	0.3
1989	Det-A	137	385	38	103	13	1	7	37	44	44	.268	.346	.361	.707	102	1	2	97	90	50	.641	1	3	-2	-0	*1/OD	-0.7
Total	14	1076	2099	251	545	77	14	44	224	292	271	.260	.352	.373	.725	104	11	18	97	95	290	.681	14	11	-2	9	1/OD3	-1.5
■ GERONIMO BERROA	Berroa, Geronimo Emiliano b: 3/18/65, Santo Domingo, D.R. BR/TR, 6', 165 lbs. Deb: 4/05/89																											
1989	Atl-N	81	136	7	36	4	0	2	9	7	32	.265	.301	.338	.639	81	-3	-4	102	70	13	.515	0	1	-1	-0	O	-0.4
■ DAMON BERRYHILL	Berryhill, Damon Scott b: 12/3/63, South Laguna, Cal. BB/TR, 6' ", 210 lbs. Deb: 9/05/87																											
1987	Chi-N	12	28	2	5	1	0	0	1	3	5	.179	.258	.214	.472	27	-3	-3	101	66	1	.360	0	1	-1	0	C	-0.2
1988	Chi-N	95	309	19	80	19	1	7	38	17	56	.259	.298	.395	.692	93	-2	-4	104	106	33	.583	1	0	0	2	C	0.4
1989	Chi-N	91	334	37	86	13	0	5	41	16	54	.257	.295	.341	.637	75	-8	-12	108	130	31	.510	1	0	0	2	C	-0.2
Total	3	198	671	58	171	33	1	12	80	36	115	.255	.295	.361	.655	81	-13	-18	106	116	66	.536	2	1	0	4	C	0.0
■ DANTE BICHETTE	Bichette, Alphonse Dante b: 11/18/63, W.Palm Beach, Fla. BR/TR, 6'3", 215 lbs. Deb: 9/05/88																											
1988	Cal-A	21	46	1	12	2	0	0	8	0	7	.261	.261	.304	.565	61	-3	-2	94	227	4	.412	0	0	0	0	O	-0.1
1989	Cal-A	48	138	13	29	7	0	3	15	6	24	.210	.243	.326	.569	60	-8	-8	99	108	11	.482	3	0	1	6	O/D	0.0
Total	2	69	184	14	41	9	0	3	23	6	31	.223	.247	.321	.568	60	-10	-10	97	137	15	.466	3	0	1	7	/OD	-0.1
■ CRAIG BIGGIO	Biggio, Craig Alan b: 12/14/65, Smithtown, N.Y. BR/TR, 5'11", 185 lbs. Deb: 6/26/88																											
1988	Hou-N	50	123	14	26	6	1	3	5	7	29	.211	.254	.350	.603	77	-5	-4	93	38	11	.566	6	1	1	-4	C	-0.4
1989	Hou-N	134	443	64	114	21	2	13	60	49	64	.257	.339	.402	.741	109	7	6	102	111	65	.749	21	3	5	4	*C/O	2.4
Total	2	184	566	78	140	27	3	16	65	56	93	.247	.322	.390	.712	102	2	2	100	96	76	.708	27	4	6	0	C/O	2.0
■ DANN BILARDELLO	Bilardello, Dann James b: 5/26/59, Santa Cruz, Cal. BR/TR, 6', 185 lbs. Deb: 4/11/83																											
1983	Cin-N	109	298	27	71	18	0	9	38	15	49	.238	.277	.389	.666	81	-8	-9	103	105	30	.565	2	1	0	-8	*C	-1.4
1984	Cin-N	68	182	16	38	7	0	2	10	19	34	.209	.287	.280	.567	57	-9	-11	106	69	14	.470	0	1	-1	-7	C	-1.7
1985	Cin-N	42	102	6	17	0	0	1	9	4	15	.167	.206	.196	.402	12	-12	-12	105	156	3	.278	0	0	0	-5	C	-1.6
1986	Mon-N	79	191	12	37	5	0	4	17	14	32	.194	.249	.283	.532	47	-14	-14	98	103	13	.434	1	0	0	-10	C	-2.2
1989	Pit-N	33	80	11	18	6	0	2	8	2	18	.225	.244	.375	.619	80	-3	-2	94	89	6	.508	1	2	-1	-1	C	-0.2
Total	5	331	853	72	181	36	0	18	82	54	148	.212	.262	.318	.579	60	-47	-48	102	101	67	.473	4	4	-1	-32	C	-7.1
■ LANCE BLANKENSHIP	Blankenship, Lance Robert b: 12/6/63, Portland, Ore. BR/TR, 6', 190 lbs. Deb: 9/04/88																											
1988	Oak-A	10	3	1	0	0	0	0	0	0	1	.000	.000	.000	.000	-99	-1	-1	95	0	0	.000	0	1	-1	0	/2D	0.0
1989	Oak-A	58	125	22	29	5	1	1	4	8	31	.232	.278	.312	.590	64	-6	-6	103	37	12	.536	5	1	1	-0	O2D	-0.5
Total	2	68	128	23	29	5	1	1	4	8	32	.227	.272	.305	.577	60	-6	-7	103	36	12	.515	5	2	0	-0	/2OD	-0.5
■ JEFF BLAUSER	Blauser, Jeffrey Michael b: 11/8/65, Los Gatos, Cal. BR/TR, 6' ", 170 lbs. Deb: 7/05/87																											
1987	Atl-N	51	165	11	40	6	3	2	15	18	34	.242	.328	.352	.679	74	-4	-6	108	93	19	.652	7	3	0	4	S	0.4
1988	Atl-N	18	67	7	16	3	1	2	7	2	11	.239	.271	.403	.674	87	-1	-1	104	90	7	.566	0	1	-1	-0	/2S	-0.1
1989	Atl-N	142	456	63	123	24	2	12	46	38	101	.270	.327	.410	.737	107	5	4	102	83	62	.675	5	2	0	-3	32S/O	0.3
Total	3	211	688	81	179	33	6	16	68	58	146	.260	.322	.395	.718	96	-0	-4	104	86	88	.658	12	6	0	1	/S32O	0.6

YEAR TM/L		G	AB	R	H	2B	3B	HR	RBI	BB	SO	AVG	OBP	SLG	PRO	/A	BR	/A	PF	CHI	RC	TA	SB	CS	SBR	FR	POS	TPR
■ **TERRY BLOCKER** Blocker, Terry Fennell b: 8/18/59, Columbia, S.C. BL/TL, 6'2", 195 lbs. Deb: 4/11/85																												
1985	NY-N	18	15	1	1	0	0	0	0	1	2	.067	.125	.067	.192	-46	-3	-3	97	0	0	.143	0	0	0	-1	/O	-0.3
1988	Atl-N	66	198	13	42	4	2	2	10	10	20	.212	.250	.283	.533	50	-12	-13	104	64	13	.411	1	1	-0	0	O	-1.5
1989	Atl-N	26	31	1	7	1	0	0	1	1	5	.226	.250	.258	.508	45	-2	-2	102	50	2	.417	1	0	0	-2	/OP	-0.3
Total	3	110	244	15	50	5	2	2	11	12	27	.205	.242	.266	.509	44	-17	-18	104	59	15	.393	2	1	0	-3	/OP	-2.1
■ **MIKE BLOWERS** Blowers, Michael Roy b: 4/24/65, Wurzburg, Germany BR/TR, 6'2", 190 lbs. Deb: 9/01/89																												
1989	NY-A	13	38	2	10	0	0	0	3	3	13	.263	.317	.263	.580	63	-2	-2	104	117	3	.448	0	0	0	-1	3	-0.2
■ **WADE BOGGS** Boggs, Wade Anthony b: 6/15/58, Omaha, Neb. BL/TR, 6'2", 190 lbs. Deb: 4/10/82																												
1982	Bos-A	104	338	51	118	14	1	5	44	35	21	.349	.410	.441	.851	121	17	12	110	107	61	.808	1	0	0	3	13/OD	1.4
1983	Bos-A	153	582	100	210	44	7	5	74	92	36	**.361**	**.449**	.486	.935	156	**51**	**50**	101	93	130	.972	3	3	-1	10	*3	5.8
1984	Bos-A	158	625	109	203	31	4	6	55	89	44	.325	.409	.416	.825	117	29	20	110	70	110	.805	3	2	-0	23	*3/D	4.4
1985	Bos-A	161	653	107	**240**	42	3	8	78	96	61	**.368**	**.452**	.478	.929	151	55	53	102	81	143	.954	2	1	0	9	*3	5.5
1986	Bos-A	149	580	107	207	47	2	8	71	**105**	44	**.357**	**.455**	.486	.942	**159**	53	53	100	80	133	**.997**	0	4	-2	-0	*3	4.4
1987	Bos-A	147	551	108	200	40	6	24	89	105	48	**.363**	**.467**	.588	**1.055**	**180**	**68**	**68**	99	86	**154**	1.177	1	3	-2	-0	*3/1D	**5.9**
1988	Bos-A	155	584	**128**	214	**45**	6	5	58	**125**	34	**.366**	**.480**	.490	**.970**	158	**66**	**58**	109	68	**140**	**1.051**	2	3	-1	-2	*3/D	5.5
1989	Bos-A	156	621	**113**	205	**51**	7	3	54	107	51	.330	**.434**	.449	.883	143	47	43	105	64	122	.896	2	6	-3	-1	*3/D	4.0
Total	8	1183	4534	823	1597	314	36	64	523	754	339	.352	.446	.480	.926	149	383	357	104	79	994	.960	14	22	-9	43	*3/1DO	36.9
■ **BARRY BONDS** Bonds, Barry Lamar b: 7/24/64, Riverside, Cal. BL/TL, 6'1", 185 lbs. Deb: 5/30/86																												
1986	Pit-N	113	413	72	92	26	3	16	48	65	102	.223	.331	.416	.748	105	3	3	100	92	64	.828	36	7	7	10	*O	1.7
1987	Pit-N	150	551	99	144	34	9	25	59	54	88	.261	.331	.492	.822	110	10	7	104	69	93	.855	32	10	4	6	*O	1.0
1988	Pit-N	144	538	97	152	30	5	24	58	72	82	.283	.369	.491	.860	148	32	33	98	73	100	.887	17	11	-2	1	*O	3.1
1989	Pit-N	159	580	96	144	34	6	19	58	93	93	.248	.353	.426	.779	130	18	22	94	81	92	.820	32	10	4	13	*O	3.9
Total	4	566	2082	364	532	124	23	84	223	284	365	.256	.347	.458	.805	124	62	65	99	78	349	.848	117	38	12	30	O	9.7
■ **BOBBY BONILLA** Bonilla, Roberto Martin Antonio b: 2/23/63, New York, N.Y. BB/TR, 6'3", 210 lbs. Deb: 4/09/86																												
1986	Chi-A	75	234	27	63	10	2	2	26	33	49	.269	.362	.355	.717	96	0	-0	101	116	32	.688	4	1	1	-0	O1	-0.2
	Pit-N	63	192	28	46	6	2	1	17	29	39	.240	.342	.307	.650	80	-4	-4	100	109	21	.600	4	4	-1	-4	O/13	-1.0
1987	Pit-N	141	466	58	140	33	3	15	77	39	64	.300	.357	.481	.838	115	12	10	104	114	78	.791	3	5	-2	-12	3O/1	-0.7
1988	Pit-N	159	584	87	160	32	7	24	100	85	82	.274	.370	.476	.846	145	32	34	98	121	106	.855	3	5	-2	-1	*3	3.2
1989	Pit-N	163	616	96	173	37	10	24	86	76	93	.281	.361	.490	.851	150	33	37	94	98	108	.839	8	8	-2	6	*3/1O	4.1
Total	4	601	2092	296	582	118	24	66	306	262	327	.278	.361	.452	.813	127	73	76	99	111	345	.792	22	23	-7	-12	3O/1	5.4
■ **ROD BOOKER** Booker, Roderick Stewart b: 9/4/58, Los Angeles, Cal. BL/TR, 6' ", 175 lbs. Deb: 4/29/87																												
1987	StL-N	44	47	9	13	1	1	0	8	7	7	.277	.370	.340	.711	91	-0	-0	99	200	7	.735	2	0	1	-1	2/3S	0.0
1988	StL-N	18	35	6	12	3	0	0	3	4	3	.343	.410	.429	.839	136	2	2	104	80	6	.840	2	2	-1	0	3/2	0.2
1989	StL-N	10	8	1	2	0	0	0	0	0	1	.250	.250	.250	.500	43	-1	-1	101	0	1	.333	0	0	0	0	/23	0.0
Total	3	72	90	16	27	4	1	0	11	11	11	.300	.376	.367	.743	104	1	1	101	138	14	.738	4	2	0	-0	/23S	0.2
■ **BOB BOONE** Boone, Robert Raymond b: 11/19/47, San Diego, Cal. BR/TR, 6'2.5", 195 lbs. Deb: 9/10/72																												
1972	Phi-N	16	51	4	14	1	0	1	4	5	7	.275	.339	.353	.692	100	-0	0	97	78	6	.615	1	0	0	-1	C	0.0
1973	Phi-N	145	521	42	136	20	2	10	61	41	36	.261	.315	.365	.680	81	-9	-14	108	114	60	.591	3	4	-2	17	*C	1.0
1974	Phi-N	146	488	41	118	24	3	3	52	35	29	.242	.298	.322	.620	71	-18	-20	103	121	45	.514	3	1	0	-11	*C	-2.5
1975	Phi-N	97	289	28	71	14	2	2	20	32	14	.246	.323	.329	.652	80	-7	-8	101	77	30	.563	1	3	-2	-4	C/3	-0.9
1976	Phi-N	121	361	40	98	18	2	4	54	45	44	.271	.354	.366	.719	97	3	-0	107	144	45	.647	2	5	-2	-8	*C/1	-0.5
1977	Phi-N	132	440	55	125	26	4	11	66	42	54	.284	.349	.436	.786	109	6	5	100	117	66	.735	5	5	-2	-1	*C/3	0.1
1978	Phi-N	132	435	48	123	18	4	12	62	46	37	.283	.353	.425	.778	110	10	7	105	111	62	.709	2	5	-2	-6	*C/1O	0.1
1979	Phi-N	119	398	38	114	21	3	9	58	49	33	.286	.367	.422	.790	118	9	11	97	120	61	.741	1	4	-2	-2	*C/3	1.0
1980	Phi-N	141	480	34	110	23	1	9	55	48	41	.229	.301	.338	.638	72	-14	-19	107	115	48	.559	3	4	-2	4	*C	-1.3
1981	Phi-N	76	227	19	48	7	0	4	24	22	16	.211	.281	.295	.576	57	-11	-14	112	119	18	.487	2	2	-1	-6	C	-2.0
1982	Cal-A	143	472	42	121	17	0	7	58	39	34	.256	.313	.337	.650	78	-14	-14	100	129	51	.547	0	2	-1	18	*C	1.1
1983	Cal-A	142	468	46	120	18	0	9	52	24	42	.256	.293	.353	.645	80	-15	-13	96	106	44	.522	4	3	-1	17	*C	1.0
1984	Cal-A	139	450	33	91	16	1	3	32	25	45	.202	.244	.262	.506	40	-37	-37	101	100	28	.391	3	3	-1	8	*C	-2.1
1985	Cal-A	150	460	37	114	17	0	5	55	37	35	.248	.308	.317	.625	71	-17	-18	101	136	45	.519	1	2	-1	7	*C	-0.5
1986	Cal-A	144	442	48	98	12	2	7	49	43	30	.222	.291	.305	.596	66	-22	-20	96	125	39	.499	1	0	0	-4	*C	-1.5
1987	Cal-A	128	389	42	94	18	0	3	33	35	36	.242	.306	.311	.617	66	-19	-18	99	101	37	.511	0	2	-1	-1	*C/D	-0.9
1988	Cal-A	122	352	38	104	17	0	5	39	29	26	.295	.352	.386	.739	113	4	6	94	103	47	.653	2	2	-1	-8	*C	0.3
1989	KC-A	131	405	33	111	13	2	1	43	49	37	.274	.355	.323	.679	97	-2	0	96	125	47	.593	3	2	-0	-8	*C	-0.2
Total	18	2224	7128	668	1810	300	26	105	817	646	596	.254	.318	.348	.665	83	-154	-165	101	116	779	.572	37	49	-18	11	*C/13DO	-7.8
■ **PAT BORDERS** Borders, Patrick Lance b: 5/14/63, Columbus, Ohio BR/TR, 6'2", 190 lbs. Deb: 4/06/88																												
1988	Tor-A	56	154	15	42	6	3	5	21	3	24	.273	.287	.448	.735	103	-0	-0	100	99	18	.615	0	0	0	-1	C/23D	0.1
1989	Tor-A	94	241	22	62	11	1	3	29	11	45	.257	.292	.349	.641	85	-7	-5	94	121	23	.524	2	1	0	-5	CD	-0.6
Total	2	150	395	37	104	17	4	8	50	14	69	.263	.290	.387	.678	92	-7	-5	96	113	41	.559	2	1	0	-5	C/D32	-0.5
■ **THAD BOSLEY** Bosley, Thaddis b: 9/17/56, Oceanside, Cal. BL/TL, 6'3", 175 lbs. Deb: 6/29/77																												
1977	Cal-A	58	212	19	63	10	2	0	19	16	32	.297	.349	.363	.713	100	-1	0	95	100	27	.631	5	4	-1	3	O	0.0
1978	Chi-A	66	219	25	59	5	1	2	13	13	32	.269	.310	.329	.639	79	-6	-6	101	66	20	.554	12	11	-3	4	O	-0.6
1979	Chi-A	36	77	13	24	1	1	1	8	9	14	.312	.384	.390	.773	107	1	1	102	93	12	.782	4	1	1	0	O	0.1
1980	Chi-A	70	147	12	33	2	0	2	14	10	27	.224	.274	.279	.553	54	-10	-9	97	116	10	.446	3	2	-0	-6	O	-1.5
1981	Mil-A	42	105	11	24	2	0	0	3	6	13	.229	.270	.248	.518	52	-7	-6	96	45	7	.395	2	1	0	-6	O/D	-1.3
1982	Sea-A	22	46	3	8	1	0	0	2	4	8	.174	.240	.196	.436	19	-5	-5	109	89	2	.400	3	1	0	-5	O	-1.0
1983	Chi-N	43	72	12	21	4	1	2	12	10	12	.292	.378	.458	.836	129	3	3	101	122	13	.846	1	1	-0	-2	O	0.1
1984	Chi-N	55	98	17	29	2	2	2	14	13	22	.296	.378	.418	.797	112	3	2	110	117	17	.831	5	1	1	-4	O	-0.2
1985	Chi-N	108	180	25	59	6	3	7	27	20	29	.328	.395	.511	.906	130	12	9	116	95	37	.936	5	1	1	-6	O	0.3
1986	Chi-N	87	120	15	33	4	1	1	9	18	24	.275	.370	.350	.720	93	1	-0	107	80	17	.700	3	0	1	-10	O	-1.0
1987	KC-A	80	140	13	39	6	1	1	16	9	26	.279	.322	.357	.679	78	-4	-4	104	120	16	.573	0	0	0	-6	OD	-1.0
1988	KC-A	15	21	1	4	0	0	0	2	2	6	.190	.261	.190	.451	28	-2	-2	103	199	1	.353	0	0	0	-2	/OD	-0.3
	Cal-A	35	75	9	21	5	0	0	7	6	12	.280	.333	.347	.680	96	-1	-0	94	107	9	.579	1	1	-0	-1	O/D	-0.2
	Yr	50	96	10	25	5	0	0	9	8	18	.260	.317	.313	.630	80	-3	-2	97	138	10	.527	1	1	-0	-3		-0.5
1989	Tex-A	37	40	5	9	2	0	1	9	3	11	.225	.279	.350	.629	74	-1	-1	102	206	4	.576	2	0	1	0	/OD	0.0
Total	13	754	1552	180	426	50	12	19	155	139	268	.274	.335	.359	.693	90	-15	-20	103	99	192	.629	46	24	-1	-42	O/D	-6.6
■ **DARYL BOSTON** Boston, Daryl Lamont b: 1/4/63, Cincinnati, Ohio BL/TL, 6'3", 185 lbs. Deb: 5/13/84																												
1984	Chi-A	35	83	8	14	3	1	0	3	4	20	.169	.207	.229	.436	18	-9	-10	111	63	5	.420	6	0	2	-3	O/D	-1.2
1985	Chi-A	95	232	20	53	13	1	3	15	14	44	.228	.272	.332	.604	65	-12	-12	100	69	20	.527	8	6	-1	1	O/D	-1.2
1986	Chi-A	56	199	29	53	11	3	5	22	21	33	.266	.336	.427	.763	106	2	2	101	89	28	.742	9	5	-0	2	O/D	0.2
1987	Chi-A	103	337	51	87	21	2	10	29	25	68	.258	.309	.421	.731	85	-4	-8	109	67	43	.686	12	6	0	3	O/D	-0.7
1988	Chi-A	105	281	37	61	12	2	15	31	21	44	.217	.272	.434	.706	97	-3	-3	97	74	32	.667	9	3	1	0	O/D	-0.2
1989	Chi-A	101	218	34	55	3	4	5	23	24	31	.252	.326	.372	.698	104	-1	1	93	93	29	.675	7	2	1	-7	O/D	-0.6
Total	6	495	1350	179	323	63	13	38	123	109	240	.239	.296	.390	.686	85	-27	-30	101	76	157	.643	51	22	2	-4	O/D	-3.7
■ **PHIL BRADLEY** Bradley, Philip Poole b: 3/11/59, Bloomington, Ind. BR/TR, 6', 185 lbs. Deb: 9/02/83																												
1983	Sea-A	23	67	8	18	2	0	0	5	8	5	.269	.347	.299	.645	80	-2	-2	100	98	8	.620	3	1	0	-1	O/D	-0.2
1984	Sea-A	124	322	49	97	12	4	0	24	34	61	.301	.373	.363	.737	103	3	3	102	82	46	.732	21	8	2	-2	*O/D	0.0
1985	Sea-A	159	641	100	192	33	8	26	88	55	129	.300	.366	.498	.863	141	29	34	95	78	116	.864	22	9	1	4	*O	3.6
1986	Sea-A	143	526	88	163	27	4	12	50	77	134	.310	.406	.445	.851	126	27	23	105	78	99	.885	21	12	-1	-3	*O	1.4

YEAR	TM/L	G	AB	R	H	2B	3B	HR	RBI	BB	SO	AVG	OBP	SLG	PRO	/A	BR	/A	PF	CHI	RC	TA	SB	CS	SBR	FR	POS	TPR
1987	Sea-A	158	603	101	179	38	10	14	67	84	119	.297	.390	.463	.853	123	25	23	103	74	113	.909	40	10	6	-4	*O	1.9
1988	Phi-N	154	569	77	150	30	5	11	56	54	106	.264	.344	.392	.736	110	9	8	101	93	78	.692	11	9	-2	6	*O	0.9
1989	Bal-A	144	545	83	151	23	10	11	55	70	103	.277	.367	.417	.783	122	16	17	99	79	87	.786	20	6	2	-8	*O/D	0.9
Total	7	905	3273	506	950	165	41	74	345	382	657	.290	.374	.434	.807	122	109	106	100	81	547	.814	138	55	8	-8	O/D	8.5

■ SCOTT BRADLEY Bradley, Scott William b: 3/22/60, Glen Ridge, N.J. BL/TR, 5'11", 185 lbs. Deb: 9/09/84

YEAR	TM/L	G	AB	R	H	2B	3B	HR	RBI	BB	SO	AVG	OBP	SLG	PRO	/A	BR	/A	PF	CHI	RC	TA	SB	CS	SBR	FR	POS	TPR
1984	NY-A	9	21	3	6	1	0	0	2	1	1	.286	.318	.333	.652	86	-1	-0	94	114	2	.533	0	0	0	-1	/OC	0.0
1985	NY-A	19	49	4	8	2	1	0	1	1	5	.163	.196	.245	.441	21	-5	-5	96	33	2	.326	0	0	0	0	/CD	-0.4
1986	Chi-A	9	21	3	6	0	0	0	0	1	0	.286	.375	.286	.661	84	-0	-0	101	0	2	.500	0	2	-1	-0	/OD	-0.1
	Sea-A	68	199	17	60	8	3	5	28	12	7	.302	.347	.447	.795	110	4	3	105	107	27	.689	1	0	0	-0	C/D	0.6
	Yr	77	220	20	66	8	3	5	28	13	7	.300	.350	.432	.782	108	4	2	105	95	28	.669	1	2	-1	-0		0.5
1987	Sea-A	102	342	34	95	15	1	5	43	15	18	.278	.314	.371	.685	80	-9	-10	103	121	36	.556	0	1	-1	6	C/3OD	0.1
1988	Sea-A	103	335	45	86	17	1	4	33	17	16	.257	.297	.349	.646	75	-9	-12	108	102	32	.525	1	1	-0	9	C/O31	0.0
1989	Sea-A	103	270	21	74	16	0	3	37	21	23	.274	.329	.367	.695	93	-2	-3	103	133	32	.604	1	1	-0	7	C/1OD	0.7
Total	6	413	1237	127	335	59	6	17	144	68	70	.271	.315	.369	.684	84	-22	-28	104	110	134	.567	3	5	-2	21	C/DO31	0.9

■ BRIAN BRADY Brady, Brian Phelan b: 7/11/62, Queens, N.Y. BL/TL, 5'11", 185 lbs. Deb: 4/16/89

YEAR	TM/L	G	AB	R	H	2B	3B	HR	RBI	BB	SO	AVG	OBP	SLG	PRO	/A	BR	/A	PF	CHI	RC	TA	SB	CS	SBR	FR	POS	TPR
1989	Cal-A	2	2	0	1	1	0	0	1	0	1	.500	.500	1.000	1.500	318	1	1	99	194	1	2.000	0	0	0	-0	/O	0.0

■ GLENN BRAGGS Braggs, Glenn Erick b: 10/17/62, San Bernardino, Cal BR/TR, 6'3", 210 lbs. Deb: 7/18/86

YEAR	TM/L	G	AB	R	H	2B	3B	HR	RBI	BB	SO	AVG	OBP	SLG	PRO	/A	BR	/A	PF	CHI	RC	TA	SB	CS	SBR	FR	POS	TPR
1986	Mil-A	58	215	19	51	8	2	4	18	11	47	.237	.278	.349	.626	69	-9	-10	102	84	20	.515	1	1	-0	0	O/D	-1.0
1987	Mil-A	132	505	67	136	28	7	13	77	47	96	.269	.336	.430	.766	100	2	-0	102	127	69	.711	12	5	1	11	*O/D	0.7
1988	Mil-A	72	272	30	71	14	0	10	42	14	60	.261	.309	.423	.732	99	0	-1	103	122	34	.664	6	4	-1	2	OD	0.0
1989	Mil-A	144	514	77	127	12	3	15	66	42	111	.247	.309	.370	.679	94	-7	-5	97	111	58	.625	17	5	2	-4	*OD	-0.8
Total	4	406	1506	193	385	62	12	42	203	114	314	.256	.314	.396	.710	93	-14	-15	101	115	181	.644	36	15	2	9	O/D	-1.1

■ MICKEY BRANTLEY Brantley, Michael Charles b: 6/17/61, Catskill, N.Y. BR/TR, 5'10", 180 lbs. Deb: 8/09/86

YEAR	TM/L	G	AB	R	H	2B	3B	HR	RBI	BB	SO	AVG	OBP	SLG	PRO	/A	BR	/A	PF	CHI	RC	TA	SB	CS	SBR	FR	POS	TPR
1986	Sea-A	27	102	12	20	3	2	3	7	10	21	.196	.268	.353	.621	65	-5	-5	105	66	9	.547	1	1	-0	2	O	-0.3
1987	Sea-A	92	351	52	106	23	2	14	54	24	44	.302	.347	.499	.845	119	10	9	103	105	62	.845	13	4	2	-0	O/D	0.7
1988	Sea-A	149	577	76	152	25	4	15	56	26	64	.263	.298	.399	.696	87	-7	-12	108	86	66	.622	18	7	1	-11	*O	-2.4
1989	Sea-A	34	108	14	17	5	0	0	8	7	7	.157	.209	.204	.412	16	-12	-12	103	141	5	.330	2	2	-1	0	O/D	-1.2
Total	4	302	1138	154	295	56	8	32	125	67	136	.259	.302	.407	.708	88	-13	-21	105	95	142	.647	34	14	2	-8	O/D	-3.2

■ SID BREAM Bream, Sid b: 8/3/60, Carlisle, Pa. BL/TL, 6'4", 215 lbs. Deb: 9/01/83

YEAR	TM/L	G	AB	R	H	2B	3B	HR	RBI	BB	SO	AVG	OBP	SLG	PRO	/A	BR	/A	PF	CHI	RC	TA	SB	CS	SBR	FR	POS	TPR
1983	LA-N	15	11	0	2	0	0	0	2	2	2	.182	.308	.182	.490	39	-1	-1	100	396	1	.400	0	0	0	0	/1	0.0
1984	LA-N	27	49	2	9	3	0	0	6	6	9	.184	.273	.245	.518	45	-3	-4	104	196	4	.463	1	0	0	1	1	-0.2
1985	LA-N	24	53	4	7	0	0	3	6	7	10	.132	.233	.302	.535	52	-4	-3	93	96	4	.500	0	0	0	0	1	-0.3
	Pit-N	26	95	14	27	7	0	3	15	11	14	.284	.358	.453	.811	122	3	3	103	122	14	.730	0	2	-1	0	1	0.1
	Yr	50	148	18	34	7	0	6	21	18	24	.230	.313	.399	.712	100	-1	-0	98	111	18	.642	0	2	-1	0		-0.2
1986	Pit-N	154	522	73	140	37	5	16	77	60	73	.268	.345	.450	.795	117	12	12	100	111	79	.767	13	7	-0	17	*1/O	2.3
1987	Pit-N	149	516	64	142	25	3	13	65	49	69	.275	.338	.411	.749	93	-2	-5	104	105	66	.673	9	8	-2	8	*1	-0.7
1988	Pit-N	148	462	50	122	37	0	10	65	47	64	.264	.333	.409	.742	115	7	8	98	119	61	.683	9	9	-3	14	*1	1.4
1989	Pit-N	19	36	3	8	3	0	0	4	12	10	.222	.417	.306	.722	117	1	2	94	146	5	.719	0	4	-2	-0	1	-0.1
Total	7	562	1744	210	457	112	8	45	240	194	251	.262	.337	.413	.749	105	13	12	100	117	233	.693	32	30	-8	39	1/O	2.5

■ BOB BRENLY Brenly, Robert Earl b: 2/25/54, Coshocton, Ohio BR/TR, 6'2", 210 lbs. Deb: 8/14/81

YEAR	TM/L	G	AB	R	H	2B	3B	HR	RBI	BB	SO	AVG	OBP	SLG	PRO	/A	BR	/A	PF	CHI	RC	TA	SB	CS	SBR	FR	POS	TPR
1981	SF-N	19	45	5	15	2	1	1	4	6	4	.333	.423	.489	.912	150	4	3	105	63	9	.906	0	1	-1	-0	C/3O	0.3
1982	SF-N	65	180	26	51	4	1	4	15	18	26	.283	.352	.383	.735	113	2	3	94	73	25	.707	6	2	1	1	C/3	0.5
1983	SF-N	104	281	36	63	12	2	7	34	37	48	.224	.319	.356	.675	86	-5	-5	101	111	30	.629	10	7	-1	3	C1/O	0.0
1984	SF-N	145	506	74	147	28	0	20	80	48	52	.291	.355	.464	.820	134	19	21	96	108	79	.764	6	9	-4	-3	*C1/O	1.8
1985	SF-N	133	440	41	97	16	1	19	56	57	62	.220	.313	.391	.704	102	-3	1	93	99	55	.657	1	4	-2	5	*C31	0.8
1986	SF-N	149	472	60	116	26	0	16	62	74	97	.246	.352	.403	.754	112	6	9	96	104	71	.757	10	6	-1	-14	*C31	-0.4
1987	SF-N	123	375	55	100	19	1	18	51	47	85	.267	.353	.467	.820	120	8	10	96	89	63	.819	10	7	-1	1	*C/13	1.8
1988	SF-N	73	206	13	39	7	0	5	22	20	40	.189	.268	.296	.564	66	-10	-9	94	116	17	.488	1	2	-1	-7	C	-1.3
1989	Tor-A	48	88	9	15	3	1	1	6	10	17	.170	.255	.261	.516	49	-6	-6	94	90	6	.453	1	0	0	-1	DC/1	-0.5
	SF-N	12	22	2	4	2	0	0	3	1	7	.182	.217	.273	.490	41	-2	-2	97	201	1	.368	0	0	0	-1	C	-0.1
Total	9	871	2615	321	647	119	7	91	333	318	438	.247	.333	.403	.736	108	12	25	96	101	356	.697	45	38	-9	-16	C/13DO	2.9

■ GEORGE BRETT Brett, George Howard b: 5/15/53, Glen Dale, W.Va. BL/TR, 6', 185 lbs. Deb: 8/02/73

YEAR	TM/L	G	AB	R	H	2B	3B	HR	RBI	BB	SO	AVG	OBP	SLG	PRO	/A	BR	/A	PF	CHI	RC	TA	SB	CS	SBR	FR	POS	TPR
1973	KC-A	13	40	2	5	2	0	0	0	0	5	.125	.125	.175	.300	-15	-6	-7	109	0	1	.200	0	0	0	-1	3	-0.8
1974	KC-A	133	457	49	129	21	5	2	47	21	38	.282	.314	.363	.677	89	-4	-8	106	107	50	.570	8	5	-1	-6	*3/S	-1.2
1975	KC-A	159	634	84	**195**	35	**13**	11	89	46	49	.308	.356	.456	.812	126	22	20	102	112	102	.766	13	10	-2	-5	*3/S	1.6
1976	KC-A	159	645	94	**215**	34	**14**	7	67	49	36	**.333**	.381	.462	.843	146	36	36	100	78	**114**	.822	21	11	-0	2	*3/S	4.0
1977	KC-A	139	564	105	176	32	13	22	88	55	24	.312	.375	.532	.907	143	33	33	100	92	108	.900	14	12	-3	20	*3/SD	4.6
1978	KC-A	128	510	79	150	**45**	8	9	62	39	35	.294	.345	.467	.812	124	16	15	102	89	83	.807	23	7	3	5	*3/S	2.2
1979	KC-A	154	645	119	**212**	42	**20**	23	107	51	36	.329	.378	.563	.941	142	43	38	105	92	134	.956	17	10	-1	16	*3/1	5.3
1980	KC-A	117	449	87	175	33	9	24	118	58	22	**.390**	**.461**	**.664**	**1.124**	**207**	**65**	**66**	98	132	**135**	**1.278**	15	6	1	3	*3/1	**6.7**
1981	KC-A	89	347	42	109	27	7	6	43	27	23	.314	.365	.484	.849	145	18	19	99	96	60	.837	14	6	1	-9	3	1.1
1982	KC-A	144	552	101	166	32	9	21	82	71	51	.301	.381	.505	.887	141	32	32	100	92	107	.895	6	1	1	-2	*3O	2.8
1983	KC-A	123	464	90	144	38	2	25	93	57	39	.310	.387	**.563**	**.949**	155	36	35	101	104	100	.967	0	1	-1	-10	*31O/D	2.3
1984	KC-A	104	377	42	107	21	3	13	69	38	37	.284	.349	.459	.808	123	11	11	99	137	58	.746	0	2	-1	4	*3	1.6
1985	KC-A	155	550	108	184	38	5	30	112	103	49	.335	.442	**.585**	**1.028**	**175**	**63**	**62**	102	114	**146**	1.153	9	1	2	14	*3/D	7.0
1986	KC-A	124	441	70	128	28	4	16	73	80	45	.290	.404	.481	.885	141	28	28	100	118	89	.925	1	2	-1	7	*3/SD	2.9
1987	KC-A	115	427	71	124	18	2	22	78	72	47	.290	.394	.496	.890	130	24	21	104	108	85	.921	6	3	0	0	1D3	1.1
1988	KC-A	157	589	90	180	42	3	24	103	82	51	.306	.393	.509	.903	146	41	39	103	106	119	.934	14	3	2	-9	*1D/S	2.5
1989	KC-A	124	457	67	129	26	3	12	80	59	47	.282	.368	.431	.799	130	16	18	96	**141**	71	.780	14	4	2	3	*1D/O	1.6
Total	17	2137	8148	1300	2528	514	120	267	1311	908	634	.310	.381	.501	.882	141	474	460	101	106	1563	.885	175	84	2	32	*31/DOS	45.3

■ GREG BRILEY Briley, Gregory "Peewee" b: 5/24/65, Bethel, N.C. BL/TR, 5'9", 170 lbs. Deb: 6/27/88

YEAR	TM/L	G	AB	R	H	2B	3B	HR	RBI	BB	SO	AVG	OBP	SLG	PRO	/A	BR	/A	PF	CHI	RC	TA	SB	CS	SBR	FR	POS	TPR
1988	Sea-A	13	36	6	9	2	0	1	4	5	6	.250	.341	.389	.730	97	0	-0	108	94	5	.679	0	1	-1	-2	O	-0.2
1989	Sea-A	115	394	52	105	22	4	13	52	39	82	.266	.340	.442	.782	115	9	8	103	97	59	.756	11	5	0	-7	*O2/D	0.0
Total	2	128	430	58	114	24	4	14	56	44	88	.265	.340	.437	.778	113	10	8	104	96	64	.749	11	6	-0	-10	O/2D	-0.2

■ GREG BROCK Brock, Gregory Allen b: 6/14/57, Mc Minnville, Ore. BL/TR, 6'3", 200 lbs. Deb: 9/01/82

YEAR	TM/L	G	AB	R	H	2B	3B	HR	RBI	BB	SO	AVG	OBP	SLG	PRO	/A	BR	/A	PF	CHI	RC	TA	SB	CS	SBR	FR	POS	TPR
1982	LA-N	18	17	1	2	1	0	0	1	1	5	.118	.167	.176	.343	-4	-2	-2	95	131	1	.267	0	0	0	0	/1	-0.2
1983	LA-N	146	455	64	102	14	2	20	66	83	81	.224	.345	.396	.741	105	4	4	100	109	64	.733	5	1	1	2	*1	0.1
1984	LA-N	88	271	33	61	6	0	14	34	39	37	.225	.323	.402	.725	99	1	-0	104	88	37	.722	8	0	2	4	1	0.4
1985	LA-N	129	438	64	110	19	0	21	66	54	72	.251	.333	.438	.772	123	8	12	93	105	65	.737	4	2	0	-0	*1	0.8
1986	LA-N	115	325	33	76	13	0	16	52	37	60	.234	.312	.422	.734	107	-1	2	94	112	42	.680	2	5	-2	6	1	0.2
1987	Mil-A	141	532	81	159	29	3	13	85	57	63	.299	.373	.438	.811	113	13	11	102	132	88	.780	5	4	-1	3	*1	0.0
1988	Mil-A	115	364	53	77	16	1	6	50	63	48	.212	.333	.310	.643	79	-7	-9	103	155	39	.617	6	2	1	9	*1/D	-0.5
1989	Mil-A	107	373	40	99	16	0	12	52	43	49	.265	.346	.405	.751	115	6	7	97	110	53	.712	6	1	1	-3	*1/D	0.0
Total	8	859	2775	369	686	114	6	102	406	377	415	.247	.340	.403	.743	106	21	24	99	117	389	.713	36	15	2	21	1/D	0.8

■ TOM BROOKENS Brookens, Thomas Dale b: 8/10/53, Chambersburg, Pa. BR/TR, 5'10", 165 lbs. Deb: 7/10/79

YEAR	TM/L	G	AB	R	H	2B	3B	HR	RBI	BB	SO	AVG	OBP	SLG	PRO	/A	BR	/A	PF	CHI	RC	TA	SB	CS	SBR	FR	POS	TPR
1979	Det-A	60	190	23	50	5	2	4	21	11	40	.263	.310	.374	.684	87	-5	-4	96	97	23	.644	10	3	1	4	32	0.3
1980	Det-A	151	509	64	140	25	9	10	66	32	71	.275	.319	.418	.738	95	-1	-4	105	106	64	.664	13	11	-3	-2	*3/2SD	-0.8
1981	Det-A	71	239	19	58	10	1	4	25	14	43	.243	.290	.343	.633	78	-6	-7	105	104	23	.545	5	3	-0	-2	3	-0.9
1982	Det-A	140	398	40	92	15	3	9	58	27	63	.231	.280	.352	.632	72	-16	-16	100	139	36	.531	5	9	-4	-4	*32/SO	-2.3

YEAR	TM/L	G	AB	R	H	2B	3B	HR	RBI	BB	SO	AVG	OBP	SLG	PRO	/A	BR	/A	PF	CHI	RC	TA	SB	CS	SBR	FR	POS	TPR
1983	Det-A	138	332	50	71	13	3	6	32	29	46	.214	.281	.325	.606	69	-15	-13	96	99	32	.556	10	4	1	-9	*3S2/D	-1.9
1984	Det-A	113	224	32	55	11	4	5	26	19	33	.246	.307	.397	.705	97	-2	-1	96	100	27	.650	6	6	-2	-6	3S2/D	-0.4
1985	Det-A	156	485	54	115	34	6	7	47	27	78	.237	.277	.375	.653	72	-17	-20	106	92	50	.582	14	5	1	-1	*3/S2CD	-2.3
1986	Det-A	98	281	42	76	11	2	3	25	20	42	.270	.321	.356	.677	89	-6	-4	95	91	32	.608	11	8	-2	-2	32SD/O	-0.5
1987	Det-A	143	444	59	107	15	3	13	59	33	63	.241	.296	.376	.673	80	-14	-13	97	114	49	.599	7	4	-0	1	*3S2	-1.1
1988	Det-A	136	441	62	107	23	5	5	38	44	74	.243	.316	.351	.667	92	-8	-4	94	89	49	.594	4	4	-1	-3	*3/2S	-0.7
1989	NY-A	66	168	14	38	6	0	4	14	11	27	.226	.274	.333	.607	67	-7	-8	104	80	14	.500	1	3	-2	-2	3/S2OD	-1.0
Total	11	1272	3711	459	909	168	38	70	411	267	580	.245	.298	.367	.665	82	-96	-95	100	103	399	.591	86	60	-10	-24	*32S/DOC	-11.6
■ **HUBIE BROOKS**	Brooks, Hubert b: 9/24/56, Los Angeles, Cal. BR/TR, 6', 178 lbs. Deb: 9/04/80																											
1980	NY-N	24	81	8	25	2	1	1	10	5	9	.309	.364	.395	.759	116	1	2	96	113	12	.690	1	1	-0	-1	3	0.1
1981	NY-N	98	358	34	110	21	2	4	38	23	65	.307	.351	.411	.761	115	7	6	101	96	50	.687	9	5	-0	-2	3/OS	0.0
1982	NY-N	126	457	40	114	21	2	2	40	28	76	.249	.300	.317	.617	74	-17	-16	99	106	43	.515	6	3	0	-15	*3	-3.4
1983	NY-N	150	586	53	147	18	4	5	58	24	96	.251	.285	.321	.606	69	-26	-25	99	120	51	.486	6	4	-1	3	*3/2	-2.8
1984	NY-N	153	561	61	159	23	2	16	73	48	79	.283	.342	.417	.759	112	9	9	100	104	75	.684	6	5	-1	-20	*3S	-1.0
1985	Mon-N	156	605	67	163	34	7	13	100	34	79	.269	.314	.413	.727	109	-0	4	94	146	71	.626	6	9	-4	-33	*S	-2.1
1986	Mon-N	80	306	50	104	18	5	14	58	25	60	.340	.393	.569	.962	166	25	26	98	113	65	.953	4	2	0	-15	S	1.9
1987	Mon-N	112	430	57	113	22	3	14	72	24	72	.263	.303	.426	.729	85	-7	-10	106	130	54	.648	4	3	-1	-16	*S	-1.3
1988	Mon-N	151	588	61	164	35	2	20	90	35	108	.279	.321	.447	.768	112	12	8	106	118	78	.683	7	3	0	-7	*O	-0.2
1989	Mon-N	148	542	56	145	30	1	14	70	39	108	.268	.321	.404	.725	104	4	2	102	110	65	.634	6	11	-5	-8	*O	-1.3
Total	10	1198	4514	487	1244	224	29	103	609	285	752	.276	.322	.407	.729	102	6	6	100	117	562	.640	55	46	-11	-113	3SO/2	-10.1
■ **BOB BROWER**	Brower, Robert Richard b: 1/10/60, Jamaica, N.Y. BR/TR, 5'11", 185 lbs. Deb: 9/03/86																											
1986	Tex-A	21	9	3	1	1	0	0	0	0	3	.111	.111	.222	.333	-12	-1	-1	96	0	-0	.300	1	2	-1	-5	O/D	-0.7
1987	Tex-A	127	303	63	79	10	3	14	46	36	66	.261	.339	.452	.791	105	4	2	104	103	47	.800	15	9	-1	-7	*O/D	-0.7
1988	Tex-A	82	201	29	45	7	0	1	11	27	38	.224	.316	.274	.589	66	-8	-9	101	75	18	.551	10	5	0	-4	OD	-1.3
1989	NY-A	26	69	9	16	3	0	2	3	6	11	.232	.293	.362	.656	80	-2	-2	104	38	7	.618	3	1	0	3	O	0.0
Total	4	256	582	104	141	21	3	17	60	69	118	.242	.323	.376	.699	88	-7	-10	103	84	73	.679	29	17	-2	-14	O/D	-2.7
■ **CHRIS BROWN**	Brown, John Christopher b: 8/15/61, Jackson, Miss. BR/TR, 6', 185 lbs. Deb: 9/03/84																											
1984	SF-N	23	84	6	24	7	0	1	11	9	19	.286	.362	.405	.766	120	2	2	96	119	12	.708	2	1	0	-4	3	-0.1
1985	SF-N	131	432	50	117	20	3	16	61	38	78	.271	.345	.442	.787	127	10	14	93	102	61	.718	2	3	-1	5	*3	1.9
1986	SF-N	116	416	57	132	16	3	7	49	33	43	.317	.380	.421	.801	126	12	14	96	102	65	.762	13	9	-2	-15	*3/S	-0.4
1987	SF-N	38	132	17	32	6	0	6	17	9	16	.242	.306	.424	.730	95	-2	-1	96	92	14	.627	1	3	-2	1	3/S	-0.1
	SD-N	44	155	17	36	3	0	6	23	11	30	.232	.296	.368	.664	77	-6	-5	97	125	16	.583	3	1	0	-0	3	-0.5
	Yr	82	287	34	68	9	0	12	40	20	46	.237	.300	.394	.694	85	-8	-7	96	110	30	.603	4	4	-1	1		-0.6
1988	SD-N	80	247	14	58	6	0	2	19	19	49	.235	.297	.283	.581	69	-10	-9	97	100	20	.465	0	0	0	-2	3	-1.1
1989	Det-A	17	57	3	11	3	0	0	4	1	17	.193	.207	.246	.453	28	-6	-5	97	111	2	.306	0	0	0	-1	3	-0.5
Total	6	449	1523	164	410	61	6	38	184	120	252	.269	.335	.392	.727	105	1	9	96	104	190	.646	21	17	-4	-16	3/S	-0.8
■ **MARTY BROWN**	Brown, Marty Leo b: 1/23/63, Lawton, Okla. BR/TR, 6'1", 190 lbs. Deb: 9/04/88																											
1988	Cin-N	10	16	0	3	1	0	0	2	1	2	.188	.235	.250	.485	37	-1	-1	105	200	1	.357	0	1	-1	0	/3	-0.1
1989	Cin-N	16	30	2	5	1	0	0	4	4	9	.167	.265	.200	.465	34	-2	-3	103	268	2	.400	0	0	0	0	3	-0.2
Total	2	26	46	2	8	2	0	0	6	5	11	.174	.255	.217	.472	35	-4	-4	104	245	3	.385	0	1	-1	1	/3	-0.3
■ **JERRY BROWNE**	Browne, Jerome Austin b: 2/13/66, Christiansted, V.I. BB/TR, 5'10", 140 lbs. Deb: 9/06/86																											
1986	Tex-A	12	24	6	10	2	0	0	3	1	4	.417	.440	.500	.940	164	2	2	96	100	4	.813	0	2	-1	-0	/2	0.1
1987	Tex-A	132	454	63	123	16	6	1	38	61	50	.271	.360	.339	.699	85	-6	-8	104	99	59	.689	27	17	-2	-2	*2/D	-0.2
1988	Tex-A	73	214	26	49	9	2	1	17	25	32	.229	.310	.304	.613	72	-7	-8	101	99	20	.554	7	5	-1	-6	2/D	-1.0
1989	Cle-A	153	598	83	179	31	4	5	45	68	64	.299	.372	.390	.761	111	13	11	104	62	90	.728	14	6	1	-41	*2/D	-2.7
Total	4	370	1290	178	361	58	12	7	103	155	150	.280	.358	.360	.718	96	2	-3	103	82	173	.684	48	30	-4	-49	2/D	-3.8
■ **MIKE BRUMLEY**	Brumley, Anthony Michael b: 4/9/63, Oklahoma City, Okla. BB/TR, 5'10", 165 lbs. Deb: 6/16/87																											
1987	Chi-N	39	104	8	21	2	2	1	9	10	30	.202	.278	.288	.567	50	-7	-8	101	109	9	.558	7	1	2	1	S/2	0.0
1989	Det-A	92	212	33	42	5	2	1	11	14	45	.198	.251	.255	.506	44	-16	-15	97	75	14	.433	8	4	0	0	S23/OD	-1.1
Total	2	131	316	41	63	7	4	2	20	24	75	.199	.260	.266	.526	46	-23	-23	98	86	23	.473	15	5	2	1	/S23DO	-1.1
■ **TOM BRUNANSKY**	Brunansky, Thomas Andrew b: 8/20/60, Covina, Cal. BR/TR, 6'4", 205 lbs. Deb: 4/09/81																											
1981	Cal-A	11	33	7	5	0	0	3	6	8	10	.152	.317	.424	.741	108	1	0	104	102	5	.821	1	0	0	3	O	0.3
1982	Min-A	127	463	77	126	30	1	20	46	71	101	.272	.378	.471	.849	131	22	22	100	70	84	.849	1	2	-1	16	*O	3.2
1983	Min-A	151	542	70	123	24	5	28	82	61	95	.227	.310	.445	.754	100	2	-1	105	101	72	.705	2	5	-2	5	*O/D	0.0
1984	Min-A	155	567	75	144	21	0	32	85	57	94	.254	.322	.460	.782	108	9	5	106	97	81	.727	4	5	-2	1	*O/D	0.0
1985	Min-A	157	567	71	137	28	4	27	90	71	86	.242	.326	.448	.774	106	7	4	103	113	83	.742	5	3	-0	-0	*O	0.1
1986	Min-A	157	593	69	152	28	1	23	75	53	98	.256	.318	.423	.742	93	0	-7	108	99	78	.689	12	4	1	3	*O/D	-0.6
1987	Min-A	155	532	83	138	22	2	32	85	74	104	.259	.354	.489	.843	127	17	20	96	97	90	.837	11	11	-3	4	*OD	1.6
1988	Min-A	14	49	5	9	1	0	1	6	7	11	.184	.286	.265	.551	52	-3	-3	106	152	4	.500	1	2	-1	-3	O/D	-0.6
	StL-N	143	523	69	128	22	4	22	79	79	82	.245	.348	.428	.776	117	16	13	104	115	79	.773	16	6	1	-1	*O	1.0
1989	StL-N	158	556	67	133	29	3	20	85	59	107	.239	.314	.410	.724	105	3	3	101	121	70	.665	5	9	-4	-3	*O/1	-0.6
Total	9	1228	4425	593	1095	205	20	208	639	540	788	.247	.332	.444	.776	109	74	57	103	103	646	.742	58	47	-11	25	*O/D1	4.4
■ **BILL BUCKNER**	Buckner, William Joseph b: 12/14/49, Vallejo, Cal. BL/TL, 6', 185 lbs. Deb: 9/21/69																											
1969	LA-N	1	1	0	0	0	0	0	0	0	0	.000	.000	.000	.000	-99	-0	-0	99	0	0	.000	0	0	0	0	H	0.0
1970	LA-N	28	68	6	13	3	1	0	4	3	7	.191	.225	.265	.490	34	-7	-6	90	86	4	.375	0	1	-1	0	O/1	-0.6
1971	LA-N	108	358	37	99	15	1	5	41	11	18	.277	.307	.366	.673	91	-5	-5	99	114	40	.568	4	1	1	-0	O1	-0.8
1972	LA-N	105	383	47	122	14	3	5	37	17	13	.319	.349	.410	.759	123	7	9	94	90	52	.668	10	3	1	-1	O1	0.5
1973	LA-N	140	575	68	158	20	0	8	46	17	34	.275	.299	.351	.650	79	-17	-17	100	87	58	.539	12	2	2	-8	1O	-3.0
1974	LA-N	145	580	83	182	30	3	7	58	30	24	.314	.352	.412	.764	122	9	14	93	91	81	.717	31	13	2	-7	*O/1	0.3
1975	LA-N	92	288	30	70	11	2	6	31	17	15	.243	.290	.358	.648	83	-9	-7	95	99	27	.560	8	3	1	0	O	-0.9
1976	LA-N	154	642	76	193	28	4	7	60	26	26	.301	.329	.389	.718	104	1	1	100	82	82	.655	28	9	3	-2	*O/1	-0.2
1977	Chi-N	122	426	40	121	27	0	11	60	21	23	.284	.319	.425	.744	86	-3	-10	114	112	52	.644	7	5	-1	4	1	-1.1
1978	Chi-N	117	446	47	144	26	1	5	74	18	17	.323	.349	.419	.768	103	7	2	110	148	59	.656	7	5	-1	8	*1	0.6
1979	Chi-N	149	591	72	168	34	7	14	66	30	28	.284	.321	.437	.758	93	2	-7	112	92	78	.675	9	4	0	16	*1	0.3
1980	Chi-N	145	578	69	187	41	3	10	68	30	18	**.324**	.357	.457	.814	118	18	14	106	97	90	.727	1	2	-1	2	1O	0.9
1981	Chi-N	106	421	45	131	**35**	3	10	75	26	16	.311	.353	.480	.832	129	17	15	104	134	65	.757	5	2	0	0	*1	1.3
1982	Chi-N	161	657	93	201	34	5	15	105	36	26	.306	.347	.441	.788	115	15	13	103	118	98	.728	15	5	2	16	*1	2.2
1983	Chi-N	153	626	79	175	**38**	6	16	66	25	30	.280	.313	.436	.749	104	2	1	101	78	83	.677	12	4	1	17	*1O	1.3
1984	Chi-N	21	43	3	9	0	0	0	2	1	1	.209	.244	.209	.454	26	-4	-5	110	87	2	.314	0	0	0	1	/1O	-0.3
	Bos-A	114	439	51	122	21	2	11	67	24	38	.278	.323	.410	.733	92	0	-6	110	128	55	.639	2	2	-1	7	*1	-0.6
1985	Bos-A	162	673	89	201	46	3	16	110	30	36	.299	.330	.447	.778	108	8	6	102	132	96	.713	18	4	3	**25**	*1	2.3
1986	Bos-A	153	629	73	168	39	2	18	102	40	25	.267	.315	.421	.736	100	-2	-1	100	122	76	.643	6	4	-1	16	*1D	0.4
1987	Bos-A	75	286	23	78	6	1	2	42	13	19	.273	.304	.322	.626	68	-13	-13	99	174	25	.480	1	3	-2	-2	1	-2.2
	Cal-A	57	183	16	56	12	1	3	32	9	7	.306	.339	.432	.770	104	1	1	99	145	26	.685	1	0	0	-0	D/1	0.0
	Yr	132	469	39	134	18	2	5	74	22	26	.286	.318	.365	.682	82	-12	-12	99	163	51	.556	2	3	-1	-2		-2.2
1988	Cal-A	19	43	1	9	0	0	0	9	4	0	.209	.277	.209	.486	41	-3	-3	94	398	3	.417	2	0	1	0	D/1	-0.2
	KC-A	89	242	18	62	14	0	3	34	13	19	.256	.294	.351	.645	77	-7	-8	103	144	24	.540	3	1	0	-1	D1	-0.9
	Yr	108	285	19	71	14	0	3	43	17	19	.249	.291	.330	.621	72	-10	-11	102	192	27	.520	5	1	1	-1		-1.1
1989	KC-A	79	176	7	38	4	1	1	16	6	11	.216	.242	.267	.509	45	-13	-12	96	124	11	.380	1	0	0	1	1D	-1.2
Total	21	2495	9354	1073	2707	498	49	173	1205	447	451	.289	.325	.409	.733	100	4	-22	102	112	1187	.645	183	73	11	93	*1OD	-1.9

YEAR	TM/L	G	AB	R	H	2B	3B	HR	RBI	BB	SO	AVG	OBP	SLG	PRO	/A	BR	/A	PF	CHI	RC	TA	SB	CS	SBR	FR	POS	TPR
■ STEVE BUECHELE Buechele, Steven Bernard b: 9/26/61, Lancaster, Cal. BR/TR, 6'2", 190 lbs. Deb: 7/19/85																												
1985	Tex-A	69	219	22	48	6	3	6	21	14	38	.219	.272	.356	.629	65	-9	-12	108	87	18	.527	3	2	-0	7	3/2	-0.6
1986	Tex-A	153	461	54	112	19	2	18	54	35	98	.243	.303	.410	.713	97	-5	-2	96	89	54	.638	5	8	-3	4	*32/O	-0.3
1987	Tex-A	136	363	45	86	20	0	13	50	28	66	.237	.293	.399	.693	79	-10	-12	104	108	42	.615	2	2	-1	-8	*32/O	-2.0
1988	Tex-A	155	503	68	126	21	4	16	58	65	79	.250	.342	.404	.746	107	6	5	101	92	71	.707	2	4	-2	8	*3/2	1.2
1989	Tex-A	155	486	60	114	22	2	16	59	36	107	.235	.294	.387	.681	88	-7	-9	102	97	50	.581	1	3	-2	15	*32/SD	0.5
Total	5	668	2032	249	486	88	11	69	242	178	388	.239	.306	.395	.701	91	-25	-29	101	95	235	.624	13	19	-8	26	3/2ODS	-1.2
■ JAY BUHNER Buhner, Jay Campbell b: 8/13/64, Louisville, Ky. BR/TR, 6'3", 205 lbs. Deb: 9/11/87																												
1987	NY-A	7	22	0	5	2	0	0	1	1	6	.227	.261	.318	.579	55	-1	-1	98	57	2	.444	0	0	0	0	/O	0.0
1988	NY-A	25	69	8	13	0	0	3	13	3	25	.188	.253	.319	.572	62	-4	-4	96	167	6	.491	0	0	0	1	O	-0.2
	Sea-A	60	192	28	43	13	1	10	25	25	68	.224	.323	.458	.781	108	4	2	108	86	29	.760	1	1	-0	8	O	0.8
	Yr	85	261	36	56	13	1	13	38	28	93	.215	.305	.421	.727	97	-0	-1	104	112	34	.687	1	1	-0	9		0.6
1989	Sea-A	58	204	27	56	15	1	9	33	19	55	.275	.342	.490	.832	128	8	7	103	103	34	.803	1	4	-2	1	O	0.5
Total	3	150	487	63	117	30	2	22	72	48	154	.240	.319	.446	.764	108	7	4	104	103	70	.722	2	5	-2	10	O	1.1
■ ERIC BULLOCK Bullock, Eric Gerald b: 2/16/60, Los Angeles, Cal. BL/TL, 5'11", 185 lbs. Deb: 8/26/85																												
1985	Hou-N	18	25	3	7	2	0	0	2	1	3	.280	.308	.360	.668	90	-1	-0	96	88	2	.526	0	1	-1	-2	/O	-0.2
1986	Hou-N	6	21	0	1	0	0	0	1	0	3	.048	.048	.048	.095	-72	-5	-5	103	399	0	.150	2	0	1	-1	/O	-0.5
1988	Min-A	16	17	3	5	0	0	0	3	3	1	.294	.400	.294	.694	92	0	-0	106	239	3	.750	1	0	0	-1	/OD	0.0
1989	Phi-N	6	4	1	0	0	0	0	0	0	2	.000	.000	.000	.000	-99	-1	-1	101	0	0	.000	0	0	0	-1	/O	-0.1
Total	4	46	67	7	13	2	0	0	6	4	9	.194	.239	.224	.463	30	-6	-6	101	217	5	.400	3	1	0	-4	/OD	-0.8
■ ELLIS BURKS Burks, Ellis Rena b: 9/11/64, Vicksburg, Miss. BR/TR, 6'2", 175 lbs. Deb: 4/30/87																												
1987	Bos-A	133	558	94	152	30	2	20	59	41	98	.272	.324	.441	.765	102	0	1	99	74	85	.765	27	6	5	9	*O/D	1.0
1988	Bos-A	144	540	93	159	37	5	18	92	62	89	.294	.370	.481	.852	125	27	20	109	123	99	.879	25	9	2	6	*O/D	2.5
1989	Bos-A	97	399	73	121	19	6	12	61	36	52	.303	.368	.471	.839	129	18	16	105	102	71	.859	21	5	3	5	O/D	2.3
Total	3	374	1497	260	432	86	13	50	212	139	239	.289	.353	.464	.817	118	45	37	104	99	255	.831	73	20	10	19	O/D	5.8
■ RANDY BUSH Bush, Robert Randall b: 10/5/58, Dover, Del. BL/TL, 6'1", 186 lbs. Deb: 5/01/82																												
1982	Min-A	55	119	13	29	6	1	4	13	8	28	.244	.308	.412	.719	95	-1	-1	100	85	16	.659	0	0	0	-1	D/O	-0.1
1983	Min-A	124	373	43	93	24	3	11	56	34	51	.249	.324	.418	.742	97	1	-2	105	116	50	.684	0	1	-1	0	*D/1	-0.1
1984	Min-A	113	311	46	69	17	1	11	43	31	60	.222	.301	.389	.690	85	-5	-7	106	111	38	.641	1	2	-1	0	D/1	-0.7
1985	Min-A	97	234	26	56	13	3	10	35	24	30	.239	.323	.449	.772	105	3	1	103	103	36	.757	3	0	1	-6	OD/1	-0.4
1986	Min-A	130	357	50	96	19	7	7	45	39	63	.269	.348	.420	.768	101	5	1	108	105	53	.731	5	3	-0	-11	*O/1D	-1.2
1987	Min-A	122	293	46	74	10	2	11	46	43	49	.253	.354	.413	.767	108	2	4	96	119	45	.776	10	3	1	-10	O/1D	-0.6
1988	Min-A	136	394	51	103	20	3	14	51	58	49	.261	.369	.434	.803	117	14	11	106	95	64	.807	8	6	-1	-9	*O/1D	-0.1
1989	Min-A	141	391	60	103	17	4	14	54	48	73	.263	.348	.435	.783	112	10	7	107	99	54	.724	5	8	-3	-5	*O1/D	-0.4
Total	8	918	2472	335	623	126	24	82	343	285	403	.252	.338	.422	.760	104	29	15	104	105	356	.728	32	23	-4	-43	OD/1	-3.6
■ BRETT BUTLER Butler, Brett Morgan b: 6/15/57, Los Angeles, Cal. BL/TL, 5'10", 160 lbs. Deb: 8/20/81																												
1981	Atl-N	40	126	17	32	2	3	0	4	19	17	.254	.352	.317	.669	91	-1	-1	100	39	17	.716	9	1	2	-0	O	0.0
1982	Atl-N	89	240	35	52	2	0	0	7	25	35	.217	.291	.225	.516	43	-17	-19	107	51	19	.508	21	8	2	-6	O	-2.4
1983	Atl-N	151	549	84	154	21	**13**	5	37	54	56	.281	.347	.393	.741	99	4	0	106	65	76	.737	39	22	-2	8	*O	0.5
1984	Cle-A	159	602	108	162	25	9	3	49	86	62	.269	.364	.355	.720	94	3	-2	106	84	87	.762	52	22	2	5	*O	0.0
1985	Cle-A	152	591	106	184	28	14	5	50	63	42	.311	.379	.431	.810	129	19	23	94	71	100	.841	47	20	2	15	*O/D	3.7
1986	Cle-A	161	587	92	163	17	**14**	4	51	70	65	.278	.359	.375	.733	104	3	5	98	93	84	.729	32	15	1	0	*O	0.1
1987	Cle-A	137	522	91	154	25	8	9	41	91	55	.295	.401	.425	.826	117	19	17	103	58	97	.897	33	16	0	9	*O	2.1
1988	SF-N	157	568	**109**	163	27	9	6	43	97	64	.287	.395	.398	.793	136	25	29	94	75	99	.867	43	20	1	-2	*O	2.6
1989	SF-N	154	594	100	168	22	4	4	36	59	69	.283	.351	.354	.704	105	3	5	97	63	78	.679	31	16	-0	6	*O	0.9
Total	9	1200	4379	742	1232	169	74	36	318	564	465	.281	.366	.378	.744	107	58	58	100	71	656	.766	307	140	8	35	*O/D	7.5
■ FRANCISCO CABRERA Cabrera, Francisco (Paulino) b: 10/10/66, Santo Domingo, D.R. BR/TR, 6'4", 195 lbs. Deb: 7/24/89																												
1989	Tor-A	3	12	1	2	1	0	0	0	1	3	.167	.231	.250	.481	38	-1	-1	94	0	1	.400	0	0	0	0	/D	0.0
	Atl-N	4	14	0	3	2	0	0	0	0	3	.214	.214	.357	.571	59	-1	-1	102	0	1	.455	0	0	0	0	/1C	0.0
Total	1	7	26	1	5	3	0	0	0	1	6	.192	.231	.286	.509	49	-2	-2	98	0	2	.429	0	0	0	0	/1CD	0.0
■ IVAN CALDERON Calderon, Ivan (Perez) b: 3/19/62, Fajardo, P.R. BR/TR, 5'11", 160 lbs. Deb: 8/10/84																												
1984	Sea-A	11	24	2	5	1	0	1	1	2	5	.208	.269	.375	.644	74	-1	-1	102	33	2	.545	1	0	0	-0	O	0.0
1985	Sea-A	67	210	37	60	16	4	8	28	19	45	.286	.351	.514	.865	141	9	11	95	84	34	.821	4	2	0	1	O/1D	1.0
1986	Sea-A	37	131	13	31	5	0	2	13	6	33	.237	.275	.321	.596	59	-7	-8	105	108	12	.510	3	1	0	-0	O	-0.8
	Chi-A	13	33	3	10	2	1	0	2	3	6	.303	.361	.424	.785	113	1	1	101	57	5	.739	0	0	0	-1	/OD	0.0
	Yr	50	164	16	41	7	1	2	15	9	39	.250	.293	.341	.635	70	-6	-7	104	97	17	.552	3	1	0	-1		-0.8
1987	Chi-A	144	542	93	159	38	2	28	83	60	109	.293	.365	.526	.891	123	26	19	109	95	102	.888	10	5	0	2	*O/D	1.6
1988	Chi-A	73	264	40	56	14	0	14	35	34	66	.212	.302	.424	.726	104	-0	1	97	96	33	.688	4	4	-1	-0	O/D	-0.1
1989	Chi-A	157	622	83	178	34	9	14	87	43	94	.286	.335	.437	.773	125	12	17	93	114	87	.699	7	1	2	1	*OD1	1.6
Total	6	502	1826	271	499	110	16	67	249	167	358	.273	.336	.461	.798	117	39	40	100	100	275	.750	29	13	1	3	O/D1	3.3
■ KEN CAMINITI Caminiti, Kenneth Gene b: 4/21/63, Hanford, Cal. BB/TR, 6'3", 200 lbs. Deb: 7/16/87																												
1987	Hou-N	63	203	10	50	7	1	3	23	12	44	.246	.288	.335	.623	70	-10	-9	93	119	19	.503	0	0	0	2	3	-0.7
1988	Hou-N	30	83	5	15	2	0	1	7	5	18	.181	.227	.241	.468	37	-7	-6	93	122	4	.352	0	0	0	-0	3	-0.6
1989	Hou-N	161	585	71	149	31	3	10	72	51	93	.255	.318	.369	.687	94	-3	-5	102	120	70	.616	4	1	1	14	*3	1.0
Total	3	254	871	86	214	40	4	14	102	68	155	.246	.303	.349	.652	83	-21	-20	99	120	93	.561	4	1	1	16	3	-0.3
■ GEORGE CANALE Canale, George Anthony b: 8/11/65, Memphis, Tenn. BL/TR, 6'1", 190 lbs. Deb: 9/03/89																												
1989	Mil-A	13	26	5	5	1	0	1	3	2	3	.192	.250	.346	.596	69	-1	-1	97	97	2	.500	0	1	-1	-0	1	-0.2
■ JOHN CANGELOSI Cangelosi, John Anthony b: 3/10/63, Brooklyn, N.Y. BB/TL, 5'8", 150 lbs. Deb: 6/03/85																												
1985	Chi-A	5	2	2	0	0	0	0	0	0	1	.000	.333	.000	.333	1	-0	-0	100	0	0	.500	0	0	0	-1	/OD	0.0
1986	Chi-A	137	438	65	103	16	3	2	32	71	61	.235	.351	.299	.650	80	-9	-10	101	95	55	.725	50	17	5	1	*O/D	-0.6
1987	Pit-N	104	182	44	50	8	3	4	18	46	33	.275	.429	.418	.846	120	9	8	104	82	39	1.035	21	6	3	-2	O	0.7
1988	Pit-N	75	118	18	30	4	1	0	8	17	16	.254	.353	.305	.658	93	-1	-0	98	89	15	.685	9	4	0	-0	O/P	0.0
1989	Pit-N	112	160	18	35	4	2	0	9	35	20	.219	.369	.269	.637	91	-1	0	94	84	19	.687	11	8	-2	-5	O	-0.7
Total	5	433	900	147	218	32	9	6	67	169	131	.242	.371	.318	.689	92	-2	-2	100	89	128	.773	91	35	6	-8	O/DP	-0.6
■ JOSE CANSECO Canseco, Jose (Capas) b: 7/2/64, Havana, Cuba BR/TR, 6'3", 195 lbs. Deb: 9/02/85																												
1985	Oak-A	29	96	16	29	3	0	5	13	4	31	.302	.330	.490	.820	130	2	3	93	83	15	.754	1	1	-0	1	O	0.3
1986	Oak-A	157	600	85	144	29	1	33	117	65	175	.240	.322	.457	.779	118	8	13	94	120	89	.762	15	7	0	-4	*O/D	0.5
1987	Oak-A	159	630	81	162	35	3	31	113	50	157	.257	.314	.470	.784	115	3	11	91	123	91	.745	15	3	3	7	*OD	1.6
1988	Oak-A	158	610	120	187	34	0	**42**	**124**	78	128	.307	.394	**.569**	.963	**175**	54	58	95	110	136	1.046	40	16	2	4	*OD	**6.2**
1989	Oak-A	65	227	40	61	9	1	17	57	23	69	.269	.341	.542	.883	140	13	12	103	130	41	.890	6	3	0	3	O/D	1.3
Total	5	568	2163	342	583	110	5	128	424	220	560	.270	.343	.503	.846	136	80	97	94	118	371	.848	77	30	5	11	O/D	9.9
■ MARK CARREON Carreon, Mark Steven b: 7/19/63, Chicago, Ill. BR/TL, 6' ", 170 lbs. Deb: 9/08/87																												
1987	NY-N	9	12	0	3	0	0	0	1	1	1	.250	.308	.250	.558	51	-1	-1	99	133	1	.400	0	1	-1	-1	/O	-0.2
1988	NY-N	7	9	5	5	2	0	1	1	2	1	.556	.636	1.111	1.747	435	4	4	90	31	7	3.000	0	0	0	-1	/O	0.2
1989	NY-N	68	133	20	41	6	0	6	16	12	17	.308	.370	.489	.859	149	7	8	97	78	24	.833	2	3	-1	-4	O	0.2
Total	3	84	154	25	49	8	0	7	18	15	19	.318	.382	.506	.889	157	10	11	96	79	31	.873	2	4	-2	-7	/O	0.2
■ GARY CARTER Carter, Gary Edmund b: 4/8/54, Culver City, Cal. BR/TR, 6'2", 205 lbs. Deb: 9/16/74																												
1974	Mon-N	9	27	5	11	0	1	1	6	1	2	.407	.429	.593	1.021	176	3	3	104	122	7	1.188	2	0	1	0	/CO	0.4

YEAR	TM/L	G	AB	R	H	2B	3B	HR	RBI	BB	SO	AVG	OBP	SLG	PRO	/A	BR	/A	PF	CHI	RC	TA	SB	CS	SBR	FR	POS	TPR
1975	Mon-N	144	503	58	136	20	1	17	68	72	83	.270	.363	.416	.778	107	11	6	108	103	80	.763	5	2	0	-9	OC/3	-0.3
1976	Mon-N	91	311	31	68	8	1	6	38	30	43	.219	.289	.309	.598	70	-12	-12	100	131	28	.504	0	2	-1	5	CO	-0.6
1977	Mon-N	154	522	86	148	29	2	31	84	58	103	.284	.361	.525	.886	137	24	25	98	92	98	.881	5	5	-2	14	*C/O	3.5
1978	Mon-N	157	533	76	136	27	1	20	72	62	70	.255	.338	.422	.760	116	8	11	96	102	77	.731	10	6	-1	25	*C/1	4.0
1979	Mon-N	141	505	74	143	26	5	22	75	40	62	.283	.342	.485	.827	120	14	13	102	97	82	.781	3	2	-0	22	*C	3.8
1980	Mon-N	154	549	76	145	25	5	29	101	58	78	.264	.336	.486	.822	128	18	19	99	115	89	.793	3	2	-0	24	*C	4.7
1981	Mon-N	100	374	48	94	20	2	16	68	35	35	.251	.317	.444	.761	115	6	6	99	132	51	.698	1	5	-3	7	*C/1	1.2
1982	Mon-N	154	557	91	163	32	1	29	97	78	64	.293	.385	.510	.895	141	37	33	105	109	107	.892	2	5	-2	21	*C	5.5
1983	Mon-N	145	541	63	146	37	3	17	79	51	57	.270	.341	.444	.784	114	11	10	102	114	80	.729	1	1	-0	29	*C/1	4.4
1984	Mon-N	159	596	75	175	32	1	27	**106**	64	57	.294	.368	.487	.854	151	30	36	91	119	108	.840	2	2	-1	11	*C1	5.2
1985	NY-N	149	555	83	156	17	1	32	100	69	46	.281	.367	.488	.855	141	28	29	97	115	97	.830	1	1	-0	5	*C/1O	4.1
1986	NY-N	132	490	81	125	14	2	24	105	62	63	.255	.346	.439	.785	120	10	13	96	**155**	72	.736	1	0	0	6	*C/1O3	2.2
1987	NY-N	139	523	55	123	18	2	20	83	42	73	.235	.293	.392	.685	81	-17	-16	99	128	58	.599	0	0	0	5	*C/1O	0.0
1988	NY-N	129	455	39	110	16	2	11	46	34	52	.242	.304	.358	.663	99	-6	-1	90	96	50	.575	0	2	-1	-11	*C/13	-0.7
1989	NY-N	50	153	14	28	8	0	2	15	12	15	.183	.242	.275	.517	49	-11	-10	97	126	10	.415	0	0	0	-4	C/1	-1.1
Total	16	2007	7194	955	1907	329	30	304	1143	768	903	.265	.341	.446	.787	118	153	164	99	114	1094	.742	36	35	-10	149	*CO/13	36.3

■ JOE CARTER Carter, Joseph b: 3/7/60, Oklahoma City, Okla. BR/TR, 6'3", 215 lbs. Deb: 7/30/83

YEAR	TM/L	G	AB	R	H	2B	3B	HR	RBI	BB	SO	AVG	OBP	SLG	PRO	/A	BR	/A	PF	CHI	RC	TA	SB	CS	SBR	FR	POS	TPR
1983	Chi-N	23	51	6	9	1	1	0	1	0	21	.176	.176	.235	.412	13	-6	-6	101	33	2	.302	1	0	0	-1	O	-0.7
1984	Cle-A	66	244	32	67	6	1	13	41	11	48	.275	.309	.467	.776	105	3	1	106	107	34	.699	2	4	-2	3	O/1	0.0
1985	Cle-A	143	489	64	128	27	0	15	59	25	74	.262	.300	.409	.709	98	-6	-3	94	96	60	.668	24	6	4	1	*O1/23D	0.0
1986	Cle-A	162	663	108	200	36	9	29	**121**	32	95	.302	.339	.514	.853	132	24	26	98	119	116	.851	29	7	5	5	*O1	2.7
1987	Cle-A	149	588	83	155	27	2	32	106	27	105	.264	.306	.480	.786	102	2	0	103	119	87	.781	31	6	6	0	1O/D	-0.3
1988	Cle-A	157	621	85	168	36	6	27	98	35	82	.271	.317	.478	.795	118	13	12	102	99	96	.789	27	5	5	7	*O	2.1
1989	Cle-A	162	651	84	158	32	4	35	105	39	112	.243	.294	.465	.759	107	6	3	104	96	89	.720	13	5	1	7	*O1/D	0.8
Total	7	862	3307	462	885	165	23	151	531	169	537	.268	.310	.468	.778	110	36	34	101	105	483	.752	127	33	18	21	O1/D32	4.6

■ STEVE CARTER Carter, Steven Jerome b: 12/3/64, Charlottesville, Va. BL/TR, 6'4", 201 lbs. Deb: 4/16/89

YEAR	TM/L	G	AB	R	H	2B	3B	HR	RBI	BB	SO	AVG	OBP	SLG	PRO	/A	BR	/A	PF	CHI	RC	TA	SB	CS	SBR	FR	POS	TPR
1989	Pit-N	9	16	2	2	1	0	1	3	2	5	.125	.222	.375	.597	72	-1	-1	94	134	1	.571	0	0	0	-1	/O	-0.1

■ JUAN CASTILLO Castillo, Juan (Bryas) b: 1/25/62, San Pedro De Macoris, D.R. BB/TR, 5'11", 162 lbs. Deb: 4/12/86

YEAR	TM/L	G	AB	R	H	2B	3B	HR	RBI	BB	SO	AVG	OBP	SLG	PRO	/A	BR	/A	PF	CHI	RC	TA	SB	CS	SBR	FR	POS	TPR
1986	Mil-A	26	54	6	9	0	1	0	5	5	12	.167	.250	.204	.454	26	-5	-6	102	181	3	.375	1	1	-0	-2	2/S3OD	-0.6
1987	Mil-A	116	321	44	72	11	4	3	28	33	76	.224	.303	.312	.614	63	-16	-17	102	102	33	.585	15	7	0	-3	2S/3	-1.0
1988	Mil-A	54	90	10	20	0	0	0	2	3	14	.222	.247	.222	.470	31	-8	-8	103	40	5	.352	2	0	1	-1	23S/OD	-0.6
1989	Mil-A	3	4	0	0	0	0	0	3	0	2	.000	.000	.000	.000	-99	-1	-1	97	0	0	.000	0	0	0	0	/2	0.0
Total	4	199	469	60	101	11	5	3	38	41	104	.215	.284	.279	.563	52	-30	-32	103	99	41	.509	18	8	1	-6	2/S3DO	-2.2

■ CARMELO CASTILLO Castillo, Monte Carmelo b: 6/8/58, San Pedro De Macoris, D.R. BR/TR, 6'1", 185 lbs. Deb: 7/17/82

YEAR	TM/L	G	AB	R	H	2B	3B	HR	RBI	BB	SO	AVG	OBP	SLG	PRO	/A	BR	/A	PF	CHI	RC	TA	SB	CS	SBR	FR	POS	TPR
1982	Cle-A	47	120	11	25	4	0	2	11	6	17	.208	.258	.292	.549	50	-8	-8	100	107	9	.443	0	0	0	-2	O/D	-1.1
1983	Cle-A	23	36	9	10	2	1	1	3	4	6	.278	.366	.472	.838	122	1	1	105	59	6	.852	1	1	-0	-2	O/D	0.0
1984	Cle-A	87	211	36	55	9	2	10	36	21	32	.261	.333	.464	.798	111	5	3	106	112	30	.735	1	3	-2	-9	O/D	-0.8
1985	Cle-A	67	184	27	45	5	1	11	25	11	40	.245	.298	.462	.760	111	0	2	94	84	24	.703	3	0	1	-4	O/D	-0.1
1986	Cle-A	85	205	34	57	9	0	8	32	9	48	.278	.312	.439	.751	105	0	1	98	112	25	.646	2	1	0	-3	OD	-0.2
1987	Cle-A	89	220	27	55	17	0	11	31	16	52	.250	.301	.477	.778	100	0	-1	103	90	33	.735	1	1	-0	-2	DO	-0.3
1988	Cle-A	66	176	12	48	8	0	4	14	5	31	.273	.297	.386	.683	88	-3	-3	102	70	19	.597	6	2	1	-7	O/D	-1.0
1989	Min-A	94	218	23	56	13	3	8	33	15	40	.257	.308	.454	.762	105	3	1	107	104	29	.686	1	2	-1	-4	OD	-0.5
Total	8	558	1370	179	351	67	7	55	185	87	266	.256	.306	.436	.742	100	-1	-4	102	96	175	.669	15	10	-2	-32	OD	-4.0

■ RICK CERONE Cerone, Richard Aldo b: 5/19/54, Newark, N.J. BR/TR, 5'11", 192 lbs. Deb: 8/17/75

YEAR	TM/L	G	AB	R	H	2B	3B	HR	RBI	BB	SO	AVG	OBP	SLG	PRO	/A	BR	/A	PF	CHI	RC	TA	SB	CS	SBR	FR	POS	TPR
1975	Cle-A	7	12	1	3	1	0	0	0	1	0	.250	.308	.333	.641	81	-0	-0	100	0	1	.556	0	0	0	0	/C	0.0
1976	Cle-A	7	16	1	2	0	0	0	1	0	2	.125	.125	.125	.250	-27	-3	-3	100	192	0	.143	0	0	0	0	/CD	-0.1
1977	Tor-A	31	100	7	20	4	0	1	10	6	12	.200	.245	.270	.515	39	-8	-9	103	132	6	.398	0	0	0	3	C	-0.4
1978	Tor-A	88	282	25	63	8	2	3	20	23	32	.223	.284	.298	.582	64	-13	-14	100	85	23	.472	0	3	-2	6	C/D	-0.6
1979	Tor-A	136	469	47	112	27	4	7	61	37	40	.239	.296	.358	.654	73	-17	-19	103	127	50	.566	1	4	-2	13	*C	-0.1
1980	NY-A	147	519	70	144	30	4	14	85	32	56	.277	.327	.432	.758	107	3	4	99	127	70	.671	1	3	-2	-1	*C	0.7
1981	NY-A	71	234	23	57	13	2	2	21	12	24	.244	.280	.342	.622	78	-7	-7	100	96	20	.487	0	2	-1	1	C	-0.4
1982	NY-A	89	300	29	68	10	0	5	28	19	27	.227	.275	.310	.585	63	-16	-15	96	104	23	.459	0	2	-1	-1	C	-1.2
1983	NY-A	80	246	18	54	7	0	2	22	15	29	.220	.267	.272	.540	50	-17	-17	99	118	18	.421	0	0	0	-3	C/3	-1.5
1984	NY-A	38	120	8	25	3	0	2	13	9	15	.208	.269	.283	.553	57	-8	-7	94	130	9	.450	1	0	0	2	C	-0.2
1985	Atl-N	96	282	15	61	9	0	3	25	29	25	.216	.292	.280	.572	57	-14	-17	106	113	20	.456	0	3	-2	4	C	-1.1
1986	Mil-A	68	216	22	56	14	0	4	18	15	28	.259	.310	.380	.690	86	-4	-4	102	76	25	.596	1	1	-0	13	C	1.1
1987	NY-A	113	284	28	69	12	1	4	23	30	46	.243	.324	.335	.658	78	-9	-8	98	86	31	.576	0	1	-1	-13	*C/P1	-1.2
1988	Bos-A	84	264	31	71	13	1	3	27	20	32	.269	.328	.360	.687	85	-3	-6	109	103	31	.593	0	0	0	-2	C/D	-0.3
1989	Bos-A	102	296	28	72	16	1	4	48	34	40	.243	.325	.345	.670	85	-4	-6	105	164	33	.590	0	0	0	-7	C/OD	-0.7
Total	15	1157	3640	353	877	167	15	54	402	282	408	.241	.299	.340	.639	75	-120	-126	101	113	361	.535	4	19	-10	15	*C/D1PO3	-6.0

■ DAVE CLARK Clark, David Earl b: 9/3/62, Tupelo, Miss. BL/TR, 6'2", 200 lbs. Deb: 9/03/86

YEAR	TM/L	G	AB	R	H	2B	3B	HR	RBI	BB	SO	AVG	OBP	SLG	PRO	/A	BR	/A	PF	CHI	RC	TA	SB	CS	SBR	FR	POS	TPR
1986	Cle-A	18	58	10	16	1	0	3	9	7	11	.276	.354	.448	.802	121	1	2	98	102	10	.791	1	0	0	1	O/D	0.2
1987	Cle-A	29	87	11	18	5	0	3	12	2	24	.207	.225	.368	.593	53	-6	-6	103	117	6	.479	1	0	0	0	OD	-0.5
1988	Cle-A	63	156	11	41	4	1	3	18	17	28	.263	.335	.359	.694	93	-1	-1	102	110	17	.584	0	2	-1	-4	DO	-0.6
1989	Cle-A	102	253	21	60	12	0	8	29	30	63	.237	.318	.379	.697	92	-1	-3	104	94	29	.624	0	2	-1	-4	DO	-0.8
Total	4	212	554	53	135	22	1	17	68	56	126	.244	.313	.379	.692	89	-7	-8	102	103	62	.605	2	4	-2	-8	D/O	-1.7

■ JACK CLARK Clark, Jack Anthony b: 11/10/55, New Brighton, Pa. BR/TR, 6'2", 175 lbs. Deb: 9/12/75

YEAR	TM/L	G	AB	R	H	2B	3B	HR	RBI	BB	SO	AVG	OBP	SLG	PRO	/A	BR	/A	PF	CHI	RC	TA	SB	CS	SBR	FR	POS	TPR
1975	SF-N	8	17	3	4	0	0	0	2	1	2	.235	.278	.235	.513	43	-1	-1	102	193	1	.462	1	0	0	0	/O3	0.0
1976	SF-N	26	102	14	23	6	2	2	10	8	18	.225	.282	.382	.664	85	-2	-2	103	75	12	.654	6	2	1	5	O	0.2
1977	SF-N	136	413	64	104	17	4	13	51	49	73	.252	.334	.407	.741	94	-1	-4	104	99	58	.722	12	4	1	4	*O	-0.1
1978	SF-N	156	592	90	181	46	8	25	98	50	72	.306	.363	.537	.900	162	36	42	92	105	109	.883	15	11	-2	11	*O	4.6
1979	SF-N	143	527	84	144	25	2	26	86	63	95	.273	.352	.476	.828	134	17	22	92	110	88	.815	11	8	-2	6	*O/3	2.2
1980	SF-N	127	437	77	124	20	8	22	82	74	52	.284	.390	.517	.907	158	31	34	96	118	87	.921	2	5	-2	-4	*O	2.4
1981	SF-N	99	385	60	103	19	2	17	53	45	45	.268	.346	.460	.805	121	13	11	105	88	59	.759	1	1	-0	6	O	1.4
1982	SF-N	157	563	90	154	30	3	27	103	90	91	.274	.375	.481	.856	147	30	34	94	122	98	.840	6	9	-4	-3	*O	2.7
1983	SF-N	135	492	82	132	25	0	20	66	74	79	.268	.365	.441	.806	121	16	15	101	100	80	.788	5	3	-0	7	*O/1	2.0
1984	SF-N	57	203	33	65	9	1	11	44	43	29	.320	.439	.537	.976	180	22	23	96	129	47	1.034	1	1	-0	-2	O/1	1.9
1985	StL-N	126	442	71	124	26	3	22	87	83	88	.281	.397	.502	.899	157	32	34	96	127	89	.928	1	4	-2	-12	*1O	1.7
1986	StL-N	65	232	34	55	12	2	9	23	45	61	.237	.363	.422	.786	112	6	5	103	78	38	.797	1	1	-0	-1	1	0.1
1987	StL-N	131	419	93	120	23	1	35	106	**136**	139	.286	**.461**	**.597**	**1.058**	**180**	**54**	**55**	99	126	127	**1.265**	1	2	-1	-7	*1/O	3.9
1988	NY-A	150	496	81	120	14	0	27	93	113	141	.242	.385	.433	.818	134	23	26	96	127	88	.849	3	2	-0	-1	*DO1	2.4
1989	SD-N	142	455	76	110	19	1	26	94	**132**	145	.242	.413	.459	.873	148	36	35	101	140	95	.975	6	2	1	4	*1O	3.1
Total	15	1658	5775	952	1563	291	37	282	998	1006	1130	.271	.380	.480	.861	141	310	328	98	114	1077	.878	72	55	-11	15	*O1D/3	28.5

■ JERALD CLARK Clark, Jerald Dwayne b: 8/10/63, Crockett, Tex. BR/TR, 6'4", 189 lbs. Deb: 9/19/88

YEAR	TM/L	G	AB	R	H	2B	3B	HR	RBI	BB	SO	AVG	OBP	SLG	PRO	/A	BR	/A	PF	CHI	RC	TA	SB	CS	SBR	FR	POS	TPR
1988	SD-N	6	15	0	3	1	0	0	3	0	4	.200	.200	.267	.467	34	-1	-1	97	300	1	.333	0	0	0	1	/O	0.0
1989	SD-N	17	41	5	8	2	0	1	7	3	9	.195	.250	.317	.567	61	-2	-2	101	176	3	.471	0	1	-1	-1	O	-0.4
Total	2	23	56	5	11	3	0	1	10	3	13	.196	.237	.304	.541	54	-3	-3	100	208	4	.435	0	1	-1	-0	/O	-0.4

■ WILL CLARK Clark, William Nuschler b: 3/17/64, New Orleans, La. BL/TL, 6'2", 190 lbs. Deb: 4/08/86

YEAR	TM/L	G	AB	R	H	2B	3B	HR	RBI	BB	SO	AVG	OBP	SLG	PRO	/A	BR	/A	PF	CHI	RC	TA	SB	CS	SBR	FR	POS	TPR
1986	SF-N	111	408	66	117	27	2	11	41	34	76	.287	.346	.444	.790	121	8	10	96	78	62	.738	4	7	-3	2	*1	0.6
1987	SF-N	150	529	89	163	29	5	35	91	49	98	.308	.372	.580	.953	154	34	37	96	90	109	.951	5	17	-9	1	*1	2.1

YEAR	TM/L	G	AB	R	H	2B	3B	HR	RBI	BB	SO	AVG	OBP	SLG	PRO	/A	BR	/A	PF	CHI	RC	TA	SB	CS	SBR	FR	POS	TPR
1988	SF-N	162	575	102	162	31	6	29	**109**	**100**	129	.282	.392	.508	.900	167	**44**	**49**	94	122	**120**	.957	9	1	2	-4	*1	4.1
1989	SF-N	159	588	**104**	196	38	9	23	111	74	103	.333	.412	.546	.958	177	56	58	97	121	**136**	1.017	8	3	1	1	*1	4.8
Total	4	582	2100	361	638	125	22	98	352	257	406	.304	.384	.524	.908	157	143	154	96	106	427	.928	26	28	-9	-1	1	11.6
■ **DAVE COCHRANE**	Cochrane, David Carter b: 1/31/63, Riverside, Cal. BB/TR, 6'2", 180 lbs. Deb: 9/02/86																											
1986	Chi-A	19	62	4	12	2	0	1	2	5	22	.194	.254	.274	.528	44	-5	-5	101	40	4	.423	0	0	0	-1	3/S	-0.5
1989	Sea-A	54	102	13	24	4	1	3	7	14	27	.235	.333	.382	.716	98	0	-0	103	57	13	.659	0	2	-1	-1	S/132OC	0.0
Total	2	73	164	17	36	6	1	4	9	19	49	.220	.304	.341	.646	78	-4	-5	102	50	17	.567	0	2	-1	-2	/S312OC	-0.5
■ **VINCE COLEMAN**	Coleman, Vincent Maurice b: 9/22/60, Jacksonville, Fla. BB/TR, 6', 170 lbs. Deb: 4/18/1885																											
1985	StL-N	151	636	107	170	20	10	1	40	50	115	.267	.321	.335	.656	87	-14	-10	96	64	79	.755	**110**	25	**18**	7	*O	1.1
1986	StL-N	154	600	94	139	13	8	0	29	60	98	.232	.304	.280	.584	60	-30	-32	103	66	67	.704	**107**	14	**24**	2	*O	-0.9
1987	StL-N	151	623	121	180	14	10	3	43	70	126	.289	.364	.358	.721	93	-5	-4	99	65	96	.858	**109**	22	**20**	3	*O	1.3
1988	StL-N	153	616	77	160	20	10	3	38	49	111	.260	.315	.339	.655	85	-9	-12	104	67	71	.698	**81**	27	8	3	*O	-0.5
1989	StL-N	145	563	94	143	21	9	2	28	50	90	.254	.317	.334	.651	86	-9	-10	101	56	70	.703	**65**	10	**14**	-10	*O	-0.8
Total	5	754	3038	493	792	88	47	9	178	279	540	.261	.325	.329	.654	82	-67	-68	100	64	383	.744	472	98	83	5	O	0.2
■ **DARNELL COLES**	Coles, Darnell b: 6/2/62, San Bernardino, Cal BR/TR, 6'1", 170 lbs. Deb: 9/04/83																											
1983	Sea-A	27	92	9	26	7	0	1	6	7	12	.283	.333	.391	.725	99	-0	-0	100	61	8	.558	0	3	-2	-1	3	-0.2
1984	Sea-A	48	143	15	23	3	1	0	6	17	26	.161	.259	.196	.455	27	-14	-14	102	85	8	.389	2	1	0	-4	3/OD	-1.7
1985	Sea-A	27	59	8	14	4	0	1	5	9	17	.237	.348	.356	.704	99	-0	0	95	83	8	.674	0	1	-1	2	S/3OD	0.2
1986	Det-A	142	521	67	142	30	2	20	86	45	84	.273	.337	.453	.790	119	10	13	95	118	81	.753	6	2	1	-4	*3/SOD	0.5
1987	Det-A	53	149	14	27	5	1	4	15	15	23	.181	.265	.309	.574	54	-10	-10	97	103	13	.508	0	1	-1	-2	3/1OSD	-1.2
	Pit-N	40	119	20	27	8	0	6	24	19	20	.227	.338	.445	.784	101	1	0	104	135	17	.755	1	3	-2	-5	O3/1	-0.7
1988	Pit-N	68	211	20	49	13	1	5	36	20	41	.232	.308	.374	.682	97	-1	-1	98	153	25	.620	1	1	-0	-4	O/13	-0.7
	Sea-A	55	195	32	57	10	1	10	34	17	26	.292	.361	.508	.869	131	10	8	108	107	35	.848	3	2	-0	-5	O/1D	0.2
1989	Sea-A	146	535	54	135	21	3	10	59	27	61	.252	.296	.359	.655	81	-12	-15	103	105	54	.552	5	4	-1	2	O31D	-1.5
Total	7	606	2024	239	500	101	9	57	271	176	310	.247	.315	.390	.705	94	-18	-18	100	111	249	.635	18	18	-5	-21	3O/D1S	-5.1
■ **DAVE COLLINS**	Collins, David S b: 10/20/52, Rapid City, S.D. BB/TL, 5'11", 175 lbs. Deb: 6/07/75																											
1975	Cal-A	93	319	41	85	13	4	3	29	36	55	.266	.343	.361	.703	104	0	2	95	92	42	.710	24	10	1	2	OD	0.3
1976	Cal-A	99	365	45	96	12	1	4	28	40	55	.263	.336	.334	.670	105	-1	3	92	85	43	.669	32	19	-2	2	OD	0.1
1977	Sea-A	120	402	46	96	9	3	5	28	33	66	.239	.301	.313	.615	71	-17	-15	96	80	41	.588	25	10	2	-2	OD	-1.7
1978	Cin-N	102	102	13	22	1	0	0	7	15	18	.216	.316	.225	.542	52	-6	-6	103	121	7	.506	7	7	-2	-2	O	-1.1
1979	Cin-N	122	396	59	126	16	4	3	35	27	48	.318	.365	.402	.766	112	5	6	97	82	58	.716	16	9	-1	-7	O1	-0.4
1980	Cin-N	144	551	94	167	20	4	3	35	53	68	.303	.367	.370	.738	105	6	5	102	69	84	.827	79	21	11	-7	*O	0.4
1981	Cin-N	95	360	63	98	18	6	3	23	41	41	.272	.356	.381	.737	108	5	5	101	66	52	.755	26	10	2	-4	O	0.0
1982	NY-A	111	348	41	88	12	3	3	25	28	49	.253	.318	.330	.648	81	-10	-8	96	81	37	.588	13	8	-1	-4	O1/D	-1.5
1983	Tor-A	118	402	55	109	12	4	1	34	43	67	.271	.345	.328	.673	80	-6	-11	108	100	51	.680	31	7	5	4	*O/1D	-0.2
1984	Tor-A	128	441	59	136	24	**15**	2	44	33	41	.308	.369	.444	.813	122	14	14	102	89	81	.934	60	14	10	-1	*O/1D	1.8
1985	Oak-A	112	379	52	95	16	4	4	29	29	37	.251	.306	.346	.651	84	-11	-8	93	80	42	.638	29	8	4	1	O	-0.3
1986	Det-A	124	419	44	113	18	2	1	27	44	49	.270	.342	.329	.671	89	-7	-5	95	76	49	.645	27	12	1	1	OD	-0.4
1987	Cin-N	57	85	19	25	5	0	0	5	11	12	.294	.388	.353	.741	95	0	-0	104	66	14	.852	9	0	3	-1	O	0.0
1988	Cin-N	99	174	12	41	6	2	0	14	11	27	.236	.289	.293	.582	64	-7	-8	105	110	16	.526	7	2	1	-3	O/1	-1.1
1989	Cin-N	78	106	12	25	4	0	0	7	10	17	.236	.302	.274	.575	64	-5	-5	103	97	9	.500	3	1	0	2	O	-0.3
Total	15	1602	4849	655	1322	186	52	32	370	454	650	.273	.340	.352	.692	94	-39	-31	99	83	626	.695	388	138	34	-19	*OD/1	-4.4
■ **SCOTT COOLBAUGH**	Coolbaugh, Scott Robert b: 6/13/66, Binghamton, N.Y. BR/TR, 5'11", 185 lbs. Deb: 9/02/89																											
1989	Tex-A	25	51	7	14	1	0	2	7	4	12	.275	.327	.412	.739	104	0	0	102	101	6	.641	0	0	0	1	3/D	0.1
■ **JOEY CORA**	Cora, Jose Manuel (Amaro) b: 5/14/65, Caguas, P.R. BB/TR, 5'8", 150 lbs. Deb: 4/06/87																											
1987	SD-N	77	241	23	57	7	2	0	13	28	26	.237	.319	.282	.601	63	-13	-12	97	76	22	.563	15	11	-2	2	2/S	-0.9
1989	SD-N	12	19	5	6	1	0	0	1	1	0	.316	.350	.368	.718	105	0	0	101	57	3	.692	1	0	0	1	/S32	0.1
Total	2	89	260	28	63	8	2	0	14	29	26	.242	.321	.288	.609	66	-13	-12	97	75	25	.571	16	11	-2	2	/2S3	-0.8
■ **HENRY COTTO**	Cotto, Henry b: 1/5/61, New York, N.Y. BR/TR, 6'2", 178 lbs. Deb: 4/05/84																											
1984	Chi-N	105	146	24	40	5	0	0	8	10	23	.274	.325	.308	.633	71	-4	-6	110	70	16	.591	9	3	1	-11	O	-1.9
1985	NY-A	34	56	4	17	1	0	1	6	3	12	.304	.339	.375	.714	99	-0	-0	96	99	7	.610	1	1	-0	-4	O	-0.4
1986	NY-A	35	80	11	17	3	0	1	6	2	17	.213	.232	.287	.519	40	-7	-7	103	92	5	.424	3	0	1	-0	O/D	-0.6
1987	NY-A	68	149	21	35	10	0	5	20	6	35	.235	.269	.403	.672	78	-5	-5	98	106	14	.577	4	2	0	-6	O	-1.1
1988	Sea-A	133	386	50	100	18	1	8	33	23	53	.259	.304	.373	.677	82	-6	-10	108	78	46	.660	27	3	6	3	*O/D	-0.2
1989	Sea-A	100	295	44	78	11	2	9	33	12	44	.264	.300	.407	.707	94	-2	-3	103	87	35	.644	10	4	1	-2	O/D	-0.5
Total	6	475	1112	154	287	48	3	24	106	56	184	.258	.298	.371	.669	81	-25	-31	105	85	122	.615	54	13	8	-19	O/D	-4.7
■ **PETE DALENA**	Dalena, Peter Martin b: 6/26/60, Fresno, Cal. BL/TR, 5'11", 200 lbs. Deb: 7/07/89																											
1989	Cle-A	5	7	0	1	1	0	0	0	0	3	.143	.143	.286	.429	17	-1	-1	104	0	0	.333	0	0	0	0	/D	0.0
■ **KAL DANIELS**	Daniels, Kalvoski b: 8/20/63, Vienna, Ga. BL/TR, 5'11", 195 lbs. Deb: 4/09/86																											
1986	Cin-N	74	181	34	58	10	4	6	23	22	30	.320	.400	.519	.919	145	13	12	104	82	40	1.031	15	2	3	-2	O	1.3
1987	Cin-N	108	368	73	123	24	1	26	64	60	62	.334	.429	.617	1.046	167	40	38	104	85	100	1.212	26	8	3	1	O	3.7
1988	Cin-N	140	495	95	144	29	1	18	64	87	94	.291	**.400**	.463	.863	139	33	30	105	96	98	.940	27	6	5	1	*O	3.3
1989	Cin-N	44	133	26	29	11	0	2	9	36	28	.218	.392	.346	.738	109	4	4	103	71	21	.826	6	4	-1	1	O	0.4
	LA-N	11	38	7	13	2	0	2	8	7	5	.342	.444	.553	.997	198	4	5	93	126	10	1.192	3	0	1	-0	O	0.5
	Yr	55	171	33	42	13	0	4	17	43	33	.246	.403	.392	.795	127	9	8	101	83	31	.896	9	4	0	1		0.9
Total	4	377	1215	235	367	76	6	54	168	212	219	.302	.409	.508	.917	148	94	88	104	89	270	1.026	77	20	11	0	O	9.2
■ **DOUG DASCENZO**	Dascenzo, Douglas Craig b: 6/30/64, Cleveland, Ohio BB/TL, 5'7", 150 lbs. Deb: 9/02/88																											
1988	Chi-N	26	75	9	16	3	0	0	4	9	4	.213	.298	.253	.551	57	-4	-4	104	84	6	.548	6	1	1	3	O	0.0
1989	Chi-N	47	139	20	23	1	0	1	12	13	13	.165	.237	.194	.431	23	-13	-15	108	161	7	.380	6	3	0	0	O	-1.6
Total	2	73	214	29	39	4	0	1	16	22	17	.182	.258	.215	.473	35	-17	-19	107	134	14	.437	12	4	1	4	/O	-1.6
■ **JEFF DATZ**	Datz, Jeffrey William b: 11/28/59, Camden, N.J. BR/TR, 6'4", 220 lbs. Deb: 9/05/89																											
1989	Det-A	7	10	0	2	0	0	0	0	1	1	.200	.333	.200	.533	55	-1	-0	97	0	1	.444	0	0	0	0	/CD	0.0
■ **JACK DAUGHERTY**	Daugherty, John Michael b: 7/3/60, Hialeah, Fla. BB/TL, 6' ", 188 lbs. Deb: 9/01/87																											
1987	Mon-N	11	10	1	1	1	0	0	1	0	3	.100	.100	.200	.300	-22	-2	-2	106	200	0	.222	0	0	0	0	/1	-0.1
1989	Tex-A	52	106	15	32	4	2	1	10	11	21	.302	.373	.406	.779	116	3	3	102	84	17	.750	2	1	0	1	1/OD	0.2
Total	2	63	116	16	33	5	2	1	11	11	24	.284	.352	.388	.739	104	1	1	103	93	17	.694	2	1	0	1	/1DO	0.1
■ **DARREN DAULTON**	Daulton, Darren Arthur b: 1/3/62, Arkansas City, Kan. BL/TR, 6', 185 lbs. Deb: 9/25/83																											
1983	Phi-N	2	3	1	1	0	0	0	0	1	1	.333	.500	.333	.833	134	0	0	101	0	1	1.000	0	0	0	0	/C	0.0
1985	Phi-N	36	103	14	21	3	1	4	11	16	37	.204	.311	.369	.680	88	-1	-2	102	88	13	.687	3	0	1	3	C	0.3
1986	Phi-N	49	138	18	31	4	0	8	21	38	41	.225	.395	.428	.823	122	7	6	104	101	26	.901	2	3	-1	2	C	0.8
1987	Phi-N	53	129	10	25	6	0	3	13	16	37	.194	.283	.310	.593	55	-8	-9	104	106	13	.538	0	0	0	3	C/1	-0.1
1988	Phi-N	58	144	13	30	6	0	1	12	17	26	.208	.292	.271	.563	62	-7	-7	101	114	12	.496	2	1	0	4	C/1	0.0
1989	Phi-N	131	368	29	74	12	2	8	44	52	58	.201	.303	.310	.613	75	-11	-11	101	128	37	.569	2	1	0	5	*C	0.3
Total	6	329	885	85	182	31	3	24	101	140	200	.206	.316	.329	.645	79	-20	-22	102	113	102	.619	9	5	-0	17	C/1	1.3
■ **MARK DAVIDSON**	Davidson, John Mark b: 2/15/61, Knoxville, Tenn. BR/TR, 6'2", 180 lbs. Deb: 6/20/86																											
1986	Min-A	36	68	5	8	3	0	0	2	6	22	.118	.189	.162	.351	-2	-10	-10	108	72	2	.297	2	3	-1	-4	O/D	-1.6
1987	Min-A	102	150	32	40	4	1	1	14	13	26	.267	.325	.327	.652	78	-5	-4	96	107	17	.612	9	2	2	-13	O/D	-1.7

YEAR	TM/L	G	AB	R	H	2B	3B	HR	RBI	BB	SO	AVG	OBP	SLG	PRO	/A	BR	/A	PF	CHI	RC	TA	SB	CS	SBR	FR	POS	TPR
1988	Min-A	100	106	22	23	7	0	1	10	10	20	.217	.291	.311	.602	65	-4	-5	106	110	9	.528	3	3	-1	-18	O/3D	-2.6
1989	Hou-N	33	65	7	13	2	1	1	5	7	14	.200	.278	.308	.585	66	-3	-3	102	87	6	.528	1	0	0	-2	O	-0.5
Total	4	271	389	66	84	16	2	3	31	36	82	.216	.284	.290	.575	57	-22	-23	102	99	34	.512	15	8	-0	-38	O/D3	-6.4

■ **ALVIN DAVIS** Davis, Alvin Glenn b: 9/9/60, Riverside, Cal. BL/TR, 6'1", 195 lbs. Deb: 4/11/84

YEAR	TM/L	G	AB	R	H	2B	3B	HR	RBI	BB	SO	AVG	OBP	SLG	PRO	/A	BR	/A	PF	CHI	RC	TA	SB	CS	SBR	FR	POS	TPR
1984	Sea-A	152	567	80	161	34	3	27	116	97	78	.284	.395	.497	.892	142	38	36	102	122	117	.938	5	4	-1	-3	*1/D	2.2
1985	Sea-A	155	578	78	166	33	1	18	78	90	71	.287	.385	.441	.826	133	23	27	95	96	101	.813	1	2	-1	-6	*1	1.0
1986	Sea-A	135	479	66	130	18	1	18	72	76	68	.271	.375	.426	.800	113	14	11	105	118	78	.780	0	3	-2	-2	*1D	0.0
1987	Sea-A	157	580	86	171	37	2	29	100	72	84	.295	.375	.516	.890	131	29	26	103	110	111	.876	0	0	0	-7	*1	0.3
1988	Sea-A	140	478	67	141	24	1	18	69	95	53	.295	.416	.462	.878	135	34	29	108	106	95	.912	1	1	-0	-4	*1D	1.8
1989	Sea-A	142	498	84	152	30	1	21	95	101	49	.305	.428	.496	.924	155	44	42	103	126	109	.978	0	1	-1	-2	*1D	3.1
Total	6	881	3180	461	921	176	9	131	530	531	403	.290	.395	.474	.869	135	182	171	102	113	610	.882	7	11	-5	-24	1/D	8.4

■ **CHILI DAVIS** Davis, Charles Theodore b: 1/17/60, Kingston, Jamaica BB/TR, 6'3", 195 lbs. Deb: 4/10/81

YEAR	TM/L	G	AB	R	H	2B	3B	HR	RBI	BB	SO	AVG	OBP	SLG	PRO	/A	BR	/A	PF	CHI	RC	TA	SB	CS	SBR	FR	POS	TPR
1981	SF-N	8	15	1	2	0	0	0	0	1	2	.133	.188	.133	.321	-7	-2	-2	105	0	0	.357	2	0	1	-1	/O	-0.2
1982	SF-N	154	641	86	167	27	6	19	76	45	115	.261	.311	.410	.721	107	-2	3	94	82	79	.668	24	13	-1	10	*O	1.2
1983	SF-N	137	486	54	113	21	2	11	59	55	108	.233	.311	.352	.662	82	-11	-12	101	117	52	.599	10	12	-4	5	*O	-1.3
1984	SF-N	137	499	87	157	21	6	21	81	42	74	.315	.369	.507	.876	150	28	30	96	103	89	.848	12	8	-1	12	*O	3.8
1985	SF-N	136	481	53	130	25	2	13	56	62	74	.270	.354	.412	.765	121	9	13	93	100	68	.735	15	7	0	0	*O	1.1
1986	SF-N	153	526	71	146	28	3	13	70	84	96	.278	.378	.416	.794	124	16	19	96	110	83	.792	16	13	-3	6	*O	1.9
1987	SF-N	149	500	80	125	22	1	24	76	72	109	.250	.347	.442	.789	112	5	8	96	106	78	.793	16	9	-1	-9	*O	-0.7
1988	Cal-A	158	600	81	161	29	3	21	93	56	118	.268	.331	.432	.762	119	9	13	94	122	82	.701	9	10	-3	-5	*O/D	0.2
1989	Cal-A	154	560	81	152	24	1	22	90	61	109	.271	.343	.436	.779	120	13	14	99	120	80	.718	3	0	1	-11	*O/D	0.2
Total	9	1186	4308	594	1153	197	24	144	601	478	805	.268	.342	.425	.766	116	65	87	96	107	610	.727	107	72	-11	6	*O/D	6.2

■ **ERIC DAVIS** Davis, Eric Keith b: 5/29/62, Los Angeles, Cal. BR/TR, 6'2", 165 lbs. Deb: 5/19/84

YEAR	TM/L	G	AB	R	H	2B	3B	HR	RBI	BB	SO	AVG	OBP	SLG	PRO	/A	BR	/A	PF	CHI	RC	TA	SB	CS	SBR	FR	POS	TPR
1984	Cin-N	57	174	33	39	10	1	10	30	24	48	.224	.322	.466	.787	112	4	3	106	106	28	.841	10	2	2	8	O	1.1
1985	Cin-N	56	122	26	30	3	3	8	18	7	39	.246	.287	.516	.803	114	2	2	105	82	19	.896	16	3	3	-1	O	0.2
1986	Cin-N	132	415	97	115	15	3	27	71	68	100	.277	.380	.523	.903	140	27	24	104	95	95	1.155	80	11	17	4	*O	4.4
1987	Cin-N	129	474	120	139	23	4	37	100	84	134	.293	.401	.593	.994	154	41	39	104	108	124	1.199	50	6	11	21	*O	**6.3**
1988	Cin-N	135	472	81	129	18	3	26	93	65	124	.273	.365	.489	.854	136	27	24	105	123	90	.936	35	3	9	-8	*O	2.2
1989	Cin-N	131	462	74	130	14	2	34	101	68	116	.281	.375	.541	.916	154	35	34	103	122	91	.958	21	7	2	-6	*O	3.0
Total	6	640	2119	431	582	83	16	142	413	316	561	.275	.371	.530	.901	142	136	125	104	110	447	1.030	212	32	44	18	O	17.2

■ **GLENN DAVIS** Davis, Glenn Earle b: 3/28/61, Jacksonville, Fla. BR/TR, 6'3", 210 lbs. Deb: 9/02/84

YEAR	TM/L	G	AB	R	H	2B	3B	HR	RBI	BB	SO	AVG	OBP	SLG	PRO	/A	BR	/A	PF	CHI	RC	TA	SB	CS	SBR	FR	POS	TPR
1984	Hou-N	18	61	6	13	5	0	2	8	4	12	.213	.262	.393	.655	88	-2	-1	93	104	7	.583	0	0	0	-0	1	-0.1
1985	Hou-N	100	350	51	95	11	0	20	64	27	68	.271	.336	.474	.810	129	10	12	96	115	53	.749	0	0	0	-2	1/O	0.7
1986	Hou-N	158	574	91	152	32	3	31	101	64	72	.265	.348	.493	.841	126	22	20	103	113	100	.827	3	1	0	2	*1	1.6
1987	Hou-N	151	578	70	145	35	2	27	93	47	84	.251	.313	.458	.771	109	-1	4	93	114	80	.713	4	1	1	3	*1	0.0
1988	Hou-N	152	561	78	152	26	0	30	99	53	77	.271	.346	.478	.823	144	24	28	93	117	91	.794	4	3	-1	-1	*1	2.0
1989	Hou-N	158	581	87	156	26	1	34	89	69	123	.269	.353	.492	.845	136	29	28	102	98	102	.839	4	2	0	3	*1	2.0
Total	6	737	2705	383	713	135	6	144	454	264	436	.264	.338	.478	.815	128	82	91	97	111	432	.782	15	7	0	4	1/O	6.2

■ **JODY DAVIS** Davis, Jody Richard b: 11/12/56, Gainesville, Ga. BR/TR, 6'4", 192 lbs. Deb: 4/21/81

YEAR	TM/L	G	AB	R	H	2B	3B	HR	RBI	BB	SO	AVG	OBP	SLG	PRO	/A	BR	/A	PF	CHI	RC	TA	SB	CS	SBR	FR	POS	TPR
1981	Chi-N	56	180	14	46	5	1	4	21	21	28	.256	.337	.361	.698	94	-0	-1	104	107	21	.617	0	1	-1	3	C	0.2
1982	Chi-N	130	418	41	109	20	2	12	52	36	92	.261	.321	.404	.725	98	0	-1	103	99	55	.652	0	1	-1	13	*C	1.2
1983	Chi-N	151	510	56	138	31	2	24	84	33	93	.271	.317	.480	.798	117	10	9	101	105	72	.718	0	2	-1	0	*C	1.4
1984	Chi-N	150	523	55	134	25	2	19	94	47	99	.256	.319	.421	.739	96	3	-3	110	136	63	.658	5	6	-2	8	*C	0.7
1985	Chi-N	142	482	47	112	30	0	17	58	48	83	.232	.302	.400	.702	82	-4	-14	116	95	57	.630	1	0	0	5	*C	-0.3
1986	Chi-N	148	528	61	132	27	2	21	74	41	110	.250	.304	.428	.732	93	-2	-6	107	104	66	.650	0	1	-1	19	*C/1	1.5
1987	Chi-N	125	428	57	106	12	2	19	51	52	91	.248	.332	.418	.750	96	-2	-2	101	88	58	.692	1	2	-1	0	*C	0.7
1988	Chi-N	88	249	19	57	9	0	6	33	29	51	.229	.312	.337	.649	83	-4	-5	104	129	25	.564	0	3	-2	2	C	-0.1
	Atl-N	2	8	2	2	0	0	1	3	0	1	.250	.250	.625	.875	138	0	0	104	153	1	.833	0	0	0	0	/C	0.0
	Yr	90	257	21	59	9	0	7	36	29	52	.230	.310	.346	.656	84	-4	-5	104	131	27	.572	0	3	-2	2		-0.1
1989	Atl-N	78	231	12	39	5	0	4	19	23	61	.169	.247	.242	.489	40	-18	-18	102	112	13	.400	0	0	0	-1	C/1	-1.5
Total	9	1070	3557	364	875	164	11	127	489	330	709	.246	.312	.405	.717	92	-17	-42	106	108	432	.638	7	16	-8	49	*C/1	3.8

■ **MIKE DAVIS** Davis, Michael Dwayne b: 6/11/59, San Diego, Cal. BL/TL, 6'2", 175 lbs. Deb: 4/10/80

YEAR	TM/L	G	AB	R	H	2B	3B	HR	RBI	BB	SO	AVG	OBP	SLG	PRO	/A	BR	/A	PF	CHI	RC	TA	SB	CS	SBR	FR	POS	TPR
1980	Oak-A	51	95	11	20	2	1	1	8	7	14	.211	.265	.284	.549	53	-6	-6	95	104	7	.462	2	1	0	-1	O/1D	-0.6
1981	Oak-A	17	20	0	1	1	0	0	0	2	4	.050	.136	.100	.236	-32	-3	-3	96	0	0	.200	0	0	0	-0	/O1D	-0.3
1982	Oak-A	23	75	12	30	4	0	1	10	2	8	.400	.416	.493	.909	156	5	5	95	100	15	.894	3	2	-0	0	O/1	0.5
1983	Oak-A	128	443	61	122	24	4	8	62	27	74	.275	.324	.402	.726	103	-1	1	96	120	56	.701	32	15	1	10	*O/D	1.0
1984	Oak-A	134	382	47	88	18	3	9	46	31	66	.230	.290	.364	.654	87	-11	-7	92	110	40	.601	14	9	-1	2	*O/D	-0.9
1985	Oak-A	154	547	92	157	34	1	24	82	50	99	.287	.349	.484	.833	135	18	23	93	98	91	.832	24	10	1	7	*O	2.9
1986	Oak-A	142	489	77	131	28	3	19	55	34	91	.268	.317	.454	.771	115	4	8	94	79	72	.770	27	4	6	7	*O	1.6
1987	Oak-A	139	494	69	131	32	1	22	72	42	94	.265	.324	.468	.792	118	4	11	91	99	72	.765	19	7	2	-10	*OD	-0.1
1988	LA-N	108	281	29	55	11	2	2	17	25	59	.196	.261	.270	.532	50	-17	-19	106	83	20	.460	7	3	0	-5	O	-2.7
1989	LA-N	67	173	21	43	7	1	5	19	16	28	.249	.312	.387	.699	107	-0	1	93	93	20	.650	6	5	-1	-4	O	-0.4
Total	10	963	2999	419	778	161	16	91	371	236	537	.259	.316	.415	.730	105	-8	15	94	98	395	.696	134	56	7	6	O/D1	1.0

■ **BUTCH DAVIS** Davis, Wallace Mc Arthur b: 6/19/58, Martin Co., N.C. BR/TR, 6', 185 lbs. Deb: 8/23/83

YEAR	TM/L	G	AB	R	H	2B	3B	HR	RBI	BB	SO	AVG	OBP	SLG	PRO	/A	BR	/A	PF	CHI	RC	TA	SB	CS	SBR	FR	POS	TPR
1983	KC-A	33	122	13	42	2	6	2	18	4	19	.344	.365	.508	.873	135	6	6	101	106	21	.814	4	3	-1	1	O	0.5
1984	KC-A	41	116	11	17	3	0	2	12	10	19	.147	.214	.224	.438	22	-12	-12	99	150	5	.385	4	3	-1	-1	O/D	-1.5
1987	Pit-N	7	7	3	1	1	0	0	0	1	3	.143	.250	.286	.536	40	-1	-1	104	0	1	.500	0	0	0	0	/O	0.0
1988	Bal-A	13	25	2	6	1	0	0	0	0	8	.240	.240	.280	.520	47	-2	-2	95	0	1	.381	1	0	0	-0	O/D	-0.1
1989	Bal-A	5	6	1	1	1	0	0	0	0	3	.167	.167	.333	.500	38	-1	-1	99	0	0	.400	0	0	0	-1	/O	0.0
Total	5	99	276	30	67	8	6	4	30	15	52	.243	.282	.359	.640	76	-10	-10	100	110	28	.554	9	6	-1	-1	/OD	-1.1

■ **ANDRE DAWSON** Dawson, Andre Fernando b: 7/10/54, Miami, Fla. BR/TR, 6'3", 180 lbs. Deb: 9/11/76

YEAR	TM/L	G	AB	R	H	2B	3B	HR	RBI	BB	SO	AVG	OBP	SLG	PRO	/A	BR	/A	PF	CHI	RC	TA	SB	CS	SBR	FR	POS	TPR
1976	Mon-N	24	85	9	20	4	1	0	7	5	13	.235	.278	.306	.584	65	-4	-4	100	106	7	.478	1	2	-1	3	O	-0.2
1977	Mon-N	139	525	64	148	26	9	19	65	34	93	.282	.328	.474	.802	114	7	8	98	87	82	.785	21	7	2	2	*O	0.7
1978	Mon-N	157	609	84	154	24	8	25	72	30	128	.253	.301	.442	.743	110	1	4	96	88	80	.717	28	11	2	14	*O	1.4
1979	Mon-N	155	639	90	176	24	12	25	92	27	115	.275	.311	.468	.779	107	5	4	102	86	91	.760	35	10	5	-2	*O	0.2
1980	Mon-N	151	577	96	178	41	7	17	87	44	69	.308	.364	.492	.856	138	27	28	99	109	105	.882	34	9	5	11	*O	3.9
1981	Mon-N	103	394	71	119	21	3	24	64	35	50	.302	.369	.553	.923	161	29	29	99	92	83	1.004	26	4	5	12	*O	4.6
1982	Mon-N	148	608	107	183	37	7	23	83	34	96	.301	.346	.498	.845	127	25	21	105	84	106	.867	39	10	6	13	*O	3.9
1983	Mon-N	159	633	104	**189**	36	10	32	113	38	81	.299	.347	.539	.886	140	32	31	102	108	113	.881	25	11	1	6	*O	3.6
1984	Mon-N	138	533	73	132	23	6	17	86	41	80	.248	.304	.409	.713	108	-3	3	91	133	65	.656	13	5	1	12	*O	1.1
1985	Mon-N	139	529	65	135	27	2	23	91	29	92	.255	.299	.444	.743	112	1	5	94	126	67	.685	13	4	2	-0	*O	0.3
1986	Mon-N	130	496	65	141	32	2	20	78	37	79	.284	.341	.478	.819	126	14	16	98	111	75	.784	18	12	-2	-3	*O	0.9
1987	Chi-N	153	621	90	178	24	2	**49**	**137**	32	103	.287	.329	.568	.897	131	25	24	101	116	111	.874	11	3	2	3	*O	2.1
1988	Chi-N	157	591	78	179	31	8	24	79	37	73	.303	.348	.504	.852	136	30	27	104	87	100	.818	12	4	1	-4	*O	2.1
1989	Chi-N	118	416	62	105	18	6	21	77	35	62	.252	.312	.476	.788	113	10	6	108	121	55	.729	8	5	-1	-0	*O	0.4
Total	14	1871	7256	1058	2037	368	83	319	1131	458	1134	.281	.330	.486	.816	124	200	202	100	103	1141	.796	284	97	27	65	*O	25.0

■ **ROB DEER** Deer, Robert George b: 9/29/60, Orange, Cal. BR/TR, 6'3", 210 lbs. Deb: 9/04/84

YEAR	TM/L	G	AB	R	H	2B	3B	HR	RBI	BB	SO	AVG	OBP	SLG	PRO	/A	BR	/A	PF	CHI	RC	TA	SB	CS	SBR	FR	POS	TPR
1984	SF-N	13	24	5	4	0	0	3	3	7	10	.167	.375	.542	.917	161	2	2	96	53	5	1.048	1	1	-0	-0	/O	0.1
1985	SF-N	78	162	22	30	5	1	8	20	23	71	.185	.286	.377	.663	90	-4	-2	93	94	19	.632	0	1	-1	-3	O1	-0.7
1986	Mil-A	134	466	75	108	17	3	33	86	72	179	.232	.338	.494	.832	121	15	14	102	106	82	.852	5	2	0	4	*O/1	1.4

YEAR	TM/L	G	AB	R	H	2B	3B	HR	RBI	BB	SO	AVG	OBP	SLG	PRO	/A	BR	/A	PF	CHI	RC	TA	SB	CS	SBR	FR	POS	TPR
1987	Mil-A	134	474	71	113	15	2	28	80	86	186	.238	.361	.456	.817	113	12	11	102	109	85	.864	12	4	1	5	*O1/D	1.2
1988	Mil-A	135	492	71	124	24	0	23	85	51	153	.252	.331	.441	.772	110	9	7	103	125	74	.753	9	5	-0	5	*O/D	0.9
1989	Mil-A	130	466	72	98	18	2	26	65	60	158	.210	.306	.425	.731	108	1	3	97	97	59	.693	4	8	-4	3	*O/D	0.0
Total	6	624	2084	316	477	79	8	121	339	299	757	.229	.331	.449	.780	112	36	34	101	107	325	.780	31	21	-3	13	O/1D	2.9
■ LUIS de los SANTOS de los Santos, Luis Manuel (Martinez) b: 12/29/66, San Cristobal, D.R. BR/TR, 6'5", 205 lbs. Deb: 9/07/88																												
1988	KC-A	11	22	1	2	1	1	0	1	4	4	.091	.231	.227	.458	28	-2	-2	103	79	1	.391	0	0	0	-0	/1D	-0.2
1989	KC-A	28	87	6	22	3	1	0	6	5	14	.253	.293	.310	.604	73	-3	-3	96	86	8	.478	0	0	0	1	1	-0.3
Total	2	39	109	7	24	4	2	0	7	9	18	.220	.280	.294	.573	63	-6	-5	97	85	8	.456	0	0	0	1	/1D	-0.5
■ RICK DEMPSEY Dempsey, John Rikard b: 9/13/49, Fayetteville, Tenn. BR/TR, 6', 190 lbs. Deb: 9/23/69																												
1969	Min-A	5	6	1	3	1	0	0	0	1	0	.500	.571	.667	1.238	240	1	1	102	0	2	1.667	0	0	0	0	/C	0.1
1970	Min-A	5	7	1	0	0	0	0	0	1	1	.000	.125	.000	.125	-64	-2	-2	98	0	0	.125	0	0	0	0	/C	-0.1
1971	Min-A	6	13	2	4	1	0	0	0	1	1	.308	.357	.385	.742	106	0	0	104	0	2	.600	0	0	0	-0	/C	0.0
1972	Min-A	25	40	0	8	1	0	0	0	6	8	.200	.304	.225	.529	55	-2	-2	107	0	3	.441	0	0	0	-2	C	-0.4
1973	NY-A	6	11	0	2	0	0	0	0	1	3	.182	.250	.182	.432	23	-1	-1	101	0	0	.300	0	0	0	0	/C	0.0
1974	NY-A	43	109	12	26	3	0	2	12	8	7	.239	.291	.321	.612	79	-3	-3	96	115	9	.500	1	0	0	3	C/OD	0.1
1975	NY-A	71	145	18	38	8	0	1	11	21	15	.262	.355	.338	.693	98	0	0	99	81	18	.625	0	0	0	3	CD/O3	0.4
1976	NY-A	21	42	1	5	0	0	0	2	5	4	.119	.213	.119	.332	-1	-5	-5	99	154	1	.270	0	0	0	1	/CO	-0.4
	Bal-A	59	174	11	37	2	0	0	10	13	17	.213	.275	.224	.499	48	-11	-11	98	98	11	.393	1	1	-0	0	C/O	-0.8
	Yr	80	216	12	42	2	0	0	12	18	21	.194	.263	.204	.466	39	-16	-16	98	115	13	.367	1	1	-0	1		-1.2
1977	Bal-A	91	270	27	61	7	4	3	34	34	34	.226	.317	.315	.632	78	-9	-7	93	143	27	.557	2	3	-1	2	C	-0.3
1978	Bal-A	136	441	41	114	25	0	6	32	48	54	.259	.331	.356	.687	103	-3	2	91	72	53	.622	7	3	0	4	*C	1.0
1979	Bal-A	124	368	48	88	23	0	6	41	38	37	.239	.310	.351	.661	80	-11	-10	97	107	39	.570	0	1	-1	1	*C	-0.3
1980	Bal-A	119	362	51	95	26	3	9	40	36	45	.262	.334	.425	.760	106	3	3	101	86	50	.703	3	1	0	4	*C/O1D	1.2
1981	Bal-A	92	251	24	54	10	1	6	15	32	36	.215	.306	.335	.641	86	-5	-4	99	84	26	.576	0	1	-1	-8	C/D	-0.9
1982	Bal-A	125	344	35	88	15	1	5	36	46	37	.256	.344	.349	.692	91	-3	-3	100	107	42	.617	0	3	-2	-6	*C/D	-0.3
1983	Bal-A	128	347	33	80	16	2	4	32	40	54	.231	.315	.323	.638	76	-11	-11	100	101	36	.563	1	1	-0	-4	*C	-0.8
1984	Bal-A	109	330	37	76	11	0	11	34	40	58	.230	.315	.364	.679	93	-5	-3	94	89	37	.607	1	2	-1	7	*C	0.9
1985	Bal-A	132	362	54	92	19	0	12	52	50	87	.254	.346	.406	.752	106	3	4	99	113	55	.725	0	1	-1	-4	*C	0.5
1986	Bal-A	122	327	42	68	15	1	13	29	45	78	.208	.309	.379	.689	88	-6	-5	99	71	41	.655	1	0	0	-8	*C	-0.5
1987	Cle-A	60	141	16	25	10	0	1	9	23	29	.177	.297	.270	.566	51	-9	-10	103	88	12	.517	0	0	0	2	C	-0.2
1988	LA-N	77	167	25	42	13	0	7	30	25	44	.251	.349	.455	.804	122	6	5	106	124	27	.791	1	0	0	-3	C	0.6
1989	LA-N	79	151	16	27	7	0	4	16	30	37	.179	.319	.305	.623	85	-3	-2	93	111	16	.605	1	0	0	1	C	0.3
Total	21	1635	4408	495	1033	213	12	90	435	544	686	.234	.321	.349	.670	88	-76	-63	98	95	509	.605	19	17	-5	-7	*C/OD13	0.1
■ DREW DENSON Denson, Andrew b: 11/16/65, Cincinnati, Ohio BB/TR, 6'5", 210 lbs. Deb: 9/13/89																												
1989	Atl-N	12	36	1	9	1	0	0	5	3	9	.250	.308	.278	.585	67	-1	-1	102	201	3	.519	1	0	0	1	1	-0.1
■ BOB DERNIER Dernier, Robert Eugene b: 1/5/57, Kansas City, Mo. BR/TR, 6', 160 lbs. Deb: 9/07/80																												
1980	Phi-N	10	7	5	4	0	0	0	1	1	0	.571	.625	.571	1.196	220	1	1	107	99	4	2.667	3	0	1	1	/O	0.3
1981	Phi-N	10	4	0	3	0	0	0	0	0	0	.750	.750	.750	1.500	291	1	1	112	0	2	2.500	2	1	0	-2	/O	0.0
1982	Phi-N	122	370	56	92	10	2	4	21	36	69	.249	.317	.319	.636	84	-10	-7	94	63	41	.666	42	12	5	6	*O	0.3
1983	Phi-N	122	221	41	51	10	0	1	15	18	21	.231	.289	.290	.578	60	-12	-12	101	89	22	.654	35	7	6	-7	*O	-1.4
1984	Chi-N	143	536	94	149	26	5	3	32	63	60	.278	.356	.362	.718	93	3	-3	110	65	75	.743	45	17	3	-2	*O	-0.7
1985	Chi-N	121	469	63	119	20	3	1	21	40	44	.254	.316	.316	.632	67	-14	-23	116	59	51	.608	31	8	5	3	*O	-1.8
1986	Chi-N	108	324	32	73	14	1	4	18	22	41	.225	.275	.312	.586	58	-17	-20	107	63	30	.577	27	2	7	-4	*O	-1.9
1987	Chi-N	93	199	38	63	4	4	8	21	19	19	.317	.379	.497	.876	129	8	8	101	68	37	.918	16	7	1	-8	O	-0.2
1988	Phi-N	68	166	19	48	3	1	1	10	9	19	.289	.330	.337	.667	91	-2	-2	101	68	19	.627	13	6	0	-2	O	-0.4
1989	Phi-N	107	187	26	32	5	0	1	13	14	28	.171	.229	.214	.443	27	-18	-18	101	122	10	.365	4	3	-1	-11	O	-3.2
Total	10	904	2483	374	634	92	16	23	152	222	301	.255	.318	.333	.652	78	-58	-74	105	70	290	.655	218	63	28	-26	O	-9.0
■ MIKE DEVEREAUX Devereaux, Michael b: 4/10/63, Casper, Wyo. BR/TR, 6' ", 195 lbs. Deb: 9/02/87																												
1987	LA-N	19	54	7	12	3	0	0	4	3	10	.222	.263	.278	.541	47	-4	-4	92	106	4	.488	3	1	0	-2	O	-0.5
1988	LA-N	30	43	4	5	1	0	0	2	2	10	.116	.156	.140	.295	-14	-6	-7	106	133	1	.205	0	1	-1	-5	O	-1.3
1989	Bal-A	122	391	55	104	14	3	8	46	36	60	.266	.331	.379	.710	101	-0	0	99	104	49	.682	22	11	0	-7	*O/D	-0.8
Total	3	171	488	66	121	18	3	8	52	41	80	.248	.309	.346	.655	84	-11	-10	99	107	54	.612	25	13	-0	-14	O/D	-2.6
■ BO DIAZ Diaz, Baudilio Jose (Seijas) b: 3/23/53, Cua, Venezuela BR/TR, 5'11", 185 lbs. Deb: 9/06/77																												
1977	Bos-A	2	1	0	0	0	0	0	0	0	1	.000	.000	.000	.000	-85	-0	-0	117	0	0	.000	0	0	0	0	/C	0.0
1978	Cle-A	44	127	12	30	4	0	2	11	4	17	.236	.260	.315	.575	65	-7	-6	93	94	10	.444	0	0	0	-2	C	-0.6
1979	Cle-A	15	32	0	5	2	0	0	1	2	6	.156	.206	.219	.425	14	-4	-4	106	55	1	.321	0	0	0	-1	C	-0.3
1980	Cle-A	76	207	15	47	11	2	3	32	7	27	.227	.252	.343	.595	60	-11	-12	102	156	14	.459	1	0	0	-4	C	-1.1
1981	Cle-A	63	182	25	57	19	0	7	38	13	23	.313	.362	.533	.895	166	12	14	93	126	32	.843	2	2	-1	-1	C/D	1.4
1982	Phi-N	144	525	69	151	29	1	18	85	36	87	.288	.337	.450	.786	126	11	15	94	117	72	.695	3	6	-3	-13	*C	0.0
1983	Phi-N	136	471	49	111	17	0	15	64	38	57	.236	.295	.367	.663	82	-12	-13	101	116	49	.572	1	4	-2	0	*C	-1.0
1984	Phi-N	27	75	5	16	4	0	1	9	5	13	.213	.262	.307	.569	58	-4	-4	102	136	5	.444	0	0	0	-1	C	-0.4
1985	Phi-N	26	76	9	16	5	1	2	16	6	7	.211	.268	.382	.650	78	-2	-3	102	182	6	.538	0	0	0	2	C	0.0
	Cin-N	51	161	12	42	8	0	3	15	15	18	.261	.328	.366	.694	89	-1	-2	105	88	19	.600	0	0	0	-7	C	-0.7
	Yr	77	237	21	58	13	1	5	31	21	25	.245	.309	.371	.680	86	-4	-5	104	122	25	.579	0	0	0	-5		-0.7
1986	Cin-N	134	474	50	129	21	0	10	56	40	52	.272	.329	.380	.709	91	-4	-6	104	108	59	.619	1	1	-0	-3	*C	-0.6
1987	Cin-N	140	496	49	134	28	1	15	82	19	73	.270	.304	.421	.725	87	-9	-11	104	129	59	.619	1	0	0	3	*C	0.3
1988	Cin-N	92	315	26	69	9	0	10	35	7	41	.219	.238	.343	.581	62	-15	-17	105	101	20	.439	0	2	-1	-1	C	-1.5
1989	Cin-N	43	132	6	27	5	0	1	8	6	7	.205	.239	.265	.504	43	-10	-10	103	85	7	.373	0	2	-1	-1	C	-0.9
Total	13	993	3274	327	834	162	5	87	452	198	429	.255	.300	.387	.687	88	-56	-59	101	117	354	.579	9	17	-8	-29	C/D	-5.4
■ MARIO DIAZ Diaz, Mario Rafael (Torres) b: 1/10/62, Humacao, P.R. BR/TR, 5'10", 145 lbs. Deb: 9/12/87																												
1987	Sea-A	11	23	4	7	0	1	0	3	0	4	.304	.304	.391	.696	82	-1	-1	103	133	3	.563	0	0	0	0	S	0.0
1988	Sea-A	28	72	6	22	5	0	0	9	3	5	.306	.333	.375	.708	91	-0	-1	108	132	8	.566	0	0	0	-0	S/213	0.0
1989	Sea-A	52	74	9	10	0	0	1	7	7	7	.135	.210	.176	.386	9	-9	-9	103	170	3	.303	0	0	0	-1	S2/3	-0.6
Total	3	91	169	19	39	5	1	1	19	10	16	.231	.274	.290	.564	55	-10	-11	105	149	14	.437	0	0	0	-1	/S231	-0.6
■ GARY DISARCINA Disarcina, Gary Thomas b: 11/19/67, Malden, Mass. BR/TR, 6'1", 170 lbs. Deb: 9/23/89																												
1989	Cal-A	2	0	0	0	0	0	0	0	0	0	—	—	—	—	—	0	0	99	—	—	—	0	0	0	0	/S	0.0
■ BENNY DISTEFANO Distefano, Benito James b: 1/23/62, Brooklyn, N.Y. BL/TL, 6'1", 195 lbs. Deb: 5/18/84																												
1984	Pit-N	45	78	10	13	1	2	3	9	5	13	.167	.226	.346	.572	62	-5	-4	94	98	5	.478	0	1	-1	-0	O1	-0.6
1986	Pit-N	31	39	3	7	1	0	1	5	1	5	.179	.200	.282	.482	31	-4	-4	100	142	2	.375	0	0	0	-1	/O1	-0.4
1988	Pit-N	16	29	6	10	3	1	1	6	3	4	.345	.406	.621	1.027	195	3	3	98	114	7	1.050	0	0	0	0	/1O	0.3
1989	Pit-N	96	154	12	38	8	0	2	15	17	30	.247	.333	.338	.671	98	-1	0	94	104	17	.598	1	0	0	-1	1/CO	-0.4
Total	4	188	300	31	68	13	3	7	35	26	52	.227	.297	.360	.657	90	-6	-4	95	108	32	.572	1	1	-0	-2	/1OC	-1.1
■ BILL DORAN Doran, William Donald b: 5/28/58, Cincinnati, Ohio BB/TR, 5'11", 175 lbs. Deb: 9/06/82																												
1982	Hou-N	26	97	11	27	3	0	0	6	4	11	.278	.307	.309	.616	74	-4	-3	99	80	10	.557	5	0	2	-0	2	0.0
1983	Hou-N	154	535	70	145	12	7	8	39	86	67	.271	.372	.364	.736	116	7	13	90	72	76	.718	12	12	-4	2	*2	1.8
1984	Hou-N	147	548	92	143	18	11	4	41	66	69	.261	.343	.356	.698	104	-1	4	93	82	70	.671	21	12	-1	9	*2S	1.8
1985	Hou-N	148	578	84	166	31	6	14	59	71	69	.287	.365	.434	.799	128	18	21	96	77	92	.789	23	15	-2	8	*2	2.9
1986	Hou-N	145	550	92	152	29	3	6	37	81	57	.276	.371	.373	.744	103	7	5	103	58	81	.773	42	19	1	-32	*2	-2.4
1987	Hou-N	162	625	82	177	23	3	16	79	82	64	.283	.369	.406	.775	113	7	13	93	92	99	.787	31	11	3	-13	*2/S	0.6

YEAR	TM/L	G	AB	R	H	2B	3B	HR	RBI	BB	SO	AVG	OBP	SLG	PRO	/A	BR	/A	PF	CHI	RC	TA	SB	CS	SBR	FR	POS	TPR
1988	Hou-N	132	480	66	119	18	1	7	53	65	60	.248	.339	.333	.672	100	-2	2	93	124	59	.653	17	4	3	-0	*2	0.9
1989	Hou-N	142	507	65	111	25	2	8	58	59	63	.219	.303	.323	.626	77	-13	-15	102	127	54	.607	22	3	5	-14	*2	-2.3
Total	8	1056	3920	562	1040	159	33	63	372	514	460	.265	.352	.371	.723	106	18	40	96	89	541	.714	173	76	6	-40	*2/S	3.3
■ BRIAN DORSETT	Dorsett, Brian Richard b: 4/9/61, Terre Haute, Ind. BR/TR, 6'3", 215 lbs. Deb: 9/08/87																											
1987	Cle-A	5	11	2	3	0	0	1	3	0	3	.273	.333	.545	.879	125	0	0	103	133	2	.875	0	0	0	0	/C	0.1
1988	Cal-A	7	11	0	1	0	0	0	2	1	5	.091	.167	.091	.258	-27	-2	-2	94	795	0	.200	0	0	0	-0	/C	-0.1
1989	NY-A	8	22	3	8	1	0	0	4	1	3	.364	.391	.409	.800	121	1	1	104	173	4	.714	0	0	0	1	/C	0.2
Total	3	20	44	5	12	1	0	1	9	2	11	.273	.319	.364	.683	88	-1	-1	101	321	6	.594	0	0	0	1	/C	0.2
■ BRIAN DOWNING	Downing, Brian Jay b: 10/9/50, Los Angeles, Cal. BR/TR, 5'10", 170 lbs. Deb: 5/31/73																											
1973	Chi-A	34	73	5	13	1	0	2	4	10	17	.178	.277	.274	.551	54	-4	-4	102	60	6	.476	0	0	0	0	OC/3D	-0.4
1974	Chi-A	108	293	41	66	12	1	10	39	51	72	.225	.344	.375	.719	105	4	3	102	110	38	.682	0	1	-1	-2	CO/D	0.2
1975	Chi-A	138	420	58	101	12	1	7	41	76	75	.240	.361	.324	.685	92	0	-2	103	100	54	.681	13	4	2	18	*C/D	2.2
1976	Chi-A	104	317	38	81	14	0	3	30	40	55	.256	.341	.328	.669	97	-0	0	99	102	39	.631	7	3	0	-2	CD	0.2
1977	Chi-A	69	169	28	48	4	2	4	25	34	21	.284	.410	.402	.812	123	7	7	99	124	30	.833	1	2	-1	6	C/OD	1.3
1978	Cal-A	133	412	42	105	15	0	7	46	52	47	.255	.347	.342	.689	93	-1	-2	102	112	49	.625	3	2	-0	-8	*C/D	-0.6
1979	Cal-A	148	509	87	166	27	3	12	75	77	57	.326	.420	.462	.881	149	30	36	93	109	99	.882	3	3	-1	-8	*CD	3.1
1980	Cal-A	30	93	5	27	6	0	2	25	12	12	.290	.371	.419	.791	121	2	3	96	217	13	.699	0	2	-1	-3	CD	0.0
1981	Cal-A	93	317	47	79	14	0	9	41	46	35	.249	.351	.379	.730	106	5	4	104	111	43	.684	1	1	-0	-4	OC/D	0.0
1982	Cal-A	158	623	109	175	37	2	28	84	86	58	.281	.373	.482	.854	132	29	29	100	77	114	.849	2	1	0	-4	*O	1.9
1983	Cal-A	113	403	68	99	15	1	19	53	62	59	.246	.353	.429	.782	119	9	11	96	92	63	.768	1	2	-1	-3	OD	0.6
1984	Cal-A	156	539	65	148	28	2	23	91	70	66	.275	.365	.462	.827	125	21	20	101	116	89	.789	0	4	-2	-3	*OD	1.0
1985	Cal-A	150	520	80	137	23	1	20	85	78	61	.263	.373	.427	.800	118	16	15	101	122	86	.797	5	3	-0	-5	*OD	0.8
1986	Cal-A	152	513	90	137	27	4	20	95	90	84	.267	.394	.452	.846	136	26	28	96	**132**	96	.871	4	4	-1	-5	*OD	1.8
1987	Cal-A	155	567	110	154	29	3	29	77	**106**	85	.272	.401	.487	.888	136	33	34	99	81	117	.944	5	5	-2	-4	*DO	2.5
1988	Cal-A	135	484	80	117	18	2	25	64	81	63	.242	.366	.442	.808	133	19	22	94	93	81	.815	3	4	-2	0	*D	2.1
1989	Cal-A	142	544	59	154	25	2	14	59	56	87	.283	.356	.414	.770	118	12	13	99	91	83	.721	0	2	-1	0	*D	1.2
Total	17	2018	6796	1012	1807	307	24	234	934	1027	954	.266	.371	.421	.792	120	207	217	99	104	1101	.777	48	43	-11	-26	OCD/3	17.9
■ ROB DUCEY	Ducey, Robert Thomas b: 5/24/65, Toronto, Ont., Can. BL/TR, 6'2", 175 lbs. Deb: 5/01/87																											
1987	Tor-A	34	48	12	9	1	0	1	6	8	10	.188	.304	.271	.574	54	-3	-3	101	150	5	.590	2	0	1	-6	O/D	-0.7
1988	Tor-A	27	54	15	17	4	1	0	6	5	7	.315	.373	.426	.799	124	2	2	100	104	9	.763	1	0	0	-4	O	-0.1
1989	Tor-A	41	76	5	16	4	0	0	7	9	25	.211	.294	.263	.557	62	-4	-3	94	136	6	.492	2	1	0	-2	O/D	-0.5
Total	3	102	178	32	42	9	1	1	19	22	42	.236	.320	.315	.635	78	-5	-5	98	130	20	.593	5	1	1	-11	/OD	-1.3
■ MARIANO DUNCAN	Duncan, Mariano (Nalasco) b: 3/13/63, San Pedro De Macoris, D.R. BB/TR, 6', 160 lbs. Deb: 4/09/85																											
1985	LA-N	142	562	74	137	24	6	6	39	38	113	.244	.295	.340	.635	83	-18	-13	93	79	60	.611	38	8	7	1	*S2	0.4
1986	LA-N	109	407	47	93	7	0	8	30	30	78	.229	.285	.305	.589	66	-21	-18	94	86	38	.613	48	13	7	-1	*S	-0.1
1987	LA-N	76	261	31	56	8	1	6	18	17	62	.215	.268	.322	.590	60	-17	-14	92	72	24	.543	11	1	3	1	S/2O	-0.2
1989	LA-N	49	84	9	21	5	1	0	8	0	15	.250	.267	.333	.601	76	-3	-3	93	115	7	.493	3	3	-1	-3	S/2O	-0.5
	Cin-N	45	174	23	43	10	1	3	13	8	36	.247	.292	.368	.660	85	-3	-4	103	76	19	.600	6	2	1	2	S/2	0.2
	Yr	94	258	32	64	15	2	3	21	8	51	.248	.284	.357	.641	84	-7	-6	98	97	26	.564	9	5	-0	-1		-0.3
Total	4	421	1488	184	350	54	9	23	108	93	304	.235	.286	.330	.616	74	-62	-52	94	81	147	.591	106	27	16	0	S/2O	-0.2
■ SHAWON DUNSTON	Dunston, Shawon Donnell b: 3/21/63, Brooklyn, N.Y. BR/TR, 6'1", 175 lbs. Deb: 4/09/85																											
1985	Chi-N	74	250	40	65	12	4	4	18	19	42	.260	.312	.388	.700	82	-2	-7	116	66	31	.665	11	3	2	14	S	1.4
1986	Chi-N	150	581	66	145	37	3	17	68	21	114	.250	.279	.411	.691	83	-12	-16	107	95	64	.611	13	11	-3	23	*S	1.8
1987	Chi-N	95	346	40	85	18	3	5	22	10	68	.246	.269	.358	.627	64	-18	-19	101	63	32	.544	12	3	2	3	S	-0.2
1988	Chi-N	155	575	69	143	23	6	9	56	16	108	.249	.272	.357	.628	76	-17	-20	104	98	55	.566	30	9	4	11	*S	0.6
1989	Chi-N	138	471	52	131	20	6	9	60	30	86	.278	.323	.403	.726	98	3	-1	108	111	59	.670	19	11	-1	10	*S	1.7
Total	5	612	2223	267	569	110	22	44	224	96	418	.256	.289	.385	.674	81	-47	-63	107	91	241	.607	85	37	3	61	S	5.3
■ LEON DURHAM	Durham, Leon b: 7/31/57, Cincinnati, Ohio BL/TL, 6'1", 185 lbs. Deb: 5/27/80																											
1980	StL-N	96	303	42	82	15	4	8	42	18	55	.271	.314	.426	.739	102	1	-0	103	109	40	.681	8	5	-1	3	O/1	-0.1
1981	Chi-N	87	328	42	95	14	6	10	35	27	53	.290	.344	.460	.804	122	10	9	104	80	50	.812	25	11	1	-3	O/1	0.5
1982	Chi-N	148	539	84	168	33	7	22	90	66	77	.312	.389	.521	.910	148	38	36	103	108	108	.952	28	14	0	-10	*O/1	2.5
1983	Chi-N	100	337	58	87	18	8	12	55	66	83	.258	.384	.466	.850	133	17	17	101	115	64	.915	12	6	0	-6	O/1	1.0
1984	Chi-N	137	473	86	132	30	4	23	96	69	86	.279	.372	.505	.877	131	28	22	110	125	90	.910	16	8	0	4	*1	2.3
1985	Chi-N	153	542	58	153	32	2	21	75	64	99	.282	.358	.465	.823	111	20	10	116	97	90	.808	7	6	-2	2	*1	0.6
1986	Chi-N	141	484	66	127	18	7	20	65	67	98	.262	.353	.452	.806	113	14	10	107	95	78	.797	8	7	-2	-7	*1	-0.4
1987	Chi-N	131	439	70	120	22	1	27	63	51	92	.273	.349	.513	.862	124	15	14	101	82	79	.850	2	2	-1	-8	*1	-0.1
1988	Chi-N	24	73	10	16	6	1	3	6	9	20	.219	.305	.452	.757	110	1	1	104	57	10	.724	0	1	-1	-0	1	0.0
	Cin-N	21	51	4	11	3	0	1	2	5	12	.216	.286	.333	.619	73	-2	-2	105	40	5	.550	0	0	0	-1	1	-0.3
	Yr	45	124	14	27	9	1	4	8	14	32	.218	.297	.403	.700	95	-0	-1	105	50	15	.653	0	1	-1	-1		-0.3
1989	StL-N	29	18	2	1	1	0	0	1	2	4	.056	.190	.111	.302	-12	-3	-3	101	201	0	.278	0	1	-1	-0	1	-0.4
Total	10	1067	3587	522	992	192	40	147	530	444	679	.277	.358	.475	.833	122	140	113	106	100	615	.837	106	61	-5	-27	1O	5.6
■ JIM DWYER	Dwyer, James Edward b: 1/3/50, Evergreen Park, Ill. BL/TL, 5'10", 165 lbs. Deb: 6/10/73																											
1973	StL-N	28	57	7	11	1	1	0	0	1	5	.193	.207	.246	.453	27	-6	-5	91	0	2	.300	0	0	0	-2	O	-0.8
1974	StL-N	74	86	13	24	1	0	2	11	11	16	.279	.367	.360	.728	101	1	0	104	115	12	.683	0	0	0	-5	O/1	-0.5
1975	StL-N	21	31	4	6	1	0	0	1	4	6	.194	.286	.226	.512	42	-2	-2	103	55	2	.423	0	0	0	-0	/O	-0.2
	Mon-N	60	175	22	50	7	1	3	20	23	30	.286	.369	.389	.757	102	3	1	108	100	28	.754	4	1	1	0	O	0.0
	Yr	81	206	26	56	8	1	3	21	27	36	.272	.356	.364	.720	94	1	-1	107	89	30	.697	4	1	1	0		-0.2
1976	Mon-N	50	92	7	17	3	1	0	5	11	10	.185	.272	.239	.511	46	-6	-6	100	87	6	.423	0	0	0	-2	O	-0.9
	NY-N	11	13	2	2	0	0	0	0	2	1	.154	.267	.154	.421	23	-1	-1	92	0	1	.364	0	0	0	-0	/O	-0.1
	Yr	61	105	9	19	3	1	0	5	13	11	.181	.271	.229	.500	43	-8	-7	99	73	7	.416	0	0	0	-2		-1.0
1977	StL-N	13	31	3	7	1	0	0	2	4	5	.226	.351	.258	.609	69	-1	-1	96	100	3	.583	0	0	0	-2	O	-0.2
1978	StL-N	34	65	8	14	3	0	1	4	9	3	.215	.320	.308	.628	80	-2	-1	95	69	7	.596	1	0	0	-5	O	-0.6
	SF-N	73	173	22	39	9	2	5	22	28	29	.225	.333	.387	.721	110	0	2	92	106	25	.748	6	0	2	2	O1	0.4
	Yr	107	238	30	53	12	2	6	26	37	32	.223	.330	.366	.695	102	-1	1	93	95	33	.706	7	0	2	-2		-0.2
1979	Bos-A	76	113	19	30	7	0	2	14	17	9	.265	.366	.381	.747	95	1	-0	107	110	15	.703	3	1	0	-2	1O	-0.3
1980	Bos-A	93	260	41	74	11	1	9	38	28	23	.285	.359	.438	.797	115	6	6	102	105	41	.766	3	2	-0	-3	OD/1	0.1
1981	Bal-A	68	134	16	30	0	1	3	10	20	19	.224	.325	.306	.631	83	-2	-2	99	78	14	.565	0	2	-1	-9	O/1D	-1.4
1982	Bal-A	71	148	28	45	4	3	6	15	27	24	.304	.411	.493	.905	147	11	11	100	66	33	.990	2	0	1	-7	O/1D	0.2
1983	Bal-A	100	196	37	56	17	1	8	38	31	29	.286	.383	.505	.888	142	12	12	100	121	39	.910	1	1	-0	-9	OD/1	0.2
1984	Bal-A	76	161	22	41	9	1	2	21	23	24	.255	.348	.360	.708	102	-0	1	94	131	21	.653	0	2	-1	-6	O/D	-0.7
1985	Bal-A	101	233	35	58	8	3	7	36	37	31	.249	.354	.399	.753	107	3	3	99	125	33	.716	0	3	-2	-6	O/D	-0.5
1986	Bal-A	94	160	18	39	13	1	8	31	23	31	.244	.346	.488	.833	126	6	6	99	121	27	.824	0	2	-1	-1	OD/1	0.3
1987	Bal-A	92	241	54	66	7	1	15	33	37	57	.274	.373	.498	.871	132	11	11	98	80	46	.900	4	1	1	-1	DO	0.9
1988	Bal-A	35	53	3	12	0	0	0	3	12	11	.226	.369	.226	.596	75	-1	-1	95	99	5	.585	0	0	0	-0	D/O	0.0
	Min-A	20	41	6	12	1	0	2	15	13	8	.293	.473	.463	.936	154	5	4	106	239	10	1.100	0	0	0	0	D	0.4
	Yr	55	94	9	24	1	0	2	18	25	19	.255	.417	.330	.746	113	3	3	99	152	15	.803	0	0	0	-0		0.4
1989	Min-A	88	225	34	71	11	0	3	23	28	23	.316	.391	.404	.796	117	8	6	107	89	36	.756	2	0	1	-0	D/O	0.7
	Mon-N	13	10	1	3	1	0	0	2	1	1	.300	.364	.400	.764	116	0	0	102	201	2	.714	0	0	0	0	H	0.0
Total	17	1291	2698	402	707	115	17	76	344	390	395	.262	.358	.402	.760	109	43	43	100	102	412	.736	26	15	-1	-57	OD/1	-3.0

YEAR	TM/L	G	AB	R	H	2B	3B	HR	RBI	BB	SO	AVG	OBP	SLG	PRO	/A	BR	/A	PF	CHI	RC	TA	SB	CS	SBR	FR	POS	TPR
■ **LENNY DYKSTRA**	Dykstra, Leonard Kyle b: 2/10/63, Santa Ana, Cal. BL/TL, 5'10", 160 lbs. Deb: 5/03/85																											
1985	NY-N	83	236	40	60	9	3	1	19	30	24	.254	.341	.331	.671	91	-3	-2	97	93	30	.681	15	2	3	9	O	0.9
1986	NY-N	147	431	77	127	27	7	8	45	58	55	.295	.378	.445	.824	132	16	19	96	83	80	.892	31	7	5	-3	*O	1.9
1987	NY-N	132	431	86	123	37	3	10	43	40	67	.285	.352	.455	.806	113	7	8	99	76	74	.845	27	7	4	-7	*O	0.0
1988	NY-N	126	429	57	116	19	3	8	33	30	43	.270	.323	.385	.707	113	1	6	90	70	56	.704	30	8	4	1	*O	0.8
1989	NY-N	56	159	27	43	12	1	3	13	23	15	.270	.370	.415	.785	129	6	6	97	70	28	.874	13	1	3	5	O	1.5
	Phi-N	90	352	39	78	20	3	4	19	37	38	.222	.297	.330	.627	78	-9	-10	101	57	35	.590	17	11	-2	11	O	0.0
	Yr	146	511	66	121	32	4	7	32	60	53	.237	.321	.356	.677	94	-4	-3	99	63	62	.672	30	12	2	16		1.5
Total	5	634	2038	326	547	124	20	34	172	218	242	.268	.342	.399	.741	110	18	27	96	75	303	.760	133	36	18	16	O	5.1
■ **JIM EISENREICH**	Eisenreich, James Michael b: 4/18/59, St.Cloud, Minn. BL/TL, 5'11", 180 lbs. Deb: 4/06/82																											
1982	Min-A	34	99	10	30	6	0	2	9	11	13	.303	.378	.424	.803	120	3	3	100	75	17	.771	0	0	0	0	O	0.2
1983	Min-A	2	7	1	2	1	0	0	0	1	1	.286	.375	.429	.804	115	0	0	105	0	1	.800	0	0	0	1	/O	0.1
1984	Min-A	12	32	1	7	1	0	0	3	2	4	.219	.265	.250	.515	41	-2	-3	106	150	2	.462	2	0	1	-0	/OD	-0.2
1987	KC-A	44	105	10	25	8	2	4	21	7	13	.238	.286	.467	.752	92	-1	-2	104	137	13	.687	1	1	-0	0	D	-0.1
1988	KC-A	82	202	26	44	8	1	1	19	6	31	.218	.240	.282	.523	44	-15	-16	103	126	14	.442	9	3	1	-8	OD	-2.3
1989	KC-A	134	475	64	139	33	7	9	59	37	44	.293	.344	.448	.792	127	13	15	96	98	73	.787	27	8	3	2	*OD	1.9
Total	6	308	920	112	247	57	10	16	111	64	106	.268	.317	.404	.721	100	-2	-2	99	106	121	.681	39	12	5	-4	O/D	-0.4
■ **KEVIN ELSTER**	Elster, Kevin Daniel b: 8/3/64, San Pedro, Cal. BR/TR, 6'2", 180 lbs. Deb: 9/02/86																											
1986	NY-N	19	30	3	5	1	0	0	0	3	8	.167	.242	.200	.442	24	-3	-3	96	0	2	.360	0	0	0	1	S	0.0
1987	NY-N	5	10	1	4	2	0	0	1	0	1	.400	.400	.600	1.000	163	1	1	99	66	2	.857	0	0	0	0	/S	0.1
1988	NY-N	149	406	41	87	11	1	9	37	35	47	.214	.282	.313	.594	78	-16	-11	90	96	37	.515	2	0	1	-4	*S	-0.4
1989	NY-N	151	458	52	106	25	2	10	55	34	77	.231	.287	.360	.648	87	-10	-8	97	114	45	.557	4	3	-1	-1	*S	-0.1
Total	4	324	904	97	202	39	3	19	93	72	133	.223	.284	.336	.621	82	-28	-22	94	101	85	.535	6	3	0	-5	S	-0.4
■ **DAVE ENGLE**	Engle, Ralph David b: 11/30/56, San Diego, Cal. BR/TR, 6'3", 210 lbs. Deb: 4/14/81																											
1981	Min-A	82	248	29	64	14	4	5	32	13	37	.258	.298	.407	.705	97	-0	-2	105	108	27	.593	0	1	-1	-4	O/3D	-0.8
1982	Min-A	58	186	20	42	7	2	4	16	10	22	.226	.269	.349	.618	68	-8	-8	100	83	16	.507	0	0	0	-0	OD	-0.9
1983	Min-A	120	374	46	114	22	4	8	43	28	39	.305	.355	.449	.804	114	10	7	105	88	57	.726	2	1	0	3	CD/O	1.3
1984	Min-A	109	391	56	104	20	1	4	38	26	22	.266	.312	.353	.665	79	-9	-11	106	103	39	.536	0	1	-1	4	CD	-0.2
1985	Min-A	70	172	28	44	8	2	7	25	21	28	.256	.337	.448	.784	109	3	2	103	101	26	.752	2	2	-1	0	DC/O	0.2
1986	Det-A	35	86	6	22	7	0	0	4	7	13	.256	.312	.337	.649	81	-3	-2	95	55	9	.545	0	0	0	0	1/OCD	-0.2
1987	Mon-N	59	84	7	19	4	0	1	14	6	11	.226	.278	.310	.587	52	-5	-6	106	193	6	.471	1	0	0	0	O/C13	-0.5
1988	Mon-N	34	37	4	8	3	0	0	1	5	5	.216	.310	.297	.607	71	-1	-1	106	36	3	.516	0	0	0	-1	/CO3	-0.1
1989	Mil-A	27	65	5	14	3	0	2	8	4	13	.215	.261	.354	.615	74	-3	-2	97	107	6	.519	0	0	0	-0	1/CD	-0.3
Total	9	594	1643	201	431	88	13	31	181	120	190	.262	.314	.388	.702	90	-17	-24	104	98	189	.600	5	5	-2	2	COD/13	-1.5
■ **JIM EPPARD**	Eppard, James Gerhard b: 4/27/60, South Bend, Ind. BL/TL, 6'2", 180 lbs. Deb: 9/08/87																											
1987	Cal-A	8	9	2	3	0	0	0	0	2	0	.333	.455	.333	.788	116	0	0	99	0	1	.714	0	0	0	-0	/O	0.0
1988	Cal-A	56	113	7	32	3	1	0	14	11	15	.283	.347	.327	.674	96	-1	-0	94	150	13	.565	0	0	0	-1	OD/1	-0.1
1989	Cal-A	12	12	0	3	0	0	0	2	1	4	.250	.308	.250	.558	60	-1	-1	99	259	1	.444	0	0	0	0	/1	0.0
Total	3	76	134	9	38	3	1	0	16	14	19	.284	.351	.321	.672	94	-1	-1	95	149	15	.564	0	0	0	-1	/O1D	-0.1
■ **NICK ESASKY**	Esasky, Nicholas Andrew b: 2/24/60, Hialeah, Fla. BR/TR, 6'3", 200 lbs. Deb: 6/19/83																											
1983	Cin-N	85	302	41	80	10	5	12	46	27	99	.265	.331	.450	.782	112	5	4	103	108	46	.751	6	2	1	-8	3	-0.6
1984	Cin-N	113	322	30	62	10	5	10	45	52	103	.193	.305	.348	.653	79	-7	-9	106	124	36	.616	1	2	-1	-5	31	-1.6
1985	Cin-N	125	413	61	108	21	0	21	66	41	102	.262	.334	.465	.799	115	11	8	105	103	63	.755	3	4	-2	-5	3O1	0.0
1986	Cin-N	102	330	35	76	17	2	12	41	47	97	.230	.328	.403	.731	96	0	-2	104	97	44	.686	0	2	-1	-2	1O/3	-0.8
1987	Cin-N	100	346	48	94	19	2	22	59	29	76	.272	.328	.529	.857	118	9	8	104	95	57	.809	0	0	0	-4	1/3O	-0.1
1988	Cin-N	122	391	40	95	17	2	15	62	48	104	.243	.332	.412	.744	107	6	4	105	120	56	.724	7	2	1	-9	*1	-1.0
1989	Bos-A	154	564	79	156	26	5	30	108	66	117	.277	.355	.500	.855	133	28	25	105	115	100	.836	1	2	-1	3	*1/O	1.7
Total	7	801	2668	334	671	120	21	122	427	310	698	.251	.333	.449	.782	111	53	38	105	109	401	.746	18	14	-3	-30	13/O	-2.4
■ **ALVARO ESPINOZA**	Espinoza, Alvaro Alberto b: 2/19/62, Valencia, Venez. BR/TR, 6', 170 lbs. Deb: 9/14/84																											
1984	Min-A	1	0	0	0	0	0	0	0	0	0	—	—	—	—	—	0	0	106	—	—	—	0	0	0	0	/S	0.0
1985	Min-A	32	57	5	15	2	0	0	9	1	9	.263	.288	.298	.586	59	-3	-3	103	210	4	.422	0	1	-1	-1	S	-0.2
1986	Min-A	37	42	4	9	1	0	0	1	1	10	.214	.233	.238	.471	27	-4	-4	108	40	2	.324	0	1	-1	-1	2S	-0.3
1988	NY-A	3	3	0	0	0	0	0	0	0	0	.000	.000	.000	.000	-99	-1	-1	96	0	0	.000	0	0	0	0	/2S	0.0
1989	NY-A	146	503	51	142	23	1	0	41	14	60	.282	.303	.332	.635	76	-15	-17	104	96	48	.489	3	3	-1	21	*S	1.5
Total	5	219	605	60	166	26	1	0	51	16	79	.274	.295	.321	.616	70	-22	-26	104	102	455	.467	3	5	-2	20	S/2	1.0
■ **CECIL ESPY**	Espy, Cecil Edward b: 1/20/63, San Diego, Cal. BB/TR, 6'3", 195 lbs. Deb: 9/02/83																											
1983	LA-N	20	11	4	3	1	0	0	1	1	2	.273	.333	.364	.697	93	-0	-0	100	99	1	.625	0	0	0	-4	O	-0.3
1987	Tex-A	14	8	1	0	0	0	0	0	1	3	.000	.111	.000	.111	-64	-2	-2	104	0	0	.333	2	0	1	-0	/O	-0.1
1988	Tex-A	123	347	46	86	17	6	2	39	20	83	.248	.291	.349	.639	77	-10	-11	101	122	37	.641	33	10	4	2	OD/SC12	-0.5
1989	Tex-A	142	475	65	122	12	7	3	31	38	99	.257	.315	.331	.645	80	-11	-12	102	73	52	.645	45	20	2	-7	*O/D	-1.9
Total	4	299	841	116	211	30	13	5	71	60	187	.251	.303	.335	.638	78	-24	-26	102	92	91	.639	80	30	6	-8	O/DSC21	-2.8
■ **DARRELL EVANS**	Evans, Darrell Wayne b: 5/26/47, Pasadena, Cal. BL/TR, 6'2", 200 lbs. Deb: 4/20/69																											
1969	Atl-N	12	26	3	6	0	0	0	1	1	8	.231	.259	.231	.490	37	-2	-2	104	67	2	.350	0	0	0	0	/3	-0.1
1970	Atl-N	12	44	4	14	1	1	0	9	7	5	.318	.423	.386	.809	114	2	1	104	218	7	.781	0	0	0	1	3	0.2
1971	Atl-N	89	260	42	63	11	1	12	38	39	54	.242	.343	.431	.774	107	6	3	110	104	39	.755	2	3	-1	3	3/O	0.6
1972	Atl-N	125	418	67	106	12	0	19	71	90	58	.254	.391	.419	.809	124	20	18	105	133	76	.853	4	2	0	6	*3	2.4
1973	Atl-N	161	595	114	167	25	8	41	104	**124**	104	.281	.407	.556	.964	146	55	44	113	88	**143**	1.055	6	3	0	7	*31	4.8
1974	Atl-N	160	571	99	137	21	3	25	79	**126**	88	.240	.383	.419	.801	118	23	19	105	93	100	.839	4	2	0	16	*3	3.3
1975	Atl-N	156	567	82	138	22	2	22	73	105	106	.243	.364	.406	.769	119	12	16	95	92	91	.790	12	3	2	23	*3/1	4.1
1976	Atl-N	44	139	11	24	0	0	1	10	30	33	.173	.320	.194	.514	43	-8	-10	111	131	11	.508	3	0	1	-1	1/3	-1.2
	SF-N	92	257	42	57	9	1	10	36	42	38	.222	.331	.381	.712	99	1	-0	103	108	36	.719	6	1	1	4	1/3	0.1
	Yr	136	396	53	81	9	1	11	46	72	71	.205	.327	.316	.643	78	-7	-10	106	116	46	.642	9	1	2	3		-1.1
1977	SF-N	144	461	64	117	18	3	17	72	69	50	.254	.355	.416	.771	102	5	2	104	119	71	.763	9	6	-1	-8	O13	-1.1
1978	SF-N	159	547	82	133	24	2	20	78	105	64	.243	.365	.404	.769	125	13	20	92	117	87	.778	4	5	-2	11	*3	2.8
1979	SF-N	160	562	68	142	23	2	17	70	91	80	.253	.359	.391	.750	113	6	11	92	108	83	.737	6	7	-2	20	*3	2.3
1980	SF-N	154	556	69	147	23	0	20	78	83	65	.264	.362	.414	.776	121	14	17	96	113	87	.779	17	5	2	17	*31	3.6
1981	SF-N	102	357	51	92	13	4	12	48	54	33	.258	.358	.417	.776	114	10	8	105	104	56	.761	2	3	-1	1	31	0.3
1982	SF-N	141	465	64	119	20	4	16	61	77	64	.256	.364	.419	.783	127	13	17	94	100	74	.779	5	4	-1	-1	31S	1.2
1983	SF-N	142	523	94	145	29	3	30	82	84	81	.277	.379	.516	.896	145	33	32	101	95	104	.923	6	6	-2	1	*13/S	2.7
1984	Det-A	131	401	60	93	11	1	16	63	77	70	.232	.356	.384	.740	109	5	7	96	124	58	.735	2	2	-1	3	D13	0.6
1985	Det-A	151	505	81	125	17	0	**40**	94	85	85	.248	.357	.519	.876	128	25	21	106	100	96	.895	0	4	-2	10	*1D/3	2.0
1986	Det-A	151	507	78	122	15	0	29	85	91	105	.241	.357	.442	.799	123	14	17	95	111	85	.812	3	2	-0	8	*1D/3	1.7
1987	Det-A	150	499	90	128	20	0	34	99	100	84	.257	.383	.501	.884	137	26	28	97	115	103	.947	6	5	-1	6	*1D/3	2.1
1988	Det-A	144	437	48	91	9	0	22	64	84	89	.208	.337	.380	.717	106	2	5	94	110	57	.692	1	4	-2	1	D1	0.1
1989	Atl-N	107	276	31	57	6	1	11	39	41	46	.207	.309	.355	.664	88	-3	-4	102	120	33	.629	0	1	-1	1	13	-0.7
Total	21	2687	8973	1344	2223	329	36	414	1354	1605	1410	.248	.364	.431	.795	119	270	270	100	108	1499	.806	98	68	-11	130	*31D/OS	31.8
■ **DWIGHT EVANS**	Evans, Dwight Michael "Dewey" b: 11/3/51, Santa Monica, Cal. BR/TR, 6'2", 180 lbs. Deb: 9/16/72																											
1972	Bos-A	18	57	2	15	3	1	1	6	7	13	.263	.344	.404	.747	116	2	1	105	96	8	.682	0	0	0	0	O	0.1
1973	Bos-A	119	282	46	63	13	1	10	32	40	52	.223	.322	.383	.705	92	-1	-3	106	91	36	.678	5	0	2	-11	*O/D	-1.5
1974	Bos-A	133	463	60	130	19	8	10	70	38	77	.281	.338	.421	.759	110	10	6	107	125	65	.691	4	4	-1	10	*O/D	1.2

YEAR	TM/L	G	AB	R	H	2B	3B	HR	RBI	BB	SO	AVG	OBP	SLG	PRO	/A	BR	/A	PF	CHI	RC	TA	SB	CS	SBR	FR	POS	TPR
1975	Bos-A	128	412	61	113	24	6	13	56	47	60	.274	.354	.456	.811	117	15	10	109	95	66	.773	3	4	-2	18	*O/D	2.4
1976	Bos-A	146	501	61	121	34	5	17	62	57	92	.242	.326	.431	.757	109	12	6	110	91	69	.716	6	7	-2	8	*O/D	0.9
1977	Bos-A	73	230	39	66	9	2	14	36	28	58	.287	.364	.526	.890	119	12	7	117	87	45	.905	4	2	0	-1	O/D	0.3
1978	Bos-A	147	497	75	123	24	2	24	63	65	119	.247	.337	.449	.786	111	12	7	107	86	74	.756	8	5	-1	6	*O/D	0.9
1979	Bos-A	152	489	69	134	24	1	21	58	69	76	.274	.365	.456	.821	112	14	9	107	78	79	.791	6	9	-4	7	*O	0.6
1980	Bos-A	148	463	72	123	37	5	18	60	64	98	.266	.361	.484	.845	127	19	18	102	84	85	.855	3	1	0	-4	*O/D	1.0
1981	Bos-A	108	412	84	122	19	4	**22**	71	**85**	85	.296	.418	.522	**.940**	**159**	**40**	**36**	106	87	**95**	**1.013**	3	2	-0	-3	*O	3.2
1982	Bos-A	162	609	122	178	37	7	32	98	112	125	.292	**.403**	.534	.937	140	48	40	110	89	134	.980	3	2	-0	1	*O/D	3.5
1983	Bos-A	126	470	74	112	19	4	22	58	70	97	.238	.339	.436	.776	110	8	7	101	89	71	.757	3	0	1	2	OD	0.9
1984	Bos-A	162	630	**121**	186	37	8	32	104	96	115	.295	.392	.532	**.924**	138	47	38	110	85	**132**	.944	3	1	0	-3	*O/D	3.0
1985	Bos-A	159	617	110	162	29	1	29	78	**114**	105	.263	.382	.454	.836	125	27	25	102	74	112	.858	7	2	1	-3	*O/D	2.0
1986	Bos-A	152	529	86	137	33	2	26	97	97	117	.259	.380	.476	.856	133	26	27	100	124	100	.882	3	3	-1	0	*O/D	2.1
1987	Bos-A	154	541	109	165	37	2	34	123	**106**	98	.305	.422	.569	.991	162	51	51	99	127	134	1.074	4	6	-2	-4	1O/D	3.3
1988	Bos-A	149	559	96	164	31	7	21	111	76	99	.293	.379	.487	.866	129	31	24	109	**140**	104	.859	5	1	1	-4	O1/D	1.6
1989	Bos-A	146	520	82	148	27	3	20	100	99	84	.285	.402	.463	.865	137	33	30	105	132	100	.885	3	3	-1	1	OD	2.9
Total	18	2382	8281	1369	2262	456	69	366	1283	1270	1570	.273	.373	.477	.850	127	406	340	106	100	1508	.852	73	52	-9	19	*O1D	28.4

■ MIKE FELDER Felder, Michael Otis b: 11/18/61, Vallejo, Cal. BB/TR, 5'8", 160 lbs. Deb: 9/11/85

YEAR	TM/L	G	AB	R	H	2B	3B	HR	RBI	BB	SO	AVG	OBP	SLG	PRO	/A	BR	/A	PF	CHI	RC	TA	SB	CS	SBR	FR	POS	TPR
1985	Mil-A	15	56	8	11	1	0	0	0	5	6	.196	.262	.214	.477	31	-5	-5	105	0	3	.438	4	1	1	1	O	-0.3
1986	Mil-A	44	155	24	37	2	4	1	13	13	16	.239	.298	.323	.620	68	-6	-7	102	100	17	.648	16	2	4	1	O/D	-0.2
1987	Mil-A	108	289	48	77	5	7	2	31	28	23	.266	.331	.353	.684	81	-7	-8	102	115	38	.735	34	8	5	1	O/2D	-0.3
1988	Mil-A	50	81	14	14	1	0	0	5	0	11	.173	.183	.185	.368	3	-10	-11	103	132	3	.343	8	2	1	-5	OD/2	-1.4
1989	Mil-A	117	315	50	76	11	3	3	23	23	38	.241	.293	.324	.617	76	-11	-10	97	81	33	.609	26	5	5	3	OD2	-0.3
Total	5	334	896	144	215	20	14	6	72	69	94	.240	.295	.314	.609	67	-40	-40	101	94	94	.617	88	18	16	1	O/D2	-2.5

■ JUNIOR FELIX Felix, Junior Francisco (Sanchez) b: 10/3/67, Laguna Sabada, D.R. BB/TR, 6', 170 lbs. Deb: 5/03/89

YEAR	TM/L	G	AB	R	H	2B	3B	HR	RBI	BB	SO	AVG	OBP	SLG	PRO	/A	BR	/A	PF	CHI	RC	TA	SB	CS	SBR	FR	POS	TPR
1989	Tor-A	110	415	62	107	14	8	9	46	33	101	.258	.317	.395	.712	106	-1	2	94	95	51	.671	18	12	-2	4	*O/D	0.2

■ FELIX FERMIN Fermin, Felix Jose (Minaya) b: 10/9/63, Mao Valverde, D.R. BR/TR, 5'11", 160 lbs. Deb: 7/08/87

YEAR	TM/L	G	AB	R	H	2B	3B	HR	RBI	BB	SO	AVG	OBP	SLG	PRO	/A	BR	/A	PF	CHI	RC	TA	SB	CS	SBR	FR	POS	TPR
1987	Pit-N	23	68	6	17	0	0	0	4	4	9	.250	.301	.250	.551	46	-5	-5	104	94	5	.407	0	0	0	-1	S	-0.3
1988	Pit-N	43	87	9	24	0	2	0	2	8	10	.276	.357	.322	.679	98	0	0	98	29	10	.627	3	1	0	-3	S	0.0
1989	Cle-A	156	484	50	115	9	1	0	21	41	27	.238	.302	.260	.563	58	-24	-27	104	65	40	.456	6	4	-1	14	*S/2	0.0
Total	3	222	639	65	156	9	3	0	27	53	46	.244	.310	.268	.578	62	-29	-32	103	63	55	.473	9	5	-0	10	S/2	-0.3

■ TONY FERNANDEZ Fernandez, Octavio Antonio (Castro) b: 8/6/62, San Pedro De Macoris, D.R. BB/TR, 6'2", 165 lbs. Deb: 9/02/83

YEAR	TM/L	G	AB	R	H	2B	3B	HR	RBI	BB	SO	AVG	OBP	SLG	PRO	/A	BR	/A	PF	CHI	RC	TA	SB	CS	SBR	FR	POS	TPR
1983	Tor-A	15	34	5	9	1	1	0	2	2	2	.265	.324	.353	.677	80	-1	-1	108	65	4	.556	0	1	-1	-0	S/D	0.0
1984	Tor-A	88	233	29	63	5	3	3	19	17	15	.270	.320	.356	.676	86	-4	-5	102	82	25	.583	5	7	-3	-3	S3/D	-0.4
1985	Tor-A	161	564	71	163	31	10	2	51	43	41	.289	.342	.390	.732	99	0	-1	101	91	75	.663	13	6	0	9	*S	2.0
1986	Tor-A	163	687	91	213	33	9	10	65	27	52	.310	.340	.428	.768	103	7	3	105	77	99	.709	25	12	0	3	*S	1.4
1987	Tor-A	146	578	90	186	29	8	5	67	51	48	.322	.382	.426	.807	114	14	13	101	109	94	.799	32	12	2	16	*S	3.5
1988	Tor-A	154	648	76	186	41	4	5	70	45	65	.287	.337	.386	.723	102	2	2	100	93	86	.660	15	5	2	11	*S	2.2
1989	Tor-A	140	573	64	147	25	9	11	64	29	51	.257	.296	.389	.685	97	-8	-4	94	93	66	.628	22	6	3	22	*S	3.3
Total	7	867	3317	426	967	165	44	36	338	214	274	.292	.338	.400	.738	102	10	8	100	91	448	.681	112	49	4	58	S/3D	12.0

■ BRUCE FIELDS Fields, Bruce Alan b: 10/6/60, Cleveland, Ohio BL/TR, 6', 185 lbs. Deb: 9/03/86

YEAR	TM/L	G	AB	R	H	2B	3B	HR	RBI	BB	SO	AVG	OBP	SLG	PRO	/A	BR	/A	PF	CHI	RC	TA	SB	CS	SBR	FR	POS	TPR
1986	Det-A	16	43	4	12	1	1	0	6	1	6	.279	.295	.349	.644	79	-1	-1	95	159	4	.531	1	1	-0	-1	O/D	-0.2
1988	Sea-A	38	67	8	18	5	0	1	5	4	11	.269	.310	.388	.698	88	-1	-1	108	69	7	.577	0	1	-1	-5	O/D	-0.7
1989	Sea-A	3	3	2	1	1	0	0	0	0	1	.333	.333	.667	1.000	170	0	0	103	0	1	1.000	0	0	0	-0	/O	0.0
Total	3	57	113	14	31	7	1	1	11	5	18	.274	.305	.381	.686	87	-2	-2	103	101	12	.570	1	2	-1	-7	/OD	-0.9

■ STEVE FINLEY Finley, Steven Allen b: 5/12/65, Union City, Tenn. BL/TL, 6'2", 175 lbs. Deb: 4/03/89

YEAR	TM/L	G	AB	R	H	2B	3B	HR	RBI	BB	SO	AVG	OBP	SLG	PRO	/A	BR	/A	PF	CHI	RC	TA	SB	CS	SBR	FR	POS	TPR
1989	Bal-A	81	217	35	54	5	2	2	25	15	30	.249	.300	.318	.618	75	-7	-7	99	130	23	.604	17	3	3	-8	O/D	-1.2

■ CARLTON FISK Fisk, Carlton Ernest "Pudge" b: 12/26/47, Bellows Falls, Vt. BR/TR, 6'3", 200 lbs. Deb: 9/18/69

YEAR	TM/L	G	AB	R	H	2B	3B	HR	RBI	BB	SO	AVG	OBP	SLG	PRO	/A	BR	/A	PF	CHI	RC	TA	SB	CS	SBR	FR	POS	TPR
1969	Bos-A	2	5	0	0	0	0	0	0	0	2	.000	.000	.000	.000	-95	-1	-1	105	0	0	.000	0	0	0	0	/C	0.0
1971	Bos-A	14	48	7	15	2	1	2	6	1	10	.313	.327	.521	.847	130	2	2	106	79	8	.765	0	0	0	0	C	0.2
1972	Bos-A	131	457	74	134	28	**9**	22	61	52	83	.293	.370	.538	.909	160	37	35	105	83	90	.914	5	2	0	17	*C	**5.9**
1973	Bos-A	135	508	65	125	21	0	26	71	37	99	.246	.310	.441	.751	103	4	1	106	94	69	.702	7	2	1	17	*C/D	2.2
1974	Bos-A	52	187	36	56	12	1	11	26	24	23	.299	.385	.551	.936	156	16	14	107	80	40	.978	5	1	1	1	C/D	1.8
1975	Bos-A	79	263	47	87	14	4	10	52	27	32	.331	.397	.529	.926	147	20	17	109	118	54	.925	4	3	-1	0	C/D	1.9
1976	Bos-A	134	487	76	124	17	5	17	58	56	71	.255	.339	.415	.754	109	12	6	110	93	70	.728	12	5	1	**18**	*C/D	3.1
1977	Bos-A	152	536	106	169	26	3	26	102	75	85	.315	.408	.521	.929	129	40	27	117	120	117	.969	7	6	-2	16	*C	4.4
1978	Bos-A	157	571	94	162	39	5	20	88	71	83	.284	.370	.475	.844	126	28	22	107	107	103	.846	7	2	1	16	*C/OD	4.4
1979	Bos-A	91	320	49	87	23	2	10	42	10	38	.272	.307	.450	.757	94	-1	-4	107	93	42	.674	3	0	1	-9	DC/O	-1.0
1980	Bos-A	131	478	73	138	25	3	18	62	36	62	.289	.355	.467	.821	121	15	14	102	89	77	.793	11	5	0	12	*C/013D	3.0
1981	Chi-A	96	338	44	89	12	0	7	45	38	37	.263	.358	.361	.719	108	5	5	100	126	45	.673	3	2	-0	-8	C/13O	0.1
1982	Chi-A	135	476	66	127	17	3	14	65	46	60	.267	.339	.403	.742	106	2	4	97	113	67	.719	17	2	4	-4	*C/1	1.1
1983	Chi-A	138	488	85	141	26	4	26	86	46	88	.289	.357	.518	.876	133	24	22	103	104	90	.870	9	6	-1	-6	*C/D	2.1
1984	Chi-A	102	359	54	83	20	1	21	43	26	60	.231	.292	.468	.760	96	2	-3	111	76	49	.724	6	0	2	-9	C/D	-0.4
1985	Chi-A	153	543	85	129	23	1	37	107	52	81	.238	.324	.488	.812	119	13	13	100	120	85	.813	17	9	-0	3	*CD	2.0
1986	Chi-A	125	457	42	101	11	0	14	63	22	92	.221	.266	.337	.603	63	-23	-24	101	131	39	.497	2	4	-2	4	CO/D	-1.8
1987	Chi-A	135	454	68	116	22	1	23	71	39	72	.256	.325	.460	.786	98	3	-2	109	102	66	.732	1	4	-2	15	*C/1OD	1.8
1988	Chi-A	76	253	37	70	8	1	19	50	37	40	.277	.380	.542	.921	159	19	20	97	104	52	.947	0	0	0	4	C	2.6
1989	Chi-A	103	375	47	110	25	2	13	68	36	60	.293	.360	.475	.835	144	16	19	93	124	61	.779	1	0	0	7	CD	3.0
Total	20	2141	7603	1155	2063	371	46	336	1166	731	1178	.271	.345	.465	.810	118	232	186	105	105	1222	.782	117	53	3	93	*CD/O13	36.4

■ MIKE FITZGERALD Fitzgerald, Michael Roy b: 7/13/60, Long Beach, Cal. BR/TR, 6', 185 lbs. Deb: 9/13/83

YEAR	TM/L	G	AB	R	H	2B	3B	HR	RBI	BB	SO	AVG	OBP	SLG	PRO	/A	BR	/A	PF	CHI	RC	TA	SB	CS	SBR	FR	POS	TPR
1983	NY-N	8	20	1	2	0	0	1	2	3	6	.100	.217	.250	.467	30	-2	-2	99	99	1	.444	0	0	0	-0	/C	-0.1
1984	NY-N	112	360	20	87	15	1	2	33	24	71	.242	.291	.306	.596	68	-15	-15	100	111	29	.469	1	0	0	-2	*C	-1.4
1985	Mon-N	108	295	25	61	7	1	5	34	38	55	.207	.301	.288	.590	70	-13	-11	94	135	26	.531	5	3	-0	-22	*C	-3.0
1986	Mon-N	73	209	20	59	13	1	6	37	27	34	.282	.367	.440	.807	125	6	7	98	134	34	.788	3	2	-0	-11	C	-0.2
1987	Mon-N	107	287	32	69	11	0	3	36	42	54	.240	.339	.310	.649	69	-10	-12	106	147	30	.582	3	4	-2	-15	*C/12	-2.0
1988	Mon-N	63	155	17	42	6	1	5	23	19	22	.271	.351	.419	.770	114	4	3	106	115	23	.723	2	2	-1	2	C/O	0.7
1989	Mon-N	100	290	33	69	18	2	7	42	35	61	.238	.324	.386	.710	100	1	0	102	127	35	.652	3	4	-2	7	C/3O	1.2
Total	7	571	1616	148	389	70	6	29	207	188	303	.241	.322	.345	.668	86	-28	-29	100	128	178	.596	17	15	-4	-42	C/O321	-4.8

■ TIM FLANNERY Flannery, Timothy Earl b: 9/29/57, Tulsa, Okla. BL/TR, 5'11", 175 lbs. Deb: 9/03/79

YEAR	TM/L	G	AB	R	H	2B	3B	HR	RBI	BB	SO	AVG	OBP	SLG	PRO	/A	BR	/A	PF	CHI	RC	TA	SB	CS	SBR	FR	POS	TPR
1979	SD-N	22	65	2	10	0	1	0	4	4	5	.154	.225	.185	.410	14	-8	-7	96	132	3	.310	0	0	0	-1	2	-0.6
1980	SD-N	95	292	15	70	12	0	0	25	18	30	.240	.284	.281	.565	62	-16	-14	93	121	23	.445	2	2	-1	1	23	-0.9
1981	SD-N	37	67	4	17	4	1	0	6	2	4	.254	.275	.343	.619	80	-2	-2	93	102	6	.510	1	0	0	-0	3/2	-0.1
1982	SD-N	122	379	40	100	11	7	0	30	30	32	.264	.321	.330	.651	90	-9	-5	92	94	42	.558	1	0	0	-22	*2/3S	-2.2
1983	SD-N	92	214	24	50	7	3	3	19	20	23	.234	.314	.336	.650	81	-6	-5	99	93	23	.582	2	2	-1	3	32/S	-0.3
1984	SD-N	86	128	24	35	3	3	2	10	12	17	.273	.350	.391	.740	109	1	2	99	70	19	.726	4	1	1	-3	23S	0.2
1985	SD-N	126	384	50	108	14	3	1	40	58	39	.281	.388	.341	.729	104	6	5	102	119	55	.702	2	5	-2	-13	*2/3	-0.9
1986	SD-N	134	368	48	103	11	2	3	28	54	61	.280	.379	.345	.724	106	3	5	95	82	50	.677	3	6	-3	-3	*23/S	0.2
1987	SD-N	106	276	23	63	5	1	0	20	42	30	.228	.334	.254	.588	61	-15	-14	97	114	25	.520	2	4	-2	2	2/3S	-1.1
1988	SD-N	79	170	16	45	5	4	0	19	24	32	.265	.369	.341	.710	108	2	3	97	131	23	.674	3	2	-0	-1	3/2S	0.2
1989	SD-N	73	130	9	30	5	0	0	8	13	20	.231	.301	.269	.570	64	-6	-6	101	92	11	.490	2	0	1	2	3/2	-0.3
Total	11	972	2473	255	631	77	25	9	209	277	293	.255	.338	.317	.655	86	-48	-37	97	104	279	.585	22	22	-7	-34	23/S	-5.8

YEAR	TM/L	G	AB	R	H	2B	3B	HR	RBI	BB	SO	AVG	OBP	SLG	PRO	/A	BR	/A	PF	CHI	RC	TA	SB	CS	SBR	FR	POS	TPR
■ **DARRIN FLETCHER** Fletcher, Darrin Glen b: 10/3/66, Elmhurst, Ill. BL/TR, 6'2", 195 lbs. Deb: 9/10/89																												
1989	LA-N	5	8	1	4	0	0	1	2	1	0	.500	.556	.875	1.431	327	2	2	93	80	4	2.000	0	0	0	0	/C	0.3
■ **SCOTT FLETCHER** Fletcher, Scott Brian b: 7/30/58, Fort Walton Beach Fla. BR/TR, 5'11", 168 lbs. Deb: 4/25/81																												
1981	Chi-N	19	46	6	10	4	0	0	1	2	4	.217	.250	.304	.554	54	-3	-3	104	28	4	.444	0	0	0	2	2/S3	0.1
1982	Chi-N	11	24	4	4	0	0	0	1	4	5	.167	.286	.167	.452	28	-2	-2	103	98	2	.450	1	0	0	-1	S	-0.2
1983	Chi-A	114	262	42	62	16	5	3	31	29	22	.237	.317	.370	.688	86	-4	-5	103	114	31	.636	5	1	1	7	*S2/3D	0.9
1984	Chi-A	149	456	46	114	13	3	3	35	46	46	.250	.329	.311	.641	71	-12	-18	111	92	51	.587	10	4	1	16	*S2/3	1.0
1985	Chi-A	119	301	38	77	8	1	2	31	35	47	.256	.333	.309	.642	77	-8	-8	100	124	31	.559	5	5	-2	5	3S2/D	-0.2
1986	Tex-A	147	530	82	159	34	5	3	50	47	59	.300	.361	.400	.761	113	7	10	96	92	76	.702	12	11	-3	2	*S32/D	1.6
1987	Tex-A	156	588	82	169	28	4	5	63	61	66	.287	.359	.374	.733	93	-1	-4	104	113	78	.672	13	12	-3	9	*S	0.8
1988	Tex-A	140	515	59	142	19	4	0	47	62	34	.276	.367	.328	.695	95	0	-0	101	117	66	.642	8	5	-1	8	*S/C	1.3
1989	Tex-A	83	314	47	75	14	1	0	22	38	41	.239	.325	.290	.615	73	-9	-10	102	90	31	.534	1	0	0	-11	S	-1.4
	Chi-A	59	232	30	63	11	1	1	21	26	19	.272	.347	.341	.688	102	-1	1	93	86	29	.615	1	1	-0	-3	2/SD	0.0
	Yr	142	546	77	138	25	2	1	43	64	60	.253	.334	.311	.646	84	-10	-9	98	89	60	.568	2	1	0	-14		-1.4
Total	9	997	3268	436	875	147	24	17	302	350	343	.268	.345	.343	.688	89	-33	-40	102	103	399	.624	56	39	-7	34	S2/3DC	3.9
■ **TOM FOLEY** Foley, Thomas Michael b: 9/9/59, Columbus, Ga. BL/TR, 6'1", 175 lbs. Deb: 4/09/83																												
1983	Cin-N	68	98	7	20	4	1	0	9	13	17	.204	.297	.265	.563	55	-5	-6	103	137	9	.506	1	0	0	-3	S/2	-0.4
1984	Cin-N	106	277	26	70	8	3	5	27	24	36	.253	.312	.357	.670	83	-5	-6	106	93	32	.597	3	2	-0	-13	S2/3	-1.0
1985	Cin-N	43	92	7	18	5	1	0	6	6	16	.196	.245	.272	.517	42	-7	-7	105	96	7	.432	1	0	0	-3	2S/3	-0.8
	Phi-N	46	158	17	42	8	0	3	17	13	18	.266	.322	.373	.695	92	-1	-2	102	100	18	.603	1	3	-2	-2	S	-0.1
	Yr	89	250	24	60	13	1	3	23	19	34	.240	.294	.336	.630	73	-8	-9	104	99	24	.538	2	3	-1	-5		-0.9
1986	Phi-N	39	61	8	18	2	1	0	5	10	11	.295	.394	.361	.755	105	1	1	104	91	10	.773	2	0	1	-1	S/23	0.3
	Mon-N	64	202	18	52	13	2	1	18	20	26	.257	.324	.356	.681	90	-3	-3	98	96	24	.641	8	3	1	1	S23	0.1
	Yr	103	263	26	70	15	3	1	23	30	37	.266	.341	.357	.699	93	-2	-2	100	95	34	.670	10	3	1	-0		0.4
1987	Mon-N	106	280	35	82	18	3	5	28	11	40	.293	.322	.432	.754	92	-2	-4	106	82	34	.650	6	10	-4	-9	S2/3	-1.0
1988	Mon-N	127	377	33	100	21	3	5	43	30	49	.265	.321	.377	.698	94	-0	-3	106	110	41	.593	2	7	-4	5	2S/3	0.3
1989	Mon-N	122	375	34	86	19	2	7	39	45	53	.229	.317	.347	.663	88	-5	-6	102	104	44	.612	2	3	-1	20	*23S/P	1.6
Total	7	721	1920	185	488	98	16	26	192	172	266	.254	.317	.363	.680	86	-27	-35	104	100	217	.604	26	28	-9	-6	S2/3P	-1.0
■ **CURT FORD** Ford, Curtis Glenn b: 10/11/60, Jackson, Miss. BL/TR, 5'10", 150 lbs. Deb: 6/22/85																												
1985	StL-N	11	12	2	6	2	0	0	3	4	1	.500	.625	.667	1.292	273	3	3	96	149	6	2.167	1	0	0	-1	/O	0.2
1986	StL-N	85	214	30	53	15	2	2	29	23	29	.248	.321	.364	.685	86	-3	-4	103	138	27	.683	13	5	1	1	O	-0.3
1987	StL-N	89	228	32	65	9	5	3	26	14	32	.285	.329	.408	.737	95	-2	-2	99	102	28	.676	11	8	-2	1	O	-0.5
1988	StL-N	92	128	11	25	6	0	1	18	8	26	.195	.243	.266	.508	44	-9	-10	104	195	8	.444	6	1	1	-5	O/1	-1.5
1989	Phi-N	108	142	13	31	5	1	1	13	16	33	.218	.302	.289	.591	69	-5	-5	101	119	12	.534	5	3	-0	-10	O/12	-1.7
Total	5	385	724	88	180	37	8	7	89	65	121	.249	.312	.351	.663	82	-17	-18	101	133	82	.621	36	17	1	-15	O/12	-3.8
■ **JULIO FRANCO** Franco, Julio Cesar (born Julio Cesar Robles (Franco)) b: 8/23/58, Hato Mayor, D.R. BR/TR, 6', 160 lbs. Deb: 4/23/82																												
1982	Phi-N	16	29	3	8	1	0	0	3	2	4	.276	.323	.310	.633	83	-1	-1	94	131	2	.458	0	2	-1	-0	S/3	0.0
1983	Cle-A	149	560	68	153	24	8	8	80	27	50	.273	.309	.387	.696	86	-8	-12	105	132	61	.632	32	12	2	-6	*S	-0.6
1984	Cle-A	160	658	82	188	22	5	3	79	43	68	.286	.335	.348	.683	84	-9	-14	106	127	73	.590	19	10	-0	3	*S/D	0.1
1985	Cle-A	160	636	97	183	33	4	6	90	54	74	.288	.347	.381	.728	105	0	5	94	132	79	.641	13	9	-2	-8	*S/2D	0.7
1986	Cle-A	149	599	80	183	30	5	10	74	32	66	.306	.341	.422	.763	110	6	7	98	110	76	.654	10	7	-1	-7	*S2/D	0.6
1987	Cle-A	128	495	86	158	24	3	8	52	57	56	.319	.393	.428	.821	116	15	13	103	85	82	.824	32	9	4	-16	*S/2D	0.6
1988	Cle-A	152	613	88	186	23	6	10	54	56	72	.303	.364	.409	.773	114	14	13	102	67	90	.734	25	11	1	-1	*2/D	2.2
1989	Tex-A	150	548	80	173	31	5	13	92	66	69	.316	.390	.462	.852	136	30	28	102	130	95	.842	21	3	5	-5	*2D	3.0
Total	8	1064	4138	584	1232	188	36	58	524	337	459	.298	.353	.403	.756	106	47	40	101	112	558	.693	152	63	8	-41	S2/D3	6.6
■ **TERRY FRANCONA** Francona, Terry Jon b: 4/22/59, Aberdeen, S.D. BL/TL, 6'1", 190 lbs. Deb: 8/19/81																												
1981	Mon-N	34	95	11	26	0	1	1	8	5	6	.274	.317	.326	.643	84	-2	-2	99	92	11	.551	1	0	0	0	O/1	-0.1
1982	Mon-N	46	131	14	42	3	0	0	9	8	11	.321	.360	.344	.703	93	-0	-1	105	78	16	.585	2	3	-1	-5	O1	-0.8
1983	Mon-N	120	230	21	59	11	1	3	22	6	20	.257	.275	.352	.628	72	-9	-10	102	97	20	.483	0	2	-1	-2	O1	-1.6
1984	Mon-N	58	214	18	74	19	2	1	18	5	12	.346	.364	.467	.831	144	8	10	91	70	35	.736	0	0	0	2	1/O	1.1
1985	Mon-N	107	281	19	75	15	1	2	31	12	12	.267	.299	.349	.648	86	-8	-6	94	119	29	.547	5	5	-2	2	1O/3	-0.7
1986	Chi-N	86	124	13	31	3	0	2	8	6	8	.250	.290	.323	.613	64	-5	-6	107	69	11	.485	0	1	-1	-7	O1	-1.6
1987	Cin-N	102	207	16	47	5	0	3	12	10	12	.227	.266	.295	.561	47	-15	-16	104	68	16	.448	2	0	1	-4	1/O	-2.3
1988	Cle-A	62	212	24	66	8	0	1	12	5	18	.311	.327	.363	.690	92	-2	-3	102	60	24	.547	0	0	0	1	D/1O	-0.1
1989	Mil-A	90	233	26	54	10	1	3	23	8	20	.232	.257	.322	.579	64	-12	-11	97	106	18	.462	2	1	0	-4	1DO/P	-1.8
Total	9	705	1727	162	474	74	6	16	143	65	119	.274	.303	.352	.655	82	-46	-44	99	87	179	.533	12	12	-4	-18	1O/DP3	-7.9
■ **LAVEL FREEMAN** Freeman, Lavel Maurice b: 2/18/63, Oakland, Cal. BL/TL, 5'9", 170 lbs. Deb: 4/07/89																												
1989	Mil-A	2	3	1	0	0	0	0	0	0	2	.000	.000	.000	.000	-99	-1	-1	97	0	0	.000	0	0	0	0	/D	0.0
■ **GARY GAETTI** Gaetti, Gary Joseph b: 8/19/58, Centralia, Ill. BR/TR, 6', 180 lbs. Deb: 9/20/81																												
1981	Min-A	9	26	4	5	0	0	2	3	0	6	.192	.192	.423	.615	70	-1	-1	105	69	2	.500	0	0	0	1	/3D	0.0
1982	Min-A	145	508	59	117	25	4	25	84	37	107	.230	.286	.443	.729	97	-4	-4	100	114	59	.645	0	4	-2	1	*3/SD	-0.7
1983	Min-A	157	584	81	143	30	3	21	78	54	121	.245	.313	.414	.727	93	-2	-6	105	106	74	.667	7	1	2	16	*3/SD	1.2
1984	Min-A	162	588	55	154	29	4	5	65	44	81	.262	.318	.350	.668	80	-12	-16	106	120	67	.592	11	5	0	14	*3/OS	0.0
1985	Min-A	160	560	71	138	31	0	20	63	37	89	.246	.301	.409	.710	89	-7	-9	103	88	66	.647	13	5	1	21	*3/O1D	0.7
1986	Min-A	157	596	91	171	34	1	34	108	52	108	.287	.350	.518	.869	124	27	20	108	111	99	.832	14	15	-5	21	*3/S2O	3.1
1987	Min-A	154	584	95	150	36	2	31	109	37	92	.257	.304	.485	.789	110	3	6	96	123	75	.715	10	7	-1	-6	*3/D	-0.3
1988	Min-A	133	468	66	141	29	2	28	88	36	85	.301	.358	.551	.909	142	30	26	106	104	89	.897	7	4	-0	-5	*3S/D	2.1
1989	Min-A	130	498	63	125	11	4	19	75	25	87	.251	.291	.404	.694	88	-6	-10	107	115	56	.607	6	2	1	10	*3/1D	0.1
Total	9	1207	4412	585	1144	225	20	185	673	322	776	.259	.315	.445	.760	102	27	5	104	110	587	.695	68	43	-5	73	*3/SDO12	6.2
■ **GREG GAGNE** Gagne, Gregory Carpenter b: 11/12/61, Fall River, Mass. BR/TR, 5'11", 185 lbs. Deb: 6/05/83																												
1983	Min-A	10	27	2	3	1	0	0	3	0	6	.111	.111	.148	.259	-28	-5	-5	105	293	1	.167	0	0	0	-1	S	-0.5
1984	Min-A	2	1	0	0	0	0	0	0	0	0	.000	.000	.000	.000	-95	-0	-0	106	0	0	.000	0	0	0	0	/H	0.0
1985	Min-A	114	293	37	66	15	3	2	23	20	57	.225	.282	.317	.599	62	-15	-16	103	92	27	.534	10	4	1	-7	*S/D	-1.4
1986	Min-A	156	472	63	118	22	6	12	54	30	108	.250	.303	.398	.701	83	-7	-12	108	96	57	.641	12	10	-2	-17	*S/2	-2.2
1987	Min-A	137	437	68	116	28	7	10	40	25	84	.265	.311	.430	.741	99	-4	-1	96	73	58	.676	6	6	-2	9	*S/O2D	1.1
1988	Min-A	149	461	70	109	20	6	14	48	27	110	.236	.289	.397	.686	85	-7	-11	106	85	50	.624	15	7	0	-13	*S/O23	-1.6
1989	Min-A	149	460	69	125	29	7	9	48	17	80	.272	.301	.424	.725	96	-1	-4	107	84	56	.645	11	4	1	-10	*S/O	0.0
Total	7	717	2151	309	537	115	29	47	216	119	445	.250	.296	.396	.691	85	-39	-50	104	88	248	.623	54	31	-2	-39	S/O2D3	-4.6
■ **ANDRES GALARRAGA** Galarraga, Andres Jose (born Andres Jose Padovani (Galarraga)) b: 6/18/61, Caracas, Venez. BR/TR, 6'3", 235 lbs. Deb: 8/23/85																												
1985	Mon-N	24	75	9	14	1	0	2	4	3	18	.187	.228	.280	.508	44	-6	-5	94	59	5	.413	1	2	-1	1	1	-0.5
1986	Mon-N	105	321	39	87	13	0	10	42	30	79	.271	.339	.405	.744	107	2	3	98	105	43	.684	6	5	-1	-5	*1	-0.7
1987	Mon-N	147	551	72	168	40	3	13	90	41	127	.305	.364	.459	.823	110	13	8	106	130	88	.770	7	10	-4	-1	*1	-0.4
1988	Mon-N	157	609	99	**184**	**42**	8	29	92	39	153	.302	.354	.540	.894	145	39	35	106	94	114	.887	13	4	2	-3	*1	2.8
1989	Mon-N	152	572	76	147	30	1	23	85	48	158	.257	.329	.434	.762	114	11	10	102	114	81	.726	12	5	1	-2	*1	-0.3
Total	5	585	2128	295	600	126	12	77	313	161	535	.282	.343	.461	.804	118	59	51	103	109	330	.763	39	26	-4	-10	1	0.9
■ **DAVE GALLAGHER** Gallagher, David Thomas b: 9/20/60, Trenton, N.J. BR/TR, 6' ", 180 lbs. Deb: 4/12/87																												
1987	Cle-A	15	36	2	4	1	1	0	1	2	5	.111	.158	.194	.352	-7	-6	-6	103	57	1	.333	2	0	1	2	O	-0.3
1988	Chi-A	101	347	59	105	15	3	5	31	29	40	.303	.356	.406	.763	116	6	7	97	81	49	.689	5	4	-1	-5	O/D	0.0
1989	Chi-A	161	601	74	160	22	2	1	46	46	79	.266	.320	.314	.635	86	-15	-10	93	99	62	.531	5	6	-2	-3	*O/D	-1.7

YEAR	TM/L	G	AB	R	H	2B	3B	HR	RBI	BB	SO	AVG	OBP	SLG	PRO	/A	BR	/A	PF	CHI	RC	TA	SB	CS	SBR	FR	POS	TPR
Total	3	277	984	135	269	38	6	6	78	77	124	.273	.327	.342	.670	93	-15	-8	95	91	112	.576	12	10	-2	-6	O/D	-2.0
■ **MIKE GALLEGO** Gallego, Michael Anthon b: 10/31/60, Whittier, Cal. BR/TR, 5'8", 160 lbs. Deb: 4/11/85																												
1985	Oak-A	76	77	13	16	5	1	1	9	12	14	.208	.322	.338	.660	87	-2	-1	93	123	9	.625	1	1	-0	-5	2S3	-0.3
1986	Oak-A	20	37	2	10	2	0	0	4	1	6	.270	.289	.324	.614	72	-2	-1	94	133	3	.448	0	2	-1	1	2/3S	0.0
1987	Oak-A	72	124	18	31	6	0	2	14	12	21	.250	.321	.347	.668	86	-4	-2	91	114	13	.566	0	1	-1	-0	23S	0.0
1988	Oak-A	129	277	38	58	8	0	2	20	34	53	.209	.298	.260	.558	61	-15	-13	95	102	23	.478	2	3	-1	0	2S3	-0.6
1989	Oak-A	133	357	45	90	14	2	3	30	35	43	.252	.329	.328	.657	83	-6	-8	103	93	39	.585	7	5	-1	-2	S2/3D	-0.1
Total	5	430	872	116	205	35	3	8	77	94	137	.235	.316	.310	.626	76	-28	-25	98	103	86	.546	10	12	-4	-6	2S/3D	-1.0
■ **RON GANT** Gant, Ronald Edwin b: 3/2/65, Victoria, Tex. BR/TR, 6' ", 172 lbs. Deb: 9/06/87																												
1987	Atl-N	21	83	9	22	4	0	2	9	1	11	.265	.274	.386	.659	67	-4	-4	108	96	7	.561	4	2	0	4	2	0.0
1988	Atl-N	146	563	85	146	28	8	19	60	46	118	.259	.319	.439	.757	110	10	7	104	84	78	.726	19	10	-0	2	*23	1.3
1989	Atl-N	75	260	26	46	8	3	9	25	20	63	.177	.238	.335	.573	61	-14	-14	102	90	21	.532	9	6	-1	2	3O	-1.4
Total	3	242	906	120	214	40	11	30	94	67	192	.236	.292	.404	.696	92	-7	-12	104	87	107	.651	32	18	-1	7	2/3O	-0.1
■ **JIM GANTNER** Gantner, James Elmer b: 1/5/53, Fond Du Lac, Wis. BL/TR, 6', 180 lbs. Deb: 9/03/76																												
1976	Mil-A	26	69	6	17	1	0	0	7	6	11	.246	.316	.261	.577	71	-2	-2	99	149	6	.491	1	0	0	-1	3/D	-0.3
1977	Mil-A	14	47	4	14	1	0	1	2	2	5	.298	.327	.383	.710	97	-1	-0	95	38	6	.629	2	1	0	0	3	0.0
1978	Mil-A	43	97	14	21	1	0	1	8	5	10	.216	.269	.258	.527	46	-7	-7	106	113	8	.447	2	0	1	-1	23/1S	-0.5
1979	Mil-A	70	208	29	59	10	3	2	22	16	17	.284	.341	.389	.730	96	-1	-1	100	97	27	.650	3	5	-2	-1	32/SP	-0.1
1980	Mil-A	132	415	47	117	21	3	4	40	30	29	.282	.332	.376	.708	99	-4	-1	95	93	50	.627	11	10	-3	-1	32/S	-0.1
1981	Mil-A	107	352	35	94	14	1	2	33	29	29	.267	.328	.330	.658	94	-4	-2	96	106	38	.559	3	6	-3	19	*2	1.8
1982	Mil-A	132	447	48	132	17	2	4	43	26	36	.295	.337	.369	.706	100	-4	-0	94	97	56	.614	6	3	0	5	*2	1.2
1983	Mil-A	161	603	85	170	23	8	11	74	38	46	.282	.331	.401	.732	110	-0	7	92	107	79	.648	5	6	-2	8	*2	1.7
1984	Mil-A	153	613	61	173	27	1	3	56	30	51	.282	.319	.344	.663	91	-14	-7	92	98	64	.542	6	5	-1	12	*2	1.0
1985	Mil-A	143	523	63	133	15	4	5	44	33	42	.254	.302	.327	.629	69	-20	-23	105	96	49	.530	11	8	-2	11	*23/S	-0.8
1986	Mil-A	139	497	58	136	25	1	7	38	26	50	.274	.318	.370	.688	86	-9	-10	102	75	56	.601	13	7	-0	-10	*2/3SD	-1.2
1987	Mil-A	81	265	37	72	14	0	4	30	19	22	.272	.332	.370	.702	85	-5	-6	102	109	32	.634	6	2	1	-4	23/D	-0.4
1988	Mil-A	155	539	67	149	28	2	0	47	34	50	.276	.323	.336	.659	82	-11	-13	103	105	60	.585	20	8	1	-5	*2/3	-0.6
1989	Mil-A	116	409	51	112	18	3	0	34	21	33	.274	.325	.333	.658	89	-7	-6	97	99	45	.597	20	6	2	10	*2/D	0.8
Total	14	1472	5084	605	1399	215	28	44	478	315	431	.275	.323	.354	.678	89	-86	-71	98	98	575	.590	109	67	-8	41	*23/SDP1	2.5
■ **DAMASO GARCIA** Garcia, Damaso Domingo (Sanchez) b: 2/7/55, Moca, D.R. BR/TR, 6'1", 165 lbs. Deb: 6/24/78																												
1978	NY-A	18	41	5	8	0	0	0	1	2	6	.195	.233	.195	.428	22	-4	-4	99	49	2	.324	1	0	0	0	2/S	-0.1
1979	NY-A	11	38	3	10	1	0	0	4	0	2	.263	.263	.289	.553	51	-3	-2	96	140	3	.448	2	0	1	1	S/3	0.1
1980	Tor-A	140	543	50	151	30	7	4	46	12	55	.278	.297	.381	.679	85	-13	-13	100	84	54	.561	13	13	-4	20	*2/D	1.0
1981	Tor-A	64	250	24	63	8	1	1	13	9	32	.252	.278	.304	.582	61	-11	-14	111	68	21	.500	13	3	2	-9	2/D	-1.9
1982	Tor-A	147	597	89	185	32	3	5	42	21	44	.310	.339	.399	.737	94	1	-6	109	64	81	.724	54	20	4	11	*2/D	1.8
1983	Tor-A	131	525	84	161	23	6	3	38	24	34	.307	.339	.390	.730	92	-0	-6	108	74	66	.670	31	17	-1	-11	*2	-1.3
1984	Tor-A	152	633	79	180	32	5	5	46	16	46	.284	.312	.374	.686	88	-10	-12	102	77	76	.654	46	12	7	-7	*2/D	-0.4
1985	Tor-A	146	600	70	169	25	4	8	65	15	41	.282	.304	.377	.680	84	-13	-14	101	109	64	.595	28	15	-1	-13	*2	-2.1
1986	Tor-A	122	424	57	119	22	0	6	46	13	32	.281	.308	.375	.683	82	-9	-11	105	103	44	.569	9	6	-1	-10	*2D/1	-1.6
1988	Atl-N	21	60	3	7	1	0	1	4	3	10	.117	.159	.183	.342	-2	-8	-8	104	114	1	.263	1	0	0	0	2	-0.7
1989	Mon-N	80	203	26	55	9	1	3	18	15	20	.271	.321	.369	.691	95	-1	-1	102	86	23	.601	5	4	-1	9	2/3	0.7
Total	11	1032	3914	490	1108	183	27	36	323	130	322	.283	.311	.371	.682	84	-71	-91	104	84	435	.609	203	90	7	-8	2/DS31	-4.5
■ **RICH GEDMAN** Gedman, Richard Leo b: 9/26/59, Worcester, Mass. BL/TR, 6', 210 lbs. Deb: 9/07/80																												
1980	Bos-A	9	24	2	5	0	0	0	1	0	5	.208	.208	.208	.417	14	-3	-3	102	78	1	.250	0	0	0	0	/CD	-0.1
1981	Bos-A	62	205	22	59	15	0	5	26	9	31	.288	.321	.434	.755	109	3	2	106	98	26	.639	0	0	0	-2	C	0.3
1982	Bos-A	92	289	30	72	17	2	4	26	10	37	.249	.279	.363	.642	68	-10	-14	110	89	25	.506	0	1	-1	-2	C	-1.1
1983	Bos-A	81	204	21	60	16	1	2	18	15	37	.294	.345	.412	.757	106	2	2	101	78	28	.671	0	1	-1	-2	C	0.2
1984	Bos-A	133	449	54	121	26	4	24	72	29	72	.269	.315	.506	.821	111	12	6	110	96	71	.772	0	0	0	-3	*C	1.1
1985	Bos-A	144	498	66	147	30	5	18	80	50	79	.295	.363	.484	.847	127	20	19	102	108	86	.815	2	0	1	7	*C	3.1
1986	Bos-A	135	462	49	119	29	0	16	65	37	61	.258	.318	.424	.742	101	0	0	100	106	59	.665	1	0	0	14	*C	2.2
1987	Bos-A	52	151	11	31	8	0	1	13	10	24	.205	.255	.278	.533	42	-12	-12	99	115	11	.426	0	0	0	0	C	-0.7
1988	Bos-A	95	299	33	69	14	0	9	39	18	49	.231	.281	.368	.649	74	-9	-12	109	113	31	.555	0	0	0	-2	C/D	-0.9
1989	Bos-A	93	260	24	55	9	0	4	16	23	47	.212	.276	.292	.568	58	-14	-15	105	71	20	.463	0	1	-1	-5	C	-1.7
Total	10	896	2841	312	738	164	12	83	356	201	442	.260	.312	.414	.726	94	-11	-28	105	98	358	.639	3	3	-1	6	C/D	2.4
■ **BOB GEREN** Geren, Robert Peter b: 9/22/61, San Diego, Cal. BR/TR, 6'3", 205 lbs. Deb: 5/17/88																												
1988	NY-A	10	10	0	1	0	0	0	0	2	3	.100	.250	.100	.350	2	-1	-1	96	0	0	.333	0	0	0	-0	C	0.0
1989	NY-A	65	205	26	59	5	1	9	27	12	44	.288	.330	.454	.784	114	4	3	104	87	28	.679	0	0	0	8	C/D	1.4
Total	2	75	215	26	60	5	1	9	27	14	47	.279	.326	.437	.763	109	3	2	104	83	28	.661	0	0	0	8	/CD	1.4
■ **KIRK GIBSON** Gibson, Kirk Harold b: 5/28/57, Pontiac, Mich. BL/TL, 6'3", 215 lbs. Deb: 9/08/79																												
1979	Det-A	12	38	3	9	3	0	1	4	1	3	.237	.256	.395	.651	75	-2	-1	96	85	3	.594	3	3	-1	-1	O	-0.3
1980	Det-A	51	175	23	46	2	1	9	16	10	45	.263	.306	.440	.746	97	-0	-1	105	60	22	.676	4	7	-3	2	O/D	-0.2
1981	Det-A	83	290	41	95	11	3	9	40	18	64	.328	.371	.479	.850	136	15	14	105	96	50	.842	17	5	2	-3	O/D	1.2
1982	Det-A	69	266	34	74	16	2	8	35	25	41	.278	.342	.444	.786	113	5	5	100	104	40	.761	9	7	-2	8	O/D	0.9
1983	Det-A	128	401	60	91	12	9	15	51	53	96	.227	.323	.414	.737	106	1	3	96	94	59	.752	14	3	2	-0	DO	0.4
1984	Det-A	149	531	92	150	23	10	27	91	63	103	.282	.367	.516	.883	147	30	32	96	104	106	.949	29	9	3	-12	*O/D	1.9
1985	Det-A	154	581	96	167	37	5	29	97	71	137	.287	.370	.518	.888	132	32	27	106	105	118	.962	30	4	7	-9	*O/D	2.2
1986	Det-A	119	441	84	118	11	2	28	86	68	107	.268	.374	.492	.866	141	22	25	95	121	88	.967	34	6	7	-12	*O/D	1.6
1987	Det-A	128	487	95	135	25	3	24	79	71	117	.277	.375	.489	.863	132	21	23	97	108	95	.934	26	7	4	1	*O/D	2.3
1988	LA-N	150	542	106	157	28	1	25	76	73	120	.290	.381	.483	.864	138	34	30	106	96	107	.940	31	4	7	4	*O	3.9
1989	LA-N	71	253	35	54	8	2	9	28	35	55	.213	.314	.368	.681	102	-2	1	93	96	31	.686	12	3	2	3	O	0.5
Total	11	1114	4005	669	1096	176	38	184	603	488	888	.274	.359	.474	.833	128	156	156	100	101	719	.875	209	58	28	-20	OD	14.4
■ **JOE GIRARDI** Girardi, Joseph Elliott b: 10/14/64, Peoria, Ill. BR/TR, 5'11", 195 lbs. Deb: 4/04/89																												
1989	Chi-N	59	157	15	39	10	0	1	14	11	26	.248	.306	.331	.637	76	-4	-5	108	102	15	.545	2	1	0	1	C	0.0
■ **DAN GLADDEN** Gladden, Clinton Daniel b: 7/7/57, San Jose, Cal. BB/TR, 5'11", 180 lbs. Deb: 9/05/83																												
1983	SF-N	18	63	6	14	2	0	1	9	5	11	.222	.279	.302	.581	60	-3	-3	101	165	4	.509	4	3	-1	3	O	0.0
1984	SF-N	86	342	71	120	17	2	4	31	33	37	.351	.411	.447	.859	147	20	21	96	71	64	.909	31	16	-0	5	O	2.3
1985	SF-N	142	502	64	122	15	8	7	41	40	78	.243	.308	.347	.654	89	-12	-8	93	85	54	.625	32	15	1	5	*O	-0.5
1986	SF-N	102	351	55	97	16	1	4	29	39	59	.276	.357	.362	.719	103	1	2	96	85	49	.736	27	10	2	8	O	1.1
1987	Min-A	121	438	69	109	21	2	8	38	38	72	.249	.313	.361	.674	82	-13	-10	96	85	50	.647	25	9	2	5	*O/D	-0.5
1988	Min-A	141	576	91	155	32	6	11	62	46	74	.269	.327	.403	.730	97	2	-2	106	82	78	.708	28	8	4	13	*O/23P	1.2
1989	Min-A	121	461	69	136	23	3	8	46	23	53	.295	.335	.410	.745	102	5	1	107	86	64	.710	23	7	3	2	*O/PD	0.3
Total	7	731	2733	425	753	126	22	43	256	224	384	.276	.336	.385	.721	100	-1	1	99	85	364	.704	170	68	10	40	O/DP32	3.9
■ **RENE GONZALES** Gonzales, Rene Adrian b: 9/3/60, Austin, Tex. BR/TR, 6'3", 180 lbs. Deb: 7/27/84																												
1984	Mon-N	29	30	5	7	1	0	0	2	2	4	.233	.303	.267	.570	67	-1	-1	91	98	3	.478	0	0	0	-2	S	0.0
1986	Mon-N	11	26	1	3	0	0	0	0	2	7	.115	.179	.115	.294	-18	-4	-4	98	0	0	.200	0	2	-1	0	/S3	-0.4
1987	Bal-A	37	60	14	16	2	1	1	7	3	11	.267	.302	.383	.685	83	-2	-2	98	107	7	.587	1	0	0	2	3/2S	0.1
1988	Bal-A	92	237	13	51	6	0	2	15	13	32	.215	.265	.266	.531	52	-16	-15	95	86	17	.424	2	0	1	1	32/1SO	-1.1
1989	Bal-A	71	166	16	36	4	0	1	11	12	30	.217	.270	.259	.529	50	-11	-11	99	93	11	.432	5	3	-0	1	23/S	-0.8
Total	5	240	519	49	113	13	1	4	35	32	84	.218	.268	.270	.538	52	-34	-32	96	87	38	.434	8	5	-1	3	3/2SO1	-2.2

YEAR	TM/L	G	AB	R	H	2B	3B	HR	RBI	BB	SO	AVG	OBP	SLG	PRO	/A	BR	/A	PF	CHI	RC	TA	SB	CS	SBR	FR	POS	TPR
■ DENNY GONZALEZ	Gonzalez, Denio Mariano (Manzueta) b: 7/22/63, Sabana Grande Boya, D.R. BR/TR, 5'11", 165 lbs. Deb: 8/06/84																											
1984	Pit-N	26	82	9	15	3	1	0	4	7	21	.183	.247	.244	.491	41	-7	-6	94	78	4	.389	1	1	-0	-0	3S/O	-0.5
1985	Pit-N	35	124	11	28	4	0	4	12	13	27	.226	.299	.355	.654	80	-3	-3	103	87	13	.584	2	4	-2	-5	3O/2	-1.0
1987	Pit-N	5	7	1	0	0	0	0	0	1	2	.000	.125	.000	.125	-61	-2	-2	104	0	0	.143	0	0	0	0	/S	-0.1
1988	Pit-N	24	32	5	6	1	0	0	1	6	10	.188	.316	.219	.535	57	-2	-1	98	57	3	.481	0	0	0	-0	S/23	0.0
1989	Cle-A	8	17	3	5	1	0	0	1	0	4	.294	.333	.353	.686	90	-0	-0	104	65	2	.583	0	0	0	0	/3D	0.0
Total	5	98	262	29	54	9	1	4	18	27	64	.206	.283	.294	.577	62	-13	-13	100	77	22	.493	3	5	-2	-5	/3SO2D	-1.6
■ JOSE GONZALEZ	Gonzalez, Jose Rafael (Gutierrez) b: 11/23/64, Puerto Plata, D.R. BR/TR, 6'2", 190 lbs. Deb: 9/02/85																											
1985	LA-N	23	11	6	3	2	0	0	0	1	3	.273	.333	.455	.788	127	0	0	93	0	1	.700	1	1	-0	-5	O	-0.5
1986	LA-N	57	93	15	20	5	1	2	6	7	29	.215	.270	.355	.625	75	-4	-3	94	61	9	.579	4	3	-1	-9	O	-1.3
1987	LA-N	19	16	2	3	2	0	0	1	1	2	.188	.235	.313	.548	48	-1	-1	92	80	2	.846	5	0	2	-1	O	-0.1
1988	LA-N	37	24	7	2	1	0	0	0	2	10	.083	.154	.125	.279	-18	-4	-4	106	0	1	.364	3	0	1	-7	O	-1.0
1989	LA-N	95	261	31	70	11	2	3	18	23	53	.268	.327	.360	.688	104	-1	1	93	70	32	.643	9	3	1	4	O	0.4
Total	5	231	405	61	98	21	3	5	25	34	97	.242	.301	.346	.646	88	-10	-7	94	63	45	.618	22	7	2	-18	O	-2.5
■ JUAN GONZALEZ	Gonzalez, Juan Alberto (Vazquez) b: 10/16/69, Vega Baja, P.R. BR/TR, 6'3", 175 lbs. Deb: 9/01/89																											
1989	Tex-A	24	60	6	9	3	0	1	7	6	17	.150	.227	.250	.477	34	-5	-5	102	151	3	.382	0	0	0	0	O	-0.5
■ MARK GRACE	Grace, Mark Eugene b: 6/28/64, Winston-Salem, N.C BL/TL, 6'2", 190 lbs. Deb: 5/02/88																											
1988	Chi-N	134	486	65	144	23	4	7	57	60	43	.296	.374	.403	.777	118	16	13	104	107	74	.725	3	3	-1	-3	*1	0.3
1989	Chi-N	142	510	74	160	28	3	13	79	80	42	.314	.407	.457	.864	135	34	28	108	124	96	.884	14	7	0	9	*1	2.8
Total	2	276	996	139	304	51	7	20	136	140	85	.305	.391	.431	.822	127	50	42	106	116	170	.806	17	10	-1	7	1	3.1
■ GARY GREEN	Green, Gary Allan b: 1/14/62, Pittsburgh, Pa. BR/TR, 6'3", 175 lbs. Deb: 9/14/86																											
1986	SD-N	13	33	2	7	1	0	0	2	1	11	.212	.235	.242	.478	34	-3	-3	95	100	2	.346	0	0	0	-2	S	-0.2
1989	SD-N	15	27	4	7	3	0	0	0	1	1	.259	.286	.370	.656	86	-1	-1	101	0	3	.524	0	1	-1	0	S/3	0.0
Total	2	28	60	6	14	4	0	0	2	2	12	.233	.258	.300	.558	57	-4	-3	98	55	5	.426	0	1	-1	-1	/S3	-0.2
■ MIKE GREENWELL	Greenwell, Michael Lewis b: 7/18/63, Louisville, Ky. BL/TR, 6', 170 lbs. Deb: 9/05/85																											
1985	Bos-A	17	31	7	10	1	0	4	8	3	4	.323	.382	.742	1.124	194	4	4	102	91	9	1.286	1	0	0	-5	O	0.0
1986	Bos-A	31	35	4	11	2	0	0	4	5	7	.314	.400	.371	.771	113	1	1	100	123	5	.720	0	0	0	-2	O/D	0.0
1987	Bos-A	125	412	71	135	31	6	19	89	35	40	.328	.389	.570	.959	152	30	30	99	122	90	.976	5	4	-1	-0	OD/C	2.5
1988	Bos-A	158	590	86	192	39	8	22	119	87	38	.325	.420	.531	.950	151	53	46	109	132	134	1.019	16	8	0	4	*OD	4.7
1989	Bos-A	145	578	87	178	36	0	14	95	56	44	.308	.372	.443	.815	123	22	19	105	131	91	.770	13	5	1	-10	*O/D	0.8
Total	5	476	1646	255	526	109	14	59	315	186	133	.320	.395	.510	.905	142	110	100	105	128	330	.917	35	17	0	-12	O/DC	8.0
■ TOMMY GREGG	Gregg, William Thomas b: 7/29/63, Boone, N.C. BL/TL, 6'1", 190 lbs. Deb: 9/14/87																											
1987	Pit-N	10	8	3	2	1	0	0	0	0	2	.250	.250	.375	.625	60	-0	-0	104	0	0	.375	0	0	0	-1	/O	-0.1
1988	Pit-N	14	15	4	3	1	0	1	3	1	4	.200	.250	.467	.717	104	-0	-0	98	120	1	.615	0	1	-1	-2	/O	-0.2
	Atl-N	11	29	1	10	3	0	0	4	2	2	.345	.387	.448	.835	133	1	1	104	123	5	.750	0	0	0	3	/O	0.4
	Yr	25	44	5	13	4	0	1	7	3	6	.295	.340	.455	.795	126	1	1	101	126	6	.697	0	1	-1	1		0.2
1989	Atl-N	102	276	24	67	8	0	6	23	18	45	.243	.289	.337	.626	77	-8	-9	102	83	26	.525	3	4	-2	-6	O1	-2.1
Total	3	137	328	32	82	13	0	7	30	21	53	.250	.295	.354	.649	83	-7	-8	102	87	32	.543	3	5	-2	-7	/O1	-2.0
■ KEN GRIFFEY	Griffey, George Kenneth Jr. "Ken" b: 11/21/69, Donora, Pa. BL/TL, 6'3", 195 lbs. Deb: 4/03/89																											
1989	Sea-A	127	455	61	120	23	0	16	61	44	83	.264	.331	.420	.751	107	6	4	103	101	65	.731	16	7	1	2	*O	0.4
■ KEN GRIFFEY	Griffey, George Kenneth Sr. "Ken" b: 4/10/50, Donora, Pa. BL/TL, 5'11", 190 lbs. Deb: 8/25/73																											
1973	Cin-N	25	86	19	33	5	1	3	14	6	10	.384	.424	.570	.994	186	8	9	93	97	21	1.073	4	2	0	-3	O	0.5
1974	Cin-N	88	227	24	57	9	5	2	19	27	43	.251	.333	.361	.695	96	-2	-1	98	83	29	.676	9	4	0	-2	O	-0.5
1975	Cin-N	132	463	95	141	15	9	4	46	67	67	.305	.394	.402	.795	116	16	13	104	92	77	.796	16	7	1	-9	*O	0.0
1976	Cin-N	148	562	111	189	28	9	6	74	62	65	.336	.403	.450	.853	138	32	30	103	107	109	.904	34	11	4	-3	*O	2.7
1977	Cin-N	154	585	117	186	35	8	12	57	69	84	.318	.390	.467	.857	129	25	25	100	78	108	.857	17	8	0	6	*O	2.6
1978	Cin-N	158	614	90	177	33	8	10	63	54	70	.288	.346	.417	.763	109	9	7	103	93	93	.743	23	5	4	2	*O	0.8
1979	Cin-N	95	380	62	120	27	4	8	32	36	39	.316	.376	.471	.848	133	16	17	97	60	68	.838	12	5	1	1	O	1.6
1980	Cin-N	146	544	89	160	28	10	13	85	62	77	.294	.367	.454	.821	126	21	20	102	125	99	.856	23	1	6	-4	*O	1.7
1981	Cin-N	101	396	65	123	21	6	2	34	39	42	.311	.374	.409	.783	121	12	12	101	76	61	.748	12	4	1	5	O	1.5
1982	NY-A	127	484	70	134	23	2	12	54	39	58	.277	.331	.407	.738	105	1	3	96	95	65	.676	10	4	1	6	*O	0.6
1983	NY-A	118	458	60	140	21	3	11	46	34	45	.306	.356	.437	.793	119	10	11	99	82	74	.752	6	1	1	-4	*1/OD	0.4
1984	NY-A	120	399	44	109	20	1	7	56	29	32	.273	.324	.381	.705	100	-3	-0	94	129	49	.615	2	2	-1	5	O1/D	0.0
1985	NY-A	127	438	68	120	28	4	10	69	41	51	.274	.336	.425	.761	111	4	6	96	127	63	.716	7	7	-2	1	*O/1D	0.4
1986	NY-A	59	198	33	60	7	0	9	26	15	24	.303	.355	.475	.830	121	7	6	103	86	31	.762	2	2	-1	0	O/D	0.4
	Atl-N	80	292	36	90	15	3	12	32	20	43	.308	.353	.503	.856	131	12	11	102	71	51	.848	12	7	-1	-4	O/1	0.5
1987	Atl-N	122	399	65	114	24	1	14	64	46	54	.286	.361	.456	.817	106	9	4	108	114	62	.766	4	7	-3	-3	*O/1	-0.5
1988	Atl-N	69	193	21	48	5	0	2	19	17	26	.249	.310	.306	.615	74	-5	-6	104	117	17	.503	1	3	-2	-5	O1	-1.5
	Cin-N	25	50	5	14	1	0	2	4	2	5	.280	.308	.420	.728	102	0	-0	105	59	7	.639	0	0	0	-1	1	0.0
	Yr	94	243	26	62	6	0	4	23	19	31	.255	.309	.329	.638	80	-5	-6	105	103	24	.529	1	3	-2	-5		-1.5
1989	Cin-N	106	236	26	62	8	3	8	30	29	42	.263	.346	.424	.770	115	6	5	103	97	36	.753	4	2	0	-8	O/1	-0.3
Total	17	2000	7004	1100	2077	353	77	147	824	694	877	.297	.361	.432	.793	118	176	171	101	96	1119	.769	198	82	10	-18	*O1/D	10.9
■ ALFREDO GRIFFIN	Griffin, Alfredo Claudino (born Alfredo Claudino Baptist (Griffin)) b: 10/6/57, Santo Domingo, D.R. BB/TR, 5'11", 160 lbs. Deb: 9/04/76																											
1976	Cle-A	12	4	0	1	0	0	0	0	0	2	.250	.250	.250	.500	47	-0	-0	100	0	0	.250	0	1	-1	0	/SD	0.0
1977	Cle-A	14	41	5	6	1	0	0	3	3	5	.146	.205	.171	.375	4	-5	-5	98	170	1	.316	2	2	-1	-2	S/D	-0.5
1978	Cle-A	5	4	1	2	1	0	0	0	2	1	.500	.667	.750	1.417	319	1	1	93	0	2	2.500	0	0	0	-0	/S	0.1
1979	Tor-A	153	624	81	179	22	10	2	31	40	59	.287	.335	.364	.699	86	-10	-13	103	44	75	.622	21	16	-3	8	*S	1.0
1980	Tor-A	155	653	63	166	26	**15**	2	41	24	58	.254	.285	.349	.634	73	-25	-25	100	60	59	.530	18	23	-8	6	*S	-1.4
1981	Tor-A	101	388	30	81	19	6	0	21	17	38	.209	.244	.289	.533	48	-24	-29	111	78	24	.425	8	12	-5	-14	S/32	-4.3
1982	Tor-A	162	539	57	130	20	8	1	48	22	48	.241	.271	.314	.584	55	-30	-36	109	112	45	.474	10	8	-2	5	*S	-1.8
1983	Tor-A	162	528	62	132	22	9	4	47	27	44	.250	.290	.348	.639	69	-19	-24	108	94	52	.539	8	11	-4	-7	*S/2D	-2.5
1984	Tor-A	140	419	53	101	8	2	4	30	4	33	.241	.250	.298	.548	50	-28	-29	102	87	31	.433	11	3	2	-5	*S2/D	-2.2
1985	Oak-A	162	614	75	166	18	7	2	64	20	50	.270	.293	.332	.626	76	-25	-19	93	123	60	.536	24	9	2	-10	*S	-1.5
1986	Oak-A	162	594	74	169	23	6	4	51	35	52	.285	.326	.364	.690	95	-9	-4	94	91	71	.641	33	16	0	-12	*S	-0.6
1987	Oak-A	144	494	69	130	23	5	3	60	28	41	.263	.308	.348	.656	82	-18	-12	91	**132**	52	.596	26	13	0	4	*S/2	-0.1
1988	LA-N	95	316	39	63	8	3	1	27	24	30	.199	.260	.253	.513	45	-21	-23	106	133	22	.433	7	5	-1	8	S	-0.9
1989	LA-N	136	506	49	125	27	2	0	29	29	57	.247	.288	.308	.596	76	-20	-15	93	76	45	.496	10	7	-1	-3	*S	-1.2
Total	14	1603	5724	658	1451	218	73	23	452	275	518	.253	.290	.329	.619	70	-232	-233	100	92	541	.528	178	126	-22	-22	*S/2D3	-15.9
■ MARQUIS GRISSOM	Grissom, Marquis Deon b: 4/17/67, Atlanta, Ga. BR/TR, 5'11", 190 lbs. Deb: 8/22/89																											
1989	Mon-N	26	74	16	19	2	0	1	2	12	21	.257	.360	.324	.685	95	0	0	102	30	10	.661	1	0	0	-3	O	-0.2
■ GREG GROSS	Gross, Gregory Eugene b: 8/1/52, York, Pa. BL/TL, 5'10", 160 lbs. Deb: 9/05/73																											
1973	Hou-N	14	39	5	9	2	1	0	1	4	4	.231	.302	.333	.636	80	-1	-1	95	31	4	.576	2	1	0	0	/O	0.0
1974	Hou-N	156	589	78	185	21	8	0	36	76	39	.314	.393	.377	.770	119	16	17	98	60	86	.712	12	20	-8	8	*O	1.2
1975	Hou-N	132	483	67	142	14	10	0	41	63	37	.294	.375	.364	.740	112	6	9	94	95	69	.681	2	2	-1	2	*O	0.7
1976	Hou-N	128	426	52	122	12	3	0	27	64	39	.286	.380	.329	.708	118	4	12	86	76	56	.648	2	6	-3	2	*O	0.7
1977	Chi-N	115	239	43	77	10	4	5	32	33	19	.322	.404	.460	.865	115	12	7	114	102	45	.846	0	1	-1	-6	O	-0.1
1978	Chi-N	124	347	34	92	12	7	1	39	33	19	.265	.329	.349	.678	81	-5	-9	110	125	41	.599	3	1	0	-9	*O	-2.2
1979	Phi-N	111	174	21	58	6	3	0	15	29	5	.333	.429	.402	.831	132	8	9	97	85	32	.860	5	2	0	-11	O	-0.3
1980	Phi-N	127	154	19	37	7	2	0	12	24	7	.240	.346	.312	.658	79	-2	-4	107	99	18	.607	1	1	-0	-21	O/1	-3.0

YEAR	TM/L	G	AB	R	H	2B	3B	HR	RBI	BB	SO	AVG	OBP	SLG	PRO	/A	BR	/A	PF	CHI	RC	TA	SB	CS	SBR	FR	POS	TPR
1981	Phi-N	83	102	14	23	6	1	0	7	15	5	.225	.325	.304	.629	71	-2	-4	112	89	10	.565	2	2	-1	-8	O	-1.4
1982	Phi-N	119	134	14	40	4	0	0	10	19	8	.299	.386	.328	.714	108	1	2	94	89	17	.650	4	3	-1	-15	O	-1.4
1983	Phi-N	136	245	25	74	12	3	0	29	34	16	.302	.389	.376	.765	112	6	5	101	125	36	.714	3	5	-2	-22	*O/1	-2.1
1984	Phi-N	112	202	19	65	9	1	0	16	24	11	.322	.396	.376	.773	116	6	6	102	82	31	.723	1	0	0	-5	O1	-0.1
1985	Phi-N	93	169	21	44	5	2	0	14	32	9	.260	.378	.314	.692	94	1	0	102	105	22	.662	1	0	0	-8	O/1	-0.9
1986	Phi-N	87	101	11	25	5	0	0	8	21	11	.248	.382	.297	.679	86	-0	-1	104	106	12	.663	1	0	0	-4	O/1P	-0.4
1987	Phi-N	114	133	14	38	4	1	1	12	25	12	.286	.403	.353	.756	98	2	1	104	96	21	.753	0	0	0	-13	O1	-1.4
1988	Phi-N	98	133	10	27	1	0	0	5	16	3	.203	.293	.211	.504	46	-9	-9	101	71	9	.413	0	0	0	-11	O1	-2.2
1989	Hou-N	60	75	2	15	0	0	0	4	11	6	.200	.310	.200	.510	48	-4	-5	102	107	5	.429	0	0	0	-3	O/1P	-0.8
Total	17	1809	3745	449	1073	130	46	7	308	523	250	.287	.375	.351	.727	103	38	38	100	91	511	.672	39	44	-15	-122	*O/1P	-13.7

■ KELLY GRUBER Gruber, Kelly Wayne b: 2/26/62, Houston, Tex. BR/TR, 6', 180 lbs. Deb: 4/20/84

YEAR	TM/L	G	AB	R	H	2B	3B	HR	RBI	BB	SO	AVG	OBP	SLG	PRO	/A	BR	/A	PF	CHI	RC	TA	SB	CS	SBR	FR	POS	TPR
1984	Tor-A	15	16	1	1	0	0	1	2	0	5	.063	.063	.250	.313	-18	-3	-3	102	114	0	.250	0	0	0	-1	3/OS	-0.2
1985	Tor-A	5	13	0	3	0	0	0	1	0	3	.231	.231	.231	.462	27	-1	-1	101	132	1	.300	0	0	0	-0	/32	-0.1
1986	Tor-A	87	143	20	28	4	1	5	15	5	27	.196	.223	.343	.566	49	-10	-11	105	93	8	.452	2	5	-2	-3	32D/OS	-1.5
1987	Tor-A	138	341	50	80	14	3	12	36	17	70	.235	.285	.399	.684	79	-11	-11	101	83	37	.628	12	2	2	0	*3S/2OD	-0.8
1988	Tor-A	158	569	75	158	33	5	16	81	38	92	.278	.331	.438	.768	114	9	9	100	111	79	.727	23	5	4	24	*3/2OS	3.8
1989	Tor-A	135	545	83	158	24	4	18	73	30	60	.290	.330	.448	.778	125	11	15	94	101	77	.709	10	5	0	17	*3O/SD	3.2
Total	6	538	1627	229	428	75	13	52	208	90	257	.263	.309	.421	.730	101	-5	-2	99	100	203	.663	47	17	4	38	3/O2SD	4.4

■ PEDRO GUERRERO Guerrero, Pedro b: 6/29/56, San Pedro De Macoris, D.R. BR/TR, 5'11", 176 lbs. Deb: 9/22/78

YEAR	TM/L	G	AB	R	H	2B	3B	HR	RBI	BB	SO	AVG	OBP	SLG	PRO	/A	BR	/A	PF	CHI	RC	TA	SB	CS	SBR	FR	POS	TPR
1978	LA-N	5	8	3	5	0	1	0	1	0	0	.625	.625	.875	1.500	318	2	2	99	57	4	2.333	0	0	0	0	/1	0.2
1979	LA-N	25	62	7	15	2	0	2	9	1	14	.242	.254	.371	.625	69	-3	-3	100	123	6	.542	2	0	1	-1	O/13	-0.4
1980	LA-N	75	183	27	59	9	1	7	31	12	31	.322	.364	.497	.861	143	9	9	97	110	33	.827	2	1	0	-2	O2/31	0.7
1981	LA-N	98	347	46	104	17	2	12	48	34	57	.300	.366	.464	.830	137	15	16	98	98	54	.765	5	9	-4	-0	O3/1	0.9
1982	LA-N	150	575	87	175	27	5	32	100	65	89	.304	.380	.536	.915	162	40	44	95	103	120	.971	22	5	4	7	*O3	5.4
1983	LA-N	160	584	87	174	28	6	32	103	72	110	.298	.377	.531	.908	149	38	38	100	106	118	.951	23	7	3	9	*3/1	4.5
1984	LA-N	144	535	85	162	29	4	16	72	49	105	.303	.362	.462	.824	125	21	18	104	101	89	.789	9	8	-2	6	3O1	2.0
1985	LA-N	137	487	99	156	22	2	33	87	83	68	.320	**.425**	**.577**	**1.002**	**191**	**53**	**57**	93	97	121	**1.098**	12	4	1	6	O31	**6.4**
1986	LA-N	31	61	7	15	3	0	5	10	2	19	.246	.281	.541	.822	129	1	2	94	83	9	.766	0	0	0	-1	O/1	0.0
1987	LA-N	152	545	89	184	25	2	27	89	74	85	.338	.421	.539	.960	166	43	49	92	100	121	.992	9	7	-2	-4	*O1	3.6
1988	LA-N	59	215	24	64	7	1	5	35	25	33	.298	.379	.409	.788	119	8	6	106	144	35	.766	2	1	0	-3	31/O	0.2
	StL-N	44	149	16	40	7	1	5	30	21	26	.268	.366	.430	.796	123	6	5	104	155	24	.795	2	0	1	-1	1/O	0.2
	Yr	103	364	40	104	14	2	10	65	46	59	.286	.373	.418	.791	120	14	12	105	150	60	.778	4	1	1	-5		0.4
1989	StL-N	162	570	60	177	**42**	1	17	117	79	84	.311	.398	.477	.875	148	38	38	101	**154**	109	.871	2	0	1	-12	*1	1.5
Total	12	1242	4321	637	1330	218	26	193	732	517	721	.308	.386	.504	.890	149	271	282	98	113	843	.901	90	42	2	4	O31/2	25.2

■ OZZIE GUILLEN Guillen, Oswaldo Jose (Barrios) b: 1/20/64, Oculare Del Tuy, Venezuela BL/TR, 5'11", 150 lbs. Deb: 4/09/85

YEAR	TM/L	G	AB	R	H	2B	3B	HR	RBI	BB	SO	AVG	OBP	SLG	PRO	/A	BR	/A	PF	CHI	RC	TA	SB	CS	SBR	FR	POS	TPR
1985	Chi-A	150	491	71	134	21	9	1	33	12	36	.273	.292	.358	.650	77	-16	-16	100	73	50	.536	7	4	-0	9	*S	0.4
1986	Chi-A	159	547	58	137	19	4	2	47	12	52	.250	.268	.311	.579	57	-32	-32	101	106	43	.446	8	4	0	12	*S/D	-1.1
1987	Chi-A	149	560	64	156	22	7	2	51	22	52	.279	.307	.354	.661	70	-19	-26	109	102	61	.583	25	8	3	17	*S	0.1
1988	Chi-A	156	566	58	148	16	7	0	39	25	40	.261	.295	.314	.610	73	-22	-20	97	89	50	.517	25	13	-0	**43**	*S	3.0
1989	Chi-A	155	597	63	151	20	8	1	54	15	48	.253	.271	.318	.589	71	-28	-23	93	111	49	.512	36	17	1	13	*S	0.4
Total	5	769	2761	314	726	98	35	6	224	86	228	.263	.286	.330	.617	69	-118	-118	100	97	253	.518	101	46	3	94	S/D	2.8

■ TONY GWYNN Gwynn, Anthony Keith b: 5/9/60, Los Angeles, Cal. BL/TL, 5'11", 185 lbs. Deb: 7/19/82

YEAR	TM/L	G	AB	R	H	2B	3B	HR	RBI	BB	SO	AVG	OBP	SLG	PRO	/A	BR	/A	PF	CHI	RC	TA	SB	CS	SBR	FR	POS	TPR
1982	SD-N	54	190	33	55	12	2	1	17	14	16	.289	.338	.389	.728	112	1	3	92	88	25	.671	8	3	1	0	O	0.3
1983	SD-N	86	304	34	94	12	2	1	37	23	21	.309	.358	.372	.730	103	1	2	99	129	39	.641	7	4	-0	6	O	0.6
1984	SD-N	158	606	88	**213**	21	10	5	71	59	23	**.351**	.411	.444	.855	142	34	35	99	104	108	.852	33	18	-1	11	*O	4.1
1985	SD-N	154	622	90	197	29	5	6	46	45	33	.317	.365	.408	.773	114	13	12	102	65	88	.695	14	11	-2	11	*O	1.8
1986	SD-N	160	642	**107**	**211**	33	7	14	59	52	35	.329	.382	.467	.849	140	28	32	95	66	113	.852	37	9	6	17	*O	5.2
1987	SD-N	157	589	119	**218**	36	13	7	54	82	35	**.370**	.450	.511	.961	159	50	52	97	71	143	1.116	56	12	10	5	*O	5.9
1988	SD-N	133	521	64	163	22	5	7	70	51	40	**.313**	.374	.415	.789	130	18	20	97	114	81	.771	26	11	1	2	*O	2.0
1989	SD-N	158	604	82	**203**	27	7	4	62	56	30	**.336**	.393	.424	.817	133	28	27	101	99	101	.823	40	16	2	-4	*O	2.5
Total	8	1060	4078	617	1354	192	51	45	416	382	233	.332	.391	.437	.828	133	173	183	98	89	697	.824	221	84	16	48	*O	22.4

■ CHRIS GWYNN Gwynn, Christopher Karlton b: 10/13/64, Los Angeles, Cal. BL/TL, 6' ", 200 lbs. Deb: 8/14/87

YEAR	TM/L	G	AB	R	H	2B	3B	HR	RBI	BB	SO	AVG	OBP	SLG	PRO	/A	BR	/A	PF	CHI	RC	TA	SB	CS	SBR	FR	POS	TPR
1987	LA-N	17	32	2	7	1	0	0	2	1	7	.219	.242	.250	.492	34	-3	-3	92	100	2	.360	0	0	0	-1	O	-0.4
1988	LA-N	12	11	1	2	0	0	0	0	1	2	.182	.250	.182	.432	24	-1	-1	106	0	1	.333	0	0	0	-2	/O	-0.2
1989	LA-N	32	68	8	16	4	1	0	7	2	9	.235	.257	.324	.581	70	-3	-3	93	128	6	.472	1	0	0	-1	O	-0.3
Total	3	61	111	11	25	5	1	0	9	4	18	.225	.252	.288	.540	54	-7	-7	94	107	8	.425	1	0	0	-4	/O	-0.9

■ JERRY HAIRSTON Hairston, Jerry Wayne b: 2/16/52, Birmingham, Ala. BB/TR, 5'10", 170 lbs. Deb: 7/26/73

YEAR	TM/L	G	AB	R	H	2B	3B	HR	RBI	BB	SO	AVG	OBP	SLG	PRO	/A	BR	/A	PF	CHI	RC	TA	SB	CS	SBR	FR	POS	TPR
1973	Chi-A	60	210	25	57	11	1	0	23	33	30	.271	.373	.333	.706	98	2	1	102	132	29	.667	0	0	0	0	O1/D	0.0
1974	Chi-A	45	109	8	25	7	0	0	8	13	18	.229	.311	.294	.605	74	-3	-3	102	98	10	.511	0	2	-1	-5	OD	-1.0
1975	Chi-A	69	219	26	62	8	0	0	23	46	23	.283	.410	.320	.729	105	5	4	103	129	33	.733	1	0	0	-1	O/D	0.2
1976	Chi-A	44	119	20	27	2	2	0	10	24	19	.227	.357	.277	.634	88	-1	-1	99	116	14	.624	1	1	-0	-4	O	-0.5
1977	Chi-A	13	26	3	8	2	0	0	4	5	7	.308	.419	.385	.804	122	1	1	99	159	4	.750	0	0	0	-1	O	0.0
	Pit-N	51	52	5	10	2	0	2	6	6	10	.192	.276	.346	.622	64	-3	-3	103	100	5	.558	0	0	0	-4	O/2	-0.6
1981	Chi-A	9	25	5	7	1	0	1	6	2	4	.280	.357	.440	.797	129	1	1	100	168	4	.778	0	0	0	-1	/O	0.0
1982	Chi-A	85	90	11	21	5	0	5	18	9	15	.233	.303	.456	.759	108	0	1	97	128	12	.694	0	0	0	-8	O/D	-0.7
1983	Chi-A	101	126	17	37	9	1	5	22	23	16	.294	.403	.500	.903	142	9	8	103	110	26	.945	0	1	-1	-8	O/D	0.0
1984	Chi-A	115	227	41	59	13	2	5	19	41	29	.260	.375	.401	.776	104	6	3	111	71	37	.785	2	1	0	-5	OD	-0.2
1985	Chi-A	95	140	9	34	8	0	2	20	29	18	.243	.380	.343	.723	100	1	1	100	147	20	.725	0	0	0	-1	D/O	0.0
1986	Chi-A	101	225	32	61	15	0	5	26	26	26	.271	.349	.404	.754	105	2	2	101	98	31	.682	0	0	0	-2	D1O	-0.2
1987	Chi-A	66	126	14	29	8	0	5	20	25	25	.230	.362	.413	.775	98	2	0	109	119	20	.772	0	0	0	-1	OD/1	-0.1
1988	Chi-A	2	2	0	0	0	0	0	0	0	0	.000	.000	.000	.000	-99	-1	-1	97	0	0	.000	0	0	0	0	/H	0.0
1989	Chi-A	3	3	0	1	0	0	0	0	0	0	.333	.333	.333	.667	95	-0	-0	93	0	0	.500	0	0	0	0	/D	0.0
Total	14	859	1699	216	438	91	6	30	205	282	240	.258	.366	.371	.737	102	22	15	103	114	245	.711	4	5	-2	-40	OD/12	-3.1

■ CHIP HALE Hale, Walter William b: 12/2/64, Samta Clara, Cal. BL/TR, 5'11", 180 lbs. Deb: 8/27/89

YEAR	TM/L	G	AB	R	H	2B	3B	HR	RBI	BB	SO	AVG	OBP	SLG	PRO	/A	BR	/A	PF	CHI	RC	TA	SB	CS	SBR	FR	POS	TPR
1989	Min-A	28	67	6	14	3	0	0	4	1	6	.209	.221	.254	.474	31	-6	-6	107	91	4	.340	0	0	0	-2	2/3D	-0.7

■ ALBERT HALL Hall, Albert b: 3/7/58, Birmingham, Ala. BB/TR, 5'11", 155 lbs. Deb: 9/12/81

YEAR	TM/L	G	AB	R	H	2B	3B	HR	RBI	BB	SO	AVG	OBP	SLG	PRO	/A	BR	/A	PF	CHI	RC	TA	SB	CS	SBR	FR	POS	TPR
1981	Atl-N	6	2	1	0	0	0	0	0	1	1	.000	.333	.000	.333	1	-0	-0	100	0	0	.500	0	0	0	-1	/O	0.0
1982	Atl-N	5	0	1	0	0	0	0	0	0	0	—	—	—	—	—	0	0	107	—	—	—	0	0	0	0	/R	0.0
1983	Atl-N	10	8	2	0	0	0	0	0	2	2	.000	.200	.000	.200	-38	-2	-2	106	0	0	.333	1	1	-0	-1	/O	-0.2
1984	Atl-N	87	142	25	37	6	1	1	9	10	18	.261	.309	.338	.647	75	-3	-5	110	69	15	.577	6	4	-1	-12	O	-2.1
1985	Atl-N	54	47	5	7	0	1	0	3	9	12	.149	.286	.191	.477	34	-4	-4	106	133	3	.432	1	1	-0	-3	O	-0.7
1986	Atl-N	16	50	6	12	2	0	0	1	5	6	.240	.309	.280	.589	62	-2	-2	102	28	5	.659	8	3	1	0	O	-0.1
1987	Atl-N	92	292	54	83	20	4	3	24	38	36	.284	.370	.411	.781	99	4	0	108	74	48	.862	33	10	4	5	O	0.7
1988	Atl-N	85	231	27	57	7	1	1	15	21	35	.247	.315	.299	.614	74	-6	-8	104	83	22	.569	15	10	-2	5	O	-0.5
1989	Pit-N	20	33	4	6	2	1	0	1	3	5	.182	.250	.303	.553	61	-2	-2	94	40	3	.593	3	0	1	-3	O	-0.4
Total	9	375	805	125	202	37	8	5	53	89	115	.251	.329	.335	.664	79	-16	-22	106	74	95	.666	67	29	3	-9	O	-3.3

■ MEL HALL Hall, Melvin b: 9/16/60, Lyons, N.Y. BL/TL, 6', 185 lbs. Deb: 9/03/81

YEAR	TM/L	G	AB	R	H	2B	3B	HR	RBI	BB	SO	AVG	OBP	SLG	PRO	/A	BR	/A	PF	CHI	RC	TA	SB	CS	SBR	FR	POS	TPR
1981	Chi-N	10	11	1	1	0	0	1	2	1	4	.091	.167	.364	.530	45	-1	-1	104	112	1	.500	0	0	0	-1	/O	-0.2
1982	Chi-N	24	80	6	21	3	2	0	4	5	17	.262	.322	.350	.672	85	-1	-2	103	56	9	.583	0	1	-1	2	O	0.0
1983	Chi-N	112	410	60	116	23	5	17	56	42	101	.283	.354	.488	.842	130	16	16	101	90	71	.826	6	6	-2	-6	*O	0.6

YEAR	TM/L	G	AB	R	H	2B	3B	HR	RBI	BB	SO	AVG	OBP	SLG	PRO	/A	BR	/A	PF	CHI	RC	TA	SB	CS	SBR	FR	POS	TPR
1984	Chi-N	48	150	25	42	11	3	4	22	12	23	.280	.333	.473	.807	113	4	3	110	104	23	.766	2	1	0	-1	O	0.0
	Cle-A	83	257	43	66	13	1	7	30	35	55	.257	.350	.397	.747	100	3	1	106	97	38	.718	1	1	-0	-1	O/D	-0.2
1985	Cle-A	23	66	7	21	6	0	0	12	8	12	.318	.392	.409	.801	127	2	3	94	176	10	.729	0	1	-1	-3	O/D	-0.1
1986	Cle-A	140	442	68	131	29	2	18	77	33	65	.296	.348	.493	.841	130	16	17	98	113	75	.807	6	2	1	-8	*O/D	0.6
1987	Cle-A	142	485	57	136	21	1	18	76	20	68	.280	.310	.439	.749	94	-3	-5	103	114	63	.664	5	4	-1	2	*OD	-0.6
1988	Cle-A	150	515	69	144	32	4	6	71	28	50	.280	.317	.392	.709	96	-3	-4	102	128	63	.620	7	3	0	-6	*O/D	-1.1
1989	NY-A	113	361	54	94	9	0	17	58	21	37	.260	.301	.427	.728	99	-0	-2	104	110	44	.634	0	0	0	-3	OD	-0.5
Total	9	845	2777	390	772	147	18	88	408	205	432	.278	.330	.439	.769	108	33	26	102	110	397	.707	27	19	-3	-25	O/D	-1.5

■ JEFF HAMILTON Hamilton, Jeffrey Robert b: 3/19/64, Flint, Mich. BR/TR, 6'3", 190 lbs. Deb: 6/28/86

YEAR	TM/L	G	AB	R	H	2B	3B	HR	RBI	BB	SO	AVG	OBP	SLG	PRO	/A	BR	/A	PF	CHI	RC	TA	SB	CS	SBR	FR	POS	TPR
1986	LA-N	71	147	22	33	5	0	5	19	2	43	.224	.235	.361	.595	66	-8	-7	94	111	12	.470	0	0	0	3	3/S	-0.5
1987	LA-N	35	83	5	18	3	0	0	1	7	22	.217	.286	.253	.539	48	-7	-6	92	19	6	.439	0	1	-1	2	3/S	-0.3
1988	LA-N	111	309	34	73	14	2	6	33	10	51	.236	.269	.353	.622	73	-10	-12	106	104	27	.500	0	2	-1	-11	*3/1S	-2.5
1989	LA-N	151	548	45	134	35	1	12	56	20	71	.245	.275	.378	.653	92	-12	-8	93	95	55	.542	0	0	0	-7	*3/P2S	-1.7
Total	4	368	1087	106	258	57	3	23	109	39	187	.237	.269	.359	.628	79	-37	-33	97	93	100	.512	0	3	-2	-13	3/S2P1	-5.0

■ BRIAN HARPER Harper, Brian David b: 10/16/59, Los Angeles, Cal. BR/TR, 6'2", 195 lbs. Deb: 9/29/79

YEAR	TM/L	G	AB	R	H	2B	3B	HR	RBI	BB	SO	AVG	OBP	SLG	PRO	/A	BR	/A	PF	CHI	RC	TA	SB	CS	SBR	FR	POS	TPR
1979	Cal-A	1	2	0	0	0	0	0	0	0	1	.000	.000	.000	.000	-99	-1	-1	93	0	0	.000	0	0	0	0	/H	0.0
1981	Cal-A	4	11	1	3	0	0	0	1	0	0	.273	.273	.273	.545	55	-1	-1	104	130	1	.500	1	0	0	0	/OD	0.0
1982	Pit-N	20	29	4	8	1	0	2	4	1	4	.276	.300	.517	.817	113	1	0	110	75	4	.727	0	0	0	-1	/O	0.0
1983	Pit-N	61	131	16	29	4	1	7	20	2	15	.221	.239	.427	.666	79	-4	-5	103	103	12	.562	0	0	0	-6	O/1	-1.1
1984	Pit-N	46	112	4	29	4	0	2	11	5	11	.259	.303	.348	.651	87	-3	-2	94	96	11	.529	0	0	0	-3	O/C	-0.6
1985	StL-N	43	52	5	13	4	0	0	8	2	3	.250	.278	.327	.605	72	-2	-2	96	187	4	.463	0	0	0	-3	O/3C1	-0.4
1986	Det-A	19	36	2	5	1	0	0	3	3	3	.139	.205	.167	.372	4	-5	-5	95	199	1	.281	0	0	0	-2	O/C1D	-0.6
1987	Oak-A	11	17	1	4	1	0	0	3	0	4	.235	.235	.294	.529	44	-1	-1	91	239	1	.357	0	0	0	-0	/OD	-0.1
1988	Min-A	60	166	15	49	11	1	3	20	10	12	.295	.346	.428	.774	109	3	2	106	99	20	.636	0	3	-2	0	C/3D	0.2
1989	Min-A	126	385	43	125	24	0	8	57	13	16	.325	.356	.449	.806	118	12	9	107	112	57	.705	2	4	-2	-11	*CD/O13	0.1
Total	10	391	941	91	265	50	2	22	127	36	69	.282	.316	.409	.726	98	-1	-4	103	115	112	.607	3	7	-3	-26	CO/D31	-2.5

■ LENNY HARRIS Harris, Leonard Anthony b: 10/28/64, Miami, Fla. BL/TR, 5'10", 195 lbs. Deb: 9/07/88

YEAR	TM/L	G	AB	R	H	2B	3B	HR	RBI	BB	SO	AVG	OBP	SLG	PRO	/A	BR	/A	PF	CHI	RC	TA	SB	CS	SBR	FR	POS	TPR
1988	Cin-N	16	43	7	16	1	0	0	8	5	4	.372	.438	.395	.833	133	3	2	105	188	9	.929	4	1	1	1	/32	0.4
1989	Cin-N	61	188	17	42	4	0	2	11	9	20	.223	.263	.277	.539	53	-11	-12	103	76	12	.459	10	6	-1	-0	2S3	-1.2
	LA-N	54	147	19	37	6	1	1	15	11	13	.252	.308	.327	.635	88	-3	-2	93	118	12	.525	4	3	-1	-2	O2/3S	-0.5
	Yr	115	335	36	79	10	1	3	26	20	33	.236	.283	.299	.581	68	-15	-14	98	97	25	.487	14	9	-1	-3		-1.7
Total	2	131	378	43	95	11	1	3	34	25	37	.251	.301	.310	.611	76	-12	-12	99	106	33	.528	18	10	-1	-2	/23OS	-1.3

■ RON HASSEY Hassey, Ronald William b: 2/27/53, Tucson, Ariz. BL/TR, 6'2", 200 lbs. Deb: 4/23/78

YEAR	TM/L	G	AB	R	H	2B	3B	HR	RBI	BB	SO	AVG	OBP	SLG	PRO	/A	BR	/A	PF	CHI	RC	TA	SB	CS	SBR	FR	POS	TPR
1978	Cle-A	25	74	5	15	0	0	2	9	5	7	.203	.262	.284	.546	57	-5	-4	93	132	6	.483	2	0	1	-2	C	-0.4
1979	Cle-A	75	223	20	64	14	0	4	32	19	19	.287	.343	.404	.747	95	0	-2	106	121	30	.659	1	0	0	-3	C/1	-0.1
1980	Cle-A	130	390	43	124	18	4	8	65	49	51	.318	.395	.446	.842	127	18	16	102	128	68	.797	0	2	-1	-7	*C/1D	1.3
1981	Cle-A	61	190	8	44	4	0	1	25	17	11	.232	.301	.268	.570	70	-8	-6	93	181	16	.461	0	1	-1	-1	C/1D	-0.5
1982	Cle-A	113	323	33	81	18	0	5	34	53	32	.251	.358	.353	.711	96	0	-0	100	105	42	.673	3	2	-0	-13	*C/1D	-0.7
1983	Cle-A	117	341	48	92	21	0	6	42	38	35	.270	.346	.384	.731	96	1	-1	105	110	45	.660	2	2	-1	-5	*C/D	-0.1
1984	Cle-A	48	149	11	38	5	1	0	19	15	26	.255	.323	.302	.625	70	-5	-6	106	168	15	.530	1	0	0	1	C/1D	-0.1
	Chi-N	19	33	5	11	0	0	2	5	4	6	.333	.405	.515	.921	143	3	2	110	85	6	.875	0	1	-1	0	/C1	0.2
1985	NY-A	92	267	31	79	16	1	13	42	28	21	.296	.369	.509	.878	144	14	15	96	95	49	.856	0	0	0	4	C/1D	2.1
1986	NY-A	64	191	23	57	14	0	6	29	24	16	.298	.382	.466	.848	127	9	8	103	108	33	.811	1	1	-0	0	C/D	1.0
	Chi-A	49	150	22	53	11	1	3	20	22	11	.353	.439	.500	.939	155	13	13	101	95	32	.942	0	0	0	0	DC	1.3
	Yr	113	341	45	110	25	1	9	49	46	27	.323	.408	.481	.889	139	21	20	102	103	65	.866	1	1	-0	0		2.3
1987	Chi-A	49	145	15	31	9	0	3	12	17	11	.214	.305	.338	.643	66	-6	-8	109	83	13	.553	0	0	0	3	CD	-0.2
1988	Oak-A	107	323	32	83	15	0	7	45	30	42	.257	.328	.368	.696	100	-2	0	95	128	39	.622	2	0	1	-7	C/D	-0.2
1989	Oak-A	97	268	29	61	12	0	5	23	24	45	.228	.294	.328	.622	72	-9	-10	103	87	25	.528	1	0	0	-0	C/1D	-0.6
Total	12	1046	3067	325	833	157	7	65	402	345	333	.272	.349	.391	.740	103	22	17	101	116	419	.672	13	9	-2	-29	C/D1	3.0

■ MICKEY HATCHER Hatcher, Michael Vaughn b: 3/15/55, Cleveland, Ohio BR/TR, 6'2", 200 lbs. Deb: 8/03/79

YEAR	TM/L	G	AB	R	H	2B	3B	HR	RBI	BB	SO	AVG	OBP	SLG	PRO	/A	BR	/A	PF	CHI	RC	TA	SB	CS	SBR	FR	POS	TPR
1979	LA-N	33	93	9	25	4	1	1	5	7	12	.269	.327	.366	.692	89	-1	-1	100	53	9	.566	1	3	-2	-1	O3	-0.4
1980	LA-N	57	84	4	19	2	0	1	5	2	12	.226	.244	.286	.530	49	-6	-6	97	73	4	.356	0	2	-1	-6	O3	-1.4
1981	Min-A	99	377	36	96	23	2	3	37	15	29	.255	.287	.350	.637	79	-9	-11	105	109	36	.521	3	1	0	-2	O/13D	-1.5
1982	Min-A	84	277	23	69	13	2	3	26	8	27	.249	.270	.343	.613	67	-13	-13	100	100	21	.464	0	2	-1	-0	OD/3	-1.5
1983	Min-A	106	375	50	119	15	3	9	47	14	19	.317	.344	.445	.789	110	7	5	105	95	54	.687	2	0	1	4	OD/13	0.8
1984	Min-A	152	576	61	174	35	5	5	69	37	34	.302	.346	.406	.753	102	6	2	106	117	78	.650	0	1	-1	10	*OD1/3	0.7
1985	Min-A	116	444	46	125	28	0	3	49	16	23	.282	.310	.365	.674	81	-10	-12	103	116	46	.539	0	0	0	4	OD/1	-0.9
1986	Min-A	115	317	40	88	13	3	3	32	19	26	.278	.318	.366	.684	80	-6	-9	108	102	36	.576	2	1	0	-3	OD1/3	-1.4
1987	LA-N	101	287	27	81	19	1	7	42	20	19	.282	.331	.429	.760	108	-1	2	92	116	39	.679	2	3	-1	4	31/O	0.2
1988	LA-N	87	191	22	56	8	0	1	25	7	7	.293	.325	.351	.676	88	-2	-3	106	143	20	.535	0	0	0	-2	O1/3	-0.6
1989	LA-N	94	224	18	66	9	2	2	25	13	16	.295	.336	.379	.716	112	1	3	93	111	27	.599	1	2	-1	-2	O3/1P	0.0
Total	11	1044	3245	336	918	169	19	38	362	158	224	.283	.319	.382	.700	91	-34	-44	102	108	369	.580	11	15	-6	7	OD13/P	-6.0

■ BILLY HATCHER Hatcher, William Augustus b: 10/4/60, Williams, Ariz. BR/TR, 5'9", 175 lbs. Deb: 9/10/84

YEAR	TM/L	G	AB	R	H	2B	3B	HR	RBI	BB	SO	AVG	OBP	SLG	PRO	/A	BR	/A	PF	CHI	RC	TA	SB	CS	SBR	FR	POS	TPR
1984	Chi-N	8	9	1	1	0	0	0	0	1	0	.111	.200	.111	.311	-10	-1	-1	110	0	0	.500	2	0	1	-0	/O	-0.1
1985	Chi-N	53	163	24	40	12	1	2	10	8	12	.245	.293	.368	.661	72	-4	-7	116	60	14	.537	2	4	-2	-1	O	-1.1
1986	Hou-N	127	419	55	108	15	4	6	36	22	52	.258	.303	.356	.658	79	-11	-13	103	86	47	.652	38	14	3	3	*O	-0.9
1987	Hou-N	141	564	96	167	28	3	11	63	42	70	.296	.354	.415	.769	111	3	8	93	83	89	.811	53	9	11	4	*O	1.7
1988	Hou-N	145	530	79	142	25	4	7	52	37	56	.268	.325	.370	.695	106	-1	3	93	98	66	.671	32	13	2	2	*O	0.4
1989	Hou-N	108	395	49	90	15	3	3	44	30	53	.228	.284	.304	.588	67	-16	-17	102	140	37	.551	22	6	3	0	*O	-1.6
	Pit-N	27	86	10	21	4	0	1	7	0	9	.244	.253	.326	.578	69	-4	-4	94	91	7	.463	2	1	0	-3	O	-0.7
	Yr	135	481	59	111	19	3	4	51	30	62	.231	.279	.308	.586	67	-20	-21	101	131	44	.535	24	7	3	-3		-2.3
Total	6	609	2166	314	569	99	15	30	212	140	252	.263	.315	.364	.679	90	-35	-31	98	96	259	.660	151	47	17	5	O	-2.3

■ CHARLIE HAYES Hayes, Charles Dewayne b: 5/29/65, Hattiesburg, Miss. BR/TR, 6', 190 lbs. Deb: 9/11/88

YEAR	TM/L	G	AB	R	H	2B	3B	HR	RBI	BB	SO	AVG	OBP	SLG	PRO	/A	BR	/A	PF	CHI	RC	TA	SB	CS	SBR	FR	POS	TPR
1988	SF-N	7	11	0	1	0	0	0	0	0	3	.091	.091	.091	.182	-51	-2	-2	94	0	0	.100	0	0	0	-1	/O3	-0.2
1989	SF-N	3	5	0	1	0	0	0	0	0	1	.200	.200	.200	.400	15	-1	-1	97	0	0	.250	0	0	0	0	/3	0.0
	Phi-N	84	299	26	77	15	1	8	43	11	49	.258	.284	.395	.679	91	-4	-4	101	124	32	.576	3	1	0	3	3	-0.1
	Yr	87	304	26	78	15	1	8	43	11	50	.257	.283	.391	.674	90	-5	-5	101	120	32	.571	3	1	0	3		-0.1
Total	2	94	315	26	79	15	1	8	43	11	53	.251	.276	.381	.657	86	-7	-7	101	118	32	.551	3	1	0	2	/3O	-0.3

■ VON HAYES Hayes, Von Francis b: 8/31/58, Stockton, Cal. BL/TR, 6'5", 185 lbs. Deb: 4/14/81

YEAR	TM/L	G	AB	R	H	2B	3B	HR	RBI	BB	SO	AVG	OBP	SLG	PRO	/A	BR	/A	PF	CHI	RC	TA	SB	CS	SBR	FR	POS	TPR
1981	Cle-A	43	109	21	28	8	2	1	17	14	10	.257	.352	.394	.746	123	2	3	93	145	17	.798	8	1	2	1	DO/3	0.6
1982	Cle-A	150	527	65	132	25	3	14	82	42	63	.250	.311	.389	.700	91	-7	-7	100	133	63	.677	32	13	2	5	*O/31	-0.5
1983	Phi-N	124	351	45	93	9	5	6	32	36	55	.265	.338	.370	.709	95	-1	-2	101	86	42	.673	20	12	-1	-3	*O	-0.8
1984	Phi-N	152	561	85	164	27	6	16	67	59	84	.292	.360	.447	.807	123	19	18	102	90	94	.852	48	13	7	7	*O	2.7
1985	Phi-N	152	570	76	150	30	4	13	70	61	99	.263	.334	.398	.733	102	3	2	102	111	79	.712	21	8	2	5	*O	0.5
1986	Phi-N	158	610	**107**	186	**46**	2	19	98	74	77	.305	.381	.480	.861	130	30	27	104	118	111	.871	24	12	0	1	*1O	2.3
1987	Phi-N	158	556	84	154	36	5	21	84	121	77	.277	.406	.473	.879	127	30	27	104	109	113	.950	16	7	1	-11	*1O	0.6
1988	Phi-N	104	367	43	100	28	2	6	45	49	59	.272	.360	.409	.768	119	11	10	101	113	57	.789	20	9	1	-3	1O/3	0.3
1989	Phi-N	154	540	93	140	27	2	26	78	101	103	.259	.380	.461	.841	138	30	30	101	102	103	.923	28	7	4	-1	*O13	3.0
Total	9	1195	4191	619	1147	236	31	122	573	557	627	.274	.361	.432	.793	117	117	107	102	109	679	.812	217	82	16	1	O1/3D	8.7

YEAR	TM/L	G	AB	R	H	2B	3B	HR	RBI	BB	SO	AVG	OBP	SLG	PRO	/A	BR	/A	PF	CHI	RC	TA	SB	CS	SBR	FR	POS	TPR
■ **MIKE HEATH**	Heath, Michael Thomas b: 2/5/55, Tampa, Fla. BR/TR, 5'11", 180 lbs. Deb: 6/03/78																											
1978	NY-A	33	92	6	21	3	1	0	8	4	9	.228	.268	.283	.551	56	-6	-5	99	122	7	.431	0	0	0	-1	C	-0.4
1979	Oak-A	74	258	19	66	8	0	3	27	17	18	.256	.309	.322	.631	80	-10	-6	89	115	23	.505	1	0	0	3	OC/3D	-0.3
1980	Oak-A	92	305	27	74	10	2	1	33	16	28	.243	.280	.298	.579	62	-17	-15	95	137	24	.456	3	3	-1	9	CD/O	-0.4
1981	Oak-A	84	301	26	71	7	1	8	30	13	36	.236	.270	.346	.615	79	-10	-9	96	93	25	.500	3	3	-1	9	C/O	0.3
1982	Oak-A	101	318	43	77	18	4	3	39	27	36	.242	.301	.352	.654	83	-9	-7	95	129	35	.595	8	3	1	7	CO/3	0.5
1983	Oak-A	96	345	45	97	17	0	6	33	18	59	.281	.319	.383	.701	96	-4	-2	96	88	39	.590	3	4	-2	-2	CO/3D	-0.2
1984	Oak-A	140	475	49	118	21	5	13	64	26	72	.248	.289	.396	.685	95	-9	-4	92	112	50	.592	7	4	-0	-3	*CO/3S	-0.2
1985	Oak-A	138	436	71	109	18	6	13	55	41	63	.250	.316	.408	.724	104	-3	2	93	100	53	.654	7	7	-2	-9	*CO3	-0.4
1986	StL-N	65	190	19	39	8	1	4	25	23	36	.205	.294	.321	.615	68	-8	-9	103	137	17	.547	2	3	-1	-4	C/O	-1.2
	Det-A	30	98	11	26	3	0	4	11	4	17	.265	.294	.418	.712	97	-1	-1	95	83	12	.662	4	1	1	3	C/3	0.4
1987	Det-A	93	270	34	76	16	0	8	33	21	42	.281	.340	.430	.770	107	1	2	97	94	38	.691	1	5	-3	-5	CO/13S2	0.0
1988	Det-A	86	219	24	54	7	2	5	18	18	32	.247	.307	.365	.672	93	-4	-2	94	75	24	.585	1	0	0	-3	C/O	-0.1
1989	Det-A	122	396	38	104	16	2	10	43	24	71	.263	.311	.389	.700	99	-3	-1	97	91	44	.608	7	1	2	8	*C/3OD	1.3
Total	12	1154	3703	412	932	152	24	78	419	252	519	.252	.302	.369	.671	89	-83	-58	95	106	393	.578	47	34	-6	13	CO/3D1S2	-0.7
■ **DANNY HEEP**	Heep, Daniel William b: 7/3/57, San Antonio, Tex. BL/TL, 5'11", 185 lbs. Deb: 8/31/79																											
1979	Hou-N	14	14	0	2	0	0	0	2	1	4	.143	.200	.143	.343	-5	-2	-2	90	396	1	.250	0	0	0	1	/O	0.0
1980	Hou-N	33	87	6	24	8	0	0	6	8	9	.276	.344	.368	.712	101	-0	0	98	74	12	.651	0	0	0	0	1	0.0
1981	Hou-N	33	96	6	24	3	0	0	11	10	11	.250	.321	.281	.602	81	-3	-2	88	160	9	.493	0	0	0	-1	1/O	-0.3
1982	Hou-N	85	198	16	47	14	1	4	22	21	31	.237	.314	.379	.692	94	-2	-2	99	99	23	.614	0	2	-1	-2	O1	-0.6
1983	NY-N	115	253	30	64	12	0	8	21	29	40	.253	.332	.395	.727	102	0	1	99	67	33	.675	3	3	-1	-5	O1	-0.6
1984	NY-N	99	199	36	46	9	2	1	12	27	22	.231	.326	.312	.638	80	-5	-5	100	72	20	.571	3	1	0	-0	O1	-0.6
1985	NY-N	95	271	26	76	17	0	7	42	27	27	.280	.348	.421	.768	117	5	6	97	124	37	.689	2	2	-1	-5	O/1	-0.1
1986	NY-N	86	195	24	55	8	2	5	33	30	31	.282	.381	.421	.801	126	6	7	96	136	31	.776	1	4	-2	-3	O	0.1
1987	LA-N	60	98	7	16	4	0	0	9	8	10	.163	.226	.204	.430	16	-12	-11	92	180	4	.330	1	0	0	-2	O/1	-1.3
1988	LA-N	95	149	14	36	2	0	0	11	22	13	.242	.343	.255	.598	70	-4	-5	106	116	14	.538	2	0	1	-3	O1/P	-0.8
1989	Bos-A	113	320	36	96	17	0	5	49	29	26	.300	.360	.400	.760	109	6	4	105	133	43	.664	0	1	-1	-12	O1/D	-1.0
Total	11	828	1880	201	486	94	5	30	218	212	224	.259	.336	.362	.698	96	-10	-7	99	114	227	.622	12	13	-4	-33	O1/DP	-5.2
■ **SCOTT HEMOND**	Hemond, Scott Mathew b: 11/18/65, Taunton, Mass. BR/TR, 6', 205 lbs. Deb: 9/09/89																											
1989	Oak-A	4	0	2	0	0	0	0	0	0	0	—	—	—	—	—	0	0	103	—	—	—	0	0	0	0	R	0.0
■ **DAVE HENDERSON**	Henderson, David Lee b: 7/21/58, Merced, Cal. BR/TR, 6'2", 210 lbs. Deb: 4/09/81																											
1981	Sea-A	59	126	17	21	3	0	6	13	16	24	.167	.266	.333	.599	72	-5	-5	100	85	11	.555	2	1	0	-3	O	-0.9
1982	Sea-A	104	324	47	82	17	1	14	48	36	67	.253	.328	.441	.769	100	4	-0	109	104	46	.718	2	5	-2	4	*O	-0.1
1983	Sea-A	137	484	50	130	24	5	17	55	28	93	.269	.310	.444	.754	105	2	2	100	82	67	.699	9	3	1	16	*O/D	1.7
1984	Sea-A	112	350	42	98	23	0	14	43	19	56	.280	.321	.466	.786	112	6	5	102	84	51	.724	5	5	-2	3	OD	0.3
1985	Sea-A	139	502	70	121	28	2	14	68	48	104	.241	.311	.388	.699	95	-7	-3	95	116	61	.641	6	1	1	-6	*O	-0.9
1986	Sea-A	103	337	51	93	19	4	14	44	37	95	.276	.351	.481	.832	119	11	9	105	86	57	.802	1	3	-2	-2	OD	0.3
	Bos-A	36	51	8	10	3	0	1	3	2	15	.196	.226	.314	.540	46	-4	-4	100	63	4	.452	1	0	0	-2	O	-0.6
	Yr	139	388	59	103	22	4	15	47	39	110	.265	.336	.459	.794	111	8	6	104	80	60	.752	2	3	-1	-4		-0.3
1987	Bos-A	75	184	30	43	10	0	8	25	22	48	.234	.316	.418	.734	94	-2	-2	99	99	25	.690	1	1	-0	-5	O/D	-0.7
	SF-N	15	21	2	5	2	0	0	1	8	5	.238	.448	.333	.782	116	1	1	96	57	5	1.063	2	0	1	-1	/O	0.1
1988	Oak-A	146	507	100	154	38	1	24	94	47	92	.304	.367	.525	.892	155	31	34	95	111	94	.860	2	4	-2	-1	*O	2.8
1989	Oak-A	152	579	77	145	24	3	15	80	54	131	.250	.318	.380	.698	93	-4	-6	103	124	69	.631	8	5	-1	-1	*O/D	-0.9
Total	9	1078	3465	494	902	191	16	127	474	317	730	.260	.325	.435	.760	108	33	31	100	101	488	.707	39	28	-5	3	*O/D	1.1
■ **RICKEY HENDERSON**	Henderson, Rickey Henley b: 12/25/58, Chicago, Ill. BR/TL, 5'10", 180 lbs. Deb: 6/24/79																											
1979	Oak-A	89	351	49	96	13	3	1	26	34	39	.274	.341	.336	.677	94	-7	-2	89	71	44	.693	33	11	3	6	O	0.4
1980	Oak-A	158	591	111	179	22	4	9	53	117	54	.303	.422	.399	.821	134	29	33	95	68	120	1.032	**100**	26	14	18	*O/D	6.1
1981	Oak-A	108	423	**89**	**135**	18	7	6	35	64	68	.319	.411	.437	.848	151	27	29	96	58	81	.968	**56**	22	4	18	*O	**5.0**
1982	Oak-A	149	536	119	143	24	4	10	51	**116**	94	.267	.399	.382	.782	122	17	21	95	83	99	**1.030**	**130**	42	**14**	6	*O/D	3.6
1983	Oak-A	145	513	105	150	25	7	9	48	**103**	80	.292	.415	.421	.836	137	27	30	96	82	109	**1.097**	**108**	19	**21**	8	*O/D	5.6
1984	Oak-A	142	502	113	147	27	4	16	58	86	81	.293	.401	.458	.860	150	29	35	92	88	103	**1.018**	**66**	18	9	6	*O	4.5
1985	NY-A	143	547	**146**	172	28	5	24	72	99	65	.314	.422	.516	.938	162	45	49	96	71	138	**1.181**	**80**	10	**18**	12	*O/D	**7.4**
1986	NY-A	153	608	**130**	160	31	5	28	74	89	81	.263	.359	.469	.828	121	21	19	103	71	112	.969	**87**	18	**15**	3	*O/D	3.2
1987	NY-A	95	358	78	104	17	3	17	37	80	52	.291	.423	.497	.920	148	26	28	98	56	84	1.107	41	8	8	3	OD	3.3
1988	NY-A	140	554	118	169	30	2	6	50	82	54	.305	.397	.399	.796	129	21	24	96	73	107	.988	**93**	13	**20**	7	*O/D	4.8
1989	NY-A	65	235	41	58	13	1	3	22	56	29	.247	.394	.349	.743	106	6	5	104	83	40	.886	25	8	3	1	O	0.8
	Oak-A	85	306	72	90	13	2	9	35	70	39	.294	.429	.438	.866	140	22	21	103	75	70	1.122	52	6	12	3	O/D	3.5
	Yr	150	541	**113**	148	26	3	12	57	**126**	68	.274	.413	.399	.813	125	29	26	104	79	110	**1.017**	**77**	14	**15**	4		4.3
Total	11	1472	5524	1171	1603	261	47	138	561	996	736	.290	.402	.429	.831	134	264	292	96	73	1108	1.016	871	201	141	92	*O/D	48.2
■ **DAVE HENGEL**	Hengel, David Lee b: 12/18/61, Oakland, Cal. BR/TR, 6', 185 lbs. Deb: 9/03/86																											
1986	Sea-A	21	63	3	12	1	0	1	6	1	13	.190	.215	.254	.469	27	-6	-7	105	126	3	.346	0	0	0	-1	D/O	-0.7
1987	Sea-A	10	19	2	6	0	0	1	4	0	4	.316	.316	.474	.789	104	0	0	103	133	2	.600	0	0	0	-2	/OD	-0.1
1988	Sea-A	26	60	3	10	1	0	2	7	1	15	.167	.180	.283	.464	26	-6	-6	108	121	3	.360	0	0	0	-1	OD	-0.7
1989	Cle-A	12	25	2	3	1	0	0	1	2	4	.120	.185	.160	.345	-2	-3	-3	104	97	1	.261	0	0	0	-1	/OD	-0.4
Total	4	69	167	10	31	3	0	4	18	4	36	.186	.209	.275	.485	31	-15	-17	105	120	9	.364	0	0	0	-5	/OD	-1.9
■ **KEITH HERNANDEZ**	Hernandez, Keith b: 10/20/53, San Francisco, Cal. BL/TL, 6', 180 lbs. Deb: 8/30/74																											
1974	StL-N	14	34	3	10	1	2	0	2	7	8	.294	.415	.441	.856	135	2	2	104	51	7	.880	0	0	0	0	/1	0.2
1975	StL-N	64	188	20	47	8	2	3	20	17	26	.250	.312	.362	.674	84	-4	-4	103	100	20	.578	0	1	-1	1	1	-0.7
1976	StL-N	129	374	54	108	21	5	7	46	49	53	.289	.376	.428	.803	123	14	13	104	98	61	.783	4	2	0	12	*1	2.0
1977	StL-N	161	560	90	163	41	4	15	91	79	88	.291	.380	.459	.839	129	20	23	96	123	95	.817	7	7	-2	4	*1	1.7
1978	StL-N	159	542	90	138	32	4	11	64	82	68	.255	.355	.389	.744	113	7	11	95	110	78	.732	13	5	1	3	*1	0.9
1979	StL-N	161	610	**116**	210	**48**	11	11	105	80	78	**.344**	**.421**	.513	.934	147	47	43	105	127	**135**	.976	11	6	-0	18	*1	5.4
1980	StL-N	159	595	**111**	191	39	8	16	99	86	73	.321	**.410**	.494	.904	147	43	41	103	121	122	.934	14	8	-1	5	*1	4.0
1981	StL-N	103	376	65	115	27	4	8	48	61	45	.306	.405	.463	.868	143	25	24	102	101	73	.905	12	5	1	6	1/O	2.8
1982	StL-N	160	579	79	173	33	6	7	94	100	67	.299	.404	.413	.817	125	27	24	103	**150**	101	.843	19	11	-1	6	*1/O	2.2
1983	StL-N	55	218	34	62	15	4	3	26	24	30	.284	.355	.431	.787	119	5	6	98	96	34	.748	1	1	-0	2	1	0.4
	NY-N	95	320	43	98	8	3	9	37	64	42	.306	.425	.434	.859	140	20	21	99	93	64	.922	8	4	0	4	1	2.1
	Yr	150	538	77	160	23	7	12	63	88	72	.297	.398	.433	.831	132	25	26	98	95	98	.851	9	5	-0	5		2.5
1984	NY-N	154	550	83	171	31	0	15	94	97	89	.311	.415	.449	.864	143	35	36	100	134	108	.887	2	3	-1	18	*1	4.9
1985	NY-N	158	593	87	183	34	4	10	91	77	59	.309	.390	.430	.820	133	25	27	97	135	100	.789	3	3	-1	15	*1	3.8
1986	NY-N	149	551	94	171	34	1	13	83	**94**	69	.310	.414	.446	.861	144	32	35	96	123	106	.876	2	1	0	16	*1	4.6
1987	NY-N	154	587	87	170	28	2	18	89	81	104	.290	.379	.436	.816	117	15	16	99	121	98	.786	0	2	-1	15	*1	2.1
1988	NY-N	95	348	43	96	16	0	11	55	31	57	.276	.337	.417	.754	128	7	10	90	126	47	.678	2	1	0	3	1	0.9
1989	NY-N	75	215	18	50	8	0	4	19	27	39	.233	.324	.326	.649	89	-3	-2	97	93	23	.576	0	3	-2	1	1	-0.7
Total	16	2045	7240	1117	2156	424	60	161	1063	1056	995	.298	.389	.440	.829	131	318	326	99	120	1273	.823	98	63	-8	127	*1/O	36.6
■ **TOM HERR**	Herr, Thomas Mitchell b: 4/4/56, Lancaster, Pa. BB/TR, 6', 175 lbs. Deb: 8/13/79																											
1979	StL-N	14	10	4	2	0	0	0	1	2	2	.200	.333	.200	.533	47	-1	-1	105	198	1	.625	1	0	0	0	/2	0.0
1980	StL-N	76	222	29	55	12	5	0	15	16	21	.248	.301	.347	.648	78	-6	-7	103	77	22	.582	9	2	2	0	2S	0.1
1981	StL-N	103	411	50	110	14	9	0	46	39	30	.268	.333	.345	.678	91	-4	-4	102	122	49	.647	23	7	3	4	*2	1.0
1982	StL-N	135	493	83	131	19	4	0	36	57	56	.266	.344	.320	.665	84	-7	-9	103	95	59	.639	25	12	0	6	*2	0.3
1983	StL-N	89	313	43	101	14	4	2	31	43	27	.323	.406	.412	.818	130	13	14	98	93	53	.789	6	8	-3	-8	2	0.6

YEAR	TM/L	G	AB	R	H	2B	3B	HR	RBI	BB	SO	AVG	OBP	SLG	PRO	/A	BR	/A	PF	CHI	RC	TA	SB	CS	SBR	FR	POS	TPR
1984	StL-N	145	558	67	154	23	2	4	49	49	56	.276	.337	.346	.682	93	-5	-4	99	90	66	.609	13	7	-0	11	*2	1.0
1985	StL-N	159	596	97	180	38	3	8	110	80	55	.302	.386	.416	.803	130	22	25	96	**155**	107	.849	31	3	8	-27	*2	0.7
1986	StL-N	152	559	48	141	30	4	2	61	73	75	.252	.344	.331	.675	84	-8	-10	103	135	69	.657	22	8	2	-22	*2	-2.8
1987	StL-N	141	510	73	134	29	0	2	83	68	62	.263	.353	.331	.684	84	-11	-9	99	**200**	65	.661	19	4	3	-10	*2	-1.3
1988	StL-N	15	50	4	13	0	0	1	3	11	4	.260	.393	.320	.713	103	1	1	104	67	8	.789	3	0	1	0	2/O	0.2
	Min-A	86	304	42	80	16	0	1	21	40	47	.263	.349	.326	.674	85	-3	-5	106	83	36	.631	10	3	1	-8	2/SD	-0.6
1989	Phi-N	151	561	65	161	25	6	2	37	54	63	.287	.353	.364	.716	104	5	4	101	75	73	.651	10	7	-1	5	*2	1.0
Total	11	1266	4587	605	1262	220	37	22	493	532	498	.275	.353	.354	.707	97	-2	-5	101	117	607	.676	172	61	15	-48	*2/SDO	0.2
■ **MARK HIGGINS**	Higgins, Mark Douglas b: 7/9/63, Miami, Fla. BR/TR, 6'2", 210 lbs. Deb: 9/07/89																											
1989	Cle-A	6	10	1	1	0	0	0	0	1	6	.100	.182	.100	.282	-18	-2	-2	104	0	0	.222	0	0	0	0	/1	-0.1
■ **GLENALLEN HILL**	Hill, Glenallen b: 3/22/65, Santa Cruz, Cal. BR/TR, 6'3", 210 lbs. Deb: 9/01/89																											
1989	Tor-A	19	52	4	15	0	0	1	7	3	12	.288	.327	.346	.673	96	-1	-0	94	130	6	.605	2	1	0	-2	O/D	-0.2
■ **TOMMY HINZO**	Hinzo, Thomas Lee b: 6/18/64, San Diego, Cal. BB/TR, 5'10", 170 lbs. Deb: 7/16/87																											
1987	Cle-A	67	257	31	68	9	3	3	21	10	47	.265	.297	.358	.655	72	-10	-11	103	88	26	.568	9	4	0	-7	2	-1.1
1989	Cle-A	18	17	4	0	0	0	0	0	2	6	.000	.105	.000	.105	-66	-4	-4	104	0	0	.158	1	2	-1	-1	/2SD	-0.4
Total	2	85	274	35	68	9	3	3	21	12	53	.248	.285	.336	.620	63	-13	-15	103	82	26	.532	10	6	-1	-7	/2DS	-1.5
■ **GLENN HOFFMAN**	Hoffman, Glenn Edward b: 7/7/58, Orange, Cal. BR/TR, 6'1", 175 lbs. Deb: 4/12/80																											
1980	Bos-A	114	312	37	89	15	4	4	42	19	41	.285	.330	.397	.728	97	-1	-2	102	120	39	.626	2	4	-2	-5	*3/S2	-0.7
1981	Bos-A	78	242	28	56	10	0	1	20	12	25	.231	.271	.285	.556	57	-12	-14	106	109	18	.423	0	1	-1	1	S/3	-0.8
1982	Bos-A	150	469	53	98	23	2	7	49	30	69	.209	.264	.311	.575	52	-28	-34	110	117	35	.464	0	4	-2	16	*S	-0.6
1983	Bos-A	143	473	56	123	24	1	4	41	30	76	.260	.307	.340	.647	77	-14	-15	101	93	51	.545	1	1	-0	-3	*S	-0.9
1984	Bos-A	64	74	8	14	4	0	0	4	5	10	.189	.241	.243	.484	31	-7	-8	110	89	4	.359	0	1	-1	-4	S/32	-0.7
1985	Bos-A	96	279	40	77	17	2	6	34	25	40	.276	.346	.416	.762	105	3	2	102	101	40	.705	2	2	-1	3	S/23	1.1
1986	Bos-A	12	23	1	5	2	0	0	1	2	3	.217	.280	.304	.584	60	-1	-1	100	57	2	.474	0	0	0	-1	S/3	-0.1
1987	Bos-A	21	55	5	11	3	0	0	6	3	9	.200	.267	.255	.521	41	-5	-5	99	171	4	.413	0	0	0	-1	S/32	-0.3
	LA-N	40	132	10	29	5	0	0	10	7	23	.220	.270	.258	.527	44	-11	-10	92	117	9	.398	0	1	-1	1	S	-0.4
1989	Cal-A	48	104	9	22	3	0	1	3	3	13	.212	.241	.269	.510	44	-8	-8	99	38	6	.376	0	2	-1	4	S3/21D	-0.2
Total	9	766	2163	247	524	106	9	23	210	136	309	.242	.293	.331	.625	69	-84	-93	103	105	207	.514	5	16	-8	12	S3/2D1	-3.6
■ **CHRIS HOILES**	Hoiles, Christopher Allen b: 3/20/65, Bowling Green, O. BR/TR, 6', 195 lbs. Deb: 4/25/89																											
1989	Bal-A	6	9	0	1	1	0	0	1	1	3	.111	.200	.222	.422	19	-1	-1	99	194	0	.375	0	0	0	0	/CD	0.0
■ **SAM HORN**	Horn, Samuel Lee b: 11/2/63, Dallas, Tex. BL/TL, 6'5", 215 lbs. Deb: 7/25/87																											
1987	Bos-A	46	158	31	44	7	0	14	34	17	55	.278	.356	.589	.945	147	10	10	99	100	32	.933	0	1	-1	0	D	0.9
1988	Bos-A	24	61	4	9	0	0	2	8	11	20	.148	.278	.246	.524	44	-4	-5	109	151	5	.491	0	0	0	0	D	-0.4
1989	Bos-A	33	54	1	8	2	0	0	4	8	16	.148	.258	.185	.443	26	-5	-5	105	155	2	.360	0	0	0	0	D/1	-0.5
Total	3	103	273	36	61	9	0	16	46	36	91	.223	.318	.432	.751	100	1	-0	102	123	38	.700	0	1	-1	0	/D1	-0.0
■ **JACK HOWELL**	Howell, Jack Robert b: 8/18/61, Tucson, Ariz. BL/TR, 6', 180 lbs. Deb: 5/20/85																											
1985	Cal-A	43	137	19	27	4	0	5	18	16	33	.197	.281	.336	.617	68	-6	-6	101	117	14	.563	1	1	-0	-3	3	-1.0
1986	Cal-A	63	151	26	41	14	2	4	21	19	28	.272	.353	.470	.823	128	5	6	96	101	27	.829	2	0	1	-2	3/OD	0.3
1987	Cal-A	138	449	64	110	18	5	23	64	57	118	.245	.333	.461	.794	109	5	6	99	93	70	.774	4	3	-1	-7	O32	-0.4
1988	Cal-A	154	500	59	127	32	2	16	63	46	130	.254	.324	.422	.746	114	4	8	94	97	67	.685	2	6	-3	-20	*3/O	-1.4
1989	Cal-A	144	474	56	108	19	4	20	52	52	125	.228	.308	.411	.720	103	-0	1	99	79	60	.663	0	3	-2	20	*3/O	1.9
Total	5	542	1711	224	413	87	13	68	218	190	434	.241	.321	.427	.748	107	8	14	97	93	237	.704	9	13	-5	-12	3O/2D	-0.6
■ **DANN HOWITT**	Howitt, Dann Paul John b: 2/13/64, Battle Creek, Mich. BL/TR, 6'5", 205 lbs. Deb: 9/15/89																											
1989	Oak-A	3	3	0	0	0	0	0	0	0	2	.000	.000	.000	.000	-97	-1	-1	103	0	0	.000	0	0	0	-0	/1O	0.0
■ **KENT HRBEK**	Hrbek, Kent Alan b: 5/21/60, Minneapolis, Minn. BL/TR, 6'4", 200 lbs. Deb: 8/24/81																											
1981	Min-A	24	67	5	16	5	0	1	7	5	9	.239	.301	.358	.660	85	-1	-1	105	101	8	.588	0	0	0	-0	1/D	-0.1
1982	Min-A	140	532	82	160	21	4	23	92	54	80	.301	.365	.485	.850	131	22	22	100	119	91	.808	3	1	0	-3	*1/D	1.6
1983	Min-A	141	515	75	153	41	5	16	84	57	71	.297	.370	.489	.860	128	24	21	105	116	91	.832	4	6	-2	-3	*1/D	0.9
1984	Min-A	149	559	80	174	31	3	27	107	65	87	.311	.387	.522	.909	141	37	33	106	121	110	.898	1	1	-0	-6	*1/D	1.7
1985	Min-A	158	593	78	165	31	2	21	93	67	87	.278	.353	.444	.797	113	14	11	103	120	93	.755	1	1	-0	1	*1/D	0.2
1986	Min-A	149	550	85	147	27	1	29	91	71	81	.267	.357	.478	.835	116	20	14	108	110	93	.814	2	2	-1	-5	*1/D	-0.1
1987	Min-A	143	477	85	136	20	1	34	90	84	60	.285	.392	.545	.937	152	33	36	96	101	103	.980	5	2	0	-11	*1/D	1.1
1988	Min-A	143	510	75	159	31	0	25	76	67	54	.312	.392	.520	.911	144	37	32	106	91	104	.915	0	3	-2	-7	*1D/O	1.7
1989	Min-A	109	375	59	102	17	0	25	84	53	35	.272	.364	.517	.881	137	22	19	107	124	73	.900	3	0	1	-3	1D	1.1
Total	9	1156	4178	624	1212	224	16	201	724	523	564	.290	.371	.496	.867	131	209	188	104	112	765	.853	19	16	-4	-37	*1/DO	8.1
■ **GLENN HUBBARD**	Hubbard, Glenn Dee b: 9/25/57, Hahn Afb, Germany BR/TR, 5'9", 150 lbs. Deb: 7/14/78																											
1978	Atl-N	44	163	15	42	4	0	2	13	10	20	.258	.309	.319	.628	68	-5	-8	112	94	17	.532	2	1	0	-2	2	-0.6
1979	Atl-N	97	325	34	75	12	0	3	29	27	43	.231	.292	.295	.587	55	-17	-21	109	109	28	.479	0	6	-4	4	2	-1.5
1980	Atl-N	117	431	55	107	21	3	9	43	49	69	.248	.325	.374	.699	93	-3	-4	101	96	53	.646	7	5	-1	7	*2	1.0
1981	Atl-N	99	361	39	85	13	5	6	33	33	59	.235	.303	.349	.652	85	-8	-7	100	92	39	.579	4	2	0	-2	2	-0.2
1982	Atl-N	145	532	75	132	25	1	9	59	59	62	.248	.327	.350	.676	83	-7	-12	107	115	65	.618	4	3	-1	23	*2	1.8
1983	Atl-N	148	517	65	136	24	6	12	70	55	71	.263	.339	.402	.741	99	3	-1	106	116	68	.672	3	9	-5	21	*2	2.2
1984	Atl-N	120	397	53	93	27	2	9	43	55	61	.234	.333	.380	.714	91	1	-4	110	97	53	.684	4	1	1	22	*2	2.3
1985	Atl-N	142	439	51	102	21	0	5	39	56	54	.232	.325	.314	.639	75	-11	-14	106	102	47	.575	4	3	-1	**57**	*2	4.4
1986	Atl-N	143	408	42	94	16	1	4	36	66	74	.230	.343	.304	.647	78	-9	-10	102	106	47	.614	3	2	-0	**34**	*2	2.6
1987	Atl-N	141	443	69	117	33	2	5	38	77	57	.264	.380	.381	.762	95	5	-1	108	82	67	.749	1	1	-0	**23**	*2	2.4
1988	Oak-A	105	294	35	75	12	2	3	33	33	50	.255	.336	.340	.676	95	-3	-1	95	120	34	.593	1	3	-2	-1	*2/D	0.3
1989	Oak-A	53	131	12	26	6	0	3	12	19	20	.198	.300	.313	.613	71	-4	-5	103	93	13	.574	2	0	1	4	2/D	0.0
Total	12	1354	4441	545	1084	214	22	70	448	539	640	.244	.330	.349	.680	84	-59	-87	105	103	529	.621	35	36	-11	188	*2/D	14.7
■ **REX HUDLER**	Hudler, Rex Allen b: 9/2/60, Tempe, Ariz. BR/TR, 6'1", 180 lbs. Deb: 9/09/84																											
1984	NY-A	9	7	2	1	1	0	0	0	1	5	.143	.333	.286	.619	78	-0	-0	94	0	1	.667	0	0	0	0	/2	0.0
1985	NY-A	20	51	4	8	0	1	0	1	1	9	.157	.173	.196	.369	1	-7	-7	96	40	2	.250	0	1	-1	1	2/1S	-0.5
1986	Bal-A	14	1	1	0	0	0	0	0	0	0	.000	.000	.000	.000	-99	-0	-0	99	0	0	1.000	1	0	0	0	2/3	0.1
1988	Mon-N	77	216	38	59	14	2	4	14	10	34	.273	.305	.412	.717	99	0	-1	106	55	28	.771	29	7	5	0	2S/O	0.7
1989	Mon-N	92	155	21	38	7	0	6	13	6	23	.245	.278	.406	.684	91	-2	-2	102	65	17	.691	15	4	2	-3	2OS	-0.1
Total	5	212	430	66	106	22	3	10	28	18	71	.247	.280	.381	.661	84	-9	-10	103	56	48	.674	45	12	6	-2	2/S031	0.2
■ **MIKE HUFF**	Huff, Michael Kale b: 8/11/63, Honolulu, Hawaii BR/TR, 6'1", 180 lbs. Deb: 8/07/89																											
1989	LA-N	12	25	4	5	1	0	1	2	3	6	.200	.310	.360	.670	98	-0	-0	93	67	3	.619	0	1	-1	0	/O	0.0
■ **TIM HULETT**	Hulett, Timothy Craig b: 1/12/60, Springfield, Ill. BR/TR, 6', 185 lbs. Deb: 9/15/83																											
1983	Chi-A	6	5	0	1	0	0	0	0	0	0	.200	.200	.200	.400	10	-1	-1	103	0	0	.500	1	0	0	0	/2	0.0
1984	Chi-A	8	7	1	0	0	0	0	0	1	4	.000	.125	.000	.125	-56	-2	-2	111	0	0	.286	1	0	0	0	/32	0.0
1985	Chi-A	141	395	52	106	19	4	5	37	30	81	.268	.326	.375	.701	91	-5	-4	100	90	48	.625	6	4	-1	4	*32/O	-0.3
1986	Chi-A	150	520	53	120	16	5	17	44	21	91	.231	.262	.379	.641	72	-21	-21	101	71	49	.541	4	1	1	-9	32	-2.8
1987	Chi-A	68	240	20	52	10	0	7	28	10	41	.217	.248	.346	.594	52	-15	-18	109	107	19	.474	0	2	-1	-0	3/2	-1.9
1989	Bal-A	33	97	12	27	5	0	3	18	10	17	.278	.346	.423	.768	117	2	2	99	140	14	.699	0	0	0	1	23	0.3
Total	6	406	1264	138	306	50	9	32	127	72	234	.242	.286	.372	.657	76	-41	-44	102	89	130	.563	12	7	-1	-5	32/O	-4.7

YEAR	TM/L	G	AB	R	H	2B	3B	HR	RBI	BB	SO	AVG	OBP	SLG	PRO	/A	BR	/A	PF	CHI	RC	TA	SB	CS	SBR	FR	POS	TPR
■ JEFF HUSON	Huson, Jeffrey Kent b: 8/15/64, Scottsdale, Ariz. BL/TR, 6'3", 180 lbs. Deb: 9/02/88																											
1988	Mon-N	20	42	7	13	2	0	0	3	4	3	.310	.370	.357	.727	104	1	0	106	80	5	.656	2	1	0	-1	S/23O	0.0
1989	Mon-N	32	74	1	12	5	0	0	2	6	6	.162	.225	.230	.455	30	-7	-7	102	47	3	.382	3	0	1	2	S/23	-0.2
Total	2	52	116	8	25	7	0	0	5	10	9	.216	.278	.276	.554	57	-6	-7	103	59	8	.470	5	1	1	1	/S23O	-0.2
■ PETE INCAVIGLIA	Incaviglia, Peter Joseph b: 4/2/64, Pebble Beach, Cal. BR/TR, 6'1", 225 lbs. Deb: 4/08/86																											
1986	Tex-A	153	540	82	135	21	2	30	88	55	185	.250	.324	.463	.787	117	8	12	96	105	82	.750	3	2	-0	-15	*OD	-0.7
1987	Tex-A	139	509	85	138	26	4	27	80	48	168	.271	.335	.497	.832	114	12	10	104	98	85	.814	9	3	1	-8	*O/D	0.0
1988	Tex-A	116	418	59	104	19	3	22	54	39	153	.249	.323	.467	.790	117	9	9	101	84	63	.762	6	4	-1	2	OD	0.9
1989	Tex-A	133	453	48	107	27	4	21	81	32	136	.236	.295	.453	.748	105	3	1	102	117	56	.679	5	7	-3	-5	*O/D	-0.8
Total	4	541	1920	274	484	93	13	100	303	174	642	.252	.320	.470	.790	113	32	31	100	101	286	.752	23	16	-3	-25	O/D	-0.6
■ ALEXIS INFANTE	Infante, Fermin Alexis (Carpio) b: 12/4/61, Barquisimeto, Venez. BR/TR, 5'10", 175 lbs. Deb: 9/27/87																											
1987	Tor-A	1	0	0	0	0	0	0	0	0	0	—	—	—	—	—	0	0	101	—	—	—	0	0	0	0	/R	0.0
1988	Tor-A	19	15	7	3	0	0	0	0	2	4	.200	.294	.200	.494	41	-1	-1	100	0	1	.385	0	0	0	1	/3SD	0.0
1989	Tor-A	20	12	1	2	0	0	0	0	0	1	.167	.167	.167	.333	-6	-2	-2	94	0	0	.300	1	0	0	0	/S32	0.0
Total	3	40	27	8	5	0	0	0	0	2	5	.185	.241	.185	.427	22	-3	-3	97	0	287	.348	1	0	0	1	/3SD2	0.0
■ DARRIN JACKSON	Jackson, Darrin Jay b: 8/22/62, Los Angeles, Cal. BR/TR, 6'1", 170 lbs. Deb: 6/17/85																											
1985	Chi-N	5	11	0	1	0	0	0	0	0	3	.091	.091	.091	.182	-42	-2	-2	116	0	0	.100	0	0	0	-0	/O	-0.2
1987	Chi-N	7	5	2	4	1	0	0	0	0	0	.800	.800	1.000	1.800	371	2	2	101	0	4	5.000	0	0	0	-2	/O	0.0
1988	Chi-N	100	188	29	50	11	3	6	20	5	28	.266	.289	.452	.741	105	1	0	104	78	24	.669	4	1	1	-8	O	-0.8
1989	Chi-N	45	83	7	19	4	0	1	8	6	17	.229	.281	.313	.594	64	-3	-4	108	111	7	.493	1	2	-1	-1	O	-0.7
	SD-N	25	87	10	18	3	0	3	12	7	17	.207	.266	.345	.611	73	-3	-3	101	126	7	.514	0	2	-1	4	O	0.0
	Yr	70	170	17	37	7	0	4	20	13	34	.218	.273	.329	.603	68	-6	-8	106	118	14	.504	1	4	-2	3		-0.7
Total	4	182	374	48	92	19	3	10	40	18	65	.246	.282	.393	.675	87	-5	-7	105	94	42	.586	5	5	-2	-7	O	-1.7
■ BO JACKSON	Jackson, Vincent Edward b: 11/30/62, Bessemer, Ala. BR/TR, 6'1", 220 lbs. Deb: 9/02/86																											
1986	KC-A	25	82	9	17	2	1	2	9	7	34	.207	.286	.329	.615	68	-4	-4	100	109	8	.582	3	1	0	-4	O/D	-0.7
1987	KC-A	116	396	46	93	17	2	22	53	30	158	.235	.297	.455	.752	93	-3	-5	104	86	55	.726	10	4	1	-7	*O/D	-1.3
1988	KC-A	124	439	63	108	16	4	25	68	25	146	.246	.288	.472	.760	106	3	1	103	98	59	.758	27	6	5	4	*O/D	0.7
1989	KC-A	135	515	86	132	15	6	32	105	39	172	.256	.312	.495	.808	130	14	16	96	123	77	.803	26	9	2	4	*OD	2.1
Total	4	400	1432	204	350	50	13	81	235	101	510	.244	.299	.467	.766	108	10	9	100	104	199	.755	66	20	8	-3	O/D	0.8
■ BROOK JACOBY	Jacoby, Brook Wallace b: 11/23/59, Philadelphia, Pa. BR/TR, 5'11", 175 lbs. Deb: 9/13/81																											
1981	Atl-N	11	10	0	2	0	0	0	1	0	3	.200	.200	.200	.400	14	-1	-1	100	196	0	.222	0	0	0	-1	/3	-0.1
1983	Atl-N	4	8	0	0	0	0	0	0	0	1	.000	.000	.000	.000	-95	-2	-2	106	0	0	.000	0	0	0	0	/3	-0.1
1984	Cle-A	126	439	64	116	19	3	7	40	32	73	.264	.319	.369	.688	85	-6	-10	106	87	50	.592	3	2	-0	-19	*3/S	-2.7
1985	Cle-A	161	606	72	166	26	3	20	87	48	120	.274	.327	.426	.753	111	3	7	94	115	81	.670	2	3	-1	-7	*3/2	-0.5
1986	Cle-A	158	583	83	168	30	4	17	80	56	137	.288	.351	.441	.791	118	12	14	98	106	88	.731	2	1	0	-13	*3	-0.2
1987	Cle-A	155	540	73	162	26	4	32	69	75	73	.300	.388	.541	.929	140	35	33	103	72	110	.930	2	3	-1	-5	*3/1D	2.1
1988	Cle-A	152	552	59	133	25	0	9	49	48	101	.241	.303	.335	.638	77	-16	-17	102	94	55	.544	2	3	-1	2	*3	-1.5
1989	Cle-A	147	519	49	141	26	5	13	64	62	90	.272	.353	.416	.769	112	12	9	104	100	75	.711	2	5	-2	-8	*3/D	-0.1
Total	8	914	3257	400	888	152	19	98	390	321	598	.273	.340	.421	.761	107	36	34	101	96	459	.692	13	17	-6	-51	3/D12S	-3.1
■ DION JAMES	James, Dion b: 11/9/62, Philadelphia, Pa. BL/TL, 6'1", 170 lbs. Deb: 9/16/83																											
1983	Mil-A	11	20	1	2	0	0	0	1	2	2	.100	.182	.100	.282	-22	-3	-3	92	195	1	.278	1	0	0	-1	/OD	-0.3
1984	Mil-A	128	387	52	114	19	5	1	30	32	41	.295	.353	.377	.730	111	2	6	92	80	50	.659	10	10	-3	-16	*O	-1.6
1985	Mil-A	18	49	5	11	1	0	0	3	6	6	.224	.309	.245	.554	52	-3	-3	105	99	4	.474	0	0	0	-1	O/D	-0.3
1987	Atl-N	134	494	80	154	37	6	10	61	70	63	.312	.399	.472	.871	120	23	17	108	98	95	.885	10	8	-2	-8	*O	0.2
1988	Atl-N	132	386	46	99	17	5	3	30	58	59	.256	.355	.350	.705	99	3	1	104	83	48	.659	9	9	-3	-5	*O	-0.9
1989	Atl-N	63	170	15	44	7	0	1	11	25	23	.259	.357	.318	.675	92	-0	-1	102	78	20	.609	1	3	-2	-1	O/1	-0.4
	Cle-A	71	245	26	75	11	0	4	29	24	26	.306	.368	.400	.768	112	6	5	104	104	35	.687	1	4	-2	-0	OD/1	0.1
Total	6	557	1751	225	499	92	16	19	165	217	220	.285	.366	.388	.754	107	28	22	102	91	253	.708	32	34	-11	-33	O/D1	-3.2
■ CHRIS JAMES	James, Donald Chris b: 10/4/62, Rusk, Tex. BR/TR, 6'1", 195 lbs. Deb: 4/23/86																											
1986	Phi-N	16	46	5	13	3	0	1	5	1	13	.283	.298	.413	.711	90	-1	-1	104	91	5	.588	0	0	0	-1	O	-0.1
1987	Phi-N	115	358	48	105	20	6	17	54	27	67	.293	.346	.525	.871	122	12	11	104	90	66	.853	3	1	0	-2	*O	0.5
1988	Phi-N	150	566	57	137	24	1	19	66	31	73	.242	.285	.389	.674	91	-8	-9	101	97	59	.583	7	4	-0	7	*O/3	-0.4
1989	Phi-N	45	179	14	37	4	0	2	19	4	23	.207	.224	.263	.487	38	-14	-15	101	153	8	.355	3	1	0	-1	O3	-1.6
	SD-N	87	303	41	80	13	2	11	46	22	45	.264	.316	.429	.745	110	4	3	101	116	38	.660	2	1	0	-2	O/3	0.0
	Yr	132	482	55	117	17	2	13	65	26	68	.243	.283	.367	.650	84	-11	-11	101	130	45	.540	5	2	0	-3		-1.6
Total	4	413	1452	165	372	64	9	50	190	85	221	.256	.300	.416	.716	97	-7	-10	102	106	177	.630	15	7	0	2	O/3	-1.6
■ STAN JAVIER	Javier, Stanley Julian Antonio (De Javier) b: 1/9/64, San Francisco De Macoris, D.R. BB/TR, 6', 185 lbs. Deb: 4/15/84																											
1984	NY-A	7	7	1	1	0	0	0	0	0	1	.143	.143	.143	.286	-22	-1	-1	94	0	0	.167	0	0	0	-2	/O	-0.2
1986	Oak-A	59	114	13	23	8	0	0	8	16	27	.202	.305	.272	.577	64	-6	-5	94	103	11	.602	8	0	2	2	O/D	-0.1
1987	Oak-A	81	151	22	28	3	1	2	9	19	33	.185	.276	.258	.535	48	-12	-10	91	80	12	.480	3	2	-0	-4	O/1D	-1.6
1988	Oak-A	125	397	49	102	13	3	2	35	32	63	.257	.316	.320	.635	83	-11	-8	95	105	42	.586	20	1	5	0	*O/1D	-0.4
1989	Oak-A	112	310	42	77	12	3	1	28	31	45	.248	.319	.316	.635	77	-8	-9	103	108	33	.589	12	2	2	-2	*O/12	-1.0
Total	5	384	979	127	231	36	7	5	80	98	169	.236	.308	.302	.610	72	-38	-34	97	101	99	.568	43	5	10	-5	O/1D2	-3.3
■ GREGG JEFFERIES	Jefferies, Gregory Scott b: 8/1/67, Burlingame, Cal. BB/TR, 5'11", 175 lbs. Deb: 9/06/87																											
1987	NY-N	6	6	0	3	1	0	0	2	0	0	.500	.500	.667	1.167	209	1	1	99	200	2	1.333	0	0	0	0	/H	0.1
1988	NY-N	29	109	19	35	8	2	6	17	8	10	.321	.368	.596	.964	191	10	11	90	83	24	1.026	5	1	1	-2	32	1.1
1989	NY-N	141	508	72	131	28	2	12	56	39	46	.258	.317	.392	.709	105	0	2	97	98	61	.662	21	6	3	-30	*23	-2.5
Total	3	176	623	91	169	37	4	18	75	47	56	.271	.327	.430	.758	121	11	14	95	96	87	.724	26	7	4	-32	2/3	-1.3
■ STAN JEFFERSON	Jefferson, Stanley b: 12/4/62, New York, N.Y. BB/TR, 5'11", 175 lbs. Deb: 9/07/86																											
1986	NY-N	14	24	6	5	1	0	1	3	2	8	.208	.296	.375	.671	88	-1	-0	96	100	3	.600	0	0	0	0	/O	0.0
1987	SD-N	116	422	59	97	8	7	8	29	39	92	.230	.298	.339	.637	71	-19	-18	97	71	45	.637	34	11	4	-5	*O	-2.2
1988	SD-N	49	111	16	16	1	2	1	4	9	22	.144	.215	.216	.431	25	-11	-11	97	59	6	.394	5	1	1	-4	O	-1.5
1989	NY-A	10	12	1	1	0	0	0	1	0	4	.083	.083	.083	.167	-51	-2	-2	104	389	0	.167	1	1	-0	-3	/OD	-0.5
	Bal-A	35	127	19	33	7	0	4	20	4	22	.260	.288	.409	.697	96	-1	-1	99	124	15	.673	9	3	1	3	O/D	0.2
	Yr	45	139	20	34	7	0	4	21	4	26	.245	.271	.381	.652	82	-4	-4	100	191	14	.618	10	4	1	0		-0.3
Total	4	224	696	101	152	17	9	14	57	54	148	.218	.279	.329	.608	67	-35	-32	97	84	68	.590	49	16	5	-8	O/D	-4.0
■ STEVE JELTZ	Jeltz, Larry Steven b: 5/28/59, Paris, France BB/TR, 5'11", 180 lbs. Deb: 7/17/83																											
1983	Phi-N	13	8	0	1	0	1	0	1	1	2	.125	.222	.375	.597	62	-0	-0	101	132	0	.444	0	0	0	0	/2S3	0.0
1984	Phi-N	28	68	7	14	0	1	1	7	7	11	.206	.280	.279	.559	57	-4	-4	102	125	5	.483	2	1	0	-2	S/3	-0.2
1985	Phi-N	89	196	17	37	4	1	0	12	26	55	.189	.284	.219	.503	42	-14	-15	102	111	13	.422	1	1	-0	-4	S	-1.2
1986	Phi-N	145	439	44	96	11	4	0	36	65	97	.219	.321	.262	.583	60	-20	-23	104	125	40	.527	6	3	0	-5	*S	-1.4
1987	Phi-N	114	293	37	68	9	6	0	12	39	54	.232	.324	.304	.628	65	-13	-14	104	54	28	.542	1	2	-1	-6	*S/O	-0.7
1988	Phi-N	148	379	39	71	11	4	0	27	59	58	.187	.297	.237	.534	54	-20	-21	101	120	29	.476	3	0	1	-4	*S	-1.3
1989	Phi-N	116	263	28	64	7	3	4	25	45	44	.243	.356	.338	.694	99	2	1	101	100	34	.671	4	2	0	4	S32/O	1.0
Total	7	653	1646	172	351	42	20	5	120	242	321	.213	.315	.272	.587	63	-71	-76	103	105	149	.524	17	9	-0	-15	S/32O	-3.8
■ DOUG JENNINGS	Jennings, James Douglas b: 9/30/64, Atlanta, Ga. BL/TL, 5'10", 175 lbs. Deb: 4/08/88																											
1988	Oak-A	71	101	9	21	6	0	1	15	21	28	.208	.355	.297	.652	89	-1	-0	95	181	12	.646	0	1	-1	-4	O1/SD	-0.5
1989	Oak-A	4	4	0	0	0	0	0	0	0	2	.000	.000	.000	.000	-97	-1	-1	103	0	0	.000	0	0	0	-1	/O	-0.1

YEAR	TM/L	G	AB	R	H	2B	3B	HR	RBI	BB	SO	AVG	OBP	SLG	PRO	/A	BR	/A	PF	CHI	RC	TA	SB	CS	SBR	FR	POS	TPR
Total	2	75	105	9	21	6	0	1	15	21	30	.200	.344	.286	.629	82	-2	-1	95	175	12	.616	0	1	-1	-5	/O1DS	-0.6
■ **HOWARD JOHNSON** Johnson, Howard Michael b: 11/29/60, Clearwater, Fla. BB/TR, 5'11", 178 lbs. Deb: 4/14/82																												
1982	Det-A	54	155	23	49	5	0	4	14	16	30	.316	.384	.426	.810	122	5	5	100	72	25	.796	7	4	-0	-3	3D/O	0.1
1983	Det-A	27	66	11	14	0	0	3	5	7	10	.212	.297	.348	.646	81	-2	-2	96	61	7	.585	0	0	0	-1	3/D	-0.2
1984	Det-A	116	355	43	88	14	1	12	50	40	67	.248	.326	.394	.720	102	-1	1	96	113	46	.685	10	6	-1	-11	*3/S1OD	-0.8
1985	NY-N	126	389	38	94	18	4	11	46	34	78	.242	.303	.393	.696	96	-4	-3	97	98	45	.633	6	4	-1	-13	*3/SO	-1.6
1986	NY-N	88	220	30	54	14	0	10	39	31	64	.245	.341	.445	.787	121	4	6	96	121	36	.817	8	1	2	-1	3S/O	0.9
1987	NY-N	157	554	93	147	22	1	36	99	83	113	.265	.366	.504	.870	129	22	23	99	104	106	.939	32	10	4	-7	*3S/O	2.3
1988	NY-N	148	495	85	114	21	1	24	68	86	104	.230	.348	.422	.770	133	14	20	90	99	78	.815	23	7	3	-7	*3/S	1.8
1989	NY-N	153	571	**104**	164	41	3	36	101	77	126	.287	.373	.559	.932	169	46	48	97	101	127	1.045	41	8	8	-20	*3S	3.9
Total	8	869	2805	427	724	135	10	136	422	374	592	.258	.348	.459	.807	128	85	99	96	101	471	.835	127	40	14	-63	3S/D01	6.4
■ **LANCE JOHNSON** Johnson, Kenneth Lance b: 7/6/63, Cincinnati, Ohio BL/TL, 5'10", 160 lbs. Deb: 7/10/87																												
1987	StL-N	33	59	4	13	2	1	0	7	4	6	.220	.270	.288	.558	49	-4	-4	99	164	5	.551	6	1	1	-5	O	-0.9
1988	Chi-A	33	124	11	23	4	1	0	6	6	11	.185	.223	.234	.457	29	-12	-11	97	84	7	.394	6	2	1	-2	O/D	-1.2
1989	Chi-A	50	180	28	54	8	2	0	16	17	24	.300	.360	.367	.727	113	2	3	93	96	27	.762	16	3	3	1	O/D	0.7
Total	3	116	363	43	90	14	4	0	29	27	41	.248	.300	.309	.609	73	-15	-13	95	103	38	.590	28	6	5	-5	O/D	-1.4
■ **WALLACE JOHNSON** Johnson, Wallace Darnell b: 12/25/56, Gary, Ind. BB/TR, 6', 173 lbs. Deb: 9/08/81																												
1981	Mon-N	11	9	1	2	0	1	0	3	1	1	.222	.300	.444	.744	110	0	0	99	294	0	.667	1	1	-0	0	/2	0.0
1982	Mon-N	36	57	5	11	0	2	0	2	5	5	.193	.258	.263	.521	44	-4	-4	105	52	4	.511	4	1	1	-1	2	-0.3
1983	Mon-N	3	2	1	1	0	0	0	0	1	0	.500	.667	.500	1.167	224	1	1	102	0	1	3.000	1	0	0	0	/H	0.1
	SF-N	7	8	0	1	0	0	0	1	0	0	.125	.125	.125	.250	-30	-1	-1	101	396	0	.143	0	0	0	-0	/2	-0.1
	Yr	10	10	1	2	0	0	0	1	1	1	.200	.273	.200	.473	33	-1	-1	101	277	1	.500	1	0	0	-0		0.0
1984	Mon-N	17	24	3	5	0	0	0	4	5	4	.208	.345	.208	.553	64	-1	-1	91	314	2	.526	0	0	0	0	/1	0.0
1986	Mon-N	61	127	13	36	3	1	1	10	7	9	.283	.321	.346	.667	86	-3	-2	98	85	14	.594	6	3	0	-1	1	-0.4
1987	Mon-N	75	85	7	21	5	0	1	14	7	6	.247	.304	.341	.646	67	-4	-4	106	175	10	.641	5	0	2	0	/1	-0.2
1988	Mon-N	86	94	7	29	5	1	0	3	12	15	.309	.387	.383	.770	115	3	2	106	33	14	.696	0	2	-1	-0	1/2	0.1
1989	Mon-N	85	114	9	31	3	1	2	17	7	12	.272	.314	.368	.682	93	-1	-1	102	143	13	.588	1	0	0	-0	1	-0.2
Total	8	381	520	46	137	16	6	4	54	45	52	.263	.322	.340	.663	83	-10	-12	102	118	60	.605	18	7	1	-2	/12	-1.0
■ **RON JONES** Jones, Ronald Glen b: 6/11/64, Seguin, Tex. BL/TR, 5'10", 195 lbs. Deb: 8/26/88																												
1988	Phi-N	33	124	15	36	6	1	8	26	2	14	.290	.302	.548	.850	138	5	5	101	115	20	.778	0	0	0	1	O	0.6
1989	Phi-N	12	31	7	9	0	0	2	4	9	1	.290	.450	.484	.934	166	3	3	101	77	7	1.042	1	0	0	2	O	0.5
Total	2	45	155	22	45	6	1	10	30	11	15	.290	.337	.535	.873	145	9	8	101	106	27	.833	1	0	0	3	/O	1.1
■ **TRACY JONES** Jones, Tracy Donald b: 3/31/61, Hawthorne, Cal. BR/TR, 6'3", 180 lbs. Deb: 4/07/86																												
1986	Cin-N	46	86	16	30	3	0	2	10	9	5	.349	.411	.453	.864	132	5	4	104	89	17	.932	7	1	2	-0	O/1	0.5
1987	Cin-N	117	359	53	104	17	3	10	44	23	40	.290	.338	.437	.775	100	1	-0	104	94	52	.784	31	8	5	-0	O	0.0
1988	Cin-N	37	83	9	19	1	0	1	9	8	6	.229	.304	.277	.581	64	-3	-4	105	138	8	.603	9	0	3	-2	O	-0.4
	Mon-N	53	141	20	47	5	1	2	15	12	12	.333	.390	.426	.815	127	6	5	106	91	23	.812	9	6	-1	-6	O	-0.2
	Yr	90	224	29	66	6	1	3	24	20	18	.295	.358	.371	.728	104	3	2	105	112	31	.728	18	6	2	-8		-0.6
1989	SF-N	40	97	5	18	4	0	0	12	5	14	.186	.233	.227	.460	33	-9	-8	97	220	4	.357	2	1	0	-6	O	-1.5
	Det-A	46	158	17	41	10	0	3	26	16	16	.259	.331	.380	.711	103	0	1	97	149	21	.655	1	1	-0	-2	O/D	-0.2
Total	4	339	924	120	259	40	4	18	116	73	93	.280	.338	.391	.728	98	1	-2	102	119	126	.710	59	17	8	-17	O/D1	-1.8
■ **TIM JONES** Jones, William Timothy b: 12/1/62, Sumter, S.C. BL/TR, 5'10", 172 lbs. Deb: 7/26/88																												
1988	StL-N	31	52	2	14	0	0	0	3	4	10	.269	.321	.269	.591	68	-2	-2	104	86	5	.550	4	1	1	1	/S23	0.0
1989	StL-N	42	75	11	22	6	0	0	7	7	8	.293	.361	.373	.735	110	1	1	101	101	10	.673	1	0	0	2	2S/3CO	0.5
Total	2	73	127	13	36	6	0	0	10	11	18	.283	.345	.331	.676	93	-1	-1	102	95	15	.621	5	1	1	3	/S23OC	0.5
■ **RICKY JORDAN** Jordan, Paul Scott b: 5/26/65, Richmond, Cal. BR/TR, 6'5", 210 lbs. Deb: 7/17/88																												
1988	Phi-N	69	273	41	84	15	1	11	43	7	39	.308	.325	.491	.816	130	9	9	101	109	41	.728	1	1	-0	-3	1	0.2
1989	Phi-N	144	523	63	149	22	3	12	75	23	62	.285	.321	.407	.728	106	3	3	101	124	62	.619	4	3	-1	-9	*1	-1.9
Total	2	213	796	104	233	37	4	23	118	30	101	.293	.323	.436	.758	114	13	12	101	119	104	.655	5	4	-1	-13	1	-1.7
■ **TERRY JORGENSEN** Jorgensen, Terry Allen b: 9/2/66, Kewaunee, Wis. BR/TR, 6'4", 208 lbs. Deb: 9/10/89																												
1989	Min-A	10	23	1	4	1	0	0	2	4	5	.174	.296	.217	.514	44	-2	-2	107	155	2	.450	0	0	0	0	/3	0.0
■ **FELIX JOSE** Jose, Domingo Felix b: 5/8/65, Santo Domingo, D.R. BB/TR, 6'1", 190 lbs. Deb: 9/02/88																												
1988	Oak-A	8	6	2	2	1	0	0	1	0	1	.333	.333	.500	.833	137	0	0	95	132	1	1.000	1	0	0	-1	/O	0.0
1989	Oak-A	20	57	3	11	2	0	0	5	4	13	.193	.246	.228	.474	33	-5	-5	103	150	3	.347	0	1	-1	-0	O	-0.5
Total	2	28	63	5	13	3	0	0	6	4	14	.206	.254	.254	.508	42	-5	-5	103	148	4	.396	1	1	-0	-1	/O	-0.5
■ **WALLY JOYNER** Joyner, Wallace Keith b: 6/16/62, Atlanta, Ga. BL/TL, 6'2", 185 lbs. Deb: 4/08/86																												
1986	Cal-A	154	593	82	172	27	3	22	100	57	58	.290	.354	.457	.811	125	16	19	96	125	96	.772	5	2	0	8	*1	1.7
1987	Cal-A	149	564	100	161	33	1	34	117	72	64	.285	.371	.528	.900	137	29	30	99	124	111	.914	8	2	1	-8	*1	0.8
1988	Cal-A	158	597	81	176	31	2	13	85	55	51	.295	.359	.419	.778	124	14	19	94	124	89	.724	8	2	1	13	*1	2.4
1989	Cal-A	159	593	78	167	30	2	16	79	46	58	.282	.340	.420	.759	115	9	11	99	110	82	.686	3	2	-0	-3	*1	-0.2
Total	4	620	2347	341	676	121	8	85	381	230	231	.288	.356	.455	.811	125	69	79	97	121	378	.772	24	8	2	11	1	4.7
■ **ED JURAK** Jurak, Edward James b: 10/24/57, Los Angeles, Cal. BR/TR, 6'2", 185 lbs. Deb: 6/30/82																												
1982	Bos-A	12	21	3	7	0	0	0	7	2	4	.333	.391	.333	.725	92	0	-0	110	400	3	.643	0	0	0	-0	3/O	0.0
1983	Bos-A	75	159	19	44	8	4	0	18	18	25	.277	.354	.377	.731	100	1	1	101	117	21	.661	1	2	-1	0	S13/2D	0.1
1984	Bos-A	47	66	6	16	3	1	1	7	12	12	.242	.359	.364	.723	91	0	-1	110	103	9	.679	0	2	-1	2	12/3S	0.0
1985	Bos-A	26	13	4	3	0	0	0	0	1	3	.231	.286	.231	.516	43	-1	-1	102	0	1	.364	0	0	0	-0	/3S1OD	0.0
1988	Oak-A	3	1	1	0	0	0	0	0	0	0	.000	.000	.000	.000	-99	-0	-0	95	0	0	.000	0	0	0	0	/3D	0.0
1989	SF-N	30	42	2	10	0	0	0	1	5	5	.238	.319	.238	.557	63	-2	-2	97	40	3	.455	0	0	0	-0	/S3201	-0.1
Total	6	193	302	35	80	11	5	1	33	38	49	.265	.349	.344	.693	90	-2	-3	103	117	37	.618	1	4	-2	1	/S312DO	0.0
■ **DAVE JUSTICE** Justice, David Christopher b: 4/14/66, Cincinnati, Ohio BL/TL, 6'3", 195 lbs. Deb: 5/24/89																												
1989	Atl-N	16	51	7	12	3	0	1	3	3	9	.235	.291	.353	.644	81	-1	-1	102	57	5	.585	2	1	0	-2	O	-0.3
■ **RON KARKOVICE** Karkovice, Ronald Joseph b: 8/8/63, Union, N.J. BR/TR, 6'1", 210 lbs. Deb: 8/17/86																												
1986	Chi-A	37	97	13	24	7	0	4	13	9	37	.247	.318	.443	.761	105	1	0	101	94	13	.711	1	0	0	1	C	0.4
1987	Chi-A	39	85	7	6	0	0	2	7	7	40	.071	.160	.141	.301	-17	-15	-16	109	155	2	.296	3	0	1	4	C/D	-0.6
1988	Chi-A	46	115	10	20	4	0	3	9	7	30	.174	.228	.287	.515	44	-9	-9	97	85	8	.459	4	2	0	2	C	-0.4
1989	Chi-A	71	182	21	48	9	2	3	24	10	56	.264	.309	.385	.694	102	-2	-0	93	118	23	.612	0	0	0	5	C/D	0.8
Total	4	193	479	51	98	20	2	12	53	33	163	.205	.264	.330	.594	64	-25	-24	98	112	46	.527	8	2	1	12	C/D	0.2
■ **PAT KEEDY** Keedy, Charles Patrick b: 1/40/58, Birmingham, Ala. BR/TR, 6'4", 205 lbs. Deb: 9/10/85																												
1985	Cal-A	3	4	1	2	1	0	1	1	0	0	.500	.500	1.500	2.000	418	2	2	101	44	2	2.000	0	1	-1	-0	/3O	0.1
1987	Chi-A	17	41	6	7	1	0	2	2	2	14	.171	.209	.341	.551	40	-3	-4	109	40	3	.500	1	0	0	-0	3/12SOD	-0.3
1989	Cle-A	9	14	3	3	2	0	0	1	2	5	.214	.313	.357	.670	85	-0	-0	104	78	2	.636	0	0	0	-1	/O31SD	0.0
Total	3	29	59	10	12	4	0	3	4	4	19	.203	.254	.424	.678	74	-2	-3	107	50	6	.625	1	1	-0	-1	/3O1DS2	-0.2
■ **ROBERTO KELLY** Kelly, Roberto Conrado (Gray) b: 10/1/64, Panama City, Pan. BR/TR, 6'2", 180 lbs. Deb: 7/29/87																												
1987	NY-A	23	52	12	14	3	0	1	7	5	15	.269	.333	.385	.718	93	-1	-0	98	121	7	.829	9	3	1	1	O/D	0.0
1988	NY-A	38	77	9	19	4	1	1	7	3	15	.247	.275	.364	.639	81	-3	-2	96	90	8	.600	5	2	0	1	O/D	-0.1
1989	NY-A	137	441	65	133	18	3	9	48	41	89	.302	.369	.417	.786	116	13	11	104	88	70	.809	35	12	3	2	*O	1.4
Total	3	198	570	86	166	25	4	11	62	49	119	.291	.354	.407	.761	110	10	8	103	92	85	.781	49	17	5	4	O/D	1.3

YEAR	TM/L	G	AB	R	H	2B	3B	HR	RBI	BB	SO	AVG	OBP	SLG	PRO	/A	BR	/A	PF	CHI	RC	TA	SB	CS	SBR	FR	POS	TPR
■ TERRY KENNEDY	Kennedy, Terrence Edward b: 6/4/56, Euclid, Ohio BL/TR, 6'3", 220 lbs. Deb: 9/04/78																											
1978	StL-N	10	29	0	5	0	0	0	2	4	3	.172	.273	.172	.445	28	-3	-3	95	159	1	.346	0	0	0	1	C	-0.1
1979	StL-N	33	109	11	31	7	0	2	17	6	20	.284	.322	.404	.725	92	-1	-1	105	135	14	.625	0	0	0	-1	C	0.0
1980	StL-N	84	248	28	63	12	3	4	34	28	34	.254	.330	.375	.705	94	-1	-2	103	128	30	.624	0	0	0	0	CO	-0.1
1981	SD-N	101	382	32	115	24	1	2	41	22	53	.301	.342	.385	.727	114	3	6	93	107	49	.620	0	2	-1	6	*C	1.2
1982	SD-N	153	562	75	166	42	1	21	97	26	91	.295	.332	.486	.818	137	17	22	92	116	90	.757	1	0	0	-5	*C1	1.9
1983	SD-N	149	549	47	156	27	2	17	98	51	89	.284	.347	.434	.781	116	11	11	99	**142**	81	.719	1	3	-2	3	*C/1	1.7
1984	SD-N	148	530	54	127	16	1	14	57	33	99	.240	.287	.353	.640	80	-16	-15	99	100	50	.530	1	2	-1	-6	*C	-1.8
1985	SD-N	143	532	54	139	27	1	10	74	31	102	.261	.302	.372	.674	86	-10	-11	102	132	55	.556	0	0	0	9	*C/1	0.3
1986	SD-N	141	432	46	114	22	1	12	57	37	74	.264	.325	.403	.728	104	-1	2	95	108	54	.644	0	3	-2	2	*C	0.5
1987	Bal-A	143	512	51	128	13	1	18	62	35	112	.250	.299	.385	.684	82	-15	-13	98	101	57	.589	1	0	0	17	*C	1.4
1988	Bal-A	85	265	20	60	10	0	3	16	15	53	.226	.270	.298	.569	62	-15	-13	95	72	19	.436	0	0	0	8	C	-0.1
1989	SF-N	125	355	19	85	15	0	5	34	35	56	.239	.308	.324	.632	83	-9	-7	97	105	35	.541	1	3	-2	-15	*C/1	-1.6
Total	12	1315	4505	437	1189	215	11	108	589	323	786	.264	.315	.388	.704	97	-39	-25	97	114	534	.608	5	13	-6	18	*C/O1	3.3
■ STEVE KIEFER	Kiefer, Steven George b: 10/18/60, Chicago, Ill. BR/TR, 6'1", 175 lbs. Deb: 9/03/84																											
1984	Oak-A	23	40	7	7	1	2	0	2	2	10	.175	.214	.300	.514	44	-3	-3	92	66	3	.471	2	1	0	-1	S/3D	-0.1
1985	Oak-A	40	66	8	13	1	1	1	10	1	18	.197	.209	.288	.497	37	-6	-5	93	180	4	.370	0	0	0	-2	3/D	-0.8
1986	Mil-A	2	6	0	0	0	0	0	0	0	4	.000	.000	.000	.000	-98	-2	-2	102	0	0	.000	0	0	0	-1	/S	-0.1
1987	Mil-A	28	99	17	20	4	0	5	17	7	28	.202	.262	.394	.656	70	-4	-5	102	128	10	.573	0	0	0	-2	3/2	-0.6
1988	Mil-A	7	10	2	3	1	0	1	1	2	3	.300	.462	.700	1.162	213	2	2	103	40	4	1.429	0	0	0	0	/23	0.2
1989	NY-A	5	8	0	1	0	0	0	0	0	5	.125	.125	.125	.250	-28	-1	-1	104	0	0	.143	0	0	0	0	/3	-0.1
Total	6	105	229	34	44	7	3	7	30	12	68	.192	.239	.341	.579	56	-15	-14	98	120	20	.495	2	1	0	-6	/3S2D	-1.5
■ JEFF KING	King, Jeffrey Wayne b: 12/26/64, Marion, Ind. BR/TR, 6'1", 175 lbs. Deb: 6/02/89																											
1989	Pit-N	75	215	31	42	13	3	5	19	20	34	.195	.270	.353	.624	82	-7	-5	94	84	21	.573	4	2	0	-1	13/2S	-1.0
■ MIKE KINGERY	Kingery, Michael Scott b: 3/29/61, St.James, Minn. BL/TL, 6', 180 lbs. Deb: 7/07/86																											
1986	KC-A	62	209	25	54	8	5	3	14	12	30	.258	.299	.388	.686	86	-4	-4	100	62	23	.617	7	3	0	-1	O	-0.6
1987	Sea-A	120	354	38	99	25	4	9	52	27	43	.280	.334	.449	.783	104	3	2	103	112	51	.728	7	9	-3	9	*O/D	0.4
1988	Sea-A	57	123	21	25	6	0	1	9	19	23	.203	.315	.276	.591	62	-5	-6	108	97	12	.570	3	1	0	0	O1	-0.6
1989	Sea-A	31	76	14	17	3	0	2	6	7	14	.224	.289	.342	.631	75	-2	-3	103	73	7	.548	1	1	-0	4	O	0.0
Total	4	270	762	98	195	42	9	15	81	65	110	.256	.317	.394	.711	89	-9	-12	103	92	94	.652	18	14	-3	11	O/1D	-0.8
■ RON KITTLE	Kittle, Ronald Dale b: 1/5/58, Gary, Indiana BR/TR, 6'4", 200 lbs. Deb: 9/02/82																											
1982	Chi-A	20	29	3	7	2	0	1	7	3	12	.241	.313	.414	.726	100	-0	-0	97	187	4	.682	0	0	0	-2	/OD	-0.1
1983	Chi-A	145	520	75	132	19	3	35	100	39	150	.254	.316	.504	.820	118	13	11	103	109	81	.791	8	3	1	-13	*O/D	-0.2
1984	Chi-A	139	466	67	100	15	0	32	74	49	137	.215	.298	.453	.750	94	1	-5	111	96	62	.710	3	6	-3	-1	*O/D	-1.2
1985	Chi-A	116	379	51	87	12	0	26	58	31	92	.230	.296	.467	.763	105	1	1	100	90	48	.695	1	4	-2	-5	OD	-0.6
1986	Chi-A	86	296	34	63	11	0	17	48	28	87	.213	.287	.422	.710	90	-4	-5	101	111	34	.648	2	1	0	1	DO	-0.4
	NY-A	30	80	8	19	2	0	4	12	7	23	.237	.299	.412	.711	89	-1	-1	103	106	11	.689	2	0	1	0	D/O	0.0
	Yr	116	376	42	82	13	0	21	60	35	110	.218	.290	.420	.710	90	-5	-6	101	110	45	.656	4	1	1	1		-0.4
1987	NY-A	59	159	21	44	5	0	12	28	10	36	.277	.324	.535	.858	126	5	5	98	92	26	.800	0	1	-1	1	D/O	0.5
1988	Cle-A	75	225	31	58	8	0	18	43	16	65	.258	.329	.533	.863	135	10	10	102	98	42	.862	0	0	0	0	D	1.0
1989	Chi-A	51	169	26	51	10	0	11	37	22	42	.302	.385	.556	.942	175	14	15	93	115	37	.967	0	1	-1	-1	1D/O	1.1
Total	8	721	2323	316	561	84	3	156	407	205	644	.241	.312	.482	.793	112	39	31	102	103	344	.753	16	16	-5	-21	OD/1	0.1
■ BRAD KOMMINSK	Komminsk, Brad Lynn b: 4/4/61, Lima, Ohio BR/TR, 6'2", 202 lbs. Deb: 9/28/83																											
1983	Atl-N	19	36	2	8	2	0	0	4	5	7	.222	.317	.278	.595	63	-2	-2	106	158	3	.517	0	0	0	-1	O	-0.3
1984	Atl-N	90	301	37	61	10	0	8	36	29	77	.203	.277	.316	.593	60	-14	-17	110	119	27	.569	18	8	1	-5	O	-2.5
1985	Atl-N	106	300	52	68	12	3	4	21	38	71	.227	.316	.327	.642	75	-8	-10	106	76	32	.602	10	8	-2	-8	O	-2.2
1986	Atl-N	5	5	1	2	0	0	0	1	0	1	.400	.400	.400	.800	119	0	0	102	199	0	.500	0	1	-1	-1	/3O	0.0
1987	Mil-A	7	15	0	1	0	0	0	0	1	7	.067	.125	.067	.192	-46	-3	-3	102	0	0	.214	1	0	0	0	/OD	-0.2
1989	Cle-A	71	198	27	47	8	2	8	33	24	55	.237	.323	.419	.742	104	2	1	104	120	28	.739	8	2	1	1	O	0.2
Total	6	298	855	119	187	32	5	20	95	97	218	.219	.301	.338	.639	74	-24	-31	107	104	91	.609	37	19	-0	-14	O/3D	-5.0
■ CHAD KREUTER	Kreuter, Chad Michael b: 8/26/64, Greenbrae, Cal. BB/TR, 6'2", 190 lbs. Deb: 9/14/88																											
1988	Tex-A	16	51	3	14	2	1	1	5	7	13	.275	.362	.412	.774	115	1	1	101	83	8	.737	0	0	0	-2	C	0.0
1989	Tex-A	87	158	16	24	3	0	5	9	27	40	.152	.276	.266	.541	52	-10	-10	102	61	13	.496	0	1	-1	-27	C	-3.5
Total	2	103	209	19	38	5	1	6	14	34	53	.182	.296	.301	.598	67	-8	-9	102	66	20	.548	0	1	-1	-29	C	-3.5
■ JOHN KRUK	Kruk, John Martin b: 2/9/61, Charleston, W.Va. BL/TL, 5'10", 170 lbs. Deb: 4/07/86																											
1986	SD-N	122	278	33	86	16	2	4	38	45	58	.309	.406	.424	.830	136	13	15	95	117	47	.797	2	4	-2	-6	O/1	0.5
1987	SD-N	138	447	72	140	14	2	20	91	73	93	.313	.410	.488	.897	141	26	28	97	133	92	.957	18	10	-1	-0	*1O	2.0
1988	SD-N	120	378	54	91	17	1	9	44	80	68	.241	.373	.362	.736	115	9	11	97	109	56	.747	5	3	-0	-0	1O	0.6
1989	SD-N	31	76	7	14	0	0	3	6	17	14	.184	.333	.303	.636	83	-1	-1	101	75	8	.597	0	0	0	0	O	0.0
	Phi-N	81	281	46	93	13	6	5	38	27	39	.331	.390	.473	.863	144	17	16	101	105	53	.845	3	0	1	-3	O/1	1.3
	Yr	112	357	53	107	13	6	8	44	44	53	.300	.377	.437	.814	131	16	15	101	98	59	.781	3	0	1	-3		1.3
Total	4	492	1460	212	424	60	11	41	217	242	272	.290	.391	.431	.822	131	63	68	98	115	255	.827	28	17	-2	-10	O1	4.4
■ JEFF KUNKEL	Kunkel, Jeffrey William b: 3/25/62, W.Palm Beach, Fla. BR/TR, 6'2", 180 lbs. Deb: 7/23/84																											
1984	Tex-A	50	142	13	29	2	3	3	7	2	35	.204	.221	.324	.545	48	-10	-10	100	51	9	.449	4	3	-1	-4	S/D	-1.0
1985	Tex-A	2	4	1	1	0	0	0	0	0	3	.250	.250	.250	.500	35	-0	-0	108	0	0	.333	0	0	0	0	/S	0.0
1986	Tex-A	8	13	3	3	0	0	1	2	0	2	.231	.231	.462	.692	87	-0	-0	96	88	1	.600	0	0	0	0	/SD	0.0
1987	Tex-A	15	32	1	7	0	0	1	2	0	10	.219	.242	.313	.555	45	-2	-3	104	61	2	.423	0	1	-1	-1	2/3O1SD	-0.3
1988	Tex-A	55	154	14	35	8	3	2	15	4	35	.227	.252	.357	.609	68	-7	-7	101	96	12	.480	0	1	-1	-3	2S/3OPD	-0.7
1989	Tex-A	108	293	39	79	21	2	8	29	20	75	.270	.323	.437	.760	110	4	3	102	74	41	.694	3	2	-0	-7	SO/23PD	0.0
Total	6	238	638	71	154	31	8	15	55	26	160	.241	.278	.386	.663	82	-16	-18	102	73	66	.565	7	7	-2	-15	S/2O3DP1	-2.0
■ RANDY KUTCHER	Kutcher, Randy Scott b: 4/20/60, Anchorage, Alaska BR/TR, 5'11", 170 lbs. Deb: 6/19/86																											
1986	SF-N	71	186	28	44	9	1	7	16	11	41	.237	.279	.409	.688	91	-4	-3	96	66	20	.620	6	5	-1	3	OS/32	-0.1
1987	SF-N	14	16	7	3	1	1	0	1	1	5	.188	.235	.375	.610	61	-1	-1	96	66	2	.615	1	0	0	-1	/O23S	0.0
1988	Bos-A	19	12	2	2	1	0	0	0	0	2	.167	.167	.250	.417	14	-1	-1	109	0	0	.273	0	1	-1	-1	/O3D	-0.2
1989	Bos-A	77	160	28	36	10	3	2	18	11	46	.225	.275	.363	.637	75	-5	-6	105	109	15	.558	3	0	1	-4	O/3CD	-0.9
Total	4	181	374	65	85	21	5	9	35	23	94	.227	.272	.382	.654	80	-11	-11	100	83	37	.581	10	6	-1	-3	O/3SD2C	-1.2
■ MIKE LAGA	Laga, Michael Russell b: 6/14/60, Ridgewood, N.J. BL/TL, 6'2", 210 lbs. Deb: 9/01/82																											
1982	Det-A	27	88	6	23	9	0	3	11	4	23	.261	.293	.466	.759	104	0	0	100	88	12	.697	1	0	0	0	1/D	0.0
1983	Det-A	12	21	2	4	0	0	0	2	1	9	.190	.227	.190	.418	17	-2	-2	96	195	1	.278	0	0	0	0	/1D	-0.1
1984	Det-A	9	11	1	6	0	0	0	1	1	2	.545	.583	.545	1.129	223	2	2	96	66	4	1.400	0	0	0	0	/1D	0.2
1985	Det-A	9	36	3	6	1	0	2	6	0	9	.167	.167	.361	.528	37	-3	-3	106	128	2	.419	0	0	0	0	/1D	-0.2
1986	Det-A	15	45	6	9	1	0	3	8	5	13	.200	.280	.422	.702	93	-1	-1	95	114	6	.667	0	0	0	1	1/D	0.0
	StL-N	18	46	7	10	4	0	3	8	5	18	.217	.308	.500	.808	115	1	1	103	100	7	.784	0	0	0	-0	1	0.0
1987	StL-N	17	29	4	4	1	0	1	4	2	7	.138	.194	.276	.469	23	-3	-3	99	145	1	.385	0	0	0	-0	1	-0.3
1988	StL-N	41	100	5	13	0	0	1	4	2	21	.130	.147	.160	.307	-11	-14	-15	104	84	2	.207	0	0	0	-0	1	-1.8
1989	SF-N	17	20	1	4	1	0	1	7	1	6	.200	.238	.400	.638	82	-1	-1	97	256	2	.563	0	0	0	0	/1	0.0
Total	8	165	396	35	79	17	0	14	51	21	108	.199	.242	.348	.590	61	-22	-22	101	113	37	.500	1	0	0	1	1/D	-2.2
■ STEVE LAKE	Lake, Steven Michael b: 3/14/57, Inglewood, Cal. BR/TR, 6'1", 180 lbs. Deb: 4/09/83																											
1983	Chi-N	38	85	9	22	4	1	1	7	2	6	.259	.284	.365	.649	78	-3	-3	101	81	7	.507	0	0	0	0	C	-0.1

YEAR	TM/L	G	AB	R	H	2B	3B	HR	RBI	BB	SO	AVG	OBP	SLG	PRO	/A	BR	/A	PF	CHI	RC	TA	SB	CS	SBR	FR	POS	TPR
1984	Chi-N	25	54	4	12	4	0	2	7	0	7	.222	.236	.407	.644	71	-2	-3	110	98	5	.548	0	0	0	1	C	0.0
1985	Chi-N	58	119	5	18	2	0	1	11	3	21	.151	.179	.193	.372	3	-15	-17	116	169	4	.269	1	0	0	1	C	-1.4
1986	Chi-N	10	19	4	8	1	0	0	4	1	2	.421	.450	.474	.924	145	1	1	107	177	4	.833	0	0	0	1	C	0.2
	StL-N	26	49	4	12	1	0	2	10	2	5	.245	.275	.388	.662	78	-1	-2	103	159	5	.538	0	0	0	-1	C	-0.1
	Yr	36	68	8	20	2	0	2	14	3	7	.294	.324	.412	.736	98	-0	-0	104	169	8	.608	0	0	0	-0		0.1
1987	StL-N	74	179	19	45	7	2	2	19	10	18	.251	.291	.346	.637	69	-8	-8	99	111	18	.529	0	0	0	-3	C	-0.6
1988	StL-N	36	54	5	15	3	0	1	4	3	15	.278	.339	.389	.728	104	1	0	104	67	8	.667	0	0	0	0	C	0.2
1989	Phi-N	58	155	9	39	5	1	2	14	12	20	.252	.305	.335	.641	82	-3	-4	101	97	15	.525	0	0	0	2	C	0.3
Total	7	325	714	59	171	27	4	11	76	33	94	.239	.278	.335	.613	66	-31	-34	104	115	65	.496	1	0	0	1	C	-1.5

■ **CARNEY LANSFORD** Lansford, Carney Ray b: 2/7/57, San Jose, Cal. BR/TR, 6'2", 195 lbs. Deb: 4/08/78

YEAR	TM/L	G	AB	R	H	2B	3B	HR	RBI	BB	SO	AVG	OBP	SLG	PRO	/A	BR	/A	PF	CHI	RC	TA	SB	CS	SBR	FR	POS	TPR
1978	Cal-A	121	453	63	133	23	2	8	52	31	67	.294	.344	.406	.750	109	6	5	102	101	65	.718	20	9	1	-25	*3/SD	-2.0
1979	Cal-A	157	654	114	188	30	5	19	79	39	115	.287	.330	.436	.766	113	3	10	93	85	91	.708	20	8	1	-24	*3	-1.0
1980	Cal-A	151	602	87	157	27	3	15	80	50	93	.261	.317	.390	.708	97	-7	-3	96	107	75	.647	14	5	1	-25	*3	-2.7
1981	Bos-A	102	399	61	134	23	3	4	52	34	28	**.336**	.391	.439	.829	131	20	17	106	115	68	.804	15	10	-2	1	3D	1.7
1982	Bos-A	128	482	65	145	28	4	11	63	46	48	.301	.364	.444	.808	109	14	7	110	108	76	.761	9	4	0	-0	*3D	0.5
1983	Oak-A	80	299	43	92	16	2	10	45	22	33	.308	.361	.475	.836	134	11	13	96	104	47	.762	3	8	-4	-6	3/S	0.2
1984	Oak-A	151	597	70	179	31	5	14	74	40	62	.300	.347	.439	.786	127	12	18	92	103	90	.725	9	3	1	-3	*3	1.8
1985	Oak-A	98	401	51	111	18	2	13	46	18	27	.277	.314	.429	.743	109	-0	3	93	83	53	.656	2	3	-1	-14	3	-1.4
1986	Oak-A	151	591	80	168	16	4	19	72	39	51	.284	.334	.421	.755	112	4	9	94	99	80	.693	16	7	1	-15	*31/2D	-1.2
1987	Oak-A	151	554	89	160	27	4	19	76	60	44	.289	.368	.455	.822	129	15	22	91	104	96	.847	27	8	3	0	*31/D	2.0
1988	Oak-A	150	556	80	155	20	2	7	57	35	35	.279	.329	.360	.689	98	-5	-2	95	105	65	.636	29	8	4	-12	*3/12D	-0.9
1989	Oak-A	148	551	81	185	28	2	2	52	51	25	.336	.401	.405	.806	123	22	20	103	94	88	.796	37	15	2	-26	*31/D	-0.4
Total	12	1588	6139	884	1807	287	38	141	748	465	628	.294	.349	.422	.771	115	95	120	97	100	892	.726	201	88	8	-151	*31/DS2	-3.4

■ **BARRY LARKIN** Larkin, Barry Louis b: 4/28/64, Cincinnati, Ohio BR/TR, 6', 185 lbs. Deb: 8/13/86

YEAR	TM/L	G	AB	R	H	2B	3B	HR	RBI	BB	SO	AVG	OBP	SLG	PRO	/A	BR	/A	PF	CHI	RC	TA	SB	CS	SBR	FR	POS	TPR
1986	Cin-N	41	159	27	45	4	3	3	19	9	21	.283	.321	.403	.724	94	-1	-1	104	106	22	.698	8	0	2	-1	S/2	0.3
1987	Cin-N	125	439	64	107	16	2	12	43	36	52	.244	.308	.371	.680	76	-14	-16	104	88	52	.650	21	6	3	-12	*S	-1.0
1988	Cin-N	151	588	91	174	32	5	12	56	41	24	.296	.350	.429	.779	116	16	13	105	75	94	.797	40	7	8	14	*S	4.8
1989	Cin-N	97	325	47	111	14	4	4	36	20	23	.342	.383	.446	.829	132	15	14	103	92	54	.783	10	5	0	5	S	2.5
Total	4	414	1511	229	437	66	14	31	154	106	120	.289	.342	.413	.755	105	17	10	104	85	221	.738	79	18	13	6	S/2	6.6

■ **GENE LARKIN** Larkin, Eugene Thomas b: 10/24/62, Flushing, N.Y. BB/TR, 6'3", 195 lbs. Deb: 5/21/87

YEAR	TM/L	G	AB	R	H	2B	3B	HR	RBI	BB	SO	AVG	OBP	SLG	PRO	/A	BR	/A	PF	CHI	RC	TA	SB	CS	SBR	FR	POS	TPR
1987	Min-A	85	233	23	62	11	2	4	28	25	31	.266	.342	.382	.724	97	-2	-1	96	111	30	.654	1	4	-2	-1	D1	-0.6
1988	Min-A	149	505	56	135	30	2	8	70	68	55	.267	.371	.382	.753	105	10	6	106	131	75	.727	3	2	-0	-4	D1	0.0
1989	Min-A	136	446	61	119	25	1	6	46	54	57	.267	.358	.368	.725	98	5	1	107	100	60	.678	5	2	0	-5	1DO	-0.8
Total	3	370	1184	140	316	66	5	18	144	147	143	.267	.360	.377	.737	101	13	6	104	115	165	.694	9	8	-2	-10	D1/O	-1.4

■ **TIM LAUDNER** Laudner, Timothy Jon b: 6/7/58, Mason City, Iowa BR/TR, 6'3", 212 lbs. Deb: 8/28/81

YEAR	TM/L	G	AB	R	H	2B	3B	HR	RBI	BB	SO	AVG	OBP	SLG	PRO	/A	BR	/A	PF	CHI	RC	TA	SB	CS	SBR	FR	POS	TPR
1981	Min-A	14	43	4	7	2	0	2	5	3	17	.163	.234	.349	.583	63	-2	-2	105	93	4	.528	0	0	0	1	C/D	0.0
1982	Min-A	93	306	37	78	19	1	7	33	34	74	.255	.329	.392	.722	97	-1	-1	100	94	39	.653	0	2	-1	3	C	0.5
1983	Min-A	62	168	20	31	9	0	6	18	15	49	.185	.251	.345	.597	59	-9	-10	105	93	15	.525	0	0	0	3	C/D	-0.4
1984	Min-A	87	262	31	54	16	1	10	35	18	78	.206	.260	.389	.649	73	-9	-11	106	106	26	.571	0	0	0	4	C/D	-0.2
1985	Min-A	72	164	16	39	5	0	7	19	12	45	.238	.294	.396	.690	84	-3	-4	103	88	19	.609	0	1	-1	-4	C/1	-0.4
1986	Min-A	76	193	21	47	10	0	10	29	24	56	.244	.336	.451	.787	104	4	1	108	99	30	.762	1	0	0	-4	C	0.2
1987	Min-A	113	288	30	55	7	1	16	43	23	80	.191	.253	.389	.642	71	-14	-13	96	107	29	.578	1	0	0	-9	*C/1D	-1.3
1988	Min-A	117	375	38	94	18	1	13	54	36	89	.251	.318	.408	.726	96	0	-3	106	112	46	.644	0	0	0	1	*C1/D	0.1
1989	Min-A	100	239	24	53	11	1	6	27	25	65	.222	.295	.351	.647	77	-6	-8	107	103	25	.570	1	0	0	-7	CD1	-1.2
Total	9	734	2038	221	458	97	5	77	263	190	553	.225	.293	.391	.684	84	-41	-50	104	101	233	.613	3	3	-1	-13	C/1D	-2.7

■ **MIKE LaVALLIERE** LaValliere, Michael Eugene b: 8/18/60, Charlotte, N.C. BL/TR, 5'10", 180 lbs. Deb: 9/09/84

YEAR	TM/L	G	AB	R	H	2B	3B	HR	RBI	BB	SO	AVG	OBP	SLG	PRO	/A	BR	/A	PF	CHI	RC	TA	SB	CS	SBR	FR	POS	TPR
1984	Phi-N	6	7	0	0	0	0	0	0	2	2	.000	.222	.000	.222	-32	-1	-1	102	0	0	.286	0	0	0	-0	/C	0.0
1985	StL-N	12	34	2	5	1	0	0	6	7	3	.147	.293	.176	.469	36	-3	-3	96	398	2	.419	0	0	0	-1	C	-0.3
1986	StL-N	110	303	18	71	10	2	3	30	36	37	.234	.318	.310	.628	72	-10	-11	103	116	31	.546	0	1	-1	-6	*C	-1.5
1987	Pit-N	121	340	33	102	19	0	1	36	43	32	.300	.380	.365	.745	95	1	-1	104	113	50	.694	0	0	0	-3	*C	0.5
1988	Pit-N	120	352	24	92	18	0	2	47	50	34	.261	.356	.330	.686	100	1	2	98	154	43	.633	3	2	-0	3	*C	1.1
1989	Pit-N	68	190	15	60	10	0	2	23	29	24	.316	.406	.400	.806	140	9	11	94	113	31	.772	0	2	-1	-3	C	1.1
Total	6	437	1226	92	330	58	2	8	142	167	132	.269	.359	.339	.698	95	-3	-3	100	133	157	.637	3	5	-2	-10	C	0.9

■ **VANCE LAW** Law, Vance Aaron b: 10/1/56, Boise, Idaho BR/TR, 6'2", 185 lbs. Deb: 6/01/80

YEAR	TM/L	G	AB	R	H	2B	3B	HR	RBI	BB	SO	AVG	OBP	SLG	PRO	/A	BR	/A	PF	CHI	RC	TA	SB	CS	SBR	FR	POS	TPR
1980	Pit-N	25	74	11	17	2	2	0	3	3	7	.230	.260	.311	.571	57	-4	-4	103	52	6	.475	2	0	1	1	2/S3	-0.1
1981	Pit-N	30	67	1	9	0	1	0	3	2	15	.134	.159	.164	.324	-8	-9	-9	96	107	1	.230	1	1	-0	-0	2/S3	-0.7
1982	Chi-A	114	359	40	101	20	1	5	54	26	46	.281	.332	.384	.716	99	-2	-1	97	141	45	.626	4	2	0	9	S32/O	1.5
1983	Chi-A	145	408	55	99	21	5	4	42	51	56	.243	.328	.348	.676	84	-7	-8	103	107	49	.621	3	1	0	10	*3/2SOD	0.2
1984	Chi-A	151	481	60	121	18	2	17	59	41	75	.252	.312	.403	.715	87	-3	-10	111	96	59	.642	4	1	1	-12	*32/OS	-1.7
1985	Mon-N	147	519	75	138	30	6	10	52	86	96	.266	.372	.405	.777	125	14	19	94	91	82	.766	6	5	-1	2	*213/O	2.1
1986	Mon-N	112	360	37	81	17	2	5	44	37	66	.225	.299	.325	.624	74	-14	-13	98	133	34	.539	3	5	-2	13	213/PO	0.0
1987	Mon-N	133	436	52	119	27	1	12	56	51	62	.273	.349	.422	.771	97	2	-1	106	102	65	.736	8	5	-1	-4	*231/P	-0.4
1988	Chi-N	151	556	73	163	29	2	11	78	55	79	.293	.360	.412	.772	116	16	13	104	121	80	.699	1	4	-2	-10	*3/O	0.1
1989	Chi-N	130	408	38	96	22	3	7	42	38	73	.235	.300	.355	.656	80	-7	-11	108	102	43	.569	2	2	-1	-22	*3/O	-3.7
Total	10	1138	3668	442	944	186	25	71	433	390	575	.257	.330	.380	.710	94	-14	-26	103	109	465	.643	34	26	-5	-12	32S/1OPD	-2.7

■ **TOM LAWLESS** Lawless, Thomas James b: 12/19/56, Erie, Pa. BR/TR, 5'11", 170 lbs. Deb: 7/15/82

YEAR	TM/L	G	AB	R	H	2B	3B	HR	RBI	BB	SO	AVG	OBP	SLG	PRO	/A	BR	/A	PF	CHI	RC	TA	SB	CS	SBR	FR	POS	TPR
1982	Cin-N	49	165	19	35	6	0	0	4	9	30	.212	.253	.248	.501	40	-13	-13	102	38	10	.471	16	5	2	3	2	-0.6
1984	Cin-N	43	80	10	20	2	0	1	2	8	12	.250	.318	.313	.631	74	-2	-3	106	28	8	.609	6	3	0	-2	2/3	-0.3
	Mon-N	11	17	1	3	1	0	0	0	0	4	.176	.176	.235	.412	16	-2	-2	91	0	0	.294	1	0	0	-1	/2	-0.1
	Yr	54	97	11	23	3	0	1	2	8	16	.237	.295	.299	.594	66	-4	-4	103	23	8	.543	7	3	0	-2		-0.4
1985	StL-N	47	58	8	12	3	1	0	8	5	4	.207	.270	.293	.563	60	-3	-3	96	187	5	.511	2	1	0	1	32	-0.1
1986	StL-N	46	39	5	11	1	0	0	3	2	8	.282	.317	.308	.625	71	-1	-2	103	100	5	.759	8	1	2	1	3/2O	0.1
1987	StL-N	19	25	5	2	1	0	0	0	3	5	.080	.179	.120	.299	-19	-4	-4	99	0	1	.333	2	0	1	-1	/23O	-0.3
1988	StL-N	54	65	9	10	2	1	1	3	7	9	.154	.236	.262	.498	41	-5	-5	104	60	5	.536	6	0	2	0	3/O21	-0.2
1989	Tor-A	59	70	20	16	1	0	0	3	7	12	.229	.299	.243	.542	58	-4	-3	94	69	7	.655	12	1	3	-4	O3D/2C	-0.4
Total	7	328	519	77	109	17	2	2	23	41	84	.210	.268	.262	.530	49	-35	-35	101	62	42	.532	53	11	9	-2	2/3ODC1	-1.9

■ **MARCUS LAWTON** Lawton, Marcus Dwayne b: 8/18/65, Gulfport, Miss. BB/TR, 6'1", 160 lbs. Deb: 8/11/89

YEAR	TM/L	G	AB	R	H	2B	3B	HR	RBI	BB	SO	AVG	OBP	SLG	PRO	/A	BR	/A	PF	CHI	RC	TA	SB	CS	SBR	FR	POS	TPR
1989	NY-A	10	14	1	3	0	0	0	0	0	3	.214	.214	.214	.429	20	-1	-2	104	0	1	.333	1	0	0	-2	/OD	-0.3

■ **RICK LEACH** Leach, Richard Max b: 5/4/57, Ann Arbor, Mich. BL/TL, 6'1", 180 lbs. Deb: 4/30/81

YEAR	TM/L	G	AB	R	H	2B	3B	HR	RBI	BB	SO	AVG	OBP	SLG	PRO	/A	BR	/A	PF	CHI	RC	TA	SB	CS	SBR	FR	POS	TPR
1981	Det-A	54	83	9	16	3	1	1	11	16	15	.193	.323	.289	.612	74	-2	-2	105	159	7	.548	0	1	-1	-4	1O/D	-0.8
1982	Det-A	82	218	23	52	7	2	3	12	21	29	.239	.305	.330	.636	74	-7	-8	100	59	24	.577	4	0	1	-1	1O/D	-0.9
1983	Det-A	99	242	22	60	17	0	3	26	19	21	.248	.305	.355	.661	85	-6	-5	96	107	25	.568	2	2	-1	2	1O/D	-0.6
1984	Tor-A	65	88	11	23	6	2	0	7	8	14	.261	.323	.375	.698	91	-1	-1	102	85	10	.603	0	0	0	-5	O1/PD	-0.7
1985	Tor-A	16	35	2	7	0	1	0	1	3	9	.200	.263	.257	.520	43	-3	-3	101	44	3	.429	0	0	0	-0	1/O	-0.3
1986	Tor-A	110	246	35	76	14	1	5	39	13	24	.309	.344	.435	.779	106	4	2	105	127	35	.682	0	0	0	-8	DO/1	-0.7
1987	Tor-A	98	195	26	55	13	1	3	25	25	25	.282	.372	.405	.777	106	3	3	101	113	30	.743	0	1	-1	-7	OD/1	-0.6
1988	Tor-A	87	199	21	55	13	1	0	23	18	27	.276	.336	.352	.688	93	-2	-1	100	131	22	.575	0	1	-1	-6	OD/1	-0.9
1989	Tex-A	110	239	32	65	14	1	1	23	32	33	.272	.360	.351	.712	99	1	1	102	103	31	.654	2	1	0	-5	DO/1	-0.5
Total	9	721	1545	181	409	87	10	16	167	155	197	.265	.334	.365	.699	92	-13	-15	101	107	188	.619	8	6	-1	-37	O1D/P	-6.0

YEAR	TM/L	G	AB	R	H	2B	3B	HR	RBI	BB	SO	AVG	OBP	SLG	PRO	/A	BR	/A	PF	CHI	RC	TA	SB	CS	SBR	FR	POS	TPR
■ **MANNY LEE**	Lee, Manuel Lora (born Manuel Lora (Lee)) b: 6/17/65, San Pedro De Macoris, D.R. BB/TR, 5'10", 145 lbs. Deb: 4/10/85																											
1985	Tor-A	64	40	9	8	0	0	0	0	2	9	.200	.238	.200	.438	21	-4	-4	101	0	1	.289	1	4	-2	-1	2/S3D	-0.4
1986	Tor-A	35	78	8	16	0	1	1	7	4	10	.205	.244	.269	.513	38	-6	-7	105	116	4	.368	0	1	-1	-1	2/S/3	-0.6
1987	Tor-A	56	121	14	31	2	3	1	11	6	13	.256	.291	.347	.638	69	-5	-5	101	98	13	.549	2	0	1	-1	2S/D	-0.1
1988	Tor-A	117	381	38	111	16	3	2	38	26	64	.291	.337	.365	.701	97	-2	-2	100	104	44	.587	3	3	-1	-3	2S/3	0.1
1989	Tor-A	99	300	27	78	9	2	3	34	20	60	.260	.306	.333	.640	85	-8	-6	94	121	30	.534	4	2	0	-1	2S3D/O	-0.3
Total	5	371	920	96	244	27	9	7	90	58	156	.265	.309	.337	.646	81	-26	-24	98	105	91	.529	10	10	-3	-6	2/S3DO	-1.3
■ **MARK LEMKE**	Lemke, Mark Alan b: 8/13/65, Utica, N.Y. BB/TR, 5'10", 167 lbs. Deb: 9/17/88																											
1988	Atl-N	16	58	8	13	4	0	0	2	4	5	.224	.274	.293	.567	60	-3	-3	104	48	4	.438	0	2	-1	1	2	-0.3
1989	Atl-N	14	55	4	10	2	1	2	10	5	7	.182	.250	.364	.614	72	-2	-2	102	164	5	.532	0	1	-1	0	2	-0.2
Total	2	30	113	12	23	6	1	2	12	9	12	.204	.262	.327	.590	66	-5	-5	103	105	9	.484	0	3	-2	1	/2	-0.5
■ **CHET LEMON**	Lemon, Chester Earl b: 2/12/55, Jackson, Miss. BR/TR, 6', 190 lbs. Deb: 9/09/75																											
1975	Chi-A	9	35	2	9	2	0	0	1	2	6	.257	.297	.314	.612	71	-1	-1	103	37	4	.538	1	0	0	-0	/3OD	-0.1
1976	Chi-A	132	451	46	111	15	5	4	38	28	65	.246	.300	.328	.629	85	-9	-9	99	91	44	.551	13	7	-0	4	*O	-0.7
1977	Chi-A	150	553	99	151	38	4	19	67	52	88	.273	.347	.459	.807	118	13	14	99	87	89	.781	8	7	-2	27	*O	3.3
1978	Chi-A	105	357	51	107	24	6	13	55	39	46	.300	.381	.510	.891	147	23	23	101	100	65	.867	5	9	-4	8	OD	2.5
1979	Chi-A	148	556	79	177	**44**	2	17	86	56	68	.318	.394	.496	.890	135	31	29	102	107	104	.869	7	11	-5	3	*O	2.1
1980	Chi-A	146	514	76	150	32	6	11	51	71	56	.292	.390	.442	.832	132	22	24	97	81	90	.827	6	6	-2	-3	*O/2D	1.6
1981	Chi-A	94	328	50	99	23	6	9	50	33	48	.302	.388	.491	.879	152	22	23	100	106	60	.858	5	8	-3	-2	O	1.5
1982	Det-A	125	436	75	116	20	1	19	52	56	69	.266	.369	.447	.816	122	15	15	100	84	72	.792	1	4	-2	0	*O/D	0.9
1983	Det-A	145	491	78	125	21	5	24	69	54	70	.255	.352	.464	.817	128	16	19	96	92	79	.786	0	7	-4	4	*O	1.7
1984	Det-A	141	509	77	146	34	6	20	76	51	83	.287	.360	.495	.855	139	23	26	96	99	86	.820	5	5	-2	7	*O/D	2.6
1985	Det-A	145	517	69	137	28	4	18	68	45	93	.265	.336	.439	.775	104	7	3	106	98	78	.729	0	2	-1	4	*O	0.4
1986	Det-A	126	403	45	101	21	3	12	53	39	53	.251	.329	.407	.736	105	0	3	95	106	52	.670	2	1	0	-4	*O	-0.4
1987	Det-A	146	470	75	130	30	3	20	75	70	82	.277	.380	.481	.860	131	20	22	97	105	86	.852	0	0	0	-4	*O	1.3
1988	Det-A	144	512	67	135	29	4	17	64	59	65	.264	.348	.436	.783	125	13	16	94	95	75	.730	1	2	-1	1	*O	1.4
1989	Det-A	127	414	45	98	19	2	7	47	46	71	.237	.325	.343	.668	91	-6	-4	97	112	47	.601	1	5	-3	-9	*OD	-1.7
Total	15	1883	6546	934	1792	380	57	210	852	701	963	.274	.357	.445	.803	122	188	200	99	96	1032	.765	55	74	-28	36	*O/D32	16.4
■ **JEFFERY LEONARD**	Leonard, Jeffery b: 9/22/55, Philadelphia, Pa. BR/TR, 6'2", 200 lbs. Deb: 9/02/77																											
1977	LA-N	11	10	1	3	0	1	0	2	1	4	.300	.364	.500	.864	129	0	0	100	160	1	.750	0	0	0	-3	O	-0.2
1978	Hou-N	8	26	2	10	2	0	0	4	1	2	.385	.407	.462	.869	150	1	2	95	132	5	.765	0	1	-1	1	/O	0.2
1979	Hou-N	134	411	47	119	15	5	0	47	46	68	.290	.364	.350	.714	106	-1	4	90	129	53	.687	23	10	1	-4	*O	-0.1
1980	Hou-N	88	216	29	46	7	5	3	20	19	46	.213	.277	.333	.610	71	-9	-9	98	98	19	.531	4	1	1	-2	O1	-1.3
1981	Hou-N	7	18	1	3	1	1	0	3	0	4	.167	.167	.333	.500	44	-2	-1	88	196	1	.467	1	0	0	-0	/1O	-0.1
	SF-N	37	127	20	39	11	3	4	26	12	21	.307	.371	.535	.907	147	9	8	105	128	23	.895	4	2	0	5	O/1	1.3
	Yr	44	145	21	42	12	4	4	29	12	25	.290	.348	.510	.858	138	7	7	102	143	24	.836	5	2	0	5		1.2
1982	SF-N	80	278	32	72	16	1	9	49	19	65	.259	.311	.421	.732	110	0	2	94	133	34	.703	18	5	2	-4	O/1	0.0
1983	SF-N	139	516	74	144	17	7	21	87	35	116	.279	.326	.461	.787	115	9	8	101	117	77	.771	26	7	4	7	*O	1.7
1984	SF-N	136	514	76	155	27	2	21	86	47	123	.302	.360	.484	.845	141	23	25	96	110	87	.826	17	7	1	5	*O	2.7
1985	SF-N	133	507	49	122	20	3	17	62	21	107	.241	.272	.393	.665	90	-13	-9	93	101	47	.566	11	6	-0	-4	*O	-1.7
1986	SF-N	89	341	48	95	11	3	6	42	20	62	.279	.324	.381	.705	98	-3	-2	96	115	44	.668	16	3	3	0	O	0.0
1987	SF-N	131	503	70	141	29	4	19	63	21	68	.280	.312	.467	.779	107	0	3	96	88	66	.710	16	7	1	-8	*O	-0.9
1988	SF-N	44	160	12	41	8	1	2	20	9	24	.256	.296	.356	.652	92	-3	-2	94	129	15	.566	7	5	-1	-4	O	-0.8
	Mil-A	94	374	45	88	19	0	8	44	16	68	.235	.272	.350	.623	71	-14	-16	103	119	34	.533	10	4	1	-0	O	-1.7
1989	Sea-A	150	566	69	144	20	1	24	93	38	125	.254	.307	.420	.728	100	1	-2	103	124	72	.660	6	1	1	1	*DO	0.0
Total	13	1281	4567	575	1222	203	37	134	648	305	903	.268	.316	.416	.732	104	-2	13	97	115	579	.676	159	59	12	-11	*OD/1	-0.9
■ **JOSE LIND**	Lind, Jose (Salgado) b: 5/1/64, Toabaja, P.R. BR/TR, 5'11", 155 lbs. Deb: 8/28/87																											
1987	Pit-N	35	143	21	46	8	4	0	11	8	12	.322	.358	.434	.791	104	2	1	104	68	21	.699	2	1	0	2	2	0.4
1988	Pit-N	154	611	82	160	24	4	2	49	42	75	.262	.309	.324	.633	84	-14	-12	98	102	63	.547	15	4	2	2	*2	-0.3
1989	Pit-N	153	578	52	134	21	3	2	48	39	64	.232	.283	.289	.572	68	-27	-23	94	118	49	.487	15	1	4	-8	*2	-2.7
Total	3	342	1332	155	340	53	11	4	108	89	151	.255	.303	.321	.623	80	-39	-34	97	105	132	.536	32	6	6	-4	2	-2.6
■ **JIM LINDEMAN**	Lindeman, James William b: 1/10/62, Evanston, Ill. BR/TR, 6'1", 200 lbs. Deb: 9/03/86																											
1986	StL-N	19	55	7	14	1	0	1	6	2	10	.255	.281	.327	.608	65	-3	-3	103	114	4	.477	1	1	-0	-1	1/3O	-0.4
1987	StL-N	75	207	20	43	13	0	8	28	11	56	.208	.258	.386	.644	69	-10	-10	99	107	20	.574	3	1	0	-1	O1	-1.3
1988	StL-N	17	43	3	9	1	0	2	7	2	9	.209	.244	.372	.617	72	-2	-2	104	127	4	.514	0	0	0	-2	O/1	-0.4
1989	StL-N	73	45	8	5	1	0	0	2	3	18	.111	.167	.133	.300	-13	-7	-7	101	134	1	.214	0	0	0	-2	1/O	-1.2
Total	4	184	350	38	71	16	0	11	43	18	93	.203	.248	.343	.591	59	-21	-21	100	114	29	.500	4	2	0	-6	/1O3	-3.3
■ **NELSON LIRIANO**	Liriano, Nelson Arturo (Bonilla) b: 6/3/64, Santo Domingo, D.R. BB/TR, 5'10", 165 lbs. Deb: 8/25/87																											
1987	Tor-A	37	158	29	38	6	2	2	10	16	22	.241	.310	.342	.652	73	-6	-6	101	57	18	.664	13	2	3	-3	2	-0.3
1988	Tor-A	103	276	36	73	6	2	3	23	11	40	.264	.298	.333	.631	77	-9	-9	100	90	27	.552	12	5	1	-2	2D/3	-0.5
1989	Tor-A	132	418	51	110	26	3	5	53	43	51	.263	.335	.376	.710	106	0	4	94	120	53	.671	16	7	1	-14	*2/D	-0.7
Total	3	272	852	116	221	38	7	10	86	70	113	.259	.319	.356	.674	90	-14	-11	97	99	99	.631	41	14	4	-20	2/D3	-1.5
■ **SCOTT LITTLE**	Little, Dennis Scott b: 1/19/63, E.St.Louis, Ill. BR/TR, 6', 198 lbs. Deb: 7/27/89																											
1989	Pit-N	3	4	0	1	0	0	0	0	0	1	.250	.250	.250	.500	46	-0	-0	94	0	0	.333	0	0	0	1	/O	0.1
■ **GREG LITTON**	Litton, Jon Gregory b: 7/13/64, New Orleans, La. BR/TR, 6', 175 lbs. Deb: 5/02/89																											
1989	SF-N	71	143	12	36	5	3	4	17	7	29	.252	.291	.413	.704	102	-1	-0	97	96	16	.598	0	2	-1	-2	32/SOC	-0.2
■ **PHIL LOMBARDI**	Lombardi, Phillip Andrew b: 2/20/63, Abilene, Tex. BR/TR, 6'2", 200 lbs. Deb: 4/26/86																											
1986	NY-A	20	36	6	10	3	0	2	6	4	7	.278	.366	.528	.894	137	2	2	103	96	6	.857	0	0	0	-1	/OC	0.1
1987	NY-A	5	8	0	1	0	0	0	0	0	2	.125	.125	.125	.250	-34	-1	-1	98	0	0	.143	0	0	0	-0	/C	0.0
1989	NY-N	18	48	4	11	1	0	1	3	5	8	.229	.302	.313	.614	79	-1	-1	97	67	4	.513	0	0	0	-1	C/1	-0.1
Total	3	43	92	10	22	4	0	3	9	9	17	.239	.314	.380	.694	94	-1	-1	99	73	11	.608	0	0	0	-2	/CO1	0.0
■ **STEVE LOMBARDOZZI**	Lombardozzi, Stephen Paul b: 4/26/60, Malden, Mass. BR/TR, 6', 175 lbs. Deb: 7/12/85																											
1985	Min-A	28	54	10	20	4	1	0	6	6	6	.370	.433	.481	.915	146	4	4	103	91	12	.972	3	2	-0	-2	2	0.2
1986	Min-A	156	453	53	103	20	5	8	33	52	76	.227	.308	.347	.655	73	-13	-18	108	73	50	.593	3	1	0	2	*2	-0.7
1987	Min-A	136	432	51	103	19	3	8	38	33	66	.238	.299	.352	.650	76	-17	-14	96	86	46	.571	5	1	1	-3	*2	-0.6
1988	Min-A	103	287	34	60	15	2	3	27	35	48	.209	.299	.307	.606	66	-11	-13	106	111	28	.543	2	5	-2	-8	2/S3	-1.8
1989	Hou-N	21	37	5	8	3	1	1	3	4	9	.216	.293	.432	.725	103	0	0	102	64	5	.690	0	0	0	-1	2/3	0.0
Total	5	444	1263	153	294	61	12	20	107	130	205	.233	.308	.348	.655	76	-37	-42	103	86	140	.590	13	9	-2	-13	2/S3	-2.9
■ **TORY LOVULLO**	Lovullo, Salvatore Anthony b: 7/25/65, Santa Monica, Cal. BB/TR, 6'1", 185 lbs. Deb: 9/10/88																											
1988	Det-A	12	21	2	8	1	1	1	2	1	2	.381	.409	.667	1.076	208	3	3	94	47	5	1.071	0	0	0	-0	/23	0.3
1989	Det-A	29	87	8	10	2	0	1	4	14	20	.115	.238	.172	.410	18	-9	-9	97	86	4	.363	0	0	0	-0	13	-1.0
Total	2	41	108	10	18	3	1	2	6	15	22	.167	.268	.269	.537	53	-7	-6	97	79	9	.468	0	0	0	-1	/132	-0.7
■ **SCOTT LUSADER**	Lusader, Scott Edward b: 9/30/64, Chicago, Ill. BL/TL, 5'10", 165 lbs. Deb: 9/01/87																											
1987	Det-A	23	47	8	15	3	1	1	8	5	7	.319	.385	.489	.874	135	2	2	97	123	9	.906	1	0	0	-4	O/D	-0.1
1988	Det-A	16	16	3	1	0	0	1	3	1	4	.063	.118	.250	.368	-0	-2	-2	94	170	0	.313	0	0	0	-0	/O	-0.2
1989	Det-A	40	103	15	26	4	0	1	8	9	21	.252	.313	.320	.633	81	-3	-2	97	86	11	.570	3	0	1	-5	O/D	-0.6
Total	3	79	166	26	42	7	1	3	19	15	32	.253	.315	.361	.676	90	-3	-2	97	105	21	.622	4	0	1	-9	/OD	-0.9

YEAR	TM/L	G	AB	R	H	2B	3B	HR	RBI	BB	SO	AVG	OBP	SLG	PRO	/A	BR	/A	PF	CHI	RC	TA	SB	CS	SBR	FR	POS	TPR
■ **FRED LYNN**	Lynn, Fredric Michael b: 2/3/52, Chicago, Ill. BL/TL, 6'1", 185 lbs. Deb: 9/05/74																											
1974	Bos-A	15	43	5	18	2	2	2	10	6	6	.419	.500	.698	1.198	227	8	8	107	109	16	1.480	0	0	0	-0	O/D	0.7
1975	Bos-A	145	528	**103**	175	**47**	7	21	105	62	90	.331	.405	**.566**	**.971**	158	49	43	109	114	120	1.014	10	5	0	5	*O	4.4
1976	Bos-A	132	507	76	159	32	8	10	65	48	67	.314	.374	.467	.842	132	28	22	110	99	88	.820	14	9	-1	7	*O/D	2.7
1977	Bos-A	129	497	81	129	29	5	18	76	51	63	.260	.332	.447	.779	94	6	-6	117	116	72	.722	2	3	-1	1	*O/D	-0.9
1978	Bos-A	150	541	75	161	33	3	22	82	75	50	.298	.384	.492	.876	135	33	28	107	100	103	.873	3	6	-3	0	*O	2.2
1979	Bos-A	147	531	116	177	42	1	39	122	82	79	**.333**	.426	**.637**	**1.063**	**170**	**62**	**57**	107	109	**147**	**1.167**	2	2	-1	1	*O	4.9
1980	Bos-A	110	415	67	125	32	3	12	61	58	39	.301	.387	.480	.866	133	21	20	102	107	80	.897	12	0	4	5	*O	2.6
1981	Cal-A	76	256	28	56	8	1	5	31	38	42	.219	.327	.316	.643	83	-4	-5	104	129	27	.589	1	2	-1	-2	O	-0.9
1982	Cal-A	138	472	89	141	38	1	21	86	58	72	.299	.379	.517	.896	143	28	28	100	114	91	.897	7	8	-3	-9	*O	1.2
1983	Cal-A	117	437	56	119	20	3	22	74	55	83	.272	.356	.483	.839	134	17	20	96	111	76	.826	2	2	-1	-7	*O/D	1.1
1984	Cal-A	142	517	84	140	28	4	23	79	77	97	.271	.367	.474	.841	129	23	22	101	106	90	.830	2	2	-1	8	*O	2.5
1985	Bal-A	124	448	59	118	12	1	23	68	53	100	.263	.343	.449	.791	116	9	10	99	102	70	.771	7	3	0	-4	*O	0.4
1986	Bal-A	112	397	67	114	13	1	23	67	53	59	.287	.374	.499	.873	138	20	21	99	102	69	.836	2	2	-1	-10	*O/D	0.7
1987	Bal-A	111	396	49	100	24	0	23	60	39	72	.253	.321	.487	.808	114	5	7	98	93	58	.759	3	7	-3	-7	*O/D	-0.5
1988	Bal-A	87	301	37	76	13	1	18	37	28	66	.252	.316	.482	.798	126	7	9	95	75	44	.748	2	2	-1	-4	O/D	0.2
	Det-A	27	90	9	20	1	0	7	19	5	16	.222	.271	.467	.738	108	-0	0	94	120	11	.667	0	0	0	0	O/D	0.0
	Yr	114	391	46	96	14	1	25	56	33	82	.246	.306	.478	.784	122	7	9	95	87	55	.729	2	2	-1	-4		0.2
1989	Det-A	117	353	44	85	11	1	11	46	47	71	.241	.332	.371	.703	101	-0	1	97	109	46	.657	1	1	-0	-3	OD	-0.3
Total	16	1879	6729	1045	1913	385	42	300	1088	835	1072	.284	.366	.488	.853	130	314	284	103	106	1209	.840	70	54	-11	-20	*O/D	21.0
■ **BARRY LYONS**	Lyons, Barry Stephen b: 6/3/60, Biloxi, Miss. BR/TR, 6'1", 205 lbs. Deb: 4/19/86																											
1986	NY-N	6	9	1	0	0	0	0	2	1	2	.000	.100	.000	.100	-73	-2	-2	96	0	0	.111	0	0	0	0	/C	-0.1
1987	NY-N	53	130	15	33	4	1	4	24	8	24	.254	.307	.392	.699	85	-3	-3	99	152	16	.622	0	0	0	1	C	0.2
1988	NY-N	50	91	5	21	7	1	0	11	3	12	.231	.255	.330	.585	74	-4	-3	90	147	7	.452	0	0	0	-2	C/1	-0.3
1989	NY-N	79	235	15	58	13	0	3	27	11	28	.247	.286	.340	.627	81	-7	-6	97	122	21	.503	0	1	-1	-7	C	-0.8
Total	4	188	465	36	112	24	2	7	64	23	66	.241	.283	.346	.629	78	-16	-14	96	133	44	.515	0	1	-1	-8	C/1	-1.0
■ **STEVE LYONS**	Lyons, Stephen John b: 6/3/60, Tacoma, Wash. BL/TR, 6'3", 190 lbs. Deb: 4/15/85																											
1985	Bos-A	133	371	52	98	14	3	5	30	32	64	.264	.324	.358	.683	85	-6	-8	102	80	44	.627	12	9	-2	-13	*O/3SD	-2.3
1986	Bos-A	59	124	20	31	7	2	1	14	12	23	.250	.316	.363	.679	86	-2	-2	100	116	13	.596	2	3	-1	-1	O	-0.5
	Chi-A	42	123	10	25	2	1	0	6	7	24	.203	.252	.236	.488	34	-11	-11	101	82	7	.382	2	3	-1	0	O/31D	-1.2
	Yr	101	247	30	56	9	3	1	20	19	47	.227	.285	.300	.584	60	-13	-13	100	103	21	.488	4	6	-2	-1		-1.7
1987	Chi-A	76	193	26	54	11	1	1	19	12	37	.280	.322	.363	.685	76	-5	-7	109	104	22	.590	3	1	0	2	3O/2D	-0.5
1988	Chi-A	145	472	59	127	28	3	5	45	32	59	.269	.317	.373	.690	95	-5	-4	97	94	57	.595	1	2	-1	12	*3O/2C1	0.8
1989	Chi-A	140	443	51	117	21	3	2	50	35	68	.264	.319	.339	.658	92	-8	-4	93	125	50	.582	9	6	-1	-11	213O/SC	-1.7
Total	5	595	1726	218	452	83	13	14	164	130	275	.262	.315	.349	.664	84	-38	-36	99	101	194	.582	29	24	-6	-11	O3/21DSC	-5.4
YEAR	TM/L	G	AB	R	H	2B	3B	HR	RBI	BB	SO	AVG	OBP	SLG	PRO	/A	BR	/A	PF	CHI	RC	TA	SB	CS	SBR	FR	POS	TPR
■ **MIKE MACFARLANE**	Macfarlane, Michael Andrew b: 4/12/64, Stockton, Cal. BR/TR, 6', 195 lbs. Deb: 7/23/87																											
1987	KC-A	8	19	0	4	1	0	0	3	2	2	.211	.286	.263	.549	46	-1	-1	104	239	1	.438	0	0	0	0	/C	0.0
1988	KC-A	70	211	25	56	15	0	4	26	21	37	.265	.335	.393	.728	100	1	0	103	109	28	.656	0	0	0	-4	C	-0.1
1989	KC-A	69	157	13	35	6	0	2	19	7	27	.223	.265	.299	.564	61	-9	-8	96	139	11	.431	0	0	0	-3	C/D	-0.7
Total	3	147	387	38	95	22	0	6	48	30	66	.245	.305	.349	.654	82	-9	-9	100	127	40	.549	0	0	0	-7	C/D	-0.8
■ **SCOTTI MADISON**	Madison, Charles Scott b: 9/12/59, Pensacola, Fla. BB/TR, 5'11", 185 lbs. Deb: 7/06/85																											
1985	Det-A	6	11	0	0	0	0	0	1	2	0	.000	.154	.000	.154	-50	-2	-2	106	0	0	.182	0	0	0	0	/CD	-0.1
1986	Det-A	2	7	0	0	0	0	0	1	0	3	.000	.000	.000	.000	-99	-2	-2	95	0	0	.000	0	0	0	0	/3D	-0.1
1987	KC-A	7	15	4	4	3	0	0	0	1	5	.267	.313	.467	.779	100	0	-0	104	0	2	.727	0	0	0	0	/1C	0.0
1988	KC-A	16	35	4	6	2	0	0	2	4	5	.171	.256	.229	.485	36	-3	-3	103	99	2	.448	1	0	0	-1	/CO1D	-0.3
1989	Cin-N	40	98	13	17	7	0	1	7	8	9	.173	.243	.276	.519	47	-7	-7	103	94	6	.419	0	1	-1	1	3	-0.7
Total	5	71	166	21	27	12	0	1	11	15	22	.163	.236	.253	.489	37	-14	-14	103	76	11	.410	1	1	-0	-0	/3DC1O	-1.2
■ **DAVE MAGADAN**	Magadan, David Joseph b: 9/30/62, Tampa, Fla. BL/TR, 6'3", 190 lbs. Deb: 9/07/86																											
1986	NY-N	10	18	3	8	0	0	0	3	3	1	.444	.524	.444	.968	177	2	2	96	149	4	1.000	0	0	0	1	/1	0.2
1987	NY-N	85	192	21	61	13	1	3	24	22	22	.318	.388	.443	.831	121	6	6	99	102	33	.787	0	0	0	-1	31	0.4
1988	NY-N	112	314	39	87	15	0	1	35	60	39	.277	.396	.334	.731	124	8	12	90	130	45	.705	0	1	-1	0	13/S	0.9
1989	NY-N	127	374	47	107	22	3	4	41	49	37	.286	.370	.393	.763	123	10	12	97	104	58	.736	1	0	0	-2	13	0.3
Total	4	334	898	110	263	50	4	8	103	134	99	.293	.386	.384	.771	124	27	32	95	114	140	.740	1	1	-0	-2	13/S	1.8
■ **TOM MAGRANN**	Magrann, Thomas Joseph b: 12/9/63, Hollywood, Fla. BR/TR, 6'3", 177 lbs. Deb: 9/07/89																											
1989	Cle-A	9	10	0	0	0	0	0	0	0	4	.000	.000	.000	.000	-97	-3	-3	104	0	0	.000	0	0	0	-0	/C	-0.2
■ **CANDY MALDONADO**	Maldonado, Candido (Guadarrama) b: 9/5/60, Humacao, P.R. BR/TR, 6', 185 lbs. Deb: 9/07/81																											
1981	LA-N	11	12	0	1	0	0	0	0	0	5	.083	.083	.083	.167	-54	-2	-2	98	0	0	.091	0	0	0	-2	/O	-0.4
1982	LA-N	6	4	0	0	0	0	0	0	1	2	.000	.200	.000	.200	-42	-1	-1	95	0	0	.250	0	0	0	-0	/O	0.0
1983	LA-N	42	62	5	12	1	1	1	6	5	14	.194	.254	.290	.544	50	-4	-4	100	113	5	.451	0	0	0	-8	O	-1.3
1984	LA-N	116	254	25	68	14	0	5	28	19	29	.268	.321	.382	.703	93	-1	-2	104	98	30	.600	0	3	-2	-14	*O/3	-2.3
1985	LA-N	121	213	20	48	7	1	5	19	19	40	.225	.289	.338	.627	80	-7	-6	93	87	21	.544	1	1	-0	-16	*O	-2.6
1986	SF-N	133	405	49	102	31	3	18	85	20	77	.252	.292	.477	.769	113	2	4	96	137	51	.690	4	4	-1	-2	*O/3	0.0
1987	SF-N	118	442	69	129	28	4	20	85	34	78	.292	.351	.509	.860	129	14	17	96	121	75	.827	8	8	-2	-7	*O	0.2
1988	SF-N	142	499	53	127	23	1	12	68	37	89	.255	.315	.377	.692	104	-2	2	94	124	57	.610	6	5	-1	-8	*O	-1.1
1989	SF-N	129	345	39	75	23	0	9	41	37	69	.217	.299	.362	.661	91	-5	-4	97	109	38	.606	4	1	1	-11	*O	-1.7
Total	9	818	2236	260	562	127	10	70	332	172	403	.251	.311	.411	.722	103	-7	3	96	116	277	.649	23	22	-6	-69	O/3	-9.2
■ **KELLY MANN**	Mann, Kelly John b: 8/17/67, Santa Monica, Cal. BR/TR, 6'3", 215 lbs. Deb: 9/04/89																											
1989	Atl-N	7	24	1	5	2	0	0	1	0	6	.208	.240	.292	.532	50	-2	-2	102	57	1	.400	0	0	0	-0	/C	0.0
■ **FRED MANRIQUE**	Manrique, Fred Eloy (Reyes) b: 5/11/61, Edo Bolivar, Venez. BR/TR, 6'1", 175 lbs. Deb: 8/23/81																											
1981	Tor-A	14	28	1	4	0	0	0	1	0	12	.143	.172	.143	.315	-8	-4	-4	111	98	1	.200	0	1	-1	-1	S/3D	-0.4
1984	Tor-A	10	9	0	3	0	0	0	1	0	1	.333	.333	.333	.667	84	-0	-0	102	133	1	.429	0	0	0	0	/2D	0.0
1985	Mon-N	9	13	5	4	1	1	1	1	1	3	.308	.357	.769	1.126	221	2	2	94	31	4	1.222	0	0	0	0	/2S3	0.2
1986	StL-N	13	17	2	3	0	0	1	1	1	1	.176	.222	.353	.575	54	-1	-1	103	44	1	.533	1	0	0	0	/32	0.0
1987	Chi-A	115	298	30	77	13	3	4	29	19	69	.258	.305	.362	.667	71	-10	-13	109	96	33	.583	5	3	-0	-4	2S/D	-0.8
1988	Chi-A	140	345	43	81	10	6	5	37	21	54	.235	.285	.342	.627	77	-12	-11	97	111	33	.536	6	5	-1	2	*2S	0.0
1989	Chi-A	65	187	23	56	13	1	2	30	8	30	.299	.335	.412	.747	118	2	4	93	141	23	.617	0	4	-2	-3	2/S3	0.0
	Tex-A	54	191	23	55	12	0	2	22	9	33	.288	.320	.382	.702	95	-1	-2	102	110	24	.614	4	1	1	-5	S2/3	-0.2
	Yr	119	378	46	111	25	1	4	52	17	63	.294	.327	.397	.724	106	1	2	97	128	46	.616	4	5	-2	-7		-0.2
Total	7	420	1088	127	283	49	11	15	122	59	203	.260	.302	.367	.669	83	-24	-26	101	110	118	.572	16	14	-4	-10	2/S3D	-1.2
■ **KIRT MANWARING**	Manwaring, Kirt Dean b: 7/15/65, Elmira, N.Y. BR/TR, 6'1", 195 lbs. Deb: 9/15/87																											
1987	SF-N	6	7	0	1	0	0	0	0	0	1	.143	.250	.143	.393	8	-1	-1	96	0	0	.286	0	0	0	0	/C	0.0
1988	SF-N	40	116	12	29	7	0	1	15	2	21	.250	.281	.336	.617	81	-4	-3	94	143	11	.494	0	1	-1	-3	C	-0.4
1989	SF-N	85	200	14	42	4	2	0	18	11	28	.210	.265	.250	.515	49	-13	-13	97	145	13	.409	2	1	0	-8	C	-1.6
Total	3	131	323	26	72	11	2	1	33	13	50	.223	.270	.279	.549	60	-18	-16	96	141	24	.435	2	2	-1	-12	C	-2.0
■ **MIKE MARSHALL**	Marshall, Michael Allen b: 1/12/60, Libertyville, Ill. BR/TR, 6'5", 215 lbs. Deb: 9/07/81																											
1981	LA-N	14	25	2	5	3	0	0	1	1	4	.200	.259	.320	.579	65	-1	-1	98	49	2	.476	0	0	0	0	/13O	-0.1
1982	LA-N	49	95	10	23	3	0	5	9	13	23	.242	.339	.432	.771	121	2	3	95	63	15	.781	2	0	1	-3	O1	0.0
1983	LA-N	140	465	47	132	17	1	17	65	43	127	.284	.351	.434	.785	116	10	10	100	102	72	.747	7	3	0	-10	*O1	-0.3

YEAR	TM/L	G	AB	R	H	2B	3B	HR	RBI	BB	SO	AVG	OBP	SLG	PRO	/A	BR	/A	PF	CHI	RC	TA	SB	CS	SBR	FR	POS	TPR
1984	LA-N	134	495	69	127	27	0	21	65	40	93	.257	.316	.438	.754	106	5	3	104	96	66	.689	4	3	-1	-15	*O1	-1.8
1985	LA-N	135	518	72	152	27	2	28	95	37	137	.293	.344	.515	.860	148	23	28	93	114	87	.807	3	10	-5	-3	*O/1	1.7
1986	LA-N	103	330	47	77	11	0	19	53	27	90	.233	.299	.439	.739	107	-1	1	94	105	42	.687	4	4	-1	-4	O	-0.5
1987	LA-N	104	402	45	118	19	0	16	72	18	79	.294	.330	.460	.790	116	3	7	92	131	55	.685	0	5	-3	-8	*O	-0.7
1988	LA-N	144	542	63	150	27	2	20	82	24	93	.277	.316	.445	.761	109	9	6	106	111	71	.673	4	1	1	-4	O1	-0.3
1989	LA-N	105	377	41	98	21	1	11	42	33	78	.260	.328	.408	.736	118	4	7	93	92	49	.664	2	5	-2	-6	*O	-0.2
Total	9	928	3249	396	882	155	6	137	484	236	724	.271	.327	.449	.777	117	54	63	98	105	458	.710	26	31	-11	-54	O1/3	-2.2
■ CARLOS MARTINEZ	Martinez, Carlos Alberto Escobar (born Carlos Alberto Escobar (Martinez)) b: 8/11/64, La Guaira, Venez. BR/TR, 6′5″, 175 lbs. Deb: 9/02/88																											
1988	Chi-A	17	55	5	9	1	0	0	0	0	12	.164	.164	.182	.345	-4	-7	-7	97	0	2	.234	1	0	0	1	3/D	-0.5
1989	Chi-A	109	350	44	105	22	0	5	32	21	57	.300	.341	.406	.747	118	4	7	93	79	45	.646	4	1	1	-4	31O/D	0.1
Total	2	126	405	49	114	23	0	5	32	21	69	.281	.319	.375	.694	101	-3	-0	93	69	47	.583	5	1	1	-3	/31OD	-0.4
■ CARMELO MARTINEZ	Martinez, Carmelo (Salgado) b: 7/28/60, Dorado, P.R. BR/TR, 6′1″, 190 lbs. Deb: 8/22/83																											
1983	Chi-N	29	89	8	23	3	0	6	16	4	19	.258	.290	.494	.785	113	1	1	101	102	12	.696	0	0	0	3	1/3O	0.2
1984	SD-N	149	488	64	122	28	2	13	66	68	82	.250	.346	.395	.742	110	6	7	99	114	70	.707	1	3	-2	13	*O/1	1.4
1985	SD-N	150	514	64	130	28	1	21	72	87	82	.253	.364	.434	.798	120	17	16	102	102	84	.786	0	4	-2	4	*O/1	1.4
1986	SD-N	113	244	28	58	10	0	9	25	35	46	.238	.336	.389	.725	104	0	2	95	82	31	.673	1	1	-0	-4	O1/3	-0.4
1987	SD-N	139	447	59	122	21	2	15	70	70	82	.273	.375	.430	.805	116	10	12	97	118	73	.792	5	5	-2	-3	O1	0.0
1988	SD-N	121	365	48	86	12	0	18	65	35	57	.236	.303	.416	.719	107	1	2	97	126	44	.648	1	1	-0	0	O1	-0.1
1989	SD-N	111	267	23	59	12	2	6	39	32	54	.221	.304	.348	.653	86	-5	-5	101	141	27	.568	0	0	0	-2	O1	-1.0
Total	7	812	2414	294	600	114	7	88	353	331	422	.249	.342	.411	.753	110	31	35	99	113	341	.710	8	14	-6	10	O1/3	1.5
■ DAVE MARTINEZ	Martinez, David b: 9/26/64, New York, N.Y. BL/TL, 5′10″, 150 lbs. Deb: 6/15/86																											
1986	Chi-N	53	108	13	15	1	1	1	7	6	22	.139	.191	.194	.386	6	-14	-15	107	116	4	.333	4	2	0	-1	O	-1.7
1987	Chi-N	142	459	70	134	18	8	8	36	57	96	.292	.373	.418	.791	108	7	7	101	67	75	.792	16	8	0	-3	*O	-0.1
1988	Chi-N	75	256	27	65	10	1	4	34	21	46	.254	.315	.348	.663	86	-3	-4	104	135	29	.607	7	3	0	3	O	-0.3
	Mon-N	63	191	24	49	3	5	2	12	17	48	.257	.317	.356	.673	88	-2	-3	106	65	23	.678	16	6	1	0	O	-0.3
	Yr	138	447	51	114	13	6	6	46	38	94	.255	.316	.351	.667	87	-5	-7	105	104	52	.638	23	9	2	3		-0.6
1989	Mon-N	126	361	41	99	16	7	3	27	27	57	.274	.325	.382	.707	99	0	-1	102	74	49	.704	23	4	5	-5	*O	-0.2
Total	4	459	1375	175	362	48	22	18	116	128	269	.263	.328	.369	.698	91	-11	-16	103	85	180	.677	66	23	6	-6	O	-2.6
■ EDGAR MARTINEZ	Martinez, Edgar b: 1/2/63, New York, N.Y. BR/TR, 6′ ″, 175 lbs. Deb: 9/12/87																											
1987	Sea-A	13	43	6	16	5	2	0	5	2	5	.372	.413	.581	.994	157	4	4	103	80	11	1.037	0	0	0	1	3/D	0.4
1988	Sea-A	14	32	0	9	4	0	0	5	4	7	.281	.361	.406	.767	106	1	0	108	153	5	.739	0	0	0	-1	3	0.0
1989	Sea-A	65	171	20	41	5	0	2	20	17	26	.240	.319	.304	.623	74	-5	-6	103	134	18	.552	2	1	0	-4	3	-0.9
Total	3	92	246	26	66	14	2	2	30	23	38	.268	.341	.366	.707	94	-0	-2	104	127	33	.647	2	1	0	-3	/3D	-0.5
■ JOHN MARZANO	Marzano, John Robert b: 2/14/63, Philadelphia, Pa. BR/TR, 5′11″, 185 lbs. Deb: 7/31/87																											
1987	Bos-A	52	168	20	41	11	0	5	24	7	41	.244	.287	.399	.685	81	-5	-5	99	117	19	.588	0	1	-1	0	C	0.0
1988	Bos-A	10	29	3	4	1	0	0	1	1	3	.138	.167	.172	.339	-4	-4	-4	109	79	1	.231	0	0	0	-0	C	-0.3
1989	Bos-A	7	18	5	8	3	0	1	3	0	2	.444	.444	.778	1.222	228	3	3	105	69	5	1.273	0	0	0	-0	/C	0.3
Total	3	69	215	28	53	15	0	6	28	8	46	.247	.283	.400	.683	81	-6	-6	101	108	24	.577	0	1	-1	0	/C	0.0
■ DON MATTINGLY	Mattingly, Donald Arthur b: 4/20/61, Evansville, Ind. BL/TL, 6′, 175 lbs. Deb: 9/08/82																											
1982	NY-A	7	12	0	2	0	0	0	1	0	1	.167	.167	.167	.333	-8	-2	-2	96	200	0	.167	0	0	0	0	/O1	-0.1
1983	NY-A	91	279	34	79	15	4	4	32	21	31	.283	.336	.409	.744	105	1	2	99	99	37	.654	0	0	0	-7	O1/2	-0.6
1984	NY-A	153	603	91	**207**	**44**	2	23	110	41	33	**.343**	.386	.537	.923	162	41	46	94	118	120	.891	1	1	-0	7	*1O	4.3
1985	NY-A	159	652	107	211	**48**	3	35	**145**	56	41	.324	.379	.567	.946	162	48	51	96	107	136	.939	2	2	-1	-12	*1	2.8
1986	NY-A	162	677	117	**238**	**53**	2	31	113	53	35	.352	.399	**.573**	**.973**	157	**57**	**54**	103	83	**150**	.969	0	0	0	-10	*1/3D	3.2
1987	NY-A	141	569	93	186	38	2	30	115	51	38	.327	.383	.559	.942	150	37	39	98	108	115	.921	1	4	-2	-3	*1/D	1.8
1988	NY-A	144	599	94	186	37	0	18	88	41	29	.311	.358	.462	.820	134	21	24	96	102	96	.756	1	0	0	-5	*1/OD	1.2
1989	NY-A	158	631	79	191	37	2	23	113	51	30	.303	.356	.477	.833	127	26	22	104	114	104	.782	3	0	1	-7	*1D/O	0.7
Total	8	1015	4022	615	1300	272	15	164	717	314	238	.323	.374	.521	.894	145	230	238	99	105	759	.857	8	7	-2	-36	1/OD32	13.3
■ LEE MAZZILLI	Mazzilli, Lee Louis b: 3/25/55, New York, N.Y. BB/TR, 6′1″, 180 lbs. Deb: 9/07/76																											
1976	NY-N	24	77	9	15	2	0	2	7	14	10	.195	.326	.299	.625	85	-2	-1	92	95	8	.652	5	4	-1	4	O	0.1
1977	NY-N	159	537	66	134	24	3	6	46	72	72	.250	.342	.339	.680	87	-11	-8	96	94	66	.661	22	15	-2	2	*O	-1.3
1978	NY-N	148	542	78	148	28	5	16	61	69	82	.273	.356	.432	.788	121	14	15	98	91	85	.783	20	13	-2	7	*O	1.6
1979	NY-N	158	597	78	181	34	4	15	79	93	74	.303	.397	.449	.846	137	28	32	95	96	115	.910	34	12	3	0	*O1	3.1
1980	NY-N	152	578	82	162	31	4	16	76	82	92	.280	.373	.431	.803	129	20	23	96	97	98	.854	41	15	3	0	1O	2.0
1981	NY-N	95	324	36	74	14	5	6	34	46	53	.228	.328	.358	.686	94	-2	-2	101	102	41	.691	17	7	1	2	O	-0.1
1982	Tex-A	58	195	23	47	8	0	4	17	28	26	.241	.339	.344	.683	95	-2	-1	93	88	24	.677	11	6	-0	-1	OD	-0.2
	NY-A	37	128	20	34	2	0	6	17	15	15	.266	.347	.422	.769	114	2	3	96	96	19	.727	2	3	-1	-2	1/OD	0.0
	Yr	95	323	43	81	10	0	10	34	43	41	.251	.342	.375	.717	103	-1	2	94	92	42	.696	13	9	-2	-3		-0.2
1983	Pit-N	109	246	37	59	9	0	5	24	49	43	.240	.370	.337	.708	95	1	0	103	97	34	.745	15	5	2	6	O/1	0.6
1984	Pit-N	111	266	37	63	11	1	4	21	40	42	.237	.339	.331	.670	94	-3	-1	94	82	33	.656	8	1	2	-11	O/1	-1.2
1985	Pit-N	92	117	20	33	8	0	1	9	29	17	.282	.425	.376	.801	123	6	5	103	76	21	.875	4	1	1	1	1/O	0.6
1986	Pit-N	61	93	18	21	2	1	1	8	26	25	.226	.395	.301	.696	95	1	1	100	103	13	.740	3	3	-1	-1	O/1	-0.1
	NY-N	39	58	10	16	3	0	2	7	12	11	.276	.417	.431	.848	140	3	4	96	90	11	.909	1	1	-0	0	O/1	0.3
	Yr	100	151	28	37	5	1	3	15	38	36	.245	.403	.351	.754	112	4	5	98	99	24	.802	4	4	-1	-1		0.2
1987	NY-N	88	124	26	38	8	1	3	24	21	14	.306	.407	.460	.867	131	6	6	99	145	24	.902	5	3	-0	-3	O1	0.1
1988	NY-N	68	116	9	17	2	0	0	12	12	16	.147	.233	.164	.396	17	-12	-11	90	253	5	.350	4	1	1	-1	O1	-1.3
1989	NY-N	48	60	10	11	2	0	2	7	17	19	.183	.364	.317	.680	100	0	1	97	113	9	.780	3	0	1	-2	O/1	-0.1
	Tor-A	28	66	12	15	3	0	4	11	17	16	.227	.400	.455	.855	149	4	5	94	102	14	.981	2	0	1	-0	D/1O	0.5
Total	14	1475	4124	571	1068	191	24	93	460	642	627	.259	.361	.385	.746	110	54	71	97	100	618	.762	197	90	5	-1	O1/D	4.6
■ LLOYD McCLENDON	McClendon, Lloyd Glenn b: 1/11/59, Gary, Ind. BR/TR, 5′10″, 190 lbs. Deb: 4/06/87																											
1987	Cin-N	45	72	8	15	5	0	2	13	4	15	.208	.250	.361	.611	57	-4	-5	104	162	7	.534	1	0	0	-0	C/13O	-0.3
1988	Cin-N	72	137	9	30	4	0	3	14	15	22	.219	.305	.314	.619	74	-4	-5	105	108	13	.566	4	0	1	-3	CO1/3	-0.6
1989	Chi-N	92	259	47	74	12	1	12	40	37	31	.286	.377	.479	.856	132	15	12	108	101	48	.875	6	4	-1	-2	O1/3C	0.8
Total	3	209	468	64	119	21	1	17	67	56	68	.254	.338	.412	.750	104	7	3	107	112	68	.725	11	4	1	-5	/O1C3	-0.1
■ ODDIBE McDOWELL	McDowell, Oddibe b: 8/25/62, Hollywood, Fla. BL/TL, 5′9″, 165 lbs. Deb: 5/19/85																											
1985	Tex-A	111	406	63	97	14	5	18	42	36	85	.239	.306	.431	.737	91	-1	-6	108	77	55	.742	25	7	3	6	*O/D	0.1
1986	Tex-A	154	572	105	152	24	7	18	49	65	112	.266	.342	.427	.768	114	7	11	96	69	83	.767	33	15	1	12	*O/D	1.9
1987	Tex-A	128	407	65	98	26	4	14	52	51	99	.241	.325	.428	.753	95	-1	-3	104	96	61	.781	24	2	6	-7	*O	-0.6
1988	Tex-A	120	437	55	108	19	5	6	37	41	89	.247	.315	.355	.669	86	-7	-8	101	87	53	.675	33	10	4	-8	*O/D	-1.3
1989	Cle-A	69	239	33	53	5	2	3	22	25	36	.222	.298	.297	.595	66	-10	-11	104	109	23	.562	12	5	1	-1	O/D	-1.1
	Atl-N	76	280	56	85	18	4	7	24	27	37	.304	.365	.471	.836	134	13	13	102	64	49	.849	15	10	-2	1	O	1.1
Total	5	658	2341	377	593	106	27	66	226	245	458	.253	.326	.406	.732	99	1	-5	102	82	323	.735	142	49	13	3	O/D	0.1
■ WILLIE McGEE	McGee, Willie Dean b: 11/2/58, San Francisco, Cal. BB/TR, 6′1″, 175 lbs. Deb: 5/10/82																											
1982	StL-N	123	422	43	125	12	8	4	56	12	58	.296	.319	.391	.710	94	-2	-4	103	124	49	.638	24	12	0	-16	*O	-2.2
1983	StL-N	147	601	75	172	22	8	5	75	26	98	.286	.316	.374	.690	92	-9	-7	98	131	73	.652	39	8	7	0	*O	-0.2
1984	StL-N	145	571	82	166	19	11	6	50	29	80	.291	.326	.394	.720	103	-0	1	99	85	74	.698	43	10	7	4	*O	0.7
1985	StL-N	152	612	114	**216**	26	**18**	10	82	34	86	**.353**	.387	.503	.890	154	37	40	96	102	123	.959	56	16	7	4	*O	4.9
1986	StL-N	124	497	65	127	22	7	7	48	37	82	.256	.308	.370	.679	84	-10	-12	103	90	53	.612	19	16	-4	9	*O	-0.9
1987	StL-N	153	620	76	177	37	11	11	105	24	90	.285	.314	.434	.748	97	-6	-4	99	147	77	.660	16	4	2	-1	*O/S	-0.9

YEAR	TM/L	G	AB	R	H	2B	3B	HR	RBI	BB	SO	AVG	OBP	SLG	PRO	/A	BR	/A	PF	CHI	RC	TA	SB	CS	SBR	FR	POS	TPR
1988	StL-N	137	562	73	164	24	6	3	50	32	84	.292	.331	.372	.703	98	1	-2	104	88	72	.684	41	6	9	3	*O	0.6
1989	StL-N	58	199	23	47	10	2	3	17	10	34	.236	.276	.352	.628	78	-6	-6	101	87	18	.556	8	6	-1	5	O	-0.3
Total	8	1039	4084	551	1194	172	71	49	483	204	612	.292	.327	.405	.733	102	5	5	100	109	540	.694	246	78	27	7	*O/S	1.7
■ **FRED McGRIFF** McGriff, Frederick Stanley b: 10/31/63, Tampa, Fla. BL/TL, 6'3", 200 lbs. Deb: 5/17/86																												
1986	Tor-A	3	5	1	1	0	0	0	0	0	2	.200	.200	.200	.400	10	-1	-1	105	0	0	.250	0	0	0	0	/1D	0.0
1987	Tor-A	107	295	58	73	16	0	20	43	60	104	.247	.376	.505	.881	131	15	14	101	82	60	.938	3	2	-0	1	D1	1.2
1988	Tor-A	154	536	100	151	35	4	34	82	79	149	.282	.378	.552	.930	158	41	41	100	84	113	.960	6	1	1	-3	*1	3.0
1989	Tor-A	161	551	98	148	27	3	**36**	92	119	132	.269	.402	.525	**.927**	**169**	**47**	**51**	94	95	121	.995	7	4	-0	-1	*1/D	4.0
Total	4	425	1387	257	373	78	7	90	217	258	387	.269	.387	.530	.917	155	102	106	98	88	294	.967	16	7	1	-3	1/D	8.2
■ **TERRY McGRIFF** McGriff, Terence Roy b: 9/23/63, Fort Pierce, Fla. BR/TR, 6'2", 190 lbs. Deb: 7/11/87																												
1987	Cin-N	34	89	6	20	3	0	2	11	8	17	.225	.289	.326	.615	60	-5	-5	104	125	8	.514	0	0	0	1	C	-0.1
1988	Cin-N	35	96	9	19	3	0	1	4	12	31	.198	.287	.260	.547	55	-5	-6	105	57	7	.475	1	0	0	-0	C	-0.3
1989	Cin-N	6	11	1	3	0	0	0	2	2	3	.273	.385	.273	.657	88	-0	-0	103	268	1	.625	0	0	0	0	/C	0.0
Total	3	75	196	16	42	6	0	3	17	22	51	.214	.294	.291	.584	60	-10	-11	104	100	17	.500	1	0	0	1	/C	-0.4
■ **BILL McGUIRE** McGuire, William Patrick b: 2/14/64, Omaha, Neb. BR/TR, 6'3", 205 lbs. Deb: 8/02/88																												
1988	Sea-A	9	16	1	3	0	0	0	2	3	2	.188	.316	.188	.503	41	-1	-1	108	265	1	.462	0	0	0	1	/C	0.0
1989	Sea-A	14	28	2	5	0	0	1	4	2	6	.179	.233	.286	.519	44	-2	-2	103	141	1	.400	0	0	0	1	C	0.0
Total	2	23	44	3	8	0	0	1	6	5	8	.182	.265	.250	.515	44	-3	-3	105	189	3	.421	0	0	0	2	/C	0.0
■ **MARK McGWIRE** McGwire, Mark David b: 10/1/63, Pomona, Cal. BR/TR, 6'5", 215 lbs. Deb: 8/22/86																												
1986	Oak-A	18	53	10	10	1	0	3	9	4	18	.189	.259	.377	.636	76	-2	-2	94	124	5	.568	0	1	-1	-2	3	-0.4
1987	Oak-A	151	557	97	161	28	4	**49**	118	71	131	.289	.374	**.618**	.992	173	45	53	91	102	131	1.045	1	1	-0	-2	*1/3O	3.3
1988	Oak-A	155	550	87	143	22	1	32	99	76	117	.260	.354	.478	.832	138	23	26	95	112	93	.813	0	0	0	-9	*1/O	0.9
1989	Oak-A	143	490	74	113	17	0	33	95	83	94	.231	.345	.467	.813	123	18	16	103	119	76	.788	1	1	-0	5	*1/D	1.0
Total	4	467	1650	268	427	68	5	117	321	234	360	.259	.355	.519	.874	143	84	93	96	111	306	.870	2	3	-1	-8	1/3OD	4.8
■ **JEFF McKNIGHT** McKnight, Jefferson Alan b: 2/18/63, Conway, Ark. BL/TR, 6', 170 lbs. Deb: 6/06/89																												
1989	NY-N	6	12	2	3	0	0	0	0	2	1	.250	.357	.250	.607	79	-0	-0	97	0	1	.500	0	0	0	0	/213S	0.0
■ **MARK McLEMORE** McLemore, Mark Tremell b: 10/4/64, San Diego, Cal. BB/TR, 5'11", 175 lbs. Deb: 9/13/86																												
1986	Cal-A	5	4	0	0	0	0	0	0	1	2	.000	.200	.000	.200	-41	-1	-1	96	0	0	.200	0	1	-1	0	/2	0.0
1987	Cal-A	138	433	61	102	13	3	3	41	48	72	.236	.312	.300	.612	65	-21	-21	99	118	45	.587	25	8	3	-6	*2/SD	-1.3
1988	Cal-A	77	233	38	56	11	2	2	16	25	28	.240	.314	.330	.644	86	-6	-4	94	77	24	.605	13	7	-0	4	2/3D	0.4
1989	Cal-A	32	103	12	25	3	1	0	14	7	19	.243	.297	.291	.589	67	-4	-4	99	181	10	.543	6	1	1	1	2/D	0.0
Total	4	252	773	111	183	27	6	5	71	81	121	.237	.310	.307	.617	71	-32	-29	98	113	78	.584	44	17	3	-1	2/SD3	-0.9
■ **KEVIN McREYNOLDS** McReynolds, Walter Kevin b: 10/16/59, Little Rock, Ark. BR/TR, 6', 205 lbs. Deb: 6/02/83																												
1983	SD-N	39	140	15	31	3	1	4	14	12	29	.221	.283	.343	.626	73	-5	-5	99	94	14	.559	2	1	0	5	O	0.0
1984	SD-N	147	525	68	146	26	6	20	75	34	69	.278	.322	.465	.787	121	11	12	99	99	72	.704	3	6	-3	11	*O	1.5
1985	SD-N	152	564	61	132	24	4	15	75	43	81	.234	.292	.371	.662	83	-13	-14	102	120	59	.577	4	0	1	15	*O	-0.1
1986	SD-N	158	560	89	161	31	6	26	96	66	83	.287	.364	.504	.867	144	27	30	95	108	103	.862	8	6	-1	-0	*O	2.7
1987	NY-N	151	590	86	163	32	5	29	95	39	70	.276	.322	.495	.817	114	8	9	99	102	93	.785	14	1	4	3	*O	0.9
1988	NY-N	147	552	82	159	30	2	27	99	38	56	.288	.338	.496	.835	152	24	30	90	114	97	.845	21	0	6	7	*O	4.2
1989	NY-N	148	545	74	148	25	3	22	85	46	74	.272	.329	.450	.779	125	13	15	97	112	80	.745	15	7	0	10	*O	2.5
Total	7	942	3476	475	940	171	27	143	539	278	462	.270	.326	.459	.785	120	65	77	97	109	518	.742	67	21	8	50	O	11.7
■ **LOUIE MEADOWS** Meadows, Michael Ray b: 4/29/61, Maysville, N.C. BL/TL, 5'11", 190 lbs. Deb: 7/03/86																												
1986	Hou-N	6	6	1	2	0	0	0	0	0	0	.333	.333	.333	.667	82	-0	-0	103	0	1	.750	1	0	0	-0	/O	0.0
1988	Hou-N	35	42	5	8	0	1	2	3	6	8	.190	.292	.381	.673	98	-0	-0	93	54	5	.703	4	2	0	0	O	0.0
1989	Hou-N	31	51	5	9	0	0	3	10	1	14	.176	.192	.353	.545	52	-3	-3	102	149	3	.455	1	2	-1	-3	O/1	-0.8
Total	3	72	99	11	19	0	1	5	13	7	22	.192	.245	.364	.609	73	-4	-4	98	98	8	.576	6	4	-1	-3	/O1	-0.8
■ **LUIS MEDINA** Medina, Luis Main b: 3/26/63, Santa Monica, Cal. BR/TL, 6'4", 200 lbs. Deb: 9/02/88																												
1988	Cle-A	16	51	10	13	0	0	6	8	2	18	.255	.309	.608	.917	148	3	3	102	65	10	.921	0	0	0	0	1	0.2
1989	Cle-A	30	83	8	17	1	0	4	8	6	35	.205	.258	.361	.620	70	-3	-4	104	74	7	.514	0	1	-1	-1	D/O1	-0.5
Total	2	46	134	18	30	1	0	10	16	8	53	.224	.278	.455	.733	100	-0	-1	103	70	17	.657	0	1	-1	-1	/D1O	-0.3
■ **FRANCISCO MELENDEZ** Melendez, Francisco Javier (Villegas) b: 1/25/64, Rio Piedras, P.R. BL/TL, 6', 190 lbs. Deb: 8/26/84																												
1984	Phi-N	21	23	0	3	0	0	0	2	1	5	.130	.167	.130	.297	-15	-3	-4	102	261	0	.190	0	0	0	0	1	-0.3
1986	Phi-N	9	8	0	2	0	0	0	0	0	2	.250	.250	.250	.500	37	-1	-1	104	0	1	.333	0	0	0	0	/1	0.0
1987	SF-N	12	16	2	5	0	0	1	1	0	3	.313	.313	.500	.813	116	0	0	96	36	3	.727	0	0	0	0	/1	0.0
1988	SF-N	23	26	1	5	0	0	0	3	3	2	.192	.276	.192	.468	39	-2	-2	94	240	1	.364	0	0	0	-0	/1O	-0.2
1989	Bal-A	9	11	1	3	0	0	0	3	1	2	.273	.333	.273	.606	74	-0	-0	99	389	1	.444	0	0	0	0	/1	0.0
Total	5	74	84	4	18	0	0	1	9	5	14	.214	.258	.250	.508	43	-6	-6	98	208	6	.377	0	0	0	-0	/1O	-0.5
■ **BOB MELVIN** Melvin, Robert Paul b: 10/28/61, Palo Alto, Cal. BR/TR, 6'4", 205 lbs. Deb: 5/25/85																												
1985	Det-A	41	82	10	18	4	1	0	4	3	21	.220	.247	.293	.540	44	-6	-7	106	66	6	.415	0	0	0	-1	C	-0.5
1986	SF-N	89	268	24	60	14	2	5	25	15	69	.224	.265	.347	.612	70	-13	-11	96	92	23	.512	3	2	-0	-5	C/3	-1.5
1987	SF-N	84	246	31	49	8	0	11	31	17	44	.199	.251	.366	.617	63	-15	-13	96	101	20	.514	0	4	-2	1	C/1	-0.8
1988	SF-N	92	273	23	64	13	1	8	27	13	46	.234	.269	.377	.647	89	-7	-5	94	85	26	.537	0	2	-1	-8	C/1	-1.0
1989	Bal-A	85	278	22	67	10	1	1	32	15	53	.241	.280	.295	.575	63	-14	-14	99	146	20	.436	1	4	-2	6	C/D	-0.5
Total	5	391	1147	110	258	49	5	25	119	63	233	.225	.265	.342	.607	69	-54	-50	97	104	95	.493	4	12	-6	-7	C/D13	-4.3
■ **ORLANDO MERCADO** Mercado, Orlando (Rodriguez) b: 11/7/61, Arecibo, P.R. BR/TR, 6', 180 lbs. Deb: 9/13/82																												
1982	Sea-A	9	17	1	2	0	0	1	6	0	5	.118	.118	.294	.412	8	-2	-2	109	300	1	.333	0	0	0	-1	/C	-0.2
1983	Sea-A	66	178	10	35	11	2	1	16	14	27	.197	.259	.298	.557	53	-12	-11	100	112	14	.473	2	2	-1	-1	C	-1.0
1984	Sea-A	30	78	5	17	3	1	0	5	4	12	.218	.265	.282	.547	50	-5	-5	102	91	6	.452	1	0	0	0	C	-0.2
1986	Tex-A	46	102	7	24	1	1	1	7	6	13	.235	.284	.294	.579	62	-6	-5	96	84	7	.440	0	1	-1	-4	C	-0.6
1987	Det-A	10	22	2	3	0	0	0	1	2	0	.136	.208	.136	.345	-5	-3	-3	97	133	1	.263	0	0	0	0	C	-0.1
	LA-N	7	5	1	3	1	0	0	1	1	1	.600	.667	.800	1.467	312	1	2	92	100	3	2.500	0	0	0	0	/C	0.2
1988	Oak-A	16	24	3	3	0	0	1	1	3	8	.125	.222	.250	.472	34	-2	-2	95	44	2	.429	0	0	0	-1	C	-0.1
1989	Min-A	19	38	1	4	0	0	0	1	4	4	.105	.190	.105	.296	-14	-6	-6	107	97	1	.265	1	0	0	-2	C	-0.6
Total	7	203	464	30	91	16	4	4	38	34	70	.196	.255	.274	.529	46	-34	-34	100	105	34	.436	4	3	-1	-7	C	-2.6
■ **MATT MERULLO** Merullo, Matthew Bates b: 8/4/65, Winchester, Mass. BL/TR, 6'2", 200 lbs. Deb: 4/12/89																												
1989	Chi-A	31	81	5	18	1	0	1	8	6	14	.222	.276	.272	.547	59	-5	-4	93	124	6	.424	0	1	-1	2	C	-0.1
■ **HENSLEY MEULENS** Meulens, Hensley Filemon "Bam-Bam" b: 6/23/67, Curaçao, Neth.Antilles BR/TR, 6'3", 190 lbs. Deb: 8/23/89																												
1989	NY-A	8	28	2	5	0	0	0	1	2	8	.179	.233	.179	.412	17	-3	-3	104	78	1	.269	0	1	-1	-1	/3	-0.4
■ **JOEY MEYER** Meyer, Tanner Joe b: 5/10/62, Honolulu, Hawaii BR/TR, 6'3", 260 lbs. Deb: 4/04/88																												
1988	Mil-A	103	327	22	86	18	0	11	45	23	88	.263	.313	.419	.732	100	1	-1	103	105	41	.641	0	1	-1	2	D1	0.0
1989	Mil-A	53	147	13	33	6	0	7	29	12	36	.224	.283	.408	.691	96	-2	-1	97	139	17	.629	1	0	0	-0	D1	-0.2
Total	2	156	474	35	119	24	0	18	74	35	124	.251	.304	.416	.720	99	-1	-2	101	116	58	.638	1	1	-0	2	/D1	-0.2
■ **KEITH MILLER** Miller, Keith Alan b: 6/12/63, Midland, Mich. BR/TR, 5'11", 175 lbs. Deb: 6/16/87																												
1987	NY-N	25	51	14	19	2	2	0	1	2	6	.373	.407	.490	.898	139	3	3	99	16	11	1.059	8	1	2	-1	2	0.4
1988	NY-N	40	70	9	15	1	1	1	5	6	10	.214	.276	.300	.576	72	-3	-2	90	83	5	.443	0	5	-3	-1	2/S3O	-0.5
1989	NY-N	57	143	15	33	7	0	1	7	5	27	.231	.262	.301	.562	63	-7	-7	97	61	12	.487	6	0	2	-5	2O/S3	-1.0

YEAR	TM/L	G	AB	R	H	2B	3B	HR	RBI	BB	SO	AVG	OBP	SLG	PRO	/A	BR	/A	PF	CHI	RC	TA	SB	CS	SBR	FR	POS	TPR
Total	3	122	264	38	67	10	3	2	13	13	43	.254	.294	.337	.631	81	-8	-7	95	58	27	.567	14	6	1	-7	/2OS3	-1.1
■ KEITH MILLER Miller, Neal Keith b: 3/7/63, Dallas, Tex. BB/TR, 5'11", 175 lbs. Deb: 4/23/88																												
1988	Phi-N	47	48	4	8	3	0	0	6	5	13	.167	.245	.229	.474	36	-4	-4	101	218	3	.400	0	0	0	-1	/O3S	-0.5
1989	Phi-N	8	10	0	3	1	0	0	0	0	3	.300	.300	.400	.700	98	-0	-0	101	0	1	.571	0	0	0	-0	/O	0.0
Total	2	55	58	4	11	4	0	0	6	5	16	.190	.254	.259	.513	47	-4	-4	101	183	4	.426	0	0	0	-2	/O3S	-0.5
■ RANDY MILLIGAN Milligan, Randy Andre b: 11/27/61, San Diego, Cal. BR/TR, 6'2", 200 lbs. Deb: 9/12/87																												
1987	NY-N	3	1	0	0	0	0	0	0	1	1	.000	.500	.000	.500	47	0	0	99	0	0	1.000	0	0	0	0	/H	0.0
1988	Pit-N	40	82	10	18	5	0	3	8	20	24	.220	.379	.390	.769	124	3	3	98	78	13	.794	1	2	-1	2	1/O	0.3
1989	Bal-A	124	365	56	98	23	5	12	45	74	75	.268	.396	.458	.853	142	22	23	99	86	68	.891	9	5	-0	5	*1	1.9
Total	3	167	448	66	116	28	5	15	53	95	100	.259	.393	.444	.837	138	25	26	99	84	81	.873	10	7	-1	7	1/O	2.2
■ KEVIN MITCHELL Mitchell, Kevin Darnell b: 1/13/62, San Diego, Cal. BR/TR, 5'10", 186 lbs. Deb: 9/04/84																												
1984	NY-N	7	14	0	3	0	0	0	1	0	3	.214	.214	.214	.429	21	-1	-1	100	131	0	.250	0	1	-1	-0	/3	-0.1
1986	NY-N	108	328	51	91	22	2	12	43	33	61	.277	.345	.466	.812	127	9	11	96	91	52	.772	3	3	-1	-1	OS/31	1.0
1987	SD-N	62	196	19	48	7	1	7	26	20	38	.245	.315	.398	.713	90	-4	-3	97	105	24	.641	0	0	0	-1	3/O	-0.3
	SF-N	69	268	49	82	13	1	15	44	28	50	.306	.376	.530	.906	142	14	15	96	99	52	.919	9	6	-1	0	3/OS	1.3
	Yr	131	464	68	130	20	2	22	70	48	88	.280	.350	.474	.824	120	10	12	96	103	76	.797	9	6	-1	-1		1.0
1988	SF-N	148	505	60	127	25	7	19	80	48	85	.251	.323	.442	.764	125	10	14	94	117	71	.717	5	5	-2	3	*3O	1.5
1989	SF-N	154	543	100	158	34	6	**47**	**125**	87	115	.291	.392	**.635**	**1.027**	**195**	**62**	**64**	97	110	136	**1.109**	3	4	-2	1	*O/3	**6.3**
Total	5	548	1854	279	509	101	17	100	319	216	352	.275	.354	.509	.863	144	90	100	96	106	336	.854	20	19	-5	2	O3/S1	9.7
■ JOHN MIZEROCK Mizerock, John Joseph b: 12/8/60, Punxsutawney, Pa. BL/TR, 5'11", 190 lbs. Deb: 4/12/83																												
1983	Hou-N	33	85	8	13	4	1	1	10	12	15	.153	.265	.259	.524	51	-6	-5	90	158	6	.473	0	0	0	-2	C	-0.5
1985	Hou-N	15	38	6	9	4	0	0	6	2	8	.237	.293	.342	.635	80	-1	-1	96	184	3	.485	0	0	0	0	C	0.0
1986	Hou-N	44	81	9	15	1	1	1	6	24	16	.185	.377	.259	.637	77	-1	-1	103	100	9	.657	0	0	0	-6	C	-0.6
1989	Atl-N	11	27	1	6	0	0	0	2	0	3	.222	.222	.222	.444	27	-3	-3	102	134	1	.286	0	0	0	-0	C	-0.1
Total	4	103	231	24	43	9	2	2	24	38	42	.186	.309	.268	.577	64	-11	-10	97	137	19	.520	0	0	0	-8	C	-1.2
■ PAUL MOLITOR Molitor, Paul Leo b: 8/22/56, St.Paul, Minn. BR/TR, 6', 185 lbs. Deb: 4/07/78																												
1978	Mil-A	125	521	73	142	26	4	6	45	19	54	.273	.303	.372	.676	84	-9	-12	106	81	59	.622	30	12	2	0	2S/3D	-0.2
1979	Mil-A	140	584	88	188	27	16	9	62	48	48	.322	.375	.469	.845	126	21	21	100	70	103	.854	33	13	2	3	*2S/D	3.2
1980	Mil-A	111	450	81	137	29	2	9	37	48	48	.304	.375	.438	.813	129	14	18	95	57	78	.857	34	7	6	-2	2S/3D	2.7
1981	Mil-A	64	251	45	67	11	0	2	19	25	29	.267	.341	.335	.675	99	-1	0	96	79	30	.632	10	6	-1	-0	OD	-0.1
1982	Mil-A	160	666	**136**	201	26	8	19	71	69	93	.302	.368	.450	.819	131	22	27	94	69	117	.851	41	9	7	3	*3/SD	3.4
1983	Mil-A	152	608	95	164	28	6	15	47	59	74	.270	.336	.410	.746	114	3	10	92	60	88	.756	41	8	8	5	*3/D	2.2
1984	Mil-A	13	46	3	10	1	0	0	6	2	8	.217	.250	.239	.489	39	-4	-3	92	222	3	.389	1	0	0	1	/3D	-0.1
1985	Mil-A	140	576	93	171	28	3	10	48	54	80	.297	.358	.408	.766	104	8	5	105	62	85	.733	21	7	2	-4	*3/D	-0.1
1986	Mil-A	105	437	62	123	24	6	9	55	40	81	.281	.342	.426	.767	106	5	4	102	89	65	.750	20	5	3	-1	3D/O	0.3
1987	Mil-A	118	465	**114**	164	**41**	5	16	75	69	67	.353	.438	.566	1.004	161	46	44	102	85	125	**1.203**	45	10	8	-4	D32	4.5
1988	Mil-A	154	609	115	190	34	6	13	60	71	54	.312	.386	.452	.837	129	29	26	103	67	112	.886	41	10	6	-4	*3D/2	2.9
1989	Mil-A	155	615	84	194	35	4	11	56	64	67	.315	.384	.439	.823	136	27	29	97	63	106	.824	27	11	2	9	*3D2	4.0
Total	12	1437	5828	989	1751	310	60	119	581	568	703	.300	.365	.435	.800	121	162	169	99	71	971	.814	344	98	44	6	32D/SO	22.7
■ KEITH MORELAND Moreland, Bobby Keith b: 5/2/54, Dallas, Tex. BR/TR, 6', 190 lbs. Deb: 10/01/78																												
1978	Phi-N	1	2	0	0	0	0	0	0	0	0	.000	.000	.000	.000	-95	-1	-1	105	0	0	.000	0	0	0	0	/C	0.0
1979	Phi-N	14	48	3	18	3	2	0	8	3	5	.375	.412	.521	.933	158	3	4	97	127	10	.903	0	0	0	-0	C	0.4
1980	Phi-N	62	159	13	50	8	0	4	29	8	14	.314	.347	.440	.788	110	4	2	107	140	22	.698	3	1	0	2	C/3O	0.5
1981	Phi-N	61	196	16	50	7	0	6	37	15	13	.255	.311	.383	.694	86	-1	-4	112	156	20	.582	1	2	-1	-3	C/31O	-0.7
1982	Chi-N	138	476	50	124	17	2	15	68	46	71	.261	.330	.399	.729	100	2	-0	103	116	61	.651	0	6	-4	8	OC/3	0.3
1983	Chi-N	154	533	76	161	30	3	16	70	68	73	.302	.384	.460	.844	132	25	24	101	96	93	.808	0	3	-2	-12	*O/C	0.8
1984	Chi-N	140	495	59	138	17	3	16	80	34	71	.279	.329	.422	.751	100	5	-1	110	124	64	.655	1	4	-2	-8	*O1/3C	-1.6
1985	Chi-N	161	587	74	180	30	3	14	106	68	58	.307	.380	.440	.819	111	23	12	116	149	100	.800	12	3	2	-10	*O13/C	0.0
1986	Chi-N	156	586	72	159	30	0	12	79	53	48	.271	.332	.384	.716	91	-3	-7	107	128	72	.627	3	6	-3	-4	*O3C1	-1.7
1987	Chi-N	153	563	63	150	29	1	27	88	39	66	.266	.314	.465	.779	102	0	-0	101	104	78	.705	3	3	-1	0	*3/1	-0.1
1988	SD-N	143	511	40	131	23	0	5	64	40	51	.256	.310	.331	.641	86	-10	-9	97	**142**	50	.527	2	3	-1	-5	1O/3	-2.1
1989	Det-A	90	318	34	95	16	0	5	35	27	33	.299	.357	.396	.754	115	5	6	97	98	42	.661	3	2	-0	0	D13/C	0.4
	Bal-A	33	107	11	23	4	0	1	10	4	12	.215	.243	.280	.524	48	-8	-7	99	118	6	.374	0	0	0	0	D	-0.7
	Yr	123	425	45	118	20	0	6	45	31	45	.278	.330	.367	.697	98	-2	-1	98	104	46	.582	3	2	-0	0		-0.3
Total	12	1306	4581	511	1279	214	14	121	674	405	515	.279	.339	.411	.751	103	45	19	105	123	616	.671	28	33	-11	-30	O3C1/D	-4.5
■ RUSS MORMAN Morman, Russell Lee b: 4/28/62, Independence, Mo. BR/TR, 6'4", 215 lbs. Deb: 8/03/86																												
1986	Chi-A	49	159	18	40	5	0	4	17	16	36	.252	.328	.358	.686	87	-2	-3	101	98	19	.613	1	0	0	-2	1	-0.6
1988	Chi-A	40	75	8	18	2	0	0	3	3	17	.240	.269	.267	.536	52	-5	-5	97	60	4	.371	0	0	0	-3	1O/D	-0.9
1989	Chi-A	37	58	5	13	2	0	0	8	6	16	.224	.297	.259	.555	62	-3	-3	93	207	5	.478	1	0	0	-1	1	-0.5
Total	3	126	292	31	71	9	0	4	28	25	69	.243	.307	.315	.622	74	-10	-10	98	111	28	.522	2	0	1	-6	1/OD	-2.0
■ JOHN MORRIS Morris, John Daniel b: 2/23/61, Freeport, N.Y. BL/TL, 6'1", 185 lbs. Deb: 8/05/86																												
1986	StL-N	39	100	8	24	0	1	1	14	7	15	.240	.290	.290	.580	59	-5	-6	103	174	8	.525	6	2	1	0	O	-0.5
1987	StL-N	101	157	22	41	6	4	3	23	11	22	.261	.314	.408	.721	91	-3	-2	99	126	20	.675	5	2	0	-14	O	-1.8
1988	StL-N	20	38	3	11	2	1	0	3	1	7	.289	.308	.395	.702	96	-0	-0	104	80	5	.593	0	0	0	-5	O	-0.5
1989	StL-N	96	117	8	28	4	1	2	14	4	22	.239	.264	.342	.606	72	-5	-5	101	122	10	.484	1	0	0	-13	O	-1.8
Total	4	256	412	41	104	12	7	6	54	23	66	.252	.294	.359	.653	78	-13	-13	101	133	43	.575	12	4	1	-31	O	-4.6
■ HAL MORRIS Morris, William Harold b: 4/9/65, Fort Rucker, Ala. BL/TL, 6'3", 200 lbs. Deb: 7/29/88																												
1988	NY-A	15	20	1	2	0	0	0	0	0	9	.100	.100	.100	.200	-46	-4	-4	96	0	0	.111	0	0	0	-0	/OD	-0.3
1989	NY-A	15	18	2	5	0	0	0	4	1	4	.278	.316	.278	.594	66	-1	-1	104	311	1	.400	0	0	0	-1	/O1D	-0.2
Total	2	30	38	3	7	0	0	0	4	1	13	.184	.205	.184	.389	10	-4	-4	100	152	1	.242	0	0	0	-2	/O1D	-0.5
■ LLOYD MOSEBY Moseby, Lloyd Anthony b: 11/5/59, Portland, Ark. BL/TR, 6'3", 200 lbs. Deb: 5/24/80																												
1980	Tor-A	114	389	44	89	24	1	9	46	25	85	.229	.282	.365	.647	76	-14	-14	100	106	37	.552	4	6	-2	1	*O/D	-1.6
1981	Tor-A	100	378	36	88	16	2	9	43	24	86	.233	.280	.357	.638	75	-9	-14	111	110	37	.566	11	8	-2	-4	*O	-2.2
1982	Tor-A	147	487	51	115	20	9	9	52	33	106	.236	.295	.370	.665	75	-13	-18	109	101	52	.596	11	7	-1	-8	*O	-3.1
1983	Tor-A	151	539	104	170	31	7	18	81	51	85	.315	.380	.499	.879	129	29	23	108	100	104	.910	27	8	3	3	*O	2.8
1984	Tor-A	158	592	97	166	28	**15**	18	92	78	122	.280	.372	.470	.841	129	26	25	102	117	110	.910	39	9	6	7	*O	3.3
1985	Tor-A	152	584	92	151	30	7	18	70	76	91	.259	.348	.426	.774	110	9	9	101	88	89	.796	37	15	2	-7	*O	0.2
1986	Tor-A	152	589	89	149	24	5	21	86	64	122	.253	.332	.418	.750	99	3	-1	105	117	86	.760	32	11	3	-5	*O/D	-0.6
1987	Tor-A	155	592	106	167	27	4	26	96	70	124	.282	.360	.473	.833	118	17	16	101	113	106	.883	39	7	8	-1	*O/D	1.7
1988	Tor-A	128	472	77	113	17	7	10	42	70	93	.239	.345	.369	.714	100	2	2	100	87	66	.749	31	8	5	-8	*O/D	-0.3
1989	Tor-A	135	502	72	111	25	3	11	43	56	101	.221	.307	.349	.655	90	-10	-6	94	85	58	.644	24	7	3	-8	*OD	-1.2
Total	10	1392	5124	768	1319	242	60	149	651	547	1015	.257	.335	.415	.750	103	40	21	103	103	744	.749	255	86	25	-29	*O/D	-1.0
■ JOHN MOSES Moses, John William b: 8/9/57, Los Angeles, Cal. BB/TL, 5'10", 165 lbs. Deb: 8/23/82																												
1982	Sea-A	22	44	7	14	5	1	1	3	4	5	.318	.375	.545	.920	136	3	2	109	44	10	1.065	5	1	1	-4	O	0.0
1983	Sea-A	93	130	19	27	4	1	0	6	12	20	.208	.280	.254	.534	48	-9	-9	100	71	9	.509	11	5	0	-7	OD	-1.6
1984	Sea-A	19	35	3	12	1	1	0	2	2	5	.343	.395	.429	.823	125	1	1	102	53	6	.826	1	0	0	-2	O/D	0.0
1985	Sea-A	33	62	4	12	0	0	0	3	2	8	.194	.219	.194	.412	15	-7	-7	95	99	2	.345	5	2	0	-5	O	-1.1
1986	Sea-A	103	399	56	102	16	3	3	34	34	65	.256	.314	.333	.647	74	-12	-15	105	101	40	.596	25	18	-3	8	O/1D	-1.2
1987	Sea-A	116	390	58	96	16	4	3	38	29	49	.246	.303	.331	.634	67	-17	-18	103	110	38	.584	23	15	-2	-6	*O/1D	-2.8

YEAR	TM/L	G	AB	R	H	2B	3B	HR	RBI	BB	SO	AVG	OBP	SLG	PRO	/A	BR	/A	PF	CHI	RC	TA	SB	CS	SBR	FR	POS	TPR
1988	Min-A	105	206	33	65	10	3	2	12	15	21	.316	.368	.422	.790	114	6	4	106	51	31	.762	11	6	-0	-11	O/D	-0.8
1989	Min-A	129	242	33	68	12	3	1	31	19	23	.281	.336	.368	.704	92	-1	-2	107	131	30	.661	14	7	0	-16	*O/1PD	-2.0
Total	8	620	1508	213	396	64	16	10	129	117	196	.263	.319	.346	.665	79	-36	-43	104	96	166	.621	95	54	-4	-43	O/1DP	-9.5

■ **RANCE MULLINIKS** Mulliniks, Steven Rance b: 1/15/56, Tulare, Cal. BL/TR, 5'11", 162 lbs. Deb: 6/18/77

YEAR	TM/L	G	AB	R	H	2B	3B	HR	RBI	BB	SO	AVG	OBP	SLG	PRO	/A	BR	/A	PF	CHI	RC	TA	SB	CS	SBR	FR	POS	TPR
1977	Cal-A	78	271	36	73	13	2	3	21	23	36	.269	.329	.365	.694	94	-4	-2	95	79	34	.617	1	1	-0	-0	S	0.6
1978	Cal-A	50	119	6	22	3	1	1	6	8	23	.185	.242	.252	.494	39	-10	-10	102	72	7	.410	2	0	1	-3	S/D	-0.8
1979	Cal-A	22	68	7	10	0	0	1	8	4	14	.147	.205	.191	.397	8	-9	-8	93	192	3	.300	0	0	0	0	S	-0.5
1980	KC-A	36	54	8	14	3	0	0	6	7	10	.259	.344	.315	.659	83	-1	-1	98	138	6	.571	0	0	0	-2	S2	0.0
1981	KC-A	24	44	6	10	3	0	0	5	2	7	.227	.261	.295	.556	61	-2	-2	99	151	3	.405	0	1	-1	-2	2/S3	-0.4
1982	Tor-A	112	311	32	76	25	0	4	35	37	49	.244	.327	.363	.690	82	-4	-8	109	112	36	.623	3	2	-0	-10	*3S	-1.8
1983	Tor-A	129	364	54	100	34	3	10	49	57	43	.275	.374	.467	.841	120	16	12	108	96	62	.817	0	2	-1	-16	*3S/2	-0.3
1984	Tor-A	125	343	41	111	21	5	3	42	33	44	.324	.385	.440	.825	126	13	13	102	105	58	.779	2	3	-1	-4	*3/S2	0.9
1985	Tor-A	129	366	55	108	26	1	10	57	55	54	.295	.387	.454	.841	128	16	16	101	115	66	.832	2	0	1	-7	*3	0.5
1986	Tor-A	117	348	50	90	22	0	11	45	43	60	.259	.342	.417	.759	101	3	1	105	101	48	.701	1	1	-0	2	*3/2D	0.0
1987	Tor-A	124	332	37	103	28	1	11	44	34	55	.310	.374	.500	.874	129	14	14	101	88	60	.837	1	1	-0	0	3D/S	1.1
1988	Tor-A	119	337	49	101	21	1	12	48	56	57	.300	.399	.475	.874	144	21	22	100	97	65	.882	1	0	0	1	*D/3	2.3
1989	Tor-A	103	273	25	65	11	2	3	29	34	40	.238	.322	.326	.648	88	-5	-3	94	115	27	.559	0	0	0	3	D3	0.0
Total	13	1168	3230	406	883	210	16	69	395	393	492	.273	.353	.412	.766	108	50	43	102	103	477	.712	13	11	-3	-39	3DS/2	1.6

■ **DALE MURPHY** Murphy, Dale Bryan b: 3/12/56, Portland, Ore. BR/TR, 6'4", 210 lbs. Deb: 9/13/76

YEAR	TM/L	G	AB	R	H	2B	3B	HR	RBI	BB	SO	AVG	OBP	SLG	PRO	/A	BR	/A	PF	CHI	RC	TA	SB	CS	SBR	FR	POS	TPR
1976	Atl-N	19	65	3	17	6	0	0	9	7	9	.262	.333	.354	.687	85	-0	-1	111	154	8	.625	0	0	0	0	C	0.0
1977	Atl-N	18	76	5	24	8	1	2	14	0	8	.316	.316	.526	.842	108	2	1	113	129	11	.714	0	1	-1	1	C	0.1
1978	Atl-N	151	530	66	120	14	3	23	79	42	145	.226	.287	.394	.681	79	-10	-17	112	115	56	.613	11	7	-1	5	*1C	-1.7
1979	Atl-N	104	384	53	106	7	2	21	57	38	67	.276	.344	.469	.813	110	10	5	109	98	60	.777	6	1	1	-3	1C	0.1
1980	Atl-N	156	569	98	160	27	2	33	89	59	133	.281	.350	.510	.859	136	26	26	101	96	101	.849	9	6	-1	-1	*O/1	1.9
1981	Atl-N	104	369	43	91	12	1	13	50	44	72	.247	.327	.390	.717	103	1	1	100	109	47	.689	14	5	1	-1	*O/1	-0.1
1982	Atl-N	162	598	113	168	23	2	36	**109**	93	134	.281	.380	.507	.887	136	38	32	107	110	118	.936	23	11	0	-2	*O	3.0
1983	Atl-N	162	589	131	178	24	4	36	**121**	90	110	.302	.396	**.540**	**.936**	149	**46**	42	106	119	**131**	**1.023**	30	4	7	-4	*O	4.3
1984	Atl-N	162	607	94	176	32	8	**36**	100	79	134	.290	.374	**.547**	.920	142	**44**	37	110	94	123	.958	19	7	2	-7	*O	2.6
1985	Atl-N	162	616	**118**	185	32	2	**37**	111	**90**	141	.300	.390	.539	.929	148	48	43	106	96	**131**	.967	10	3	1	-13	*O	2.8
1986	Atl-N	160	614	89	163	29	7	29	83	75	141	.265	.347	.477	.825	123	20	18	102	84	102	.806	7	7	-2	-11	*O	0.2
1987	Atl-N	159	566	115	167	27	1	44	105	115	136	.295	.420	.580	1.000	149	53	47	108	97	**143**	1.120	16	6	1	9	*O	4.9
1988	Atl-N	156	592	77	134	35	4	24	77	74	125	.226	.314	.421	.735	105	6	3	104	92	72	.674	3	5	-2	12	*O	1.0
1989	Atl-N	154	574	60	131	16	0	20	84	65	142	.228	.309	.361	.670	89	-7	-8	102	134	64	.603	3	2	-0	5	*O	-0.5
Total	14	1829	6749	1065	1820	292	37	354	1088	871	1497	.270	.355	.481	.837	124	277	228	106	104	1166	.834	151	65	6	-8	*O1/C	18.6

■ **DWAYNE MURPHY** Murphy, Dwayne Keith b: 3/18/55, Merced, Cal. BL/TR, 6'1", 185 lbs. Deb: 4/08/78

YEAR	TM/L	G	AB	R	H	2B	3B	HR	RBI	BB	SO	AVG	OBP	SLG	PRO	/A	BR	/A	PF	CHI	RC	TA	SB	CS	SBR	FR	POS	TPR
1978	Oak-A	60	52	15	10	2	0	0	5	7	14	.192	.288	.231	.519	47	-3	-4	101	165	4	.442	0	1	-1	-9	O/D	-1.4
1979	Oak-A	121	388	57	99	10	4	11	40	84	80	.255	.389	.387	.776	124	9	16	89	89	62	.806	15	11	-2	4	*O	1.2
1980	Oak-A	159	573	86	157	18	2	13	68	102	96	.274	.386	.380	.766	117	13	17	95	99	90	.786	26	15	-1	17	*O	2.9
1981	Oak-A	107	390	58	98	10	3	15	60	73	91	.251	.372	.408	.780	130	15	17	96	102	64	.808	10	4	1	7	*O/D	2.3
1982	Oak-A	151	543	84	129	15	1	27	94	94	122	.238	.353	.418	.771	116	10	14	95	117	88	.814	26	8	3	15	*O/SD	2.6
1983	Oak-A	130	471	55	107	17	2	17	75	62	105	.227	.317	.380	.697	95	-6	-3	96	135	55	.644	7	5	-1	3	*O/D	-0.1
1984	Oak-A	153	559	93	143	18	2	33	88	74	111	.256	.346	.472	.818	135	18	24	92	102	90	.791	4	5	-2	11	*O	2.9
1985	Oak-A	152	523	77	122	21	3	20	59	84	123	.233	.343	.400	.742	110	3	8	93	89	73	.714	4	5	-2	1	*O	0.5
1986	Oak-A	98	329	50	83	11	3	9	39	56	80	.252	.368	.386	.754	114	5	8	94	103	51	.757	3	1	0	7	O/D	1.2
1987	Oak-A	82	219	39	51	7	0	8	35	58	61	.233	.394	.374	.768	117	5	8	91	132	36	.814	4	4	-1	4	O/12	0.8
1988	Det-A	49	144	14	36	5	0	4	19	24	26	.250	.361	.368	.729	111	2	3	94	116	21	.725	1	1	-0	6	O/D	0.8
1989	Phi-N	98	156	20	34	5	0	9	27	29	44	.218	.341	.423	.764	116	4	4	101	117	24	.760	0	1	-1	-7	O	-0.4
Total	12	1360	4347	648	1069	139	20	166	609	747	953	.246	.359	.402	.761	117	74	113	94	108	659	.761	100	61	-7	58	*O/D21S	13.3

■ **EDDIE MURRAY** Murray, Eddie Clarence b: 2/24/56, Los Angeles, Cal. BB/TR, 6'2", 190 lbs. Deb: 4/07/77

YEAR	TM/L	G	AB	R	H	2B	3B	HR	RBI	BB	SO	AVG	OBP	SLG	PRO	/A	BR	/A	PF	CHI	RC	TA	SB	CS	SBR	FR	POS	TPR
1977	Bal-A	160	611	81	173	29	2	27	88	48	104	.283	.336	.470	.806	126	13	18	93	100	90	.729	0	1	-1	-2	*D1/O	1.3
1978	Bal-A	161	610	85	174	32	3	27	95	70	97	.285	.360	.480	.840	148	27	34	91	106	104	.811	6	5	-1	1	*1/3D	2.8
1979	Bal-A	159	606	90	179	30	2	25	99	72	78	.295	.372	.475	.847	130	23	25	97	111	107	.836	10	2	2	-2	*1	1.6
1980	Bal-A	158	621	100	186	36	2	32	116	54	71	.300	.357	.519	.876	136	30	29	101	115	111	.846	7	2	1	-8	*1/D	1.2
1981	Bal-A	99	378	57	111	21	2	**22**	**78**	40	43	.294	.363	.534	.897	157	26	26	99	121	70	.875	2	3	-1	9	1	3.2
1982	Bal-A	151	550	87	174	30	1	32	110	70	82	.316	.395	.549	.944	156	42	43	100	113	116	.962	7	2	1	1	*1/D	4.0
1983	Bal-A	156	582	115	178	30	3	33	111	86	90	.306	.398	.538	.936	154	45	45	100	112	**133**	1.002	5	1	1	2	*1/D	4.0
1984	Bal-A	162	588	97	180	26	3	29	110	**107**	87	.306	**.415**	.509	.923	**163**	**47**	**51**	94	120	130	.998	10	2	2	7	*1/D	5.0
1985	Bal-A	156	583	111	173	37	1	31	124	84	68	.297	.387	.523	.910	148	38	39	99	131	122	.943	5	2	0	12	*1/D	4.1
1986	Bal-A	137	495	61	151	25	1	17	84	78	49	.305	.400	.463	.862	137	27	27	99	127	92	.859	3	0	1	-2	*1D	1.8
1987	Bal-A	160	618	89	171	28	3	30	91	73	80	.277	.353	.477	.830	121	17	18	98	100	103	.795	1	2	-1	10	*1/D	1.1
1988	Bal-A	161	603	75	171	27	2	28	84	75	78	.284	.363	.474	.837	139	26	30	95	96	101	.806	5	2	0	11	*1D	3.6
1989	LA-N	160	594	66	147	29	1	20	88	87	85	.247	.346	.401	.746	122	11	16	93	126	85	.726	7	2	1	14	*1/3	1.9
Total	13	1980	7439	1114	2168	380	26	353	1278	944	1012	.291	.373	.492	.864	141	372	404	97	113	1363	.856	68	26	5	53	*1D/3O	35.6

■ **GREG MYERS** Myers, Gregory Richard b: 4/14/66, Riverside, Cal. BL/TR, 6'1", 200 lbs. Deb: 9/12/87

YEAR	TM/L	G	AB	R	H	2B	3B	HR	RBI	BB	SO	AVG	OBP	SLG	PRO	/A	BR	/A	PF	CHI	RC	TA	SB	CS	SBR	FR	POS	TPR
1987	Tor-A	7	9	1	1	0	0	0	0	0	3	.111	.111	.111	.222	-40	-2	-2	101	0	-0	.100	0	0	0	0	/C	0.0
1989	Tor-A	17	44	0	5	2	0	0	1	2	9	.114	.152	.159	.311	-13	-7	-6	94	56	1	.214	0	1	-1	-1	C/D	-0.7
Total	2	24	53	1	6	2	0	0	1	2	12	.113	.145	.151	.296	-18	-8	-8	95	46	1	.192	0	1	-1	-1	/CD	-0.7

■ **ROB NELSON** Nelson, Robert Augustus b: 5/17/64, Pasadena, Cal. BL/TL, 6'4", 215 lbs. Deb: 9/09/86

YEAR	TM/L	G	AB	R	H	2B	3B	HR	RBI	BB	SO	AVG	OBP	SLG	PRO	/A	BR	/A	PF	CHI	RC	TA	SB	CS	SBR	FR	POS	TPR
1986	Oak-A	5	9	1	2	1	0	0	0	1	4	.222	.300	.333	.633	78	-0	-0	94	0	1	.571	0	0	0	0	/1D	0.0
1987	Oak-A	7	24	1	4	1	0	0	0	0	12	.167	.167	.208	.375	-1	-3	-3	91	0	1	.250	0	0	0	0	/1	-0.3
	SD-N	10	11	0	1	0	0	0	1	1	8	.091	.167	.091	.258	-30	-2	-2	97	399	0	.200	0	0	0	0	/1	-0.1
1988	SD-N	7	21	4	4	0	0	1	3	2	9	.190	.261	.333	.594	71	-1	-1	97	120	2	.529	0	0	0	0	/1	0.0
1989	SD-N	42	82	6	16	0	1	3	7	20	29	.195	.353	.329	.682	96	0	0	101	78	10	.676	1	3	-2	1	1	-0.2
Total	4	71	147	12	27	2	1	4	11	24	62	.184	.298	.293	.591	68	-6	-6	98	91	14	.544	1	3	-2	1	/1D	-0.6

■ **AL NEWMAN** Newman, Albert Dwayne b: 6/30/60, Kansas City, Mo. BB/TR, 5'9", 175 lbs. Deb: 6/14/85

YEAR	TM/L	G	AB	R	H	2B	3B	HR	RBI	BB	SO	AVG	OBP	SLG	PRO	/A	BR	/A	PF	CHI	RC	TA	SB	CS	SBR	FR	POS	TPR
1985	Mon-N	25	29	7	5	1	0	0	1	3	4	.172	.250	.207	.457	31	-3	-2	94	66	2	.440	2	1	0	-0	2/S	-0.2
1986	Mon-N	95	185	23	37	3	0	1	8	21	20	.200	.282	.232	.514	44	-14	-13	98	69	12	.460	11	11	-3	3	2S	-1.0
1987	Min-A	110	307	44	68	15	5	0	29	34	27	.221	.299	.303	.602	64	-17	-15	96	124	28	.557	15	11	-2	2	S23/OD	-0.8
1988	Min-A	105	260	35	58	7	0	0	19	29	34	.223	.301	.250	.551	53	-14	-17	106	116	22	.507	12	3	2	-5	32S/D	-1.7
1989	Min-A	141	446	62	113	18	2	0	38	59	46	.253	.343	.303	.646	78	-8	-11	107	110	52	.635	25	12	0	-13	23S/OD	-2.0
Total	5	476	1227	171	281	44	7	1	95	146	131	.229	.312	.279	.591	63	-55	-58	102	108	116	.555	65	38	-3	-14	2S3/DO	-5.7

■ **CARL NICHOLS** Nichols, Carl Edward b: 10/14/62, Los Angeles, Cal. BR/TR, 6', 184 lbs. Deb: 9/14/86

YEAR	TM/L	G	AB	R	H	2B	3B	HR	RBI	BB	SO	AVG	OBP	SLG	PRO	/A	BR	/A	PF	CHI	RC	TA	SB	CS	SBR	FR	POS	TPR
1986	Bal-A	5	5	0	0	0	0	0	0	1	4	.000	.167	.000	.167	-50	-1	-1	99	0	0	.200	0	0	0	0	/C	0.0
1987	Bal-A	13	21	4	8	1	0	0	3	1	4	.381	.409	.429	.838	127	1	1	98	133	4	.769	0	0	0	1	C	0.3
1988	Bal-A	18	47	2	9	1	0	0	1	3	10	.191	.240	.213	.453	29	-4	-4	95	40	2	.317	0	0	0	2	C/O	-0.1
1989	Hou-N	8	13	0	1	0	0	0	2	0	3	.077	.077	.077	.154	-55	-3	-3	102	805	0	.083	0	0	0	0	/C	-0.1
Total	4	44	86	6	18	2	0	0	6	5	21	.209	.253	.233	.485	37	-7	-7	97	169	6	.352	0	0	0	3	/CO	0.1

■ **TOM NIETO** Nieto, Thomas Andrew b: 10/27/60, Downey, Cal. BR/TR, 6'1", 193 lbs. Deb: 5/10/84

YEAR	TM/L	G	AB	R	H	2B	3B	HR	RBI	BB	SO	AVG	OBP	SLG	PRO	/A	BR	/A	PF	CHI	RC	TA	SB	CS	SBR	FR	POS	TPR
1984	StL-N	33	86	7	24	4	0	3	12	5	18	.279	.319	.430	.749	110	1	1	99	102	11	.646	0	0	0	1	C	0.2
1985	StL-N	95	253	15	57	10	2	0	34	26	37	.225	.305	.281	.586	68	-11	-10	96	191	21	.483	0	2	-1	-10	C	-1.8

YEAR	TM/L	G	AB	R	H	2B	3B	HR	RBI	BB	SO	AVG	OBP	SLG	PRO	/A	BR	/A	PF	CHI	RC	TA	SB	CS	SBR	FR	POS	TPR
1986	Mon-N	30	65	5	13	3	1	1	7	6	21	.200	.278	.323	.601	67	-3	-3	98	116	5	.500	0	1	-1	-3	C	-0.5
1987	Min-A	41	105	7	21	7	1	1	12	8	24	.200	.276	.314	.590	59	-6	-6	96	133	10	.518	0	0	0	-4	C/D	-0.5
1988	Min-A	24	60	1	4	0	0	0	0	1	17	.067	.097	.067	.163	-50	-12	-13	106	0	0	.103	0	0	0	0	C	-1.1
1989	Phi-N	11	20	1	3	0	0	0	0	6	7	.150	.370	.150	.520	54	-1	-1	101	0	2	.588	0	0	0	1	C	0.1
Total	6	234	589	36	122	24	4	5	65	52	124	.207	.282	.287	.568	59	-33	-31	98	134	49	.471	0	3	-2	-15	C/D	-3.6
■ **OTIS NIXON**	Nixon, Otis Junior b: 1/9/59, Columbus Co., N.C. BB/TR, 6'2", 180 lbs. Deb: 9/09/83																											
1983	NY-A	13	14	2	2	0	0	0	0	1	5	.143	.200	.143	.343	-4	-2	-2	99	0	1	.417	2	0	1	-1	/O	-0.1
1984	Cle-A	49	91	16	14	0	0	0	1	8	11	.154	.222	.154	.376	6	-11	-12	106	28	3	.400	12	6	0	-3	O	-1.6
1985	Cle-A	104	162	34	38	4	0	3	9	8	27	.235	.271	.315	.585	63	-9	-8	94	59	12	.577	20	11	-1	-8	OD	-1.6
1986	Cle-A	105	95	33	25	4	1	0	8	13	12	.263	.352	.326	.678	89	-1	-1	98	103	13	.870	23	6	3	-24	O/D	-2.3
1987	Cle-A	19	17	2	1	0	0	0	1	3	4	.059	.200	.059	.259	-25	-3	-3	103	399	0	.316	2	3	-1	-3	O/D	-0.7
1988	Mon-N	90	271	47	66	8	2	0	15	28	42	.244	.314	.288	.602	70	-8	-10	106	77	30	.697	46	13	6	2	O	-0.4
1989	Mon-N	126	258	41	56	7	2	0	21	33	36	.217	.306	.260	.566	62	-11	-12	102	126	24	.628	37	12	4	-7	O	-1.7
Total	7	506	908	175	202	23	5	3	55	94	137	.222	.295	.269	.564	59	-47	-48	102	91	84	.627	142	51	12	-43	O/D	-8.4
■ **DONELL NIXON**	Nixon, Robert Donell b: 12/31/61, Evergreen, N.C. BR/TR, 6'1", 185 lbs. Deb: 4/07/87																											
1987	Sea-A	46	132	17	33	4	0	3	12	13	28	.250	.327	.348	.675	78	-3	-4	103	87	16	.752	21	7	2	2	O/D	0.0
1988	SF-N	59	78	15	27	3	0	0	6	10	12	.346	.420	.385	.805	141	4	4	94	80	12	.850	11	8	-2	-8	O	-0.6
1989	SF-N	95	166	23	44	2	0	1	15	11	30	.265	.311	.295	.606	76	-5	-5	97	116	15	.543	10	3	1	-11	O	-1.6
Total	3	200	376	55	104	9	0	4	33	34	70	.277	.340	.332	.672	90	-5	-4	98	98	43	.681	42	18	2	-17	O/D	-2.2
■ **JUNIOR NOBOA**	Noboa, Miliciades Arturo (Diaz) b: 11/10/64, Azua, D.R. BR/TR, 5'10", 155 lbs. Deb: 8/22/84																											
1984	Cle-A	23	11	3	4	0	0	0	0	0	2	.364	.364	.364	.727	96	0	-0	106	0	1	.625	1	0	0	0	2/D	0.1
1987	Cle-A	39	80	7	18	2	1	0	7	3	6	.225	.253	.275	.528	40	-7	-7	103	127	6	.413	1	0	0	-2	2/S3D	-0.6
1988	Cal-A	21	16	4	1	0	0	0	0	0	1	.063	.063	.063	.125	-69	-3	-3	94	0	-0	.059	0	0	0	0	/2S3	-0.1
1989	Mon-N	21	44	3	10	0	0	0	1	1	3	.227	.244	.227	.472	35	-4	-4	102	40	3	.324	0	0	0	2	2/S3	-0.1
Total	4	104	151	17	33	2	1	0	8	4	12	.219	.239	.245	.484	32	-14	-14	102	80	10	.352	2	0	1	0	/2S3D	-0.7
■ **MATT NOKES**	Nokes, Matthew Dodge b: 10/31/63, San Diego, Cal. BL/TR, 6'1", 185 lbs. Deb: 9/03/85																											
1985	SF-N	19	53	3	11	2	0	2	5	1	9	.208	.236	.358	.595	69	-3	-2	93	80	4	.477	0	0	0	1	C	0.0
1986	Det-A	7	24	2	8	1	0	1	2	1	1	.333	.360	.500	.860	139	1	1	95	53	4	.765	0	0	0	1	/C	0.2
1987	Det-A	135	461	69	133	14	2	32	87	35	70	.289	.347	.536	.882	134	19	21	97	101	82	.848	2	1	0	-2	*CD/O3	2.6
1988	Det-A	122	382	53	96	18	0	16	53	34	58	.251	.314	.424	.738	111	2	4	94	100	49	.661	0	1	-1	1	*C/D	0.9
1989	Det-A	87	268	15	67	10	0	9	39	17	37	.250	.300	.388	.688	95	-3	-2	97	116	30	.596	1	0	0	4	CD	0.4
Total	5	370	1188	142	315	45	2	60	186	88	175	.265	.321	.458	.779	116	15	22	96	102	169	.710	3	2	-0	4	C/DO3	4.1
YEAR	TM/L	G	AB	R	H	2B	3B	HR	RBI	BB	SO	AVG	OBP	SLG	PRO	/A	BR	/A	PF	CHI	RC	TA	SB	CS	SBR	FR	POS	TPR
■ **KEN OBERKFELL**	Oberkfell, Kenneth Ray b: 5/4/56, Highland, Ill. BL/TR, 6', 175 lbs. Deb: 8/22/77																											
1977	StL-N	9	9	0	1	0	0	0	1	0	3	.111	.111	.111	.222	-42	-2	-2	96	400	0	.125	0	0	0	0	/2	0.0
1978	StL-N	24	50	7	6	1	0	0	0	3	1	.120	.170	.140	.310	-13	-8	-7	95	0	1	.222	0	0	0	0	2/3	-0.5
1979	StL-N	135	369	53	111	19	5	1	35	57	35	.301	.400	.388	.788	111	11	9	105	95	60	.776	4	1	1	5	*23/S	2.2
1980	StL-N	116	422	58	128	27	6	3	46	51	23	.303	.380	.417	.797	119	14	12	103	104	66	.751	4	4	-1	-5	*23	1.4
1981	StL-N	102	376	43	110	12	6	2	45	37	28	.293	.356	.372	.728	105	4	3	102	123	49	.674	13	5	1	11	*3/S	1.1
1982	StL-N	137	470	55	136	22	5	2	34	40	31	.289	.346	.370	.717	97	1	-1	103	74	58	.638	11	9	-2	7	*3/2	0.1
1983	StL-N	151	488	62	143	26	5	3	38	61	27	.293	.373	.385	.758	113	9	10	98	76	71	.722	12	6	0	1	*32/S	0.8
1984	StL-N	50	152	17	47	11	1	0	11	16	10	.309	.379	.395	.773	119	4	4	99	72	22	.709	1	2	-1	5	3/2S	0.9
	Atl-N	50	172	21	40	8	1	1	10	15	17	.233	.294	.308	.602	63	-7	-9	110	71	15	.496	1	3	-2	-0	3/2	-1.1
	Yr	100	324	38	87	19	2	1	21	31	27	.269	.334	.349	.683	88	-3	-5	104	72	37	.590	2	5	-2	5		-0.2
1985	Atl-N	134	412	30	112	19	4	3	35	51	38	.272	.360	.359	.720	96	3	-0	106	89	54	.660	1	2	-1	-4	*32	-0.4
1986	Atl-N	151	503	62	136	24	3	5	48	83	40	.270	.376	.360	.736	102	6	5	102	100	72	.715	7	4	-0	15	*32	1.7
1987	Atl-N	135	508	59	142	29	2	3	48	48	29	.280	.344	.362	.706	81	-8	-14	108	105	63	.620	3	3	-1	-4	*32	-1.9
1988	Atl-N	120	422	42	117	20	4	3	40	32	28	.277	.331	.365	.696	95	-0	-2	104	100	51	.608	4	5	-2	-6	*3/2	-1.0
	Pit-N	20	54	7	12	2	0	0	2	5	6	.222	.288	.259	.547	60	-3	-3	98	57	4	.432	0	0	0	0	2/S31	-0.1
	Yr	140	476	49	129	22	4	3	42	37	34	.271	.326	.353	.679	92	-3	-5	103	95	55	.586	4	5	-2	-6		-1.1
1989	Pit-N	14	40	2	5	1	0	0	2	2	2	.125	.167	.150	.317	-9	-6	-5	94	134	1	.229	0	0	0	-0	/12	-0.6
	SF-N	83	116	17	37	5	1	2	15	8	8	.319	.373	.431	.804	133	4	5	97	108	18	.714	0	1	-1	0	3/12	0.4
	Yr	97	156	19	42	6	1	2	17	10	10	.269	.321	.359	.680	98	-1	-1	97	113	17	.571	0	1	-1	-0		-0.2
Total	13	1431	4563	535	1283	226	43	28	410	509	326	.281	.356	.368	.724	98	22	4	103	94	607	.662	61	45	-9	26	*32/1S	3.0
■ **CHARLIE O'BRIEN**	O'Brien, Charles Hugh b: 5/1/60, Tulsa, Okla. BR/TR, 6'2", 195 lbs. Deb: 6/02/85																											
1985	Oak-A	16	11	3	3	1	0	0	1	3	3	.273	.429	.364	.792	129	0	1	93	99	2	.875	0	0	0	-0	C	0.1
1987	Mil-A	10	35	2	7	3	1	0	0	4	4	.200	.282	.343	.625	64	-2	-2	102	0	3	.552	0	1	-1	2	C	0.0
1988	Mil-A	40	118	12	26	6	0	2	9	5	16	.220	.252	.322	.574	58	-7	-7	103	81	9	.448	0	1	-1	4	C	-0.1
1989	Mil-A	62	188	22	44	10	0	6	35	21	11	.234	.339	.383	.722	107	1	2	97	151	23	.658	0	0	0	9	C	1.4
Total	4	128	352	39	80	20	1	8	45	33	34	.227	.310	.358	.668	87	-7	-6	99	112	38	.583	0	2	-1	15	C	1.4
■ **PETE O'BRIEN**	O'Brien, Peter Michael b: 2/9/58, Santa Monica, Cal. BL/TR, 6'1", 185 lbs. Deb: 9/03/82																											
1982	Tex-A	20	67	13	16	4	1	4	13	6	8	.239	.301	.507	.809	126	1	2	93	115	11	.804	1	0	0	-1	O/1D	0.1
1983	Tex-A	154	524	53	124	24	5	8	53	58	62	.237	.314	.347	.661	81	-13	-13	101	103	57	.591	5	4	-1	9	*1O/D	-1.0
1984	Tex-A	142	520	57	149	26	2	18	80	53	50	.287	.353	.448	.801	120	14	14	100	113	80	.747	3	5	-2	-0	*1/O	0.2
1985	Tex-A	159	573	69	153	34	3	22	92	69	53	.267	.347	.452	.799	108	13	7	108	119	85	.746	5	10	-5	-6	*1	-1.3
1986	Tex-A	156	551	86	160	23	3	23	90	87	66	.290	.387	.468	.855	139	27	31	96	116	98	.843	4	4	-1	2	*1	2.0
1987	Tex-A	159	569	84	163	26	1	23	88	59	61	.286	.354	.457	.810	110	11	9	104	109	91	.761	0	4	-2	17	*1/OD	0.6
1988	Tex-A	156	547	57	149	24	1	16	71	72	73	.272	.357	.408	.765	112	11	10	101	106	80	.715	1	4	-2	13	*1/D	1.2
1989	Cle-A	155	555	75	144	24	1	12	55	83	48	.259	.358	.371	.729	102	7	4	104	94	77	.697	3	1	0	5	*1/D	0.0
Total	8	1101	3906	494	1058	185	17	126	542	487	421	.271	.352	.424	.776	110	72	63	102	109	580	.730	22	32	-13	40	*1/OD	1.8
■ **RON OESTER**	Oester, Ronald John b: 5/5/56, Cincinnati, Ohio BB/TR, 6'2", 185 lbs. Deb: 9/10/78																											
1978	Cin-N	6	8	1	3	0	0	0	1	0	2	.375	.375	.375	.750	107	0	0	103	132	1	.600	0	0	0	0	/S	0.1
1979	Cin-N	6	3	0	0	0	0	0	0	0	1	.000	.000	.000	.000	-99	-1	-1	97	0	0	.000	0	0	0	0	/S	0.0
1980	Cin-N	100	303	40	84	16	2	2	20	26	44	.277	.336	.363	.699	94	-2	-2	102	68	37	.627	6	2	1	-6	2S/3	0.0
1981	Cin-N	105	354	45	96	16	7	5	42	42	49	.271	.348	.398	.747	110	6	5	101	108	48	.683	2	5	-2	5	*2/S	1.7
1982	Cin-N	151	549	63	143	19	4	9	47	35	82	.260	.305	.359	.664	83	-12	-13	102	84	56	.554	5	6	-2	10	*2S3	0.1
1983	Cin-N	157	549	63	145	23	5	11	58	49	106	.264	.326	.384	.710	93	-3	-5	103	96	66	.622	2	2	-1	-24	*2	-2.4
1984	Cin-N	150	553	54	134	26	3	3	38	41	97	.242	.296	.316	.612	68	-21	-24	106	83	50	.513	7	2	1	-12	*2/S	-3.3
1985	Cin-N	152	526	59	155	26	3	1	34	51	65	.295	.357	.361	.718	96	2	-1	105	72	68	.641	5	0	2	4	*2	0.6
1986	Cin-N	153	523	52	135	23	2	8	44	52	84	.258	.326	.356	.682	84	-8	-11	104	84	59	.608	9	2	2	15	*2	0.8
1987	Cin-N	69	237	28	60	9	6	2	23	22	51	.253	.317	.367	.684	78	-7	-8	104	99	26	.590	2	3	-1	-2	2	-0.8
1988	Cin-N	54	150	20	42	7	0	0	10	9	24	.280	.321	.327	.647	82	-3	-4	105	82	15	.518	0	2	-1	0	2/S	-0.2
1989	Cin-N	109	305	23	75	15	0	1	14	32	47	.246	.318	.305	.622	76	-8	-9	103	59	29	.525	1	0	0	-3	*2/S	-1.0
Total	12	1212	4060	448	1072	180	32	42	331	359	652	.264	.324	.355	.680	86	-56	-73	104	84	454	.590	39	24	-3	-12	*2/S3	-4.4
■ **JOHN OLERUD**	Olerud, John Garrett b: 8/5/68, Bellevue, Wash. BL/TL, 6'5", 205 lbs. Deb: 9/03/89																											
1989	Tor-A	6	8	2	3	0	0	0	0	0	1	.375	.375	.375	.750	119	0	0	94	0	1	.600	0	0	0	0	/1D	0.0
■ **JOE OLIVER**	Oliver, Joseph Melton b: 7/24/65, Memphis, Tenn. BR/TR, 6'3", 215 lbs. Deb: 7/15/89																											
1989	Cin-N	49	151	13	41	8	0	3	23	6	28	.272	.304	.384	.688	93	-1	-2	103	138	17	.575	0	0	0	-1	C	0.0

YEAR	TM/L	G	AB	R	H	2B	3B	HR	RBI	BB	SO	AVG	OBP	SLG	PRO	/A	BR	/A	PF	CHI	RC	TA	SB	CS	SBR	FR	POS	TPR

■ GREG OLSON Olson, Gregory William b: 9/6/60, Marshall, Minn. BR/TR, 6', 200 lbs. Deb: 6/27/89

| | | | | | | | | | | | | | | | | | | | | | | | | | | | | |
|1989|Min-A|3|2|0|1|0|0|0|0|0|0|.500|.500|.500|1.000|171|0|0|107|0|1|1.000|0|0|0|0|/C|0.0|

■ TOM O'MALLEY O'Malley, Thomas Patrick b: 12/25/60, Orange, N.J. BL/TR, 6', 180 lbs. Deb: 5/08/82

1982	SF-N	92	291	26	80	12	4	2	27	33	39	.275	.351	.364	.715	107	1	3	94	95	35	.622	0	3	-2	-3	3/2S	-0.2
1983	SF-N	135	410	40	106	16	1	5	45	52	47	.259	.348	.339	.687	90	-3	-4	101	116	49	.616	2	4	-2	-1	*3	-1.0
1984	SF-N	13	25	2	3	0	0	0	2	2	2	.120	.185	.120	.305	-13	-4	-4	96	0	1	.227	0	0	0	-1	/3	-0.4
	Chi-A	12	16	0	2	0	0	0	3	0	5	.125	.125	.125	.250	-28	-3	-3	111	598	0	.133	0	0	0	-0	/3	-0.2
1985	Bal-A	8	14	1	1	0	0	1	2	0	2	.071	.071	.286	.357	-8	-2	-2	99	113	0	.286	0	0	0	0	/3	-0.1
1986	Bal-A	56	181	19	46	9	0	1	18	17	21	.254	.318	.320	.639	76	-6	-6	99	118	18	.536	0	1	-1	1	3	-0.6
1987	Tex-A	45	117	10	32	8	0	1	12	15	9	.274	.356	.368	.724	90	-1	-1	104	104	14	.630	0	0	0	-2	3/2	-0.3
1988	Mon-N	14	27	3	7	0	0	0	2	3	4	.259	.333	.259	.593	68	-1	-1	106	114	3	.500	0	0	0	-0	/3	0.0
1989	NY-N	9	11	2	6	2	0	0	8	0	2	.545	.545	.727	1.273	271	2	2	97	403	4	1.600	0	0	0	-1	/3	0.2
Total	8	384	1092	103	283	47	5	10	117	122	131	.259	.336	.339	.675	88	-16	-15	99	115	124	.585	2	8	-4	-6	3/2S	-2.6

■ PAUL O'NEILL O'Neill, Paul Andrew b: 2/25/63, Columbus, Ohio BL/TR, 6'4", 200 lbs. Deb: 9/03/85

1985	Cin-N	5	12	1	4	1	0	0	1	0	2	.333	.333	.417	.750	103	0	0	105	80	2	.625	0	0	0	1	/O	0.1
1986	Cin-N	3	2	0	0	0	0	0	0	1	1	.000	.333	.000	.333	-0	-0	-0	104	0	0	.500	0	0	0	0	/H	0.0
1987	Cin-N	84	160	24	41	14	1	7	28	18	29	.256	.331	.488	.819	110	3	2	104	113	26	.797	2	1	0	-2	O/1P	-0.1
1988	Cin-N	145	485	58	122	25	3	16	73	38	65	.252	.309	.414	.723	100	2	-0	105	117	61	.662	8	6	-1	-1	*O1	-0.7
1989	Cin-N	117	428	49	118	24	2	15	74	46	64	.276	.349	.446	.795	122	14	13	103	129	69	.804	20	5	3	1	*O	1.6
Total	5	354	1087	132	285	64	6	38	176	103	161	.262	.328	.437	.765	110	19	14	104	120	157	.736	30	12	2	-1	O/1P	0.9

■ JOSE OQUENDO Oquendo, Jose Manuel (Contreras) b: 7/4/63, Rio Piedras, P.R. BB/TR, 5'10", 160 lbs. Deb: 5/02/83

1983	NY-N	120	328	29	70	7	0	1	17	19	60	.213	.261	.244	.505	41	-26	-26	99	81	19	.394	8	9	-3	-1	*S	-1.9
1984	NY-N	81	189	23	42	5	0	0	10	15	26	.222	.286	.249	.535	52	-12	-12	100	83	16	.493	10	1	2	-3	S	-0.4
1986	StL-N	76	138	20	41	4	1	0	13	15	20	.297	.366	.341	.707	93	-0	-1	103	110	17	.621	2	3	-1	-3	S2/3O	-0.1
1987	StL-N	116	248	43	71	9	0	1	24	54	29	.286	.414	.335	.749	103	4	4	99	111	38	.754	4	4	-1	-2	O2S/31P	0.2
1988	StL-N	148	451	36	125	10	1	7	46	52	40	.277	.352	.350	.702	98	3	1	104	103	57	.629	4	6	-2	5	2310S/PC	0.5
1989	StL-N	163	556	59	162	28	7	1	48	79	59	.291	.380	.372	.752	115	14	14	101	94	81	.703	3	5	-2	21	*2/S1	3.6
Total	6	704	1910	210	511	63	9	10	158	234	234	.268	.349	.326	.674	89	-17	-19	101	96	227	.607	31	28	-8	17	2S/031PC	1.9

■ JOE ORSULAK Orsulak, Joseph Michael b: 5/31/62, Parsippany, N.J. BL/TL, 6'1", 185 lbs. Deb: 9/01/83

1983	Pit-N	7	11	0	2	0	0	0	1	0	2	.182	.182	.182	.364	1	-1	-1	103	198	0	.200	0	1	-1	0	/O	-0.1
1984	Pit-N	32	67	12	17	1	2	0	3	1	7	.254	.275	.328	.604	73	-3	-2	94	53	6	.529	3	1	0	-1	O	-0.4
1985	Pit-N	121	397	54	119	14	6	0	21	26	27	.300	.344	.365	.710	96	-1	-2	103	58	51	.667	24	11	1	5	*O	0.1
1986	Pit-N	138	401	60	100	19	6	2	19	28	38	.249	.300	.342	.642	77	-13	-13	100	53	42	.601	24	11	1	-3	*O	-1.8
1988	Bal-A	125	379	48	109	21	3	8	27	23	30	.288	.333	.422	.755	116	4	7	95	58	51	.684	9	8	-2	-4	*O	0.0
1989	Bal-A	123	390	59	111	22	5	7	55	41	35	.285	.356	.421	.776	119	10	10	99	116	59	.731	5	3	-0	5	*O/D	1.3
Total	6	546	1645	233	458	77	22	17	126	119	139	.278	.330	.383	.713	100	-4	-2	99	71	209	.660	65	35	-2	3	O/D	-0.9

■ JUNIOR ORTIZ Ortiz, Adalberto Colon b: 10/24/59, Humacao, P.R. BR/TR, 5'11", 174 lbs. Deb: 9/20/82

1982	Pit-N	7	15	1	3	1	0	0	0	1	3	.200	.250	.267	.517	40	-1	-1	110	0	1	.385	0	0	0	0	/C	0.0
1983	Pit-N	5	8	1	1	0	0	0	0	1	0	.125	.222	.125	.347	-1	-1	-1	103	0	0	.286	0	0	0	0	/C	0.0
	NY-N	68	185	10	47	5	0	0	12	3	34	.254	.270	.281	.551	54	-12	-12	99	91	14	.410	1	0	0	-2	C	-1.1
	Yr	73	193	11	48	5	0	0	12	4	34	.249	.268	.275	.542	51	-13	-13	99	85	15	.404	1	0	0	-2		-1.1
1984	NY-N	40	91	6	18	3	0	0	11	5	15	.198	.240	.231	.470	33	-8	-8	100	205	5	.360	1	0	0	-0	C	-0.7
1985	Pit-N	23	72	4	21	2	0	1	5	3	17	.292	.320	.361	.681	88	-1	-1	103	69	8	.577	1	0	0	4	C	0.4
1986	Pit-N	49	110	11	37	6	0	0	14	9	13	.336	.387	.391	.777	115	2	2	100	130	16	.667	0	1	-1	4	C	0.7
1987	Pit-N	75	192	16	52	8	1	1	22	15	23	.271	.324	.339	.662	73	-6	-8	104	129	20	.541	0	2	-1	-1	C	-0.3
1988	Pit-N	49	118	8	33	6	0	2	18	9	9	.280	.341	.381	.722	110	1	1	98	141	13	.600	1	4	-2	1	C	0.2
1989	Pit-N	91	230	16	50	6	1	1	22	20	25	.217	.286	.265	.551	62	-12	-10	94	138	17	.445	2	2	-1	-3	C	-0.8
Total	8	407	1021	73	262	37	2	5	104	66	134	.257	.305	.311	.616	72	-38	-37	99	126	94	.495	6	9	-4	-2	C	-1.6

■ JOHN ORTON Orton, John Andrew b: 12/8/65, Santa Cruz, Cal. BR/TR, 6'1", 195 lbs. Deb: 8/20/89

| | | | | | | | | | | | | | | | | | | | | | | | | | | | | |
|1989|Cal-A|16|39|4|7|1|0|0|4|2|17|.179|.220|.205|.425|21|-4|-4|99|194|2|.313|0|0|0|2|C|-0.1|

■ SPIKE OWEN Owen, Spike Dee b: 4/19/61, Cleburne, Tex. BB/TR, 5'9", 165 lbs. Deb: 6/25/83

1983	Sea-A	80	306	36	60	11	3	2	21	24	44	.196	.259	.271	.530	46	-22	-22	100	89	23	.469	10	6	-1	13	S	-0.4
1984	Sea-A	152	530	67	130	18	8	3	43	46	63	.245	.309	.326	.636	74	-17	-18	102	96	56	.576	16	8	0	17	*S	1.0
1985	Sea-A	118	352	41	91	10	6	6	37	34	27	.259	.324	.372	.696	95	-5	-2	95	98	44	.649	11	5	0	15	*S	2.2
1986	Sea-A	112	402	46	99	22	6	0	35	34	42	.246	.307	.331	.637	71	-14	-16	105	107	40	.533	1	3	-2	29	*S	1.7
	Bos-A	42	126	21	23	2	1	1	10	17	9	.183	.285	.238	.523	45	-9	-9	100	121	9	.481	3	1	0	-5	S	-1.1
	Yr	154	528	67	122	24	7	1	45	51	51	.231	.301	.309	.610	65	-23	-26	104	111	49	.520	4	4	-1	24		0.6
1987	Bos-A	132	437	50	113	17	7	2	48	53	43	.259	.340	.343	.683	84	-9	-9	99	123	52	.630	11	8	-2	-10	*S	-1.3
1988	Bos-A	89	257	40	64	14	1	5	18	27	27	.249	.325	.370	.695	86	-2	-5	109	65	31	.617	0	1	-1	-1	S/D	-0.1
1989	Mon-N	142	437	52	102	17	4	6	41	76	44	.233	.351	.332	.683	94	1	-1	102	101	53	.652	3	2	-0	4	*S	1.2
Total	7	867	2847	353	682	111	36	25	253	311	299	.240	.317	.330	.647	78	-77	-82	101	100	308	.586	55	34	-4	62	S/D	3.1

■ MIKE PAGLIARULO Pagliarulo, Michael Timothy b: 3/15/60, Medford, Mass. BL/TR, 6'1", 205 lbs. Deb: 7/07/84

1984	NY-A	67	201	24	48	15	3	7	34	15	46	.239	.292	.448	.739	108	-0	1	94	122	25	.665	0	0	0	5	3	0.7
1985	NY-A	138	380	55	91	16	2	19	62	45	86	.239	.326	.442	.768	113	4	6	96	109	56	.736	0	0	0	-12	*3	-0.9
1986	NY-A	149	504	71	120	24	3	28	71	54	120	.238	.317	.464	.781	107	6	4	103	89	74	.749	4	1	1	8	*3/S	0.9
1987	NY-A	150	522	76	122	26	3	32	87	53	111	.234	.307	.479	.786	108	2	4	98	102	75	.743	1	3	-2	6	*3/1	0.5
1988	NY-A	125	444	46	96	20	1	15	67	37	104	.216	.280	.367	.647	83	-13	-11	92	131	46	.575	1	1	-0	-3	*3	-0.7
1989	NY-A	74	223	19	44	10	0	4	16	19	43	.197	.266	.296	.562	56	-12	-14	104	80	18	.484	1	1	-0	-3	3/D	-1.6
	SD-N	50	148	12	29	7	0	3	18	6	39	.196	.287	.304	.591	69	-6	-6	101	104	14	.541	2	0	1	2	3	-0.3
Total	6	753	2422	303	550	118	12	108	351	241	549	.227	.301	.419	.720	97	-19	-15	99	105	309	.668	9	5	-0	1	3/SD1	-1.4

■ TOM PAGNOZZI Pagnozzi, Thomas Alan b: 7/30/62, Tucson, Ariz. BR/TR, 6', 190 lbs. Deb: 4/12/87

1987	StL-N	27	48	8	9	1	0	2	9	4	13	.188	.250	.333	.583	54	-3	-3	99	163	4	.538	1	0	0	-1	C/1	-0.1
1988	StL-N	81	195	17	55	9	0	0	15	11	32	.282	.320	.328	.649	83	-3	-4	104	94	20	.517	0	1	0	1	C1/3	-0.3
1989	StL-N	52	80	3	12	2	0	0	3	6	19	.150	.218	.175	.393	14	-9	-9	101	86	2	.280	0	1	0	1	C/13	-0.5
Total	3	160	323	28	76	12	0	2	27	21	64	.235	.284	.291	.575	62	-16	-16	102	102	26	.452	1	2	0	1	/C13	-0.9

■ REY PALACIOS Palacios, Robert Rey b: 11/8/62, Brooklyn, N.Y. BR/TR, 5'10", 190 lbs. Deb: 9/08/88

1988	KC-A	5	11	2	1	0	0	0	0	0	4	.091	.091	.091	.182	-47	-2	-2	103	0	0	.091	0	0	0	0	/3	-0.1
1989	KC-A	47	47	12	8	1	0	1	8	2	14	.170	.220	.277	.497	41	-4	-4	96	194	3	.390	0	1	-1	-1	31C/O	-0.5
Total	2	60	58	14	9	2	0	1	8	2	18	.155	.197	.241	.438	23	-6	-6	97	159	3	.327	0	1	-1	-1	/31CO	-0.6

■ RAFAEL PALMEIRO Palmeiro, Rafael (Corrales) b: 9/24/64, Havana, Cuba BL/TL, 6', 175 lbs. Deb: 9/08/86

1986	Chi-N	22	73	9	18	4	0	3	12	4	6	.247	.295	.425	.720	90	-1	-1	107	120	8	.617	1	1	0	0	O	-0.1
1987	Chi-N	84	221	32	61	15	1	14	30	20	26	.276	.339	.543	.882	128	8	8	101	74	40	.861	2	2	-1	-4	O1	0.0
1988	Chi-N	152	580	75	178	41	5	8	53	38	34	.307	.353	.436	.789	120	18	15	104	81	89	.737	12	2	2	-0	*O/1	1.4
1989	Tex-A	156	559	76	154	23	4	8	64	63	48	.275	.355	.374	.729	103	6	4	102	109	74	.662	4	3	-1	9	*1/D	0.3
Total	4	414	1433	192	411	83	10	33	159	125	114	.287	.349	.428	.776	113	31	26	103	93	210	.720	19	8	1	5	O1/D	1.6

■ DEAN PALMER Palmer, Dean William b: 12/27/68, Tallahassee, Fla. BR/TR, 6'1", 175 lbs. Deb: 9/01/89

| | | | | | | | | | | | | | | | | | | | | | | | | | | | | |
|1989|Tex-A|16|19|0|2|2|0|0|1|0|12|.105|.105|.211|.316|-13|-3|-3|102|97|0|.235|0|0|0|-0|/3SOD|-0.2|

YEAR	TM/L	G	AB	R	H	2B	3B	HR	RBI	BB	SO	AVG	OBP	SLG	PRO	/A	BR	/A	PF	CHI	RC	TA	SB	CS	SBR	FR	POS	TPR
■ **AL PARDO**		Pardo, Alberto Judas b: 9/8/62, Oviedo, Spain BB/TR, 6'2", 187 lbs. Deb: 7/03/85																										
1985	Bal-A	34	75	3	10	1	0	0	1	3	15	.133	.167	.147	.313	-13	-12	-11	99	36	2	.215	0	0	0	-1	C	-1.0
1986	Bal-A	16	51	3	7	1	0	1	3	0	14	.137	.137	.216	.353	-5	-7	-7	99	85	1	.239	0	0	0	-1	C/D	-0.6
1988	Phi-N	2	2	0	0	0	0	0	0	0	2	.000	.000	.000	.000	-99	-1	-1	101	0	0	.000	0	0	0	0	/C	0.0
1989	Phi-N	1	1	0	0	0	0	0	0	0	0	.000	.000	.000	.000	-99	-0	-0	101	0	0	.000	0	0	0	0	/C	0.0
Total	4	53	129	6	17	2	0	1	4	3	31	.132	.152	.171	.322	-12	-20	-19	99	54	3	.219	0	0	0	-1	/CD	-1.6
■ **MARK PARENT**		Parent, Mark Allen b: 9/16/61, Ashland, Ore. BR/TR, 6'5", 215 lbs. Deb: 9/20/86																										
1986	SD-N	8	14	1	2	0	0	0	0	1	3	.143	.200	.143	.343	-4	-2	-2	95	0	0	.231	0	0	0	0	/C	-0.1
1987	SD-N	12	25	0	2	0	0	0	2	0	9	.080	.080	.080	.160	-59	-6	-5	97	399	0	.087	0	0	0	0	C	-0.3
1988	SD-N	41	118	9	23	3	0	6	15	6	23	.195	.234	.373	.607	74	-5	-5	97	97	10	.521	0	0	0	4	C	0.2
1989	SD-N	52	141	12	27	4	0	7	21	8	34	.191	.235	.369	.604	70	-6	-6	101	116	11	.513	1	0	0	6	C/1	0.3
Total	4	113	298	22	54	7	0	13	38	15	69	.181	.220	.336	.556	56	-18	-18	99	125	22	.462	1	0	0	10	/C1	0.1
■ **DAVE PARKER**		Parker, David Gene b: 6/9/51, Calhoun, Miss. BL/TR, 6'5", 230 lbs. Deb: 7/12/73																										
1973	Pit-N	54	139	17	40	9	1	4	14	2	27	.288	.308	.453	.761	118	1	2	92	75	18	.667	1	1	-0	1	O	0.1
1974	Pit-N	73	220	27	62	10	3	4	29	10	53	.282	.322	.409	.731	106	0	1	98	110	28	.646	3	3	-1	2	O/1	0.0
1975	Pit-N	148	558	75	172	35	10	25	101	38	89	.308	.358	**.541**	.899	148	32	32	99	106	101	.861	8	6	-1	7	*O	3.3
1976	Pit-N	138	537	82	168	28	10	13	90	30	80	.313	.351	.475	.826	132	21	21	100	125	85	.781	19	7	2	5	*O	2.4
1977	Pit-N	159	637	107	**215**	**44**	8	21	88	58	107	**.338**	.399	.531	.929	143	42	40	103	84	130	.938	17	19	-6	30	*O/2	5.8
1978	Pit-N	148	581	102	194	32	12	30	117	57	92	**.334**	.395	**.585**	**.981**	162	**53**	**49**	105	104	**134**	1.042	20	7	2	5	*O	**5.2**
1979	Pit-N	158	622	109	193	45	7	25	94	67	101	.310	.385	.526	.911	138	39	35	106	89	131	.961	20	4	4	9	*O	4.4
1980	Pit-N	139	518	71	153	31	1	17	79	25	69	.295	.330	.458	.788	114	10	8	103	111	75	.721	10	7	-1	-2	*O	0.0
1981	Pit-N	67	240	29	62	14	3	9	48	9	25	.258	.291	.454	.745	114	1	2	96	139	30	.681	6	2	1	-6	O	-0.4
1982	Pit-N	73	244	41	66	19	3	6	29	22	45	.270	.333	.447	.780	106	5	2	110	90	34	.732	7	5	-1	-3	O	-0.2
1983	Pit-N	144	552	68	154	29	4	12	69	28	89	.279	.314	.411	.725	97	-2	-4	103	106	67	.639	12	9	-2	1	*O	-0.7
1984	Cin-N	156	607	73	173	28	0	16	94	41	89	.285	.331	.410	.741	102	5	1	106	131	80	.668	11	10	-3	0	*O	-0.7
1985	Cin-N	160	635	88	198	**42**	4	34	**125**	52	80	.312	.367	.551	.918	146	43	39	105	106	112	.861	5	13	-6	7	*O	3.7
1986	Cin-N	162	637	89	174	31	3	31	116	56	126	.273	.333	.477	.810	116	16	12	104	123	94	.743	1	6	-3	-6	*O	0.0
1987	Cin-N	153	589	77	149	28	0	26	97	44	104	.253	.314	.433	.747	92	-5	-8	104	123	77	.687	7	3	0	6	*O/1	-0.7
1988	Oak-A	101	377	43	97	18	1	12	55	32	70	.257	.315	.406	.721	106	-0	2	95	118	49	.651	0	1	-1	-2	DO/1	0.0
1989	Oak-A	144	553	56	146	27	0	22	97	38	91	.264	.313	.432	.745	104	4	2	103	131	68	.650	0	0	0	0	*D/O	0.2
Total	17	2177	8246	1154	2416	470	70	307	1342	609	1337	.293	.345	.479	.824	123	263	235	103	111	1314	.777	147	103	-18	54	*OD/12	22.4
■ **LANCE PARRISH**		Parrish, Lance Michael b: 6/15/56, Clairton, Pa. BR/TR, 6'3", 210 lbs. Deb: 9/05/77																										
1977	Det-A	12	46	10	9	2	0	3	7	5	12	.196	.275	.435	.709	86	-1	-1	105	101	5	.641	0	0	0	2	C	0.1
1978	Det-A	85	288	37	63	11	3	14	41	11	71	.219	.255	.424	.679	81	-6	-9	108	99	29	.584	0	0	0	5	C	0.0
1979	Det-A	143	493	65	136	26	3	19	65	49	105	.276	.344	.456	.800	118	9	11	96	90	73	.744	6	7	-2	5	*C	1.9
1980	Det-A	144	553	79	158	34	6	24	82	31	109	.286	.327	.499	.826	117	15	11	105	94	80	.747	6	4	-1	8	*CD/1O	2.3
1981	Det-A	96	348	39	85	18	2	10	46	34	52	.244	.312	.394	.705	97	0	-2	105	110	38	.613	2	3	-1	1	C/D	0.2
1982	Det-A	133	486	75	138	19	2	32	87	40	99	.284	.340	.529	.868	134	21	21	100	101	86	.843	3	4	-2	10	*C/O	3.6
1983	Det-A	155	605	80	163	42	3	27	114	44	106	.269	.320	.483	.803	123	12	16	96	127	86	.725	1	3	-2	2	*CD	2.2
1984	Det-A	147	578	75	137	16	2	33	98	41	120	.237	.290	.443	.733	103	-3	0	96	117	71	.660	2	3	-1	-5	*CD	0.2
1985	Det-A	140	549	64	150	27	1	28	98	41	90	.273	.326	.479	.805	110	11	7	106	119	82	.742	2	6	-3	-4	*CD	0.5
1986	Det-A	91	327	53	84	6	1	22	62	38	83	.257	.343	.483	.826	129	10	12	95	112	57	.817	0	0	0	9	C/D	2.5
1987	Phi-N	130	466	42	114	21	0	17	67	47	104	.245	.315	.399	.714	84	-9	-11	104	115	53	.622	0	1	-1	13	*C	1.1
1988	Phi-N	123	424	44	91	17	2	15	60	47	93	.215	.296	.370	.666	89	-6	-6	101	121	46	.599	0	0	0	13	*C/1	1.3
1989	Cal-A	124	433	48	103	12	1	17	50	42	104	.238	.308	.388	.696	96	-3	-3	99	90	51	.625	1	1	-0	15	*C/D	1.8
Total	13	1523	5596	711	1431	251	26	261	877	470	1148	.256	.316	.450	.766	108	51	46	101	108	758	.696	23	32	-12	74	*CD/O1	17.7
■ **DAN PASQUA**		Pasqua, Daniel Anthony b: 10/17/61, Yonkers, N.Y. BL/TL, 6', 203 lbs. Deb: 5/30/85																										
1985	NY-A	60	148	17	31	3	1	9	25	16	38	.209	.291	.426	.717	97	-2	-1	96	110	19	.678	0	0	0	-0	OD	-0.1
1986	NY-A	102	280	44	82	17	0	16	45	47	78	.293	.400	.525	.925	146	21	20	103	92	62	.985	2	0	1	-4	O/1D	1.3
1987	NY-A	113	318	42	74	7	1	17	42	40	99	.233	.320	.421	.742	98	-2	-1	98	91	43	.692	0	2	-1	-5	OD1	-0.9
1988	Chi-A	129	422	48	96	16	2	20	50	46	100	.227	.308	.417	.725	104	-0	1	97	84	54	.673	1	0	0	4	*O/1D	0.3
1989	Chi-A	73	246	26	61	9	1	11	47	25	58	.248	.320	.427	.747	117	2	5	93	135	35	.706	1	2	-1	2	O/D	0.5
Total	5	477	1414	177	344	52	5	73	209	174	373	.243	.330	.442	.772	113	19	24	98	98	213	.741	4	4	-1	-3	O/D1	1.1
■ **BILL PECOTA**		Pecota, William Joseph b: 2/16/60, Redwood City, Cal. BR/TR, 6'2", 195 lbs. Deb: 9/19/86																										
1986	KC-A	12	29	3	6	2	0	0	2	3	3	.207	.303	.276	.579	60	-2	-2	100	100	2	.462	0	2	-1	1	3/SD	-0.1
1987	KC-A	66	156	22	43	5	1	3	14	15	25	.276	.343	.378	.721	89	-1	-2	104	82	21	.690	5	0	2	6	S32/D	0.7
1988	KC-A	90	178	25	37	3	3	1	15	18	34	.208	.288	.275	.563	57	-10	-10	103	115	16	.528	7	2	1	-3	S31/O2C	-1.0
1989	KC-A	65	83	21	17	4	2	3	5	7	9	.205	.275	.410	.684	94	-1	-1	96	45	9	.671	5	0	2	-8	SO2/31	-0.4
Total	4	233	446	71	103	14	6	7	36	43	71	.231	.306	.336	.642	75	-14	-15	102	89	49	.604	17	4	3	-4	S/32O1DC	-0.8
■ **AL PEDRIQUE**		Pedrique, Alfredo Jose (Garcia) b: 8/11/60, Aragua, Venez. BR/TR, 6', 155 lbs. Deb: 4/14/87																										
1987	NY-N	5	6	1	0	0	0	0	0	1	2	.000	.143	.000	.143	-59	-1	-1	99	0	0	.167	0	0	0	0	/S2	0.0
	Pit-N	88	246	23	74	10	1	1	27	18	27	.301	.356	.362	.718	87	-3	-4	104	117	31	.628	5	4	-1	-4	S/32	0.0
	Yr	93	252	24	74	10	1	1	27	19	29	.294	.350	.353	.704	84	-4	-5	104	111	30	.614	5	4	-1	-4		0.0
1988	Pit-N	50	128	7	23	5	0	0	4	8	17	.180	.234	.219	.452	31	-11	-11	98	57	6	.339	0	0	0	-4	S/3	-1.2
1989	Det-A	31	69	1	14	3	0	0	5	2	15	.203	.225	.246	.472	34	-6	-6	97	114	3	.317	0	0	0	0	3S/2	-0.4
Total	3	174	449	32	111	18	1	1	36	29	61	.247	.299	.298	.597	63	-22	-22	101	98	39	.480	5	4	-1	-8	S/32	-1.6
■ **TONY PENA**		Pena, Antonio Francisco (Padilla) b: 6/4/57, Monte Cristi, D.R. BR/TR, 6', 175 lbs. Deb: 9/01/80																										
1980	Pit-N	8	21	1	9	1	1	0	1	0	4	.429	.429	.571	1.000	171	2	2	103	33	4	.857	0	1	-1	0	/C	0.2
1981	Pit-N	66	210	16	63	9	1	2	17	8	23	.300	.329	.381	.710	105	-0	1	96	78	25	.588	1	2	-1	4	C	0.5
1982	Pit-N	138	497	53	147	28	4	11	63	17	57	.296	.324	.435	.759	100	5	-1	110	99	63	.642	2	5	-2	4	*C	0.2
1983	Pit-N	151	542	51	163	22	3	15	70	31	73	.301	.339	.435	.774	110	8	6	103	101	75	.684	6	7	-2	10	*C	1.9
1984	Pit-N	147	546	77	156	27	2	15	78	36	79	.286	.334	.425	.759	119	8	11	94	113	74	.689	12	8	-1	19	*C	3.4
1985	Pit-N	147	546	53	136	27	2	10	59	29	67	.249	.287	.361	.648	78	-16	-17	103	106	51	.545	12	8	-1	33	*C/1	2.1
1986	Pit-N	144	510	56	147	26	2	10	52	53	69	.288	.356	.406	.762	110	7	7	100	89	68	.685	9	10	-3	20	*C/1	2.7
1987	StL-N	116	384	40	82	13	4	5	44	36	54	.214	.283	.307	.590	57	-24	-24	99	132	30	.500	6	1	1	-9	*C/1O	-2.1
1988	StL-N	149	505	55	133	23	1	10	51	33	60	.263	.310	.372	.682	91	-4	-6	104	94	56	.591	6	2	1	5	*C1	0.6
1989	StL-N	141	424	36	110	17	2	4	37	35	33	.259	.319	.337	.656	87	-6	-7	101	96	41	.551	5	3	-0	6	*C/O	0.9
Total	10	1207	4185	438	1146	193	22	82	472	278	519	.274	.321	.389	.710	96	-21	-27	101	101	486	.614	59	47	-11	92	*C/1O	10.4
■ **TERRY PENDLETON**		Pendleton, Terry Lee b: 7/16/60, Los Angeles, Cal. BB/TR, 5'9", 178 lbs. Deb: 7/18/84																										
1984	StL-N	67	262	37	85	16	3	1	33	16	32	.324	.363	.420	.783	121	6	7	99	121	40	.772	20	5	3	11	3	2.1
1985	StL-N	149	559	56	134	16	3	5	69	37	75	.240	.287	.306	.593	69	-26	-23	96	151	45	.495	17	12	-2	26	*3	0.2
1986	StL-N	159	578	56	138	26	5	1	59	34	59	.239	.282	.306	.588	60	-30	-32	103	133	50	.515	24	6	4	24	*3/O	-0.8
1987	StL-N	159	583	82	167	29	4	12	96	70	74	.286	.365	.412	.777	107	6	7	99	142	86	.742	19	12	-2	16	*3	2.0
1988	StL-N	110	391	44	99	20	2	6	53	21	51	.253	.295	.361	.655	84	-7	-9	104	136	39	.549	3	3	-1	9	*3	0.0
1989	StL-N	162	613	83	162	28	5	13	74	44	81	.264	.314	.390	.703	100	-1	-1	101	114	72	.619	9	5	-0	**28**	*3	2.6
Total	6	806	2986	358	785	135	22	38	384	222	372	.263	.315	.361	.676	88	-52	-51	100	133	332	.601	92	43	2	114	3/O	6.1
■ **GERALD PERRY**		Perry, Gerald June b: 10/30/60, Savannah, Ga. BL/TR, 5'11", 180 lbs. Deb: 8/11/83																										
1983	Atl-N	27	39	5	14	2	0	1	6	5	4	.359	.432	.487	.919	146	3	3	106	108	8	.889	0	1	-1	-0	/1O	0.1
1984	Atl-N	122	347	52	92	12	2	7	47	61	38	.265	.378	.372	.750	102	8	3	110	123	50	.750	15	12	-3	-7	1O	-1.0
1985	Atl-N	110	238	22	51	5	0	3	13	23	28	.214	.284	.273	.557	53	-14	-15	106	70	18	.487	9	5	-0	0	1/O	-1.8

YEAR	TM/L	G	AB	R	H	2B	3B	HR	RBI	BB	SO	AVG	OBP	SLG	PRO	/A	BR	/A	PF	CHI	RC	TA	SB	CS	SBR	FR	POS	TPR
1986	Atl-N	29	70	6	19	2	0	2	11	8	4	.271	.346	.386	.732	100	0	0	102	133	8	.625	0	1	-1	-5	O/1	-0.6
1987	Atl-N	142	533	77	144	35	2	12	74	48	63	.270	.332	.411	.742	88	-4	-10	108	118	69	.733	42	16	3	-5	*1/O	-1.9
1988	Atl-N	141	547	61	164	29	1	8	74	36	49	.300	.344	.400	.745	108	9	6	104	129	70	.687	29	14	0	2	*1	0.1
1989	Atl-N	72	266	24	67	11	0	4	21	32	28	.252	.339	.338	.677	92	-1	-2	102	88	31	.643	10	6	-1	4	1	-0.4
Total	7	643	2040	247	551	96	5	37	246	213	214	.270	.341	.376	.718	94	1	-15	106	112	255	.681	105	55	-1	-12	1/O	-5.5
■ **GENO PETRALLI**	Petralli, Eugene James b: 9/25/59, Sacramento, Cal. BB/TR, 6'2", 185 lbs. Deb: 9/04/82																											
1982	Tor-A	16	44	3	16	2	0	0	1	4	6	.364	.417	.409	.826	118	2	1	109	22	8	.759	0	0	0	-1	C/3	0.0
1983	Tor-A	6	4	0	0	0	0	0	0	1	1	.000	.200	.000	.200	-36	-1	-1	108	0	0	.250	0	0	0	0	/CD	0.0
1984	Tor-A	3	3	0	0	0	0	0	0	0	0	.000	.000	.000	.000	-99	-1	-1	102	0	0	.000	0	0	0	0	/CD	0.0
1985	Tex-A	42	100	7	27	2	0	0	11	8	12	.270	.330	.290	.620	66	-4	-5	108	150	10	.506	1	0	0	-2	C	-0.3
1986	Tex-A	69	137	17	35	9	3	2	18	5	14	.255	.282	.409	.690	90	-3	-2	96	116	14	.587	3	0	1	-2	C3/2D	0.0
1987	Tex-A	101	202	28	61	11	2	7	31	27	29	.302	.390	.480	.870	126	9	8	104	105	38	.857	0	2	-1	-15	C3/12OD	-0.2
1988	Tex-A	129	351	35	99	14	2	7	36	41	52	.282	.360	.393	.754	110	6	5	101	90	49	.683	0	1	-1	-10	CD/312	0.0
1989	Tex-A	70	184	18	56	7	0	4	23	17	24	.304	.369	.408	.777	116	5	4	102	103	28	.707	0	0	0	-16	CD	-0.8
Total	8	436	1025	108	294	45	7	20	120	103	138	.287	.356	.403	.759	107	14	11	102	101	145	.687	4	3	-1	-45	C/D312O	-1.3
■ **GARY PETTIS**	Pettis, Gary George b: 4/3/58, Oakland, Cal. BB/TR, 6'1", 165 lbs. Deb: 9/13/82																											
1982	Cal-A	10	5	5	1	0	0	1	1	0	2	.200	.200	.800	1.000	159	0	0	100	57	1	1.000	0	0	0	-2	/O	-0.1
1983	Cal-A	22	85	19	25	2	3	3	6	7	15	.294	.348	.494	.842	134	3	4	96	49	15	.891	8	3	1	4	O	0.8
1984	Cal-A	140	397	63	90	11	6	2	29	60	115	.227	.333	.300	.632	75	-11	-12	101	92	46	.701	48	17	4	-7	*O	-1.8
1985	Cal-A	125	443	67	114	10	8	1	32	62	125	.257	.349	.323	.671	85	-7	-7	101	89	61	.761	56	9	11	12	*O	1.4
1986	Cal-A	154	539	93	139	23	4	5	58	69	132	.258	.342	.343	.685	92	-7	-4	96	118	71	.724	50	13	7	13	*O/D	1.1
1987	Cal-A	133	394	49	82	13	2	1	17	52	124	.208	.302	.259	.561	52	-26	-26	99	65	35	.551	24	5	4	12	*O	-1.1
1988	Det-A	129	458	65	96	14	4	3	36	47	85	.210	.285	.277	.562	62	-25	-22	94	107	42	.584	44	10	7	5	*O/D	-1.1
1989	Det-A	119	444	77	114	8	6	1	18	84	106	.257	.375	.309	.684	97	1	3	97	44	58	.735	43	15	4	0	*O	0.5
Total	8	832	2765	438	661	81	33	17	197	381	704	.239	.332	.311	.643	80	-71	-64	98	86	330	.684	273	72	39	36	O/D	-0.3
■ **MARTY PEVEY**	Pevey, Marty Ashley b: 12/25/62, Statesboro, Ga. BL/TR, 6'1", 185 lbs. Deb: 5/16/89																											
1989	Mon-N	13	41	2	9	1	1	0	3	0	8	.220	.220	.293	.512	44	-3	-3	102	101	2	.364	0	0	0	1	C/O	-0.1
■ **KEN PHELPS**	Phelps, Kenneth Allen b: 8/6/54, Seattle, Wash. BL/TL, 6'1", 209 lbs. Deb: 9/20/80																											
1980	KC-A	3	4	0	0	0	0	0	0	0	2	.000	.000	.000	.000	-99	-1	-1	98	0	0	.000	0	0	0	0	/1	0.0
1981	KC-A	21	22	1	3	0	1	0	1	1	13	.136	.174	.227	.401	15	-2	-2	99	78	1	.316	0	0	0	0	/1D	-0.2
1982	Mon-N	10	8	0	2	0	0	0	0	0	3	.250	.333	.250	.583	62	-0	-0	105	0	1	.500	0	0	0	0	H	0.0
1983	Sea-A	50	127	10	30	4	1	7	16	13	25	.236	.307	.449	.756	106	1	1	100	80	19	.722	0	0	0	1	1D	0.0
1984	Sea-A	101	290	52	70	9	0	24	51	61	73	.241	.382	.521	.903	144	20	19	102	91	63	.982	3	3	-1	-0	D/1	1.7
1985	Sea-A	61	116	18	24	3	0	9	24	24	33	.207	.343	.466	.808	126	3	4	95	117	20	.860	2	0	1	0	D/1	0.4
1986	Sea-A	125	344	69	85	16	4	24	64	88	96	.247	.409	.526	.935	146	29	26	105	101	81	1.041	2	3	-1	-1	1D	1.9
1987	Sea-A	120	332	68	86	13	1	27	68	80	75	.259	.414	.548	.962	150	29	27	103	103	81	1.067	1	1	-0	0	*D/1	2.5
1988	Sea-A	72	190	37	54	8	0	14	32	51	35	.284	.438	.547	.985	162	21	19	108	87	50	1.129	1	0	0	0	D/1	1.9
	NY-A	45	107	17	24	5	0	10	22	19	26	.224	.341	.551	.893	152	6	7	96	98	20	.907	0	0	0	0	D/1	0.7
	Yr	117	297	54	78	13	0	24	54	70	61	.263	.405	.549	.954	160	28	26	103	92	70	1.044	1	0	0	0		2.6
1989	NY-A	86	185	26	46	3	0	7	29	27	47	.249	.344	.378	.723	99	1	0	104	124	26	.688	0	0	0	-0	D/1	0.0
	Oak-A	11	9	0	1	1	0	0	0	4	0	.111	.385	.222	.607	73	-0	-0	103	0	1	.750	0	0	0	0	/1D	0.0
	Yr	97	194	26	47	4	0	7	29	31	47	.242	.347	.371	.718	98	1	0	104	111	27	.691	0	0	0	-0		0.0
Total	10	705	1734	298	425	62	7	122	307	368	428	.245	.383	.500	.883	137	107	100	103	98	362	.946	9	7	-2	-1	D1	8.9
■ **TONY PHILLIPS**	Phillips, Keith Anthony b: 4/25/59, Atlanta, Ga. BB/TR, 5'9", 155 lbs. Deb: 5/10/82																											
1982	Oak-A	40	81	11	17	2	2	0	8	12	26	.210	.326	.284	.610	73	-3	-2	95	139	8	.582	2	3	-1	-5	S	-0.4
1983	Oak-A	148	412	54	102	12	3	4	35	48	70	.248	.329	.320	.649	83	-10	-8	96	95	48	.619	16	5	2	-17	*S2/3D	-1.4
1984	Oak-A	154	451	62	120	24	3	4	37	42	86	.266	.329	.359	.688	99	-6	-1	92	85	55	.626	10	6	-1	-21	S2/O	-1.0
1985	Oak-A	42	161	23	45	12	2	4	17	13	34	.280	.333	.453	.787	122	3	4	93	84	25	.748	3	2	-0	-8	32	-0.3
1986	Oak-A	118	441	76	113	14	5	5	52	76	82	.256	.369	.345	.714	104	1	5	94	110	63	.724	15	10	-2	1	23/OSD	0.9
1987	Oak-A	111	379	48	91	20	0	10	46	57	76	.240	.339	.372	.711	98	-5	0	91	109	49	.677	7	6	-2	-2	23/SOD	0.3
1988	Oak-A	79	212	32	43	8	4	2	17	36	50	.203	.321	.307	.628	81	-6	-4	95	95	22	.576	0	2	-1	-8	O23/S1	-1.1
1989	Oak-A	143	451	48	118	15	6	4	47	58	66	.262	.350	.350	.698	94	0	-2	103	108	53	.617	3	8	-4	-3	23SO/1	-0.6
Total	8	835	2588	354	649	107	25	33	259	342	490	.251	.341	.350	.690	95	-25	-7	95	101	323	.649	56	42	-8	-62	2S3/O1D	-3.6
■ **GUS POLIDOR**	Polidor, Gustavo Adolfo (Gonzalez) b: 10/26/61, Caracas, Venezuela BR/TR, 6', 170 lbs. Deb: 9/07/85																											
1985	Cal-A	2	1	1	1	0	0	0	0	0	0	1.000	1.000	1.000	2.000	446	0	0	101	0	1	—	0	0	0	-0	/SO	0.0
1986	Cal-A	6	19	1	5	1	0	0	1	1	0	.263	.300	.316	.616	71	-1	-1	96	66	1	.438	0	0	0	0	/2S3	0.0
1987	Cal-A	63	137	12	36	3	0	2	15	2	15	.263	.279	.328	.607	62	-8	-7	99	117	12	.462	0	0	0	-4	S3/2	-0.8
1988	Cal-A	54	81	4	12	3	0	0	4	3	11	.148	.179	.185	.364	2	-11	-10	94	106	3	.254	0	0	0	1	S3/21	-0.7
1989	Mil-A	79	175	15	34	7	0	0	14	6	18	.194	.230	.234	.464	32	-16	-15	97	133	9	.354	3	0	1	2	32S/D	-0.9
Total	5	204	413	33	88	14	0	2	34	12	44	.213	.241	.262	.502	40	-34	-33	97	119	26	.373	3	0	1	-2	/S32D1O	-2.4
■ **LUIS POLONIA**	Polonia, Luis Andrew (Almonte) b: 12/10/64, Santiago, D.R. BB/TL, 5'8", 155 lbs. Deb: 4/24/87																											
1987	Oak-A	125	435	78	125	16	10	4	49	32	64	.287	.336	.398	.734	104	-3	2	91	106	61	.729	29	7	5	-6	*OD	-0.1
1988	Oak-A	84	288	51	84	11	4	2	27	21	40	.292	.340	.378	.718	106	0	2	95	93	38	.713	24	9	2	-1	O/D	0.1
1989	Oak-A	59	206	31	59	6	4	1	17	9	15	.286	.316	.369	.685	89	-2	-3	103	84	23	.628	13	4	2	3	O	0.0
	NY-A	66	227	39	71	11	2	2	29	16	29	.313	.363	.405	.769	112	5	4	104	115	32	.708	9	4	0	2	O/D	0.5
	Yr	125	433	70	130	17	6	3	46	25	44	.300	.341	.388	.729	101	3	1	104	101	55	.670	22	8	2	4		0.5
Total	3	334	1156	199	339	44	20	9	122	78	148	.293	.339	.389	.728	103	-0	5	97	101	155	.703	75	24	8	-2	O/D	0.5
■ **JIM PRESLEY**	Presley, James Arthur b: 10/23/61, Pensacola, Fla. BR/TR, 6'1", 200 lbs. Deb: 6/24/84																											
1984	Sea-A	70	251	27	57	12	1	10	36	6	63	.227	.248	.402	.650	75	-9	-10	102	110	24	.548	1	1	-0	-7	3/D	-1.5
1985	Sea-A	155	570	71	157	33	1	28	84	44	100	.275	.328	.484	.813	126	13	17	95	94	80	.727	2	2	-1	6	*3	1.7
1986	Sea-A	155	616	83	163	33	4	27	107	32	172	.265	.305	.463	.768	101	4	-1	105	123	80	.676	0	4	-2	8	*3	0.1
1987	Sea-A	152	575	78	142	23	6	24	88	38	157	.247	.298	.433	.731	89	-8	-10	103	112	72	.654	2	0	1	10	*3/SD	-0.1
1988	Sea-A	150	544	50	125	26	0	14	62	36	114	.230	.283	.355	.637	72	-17	-22	108	107	52	.539	3	5	-2	-13	*3/D	-3.7
1989	Sea-A	117	390	42	92	20	1	12	41	21	107	.236	.277	.385	.661	82	-9	-11	103	86	39	.555	0	0	0	-5	31/D	-1.8
Total	6	799	2946	351	736	147	13	115	418	177	713	.250	.296	.426	.721	93	-27	-36	102	106	345	.628	8	12	-5	-1	3/1DS	-5.3
■ **TOM PRINCE**	Prince, Thomas Albert b: 8/13/64, Kankakee, Ill. BR/TR, 5'11", 185 lbs. Deb: 9/22/87																											
1987	Pit-N	4	9	1	2	1	0	1	2	0	2	.222	.222	.667	.889	119	0	0	104	89	1	.857	0	0	0	0	/C	0.0
1988	Pit-N	29	74	3	13	2	0	0	6	4	15	.176	.218	.203	.421	22	-7	-7	98	160	3	.288	0	0	0	1	C	-0.5
1989	Pit-N	21	52	1	7	4	0	0	5	6	12	.135	.224	.212	.436	27	-5	-5	94	183	2	.383	1	1	-0	-1	C	-0.4
Total	3	54	135	5	22	7	0	1	13	10	29	.163	.221	.237	.458	32	-12	-12	97	165	6	.358	1	1	-0	-0	/C	-0.9
■ **KIRBY PUCKETT**	Puckett, Kirby b: 3/14/61, Chicago, Ill. BR/TR, 5'8", 178 lbs. Deb: 5/08/84																											
1984	Min-A	128	557	63	165	12	5	0	31	16	69	.296	.321	.336	.656	78	-14	-17	106	57	58	.539	14	7	0	22	*O	0.1
1985	Min-A	161	691	80	199	29	13	4	74	41	87	.288	.332	.385	.716	93	-4	-7	103	91	88	.647	21	12	-1	14	*O	0.4
1986	Min-A	161	680	119	223	37	6	31	96	34	99	.328	.366	.537	.903	132	38	31	108	74	127	.882	20	12	-1	3	*O	2.7
1987	Min-A	157	624	96	**207**	32	5	28	99	32	91	.332	.370	.534	.904	143	32	35	96	100	116	.870	12	7	-1	-1	*O/D	2.7
1988	Min-A	158	657	109	**234**	42	5	24	121	23	83	.356	.380	.545	.925	147	46	41	106	108	126	.870	6	7	-2	13	*O	4.9
1989	Min-A	159	635	75	**215**	45	4	9	85	41	59	**.339**	.381	.465	.846	129	30	25	107	109	107	.787	11	4	1	13	*O/D	3.7
Total	6	924	3844	542	1243	197	38	96	506	187	488	.323	.359	.469	.828	121	128	108	104	90	622	.767	84	49	-4	64	O/D	14.5

YEAR	TM/L	G	AB	R	H	2B	3B	HR	RBI	BB	SO	AVG	OBP	SLG	PRO	/A	BR	/A	PF	CHI	RC	TA	SB	CS	SBR	FR	POS	TPR
■ **TERRY PUHL**	Puhl, Terry Stephen b: 7/8/56, Melville, Sask., Can BL/TR, 6'2", 195 lbs. Deb: 7/12/77																											
1977	Hou-N	60	229	40	69	13	5	0	10	30	31	.301	.385	.402	.786	120	5	7	93	42	39	.811	10	1	2	0	O	0.8
1978	Hou-N	149	585	87	169	25	6	3	35	48	46	.289	.347	.368	.714	105	0	4	95	60	75	.678	32	14	1	20	*O	2.0
1979	Hou-N	157	600	87	172	22	4	8	49	58	46	.287	.353	.377	.730	110	1	8	90	75	80	.696	30	22	-4	-6	*O	-0.6
1980	Hou-N	141	535	75	151	24	5	13	55	60	52	.282	.359	.419	.778	119	12	14	98	88	85	.791	27	11	2	14	*O	2.5
1981	Hou-N	96	350	43	88	19	4	3	28	31	49	.251	.319	.354	.674	103	-4	1	88	88	44	.673	22	4	4	3	O	0.5
1982	Hou-N	145	507	64	133	17	9	8	50	51	49	.262	.332	.379	.711	99	-1	-0	99	93	66	.674	17	9	-0	-2	*O	-0.3
1983	Hou-N	137	465	66	136	25	7	8	44	36	48	.292	.346	.428	.774	126	8	13	90	78	70	.759	24	11	1	-5	*O	0.6
1984	Hou-N	132	449	66	135	19	7	9	55	59	45	.301	.383	.434	.817	140	19	23	93	99	77	.820	13	8	-1	-3	*O	1.5
1985	Hou-N	57	194	34	55	14	3	2	23	18	23	.284	.347	.418	.765	118	3	4	96	107	30	.752	6	2	1	-0	O	0.3
1986	Hou-N	81	172	17	42	10	0	3	14	15	24	.244	.305	.355	.659	79	-5	-5	103	80	18	.572	3	2	-0	-4	O	-1.0
1987	Hou-N	90	122	9	28	5	0	2	15	11	16	.230	.293	.320	.613	67	-7	-5	93	133	11	.520	1	1	-0	-6	O	-1.2
1988	Hou-N	113	234	42	71	7	2	3	19	35	30	.303	.396	.389	.785	135	10	11	93	76	42	.892	22	4	4	-8	O	0.6
1989	Hou-N	121	354	41	96	25	4	0	27	45	39	.271	.355	.364	.719	104	4	3	102	84	46	.674	9	8	-2	-1	*O/1	-0.1
Total	13	1479	4796	671	1345	225	56	62	424	497	498	.280	.351	.389	.741	112	45	78	94	82	683	.723	216	97	7	2	*O/1	5.6
■ **LUIS QUINONES**	Quinones, Luis Raul b: 4/28/62, Ponce, P.R. BB/TR, 5'11", 165 lbs. Deb: 5/27/83																											
1983	Oak-A	19	42	5	8	2	1	0	4	1	4	.190	.209	.286	.495	36	-4	-4	96	130	2	.400	1	1	-0	-3	/23OSD	-0.5
1986	SF-N	71	106	13	19	1	3	0	11	3	17	.179	.209	.245	.454	26	-11	-10	96	169	6	.371	3	1	0	-1	S3/2	-0.8
1987	Chi-N	49	101	12	22	6	0	0	8	10	16	.218	.288	.277	.566	50	-7	-7	101	114	9	.481	0	0	0	1	S/23	-0.2
1988	Cin-N	23	52	4	12	3	0	1	11	2	11	.231	.259	.346	.605	69	-2	-2	105	209	5	.512	1	1	-0	1	/S23	0.0
1989	Cin-N	97	340	43	83	13	4	12	34	25	46	.244	.302	.412	.713	99	0	-1	103	79	42	.644	2	4	-2	0	23/S	-0.1
Total	5	259	641	77	144	25	8	13	68	41	94	.225	.276	.349	.625	73	-24	-25	101	113	64	.543	7	7	-2	-1	/3S2DO	-1.6
■ **REY QUINONES**	Quinones, Rey Francisco (Santiago) b: 11/11/63, Rio Pedras, P.R. BR/TR, 5'11", 160 lbs. Deb: 5/17/86																											
1986	Bos-A	62	190	26	45	12	1	2	15	19	26	.237	.316	.342	.658	81	-5	-5	100	84	20	.584	3	2	-0	-6	S	-0.7
	Sea-A	36	122	6	23	4	0	0	7	5	31	.189	.220	.221	.442	20	-13	-14	105	103	6	.330	1	1	-0	8	S	-0.3
	Yr	98	312	32	68	16	1	2	22	24	57	.218	.280	.295	.575	57	-18	-19	102	92	26	.484	4	3	-1	2		-1.0
1987	Sea-A	135	478	55	132	18	2	12	56	26	71	.276	.319	.397	.716	87	-7	-9	103	101	57	.609	1	3	-2	-0	*S	-0.4
1988	Sea-A	140	499	63	124	30	3	12	52	23	71	.248	.286	.393	.678	82	-9	-14	108	91	52	.569	0	3	-2	-0	*S/D	-0.9
1989	Sea-A	7	19	2	2	0	0	0	0	1	1	.105	.150	.105	.255	-26	-3	-3	103	0	0	.176	0	0	0	-0	/S	-0.2
	Pit-N	71	225	21	47	11	0	3	29	15	40	.209	.261	.298	.559	63	-12	-10	94	154	17	.449	0	2	-1	-9	S	-1.7
Total	4	451	1533	173	373	75	6	29	159	89	240	.243	.290	.357	.646	75	-50	-55	103	102	153	.539	5	11	-5	-8	S/D	-4.2
■ **CARLOS QUINTANA**	Quintana, Carlos Narcis (Hernand b: 8/26/65, Estado Miranda, Ven BR/TR, 6', 175 lbs. Deb: 9/16/88																											
1988	Bos-A	5	6	1	2	0	0	0	2	2	3	.333	.500	.333	.833	127	1	0	109	398	1	1.000	0	0	0	-0	/OD	0.0
1989	Bos-A	34	77	6	16	5	0	0	6	7	12	.208	.274	.273	.547	52	-5	-5	105	111	5	.424	0	0	0	-5	O/1D	-0.9
Total	2	39	83	7	18	5	0	0	8	9	15	.217	.293	.277	.571	59	-4	-5	105	136	6	.457	0	0	0	-5	/OD1	-0.9
■ **JAMIE QUIRK**	Quirk, James Patrick b: 10/22/54, Whittier, Cal. BL/TR, 6'4", 190 lbs. Deb: 9/04/75 C																											
1975	KC-A	14	39	2	10	0	0	1	5	2	7	.256	.293	.333	.626	75	-1	-1	102	120	4	.500	0	0	0	-0	O/3D	-0.1
1976	KC-A	64	114	11	28	6	0	1	15	2	22	.246	.259	.325	.583	70	-5	-5	100	144	8	.429	0	0	0	0	DS3/1	-0.3
1977	Mil-A	93	221	16	48	14	1	3	13	8	47	.217	.251	.330	.581	60	-14	-12	95	63	17	.466	0	1	-1	0	DO/3	-1.2
1978	KC-A	17	29	3	6	2	0	0	2	5	4	.207	.324	.276	.599	69	-1	-1	102	99	3	.565	0	0	0	0	3/SD	0.0
1979	KC-A	51	79	8	24	6	1	1	11	5	13	.304	.353	.443	.796	107	1	1	105	111	13	.745	0	0	0	0	/CS3D	0.2
1980	KC-A	62	163	13	45	5	0	5	21	7	24	.276	.310	.399	.709	94	-2	-2	98	102	18	.598	3	2	-0	-1	3C/O1D	-0.1
1981	KC-A	46	100	8	25	7	0	0	10	6	17	.250	.299	.320	.619	79	-3	-3	99	122	8	.476	0	2	-1	-2	C/32O	-0.4
1982	KC-A	36	78	8	18	3	0	1	5	3	15	.231	.259	.308	.567	55	-5	-5	100	74	6	.435	0	0	0	-2	C/13O	-0.5
1983	StL-N	48	86	3	18	2	1	2	11	6	27	.209	.269	.326	.594	65	-4	-4	98	128	7	.500	0	0	0	-0	C/3S	-0.3
1984	Chi-A	3	2	0	0	0	0	0	1	0	2	.000	.000	.000	.000	-90	-1	-1	111	0	0	.000	0	0	0	-0	/3	0.0
	Cle-A	1	1	1	1	0	0	1	1	0	0	1.000	1.000	4.000	5.000	1142	1	1	106	57	4	—	0	0	0	0	/C	0.1
	Yr	4	3	1	1	0	0	1	2	0	2	.333	.333	1.333	1.667	308	1	1	109	14	1	2.000	0	0	0	-0		0.1
1985	KC-A	19	57	3	16	3	1	0	4	2	9	.281	.305	.368	.674	82	-1	-1	102	76	6	.548	0	0	0	1	C/1	0.0
1986	KC-A	80	219	24	47	10	0	8	26	17	41	.215	.274	.370	.644	74	-8	-8	100	99	22	.559	0	1	-1	5	C3/1O	-0.2
1987	KC-A	109	296	24	70	17	0	5	33	28	56	.236	.311	.345	.656	72	-10	-12	104	113	32	.577	1	0	0	-1	*C/S	-0.3
1988	KC-A	84	196	22	47	7	1	8	25	28	41	.240	.338	.408	.746	105	2	2	103	96	27	.705	1	5	-3	-6	C/13	-0.3
1989	NY-A	13	24	0	2	0	0	0	0	3	5	.083	.185	.083	.269	-21	-4	-4	104	0	0	.208	0	1	-1	1	/CD	-0.3
	Oak-A	9	10	1	2	0	0	1	1	0	4	.200	.200	.500	.700	88	-0	-0	103	49	1	.625	0	0	0	0	/3C1SO	0.0
	Bal-A	25	51	5	11	2	0	0	9	9	11	.216	.333	.255	.588	69	-2	-2	99	269	4	.500	0	1	-1	2	C	0.1
	Yr	47	85	6	15	2	0	1	10	12	20	.176	.278	.235	.514	46	-6	-6	101	153	5	.421	0	2	-1	3		-0.2
Total	15	774	1765	152	418	84	5	37	193	131	345	.237	.294	.353	.647	77	-56	-57	101	105	180	.549	5	13	-6	-2	C3/DOS12	-3.6
■ **TIM RAINES**	Raines, Timothy b: 9/16/59, Sanford, Fla. BB/TR, 5'8", 160 lbs. Deb: 9/11/79																											
1979	Mon-N	6	0	3	0	0	0	0	0	0	0	—	—	—	—	—	0	0	102	—	—	—	2	0	1	0	/R	0.1
1980	Mon-N	15	20	5	1	0	0	0	0	6	3	.050	.269	.050	.319	-6	-3	-3	99	0	1	.632	5	0	2	-0	/2O	0.0
1981	Mon-N	88	313	61	95	13	7	5	37	45	31	.304	.394	.438	.832	137	16	17	99	101	64	1.081	**71**	11	**15**	-1	O/2	2.9
1982	Mon-N	156	647	90	179	32	8	4	43	75	83	.277	.354	.369	.723	97	4	-0	105	58	96	.804	**78**	16	**14**	0	*O2	1.4
1983	Mon-N	156	615	**133**	183	32	8	11	71	97	70	.298	.395	.429	.824	126	27	26	102	84	120	.989	**90**	14	**19**	13	*O/2	5.6
1984	Mon-N	160	622	106	192	**38**	9	8	60	87	69	.309	.395	.437	.833	146	30	37	91	70	124	**.975**	**75**	10	**17**	2	*O/2	5.1
1985	Mon-N	150	575	115	184	30	13	11	41	81	60	.320	.407	.475	.881	156	38	42	94	47	124	1.044	70	9	16	2	*O	5.7
1986	Mon-N	151	580	91	194	35	10	9	62	78	60	**.334**	**.415**	.476	.891	149	38	40	98	78	**130**	**1.062**	70	9	16	3	*O	**5.7**
1987	Mon-N	139	530	**123**	175	34	8	18	68	90	52	.330	.431	.526	.958	143	43	39	106	72	132	1.146	50	5	12	-2	*O	4.2
1988	Mon-N	109	429	66	116	19	7	12	48	53	44	.270	.353	.431	.785	118	14	11	106	77	69	.832	33	7	6	-7	*O	0.8
1989	Mon-N	145	517	76	148	29	6	9	60	93	48	.286	.398	.418	.816	131	27	25	102	105	96	.915	41	9	7	-16	*O	1.5
Total	11	1275	4848	869	1467	262	76	87	490	705	520	.303	.394	.442	.835	132	234	233	100	75	1136	.975	585	90	122	-5	*O/2	33.0
■ **RAFAEL RAMIREZ**	Ramirez, Rafael Emilio (Peguero) b: 2/18/59, San Pedro De Macoris, D.R. BR/TR, 6', 170 lbs. Deb: 8/04/80																											
1980	Atl-N	50	165	17	44	6	1	2	11	2	33	.267	.292	.352	.644	78	-5	-5	101	68	17	.532	2	1	0	-0	S	0.0
1981	Atl-N	95	307	30	67	16	2	2	20	24	47	.218	.277	.303	.580	65	-15	-14	100	79	27	.508	7	3	0	-5	S	-0.9
1982	Atl-N	157	609	74	169	24	4	10	52	36	49	.278	.321	.379	.700	89	-5	-10	107	83	73	.640	27	14	-0	19	*S	2.1
1983	Atl-N	152	622	82	185	13	5	7	58	36	48	.297	.338	.368	.706	90	-4	-8	106	88	76	.619	16	12	-2	7	*S	1.1
1984	Atl-N	145	591	51	157	22	4	2	48	26	70	.266	.298	.327	.624	69	-20	-26	110	91	53	.509	14	17	-6	1	*S	-1.5
1985	Atl-N	138	568	54	141	25	4	5	58	20	63	.248	.274	.333	.607	65	-25	-29	106	120	45	.465	2	6	-3	12	*S	-0.9
1986	Atl-N	134	496	57	119	21	1	8	33	21	60	.240	.275	.335	.610	66	-23	-24	102	71	42	.521	19	8	1	21	S3/O	0.4
1987	Atl-N	56	179	22	47	12	0	1	21	8	16	.263	.302	.346	.648	66	-8	-9	108	129	18	.565	6	3	0	3	S3	-0.1
1988	Hou-N	155	566	51	156	30	5	6	59	18	61	.276	.302	.378	.680	101	-6	-2	93	104	60	.556	3	2	-0	-12	*S	-0.2
1989	Hou-N	151	537	46	132	20	2	6	54	29	64	.246	.284	.324	.608	72	-19	-20	102	113	49	.498	3	1	0	-30	*S	-4.4
Total	10	1233	4640	484	1217	189	28	49	414	220	511	.262	.298	.347	.645	77	-128	-148	104	95	461	.543	99	67	-11	16	*S/3O	-4.4
■ **DOMINGO RAMOS**	Ramos, Domingo Antonio (De Ramos) b: 3/29/58, Santiago, D.R. BR/TR, 5'10", 154 lbs. Deb: 9/08/78																											
1978	NY-A	1	0	0	0	0	0	0	0	0	0	—	—	—	—	—	0	0	99	—	—	—	0	0	0	0	/S	0.0
1980	Tor-A	5	16	0	2	0	0	0	0	2	5	.125	.222	.125	.347	-2	-2	-2	100	0	1	.286	0	0	0	0	/2SD	-0.1
1982	Sea-A	8	26	3	4	2	0	0	1	3	2	.154	.241	.231	.472	28	-2	-3	109	67	2	.409	0	0	0	1	/S	-0.1
1983	Sea-A	53	127	14	36	4	0	2	10	7	12	.283	.326	.362	.688	90	-2	-2	100	75	14	.594	3	1	0	4	S/23D	0.4
1984	Sea-A	59	81	6	15	2	0	0	2	5	12	.185	.233	.210	.442	23	-8	-9	102	47	3	.333	2	2	-1	-2	3S/12	-0.9
1985	Sea-A	75	168	19	33	6	0	1	15	17	23	.196	.270	.250	.520	46	-13	-12	95	132	12	.421	0	1	-1	5	S21/3	-0.4
1986	Sea-A	49	99	8	18	2	0	0	5	8	13	.182	.250	.202	.452	24	-10	-11	105	100	4	.326	0	1	-1	7	S2/3D	-0.2
1987	Sea-A	42	103	9	32	6	0	2	11	3	12	.311	.336	.427	.764	99	0	-0	103	88	14	.658	0	1	-1	1	S/32D	0.2

YEAR	TM/L	G	AB	R	H	2B	3B	HR	RBI	BB	SO	AVG	OBP	SLG	PRO	/A	BR	/A	PF	CHI	RC	TA	SB	CS	SBR	FR	POS	TPR
1988	Cle-A	22	46	7	12	1	0	0	5	3	7	.261	.320	.283	.603	69	-2	-2	102	153	5	.500	0	0	0	-0	2/1S3	0.0
	Cal-A	10	15	3	2	0	0	0	0	0	0	.133	.133	.133	.267	-27	-2	-2	94	0	0	.133	0	0	0	-1	/3O	-0.2
	Yr	32	61	10	14	1	0	0	5	3	7	.230	.277	.246	.523	48	-4	-4	99	110	4	.388	0	0	0	-1		-0.2
1989	Chi-N	85	179	18	47	6	2	1	19	17	23	.263	.333	.335	.669	85	-2	-3	108	121	18	.559	1	1	-0	0	S3	0.0
Total	10	409	860	87	201	29	2	6	68	65	109	.234	.292	.293	.585	61	-43	-45	102	99	533	.471	6	7	-2	15	S3/21DO	-1.3

■ WILLIE RANDOLPH Randolph, Willie Larry b: 7/6/54, Holly Hill, S.C. BR/TR, 5'11", 165 lbs. Deb: 7/29/75

YEAR	TM/L	G	AB	R	H	2B	3B	HR	RBI	BB	SO	AVG	OBP	SLG	PRO	/A	BR	/A	PF	CHI	RC	TA	SB	CS	SBR	FR	POS	TPR
1975	Pit-N	30	61	9	10	1	0	0	3	7	6	.164	.250	.180	.430	21	-6	-6	99	105	3	.352	1	0	0	1	2/3	-0.3
1976	NY-A	125	430	59	115	15	4	1	40	58	39	.267	.358	.328	.686	102	3	4	99	109	55	.709	37	12	4	10	*2	2.5
1977	NY-A	147	551	91	151	28	11	4	40	64	53	.274	.351	.387	.737	102	2	3	99	75	77	.698	13	6	0	8	*2	2.2
1978	NY-A	134	499	87	139	18	6	3	42	82	51	.279	.385	.357	.741	111	10	11	99	85	78	.792	36	7	7	4	*2	2.9
1979	NY-A	153	574	98	155	15	13	5	61	95	39	.270	.376	.368	.744	106	5	9	96	92	82	.753	33	12	3	12	*2	2.9
1980	NY-A	138	513	99	151	23	7	7	46	**119**	45	.294	.429	.407	.836	132	29	29	99	69	105	.965	30	5	6	-3	*2	3.9
1981	NY-A	93	357	59	83	14	3	2	24	57	24	.232	.338	.305	.643	86	-4	-4	100	71	40	.623	14	5	1	-1	2	-0.1
1982	NY-A	144	553	85	155	21	4	3	36	75	35	.280	.369	.349	.718	102	2	5	96	69	75	.683	16	9	-1	3	*2/D	1.5
1983	NY-A	104	420	73	117	21	1	2	38	53	32	.279	.361	.348	.708	97	-0	0	99	86	55	.667	12	4	1	5	*2	0.9
1984	NY-A	142	564	86	162	24	2	2	31	86	42	.287	.382	.348	.729	110	6	11	94	54	79	.690	10	6	-1	13	*2	3.0
1985	NY-A	143	497	75	137	21	2	5	40	85	39	.276	.386	.356	.742	109	7	10	96	84	69	.718	16	9	-1	5	*2	1.9
1986	NY-A	141	492	76	136	15	2	5	50	94	49	.276	.396	.346	.741	102	9	6	103	114	77	.764	15	2	3	-5	*2/D	1.2
1987	NY-A	120	449	96	137	24	2	7	67	82	25	.305	.415	.414	.829	125	18	20	98	114	82	.857	11	1	3	2	*2/D	3.1
1988	NY-A	110	404	43	93	20	1	2	34	55	39	.230	.325	.300	.625	80	-11	-9	96	113	42	.572	8	4	0	11	*2	0.9
1989	LA-N	145	549	62	155	18	0	2	36	71	51	.282	.369	.326	.695	108	3	8	93	75	69	.635	7	6	-2	-4	*2	0.4
Total	15	1869	6913	1098	1896	278	58	50	588	1083	569	.274	.375	.353	.728	106	73	97	97	85	988	.721	259	88	25	59	*2/D3	26.9

■ JOHNNY RAY Ray, John Cornelius b: 3/1/57, Chouteau, Okla. BB/TR, 5'11", 170 lbs. Deb: 9/02/81

YEAR	TM/L	G	AB	R	H	2B	3B	HR	RBI	BB	SO	AVG	OBP	SLG	PRO	/A	BR	/A	PF	CHI	RC	TA	SB	CS	SBR	FR	POS	TPR
1981	Pit-N	31	102	10	25	11	0	0	6	6	9	.245	.287	.353	.640	84	-3	-2	96	65	10	.525	0	0	0	0	2	0.0
1982	Pit-N	162	647	79	182	30	7	7	63	36	34	.281	.320	.382	.702	87	-5	-13	110	98	80	.625	16	7	1	8	*2	0.3
1983	Pit-N	151	576	68	163	**38**	7	5	53	35	26	.283	.324	.399	.723	97	-2	-4	103	91	73	.654	18	9	0	20	*2/3	2.2
1984	Pit-N	155	555	75	173	**38**	6	6	67	37	31	.312	.358	.434	.792	129	15	19	94	103	83	.723	11	6	-0	-7	*2	1.6
1985	Pit-N	154	594	67	163	33	3	7	70	46	24	.274	.328	.375	.703	94	-3	-5	103	121	71	.627	13	9	-2	-11	*2	-1.7
1986	Pit-N	155	579	67	174	33	0	7	78	58	47	.301	.367	.394	.761	110	9	9	100	132	79	.678	6	9	-4	9	*2	1.7
1987	Pit-N	123	472	48	129	19	3	5	54	41	36	.273	.331	.358	.689	79	-11	-14	104	124	53	.590	4	2	0	11	*2	0.0
	Cal-A	30	127	16	44	11	0	0	15	3	10	.346	.362	.433	.795	112	2	2	99	115	19	.667	0	0	0	-1	2/D	0.3
1988	Cal-A	153	602	75	184	42	7	6	83	36	38	.306	.349	.429	.777	124	12	17	94	127	90	.704	4	1	1	3	*2O/D	2.7
1989	Cal-A	134	530	52	153	16	3	5	62	36	30	.289	.334	.358	.692	97	-3	-2	99	113	62	.589	6	3	0	7	*2	0.7
Total	9	1248	4784	557	1390	271	36	48	551	334	285	.291	.338	.392	.731	101	11	7	101	112	618	.647	78	46	-4	39	*2/OD3	7.8

■ RANDY READY Ready, Randy Max b: 1/8/60, Fremont, Cal. BR/TR, 5'11", 180 lbs. Deb: 9/04/83

YEAR	TM/L	G	AB	R	H	2B	3B	HR	RBI	BB	SO	AVG	OBP	SLG	PRO	/A	BR	/A	PF	CHI	RC	TA	SB	CS	SBR	FR	POS	TPR
1983	Mil-A	12	37	8	15	3	2	1	6	6	3	.405	.488	.676	1.164	236	6	7	92	84	12	1.348	0	1	-1	0	/3D	0.6
1984	Mil-A	37	123	13	23	6	1	3	13	14	18	.187	.270	.325	.595	70	-6	-5	92	108	11	.529	0	0	0	3	3	-0.1
1985	Mil-A	48	181	29	48	9	5	1	21	14	23	.265	.321	.387	.708	89	-2	-3	105	121	22	.612	0	0	0	4	O/32D	0.1
1986	Mil-A	23	79	8	15	4	0	1	4	9	9	.190	.273	.278	.551	50	-5	-5	102	65	6	.493	2	0	1	-2	O/23D	-0.6
	SD-N	1	3	0	0	0	0	0	0	0	1	.000	.000	.000	.000	-99	-1	-1	95	0	0	.000	0	0	0	0	/3	0.0
1987	SD-N	124	350	69	108	26	6	12	54	67	44	.309	.424	.520	.944	154	27	29	97	99	81	1.028	7	3	0	1	32O	2.9
1988	SD-N	114	331	43	88	16	2	7	39	39	38	.266	.349	.390	.738	115	6	7	97	104	48	.714	6	2	1	-2	32O	0.6
1989	SD-N	28	67	4	17	2	1	0	5	11	6	.254	.359	.313	.672	93	-0	-0	101	96	8	.615	0	0	0	1	3/2O	0.1
	Phi-N	72	187	33	50	11	1	8	21	31	31	.267	.377	.465	.843	139	10	10	101	76	35	.873	4	3	-1	-1	O3/2	0.9
	Yr	100	254	37	67	13	2	8	26	42	37	.264	.372	.425	.798	127	10	10	101	83	43	.804	4	3	-1	1		1.0
Total	7	459	1358	207	364	77	18	33	163	191	173	.268	.362	.424	.786	119	35	38	98	98	224	.773	19	9	0	5	3O/2D	4.5

■ GARY REDUS Redus, Gary Eugene b: 11/1/56, Athens, Ala. BR/TR, 6'1", 180 lbs. Deb: 9/07/82

YEAR	TM/L	G	AB	R	H	2B	3B	HR	RBI	BB	SO	AVG	OBP	SLG	PRO	/A	BR	/A	PF	CHI	RC	TA	SB	CS	SBR	FR	POS	TPR
1982	Cin-N	20	83	12	18	3	2	1	7	5	21	.217	.261	.337	.599	65	-4	-4	102	78	8	.657	11	2	2	0	O	-0.1
1983	Cin-N	125	453	90	112	20	9	17	51	71	111	.247	.353	.444	.797	116	12	11	103	85	76	.870	39	14	3	5	*O	1.8
1984	Cin-N	123	394	69	100	21	3	7	22	52	71	.254	.342	.376	.718	96	2	-1	106	51	58	.806	48	11	8	-3	*O	0.0
1985	Cin-N	101	246	51	62	14	4	6	28	44	52	.252	.368	.415	.782	113	7	6	105	93	45	.995	48	12	7	-6	O	0.5
1986	Phi-N	90	340	62	84	22	4	11	33	47	78	.247	.344	.432	.776	108	6	4	104	77	55	.838	25	7	3	5	O	1.1
1987	Chi-A	130	475	78	112	26	6	12	48	69	90	.236	.333	.392	.724	85	-4	-11	109	91	69	.806	52	11	9	7	*O/D	0.2
1988	Chi-A	77	262	42	69	10	4	6	34	33	52	.263	.350	.401	.751	113	4	5	97	112	42	.830	26	2	7	2	O/D	1.2
	Pit-N	30	71	12	14	2	0	2	4	15	19	.197	.345	.310	.655	91	-0	-0	98	57	9	.717	5	2	0	1	O	0.1
1989	Pit-N	98	279	42	79	18	7	6	33	40	51	.283	.375	.462	.837	147	14	17	94	90	52	.924	25	6	4	-4	1O	1.1
Total	8	794	2603	458	650	136	39	68	260	376	545	.250	.347	.410	.757	106	37	26	103	83	414	.846	279	67	44	8	O/1D	5.9

■ JEFF REED Reed, Jeffrey Scott b: 11/12/62, Joliet, Ill. BL/TR, 6'2", 190 lbs. Deb: 4/05/84

YEAR	TM/L	G	AB	R	H	2B	3B	HR	RBI	BB	SO	AVG	OBP	SLG	PRO	/A	BR	/A	PF	CHI	RC	TA	SB	CS	SBR	FR	POS	TPR
1984	Min-A	18	21	3	3	3	0	0	1	2	6	.143	.217	.286	.503	36	-2	-2	106	66	1	.444	0	0	0	0	C	0.0
1985	Min-A	7	10	2	2	0	0	0	0	0	3	.200	.200	.200	.400	10	-1	-1	103	0	0	.250	0	0	0	0	/C	0.0
1986	Min-A	68	165	13	39	6	1	2	9	16	19	.236	.308	.321	.629	67	-6	-8	108	61	17	.555	1	0	0	-4	C	-0.7
1987	Mon-N	75	207	15	44	11	0	1	21	12	20	.213	.259	.280	.539	40	-17	-19	106	137	14	.413	0	1	-1	-9	C	-2.2
1988	Mon-N	43	123	10	27	3	2	0	9	13	22	.220	.294	.276	.571	61	-5	-6	106	106	10	.485	1	0	0	2	C	-0.1
	Cin-N	49	142	10	33	6	0	1	7	15	19	.232	.306	.296	.602	70	-5	-5	105	62	13	.514	0	0	0	-0	C	-0.3
	Yr	92	265	20	60	9	2	1	16	28	41	.226	.300	.287	.587	66	-10	-12	105	84	24	.500	1	0	0	2		-0.4
1989	Cin-N	102	287	16	64	11	0	3	23	34	46	.223	.310	.293	.602	71	-9	-10	103	100	27	.524	0	0	0	-2	C	-0.5
Total	6	362	955	69	212	40	3	7	70	92	135	.222	.293	.292	.585	61	-45	-52	105	94	84	.493	2	1	0	-13	C	-3.8

■ JODY REED Reed, Jody Eric b: 7/26/62, Tampa, Fla. BR/TR, 5'9", 170 lbs. Deb: 9/12/87

YEAR	TM/L	G	AB	R	H	2B	3B	HR	RBI	BB	SO	AVG	OBP	SLG	PRO	/A	BR	/A	PF	CHI	RC	TA	SB	CS	SBR	FR	POS	TPR
1987	Bos-A	9	30	4	9	1	1	0	8	4	0	.300	.382	.400	.782	110	1	1	99	266	5	.773	1	1	-0	0	/S23	0.0
1988	Bos-A	109	338	60	99	23	1	1	28	45	21	.293	.382	.376	.758	104	8	4	109	86	51	.717	1	3	-2	-1	S2/3	0.6
1989	Bos-A	146	524	76	151	42	2	3	40	73	44	.288	.379	.393	.772	113	15	12	105	74	81	.736	4	5	-2	3	S2/3OD	2.1
Total	3	264	892	140	259	66	4	4	76	122	65	.290	.381	.387	.767	109	23	16	106	85	137	.730	6	9	-4	2	S/23DO	2.7

■ KEVIN REIMER Reimer, Kevin Michael b: 6/28/64, Macon, Ga. BL/TR, 6'2", 215 lbs. Deb: 9/13/88

YEAR	TM/L	G	AB	R	H	2B	3B	HR	RBI	BB	SO	AVG	OBP	SLG	PRO	/A	BR	/A	PF	CHI	RC	TA	SB	CS	SBR	FR	POS	TPR
1988	Tex-A	12	25	2	3	0	0	1	2	0	6	.120	.120	.240	.360	-2	-3	-3	101	88	1	.273	0	0	0	-0	/OD	-0.3
1989	Tex-A	3	5	0	0	0	0	0	0	0	1	.000	.000	.000	.000	-98	-1	-1	102	0	0	.000	0	0	0	0	/D	0.0
Total	2	15	30	2	3	0	0	1	2	0	7	.100	.100	.200	.300	-18	-5	-5	101	74	1	.214	0	0	0	-0	/DO	-0.3

■ GIL REYES Reyes, Gilberto R. (Polanco) b: 12/10/63, Santo Domingo, D.R. BR/TR, 6'2", 200 lbs. Deb: 6/11/83

YEAR	TM/L	G	AB	R	H	2B	3B	HR	RBI	BB	SO	AVG	OBP	SLG	PRO	/A	BR	/A	PF	CHI	RC	TA	SB	CS	SBR	FR	POS	TPR
1983	LA-N	19	31	1	5	2	0	0	0	0	5	.161	.188	.226	.413	14	-4	-4	100	0	1	.276	0	0	0	-1	C	-0.3
1984	LA-N	4	5	0	0	0	0	0	0	0	3	.000	.000	.000	.000	-96	-1	-1	104	0	0	.000	0	0	0	0	/C	0.0
1985	LA-N	6	1	0	0	0	0	0	0	1	1	.000	.667	.000	.667	110	0	0	93	0	0	2.000	0	0	0	0	/C	0.1
1987	LA-N	1	0	0	0	0	0	0	0	0	0	—	—	—	—	—	0	0	92	—	—	—	0	0	0	0	/C	0.0
1988	LA-N	5	9	1	1	0	0	0	0	0	3	.111	.111	.111	.222	-34	-2	-2	106	0	0	.125	0	0	0	-0	/C	-0.1
1989	Mon-N	4	5	0	1	0	0	0	1	0	1	.200	.200	.200	.400	14	-1	-1	102	403	0	.250	0	0	0	0	/C	0.0
Total	6	39	51	2	7	2	0	0	1	1	13	.137	.185	.176	.362	2	-7	-7	101	37	2	.255	0	0	0	-1	/C	-0.3

■ CRAIG REYNOLDS Reynolds, Gordon Craig b: 12/27/52, Houston, Tex. BL/TR, 6'1", 175 lbs. Deb: 8/01/75

YEAR	TM/L	G	AB	R	H	2B	3B	HR	RBI	BB	SO	AVG	OBP	SLG	PRO	/A	BR	/A	PF	CHI	RC	TA	SB	CS	SBR	FR	POS	TPR
1975	Pit-N	31	76	8	17	3	0	0	4	3	5	.224	.253	.263	.516	44	-6	-6	99	77	5	.377	0	1	-1	-1	S	-0.3
1976	Pit-N	7	4	1	1	0	0	1	1	0	0	.250	.250	1.000	1.250	242	1	1	100	55	1	1.333	0	0	0	0	/S2	0.1
1977	Sea-A	135	420	41	104	12	3	4	28	15	23	.248	.279	.319	.598	65	-22	-20	96	76	36	.479	6	6	-2	4	*S	-0.1
1978	Sea-A	148	548	57	160	16	7	5	44	36	41	.292	.339	.374	.713	99	0	-1	102	84	71	.636	9	6	-1	8	*S	1.9
1979	Hou-N	146	555	63	147	20	9	0	39	21	49	.265	.294	.333	.627	78	-23	-16	90	88	57	.529	12	6	0	-7	*S	-0.8

YEAR	TM/L	G	AB	R	H	2B	3B	HR	RBI	BB	SO	AVG	OBP	SLG	PRO	/A	BR	/A	PF	CHI	RC	TA	SB	CS	SBR	FR	POS	TPR
1980	Hou-N	137	381	34	86	9	6	3	28	20	39	.226	.264	.304	.569	60	-22	-21	98	89	32	.460	2	1	0	5	*S	0.0
1981	Hou-N	87	323	43	84	10	**12**	4	31	12	31	.260	.287	.402	.689	106	-4	0	88	87	35	.585	3	3	-1	-1	S	0.8
1982	Hou-N	54	118	16	30	2	3	1	7	11	9	.254	.323	.347	.671	88	-2	-2	99	62	14	.622	3	1	0	2	S/3	0.4
1983	Hou-N	65	98	10	21	3	0	1	6	6	10	.214	.260	.276	.535	54	-7	-6	90	79	7	.423	0	1	-1	1	23/SO	-0.4
1984	Hou-N	146	527	61	137	15	11	6	60	22	53	.260	.290	.364	.654	89	-13	-9	93	114	57	.559	7	1	2	16	*S/3	2.5
1985	Hou-N	107	379	43	103	18	8	4	32	12	30	.272	.294	.393	.687	94	-6	-4	96	79	42	.581	4	4	-1	9	*S/2	1.2
1986	Hou-N	114	313	32	78	7	3	6	41	12	31	.249	.277	.348	.625	69	-13	-14	103	129	28	.508	3	1	0	-5	S/13OP	-0.9
1987	Hou-N	135	374	35	95	17	3	4	28	30	44	.254	.309	.348	.657	79	-14	-11	93	79	42	.581	5	1	1	-18	*S/3	-1.2
1988	Hou-N	78	161	20	41	7	0	1	14	8	23	.255	.290	.317	.607	79	-5	-4	93	104	15	.512	3	0	1	-1	S321	-0.3
1989	Hou-N	101	189	16	38	4	0	2	14	19	18	.201	.274	.254	.528	51	-12	-12	102	104	14	.444	1	0	0	-6	2S3/1PO	-1.7
Total	15	1491	4466	480	1142	143	65	42	377	227	406	.256	.293	.345	.638	80	-148	-124	96	91	457	.539	58	32	-2	7	*S/231OP	1.2
■ **HAROLD REYNOLDS** Reynolds, Harold Craig b: 11/26/60, Eugene, Ore. BB/TR, 5'11", 165 lbs. Deb: 9/02/83																												
1983	Sea-A	20	59	8	12	4	1	0	1	2	9	.203	.230	.305	.535	46	-4	-4	100	22	3	.400	0	2	-1	1	2	-0.3
1984	Sea-A	10	10	3	3	0	0	0	0	0	1	.300	.364	.300	.664	84	-0	-0	102	0	1	.625	1	1	-0	0	/2	0.0
1985	Sea-A	67	104	15	15	3	1	0	6	17	14	.144	.264	.192	.457	29	-10	-9	95	119	7	.440	3	2	-0	4	2	-0.2
1986	Sea-A	126	445	46	99	19	4	1	24	29	42	.222	.275	.290	.565	52	-27	-30	105	74	37	.525	30	12	2	**29**	*2	0.7
1987	Sea-A	160	530	73	146	31	8	1	35	39	34	.275	.327	.370	.697	83	-10	-12	103	70	67	.723	**60**	20	6	20	*2	2.3
1988	Sea-A	158	598	61	169	26	**11**	4	41	51	51	.283	.341	.383	.724	95	2	-3	108	72	74	.679	35	29	-7	8	*2	0.8
1989	Sea-A	153	613	87	184	24	9	0	43	55	45	.300	.361	.369	.729	103	6	4	103	71	83	.685	25	18	-3	**26**	*2/D	2.9
Total	7	694	2359	293	628	107	34	6	150	193	196	.266	.325	.348	.673	82	-44	-57	104	72	272	.640	154	84	-4	87	2/D	6.2
■ **R.J. REYNOLDS** Reynolds, Robert James b: 4/19/59, Sacramento, Cal. BB/TR, 6', 190 lbs. Deb: 9/01/83																												
1983	LA-N	24	55	5	13	0	0	2	11	3	11	.236	.276	.345	.621	71	-2	-2	100	174	6	.628	5	0	2	-1	O	-0.1
1984	LA-N	73	240	23	62	12	2	2	24	14	38	.258	.302	.350	.652	80	-6	-7	104	104	24	.561	7	5	-1	-1	O	-1.1
1985	LA-N	73	207	22	55	10	4	0	25	13	31	.266	.312	.353	.665	92	-4	-2	93	136	23	.589	6	3	0	-1	O	-0.4
	Pit-N	31	130	22	40	5	3	3	17	9	18	.308	.357	.462	.819	124	4	4	103	85	22	.863	12	2	2	3	O	0.8
	Yr	104	337	44	95	15	7	3	42	22	49	.282	.330	.395	.724	106	0	2	96	122	45	.692	18	5	2	2		0.4
1986	Pit-N	118	402	63	108	30	2	9	48	40	78	.269	.336	.420	.757	107	4	4	100	100	55	.722	16	9	-1	-9	*O	-0.8
1987	Pit-N	117	335	47	87	24	1	7	51	34	80	.260	.328	.400	.728	88	-4	-6	104	131	46	.717	14	1	4	-8	O	-1.3
1988	Pit-N	130	323	35	80	14	2	6	51	20	62	.248	.292	.359	.651	88	-6	-6	98	152	35	.604	15	2	3	-8	O	-1.3
1989	Pit-N	125	363	45	98	16	2	6	48	34	66	.270	.334	.375	.709	109	1	4	94	125	45	.682	22	5	4	2	O	0.8
Total	7	691	2055	262	543	111	16	35	275	167	384	.264	.321	.385	.706	97	-13	-12	99	123	256	.669	97	27	13	-23	O	-3.4
■ **JIM RICE** Rice, James Edward b: 3/8/53, Anderson, S.C. BR/TR, 6'2", 200 lbs. Deb: 8/19/74																												
1974	Bos-A	24	67	6	18	2	1	1	13	4	12	.269	.319	.373	.693	93	-0	-1	107	183	8	.588	0	0	0	-1	D/O	-0.1
1975	Bos-A	144	564	92	174	29	4	22	102	36	122	.309	.354	.491	.845	126	25	19	109	121	92	.790	10	5	0	-4	OD	1.3
1976	Bos-A	153	581	75	164	25	8	25	85	28	123	.282	.320	.482	.802	120	20	13	110	94	83	.727	8	5	-1	-3	OD	0.8
1977	Bos-A	160	644	104	206	29	15	**39**	114	53	120	.320	.379	**.593**	.972	136	51	36	117	87	136	.968	5	4	-1	0	*DO	3.4
1978	Bos-A	163	677	121	**213**	25	**15**	**46**	**139**	58	126	.315	.373	**.600**	**.973**	158	**59**	**52**	107	89	**147**	.983	7	5	-1	6	*OD	**5.5**
1979	Bos-A	158	619	117	201	39	6	39	130	57	97	.325	.385	.596	.981	149	50	44	107	109	138	1.002	9	4	0	-3	*OD	3.5
1980	Bos-A	124	504	81	148	22	6	24	86	30	87	.294	.338	.504	.842	125	17	16	102	109	81	.789	8	3	1	3	*OD	1.7
1981	Bos-A	108	451	51	128	18	1	17	62	34	76	.284	.338	.441	.779	116	12	9	106	93	64	.702	2	2	-1	3	*O	0.9
1982	Bos-A	145	573	86	177	24	5	24	97	55	98	.309	.376	.494	.870	124	29	21	110	116	98	.810	0	1	-1	-5	*O	1.1
1983	Bos-A	155	626	90	191	34	1	**39**	**126**	52	102	.305	.364	.550	.914	146	39	38	101	103	113	.859	0	2	-1	14	*O/D	4.8
1984	Bos-A	159	657	98	184	25	7	28	122	44	102	.280	.326	.467	.793	106	13	4	110	120	88	.699	4	0	1	8	*O/D	0.8
1985	Bos-A	140	546	85	159	20	3	27	103	51	75	.291	.354	.487	.841	125	20	18	102	125	83	.761	2	0	1	-6	*O/D	1.0
1986	Bos-A	157	618	98	200	39	2	20	110	62	78	.324	.389	.490	.879	139	34	34	100	128	115	.842	0	1	-1	-8	*O/D	2.0
1987	Bos-A	108	404	66	112	14	0	13	62	45	77	.277	.360	.408	.768	105	4	4	99	124	55	.692	1	1	-0	1	OD	0.2
1988	Bos-A	135	485	57	128	18	3	15	72	48	89	.264	.334	.406	.740	97	4	-2	109	121	63	.662	1	1	-0	-2	*DO	-0.4
1989	Bos-A	56	209	22	49	10	2	3	28	13	39	.234	.283	.344	.627	73	-7	-8	105	137	20	.530	1	0	0	0	D	-0.7
Total	16	2089	8225	1249	2452	373	79	382	1451	670	1423	.298	.356	.502	.858	126	369	299	107	111	1382	.804	58	34	-3	2	*OD	25.8
■ **JEFF RICHARDSON** Richardson, Jeffrey Scott b: 8/26/65, Grand Island, Neb. BR/TR, 6'2", 175 lbs. Deb: 7/14/89																												
1989	Cin-N	53	125	10	21	4	0	2	11	10	23	.168	.235	.248	.483	37	-10	-11	103	120	8	.402	1	0	0	2	S/3	-0.6
■ **ROB RICHIE** Richie, Robert Eugene b: 9/5/65, Reno, Nev. BL/TR, 6'2", 190 lbs. Deb: 8/19/89																												
1989	Det-A	19	49	6	13	4	2	1	10	5	10	.265	.333	.490	.823	133	2	2	97	144	7	.744	0	1	-1	-1	O/D	0.0
■ **ERNIE RILES** Riles, Ernest b: 10/2/60, Cairo, Ga. BL/TR, 6'1", 180 lbs. Deb: 5/14/85																												
1985	Mil-A	116	448	54	128	12	7	5	45	36	54	.286	.342	.377	.719	92	-2	-4	105	103	55	.618	2	2	-1	-10	*S/D	-0.6
1986	Mil-A	145	524	69	132	24	2	9	47	54	80	.252	.323	.357	.680	84	-10	-11	102	89	59	.603	7	7	-2	-25	*S	-3.0
1987	Mil-A	83	276	38	72	11	1	4	38	30	47	.261	.336	.351	.687	82	-6	-7	102	139	33	.612	3	4	-2	-7	3S	-1.4
1988	Mil-A	41	127	7	32	6	1	1	9	7	26	.252	.291	.339	.630	73	-4	-5	103	78	12	.520	2	2	-1	-2	3/SD	-0.6
	SF-N	79	187	26	55	7	2	3	28	10	33	.294	.330	.401	.731	116	2	3	94	133	23	.619	1	2	-1	1	32S	0.5
1989	SF-N	122	302	43	84	13	2	7	40	28	50	.278	.343	.404	.747	116	5	6	97	113	39	.658	0	6	-4	-2	32/SO	0.0
Total	5	586	1864	237	503	73	15	29	207	165	290	.270	.331	.372	.703	93	-14	-18	101	107	221	.613	15	23	-9	-45	S3/2DO	-5.1
■ **CAL RIPKEN** Ripken, Calvin Edwin Jr. b: 8/24/60, Havre De Grace, Md. BR/TR, 6'4", 200 lbs. Deb: 8/10/81																												
1981	Bal-A	23	39	1	5	0	0	0	0	1	8	.128	.150	.128	.278	-19	-6	-6	99	0	0	.158	0	0	0	0	S/3	-0.4
1982	Bal-A	160	598	90	158	32	5	28	93	46	95	.264	.320	.475	.795	115	10	10	100	103	87	.732	3	3	-1	-7	S3	0.9
1983	Bal-A	162	663	**121**	**211**	**47**	2	27	102	58	97	.318	.373	.517	.890	142	37	37	100	90	120	.835	0	4	-2	16	*S	**5.8**
1984	Bal-A	162	641	103	195	37	7	27	86	71	89	.304	.375	.510	.885	151	37	41	94	81	122	.868	2	1	0	**39**	*S	**9.0**
1985	Bal-A	161	642	116	181	32	5	26	110	67	68	.282	.351	.469	.820	123	19	20	99	111	96	.748	2	3	-1	7	*S	3.7
1986	Bal-A	162	627	98	177	35	1	25	81	70	60	.282	.358	.461	.819	123	20	21	99	94	102	.779	4	2	0	10	*S	3.8
1987	Bal-A	162	624	97	157	28	3	27	98	81	77	.252	.339	.436	.774	107	4	6	98	107	90	.727	3	5	-2	-3	*S	0.7
1988	Bal-A	161	575	87	152	25	1	23	81	102	69	.264	.377	.431	.808	132	23	27	95	98	99	.814	2	2	-1	-1	*S	3.2
1989	Bal-A	162	646	80	166	30	0	21	93	57	72	.257	.320	.401	.721	103	1	2	99	108	79	.639	3	2	-0	5	*S	2.0
Total	9	1315	5055	793	1402	266	24	204	744	553	635	.277	.350	.461	.811	124	145	158	98	98	794	.760	19	22	-8	65	*S/3	28.7
■ **BILLY RIPKEN** Ripken, William Oliver b: 12/16/64, Havre De Grace, Md. BR/TR, 6'1", 180 lbs. Deb: 7/11/87																												
1987	Bal-A	58	234	27	72	9	0	2	20	21	23	.308	.365	.372	.737	99	-0	0	98	82	33	.675	4	1	1	-3	2	0.2
1988	Bal-A	150	512	52	106	18	1	2	34	33	63	.207	.262	.258	.520	48	-37	-33	95	100	35	.422	8	2	1	-0	*2/3	-2.3
1989	Bal-A	115	318	31	76	11	2	2	26	22	53	.239	.288	.305	.593	68	-14	-13	99	98	27	.469	1	2	-1	6	*2	-0.6
Total	3	323	1064	110	254	38	3	6	80	76	139	.239	.293	.297	.590	66	-51	-46	97	95	94	.486	13	5	1	3	2/3	-2.7
■ **LUIS RIVERA** Rivera, Luis Antonio (Pedraza) b: 1/3/64, Cidra, P.R. BR/TR, 5'11", 165 lbs. Deb: 8/03/86																												
1986	Mon-N	55	166	20	34	11	1	0	13	17	33	.205	.286	.283	.570	59	-9	-9	98	110	15	.500	1	1	-0	-8	S	-1.2
1987	Mon-N	18	32	0	5	2	0	0	1	1	8	.156	.182	.219	.401	5	-4	-5	106	57	1	.296	0	0	0	-1	S	-0.3
1988	Mon-N	123	371	35	83	17	3	4	30	24	69	.224	.273	.318	.591	65	-15	-17	106	92	30	.485	3	4	-2	-9	*S	-2.0
1989	Bos-A	93	323	35	83	17	1	5	29	20	60	.257	.302	.362	.665	83	-6	-8	105	85	34	.560	2	3	-1	-6	S/2D	-0.8
Total	4	289	892	90	205	47	5	9	73	62	170	.230	.283	.324	.607	68	-35	-39	104	92	80	.507	6	8	-3	-24	S/D2	-4.3
■ **BIP ROBERTS** Roberts, Leon Joseph b: 10/27/63, Berkeley, Cal. BB/TR, 5'7", 150 lbs. Deb: 4/07/86																												
1986	SD-N	101	241	34	61	5	2	1	12	14	29	.253	.294	.303	.597	68	-11	-10	95	63	20	.521	14	12	-3	-1	2	-1.3
1988	SD-N	5	9	1	3	0	0	0	0	1	2	.333	.400	.333	.733	116	0	0	97	0	1	.500	0	2	-1	0	/32	0.0
1989	SD-N	117	329	81	99	15	8	3	25	49	45	.301	.393	.422	.816	132	16	16	101	68	58	.861	21	11	-0	-2	O3S/2	1.4
Total	3	223	579	116	163	20	10	4	37	64	76	.282	.354	.371	.725	106	5	6	98	65	79	.706	35	25	-5	-3	/2O3S	0.1

YEAR	TM/L	G	AB	R	H	2B	3B	HR	RBI	BB	SO	AVG	OBP	SLG	PRO	/A	BR	/A	PF	CHI	RC	TA	SB	CS	SBR	FR	POS	TPR
■ BILLY ROBIDOUX	Robidoux, William Joseph b: 1/13/64, Ware, Mass. BL/TR, 6'1", 200 lbs. Deb: 9/11/85																											
1985	Mil-A	18	51	5	9	2	0	3	8	12	16	.176	.333	.392	.725	94	0	-0	105	109	7	.744	0	0	0	-1	O/1D	-0.1
1986	Mil-A	56	181	15	41	8	0	1	21	33	36	.227	.346	.287	.633	74	-5	-5	102	155	19	.574	0	0	0	-2	1D	-1.0
1987	Mil-A	23	62	9	12	0	0	0	4	8	17	.194	.286	.194	.479	31	-6	-6	102	133	4	.392	0	1	-1	0	1D	-0.6
1988	Mil-A	33	91	9	23	5	0	0	5	8	14	.253	.313	.308	.621	72	-3	-3	103	71	8	.514	1	1	-0	2	1/D	-0.2
1989	Chi-A	16	39	2	5	2	0	0	1	4	9	.128	.209	.179	.389	11	-5	-4	93	56	2	.324	0	0	0	-1	1/O	-0.6
Total	5	146	424	40	90	17	0	4	39	65	92	.212	.317	.281	.598	65	-18	-19	102	120	40	.532	1	2	-1	-2	1/DO	-2.5
■ VIC RODRIGUEZ	Rodriguez, Victor Manuel (Rivera) b: 7/14/61, New York, N.Y. BR/TR, 5'11", 173 lbs. Deb: 9/05/84																											
1984	Bal-A	11	17	4	7	3	0	0	2	0	2	.412	.412	.588	1.000	183	2	2	94	80	4	1.000	0	0	0	-0	/2D	0.2
1989	Min-A	6	11	2	5	2	0	0	0	0	1	.455	.455	.636	1.091	192	1	1	107	0	3	1.167	0	0	0	0	/3	0.2
Total	2	17	28	6	12	5	0	0	2	0	3	.429	.429	.607	1.036	187	3	3	99	48	7	1.063	0	0	0	0	/23D	0.4
■ ED ROMERO	Romero, Edgardo Ralph (Rivera) b: 12/9/57, Santurce, P.R. BR/TR, 5'11", 160 lbs. Deb: 7/16/77																											
1977	Mil-A	10	25	4	7	1	0	0	2	4	3	.280	.379	.320	.699	98	-0	0	95	99	3	.632	0	0	0	-0	S	0.1
1980	Mil-A	42	104	20	27	7	0	1	10	9	11	.260	.319	.356	.674	89	-2	-1	95	97	12	.600	2	0	1	0	S2/3	0.2
1981	Mil-A	44	91	6	18	3	0	1	10	4	9	.198	.232	.264	.495	44	-7	-6	96	145	4	.354	0	2	-1	8	S2/3	0.2
1982	Mil-A	52	144	18	36	8	0	1	7	8	16	.250	.289	.326	.616	73	-6	-5	94	56	13	.491	0	0	0	1	2S/3O	0.0
1983	Mil-A	59	145	17	46	7	0	1	18	8	8	.317	.353	.386	.739	113	1	2	92	119	20	.644	1	0	0	-2	SO/32D	0.1
1984	Mil-A	116	357	36	90	12	0	1	31	29	25	.252	.310	.294	.604	74	-15	-11	92	114	31	.489	3	3	-1	5	3S2/1OD	-0.1
1985	Mil-A	88	251	24	63	11	1	0	21	26	20	.251	.321	.303	.624	69	-9	-11	105	110	26	.536	1	1	-0	-2	S2O/3	-0.8
1986	Bos-A	100	233	41	49	11	0	2	23	18	16	.210	.273	.283	.556	53	-15	-15	100	127	19	.466	2	0	1	-8	S3/2O	-1.7
1987	Bos-A	88	235	23	64	5	0	0	14	18	22	.272	.324	.294	.618	67	-11	-10	99	81	21	.478	0	2	-1	6	2S3/1	-0.3
1988	Bos-A	31	75	3	18	3	0	0	5	3	8	.240	.278	.280	.558	52	-4	-5	109	95	5	.410	0	0	0	-0	3/S/21D	-0.4
1989	Bos-A	46	113	14	24	4	0	0	6	7	7	.212	.264	.248	.512	43	-8	-9	105	83	7	.391	0	2	-1	3	23S	-0.5
	Atl-N	7	19	1	5	1	0	1	1	0	0	.263	.263	.474	.737	104	0	-0	102	34	2	.600	0	0	0	0	/2S3	0.0
	Mil-A	15	50	3	10	3	0	0	3	0	10	.200	.200	.260	.460	30	-5	-5	97	90	2	.302	0	0	0	1	2/3SD	-0.2
Total	11	698	1842	210	457	76	1	8	151	134	155	.248	.301	.303	.604	68	-81	-76	98	103	166	.489	9	10	-3	11	S23/O1D	-3.4
■ KEVIN ROMINE	Romine, Kevin Andrew b: 5/23/61, Exeter, N.H. BR/TR, 5'11", 185 lbs. Deb: 9/05/85																											
1985	Bos-A	24	28	3	6	2	0	0	1	1	4	.214	.241	.286	.527	43	-2	-2	102	50	2	.435	1	0	0	-5	O/D	-0.7
1986	Bos-A	35	35	6	9	2	0	0	2	3	9	.257	.316	.314	.630	74	-1	-1	100	72	4	.593	2	0	1	-4	O	-0.4
1987	Bos-A	9	24	5	7	2	0	0	2	2	6	.292	.346	.375	.721	93	-0	-0	99	89	3	.647	0	0	0	0	/OD	0.0
1988	Bos-A	57	78	17	15	2	1	1	6	7	15	.192	.259	.282	.541	47	-5	-6	109	95	6	.470	2	0	1	-10	O/D	-1.6
1989	Bos-A	92	274	30	75	13	0	1	23	21	53	.274	.330	.332	.662	83	-4	-6	105	95	28	.545	1	1	-0	0	O/D	-0.6
Total	5	217	439	61	112	21	1	2	34	34	87	.255	.312	.321	.633	74	-13	-16	105	90	43	.532	6	1	1	-19	O/D	-3.3
■ ROLANDO ROOMES	Roomes, Rolando Audley b: 2/15/62, Kingston, Jamaica BR/TR, 6'3", 180 lbs. Deb: 4/12/88																											
1988	Chi-N	17	16	3	3	0	0	0	0	0	4	.188	.188	.188	.375	8	-2	-2	104	0	0	.214	0	1	-1	-1	/O	-0.3
1989	Cin-N	107	315	36	83	18	5	7	34	13	100	.263	.299	.419	.718	100	0	-1	103	89	38	.661	12	8	-1	0	*O	-0.3
Total	2	124	331	39	86	18	5	7	34	13	104	.260	.294	.408	.702	96	-2	-3	103	85	39	.637	12	9	-2	-1	O	-0.6
■ BOBBY ROSE	Rose, Robert Richard b: 3/15/67, Covina, Cal. BR/TR, 5'11", 170 lbs. Deb: 8/12/89																											
1989	Cal-A	14	38	4	8	1	2	1	3	2	10	.211	.268	.421	.689	93	-1	-1	99	61	4	.594	0	0	0	2	3/2	0.1
■ JOHN RUSSELL	Russell, John William b: 1/5/61, Oklahoma City, Okla. BR/TR, 6', 200 lbs. Deb: 6/22/84																											
1984	Phi-N	39	99	11	28	8	1	2	11	12	33	.283	.360	.444	.805	123	3	3	102	86	16	.757	0	1	-1	-1	O/C	0.0
1985	Phi-N	81	216	22	47	12	0	9	23	18	72	.218	.278	.398	.676	85	-5	-5	102	81	24	.609	2	0	1	-5	O1	-1.1
1986	Phi-N	93	315	35	76	21	2	13	60	25	103	.241	.303	.444	.748	99	0	-1	104	134	42	.683	0	1	-1	4	C	0.5
1987	Phi-N	24	62	5	9	1	0	3	8	3	17	.145	.185	.306	.491	26	-7	-7	104	114	2	.379	0	1	-1	1	O/C	-0.6
1988	Phi-N	22	49	5	12	1	0	2	4	3	15	.245	.302	.388	.690	95	-0	-0	101	64	5	.590	0	0	0	2	C	0.2
1989	Atl-N	74	159	14	29	2	0	2	9	8	53	.182	.226	.233	.459	31	-14	-15	102	84	8	.343	0	0	0	-4	CO/13P	-1.6
Total	6	333	900	92	201	45	3	31	115	69	293	.223	.282	.383	.666	81	-22	-25	103	102	96	.581	2	3	-1	-2	CO/13P	-2.6
■ MARK RYAL	Ryal, Mark Dwayne b: 4/28/60, Henryetta, Okla. BL/TL, 6'1", 185 lbs. Deb: 9/07/82																											
1982	KC-A	6	13	0	1	0	0	0	0	1	3	.077	.143	.077	.220	-38	-2	-2	100	0	0	.167	0	0	0	-1	/O	-0.2
1985	Chi-A	12	33	4	5	3	0	0	3	3	3	.152	.222	.242	.465	27	-3	-3	100	149	2	.367	0	0	0	-1	O	-0.4
1986	Cal-A	13	32	6	12	0	0	2	5	2	4	.375	.412	.563	.974	170	3	3	96	83	7	1.000	1	0	0	-1	/O1D	0.2
1987	Cal-A	58	100	7	20	6	0	5	18	3	15	.200	.223	.410	.633	64	-6	-5	99	128	8	.524	0	0	0	-5	O/1D	-1.0
1989	Phi-N	29	33	2	8	2	0	0	5	1	6	.242	.265	.303	.568	61	-2	-2	101	201	3	.440	0	0	0	-1	/1O	-0.2
Total	5	118	211	19	46	11	0	7	31	10	31	.218	.253	.370	.623	67	-10	-10	99	128	19	.517	1	0	0	-9	/O1D	-1.6
YEAR	TM/L	G	AB	R	H	2B	3B	HR	RBI	BB	SO	AVG	OBP	SLG	PRO	/A	BR	/A	PF	CHI	RC	TA	SB	CS	SBR	FR	POS	TPR
■ CHRIS SABO	Sabo, Christopher Andrew b: 1/19/62, Detroit, Mich. BR/TR, 5'11", 185 lbs. Deb: 4/04/88																											
1988	Cin-N	137	538	74	146	40	2	11	44	29	52	.271	.316	.414	.730	103	4	1	105	73	69	.727	46	14	5	16	*3/S	2.3
1989	Cin-N	82	304	40	79	21	1	6	29	25	33	.260	.318	.395	.713	100	1	-0	103	86	38	.678	14	9	-1	2	3	0.0
Total	2	219	842	114	225	61	3	17	73	54	85	.267	.317	.407	.724	102	5	1	105	78	108	.709	60	23	4	17	3/S	2.3
■ MARK SALAS	Salas, Mark Bruce b: 3/8/61, Montebello, Cal. BL/TR, 6', 180 lbs. Deb: 6/19/84																											
1984	StL-N	14	20	1	2	1	0	0	1	0	3	.100	.100	.150	.250	-31	-3	-3	99	131	0	.167	0	0	0	-1	/CO	-0.4
1985	Min-A	120	360	51	108	20	5	9	41	18	37	.300	.335	.458	.793	111	6	5	103	85	53	.708	0	1	-1	-8	*C/D	0.1
1986	Min-A	91	258	28	60	7	4	8	33	18	32	.233	.285	.384	.669	75	-7	-10	108	107	27	.585	3	1	0	-4	C/D	-0.9
1987	Min-A	22	45	8	17	2	0	3	9	5	6	.378	.440	.622	1.062	186	5	5	96	97	12	1.138	0	1	-1	-1	C	0.4
	NY-A	50	115	13	23	4	0	3	12	10	17	.200	.281	.313	.594	60	-7	-6	98	106	11	.521	0	0	0	-4	C/OD	-0.7
	Yr	72	160	21	40	6	0	6	21	15	23	.250	.326	.400	.726	95	-2	-1	97	105	21	.667	0	1	-1	-6		-0.3
1988	Chi-A	75	196	17	49	7	0	3	9	12	17	.250	.303	.332	.635	80	-6	-5	97	48	20	.533	0	0	0	3	C/D	0.0
1989	Cle-A	30	77	4	17	4	1	2	7	5	13	.221	.277	.377	.654	80	-2	-2	104	78	8	.565	0	0	0	0	D/C	-0.1
Total	6	402	1071	122	276	45	10	28	112	68	125	.258	.307	.397	.704	89	-14	-17	102	87	130	.616	3	3	-1	-16	C/DO	-1.6
■ LUIS SALAZAR	Salazar, Luis Ernesto (Garcia) b: 5/19/56, Barcelona, Venez. BR/TR, 6', 185 lbs. Deb: 8/15/80																											
1980	SD-N	44	169	28	57	4	7	1	25	9	25	.337	.374	.462	.836	142	7	8	93	129	29	.839	11	2	2	1	3/O	1.2
1981	SD-N	109	400	37	121	19	6	3	38	16	72	.303	.331	.403	.733	115	3	6	93	90	51	.643	11	8	-2	1	3O	0.0
1982	SD-N	145	524	55	127	15	5	8	62	23	80	.242	.277	.336	.613	77	-22	-16	92	124	48	.560	32	9	4	11	*3S/O	-0.2
1983	SD-N	134	481	52	124	16	2	14	45	17	80	.258	.286	.387	.673	85	-12	-11	99	80	53	.621	24	9	2	16	*3S	0.4
1984	SD-N	93	228	20	55	7	2	3	17	6	38	.241	.261	.329	.590	66	-11	-11	99	79	17	.497	11	7	-1	-2	3O/S	-1.4
1985	Chi-A	122	327	39	80	18	2	10	45	12	60	.245	.271	.404	.675	82	-9	-9	100	110	35	.617	14	4	2	-9	O3/1D	-1.8
1986	Chi-A	4	7	1	1	0	0	0	0	1	3	.143	.250	.143	.393	11	-1	-1	101	0	0	.333	0	0	0	0	/D	0.0
1987	SD-N	84	189	13	48	5	0	3	17	14	30	.254	.305	.328	.633	70	-9	-8	97	96	19	.541	3	3	-1	-2	3SO/P1	-0.8
1988	Det-A	130	452	61	122	14	1	12	62	21	70	.270	.307	.385	.692	98	-5	-2	94	117	52	.595	6	0	2	-5	OS3/21	-0.4
1989	SD-N	95	246	27	66	7	2	8	22	11	44	.268	.302	.411	.713	101	-0	-0	101	71	29	.610	1	3	-2	2	3O/S1	0.0
	Chi-N	26	80	7	26	5	0	1	12	4	13	.325	.357	.425	.782	113	2	1	108	131	11	.667	0	1	-1	-2	3/O	-0.1
	Yr	121	326	34	92	12	2	9	34	15	57	.282	.316	.414	.730	105	2	1	102	84	40	.623	1	4	-2	0		-0.1
Total	10	986	3103	340	827	110	27	63	345	134	515	.267	.299	.380	.679	92	-57	-43	96	101	344	.605	113	46	6	11	3OS/1D2P	-3.1
■ JUAN SAMUEL	Samuel, Juan Milton b: 12/9/60, San Pedro De Macoris, , D.R. BR/TR, 5'11", 170 lbs. Deb: 8/24/83																											
1983	Phi-N	18	65	14	18	1	2	2	5	4	16	.277	.329	.446	.775	112	1	1	101	58	9	.740	3	2	-0	2	2	0.3
1984	Phi-N	160	701	105	191	36	**19**	15	69	28	168	.272	.307	.442	.749	106	5	3	102	67	99	.785	72	15	13	-16	*2	0.4
1985	Phi-N	161	663	101	175	31	13	19	74	33	141	.264	.305	.436	.741	103	2	0	102	82	87	.740	53	19	5	1	*2	0.6
1986	Phi-N	145	591	90	157	36	12	16	78	26	142	.266	.306	.448	.754	101	2	-1	104	105	80	.748	42	14	4	-8	*2	-0.2
1987	Phi-N	160	655	113	178	37	**15**	28	100	60	162	.272	.338	.502	.840	114	16	12	104	85	109	.851	35	15	2	-17	*2	0.0

YEAR	TM/L	G	AB	R	H	2B	3B	HR	RBI	BB	SO	AVG	OBP	SLG	PRO	/A	BR	/A	PF	CHI	RC	TA	SB	CS	SBR	FR	POS	TPR
1988	Phi-N	157	629	68	153	32	9	12	67	39	151	.243	.300	.380	.680	93	-6	-7	101	94	73	.654	33	10	4	-22	*2/O3	-2.1
1989	Phi-N	51	199	32	49	3	1	8	20	18	45	.246	.312	.392	.704	99	-0	-0	101	76	26	.697	11	3	2	2	O	0.2
	NY-N	86	333	37	76	13	1	3	28	24	75	.228	.300	.300	.600	75	-12	-10	97	109	33	.609	31	9	4	3	O	-0.4
	Yr	137	532	69	125	16	2	11	48	42	120	.235	.304	.335	.639	84	-12	-11	98	97	58	.641	42	12	5	4		-0.2
Total	7	938	3836	560	997	189	72	103	441	232	900	.260	.311	.427	.738	101	7	-3	102	87	516	.740	280	87	32	-55	2O/3	-1.2

■ **RYNE SANDBERG** Sandberg, Ryne Dee b: 9/18/59, Spokane, Wash. BR/TR, 6'1", 175 lbs. Deb: 9/02/81

YEAR	TM/L	G	AB	R	H	2B	3B	HR	RBI	BB	SO	AVG	OBP	SLG	PRO	/A	BR	/A	PF	CHI	RC	TA	SB	CS	SBR	FR	POS	TPR
1981	Phi-N	13	6	2	1	0	0	0	0	0	1	.167	.167	.167	.333	-5	-1	-1	112	0	0	.200	0	0	0	-0	/S2	0.0
1982	Chi-N	156	635	103	172	33	5	7	54	36	90	.271	.314	.372	.686	88	-8	-11	103	79	75	.639	32	12	2	-4	*32	-1.4
1983	Chi-N	158	633	94	165	25	4	8	48	51	79	.261	.319	.351	.669	85	-13	-13	101	74	75	.643	37	11	5	**41**	*2/S	3.9
1984	Chi-N	156	636	**114**	200	36	**19**	19	84	52	101	.314	.369	.520	.889	134	38	30	110	75	**126**	.929	32	7	5	23	*2	**6.5**
1985	Chi-N	153	609	113	186	31	6	26	83	57	97	.305	.366	.504	.870	121	32	20	116	83	117	.944	54	11	10	8	*2/S	4.0
1986	Chi-N	154	627	68	178	28	5	14	76	46	79	.284	.333	.411	.744	98	2	-2	107	97	86	.718	34	11	4	8	*2	1.1
1987	Chi-N	132	523	81	154	25	2	16	59	59	79	.294	.368	.442	.810	113	11	10	101	81	89	.819	21	2	5	12	*2	2.9
1988	Chi-N	155	618	77	163	23	8	19	69	54	91	.264	.324	.419	.743	107	8	5	104	84	82	.708	25	10	2	10	*2	2.3
1989	Chi-N	157	606	**104**	176	25	5	30	76	59	85	.290	.357	.497	.854	131	32	26	108	83	109	.854	15	5	2	7	*2	3.8
Total	9	1234	4893	756	1395	226	54	139	549	414	702	.285	.343	.439	.782	110	101	65	106	82	759	.776	250	69	34	103	*23/S	23.1

■ **DEION SANDERS** Sanders, Deion Luwynn b: 8/9/67, Ft.Myers, Fla. BL/TL, 6'1", 195 lbs. Deb: 6/01/89

YEAR	TM/L	G	AB	R	H	2B	3B	HR	RBI	BB	SO	AVG	OBP	SLG	PRO	/A	BR	/A	PF	CHI	RC	TA	SB	CS	SBR	FR	POS	TPR
1989	NY-A	14	47	7	11	2	0	2	7	3	8	.234	.280	.404	.684	87	-1	-1	104	109	6	.639	1	0	0	0	O	0.0

■ **BENITO SANTIAGO** Santiago, Benito (Rivera) b: 3/9/65, Ponce, P.R. BR/TR, 6'1", 180 lbs. Deb: 9/14/86

YEAR	TM/L	G	AB	R	H	2B	3B	HR	RBI	BB	SO	AVG	OBP	SLG	PRO	/A	BR	/A	PF	CHI	RC	TA	SB	CS	SBR	FR	POS	TPR
1986	SD-N	17	62	10	18	2	0	3	6	2	12	.290	.313	.468	.780	118	1	1	95	64	9	.689	0	1	-1	0	C	0.1
1987	SD-N	146	546	64	164	33	2	18	79	16	112	.300	.326	.467	.793	111	4	6	97	104	77	.732	21	12	-1	8	*C	2.4
1988	SD-N	139	492	49	122	22	2	10	46	24	82	.248	.284	.362	.646	87	-11	-10	97	90	46	.552	15	7	0	15	*C	1.4
1989	SD-N	129	462	50	109	16	3	16	62	26	89	.236	.278	.387	.666	88	-8	-9	101	112	47	.590	11	6	-0	16	*C	1.7
Total	4	431	1562	173	413	73	7	47	193	68	295	.264	.298	.410	.708	97	-15	-11	98	100	179	.629	47	26	-2	39	C	5.6

■ **NELSON SANTOVENIA** Santovenia, Nelson Gil (Mayol) b: 7/27/61, Pinar Del Rio, Cuba BR/TR, 6'3", 195 lbs. Deb: 9/16/87

YEAR	TM/L	G	AB	R	H	2B	3B	HR	RBI	BB	SO	AVG	OBP	SLG	PRO	/A	BR	/A	PF	CHI	RC	TA	SB	CS	SBR	FR	POS	TPR
1987	Mon-N	2	1	0	0	0	0	0	0	0	0	.000	.000	.000	.000	-94	-0	-0	106	0	0	.000	0	0	0	0	/C	0.0
1988	Mon-N	92	309	26	73	20	2	8	41	24	77	.236	.298	.392	.689	91	-2	-4	106	113	36	.617	2	3	-1	4	C/1	0.4
1989	Mon-N	97	304	30	76	14	1	5	31	24	37	.250	.311	.352	.663	87	-4	-5	102	102	31	.564	2	1	0	8	C/1	1.0
Total	3	191	614	56	149	34	3	13	72	48	114	.243	.304	.371	.675	89	-7	-9	104	107	67	.590	4	4	-1	13	C/1	1.4

■ **MACKEY SASSER** Sasser, Mack Daniel b: 8/3/62, Fort Gaines, Ga. BL/TR, 6'1", 190 lbs. Deb: 7/17/87

YEAR	TM/L	G	AB	R	H	2B	3B	HR	RBI	BB	SO	AVG	OBP	SLG	PRO	/A	BR	/A	PF	CHI	RC	TA	SB	CS	SBR	FR	POS	TPR
1987	SF-N	2	4	0	0	0	0	0	0	0	0	.000	.000	.000	.000	-99	-1	-1	96	0	0	.000	0	0	0	0	/C	0.0
	Pit-N	12	23	2	5	0	0	0	2	0	2	.217	.217	.217	.435	15	-3	-3	104	160	1	.263	0	0	0	0	/C	-0.2
	Yr	14	27	2	5	0	0	0	2	0	2	.185	.185	.185	.370	-1	-4	-4	103	137	1	.217	0	0	0	0		-0.2
1988	NY-N	60	123	9	35	10	1	1	17	6	9	.285	.318	.407	.724	118	1	2	90	128	15	.609	0	0	0	-4	C/3O	0.1
1989	NY-N	72	182	17	53	14	2	1	22	7	15	.291	.317	.407	.724	110	1	1	97	115	22	.609	0	1	-1	-5	C/3	0.0
Total	3	146	332	28	93	24	3	2	41	13	26	.280	.307	.389	.696	102	-2	-0	95	122	38	.573	0	1	-1	-9	C/3O	-0.1

■ **STEVE SAX** Sax, Stephen Louis b: 1/29/60, Sacramento, Cal. BR/TR, 5'11", 185 lbs. Deb: 8/18/81

YEAR	TM/L	G	AB	R	H	2B	3B	HR	RBI	BB	SO	AVG	OBP	SLG	PRO	/A	BR	/A	PF	CHI	RC	TA	SB	CS	SBR	FR	POS	TPR
1981	LA-N	31	119	15	33	2	0	2	9	7	14	.277	.317	.345	.662	90	-2	-2	98	77	12	.570	5	7	-3	1	2	-0.1
1982	LA-N	150	638	88	180	23	7	4	47	49	53	.282	.335	.359	.694	100	-5	-0	95	68	79	.676	49	19	3	-6	*2	0.4
1983	LA-N	155	623	94	175	18	5	5	41	58	73	.281	.343	.350	.693	92	-5	-5	100	61	76	.685	56	30	-1	-24	*2	-2.6
1984	LA-N	145	569	70	138	24	4	1	35	47	53	.243	.301	.304	.606	68	-22	-24	104	75	51	.552	34	19	-1	13	*2	-0.8
1985	LA-N	136	488	62	136	8	4	1	42	54	43	.279	.354	.318	.672	96	-5	-1	93	108	56	.632	27	11	2	-10	*2/3	-0.8
1986	LA-N	157	633	91	210	43	4	6	56	59	58	.332	.391	.441	.832	137	26	30	94	66	110	.843	40	17	2	-4	*2	3.1
1987	LA-N	157	610	84	171	22	7	6	46	44	61	.280	.332	.369	.701	93	-13	-6	92	80	76	.667	37	11	5	5	*2/3O	0.6
1988	LA-N	160	632	70	175	19	4	5	57	45	51	.277	.326	.343	.669	87	-6	-10	106	94	73	.635	42	12	5	-17	*2	-1.8
1989	NY-A	158	651	88	205	26	3	5	63	52	44	.315	.366	.387	.754	108	12	8	104	81	91	.722	43	17	3	-6	*2	0.7
Total	9	1249	4963	662	1423	185	38	35	396	415	450	.287	.344	.360	.704	98	-19	-10	99	78	623	.675	333	143	14	-49	*2/3O	-1.3

■ **JEFF SCHAEFER** Schaefer, Jeffrey Scott b: 5/31/60, Patchogue, N.Y. BR/TR, 5'10", 170 lbs. Deb: 4/07/89

YEAR	TM/L	G	AB	R	H	2B	3B	HR	RBI	BB	SO	AVG	OBP	SLG	PRO	/A	BR	/A	PF	CHI	RC	TA	SB	CS	SBR	FR	POS	TPR
1989	Chi-A	15	10	2	1	0	0	0	0	0	2	.100	.100	.100	.200	-47	-2	-2	93	0	0	.200	1	1	-0	0	/S23D	0.0

■ **MIKE SCHMIDT** Schmidt, Michael Jack b: 9/27/49, Dayton, Ohio BR/TR, 6'2", 195 lbs. Deb: 9/12/72

YEAR	TM/L	G	AB	R	H	2B	3B	HR	RBI	BB	SO	AVG	OBP	SLG	PRO	/A	BR	/A	PF	CHI	RC	TA	SB	CS	SBR	FR	POS	TPR
1972	Phi-N	13	34	2	7	0	0	1	3	5	15	.206	.325	.294	.619	79	-1	-1	97	95	4	.593	0	0	0	1	3/2	0.0
1973	Phi-N	132	367	43	72	11	0	18	52	62	136	.196	.326	.373	.700	87	-2	-6	108	109	48	.708	8	2	1	5	*3/21S	-0.2
1974	Phi-N	162	568	108	160	28	7	**36**	116	106	138	.282	.398	**.546**	.944	157	**48**	46	103	113	**130**	1.045	23	12	-0	26	*3	**7.0**
1975	Phi-N	158	562	93	140	34	3	**38**	95	101	180	.249	.367	.523	.890	143	34	33	101	95	113	.971	29	12	2	**26**	*3S	6.2
1976	Phi-N	160	584	112	153	31	4	**38**	107	100	149	.262	.380	.524	.904	144	43	37	107	94	121	.964	14	9	-1	**25**	*3	**6.1**
1977	Phi-N	154	544	114	149	27	11	38	101	104	122	.274	.399	.574	.972	157	46	45	100	101	129	1.065	15	8	-0	29	*3/S2	**7.2**
1978	Phi-N	145	513	93	129	27	2	21	78	91	103	.251	.368	.435	.803	117	18	15	105	115	90	.855	19	6	2	11	*3/S	2.8
1979	Phi-N	160	541	109	137	25	4	45	114	**120**	115	.253	.392	.564	.955	162	45	47	97	109	123	**1.036**	9	5	-0	20	*3/S	**6.1**
1980	Phi-N	150	548	104	157	25	8	**48**	**121**	89	119	.286	.388	**.624**	**1.012**	**166**	**56**	**51**	107	104	**137**	**1.107**	12	5	1	21	*3	**7.4**
1981	Phi-N	102	354	**78**	112	19	2	**31**	**91**	**73**	71	.316	**.439**	**.644**	**1.083**	**182**	**50**	**45**	112	118	**102**	**1.243**	12	4	1	22	*3	**6.6**
1982	Phi-N	148	514	108	144	26	3	35	87	**107**	131	.280	**.407**	**.547**	**.954**	**176**	**47**	**52**	94	94	118	**1.044**	14	7	0	18	*3	**6.8**
1983	Phi-N	154	534	104	136	16	4	**40**	109	**128**	148	.255	**.402**	.524	.926	**153**	43	**43**	101	114	117	1.005	7	8	-3	21	*3/S	**5.7**
1984	Phi-N	151	528	93	146	23	3	**36**	**106**	92	116	.277	.388	.536	**.924**	**154**	41	**40**	102	108	108	.950	5	7	-3	13	*3/1S	5.1
1985	Phi-N	158	549	89	152	31	5	33	93	87	117	.277	.379	.532	.911	149	39	37	102	97	113	.934	1	3	-2	-2	*13/S	3.2
1986	Phi-N	160	552	97	160	29	1	**37**	**119**	89	84	.290	.395	**.547**	**.942**	**151**	**44**	**41**	104	117	122	.993	1	2	-1	-3	*31	3.4
1987	Phi-N	147	522	88	153	28	0	35	113	83	80	.293	.392	.548	.940	140	35	32	104	122	111	.964	2	1	0	10	*3/1S	4.0
1988	Phi-N	108	390	52	97	21	2	12	62	49	42	.249	.342	.405	.747	112	7	7	101	135	55	.711	3	0	1	-2	*3/1	0.5
1989	Phi-N	42	148	19	30	7	0	6	28	21	17	.203	.302	.372	.673	91	-2	-2	101	163	16	.608	0	1	-1	1	3	-0.1
Total	18	2404	8352	1506	2234	408	59	548	1595	1507	1883	.267	.384	.527	.912	147	592	561	103	109	1757	.968	174	92	-3	242	*31/S2	77.8

■ **DICK SCHOFIELD** Schofield, Richard Craig b: 11/21/62, Springfield, Ill. BR/TR, 5'10", 175 lbs. Deb: 9/08/83

YEAR	TM/L	G	AB	R	H	2B	3B	HR	RBI	BB	SO	AVG	OBP	SLG	PRO	/A	BR	/A	PF	CHI	RC	TA	SB	CS	SBR	FR	POS	TPR
1983	Cal-A	21	54	4	11	2	0	3	4	6	8	.204	.295	.407	.702	95	-1	-0	96	50	6	.644	0	0	0	3	S	0.3
1984	Cal-A	140	400	39	77	10	3	4	21	33	79	.192	.264	.262	.527	46	-29	-30	101	72	29	.449	5	2	0	7	*S	-1.1
1985	Cal-A	147	438	50	96	19	3	8	41	35	70	.219	.289	.331	.620	69	-19	-19	101	96	43	.562	11	4	1	16	*S	0.9
1986	Cal-A	139	458	67	114	17	6	13	57	48	55	.249	.327	.397	.724	101	-2	1	96	103	63	.723	23	5	4	10	*S	2.1
1987	Cal-A	134	479	52	120	17	3	9	46	37	63	.251	.307	.355	.662	76	-16	-16	99	95	56	.623	19	3	4	-20	*S/2D	-2.4
1988	Cal-A	155	527	61	126	11	6	6	34	40	57	.239	.304	.317	.621	79	-18	-14	94	73	55	.574	20	5	3	21	*S	1.8
1989	Cal-A	91	302	42	69	11	2	4	26	28	47	.228	.300	.318	.618	75	-10	-9	99	95	31	.567	9	3	1	3	S	0.1
Total	7	827	2658	315	613	87	23	47	229	227	379	.231	.299	.334	.633	75	-94	-87	98	88	285	.587	87	22	13	39	S/2D	1.7

■ **BILL SCHROEDER** Schroeder, Alfred William b: 9/7/58, Baltimore, Md. BR/TR, 6'2", 200 lbs. Deb: 7/13/83

YEAR	TM/L	G	AB	R	H	2B	3B	HR	RBI	BB	SO	AVG	OBP	SLG	PRO	/A	BR	/A	PF	CHI	RC	TA	SB	CS	SBR	FR	POS	TPR
1983	Mil-A	23	73	7	13	2	1	3	7	3	23	.178	.221	.356	.577	61	-5	-4	92	78	6	.492	0	1	-1	1	C	-0.1
1984	Mil-A	61	210	29	54	6	0	14	25	8	54	.257	.291	.486	.777	121	2	4	92	69	27	.687	0	1	-1	7	C/1D	1.4
1985	Mil-A	53	194	18	47	8	0	8	25	12	61	.242	.293	.407	.700	85	-3	-4	105	98	22	.608	0	1	-1	4	C/1D	0.1
1986	Mil-A	64	217	32	46	14	0	7	19	9	59	.212	.263	.373	.636	70	-9	-10	102	74	22	.557	1	0	0	5	C1D	-0.2
1987	Mil-A	75	250	35	83	12	0	14	42	16	56	.332	.379	.548	.927	140	15	14	102	94	52	.936	5	2	0	10	C/1D	2.7
1988	Mil-A	41	122	9	19	2	0	5	10	6	36	.156	.208	.295	.503	38	-10	-11	103	78	6	.404	0	0	0	3	C1/D	-0.6
1989	Cal-A	41	138	16	28	2	0	6	15	3	44	.203	.220	.348	.568	58	-8	-8	99	88	10	.451	0	0	0	5	C/1	-0.2
Total	7	358	1204	146	290	46	1	57	143	57	333	.241	.284	.423	.707	91	-19	-19	100	83	144	.622	6	5	-1	35	C/1D	3.1

■ **RICH SCHU** Schu, Rick Spencer b: 1/26/62, Philadelphia, Pa. BR/TR, 6', 170 lbs. Deb: 9/01/84

YEAR	TM/L	G	AB	R	H	2B	3B	HR	RBI	BB	SO	AVG	OBP	SLG	PRO	/A	BR	/A	PF	CHI	RC	TA	SB	CS	SBR	FR	POS	TPR
1984	Phi-N	17	29	12	8	2	1	2	5	6	6	.276	.400	.621	1.021	180	3	3	102	82	8	1.143	0	0	0	1	3	0.4

YEAR	TM/L	G	AB	R	H	2B	3B	HR	RBI	BB	SO	AVG	OBP	SLG	PRO	/A	BR	/A	PF	CHI	RC	TA	SB	CS	SBR	FR	POS	TPR
1985	Phi-N	112	416	54	105	21	4	7	24	38	78	.252	.318	.373	.691	91	-4	-5	102	55	49	.627	8	6	-1	-7	*3	-1.3
1986	Phi-N	92	208	32	57	10	1	8	25	18	44	.274	.338	.447	.785	110	4	3	104	85	32	.747	2	2	-1	-1	3	0.0
1987	Phi-N	92	196	24	46	6	3	7	23	20	36	.235	.312	.403	.715	84	-4	-5	104	92	25	.660	0	2	-1	2	31	-0.6
1988	Bal-A	89	270	22	69	9	4	4	20	21	49	.256	.316	.363	.679	94	-4	-2	95	72	30	.604	6	4	-1	2	3/1D	0.0
1989	Bal-A	1	0	0	0	0	0	0	0	0	0	—	—	—	—	—	0	0	99	—	—	—	0	0	0	0	/2	0.0
	Det-A	98	266	25	57	11	0	7	21	24	37	.214	.279	.335	.614	74	-10	-9	97	74	24	.525	1	2	-1	-2	3/21SD	-1.2
	Yr	99	266	25	57	11	0	7	21	24	37	.214	.279	.335	.614	74	-10	-9	97	73	24	.525	1	2	-1	-2		-1.2
Total	6	501	1385	169	342	59	13	35	118	127	250	.247	.314	.384	.698	92	-15	-16	100	72	198	.634	17	16	-5	-6	3/1D2S	-2.7
■ **JEFF SCHULZ**	Schulz, Jeffrey Alan b: 6/2/61, Evansville, Ind. BL/TR, 6'1", 190 lbs. Deb: 9/02/89																											
1989	KC-A	7	9	0	2	0	0	0	1	0	2	.222	.222	.222	.444	27	-1	-1	96	194	0	.286	0	0	0	-1	/O	-0.1
■ **MIKE SCIOSCIA**	Scioscia, Michael Lorri b: 11/27/58, Upper Darby, Pa. BL/TR, 6'2", 200 lbs. Deb: 4/20/80																											
1980	LA-N	54	134	8	34	5	1	1	8	12	9	.254	.315	.328	.643	82	-4	-3	97	67	15	.559	1	0	0	-7	C	-0.9
1981	LA-N	93	290	27	80	10	0	2	29	36	18	.276	.358	.331	.689	98	-0	1	98	112	34	.605	0	2	-1	-8	C	-0.7
1982	LA-N	129	365	31	80	11	1	5	38	44	31	.219	.305	.296	.601	73	-15	-12	95	121	34	.529	2	0	1	-16	*C	-2.7
1983	LA-N	12	35	3	11	3	0	1	7	5	2	.314	.400	.486	.886	144	2	2	100	138	7	.880	0	0	0	-1	C	0.2
1984	LA-N	114	341	29	93	18	0	5	38	52	26	.273	.371	.370	.740	105	6	4	104	106	48	.699	2	1	0	-5	*C	0.2
1985	LA-N	141	429	47	127	26	3	7	53	77	21	.296	.409	.420	.829	142	22	26	93	105	78	.841	3	3	-1	-1	*C	3.0
1986	LA-N	122	374	36	94	18	1	5	26	62	23	.251	.362	.345	.707	102	0	3	94	72	49	.670	3	3	-1	0	*C	0.5
1987	LA-N	142	461	44	122	26	1	6	38	55	23	.265	.344	.364	.709	96	-7	-2	92	82	58	.649	7	4	-0	-2	*C	0.7
1988	LA-N	130	408	29	105	18	0	3	35	38	31	.257	.321	.324	.644	80	-7	-10	106	99	40	.531	0	3	-2	-8	*C	-1.4
1989	LA-N	133	408	40	102	16	0	10	44	52	29	.250	.339	.363	.702	109	1	5	93	99	52	.651	0	2	-1	2	*C	1.6
Total	10	1070	3245	294	848	151	7	45	316	433	213	.261	.351	.354	.705	101	-0	14	96	98	413	.647	18	18	-5	-47	*C	0.5
■ **DICK SCOTT**	Scott, Richard Edward b: 7/19/62, Ellsworth, Maine BR/TR, 6'1", 170 lbs. Deb: 5/19/89																											
1989	Oak-A	3	2	0	0	0	0	0	1	0	0	.000	.000	.000	.000	-97	-1	-1	103	0	0	.000	0	0	0	0	/S	0.0
■ **KEVIN SEITZER**	Seitzer, Kevin Lee b: 3/26/62, Springfield, Ill. BR/TR, 5'11", 180 lbs. Deb: 9/03/86																											
1986	KC-A	28	96	16	31	4	1	2	11	19	14	.323	.440	.448	.888	144	7	7	100	95	21	.969	0	0	0	1	1/O3	0.6
1987	KC-A	161	641	105	**207**	33	8	15	83	80	85	.323	.400	.470	.869	126	31	27	104	85	120	.861	12	7	-1	5	*31/OD	2.4
1988	KC-A	149	559	90	170	32	5	5	60	72	64	.304	.389	.406	.795	119	20	18	103	95	89	.765	10	8	-2	8	*3/OD	2.5
1989	KC-A	160	597	78	168	17	2	4	48	102	76	.281	.391	.337	.727	111	11	14	96	77	85	.717	17	8	0	-6	*3/SO1	0.9
Total	4	498	1893	289	576	86	16	26	202	273	239	.304	.396	.408	.804	121	68	66	101	86	315	.790	39	23	-2	8	3/1OSD	6.4
■ **MIKE SHARPERSON**	Sharperson, Michael Tyrone b: 10/4/61, Orangeburg, S.C. BR/TR, 6'1", 175 lbs. Deb: 4/06/87																											
1987	Tor-A	32	96	4	20	4	1	0	9	7	15	.208	.269	.271	.540	44	-8	-8	101	138	7	.456	2	1	0	-3	2	-0.7
	LA-N	10	33	7	9	2	0	0	1	4	5	.273	.351	.333	.685	90	-1	-0	92	36	4	.600	0	0	0	0	/32	0.0
1988	LA-N	46	59	8	16	1	0	0	4	1	12	.271	.295	.288	.583	64	-2	-3	106	94	5	.422	0	1	-1	-1	2/3S	-0.3
1989	LA-N	27	28	2	7	3	0	0	5	4	7	.250	.344	.357	.701	109	0	0	93	201	3	.609	0	1	-1	0	/213S	0.0
Total	3	115	216	21	52	10	1	0	19	16	39	.241	.299	.296	.595	64	-11	-10	100	119	19	.488	2	3	-1	-3	/23S1	-1.0
■ **DANNY SHEAFFER**	Sheaffer, Danny Todd b: 8/2/61, Jacksonville, Fla. BR/TR, 6' ", 185 lbs. Deb: 4/09/87																											
1987	Bos-A	25	66	5	8	1	0	1	5	0	14	.121	.121	.182	.303	-21	-11	-11	99	133	1	.200	0	0	0	0	C	-0.8
1989	Cle-A	7	16	1	1	0	0	0	0	2	2	.063	.167	.063	.229	-32	-3	-3	104	0	0	.200	0	0	0	0	/3OD	-0.2
Total	2	32	82	6	9	1	0	1	5	2	16	.110	.131	.159	.289	-22	-14	-14	100	105	1	.200	0	0	0	0	/CD3O	-1.0
■ **LARRY SHEETS**	Sheets, Larry Kent b: 12/6/59, Staunton, Va. BL/TR, 6'3", 217 lbs. Deb: 9/18/84																											
1984	Bal-A	8	16	3	7	1	0	1	2	1	3	.438	.471	.688	1.158	229	2	3	94	57	5	1.333	0	0	0	0	/O	0.2
1985	Bal-A	113	328	43	86	8	0	17	50	28	52	.262	.324	.442	.766	109	3	3	99	101	43	.678	0	1	-1	-3	D/O1	0.0
1986	Bal-A	112	338	42	92	17	1	18	60	21	56	.272	.319	.488	.807	118	7	7	99	109	47	.725	2	0	1	-1	DO/C13	0.5
1987	Bal-A	135	469	74	148	23	0	31	94	31	67	.316	.362	.563	.925	144	26	28	98	105	90	.885	1	1	-0	-5	*O/1D	1.7
1988	Bal-A	136	452	38	104	19	1	10	47	42	72	.230	.304	.343	.647	85	-11	-9	95	103	45	.559	1	6	-3	-1	OD/1	-1.4
1989	Bal-A	102	304	33	74	12	1	7	33	26	58	.243	.309	.359	.668	89	-5	-5	99	99	34	.591	1	1	-0	0	D	-0.4
Total	6	606	1907	233	511	80	3	84	286	149	308	.268	.326	.445	.771	112	22	28	98	103	264	.695	5	9	-4	-10	DO/1C3	0.6
■ **GARY SHEFFIELD**	Sheffield, Gary Antonian b: 11/18/68, Tampa, Fla. BR/TR, 5'11", 190 lbs. Deb: 9/03/88																											
1988	Mil-A	24	80	12	19	1	0	4	12	7	7	.237	.299	.400	.699	91	-1	-1	103	108	8	.627	3	1	0	-2	S	-0.1
1989	Mil-A	95	368	34	91	18	0	5	32	27	33	.247	.306	.337	.643	84	-9	-8	97	95	39	.575	10	6	-1	-1	S3/D	-0.2
Total	2	119	448	46	110	19	0	9	44	34	40	.246	.305	.348	.653	85	-10	-9	98	97	47	.585	13	7	-0	-3	/S3D	-0.3
■ **JOHN SHELBY**	Shelby, John T. b: 2/23/58, Lexington, Ky. BB/TR, 6'1", 175 lbs. Deb: 9/15/81																											
1981	Bal-A	7	2	2	0	0	0	0	0	0	1	.000	.000	.000	.000	-99	-1	-1	99	0	0	1.000	2	0	1	-2	/O	-0.1
1982	Bal-A	26	35	8	11	3	0	1	2	0	5	.314	.314	.486	.800	116	1	1	100	40	5	.680	0	1	-1	-6	O	-0.6
1983	Bal-A	126	325	52	84	15	2	5	27	18	64	.258	.297	.363	.660	81	-9	-9	100	79	37	.616	15	2	3	-7	*O/D	-1.3
1984	Bal-A	128	383	44	80	12	5	6	30	20	71	.209	.248	.313	.561	57	-24	-22	94	87	31	.489	12	4	1	1	*O	-2.3
1985	Bal-A	69	205	28	58	6	2	7	27	7	44	.283	.307	.434	.741	101	-1	-0	99	97	26	.664	5	1	1	5	O/2D	0.4
1986	Bal-A	135	404	54	92	14	4	11	49	18	75	.228	.264	.364	.628	70	-18	-17	99	108	39	.576	18	6	2	-5	*O/D	-2.3
1987	Bal-A	21	32	4	6	0	0	1	3	1	13	.188	.212	.281	.493	31	-3	-3	98	100	2	.370	0	1	-1	-3	O/D	-0.6
	LA-N	120	476	61	132	26	0	21	69	31	97	.277	.323	.464	.787	115	2	7	92	93	70	.749	16	6	1	5	*O	0.8
1988	LA-N	140	494	65	130	23	6	10	64	44	128	.263	.323	.395	.718	99	3	-1	106	116	62	.668	16	5	2	-1	*O	-0.3
1989	LA-N	108	345	28	63	11	1	1	12	25	92	.183	.238	.229	.467	37	-29	-27	93	59	18	.386	10	7	-1	-5	O	-3.6
Total	9	880	2701	346	656	110	20	63	283	164	590	.243	.287	.368	.655	82	-79	-71	98	92	290	.593	94	33	8	-18	O/D2	-9.9
■ **PAT SHERIDAN**	Sheridan, Patrick Arthur b: 12/4/57, Ann Arbor, Mich. BL/TR, 6'3", 175 lbs. Deb: 9/16/81																											
1981	KC-A	3	1	0	0	0	0	0	0	0	1	.000	.000	.000	.000	-99	-0	-0	99	0	0	.000	0	0	0	-1	/O	0.0
1983	KC-A	109	333	43	90	12	2	7	36	20	64	.270	.312	.381	.693	88	-5	-6	101	95	41	.639	12	3	2	3	*O	-0.1
1984	KC-A	138	481	64	136	24	4	8	53	41	91	.283	.340	.399	.740	105	3	3	99	100	68	.709	19	6	2	-2	*O	-0.1
1985	KC-A	78	206	18	47	9	2	3	17	23	38	.228	.309	.335	.644	75	-7	-7	102	86	23	.627	11	3	2	-6	O/D	-1.2
1986	Det-A	98	236	41	56	9	1	6	19	21	57	.237	.302	.360	.662	84	-6	-5	95	73	27	.627	9	2	2	-6	O/D	-1.1
1987	Det-A	141	421	57	109	19	3	6	49	44	90	.259	.330	.361	.692	87	-9	-7	97	115	50	.648	18	13	-2	-8	*O	-2.0
1988	Det-A	127	347	47	88	9	5	11	47	44	64	.254	.341	.403	.744	114	4	7	94	108	48	.716	8	6	-1	-8	*O/D	-0.4
1989	Det-A	50	120	16	29	3	0	3	15	17	21	.242	.336	.342	.677	94	-1	-1	97	117	15	.667	4	0	1	-4	O/D	-0.3
	SF-N	70	161	20	33	3	4	3	14	13	45	.205	.264	.329	.594	71	-7	-6	97	91	15	.538	4	1	1	-5	O	-1.2
Total	8	814	2306	306	588	88	21	47	250	223	471	.255	.322	.373	.695	93	-28	-22	98	100	286	.658	85	34	5	-38	O/D	-6.4
■ **CRAIG SHIPLEY**	Shipley, Craig Barry b: 1/7/63, Parramatta, Australia BR/TR, 6'1", 175 lbs. Deb: 6/22/86																											
1986	LA-N	12	27	3	3	1	0	0	4	2	5	.111	.200	.148	.348	-3	-4	-4	94	399	1	.280	0	0	0	0	S/23	-0.2
1987	LA-N	26	35	3	9	1	0	0	2	0	6	.257	.257	.286	.543	48	-3	-2	92	80	2	.357	0	0	0	0	S/3	0.0
1989	NY-N	4	7	3	1	0	0	0	0	0	1	.143	.143	.143	.286	-19	-1	-1	97	0	0	.167	0	0	0	0	/S3	0.0
Total	3	42	69	9	13	2	0	0	6	2	12	.188	.222	.217	.440	21	-8	-7	93	205	3	.305	0	0	0	0	/S32	-0.2
■ **RUBEN SIERRA**	Sierra, Ruben Angel (Garcia) b: 10/6/65, Rio Piedras, P.R. BB/TR, 6'1", 175 lbs. Deb: 6/01/86																											
1986	Tex-A	113	382	50	101	13	10	16	55	22	65	.264	.306	.476	.783	115	4	6	96	95	51	.714	7	8	-3	-1	*O/D	0.0
1987	Tex-A	158	643	97	169	35	4	30	109	39	114	.263	.307	.470	.777	99	1	-2	104	107	85	.714	16	11	-2	3	*O	-0.4
1988	Tex-A	156	615	77	156	32	2	23	91	44	91	.254	.305	.424	.729	101	-0	-1	101	116	77	.678	18	4	3	2	*O/D	0.2
1989	Tex-A	162	634	101	194	35	**14**	29	**119**	43	82	.306	.352	**.543**	.895	145	37	36	102	114	122	.884	8	2	1	4	*O	3.8
Total	4	589	2274	325	620	115	30	98	374	148	352	.273	.319	.479	.798	115	42	38	101	109	335	.748	49	25	-0	8	O/D	3.6
■ **MATT SINATRO**	Sinatro, Matthew Stephen b: 3/22/60, Hartford, Conn. BR/TR, 5'9", 174 lbs. Deb: 9/22/81																											
1981	Atl-N	12	32	4	9	1	1	0	4	5	4	.281	.378	.375	.753	115	1	1	100	131	5	.783	1	0	0	2	C	0.3

YEAR	TM/L	G	AB	R	H	2B	3B	HR	RBI	BB	SO	AVG	OBP	SLG	PRO	/A	BR	/A	PF	CHI	RC	TA	SB	CS	SBR	FR	POS	TPR
1982	Atl-N	37	81	10	11	2	0	1	4	4	9	.136	.176	.198	.374	4	-10	-11	107	83	2	.270	0	1	-1	0	C	-1.1
1983	Atl-N	7	12	0	2	0	0	0	2	2	1	.167	.286	.167	.452	27	-1	-1	106	396	1	.400	0	0	0	0	/C	0.0
1984	Atl-N	2	4	0	0	0	0	0	0	0	0	.000	.000	.000	.000	-91	-1	-1	110	0	0	.000	0	0	0	0	/C	0.0
1987	Oak-A	6	3	0	0	0	0	0	0	0	1	.000	.000	.000	.000	-99	-1	-1	91	0	0	.000	0	0	0	0	/C	0.0
1988	Oak-A	10	9	1	3	2	0	0	5	0	1	.333	.333	.556	.889	152	0	1	95	398	1	.625	0	0	0	-0	/C	0.1
1989	Det-A	13	25	2	3	0	0	0	1	1	3	.120	.185	.120	.305	-13	-4	-4	97	130	1	.217	0	0	0	1	C	-0.1
Total	7	87	166	17	28	5	1	1	16	12	19	.169	.229	.229	.458	28	-16	-16	103	137	9	.356	1	1	-0	2	/C	-0.8
■ **JOEL SKINNER** Skinner, Joel Patrick b: 2/21/61, La Jolla, Cal. BR/TR, 6'4", 198 lbs. Deb: 6/12/83																												
1983	Chi-A	6	11	2	3	0	0	0	1	0	1	.273	.273	.273	.545	49	-1	-1	103	130	0	.300	0	0	0	-0	/C	0.0
1984	Chi-A	43	80	4	17	2	0	0	3	7	19	.213	.276	.237	.513	39	-6	-7	111	63	5	.415	1	0	0	-4	C	-0.7
1985	Chi-A	22	44	9	15	4	1	1	5	5	13	.341	.408	.545	.954	158	4	4	100	73	9	.935	0	0	0	0	C	0.5
1986	NY-A	54	166	6	43	4	0	1	17	7	40	.259	.289	.301	.590	60	-9	-9	103	128	13	.435	0	4	-2	0	C	-0.8
	Chi-A	60	149	17	30	5	1	4	20	9	43	.201	.252	.329	.580	57	-9	-9	101	131	13	.496	1	0	0	1	C	-0.4
	Yr	114	315	23	73	9	1	5	37	16	83	.232	.271	.314	.585	59	-18	-18	102	130	25	.464	1	4	-2	1		-1.2
1987	NY-A	64	139	9	19	4	0	3	14	8	46	.137	.189	.230	.419	11	-18	-17	98	136	5	.318	0	0	0	-5	C	-1.6
1988	NY-A	88	251	23	57	15	0	4	23	14	72	.227	.268	.335	.603	71	-11	-10	96	95	22	.490	0	0	0	-6	C/O1	-1.2
1989	Cle-A	79	178	10	41	10	0	1	13	9	42	.230	.271	.303	.575	60	-9	-10	104	89	14	.461	1	1	-0	-4	C	-1.1
Total	7	416	1018	80	225	44	2	14	96	59	276	.221	.266	.309	.575	58	-59	-60	101	107	81	.459	3	5	-2	-18	C/O1	-5.3
■ **DON SLAUGHT** Slaught, Donald Martin b: 9/11/58, Long Beach, Cal. BR/TR, 6'1", 190 lbs. Deb: 7/06/82																												
1982	KC-A	43	115	14	32	6	0	3	8	9	12	.278	.331	.409	.739	102	0	0	100	57	15	.651	0	0	0	-3	C	0.0
1983	KC-A	83	276	21	86	13	4	0	28	11	27	.312	.338	.388	.726	98	-1	-1	101	102	34	.608	3	1	0	6	C/D	0.9
1984	KC-A	124	409	48	108	27	4	4	42	20	55	.264	.302	.379	.681	88	-8	-7	99	100	46	.573	0	0	0	-1	*C/D	0.0
1985	Tex-A	102	343	34	96	17	4	8	35	20	41	.280	.331	.423	.753	97	2	-2	108	82	46	.680	5	4	-1	-6	*C	-0.3
1986	Tex-A	95	314	39	83	17	1	13	46	16	59	.264	.310	.449	.759	110	1	3	96	102	42	.685	3	2	-0	-8	C/D	0.0
1987	Tex-A	95	237	25	53	15	2	8	16	24	51	.224	.298	.405	.703	82	-5	-7	104	53	27	.624	0	3	-2	-16	C/D	-1.6
1988	NY-A	97	322	33	91	25	1	9	43	24	54	.283	.338	.450	.788	124	7	9	96	99	47	.718	1	0	0	-6	C/D	0.7
1989	NY-A	117	350	34	88	21	3	5	38	30	57	.251	.319	.371	.691	90	-3	-5	104	102	41	.610	1	1	-0	13	*C/D	1.2
Total	8	756	2366	248	637	141	19	50	256	154	356	.269	.320	.408	.728	98	-6	-9	101	91	298	.641	13	11	-3	-21	C/D	0.9
■ **GREG SMITH** Smith, Gregory Allen b: 4/5/67, Baltimore, Md. BB/TR, 5'11", 170 lbs. Deb: 9/02/89																												
1989	Chi-N	4	5	1	2	0	0	0	2	0	0	.400	.500	.400	.900	148	0	0	108	403	1	1.000	0	0	0	0	/2	0.1
■ **DWIGHT SMITH** Smith, John Dwight b: 11/8/63, Tallahassee, Fla. BL/TR, 5'11", 175 lbs. Deb: 5/01/89																												
1989	Chi-N	109	343	52	111	19	6	9	52	31	51	.324	.383	.493	.876	137	21	18	108	107	66	.879	9	4	0	-1	*O	1.7
■ **LONNIE SMITH** Smith, Lonnie b: 12/22/55, Chicago, Ill. BR/TR, 5'9", 170 lbs. Deb: 9/02/78																												
1978	Phi-N	17	4	6	0	0	0	0	0	4	3	.000	.500	.000	.500	48	0	0	105	0	2	2.000	4	0	1	-3	O	-0.1
1979	Phi-N	17	30	4	5	2	0	0	3	1	7	.167	.194	.233	.427	16	-4	-3	97	170	1	.385	2	1	0	-0	O	-0.3
1980	Phi-N	100	298	69	101	14	4	3	20	26	48	.339	.399	.443	.842	125	15	12	107	56	54	.907	33	13	2	-11	O	0.0
1981	Phi-N	62	176	40	57	14	3	2	11	18	14	.324	.402	.472	.874	131	11	9	112	48	35	.977	21	10	0	4	O	1.2
1982	StL-N	156	592	**120**	182	35	8	8	69	64	74	.307	.383	.434	.818	124	24	21	103	102	102	.890	68	26	5	6	*O	3.2
1983	StL-N	130	492	83	158	31	5	8	45	41	55	.321	.384	.453	.837	134	21	22	98	76	85	.871	43	18	2	-1	*O	2.2
1984	StL-N	145	504	77	126	20	4	6	49	70	90	.250	.352	.341	.693	97	-1	0	99	107	70	.756	50	13	7	-11	*O	-0.8
1985	StL-N	28	96	15	25	2	2	0	7	15	20	.260	.377	.323	.700	102	1	1	96	92	13	.772	12	6	0	-2	O	-0.1
	KC-A	120	448	77	115	23	4	6	41	41	69	.257	.325	.366	.691	87	-7	-8	102	95	60	.728	40	7	8	-9	*O	-0.9
1986	KC-A	134	508	80	146	25	7	8	44	46	78	.287	.358	.411	.770	110	8	8	100	80	77	.764	26	9	2	-2	*OD	0.5
1987	KC-A	48	167	26	42	7	1	3	8	24	31	.251	.359	.359	.718	89	-1	-2	104	49	24	.746	9	4	0	-3	OD	-0.4
1988	Atl-N	43	114	14	27	3	0	3	9	10	25	.237	.298	.342	.640	80	-2	-3	104	75	12	.596	4	2	0	-2	O	-0.6
1989	Atl-N	134	482	89	152	34	4	21	79	76	95	.315	**.420**	.533	.953	167	47	46	102	105	113	1.057	25	12	0	4	*O	5.0
Total	12	1134	3911	700	1136	210	42	68	385	436	609	.290	.371	.418	.789	117	112	103	102	87	648	.838	337	121	29	-28	*O/D	8.9
■ **OZZIE SMITH** Smith, Osborne Earl b: 12/26/54, Mobile, Ala. BB/TR, 5'11", 150 lbs. Deb: 4/07/78																												
1978	SD-N	159	590	69	152	17	6	1	46	47	43	.258	.312	.312	.624	81	-19	-14	93	103	61	.588	40	12	5	33	*S	3.8
1979	SD-N	156	587	77	124	18	6	0	27	37	37	.211	.260	.262	.523	45	-46	-43	96	74	42	.459	28	7	4	24	*S	0.0
1980	SD-N	158	609	67	140	18	5	0	35	71	49	.230	.315	.276	.591	71	-25	-20	93	73	62	.611	57	15	8	**43**	*S	5.0
1981	SD-N	110	450	53	100	11	2	0	21	41	37	.222	.294	.256	.550	61	-24	-21	93	62	36	.495	22	12	-1	**28**	*S	1.9
1982	StL-N	140	488	58	121	24	1	2	43	68	32	.248	.342	.314	.656	82	-8	-10	103	108	58	.649	25	5	5	**34**	*S	4.0
1983	StL-N	159	552	69	134	30	6	3	50	64	36	.243	.323	.335	.658	84	-12	-11	98	104	65	.653	34	7	6	20	*S	3.0
1984	StL-N	124	412	53	106	20	5	1	44	56	17	.257	.349	.337	.686	95	-2	-1	99	124	55	.723	35	7	6	**31**	*S	5.1
1985	StL-N	158	537	70	148	22	3	6	54	65	27	.276	.356	.361	.717	106	3	5	96	104	73	.712	31	8	5	14	*S	3.8
1986	StL-N	153	514	67	144	19	4	0	54	79	27	.280	.378	.333	.711	95	2	0	103	128	73	.733	31	7	5	-11	*S	0.8
1987	StL-N	158	600	104	182	40	4	0	75	89	36	.303	.394	.383	.778	109	10	11	99	125	102	.833	43	9	8	22	*S	5.8
1988	StL-N	153	575	80	155	27	1	3	51	74	43	.270	.354	.336	.689	95	2	-1	104	97	80	.745	57	9	**12**	**24**	*S	4.8
1989	StL-N	155	593	82	162	30	8	2	50	55	37	.273	.337	.361	.698	99	0	-0	101	88	76	.670	29	7	5	6	*S	2.0
Total	12	1783	6507	849	1668	276	51	18	550	746	421	.256	.335	.323	.658	86	-120	-104	98	99	783	.653	432	105	67	267	*S	40.0
■ **VAN SNIDER** Snider, Van Voorhees b: 8/11/63, Birmingham, Ala. BL/TR, 6'3", 185 lbs. Deb: 9/02/88																												
1988	Cin-N	11	28	4	6	1	0	1	6	0	13	.214	.214	.357	.571	58	-2	-2	105	185	2	.435	0	1	-1	-0	/O	-0.2
1989	Cin-N	8	7	1	1	0	0	0	0	0	5	.143	.143	.143	.286	-17	-1	-1	103	0	0	.167	0	0	0	-1	/O	-0.2
Total	2	19	35	5	7	1	0	1	6	0	18	.200	.200	.314	.514	43	-3	-3	105	148	2	.379	0	1	-1	-2	/O	-0.4
■ **CORY SNYDER** Snyder, James Cory b: 11/11/62, Inglewood, Cal. BR/TR, 6'4", 175 lbs. Deb: 6/13/86																												
1986	Cle-A	103	416	58	113	21	1	24	69	16	123	.272	.299	.500	.799	116	6	7	98	104	58	.720	2	3	-1	-4	OS3/D	0.1
1987	Cle-A	157	577	74	136	24	2	33	82	31	166	.236	.276	.456	.732	88	-10	-12	103	92	74	.674	5	1	1	5	*OS	-0.8
1988	Cle-A	142	511	71	139	24	3	26	75	42	101	.272	.329	.483	.812	122	15	14	102	94	79	.766	5	1	1	11	*O	2.3
1989	Cle-A	132	489	49	105	17	0	18	59	23	134	.215	.253	.360	.613	68	-21	-23	104	102	41	.517	6	5	-1	17	*O/SD	-0.8
Total	4	534	1993	252	493	86	6	101	285	112	524	.247	.289	.449	.737	98	-10	-14	102	97	252	.666	18	10	-1	28	O/S3D	0.8
■ **PAUL SORRENTO** Sorrento, Paul Anthony b: 11/17/65, Somerville, Mass. BL/TR, 6'2", 195 lbs. Deb: 9/08/89																												
1989	Min-A	14	21	2	5	0	0	0	1	5	4	.238	.385	.238	.623	74	-0	-0	107	78	2	.625	0	0	0	0	/1D	0.0
■ **SAM SOSA** Sosa, Samuel b: 11/10/68, San Pedro De Macoris, D.R. BR/TR, 6', 165 lbs. Deb: 6/16/89																												
1989	Tex-A	25	84	8	20	3	0	1	3	0	20	.238	.238	.310	.548	52	-5	-6	102	40	5	.377	0	2	-1	-1	O	-0.7
	Chi-A	33	99	19	27	5	0	3	10	11	27	.273	.357	.414	.771	126	2	3	93	78	15	.782	7	3	0	-3	O/D	0.0
	Yr	58	183	27	47	8	0	4	13	11	47	.257	.306	.366	.672	91	-3	-2	97	62	19	.592	7	5	-1	-4		-0.7
■ **CHRIS SPEIER** Speier, Chris Edward b: 6/28/50, Alameda, Cal. BR/TR, 6'1", 175 lbs. Deb: 4/07/71																												
1971	SF-N	157	601	74	141	17	6	8	46	56	90	.235	.307	.323	.630	79	-16	-16	100	91	58	.541	4	7	-3	-4	*S	-0.2
1972	SF-N	150	562	74	151	25	2	15	71	82	92	.269	.365	.400	.765	117	15	15	100	104	87	.754	9	4	0	-0	*S	3.4
1973	SF-N	153	542	58	135	17	4	11	71	66	69	.249	.333	.356	.689	87	-6	-9	105	129	63	.616	4	5	-2	-10	*S/2	0.0
1974	SF-N	141	501	55	125	19	5	9	53	62	64	.250	.337	.361	.698	88	-3	-7	108	100	64	.649	3	2	-0	6	*S/2	1.4
1975	SF-N	141	487	60	132	30	5	10	69	70	50	.271	.364	.415	.779	114	11	10	102	117	73	.743	4	5	-2	3	*S/3	2.8
1976	SF-N	145	495	51	112	18	4	3	40	60	52	.226	.315	.297	.612	72	-15	-17	103	101	47	.531	2	2	-1	6	*S/231	0.1
1977	SF-N	6	17	1	3	1	0	0	0	0	3	.176	.176	.235	.412	9	-2	-2	104	0	1	.286	0	0	0	0	/S	-0.1
	Mon-N	139	531	58	125	30	6	5	38	67	78	.235	.322	.343	.665	80	-15	-14	98	82	59	.595	1	2	-1	-5	*S	0.0
	Yr	145	548	59	128	31	6	5	38	67	81	.234	.318	.339	.658	78	-18	-16	99	78	60	.585	1	2	-1	-5		-0.1
1978	Mon-N	150	501	47	126	18	3	5	51	60	75	.251	.333	.329	.662	89	-8	-6	96	115	56	.584	1	0	0	0	*S	0.7
1979	Mon-N	113	344	31	78	13	1	7	26	43	45	.227	.318	.331	.649	76	-10	-11	102	76	35	.573	0	0	0	-8	*S	-0.8

YEAR	TM/L	G	AB	R	H	2B	3B	HR	RBI	BB	SO	AVG	OBP	SLG	PRO	/A	BR	/A	PF	CHI	RC	TA	SB	CS	SBR	FR	POS	TPR
1980	Mon-N	128	388	35	103	14	4	1	32	52	38	.265	.352	.330	.682	92	-3	-2	99	97	45	.604	0	3	-2	-4	*S/3	0.7
1981	Mon-N	96	307	33	69	10	2	2	25	38	29	.225	.310	.290	.600	72	-11	-10	99	103	27	.514	1	2	-1	-9	S	-1.0
1982	Mon-N	156	530	41	136	26	4	7	60	47	67	.257	.318	.360	.679	85	-7	-11	105	111	58	.581	1	6	-3	-21	*S	-2.4
1983	Mon-N	88	261	31	67	12	2	2	22	29	37	.257	.336	.341	.677	86	-4	-4	102	92	31	.613	2	1	0	-12	S3/2	-0.9
1984	Mon-N	25	40	1	6	0	0	0	1	1	8	.150	.171	.150	.321	-10	-6	-5	91	65	1	.200	0	0	0	-1	S/3	-0.4
	StL-N	38	118	9	21	7	1	3	8	9	19	.178	.242	.331	.573	60	-7	-7	99	65	9	.485	0	0	0	7	S/3	0.4
	Yr	63	158	10	27	7	1	3	9	10	27	.171	.225	.285	.510	44	-12	-12	96	66	9	.412	0	0	0	6		0.0
	Min-A	12	33	2	7	0	0	0	1	3	7	.212	.278	.212	.490	36	-3	-3	106	57	2	.370	0	0	0	-2	S	-0.3
1985	Chi-N	106	218	16	53	11	0	4	24	17	34	.243	.298	.349	.646	69	-6	-10	116	109	21	.537	1	3	-2	6	S32	0.0
1986	Chi-N	95	155	21	44	8	0	6	23	15	32	.284	.351	.452	.802	112	4	3	107	104	24	.752	2	2	-1	1	3S/2	0.4
1987	SF-N	111	317	39	79	13	0	11	39	42	51	.249	.343	.394	.737	98	-2	-0	96	98	43	.702	4	7	-3	4	23S	0.3
1988	SF-N	82	171	26	37	9	1	3	18	23	39	.216	.313	.333	.646	91	-3	-2	94	109	17	.583	3	3	-1	0	23/S	0.0
1989	SF-N	28	37	7	9	4	0	0	2	5	9	.243	.333	.351	.685	99	-0	0	97	62	4	.600	0	0	0	0	/3S21	0.1
Total	19	2260	7156	770	1759	302	50	112	720	847	988	.246	.329	.349	.678	87	-97	-110	101	101	826	.607	42	54	-20	-42	*S32/1	4.2
■ **BILL SPIERS**	Spiers, William James b: 6/5/66, Orangeburg, S.C. BL/TR, 6'2", 190 lbs. Deb: 4/07/89																											
1989	Mil-A	114	345	44	88	9	3	4	33	21	63	.255	.300	.333	.633	81	-10	-9	97	101	37	.563	10	2	2	-2	S3/21D	-0.1
■ **HARRY SPILMAN**	Spilman, William Harry b: 7/18/54, Albany, Ga. BL/TR, 6'1", 180 lbs. Deb: 9/11/78																											
1978	Cin-N	4	4	1	1	0	0	0	0	0	1	.250	.250	.250	.500	39	-0	-0	103	0	0	.333	0	0	0	0	H	0.0
1979	Cin-N	43	56	7	12	3	0	0	5	7	5	.214	.323	.268	.591	65	-3	-2	97	132	5	.533	0	0	0	-0	1/3	-0.3
1980	Cin-N	65	101	14	27	4	0	4	19	9	19	.267	.333	.426	.759	109	1	1	102	137	14	.697	0	0	0	-1	1/OC3	0.0
1981	Cin-N	23	24	4	4	1	0	0	3	3	7	.167	.259	.208	.468	34	-2	-2	101	236	1	.381	0	0	0	-1	/31	-0.2
	Hou-N	28	34	5	10	0	0	0	1	2	3	.294	.333	.294	.627	90	-1	-0	88	39	3	.462	0	1	-1	-0	1	-0.1
	Yr	51	58	9	14	1	0	0	4	5	10	.241	.302	.259	.560	64	-3	-2	94	132	4	.426	0	1	-1	-1		-0.3
1982	Hou-N	38	61	7	17	2	0	3	11	5	10	.279	.333	.459	.792	121	1	1	99	117	9	.733	0	0	0	-0	1	0.0
1983	Hou-N	42	78	7	13	3	0	1	9	5	12	.167	.217	.244	.460	30	-8	-7	90	162	4	.358	0	0	0	-1	1/C	-0.8
1984	Hou-N	32	72	14	19	2	0	2	15	12	10	.264	.369	.375	.744	118	1	2	93	178	11	.722	0	0	0	-0	1/C	0.1
1985	Hou-N	44	66	3	9	1	0	1	4	3	7	.136	.174	.197	.371	4	-9	-8	96	100	2	.271	0	0	0	-0	1/C	-0.9
1986	Det-A	24	49	6	12	2	0	3	8	3	8	.245	.288	.469	.758	108	0	0	95	100	6	.684	0	0	0	0	D/3C1	0.0
	SF-N	58	94	12	27	7	0	2	22	12	13	.287	.368	.426	.793	123	2	3	96	191	16	.776	0	0	0	-0	1/3C2O	0.2
1987	SF-N	83	90	5	24	5	0	1	14	9	20	.267	.333	.356	.689	86	-2	-2	96	160	10	.600	1	1	-0	0	3/1C	-0.1
1988	SF-N	40	40	4	7	1	1	1	3	4	6	.175	.250	.325	.575	68	-2	-2	94	75	3	.515	0	0	0	0	/1CO	-0.1
	Hou-N	7	5	0	0	0	0	0	0	0	3	.000	.000	.000	.000	-99	-1	-1	93	0	0	.000	0	0	0	0	/1	0.0
	Yr	47	45	4	7	1	1	1	3	4	9	.156	.224	.289	.513	49	-3	-3	94	65	3	.447	0	0	0	0		-0.1
1989	Hou-N	32	36	7	10	3	0	0	3	7	2	.278	.395	.361	.756	115	1	1	102	93	5	.741	0	0	0	0	/1C	0.1
Total	12	563	810	96	192	34	1	18	117	81	126	.237	.309	.348	.657	85	-20	-16	96	137	92	.577	1	2	-1	-4	1/3CDO2	-2.1
■ **STEVE STANICEK**	Stanicek, Stephen Blair b: 6/19/61, Lake Forest, Ill. BR/TR, 6' ", 190 lbs. Deb: 9/16/87																											
1987	Mil-A	4	7	2	2	0	0	0	0	0	2	.286	.286	.286	.571	52	-0	-0	102	0	1	.400	0	0	0	0	/D	0.0
1989	Phi-N	9	9	0	1	0	0	0	1	0	3	.111	.111	.111	.222	-36	-2	-2	101	403	0	.125	0	0	0	0	H	-0.1
Total	2	13	16	2	3	0	0	0	1	0	5	.188	.188	.188	.375	4	-2	-2	102	226	1	.231	0	0	0	0	/D	-0.1
■ **MIKE STANLEY**	Stanley, Robert Michael b: 6/25/63, Ft.Lauderdale, Fla BR/TR, 6'1", 185 lbs. Deb: 6/24/86																											
1986	Tex-A	15	30	4	10	3	0	1	1	3	7	.333	.394	.533	.927	158	2	2	96	21	7	1.000	1	0	0	-1	/3COD	0.2
1987	Tex-A	78	216	34	59	8	1	6	37	31	48	.273	.367	.403	.770	102	2	1	104	141	33	.748	3	0	1	-12	C1/OD	-0.5
1988	Tex-A	94	249	21	57	8	0	3	27	37	62	.229	.329	.297	.626	76	-7	-7	101	129	26	.561	0	0	0	-7	CD/13	-1.1
1989	Tex-A	67	122	9	30	3	1	1	11	12	29	.246	.324	.311	.635	78	-3	-3	102	104	12	.546	1	0	0	-5	CD/13	-0.6
Total	4	254	617	68	156	22	2	11	76	83	146	.253	.344	.348	.693	89	-5	-7	102	123	78	.640	5	0	2	-24	C/D13O	-2.0
■ **JIM STEELS**	Steels, James Earl b: 5/30/61, Jackson, Miss. BL/TL, 5'10", 185 lbs. Deb: 4/06/87																											
1987	SD-N	62	68	9	13	1	1	0	6	11	14	.191	.304	.235	.539	47	-5	-5	97	150	5	.508	3	2	-0	-6	O	-1.1
1988	Tex-A	36	53	4	10	1	0	0	5	0	15	.189	.189	.208	.396	11	-6	-6	101	181	2	.302	2	0	1	-5	O/1D	-1.1
1989	SF-N	13	12	0	1	0	0	0	0	2	4	.083	.214	.083	.298	-12	-2	-2	97	0	0	.273	0	0	0	-0	/1O	-0.1
Total	3	111	133	13	24	2	1	0	11	13	33	.180	.253	.211	.464	28	-13	-13	98	147	8	.407	5	2	0	-11	/O1D	-2.3
■ **TERRY STEINBACH**	Steinbach, Terry Lee b: 3/2/62, New Ulm, Minn. BR/TR, 6'1", 195 lbs. Deb: 9/12/86																											
1986	Oak-A	6	15	3	5	0	0	2	4	1	0	.333	.375	.733	1.108	207	2	2	94	94	4	1.200	0	0	0	-0	/C	0.2
1987	Oak-A	122	391	66	111	16	3	16	56	32	66	.284	.352	.463	.815	126	8	13	91	98	62	.764	1	2	-1	-3	*C3/1D	1.6
1988	Oak-A	104	351	42	93	19	1	9	51	33	47	.265	.338	.402	.740	112	3	6	95	121	47	.675	3	0	1	-8	C1/3OD	0.1
1989	Oak-A	130	454	37	124	13	1	7	42	30	66	.273	.321	.352	.673	87	-6	-8	103	92	49	.558	1	2	-1	-2	*CO1/3D	-0.7
Total	4	362	1211	148	333	48	5	34	153	96	179	.275	.337	.407	.744	108	7	13	97	102	162	.665	5	4	-1	-13	C/13DO	1.2
■ **PHIL STEPHENSON**	Stephenson, Phillip Raymond b: 9/19/60, Guthrie, Okla. BL/TL, 6'1", 195 lbs. Deb: 4/05/89																											
1989	Chi-N	17	21	0	3	0	0	0	0	2	3	.143	.217	.143	.360	5	-3	-3	108	0	1	.333	1	0	0	-1	/O	-0.2
	SD-N	10	17	4	6	0	0	2	2	3	2	.353	.450	.706	1.156	224	3	3	101	45	6	1.364	0	0	0	0	/1	0.2
	Yr	27	38	4	9	0	0	2	2	5	5	.237	.326	.395	.720	100	0	0	106	17	6	.724	1	0	0	-1		0.0
■ **KURT STILLWELL**	Stillwell, Kurt Andrew b: 6/4/65, Glendale, Cal. BB/TR, 5'11", 165 lbs. Deb: 4/13/86																											
1986	Cin-N	104	279	31	64	6	1	0	26	30	47	.229	.309	.258	.567	56	-15	-17	104	144	24	.495	6	2	1	-3	S	-1.1
1987	Cin-N	131	395	54	102	20	7	4	33	32	50	.258	.317	.375	.692	80	-10	-12	104	82	46	.612	4	6	-2	-7	S23	-1.4
1988	KC-A	128	459	63	115	28	5	10	53	47	76	.251	.324	.399	.723	98	1	-1	103	101	60	.671	6	5	-1	-4	*S	0.0
1989	KC-A	130	463	52	121	20	7	7	54	42	64	.261	.327	.380	.707	103	-1	2	96	109	60	.655	9	6	-1	-18	*S	-0.6
Total	4	493	1596	200	402	74	20	21	166	151	237	.252	.320	.363	.683	87	-26	-28	101	106	190	.620	25	19	-4	-32	S/23	-3.1
■ **JEFF STONE**	Stone, Jeffrey Glen b: 12/26/60, Kennett, Mo. BL/TR, 6', 175 lbs. Deb: 9/09/83																											
1983	Phi-N	9	4	2	3	0	2	0	3	0	1	.750	.750	1.750	2.500	568	2	2	101	170	7	11.000	4	0	1	-0	/O	0.3
1984	Phi-N	51	185	27	67	4	6	1	15	9	26	.362	.398	.465	.863	139	10	10	102	67	37	.992	27	5	5	-5	O	0.9
1985	Phi-N	88	264	36	70	4	3	3	11	15	50	.265	.307	.337	.644	78	-7	-8	102	45	28	.594	15	5	2	-9	O	-1.7
1986	Phi-N	82	249	32	69	6	4	6	19	20	52	.277	.341	.406	.746	101	2	0	104	64	36	.762	19	6	2	3	O	0.5
1987	Phi-N	66	125	19	32	7	1	1	16	8	38	.256	.316	.352	.668	74	-4	-5	104	136	14	.604	3	1	0	-1	O	-0.6
1988	Bal-A	26	61	4	10	1	0	0	1	4	11	.164	.215	.180	.396	13	-7	-7	95	36	2	.345	4	1	1	-3	O/D	-0.8
1989	Tex-A	22	36	5	6	1	2	0	5	3	5	.167	.250	.306	.556	54	-2	-2	102	177	2	.515	2	1	0	-1	D/O	-0.3
	Bos-A	18	15	3	3	0	0	0	1	1	2	.200	.250	.200	.450	27	-1	-1	105	130	1	.385	1	0	0	-3	O/D	-0.4
	Yr	40	51	8	9	1	2	0	6	4	7	.176	.250	.275	.525	46	-4	-4	103	160	3	.478	3	1	0	-4		-0.7
Total	7	362	939	128	260	23	18	11	71	60	185	.277	.328	.375	.703	92	-8	-11	102	73	128	.697	75	19	11	-18	O/D	-2.1
■ **DOUG STRANGE**	Strange, Joseph Douglas b: 4/13/64, Greenville, S.C. BB/TR, 6'2", 170 lbs. Deb: 7/13/89																											
1989	Det-A	64	196	16	42	4	1	1	14	17	36	.214	.280	.260	.541	55	-12	-11	97	101	14	.442	3	3	-1	-1	3/2SD	-1.2
■ **DARRYL STRAWBERRY**	Strawberry, Darryl Eugene b: 3/12/62, Los Angeles, Cal. BL/TL, 6'6", 190 lbs. Deb: 5/06/83																											
1983	NY-N	122	420	63	108	15	7	26	74	47	128	.257	.338	.512	.849	134	17	17	99	102	74	.882	19	6	2	0	*O	1.8
1984	NY-N	147	522	75	131	27	4	26	97	75	131	.251	.345	.467	.812	126	18	18	100	125	87	.850	27	8	3	6	*O	2.3
1985	NY-N	111	393	78	109	15	4	29	79	73	96	.277	.392	.557	.949	167	34	35	97	109	87	1.049	26	11	1	1	*O	3.5
1986	NY-N	136	475	76	123	27	5	27	93	72	141	.259	.363	.507	.871	144	24	27	96	117	92	.943	28	12	1	-1	*O	2.6
1987	NY-N	154	532	108	151	32	5	39	104	97	122	.284	.401	.583	.984	159	45	46	99	99	132	1.134	36	12	4	-2	*O	4.1
1988	NY-N	153	543	101	146	27	3	**39**	101	85	127	.269	.371	**.545**	**.916**	**177**	42	48	90	104	111	**.990**	29	14	0	2	*O	**4.9**
1989	NY-N	134	476	69	107	26	1	29	77	61	105	.225	.314	.466	.781	125	11	13	97	102	72	.782	11	4	1	4	*O	1.7
Total	7	957	3361	570	875	169	29	215	625	510	850	.260	.361	.520	.881	148	191	205	97	108	655	.947	176	67	13	10	O	20.9

YEAR	TM/L	G	AB	R	H	2B	3B	HR	RBI	BB	SO	AVG	OBP	SLG	PRO	/A	BR	/A	PF	CHI	RC	TA	SB	CS	SBR	FR	POS	TPR
■ **FRANKLIN STUBBS** Stubbs, Franklin Lee b: 10/21/60, Richland, N.C. BL/TL, 6'2", 215 lbs. Deb: 4/28/84																												
1984	LA-N	87	217	22	42	2	3	8	17	24	63	.194	.274	.341	.615	69	-9	-10	104	68	22	.565	2	2	-1	-1	1O	-1.4
1985	LA-N	10	9	0	2	0	0	0	2	0	3	.222	.222	.222	.444	27	-1	-1	93	398	0	.286	0	0	0	0	/1	0.0
1986	LA-N	132	420	55	95	11	1	23	58	37	107	.226	.292	.421	.713	100	-5	-2	94	94	51	.666	7	1	2	-9	*O1	-1.2
1987	LA-N	129	386	48	90	16	3	16	52	31	85	.233	.292	.415	.706	92	-10	-6	92	100	47	.658	8	1	2	7	*1O	-0.3
1988	LA-N	115	242	30	54	13	0	8	34	23	61	.223	.293	.376	.669	86	-3	-5	106	118	28	.646	11	3	2	0	1O	-0.7
1989	LA-N	69	103	11	30	6	0	4	15	16	27	.291	.387	.466	.853	154	6	7	93	101	18	.859	3	2	-0	2	O/1	0.8
Total	6	542	1377	166	313	48	7	59	178	131	346	.227	.296	.401	.697	93	-21	-16	97	98	165	.655	31	9	4	-1	1O	-2.8
■ **JIM SUNDBERG** Sundberg, James Howard b: 5/18/51, Galesburg, Ill. BR/TR, 6', 190 lbs. Deb: 4/04/74																												
1974	Tex-A	132	368	45	91	13	3	3	36	62	61	.247	.356	.323	.679	101	1	3	96	111	43	.616	2	4	-2	9	*C	1.5
1975	Tex-A	155	472	45	94	9	0	6	36	51	77	.199	.283	.256	.539	53	-28	-28	100	100	35	.453	3	1	0	6	*C	-1.7
1976	Tex-A	140	448	33	102	24	2	3	34	37	61	.228	.287	.310	.597	73	-14	-16	102	88	39	.488	0	0	0	17	*C	0.6
1977	Tex-A	149	453	61	132	20	3	6	65	53	77	.291	.368	.389	.757	102	6	3	105	133	67	.702	2	3	-1	0	*C	0.5
1978	Tex-A	149	518	54	144	23	6	6	58	64	70	.278	.361	.380	.741	113	7	10	96	109	69	.670	2	5	-2	16	*C/D	2.8
1979	Tex-A	150	495	50	136	23	4	5	64	51	51	.275	.348	.368	.716	94	-3	-3	100	125	62	.636	3	3	-1	9	*C	1.1
1980	Tex-A	151	505	59	138	24	1	10	63	64	67	.273	.356	.384	.740	103	3	3	100	110	69	.680	2	2	-1	15	*C	2.5
1981	Tex-A	102	339	42	94	17	2	3	28	50	48	.277	.372	.366	.738	124	8	12	91	84	48	.694	2	5	-2	11	C/O	2.5
1982	Tex-A	139	470	37	118	22	5	10	47	49	57	.251	.323	.383	.706	100	-4	0	93	91	57	.629	2	6	-3	20	*C/O	2.4
1983	Tex-A	131	378	30	76	14	0	2	28	35	64	.201	.272	.254	.526	45	-27	-28	101	107	26	.424	0	4	-2	-4	*C	-2.7
1984	Mil-A	110	348	43	91	19	4	7	43	38	63	.261	.334	.399	.734	111	1	5	92	107	48	.677	1	1	-0	14	*C	2.5
1985	KC-A	115	367	38	90	12	4	10	35	33	67	.245	.309	.381	.691	86	-6	-7	102	82	42	.604	0	2	-1	10	*C	0.6
1986	KC-A	140	429	41	91	9	1	12	42	57	91	.212	.305	.322	.626	72	-16	-16	100	96	44	.566	1	1	-0	12	*C	0.2
1987	Chi-N	61	139	9	28	2	0	4	15	19	40	.201	.306	.302	.608	61	-7	-8	101	111	13	.553	0	0	0	0	C	-0.2
1988	Chi-N	24	54	8	13	1	0	2	9	8	15	.241	.339	.370	.709	99	0	0	104	138	7	.667	0	0	0	1	C	0.2
	Tex-A	38	91	13	26	4	0	4	13	5	17	.286	.323	.462	.784	116	2	2	101	96	13	.701	0	0	0	-3	C	0.0
1989	Tex-A	76	147	13	29	7	1	2	8	23	37	.197	.306	.299	.605	69	-5	-6	102	62	15	.554	0	0	0	-21	C/D	-2.4
Total	16	1962	6021	621	1493	243	36	95	624	699	963	.248	.328	.348	.676	89	-85	-75	99	103	698	.600	20	37	-16	110	*C/OD	10.4
■ **B.J. SURHOFF** Surhoff, William James b: 8/4/64, Bronx, N.Y. BL/TR, 6'1", 185 lbs. Deb: 4/08/87																												
1987	Mil-A	115	395	50	118	22	3	7	68	36	30	.299	.357	.423	.780	104	4	3	102	144	56	.713	11	10	-3	18	C3/1D	2.4
1988	Mil-A	139	493	47	121	21	0	5	38	31	49	.245	.294	.318	.613	69	-19	-21	103	90	46	.544	21	6	3	8	*C3/1SO	-0.5
1989	Mil-A	126	436	42	108	17	4	5	55	25	29	.248	.293	.339	.633	81	-13	-11	97	134	41	.546	14	12	-3	15	*CD/3	0.6
Total	3	380	1324	139	347	60	7	17	161	92	108	.262	.313	.356	.669	84	-28	-29	101	121	143	.593	46	28	-3	41	C/3D1OS	2.5
YEAR	TM/L	G	AB	R	H	2B	3B	HR	RBI	BB	SO	AVG	OBP	SLG	PRO	/A	BR	/A	PF	CHI	RC	TA	SB	CS	SBR	FR	POS	TPR
■ **PAT TABLER** Tabler, Patrick Sean b: 2/2/58, Hamilton, Ohio BR/TR, 6'3", 175 lbs. Deb: 8/21/81																												
1981	Chi-N	35	101	11	19	3	1	1	5	13	26	.188	.281	.267	.548	54	-6	-6	104	65	7	.460	0	1	-1	5	2	0.1
1982	Chi-N	25	85	9	20	4	2	1	7	6	20	.235	.293	.365	.658	80	-2	-2	103	81	9	.559	0	0	0	-2	3	-0.4
1983	Cle-A	124	430	56	125	23	5	6	65	56	63	.291	.374	.409	.783	110	11	8	105	134	63	.719	2	4	-2	-6	O3/2D	0.0
1984	Cle-A	144	473	66	137	21	3	10	68	47	62	.290	.358	.410	.768	106	8	5	106	121	68	.700	3	1	0	-10	1O3/2D	-0.9
1985	Cle-A	117	404	47	111	18	3	5	59	27	55	.275	.323	.371	.695	95	-6	-3	94	142	43	.570	0	6	-4	3	1D/32	-0.9
1986	Cle-A	130	473	61	154	29	2	6	48	29	75	.326	.368	.433	.802	121	12	14	98	87	74	.725	3	1	0	-1	*1D	0.5
1987	Cle-A	151	553	66	170	34	3	11	86	51	84	.307	.372	.439	.812	112	13	11	103	127	93	.780	5	2	0	0	1D	0.2
1988	Cle-A	41	143	16	32	5	1	1	17	23	27	.224	.335	.294	.629	77	-3	-4	102	159	15	.588	1	0	0	0	D1	-0.3
	KC-A	89	301	37	93	17	2	1	49	23	41	.309	.362	.389	.751	107	4	3	103	162	42	.664	2	3	-1	-3	DO/13	-0.1
	Yr	130	444	53	125	22	3	2	66	46	68	.282	.353	.358	.711	97	1	-0	103	162	57	.637	3	3	-1	-3		-0.4
1989	KC-A	123	390	36	101	11	1	2	42	37	42	.259	.326	.308	.634	83	-10	-7	96	130	39	.525	0	0	0	0	OD1/23	-0.9
Total	9	979	3353	405	962	165	23	44	446	312	495	.287	.351	.389	.741	103	22	18	101	125	453	.660	16	18	-6	-12	1OD/32	-2.7
■ **DAN TARTABULL** Tartabull, Danilo (Mora) b: 10/30/62, San Juan, P.R. BR/TR, 6'1.5", 185 lbs. Deb: 9/07/84																												
1984	Sea-A	10	20	3	6	1	0	2	7	2	3	.300	.391	.650	1.041	178	2	2	102	147	5	1.143	0	0	0	1	/S2	0.3
1985	Sea-A	19	61	8	20	7	1	1	7	8	14	.328	.406	.525	.930	161	5	5	95	79	14	.976	1	0	0	2	S/3	0.8
1986	Sea-A	137	511	76	138	25	6	25	96	61	157	.270	.349	.489	.838	120	18	15	105	125	85	.808	4	8	-4	-1	*O2/3D	0.8
1987	KC-A	158	582	95	180	27	3	34	101	79	136	.309	.393	.541	.934	140	39	35	104	102	124	.962	9	4	0	-10	*O/D	2.0
1988	KC-A	146	507	80	139	38	3	26	102	76	119	.274	.373	.515	.888	142	32	30	103	122	99	.911	8	5	-1	-8	*OD	1.9
1989	KC-A	133	441	54	118	22	0	18	62	69	123	.268	.370	.440	.810	133	17	20	96	99	74	.801	4	2	0	-8	OD	1.1
Total	6	603	2122	316	601	120	13	106	375	295	552	.283	.373	.502	.875	135	113	107	102	111	401	.880	26	19	-4	-24	O/D2S3	6.9
■ **GARRY TEMPLETON** Templeton, Garry Lewis b: 3/24/56, Lockney, Tex. BB/TR, 5'11", 175 lbs. Deb: 8/09/76																												
1976	StL-N	53	213	32	62	8	2	1	17	7	33	.291	.317	.362	.678	89	-3	-4	104	87	24	.604	11	7	-1	2	S	0.3
1977	StL-N	153	621	94	200	19	**18**	8	79	15	70	.322	.339	.449	.788	114	6	10	96	111	85	.711	28	24	-6	3	*S	2.7
1978	StL-N	155	647	82	181	31	**13**	2	47	22	87	.280	.304	.377	.682	94	-11	-7	95	66	74	.622	34	11	4	27	*S	3.8
1979	StL-N	154	672	105	**211**	32	**19**	9	62	18	91	.314	.333	.458	.791	109	10	6	105	70	100	.737	26	10	2	**26**	*S	5.0
1980	StL-N	118	504	83	161	19	9	4	43	18	43	.319	.343	.417	.760	108	6	5	103	74	66	.698	31	15	0	31	*S	5.0
1981	StL-N	80	333	47	96	16	8	1	33	14	55	.288	.317	.393	.710	99	-1	-1	102	102	37	.605	8	12	-5	14	S	1.7
1982	SD-N	141	563	76	139	25	8	6	64	26	82	.247	.281	.352	.633	83	-19	-14	92	123	49	.549	27	16	-2	-22	*S	-2.8
1983	SD-N	126	460	39	121	20	2	3	40	21	57	.263	.295	.335	.630	75	-17	-16	99	99	42	.529	16	6	1	-15	*S	-1.9
1984	SD-N	148	493	40	127	19	3	2	35	39	81	.258	.313	.320	.634	80	-14	-13	99	84	48	.544	8	3	1	-23	*S	-1.9
1985	SD-N	148	546	63	154	30	2	6	55	41	88	.282	.333	.377	.711	97	-1	-2	102	100	69	.655	16	6	1	-9	*S	0.2
1986	SD-N	147	510	42	126	21	2	2	44	35	86	.247	.297	.308	.605	70	-23	-20	95	108	44	.506	10	5	0	-21	*S	-2.8
1987	SD-N	148	510	42	113	13	5	5	48	42	92	.222	.282	.296	.578	55	-34	-32	97	115	42	.501	14	3	2	1	*S	-1.0
1988	SD-N	110	362	35	90	15	7	3	36	20	50	.249	.288	.354	.642	85	-8	-7	97	105	36	.557	8	2	1	-4	*S/3	-0.2
1989	SD-N	142	506	43	129	26	3	6	40	23	80	.255	.287	.354	.641	82	-13	-13	101	83	47	.514	1	3	-2	11	*S	0.5
Total	14	1823	6940	823	1910	294	101	58	643	341	995	.275	.310	.372	.682	90	-121	-109	99	94	764	.599	238	123	-2	23	*S/3	8.6
■ **MICKEY TETTLETON** Tettleton, Mickey Lee b: 9/16/60, Oklahoma City, Okla. BB/TR, 6'2", 200 lbs. Deb: 6/30/84																												
1984	Oak-A	33	76	10	20	2	1	1	5	11	21	.263	.356	.355	.712	107	0	1	92	66	10	.644	0	0	0	1	C	0.4
1985	Oak-A	78	211	23	53	12	0	3	15	28	59	.251	.344	.351	.695	98	-2	0	93	72	26	.639	2	2	-1	-4	C/D	0.0
1986	Oak-A	90	211	26	43	9	0	10	35	39	51	.204	.331	.389	.719	103	-1	1	94	124	31	.750	7	1	2	-8	C	0.0
1987	Oak-A	82	211	19	41	3	0	8	26	30	65	.194	.295	.322	.617	71	-11	-8	91	113	22	.569	1	1	-0	-2	C/1D	-0.3
1988	Bal-A	86	283	31	74	11	1	11	37	28	70	.261	.332	.424	.756	116	4	5	95	96	38	.685	0	1	-1	9	C	1.7
1989	Bal-A	117	411	72	106	21	2	26	65	73	117	.258	.371	.509	.880	147	26	26	99	93	80	.908	3	2	-0	6	CD	3.5
Total	6	486	1403	181	337	58	4	59	183	209	383	.240	.341	.413	.755	113	16	27	95	97	207	.731	13	7	-0	2	C/D1	5.3
■ **TIM TEUFEL** Teufel, Timothy Shawn b: 7/7/58, Greenwich, Conn. BR/TR, 6', 175 lbs. Deb: 9/03/83																												
1983	Min-A	21	78	11	24	7	1	3	6	2	8	.308	.325	.538	.863	126	3	3	105	47	13	.800	0	0	0	0	2/SD	0.3
1984	Min-A	157	568	76	149	30	3	14	61	76	73	.262	.351	.400	.751	102	7	3	106	96	79	.695	1	3	-2	-11	*2	-0.1
1985	Min-A	138	434	58	113	24	3	10	50	48	70	.260	.338	.399	.737	98	1	-1	103	98	58	.677	4	2	0	-19	*2/D	-1.4
1986	NY-N	93	279	35	69	20	1	4	31	32	42	.247	.327	.369	.696	96	-3	-2	96	107	34	.628	1	2	-1	-9	2/13	-1.0
1987	NY-N	97	299	55	92	29	0	14	61	44	53	.308	.400	.545	.945	150	21	22	99	119	66	.981	3	2	-0	-8	2/1	1.5
1988	NY-N	90	273	35	64	20	0	4	31	29	41	.234	.310	.352	.662	99	-4	-0	90	115	30	.583	0	1	-1	-0	2/1	0.1
1989	NY-N	83	219	27	56	7	2	2	15	32	50	.256	.353	.333	.687	101	0	1	97	76	27	.629	1	3	-2	-6	21	-0.8
Total	7	679	2150	297	567	137	10	51	255	263	337	.264	.347	.408	.755	108	26	25	100	100	306	.702	10	13	-5	-53	2/1D3S	-1.4
■ **ANDRES THOMAS** Thomas, Andres Perez (born Andres Perez (Thomas)) b: 11/10/63, Boca Chica, D.R. BR/TR, 6'1", 170 lbs. Deb: 9/03/85																												
1985	Atl-N	15	18	6	5	0	0	0	2	0	2	.278	.278	.278	.556	52	-1	-1	106	159	1	.357	0	0	0	0	S	0.0
1986	Atl-N	102	323	26	81	17	2	6	32	8	49	.251	.269	.372	.640	73	-12	-13	102	92	26	.504	4	6	-2	20	S	1.5

YEAR	TM/L	G	AB	R	H	2B	3B	HR	RBI	BB	SO	AVG	OBP	SLG	PRO	/A	BR	/A	PF	CHI	RC	TA	SB	CS	SBR	FR	POS	TPR
1987	Atl-N	82	324	29	75	11	0	5	39	14	50	.231	.268	.312	.579	49	-22	-26	108	137	25	.471	6	5	-1	8	S	-0.9
1988	Atl-N	153	606	54	153	22	2	13	68	14	95	.252	.271	.360	.630	76	-18	-21	104	112	54	.507	7	3	0	-9	*S	-2.0
1989	Atl-N	141	554	41	118	18	0	13	57	12	62	.213	.230	.316	.546	53	-34	-35	102	109	35	.417	3	3	-1	3	*S	-2.6
Total	5	493	1825	156	432	68	4	37	198	48	258	.237	.257	.339	.597	63	-87	-96	104	113	141	.471	20	17	-4	22	S	-4.0
■ **MILT THOMPSON** Thompson, Milton Bernard b: 1/5/59, Washington, D.C. BL/TR, 5'11", 170 lbs. Deb: 9/04/84																												
1984	Atl-N	25	99	16	30	1	0	2	4	11	11	.303	.373	.374	.746	101	2	1	110	32	16	.861	14	2	3	2	O	0.5
1985	Atl-N	73	182	17	55	7	2	0	6	7	36	.302	.339	.363	.701	90	-1	-2	106	36	23	.644	9	4	0	-4	O	-0.7
1986	Phi-N	96	299	38	75	7	1	6	23	26	62	.251	.313	.341	.654	77	-8	-10	104	76	34	.638	19	4	3	-1	O	-0.8
1987	Phi-N	150	527	86	159	26	9	7	43	42	87	.302	.353	.425	.778	101	4	1	104	71	85	.815	46	10	8	-0	*O	0.2
1988	Phi-N	122	378	53	109	16	2	2	33	39	59	.288	.356	.357	.714	104	4	3	101	94	48	.671	17	9	-0	1	*O	0.0
1989	StL-N	155	545	60	158	28	8	4	68	39	91	.290	.342	.393	.734	109	7	6	101	124	73	.698	27	8	3	-7	*O	0.0
Total	6	621	2030	270	586	85	22	21	177	164	346	.289	.345	.383	.728	99	7	-1	103	85	280	.716	132	37	17	-10	O	-0.8
■ **ROB THOMPSON** Thompson, Robert Randall b: 5/10/62, W.Palm Beach, Fla. BR/TR, 5'11", 165 lbs. Deb: 4/08/86																												
1986	SF-N	149	549	73	149	27	3	7	47	42	112	.271	.329	.370	.699	96	-6	-3	96	85	64	.615	12	15	-5	-1	*2/S	-0.7
1987	SF-N	132	420	62	110	26	5	10	44	40	91	.262	.338	.419	.757	103	-1	2	96	85	58	.729	16	11	-2	4	*2	0.6
1988	SF-N	138	477	66	126	24	6	7	48	40	111	.264	.326	.384	.710	110	2	5	94	96	62	.664	14	5	1	-6	*2	0.4
1989	SF-N	148	547	91	132	26	**11**	13	50	51	133	.241	.321	.400	.721	108	3	5	97	83	75	.697	12	2	2	-1	*2	0.9
Total	4	567	1993	292	517	103	25	37	189	173	447	.259	.328	.392	.720	104	-1	9	96	87	259	.674	54	33	-4	-5	2/S	1.2
■ **DICKIE THON** Thon, Richard William b: 6/20/58, South Bend, Ind BR/TR, 5'11", 160 lbs. Deb: 5/22/79																												
1979	Cal-A	35	56	6	19	3	0	0	8	5	10	.339	.393	.393	.786	122	1	2	93	140	8	.692	0	0	0	0	2/S3	0.4
1980	Cal-A	80	267	32	68	12	2	0	15	10	28	.255	.284	.315	.599	67	-13	-12	96	70	23	.488	7	5	-1	-4	S2D3/1	-1.3
1981	Hou-N	49	95	13	26	6	0	0	3	9	13	.274	.337	.337	.673	104	-1	0	88	37	11	.644	6	1	1	-3	2S/3	0.2
1982	Hou-N	136	496	73	137	31	**10**	3	36	37	48	.276	.328	.397	.725	103	1	1	99	70	69	.733	37	8	6	9	*S/32	2.6
1983	Hou-N	154	619	81	177	28	9	20	79	54	73	.286	.345	.457	.802	134	16	23	90	88	95	.794	34	16	1	18	*S	5.6
1984	Hou-N	5	17	3	6	0	1	0	1	0	4	.353	.389	.471	.859	152	1	1	93	49	2	.692	0	1	-1	1	/S	0.2
1985	Hou-N	84	251	26	63	6	1	6	29	18	50	.251	.301	.355	.656	86	-6	-5	96	108	27	.596	8	3	1	6	S	0.8
1986	Hou-N	106	278	24	69	13	1	3	21	29	49	.248	.319	.335	.654	78	-7	-8	103	82	28	.577	6	5	-1	-7	*S	-0.5
1987	Hou-N	32	66	6	14	1	0	1	3	16	13	.212	.366	.273	.639	78	-2	-1	93	57	8	.698	3	0	1	-2	S	0.1
1988	SD-N	95	258	36	68	12	2	1	18	33	49	.264	.349	.337	.687	100	0	1	97	80	34	.707	19	4	3	-2	S/23	0.8
1989	Phi-N	136	435	45	118	18	4	15	60	33	81	.271	.323	.434	.757	114	7	7	101	103	61	.699	6	3	0	9	*S	2.4
Total	11	912	2838	345	765	130	30	49	273	244	418	.270	.329	.388	.717	103	-3	9	96	84	368	.682	126	46	10	25	S/23D1	11.3
■ **LOU THORNTON** Thornton, Louis b: 4/26/63, Montgomery, Ala. BL/TR, 6'2", 185 lbs. Deb: 4/08/85																												
1985	Tor-A	56	72	18	17	1	1	1	8	2	24	.236	.267	.319	.586	59	-4	-4	101	122	6	.474	1	0	0	-8	OD	-1.1
1987	Tor-A	12	2	5	1	0	0	0	0	1	0	.500	.667	.500	1.167	216	1	0	101	0	0	.667	0	1	-1	-2	/OD	-0.1
1988	Tor-A	11	2	1	0	0	0	0	0	0	0	.000	.000	.000	.000	-99	-1	-1	100	0	0	.000	0	0	0	-4	O/D	-0.4
1989	NY-N	13	13	5	4	1	0	0	1	0	1	.308	.308	.385	.692	100	-0	-0	97	80	2	.778	2	0	1	-1	/O	0.0
Total	4	92	89	29	22	2	1	1	9	3	25	.247	.280	.326	.605	66	-4	-4	100	110	8	.507	3	1	0	-14	/OD	-1.6
■ **GARY THURMAN** Thurman, Gary Montez b: 11/12/64, Indianapolis, Ind. BR/TR, 5'10", 170 lbs. Deb: 8/30/87																												
1987	KC-A	27	81	12	24	2	0	0	5	8	20	.296	.360	.321	.681	81	-2	-2	104	77	10	.683	7	2	1	5	O	0.3
1988	KC-A	35	66	6	11	1	0	0	2	4	20	.167	.214	.182	.396	12	-8	-8	103	66	3	.375	5	1	1	-7	O/D	-1.4
1989	KC-A	72	87	24	17	2	1	0	5	15	26	.195	.314	.241	.555	61	-4	-4	96	93	11	.743	16	0	5	-15	O/D	-1.4
Total	3	134	234	42	52	5	1	0	12	27	66	.222	.303	.252	.555	55	-14	-14	101	80	24	.613	28	3	7	-17	O/D	-2.5
■ **RON TINGLEY** Tingley, Ronald Irvin b: 5/27/59, Presque Isle, Maine BR/TR, 6'2", 160 lbs. Deb: 9/25/82																												
1982	SD-N	8	20	0	2	0	0	0	0	0	7	.100	.100	.100	.200	-48	-4	-4	92	0	0	.111	0	0	0	-0	/C	-0.3
1988	Cle-A	9	24	1	4	0	0	1	2	2	8	.167	.231	.292	.522	45	-2	-2	102	79	1	.429	0	0	0	1	/C	0.0
1989	Cal-A	4	3	0	1	0	0	0	0	1	0	.333	.500	.333	.833	141	0	0	99	0	1	1.000	0	0	0	0	/C	0.1
Total	3	21	47	1	7	0	0	1	2	3	15	.149	.200	.213	.413	16	-5	-5	97	41	2	.317	0	0	0	1	/C	-0.2
■ **WAYNE TOLLESON** Tolleson, Jimmy Wayne b: 11/22/59, Spartanburg, S.C. BB/TR, 5'9", 160 lbs. Deb: 9/01/81																												
1981	Tex-A	14	24	6	4	0	0	0	1	1	5	.167	.200	.167	.367	7	-3	-3	91	98	1	.350	2	0	1	2	/3S	0.0
1982	Tex-A	38	70	6	8	1	0	0	2	5	14	.114	.173	.129	.302	-17	-11	-10	93	89	2	.234	1	1	-0	0	S/32	-0.7
1983	Tex-A	134	470	64	122	13	2	3	20	40	68	.260	.320	.315	.635	75	-15	-15	101	51	51	.609	33	10	4	-2	*2S/D	-0.7
1984	Tex-A	118	338	35	72	9	2	0	9	27	47	.213	.277	.251	.529	47	-24	-24	100	42	25	.486	22	4	4	-16	*2/S3OD	-2.9
1985	Tex-A	123	323	45	101	9	5	1	18	21	46	.313	.355	.381	.735	94	1	-3	108	57	43	.688	21	12	-1	-3	S23/D	0.0
1986	Chi-A	81	260	39	65	7	3	3	29	38	43	.250	.346	.335	.680	87	-3	-4	101	123	33	.676	13	6	0	-4	3S/OD	-0.7
	NY-A	60	215	22	61	9	2	0	14	14	33	.284	.333	.344	.678	83	-4	-5	103	77	25	.584	4	4	-1	3	S/32	0.0
	Yr	141	475	61	126	16	5	3	43	52	76	.265	.340	.339	.679	85	-7	-8	102	104	58	.636	17	10	-1	-1		-0.7
1987	NY-A	121	349	48	77	4	0	1	22	43	72	.221	.306	.241	.547	50	-24	-23	98	101	29	.475	5	3	-0	-4	*S/3	-2.1
1988	NY-A	21	59	8	15	2	0	0	5	8	12	.254	.343	.288	.631	82	-1	-1	96	117	7	.578	1	0	0	1	2/3S	0.1
1989	NY-A	79	140	16	23	5	2	1	9	16	23	.164	.255	.250	.505	41	-11	-11	104	92	10	.471	5	1	1	1	3S2/D	-0.7
Total	9	789	2248	289	548	59	16	9	129	213	363	.244	.311	.296	.608	67	-95	-99	101	75	224	.558	107	41	8	-22	S23/DO	-7.7
■ **JIM TRABER** Traber, James Joseph b: 12/26/61, Columbus, Ohio BL/TL, 6', 194 lbs. Deb: 9/21/84																												
1984	Bal-A	10	21	3	5	0	0	0	2	2	4	.238	.304	.238	.542	56	-1	-1	94	159	2	.412	0	0	0	0	/D	0.0
1986	Bal-A	65	212	28	54	7	0	13	44	18	31	.255	.328	.472	.799	117	4	5	99	126	32	.750	0	0	0	1	1D/O	0.3
1988	Bal-A	103	352	25	78	6	0	10	45	19	42	.222	.263	.324	.587	67	-18	-16	95	124	28	.475	1	2	-1	6	1DO	-1.3
1989	Bal-A	86	234	14	49	8	0	4	26	19	41	.209	.269	.295	.564	59	-13	-13	99	125	18	.472	4	3	-1	3	1/D	-1.5
Total	4	264	819	70	186	21	0	27	117	58	118	.227	.283	.352	.635	78	-28	-25	97	126	79	.541	5	5	-2	10	1/DO	-2.5
■ **ALAN TRAMMELL** Trammell, Alan Stuart b: 2/21/58, Garden Grove, Cal. BR/TR, 6', 165 lbs. Deb: 9/09/77																												
1977	Det-A	19	43	6	8	0	0	0	0	4	12	.186	.255	.186	.441	22	-5	-5	105	0	2	.333	0	0	0	0	S	-0.1
1978	Det-A	139	448	49	120	14	6	2	34	45	56	.268	.337	.339	.677	84	-5	-9	108	85	52	.592	3	1	0	-0	*S	0.2
1979	Det-A	142	460	68	127	11	4	6	50	43	55	.276	.338	.357	.694	91	-7	-5	96	106	56	.635	17	14	-3	-9	*S	0.0
1980	Det-A	146	560	107	168	21	5	9	65	69	63	.300	.380	.404	.783	109	14	9	105	106	87	.749	12	12	-4	-22	*S	-0.4
1981	Det-A	105	392	52	101	15	3	2	31	49	31	.258	.345	.327	.671	90	-1	-4	105	87	47	.625	10	3	1	11	*S	1.6
1982	Det-A	157	489	66	126	34	3	9	57	52	47	.258	.329	.395	.724	97	-1	-2	100	104	67	.702	19	8	1	-3	*S	1.0
1983	Det-A	142	505	83	161	31	2	14	66	57	64	.319	.388	.471	.859	141	25	28	96	94	96	.900	30	10	3	-10	*S	2.9
1984	Det-A	139	555	85	174	34	5	14	69	60	63	.314	.383	.468	.852	140	27	30	96	88	100	.851	19	13	-2	-2	*SD	3.4
1985	Det-A	149	605	79	156	21	7	13	57	50	71	.258	.317	.380	.697	84	-9	-14	106	74	76	.643	14	5	1	-15	*S	-1.6
1986	Det-A	151	574	107	159	33	7	21	75	59	57	.277	.350	.469	.818	127	17	20	95	95	95	.825	25	12	0	8	*S/D	3.5
1987	Det-A	151	597	109	205	34	3	28	105	60	47	.343	.406	.551	.957	156	45	47	97	108	137	1.020	21	2	5	-4	*S	5.1
1988	Det-A	128	466	73	145	24	1	15	69	46	46	.311	.378	.464	.841	142	22	25	94	107	79	.805	7	4	-0	-10	*S	2.1
1989	Det-A	121	449	54	109	20	3	5	43	45	45	.243	.317	.334	.651	86	-9	-8	97	107	50	.595	10	2	2	4	*S/D	0.8
Total	13	1689	6143	938	1759	292	49	138	721	639	657	.286	.356	.417	.774	113	112	114	100	96	944	.747	187	86	5	-52	*S/D	18.5
■ **JEFF TREADWAY** Treadway, Hugh Jeffery b: 1/22/63, Columbus, Ga. BL/TR, 5'10", 170 lbs. Deb: 9/04/87																												
1987	Cin-N	23	84	9	28	4	0	2	4	2	6	.333	.356	.452	.809	109	1	1	104	37	14	.737	1	0	0	-0	2	0.1
1988	Cin-N	103	301	30	76	19	4	2	23	27	30	.252	.320	.362	.682	91	-2	-4	105	80	36	.616	2	0	1	0	2/3	0.0
1989	Atl-N	134	473	58	131	18	3	8	40	30	38	.277	.320	.378	.699	97	-1	-2	102	81	56	.601	3	2	-0	-1	*2/3	-0.2
Total	3	260	858	97	235	41	7	12	67	59	74	.274	.324	.380	.704	96	-1	-5	104	76	106	.618	6	2	1	-1	2/3	-0.1
■ **ALEX TREVINO** Trevino, Alejandro (Castro) b: 8/26/57, Monterrey, Mex. BR/TR, 5'10", 165 lbs. Deb: 9/11/78																												
1978	NY-N	6	12	3	3	0	0	0	0	1	2	.250	.308	.250	.558	58	-1	-1	98	0	1	.400	0	0	0	0	/C3	0.0
1979	NY-N	79	207	24	56	11	1	0	20	20	27	.271	.338	.333	.671	88	-4	-3	95	115	22	.571	2	2	-1	6	C3/2	0.3

YEAR	TM/L	G	AB	R	H	2B	3B	HR	RBI	BB	SO	AVG	OBP	SLG	PRO	/A	BR	/A	PF	CHI	RC	TA	SB	CS	SBR	FR	POS	TPR
1980	NY-N	106	355	26	91	11	2	0	37	13	41	.256	.285	.299	.583	66	-18	-16	96	138	27	.432	0	3	-2	7	C3/2	-0.9
1981	NY-N	56	149	17	39	2	0	0	10	13	19	.262	.325	.275	.600	71	-5	-5	101	96	14	.509	3	0	1	2	C/2O3	-0.1
1982	Cin-N	120	355	24	89	10	3	1	33	34	34	.251	.321	.304	.626	74	-11	-12	102	117	33	.523	3	1	0	-5	*C/3	-1.6
1983	Cin-N	74	167	14	36	8	1	1	13	17	20	.216	.288	.293	.581	60	-9	-9	103	99	14	.493	0	0	0	-6	C/32	-1.3
1984	Cin-N	6	6	0	1	0	0	0	0	0	2	.167	.167	.167	.333	-6	-1	-1	106	0	0	.200	0	0	0	0	/C	0.0
	Atl-N	79	266	36	65	16	0	3	28	16	27	.244	.290	.338	.628	69	-9	-12	110	111	26	.541	5	2	0	6	C	-0.2
	Yr	85	272	36	66	16	0	3	28	16	29	.243	.287	.335	.622	68	-10	-13	109	103	26	.533	5	2	0	6		-0.2
1985	SF-N	57	157	17	34	10	1	6	19	20	24	.217	.305	.408	.713	105	-1	0	93	92	19	.656	0	0	0	2	C/3	0.5
1986	LA-N	89	202	31	53	13	0	4	26	27	35	.262	.352	.386	.738	110	1	3	94	115	28	.684	0	0	0	0	C/1	0.4
1987	LA-N	72	144	16	32	7	1	3	16	6	28	.222	.273	.347	.620	69	-8	-6	92	108	12	.513	1	0	0	-1	C/O3	-0.3
1988	Hou-N	78	193	19	48	17	0	2	13	24	29	.249	.341	.368	.709	111	1	3	93	67	24	.665	5	2	0	-6	C/O	0.1
1989	Hou-N	59	131	15	38	7	1	2	16	7	18	.290	.331	.405	.736	107	1	1	102	109	17	.635	0	0	0	1	C/13	0.4
Total	12	881	2344	242	585	112	10	22	231	198	306	.250	.312	.334	.646	81	-61	-57	99	108	238	.551	19	10	-0	7	C/3201	-2.7
■ MANNY TRILLO	Trillo, Jesus Manuel Marcano (born Jesus Manuel Marcano (Trillo)) b: 12/25/50, Caripito, Ven. BR/TR, 6'1", 150 lbs. Deb: 6/28/73																											
1973	Oak-A	17	12	0	3	2	0	0	3	0	4	.250	.250	.417	.667	97	-0	-0	87	236	1	.500	0	0	0	-0	2	0.0
1974	Oak-A	21	33	3	5	0	0	0	2	2	8	.152	.222	.152	.374	9	-4	-4	100	157	1	.286	0	0	0	-0	2	-0.3
1975	Chi-N	154	545	55	135	12	2	7	70	45	78	.248	.309	.316	.624	71	-19	-22	104	143	53	.518	1	7	-4	19	*2/S	0.0
1976	Chi-N	158	582	42	139	24	3	4	59	53	70	.239	.306	.311	.617	69	-18	-25	109	120	55	.545	17	6	2	17	*2/S	0.1
1977	Chi-N	152	504	51	141	18	5	7	57	44	58	.280	.344	.377	.721	82	-4	-13	114	108	62	.629	3	5	-2	36	*2	2.9
1978	Chi-N	152	552	53	144	17	5	4	55	50	67	.261	.325	.332	.656	76	-11	-18	110	114	59	.553	0	7	-4	**34**	*2	2.2
1979	Phi-N	118	431	40	112	22	1	6	42	20	59	.260	.299	.357	.656	81	-14	-12	97	99	42	.537	4	7	-3	4	*2	-0.2
1980	Phi-N	141	531	68	155	25	9	7	43	32	46	.292	.336	.412	.748	100	5	0	107	72	70	.663	8	3	1	17	*2	2.8
1981	Phi-N	94	349	37	100	14	3	6	36	26	37	.287	.341	.395	.737	97	4	-1	112	92	48	.683	10	4	1	10	2	1.7
1982	Phi-N	149	549	52	149	24	1	0	39	33	53	.271	.316	.319	.635	83	-16	-11	94	89	52	.517	8	10	-4	8	*2	0.0
1983	Cle-A	88	320	33	87	13	1	1	29	21	46	.272	.317	.328	.645	74	-9	-12	105	107	30	.510	1	3	-2	12	2	0.2
	Mon-N	31	121	16	32	8	0	2	16	10	18	.264	.331	.380	.711	95	-1	-1	102	129	16	.637	0	0	0	-2	2	-0.1
1984	SF-N	98	401	45	102	21	1	4	36	25	55	.254	.303	.342	.645	84	-11	-9	96	91	41	.537	0	0	0	3	2/3	-0.2
1985	SF-N	125	451	36	101	16	2	3	25	40	44	.224	.289	.288	.577	66	-23	-19	93	73	40	.486	2	0	1	-3	*2/3	-2.1
1986	Chi-N	81	152	22	45	10	0	1	19	16	21	.296	.363	.382	.745	99	1	0	107	124	21	.667	0	2	-1	-2	31/2	-0.4
1987	Chi-N	108	214	27	63	8	0	8	26	25	37	.294	.368	.444	.812	113	5	4	101	87	34	.750	0	3	-2	-2	132/S	0.0
1988	Chi-N	76	164	15	41	5	0	1	14	8	32	.250	.285	.299	.584	65	-7	-8	104	108	15	.472	2	0	1	0	132/S	-0.7
1989	Cin-N	17	39	3	8	0	0	0	0	2	9	.205	.262	.205	.467	34	-3	-3	103	0	2	.355	0	0	0	-0	2/1S	-0.3
Total	17	1780	5950	598	1562	239	33	61	571	452	742	.263	.318	.345	.663	81	-126	-154	104	103	641	.565	56	57	-17	151	*23/1S	5.6
■ JOSE URIBE	Uribe, Jose Altagracia (Played under real name of Jose Altagracia Gonzalez (Uribe) in 1984) b: 1/21/59, San Cristobal, D.R. BB/TR, 5'10", 155 lbs. Deb: 9/13/84																											
1984	StL-N	8	19	4	4	0	0	0	3	0	2	.211	.211	.211	.421	19	-2	-2	99	294	1	.313	1	0	0	1	/S2	0.0
1985	SF-N	147	476	46	113	20	4	3	26	30	57	.237	.285	.315	.601	73	-21	-17	93	65	44	.514	8	2	1	-3	*S/2	-0.7
1986	SF-N	157	453	46	101	15	1	3	43	61	76	.223	.315	.280	.596	68	-20	-17	96	126	43	.575	22	11	0	6	*S	0.3
1987	SF-N	95	309	44	90	16	5	5	30	24	35	.291	.344	.424	.768	106	1	2	96	82	48	.757	12	2	2	16	S	3.1
1988	SF-N	141	493	47	124	10	7	3	35	36	69	.252	.302	.318	.621	83	-14	-10	94	86	48	.542	14	10	-2	-2	*S	-0.4
1989	SF-N	151	453	34	100	12	6	1	30	34	74	.221	.275	.280	.556	61	-24	-22	97	93	34	.456	6	6	-2	5	*S	-1.0
Total	6	699	2203	221	532	73	23	15	167	185	313	.241	.301	.316	.617	76	-79	-67	95	93	218	.550	63	31	0	23	S/2	1.3
■ DAVE VALLE	Valle, David b: 10/30/60, Bayside, N.Y. BR/TR, 6'2", 200 lbs. Deb: 9/07/84																											
1984	Sea-A	13	27	4	8	1	0	1	4	1	5	.296	.321	.444	.766	107	0	0	102	106	4	.684	0	0	0	0	C	0.1
1985	Sea-A	31	70	2	11	1	0	0	4	1	17	.157	.181	.171	.352	-3	-10	-9	95	132	2	.233	0	0	0	-2	C	-0.9
1986	Sea-A	22	53	10	18	3	0	5	15	7	7	.340	.417	.679	1.096	184	7	6	105	117	14	1.162	0	0	0	0	C/1	0.6
1987	Sea-A	95	324	40	83	16	3	12	53	15	46	.256	.295	.435	.731	89	-5	-6	103	119	38	.634	2	0	1	6	CD/1O	0.5
1988	Sea-A	93	290	29	67	15	2	10	50	18	38	.231	.297	.400	.697	87	-3	-6	108	136	31	.603	0	1	-1	8	C/1D	0.5
1989	Sea-A	94	316	32	75	10	3	7	34	29	32	.237	.313	.354	.668	85	-5	-6	103	101	34	.579	0	0	0	9	C	0.7
Total	6	348	1080	117	262	46	8	35	160	71	145	.243	.301	.397	.698	87	-16	-21	104	119	123	.605	2	1	0	21	C/D1O	1.5
■ ANDY VAN SLYKE	Van Slyke, Andrew James b: 12/21/60, Utica, N.Y. BL/TR, 6'1", 190 lbs. Deb: 6/17/83																											
1983	StL-N	101	309	51	81	15	5	8	38	46	64	.262	.360	.421	.780	118	7	8	98	98	50	.828	21	7	2	-4	O3/1	0.3
1984	StL-N	137	361	45	88	16	4	7	50	63	71	.244	.356	.368	.725	105	4	4	99	127	54	.792	28	5	5	-9	O31	-0.3
1985	StL-N	146	424	61	110	25	6	13	55	47	54	.259	.336	.439	.775	120	8	10	96	97	66	.823	34	6	7	-4	*O/1	1.0
1986	StL-N	137	418	48	113	23	7	13	61	47	85	.270	.345	.452	.798	115	10	8	103	107	68	.819	21	8	2	1	*O1	0.7
1987	Pit-N	157	564	93	165	36	11	21	82	56	122	.293	.361	.507	.868	122	21	18	104	96	108	.920	34	8	5	13	*O/1	3.0
1988	Pit-N	154	587	101	169	23	**15**	25	100	57	126	.288	.352	.506	.858	147	31	33	98	114	107	.885	30	9	4	8	*O	4.3
1989	Pit-N	130	476	64	113	18	9	9	53	47	100	.237	.310	.370	.680	100	-4	-1	94	107	55	.637	16	4	2	7	*O/1	0.7
Total	7	962	3139	463	839	156	57	96	439	363	622	.267	.345	.445	.791	120	77	81	99	106	508	.818	184	47	27	13	O/13	9.7
■ GARY VARSHO	Varsho, Gary Andrew b: 6/20/61, Marshfield, Wis. BL/TR, 5'11", 190 lbs. Deb: 7/06/88																											
1988	Chi-N	46	73	6	20	3	0	0	5	1	6	.274	.284	.315	.599	69	-3	-3	104	87	7	.547	5	0	2	-2	O	-0.4
1989	Chi-N	61	87	10	16	4	2	0	6	4	13	.184	.220	.276	.496	38	-7	-8	108	101	6	.437	3	0	1	-3	O	-1.0
Total	2	107	160	16	36	7	2	0	11	5	19	.225	.248	.294	.542	51	-10	-11	107	94	13	.484	8	0	2	-6	/O	-1.4
■ GREG VAUGHN	Vaughn, Gregory Lamont b: 7/3/65, Sacramento, Cal. BR/TR, 6', 195 lbs. Deb: 8/10/89																											
1989	Mil-A	38	113	18	30	3	0	5	23	13	23	.265	.341	.425	.766	119	2	3	97	142	18	.774	4	1	1	-4	OD	0.0
■ RANDY VELARDE	Velarde, Randy Lee b: 11/24/62, Midland, Tex. BR/TR, 6' ", 185 lbs. Deb: 8/20/87																											
1987	NY-A	8	22	1	4	0	0	0	1	0	6	.182	.182	.182	.364	-3	-3	-3	98	100	1	.211	0	0	0	-0	/S	-0.2
1988	NY-A	48	115	18	20	6	0	5	12	8	24	.174	.240	.357	.597	68	-6	-5	96	85	9	.525	1	1	-0	1	2S3	-0.1
1989	NY-A	33	100	12	34	4	2	2	11	7	14	.340	.389	.480	.869	138	6	5	104	79	18	.812	0	3	-2	-1	3/S	0.3
Total	3	89	237	31	58	10	2	7	24	15	44	.245	.298	.392	.690	92	-3	-3	99	84	28	.599	1	4	-2	0	/3S2	0.0
■ MAX VENABLE	Venable, William Mc Kinley b: 6/6/57, Phoenix, Ariz. BL/TR, 5'10", 185 lbs. Deb: 4/08/79																											
1979	SF-N	55	85	12	14	1	1	0	3	10	18	.165	.260	.200	.460	30	-8	-8	92	70	5	.419	3	3	-1	-4	O	-1.2
1980	SF-N	64	138	13	37	5	0	0	10	15	22	.268	.340	.304	.644	85	-3	-2	96	94	16	.613	8	2	1	-5	O	-0.7
1981	SF-N	18	32	2	6	0	2	0	1	4	3	.188	.278	.313	.590	64	-1	-2	105	39	3	.630	3	1	0	0	/O	0.0
1982	SF-N	71	125	17	28	2	1	1	7	7	16	.224	.265	.280	.545	56	-8	-7	94	72	9	.500	9	3	1	-4	O	-1.0
1983	SF-N	94	228	28	50	7	4	6	27	22	34	.219	.296	.364	.660	81	-6	-6	101	106	27	.672	15	2	3	5	O	0.1
1984	Mon-N	38	71	7	17	2	0	2	7	3	7	.239	.280	.352	.632	84	-2	-2	91	88	7	.556	1	0	0	-5	O	-0.6
1985	Cin-N	77	135	21	39	12	3	0	10	6	17	.289	.319	.422	.741	100	1	-0	105	70	18	.733	11	3	2	-1	O	0.0
1986	Cin-N	108	147	17	31	7	1	2	15	17	24	.211	.293	.313	.606	64	-7	-7	104	115	15	.593	7	2	1	-11	O	-1.8
1987	Cin-N	7	7	2	1	0	0	0	2	0	0	.143	.143	.143	.286	-23	-1	-1	104	798	0	.167	0	0	0	-1	/O	-0.1
1989	Cal-A	20	53	7	19	4	0	0	4	1	16	.358	.370	.434	.804	128	2	2	99	68	9	.706	0	0	0	-2	O	0.0
Total	10	552	1021	126	242	40	12	11	86	85	157	.237	.299	.332	.631	76	-35	-33	99	93	110	.604	57	16	8	-27	O	-5.3
■ ROBIN VENTURA	Ventura, Robin Mark b: 7/14/67, Santa Maria, Cal. BL/TR, 6'1", 185 lbs. Deb: 9/12/89																											
1989	Chi-A	16	45	5	8	3	0	0	7	8	6	.178	.315	.244	.559	64	-2	-2	93	247	4	.526	0	0	0	-1	3	-0.1
■ OZZIE VIRGIL	Virgil, Osvaldo Jose Jr. b: 12/7/56, Mayaguez, P.R. BR/TR, 6'1", 180 lbs. Deb: 10/05/80																											
1980	Phi-N	1	5	1	1	1	0	0	0	0	1	.200	.200	.400	.600	59	-0	-0	107	0	0	.500	0	0	0	0	/C	0.0
1981	Phi-N	6	6	0	0	0	0	0	0	0	2	.000	.000	.000	.000	-89	-2	-2	112	0	0	.000	0	0	0	0	/C	-0.1
1982	Phi-N	49	101	11	24	6	0	3	8	10	26	.238	.306	.386	.692	99	-1	-0	94	65	11	.605	0	1	-1	-3	C	-0.3
1983	Phi-N	55	140	11	30	7	0	6	23	8	34	.214	.272	.393	.664	81	-4	-4	101	125	12	.550	0	2	-1	0	C	-0.3
1984	Phi-N	141	456	61	119	21	2	18	68	45	91	.261	.334	.434	.768	112	8	7	102	106	62	.697	1	1	-0	-8	*C	0.3

YEAR	TM/L	G	AB	R	H	2B	3B	HR	RBI	BB	SO	AVG	OBP	SLG	PRO	/A	BR	/A	PF	CHI	RC	TA	SB	CS	SBR	FR	POS	TPR
1985	Phi-N	131	426	47	105	16	3	19	55	49	85	.246	.331	.432	.763	110	6	5	102	91	59	.710	0	0	0	11	*C	2.1
1986	Atl-N	114	359	45	80	9	0	15	48	63	73	.223	.345	.373	.718	96	0	-1	102	109	49	.701	1	0	0	17	*C	1.9
1987	Atl-N	123	429	57	106	13	1	27	72	47	81	.247	.331	.471	.802	101	5	0	108	103	63	.749	0	1	-1	19	*C	2.8
1988	Atl-N	107	320	23	82	10	0	9	31	22	54	.256	.314	.372	.686	92	-2	-3	104	85	36	.597	2	0	1	-1	C	0.1
1989	Tor-A	9	11	2	2	1	0	1	2	4	3	.182	.400	.545	.945	174	1	1	94	86	3	1.111	0	0	0	0	/CD	0.1
Total	10	736	2253	258	549	84	6	98	307	248	450	.244	.326	.417	.743	101	12	3	103	99	296	.682	4	5	-2	35	C/D	6.6
■ **JOSE VIZCAINO**	Vizcaino, Jose Luis (Pimental) b: 3/26/68, San Cristobal, D.R. BB/TR, 6'1", 150 lbs. Deb: 9/10/89																											
1989	LA-N	7	10	2	2	0	0	0	0	0	1	.200	.200	.200	.400	16	-1	-1	93	0	0	.250	0	0	0	0	/S	0.0
■ **OMAR VIZQUEL**	Vizquel, Omar Enrique (Gonzalez) b: 5/15/67, Caracas, Venez. BB/TR, 5'9", 155 lbs. Deb: 4/03/89																											
1989	Sea-A	143	387	45	85	7	3	1	20	28	40	.220	.274	.261	.535	50	-24	-26	103	75	28	.420	1	4	-2	-10	*S	-2.6
■ **GREG WALKER**	Walker, Gregory Lee b: 10/6/59, Douglas, Ga. BL/TR, 6'3", 205 lbs. Deb: 9/18/82																											
1982	Chi-A	11	17	3	7	2	1	2	7	2	3	.412	.474	1.000	1.474	300	4	4	97	122	8	1.900	0	0	0	0	/D	0.4
1983	Chi-A	118	307	32	83	16	3	10	55	28	57	.270	.335	.440	.775	108	4	3	103	130	46	.732	2	1	0	-1	1D	0.0
1984	Chi-A	136	442	62	130	29	2	24	75	35	66	.294	.349	.532	.880	126	22	16	111	97	79	.859	8	5	-1	-6	*1D	0.4
1985	Chi-A	163	601	77	155	38	4	24	92	44	100	.258	.311	.454	.765	106	3	4	100	108	81	.698	5	2	0	-1	*1/D	-0.6
1986	Chi-A	78	282	37	78	10	6	13	51	29	44	.277	.348	.493	.841	126	10	10	101	121	48	.814	1	2	-1	-3	1/D	0.0
1987	Chi-A	157	566	85	145	33	2	27	94	75	112	.256	.348	.465	.813	105	12	5	109	116	93	.795	2	1	0	-11	*1/D	-2.0
1988	Chi-A	99	377	45	93	22	1	8	42	29	77	.247	.306	.374	.680	92	-6	-5	97	107	43	.592	0	1	-1	-10	1	-2.0
1989	Chi-A	77	233	25	49	14	0	5	26	23	50	.210	.290	.335	.624	81	-8	-6	93	109	22	.542	0	0	0	-3	1D	-1.1
Total	8	839	2825	366	740	164	19	113	442	265	509	.262	.329	.453	.783	109	43	32	103	112	421	.734	18	12	-2	-34	1/D	-4.9
■ **LARRY WALKER**	Walker, Larry Kenneth Robert b: 12/1/66, Maple River, B.C., Canada BL/TR, 6'2", 185 lbs. Deb: 8/16/89																											
1989	Mon-N	20	47	4	8	0	0	0	4	5	13	.170	.264	.170	.434	26	-4	-4	102	201	3	.375	1	1	-0	-0	O	-0.5
■ **TIM WALLACH**	Wallach, Timothy Charles b: 9/14/57, Huntington Park, Cal. BR/TR, 6'3", 220 lbs. Deb: 9/06/80																											
1980	Mon-N	5	11	1	2	0	0	1	2	1	5	.182	.250	.455	.705	93	-0	-0	99	99	1	.667	0	0	0	-1	/O1	0.0
1981	Mon-N	71	212	19	50	9	1	4	13	15	37	.236	.299	.344	.643	83	-5	-5	99	60	22	.554	0	1	-1	-4	O13	-1.2
1982	Mon-N	158	596	89	160	31	3	28	97	36	81	.268	.314	.471	.786	111	11	7	105	106	84	.719	6	4	-1	-8	*3/O1	-0.4
1983	Mon-N	156	581	54	156	33	3	19	70	55	97	.269	.338	.434	.772	111	9	8	102	91	85	.716	0	3	-2	-9	*3	-0.8
1984	Mon-N	160	582	55	143	25	4	18	72	50	101	.246	.313	.395	.708	107	-3	3	91	101	70	.633	3	7	-3	17	*3/S	1.7
1985	Mon-N	155	569	70	148	36	3	22	81	38	79	.260	.312	.450	.762	118	6	10	94	102	73	.689	9	9	-3	37	*3	4.6
1986	Mon-N	134	480	50	112	22	1	18	71	44	72	.233	.311	.396	.707	96	-5	-4	98	118	57	.649	8	4	0	13	*3	0.7
1987	Mon-N	153	593	89	177	**42**	4	26	123	37	98	.298	.347	.514	.861	117	19	14	106	136	105	.838	9	5	-0	-0	*3/P	1.2
1988	Mon-N	159	592	52	152	32	5	12	69	38	88	.257	.305	.389	.693	93	-3	-7	106	106	64	.587	2	6	-3	11	*3/2	0.1
1989	Mon-N	154	573	76	159	**42**	0	13	77	58	81	.277	.345	.419	.764	115	13	11	102	118	77	.683	3	7	-3	6	*3/P	1.4
Total	10	1305	4789	555	1259	272	24	161	675	372	739	.263	.322	.431	.753	108	41	39	100	107	637	.682	40	46	-16	61	*3/O1P2S	7.3
■ **DENNIS WALLING**	Walling, Dennis Martin b: 4/17/54, Neptune, N.J. BL/TR, 6', 180 lbs. Deb: 9/07/75																											
1975	Oak-A	6	8	0	1	1	0	0	2	0	4	.125	.125	.250	.375	4	-1	-1	93	384	0	.286	0	0	0	-1	/O	-0.1
1976	Oak-A	3	11	1	3	0	0	0	0	0	3	.273	.273	.273	.545	60	-1	-1	100	0	1	.375	0	0	0	0	/O	0.0
1977	Hou-N	6	21	1	6	0	1	0	6	2	4	.286	.348	.381	.729	103	-0	0	93	306	3	.625	0	1	-1	1	/O	0.0
1978	Hou-N	120	247	30	62	11	3	3	36	30	24	.251	.335	.356	.691	98	-2	-0	95	147	32	.677	9	2	2	-1	O	-0.2
1979	Hou-N	82	147	21	48	8	4	3	31	17	21	.327	.396	.497	.893	157	9	10	90	150	29	.903	3	2	-0	-4	O	0.5
1980	Hou-N	100	284	30	85	6	5	3	29	35	26	.299	.376	.387	.763	116	6	7	98	96	43	.730	4	3	-1	-4	1O	-0.1
1981	Hou-N	65	158	23	37	6	0	5	23	28	17	.234	.349	.367	.717	117	1	4	88	124	22	.704	2	1	0	-4	1O	-0.1
1982	Hou-N	85	146	22	30	4	1	1	14	23	19	.205	.314	.267	.581	65	-6	-6	99	131	12	.532	4	2	0	-4	O1	-1.1
1983	Hou-N	100	135	24	40	5	3	3	19	15	16	.296	.367	.444	.811	137	4	6	90	109	22	.786	2	2	-1	-4	13O	-0.1
1984	Hou-N	87	249	37	70	11	5	3	31	16	28	.281	.327	.402	.729	112	1	3	93	111	33	.674	7	1	2	2	31/O	0.5
1985	Hou-N	119	345	44	93	20	1	7	45	25	26	.270	.319	.394	.713	102	-1	0	96	114	42	.634	5	2	0	-5	31O	-0.6
1986	Hou-N	130	382	54	119	23	1	13	58	36	31	.312	.371	.479	.850	129	16	15	103	104	67	.809	1	1	-0	2	*3O/1	1.5
1987	Hou-N	110	325	45	92	21	4	5	33	39	37	.283	.360	.418	.778	114	3	6	93	87	50	.741	5	1	1	2	31/O	0.7
1988	Hou-N	65	176	19	43	10	2	1	20	15	18	.244	.304	.341	.645	91	-3	-2	93	127	19	.563	1	0	0	-1	3/1O	-0.2
	StL-N	19	58	3	13	3	0	0	1	2	7	.224	.250	.276	.526	49	-4	-4	104	25	4	.413	1	0	0	-2	O/31	-0.6
	Yr	84	234	22	56	13	2	1	21	17	25	.239	.291	.325	.616	80	-7	-6	96	105	23	.525	2	0	1	-3		-0.8
1989	StL-N	69	79	9	24	7	0	1	11	14	12	.304	.409	.430	.839	139	5	5	101	120	15	.857	0	0	0	-1	1/3O	0.2
Total	15	1166	2771	363	766	136	30	48	359	297	293	.276	.347	.399	.746	112	27	43	95	115	395	.699	44	18	2	-24	3O1	0.3
■ **JEROME WALTON**	Walton, Jerome O'Terrell b: 7/8/65, Newnan, Ga. BR/TR, 6'1", 175 lbs. Deb: 4/04/89																											
1989	Chi-N	116	475	64	139	23	3	5	46	27	77	.293	.339	.385	.724	98	4	-1	108	83	64	.688	24	7	3	-3	*O	-0.1
■ **GARY WARD**	Ward, Gary Lamell b: 12/6/53, Los Angeles, Cal. BR/TR, 6'2", 195 lbs. Deb: 9/03/79																											
1979	Min-A	10	14	2	4	0	0	0	1	3	3	.286	.412	.286	.697	85	0	-0	109	96	2	.636	0	1	-1	-1	/O	-0.1
1980	Min-A	13	41	11	19	6	2	1	10	3	6	.463	.500	.780	1.280	226	8	7	109	111	16	1.591	0	0	0	-3	O	0.4
1981	Min-A	85	295	42	78	7	6	3	29	28	48	.264	.328	.359	.687	93	-1	-2	105	101	34	.607	5	2	0	7	O/D	0.3
1982	Min-A	152	570	85	165	33	7	28	91	37	105	.289	.334	.519	.853	130	21	21	100	98	95	.822	13	1	3	11	*O/D	3.0
1983	Min-A	157	623	76	173	34	5	19	88	44	98	.278	.328	.440	.768	104	7	3	105	110	85	.693	8	1	2	**23**	*O/D	2.5
1984	Tex-A	155	602	97	171	21	7	21	79	55	95	.284	.344	.447	.791	117	13	13	100	101	87	.723	7	5	-1	-5	*O/D	0.3
1985	Tex-A	154	593	77	170	28	7	15	70	39	97	.287	.332	.433	.765	99	5	-1	108	97	82	.719	26	7	4	0	*O/D	0.1
1986	Tex-A	105	380	54	120	15	2	5	51	31	72	.316	.373	.405	.779	119	8	10	96	123	56	.723	12	8	-1	-2	*O/D	0.4
1987	NY-A	146	529	65	131	22	1	16	78	33	101	.248	.293	.384	.677	80	-17	-15	98	127	55	.587	9	1	2	-1	OD1	-1.7
1988	NY-A	91	231	26	52	8	0	4	24	24	41	.225	.304	.312	.615	76	-8	-7	96	114	21	.521	0	1	-1	1	O1/3D	-0.8
1989	NY-A	8	17	3	5	1	0	0	1	3	5	.294	.400	.353	.753	109	0	0	104	65	2	.692	0	0	0	-1	/OD	0.0
	Det-A	105	275	24	69	10	2	9	29	21	54	.251	.304	.400	.704	100	-2	-1	97	82	30	.603	1	3	-2	-1	O1D	-0.5
	Yr	113	292	27	74	11	2	9	30	24	59	.253	.310	.397	.707	100	-1	-1	98	82	33	.608	1	3	-2	-2		-0.5
Total	11	1181	4170	562	1157	185	39	121	551	321	725	.277	.331	.428	.758	106	35	28	101	106	564	.690	81	30	6	28	*O/D13	3.9
■ **CLAUDELL WASHINGTON**	Washington, Claudell b: 8/31/54, Los Angeles, Cal. BL/TL, 6', 190 lbs. Deb: 7/05/74																											
1974	Oak-A	73	221	16	63	10	5	0	19	13	44	.285	.328	.376	.703	101	0	0	100	90	24	.599	6	8	-3	-1	DO	-0.4
1975	Oak-A	148	590	86	182	24	7	10	77	32	80	.308	.349	.424	.773	126	12	17	93	112	85	.752	40	15	3	0	*O	1.7
1976	Oak-A	134	490	65	126	20	6	5	53	30	90	.257	.304	.353	.657	92	-6	-6	100	111	49	.612	37	20	-1	1	*O/D	-0.8
1977	Tex-A	129	521	63	148	31	2	12	68	25	112	.284	.321	.420	.741	96	-1	-4	105	112	68	.685	21	8	2	3	*O/D	-0.2
1978	Tex-A	12	42	1	7	0	0	0	2	1	12	.167	.186	.167	.353	-0	-6	-5	96	113	1	.216	0	1	-1	-1	/OD	-0.7
	Chi-A	86	314	33	83	16	5	6	31	12	57	.264	.294	.404	.698	94	-3	-4	101	86	34	.597	5	5	-2	-1	O/D	-0.8
	Yr	98	356	34	90	16	5	6	33	13	69	.253	.281	.376	.657	83	-9	-9	100	90	34	.546	5	6	-2	-3		-1.5
1979	Chi-A	131	471	79	132	33	5	13	66	28	93	.280	.325	.454	.779	105	4	2	102	102	65	.733	19	11	-1	1	*O	-0.1
1980	Chi-A	32	90	15	26	4	2	1	12	5	19	.289	.333	.411	.744	106	0	1	97	117	11	.662	4	2	0	-2	O/D	-0.1
	NY-N	79	284	38	78	16	4	10	42	20	63	.275	.325	.465	.789	123	6	7	96	105	42	.787	17	5	2	4	O	1.1
1981	Atl-N	85	320	37	93	22	3	5	37	15	47	.291	.330	.425	.755	114	4	5	100	102	44	.699	12	6	0	-4	O	-0.1
1982	Atl-N	150	563	94	150	24	6	16	80	50	107	.266	.333	.416	.748	101	6	1	107	118	80	.748	33	10	4	-9	*O	-0.6
1983	Atl-N	134	496	75	138	24	8	9	44	35	103	.278	.326	.413	.739	98	1	-2	106	77	67	.721	31	9	4	-3	*O	-0.3
1984	Atl-N	120	416	62	119	21	2	17	61	59	77	.286	.376	.469	.845	124	21	16	110	99	73	.871	21	9	1	-9	*O	0.4
1985	Atl-N	122	398	62	110	14	6	15	43	40	66	.276	.344	.455	.799	114	11	8	106	76	61	.779	14	4	2	-15	O	-0.8
1986	Atl-N	40	137	17	37	11	0	5	14	14	26	.270	.338	.460	.798	115	3	3	102	73	18	.730	4	7	-3	-6	O	-0.6
	NY-A	54	135	19	32	5	0	6	16	7	33	.237	.285	.407	.692	84	-3	-3	103	87	16	.654	6	1	1	-5	O	-0.7
1987	NY-A	102	312	42	87	17	0	9	44	27	54	.279	.336	.420	.756	102	0	1	98	111	46	.734	10	1	2	4	OD	0.5
1988	NY-A	126	455	62	140	22	3	11	64	24	74	.308	.345	.442	.787	124	10	13	96	109	68	.738	15	6	1	-2	*O	1.0

YEAR	TM/L	G	AB	R	H	2B	3B	HR	RBI	BB	SO	AVG	OBP	SLG	PRO	/A	BR	/A	PF	CHI	RC	TA	SB	CS	SBR	FR	POS	TPR
1989	Cal-A	110	418	53	114	18	4	13	42	27	84	.273	.320	.428	.748	111	4	5	99	79	57	.699	13	5	1	-4	*O/D	0.0
Total	16	1867	6673	919	1865	332	68	163	815	464	1241	.279	.330	.423	.753	107	63	53	101	100	909	.715	308	133	13	-47	*O/D	-1.5

■ **RON WASHINGTON** Washington, Ronald b: 4/29/52, New Orleans, La. BR/TR, 5'11", 155 lbs. Deb: 9/10/77

YEAR	TM/L	G	AB	R	H	2B	3B	HR	RBI	BB	SO	AVG	OBP	SLG	PRO	/A	BR	/A	PF	CHI	RC	TA	SB	CS	SBR	FR	POS	TPR
1977	LA-N	10	19	4	7	0	0	0	1	0	2	.368	.400	.368	.768	108	0	0	100	57	2	.643	1	1	-0	0	S	0.2
1981	Min-A	28	84	8	19	3	1	0	5	4	14	.226	.270	.286	.555	57	-4	-5	105	82	7	.493	4	1	1	-3	S/O	-0.5
1982	Min-A	119	451	48	122	17	6	5	39	14	79	.271	.292	.368	.661	80	-13	-13	100	88	45	.534	3	3	-1	-19	S2/3	-2.3
1983	Min-A	99	317	28	78	7	3	4	26	22	50	.246	.297	.325	.622	68	-12	-15	105	88	30	.542	10	5	0	-18	S2/3D	-2.7
1984	Min-A	88	197	25	58	11	5	3	23	4	31	.294	.312	.447	.759	102	1	-0	106	95	26	.653	1	1	-0	-8	S/23D	-0.1
1985	Min-A	70	135	24	37	6	4	1	14	8	15	.274	.315	.400	.715	91	-1	-2	103	97	17	.657	5	1	1	-3	S2/31D	0.0
1986	Min-A	48	74	15	19	3	0	4	11	3	21	.257	.286	.459	.745	92	-0	-1	108	95	9	.667	1	2	-1	0	2D/S3	0.0
1987	Bal-A	26	79	7	16	3	1	1	6	1	15	.203	.213	.304	.516	36	-7	-7	98	89	4	.379	0	1	-1	1	3/2OSD	-0.6
1988	Cle-A	69	223	30	57	14	2	2	21	9	35	.256	.300	.363	.663	83	-5	-5	102	96	24	.573	3	3	-1	-9	S/32D	-1.2
1989	Hou-N	7	7	1	1	1	0	0	0	0	4	.143	.143	.286	.429	19	-1	-1	102	0	0	.333	0	0	0	0	/23	0.0
Total	10	564	1586	190	414	65	22	20	146	65	266	.261	.294	.368	.662	79	-43	-48	103	90	165	.561	28	18	-2	-59	S2/3DO1	-7.2

■ **JIM WEAVER** Weaver, James Francis b: 10/10/59, Kingston, N.Y. BL/TL, 6'3", 190 lbs. Deb: 4/10/85

YEAR	TM/L	G	AB	R	H	2B	3B	HR	RBI	BB	SO	AVG	OBP	SLG	PRO	/A	BR	/A	PF	CHI	RC	TA	SB	CS	SBR	FR	POS	TPR
1985	Det-A	12	7	2	1	1	0	0	0	1	4	.143	.250	.286	.536	44	-1	-1	106	0	0	.429	0	1	-1	-2	/OD	-0.2
1987	Sea-A	7	4	2	0	0	0	0	0	2	3	.000	.333	.000	.333	0	-0	-1	103	0	0	.600	1	1	-0	0	/O	0.0
1989	SF-N	12	20	2	4	3	0	0	2	0	7	.200	.200	.350	.550	56	-1	-1	97	115	2	.500	1	0	0	-2	/O	-0.2
Total	3	31	31	6	5	4	0	0	2	3	14	.161	.235	.290	.526	46	-2	-2	100	68	2	.500	2	2	-1	-4	/OD	-0.4

■ **LENNY WEBSTER** Webster, Leonard Irell b: 2/10/65, New Orleans, La. BR/TR, 5'9", 185 lbs. Deb: 9/01/89

YEAR	TM/L	G	AB	R	H	2B	3B	HR	RBI	BB	SO	AVG	OBP	SLG	PRO	/A	BR	/A	PF	CHI	RC	TA	SB	CS	SBR	FR	POS	TPR
1989	Min-A	14	20	3	6	2	0	0	1	3	2	.300	.391	.400	.791	116	1	1	107	49	3	.786	0	0	0	-1	C	0.0

■ **MITCH WEBSTER** Webster, Mitchell Dean b: 5/16/59, Larned, Kan. BB/TL, 6', 185 lbs. Deb: 9/02/83

YEAR	TM/L	G	AB	R	H	2B	3B	HR	RBI	BB	SO	AVG	OBP	SLG	PRO	/A	BR	/A	PF	CHI	RC	TA	SB	CS	SBR	FR	POS	TPR
1983	Tor-A	11	11	2	2	0	0	0	0	1	1	.182	.250	.182	.432	19	-1	-1	108	0	1	.333	0	0	0	-2	/OD	-0.3
1984	Tor-A	26	22	9	5	2	1	0	4	1	7	.227	.261	.409	.670	81	-1	-1	102	177	2	.556	0	0	0	-2	O/1D	-0.2
1985	Tor-A	4	1	0	0	0	0	0	0	0	0	.000	.000	.000	.000	-99	-0	-0	101	0	0	.000	0	1	-1	-1	/OD	-0.1
	Mon-N	74	212	32	58	8	2	11	30	20	33	.274	.336	.486	.822	136	7	9	94	88	33	.831	15	9	-1	2	O	0.9
1986	Mon-N	151	576	89	167	31	**13**	8	49	57	78	.290	.358	.431	.788	119	13	15	98	76	90	.797	36	15	2	5	*O	1.9
1987	Mon-N	156	588	101	165	30	8	15	63	70	95	.281	.363	.435	.798	104	10	5	106	89	99	.831	33	10	4	-3	*O	0.0
1988	Chi-N	70	264	36	70	11	6	4	26	19	50	.265	.322	.398	.719	101	2	0	104	94	35	.685	10	4	1	-1	O	-0.1
	Mon-N	81	259	33	66	5	2	2	13	36	37	.255	.357	.313	.669	89	-0	-2	106	61	31	.650	12	10	-2	2	O	-0.4
	Yr	151	523	69	136	16	8	6	39	55	87	.260	.340	.356	.695	95	1	-2	105	77	66	.667	22	14	-2	1		-0.5
1989	Chi-N	98	272	40	70	12	4	3	19	30	55	.257	.333	.364	.697	92	0	-3	108	71	36	.696	14	2	3	2	O	0.2
Total	7	671	2205	342	603	99	36	43	204	234	356	.273	.348	.410	.758	106	29	21	103	81	327	.760	120	51	5	2	O/D1	1.9

■ **WALT WEISS** Weiss, Walter William b: 11/28/63, Tuxedo, N.Y. BB/TR, 6', 175 lbs. Deb: 7/12/87

YEAR	TM/L	G	AB	R	H	2B	3B	HR	RBI	BB	SO	AVG	OBP	SLG	PRO	/A	BR	/A	PF	CHI	RC	TA	SB	CS	SBR	FR	POS	TPR
1987	Oak-A	16	26	3	12	4	0	0	1	2	2	.462	.500	.615	1.115	214	4	4	91	25	7	1.188	1	2	-1	0	S/D	0.3
1988	Oak-A	147	452	44	113	17	3	3	39	35	56	.250	.317	.321	.637	83	-12	-9	95	101	47	.548	4	4	-1	8	*S	0.4
1989	Oak-A	84	236	30	55	11	0	3	21	21	39	.233	.298	.318	.616	71	-8	-9	103	97	23	.551	6	1	1	-3	S	-0.3
Total	3	247	714	77	180	32	3	6	61	58	97	.252	.317	.331	.648	84	-17	-14	98	97	77	.568	11	7	-1	5	S/D	0.4

■ **BRAD WELLMAN** Wellman, Brad Eugene b: 8/17/59, Lodi, Cal. BR/TR, 6', 170 lbs. Deb: 9/04/82

YEAR	TM/L	G	AB	R	H	2B	3B	HR	RBI	BB	SO	AVG	OBP	SLG	PRO	/A	BR	/A	PF	CHI	RC	TA	SB	CS	SBR	FR	POS	TPR
1982	SF-N	6	4	1	1	0	0	0	0	0	1	.250	.250	.250	.500	43	-0	-0	94	0	0	.333	0	0	0	0	/2	0.0
1983	SF-N	82	182	15	39	3	0	1	16	22	39	.214	.299	.247	.546	52	-11	-11	101	132	14	.477	5	3	-0	-8	2/S	-1.7
1984	SF-N	93	265	23	60	9	1	2	25	19	41	.226	.278	.291	.569	62	-14	-13	96	118	21	.486	10	5	0	3	2S/3	-0.4
1985	SF-N	71	174	16	41	11	1	0	16	4	33	.236	.269	.310	.580	66	-9	-8	93	118	14	.486	5	2	0	0	23/S	-0.6
1986	SF-N	12	13	0	2	0	0	0	1	1	2	.154	.214	.154	.368	3	-2	-2	96	199	0	.273	0	0	0	0	/S23	0.0
1987	LA-N	3	4	1	1	0	0	0	1	0	1	.250	.250	.250	.500	36	-0	-0	92	399	0	.333	0	0	0	0	/2S3	0.0
1988	KC-A	71	107	11	29	3	0	1	6	6	23	.271	.322	.327	.649	80	-2	-3	103	63	11	.543	1	2	-1	3	2S/3D	0.3
1989	KC-A	103	178	30	41	4	0	2	12	7	36	.230	.263	.287	.550	57	-11	-10	96	82	12	.435	5	3	-0	3	2S/3D	-0.3
Total	8	441	927	97	214	30	2	6	77	59	176	.231	.282	.287	.569	61	-50	-47	97	109	73	.476	26	15	-1	1	2/S3D	-2.7

■ **JEFF WETHERBY** Wetherby, Jeffrey Barrett b: 10/18/63, Granada Hills, Cal. BL/TL, 6'2", 195 lbs. Deb: 6/07/89

YEAR	TM/L	G	AB	R	H	2B	3B	HR	RBI	BB	SO	AVG	OBP	SLG	PRO	/A	BR	/A	PF	CHI	RC	TA	SB	CS	SBR	FR	POS	TPR
1989	Atl-N	52	48	5	10	2	1	1	7	4	6	.208	.269	.354	.623	75	-2	-2	102	141	4	.550	1	0	0	-2	/O	-0.3

■ **LOU WHITAKER** Whitaker, Louis Rodman b: 5/12/57, Brooklyn, N.Y. BL/TR, 5'11", 160 lbs. Deb: 9/09/77

YEAR	TM/L	G	AB	R	H	2B	3B	HR	RBI	BB	SO	AVG	OBP	SLG	PRO	/A	BR	/A	PF	CHI	RC	TA	SB	CS	SBR	FR	POS	TPR
1977	Det-A	11	32	5	8	1	0	0	2	4	6	.250	.333	.281	.615	66	-1	-1	105	88	3	.577	2	2	-1	0	/2	0.0
1978	Det-A	139	484	71	138	12	7	3	58	61	65	.285	.366	.357	.724	97	5	-0	108	128	66	.669	7	7	-2	22	*2/D	2.7
1979	Det-A	127	423	75	121	14	8	3	42	78	66	.286	.398	.378	.777	115	10	12	96	101	69	.804	20	10	0	9	*2	2.6
1980	Det-A	145	477	68	111	19	1	1	45	73	79	.233	.335	.283	.618	67	-16	-20	105	127	50	.570	8	4	0	-1	*2	-1.2
1981	Det-A	109	335	48	88	14	4	5	36	40	42	.263	.343	.373	.716	101	3	1	105	101	45	.671	5	3	-0	5	*2	1.0
1982	Det-A	152	560	76	160	22	8	15	65	48	58	.286	.343	.434	.777	111	9	8	100	92	85	.737	11	3	2	15	*2/D	3.2
1983	Det-A	161	643	94	206	40	6	12	72	67	70	.320	.385	.457	.842	137	28	32	96	82	114	.829	17	10	-1	-7	*2	2.9
1984	Det-A	143	558	90	161	25	1	13	56	62	63	.289	.360	.407	.766	116	10	13	96	89	83	.718	6	5	-1	-1	*2	1.8
1985	Det-A	152	609	102	170	29	8	21	73	80	56	.279	.365	.456	.821	116	20	15	106	75	107	.821	6	4	-1	-7	*2	1.3
1986	Det-A	144	584	95	157	26	6	20	73	63	70	.269	.340	.437	.777	116	9	12	95	89	82	.727	13	8	-1	1	*2	1.9
1987	Det-A	149	604	110	160	38	6	16	59	71	108	.265	.343	.427	.770	107	4	6	97	74	93	.756	13	5	1	-4	*2	1.3
1988	Det-A	115	403	54	111	18	2	12	55	66	61	.275	.377	.419	.797	130	14	17	94	113	67	.790	2	0	1	-8	*2	1.7
1989	Det-A	148	509	77	128	21	1	28	85	89	59	.251	.366	.462	.828	136	23	25	97	110	91	.852	6	3	0	6	*2/D	3.3
Total	13	1695	6221	965	1719	279	58	149	721	802	803	.276	.360	.412	.772	112	117	121	100	97	956	.747	116	64	-4	31	*2/D	22.5

■ **DEVON WHITE** White, Devon Markes b: 12/29/62, Kingston, Jamaica BB/TR, 6'1", 170 lbs. Deb: 9/02/85

YEAR	TM/L	G	AB	R	H	2B	3B	HR	RBI	BB	SO	AVG	OBP	SLG	PRO	/A	BR	/A	PF	CHI	RC	TA	SB	CS	SBR	FR	POS	TPR
1985	Cal-A	21	7	7	1	0	0	0	0	1	3	.143	.333	.143	.476	36	-1	-1	101	0	1	.857	3	1	0	-5	O	-0.4
1986	Cal-A	29	51	8	12	1	1	1	3	6	8	.235	.316	.353	.669	86	-1	-1	96	57	7	.769	6	0	2	-3	O	-0.2
1987	Cal-A	159	639	103	168	33	5	24	87	39	135	.263	.307	.443	.750	97	-4	-4	99	104	87	.727	32	11	3	12	*O	0.6
1988	Cal-A	122	455	76	118	22	2	11	51	23	84	.259	.298	.389	.687	96	-7	-3	94	98	52	.626	17	8	0	10	*O	0.5
1989	Cal-A	156	636	86	156	18	13	12	56	31	129	.245	.283	.371	.654	84	-16	-15	99	77	64	.616	44	16	4	10	*O/D	-0.3
Total	5	487	1788	280	455	74	21	48	197	100	359	.254	.297	.400	.696	92	-29	-24	98	91	211	.663	102	36	9	24	O/D	0.2

■ **FRANK WHITE** White, Frank b: 9/4/50, Greenville, Miss. BR/TR, 5'11", 165 lbs. Deb: 6/12/73

YEAR	TM/L	G	AB	R	H	2B	3B	HR	RBI	BB	SO	AVG	OBP	SLG	PRO	/A	BR	/A	PF	CHI	RC	TA	SB	CS	SBR	FR	POS	TPR
1973	KC-A	51	139	20	31	6	1	0	5	8	23	.223	.265	.281	.546	49	-9	-10	109	50	11	.455	3	1	0	8	S2	0.4
1974	KC-A	99	204	19	45	6	3	1	18	5	33	.221	.239	.294	.533	50	-13	-14	106	112	13	.407	3	4	-2	-1	2S3/D	-1.2
1975	KC-A	111	304	43	76	10	2	7	36	20	39	.250	.298	.365	.664	85	-6	-7	102	105	34	.609	11	3	2	-1	2S/3CD	0.0
1976	KC-A	152	446	39	102	17	6	2	46	19	42	.229	.265	.307	.572	67	-19	-19	100	124	37	.499	20	11	-1	4	*2S	-0.6
1977	KC-A	152	474	59	116	21	5	5	50	25	67	.245	.285	.342	.627	70	-20	-20	100	112	49	.578	23	5	4	-2	*2/S	-0.5
1978	KC-A	143	461	66	127	24	6	7	50	26	59	.275	.318	.399	.717	98	-1	-2	102	96	59	.653	13	10	-2	-16	*2	-1.2
1979	KC-A	127	467	73	124	26	4	10	48	25	54	.266	.304	.403	.707	84	-8	-12	105	86	56	.669	28	8	4	-10	*2	-1.2
1980	KC-A	154	560	70	148	23	4	7	60	19	69	.264	.291	.357	.648	78	-19	-18	98	106	57	.559	19	6	2	-5	*2	-1.2
1981	KC-A	94	364	35	91	17	1	9	38	19	50	.250	.287	.376	.664	91	-6	-5	99	96	37	.561	4	2	0	-15	2	-1.8
1982	KC-A	145	524	71	156	45	6	11	56	16	65	.298	.321	.469	.790	114	8	8	100	82	73	.708	10	7	-1	-11	*2	0.3
1983	KC-A	146	549	52	143	35	6	11	77	20	51	.260	.286	.406	.693	87	-10	-11	101	120	58	.597	13	5	1	14	*2	0.8
1984	KC-A	129	479	58	130	22	5	17	56	27	72	.271	.313	.445	.758	108	3	4	99	86	63	.677	5	5	-2	16	*2	2.4
1985	KC-A	149	563	62	140	25	1	22	69	28	86	.249	.285	.414	.699	87	-10	-12	102	93	65	.625	10	4	1	15	*2	1.0
1986	KC-A	151	566	76	154	37	3	22	84	43	88	.272	.326	.465	.790	113	9	9	100	108	84	.732	4	4	-1	8	*2/S3	2.3
1987	KC-A	154	563	67	138	32	2	17	78	51	86	.245	.310	.400	.710	84	-11	-14	104	115	67	.628	1	3	-2	13	*2/D	0.8
1988	KC-A	150	537	48	126	25	1	8	58	21	67	.235	.269	.330	.598	65	-25	-27	103	117	44	.486	7	3	0	17	*2/D	0.0

YEAR	TM/L	G	AB	R	H	2B	3B	HR	RBI	BB	SO	AVG	OBP	SLG	PRO	/A	BR	/A	PF	CHI	RC	TA	SB	CS	SBR	FR	POS	TPR
1989	KC-A	135	418	34	107	22	1	2	36	30	52	.256	.309	.328	.637	83	-11	-9	96	98	43	.538	3	2	-0	18	*2/O	1.1
Total	17	2242	7618	892	1954	393	57	158	865	402	1003	.256	.296	.385	.681	86	-148	-159	101	103	848	.601	177	83	3	52	*2S/3DOC	1.4
■ **ED WHITED**	Whited, Edward Morris b: 2/9/64, Bristol, Pa. BR/TR, 6'3", 195 lbs. Deb: 7/05/89																											
1989	Atl-N	36	74	5	12	3	0	1	4	6	15	.162	.225	.243	.468	33	-6	-7	102	77	4	.391	1	0	0	-1	3/1	-0.8
■ **ERNIE WHITT**	Whitt, Leo Ernest b: 6/13/52, Detroit, Mich. BL/TR, 6'2", 200 lbs. Deb: 9/12/76																											
1976	Bos-A	8	18	4	4	2	0	1	3	2	2	.222	.300	.500	.800	119	1	0	110	96	3	.786	0	0	0	1	/C	0.1
1977	Tor-A	23	41	4	7	3	0	0	6	2	12	.171	.209	.244	.453	22	-4	-5	103	238	2	.343	0	0	0	1	C	-0.2
1978	Tor-A	2	4	0	0	0	0	0	0	1	1	.000	.200	.000	.200	-39	-1	-1	100	0	0	.250	0	0	0	0	/C	0.0
1980	Tor-A	106	295	23	70	12	2	6	34	22	30	.237	.290	.353	.643	75	-10	-10	100	109	27	.531	1	3	-2	0	*C	-0.6
1981	Tor-A	74	195	16	46	9	0	1	16	20	30	.236	.307	.297	.604	67	-6	-9	111	103	19	.542	5	2	0	6	C	0.0
1982	Tor-A	105	284	28	74	14	2	11	42	26	34	.261	.323	.440	.763	99	2	-1	109	106	40	.713	3	1	0	-9	C/D	-0.4
1983	Tor-A	123	344	53	88	15	2	17	56	50	55	.256	.350	.459	.810	111	10	6	108	105	55	.786	1	1	-0	-11	*C	0.0
1984	Tor-A	124	315	35	75	12	1	15	46	43	49	.238	.331	.425	.757	106	3	3	102	102	44	.712	0	3	-2	-18	*C	-0.9
1985	Tor-A	139	412	55	101	21	2	19	64	47	59	.245	.324	.444	.768	107	4	3	101	106	58	.722	3	6	-3	-8	*C	-0.1
1986	Tor-A	131	395	48	106	19	2	16	56	35	39	.268	.328	.448	.776	104	5	2	105	99	56	.704	0	1	-1	-25	*C	-1.5
1987	Tor-A	135	446	57	120	24	1	19	75	44	50	.269	.336	.455	.791	107	5	4	101	115	64	.721	0	1	-1	-2	*C	1.1
1988	Tor-A	127	398	63	100	11	2	16	70	61	38	.251	.352	.410	.762	113	8	8	100	132	59	.741	4	2	0	-2	*C	1.1
1989	Tor-A	129	385	42	101	24	1	11	53	52	53	.262	.350	.416	.766	122	8	11	94	107	56	.731	5	4	-1	-10	*C/D	0.5
Total	13	1226	3532	428	892	166	15	132	521	405	452	.253	.330	.420	.750	103	24	13	102	110	484	.696	22	24	-8	-78	*C/D	-0.9
■ **CURTIS WILKERSON**	Wilkerson, Curtis Vernon b: 4/26/61, Petersburgh, Va. BB/TR, 5'9", 158 lbs. Deb: 9/10/83																											
1983	Tex-A	16	35	7	6	0	1	0	1	2	5	.171	.216	.229	.445	22	-4	-4	101	49	2	.448	3	0	1	-0	/S23	-0.2
1984	Tex-A	153	484	47	120	12	0	1	26	22	72	.248	.283	.279	.562	56	-28	-28	100	75	38	.449	12	10	-2	-14	*S2	-3.3
1985	Tex-A	129	360	35	88	11	6	0	22	22	63	.244	.295	.308	.604	61	-17	-21	108	79	33	.528	14	7	0	-6	*S2/D	-1.7
1986	Tex-A	110	236	27	56	10	3	0	15	11	42	.237	.274	.305	.579	61	-14	-12	96	83	19	.492	9	7	-2	-2	2S/D	-0.9
1987	Tex-A	85	138	28	37	5	3	2	14	6	16	.268	.308	.391	.700	82	-3	-4	104	93	16	.642	6	3	0	1	S23/D	0.0
1988	Tex-A	117	338	41	99	12	5	0	28	26	43	.293	.347	.358	.705	97	-0	-1	101	92	42	.632	9	4	0	-7	2S/3D	-0.1
1989	Chi-N	77	160	18	39	4	2	1	10	8	33	.244	.280	.313	.592	64	-7	-8	108	76	14	.492	4	2	0	-4	32/SO	-1.1
Total	7	687	1751	203	445	54	20	4	116	97	274	.254	.297	.315	.612	68	-72	-78	102	81	164	.524	57	33	-3	-32	S2/3DO	-7.3
■ **DANA WILLIAMS**	Williams, Dana Lamont b: 3/20/63, Weirton, W.Va. BR/TR, 5'10", 170 lbs. Deb: 6/21/89																											
1989	Bos-A	8	5	1	1	1	0	0	0	0	1	.200	.333	.400	.733	101	0	0	105	0	1	.750	0	0	0	0	/OD	0.0
■ **EDDIE WILLIAMS**	Williams, Edward Laquan b: 11/1/64, Shreveport, La. BR/TR, 6', 175 lbs. Deb: 4/18/86																											
1986	Cle-A	5	7	2	1	0	0	0	1	0	3	.143	.143	.143	.286	-22	-1	-1	98	398	0	.167	0	0	0	-2	/O	-0.2
1987	Cle-A	22	64	9	11	4	0	1	4	9	19	.172	.284	.281	.565	50	-4	-5	103	76	5	.509	0	0	0	-1	3	-0.5
1988	Cle-A	10	21	3	4	0	0	0	1	0	3	.190	.227	.190	.418	18	-2	-2	102	99	1	.278	0	0	0	0	3	-0.1
1989	Chi-A	66	201	25	55	8	0	3	10	18	31	.274	.345	.358	.704	106	0	2	93	48	25	.625	1	2	-1	-1	3	0.0
Total	4	103	293	39	71	12	0	4	16	27	56	.242	.319	.324	.643	83	-8	-6	96	65	31	.558	1	2	-1	-4	/3O	-0.8
■ **KEN WILLIAMS**	Williams, Kenneth Royal b: 4/6/64, Berkeley, Cal. BR/TR, 6'2", 187 lbs. Deb: 9/02/86																											
1986	Chi-A	15	31	2	4	0	0	1	1	1	11	.129	.182	.226	.408	11	-4	-4	101	40	1	.345	1	1	-0	0	O/D	-0.3
1987	Chi-A	116	391	48	110	18	2	11	50	10	83	.281	.315	.422	.737	87	-4	-8	109	101	50	.693	21	10	0	0	*O	-1.0
1988	Chi-A	73	220	18	35	4	2	8	28	10	64	.159	.223	.305	.527	47	-16	-16	97	122	15	.474	6	5	-1	-0	O3/D	-1.7
1989	Det-A	94	258	29	53	5	1	6	23	18	63	.205	.270	.302	.573	63	-13	-13	97	93	21	.512	9	4	0	6	O/1D	-0.7
Total	4	298	900	97	202	27	5	26	102	39	221	.224	.274	.352	.627	69	-38	-41	102	102	87	.568	37	20	-1	6	O/3D1	-3.7
■ **MATT WILLIAMS**	Williams, Matthew Derrick b: 11/28/65, Bishop, Cal. BR/TR, 6'2", 205 lbs. Deb: 4/11/87																											
1987	SF-N	84	245	28	46	9	2	8	21	16	68	.188	.240	.339	.579	53	-18	-17	96	78	19	.502	4	3	-1	12	S3	0.2
1988	SF-N	52	156	17	32	6	1	8	19	8	41	.205	.253	.410	.663	93	-3	-2	94	86	14	.561	0	1	-1	5	3/S	0.2
1989	SF-N	84	292	31	59	18	1	18	50	14	72	.202	.244	.455	.699	99	-4	-3	97	108	30	.625	1	2	-1	-0	3S	-0.2
Total	3	220	693	76	137	33	4	34	90	38	181	.198	.245	.404	.649	80	-25	-22	96	92	63	.566	5	6	-2	16	3S	0.2
■ **CRAIG WILSON**	Wilson, Craig b: 11/28/64, Annapolis, Md. BR/TR, 5'11", 175 lbs. Deb: 9/06/89																											
1989	StL-N	6	4	1	1	0	0	0	1	1	2	.250	.400	.250	.650	89	0	0	101	403	1	.667	0	0	0	0	/3	0.0
■ **GLENN WILSON**	Wilson, Glenn Dwight b: 12/22/58, Baytown, Tex. BR/TR, 6'1", 190 lbs. Deb: 4/15/82																											
1982	Det-A	84	322	39	94	15	1	12	34	15	51	.292	.323	.457	.780	111	4	4	100	76	44	.686	2	3	-1	3	O/D	0.3
1983	Det-A	144	503	55	135	25	6	11	65	25	79	.268	.307	.408	.715	99	-5	-2	96	107	61	.619	1	1	-0	-11	*O	-1.4
1984	Phi-N	132	341	28	82	21	3	6	31	17	56	.240	.279	.372	.651	80	-9	-10	102	84	33	.559	7	1	2	-13	*O/3	-2.6
1985	Phi-N	161	608	73	167	39	5	14	102	35	117	.275	.314	.424	.738	103	2	0	102	138	73	.640	7	4	-0	16	*O	1.3
1986	Phi-N	155	584	70	158	30	4	15	84	42	91	.271	.324	.413	.736	98	0	-3	104	119	76	.661	5	1	1	18	*O	1.3
1987	Phi-N	154	569	55	150	21	2	14	54	38	82	.264	.311	.381	.692	79	-15	-18	104	85	62	.585	3	6	-3	12	*O/P	-1.4
1988	Sea-A	78	284	28	71	10	1	3	17	15	52	.250	.288	.324	.612	66	-11	-14	108	68	23	.476	1	1	-0	-1	O/D	-1.6
	Pit-N	37	126	11	34	8	0	2	15	3	18	.270	.292	.381	.673	94	-2	-1	98	111	13	.542	0	0	0	-1	O	-0.3
1989	Pit-N	100	330	42	93	20	4	9	49	32	39	.282	.347	.448	.796	134	11	13	94	113	49	.731	1	4	-2	-2	O1	0.7
	Hou-N	28	102	8	22	6	0	2	15	5	14	.216	.252	.333	.586	65	-5	-5	102	154	8	.464	0	1	-1	4	O	-0.1
	Yr	128	432	50	115	26	4	11	64	37	53	.266	.326	.421	.747	117	6	8	96	123	56	.664	1	5	-3	2		0.6
Total	8	1073	3769	409	1006	195	26	88	466	227	599	.267	.310	.402	.713	95	-30	-36	101	105	443	.615	27	22	-5	24	*O/1D3P	-3.8
■ **JIM WILSON**	Wilson, James George b: 12/29/60, Corvallis, Ore. BR/TR, 6'3", 230 lbs. Deb: 9/13/85																											
1985	Cle-A	4	14	2	5	0	0	0	4	1	3	.357	.400	.357	.757	116	0	0	94	317	2	.667	0	0	0	0	/1D	0.0
1989	Sea-A	5	8	0	0	0	0	0	0	0	3	.000	.000	.000	.000	-97	-2	-2	103	0	0	.000	0	0	0	0	/D	-0.1
Total	2	9	22	2	5	0	0	0	4	1	6	.227	.261	.227	.488	37	-2	-2	97	207	2	.353	0	0	0	0	/D1	-0.1
■ **MOOKIE WILSON**	Wilson, William Hayward b: 2/9/56, Bamberg, S.C. BB/TR, 5'10", 170 lbs. Deb: 9/02/80																											
1980	NY-N	27	105	16	26	5	3	0	4	12	19	.248	.325	.352	.677	93	-1	-1	96	41	12	.651	7	7	-2	4	O	0.0
1981	NY-N	92	328	49	89	8	8	3	14	20	59	.271	.317	.372	.689	94	-3	-3	101	43	38	.661	24	12	0	2	O	-0.3
1982	NY-N	159	639	90	178	25	9	5	55	32	102	.279	.315	.369	.684	92	-9	-8	99	91	78	.680	58	16	8	9	*O	0.8
1983	NY-N	152	638	91	176	25	6	7	51	18	103	.276	.300	.367	.667	85	-15	-14	99	70	71	.640	54	16	7	4	*O	-0.6
1984	NY-N	154	587	88	162	28	10	10	54	26	90	.276	.309	.409	.718	100	-2	-2	100	80	78	.715	46	9	8	11	*O	1.2
1985	NY-N	93	337	56	93	16	8	6	26	28	52	.276	.332	.424	.756	113	4	5	97	66	46	.744	24	9	2	-1	O	0.4
1986	NY-N	123	381	61	110	17	5	9	45	32	72	.289	.345	.430	.776	118	6	8	96	94	58	.784	25	7	3	4	*O	1.4
1987	NY-N	124	385	58	115	19	7	9	34	35	85	.299	.360	.455	.815	116	8	8	99	67	66	.838	21	6	3	0	*O	0.7
1988	NY-N	112	378	61	112	17	5	8	41	27	63	.296	.346	.431	.778	135	10	14	90	88	55	.734	15	4	2	1	*O	1.6
1989	NY-N	80	249	22	51	10	1	3	18	10	47	.205	.238	.289	.528	52	-16	-15	97	89	17	.446	7	4	-0	3	O	-1.4
	Tor-A	54	238	32	71	9	1	2	17	3	37	.298	.313	.370	.683	97	-3	-1	94	62	28	.607	12	1	3	-1	O	0.0
Total	10	1170	4265	624	1183	179	63	62	359	243	729	.277	.319	.392	.712	100	-22	-9	97	75	546	.691	293	91	33	37	*O	3.8
■ **WILLIE WILSON**	Wilson, Willie James b: 7/9/55, Montgomery, Ala. BB/TR, 6'3", 190 lbs. Deb: 9/04/76																											
1976	KC-A	12	6	0	1	0	0	0	0	0	2	.167	.167	.167	.333	-2	-1	-1	100	0	0	.500	2	1	0	-1	/O	-0.1
1977	KC-A	13	34	10	11	2	0	0	1	1	8	.324	.343	.382	.725	97	-0	-0	100	30	4	.741	6	3	0	1	/OD	0.0
1978	KC-A	127	198	43	43	8	2	0	16	16	33	.217	.282	.278	.560	57	-11	-11	102	115	18	.704	46	12	7	-13	*O/D	-2.0
1979	KC-A	154	588	113	185	18	13	6	49	28	92	.315	.353	.420	.773	102	6	2	105	73	99	.877	**83**	12	**18**	14	*O	2.7
1980	KC-A	161	705	**133**	**230**	28	**15**	3	49	28	81	.326	.357	.421	.779	114	11	13	98	55	117	.838	79	10	**18**	5	*O	3.2
1981	KC-A	102	439	54	133	10	7	1	32	18	42	.303	.336	.364	.701	103	1	1	99	68	56	.677	34	8	5	22	*O	2.8
1982	KC-A	136	585	87	194	19	**15**	3	46	26	81	**.332**	.366	.431	.797	118	14	14	100	62	96	.791	37	11	5	-2	*O	1.3
1983	KC-A	137	576	90	159	22	8	2	33	33	75	.276	.316	.352	.669	83	-13	-14	101	55	72	.690	59	8	13	-10	*O	-1.2

YEAR	TM/L	G	AB	R	H	2B	3B	HR	RBI	BB	SO	AVG	OBP	SLG	PRO	/A	BR	/A	PF	CHI	RC	TA	SB	CS	SBR	FR	POS	TPR
1984	KC-A	128	541	81	163	24	9	2	44	39	56	.301	.352	.390	.742	106	4	5	99	70	82	.769	47	5	**11**	2	*O	1.4
1985	KC-A	141	605	87	168	25	**21**	4	43	29	94	.278	.316	.408	.724	95	-4	-5	102	57	80	.714	43	11	6	-4	*O	-0.4
1986	KC-A	156	631	77	170	20	7	9	44	31	97	.269	.313	.366	.679	85	-13	-13	100	65	76	.642	34	8	5	-3	*O	-1.5
1987	KC-A	146	610	97	170	18	**15**	4	30	32	88	.279	.321	.377	.698	82	-13	-16	104	44	78	.711	59	11	**11**	-4	*O/D	-1.2
1988	KC-A	147	591	81	155	17	**11**	1	37	22	106	.262	.291	.333	.624	72	-21	-23	103	78	61	.571	35	7	6	-6	*O	-2.4
1989	KC-A	112	383	58	97	17	7	3	43	27	78	.253	.304	.358	.662	90	-8	-6	96	117	43	.630	24	6	4	-7	*O/D	-1.0
Total	14	1672	6492	1011	1879	228	130	38	467	330	933	.289	.329	.382	.711	94	-46	-55	101	67	882	.721	588	113	109	-5	*O/D	1.6
■ **HERM WINNINGHAM**	Winningham, Herman Son b: 12/1/61, Orangeburg, S.C. BL/TR, 6'1", 170 lbs. Deb: 9/01/84																											
1984	NY-N	14	27	5	11	1	1	0	5	1	7	.407	.429	.519	.947	165	2	2	100	140	6	1.000	2	1	0	-3	O	0.0
1985	Mon-N	125	312	30	74	6	5	3	21	28	72	.237	.300	.317	.617	78	-11	-9	94	77	32	.593	20	9	1	-10	*O	-2.2
1986	Mon-N	90	185	23	40	6	3	4	11	18	51	.216	.286	.346	.632	75	-7	-6	98	58	17	.603	12	7	-1	-5	O/S	-1.3
1987	Mon-N	137	347	34	83	20	3	4	41	34	68	.239	.307	.349	.656	69	-13	-16	106	123	37	.648	29	10	3	-5	*O	-2.3
1988	Mon-N	47	90	10	21	2	1	0	6	12	18	.233	.324	.278	.601	70	-3	-3	106	96	8	.539	4	5	-2	-2	O	-0.7
	Cin-N	53	113	6	26	1	3	0	15	5	27	.230	.263	.292	.555	56	-6	-7	105	182	9	.511	8	3	1	-2	O	-1.0
	Yr	100	203	16	47	3	4	0	21	17	45	.232	.291	.286	.577	63	-9	-10	105	142	17	.524	12	8	-1	-4		-1.7
1989	Cin-N	115	251	40	63	11	3	3	13	24	50	.251	.316	.355	.671	89	-3	-4	103	53	29	.641	14	5	1	-4	O	-0.8
Total	6	581	1325	148	318	47	19	14	112	122	293	.240	.304	.336	.640	76	-41	-43	101	93	137	.614	89	40	3	-30	O/S	-8.3
■ **MATT WINTERS**	Winters, Matthew Littleton b: 3/18/60, Buffalo, N.Y. BL/TR, 6'3", 215 lbs. Deb: 5/30/89																											
1989	KC-A	42	107	14	25	6	0	2	9	14	23	.234	.322	.346	.668	92	-1	-1	96	81	12	.600	0	0	0	-5	O/D	-0.5
■ **TRACY WOODSON**	Woodson, Tracy Michael b: 10/5/62, Richmond, Va. BR/TR, 6'3", 215 lbs. Deb: 4/07/87																											
1987	LA-N	53	136	14	31	8	1	1	11	9	21	.228	.286	.324	.609	67	-8	-6	92	93	12	.519	1	1	-0	3	3/1	-0.3
1988	LA-N	64	173	15	43	4	1	3	15	7	32	.249	.282	.335	.617	72	-6	-7	106	90	15	.493	1	2	-1	-2	31	-1.1
1989	LA-N	4	6	0	0	0	0	0	0	0	1	.000	.000	.000	.000	-99	-2	-1	93	0	0	.000	0	0	0	0	/3	-0.1
Total	3	121	315	29	74	12	2	4	26	16	54	.235	.278	.324	.602	66	-15	-14	100	90	28	.488	2	3	-1	1	/31	-1.5
■ **CRAIG WORTHINGTON**	Worthington, Craig Richard b: 4/17/65, Los Angeles, Cal. BR/TR, 6', 160 lbs. Deb: 4/26/88																											
1988	Bal-A	26	81	5	15	2	0	2	4	9	24	.185	.267	.284	.551	57	-5	-4	95	55	6	.485	1	0	0	1	3	-0.3
1989	Bal-A	145	497	57	123	23	0	15	70	61	114	.247	.335	.384	.719	103	2	3	99	118	65	.666	1	2	-1	-11	*3	-0.8
Total	2	171	578	62	138	25	0	17	74	70	138	.239	.325	.370	.695	97	-3	-2	98	109	72	.639	2	2	-1	-10	3	-1.1
■ **RICK WRONA**	Wrona, Richard James b: 12/10/63, Tulsa, Okla. BR/TR, 6'1", 185 lbs. Deb: 9/03/88																											
1988	Chi-N	4	6	0	0	0	0	0	0	0	1	.000	.000	.000	.000	-96	-2	-2	104	0	0	.000	0	0	0	0	/C	-0.1
1989	Chi-N	38	92	11	26	2	1	2	14	2	21	.283	.305	.391	.697	90	-1	-1	108	134	11	.582	0	0	0	1	C	0.2
Total	2	42	98	11	26	2	1	2	14	2	22	.265	.287	.367	.654	80	-2	-3	108	126	11	.534	0	0	0	1	/C	0.1
■ **MARVELL WYNNE**	Wynne, Marvell b: 12/17/59, Chicago, Ill. BL/TL, 5'11", 175 lbs. Deb: 6/15/83																											
1983	Pit-N	103	366	66	89	16	2	7	26	38	52	.243	.319	.355	.675	84	-6	-8	103	69	43	.631	12	10	-2	-5	*O	-1.7
1984	Pit-N	154	653	77	174	24	11	0	39	42	81	.266	.311	.337	.648	87	-16	-12	94	60	67	.565	24	19	-4	-3	*O	-2.5
1985	Pit-N	103	337	21	69	6	3	2	18	18	48	.205	.247	.258	.505	40	-26	-27	103	77	21	.413	10	5	0	1	O	-3.0
1986	SD-N	137	288	34	76	19	2	7	37	15	45	.264	.303	.417	.719	101	-2	-1	95	105	32	.645	11	11	-3	-9	*O	-1.5
1987	SD-N	98	188	17	47	8	2	2	24	20	37	.250	.322	.346	.668	80	-6	-5	97	135	21	.632	11	6	-0	-7	O	-1.5
1988	SD-N	128	333	37	88	13	4	11	42	31	62	.264	.327	.426	.753	118	6	7	97	96	47	.698	3	4	-2	-1	*O	0.1
1989	SD-N	105	294	19	74	11	1	6	35	12	41	.252	.283	.357	.641	82	-8	-8	101	115	30	.545	4	1	1	-4	O	-1.2
	Chi-N	20	48	8	9	2	1	1	4	1	7	.188	.220	.333	.553	52	-3	-3	108	85	4	.513	2	0	1	-2	O	-0.4
	Yr	125	342	27	83	13	2	7	39	13	48	.243	.275	.354	.628	77	-10	-11	102	111	34	.540	6	1	1	-6		-1.6
Total	7	848	2507	279	626	99	26	36	225	177	373	.250	.301	.353	.654	84	-62	-57	98	86	263	.581	77	56	-11	-29	O	-11.7
■ **ERIC YELDING**	Yelding, Eric Girard b: 2/22/65, Montrose, Ala. BR/TR, 6'1", 170 lbs. Deb: 4/09/89																											
1989	Hou-N	70	90	19	21	2	0	0	9	7	19	.233	.296	.256	.551	58	-5	-5	102	158	7	.553	11	5	0	-4	S2/O	-0.7
■ **GERALD YOUNG**	Young, Gerald Anthony b: 10/22/64, Tele, Honduras BB/TR, 6'2", 185 lbs. Deb: 7/08/87																											
1987	Hou-N	71	274	44	88	9	2	1	15	26	27	.321	.382	.380	.762	111	2	5	93	59	44	.801	26	9	2	7	O	1.1
1988	Hou-N	149	576	79	148	21	9	0	37	66	66	.257	.336	.325	.661	97	-5	-1	93	76	67	.690	65	27	3	5	*O	0.4
1989	Hou-N	146	533	71	124	17	3	0	38	74	60	.233	.328	.276	.604	73	-15	-16	102	110	51	.583	34	25	-5	19	*O	-0.4
Total	3	366	1383	194	360	47	14	1	90	166	153	.260	.342	.317	.659	90	-18	-12	97	86	162	.667	125	61	1	32	O	1.1
■ **MIKE YOUNG**	Young, Michael Darren b: 3/20/60, Oakland, Cal. BB/TR, 6'2", 195 lbs. Deb: 9/14/82																											
1982	Bal-A	6	2	2	0	0	0	0	0	0	1	.000	.000	.000	.000	-99	-1	-1	100	0	0	.000	0	0	0	-0	/OD	0.0
1983	Bal-A	25	36	5	6	2	1	0	2	2	8	.167	.231	.278	.509	39	-3	-3	100	78	2	.452	1	0	0	-5	O/D	-0.7
1984	Bal-A	123	401	59	101	17	2	17	52	58	110	.252	.356	.431	.788	124	10	13	94	94	66	.795	6	2	1	-8	*O/D	0.2
1985	Bal-A	139	450	72	123	22	1	28	81	48	104	.273	.349	.513	.862	134	19	20	99	102	78	.833	1	5	-3	0	OD	1.6
1986	Bal-A	117	369	43	93	15	1	9	42	49	90	.252	.344	.371	.716	97	-1	-0	99	102	47	.662	3	1	0	-1	OD	-0.2
1987	Bal-A	110	363	46	87	10	1	16	39	46	91	.240	.328	.405	.733	96	-3	-2	98	80	48	.707	10	7	-1	-4	OD	-0.7
1988	Phi-N	75	146	13	33	14	0	1	14	26	43	.226	.347	.342	.689	97	1	0	101	106	19	.675	0	0	0	-3	O	-0.4
	Mil-A	8	14	2	0	0	0	0	0	2	5	.000	.176	.000	.176	-45	-3	-3	103	0	0	.214	0	0	0	-1	/OD	-0.3
1989	Cle-A	32	59	2	11	0	0	1	5	6	13	.186	.273	.237	.510	43	-4	-4	104	114	4	.469	2	0	1	-0	D/O	-0.3
Total	8	635	1840	244	454	80	6	72	235	237	465	.247	.339	.414	.753	107	16	21	98	95	266	.725	23	15	-2	-22	OD	-0.8
■ **JOEL YOUNGBLOOD**	Youngblood, Joel Randolph b: 8/28/51, Houston, Tex. BR/TR, 6', 180 lbs. Deb: 4/13/76																											
1976	Cin-N	55	57	8	11	1	1	0	1	2	8	.193	.233	.246	.479	35	-5	-5	103	27	3	.383	1	0	0	-0	/O3C2	-0.5
1977	StL-N	25	27	1	5	2	0	0	1	3	5	.185	.267	.259	.526	44	-2	-2	96	57	1	.400	0	2	-1	-3	O/3	-0.6
	NY-N	70	182	16	46	11	1	0	11	13	40	.253	.303	.324	.627	71	-8	-7	96	75	16	.503	1	3	-2	-2	2O3	-0.9
	Yr	95	209	17	51	13	1	0	12	16	45	.244	.298	.316	.614	67	-10	-9	96	71	17	.488	1	5	-3	-5		-1.5
1978	NY-N	113	266	40	67	12	8	7	30	16	39	.252	.297	.436	.733	104	-0	0	98	87	35	.675	4	0	1	1	O2/3S	0.3
1979	NY-N	158	590	90	162	37	5	16	60	60	84	.275	.349	.436	.784	119	10	14	95	83	90	.763	18	13	-2	11	*O23	1.9
1980	NY-N	146	514	58	142	26	2	8	69	52	69	.276	.345	.381	.726	107	2	5	96	127	67	.672	14	11	-2	21	*O3/2	1.9
1981	NY-N	43	143	16	50	10	2	4	25	12	19	.350	.408	.531	.939	164	12	12	101	114	28	.902	2	5	-2	0	O	0.9
1982	NY-N	80	202	21	52	12	0	3	21	8	37	.257	.302	.361	.664	86	-4	-4	99	100	20	.544	0	4	-2	-5	O/2S3	-1.2
	Mon-N	40	90	16	18	2	0	0	8	9	21	.200	.294	.222	.516	44	-6	-7	105	157	6	.453	2	1	0	-4	O	-1.1
	Yr	120	292	37	70	14	0	3	29	17	58	.240	.300	.318	.618	72	-10	-11	101	120	27	.515	2	5	-2	-9		-2.3
1983	SF-N	124	373	59	109	20	3	17	53	33	59	.292	.358	.499	.856	134	17	16	101	88	64	.828	7	4	-0	-11	23O	0.6
1984	SF-N	134	469	50	119	17	1	10	51	48	86	.254	.328	.358	.686	96	-4	-2	96	103	56	.618	5	6	-2	-19	*3O/2	-2.4
1985	SF-N	95	230	24	62	6	0	4	24	30	37	.270	.356	.348	.704	105	0	2	93	104	29	.648	3	2	-0	1	O/3	0.1
1986	SF-N	97	184	20	47	12	0	5	28	18	34	.255	.325	.402	.727	104	-0	1	96	125	25	.671	1	1	-0	-6	O/132S	-0.6
1987	SF-N	69	91	9	23	3	0	3	11	5	13	.253	.299	.385	.684	83	-3	-2	96	100	10	.583	1	1	-0	-2	O/3	-0.5
1988	SF-N	83	123	12	31	4	0	0	16	10	17	.252	.313	.285	.598	77	-4	-3	94	183	11	.480	1	1	-0	-10	O	-1.5
1989	Cin-N	76	118	13	25	5	0	3	13	13	21	.212	.301	.331	.631	78	-3	-3	103	109	11	.540	0	1	-1	-11	O	-1.6
Total	14	1408	3659	453	969	180	23	80	422	332	589	.265	.332	.392	.724	103	1	14	97	103	471	.659	60	55	-15	-39	O32/1SC	-5.2
■ **ROBIN YOUNT**	Yount, Robin R. b: 9/16/55, Danville, Ill. BR/TR, 6', 165 lbs. Deb: 4/05/74																											
1974	Mil-A	107	344	48	86	14	5	3	26	12	46	.250	.277	.346	.623	77	-10	-11	102	80	31	.517	7	7	-2	-8	*S	-1.3
1975	Mil-A	147	558	67	149	28	2	8	52	33	69	.267	.309	.367	.677	90	-8	-8	100	92	64	.596	12	4	1	-16	*S	-0.8
1976	Mil-A	161	638	59	161	19	3	2	54	38	69	.252	.294	.301	.595	75	-21	-20	99	111	55	.491	16	11	-2	-5	*S/O	-1.8
1977	Mil-A	154	605	66	174	34	4	4	49	41	80	.288	.335	.377	.712	98	-5	-1	95	78	77	.639	16	7	1	-6	*S	1.1
1978	Mil-A	127	502	66	147	23	9	9	71	24	43	.293	.326	.428	.755	105	5	2	106	123	71	.701	16	5	2	21	*S	3.5
1979	Mil-A	149	577	72	154	26	5	8	51	35	52	.267	.310	.371	.681	83	-15	-15	100	87	63	.585	11	8	-2	3	*S	0.5
1980	Mil-A	143	611	121	179	**49**	10	23	87	26	67	.293	.323	.519	.842	134	19	23	95	78	101	.818	20	5	3	3	*S/D	3.8

YEAR	TM/L	G	AB	R	H	2B	3B	HR	RBI	BB	SO	AVG	OBP	SLG	PRO	/A	BR	/A	PF	CHI	RC	TA	SB	CS	SBR	FR	POS	TPR
1981	Mil-A	96	377	50	103	15	5	10	49	22	37	.273	.317	.419	.736	115	4	6	96	108	51	.667	4	1	1	25	S/D	3.9
1982	Mil-A	156	635	129	**210**	**46**	12	29	114	54	63	.331	.384	**.578**	**.962**	**170**	**50**	**55**	94	97	**136**	.975	14	3	2	-3	*S/D	**6.6**
1983	Mil-A	149	578	102	178	42	**10**	17	80	72	58	.308	.387	.503	.891	**156**	35	41	92	88	115	.909	12	5	1	-7	*S/D	4.2
1984	Mil-A	160	624	105	186	27	7	16	80	67	67	.298	.367	.441	.808	133	20	26	92	95	99	.769	14	4	2	5	*SD	4.2
1985	Mil-A	122	466	76	129	26	3	15	68	49	56	.277	.348	.442	.790	110	9	7	105	114	73	.765	10	4	1	-10	*OD/1	-0.4
1986	Mil-A	140	522	82	163	31	7	9	46	62	73	.312	.389	.450	.840	126	23	21	102	74	94	.845	14	5	1	6	*O/1D	2.3
1987	Mil-A	158	635	99	198	25	9	21	103	76	94	.312	.386	.479	.865	126	28	25	102	108	120	.879	19	9	0	1	*O/D	2.1
1988	Mil-A	162	621	92	190	38	**11**	13	91	63	63	.306	.373	.465	.838	129	28	25	103	106	106	.827	22	4	4	8	*O/D	3.5
1989	Mil-A	160	614	101	195	38	9	21	103	63	71	.318	.387	.511	.898	156	41	44	97	102	**125**	.933	19	3	4	-1	*OD	**4.5**
Total	16	2291	8907	1335	2602	481	111	208	1124	737	1008	.292	.348	.441	.789	119	203	221	98	96	1381	.750	226	85	17	17	*SOD/1	35.9

■ **TODD ZEILE**   Zeile, Todd Edward   b: 9/9/65, Van Nuys, Cal.   BR/TR, 6'1", 190 lbs.   Deb: 8/18/89

YEAR	TM/L	G	AB	R	H	2B	3B	HR	RBI	BB	SO	AVG	OBP	SLG	PRO	/A	BR	/A	PF	CHI	RC	TA	SB	CS	SBR	FR	POS	TPR
1989	StL-N	28	82	7	21	3	1	1	8	9	14	.256	.330	.354	.683	95	-0	-0	101	101	10	.613	0	0	0	1	C	0.2

■ **PAUL ZUVELLA**   Zuvella, Paul   b: 10/31/58, San Mateo, Cal.   BR/TR, 6', 173 lbs.   Deb: 9/04/82

YEAR	TM/L	G	AB	R	H	2B	3B	HR	RBI	BB	SO	AVG	OBP	SLG	PRO	/A	BR	/A	PF	CHI	RC	TA	SB	CS	SBR	FR	POS	TPR
1982	Atl-N	2	1	0	0	0	0	0	0	0	0	.000	.000	.000	.000	-93	-0	-0	107	0	0	.000	0	0	0	0	/S	0.0
1983	Atl-N	3	5	0	0	0	0	0	0	2	1	.000	.375	.000	.375	12	-0	-0	106	0	0	.600	0	0	0	0	/S	0.0
1984	Atl-N	11	25	2	5	1	0	0	1	2	3	.200	.259	.240	.499-	37	-2	-2	110	65	2	.400	0	0	0	1	/2S	0.0
1985	Atl-N	81	190	16	48	8	1	0	4	16	14	.253	.311	.305	.616	69	-7	-8	106	27	19	.524	2	0	1	12	2S/3	0.8
1986	NY-A	21	48	2	4	1	0	0	2	5	4	.083	.170	.104	.274	-22	-8	-8	103	159	1	.222	0	0	0	1	S	-0.5
1987	NY-A	14	34	2	6	0	0	0	0	0	4	.176	.176	.176	.353	-6	-5	-5	98	0	1	.207	0	0	0	0	/2S3	-0.3
1988	Cle-A	51	130	9	30	5	1	0	7	8	13	.231	.275	.285	.560	56	-7	-8	102	75	10	.437	0	0	0	-8	S	-1.3
1989	Cle-A	24	58	10	16	2	0	2	6	1	11	.276	.300	.414	.714	96	-0	-1	104	78	7	.619	0	0	0	0	S/3D	0.1
Total	8	207	491	41	109	17	2	2	20	34	50	.222	.275	.277	.552	52	-30	-32	104	59	41	.446	2	0	1	6	S/23D	-1.2

The Pitcher Register

The Pitcher Register contains the most important career pitching statistics of every man who pitched in a major league game in 1989, without exception. The pitchers are listed alphabetically by surname and, when more than one pitcher bears the name, alphabetically by *given* name, not by "use name." Each page of the Pitcher Register is topped at the corner by a finding aid: in capital letters, the surname of, first, the pitcher whose entry heads up the page and, second, the pitcher whose entry concludes it. Another finding aid is the use of boldface numerals to indicate a league-leading total in those categories in which a pitcher is truly attempting to excel (no boldface is given to the "leaders" in losses); games started (innings pitched is the better mark of endurance); hits allowed (the most would produce an absurd leader while the fewest would tend to reward a man for pitching fewer innings—hits per nine innings is the better category in which to cite leaders); or (using the same reasoning as for hits allowed) in home runs against or bases on balls. Pitcher batting and pitcher defense, because the win denominated numbers they produce are so small, are also not sorted for single-season leaders (although the all-time leaders in these categories, single season and lifetime, will be found in a separate section called "All-Time Leaders").

The record for a man who pitched in more than one season is given in a line for each season, plus a career total line. If he pitched for more than one team in a given year, his totals for each team are stated on separate lines. And if the teams for which he pitched in his "traded year" are in the same league, then his full record is stated in both separate and combined fashion.

For a key to the team and league abbreviations used in the Pitcher Register, flip back to page 19 of this volume.

While fractional innings are calculated for teams in the Annual Record, they are rounded off to the nearest whole inning for individuals, in accordance with baseball scoring practice from 1976 through 1981 (for the previous century, fractional innings were simply lopped off). In this book, as in *Total Baseball*, our database conforms to the 1976–1981 practice for all of pitching history, excepting those men who pitched only one third of an inning in an entire season; rounding off their figures would produce an innings-pitched figure of zero, which in turn would produce a meaningless ERA. Accordingly, our policy regarding this relative handful of pitchers conforms to a 1978 ruling by the Baseball Playing Rules Committee that such fractional innings be stated.

Looking at the biographical line for any pitcher, we see first his use name in full capitals, then his given name and nickname (and any other name he may have used or been born with, such as the matronymic of a Latin American pitcher). His date and place of birth follow "b." Then come his manner of batting and throwing, abbreviated in the usual manner. Next is the pitcher's debut date in the major leagues.

The explanations for the statistical column heads follow; for more detail or technical information about formulas and calculations, see the final page of this book or the Glossary in *Total Baseball*.

YEAR   Year in which a man pitched (When a space in the column is blank, this indicates that the man has pitched for two or more clubs in the last year stated in the column; if those clubs were in the same league, then the man will also have a combined total line, beginning with the abbreviation "Yr" placed in the TM/L column.)

TM/L   Team and League

Yr   See comments for YEAR

W   Wins

L   Losses

PCT   Win Percentage (Wins divided by decisions.)

G   Games pitched

GS   Games Started

CG   Complete Games

SHO   Shutouts (Complete-game shutouts only.)

SV   Saves

IP   Innings Pitched

H   Hits allowed

H/G   Hits allowed per Game (Game defined as nine innings.)

HR   Home Runs allowed

BB   Bases on Balls allowed

BB/G   Bases on Balls per Game

SO   Strikeouts

SO/G   Strikeouts per Game

ERA   Earned Run Average

/A   Normalized to league average and park-adjusted (A mark of 100 is a league-average performance and plus-100 figures are better than average.)

OAVG   Opponents' Batting Average

OOBP   Opponents' On-Base Percentage

PR   Pitching Runs (Linear Weights measure of runs saved *beyond* what a league-average pitcher might have saved, defined as zero. Also, this column and the adjusted one to its right will each contain a pair of single-season leaders, the figures shown in boldface: the top mark in Starters' Runs and the top mark in Relievers' Runs. The former category is reserved for men who averaged more than three innings per game pitched, while the latter category is for those who averaged less than three innings per game pitched.)

PF   Park Factor (A measure of run scoring at the pitcher's home park in a given year or, in the Totals line, of all his various home parks; above 100 signifies a park or aggregate of parks favorable to hitters, below 100 signifies a park or aggregate of parks unfavorable to hitters. Park Factors for batters and pitchers are calculated differently and vary somewhat.)

CPI   Clutch Pitching Index (Expected runs over actual runs, with 100 being a league-average performance and marks over 100 being superior; see final page for formula.)

WAT   Wins Above Team (The number of wins a pitcher collects beyond those expected for an average pitcher on his team, based on the team's won-lost record. See final page for the equation.)

PB   Pitcher Batting (Expressed in Batting Wins, which are park-adjusted Batting Runs divided by the number of runs required to create an additional win beyond league average, with that average defined as zero.)

PD   Pitcher Defense (Expressed in Fielding Wins, which are Fielding Runs divided by the number of runs required to create an additional win beyond league average, with that average defined as zero.)

TPI   Total Pitcher Index (The sum of a pitcher's Adjusted Pitcher Runs, Pitcher Batting—zero in the American League since 1973—and Pitcher Fielding, all divided by the Runs per Win factor for that year, generally around 10.)

Total   The lifetime record is shown alongside the notation "Total x," where x stands for the number of years played.

YEAR	TM/L	W	L	PCT	G	GS	CG	SHO	SV	IP	H	H/G	HR	BB	BB/G	SO	SO/G	ERA	/A	OAVG	OOBP	PR	/A	PF	CPI	WAT	PB	PD	TPI
■ DON AASE	Aase, Donald William b: 9/8/54, Orange, Cal. BR/TR, 6'3", 190 lbs. Deb: 7/26/77																												
1977	Bos-A	6	2	.750	13	13	4	2	0	92	85	8.3	6	19	1.9	49	4.8	3.13	151	.244	.282	10	16	116	87	1.5	0	-0	1.7
1978	Cal-A	11	8	.579	29	29	6	1	0	179	185	9.3	14	80	4.0	93	4.7	4.02	95	.270	.345	-5	-4	101	104	1.0	0	0	-0.3
1979	Cal-A	9	10	.474	37	28	7	1	2	185	200	9.7	19	77	3.7	96	4.7	4.82	80	.277	.340	-12	-19	92	93	-1.3	0	-2	-2.0
1980	Cal-A	8	13	.381	40	21	5	1	2	175	193	9.9	13	66	3.4	74	3.8	4.06	96	.287	.342	-0	-3	97	109	-0.6	0	-1	-0.3
1981	Cal-A	4	4	.500	39	0	0	0	11	65	56	7.8	4	24	3.3	38	5.3	2.35	161	.234	.302	9	10	104	127	0.3	0	-0	1.1
1982	Cal-A	3	3	.500	24	0	0	0	4	52	45	7.8	5	23	4.0	40	6.9	3.46	116	.243	.321	4	3	99	109	-0.3	0	-0	0.3
1984	Cal-A	4	1	.800	23	0	0	0	8	39	30	6.9	1	19	4.4	28	6.5	1.62	251	.221	.306	10	11	101	175	1.5	0	-0	1.1
1985	Bal-A	10	6	.625	54	0	0	0	14	88	83	8.5	6	35	3.6	67	6.9	3.78	108	.258	.325	4	3	98	103	2.0	0	0	0.3
1986	Bal-A	6	7	.462	66	0	0	0	34	82	71	7.8	6	28	3.1	67	7.4	2.96	140	.234	.294	11	11	99	101	0.1	0	0	1.1
1987	Bal-A	1	0	1.000	7	0	0	0	2	8	8	9.0	1	4	4.5	3	3.4	2.25	197	.276	.364	2	2	99	226	0.5	0	0	0.2
1988	Bal-A	0	0	—	35	0	0	0	0	47	40	7.7	4	37	7.1	28	5.4	4.02	96	.240	.368	-0	-1	97	115	0.0	0	-1	-0.1
1989	NY-N	1	5	.167	49	0	0	0	2	59	56	8.5	5	26	4.0	34	5.2	3.97	84	.245	.318	-3	-4	95	93	-2.0	-1	0	-0.4
Total	12	63	59	.516	416	91	22	5	79	1071	1052	8.8	84	438	3.7	617	5.2	3.76	106	.260	.328	29	26	99	106	2.7	-1	-4	2.7
■ JIM ABBOTT	Abbott, James Anthony b: 9/19/67, Flint, Mich. BL/TL, 6'3", 200 lbs. Deb: 4/08/89																												
1989	Cal-A	12	12	.500	29	29	4	2	0	181	190	9.4	13	74	3.7	115	5.7	3.93	97	.274	.340	-1	-3	98	109	-1.4	0	-1	-0.3
■ JIM ACKER	Acker, James Justin b: 9/24/58, Freer, Tex. BR/TR, 6'2", 210 lbs. Deb: 4/07/83																												
1983	Tor-A	5	1	.833	38	5	0	0	1	98	103	9.5	7	38	3.5	44	4.0	4.32	102	.273	.350	-3	1	108	101	1.9	0	1	0.2
1984	Tor-A	3	5	.375	32	3	0	0	1	72	79	9.9	3	25	3.1	33	4.1	4.38	92	.286	.353	-3	-3	101	99	-1.2	0	-0	-0.2
1985	Tor-A	7	2	.778	61	0	0	0	10	86	86	9.0	7	43	4.5	42	4.4	3.24	127	.268	.357	9	8	99	141	2.0	0	1	1.0
1986	Tor-A	2	4	.333	23	5	0	0	0	60	63	9.4	6	22	3.3	32	4.8	4.35	100	.281	.336	-1	0	104	107	-1.0	0	1	0.1
	Atl-N	3	8	.273	21	14	0	0	0	95	100	9.5	7	26	2.5	37	3.5	3.79	102	.274	.316	-1	1	103	101	-2.1	-1	0	0.0
1987	Atl-N	4	9	.308	68	0	0	0	14	115	109	8.5	11	51	4.0	68	5.3	4.15	108	.253	.334	-1	4	109	98	-1.8	0	1	0.6
1988	Atl-N	0	4	.000	21	1	0	0	0	42	45	9.6	6	14	3.0	25	5.4	4.71	78	.280	.326	-6	-5	107	102	-1.9	1	0	-0.3
1989	Atl-N	0	6	.000	59	0	0	0	2	98	84	7.7	5	20	1.8	68	6.2	2.66	136	.237	.274	9	11	104	100	-2.9	-0	1	1.2
	Tor-A	2	1	.667	14	0	0	0	0	28	24	7.7	1	12	3.9	24	7.7	1.61	226	.235	.319	7	6	93	195	0.4	0	1	0.8
Total	7	26	40	.394	337	28	0	0	28	694	693	9.0	53	251	3.3	373	4.8	3.77	108	.266	.330	11	23	104	110	-6.6	0	7	3.4
■ JUAN AGOSTO	Agosto, Juan Roberto (Gonzalez) b: 2/23/58, Rio Piedras, P.R. BL/TL, 6', 175 lbs. Deb: 9/07/81																												
1981	Chi-A	0	0	—	2	0	0	0	0	6	5	7.5	1	0	0.0	3	4.5	4.50	80	.238	.273	-1	-1	99	76	0.0	0	0	0.0
1982	Chi-A	0	0	—	1	0	0	0	0	2	7	31.5	0	0	0.0	1	4.5	18.00	22	.538	.538	-3	-3	97	78	0.0	0	0	-0.2
1983	Chi-A	2	2	.500	39	0	0	0	7	42	41	8.8	2	11	2.4	29	6.2	4.07	102	.283	.319	0	0	102	100	-0.3	0	0	0.1
1984	Chi-A	2	1	.667	49	0	0	0	7	55	54	8.8	2	34	5.6	26	4.3	3.11	143	.270	.374	5	8	111	148	0.6	0	2	1.1
1985	Chi-A	4	3	.571	54	0	0	0	1	60	45	6.8	3	23	3.5	39	5.8	3.60	115	.210	.289	4	4	100	73	0.4	0	2	0.5
1986	Chi-A	0	2	.000	9	0	0	0	0	5	6	10.8	0	4	7.2	3	5.4	7.20	59	.300	.417	-2	-2	101	76	-0.9	0	-0	-0.1
	Min-A	1	2	.333	17	1	0	0	1	20	43	19.3	1	14	6.3	9	4.0	9.00	51	.443	.513	-11	-10	109	120	-0.3	0	0	-0.8
	Yr	1	4	.200	26	1	0	0	1	25	49	17.6	1	18	6.5	12	4.3	8.64	52	.419	.496	-12	-11	108	120	-1.2	0	0	-0.9
1987	Hou-N	1	1	.500	27	0	0	0	2	27	26	8.7	1	10	3.3	6	2.0	2.67	142	.248	.305	4	3	93	115	0.1	-0	1	0.4
1988	Hou-N	10	2	.833	75	0	0	0	4	92	74	7.2	6	30	2.9	33	3.2	2.25	143	.226	.280	12	10	93	126	4.1	-0	4	1.5
1989	Hou-N	4	5	.444	71	0	0	0	1	83	81	8.8	3	32	3.5	46	5.0	2.93	123	.256	.319	5	6	103	120	-0.7	0	1	0.8
Total	9	24	18	.571	344	1	0	0	23	392	382	8.8	19	158	3.6	195	4.5	3.47	111	.262	.329	15	16	101	114	3.0	-1	11	3.3
■ RICK AGUILERA	Aguilera, Richard Warren b: 12/31/61, San Gabriel, Cal. BR/TR, 6'4", 195 lbs. Deb: 6/12/85																												
1985	NY-N	10	7	.588	21	19	2	0	0	122	118	8.7	8	37	2.7	74	5.5	3.25	106	.258	.310	5	3	95	107	-0.2	3	-0	0.5
1986	NY-N	10	7	.588	28	20	2	0	0	142	145	9.2	15	36	2.3	104	6.6	3.87	90	.263	.311	-2	-6	93	99	-1.0	2	2	-0.2
1987	NY-N	11	3	.786	18	17	1	0	0	115	124	9.7	12	33	2.6	77	6.0	3.60	110	.276	.324	6	5	97	118	3.7	3	2	1.0
1988	NY-N	0	4	.000	11	3	0	0	0	25	29	10.4	2	10	3.6	16	5.8	6.84	44	.296	.360	-9	-11	88	73	-1.9	0	0	-0.9
1989	NY-N	6	6	.500	36	0	0	0	7	69	59	7.7	3	21	2.7	80	10.4	2.35	142	.231	.289	9	8	95	117	-0.3	-0	-0	0.7
	Min-A	3	5	.375	11	11	3	0	0	76	71	8.4	5	17	2.0	57	6.8	3.20	130	.245	.287	6	8	106	90	-0.9	0	1	0.9
Total	5	40	32	.556	125	70	8	0	7	549	546	9.0	45	154	2.5	408	6.7	3.52	103	.260	.310	14	6	96	104	-0.6	8	5	2.0
■ DARREL AKERFELDS	Akerfelds, Darrel Wayne b: 6/12/62, Denver, Colo. BR/TR, 6'2", 210 lbs. Deb: 8/01/86																												
1986	Oak-A	0	0	—	2	0	0	0	0	5	7	12.6	2	3	5.4	5	9.0	7.20	55	.304	.385	-2	-2	94	111	0.0	0	0	-0.1
1987	Cle-A	2	6	.250	16	13	1	0	0	75	84	10.1	18	38	4.6	42	5.0	6.72	70	.284	.372	-19	-17	105	94	-1.3	0	-0	-1.5
1989	Tex-A	0	1	.000	6	0	0	0	0	11	11	9.0	1	5	4.1	9	7.4	3.27	122	.250	.320	1	1	103	114	-0.4	0	0	0.1
Total	3	2	7	.222	24	13	1	0	0	91	102	10.1	21	46	4.5	56	5.5	6.33	72	.281	.366	-20	-18	104	97	-1.7	0	-0	-1.5
■ JAY ALDRICH	Aldrich, Jay Robert b: 4/14/61, Alexandria, La. BR/TR, 6'3", 210 lbs. Deb: 6/05/87																												
1987	Mil-A	3	1	.750	31	0	0	0	0	58	71	11.0	8	13	2.0	22	3.4	4.97	92	.306	.340	-3	-3	102	105	0.9	0	-1	-0.2
1989	Mil-A	1	0	1.000	16	0	0	0	1	26	24	8.3	3	13	4.5	12	4.2	3.81	98	.253	.345	0	-0	96	116	0.5	0	0	0.0
	Atl-N	1	2	.333	8	0	0	0	0	12	7	5.3	0	6	4.5	7	5.3	2.25	161	.167	.260	2	2	104	61	-0.1	-0	-0	0.2
Total	2	5	3	.625	55	0	0	0	1	96	102	9.6	11	32	3.0	41	3.8	4.31	98	.276	.332	-1	-1	101	103	1.3	-0	-1	0.0
■ DOYLE ALEXANDER	Alexander, Doyle Lafayette b: 9/4/50, Cordova, Ala. BR/TR, 6'3", 190 lbs. Deb: 6/26/71																												
1971	LA-N	6	6	.500	17	12	4	0	0	92	105	10.3	6	18	1.8	30	2.9	3.82	89	.282	.314	-4	-4	98	96	-0.5	2	-1	-0.2
1972	Bal-A	6	8	.429	35	9	2	2	2	106	78	6.6	5	30	2.5	49	4.2	2.46	120	.203	.258	7	6	96	72	-1.2	-1	2	0.7
1973	Bal-A	12	8	.600	29	26	10	0	0	175	169	8.7	19	52	2.7	63	3.2	3.86	104	.258	.314	-1	3	105	98	0.0	0	1	0.4
1974	Bal-A	6	9	.400	30	12	2	0	0	114	127	10.0	7	43	3.4	40	3.2	4.03	83	.290	.350	-5	-9	92	110	-2.2	0	3	-0.5
1975	Bal-A	8	8	.500	32	11	3	1	1	133	127	8.6	7	47	3.2	46	3.1	3.05	111	.251	.312	11	5	89	105	-0.9	0	2	0.7
1976	Bal-A	3	4	.429	11	6	2	1	0	64	58	8.2	3	24	3.4	17	2.4	3.52	98	.247	.309	0	-1	97	91	-0.7	0	1	0.1
	NY-A	10	5	.667	19	19	5	2	0	137	114	7.5	9	39	2.6	41	2.7	3.28	104	.229	.285	4	2	97	83	1.2	0	-2	0.0
	Yr	13	9	.591	30	25	7	3	0	201	172	7.7	12	63	2.8	58	2.6	3.36	102	.234	.293	4	2	97	83	0.5	0	-1	0.1
1977	Tex-A	17	11	.607	34	34	12	1	0	237	221	8.4	24	82	3.1	82	3.1	3.65	116	.246	.307	11	15	104	95	1.1	0	1	1.6
1978	Tex-A	9	10	.474	31	28	7	1	0	191	198	9.3	18	71	3.3	81	3.8	3.86	94	.270	.328	-2	-5	96	105	-1.2	0	2	-0.3
1979	Tex-A	5	7	.417	23	18	0	0	0	113	114	9.1	3	69	5.5	50	4.0	4.46	94	.268	.362	-3	-3	99	95	-1.1	0	2	-0.1
1980	Atl-N	14	11	.560	35	35	7	1	0	232	227	8.8	20	74	2.9	114	4.4	4.19	87	.256	.311	-15	-14	101	85	1.7	1	3	-1.0
1981	SF-N	11	7	.611	24	24	1	1	0	152	156	9.2	11	44	2.6	77	4.6	2.90	126	.263	.313	10	13	105	122	2.2	1	-2	1.4
1982	NY-A	1	7	.125	16	11	0	0	0	67	81	10.9	14	14	1.9	26	3.5	6.04	65	.298	.324	-15	-16	97	88	-2.9	0	-0	-1.4
1983	NY-A	0	2	.000	8	5	0	0	0	28	31	10.0	6	7	2.3	17	5.5	6.43	62	.277	.314	-7	-8	98	76	-0.9	0	-0	-0.7
	Tor-A	7	6	.538	17	15	5	0	0	117	126	9.7	14	26	2.0	46	3.5	3.92	112	.279	.317	2	6	108	108	0.0	0	0	0.6
	Yr	7	8	.467	25	20	5	0	0	145	157	9.7	20	33	2.0	63	3.9	4.41	98	.278	.317	-5	-2	106	108	-0.9	0	0	-0.1
1984	Tor-A	17	6	**.739**	36	35	11	2	0	262	238	8.2	21	59	2.0	139	4.8	3.13	129	.242	.283	25	27	101	94	5.3	0	-0	2.7
1985	Tor-A	17	10	.630	36	36	6	1	0	261	268	9.2	28	67	2.3	142	4.9	3.45	119	.266	.313	20	19	99	115	0.6	0	0	2.0
1986	Tor-A	5	4	.556	17	17	3	0	0	111	120	9.7	18	20	1.6	65	5.3	4.46	98	.273	.306	-3	-1	104	96	0.3	0	-1	-0.1
	Atl-N	6	6	.500	17	17	2	0	0	117	135	10.4	9	17	1.3	74	5.7	3.85	100	.287	.306	-2	0	103	99	0.6	1	-1	0.0
1987	Atl-N	5	10	.333	16	16	3	0	0	118	115	8.8	21	27	2.1	64	4.9	4.12	108	.257	.299	-0	5	109	100	-1.7	-3	-2	0.0
	Det-A	9	0	1.000	11	11	3	3	0	88	63	6.4	3	26	2.7	44	4.5	1.53	279	.201	.262	29	27	96	122	4.5	0	0	2.9
1988	Det-A	14	11	.560	34	34	5	1	0	229	260	10.2	30	46	1.8	126	5.0	4.32	86	.282	.316	-9	-15	94	101	0.5	0	-3	-1.7
1989	Det-A	6	18	.250	33	33	5	1	0	223	245	9.9	28	76	3.1	95	3.8	4.44	87	.280	.334	-14	-14	99	104	-4.1	0	0	-1.3
Total	19	194	174	.527	561	464	98	18	3	3367	3376	9.0	324	978	2.6	1528	4.1	3.76	103	.261	.311	41	37	100	99	0.6	1	8	5.8
■ NEIL ALLEN	Allen, Neil Patrick b: 1/24/58, Kansas City, Kan. BR/TR, 6'3", 185 lbs. Deb: 4/15/79																												
1979	NY-N	6	10	.375	50	5	0	0	8	99	100	9.1	4	47	4.3	65	5.9	3.55	102	.268	.341	2	1	96	110	-0.2	-2	0	0.0
1980	NY-N	7	10	.412	59	0	0	0	22	97	87	8.1	7	40	3.7	79	7.3	3.71	94	.244	.312	-1	-2	97	92	0.0	-0	-1	-0.3
1981	NY-N	7	6	.538	43	0	0	0	18	67	64	8.6	4	26	3.5	50	6.7	2.96	121	.259	.315	4	5	103	124	1.7	1	1	0.7
1982	NY-N	3	7	.300	50	0	0	0	19	65	65	9.0	5	30	4.2	59	8.2	3.05	118	.266	.344	4	4	100	138	-1.2	1	-0	0.4

YEAR	TM/L	W	L	PCT	G	GS	CG	SHO	SV	IP	H	H/G	HR	BB	BB/G	SO	SO/G	ERA	/A	OAVG	OOBP	PR	/A	PF	CPI	WAT	PB	PD	TPI
1983	NY-N	2	7	.222	21	4	1	1	2	54	57	9.5	6	36	6.0	32	5.3	4.50	81	.278	.378	-5	-5	100	117	-2.1	-1	-0	-0.6
	StL-N	10	6	.625	25	18	4	2	0	122	122	9.0	6	48	3.5	74	5.5	3.69	97	.265	.331	-1	-2	98	100	2.3	-1	-0	-0.2
	Yr	12	13	.480	46	22	5	3	2	176	179	9.2	12	84	4.3	106	5.4	3.94	91	.268	.346	-6	-7	99	100	0.2	-1	-1	-0.8
1984	StL-N	9	6	.600	57	1	0	0	3	119	105	7.9	6	49	3.7	66	5.0	3.55	100	.239	.311	1	-0	99	88	1.4	1	1	0.2
1985	StL-N	1	4	.200	23	1	0	0	2	29	32	9.9	3	17	5.3	10	3.1	5.59	60	.283	.370	-6	-7	93	94	-1.6	-0	0	-0.7
	NY-A	1	0	1.000	17	0	0	0	1	29	26	8.1	1	13	4.0	16	5.0	2.79	140	.234	.315	4	4	94	107	0.5	0	0	0.3
1986	Chi-A	7	2	.778	22	17	2	2	0	113	101	8.0	8	38	3.0	57	4.5	3.82	111	.244	.303	5	5	101	87	2.8	0	-0	0.5
1987	Chi-A	0	7	.000	15	10	0	0	0	50	74	13.3	6	26	4.7	26	4.7	7.02	69	.365	.432	-14	-12	109	110	-3.4	0	-0	-1.0
	NY-A	0	1	.000	8	1	0	0	0	25	23	8.3	2	10	3.6	16	5.8	3.60	121	.242	.311	2	2	97	95	-0.4	0	-0	0.2
	Yr	0	8	.000	23	11	0	0	0	75	97	11.6	8	36	4.3	42	5.0	5.88	80	.321	.389	-12	-10	105	95	-3.8	0	-0	-0.8
1988	NY-A	5	3	.625	41	2	0	1	0	117	121	9.3	14	37	2.8	61	4.7	3.85	99	.268	.317	2	-1	96	110	0.9	0	-2	-0.2
1989	Cle-A	0	1	.000	3	0	0	0	0	3	8	24.0	1	0	0.0	0	0.0	15.00	27	.500	.471	-4	-4	104	88	-0.4	0	0	-0.2
Total	11	58	70	.453	434	59	7	6	75	989	985	9.0	73	417	3.8	611	5.6	3.88	97	.264	.332	-8	-13	99	104	0.3	-1	-2	-0.9

■ JOSE ALVAREZ Alvarez, Jose Lino b: 4/12/56, Tampa, Fla. BR/TR, 5'10", 170 lbs. Deb: 10/01/81

YEAR	TM/L	W	L	PCT	G	GS	CG	SHO	SV	IP	H	H/G	HR	BB	BB/G	SO	SO/G	ERA	/A	OAVG	OOBP	PR	/A	PF	CPI	WAT	PB	PD	TPI
1981	Atl-N	0	0	—	1	0	0	0	0	2	0	0.0	0	0	0.0	2	9.0	0.00	—	.000	.000	1	1	100	0	0.0	0	0	0.1
1982	Atl-N	0	0	—	7	0	0	0	0	8	8	9.0	1	2	2.3	6	6.8	4.50	85	.308	.345	-1	-1	107	113	0.0	0	0	0.0
1988	Atl-N	5	6	.455	60	0	0	0	3	102	88	7.8	7	53	4.7	81	7.1	3.00	123	.240	.337	5	8	107	130	1.0	1	1	1.1
1989	Atl-N	3	3	.500	30	0	0	0	2	50	44	7.9	4	24	4.3	45	8.1	2.88	126	.237	.318	3	4	104	126	0.5	-0	1	0.5
Total	4	8	9	.471	98	0	0	0	5	162	140	7.8	12	79	4.4	134	7.4	3.00	123	.240	.328	9	12	106	126	1.5	1	2	1.7

■ WILSON ALVAREZ Alvarez, Wilson Eduardo b: 3/24/70, Maracaibo, Venez. BL/TL, 6'1", 175 lbs. Deb: 7/24/89

YEAR	TM/L	W	L	PCT	G	GS	CG	SHO	SV	IP	H	H/G	HR	BB	BB/G	SO	SO/G	ERA	/A	OAVG	OOBP	PR	/A	PF	CPI	WAT	PB	PD	TPI
1989	Tex-A	0	1	.000	1	1	0	0	0	0	3	—	2	2	—	0	—	∞	—	1.000	1.000	-3	-3	103	132	-0.4	0	0	-0.2

■ LARRY ANDERSEN Andersen, Larry Eugene b: 5/6/53, Portland, Ore. BR/TR, 6'3", 200 lbs. Deb: 9/05/75

YEAR	TM/L	W	L	PCT	G	GS	CG	SHO	SV	IP	H	H/G	HR	BB	BB/G	SO	SO/G	ERA	/A	OAVG	OOBP	PR	/A	PF	CPI	WAT	PB	PD	TPI
1975	Cle-A	0	0	—	3	0	0	0	0	6	4	6.0	0	2	3.0	4	6.0	4.50	84	.200	.261	-0	-0	100	39	0.0	0	0	0.0
1977	Cle-A	0	1	.000	11	0	0	0	0	14	10	6.4	1	9	5.8	8	5.1	3.21	124	.200	.306	1	1	98	92	-0.4	0	1	0.2
1979	Cle-A	0	0	—	8	0	0	0	0	17	25	13.2	3	4	2.1	7	3.7	7.41	61	.357	.377	-6	-6	106	93	0.0	0	0	-0.4
1981	Sea-A	3	3	.500	41	0	0	0	5	68	57	7.5	4	18	2.4	40	5.3	2.65	140	.228	.282	8	8	101	98	0.5	0	0	0.8
1982	Sea-A	0	0	—	40	1	0	0	1	80	100	11.2	16	23	2.6	32	3.6	5.96	75	.311	.359	-17	-13	110	100	0.0	0	1	-1.1
1983	Phi-N	1	0	1.000	17	0	0	0	0	26	19	6.6	0	9	3.1	14	4.8	2.42	150	.200	.264	4	4	100	62	0.5	-0	0	0.4
1984	Phi-N	3	7	.300	64	0	0	0	4	91	85	8.4	5	25	2.5	54	5.3	2.37	153	.248	.293	12	13	101	126	-2.0	-0	0	1.3
1985	Phi-N	3	3	.500	57	0	0	0	3	73	78	9.6	5	26	3.2	50	6.2	4.32	85	.274	.336	-6	-5	102	94	0.2	-0	2	-0.3
1986	Phi-N	0	0	—	10	0	0	0	0	13	19	13.2	0	3	2.1	9	6.2	4.15	93	.388	.400	-1	-0	104	150	0.0	0	0	0.0
	Hou-N	2	1	.667	38	0	0	0	1	65	64	8.9	2	23	3.2	33	4.6	2.77	137	.276	.328	7	7	102	140	0.3	-1	0	0.7
	Yr	2	1	.667	48	0	0	0	1	78	83	9.6	2	26	3.0	42	4.8	3.00	127	.294	.341	6	7	102	140	0.3	0	0	0.7
1987	Hou-N	9	5	.643	67	0	0	0	5	102	95	8.4	7	41	3.6	94	8.3	3.44	110	.246	.314	7	4	93	101	2.4	0	-0	0.4
1988	Hou-N	2	4	.333	53	0	0	0	5	83	82	8.9	3	20	2.2	66	7.2	2.93	110	.254	.294	5	3	93	102	-1.0	1	-0	0.3
1989	Hou-N	4	4	.500	60	0	0	0	3	88	63	6.4	2	24	2.5	85	8.7	1.53	234	.198	.248	**19**	**20**	103	105	-0.1	0	1	2.3
Total	12	27	28	.491	469	1	0	0	27	726	701	8.7	48	227	2.8	496	6.1	3.32	113	.256	.308	34	35	100	106	0.4	-1	5	4.6

■ ALLAN ANDERSON Anderson, Allan Lee b: 1/7/64, Lancaster, Ohio BL/TL, 5'11.5", 178 lbs. Deb: 6/11/86

YEAR	TM/L	W	L	PCT	G	GS	CG	SHO	SV	IP	H	H/G	HR	BB	BB/G	SO	SO/G	ERA	/A	OAVG	OOBP	PR	/A	PF	CPI	WAT	PB	PD	TPI
1986	Min-A	3	6	.333	21	10	1	0	0	84	106	11.4	11	30	3.2	51	5.5	5.57	82	.316	.369	-13	-9	109	103	-1.0	0	0	-0.8
1987	Min-A	1	0	1.000	4	2	0	0	0	12	20	15.0	3	10	7.5	3	2.3	11.25	38	.392	.492	-9	-9	96	92	0.5	0	-0	-0.7
1988	Min-A	16	9	.640	30	30	3	1	0	202	199	8.9	14	37	**1.6**	83	3.7	**2.45**	**171**	.261	.298	34	39	105	**138**	2.6	0	0	4.3
1989	Min-A	17	10	.630	33	33	4	1	0	197	214	9.8	15	53	2.4	69	3.2	3.79	109	.275	.324	2	8	106	104	4.1	0	-1	0.7
Total	4	37	25	.597	88	75	8	2	0	495	539	9.8	43	130	2.4	206	3.7	3.73	114	.280	.327	14	28	106	117	6.2	0	-0	3.5

■ KEVIN APPIER Appier, Robert Kevin b: 12/6/67, Lancaster, Cal. BR/TR, 6'2", 180 lbs. Deb: 6/14/89

YEAR	TM/L	W	L	PCT	G	GS	CG	SHO	SV	IP	H	H/G	HR	BB	BB/G	SO	SO/G	ERA	/A	OAVG	OOBP	PR	/A	PF	CPI	WAT	PB	PD	TPI
1989	KC-A	1	4	.200	6	5	0	0	0	22	34	13.9	3	12	4.9	10	4.1	9.00	41	.374	.434	-12	-13	95	88	-1.5	0	-1	-1.1

■ LUIS AQUINO Aquino, Luis Antonio (Colon) b: 5/19/64, Santurce, P.R. BR/TR, 6', 155 lbs. Deb: 8/08/86

YEAR	TM/L	W	L	PCT	G	GS	CG	SHO	SV	IP	H	H/G	HR	BB	BB/G	SO	SO/G	ERA	/A	OAVG	OOBP	PR	/A	PF	CPI	WAT	PB	PD	TPI
1986	Tor-A	1	1	.500	7	0	0	0	0	11	14	11.5	2	3	2.5	5	4.1	6.55	67	.304	.340	-3	-3	104	84	0.0	0	0	-0.2
1988	KC-A	1	0	1.000	7	5	1	1	0	29	33	10.2	1	17	5.3	11	3.4	2.79	146	.282	.375	4	4	103	169	0.5	0	-0	0.4
1989	KC-A	6	8	.429	34	16	2	1	0	141	148	9.4	6	35	2.2	68	4.3	3.51	105	.271	.316	6	3	95	100	-1.7	0	1	0.4
Total	3	8	9	.471	48	21	3	2	0	181	195	9.7	9	55	2.7	84	4.2	3.58	106	.275	.328	7	4	97	110	-1.2	0	1	0.6

■ JACK ARMSTRONG Armstrong, Jack William b: 3/7/65, Englewood, N.J. BR/TR, 6'5", 220 lbs. Deb: 6/21/88

YEAR	TM/L	W	L	PCT	G	GS	CG	SHO	SV	IP	H	H/G	HR	BB	BB/G	SO	SO/G	ERA	/A	OAVG	OOBP	PR	/A	PF	CPI	WAT	PB	PD	TPI
1988	Cin-N	4	7	.364	14	13	0	0	0	65	63	8.7	8	38	5.3	45	6.2	5.82	62	.256	.345	-17	-16	105	80	-1.8	-1	1	-1.5
1989	Cin-N	2	3	.400	9	8	0	0	0	43	40	8.4	5	21	4.4	23	4.8	4.60	79	.245	.326	-5	-5	104	88	-0.2	-1	0	-0.4
Total	2	6	10	.375	23	21	0	0	0	108	103	8.6	13	59	4.9	68	5.7	5.33	68	.252	.338	-22	-20	104	83	-2.0	-2	1	-1.9

■ BRAD ARNSBERG Arnsberg, Bradley James b: 8/20/63, Seattle, Wash. BR/TR, 6'4", 205 lbs. Deb: 9/06/86

YEAR	TM/L	W	L	PCT	G	GS	CG	SHO	SV	IP	H	H/G	HR	BB	BB/G	SO	SO/G	ERA	/A	OAVG	OOBP	PR	/A	PF	CPI	WAT	PB	PD	TPI
1986	NY-A	0	0	—	2	1	0	0	0	8	13	14.6	1	1	1.1	3	3.4	3.38	127	.342	.359	1	1	103	173	0.0	0	-0	0.1
1987	NY-A	1	3	.250	6	2	0	0	0	19	22	10.4	5	13	6.2	14	6.6	5.68	77	.289	.385	-3	-3	97	121	-1.0	0	1	-0.1
1989	Tex-A	2	1	.667	16	1	0	0	1	48	45	8.4	6	22	4.1	26	4.9	4.13	97	.247	.335	-1	-1	103	102	0.5	0	1	0.0
Total	3	3	4	.429	24	4	0	0	1	75	80	9.6	12	36	4.3	43	5.2	4.44	93	.270	.351	-3	-3	101	114	-0.5	0	1	0.0

■ PAUL ASSENMACHER Assenmacher, Paul Andre b: 12/10/60, Detroit, Mich. BL/TL, 6'3", 195 lbs. Deb: 4/12/86

YEAR	TM/L	W	L	PCT	G	GS	CG	SHO	SV	IP	H	H/G	HR	BB	BB/G	SO	SO/G	ERA	/A	OAVG	OOBP	PR	/A	PF	CPI	WAT	PB	PD	TPI
1986	Atl-N	7	3	.700	61	0	0	0	7	68	61	8.1	5	26	3.4	56	7.4	2.51	153	.241	.303	9	10	103	130	2.4	-0	1	1.2
1987	Atl-N	1	1	.500	52	0	0	0	2	55	58	9.5	8	24	3.9	39	6.4	5.07	88	.260	.331	-6	-4	109	87	0.1	-0	-1	-0.4
1988	Atl-N	8	7	.533	64	0	0	0	5	79	72	8.2	4	32	3.6	71	8.1	3.08	120	.251	.319	3	5	107	116	2.4	1	0	0.7
1989	Atl-N	1	3	.250	49	0	0	0	0	58	55	8.5	2	16	2.5	64	9.9	3.57	102	.249	.291	-0	0	104	83	-0.6	-0	0	0.1
	Chi-N	2	1	.667	14	0	0	0	0	19	19	9.0	1	12	5.7	15	7.1	5.21	72	.275	.369	-4	-3	107	92	0.3	-0	0	-0.2
	Yr	3	4	.429	63	0	0	0	0	77	74	8.6	3	28	3.3	79	9.2	3.97	92	.253	.308	-4	-3	105	92	-0.3	-0	1	-0.1
Total	4	19	15	.559	240	0	0	0	14	279	265	8.5	20	110	3.5	245	7.9	3.58	108	.252	.316	2	9	106	105	4.6	-0	1	1.4

■ KEITH ATHERTON Atherton, Keith Rowe b: 2/19/59, Mathews, Va. BR/TR, 6'4", 200 lbs. Deb: 7/14/83

YEAR	TM/L	W	L	PCT	G	GS	CG	SHO	SV	IP	H	H/G	HR	BB	BB/G	SO	SO/G	ERA	/A	OAVG	OOBP	PR	/A	PF	CPI	WAT	PB	PD	TPI
1983	Oak-A	2	5	.286	29	0	0	0	4	68	53	7.0	7	23	3.0	40	5.3	2.78	141	.215	.278	10	9	96	102	-1.2	0	-1	0.8
1984	Oak-A	7	6	.538	57	0	0	0	2	104	110	9.5	13	39	3.4	58	5.0	4.33	85	.274	.333	-4	-7	92	105	0.8	0	-2	-0.9
1985	Oak-A	4	7	.364	56	0	0	0	3	105	89	7.6	17	42	3.6	77	6.6	4.29	90	.231	.301	-2	-5	93	89	-1.3	0	-2	-0.6
1986	Oak-A	1	2	.333	13	0	0	0	0	15	18	10.8	2	11	6.6	8	4.8	6.00	65	.295	.387	-3	-3	94	102	-0.3	0	-0	-0.3
	Min-A	5	8	.385	47	0	0	0	10	82	82	9.0	9	35	3.8	59	6.5	3.73	123	.264	.331	4	8	109	116	-0.8	0	-0	0.7
	Yr	6	10	.375	60	0	0	0	10	97	100	9.3	11	46	4.3	67	6.2	4.08	110	.267	.341	1	4	107	116	-1.1	0	-0	0.4
1987	Min-A	7	5	.583	59	0	0	0	2	79	81	9.2	10	30	3.4	51	5.8	4.56	94	.262	.330	-1	-2	96	96	0.8	0	0	-0.1
1988	Min-A	7	5	.583	49	0	0	0	3	74	65	7.9	10	22	2.7	43	5.2	3.41	123	.235	.288	5	6	105	102	0.3	0	-0	0.6
1989	Cle-A	0	3	.000	32	0	0	0	2	39	48	11.1	7	13	3.0	13	3.0	4.15	98	.293	.343	-1	-0	104	127	-1.4	0	-1	0.0
Total	7	33	41	.446	342	0	0	0	26	566	546	8.7	75	215	3.4	349	5.5	3.99	102	.253	.317	8	4	98	103	-3.1	0	-6	0.2

■ DON AUGUST August, Donald Glenn b: 7/3/63, Inglewood, Cal. BB/TR, 6'3", 190 lbs. Deb: 6/02/88

YEAR	TM/L	W	L	PCT	G	GS	CG	SHO	SV	IP	H	H/G	HR	BB	BB/G	SO	SO/G	ERA	/A	OAVG	OOBP	PR	/A	PF	CPI	WAT	PB	PD	TPI
1988	Mil-A	13	7	.650	24	22	6	1	0	148	137	8.3	12	48	2.9	66	4.0	3.10	132	.245	.301	14	16	103	107	2.7	0	2	1.9
1989	Mil-A	12	12	.500	31	25	2	1	0	142	175	11.1	17	58	3.7	51	3.2	5.32	70	.302	.363	-23	-25	96	101	0.0	0	1	-2.2
Total	2	25	19	.568	55	47	8	2	0	290	312	9.7	29	106	3.3	117	3.6	4.19	93	.274	.333	-8	-9	100	104	2.7	0	3	-0.3

■ SCOTT BAILES Bailes, Scott Alan b: 12/18/61, Chillicothe, Ohio BL/TL, 6'2", 170 lbs. Deb: 4/09/86

YEAR	TM/L	W	L	PCT	G	GS	CG	SHO	SV	IP	H	H/G	HR	BB	BB/G	SO	SO/G	ERA	/A	OAVG	OOBP	PR	/A	PF	CPI	WAT	PB	PD	TPI
1986	Cle-A	10	10	.500	62	10	0	0	7	113	123	9.8	12	43	3.4	60	4.8	4.94	83	.276	.334	-9	-11	98	90	-0.3	0	-1	-1.0
1987	Cle-A	7	8	.467	39	17	0	0	6	120	145	10.9	21	47	3.5	65	4.9	4.65	101	.296	.356	-2	0	105	122	1.2	0	0	0.0
1988	Cle-A	9	14	.391	37	21	5	2	0	145	149	9.2	22	46	2.9	53	3.3	4.90	83	.266	.319	-15	-14	102	90	-2.3	0	-0	-1.3
1989	Cle-A	5	9	.357	34	11	0	0	0	114	116	9.2	7	29	2.3	47	3.7	4.26	95	.269	.313	-5	-3	104	86	-1.5	0	0	-0.2
Total	4	31	41	.431	172	59	5	2	13	492	533	9.8	62	165	3.0	225	4.1	4.70	90	.277	.331	-31	-26	102	97	-2.9	0	-1	-2.5

YEAR	TM/L	W	L	PCT	G	GS	CG	SHO	SV	IP	H	H/G	HR	BB	BB/G	SO	SO/G	ERA	/A	OAVG	OOBP	PR	/A	PF	CPI	WAT	PB	PD	TPI
■ **DOUG BAIR**		Bair, Charles Douglas b: 8/22/49, Defiance, Ohio BR/TR, 6', 170 lbs. Deb: 9/13/76																											
1976	Pit-N	0	0	—	4	0	0	0	0	6	4	6.0	0	5	7.5	4	6.0	6.00	58	.174	.321	-2	-2	99	34	0.0	0	0	-0.1
1977	Oak-A	4	6	.400	45	0	0	0	8	83	78	8.5	11	57	6.2	68	7.4	3.47	113	.253	.358	6	4	97	140	0.1	0	1	0.5
1978	Cin-N	7	6	.538	70	0	0	0	28	100	87	7.8	6	38	3.4	91	8.2	1.98	185	.236	.300	18	19	102	152	-0.3	-0	-1	1.9
1979	Cin-N	11	7	.611	65	0	0	0	16	94	93	8.9	7	51	4.9	86	8.2	4.31	84	.256	.342	-6	-7	96	95	1.2	-1	-0	-0.8
1980	Cin-N	3	6	.333	61	0	0	0	6	85	91	9.6	7	39	4.1	62	6.6	4.24	86	.277	.347	-6	-6	101	105	-1.7	-0	2	-0.3
1981	Cin-N	2	2	.500	24	0	0	0	0	39	42	9.7	5	17	3.9	16	3.7	5.77	61	.271	.339	-10	-10	101	79	-0.3	1	-1	-0.9
	StL-N	2	0	1.000	11	0	0	0	1	16	13	7.3	0	2	1.1	14	7.9	3.38	104	.224	.250	0	0	101	47	1.0	-0	0	0.0
	Yr	4	2	.667	35	0	0	0	1	55	55	9.0	5	19	3.1	30	4.9	5.07	69	.258	.316	-10	-10	101	47	0.7	1	-1	-0.9
1982	StL-N	5	3	.625	63	0	0	0	8	92	69	6.8	7	36	3.5	68	6.7	2.54	145	.211	.285	11	12	102	104	0.6	-1	0	1.2
1983	StL-N	1	1	.500	26	0	0	0	1	30	24	7.2	4	13	3.9	21	6.3	3.00	119	.224	.303	2	2	98	115	0.0	-0	-0	0.2
	Det-A	7	3	.700	27	1	0	0	4	56	51	8.2	8	19	3.1	39	6.3	3.86	100	.242	.305	1	-0	95	98	1.6	0	-0	0.0
1984	Det-A	5	3	.625	47	1	0	0	4	94	82	7.9	10	36	3.4	57	5.5	3.73	101	.238	.304	3	0	94	93	0.0	0	1	0.1
1985	Det-A	2	0	1.000	21	3	0	0	0	49	54	9.9	3	25	4.6	30	5.5	6.24	70	.281	.357	-11	-10	106	75	1.0	0	1	-0.8
	StL-N	0	0	—	2	0	0	0	0	2	1	4.5	0	2	9.0	0	0.0	0.00	—	.167	.375	1	1	93	0	0.0	0	0	0.1
1986	Oak-A	2	3	.400	31	0	0	0	4	45	37	7.4	5	18	3.6	40	8.0	3.00	131	.224	.291	6	5	94	107	-0.3	0	0	0.5
1987	Phi-N	2	0	1.000	11	0	0	0	0	14	17	10.9	4	5	3.2	10	6.4	5.79	74	.309	.361	-3	-2	105	116	1.0	-0	-0	-0.2
1988	Tor-A	0	0	—	10	0	0	0	0	13	14	9.7	2	3	2.1	8	5.5	4.15	95	.280	.309	-0	-0	99	110	0.0	0	0	0.0
1989	Pit-N	2	3	.400	44	0	0	0	1	67	52	7.0	4	28	3.8	56	7.5	2.28	145	.211	.290	9	8	94	114	-0.2	0	1	0.9
Total	14	55	43	.561	562	5	0	0	81	885	809	8.2	83	394	4.0	670	6.8	3.60	104	.244	.319	19	13	99	107	3.7	-2	3	2.3
■ **JEFF BALLARD**		Ballard, Jeffrey Scott b: 8/13/63, Billings, Mont. BL/TL, 6'3", 195 lbs. Deb: 5/09/87																											
1987	Bal-A	2	8	.200	14	14	0	0	0	70	100	12.9	15	35	4.5	27	3.5	6.56	68	.344	.413	-16	-16	99	116	-2.6	0	0	-1.4
1988	Bal-A	8	12	.400	25	25	6	1	0	153	167	9.8	15	42	2.5	41	2.4	4.41	88	.278	.329	-7	-9	97	97	1.1	0	-2	-1.0
1989	Bal-A	18	8	.692	35	35	4	1	0	215	240	10.0	16	57	2.4	62	2.6	3.43	112	.287	.330	11	10	99	123	4.9	0	4	1.4
Total	3	28	28	.500	74	74	10	2	0	438	507	10.4	46	134	2.8	130	2.7	4.27	92	.294	.344	-13	-16	98	113	3.4	0	2	-1.0
■ **SCOTT BANKHEAD**		Bankhead, Michael Scott b: 7/31/63, Raleigh, N.C. BR/TR, 5'10", 175 lbs. Deb: 5/25/86																											
1986	KC-A	8	9	.471	24	17	0	0	0	121	121	9.0	14	37	2.8	94	7.0	4.61	91	.259	.311	-6	-6	100	85	0.0	0	-0	-0.5
1987	Sea-A	9	8	.529	27	25	2	0	0	149	168	10.1	35	37	2.2	95	5.7	5.44	85	.283	.324	-16	-14	103	98	0.9	0	-2	-1.4
1988	Sea-A	7	9	.438	21	21	2	1	0	135	115	7.7	8	38	2.5	102	6.8	3.07	140	.224	.276	14	19	108	80	0.2	0	-1	1.8
1989	Sea-A	14	6	.700	33	33	3	2	0	210	187	8.0	19	63	2.7	140	6.0	3.34	121	.239	.294	13	16	104	95	4.9	0	-2	1.5
Total	4	38	32	.543	105	96	7	3	0	615	591	8.6	76	175	2.6	431	6.3	4.04	106	.251	.301	5	15	104	90	6.0	0	-5	1.4
■ **FLOYD BANNISTER**		Bannister, Floyd Franklin b: 6/10/55, Pierre, S.D. BL/TL, 6'1", 190 lbs. Deb: 4/19/77																											
1977	Hou-N	8	9	.471	24	23	4	1	0	143	138	8.7	11	68	4.3	112	7.0	4.03	90	.254	.338	-2	-7	92	96	-0.5	0	-1	-0.7
1978	Hou-N	3	9	.250	28	16	2	2	0	110	120	9.8	13	63	5.2	94	7.7	4.83	70	.280	.367	-15	-17	95	107	-2.7	0	-2	-1.9
1979	Sea-A	10	15	.400	30	30	6	2	0	182	185	9.1	25	68	3.4	115	5.7	4.05	105	.260	.324	4	5	101	103	-0.4	0	-2	0.2
1980	Sea-A	9	13	.409	32	32	8	0	0	218	200	8.3	24	66	2.7	155	6.4	3.47	122	.239	.292	14	19	105	91	0.9	0	-1	1.9
1981	Sea-A	9	9	.500	21	20	5	2	0	121	128	9.5	14	39	2.9	85	6.3	4.46	83	.268	.326	-11	-10	101	92	1.7	0	-1	-1.0
1982	Sea-A	12	13	.480	35	35	5	3	0	247	225	8.2	32	77	2.8	**209**	7.6	3.43	131	.243	.298	18	29	110	105	0.3	0	-1	3.0
1983	Chi-A	16	10	.615	34	34	5	2	0	217	191	7.9	19	71	2.9	193	**8.0**	3.36	123	.233	.293	17	19	102	90	0.2	0	-1	1.8
1984	Chi-A	14	11	.560	34	33	4	0	0	218	211	8.7	30	80	3.3	152	6.3	4.83	92	.252	.317	-20	-9	111	84	2.7	0	-2	-1.1
1985	Chi-A	10	14	.417	34	34	4	1	0	211	211	9.0	30	100	4.3	198	**8.4**	4.86	85	.261	.339	-17	-17	100	97	-2.7	0	-1	-1.7
1986	Chi-A	10	14	.417	28	27	6	1	0	165	162	8.8	17	48	2.6	92	5.0	3.55	120	.259	.308	12	13	101	106	-0.8	0	-1	1.2
1987	Chi-A	16	11	.593	34	34	11	2	0	229	216	8.5	38	49	1.9	124	4.9	3.58	136	.246	.282	23	32	109	102	3.5	0	-3	2.9
1988	KC-A	12	13	.480	31	31	2	0	0	189	182	8.7	22	68	3.2	113	5.4	4.33	94	.248	.313	-8	-5	103	88	-1.1	0	-0	-0.5
1989	KC-A	4	1	.800	14	14	0	0	0	75	87	10.4	8	18	2.2	35	4.2	4.68	79	.290	.328	-7	-8	95	95	1.4	0	1	-0.6
Total	13	133	142	.484	379	363	62	16	0	2325	2256	8.7	283	815	3.2	1677	6.5	4.03	104	.253	.314	9	41	103	96	2.5	1	-14	3.5
■ **JOHN BARFIELD**		Barfield, John David b: 10/15/64, Pine Bluff, Ark. BL/TL, 6'1", 185 lbs. Deb: 9/07/89																											
1989	Tex-A	0	1	.000	4	2	0	0	0	12	15	11.3	0	4	3.0	9	6.8	6.00	67	.319	.365	-3	-3	103	78	-0.4	0	0	-0.2
■ **JOSE BAUTISTA**		Bautista, Jose Joaquin (Arias) b: 7/25/64, Bani, D.R. BR/TR, 6'1", 177 lbs. Deb: 4/09/88																											
1988	Bal-A	6	15	.286	33	25	3	0	0	172	171	8.9	21	45	2.4	76	4.0	4.29	90	.258	.309	-6	-8	97	91	-1.6	0	-1	-0.8
1989	Bal-A	3	4	.429	15	10	0	0	0	78	84	9.7	17	15	1.7	30	3.5	5.31	72	.274	.308	-12	-13	99	89	-0.6	0	-1	-1.2
Total	2	9	19	.321	48	35	3	0	0	250	255	9.2	38	60	2.2	106	3.8	4.61	84	.263	.309	-18	-21	98	90	-2.2	0	-2	-2.0
■ **DAVE BEARD**		Beard, Charles David b: 10/2/59, Atlanta, Ga. BL/TR, 6'5", 190 lbs. Deb: 7/16/80																											
1980	Oak-A	0	1	.000	13	0	0	0	1	16	12	6.8	0	7	3.9	12	6.8	3.38	113	.218	.313	1	1	94	76	-0.4	0	0	0.1
1981	Oak-A	1	1	.500	8	0	0	0	3	13	9	6.2	1	4	2.8	15	10.4	2.77	126	.191	.264	1	1	95	75	-0.1	0	0	0.1
1982	Oak-A	10	9	.526	54	2	0	0	11	92	85	8.3	9	35	3.4	73	7.1	3.42	115	.244	.305	7	5	96	104	1.9	0	-0	0.5
1983	Oak-A	5	5	.500	43	0	0	0	10	61	55	8.1	8	36	5.3	40	5.9	5.61	70	.246	.347	-10	-11	96	82	0.4	0	-1	-1.2
1984	Sea-A	3	2	.600	43	0	0	0	5	76	88	10.4	15	33	3.9	40	4.7	5.80	71	.291	.357	-15	-14	103	100	0.7	0	0	-1.3
1985	Chi-N	0	0	—	9	0	0	0	0	13	16	11.1	2	7	4.8	4	2.8	6.23	67	.314	.390	-4	-3	117	100	0.0	0	0	-0.2
1989	Det-A	0	2	.000	2	1	0	0	0	5	9	16.2	2	2	3.6	1	1.8	5.40	71	.375	.444	-1	-1	99	193	-0.9	0	0	0.0
Total	7	19	20	.487	172	3	0	0	30	276	274	8.9	37	124	4.0	185	6.0	4.70	85	.261	.335	-21	-22	99	96	1.6	0	-1	-2.0
■ **BLAINE BEATTY**		Beatty, Gordon Blaine b: 4/25/64, Victoria, Tex. BL/TL, 6'2", 185 lbs. Deb: 9/16/89																											
1989	NY-N	0	0	—	2	1	0	0	0	6	5	7.5	1	2	3.0	3	4.5	1.50	222	.217	.280	1	1	95	216	0.0	0	0	0.2
■ **STEVE BEDROSIAN**		Bedrosian, Stephen Wayne b: 12/6/57, Methuen, Mass. BR/TR, 6'3", 200 lbs. Deb: 8/14/81																											
1981	Atl-N	1	2	.333	15	1	0	0	0	24	15	5.6	2	15	5.6	9	3.4	4.50	78	.169	.292	-3	-3	100	49	-0.3	-0	-0	-0.2
1982	Atl-N	8	6	.571	64	3	0	0	11	138	102	6.7	7	57	3.7	123	8.0	2.41	159	.206	.287	18	22	107	100	0.4	-2	-0	2.1
1983	Atl-N	9	10	.474	70	1	0	0	19	120	100	7.5	11	51	3.8	114	8.6	3.60	105	.229	.308	0	3	104	91	-1.3	-1	0	0.2
1984	Atl-N	9	6	.600	40	4	0	0	11	84	65	7.0	5	33	3.5	81	8.7	2.36	167	.210	.287	12	15	110	104	1.7	-1	-1	1.4
1985	Atl-N	7	15	.318	37	37	0	0	0	207	198	8.6	17	111	4.8	134	5.8	3.83	102	.254	.346	-5	2	108	109	-2.6	-4	-2	-0.3
1986	Phi-N	8	6	.571	68	0	0	0	29	90	79	7.9	12	34	3.4	82	8.2	3.40	114	.232	.297	3	5	104	101	0.6	0	-1	0.5
1987	Phi-N	5	3	.625	65	0	0	0	**40**	89	79	8.0	11	28	2.8	74	7.5	2.83	151	.237	.295	12	14	105	119	1.1	-0	-1	1.3
1988	Phi-N	6	6	.500	57	0	0	0	28	74	75	9.1	6	27	3.3	61	7.4	3.77	94	.257	.317	-3	-2	103	98	1.0	-0	-0	-0.1
1989	Phi-N	2	3	.400	28	0	0	0	6	34	21	5.6	7	17	4.5	24	6.4	3.18	113	.183	.289	1	2	102	111	0.0	0	-0	0.1
	SF-N	1	4	.200	40	0	0	0	17	51	35	6.2	5	22	3.9	34	6.0	2.65	127	.192	.275	5	4	96	95	-1.5	-0	-1	0.3
	Yr	3	7	.300	68	0	0	0	23	85	56	5.9	12	39	4.1	58	6.1	2.86	121	.187	.278	6	6	98	95	-1.5	0	-2	0.4
Total	9	56	61	.479	484	46	0	0	161	911	769	7.6	83	395	3.9	736	7.3	3.23	119	.228	.308	42	61	105	102	-0.9	-9	-6	5.3
■ **TIM BELCHER**		Belcher, Timothy Wayne b: 10/19/61, Mount Gilead, Ohio BR/TR, 6'3", 210 lbs. Deb: 9/06/87																											
1987	LA-N	4	2	.667	6	5	0	0	0	34	30	7.9	2	7	1.9	23	6.1	2.38	158	.240	.274	6	5	92	113	1.2	0	0	0.5
1988	LA-N	12	6	.667	36	27	4	1	4	180	143	7.2	8	51	2.6	152	7.6	2.90	125	.217	.273	11	15	105	79	2.0	-2	-1	1.3
1989	LA-N	15	12	.556	39	30	**10**	**8**	1	230	182	7.1	20	80	3.1	200	7.8	2.82	115	.217	.287	17	11	93	102	2.3	-2	-1	0.8
Total	3	31	20	.608	81	62	14	9	5	444	355	7.2	30	138	2.8	375	7.6	2.82	122	.219	.280	35	31	98	93	5.5	-3	-2	2.6
■ **STAN BELINDA**		Belinda, Stanley Peter b: 8/6/66, Huntingdon, Pa. BR/TR, 6'3", 185 lbs. Deb: 9/08/89																											
1989	Pit-N	0	1	.000	8	0	0	0	0	10	13	11.7	0	2	1.8	10	9.0	6.30	52	.295	.326	-3	-3	94	58	-0.4	0	-0	-0.3
■ **ANDY BENES**		Benes, Andrew Charles b: 8/20/67, Evansville, Ind. BR/TR, 6'6", 235 lbs. Deb: 8/11/89																											
1989	SD-N	6	3	.667	10	10	0	0	0	67	51	6.9	7	31	4.2	66	8.9	3.49	101	.213	.296	0	0	101	92	1.2	2	0	0.2
■ **JUAN BERENGUER**		Berenguer, Juan Bautista b: 11/30/54, Aguadulce, Pan. BR/TR, 5'11", 186 lbs. Deb: 8/17/78																											
1978	NY-N	0	2	.000	5	3	0	0	0	13	17	11.8	1	11	7.6	8	5.5	8.31	43	.327	.446	-7	-7	99	85	-0.9	-0	0	-0.6
1979	NY-N	1	1	.500	5	5	0	0	0	31	28	8.1	2	12	3.5	25	7.3	2.90	124	.252	.325	3	2	96	124	0.2	0	-1	0.2

YEAR	TM/L	W	L	PCT	G	GS	CG	SHO	SV	IP	H	H/G	HR	BB	BB/G	SO	SO/G	ERA	/A	OAVG	OOBP	PR	/A	PF	CPI	WAT	PB	PD	TPI
1980	NY-N	0	1	.000	6	0	0	0	0	9	9	9.0	1	10	10.0	7	7.0	6.00	58	.250	.413	-2	-2	97	94	-0.4	0	0	-0.1
1981	KC-A	0	4	.000	8	3	0	0	0	20	22	9.9	4	16	7.2	20	9.0	8.55	42	.289	.412	-11	-11	99	81	-1.9	0	-1	-1.0
	Tor-A	2	9	.182	12	11	1	0	0	71	62	7.9	7	35	4.4	29	3.7	4.31	96	.235	.325	-5	-1	113	86	-2.7	0	-1	-0.1
	Yr	2	13	.133	20	14	1	0	0	91	84	8.3	11	51	5.0	49	4.8	5.24	77	.243	.341	-16	-12	110	86	-4.6	0	-1	-1.1
1982	Det-A	0	0	—	2	1	0	0	0	7	5	6.4	0	9	11.6	8	10.3	6.43	63	.200	.412	-2	-2	100	66	0.0	0	-0	-0.1
1983	Det-A	9	5	.643	37	19	2	1	1	158	110	6.3	19	71	4.0	129	7.3	3.13	123	.193	.288	17	13	95	88	1.3	0	-2	1.1
1984	Det-A	11	10	.524	31	27	2	1	0	168	146	7.8	14	79	4.2	118	6.3	3.48	108	.232	.319	10	5	94	99	-2.1	0	-1	0.4
1985	Det-A	5	6	.455	31	13	0	0	0	95	96	9.1	12	48	4.5	82	7.8	5.59	79	.259	.342	-15	-13	106	81	-0.7	0	1	-1.1
1986	SF-N	2	3	.400	46	4	0	0	4	73	64	7.9	4	44	5.4	72	8.9	2.71	130	.242	.350	8	7	95	143	-0.5	-0	-1	0.6
1987	Min-A	8	1	.889	47	6	0	0	4	112	100	8.0	10	47	3.8	110	8.8	3.94	109	.238	.311	7	4	96	88	3.5	0	-1	0.3
1988	Min-A	8	4	.667	57	1	0	0	2	100	74	6.7	7	61	5.5	99	8.9	3.96	106	.207	.318	0	3	105	81	1.5	0	0	0.3
1989	Min-A	9	3	.750	56	0	0	0	3	106	96	8.2	11	47	4.0	93	7.9	3.48	119	.246	.321	5	8	106	112	3.2	0	-1	0.7
Total	12	55	49	.529	343	93	5	2	14	963	829	7.7	92	490	4.6	800	7.5	3.93	101	.233	.325	7	6	100	96	0.5	-0	-7	0.6

■ **MIKE BIELECKI** Bielecki, Michael Joseph b: 7/31/59, Baltimore, Md. BR/TR, 6'3", 200 lbs. Deb: 9/14/84

YEAR	TM/L	W	L	PCT	G	GS	CG	SHO	SV	IP	H	H/G	HR	BB	BB/G	SO	SO/G	ERA	/A	OAVG	OOBP	PR	/A	PF	CPI	WAT	PB	PD	TPI
1984	Pit-N	0	0	—	4	0	0	0	0	4	4	9.0	0	0	0.0	1	2.3	0.00	—	.250	.235	2	1	94	0	0.0	0	0	0.2
1985	Pit-N	2	3	.400	12	7	0	0	0	46	45	8.8	5	31	6.1	22	4.3	4.50	83	.257	.365	-5	-4	104	107	0.2	-1	1	-0.3
1986	Pit-N	6	11	.353	31	27	0	0	0	149	149	9.0	10	83	5.0	83	5.0	4.65	80	.262	.351	-15	-15	101	92	-0.9	-3	-1	-1.8
1987	Pit-N	2	3	.400	8	8	2	0	0	46	43	8.4	6	12	2.3	25	4.9	4.70	91	.250	.292	-3	-2	105	79	-0.4	-1	-0	-0.2
1988	Chi-N	2	2	.500	19	5	0	0	0	48	55	10.3	4	16	3.0	33	6.2	3.38	107	.284	.330	0	1	105	129	0.1	-0	-0	0.1
1989	Chi-N	18	7	**.720**	33	33	4	3	0	212	187	7.9	16	81	3.4	147	6.2	3.14	120	.237	.304	8	15	107	104	4.8	-5	-1	0.9
Total	6	30	26	.536	107	80	6	3	0	505	483	8.6	41	223	4.0	311	5.5	3.85	98	.252	.325	-13	-3	104	100	3.8	-11	-1	-1.1

■ **MIKE BIRKBECK** Birkbeck, Michael Lawrence b: 3/10/61, Orrville, Ohio BR/TR, 6'1", 190 lbs. Deb: 8/17/86

YEAR	TM/L	W	L	PCT	G	GS	CG	SHO	SV	IP	H	H/G	HR	BB	BB/G	SO	SO/G	ERA	/A	OAVG	OOBP	PR	/A	PF	CPI	WAT	PB	PD	TPI
1986	Mil-A	1	1	.500	7	4	0	0	0	22	24	9.8	0	12	4.9	13	5.3	4.50	96	.282	.371	-1	-0	103	95	0.0	0	-0	0.0
1987	Mil-A	1	4	.200	10	10	1	0	0	45	63	12.6	8	19	3.8	25	5.0	6.20	74	.335	.390	-9	-8	102	111	-1.5	0	1	-0.6
1988	Mil-A	10	8	.556	23	23	0	0	0	124	141	10.2	10	37	2.7	64	4.6	4.72	87	.285	.333	-10	-9	103	92	0.4	0	2	-0.6
1989	Mil-A	0	4	.000	9	9	1	0	0	45	57	11.4	4	22	4.4	31	6.2	5.40	69	.310	.383	-8	-8	96	106	-1.9	0	-0	-0.7
Total	4	12	17	.414	49	46	2	0	0	236	285	10.9	22	90	3.4	133	5.1	5.11	81	.300	.358	-27	-26	101	98	-3.0	0	2	-1.9

■ **TIM BIRTSAS** Birtsas, Timothy Dean b: 9/5/60, Pontiac, Mich. BL/TL, 6'7", 240 lbs. Deb: 5/03/85

YEAR	TM/L	W	L	PCT	G	GS	CG	SHO	SV	IP	H	H/G	HR	BB	BB/G	SO	SO/G	ERA	/A	OAVG	OOBP	PR	/A	PF	CPI	WAT	PB	PD	TPI
1985	Oak-A	10	6	.625	29	25	2	0	0	141	124	7.9	18	91	5.8	94	6.0	4.02	96	.238	.349	2	-2	93	112	2.5	0	-2	-0.4
1986	Oak-A	0	0	—	2	0	0	0	0	2	2	9.0	1	4	18.0	1	4.5	22.50	17	.286	.500	-4	-4	94	55	0.0	0	0	-0.3
1988	Cin-N	1	3	.250	36	4	0	0	0	64	61	8.6	6	24	3.4	38	5.3	4.22	86	.250	.318	-5	-4	105	91	-1.0	-1	-1	-0.5
1989	Cin-N	2	2	.500	42	1	0	0	1	70	68	8.7	5	27	3.5	57	7.3	3.73	97	.261	.327	-2	-1	104	107	0.1	1	-1	0.0
Total	4	13	11	.542	109	30	2	0	1	277	255	8.3	30	146	4.7	190	6.2	4.13	91	.247	.338	-9	-11	99	105	1.6	0	-4	-1.2

■ **JEFF BITTIGER** Bittiger, Jeffrey Scott b: 4/13/62, Jersey City, N.J. BR/TR, 5'10", 175 lbs. Deb: 9/02/86

YEAR	TM/L	W	L	PCT	G	GS	CG	SHO	SV	IP	H	H/G	HR	BB	BB/G	SO	SO/G	ERA	/A	OAVG	OOBP	PR	/A	PF	CPI	WAT	PB	PD	TPI
1986	Phi-N	1	1	.500	3	3	0	0	0	15	16	9.6	2	7	4.2	8	4.8	5.40	72	.271	.353	-3	-3	104	91	0.0	1	0	0.0
1987	Min-A	1	0	1.000	3	1	0	0	0	8	11	12.4	2	0	0.0	5	5.6	5.63	76	.314	.333	-1	-1	96	105	0.5	0	0	0.0
1988	Chi-A	2	4	.333	25	7	0	0	0	62	59	8.6	11	29	4.2	33	4.8	4.21	93	.255	.328	-2	-2	99	113	-0.7	0	-1	-0.2
1989	Chi-A	0	1	.000	2	1	0	0	0	10	9	8.1	2	6	5.4	7	6.3	6.30	58	.257	.366	-3	-3	93	86	-0.4	0	-0	-0.2
Total	4	4	6	.400	33	12	0	0	0	95	95	9.0	17	42	4.0	53	5.0	4.74	83	.264	.337	-8	-9	99	106	-0.6	1	-1	-0.4

■ **BUDDY BLACK** Black, Harry Ralston b: 6/30/57, San Mateo, Cal. BL/TL, 6'2", 180 lbs. Deb: 9/05/81

YEAR	TM/L	W	L	PCT	G	GS	CG	SHO	SV	IP	H	H/G	HR	BB	BB/G	SO	SO/G	ERA	/A	OAVG	OOBP	PR	/A	PF	CPI	WAT	PB	PD	TPI
1981	Sea-A	0	0	—	2	0	0	0	0	1	2	18.0	0	3	27.0	0	0.0	0.00	—	.500	.714	0	0	101	0	0.0	0	0	0.1
1982	KC-A	4	6	.400	22	14	0	0	0	88	92	9.4	10	34	3.5	40	4.1	4.60	88	.269	.334	-5	-5	100	95	-1.4	0	0	-0.4
1983	KC-A	10	7	.588	24	24	3	0	0	161	159	8.9	19	43	2.4	58	3.2	3.80	109	.257	.304	5	6	102	99	1.8	0	2	0.8
1984	KC-A	17	12	.586	35	35	8	1	0	257	226	7.9	22	64	2.2	140	4.9	3.12	127	.233	**.281**	25	24	99	89	2.4	0	3	2.8
1985	KC-A	10	15	.400	33	33	5	2	0	206	216	9.4	17	59	2.6	122	5.3	4.33	97	.268	.320	-4	-3	101	91	-3.9	0	-1	-0.3
1986	KC-A	5	10	.333	56	4	0	0	9	121	100	7.4	14	43	3.2	68	5.1	3.20	131	.225	.298	13	13	100	103	-2.2	0	0	1.4
1987	KC-A	8	6	.571	29	18	0	0	1	122	126	9.3	16	35	2.6	61	4.5	3.61	128	.265	.319	12	14	104	116	0.9	0	-0	1.3
1988	KC-A	2	1	.667	17	0	0	0	0	22	23	9.4	2	11	4.5	19	7.8	4.91	83	.267	.347	-2	-2	103	91	0.5	0	-0	-0.2
	Cle-A	2	3	.400	16	7	0	0	1	59	59	9.0	6	23	3.5	44	6.7	5.03	81	.262	.331	-7	-6	102	86	-0.3	0	1	-0.5
	Yr	4	4	.500	33	7	0	0	1	81	82	9.1	8	34	3.8	63	7.0	5.00	81	.264	.335	-9	-8	102	86	0.2	0	1	-0.7
1989	Cle-A	12	11	.522	33	32	6	3	0	222	213	8.6	14	52	2.1	88	3.6	3.36	121	.252	.292	13	17	104	91	1.7	0	-0	1.7
Total	9	70	71	.496	267	167	22	6	11	1259	1216	8.7	120	367	2.6	640	4.6	3.72	111	.252	.306	50	59	102	95	-0.5	0	4	6.7

■ **KEVIN BLANKENSHIP** Blankenship, Kevin De Wayne b: 1/26/63, Anaheim, Cal. BR/TR, 6', 180 lbs. Deb: 9/20/88

YEAR	TM/L	W	L	PCT	G	GS	CG	SHO	SV	IP	H	H/G	HR	BB	BB/G	SO	SO/G	ERA	/A	OAVG	OOBP	PR	/A	PF	CPI	WAT	PB	PD	TPI
1988	Atl-N	0	1	.000	2	2	0	0	0	11	7	5.7	0	7	5.7	5	4.1	3.27	113	.194	.341	0	1	107	88	-0.4	-0	-0	0.0
	Chi-N	1	0	1.000	1	1	0	0	0	5	7	12.6	2	1	1.8	4	7.2	7.20	50	.318	.348	-2	-2	105	103	0.5	-0	-0	-0.1
	Yr	1	1	.500	3	3	0	0	0	16	14	7.9	2	8	4.5	9	5.1	4.50	82	.237	.328	-2	-1	106	103	0.1	-0	-0	-0.1
1989	Chi-N	0	0	—	2	0	0	0	0	5	4	7.2	0	2	3.6	2	3.6	1.80	209	.200	.273	1	1	107	86	0.0	-0	0	0.1
Total	2	1	1	.500	5	3	0	0	0	21	18	7.7	2	10	4.3	11	4.7	3.86	96	.231	.326	-1	-0	107	91	0.1	-1	-0	0.0

■ **TERRY BLOCKER** Blocker, Terry Fennell b: 8/18/59, Columbia, S.C. BL/TL, 6'2", 195 lbs. Deb: 4/11/85

YEAR	TM/L	W	L	PCT	G	GS	CG	SHO	SV	IP	H	H/G	HR	BB	BB/G	SO	SO/G	ERA	/A	OAVG	OOBP	PR	/A	PF	CPI	WAT	PB	PD	TPI
1989	Atl-N	0	0	—	1	0	0	0	0	1	0	0.0	0	2	18.0	0	0.0	0.00	—	.000	.500	0	0	104	0	0.0	0	0	0.0

■ **BERT BLYLEVEN** Blyleven, Rik Aalbert b: 4/6/51, Zeist, Holland BR/TR, 6'3", 200 lbs. Deb: 6/05/70

YEAR	TM/L	W	L	PCT	G	GS	CG	SHO	SV	IP	H	H/G	HR	BB	BB/G	SO	SO/G	ERA	/A	OAVG	OOBP	PR	/A	PF	CPI	WAT	PB	PD	TPI
1970	Min-A	10	9	.526	27	25	5	1	0	164	143	7.8	17	47	2.6	135	7.4	3.18	113	.232	.284	10	7	97	93	-1.3	-1	-2	0.5
1971	Min-A	16	15	.516	38	38	17	5	0	278	267	8.6	21	59	1.9	224	7.3	2.82	128	.255	.294	20	25	104	111	1.9	-3	-0	2.4
1972	Min-A	17	17	.500	39	38	11	3	0	287	247	7.7	22	69	2.2	228	7.1	2.73	121	.233	.282	11	18	107	99	0.0	-1	1	2.2
1973	Min-A	20	17	.541	40	40	25	**9**	0	325	296	8.2	16	67	1.9	258	7.1	2.52	156	.242	.282	**47**	51	103	103	1.9	0	-2	5.5
1974	Min-A	17	17	.500	37	37	19	3	0	281	244	7.8	14	77	2.5	249	8.0	2.66	138	.233	.287	30	31	101	97	-0.2	0	0	3.4
1975	Min-A	15	10	.600	35	35	20	3	0	276	219	7.1	24	84	2.7	233	7.6	3.00	135	.219	.278	24	33	107	87	3.3	0	3	3.8
1976	Min-A	4	5	.444	12	12	4	0	0	95	101	9.6	3	35	3.3	75	7.1	3.13	110	.283	.345	4	3	98	131	-0.6	0	0	0.4
	Tex-A	9	11	.450	24	24	14	6	0	202	182	8.1	11	46	2.0	144	6.4	2.76	131	.242	.288	17	19	103	102	-0.4	0	2	2.3
	Yr	13	16	.448	36	36	18	6	0	297	283	8.6	14	81	2.5	219	6.6	2.88	124	.254	.304	21	22	101	102	-1.0	0	2	2.7
1977	Tex-A	14	12	.538	30	30	15	5	0	235	181	6.9	20	69	2.6	182	7.0	2.72	**155**	.214	.275	35	**39**	104	93	-1.0	0	0	**4.2**
1978	Pit-N	14	10	.583	34	34	11	4	0	244	217	8.0	17	66	2.4	182	6.7	3.02	124	.235	.286	15	20	105	92	1.1	-3	1	2.0
1979	Pit-N	12	5	.706	37	37	4	0	0	237	238	9.0	21	92	3.5	172	6.5	3.61	108	.265	.330	4	7	104	112	2.4	-3	-2	0.3
1980	Pit-N	8	13	.381	34	32	5	2	0	217	219	9.1	20	59	2.4	168	7.0	3.82	97	.262	.307	-5	-2	103	94	-2.9	-4	-0	-0.6
1981	Cle-A	11	7	.611	20	20	9	1	0	159	145	8.2	9	40	2.3	107	6.1	2.89	119	.245	.295	14	9	93	102	2.2	0	-1	0.8
1982	Cle-A	2	2	.500	4	4	0	0	0	20	16	7.2	2	11	4.9	19	8.5	4.95	83	.211	.303	-2	-2	101	62	0.1	0	0	-0.1
1983	Cle-A	7	10	.412	24	24	5	0	0	156	160	9.2	8	44	2.5	123	7.1	3.92	110	.267	.324	3	7	106	95	-0.3	0	1	0.8
1984	Cle-A	19	7	.731	33	32	12	4	0	245	204	7.5	19	74	2.7	170	6.2	2.87	**148**	.224	.283	31	**37**	106	94	**7.0**	0	0	**4.0**
1985	Cle-A	9	11	.450	23	23	15	4	0	180	163	8.1	14	49	2.5	129	6.4	3.25	122	.240	.295	18	14	95	96	1.4	0	-1	1.3
	Min-A	8	5	.615	14	14	9	1	0	114	101	8.0	9	26	2.1	77	6.1	3.00	144	.237	.280	15	17	104	96	1.8	0	-0	1.7
	Yr	17	16	.515	37	37	**24**	**5**	0	**294**	264	8.1	23	75	2.3	**206**	6.3	3.15	130	.236	.283	33	31	99	96	3.2	0	-1	3.0
1986	Min-A	17	14	.548	36	36	16	3	0	**272**	262	8.7	50	58	1.9	215	7.1	4.00	114	.250	.293	6	17	109	98	3.6	0	-1	1.6
1987	Min-A	15	12	.556	37	37	8	1	0	267	249	8.4	46	101	3.4	196	6.6	4.01	107	.249	.320	14	8	96	109	1.0	0	1	0.9
1988	Min-A	10	17	.370	33	33	7	0	0	207	240	10.4	21	51	2.2	145	6.3	5.43	77	.294	.343	-34	-29	105	88	-5.1	0	-1	-2.8
1989	Cal-A	17	5	.773	33	33	8	**5**	0	241	225	8.4	14	44	1.6	131	4.9	2.73	139	.248	.285	31	29	98	106	5.7	0	1	3.2
Total	20	271	231	.540	644	638	239	60	0	4702	4319	8.3	398	1268	2.4	3562	6.8	3.22	121	.245	.296	307	361	103	99	21.6	-14	2	37.8

■ **RANDY BOCKUS** Bockus, Randy Walter b: 10/5/60, Canton, Ohio BL/TR, 6'2", 190 lbs. Deb: 9/10/86

YEAR	TM/L	W	L	PCT	G	GS	CG	SHO	SV	IP	H	H/G	HR	BB	BB/G	SO	SO/G	ERA	/A	OAVG	OOBP	PR	/A	PF	CPI	WAT	PB	PD	TPI
1986	SF-N	0	0	—	5	0	0	0	0	7	7	9.0	1	6	7.7	4	5.1	2.57	137	.241	.361	1	1	95	191	0.0	-0	1	0.1
1987	SF-N	1	0	1.000	12	0	0	0	0	17	17	9.0	2	4	2.1	9	4.8	3.71	104	.266	.309	1	0	95	105	0.5	-0	0	0.0
1988	SF-N	1	1	.500	20	0	0	0	0	32	35	9.8	2	13	3.7	18	5.1	4.78	67	.297	.355	-5	-6	93	102	0.0	0	0	-0.5

YEAR	TM/L	W	L	PCT	G	GS	CG	SHO	SV	IP	H	H/G	HR	BB	BB/G	SO	SO/G	ERA	/A	OAVG	OOBP	PR	/A	PF	CPI	WAT	PB	PD	TPI
1989	Det-A	0	0	—	2	0	0	0	0	5	7	12.6	0	2	3.6	2	3.6	5.40	71	.333	.391	-1	-1	99	98	0.0	0	-0	0.0
Total 4		2	1	.667	39	0	0	0	0	61	66	9.7	5	25	3.7	33	4.9	4.28	82	.284	.347	-4	-5	94	113	0.5	-0	1	-0.4
■ **MIKE BODDICKER**	Boddicker, Michael James b: 8/23/57, Cedar Rapids, Iowa BR/TR, 5'11", 172 lbs. Deb: 10/04/80																												
1980	Bal-A	0	1	.000	1	1	0	0	0	7	6	7.7	1	5	6.4	4	5.1	6.43	62	.207	.324	-2	-2	99	52	-0.4	0	-0	-0.1
1981	Bal-A	0	0	—	2	0	0	0	0	6	6	9.0	1	2	3.0	2	3.0	4.50	81	.261	.320	-1	-1	99	96	0.0	0	-0	0.0
1982	Bal-A	1	0	1.000	7	0	0	0	0	26	25	8.7	2	12	4.2	20	6.9	3.46	117	.258	.336	2	2	99	115	0.5	0	0	0.2
1983	Bal-A	16	8	.667	27	26	10	**5**	0	179	141	**7.1**	13	52	2.6	120	6.0	2.77	146	**.216**	.271	26	25	99	88	2.1	0	3	3.0
1984	Bal-A	**20**	11	.645	34	34	16	4	0	261	218	7.5	23	81	2.8	128	4.4	**2.79**	135	.228	.289	**35**	28	94	105	4.6	0	6	3.6
1985	Bal-A	12	17	.414	32	32	9	2	0	203	227	10.1	13	89	3.9	135	6.0	4.08	100	.286	.357	2	-0	98	115	-3.2	0	6	0.5
1986	Bal-A	14	12	.538	33	33	7	0	0	218	214	8.8	30	74	3.1	175	7.2	4.71	88	.255	.320	-13	-13	99	88	2.4	0	3	-0.9
1987	Bal-A	10	12	.455	33	33	7	2	0	226	212	8.4	29	78	3.1	152	6.1	4.18	106	.248	.313	7	7	99	94	0.9	0	4	0.9
1988	Bal-A	6	12	.333	21	21	4	0	0	147	149	9.1	14	51	3.1	100	6.1	3.86	100	.265	.332	2	0	97	109	0.0	0	-1	0.0
	Bos-A	7	3	.700	15	14	1	1	0	89	85	8.6	3	26	2.6	56	5.7	2.63	163	.257	.312	13	16	108	126	1.7	0	2	2.0
	Yr	13	15	.464	36	35	5	1	0	236	234	8.9	17	77	2.9	156	5.9	3.39	119	.256	.314	15	17	101	126	1.7	0	1	2.0
1989	Bos-A	15	11	.577	34	34	3	2	0	212	217	9.2	19	71	3.0	145	6.2	3.99	102	.267	.327	-2	2	104	102	2.0	0	1	0.3
Total 10		101	87	.537	239	228	57	16	0	1574	1500	8.6	148	541	3.1	1037	5.9	3.71	110	.252	.316	70	64	99	101	10.6	0	24	9.5
■ **JOE BOEVER**	Boever, Joseph Martin b: 10/4/60, Kirkwood, Mo. BR/TR, 6'1", 200 lbs. Deb: 7/19/85																												
1985	StL-N	0	0	—	13	0	0	0	0	16	17	9.6	3	4	2.3	20	11.3	4.50	75	.270	.304	-2	-2	93	99	0.0	0	-0	-0.2
1986	StL-N	0	1	.000	11	0	0	0	0	22	19	7.8	2	11	4.5	8	3.3	1.64	235	.232	.323	5	5	103	213	-0.4	0	-0	0.6
1987	Atl-N	1	0	1.000	14	0	0	0	0	18	29	14.5	4	12	6.0	18	9.0	7.50	59	.367	.441	-7	-6	109	118	0.5	0	-0	-0.5
1988	Atl-N	0	2	.000	16	0	0	0	1	20	12	5.4	1	1	0.4	7	3.1	1.80	205	.182	.200	4	4	107	66	-0.9	0	0	0.5
1989	Atl-N	4	11	.267	66	0	0	0	21	82	78	8.6	6	34	3.7	68	7.5	3.95	92	.252	.324	-4	-3	104	95	-2.5	-0	1	-0.1
Total 5		5	14	.263	120	0	0	0	22	158	155	8.8	16	62	3.5	121	6.9	3.82	98	.259	.325	-4	-1	104	111	-3.3	0	1	0.3
■ **TOM BOLTON**	Bolton, Thomas Edward b: 5/6/62, Nashville, Tenn. BL/TL, 6'2", 172 lbs. Deb: 5/17/87																												
1987	Bos-A	1	0	1.000	29	0	0	0	0	62	83	12.0	5	27	3.9	49	7.1	4.35	102	.329	.390	1	0	99	139	0.5	0	0	0.1
1988	Bos-A	1	3	.250	28	0	0	0	1	30	35	10.5	1	14	4.2	21	6.3	4.80	89	.285	.350	-3	-2	108	90	-1.0	0	1	0.0
1989	Bos-A	0	4	.000	4	4	0	0	0	17	21	11.1	1	10	5.3	9	4.8	8.47	48	.292	.373	-9	-8	104	59	-1.9	0	0	-0.7
Total 3		2	7	.222	61	4	0	0	1	109	139	11.5	7	51	4.2	79	6.5	5.12	85	.311	.376	-11	-9	102	113	-2.4	0	1	-0.6
■ **GREG BOOKER**	Booker, Gregory Scott b: 6/22/60, Lynchburg, Va. BR/TR, 6'6", 230 lbs. Deb: 9/11/83																												
1983	SD-N	0	1	.000	6	1	0	0	0	12	18	13.5	2	9	6.8	5	3.8	7.50	48	.375	.466	-5	-5	99	115	-0.4	-0	0	-0.4
1984	SD-N	1	1	.500	32	1	0	0	0	57	67	10.6	4	27	4.3	28	4.4	3.32	106	.295	.359	2	1	98	148	0.0	1	0	0.2
1985	SD-N	0	1	.000	17	0	0	0	0	22	20	8.2	3	17	7.0	7	2.9	6.95	52	.247	.373	-8	-8	101	74	-0.4	-0	-0	-0.8
1986	SD-N	1	0	1.000	9	0	0	0	0	11	10	8.2	0	4	3.3	7	5.7	1.64	218	.233	.298	3	2	96	141	0.5	0	-0	0.2
1987	SD-N	1	1	.500	44	0	0	0	1	68	62	8.2	5	30	4.0	17	2.3	3.18	126	.246	.330	7	6	98	118	0.2	-1	-0	0.5
1988	SD-N	2	2	.500	34	2	0	0	0	64	68	9.6	5	19	2.7	43	6.0	3.38	99	.278	.324	1	-0	97	122	0.0	1	1	0.1
1989	SD-N	0	1	.000	11	0	0	0	0	19	15	7.1	2	10	4.7	8	3.8	4.26	83	.224	.316	-2	-2	101	86	-0.4	0	0	-0.1
	Min-A	0	0	—	6	0	0	0	0	9	11	11.0	1	2	2.0	3	3.0	4.00	104	.306	.342	-0	0	106	121	0.0	0	1	0.1
Total 7		5	7	.417	159	4	0	0	1	262	271	9.3	22	118	4.1	118	4.1	3.81	95	.271	.344	-3	-5	98	120	-0.5	1	1	-0.2
■ **CHRIS BOSIO**	Bosio, Christopher Louis b: 4/3/63, Carmichael, Cal. BR/TR, 6'3", 220 lbs. Deb: 8/03/86																												
1986	Mil-A	0	4	.000	10	4	0	0	0	35	41	10.5	9	13	3.3	29	7.5	6.94	62	.293	.351	-11	-10	103	87	-1.9	0	0	-0.8
1987	Mil-A	11	8	.579	46	19	2	1	2	170	187	9.9	18	50	2.6	150	7.9	5.24	87	.276	.324	-15	-13	102	81	0.4	0	1	-1.0
1988	Mil-A	7	15	.318	38	22	9	1	6	182	190	9.4	13	38	1.9	84	4.2	3.36	121	.268	.300	12	15	103	105	-4.8	0	3	1.8
1989	Mil-A	15	10	.600	33	33	8	2	0	235	225	8.6	16	48	1.8	173	6.6	2.95	127	.249	.288	25	21	96	101	2.9	0	1	2.3
Total 4		33	37	.471	127	78	19	4	8	622	643	9.3	56	149	2.2	436	6.3	3.92	104	.264	.305	12	12	100	96	-3.4	0	5	2.3
■ **OIL CAN BOYD**	Boyd, Dennis Ray b: 10/6/59, Meridian, Miss. BR/TR, 6'1", 155 lbs. Deb: 9/13/82																												
1982	Bos-A	0	1	.000	3	1	0	0	0	8	11	12.4	2	2	2.3	2	2.3	5.63	80	.314	.351	-1	-1	110	110	-0.4	0	0	0.0
1983	Bos-A	4	8	.333	15	13	5	0	0	99	103	9.4	9	23	2.1	43	3.9	3.27	127	.269	.308	9	10	102	115	-1.8	0	-1	0.9
1984	Bos-A	12	12	.500	29	26	10	3	0	198	207	9.4	18	53	2.4	134	6.1	4.36	101	.269	.313	-8	1	110	87	-0.7	0	2	0.3
1985	Bos-A	15	13	.536	35	35	13	3	0	272	273	9.0	26	67	2.2	154	5.1	3.71	114	.261	.304	13	15	102	99	1.2	0	3	1.9
1986	Bos-A	16	10	.615	30	30	10	0	0	214	222	9.3	32	45	1.9	129	5.4	3.79	109	.265	.301	10	8	99	106	0.9	0	1	0.9
1987	Bos-A	1	3	.250	7	7	0	0	0	37	47	11.4	6	9	2.2	12	2.9	5.84	76	.315	.347	-6	-6	99	99	-0.9	0	1	-0.3
1988	Bos-A	9	7	.563	23	23	1	0	0	130	147	10.2	25	41	2.8	71	4.9	5.33	80	.289	.339	-20	-15	108	101	0.3	0	-1	-1.5
1989	Bos-A	3	2	.600	10	10	0	0	0	59	57	8.7	8	19	2.9	26	4.0	4.42	92	.253	.309	-3	-2	104	88	0.5	0	1	-0.1
Total 8		60	56	.517	152	145	39	6	0	1017	1067	9.4	126	259	2.3	571	5.1	4.15	102	.270	.312	-6	10	103	99	-0.9	0	6	2.1
■ **JEFF BRANTLEY**	Brantley, Jeffrey Hoke b: 9/5/63, Florence, Ala. BR/TR, 5'11", 180 lbs. Deb: 8/05/88																												
1988	SF-N	0	1	.000	9	1	0	0	1	21	22	9.4	2	6	2.6	11	4.7	5.57	58	.275	.330	-5	-5	93	76	-0.4	0	1	-0.4
1989	SF-N	7	1	.875	59	1	0	0	0	97	101	9.4	10	37	3.4	69	6.4	4.08	82	.271	.332	-6	-8	96	108	2.9	-1	0	-0.8
Total 2		7	2	.778	68	2	0	0	1	118	123	9.4	12	43	3.3	80	6.1	4.35	77	.272	.331	-11	-13	95	102	2.5	-0	1	-1.2
■ **KEVIN BROWN**	Brown, James Kevin b: 3/14/65, Milledgeville, Ga. BR/TR, 6'4", 195 lbs. Deb: 9/30/86																												
1986	Tex-A	1	0	1.000	1	1	0	0	0	5	6	10.8	0	0	0.0	4	7.2	3.60	111	.316	.316	0	0	95	103	0.5	0	0	0.0
1988	Tex-A	1	1	.500	4	4	1	0	0	23	33	12.9	2	8	3.1	12	4.7	4.30	94	.330	.382	-1	-1	102	137	0.1	0	-0	0.0
1989	Tex-A	12	9	.571	28	28	7	0	0	191	167	7.9	10	70	3.3	104	4.9	3.35	119	.234	.302	12	14	103	88	1.4	0	3	1.8
Total 3		14	10	.583	33	33	8	0	0	219	206	8.5	12	78	3.2	120	4.9	3.45	116	.247	.312	11	13	102	93	2.0	0	3	1.8
■ **TOM BROWNING**	Browning, Thomas Leo b: 4/28/60, Casper, Wyoming BL/TL, 6'1", 190 lbs. Deb: 9/09/84																												
1984	Cin-N	1	0	1.000	3	3	0	0	0	23	27	10.6	0	5	2.0	14	5.5	1.57	246	.303	.337	5	6	107	248	0.5	-0	0	0.7
1985	Cin-N	20	9	.690	38	38	6	4	0	261	242	8.3	29	73	2.5	155	5.3	3.55	106	.245	.294	1	7	105	95	5.1	2	-2	0.8
1986	Cin-N	14	13	.519	39	39	4	2	0	243	225	8.3	26	70	2.6	147	5.4	3.81	102	.245	.291	-2	2	104	88	-0.3	-1	-3	-0.1
1987	Cin-N	10	13	.435	32	31	2	0	0	183	201	9.9	27	61	3.0	117	5.8	5.02	84	.284	.338	-19	-16	103	98	-2.0	1	-2	-1.6
1988	Cin-N	18	5	.783	36	36	5	2	0	251	205	7.4	36	64	2.3	124	4.4	3.41	106	.224	.276	1	6	105	94	6.5	0	-3	0.5
1989	Cin-N	15	12	.556	37	37	9	2	0	250	241	8.7	31	64	2.3	118	4.2	3.38	107	.255	.299	3	7	104	111	2.7	-3	-1	0.2
Total 6		78	52	.600	185	184	26	10	0	1211	1141	8.5	149	337	2.5	675	5.0	3.72	102	.250	.298	-10	11	104	100	12.5	-1	-10	0.5
■ **BOB BUCHANAN**	Buchanan, Robert Gordon b: 5/3/61, Ridley Park, Pa. BL/TL, 6'1", 185 lbs. Deb: 7/13/85																												
1985	Cin-N	1	0	1.000	14	0	0	0	0	16	25	14.1	4	9	5.1	3	1.7	8.44	45	.368	.442	-9	-8	105	103	0.5	-0	0	-0.8
1989	KC-A	0	0	—	2	0	0	0	0	3	5	15.0	1	3	9.0	3	9.0	18.00	21	.333	.444	-5	-5	95	53	0.0	0	0	-0.3
Total 2		1	0	1.000	16	0	0	0	0	19	30	14.2	5	12	5.7	6	2.8	9.95	38	.361	.442	-13	-13	103	95	0.5	-0	0	-1.1
■ **DE WAYNE BUICE**	Buice, De Wayne Allison b: 8/20/57, Lynwood, Cal. BR/TR, 6', 170 lbs. Deb: 4/25/87																												
1987	Cal-A	6	7	.462	57	0	0	0	17	114	87	6.9	12	40	3.2	109	8.6	3.39	131	.213	.282	14	13	100	86	0.0	0	0	1.3
1988	Cal-A	2	4	.333	32	0	0	0	3	41	45	9.9	5	19	4.2	38	8.3	5.93	63	.287	.350	-9	-10	95	87	-0.8	0	0	-0.8
1989	Tor-A	1	0	1.000	7	0	0	0	0	17	13	6.9	2	13	6.9	10	5.3	5.82	62	.220	.351	-4	-4	93	74	0.5	0	0	-0.3
Total 3		9	11	.450	96	0	0	0	20	172	145	7.6	19	72	3.8	157	8.2	4.24	99	.232	.307	1	-1	98	85	-0.3	0	0	0.2
■ **TIM BURKE**	Burke, Timothy Philip b: 2/19/59, Omaha, Neb. BR/TR, 6'3", 205 lbs. Deb: 4/08/85																												
1985	Mon-N	9	4	.692	**78**	0	0	0	8	120	86	6.5	9	44	3.3	87	6.5	2.40	141	.204	.284	**16**	13	94	107	2.4	-0	1	1.4
1986	Mon-N	9	7	.563	68	2	0	0	4	101	103	9.2	7	46	4.1	82	7.3	2.94	124	.262	.339	9	8	98	138	1.3	-0	1	0.9
1987	Mon-N	7	0	1.000	55	0	0	0	18	91	64	6.3	3	17	1.7	58	5.7	1.19	364	.196	.229	**29**	**32**	106	112	3.5	-1	1	**3.2**
1988	Mon-N	3	5	.375	61	0	0	0	18	82	84	9.2	7	25	2.7	42	4.6	3.40	107	.272	.320	0	2	105	121	-0.9	-0	0	0.2
1989	Mon-N	9	3	.750	68	0	0	0	28	85	68	7.2	6	22	2.3	54	5.7	2.54	141	.225	.270	9	10	102	105	3.1	-0	1	1.1
Total 5		37	19	.661	330	2	0	0	76	479	405	7.6	32	154	2.9	323	6.1	2.48	149	.231	.291	64	64	100	117	9.4	-2	4	6.8

YEAR	TM/L	W	L	PCT	G	GS	CG	SHO	SV	IP	H	H/G	HR	BB	BB/G	SO	SO/G	ERA	/A	OAVG	OOBP	PR	/A	PF	CPI	WAT	PB	PD	TPI
■ **TODD BURNS**	Burns, Todd Edward b: 7/6/63, Maywood, Cal. BR/TR, 6'2", 186 lbs. Deb: 5/31/88																												
1988	Oak-A	8	2	.800	17	14	2	0	1	103	93	8.1	8	34	3.0	57	5.0	3.15	118	.241	.301	9	6	93	103	2.3	0	-1	0.6
1989	Oak-A	6	5	.545	50	2	0	0	8	96	66	6.2	3	28	2.6	49	4.6	2.25	176	.196	.254	18	18	102	77	-0.5	0	-1	1.8
Total	2	14	7	.667	67	16	2	0	9	199	159	7.2	11	62	2.8	106	4.8	2.71	141	.220	.279	27	25	97	90	1.8	0	-2	2.4
■ **GREG CADARET**	Cadaret, Gregory James b: 2/27/62, Detroit, Mich. BL/TL, 6'3", 200 lbs. Deb: 7/05/87																												
1987	Oak-A	6	2	.750	29	0	0	0	0	40	37	8.3	6	24	5.4	30	6.7	4.50	90	.252	.352	-0	-2	91	110	2.1	0	1	0.0
1988	Oak-A	5	2	.714	58	0	0	0	3	72	60	7.5	2	36	4.5	64	8.0	2.88	129	.226	.312	9	7	93	103	0.7	0	0	0.7
1989	Oak-A	0	0	—	26	0	0	0	0	28	21	6.8	0	19	6.1	14	4.5	2.25	176	.214	.336	5	5	102	134	0.0	0	1	0.6
	NY-A	5	5	.500	20	13	3	1	0	92	109	10.7	7	38	3.7	66	6.5	4.60	89	.298	.362	-7	-5	105	108	0.4	0	0	-0.4
	Yr	5	5	.500	46	13	3	1	0	120	130	9.8	7	57	4.3	80	6.0	4.05	100	.279	.356	-2	0	104	108	0.4	0	1	0.2
Total	3	16	9	.640	133	13	3	1	3	232	227	8.8	15	117	4.5	174	6.8	3.76	105	.259	.342	7	5	99	110	3.2	0	2	0.9
■ **ERNIE CAMACHO**	Camacho, Ernest Carlos b: 2/1/55, Salinas, Cal. BR/TR, 6'1", 180 lbs. Deb: 5/22/80																												
1980	Oak-A	0	0	—	5	0	0	0	0	12	20	15.0	2	5	3.8	9	6.8	6.75	56	.364	.426	-4	-4	94	116	0.0	0	-0	-0.3
1981	Pit-N	0	1	.000	7	3	0	0	0	22	23	9.4	0	15	6.1	11	4.5	4.91	68	.295	.396	-3	-4	96	101	-0.4	-0	0	-0.4
1983	Cle-A	0	1	.000	4	0	0	0	0	5	5	9.0	1	2	3.6	2	3.6	5.40	80	.250	.348	-1	-1	106	92	-0.4	0	-0	0.0
1984	Cle-A	5	9	.357	69	0	0	0	23	100	83	7.5	6	37	3.3	48	4.3	2.43	174	.229	.294	17	20	106	120	-1.6	0	-0	2.0
1985	Cle-A	0	1	.000	2	0	0	0	0	3	4	12.0	0	1	3.0	2	6.0	9.00	44	.333	.333	-2	-2	95	58	-0.4	0	0	-0.1
1986	Cle-A	2	4	.333	51	0	0	0	20	57	60	9.5	1	31	4.9	36	5.7	4.11	100	.269	.348	1	-0	98	100	-1.0	0	1	0.1
1987	Cle-A	0	1	.000	15	0	0	0	1	14	21	13.5	1	5	3.2	9	5.8	9.00	52	.350	.420	-7	-7	105	77	-0.4	0	1	-0.5
1988	Hou-N	0	3	.000	13	0	0	0	1	18	25	12.5	1	12	6.0	13	6.5	7.50	43	.352	.435	-8	-9	93	93	-1.4	-0	0	-0.8
1989	SF-N	3	0	1.000	13	0	0	0	0	16	10	5.6	1	11	6.2	14	7.9	2.81	119	.175	.300	1	1	96	90	1.5	-0	1	0.2
Total	9	10	20	.333	179	3	0	0	45	247	251	9.1	13	119	4.3	144	5.2	4.15	96	.268	.345	-5	-4	101	106	-4.1	-1	2	0.2
■ **MIKE CAMPBELL**	Campbell, Michael Thomas b: 2/17/64, Seattle, Wash. BR/TR, 6'3", 210 lbs. Deb: 7/04/87																												
1987	Sea-A	1	4	.200	9	9	1	0	0	49	41	7.5	9	25	4.6	35	6.4	4.78	96	.224	.316	-2	-1	103	87	-1.4	0	0	0.0
1988	Sea-A	6	10	.375	20	20	2	0	0	115	128	10.0	18	43	3.4	63	4.9	5.87	73	.280	.337	-24	-20	108	84	-0.9	0	-1	-1.9
1989	Sea-A	1	2	.333	5	5	0	0	0	21	28	12.0	4	10	4.3	6	2.6	7.29	55	.301	.369	-8	-8	104	82	-0.3	0	-0	-0.7
Total	3	8	16	.333	34	34	3	0	0	185	197	9.6	31	78	3.8	104	5.1	5.74	76	.269	.336	-34	-28	106	85	-2.6	0	-1	-2.6
■ **JOHN CANDELARIA**	Candelaria, John Robert "Candy Man" b: 11/6/53, New York, N.Y. BL/TL, 6'7", 205 lbs. Deb: 6/08/75																												
1975	Pit-N	8	6	.571	18	18	4	1	0	121	95	7.1	8	36	2.7	95	7.1	2.75	129	.212	.268	12	11	98	78	0.0	-0	-1	0.9
1976	Pit-N	16	7	.696	32	31	11	4	1	220	173	7.1	22	60	2.5	138	5.6	3.15	111	.216	.267	9	8	99	82	3.8	3	-1	1.1
1977	Pit-N	20	5	**.800**	33	33	6	1	0	231	197	7.7	29	50	**1.9**	133	5.2	**2.34**	**170**	.232	.272	**40**	42	102	**126**	6.9	4	-1	4.9
1978	Pit-N	12	11	.522	30	29	3	1	1	189	191	9.1	15	49	2.3	94	4.5	3.24	116	.261	.308	7	11	105	108	-0.5	3	-2	1.4
1979	Pit-N	14	9	.609	33	30	8	0	0	207	201	8.7	25	41	1.8	101	4.4	3.22	121	.253	.288	12	15	104	104	0.1	-1	0	1.6
1980	Pit-N	11	14	.440	35	34	7	0	1	233	246	9.5	14	50	1.9	97	3.7	4.02	93	.276	.309	-11	-8	103	90	-1.9	2	-0	-0.6
1981	Pit-N	2	2	.500	6	6	0	0	0	41	42	9.2	3	11	2.4	14	3.1	3.51	96	.271	.315	-0	-1	96	106	0.2	0	0	0.0
1982	Pit-N	12	7	.632	31	30	1	1	1	175	166	8.5	13	37	1.9	133	6.8	2.93	135	.255	.294	13	20	110	109	2.5	3	-1	2.4
1983	Pit-N	15	8	.652	33	32	2	0	0	198	191	8.7	15	45	2.0	157	7.1	3.23	116	.257	.299	9	11	103	101	3.6	-0	-2	1.0
1984	Pit-N	12	11	.522	33	28	3	1	2	185	179	8.7	19	34	1.7	133	6.5	2.72	124	.256	.285	18	13	94	122	1.4	1	-2	1.2
1985	Pit-N	2	4	.333	37	0	0	0	9	54	57	9.5	7	14	2.3	47	7.8	3.67	102	.275	.314	-0	1	104	117	-0.1	-0	-0	0.0
	Cal-A	7	3	.700	13	13	1	1	0	71	70	8.9	7	24	3.0	53	6.7	3.80	110	.262	.322	3	3	101	108	1.7	0	-1	0.2
1986	Cal-A	10	2	.833	16	16	1	1	0	92	68	6.7	4	26	2.5	81	7.9	2.54	157	.206	.266	17	15	95	81	3.8	0	-0	1.5
1987	Cal-A	8	6	.571	20	20	0	0	0	117	127	9.8	17	20	1.5	74	5.7	4.69	95	.279	.304	-3	-3	100	92	1.5	0	1	-0.1
	NY-N	2	0	1.000	3	3	0	0	0	12	17	12.8	1	3	2.3	10	7.5	6.00	66	.333	.351	-3	-3	97	93	1.0	0	0	-0.2
1988	NY-A	13	7	.650	25	24	6	2	1	157	150	8.6	18	23	1.3	121	6.9	3.38	112	.248	.273	10	7	96	93	2.8	0	0	0.7
1989	NY-A	3	3	.500	10	6	1	0	0	49	49	9.0	8	12	2.2	37	6.8	5.14	80	.258	.296	-7	-6	105	78	0.2	0	-0	-0.5
	Mon-N	0	2	.000	12	0	0	0	0	16	17	9.6	3	4	2.3	14	7.9	3.38	106	.283	.309	0	0	102	147	-0.9	0	-0	0.0
Total	15	167	107	.609	420	353	54	13	16	2368	2236	8.5	228	539	2.0	1532	5.8	3.27	116	.250	.290	127	138	101	101	26.1	14	-10	15.5
■ **TOM CANDIOTTI**	Candiotti, Thomas Caesar b: 8/31/57, Walnut Creek, Cal. BR/TR, 6'3", 205 lbs. Deb: 8/08/83																												
1983	Mil-A	4	4	.500	10	8	2	1	0	56	62	10.0	4	16	2.6	21	3.4	3.21	115	.291	.343	5	3	91	139	-0.2	0	-0	0.3
1984	Mil-A	2	2	.500	8	6	0	0	0	32	38	10.7	5	10	2.8	23	6.5	5.34	69	.277	.327	-5	-6	93	84	0.3	0	-0	-0.5
1986	Cle-A	16	12	.571	36	34	**17**	3	0	252	234	8.4	18	106	3.8	167	6.0	3.57	115	.246	.323	17	15	98	100	1.8	0	3	1.7
1987	Cle-A	7	18	.280	32	32	7	2	0	202	193	8.6	28	93	4.1	111	4.9	4.77	98	.250	.327	-7	-2	105	90	-3.5	0	0	-0.1
1988	Cle-A	14	8	.636	31	31	11	1	0	217	225	9.3	15	53	2.2	137	5.7	3.28	124	.272	.315	17	19	102	116	3.6	0	2	2.2
1989	Cle-A	13	10	.565	31	31	4	0	0	206	188	8.2	10	55	2.4	124	5.4	3.10	131	.242	.292	18	22	104	91	2.7	0	4	2.7
Total	6	56	54	.509	148	142	41	7	0	965	940	8.8	80	333	3.1	583	5.4	3.69	113	.255	.317	46	51	101	101	4.7	0	8	6.3
■ **JOSE CANO**	Cano, Joselito (Soriano) b: 3/7/62, Boca De Soco, D.R. BR/TR, 6'3", 175 lbs. Deb: 8/28/89																												
1989	Hou-N	1	1	.500	6	3	1	0	0	23	24	9.4	2	7	2.7	8	3.1	5.09	71	.267	.313	-4	-4	103	76	0.0	-1	-0	-0.4
■ **DON CARMAN**	Carman, Donald Wayne b: 8/14/59, Oklahoma City, Okla BL/TL, 6'3", 195 lbs. Deb: 10/01/83																												
1983	Phi-N	0	0	—	1	0	0	0	1	1	0	0.0	0	0	0.0	0	0.0	0.00	—	.000	.000	0	0	100	0	0.0	0	0	0.0
1984	Phi-N	0	1	.000	11	0	0	0	0	13	14	9.7	2	6	4.2	16	11.1	5.54	66	.255	.328	-3	-3	101	77	-0.4	-0	-0	-0.2
1985	Phi-N	9	4	.692	71	0	0	0	7	86	52	5.4	6	38	4.0	87	9.1	2.09	176	.178	.269	14	15	102	100	2.9	-0	0	1.6
1986	Phi-N	10	5	.667	50	14	2	1	1	134	113	7.6	11	52	3.5	98	6.6	3.22	120	.234	.308	7	10	104	103	2.3	-3	2	0.9
1987	Phi-N	13	11	.542	35	35	3	2	0	211	194	8.3	34	69	2.9	125	5.3	4.22	101	.244	.302	-3	1	105	93	1.3	-3	-3	-0.4
1988	Phi-N	10	14	.417	36	32	2	0	0	201	211	9.4	20	70	3.1	116	5.2	4.30	83	.270	.326	-19	-17	103	98	0.3	-5	-3	-2.4
1989	Phi-N	5	15	.250	49	20	0	0	0	149	152	9.2	21	86	5.2	81	4.9	5.26	68	.260	.353	-29	-28	102	93	-4.2	-3	-1	-3.2
Total	7	47	50	.485	253	101	7	3	9	795	736	8.3	94	321	3.6	523	5.9	4.05	94	.246	.317	-32	-21	103	96	2.2	-15	-5	-3.7
■ **CRIS CARPENTER**	Carpenter, Cris Howell b: 4/5/65, St.Augustine, Fla. BR/TR, 6'1", 195 lbs. Deb: 5/14/88																												
1988	StL-N	2	3	.400	8	8	1	0	0	48	56	10.5	3	9	1.7	24	4.5	4.69	77	.298	.325	-7	-6	105	91	-0.3	-0	-0	-0.6
1989	StL-N	4	4	.500	36	5	0	0	0	68	70	9.3	4	26	3.4	35	4.6	3.18	111	.262	.323	2	3	100	120	-0.1	1	0	0.4
Total	2	6	7	.462	44	13	1	0	0	116	126	9.8	7	35	2.7	59	4.6	3.80	94	.277	.324	-4	-3	102	108	-0.4	1	-0	-0.2
■ **CHUCK CARY**	Cary, Charles Douglas b: 3/3/60, Whittier, Cal. BL/TL, 6'4", 210 lbs. Deb: 8/22/85																												
1985	Det-A	0	1	.000	16	0	0	0	2	24	16	6.0	2	8	3.0	22	8.3	3.38	130	.190	.274	2	3	106	70	-0.4	0	-0	0.2
1986	Det-A	1	2	.333	22	0	0	0	0	32	33	9.3	3	15	4.2	21	5.9	3.38	117	.273	.343	3	2	95	135	-0.5	0	-0	0.2
1987	Atl-N	1	1	.500	13	0	0	0	1	17	17	9.0	3	4	2.1	15	7.9	3.71	120	.266	.314	1	1	109	121	0.1	-0	0	0.1
1988	Atl-N	0	0	—	7	0	0	0	0	8	8	9.0	1	4	4.5	7	7.9	6.75	55	.250	.333	-3	-3	107	67	0.0	0	0	-0.2
1989	NY-A	4	4	.500	22	11	2	0	0	99	78	7.1	13	29	2.6	79	7.2	3.27	125	.209	.265	7	9	105	79	0.3	0	-2	0.7
Total	5	6	8	.429	80	11	2	0	3	180	152	7.6	22	60	3.0	144	7.2	3.50	118	.226	.289	10	13	104	91	-0.5	-0	-3	1.0
■ **TONY CASTILLO**	Castillo, Antonio Jose b: 3/1/63, Quibor, Venez. BL/TL, 5'10", 177 lbs. Deb: 8/14/88																												
1988	Tor-A	1	0	1.000	14	0	0	0	0	15	10	6.0	2	2	1.2	14	8.4	3.00	131	.200	.222	2	2	99	79	0.5	0	0	0.2
1989	Tor-A	1	1	.500	17	0	0	0	1	18	23	11.5	0	10	5.0	10	5.0	6.00	60	.333	.395	-4	-5	93	98	0.0	0	-0	-0.4
	Atl-N	0	1	.000	12	0	0	0	0	9	8	8.0	0	4	4.0	5	5.0	5.00	73	.222	.293	-1	-1	104	46	-0.4	-0	0	0.0
Total	2	2	2	.500	43	0	0	0	1	42	41	8.8	2	16	3.4	29	6.2	4.71	79	.265	.320	-4	-5	97	80	0.1	-0	0	-0.2
■ **JOHN CERUTTI**	Cerutti, John Joseph b: 4/28/60, Albany, N.Y. BL/TL, 6'2", 195 lbs. Deb: 9/01/85																												
1985	Tor-A	0	2	.000	4	1	0	0	0	7	10	12.9	1	4	5.1	5	6.4	5.14	80	.323	.417	-1	-1	99	136	-0.9	0	0	0.0
1986	Tor-A	9	4	.692	34	20	2	1	1	145	150	9.3	25	47	2.9	89	5.5	4.16	105	.268	.321	0	3	104	111	2.4	0	0	0.3
1987	Tor-A	11	4	.733	44	21	2	0	0	151	144	8.6	30	59	3.5	92	5.5	4.41	101	.251	.320	1	1	99	104	2.8	0	-2	0.0
1988	Tor-A	6	7	.462	46	12	0	0	1	124	120	8.7	12	42	3.0	65	4.7	3.12	126	.256	.315	12	11	99	124	-0.9	0	3	1.4
1989	Tor-A	11	11	.500	33	31	3	1	0	205	214	9.4	19	53	2.3	69	3.0	3.07	118	.273	.319	19	13	93	**130**	-1.0	0	3	1.6
Total	5	37	28	.569	161	85	7	2	2	632	638	9.1	87	205	2.9	320	4.6	3.67	110	.264	.320	31	26	98	118	2.4	0	4	3.3

YEAR	TM/L	W	L	PCT	G	GS	CG	SHO	SV	IP	H	H/G	HR	BB	BB/G	SO	SO/G	ERA	/A	OAVG	OOBP	PR	/A	PF	CPI	WAT	PB	PD	TPI
■ **NORM CHARLTON**	Charlton, Norman Wood b: 1/6/63, Fort Polk, La. BB/TL, 6'3", 195 lbs. Deb: 8/19/88																												
1988	Cin-N	4	5	.444	10	10	0	0	0	61	60	8.9	6	20	3.0	39	5.8	3.98	91	.256	.317	-4	-2	105	97	-0.7	-1	-0	-0.3
1989	Cin-N	8	3	.727	69	0	0	0	0	95	67	6.3	5	40	3.8	98	9.3	2.94	124	.197	.277	6	7	104	79	2.8	-1	-0	0.7
Total	2	12	8	.600	79	10	0	0	0	156	127	7.3	11	60	3.5	137	7.9	3.35	108	.221	.293	2	5	104	86	2.1	-2	-0	0.4
■ **JIM CLANCY**	Clancy, James b: 12/18/55, Chicago, Ill. BR/TR, 6'2", 185 lbs. Deb: 7/26/77																												
1977	Tor-A	4	9	.308	13	13	4	1	0	77	80	9.4	7	47	5.5	44	5.1	5.03	85	.280	.367	-8	-7	105	100	-0.5	0	1	-0.5
1978	Tor-A	10	12	.455	31	30	7	0	0	194	199	9.2	10	91	4.2	106	4.9	4.08	95	.270	.344	-7	-5	102	99	1.7	0	1	-0.4
1979	Tor-A	2	7	.222	12	11	2	0	0	64	65	9.1	8	31	4.4	33	4.6	5.48	82	.272	.345	-9	-7	106	87	-1.4	0	0	-0.6
1980	Tor-A	13	16	.448	34	34	15	2	0	251	217	7.8	19	128	4.6	152	5.5	3.30	124	.233	.323	21	22	101	103	1.0	0	0	2.2
1981	Tor-A	6	12	.333	22	22	2	0	0	125	126	9.1	12	64	4.6	56	4.0	4.90	85	.262	.351	-17	-11	113	90	-0.4	0	-3	-1.2
1982	Tor-A	16	14	.533	40	40	11	3	0	267	251	8.5	26	77	2.6	139	4.7	3.71	120	.248	.300	11	22	109	91	1.8	0	-2	2.0
1983	Tor-A	15	11	.577	34	34	11	1	0	223	238	9.6	23	61	2.5	99	4.0	3.91	112	.271	.314	4	12	108	102	0.9	0	-2	0.9
1984	Tor-A	13	15	.464	36	36	5	0	0	220	249	10.2	25	88	3.6	118	4.8	5.11	79	.287	.352	-27	-26	101	95	-2.4	0	0	-2.4
1985	Tor-A	9	6	.600	23	23	1	0	0	129	117	8.2	15	37	2.6	66	4.6	3.77	109	.241	.292	5	5	99	90	-0.1	0	-1	0.4
1986	Tor-A	14	14	.500	34	34	6	3	0	219	202	8.3	24	63	2.6	126	5.2	3.95	111	.243	.295	6	10	104	85	-0.9	0	1	1.1
1987	Tor-A	15	11	.577	37	37	5	1	0	241	234	8.7	24	80	3.0	180	6.7	3.55	125	.255	.313	25	24	99	106	-0.3	0	2	2.5
1988	Tor-A	11	13	.458	36	31	4	0	1	196	207	9.5	26	47	2.2	118	5.4	4.50	87	.272	.318	-11	-12	99	96	-1.9	0	-1	-1.2
1989	Hou-N	7	14	.333	33	26	1	0	0	147	155	9.5	13	66	4.0	91	5.6	5.08	71	.269	.337	-26	-24	103	85	-4.2	-0	-3	-2.7
Total	13	135	154	.467	385	371	74	11	1	2353	2340	9.0	232	880	3.4	1328	5.1	4.16	100	.260	.323	-33	4	104	95	-6.7	-0	-7	0.1
■ **TERRY CLARK**	Clark, Terry Lee b: 10/18/60, Los Angeles, Cal. BR/TR, 6'2", 190 lbs. Deb: 7/07/88																												
1988	Cal-A	6	6	.500	15	15	2	1	0	94	120	11.5	8	31	3.0	39	3.7	5.07	74	.323	.368	-11	-14	95	108	0.4	0	0	-1.2
1989	Cal-A	0	2	.000	4	2	0	0	0	11	13	10.6	0	3	2.5	7	5.7	4.91	77	.310	.333	-1	-1	98	87	-0.9	0	0	0.0
Total	2	6	8	.429	19	17	2	1	0	105	133	11.4	8	34	2.9	46	3.9	5.06	74	.321	.365	-13	-15	95	106	-0.5	0	0	-1.2
■ **STAN CLARKE**	Clarke, Stanley Martin b: 8/9/60, Toledo, Ohio BL/TL, 6'1", 180 lbs. Deb: 6/07/83																												
1983	Tor-A	1	1	.500	10	0	0	0	0	11	10	8.2	2	5	4.1	7	5.7	3.27	134	.256	.326	1	1	108	149	0.0	0	0	0.1
1985	Tor-A	0	0	—	4	0	0	0	0	4	3	6.8	1	2	4.5	2	4.5	4.50	91	.214	.313	-0	-0	99	100	0.0	0	0	0.0
1986	Tor-A	0	1	.000	10	0	0	0	0	13	18	12.5	4	10	6.9	9	6.2	9.00	49	.375	.452	-7	-7	104	109	-0.4	0	0	-0.5
1987	Sea-A	2	2	.500	22	0	0	0	0	23	31	12.1	7	10	3.9	13	5.1	5.48	84	.333	.383	-3	-2	103	143	0.1	0	-0	-0.1
1989	KC-A	0	2	.000	2	2	0	0	0	7	14	18.0	2	4	5.1	2	2.6	15.43	24	.438	.500	-9	-9	95	74	-0.9	0	0	-0.7
Total	5	3	6	.333	48	2	0	0	0	58	76	11.8	16	31	4.8	33	5.1	6.98	63	.336	.401	-18	-17	103	125	-1.2	0	0	-1.2
■ **MARTY CLARY**	Clary, Martin Keith b: 4/3/62, Detroit, Mich. BR/TR, 6'4", 190 lbs. Deb: 9/05/87																												
1987	Atl-N	0	1	.000	7	1	0	0	0	15	20	12.0	2	4	2.4	7	4.2	6.00	74	.328	.368	-3	-3	109	100	-0.4	-0	-0	-0.2
1989	Atl-N	4	3	.571	18	17	2	1	0	109	103	8.5	6	31	2.6	30	2.5	3.14	116	.249	.299	4	6	104	101	1.1	0	0	0.7
Total	2	4	4	.500	25	18	2	1	0	124	123	8.9	8	35	2.5	37	2.7	3.48	107	.259	.308	1	3	104	101	0.7	0	0	0.5
■ **ROGER CLEMENS**	Clemens, William Roger b: 8/4/62, Dayton, Ohio BR/TR, 6'4", 205 lbs. Deb: 5/15/84																												
1984	Bos-A	9	4	.692	21	20	5	1	0	133	146	9.9	13	29	2.0	126	8.5	4.33	101	.271	.308	-5	1	110	86	2.4	0	0	0.1
1985	Bos-A	7	5	.583	15	15	3	1	0	98	83	7.6	5	37	3.4	74	6.8	3.31	127	.228	.302	9	10	102	88	1.1	0	0	1.0
1986	Bos-A	**24**	4	**.857**	33	33	10	1	0	254	179	**6.3**	21	67	2.4	238	8.4	**2.48**	**166**	**.195**	**.251**	**48**	**46**	99	79	**9.7**	0	-1	4.8
1987	Bos-A	**20**	9	**.690**	36	36	**18**	**7**	0	282	248	7.9	19	83	2.6	256	8.2	2.97	149	.235	.294	47	46	99	100	**6.5**	0	-2	4.4
1988	Bos-A	18	12	.600	35	35	**14**	**8**	0	264	217	7.4	17	62	2.1	**291**	**9.9**	2.93	146	.220	.268	31	40	108	80	2.0	0	-2	4.1
1989	Bos-A	17	11	.607	35	35	8	3	0	253	215	7.6	20	93	3.3	230	8.2	3.13	130	.231	.303	21	26	104	101	3.2	0	-1	2.7
Total	6	95	45	.679	175	174	58	21	0	1284	1088	7.6	95	371	2.6	1215	8.5	3.06	139	.227	.284	151	170	103	90	24.9	0	-5	17.1
■ **PAT CLEMENTS**	Clements, Patrick Brian b: 2/2/62, Mc Cloud, Cal. BR/TL, 6', 175 lbs. Deb: 4/09/85																												
1985	Cal-A	5	0	1.000	41	0	0	0	1	62	47	6.8	4	25	3.6	19	2.8	3.34	125	.218	.300	6	6	101	90	2.5	0	1	0.7
	Pit-N	0	2	.000	27	0	0	0	2	34	39	10.3	2	15	4.0	17	4.5	3.71	101	.289	.353	-0	0	104	122	-0.9	0	-1	0.0
1986	Pit-N	0	4	.000	65	0	0	0	2	61	53	7.8	1	32	4.7	31	4.6	2.80	134	.251	.340	6	6	101	133	-1.9	-1	1	0.7
1987	NY-A	3	3	.500	55	0	0	0	7	80	91	10.2	4	30	3.4	36	4.0	4.95	88	.299	.357	-4	-5	97	98	-0.2	0	1	-0.4
1988	NY-A	0	0	—	6	1	0	0	0	8	12	13.5	1	4	4.5	3	3.4	6.75	56	.343	.390	-2	-3	96	102	0.0	0	-0	-0.2
1989	SD-N	4	1	.800	23	1	0	0	0	39	39	9.0	4	15	3.5	18	4.2	3.92	90	.267	.323	-2	-2	101	109	1.4	-1	0	-0.1
Total	5	12	10	.545	217	2	0	0	12	284	281	8.9	16	121	3.8	124	3.9	3.90	102	.268	.338	3	3	100	108	0.9	-1	2	0.7
■ **BRYAN CLUTTERBUCK**	Clutterbuck, Bryan Richard b: 12/17/59, Detroit, Mich. BR/TR, 6'4", 223 lbs. Deb: 7/18/86																												
1986	Mil-A	0	1	.000	20	0	0	0	0	57	68	10.7	8	16	2.5	38	6.0	4.26	101	.296	.344	-0	0	103	118	-0.4	0	-0	0.0
1989	Mil-A	2	5	.286	14	11	1	0	0	67	73	9.8	11	16	2.1	29	3.9	4.16	90	.269	.306	-2	-3	96	102	-1.4	0	-2	-0.4
Total	2	2	6	.250	34	11	1	0	0	124	141	10.2	19	32	2.3	67	4.9	4.21	95	.281	.323	-3	-3	99	109	-1.8	0	-2	-0.4
■ **PAT COMBS**	Combs, Patrick Dennis b: 10/29/66, Newport, R.I. BL/TL, 6'3", 200 lbs. Deb: 9/05/89																												
1989	Phi-N	4	0	1.000	6	6	1	1	0	39	36	8.3	2	6	1.4	30	6.9	2.08	172	.248	.275	6	7	102	132	2.0	0	-1	0.7
■ **KEITH COMSTOCK**	Comstock, Keith Martin b: 12/23/55, San Francisco, Cal. BL/TL, 6', 174 lbs. Deb: 4/03/84																												
1984	Min-A	0	0	—	4	0	0	0	0	6	6	9.0	2	4	6.0	2	3.0	9.00	47	.261	.357	-3	-3	106	73	0.0	0	0	-0.2
1987	SF-N	2	0	1.000	15	0	0	0	1	21	19	8.1	1	10	4.3	21	9.0	3.00	129	.253	.333	3	2	95	126	1.0	-0	0	0.2
	SD-N	0	1	.000	26	0	0	0	0	36	33	8.3	4	21	5.3	38	9.5	5.50	73	.252	.344	-6	-6	98	82	-0.4	-0	-1	-0.6
	Yr	2	1	.667	41	0	0	0	1	57	52	8.2	5	31	4.9	59	9.3	4.58	86	.251	.340	-3	-4	97	82	0.6	-0	-1	-0.4
1988	SD-N	0	0	—	7	0	0	0	0	8	8	9.0	1	3	3.4	9	10.1	6.75	50	.250	.314	-3	-3	97	57	0.0	0	0	-0.2
1989	Sea-A	1	2	.333	31	0	0	0	0	26	26	9.0	2	10	3.5	22	7.6	2.77	145	.268	.324	3	4	104	146	-0.3	0	0	0.4
Total	4	3	3	.500	83	0	0	0	1	97	92	8.5	10	48	4.5	92	8.5	4.55	87	.257	.335	-6	-7	99	106	0.3	-0	-0	-0.4
■ **DAVID CONE**	Cone, David Bryan b: 1/2/63, Kansas City, Mo. BL/TR, 6'1", 180 lbs. Deb: 6/08/86																												
1986	KC-A	0	0	—	11	0	0	0	0	23	29	11.3	2	13	5.1	21	8.2	5.48	77	.309	.398	-3	-3	100	106	0.0	0	-0	-0.2
1987	NY-N	5	6	.455	21	13	1	0	1	99	87	7.9	11	44	4.0	68	6.2	3.73	106	.239	.324	4	3	97	104	-1.1	-1	-0	0.1
1988	NY-N	20	3	**.870**	35	28	8	4	0	231	178	6.9	10	80	3.1	213	8.3	2.22	137	.213	.280	32	21	88	108	**7.9**	2	-1	2.2
1989	NY-N	14	8	.636	34	33	7	2	0	220	183	7.5	20	74	3.0	190	7.8	3.52	95	.223	.287	-0	-4	95	83	2.6	4	-2	-0.3
Total	4	39	17	.696	101	74	16	6	1	573	477	7.5	43	211	3.3	492	7.7	3.11	108	.225	.296	32	15	93	98	9.4	4	-4	1.8
■ **DENNIS COOK**	Cook, Dennis Bryan b: 10/4/62, La Marque, Tex. BL/TL, 6'3", 185 lbs. Deb: 9/12/88																												
1988	SF-N	2	1	.667	4	4	1	1	0	22	9	3.7	1	11	4.5	13	5.3	2.86	113	.125	.233	1	1	93	34	0.5	1	-1	0.1
1989	SF-N	1	0	1.000	2	2	1	0	0	15	13	7.8	1	5	3.0	9	5.4	1.80	187	.245	.310	3	3	96	187	0.5	1	0	0.4
	Phi-N	6	8	.429	21	16	1	1	0	106	97	8.2	17	33	2.8	58	4.9	3.99	90	.243	.299	-6	-5	102	98	0.2	1	-1	-0.4
	Yr	7	8	.467	23	18	2	1	0	121	110	8.2	18	38	2.8	67	5.0	3.72	96	.243	.301	-3	-2	102	98	0.7	1	-1	0.0
Total	2	9	9	.500	27	22	3	2	0	143	119	7.5	19	49	3.1	80	5.0	3.59	98	.227	.291	-1	-1	100	97	1.2	2	-1	0.1
■ **MIKE COOK**	Cook, Michael Horace b: 8/14/63, Charleston, S.C. BR/TR, 6'3", 200 lbs. Deb: 7/01/86																												
1986	Cal-A	0	2	.000	5	1	0	0	0	9	13	13.0	3	7	7.0	6	6.0	9.00	44	.333	.435	-5	-5	95	99	-0.9	0	0	-0.4
1987	Cal-A	1	2	.333	16	1	0	0	0	34	34	9.0	7	18	4.8	27	7.1	5.56	80	.264	.351	-4	-4	100	96	-0.3	0	1	-0.2
1988	Cal-A	0	1	.000	3	0	0	0	0	4	4	9.0	0	1	2.3	2	4.5	4.50	84	.308	.400	-0	-0	95	110	-0.4	0	0	0.0
1989	Min-A	0	1	.000	15	0	0	0	0	21	22	9.4	1	17	7.3	15	6.4	5.14	81	.268	.392	-3	-2	106	99	-0.4	0	-0	-0.2
Total	4	1	6	.143	39	2	0	0	0	68	73	9.7	11	43	5.7	50	6.6	5.82	73	.278	.379	-12	-12	101	98	-2.0	0	1	-0.8
■ **SHERM CORBETT**	Corbett, Sherman Stanley b: 11/3/62, New Braunfels, Tex. BL/TL, 6'4", 205 lbs. Deb: 5/29/88																												
1988	Cal-A	2	1	.667	34	0	0	0	1	46	47	9.2	2	23	4.5	28	5.5	4.11	92	.273	.343	-1	-2	95	105	0.6	0	0	-0.1
1989	Cal-A	0	0	—	4	0	0	0	0	5	3	5.4	1	1	1.8	3	5.4	3.60	106	.158	.200	0	0	98	40	0.0	0	-0	0.0
Total	2	2	1	.667	38	0	0	0	1	51	50	8.8	3	24	4.2	31	5.5	4.06	93	.262	.330	-1	-2	95	99	0.6	0	-0	-0.1

YEAR	TM/L	W	L	PCT	G	GS	CG	SHO	SV	IP	H	H/G	HR	BB	BB/G	SO	SO/G	ERA	/A	OAVG	OOBP	PR	/A	PF	CPI	WAT	PB	PD	TPI
■ JIM CORSI	Corsi, James Bernard b: 9/9/61, Newton, Mass. BR/TR, 6'1", 210 lbs. Deb: 6/28/88																												
1988	Oak-A	0	1	.000	11	1	0	0	0	21	20	8.6	1	6	2.6	10	4.3	3.86	96	.260	.292	0	-0	93	88	-0.4	0	-0	0.0
1989	Oak-A	1	2	.333	22	0	0	0	0	38	26	6.2	2	10	2.4	21	5.0	1.89	210	.194	.248	8	9	102	95	-0.6	0	0	0.9
Total	2	1	3	.250	33	1	0	0	0	59	46	7.0	3	16	2.4	31	4.7	2.59	149	.218	.265	9	8	99	93	-1.0	0	-0	0.9
■ JOHN COSTELLO	Costello, John Reilly b: 12/24/60, Bronx, N.Y. BR/TR, 6'1", 190 lbs. Deb: 6/02/88																												
1988	StL-N	5	2	.714	36	0	0	0	1	50	44	7.9	3	25	4.5	38	6.8	1.80	201	.235	.322	9	10	105	190	1.7	-1	-1	1.0
1989	StL-N	5	4	.556	48	0	0	0	3	62	48	7.0	5	20	2.9	40	5.8	3.34	105	.213	.278	1	1	100	80	0.3	-1	-1	0.0
Total	2	10	6	.625	84	0	0	0	4	112	92	7.4	8	45	3.6	78	6.3	2.65	134	.223	.298	10	11	102	129	2.0	-1	-2	1.0
■ STEVE CRAWFORD	Crawford, Steven Ray b: 4/29/58, Pryor, Okla. BR/TR, 6'5", 225 lbs. Deb: 9/02/80																												
1980	Bos-A	2	0	1.000	6	4	2	0	0	32	41	11.5	3	8	2.3	10	2.8	3.66	113	.306	.345	1	2	102	128	1.0	0	-0	0.1
1981	Bos-A	0	5	.000	14	11	0	0	0	58	69	10.7	10	18	2.8	29	4.5	4.97	78	.301	.350	-8	-7	106	112	-2.4	0	0	-0.6
1982	Bos-A	1	0	1.000	5	0	0	0	0	9	14	14.0	0	0	0.0	2	2.0	2.00	224	.341	.341	2	2	110	223	0.5	0	0	0.2
1984	Bos-A	5	0	1.000	35	0	0	0	1	62	69	10.0	6	21	3.0	21	3.0	3.34	132	.286	.340	5	7	110	136	2.5	0	-0	0.7
1985	Bos-A	6	5	.545	44	1	0	0	12	91	103	10.2	5	28	2.8	58	5.7	3.76	112	.289	.332	4	5	102	113	0.5	0	1	0.5
1986	Bos-A	0	2	.000	40	0	0	0	4	57	69	10.9	5	19	3.0	32	5.1	3.95	105	.308	.355	2	1	99	129	-0.9	0	0	0.1
1987	Bos-A	5	4	.556	29	0	0	0	0	73	91	11.2	13	32	3.9	43	5.3	5.30	83	.314	.386	-7	-7	99	120	0.7	0	0	-0.5
1989	KC-A	3	1	.750	25	0	0	0	0	54	48	8.0	2	19	3.2	33	5.5	2.83	131	.242	.313	6	5	95	111	0.9	0	2	0.7
Total	8	22	17	.564	198	16	2	0	17	436	504	10.4	44	145	3.0	228	4.7	3.98	104	.294	.347	5	8	102	122	2.8	0	2	1.2
■ TIM CREWS	Crews, Stanley Timothy b: 4/3/61, Tampa, Fla. BR/TR, 6' ", 180 lbs. Deb: 7/27/87																												
1987	LA-N	1	1	.500	20	0	0	0	3	29	30	9.3	2	8	2.5	20	6.2	2.48	152	.268	.323	5	4	92	154	0.1	-0	0	0.4
1988	LA-N	4	0	1.000	42	0	0	0	0	72	77	9.6	3	16	2.0	45	5.6	3.13	116	.278	.309	3	4	105	116	2.0	0	-1	0.3
1989	LA-N	0	1	.000	44	0	0	0	1	62	69	10.0	7	23	3.3	56	8.1	3.19	102	.284	.342	2	0	93	151	-0.4	0	-0	0.0
Total	3	5	2	.714	106	0	0	0	4	163	176	9.7	12	47	2.6	121	6.7	3.04	116	.278	.324	10	9	98	136	1.7	-0	-1	0.7
■ CHUCK CRIM	Crim, Charles Robert b: 7/23/61, Van Nuys, Cal. BR/TR, 6' ", 175 lbs. Deb: 4/08/87																												
1987	Mil-A	6	8	.429	53	5	0	0	12	130	133	9.2	15	39	2.7	56	3.9	3.67	124	.266	.319	12	13	102	112	-1.7	0	-0	1.2
1988	Mil-A	7	6	.538	**70**	0	0	0	9	105	95	8.1	11	28	2.4	58	5.0	2.91	140	.247	.294	12	14	103	121	0.0	0	0	1.4
1989	Mil-A	9	7	.563	**76**	0	0	0	7	118	114	8.7	7	36	2.7	59	4.5	2.82	133	.259	.312	14	12	96	124	1.1	0	-1	1.1
Total	3	22	21	.512	199	5	0	0	28	353	342	8.7	33	103	2.6	173	4.4	3.16	131	.258	.309	38	38	100	119	-0.6	0	-1	3.7
■ STEVE CUMMINGS	Cummings, Steven Brent b: 7/15/64, Houston, Tex. BB/TR, 6'2", 200 lbs. Deb: 6/24/89																												
1989	Tor-A	2	0	1.000	5	2	0	0	0	21	18	7.7	1	11	4.7	8	3.4	3.00	121	.231	.333	2	1	93	112	1.0	0	0	0.1
■ RON DARLING	Darling, Ronald Maurice b: 8/19/60, Honolulu, Hawaii BR/TR, 6'3", 195 lbs. Deb: 9/06/83																												
1983	NY-N	1	3	.250	5	5	1	0	0	35	31	8.0	0	17	4.4	23	5.9	2.83	128	.248	.345	3	3	100	121	-0.7	-1	0	0.3
1984	NY-N	12	9	.571	33	33	2	2	0	206	179	7.8	17	104	4.5	136	5.9	3.80	95	.235	.326	-5	-5	100	95	0.4	-1	2	-0.3
1985	NY-N	16	6	.727	36	35	4	2	0	248	214	7.8	21	114	4.1	167	6.1	2.90	118	.235	.317	19	15	95	**120**	3.8	2	3	2.2
1986	NY-N	15	6	.714	34	34	4	2	0	237	203	7.7	21	81	3.1	184	7.0	2.81	123	.234	.297	24	17	93	113	1.7	-2	4	2.0
1987	NY-N	12	8	.600	32	32	2	0	0	208	183	7.9	24	96	4.2	167	7.2	4.28	93	.233	.316	-5	-7	97	85	0.8	0	3	-0.3
1988	NY-N	17	9	.654	34	34	7	4	0	241	218	8.1	24	60	2.2	161	6.0	3.25	93	.245	.291	5	-6	88	104	1.2	6	0	0.0
1989	NY-N	14	14	.500	33	33	4	0	0	217	214	8.9	19	70	2.9	153	6.3	3.53	95	.258	.311	-1	-5	95	107	-1.1	1	2	-0.2
Total	7	87	55	.613	207	206	24	10	0	1392	1242	8.0	126	542	3.5	991	6.4	3.38	102	.241	.311	42	12	95	105	6.1	6	14	3.7
■ DANNY DARWIN	Darwin, Daniel Wayne b: 10/25/55, Bonham, Tex. BR/TR, 6'3", 185 lbs. Deb: 9/08/78																												
1978	Tex-A	1	0	1.000	3	1	0	0	0	9	11	11.0	0	1	1.0	8	8.0	4.00	90	.324	.333	-0	-0	96	102	0.5	0	-0	0.0
1979	Tex-A	4	4	.500	20	6	1	0	0	78	50	5.8	5	30	3.5	58	6.7	4.04	104	.186	.272	2	1	99	53	0.0	0	-1	0.0
1980	Tex-A	13	4	.765	53	2	0	0	8	110	98	8.0	4	50	4.1	104	8.5	2.62	155	.243	.321	17	18	100	124	4.9	0	-0	1.8
1981	Tex-A	9	9	.500	22	22	6	2	0	146	115	7.1	12	57	3.5	98	6.0	3.64	91	.218	.296	0	-6	90	81	-0.7	0	-1	-0.6
1982	Tex-A	10	8	.556	56	1	0	0	7	89	95	9.6	6	37	3.7	61	6.2	3.44	112	.279	.340	6	4	94	128	2.6	0	1	0.5
1983	Tex-A	8	13	.381	28	26	9	2	0	183	175	8.6	9	62	3.0	92	4.5	3.49	118	.250	.308	12	13	101	93	-2.2	0	-1	1.2
1984	Tex-A	8	12	.400	35	32	5	1	0	224	249	10.0	19	54	2.2	123	4.9	3.94	102	.279	.321	2	2	101	101	-0.7	0	-2	0.0
1985	Mil-A	8	18	.308	39	29	11	1	2	218	212	8.8	34	65	2.7	125	5.2	3.80	115	.254	.306	8	14	106	108	-4.3	0	-3	1.1
1986	Mil-A	6	8	.429	27	14	5	1	0	130	120	8.3	13	35	2.4	80	5.5	3.53	122	.246	.294	9	11	103	95	-0.7	0	1	1.2
	Hou-N	5	2	.714	12	8	1	0	0	54	50	8.3	3	9	1.5	40	6.7	2.33	162	.239	.266	8	9	102	103	1.1	-1	-0	0.8
1987	Hou-N	9	10	.474	33	30	3	1	0	196	184	8.4	17	69	3.2	134	6.2	3.58	106	.246	.310	11	5	93	97	0.1	2	-2	0.5
1988	Hou-N	8	13	.381	44	20	3	0	3	192	189	8.9	20	48	2.3	129	6.0	3.84	84	.259	.303	-8	-13	93	98	-2.8	-1	2	-1.2
1989	Hou-N	11	4	.733	68	0	0	0	7	122	92	6.8	8	33	2.4	104	7.7	2.36	152	.212	.263	15	17	103	100	3.4	-1	-1	1.6
Total	12	100	105	.488	440	191	44	8	27	1751	1640	8.4	150	550	2.8	1156	5.9	3.51	111	.248	.304	83	73	99	99	1.2	-0	-8	6.9
■ BOB DAVIDSON	Davidson, Robert Banks b: 1/6/63, Bad Kurznach, W.Ger. BR/TR, 6', 185 lbs. Deb: 7/15/89																												
1989	NY-A	0	0	—	1	0	0	0	0	1	1	9.0	1	1	9.0	0	0.0	18.00	23	.250	.400	-2	-2	105	68	0.0	0	0	0.0
■ STORM DAVIS	Davis, George Earl b: 12/26/61, Dallas, Tex. BR/TR, 6'4", 207 lbs. Deb: 4/29/82																												
1982	Bal-A	8	4	.667	29	8	1	0	0	101	96	8.6	8	28	2.5	67	6.0	3.48	116	.257	.301	7	6	99	100	1.3	0	-0	0.6
1983	Bal-A	13	7	.650	34	29	6	1	0	200	180	8.1	14	64	2.9	125	5.6	3.60	112	.238	.296	11	9	99	84	1.3	0	-1	0.8
1984	Bal-A	14	9	.609	35	31	10	2	1	225	205	8.2	7	71	2.8	105	4.2	3.12	121	.247	.304	22	16	94	96	2.3	0	-3	1.3
1985	Bal-A	10	8	.556	31	28	8	1	0	175	172	8.8	11	70	3.6	93	4.8	4.53	90	.256	.324	-7	-9	98	81	0.8	0	-1	-0.8
1986	Bal-A	9	12	.429	25	25	2	0	0	154	166	9.7	16	49	2.9	96	5.6	3.62	115	.275	.327	10	9	99	116	-0.5	0	1	1.0
1987	SD-N	2	7	.222	21	10	0	0	0	63	70	10.0	5	36	5.1	37	5.3	6.14	65	.280	.370	-14	-15	98	80	-2.0	-1	0	-1.4
	Oak-A	1	1	.500	5	5	0	0	0	30	28	8.4	3	11	3.3	28	8.4	3.30	123	.241	.305	4	3	91	103	0.0	0	-1	0.2
1988	Oak-A	16	7	.696	33	33	1	0	0	202	211	9.4	16	91	4.1	127	5.7	3.70	100	.274	.347	6	0	93	121	2.0	0	-2	-0.1
1989	Oak-A	19	7	.731	31	31	1	0	0	169	187	10.0	19	68	3.6	91	4.8	4.37	91	.288	.352	-9	-7	102	113	4.5	0	-2	-0.8
Total	8	92	62	.597	244	200	29	4	1	1319	1315	9.0	99	488	3.3	769	5.2	3.86	102	.262	.325	28	12	97	100	9.7	-1	-7	0.8
■ JOHN DAVIS	Davis, John Kirk b: 1/5/63, Chicago, Ill. BR/TR, 6'7", 215 lbs. Deb: 7/24/87																												
1987	KC-A	5	2	.714	27	0	0	0	2	44	29	5.9	0	26	5.3	24	4.9	2.25	206	.195	.315	11	12	104	114	1.5	0	0	1.2
1988	Chi-A	2	5	.286	34	1	0	0	1	64	77	10.8	5	50	7.0	37	5.2	6.61	59	.297	.411	-19	-19	99	93	-1.2	0	-0	-1.8
1989	Chi-A	0	1	.000	4	0	0	0	1	6	5	7.5	2	2	3.0	5	7.5	4.50	81	.217	.280	-0	-1	93	99	-0.4	0	0	0.0
Total	3	7	8	.467	65	1	0	0	4	114	111	8.8	7	78	6.2	66	5.2	4.82	87	.258	.371	-8	-8	100	101	-0.1	0	0	-0.6
■ MARK DAVIS	Davis, Mark William b: 10/19/60, Livermore, Cal. BL/TL, 6'3", 180 lbs. Deb: 9/12/80																												
1980	Phi-N	0	0	—	2	1	0	0	0	7	4	5.1	0	5	6.4	5	6.4	2.57	149	.160	.300	1	1	106	62	0.0	0	-0	0.1
1981	Phi-N	1	4	.200	9	9	0	0	0	43	49	10.3	7	24	5.0	29	6.1	7.74	50	.299	.376	-20	-18	112	77	-1.5	-0	-0	-1.7
1983	SF-N	6	4	.600	20	20	2	2	0	111	93	7.5	14	50	4.1	83	6.7	3.49	105	.227	.311	2	2	101	101	1.2	0	-1	0.2
1984	SF-N	5	17	.227	46	27	1	0	0	175	201	10.3	25	54	2.8	124	6.4	5.35	66	.293	.339	-34	-36	98	94	-5.2	0	-2	-3.6
1985	SF-N	5	12	.294	77	1	0	0	7	114	89	7.0	13	41	3.2	131	10.3	3.55	96	.219	.286	1	-2	95	87	-2.0	1	-1	-0.1
1986	SF-N	5	7	.417	67	2	0	0	4	84	63	6.8	6	34	3.6	90	9.6	3.00	118	.212	.287	7	5	95	91	-1.1	0	-0	0.5
1987	SF-N	4	5	.444	20	11	1	0	0	71	72	9.1	9	28	3.5	51	6.5	4.69	83	.273	.346	-5	-6	95	102	-0.8	2	-0	-0.5
	SD-N	5	3	.625	43	0	0	0	2	62	51	7.4	5	31	4.5	47	6.8	3.19	125	.224	.317	6	6	98	104	1.5	0	0	0.6
	Yr	9	8	.529	63	11	1	0	2	133	123	8.3	14	59	4.0	98	6.6	3.99	98	.247	.325	1	-1	96	104	0.7	2	0	0.1
1988	SD-N	5	10	.333	62	0	0	0	28	98	70	6.4	2	42	3.9	102	9.4	2.02	166	.199	.279	16	15	97	102	-2.7	1	2	2.0
1989	SD-N	4	3	.571	70	0	0	0	**44**	93	66	6.4	6	31	3.0	92	8.9	1.84	191	.200	.268	17	17	101	123	0.2	-1	-1	1.6
Total	9	40	65	.381	416	71	4	2	85	858	758	8.0	87	340	3.6	754	7.9	3.77	95	.240	.310	-10	-17	98	98	-10.4	4	-2	-0.9
■ STEVE DAVIS	Davis, Steven Kennon b: 8/4/60, San Antonio, Tex. BL/TL, 6'1", 195 lbs. Deb: 8/25/85																												
1985	Tor-A	2	1	.667	10	5	0	0	0	28	23	7.4	5	13	4.2	22	7.1	3.54	116	.223	.308	2	2	99	111	0.2	0	0	0.2
1986	Tor-A	0	0	—	3	0	0	0	0	4	8	18.0	2	5	11.3	5	11.3	15.75	28	.471	.591	-5	-5	104	100	0.0	0	0	-0.4

YEAR TM/L	W	L	PCT	G	GS	CG	SHO	SV	IP	H	H/G	HR	BB	BB/G	SO	SO/G	ERA	/A	OAVG	OOBP	PR	/A	PF	CPI	WAT	PB	PD	TPI
1989 Cle-A	1	1	.500	12	2	0	0	0	26	34	11.8	2	14	4.8	12	4.2	7.96	51	.318	.397	-12	-11	104	73	0.1	0	-0	-1.0
Total 3	3	2	.600	25	7	0	0	0	58	65	10.1	9	32	5.0	39	6.1	6.36	65	.286	.373	-15	-15	102	93	0.3	0	-0	-1.2
■ BILL DAWLEY	Dawley, William Chester b: 2/6/58, Norwich, Conn. BR/TR, 6'5", 235 lbs. Deb: 4/15/83																											
1983 Hou-N	6	6	.500	48	0	0	0	14	80	51	5.7	9	22	2.5	60	6.7	2.81	116	.185	.243	7	4	90	71	-0.2	0	-1	0.3
1984 Hou-N	11	4	.733	60	0	0	0	5	98	82	7.5	5	35	3.2	47	4.3	1.93	171	.234	.291	18	15	92	151	3.7	1	-1	1.6
1985 Hou-N	5	3	.625	49	0	0	0	2	81	76	8.4	7	37	4.1	48	5.3	3.56	97	.259	.326	0	-1	96	114	1.0	0	0	0.0
1986 Chi-A	0	7	.000	46	0	0	0	2	98	91	8.4	10	28	2.6	66	6.1	3.31	128	.247	.296	10	10	101	104	-3.4	0	-1	0.9
1987 StL-N	5	8	.385	60	0	0	0	2	97	93	8.6	15	38	3.5	65	6.0	4.45	89	.259	.325	-4	-5	97	101	-2.3	1	1	-0.3
1988 Phi-N	0	2	.000	8	0	0	0	0	9	16	16.0	3	4	4.0	3	3.0	13.00	27	.381	.426	-10	-9	103	75	-0.9	0	-0	-0.9
1989 Oak-A	0	0	—	4	0	0	0	0	9	11	11.0	0	2	2.0	3	3.0	4.00	99	.297	.341	-0	-0	102	101	0.0	0	-0	0.0
Total 7	27	30	.474	275	0	0	0	25	472	420	8.0	49	166	3.2	292	5.6	3.41	107	.243	.302	22	13	96	109	-2.1	3	-2	1.6
■ KEN DAYLEY	Dayley, Kenneth Grant b: 2/25/59, Jerome, Idaho BL/TL, 6', 171 lbs. Deb: 5/13/82																											
1982 Atl-N	5	6	.455	20	11	0	0	0	71	79	10.0	9	25	3.2	34	4.3	4.56	84	.286	.332	-8	-6	107	104	-0.9	1	-1	-0.6
1983 Atl-N	5	8	.385	24	16	0	0	0	105	100	8.6	12	39	3.3	70	6.0	4.29	89	.257	.323	-8	-6	104	93	-1.9	2	-2	-0.6
1984 Atl-N	0	3	.000	4	4	0	0	0	19	28	13.3	5	6	2.8	10	4.7	5.21	76	.341	.380	-3	-3	110	143	-1.4	1	0	-0.1
StL-N	0	2	.000	3	2	0	0	0	5	16	28.8	1	5	9.0	0	0.0	18.00	20	.615	.656	-8	-8	99	106	-0.9	0	-0	-0.7
Yr	0	5	.000	7	6	0	0	0	24	44	16.5	6	11	4.1	10	3.8	7.88	49	.404	.444	-11	-11	107	106	-2.3	1	0	-0.8
1985 StL-N	4	4	.500	57	0	0	0	11	65	65	9.0	2	18	2.5	62	8.6	2.77	121	.263	.306	6	4	93	115	-0.7	1	2	0.7
1986 StL-N	0	3	.000	31	0	0	0	5	39	42	9.7	1	11	2.5	33	7.6	3.23	119	.275	.318	2	3	103	109	-1.4	0	0	0.3
1987 StL-N	9	5	.643	53	0	0	0	4	61	52	7.7	2	33	4.9	63	9.3	2.66	150	.234	.335	10	9	97	128	1.0	0	-1	0.8
1988 StL-N	2	7	.222	54	0	0	0	5	55	48	7.9	2	19	3.1	38	6.2	2.78	130	.239	.301	4	5	105	107	-2.3	-0	-0	0.5
1989 StL-N	4	3	.571	71	0	0	0	12	75	63	7.6	3	30	3.6	40	4.8	2.88	122	.228	.300	5	5	100	98	0.3	-1	-2	0.3
Total 8	29	41	.414	317	33	0	0	37	495	493	9.0	37	186	3.4	350	6.4	3.64	102	.263	.325	1	4	102	107	-8.2	3	-4	0.6
■ JOSE DeJESUS	DeJesus, Jose Luis b: 1/6/65, Brooklyn, N.Y. BR/TR, 6'5", 175 lbs. Deb: 9/09/88																											
1988 KC-A	0	1	.000	2	1	0	0	0	3	6	18.0	0	5	15.0	2	6.0	24.00	17	.429	.579	-7	-7	103	51	-0.4	0	0	-0.5
1989 KC-A	0	0	—	3	1	0	0	0	8	7	7.9	1	8	9.0	2	2.3	4.50	82	.241	.405	-1	-1	95	122	0.0	0	0	0.0
Total 2	0	1	.000	5	2	0	0	0	11	13	10.6	1	13	10.6	4	3.3	9.82	39	.302	.464	-7	-7	97	102	-0.4	0	0	-0.5
■ JOSE DeLEON	DeLeon, Jose (Chestaro) b: 12/20/60, La Vega, D.R. BR/TR, 6'3", 210 lbs. Deb: 7/23/83																											
1983 Pit-N	7	3	.700	15	15	3	2	0	108	75	6.3	5	47	3.9	118	9.8	2.83	132	.196	.281	10	11	103	75	2.0	-1	-1	1.0
1984 Pit-N	7	13	.350	30	28	5	1	0	192	147	6.9	10	92	4.3	153	7.2	3.75	90	.214	.304	-3	-8	94	75	-2.6	-3	-3	-1.4
1985 Pit-N	2	19	.095	31	25	1	0	3	163	138	7.6	15	89	4.9	149	8.2	4.69	80	.231	.329	-20	-17	104	78	-7.9	-2	-1	-1.9
1986 Pit-N	1	3	.250	9	1	0	0	1	16	17	9.6	2	17	9.6	11	6.2	8.44	44	.266	.422	-8	-8	101	75	-0.6	0	0	-0.7
Chi-A	4	5	.444	13	13	1	0	0	79	49	5.6	7	42	4.8	68	7.7	2.96	143	.179	.292	11	11	101	86	0.0	0	0	1.2
1987 Chi-A	11	12	.478	33	31	2	0	0	206	177	7.7	24	97	4.2	153	6.7	4.02	121	.230	.319	10	19	109	93	0.1	0	-3	1.5
1988 StL-N	13	10	.565	34	34	3	1	0	225	198	7.9	13	86	3.4	208	8.3	3.68	98	.237	.304	-6	-2	105	86	2.4	-1	-2	-0.4
1989 StL-N	16	12	.571	36	36	5	3	0	245	173	**6.4**	16	80	2.9	**201**	7.4	3.05	115	**.197**	.266	12	13	100	71	1.4	-4	-4	0.5
Total 7	61	77	.442	201	183	20	7	4	1234	974	7.1	92	550	4.0	1061	7.7	3.70	103	.217	.302	6	18	102	80	-5.2	-10	-13	-0.2
■ LUIS DeLEON	DeLeon, Luis Antonio (Tricoche) b: 8/19/58, Ponce, P.R. BR/TR, 6'1", 153 lbs. Deb: 9/06/81																											
1981 StL-N	0	1	.000	10	0	0	0	0	15	11	6.6	1	3	1.8	8	4.8	2.40	147	.200	.237	2	2	101	68	-0.4	-0	-0	0.2
1982 SD-N	9	5	.643	61	0	0	0	15	102	77	6.8	10	16	1.4	60	5.3	2.03	163	.212	.241	18	14	92	106	2.1	0	1	1.6
1983 SD-N	6	6	.500	63	0	0	0	13	111	89	7.2	8	27	2.2	90	7.3	2.68	135	.224	.265	12	11	99	92	0.0	-0	-2	1.0
1984 SD-N	2	2	.500	32	0	0	0	0	43	44	9.2	12	12	2.5	44	9.2	5.44	65	.256	.314	-9	-9	98	94	-0.1	-0	0	-0.9
1985 SD-N	0	3	.000	29	0	0	0	3	39	39	9.0	6	10	2.3	31	7.2	4.15	88	.267	.319	-2	-2	101	107	-1.4	0	-0	-0.2
1987 Bal-A	0	2	.000	11	0	0	0	1	21	19	8.1	1	8	3.4	13	5.6	4.71	94	.253	.326	-1	-1	99	82	-0.9	0	-0	0.0
1989 Sea-A	0	0	—	1	1	0	0	0	4	5	11.3	1	1	2.3	2	4.5	2.25	179	.313	.389	1	1	104	306	0.0	0	0	0.1
Total 7	17	19	.472	207	1	0	0	32	335	284	7.6	39	77	2.1	248	6.7	3.12	114	.232	.276	21	16	97	99	-0.7	-0	-1	1.8
■ JIM DESHAIES	Deshaies, James Joseph b: 6/23/60, Massena, N.Y. BL/TL, 6'4", 222 lbs. Deb: 8/07/84																											
1984 NY-A	0	1	.000	2	2	0	0	0	7	14	18.0	1	7	9.0	5	6.4	11.57	32	.438	.525	-6	-6	93	100	-0.4	0	0	-0.4
1985 Hou-N	0	0	—	2	0	0	0	0	3	1	3.0	0	0	0.0	2	6.0	0.00	—	.100	.100	1	1	96	0	0.0	0	0	0.1
1986 Hou-N	12	5	.706	26	26	1	1	0	144	124	7.8	16	59	3.7	128	8.0	3.25	116	.234	.309	8	9	102	107	2.6	-2	-1	0.6
1987 Hou-N	11	6	.647	26	25	1	0	0	152	149	8.8	22	57	3.4	104	6.2	4.62	82	.257	.318	-9	-14	93	91	3.1	0	-1	-1.4
1988 Hou-N	11	14	.440	31	31	3	2	0	207	164	7.1	20	72	3.1	127	5.5	3.00	108	.218	.281	10	5	93	97	-1.8	-3	-2	-0.1
1989 Hou-N	15	10	.600	34	34	6	3	0	226	180	7.2	15	79	3.1	153	6.1	2.91	124	.217	.283	15	17	103	92	2.1	-3	-1	1.5
Total 6	49	36	.576	121	118	11	6	0	739	632	7.7	74	274	3.3	519	6.3	3.42	104	.231	.298	19	12	98	96	5.6	-8	-5	0.3
■ ROB DIBBLE	Dibble, Robert Keith b: 1/24/64, Bridgeport, Conn. BL/TR, 6'4", 230 lbs. Deb: 6/29/88																											
1988 Cin-N	1	1	.500	37	0	0	0	0	59	43	6.6	2	21	3.2	59	9.0	1.83	198	.207	.277	11	12	105	123	0.0	-0	-1	1.1
1989 Cin-N	10	5	.667	74	0	0	0	2	99	62	5.6	4	39	3.5	141	12.8	2.09	174	.176	.259	16	17	104	79	3.0	-1	-1	1.6
Total 2	11	6	.647	111	0	0	0	2	158	105	6.0	6	60	3.4	200	11.4	1.99	182	.188	.266	26	29	104	96	3.0	-1	-2	2.7
■ GORDON DILLARD	Dillard, Gordon Lee b: 5/20/64, Salinas, Cal. BL/TL, 6'1", 190 lbs. Deb: 8/12/88																											
1988 Bal-A	0	0	—	2	1	0	0	0	3	3	9.0	1	4	12.0	2	6.0	6.00	65	.273	.467	-1	-1	97	148	0.0	0	0	0.0
1989 Phi-N	0	0	—	5	0	0	0	0	4	7	15.8	0	0	0.0	2	4.5	6.75	53	.368	.368	-1	-1	102	82	0.0	0	0	0.0
Total 2	0	0	—	7	1	0	0	0	7	10	12.9	1	4	5.1	4	5.1	6.43	58	.333	.412	-2	-2	100	110	0.0	0	0	0.0
■ FRANK DiPINO	DiPino, Frank Michael b: 10/22/56, Syracuse, N.Y. BL/TL, 5'10", 175 lbs. Deb: 9/14/81																											
1981 Mil-A	0	0	—	2	0	0	0	0	2	0	0.0	0	3	13.5	3	13.5	0.00	—	.000	.300	1	1	95	0	0.0	0	0	0.1
1982 Hou-N	2	2	.500	6	6	0	0	0	28	32	10.3	1	11	3.5	25	8.0	6.11	59	.302	.352	-8	-8	100	75	0.1	-1	-0	-0.8
1983 Hou-N	3	4	.429	53	0	0	0	20	71	52	6.6	2	20	2.5	67	8.5	2.66	123	.205	.262	8	5	90	66	-0.6	1	1	0.6
1984 Hou-N	4	9	.308	57	0	0	0	14	75	74	8.9	3	36	4.3	65	7.8	3.36	98	.260	.337	2	-1	92	113	-2.5	-1	0	0.0
1985 Hou-N	3	7	.300	54	0	0	0	6	76	69	8.2	7	43	5.1	49	5.8	4.03	86	.248	.347	-4	-5	96	104	-2.1	-0	-1	-0.6
1986 Hou-N	1	3	.250	31	0	0	0	3	40	27	6.1	5	16	3.6	27	6.1	3.60	105	.189	.269	1	1	102	72	-1.1	0	0	0.1
Chi-N	2	4	.333	30	0	0	0	0	40	47	10.6	6	14	3.1	43	9.7	5.17	78	.297	.343	-6	-5	108	101	-0.6	-0	1	-0.3
Yr	3	7	.300	61	0	0	0	3	80	74	8.3	11	30	3.4	70	7.9	4.39	89	.243	.301	-6	-4	105	101	-1.7	0	2	-0.2
1987 Chi-N	3	3	.500	69	0	0	0	4	80	75	8.4	7	34	3.8	61	6.9	3.15	132	.252	.321	8	9	102	122	0.2	0	1	1.0
1988 Chi-N	2	3	.400	63	0	0	0	6	90	102	10.2	6	32	3.2	69	6.9	5.00	72	.285	.337	-15	-14	105	87	-0.3	-0	-0	-1.5
1989 StL-N	9	0	1.000	67	0	0	0	0	88	73	7.5	6	20	2.0	44	4.5	2.45	143	.227	.268	10	10	100	104	4.5	-1	0	1.0
Total 9	29	35	.453	432	6	0	0	53	590	551	8.4	43	229	3.5	453	6.9	3.71	97	.250	.315	-4	-7	99	96	-2.4	-2	1	-0.4
■ JOHN DOPSON	Dopson, John Robert b: 7/14/63, Baltimore, Md. BL/TR, 6'4", 205 lbs. Deb: 9/04/85																											
1985 Mon-N	0	2	.000	4	3	0	0	0	13	25	17.3	4	4	2.8	4	2.8	11.08	30	.379	.414	-11	-11	94	83	-0.9	0	0	-0.9
1988 Mon-N	3	11	.214	26	26	1	0	0	169	150	8.0	15	58	3.1	101	5.4	3.04	119	.235	.297	8	11	105	105	-4.1	-3	-2	0.7
1989 Bos-A	12	8	.600	29	28	2	0	0	169	166	8.8	14	69	3.7	95	5.1	3.99	102	.257	.326	-2	1	104	96	2.0	0	3	0.4
Total 3	15	21	.417	59	57	3	0	0	351	341	8.7	33	131	3.4	200	5.1	3.79	101	.252	.316	-5	1	104	100	-3.0	-3	1	0.2
■ RICHARD DOTSON	Dotson, Richard Elliott b: 1/10/59, Cincinnati, Ohio BR/TR, 6'1", 190 lbs. Deb: 9/04/79																											
1979 Chi-A	2	0	1.000	5	5	1	1	0	24	28	10.5	0	6	2.3	13	4.9	3.75	116	.286	.318	1	2	103	91	1.0	0	0	0.2
1980 Chi-A	12	10	.545	33	32	8	0	0	198	185	8.4	20	87	4.0	109	5.0	4.27	93	.247	.322	-5	-7	98	89	2.4	0	1	-0.5
1981 Chi-A	9	8	.529	24	24	5	**4**	0	141	145	9.3	13	49	3.1	73	4.7	3.77	96	.270	.331	-2	-2	99	110	0.4	0	-0	-0.2
1982 Chi-A	11	15	.423	34	31	3	1	0	197	219	10.0	19	73	3.3	109	5.0	3.84	103	.282	.343	5	2	97	119	-3.1	0	-1	0.2
1983 Chi-A	22	7	**.759**	35	35	8	1	0	240	209	7.8	19	106	4.0	137	5.1	3.23	128	.240	.324	23	24	102	113	**6.2**	0	4	3.0
1984 Chi-A	14	15	.483	32	32	14	1	0	246	216	7.9	24	103	3.8	120	4.4	3.59	124	.238	.315	11	23	111	100	0.8	0	-0	2.4
1985 Chi-A	3	4	.429	9	9	0	0	0	52	53	9.2	5	17	2.9	33	5.7	4.50	92	.261	.323	-2	-2	100	89	-0.6	0	-0	-0.1
1986 Chi-A	10	17	.370	34	34	3	1	0	197	226	10.3	24	69	3.2	110	5.0	5.48	77	.289	.345	-28	-27	101	88	-2.5	0	-1	-2.6

YEAR	TM/L	W	L	PCT	G	GS	CG	SHO	SV	IP	H	H/G	HR	BB	BB/G	SO	SO/G	ERA	/A	OAVG	OOBP	PR	/A	PF	CPI	WAT	PB	PD	TPI
1987	Chi-A	11	12	.478	31	31	7	2	0	211	201	8.6	24	86	3.7	114	4.9	4.18	116	.249	.319	7	16	109	93	0.1	0	2	1.7
1988	NY-A	12	9	.571	32	29	4	0	0	171	178	9.4	27	72	3.8	77	4.1	5.00	76	.266	.336	-19	-23	96	95	1.1	0	-1	-2.3
1989	NY-A	2	5	.286	11	9	1	0	0	52	69	11.9	8	17	2.9	14	2.4	5.54	74	.317	.364	-10	-8	105	105	-1.3	0	-1	-0.8
	Chi-A	3	7	.300	17	17	1	0	0	100	112	10.1	8	41	3.7	55	5.0	3.87	94	.282	.343	0	-3	93	115	-1.5	0	0	-0.2
	Yr	5	12	.294	28	26	2	0	0	152	181	10.7	16	58	3.4	69	4.1	4.44	85	.293	.349	-9	-11	97	115	-2.8	0	-1	-1.0
Total	11	111	109	.505	297	288	55	11	0	1829	1841	9.1	191	726	3.6	964	4.7	4.16	99	.262	.330	-18	-5	102	101	3.0	0	2	0.8
■ KELLY DOWNS	Downs, Kelly Robert b: 10/25/60, Ogden, Utah BR/TR, 6'4", 195 lbs. Deb: 7/29/86																												
1986	SF-N	4	4	.500	14	14	1	0	0	88	78	8.0	5	30	3.1	64	6.5	2.76	128	.236	.298	9	7	95	107	0.0	0	0	0.7
1987	SF-N	12	9	.571	41	28	4	3	1	186	185	9.0	14	67	3.2	137	6.6	3.63	107	.258	.321	9	5	95	102	0.4	-0	-4	0.0
1988	SF-N	13	9	.591	27	26	6	3	0	168	140	7.5	11	47	2.5	118	6.3	3.32	97	.225	.277	2	-2	93	80	2.0	2	0	0.0
1989	SF-N	4	8	.333	18	15	0	0	0	83	82	8.9	7	26	2.8	49	5.3	4.77	70	.261	.312	-12	-13	96	79	-2.5	-1	-1	-1.4
Total	4	33	30	.524	100	83	11	6	1	525	485	8.3	37	170	2.9	368	6.3	3.57	99	.244	.302	10	-2	94	92	-0.1	1	-4	-0.7
■ DOUG DRABEK	Drabek, Douglas Dean b: 7/25/62, Victoria, Tex. BR/TR, 6'1", 185 lbs. Deb: 5/30/86																												
1986	NY-A	7	8	.467	27	21	0	0	0	132	126	8.6	13	50	3.4	76	5.2	4.09	105	.251	.319	1	3	103	93	-1.2	0	-1	0.1
1987	Pit-N	11	12	.478	29	28	1	1	0	176	165	8.4	22	46	2.4	120	6.1	3.89	110	.247	.293	4	7	105	90	-0.3	-1	1	0.7
1988	Pit-N	15	7	.682	33	32	3	1	0	219	194	8.0	21	50	2.1	127	5.2	3.08	109	.239	.284	9	7	97	101	3.9	3	-1	0.9
1989	Pit-N	14	12	.538	35	34	8	5	0	244	215	7.9	21	69	2.5	123	4.5	2.80	118	.238	.289	19	14	94	112	2.3	-2	0	1.2
Total	4	47	39	.547	124	115	12	7	0	771	700	8.2	77	215	2.5	446	5.2	3.35	110	.243	.294	33	30	99	101	4.7	0	-2	2.9
■ DAVE DRAVECKY	Dravecky, David Francis b: 2/14/56, Youngstown, Ohio BR/TL, 6'1", 195 lbs. Deb: 6/15/82																												
1982	SD-N	5	3	.625	31	10	0	0	2	105	86	7.4	8	33	2.8	59	5.1	2.57	128	.225	.282	12	9	92	105	1.0	-0	2	1.0
1983	SD-N	14	10	.583	28	28	9	1	0	184	181	8.9	18	44	2.2	74	3.6	3.57	101	.262	.302	1	1	99	100	2.3	-2	1	0.0
1984	SD-N	9	8	.529	50	14	3	2	8	157	125	7.2	12	51	2.9	71	4.1	2.92	120	.222	.285	12	10	98	95	-0.5	-0	-2	0.8
1985	SD-N	13	11	.542	34	31	7	2	0	215	200	8.4	18	57	2.4	105	4.4	2.93	125	.249	.295	16	17	101	111	0.8	-1	-1	1.7
1986	SD-N	9	11	.450	26	26	3	1	0	161	149	8.3	17	54	3.0	87	4.9	3.07	116	.246	.301	12	9	96	**115**	-0.1	0	0	1.0
1987	SD-N	3	7	.300	30	10	1	0	0	79	71	8.1	10	31	3.5	60	6.8	3.76	106	.240	.313	3	2	98	101	-1.2	0	0	0.2
	SF-N	7	5	.583	18	18	4	3	0	112	115	9.2	8	33	2.7	78	6.3	3.21	120	.272	.322	11	8	95	122	0.4	0	1	1.0
	Yr	10	12	.455	48	28	5	3	0	191	186	8.8	18	64	3.0	138	6.5	3.44	114	.257	.315	14	10	96	122	-0.8	0	1	1.2
1988	SF-N	2	2	.500	7	7	1	0	0	37	33	8.0	4	8	1.9	19	4.6	3.16	102	.243	.272	1	0	93	102	0.0	-0	0	0.0
1989	SF-N	2	0	1.000	2	2	0	0	0	13	8	5.5	2	4	2.8	5	3.5	3.46	97	.182	.260	0	-0	96	78	1.0	1	0	0.1
Total	8	64	57	.529	226	146	28	9	10	1063	968	8.2	97	315	2.7	558	4.7	3.13	115	.245	.297	68	56	97	106	3.7	-2	1	5.8
■ TIM DRUMMOND	Drummond, Timothy Darnell b: 12/24/64, La Plata, Md. BR/TR, 6'3", 170 lbs. Deb: 9/12/87																												
1987	Pit-N	0	0	—	6	0	0	0	0	6	5	7.5	0	3	4.5	5	7.5	4.50	95	.227	.308	-0	-0	105	61	0.0	-0	0	0.0
1989	Min-A	0	0	—	8	0	0	0	1	16	16	9.0	0	8	4.5	9	5.1	3.94	105	.246	.347	-0	0	106	85	0.0	0	-0	0.0
Total	2	0	0	—	14	0	0	0	1	22	21	8.6	0	11	4.5	14	5.7	4.09	102	.241	.337	-0	0	106	78	0.0	-0	-0	0.0
■ BRIAN DuBOIS	DuBois, Brian Andrew b: 4/18/67, Joliet, Ill. BL/TL, 5'10", 165 lbs. Deb: 8/17/89																												
1989	Det-A	0	4	.000	6	5	0	0	1	36	29	7.3	2	17	4.3	13	3.3	1.75	221	.218	.314	9	8	99	170	-1.9	0	-0	0.9
■ MIKE DUNNE	Dunne, Michael Dennis b: 10/27/62, South Bend, Ind. BR/TR, 6'4", 190 lbs. Deb: 6/05/87																												
1987	Pit-N	13	6	.684	23	23	5	1	0	163	143	7.9	10	68	3.8	72	4.0	3.04	**141**	.240	.312	19	22	105	110	3.9	-1	2	2.5
1988	Pit-N	7	11	.389	30	28	1	0	0	170	163	8.6	15	88	4.7	70	3.7	3.92	86	.255	.340	-9	-11	97	109	-2.5	-1	0	-1.1
1989	Pit-N	1	1	.500	3	3	0	0	0	14	21	13.5	1	9	5.8	4	2.6	7.71	43	.328	.413	-7	-7	94	87	0.1	0	0	-0.5
	Sea-A	2	9	.182	15	15	1	0	0	85	104	11.0	7	37	3.9	38	4.0	5.29	76	.307	.370	-13	-12	104	100	-3.3	0	0	-1.0
Total	3	23	27	.460	71	69	7	1	0	432	431	9.0	33	202	4.2	184	3.8	3.98	96	.263	.339	-10	-8	101	107	-1.8	-1	3	-0.1
■ MIKE DYER	Dyer, Michael Lawrence b: 9/8/66, Upland, Cal. BR/TR, 6'3", 195 lbs. Deb: 6/29/89																												
1989	Min-A	4	7	.364	16	12	1	0	0	71	74	9.4	2	37	4.7	37	4.7	4.82	86	.273	.356	-7	-5	106	88	-1.4	0	-1	-0.6
■ LOGAN EASLEY	Easley, Kenneth Logan b: 11/4/61, Salt Lake City, Utah BR/TR, 6'1", 185 lbs. Deb: 4/09/87																												
1987	Pit-N	1	1	.500	17	0	0	0	1	26	23	8.0	5	17	5.9	21	7.3	5.54	77	.242	.347	-4	-4	105	93	0.0	-0	1	-0.2
1989	Pit-N	1	0	1.000	10	0	0	0	1	12	8	6.0	1	7	5.3	6	4.5	4.50	73	.190	.314	-1	-2	94	68	0.5	-0	0	-0.1
Total	2	2	1	.667	27	0	0	0	2	38	31	7.3	6	24	5.7	27	6.4	5.21	76	.226	.337	-6	-5	101	85	0.5	-0	1	-0.3
■ GARY EAVE	Eave, Gary Louis b: 7/22/63, Monroe, La. BR/TR, 6'4", 200 lbs. Deb: 4/12/88																												
1988	Atl-N	0	0	—	5	0	0	0	0	5	7	12.6	0	3	5.4	0	0.0	9.00	41	.333	.417	-3	-3	107	66	0.0	0	-0	-0.2
1989	Atl-N	2	0	1.000	3	3	0	0	0	21	15	6.4	0	12	5.1	9	3.9	1.29	282	.200	.318	5	5	104	193	1.0	-1	-1	0.5
Total	2	2	0	1.000	8	3	0	0	0	26	22	7.6	0	15	5.2	9	3.1	2.77	131	.229	.339	2	3	104	168	1.0	-1	-1	0.3
■ DENNIS ECKERSLEY	Eckersley, Dennis Lee b: 10/3/54, Oakland, Cal. BR/TR, 6'2", 190 lbs. Deb: 4/12/75																												
1975	Cle-A	13	7	.650	34	24	6	2	2	187	147	7.1	16	90	4.3	152	7.3	2.60	145	.215	.307	25	24	100	116	3.3	0	-3	2.3
1976	Cle-A	13	12	.520	36	30	9	3	1	199	155	7.0	13	78	3.5	200	9.0	3.44	102	.214	.290	2	2	100	76	0.3	0	-1	0.1
1977	Cle-A	14	13	.519	33	33	12	3	0	247	214	7.8	31	54	2.0	191	7.0	3.53	113	.231	**.273**	15	13	98	83	2.2	0	-3	0.9
1978	Bos-A	20	8	.714	35	35	16	3	0	268	258	8.7	30	71	2.4	162	5.4	2.99	134	.251	.300	24	30	106	115	4.4	0	-1	3.1
1979	Bos-A	17	10	.630	33	33	17	2	0	247	234	8.5	29	59	2.1	150	5.5	2.99	**150**	.250	.294	34	**41**	106	**116**	2.2	0	1	**4.3**
1980	Bos-A	12	14	.462	30	30	8	0	0	198	188	8.5	25	44	2.0	121	5.5	4.27	97	.248	.286	-5	-3	102	78	-1.6	0	-1	-0.4
1981	Bos-A	9	8	.529	23	23	8	2	0	154	160	9.4	9	35	2.0	79	4.6	4.27	91	.267	.305	-10	-7	106	79	-0.2	0	-1	-0.7
1982	Bos-A	13	13	.500	33	33	11	3	0	224	228	9.2	31	43	1.7	127	5.1	3.74	120	.261	.295	9	19	110	100	-1.3	0	-1	1.8
1983	Bos-A	9	13	.409	28	28	2	0	0	176	223	11.4	27	39	2.0	77	3.9	5.63	74	.303	.341	-30	-29	102	92	-1.8	0	-1	-2.7
1984	Bos-A	4	4	.500	9	9	2	0	0	65	71	9.8	10	13	1.8	33	4.6	4.98	88	.284	.315	-7	-4	110	91	-0.1	0	1	-0.2
	Chi-N	10	8	.556	24	24	2	0	0	160	152	8.5	11	36	2.0	81	4.6	3.04	129	.250	.290	10	15	109	101	-0.6	-3	1	1.5
1985	Chi-N	11	7	.611	25	25	6	2	0	169	145	7.7	15	19	1.0	117	6.2	3.09	136	.229	.252	10	21	117	75	2.5	0	0	2.4
1986	Chi-N	6	11	.353	33	32	1	0	0	201	226	10.1	21	43	**1.9**	137	6.1	4.57	88	.285	.316	-19	-12	108	92	-1.7	2	0	-1.0
1987	Oak-A	6	8	.429	54	2	0	0	16	116	99	7.7	11	17	1.3	113	8.8	3.03	134	.228	.259	19	13	91	84	-1.0	0	-0	1.2
1988	Oak-A	4	2	.667	60	0	0	0	**45**	73	52	6.4	5	11	1.4	70	8.6	2.34	158	.198	.229	13	11	93	70	0.2	0	-1	1.0
1989	Oak-A	4	0	1.000	51	0	0	0	33	58	32	5.0	5	3	0.5	55	8.5	1.55	256	.162	.175	15	16	102	48	2.0	0	-0	1.6
Total	15	165	138	.545	541	361	100	20	97	2742	2584	8.5	289	655	2.1	1865	6.1	3.56	114	.247	.291	102	151	104	93	8.8	-1	-11	15.2
■ WAYNE EDWARDS	Edwards, Wayne Maurice b: 3/7/64, Burbank, Cal. BL/TL, 6'5", 185 lbs. Deb: 9/11/89																												
1989	Chi-A	0	0	—	7	0	0	0	0	7	7	9.0	1	3	3.9	9	11.6	3.86	94	.269	.333	0	-0	93	122	0.0	0	0	0.0
■ MARK EICHHORN	Eichhorn, Mark Anthony b: 11/21/60, San Jose, Cal. BR/TR, 6'4", 200 lbs. Deb: 8/30/82																												
1982	Tor-A	0	3	.000	7	7	0	0	0	38	40	9.5	4	14	3.3	16	3.8	5.45	82	.260	.316	-6	-4	109	70	-1.4	0	-1	-0.4
1986	Tor-A	14	6	.700	69	0	0	0	10	157	105	6.0	8	45	2.6	166	9.5	1.72	254	.191	.257	**43**	**46**	104	108	3.9	0	2	**4.9**
1987	Tor-A	10	6	.625	**89**	0	0	0	4	128	110	7.7	14	52	3.7	96	6.8	3.16	140	.234	.311	19	18	99	115	0.7	0	2	1.9
1988	Tor-A	0	3	.000	37	0	0	0	1	67	79	10.6	3	27	3.6	28	3.8	4.16	94	.304	.371	-1	-2	99	123	-1.4	0	1	0.0
1989	Atl-N	5	5	.500	45	0	0	0	0	68	70	9.3	6	19	2.5	49	6.5	4.37	83	.275	.315	-7	-6	104	94	0.9	-0	2	-0.3
Total	5	29	23	.558	247	7	0	0	15	458	404	7.9	35	157	3.1	355	7.0	3.18	133	.239	.304	48	53	102	107	2.7	-0	6	6.1
■ DAVE EILAND	Eiland, David William b: 7/5/66, Dade City, Fla. BR/TR, 6'3", 210 lbs. Deb: 8/03/88																												
1988	NY-A	0	0	—	3	3	0	0	0	13	15	10.4	6	4	2.8	7	4.8	6.23	61	.294	.368	-3	-4	96	128	0.0	0	0	-0.2
1989	NY-A	1	3	.250	6	6	0	0	0	34	44	11.6	5	13	3.4	11	2.9	5.82	70	.328	.388	-7	-7	105	110	-0.8	0	-1	-0.6
Total	2	1	3	.250	9	9	0	0	0	47	59	11.3	11	17	3.3	18	3.4	5.94	68	.319	.383	-11	-10	103	115	-0.8	0	-0	-0.8
■ STEVE FARR	Farr, Steven Michael b: 12/12/56, La Plata, Md. BR/TR, 5'10", 198 lbs. Deb: 5/16/84																												
1984	Cle-A	3	11	.214	31	16	0	0	1	116	106	8.2	14	46	3.6	83	6.4	4.58	93	.245	.322	-7	-4	106	85	-3.8	0	1	-0.3
1985	KC-A	2	1	.667	16	3	0	0	1	38	34	8.1	2	20	4.7	36	8.5	3.08	137	.245	.341	5	5	101	126	0.4	0	0	0.5
1986	KC-A	8	4	.667	56	0	0	0	8	109	90	7.4	10	39	3.2	83	6.9	3.14	134	.228	.300	13	13	100	102	2.3	0	1	1.3

YEAR	TM/L	W	L	PCT	G	GS	CG	SHO	SV	IP	H	H/G	HR	BB	BB/G	SO	SO/G	ERA	/A	OAVG	OOBP	PR	/A	PF	CPI	WAT	PB	PD	TPI
1987	KC-A	4	3	.571	47	0	0	0	1	91	97	9.6	9	44	4.4	88	8.7	4.15	112	.270	.350	3	5	104	110	0.4	0	-1	0.3
1988	KC-A	5	4	.556	62	1	0	0	20	83	74	8.0	5	30	3.3	72	7.8	2.49	163	.240	.308	14	15	103	130	0.3	0	-1	1.4
1989	KC-A	2	5	.286	51	2	0	0	18	63	75	10.7	5	22	3.1	56	8.0	4.14	89	.296	.351	-2	-3	95	114	-1.7	0	-0	-0.3
Total	6	24	28	.462	263	22	0	0	49	500	476	8.6	45	201	3.6	418	7.5	3.67	114	.252	.326	25	30	102	108	-2.1	0	-1	2.9

■ **JOHN FARRELL** Farrell, John Edward b: 8/4/62, Monmouth Beach, N.J. BR/TR, 6'4", 210 lbs. Deb: 8/18/87

YEAR	TM/L	W	L	PCT	G	GS	CG	SHO	SV	IP	H	H/G	HR	BB	BB/G	SO	SO/G	ERA	/A	OAVG	OOBP	PR	/A	PF	CPI	WAT	PB	PD	TPI
1987	Cle-A	5	1	.833	10	9	1	0	0	69	68	8.9	7	22	2.9	28	3.7	3.39	138	.256	.320	8	10	105	115	2.2	0	-0	0.9
1988	Cle-A	14	10	.583	31	30	4	0	0	210	216	9.3	15	67	2.9	92	3.9	4.24	96	.269	.326	-6	-4	102	94	2.7	0	-0	-0.4
1989	Cle-A	9	14	.391	31	31	7	2	0	208	196	8.5	14	71	3.1	132	5.7	3.63	112	.244	.306	6	10	104	89	-1.6	0	-1	0.8
Total	3	28	25	.528	72	70	12	2	0	487	480	8.9	36	160	3.0	252	4.7	3.86	107	.256	.317	8	15	103	95	3.3	0	-2	1.3

■ **SID FERNANDEZ** Fernandez, Charles Sidney b: 10/12/62, Honolulu, Hawaii BL/TL, 6'1", 220 lbs. Deb: 9/20/83

YEAR	TM/L	W	L	PCT	G	GS	CG	SHO	SV	IP	H	H/G	HR	BB	BB/G	SO	SO/G	ERA	/A	OAVG	OOBP	PR	/A	PF	CPI	WAT	PB	PD	TPI
1983	LA-N	0	1	.000	2	1	0	0	0	6	7	10.5	0	7	10.5	9	13.5	6.00	60	.280	.455	-2	-2	100	104	-0.4	0	0	0.0
1984	NY-N	6	6	.500	15	15	0	0	0	90	74	7.4	8	34	3.4	62	6.2	3.50	103	.226	.291	1	1	100	87	-0.5	-0	-2	0.0
1985	NY-N	9	9	.500	26	26	3	0	0	170	108	**5.7**	14	80	4.2	180	**9.5**	2.81	122	**.181**	.277	15	12	95	79	-1.6	2	-0	1.4
1986	NY-N	16	6	.727	32	31	2	1	1	204	161	7.1	13	91	4.0	200	8.8	3.53	98	.216	.297	4	-1	93	79	2.3	2	-3	-0.2
1987	NY-N	12	8	.600	28	27	3	1	0	156	130	7.5	16	67	3.9	134	7.7	3.81	104	.224	.308	5	3	97	87	0.8	1	-2	0.1
1988	NY-N	12	10	.545	31	31	1	1	0	187	127	**6.1**	15	70	3.4	189	9.1	3.03	100	**.191**	.270	9	0	88	75	-1.5	6	-3	0.2
1989	NY-N	14	5	.737	35	32	6	2	0	219	157	6.5	21	75	3.1	198	8.1	2.84	118	.198	.270	16	12	95	85	4.4	4	-4	1.3
Total	7	69	45	.605	169	163	15	5	1	1032	764	6.7	87	424	3.7	972	8.5	3.23	107	.205	.286	49	24	94	82	3.5	14	-13	2.8

■ **MIKE FETTERS** Fetters, Michael Lee b: 12/19/64, Van Nuys, Cal. BR/TR, 6'4", 200 lbs. Deb: 9/01/89

YEAR	TM/L	W	L	PCT	G	GS	CG	SHO	SV	IP	H	H/G	HR	BB	BB/G	SO	SO/G	ERA	/A	OAVG	OOBP	PR	/A	PF	CPI	WAT	PB	PD	TPI
1989	Cal-A	0	0	—	1	0	0	0	0	3	5	15.0	1	1	3.0	4	12.0	9.00	42	.333	.375	-2	-2	98	86	0.0	0	0	-0.1

■ **TOM FILER** Filer, Thomas Carson b: 12/1/56, Philadelphia, Pa. BR/TR, 6'1", 195 lbs. Deb: 6/08/82

YEAR	TM/L	W	L	PCT	G	GS	CG	SHO	SV	IP	H	H/G	HR	BB	BB/G	SO	SO/G	ERA	/A	OAVG	OOBP	PR	/A	PF	CPI	WAT	PB	PD	TPI
1982	Chi-N	1	2	.333	8	8	0	0	0	41	50	11.0	5	18	4.0	15	3.3	5.49	68	.301	.364	-9	-8	104	97	-0.3	-1	2	-0.6
1985	Tor-A	7	0	1.000	11	9	0	0	0	49	38	7.0	6	18	3.3	24	4.4	3.86	107	.222	.292	2	1	99	87	3.5	0	-0	0.1
1988	Mil-A	5	8	.385	19	16	2	1	0	102	108	9.5	8	33	2.9	39	3.4	4.41	93	.281	.329	-5	-4	103	98	-1.9	0	3	0.0
1989	Mil-A	7	3	.700	13	13	0	0	0	72	74	9.3	6	23	2.9	20	2.5	3.63	103	.271	.334	2	1	96	114	2.1	0	1	0.2
Total	4	20	13	.606	51	46	2	1	0	264	270	9.2	25	92	3.1	98	3.3	4.26	93	.271	.330	-10	-9	100	100	3.4	-1	5	-0.3

■ **CHUCK FINLEY** Finley, Charles Edward b: 11/26/62, Monroe, La. BL/TL, 6'6", 220 lbs. Deb: 5/29/86

YEAR	TM/L	W	L	PCT	G	GS	CG	SHO	SV	IP	H	H/G	HR	BB	BB/G	SO	SO/G	ERA	/A	OAVG	OOBP	PR	/A	PF	CPI	WAT	PB	PD	TPI
1986	Cal-A	3	1	.750	25	0	0	0	0	46	40	7.8	2	23	4.5	37	7.2	3.33	120	.235	.323	4	3	95	100	0.9	0	1	0.4
1987	Cal-A	2	7	.222	35	3	0	0	0	91	102	10.1	7	43	4.3	63	6.2	4.65	96	.287	.365	-2	-2	100	106	-2.3	0	-0	-0.1
1988	Cal-A	9	15	.375	31	31	2	0	0	194	191	8.9	15	82	3.8	111	5.1	4.18	90	.263	.336	-4	-9	95	100	-2.5	0	-1	-0.9
1989	Cal-A	16	9	.640	29	29	9	1	0	200	171	7.7	13	82	3.7	156	7.0	2.57	148	.233	.308	29	27	98	124	2.6	0	-3	2.6
Total	4	30	32	.484	120	63	11	1	0	531	504	8.5	37	230	3.9	367	6.2	3.58	109	.254	.330	28	20	97	110	-1.3	0	-3	2.0

■ **JEFF FISCHER** Fischer, Jeffrey Thomas b: 8/17/63, W.Palm Beach, Fla. BR/TR, 6'3", 185 lbs. Deb: 6/19/87

YEAR	TM/L	W	L	PCT	G	GS	CG	SHO	SV	IP	H	H/G	HR	BB	BB/G	SO	SO/G	ERA	/A	OAVG	OOBP	PR	/A	PF	CPI	WAT	PB	PD	TPI
1987	Mon-N	0	1	.000	4	2	0	0	0	14	21	13.5	3	5	3.2	6	3.9	8.36	52	.362	.394	-7	-6	106	92	-0.4	0	0	-0.5
1989	LA-N	0	0	—	2	0	0	0	0	3	7	21.0	1	0	0.0	2	6.0	15.00	22	.438	.412	-4	-4	93	73	0.0	0	0	-0.3
Total	2	0	1	.000	6	2	0	0	0	17	28	14.8	4	5	2.6	8	4.2	9.53	43	.378	.398	-10	-10	103	89	-0.4	0	0	-0.8

■ **BRIAN FISHER** Fisher, Brian Kevin b: 3/18/62, Honolulu, Hawaii BR/TR, 6'4", 210 lbs. Deb: 5/07/85

YEAR	TM/L	W	L	PCT	G	GS	CG	SHO	SV	IP	H	H/G	HR	BB	BB/G	SO	SO/G	ERA	/A	OAVG	OOBP	PR	/A	PF	CPI	WAT	PB	PD	TPI
1985	NY-A	4	4	.500	55	0	0	0	14	98	77	7.1	4	29	2.7	85	7.8	2.39	163	.216	.271	19	16	94	94	-0.6	0	0	1.7
1986	NY-A	9	5	.643	62	0	0	0	6	97	105	9.7	14	37	3.4	67	6.2	4.92	87	.277	.337	-8	-7	103	97	1.5	0	-1	-0.7
1987	Pit-N	11	9	.550	37	26	6	3	0	185	185	9.0	27	72	3.5	117	5.7	4.52	94	.262	.330	-9	-5	105	99	1.2	4	-1	-0.2
1988	Pit-N	8	10	.444	33	22	1	1	1	146	157	9.7	13	57	3.5	66	4.1	4.62	73	.277	.340	-19	-21	97	97	-1.5	-2	-2	-2.5
1989	Pit-N	0	3	.000	9	3	0	0	1	17	25	13.2	2	10	5.3	8	4.2	7.94	42	.329	.398	-8	-9	94	84	-1.4	-1	-0	-0.9
Total	5	32	31	.508	196	51	7	4	22	543	549	9.1	60	205	3.4	343	5.7	4.34	90	.263	.326	-25	-25	100	97	-0.8	2	-5	-2.6

■ **MIKE FLANAGAN** Flanagan, Michael Kendall b: 12/16/51, Manchester, N.H. BL/TL, 6', 185 lbs. Deb: 9/05/75

YEAR	TM/L	W	L	PCT	G	GS	CG	SHO	SV	IP	H	H/G	HR	BB	BB/G	SO	SO/G	ERA	/A	OAVG	OOBP	PR	/A	PF	CPI	WAT	PB	PD	TPI
1975	Bal-A	0	1	.000	2	1	0	0	0	10	9	8.1	0	6	5.4	7	6.3	2.70	125	.250	.357	1	1	89	131	-0.4	0	0	0.1
1976	Bal-A	3	5	.375	20	10	4	0	0	85	83	8.8	7	33	3.5	56	5.9	4.13	83	.260	.324	-6	-7	97	92	-1.2	0	0	-0.6
1977	Bal-A	15	10	.600	36	33	15	2	1	235	235	9.0	17	70	2.7	149	5.7	3.64	103	.266	.315	11	3	92	100	0.0	0	-0	0.3
1978	Bal-A	19	15	.559	40	40	17	2	0	281	271	8.7	22	87	2.8	167	5.3	4.04	85	.257	.311	-8	-19	91	86	0.0	0	-2	-2.0
1979	Bal-A	**23**	9	.719	39	38	16	**5**	0	266	245	8.3	23	70	2.4	190	6.4	3.08	132	.245	.293	34	29	96	102	4.1	0	-0	2.8
1980	Bal-A	16	13	.552	37	37	12	2	0	251	278	10.0	27	71	2.5	128	4.6	4.12	97	.287	.330	-2	-3	99	107	-1.7	0	0	-0.2
1981	Bal-A	9	6	.600	20	20	3	2	0	116	108	8.4	11	37	2.9	72	5.6	4.19	87	.244	.305	-7	-7	99	79	0.8	0	1	-0.5
1982	Bal-A	15	11	.577	36	35	11	1	0	236	233	8.9	24	76	2.9	103	3.9	3.97	102	.259	.316	3	2	99	96	0.0	0	0	0.2
1983	Bal-A	12	4	.750	20	20	3	1	0	125	135	9.7	10	31	2.2	50	3.6	3.31	122	.278	.318	11	10	99	121	3.1	0	-1	0.9
1984	Bal-A	13	13	.500	34	34	10	2	0	227	213	8.4	24	81	3.2	115	4.6	3.53	107	.250	.312	12	6	94	105	-0.6	0	-1	0.5
1985	Bal-A	4	5	.444	15	15	1	0	0	86	101	10.6	14	28	2.9	42	4.4	5.13	79	.297	.346	-9	-10	98	106	-0.6	0	-0	-0.9
1986	Bal-A	7	11	.389	29	28	2	0	0	172	179	9.4	15	66	3.5	96	5.0	4.24	98	.270	.329	-1	-1	99	98	-1.3	0	-2	-0.3
1987	Bal-A	3	6	.333	16	16	4	0	0	95	102	9.7	9	36	3.4	50	4.7	4.93	90	.278	.337	-5	-5	99	91	-0.8	0	-0	-0.4
	Tor-A	3	2	.600	7	7	0	0	0	49	46	8.4	3	15	2.8	43	7.9	2.39	186	.237	.292	11	11	99	115	0.0	0	-0	1.1
	Yr	6	8	.429	23	23	4	0	0	144	148	9.3	12	51	3.2	93	5.8	4.06	109	.263	.321	7	6	99	115	-0.8	0	-0	0.7
1988	Tor-A	13	13	.500	34	34	2	1	0	211	220	9.4	23	80	3.4	99	4.2	4.18	94	.271	.334	-5	-6	99	107	-1.0	0	1	-0.5
1989	Tor-A	8	10	.444	30	30	1	1	0	172	186	9.7	10	47	2.5	47	2.5	3.92	92	.283	.328	-1	-6	93	103	-1.8	0	1	-0.4
Total	15	163	134	.549	415	398	101	19	1	2617	2644	9.1	239	834	2.9	1414	4.9	3.89	100	.265	.319	40	-4	96	100	-1.4	0	-3	0.1

■ **TOM FOLEY** Foley, Thomas Michael b: 9/9/59, Columbus, Ga. BL/TR, 6'1", 175 lbs. Deb: 4/09/83

YEAR	TM/L	W	L	PCT	G	GS	CG	SHO	SV	IP	H	H/G	HR	BB	BB/G	SO	SO/G	ERA	/A	OAVG	OOBP	PR	/A	PF	CPI	WAT	PB	PD	TPI
1989	Mon-N	0	0	—	1	0	0	0	0	0	1	—	1	0	—	0	—	∞	—	.500	.500	-1	-1	102	116	0.0	0	0	0.0

■ **BOB FORSCH** Forsch, Robert Herbert b: 1/13/50, Sacramento, Cal. BR/TR, 6'4", 200 lbs. Deb: 7/07/74

YEAR	TM/L	W	L	PCT	G	GS	CG	SHO	SV	IP	H	H/G	HR	BB	BB/G	SO	SO/G	ERA	/A	OAVG	OOBP	PR	/A	PF	CPI	WAT	PB	PD	TPI
1974	StL-N	7	4	.636	19	14	5	2	0	100	84	7.6	5	34	3.1	39	3.5	2.97	126	.230	.292	7	9	103	90	1.3	1	-0	1.1
1975	StL-N	15	10	.600	34	34	7	4	0	230	213	8.3	14	70	2.7	108	4.2	2.86	132	.244	.299	20	23	103	103	2.7	10	1	3.8
1976	StL-N	8	10	.444	33	32	2	0	0	194	209	9.7	17	71	3.3	76	3.5	3.94	93	.277	.335	-9	-6	105	108	0.0	1	0	-0.4
1977	StL-N	20	7	.741	35	35	8	2	0	217	210	8.7	20	69	2.9	95	3.9	3.48	107	.251	.308	10	6	95	99	6.9	0	-1	0.5
1978	StL-N	11	17	.393	34	34	7	3	0	234	205	7.9	15	97	3.7	114	4.4	3.69	93	.238	.313	-3	-7	96	88	-1.2	3	1	-0.3
1979	StL-N	11	11	.500	33	32	7	1	0	219	215	8.8	16	52	2.1	92	3.8	3.82	102	.262	.302	-2	2	104	89	-0.6	-1	1	0.2
1980	StL-N	11	10	.524	31	31	8	0	0	215	225	9.4	12	33	**1.4**	87	3.6	3.77	98	.273	.298	-4	-2	102	88	1.5	9	2	1.0
1981	StL-N	10	5	.667	20	20	1	0	0	124	106	7.7	7	29	2.1	41	3.0	3.19	110	.232	.277	4	5	101	81	1.8	-1	0	0.4
1982	StL-N	15	9	.625	36	34	6	2	1	233	238	9.2	16	54	2.1	69	2.7	3.48	106	.268	.308	3	6	102	101	1.8	3	-2	0.7
1983	StL-N	10	12	.455	34	30	6	2	0	187	190	9.1	23	54	2.6	56	2.7	4.28	83	.266	.313	-13	-15	98	94	-0.8	5	-0	-1.1
1984	StL-N	2	5	.286	16	11	1	0	0	52	64	11.1	6	19	3.3	21	3.6	6.06	58	.303	.356	-14	-15	99	85	-1.5	1	0	-1.2
1985	StL-N	9	6	.600	34	19	3	1	2	136	132	8.7	11	47	3.1	48	3.2	3.90	86	.258	.319	-5	-8	93	94	-0.2	4	-0	-0.4
1986	StL-N	14	10	.583	33	33	3	0	0	230	211	8.3	19	68	2.7	104	4.1	3.25	118	.247	.299	12	15	103	101	2.5	3	-1	1.9
1987	StL-N	11	7	.611	33	30	2	1	0	179	189	9.5	15	45	2.3	89	4.5	4.32	92	.273	.315	-5	-7	97	90	0.6	9	-1	0.1
1988	StL-N	9	4	.692	30	12	1	1	0	109	111	9.2	8	38	3.1	40	3.3	3.72	97	.270	.324	-3	-1	105	109	2.9	2	-2	0.0
	Hou-N	1	4	.200	6	6	0	0	0	28	42	13.5	2	6	1.9	14	4.5	6.43	50	.359	.376	-9	-10	93	99	-1.4	0	-0	-0.9
	Yr	10	8	.556	36	18	1	1	0	137	153	10.1	10	44	2.9	54	3.5	4.27	83	.287	.334	-12	-11	102	99	1.5	2	-2	-0.9
1989	Hou-N	4	5	.444	37	15	0	0	0	108	133	11.1	10	46	3.8	40	3.3	5.33	67	.303	.364	-22	-21	103	99	-0.7	-0	-1	-2.2
Total	16	168	136	.553	498	422	67	19	3	2795	2777	8.9	216	832	2.7	1133	3.6	3.76	98	.261	.312	-32	-26	101	95	15.6	48	-2	3.2

■ **TONY FOSSAS** Fossas, Emilio Antonio (Morejon) b: 9/23/57, Havana, Cuba BL/TL, 6', 195 lbs. Deb: 5/15/88

YEAR	TM/L	W	L	PCT	G	GS	CG	SHO	SV	IP	H	H/G	HR	BB	BB/G	SO	SO/G	ERA	/A	OAVG	OOBP	PR	/A	PF	CPI	WAT	PB	PD	TPI
1988	Tex-A	0	0	—	5	0	0	0	0	6	11	16.5	0	2	3.0	0	0.0	4.50	90	.423	.464	-0	-0	102	178	0.0	0	0	0.0
1989	Mil-A	2	2	.500	51	0	0	0	1	61	57	8.4	3	22	3.2	42	6.2	3.54	106	.256	.313	2	1	96	99	0.0	0	0	0.2
Total	2	2	2	.500	56	0	0	0	1	67	68	9.1	3	24	3.2	42	5.6	3.63	104	.273	.327	2	1	97	106	0.0	0	0	0.2

YEAR	TM/L	W	L	PCT	G	GS	CG	SHO	SV	IP	H	H/G	HR	BB	BB/G	SO	SO/G	ERA	/A	OAVG	OOBP	PR	/A	PF	CPI	WAT	PB	PD	TPI
■ JOHN FRANCO		Franco, John Anthony b: 9/17/60, Brooklyn, N.Y. BL/TL, 5'10", 170 lbs. Deb: 4/24/84																											
1984	Cin-N	6	2	.750	54	0	0	0	4	79	74	8.4	3	36	4.1	55	6.3	2.62	147	.256	.334	9	11	107	141	2.3	-0	1	1.2
1985	Cin-N	12	3	.800	67	0	0	0	12	99	83	7.5	5	40	3.6	61	5.5	2.18	173	.234	.305	16	**18**	105	141	4.3	0	2	2.1
1986	Cin-N	6	6	.500	74	0	0	0	29	101	90	8.0	7	44	3.9	84	7.5	2.94	132	.242	.317	9	11	104	119	-0.3	-0	1	1.2
1987	Cin-N	8	5	.615	68	0	0	0	32	82	76	8.3	6	27	3.0	61	6.7	2.52	167	.245	.299	14	15	103	128	1.4	-0	-1	1.4
1988	Cin-N	6	6	.500	70	0	0	0	**39**	86	60	6.3	3	27	2.8	46	4.8	1.57	231	.198	.259	**18**	**20**	105	120	-0.4	-0	1	2.2
1989	Cin-N	4	8	.333	60	0	0	0	32	81	77	8.6	3	36	4.0	60	6.7	3.11	117	.258	.328	4	5	104	119	-1.7	0	1	0.7
Total	6	42	30	.583	393	0	0	0	148	528	460	7.8	27	210	3.6	367	6.3	2.49	154	.239	.307	69	79	105	128	5.6	-0	5	8.8
■ TERRY FRANCONA		Francona, Terry Jon b: 4/22/59, Aberdeen, S.D. BL/TL, 6'1", 190 lbs. Deb: 8/19/81																											
1989	Mil-A	0	0	—	1	0	0	0	0	1	0	0.0	0	0	0.0	1	9.0	0.00	—	.000	.000	0	0	96	0	0.0	1	0	0.0
■ WILLIE FRASER		Fraser, William Patrick b: 5/26/64, New York, N.Y. BR/TR, 6'3", 200 lbs. Deb: 9/10/86																											
1986	Cal-A	0	0	—	1	1	0	0	0	4	6	13.5	0	1	2.3	2	4.5	9.00	44	.353	.350	-2	-2	95	61	0.0	0	0	-0.1
1987	Cal-A	10	10	.500	36	23	5	1	1	177	160	8.1	26	63	3.2	106	5.4	3.92	114	.240	.308	11	11	100	99	0.8	0	-3	0.7
1988	Cal-A	12	13	.480	34	32	2	0	0	195	203	9.4	33	80	3.7	86	4.0	5.40	70	.267	.339	-31	-35	95	91	0.5	0	-1	-3.4
1989	Cal-A	4	7	.364	44	0	0	0	2	92	80	7.8	6	23	2.3	46	4.5	3.23	118	.235	.288	7	6	98	89	-1.9	0	0	0.6
Total	4	26	30	.464	115	56	7	1	3	468	449	8.6	65	167	3.2	240	4.6	4.44	91	.252	.318	-15	-22	97	93	-0.6	0	-3	-2.2
■ MARVIN FREEMAN		Freeman, Marvin b: 4/10/63, Chicago, Ill. BR/TR, 6'7", 200 lbs. Deb: 9/16/86																											
1986	Phi-N	2	0	1.000	3	3	0	0	0	16	6	3.4	0	10	5.6	8	4.5	2.25	172	.120	.262	3	3	104	44	1.0	-1	-0	0.2
1988	Phi-N	2	3	.400	11	11	0	0	0	52	55	9.5	2	43	7.4	37	6.4	6.06	59	.276	.398	-15	-14	103	87	0.0	0	0	-1.3
1989	Phi-N	0	0	—	1	1	0	0	0	3	2	6.0	0	5	15.0	0	0.0	6.00	60	.182	.438	-1	-1	102	81	0.0	-0	0	0.0
Total	3	4	3	.571	15	15	0	0	0	71	63	8.0	2	58	7.4	45	5.7	5.20	70	.242	.374	-13	-12	103	77	1.0	-1	-0	-1.1
■ STEVE FREY		Frey, Steven Francis b: 7/29/63, Meadowbrook, Pa. BR/TL, 5'9", 170 lbs. Deb: 5/10/89																											
1989	Mon-N	3	2	.600	20	0	0	0	0	21	29	12.4	4	11	4.7	15	6.4	5.57	64	.326	.398	-5	-5	102	127	0.5	0	-0	-0.4
■ TODD FROHWIRTH		Frohwirth, Todd Gerard b: 9/28/62, Milwaukee, Wis. BR/TR, 6'4", 190 lbs. Deb: 8/10/87																											
1987	Phi-N	1	0	1.000	10	0	0	0	0	11	12	9.8	0	2	1.6	9	7.4	0.00	—	.293	.326	5	5	105	0	0.5	-0	0	0.5
1988	Phi-N	1	2	.333	12	0	0	0	0	12	16	12.0	2	11	8.3	11	8.3	8.25	43	.327	.435	-6	-6	103	95	-0.2	0	1	-0.5
1989	Phi-N	1	0	1.000	45	0	0	0	0	63	56	8.0	4	18	2.6	39	5.6	3.57	100	.240	.298	-0	0	102	88	0.5	-0	0	0.0
Total	3	3	2	.600	67	0	0	0	0	86	84	8.8	6	31	3.2	59	6.2	3.77	97	.260	.325	-2	-1	103	78	0.8	-0	1	0.0
■ MIGUEL GARCIA		Garcia, Miguel Angel (Silfontes) b: 4/3/67, Caracas, Venez. BL/TL, 5'11", 173 lbs. Deb: 4/30/87																											
1987	Cal-A	0	0	—	1	0	0	0	0	2	3	13.5	0	3	13.5	0	0.0	13.50	33	.375	.545	-2	-2	100	72	0.0	0	0	-0.1
	Pit-N	0	0	—	1	0	0	0	0	1	0	0.0	0	0	0.0	0	0.0	0.00	—	.000	.000	0	0	105	0	0.0	0	0	0.0
1988	Pit-N	0	0	—	1	0	0	0	0	2	3	13.5	1	2	9.0	2	9.0	4.50	75	.375	.500	-0	-0	97	298	0.0	0	0	0.0
1989	Pit-N	0	2	.000	11	0	0	0	0	16	25	14.1	2	7	3.9	9	5.1	8.44	39	.357	.410	-9	-9	94	85	-0.9	0	0	-0.8
Total	3	0	2	.000	14	0	0	0	0	21	31	13.3	3	12	5.1	11	4.7	8.14	42	.352	.427	-11	-11	96	100	-0.9	0	0	-0.9
■ MARK GARDNER		Gardner, Mark Allan b: 3/1/62, Los Angeles, Cal. BR/TR, 6'1", 190 lbs. Deb: 5/16/89																											
1989	Mon-N	0	3	.000	7	4	0	0	0	26	26	9.0	2	11	3.8	21	7.3	5.19	69	.250	.333	-5	-5	102	74	-1.4	-0	0	-0.4
■ WES GARDNER		Gardner, Wesley Brian b: 4/29/61, Benton, Ark. BR/TR, 6'4", 197 lbs. Deb: 7/29/84																											
1984	NY-N	1	1	.500	21	0	0	0	1	25	34	12.2	0	8	2.9	19	6.8	6.48	56	.321	.362	-8	-8	100	72	0.0	-0	0	-0.7
1985	NY-N	0	2	.000	9	0	0	0	0	12	18	13.5	1	8	6.0	11	8.3	5.25	65	.375	.426	-2	-2	95	149	-0.9	0	0	-0.1
1986	Bos-A	0	0	—	1	0	0	0	0	1	1	9.0	0	0	0.0	1	9.0	9.00	46	.333	.250	-1	-1	99	47	0.0	0	0	0.0
1987	Bos-A	3	6	.333	49	1	0	0	10	90	98	9.8	17	42	4.2	70	7.0	5.40	82	.279	.354	-9	-10	99	102	-1.3	0	-1	-1.0
1988	Bos-A	8	6	.571	36	18	1	0	2	149	119	7.2	17	64	3.9	106	6.4	3.50	122	.220	.300	8	13	108	95	0.4	0	-0	1.3
1989	Bos-A	3	7	.300	22	16	0	0	0	86	97	10.2	10	47	4.9	81	8.5	5.97	68	.287	.369	-20	-18	104	89	-2.1	0	-1	-1.7
Total	6	15	22	.405	138	35	1	0	13	363	367	9.1	45	169	4.2	288	7.1	4.83	87	.264	.340	-32	-26	104	95	-3.9	-0	-2	-2.2
■ SCOTT GARRELTS		Garrelts, Scott William b: 10/30/61, Urbana, Ill. BR/TR, 6'4", 195 lbs. Deb: 10/02/82																											
1982	SF-N	0	0	—	1	0	0	0	0	2	3	13.5	0	2	9.0	4	18.0	13.50	25	.333	.455	-2	-2	94	51	0.0	0	0	-0.1
1983	SF-N	2	2	.500	5	5	1	1	0	36	33	8.3	4	19	4.8	16	4.0	2.50	147	.254	.351	5	5	101	178	0.0	0	0	0.6
1984	SF-N	2	3	.400	21	3	0	0	0	43	45	9.4	6	34	7.1	32	6.7	5.65	62	.274	.388	-10	-10	98	103	0.0	-0	-0	-1.0
1985	SF-N	9	6	.600	74	0	0	0	13	106	76	6.5	2	58	4.9	106	9.0	2.29	149	.198	.302	15	13	95	101	2.8	1	2	1.7
1986	SF-N	13	9	.591	53	18	2	0	10	174	144	7.4	17	74	3.8	125	6.5	3.10	114	.231	.307	12	8	95	110	2.0	2	2	1.2
1987	SF-N	11	7	.611	64	0	0	0	12	106	70	5.9	10	55	4.7	127	10.8	3.23	120	.192	.292	10	8	95	87	1.2	0	-0	0.7
1988	SF-N	5	9	.357	65	0	0	0	13	98	80	7.3	3	46	4.2	86	7.9	3.58	90	.226	.310	-1	-4	93	83	-2.2	-1	-0	-0.5
1989	SF-N	14	5	.737	30	29	2	1	0	193	149	6.9	11	46	2.1	119	5.5	**2.28**	147	.212	**.255**	26	23	96	92	4.0	1	-0	2.5
Total	8	56	41	.577	313	55	5	2	48	758	600	7.1	53	334	4.0	615	7.3	3.00	116	.220	.300	55	40	95	100	7.8	3	3	5.1
■ PAUL GIBSON		Gibson, Paul Marshall b: 1/4/60, Southampton, N.Y. BL/TL, 6', 165 lbs. Deb: 4/08/88																											
1988	Det-A	4	2	.667	40	1	0	0	0	92	83	8.1	6	34	3.3	50	4.9	2.93	127	.240	.305	11	8	94	111	0.8	0	0	0.8
1989	Det-A	4	8	.333	45	13	0	0	0	132	129	8.8	11	57	3.9	77	5.3	4.64	83	.259	.335	-11	-11	99	88	-0.4	0	-0	-1.1
Total	2	8	10	.444	85	14	0	0	0	224	212	8.5	17	91	3.7	127	5.1	3.94	97	.251	.323	-0	-3	97	98	0.4	0	-0	-0.3
■ BYRON GIDEON		Gideon, Byron Brett b: 8/8/63, Ozona, Tex. BR/TR, 6'2", 200 lbs. Deb: 7/05/87																											
1987	Pit-N	1	5	.167	29	0	0	0	3	37	34	8.3	6	10	2.4	31	7.5	4.62	92	.243	.294	-2	-1	105	81	-1.9	1	0	0.0
1989	Mon-N	0	0	—	4	0	0	0	0	5	5	9.0	1	5	9.0	2	3.6	1.80	199	.294	.455	1	1	102	416	0.0	0	-0	0.1
Total	2	1	5	.167	33	0	0	0	3	42	39	8.4	7	15	3.2	33	7.1	4.29	98	.248	.314	-1	-0	104	121	-1.9	1	-0	0.1
■ DAN GLADDEN		Gladden, Clinton Daniel b: 7/7/57, San Jose, Cal. BB/TR, 5'11", 180 lbs. Deb: 9/05/83																											
1988	Min-A	0	0	—	1	0	0	0	0	1	0	0.0	0	0	0.0	0	0.0	0.00	—	.000	.000	0	0	105	0	0.0	1	0	0.0
1989	Min-A	0	0	—	1	0	0	0	0	1	2	18.0	0	1	9.0	0	0.0	9.00	46	.400	.500	-1	-1	106	105	0.0	1	0	0.0
Total	2	0	0	—	2	0	0	0	0	2	2	9.0	0	1	4.5	0	0.0	4.50	93	.250	.333	-0	-0	106	52	0.0	2	0	0.0
■ TOM GLAVINE		Glavine, Thomas Michael b: 3/25/66, Concord, Mass. BL/TL, 6'", 175 lbs. Deb: 8/17/87																											
1987	Atl-N	2	4	.333	9	9	0	0	0	50	55	9.9	5	33	5.9	20	3.6	5.58	80	.279	.382	-8	-6	109	97	-0.6	-0	1	-0.5
1988	Atl-N	7	17	.292	34	34	1	0	0	195	201	9.3	12	63	2.9	84	3.9	4.57	81	.270	.322	-24	-19	107	86	-1.8	1	2	-1.6
1989	Atl-N	14	8	.636	29	29	6	4	0	186	172	8.3	20	40	1.9	90	4.4	3.68	99	.243	.279	-4	-1	104	87	4.8	0	1	0.1
Total	3	23	29	.442	72	72	7	4	0	431	428	8.9	37	136	2.8	194	4.1	4.30	87	.259	.312	-36	-26	106	88	2.4	1	3	-2.0
■ JERRY GLEATON		Gleaton, Jerry Don b: 9/14/57, Brownwood, Tex. BL/TL, 6'3", 205 lbs. Deb: 7/11/79																											
1979	Tex-A	0	1	.000	5	2	0	0	0	10	15	13.5	0	2	1.8	2	1.8	6.30	67	.375	.400	-2	-2	99	99	-0.4	0	0	-0.1
1980	Tex-A	0	0	—	5	0	0	0	0	7	5	6.4	0	4	5.1	2	2.6	2.57	158	.208	.300	1	1	100	99	0.0	0	0	0.1
1981	Sea-A	4	7	.364	20	13	1	0	0	85	88	9.3	10	38	4.0	31	3.3	4.76	78	.273	.347	-10	-10	101	98	-0.5	0	-1	-1.0
1982	Sea-A	0	0	—	3	0	0	0	0	5	7	12.6	3	2	3.6	1	1.8	12.60	36	.333	.417	-5	-5	110	83	0.0	0	0	-0.3
1984	Chi-A	1	2	.333	11	1	0	0	2	18	20	10.0	2	6	3.0	4	2.0	3.50	127	.286	.333	1	2	111	135	-0.3	0	-0	0.1
1985	Chi-A	1	0	1.000	31	0	0	0	1	30	37	11.1	3	13	3.9	22	6.6	5.70	73	.316	.370	-5	-5	100	101	0.5	0	-0	-0.4
1987	KC-A	4	4	.500	48	0	0	0	5	51	38	6.7	4	28	4.9	44	7.8	4.24	110	.216	.314	1	2	104	80	0.0	0	1	0.3
1988	KC-A	0	4	.000	42	0	0	0	3	38	33	7.8	2	17	4.0	29	6.9	3.55	115	.232	.323	2	2	103	94	-1.9	0	-0	0.2
1989	KC-A	0	0	—	15	0	0	0	0	14	20	12.9	0	6	3.9	9	5.8	5.79	64	.345	.394	-3	-3	95	99	0.0	0	0	-0.2
Total	9	10	18	.357	180	16	1	0	11	258	263	9.2	24	116	4.0	144	5.0	4.71	87	.271	.344	-20	-18	102	97	-2.6	0	0	-1.3
■ GERMAN GONZALEZ		Gonzalez, German Jose (Caraballo) b: 3/7/62, Rio Caribe, Venez. BR/TR, 6', 170 lbs. Deb: 8/05/88																											
1988	Min-A	0	0	—	16	0	0	0	1	21	20	8.6	4	8	3.4	19	8.1	3.43	122	.244	.315	1	2	105	127	0.0	0	0	0.2
1989	Min-A	3	2	.600	22	0	0	0	0	29	32	9.9	2	11	3.4	25	7.8	4.66	89	.274	.351	-2	-2	106	94	0.5	0	-0	-0.1
Total	2	3	2	.600	38	0	0	0	1	50	52	9.4	6	19	3.4	44	7.9	4.14	101	.261	.336	-1	0	106	108	0.5	0	0	0.1

YEAR	TM/L	W	L	PCT	G	GS	CG	SHO	SV	IP	H	H/G	HR	BB	BB/G	SO	SO/G	ERA	/A	OAVG	OOBP	PR	/A	PF	CPI	WAT	PB	PD	TPI
■ **DWIGHT GOODEN**	Gooden, Dwight Eugene b: 11/16/64, Tampa, Fla. BR/TR, 6'2", 190 lbs. Deb: 4/07/84																												
1984	NY-N	17	9	.654	31	31	7	3	0	218	161	**6.6**	7	73	3.0	**276**	**11.4**	2.60	138	**.202**	**.268**	24	24	100	71	3.3	1	1	2.8
1985	NY-N	**24**	4	.857	35	35	**16**	8	0	**277**	198	6.4	13	69	2.2	**268**	8.7	**1.53**	**225**	.201	.253	**64**	**59**	95	115	**9.5**	6	2	**7.9**
1986	NY-N	17	6	.739	33	33	12	2	0	250	197	7.1	17	80	2.9	200	7.2	2.84	122	.215	.275	24	17	93	85	2.8	-2	3	1.8
1987	NY-N	15	7	**.682**	25	25	7	3	0	180	162	8.1	11	53	2.7	148	7.4	3.20	124	.244	.297	18	15	97	96	3.2	2	-0	1.7
1988	NY-N	18	9	.667	34	34	10	3	0	248	242	8.8	8	57	2.1	175	6.4	3.19	95	.256	.298	7	-4	88	95	1.8	3	5	0.2
1989	NY-N	9	4	.692	19	17	0	0	1	118	93	7.1	9	47	3.6	101	7.7	2.90	115	.211	.286	8	6	95	92	2.3	1	0	0.8
Total	6	100	39	.719	177	175	52	19	1	1291	1053	7.3	65	379	2.6	1168	8.1	2.64	131	.221	.278	145	116	95	93	22.9	11	10	15.2
■ **TOM GORDON**	Gordon, Thomas b: 11/18/67, Sebring, Fla. BR/TR, 5'9", 160 lbs. Deb: 9/08/88																												
1988	KC-A	0	2	.000	5	2	0	0	0	16	16	9.0	1	7	3.9	18	10.1	5.06	81	.267	.343	-2	-2	103	81	-0.9	0	0	-0.1
1989	KC-A	17	9	.654	49	16	1	1	1	163	122	6.7	10	86	4.7	153	8.4	3.64	102	.210	.309	4	1	95	80	3.0	0	3	0.3
Total	2	17	11	.607	54	18	1	1	1	179	138	6.9	11	93	4.7	171	8.6	3.77	99	.215	.312	3	-1	96	80	2.1	0	3	0.2
■ **RICH GOSSAGE**	Gossage, Richard Michael "Goose" b: 7/5/51, Colorado Springs, Colo. BR/TR, 6'3", 180 lbs. Deb: 4/16/72																												
1972	Chi-A	7	1	.875	36	1	0	0	2	80	72	8.1	2	44	4.9	57	6.4	4.27	76	.247	.341	-11	-9	106	83	2.9	-2	-0	-1.2
1973	Chi-A	0	4	.000	20	4	1	0	0	50	57	10.3	9	37	6.7	33	5.9	7.38	53	.311	.418	-20	-19	103	96	-1.9	0	-0	-1.8
1974	Chi-A	4	6	.400	39	3	0	0	1	89	92	9.3	4	47	4.8	64	6.5	4.15	89	.272	.355	-5	-4	102	102	-1.0	0	0	-0.3
1975	Chi-A	9	8	.529	62	0	0	0	**26**	142	99	6.3	3	70	4.4	130	8.2	1.84	214	.201	.299	**31**	**33**	104	128	1.1	0	1	3.6
1976	Chi-A	9	17	.346	31	29	15	0	1	224	214	8.6	16	90	3.6	135	5.4	3.94	91	.254	.327	-10	-9	101	95	-1.9	0	-1	-0.9
1977	Pit-N	11	9	.550	72	0	0	0	26	133	78	5.3	9	49	3.3	151	10.2	1.62	245	.170	.247	**34**	35	102	95	-0.7	1	-1	3.6
1978	NY-A	10	11	.476	63	0	0	0	**27**	134	87	5.8	9	59	4.0	122	8.2	2.01	182	.187	.273	**26**	**25**	97	105	-2.5	0	-1	2.4
1979	NY-A	5	3	.625	36	0	0	0	18	58	48	7.4	5	19	2.9	41	6.4	2.64	152	.227	.286	10	9	95	109	0.6	0	-1	0.8
1980	NY-A	6	2	.750	64	0	0	0	**33**	99	74	6.7	5	37	3.4	103	9.4	2.27	174	.211	.279	19	18	98	104	1.3	0	-1	1.8
1981	NY-A	3	2	.600	32	0	0	0	20	47	22	4.2	2	14	2.7	48	9.2	0.77	473	.141	.214	15	15	99	91	0.3	0	0	1.6
1982	NY-A	4	5	.444	56	0	0	0	30	93	63	6.1	5	28	2.7	102	9.9	2.23	177	.196	.256	19	18	97	88	-0.3	0	-1	1.7
1983	NY-A	13	5	.722	57	0	0	0	22	87	82	8.5	5	25	2.6	90	9.3	2.28	175	.248	.294	17	17	98	137	3.5	0	-2	1.5
1984	SD-N	10	6	.625	62	0	0	0	25	102	75	6.6	6	36	3.2	84	7.4	2.91	121	.204	.272	8	7	98	76	1.2	0	-1	0.6
1985	SD-N	5	3	.625	50	0	0	0	26	79	64	7.3	1	17	1.9	52	5.9	1.82	200	.226	.266	16	16	101	112	1.0	-1	-1	1.5
1986	SD-N	5	7	.417	45	0	0	0	21	65	69	9.6	8	20	2.8	63	8.7	4.43	81	.273	.324	-5	-6	96	98	-0.5	-1	-1	-0.7
1987	SD-N	5	4	.556	40	0	0	0	11	52	47	8.1	4	19	3.3	44	7.6	3.12	128	.244	.304	6	5	98	108	1.2	-0	-0	0.4
1988	Chi-N	4	4	.500	46	0	0	0	13	44	50	10.2	3	15	3.1	30	6.1	4.30	84	.291	.351	-4	-3	105	109	0.2	-0	0	-0.3
1989	SF-N	2	1	.667	31	0	0	0	4	44	32	6.5	2	27	5.5	24	4.9	2.66	126	.212	.324	4	3	96	121	0.3	-0	-1	0.3
	NY-A	1	0	1.000	11	0	0	0	1	14	14	9.0	0	3	1.9	6	3.9	3.86	106	.275	.321	0	0	105	88	0.5	0	0	0.0
Total	18	113	98	.536	853	37	16	0	307	1636	1339	7.4	98	656	3.6	1379	7.6	2.92	128	.227	.300	150	150	100	102	5.3	-3	-11	14.6
■ **JIM GOTT**	Gott, James William b: 8/3/59, Hollywood, Cal. BR/TR, 6'4", 215 lbs. Deb: 4/09/82																												
1982	Tor-A	5	10	.333	30	23	1	1	0	136	134	8.9	15	66	4.4	82	5.4	4.43	100	.255	.338	-5	0	109	95	-2.4	0	-0	0.0
1983	Tor-A	9	14	.391	34	30	6	1	0	177	195	9.9	15	68	3.5	121	6.2	4.73	93	.280	.345	-13	-7	108	95	-3.6	0	-1	-0.7
1984	Tor-A	7	6	.538	35	12	1	1	2	110	93	7.6	7	49	4.0	73	6.0	4.01	101	.233	.313	-0	0	101	82	0.0	0	-1	0.0
1985	SF-N	7	10	.412	26	26	2	0	0	148	144	8.8	10	51	3.1	78	4.7	3.89	88	.254	.312	-5	-8	95	88	0.4	4	1	-0.3
1986	SF-N	0	0	—	9	2	0	0	1	13	16	11.1	0	13	9.0	9	6.2	7.62	46	.314	.439	-6	-6	95	84	0.0	0	0	-0.5
1987	SF-N	1	0	1.000	30	3	0	0	0	56	53	8.5	4	32	5.1	63	10.1	4.50	86	.244	.344	-3	-4	95	87	0.5	1	0	-0.2
	Pit-N	0	2	.000	25	0	0	0	13	31	28	8.1	0	8	2.3	27	7.8	1.45	294	.233	.279	9	10	105	143	-0.9	-0	-0	0.9
	Yr	1	2	.333	55	3	0	0	13	87	81	8.4	4	40	4.1	90	9.3	3.41	118	.238	.317	6	6	98	143	-0.4	1	-0	0.7
1988	Pit-N	6	6	.500	67	0	0	0	34	77	68	7.9	9	22	2.6	76	8.9	3.51	96	.243	.293	-0	-1	97	102	-0.3	-0	-0	-0.1
1989	Pit-N	0	0	—	1	0	0	0	0	1	1	9.0	0	1	9.0	1	9.0	0.00	—	.333	.500	0	0	94	0	0.0	0	0	0.0
Total	8	35	48	.422	257	96	10	3	50	749	732	8.8	60	310	3.7	530	6.4	4.17	95	.256	.327	-22	-16	102	93	-6.3	5	-1	-0.9
■ **MAURO GOZZO**	Gozzo, Mauro Paul b: 3/7/66, New Britain, Conn. BR/TR, 6'2", 210 lbs. Deb: 8/08/89																												
1989	Tor-A	4	1	.800	9	3	0	0	0	32	35	9.8	1	9	2.5	10	2.8	4.78	76	.289	.338	-3	-4	93	85	1.4	0	-0	-0.3
■ **MARK GRANT**	Grant, Mark Andrew b: 10/24/63, Aurora, Ill. BR/TR, 6'2", 195 lbs. Deb: 4/27/84																												
1984	SF-N	1	4	.200	11	10	0	0	1	54	56	9.3	6	19	3.2	32	5.3	6.33	55	.272	.329	-16	-17	98	68	-1.2	-1	-0	-1.7
1986	SF-N	0	1	.000	4	1	0	0	0	10	6	5.4	0	5	4.5	5	4.5	3.60	98	.176	.282	0	-0	95	45	-0.4	-0	0	0.0
1987	SF-N	1	2	.333	16	8	0	0	1	61	66	9.7	6	21	3.1	32	4.7	3.54	109	.282	.333	4	2	95	128	-0.5	-0	-1	0.1
	SD-N	6	7	.462	17	17	2	1	0	102	104	9.2	16	52	4.6	58	5.1	4.68	85	.263	.342	-7	-8	98	103	0.7	-1	-1	-0.8
	Yr	7	9	.438	33	25	2	1	1	163	170	9.4	22	73	4.0	90	5.0	4.25	93	.269	.338	-3	-6	97	103	0.2	-0	-1	-0.7
1988	SD-N	2	8	.200	33	11	0	0	0	98	97	8.9	14	36	3.3	61	5.6	3.67	91	.268	.329	-2	-3	97	126	-3.0	-1	0	-0.4
1989	SD-N	8	2	.800	50	0	0	0	2	116	105	8.1	11	32	2.5	69	5.4	3.34	105	.248	.300	2	2	101	105	2.9	-0	-0	0.2
Total	5	18	24	.429	131	47	2	1	4	441	434	8.9	53	165	3.4	257	5.2	4.12	88	.262	.325	-20	-24	98	106	-1.5	-4	-2	-2.6
■ **TOMMY GREENE**	Greene, Ira Thomas b: 4/6/67, Lumberton, N.C. BR/TR, 6'5", 225 lbs. Deb: 9/10/89																												
1989	Atl-N	1	2	.333	4	4	1	1	0	26	22	7.6	5	6	2.1	17	5.9	4.15	87	.234	.272	-2	-2	104	89	-0.1	-1	-0	-0.1
■ **MIKE GRIFFIN**	Griffin, Michael Leroy b: 6/26/57, Colusa, Cal. BR/TR, 6'4", 195 lbs. Deb: 9/17/79																												
1979	NY-A	0	0	—	3	0	0	0	1	4	5	11.3	0	2	4.5	5	11.3	4.50	89	.313	.368	-0	-0	95	110	0.0	0	0	0.0
1980	NY-A	2	4	.333	13	9	0	0	0	54	64	10.7	6	23	3.8	25	4.2	4.83	82	.287	.352	-5	-5	98	99	-1.4	0	0	-0.4
1981	NY-A	0	0	—	2	0	0	0	0	4	5	11.3	0	0	0.0	4	9.0	2.25	161	.278	.278	1	1	99	106	0.0	0	0	0.1
	Chi-N	2	5	.286	16	9	0	0	1	52	64	11.1	4	9	1.6	20	3.5	4.50	83	.302	.320	-6	-5	106	95	-0.7	-0	0	-0.4
1982	SD-N	0	1	.000	7	0	0	0	0	10	9	8.1	0	3	2.7	4	3.6	3.60	92	.237	.293	0	-0	92	64	-0.4	-0	0	0.0
1987	Bal-A	3	5	.375	23	6	1	0	1	74	78	9.5	9	33	4.0	42	5.1	4.38	101	.269	.344	1	1	99	107	-0.3	0	-1	0.0
1989	Cin-N	0	0	—	3	0	0	0	0	4	10	22.5	0	3	6.8	1	2.3	13.50	27	.500	.500	-4	-4	104	92	0.0	0	0	-0.3
Total	6	7	15	.318	67	24	1	0	3	202	235	10.5	19	73	3.3	101	4.5	4.63	87	.288	.342	-14	-13	100	99	-2.8	-0	-0	-1.0
■ **JASON GRIMSLEY**	Grimsley, Jason Alan b: 8/7/67, Cleveland, Tex. BR/TR, 6'3", 180 lbs. Deb: 9/08/89																												
1989	Phi-N	1	3	.250	4	4	0	0	0	18	19	9.5	2	19	9.5	7	3.5	6.00	60	.268	.418	-5	-5	102	103	-0.7	-1	0	-0.4
■ **GREG GROSS**	Gross, Gregory Eugene b: 8/1/52, York, Pa. BL/TL, 5'10", 160 lbs. Deb: 9/05/73																												
1986	Phi-N	0	0	—	1	0	0	0	0	1	1	9.0	0	1	9.0	2	18.0	0.00	—	.333	.500	0	0	104	0	0.0	0	0	0.0
1989	Hou-N	0	0	—	1	0	0	0	0	1	3	27.0	0	1	9.0	1	9.0	18.00	20	.500	.571	-2	-2	103	80	0.0	0	0	-0.1
Total	2	0	0	—	2	0	0	0	0	2	4	18.0	0	2	9.0	3	13.5	9.00	41	.444	.545	-1	-1	103	40	0.0	0	0	-0.1
■ **KEVIN GROSS**	Gross, Kevin Frank b: 6/8/61, Downey, Cal. BR/TR, 6'5", 203 lbs. Deb: 6/25/83																												
1983	Phi-N	4	6	.400	17	17	1	1	0	96	100	9.4	13	35	3.3	66	6.2	3.56	102	.265	.330	1	1	100	120	-1.4	-1	0	0.0
1984	Phi-N	8	5	.615	44	14	1	0	1	129	140	9.8	8	44	3.1	84	5.9	4.12	89	.277	.334	-8	-7	101	99	1.6	-2	1	-0.7
1985	Phi-N	15	13	.536	38	31	6	2	0	206	194	8.5	11	81	3.5	151	6.6	3.41	108	.251	.323	4	6	102	102	2.2	0	1	0.8
1986	Phi-N	12	12	.500	37	36	7	2	0	242	240	8.9	28	94	3.5	154	5.7	4.02	96	.259	.329	-8	-4	104	104	-0.8	3	-1	0.0
1987	Phi-N	9	16	.360	34	33	3	1	0	201	205	9.2	26	87	3.9	110	4.9	4.34	98	.267	.344	-6	-2	105	108	-3.7	2	-2	0.0
1988	Phi-N	12	14	.462	33	33	5	1	0	232	209	8.1	18	89	3.5	162	6.3	3.69	97	.239	.312	-6	-3	103	93	1.5	1	-0	-0.2
1989	Mon-N	11	12	.478	31	31	4	3	0	201	188	8.4	20	88	3.9	158	7.1	4.39	82	.247	.325	-20	-18	102	90	-0.5	1	-0	-1.7
Total	7	71	78	.477	234	195	27	10	1	1307	1276	8.8	124	518	3.6	885	6.1	3.95	95	.256	.327	-42	-27	103	101	-1.1	4	-0	-1.8
■ **CECILIO GUANTE**	Guante, Cecilio (Magallane) b: 2/1/60, Villa Mella, D.R. BR/TR, 6'3", 200 lbs. Deb: 5/01/82																												
1982	Pit-N	0	0	—	10	0	0	0	0	27	28	9.3	1	5	1.7	26	8.7	3.33	119	.264	.299	1	2	110	95	0.0	-1	-0	0.1
1983	Pit-N	2	6	.250	49	0	0	0	9	100	90	8.1	5	46	4.1	82	7.4	3.33	112	.241	.320	3	5	103	98	-2.0	-1	-1	0.3
1984	Pit-N	2	3	.400	27	0	0	0	2	41	32	7.0	3	16	3.5	30	6.6	2.63	128	.224	.301	4	3	94	118	-0.2	-0	-1	0.2
1985	Pit-N	4	6	.400	63	0	0	0	5	109	84	6.9	5	40	3.3	92	7.6	2.72	138	.214	.290	11	13	104	91	0.4	-1	-0	1.1
1986	Pit-N	5	2	.714	52	0	0	0	4	78	65	7.5	11	29	3.3	63	7.3	3.35	112	.225	.298	3	3	101	103	1.9	-0	-2	0.2
1987	NY-A	3	2	.600	23	0	0	0	1	44	42	8.6	8	20	4.1	46	9.4	5.73	76	.247	.323	-6	-7	97	79	0.3	0	-1	-0.6

YEAR	TM/L	W	L	PCT	G	GS	CG	SHO	SV	IP	H	H/G	HR	BB	BB/G	SO	SO/G	ERA	/A	OAVG	OOBP	PR	/A	PF	CPI	WAT	PB	PD	TPI
1988	NY-A	5	6	.455	56	0	0	0	11	75	59	7.1	10	22	2.6	61	7.3	2.88	132	.213	.280	9	8	96	105	-0.7	0	-1	0.6
	Tex-A	0	0	—	7	0	0	0	1	5	8	14.4	1	4	7.2	4	7.2	1.80	226	.400	.500	1	1	102	552	0.0	0	-0	0.1
	Yr	5	6	.455	63	0	0	0	12	80	67	7.5	11	26	2.9	65	7.3	2.81	136	.221	.281	10	9	96	552	-0.7	0	-2	0.7
1989	Tex-A	6	6	.500	50	0	0	0	2	69	66	8.6	7	36	4.7	69	9.0	3.91	102	.249	.341	-0	1	103	108	-0.1	0	-1	0.0
Total	8	27	31	.466	337	0	0	0	35	548	474	7.8	51	218	3.6	473	7.8	3.35	114	.233	.308	26	29	101	103	-0.4	-3	-7	2.0
■ **MARK GUBICZA** Gubicza, Mark Steven b: 8/14/62, Philadelphia, Pa. BR/TR, 6'6", 215 lbs. Deb: 4/06/84																													
1984	KC-A	10	14	.417	29	29	4	2	0	189	172	8.2	13	75	3.6	111	5.3	4.05	98	.243	.315	-1	-2	99	84	-2.6	0	2	0.0
1985	KC-A	14	10	.583	29	28	0	0	0	177	160	8.1	14	77	3.9	99	5.0	4.07	103	.238	.318	2	3	101	86	0.7	0	2	0.4
1986	KC-A	12	6	.667	35	24	3	2	0	181	155	7.7	8	84	4.2	118	5.9	3.63	116	.233	.319	11	11	100	89	3.6	0	2	1.4
1987	KC-A	13	18	.419	35	35	10	2	0	242	231	8.6	18	120	4.5	166	6.2	3.98	117	.259	.345	13	18	104	107	-3.2	0	4	2.1
1988	KC-A	20	8	.714	35	35	8	4	0	270	237	7.9	11	83	2.8	183	6.1	2.70	151	.234	.293	38	41	103	102	6.3	0	3	**4.8**
1989	KC-A	15	11	.577	36	36	8	2	0	255	252	8.9	10	63	2.2	173	6.1	3.04	122	.259	.302	24	19	95	104	0.3	0	2	2.2
Total	6	84	67	.556	199	187	33	12	0	1314	1207	8.3	74	502	3.4	850	5.8	3.51	118	.245	.315	87	90	100	97	5.1	0	15	10.9
■ **LEE GUETTERMAN** Guetterman, Arthur Lee b: 11/22/58, Chattanooga, Tenn. BL/TL, 6'8", 225 lbs. Deb: 9/12/84																													
1984	Sea-A	0	0	—	3	0	0	0	0	4	9	20.3	0	2	4.5	2	4.5	4.50	92	.450	.500	-0	-0	103	219	0.0	0	0	0.0
1986	Sea-A	0	4	.000	41	4	1	0	0	76	108	12.8	7	30	3.6	38	4.5	7.34	61	.347	.402	-27	-24	106	90	-1.9	0	0	-2.2
1987	Sea-A	11	4	.733	25	17	2	1	0	113	117	9.3	13	35	2.8	42	3.3	3.82	120	.267	.319	8	10	103	108	3.8	0	1	1.0
1988	NY-A	1	2	.333	20	2	0	0	0	41	49	10.8	2	14	3.1	15	3.3	4.61	82	.306	.362	-3	-4	96	105	-0.5	0	-0	-0.3
1989	NY-A	5	5	.500	70	0	0	0	13	103	98	8.6	6	26	2.3	51	4.5	2.45	167	.258	.301	17	19	105	134	0.4	0	2	2.1
Total	5	17	15	.531	159	23	3	1	13	337	381	10.2	28	107	2.9	148	4.0	4.30	100	.291	.342	-5	0	104	113	1.8	0	3	0.6
■ **MARK GUTHRIE** Guthrie, Mark Andrew b: 9/22/65, Buffalo, N.Y. BR/TR, 5'11", 192 lbs. Deb: 7/25/89																													
1989	Min-A	2	4	.333	13	8	0	0	0	57	66	10.4	7	21	3.3	38	6.0	4.58	90	.292	.346	-4	-3	106	109	-0.9	0	-0	-0.2
■ **DREW HALL** Hall, Andrew Clark b: 3/27/63, Louisville, Ky. BL/TL, 6'5", 200 lbs. Deb: 9/14/86																													
1986	Chi-N	1	2	.333	5	4	1	0	1	24	24	9.0	3	10	3.8	21	7.9	4.50	89	.267	.337	-2	-1	108	99	-0.3	0	-0	-0.1
1987	Chi-N	1	1	.500	21	0	0	0	0	33	40	10.9	4	14	3.8	20	5.5	6.82	61	.308	.367	-10	-10	102	82	0.1	-0	-0	-0.9
1988	Chi-N	1	1	.500	19	0	0	0	1	22	26	10.6	4	9	3.7	22	9.0	7.77	47	.295	.350	-11	-10	105	75	0.0	0	0	-0.9
1989	Tex-A	2	1	.667	38	0	0	0	0	58	42	6.5	3	33	5.1	45	7.0	3.72	107	.207	.322	1	2	103	82	0.5	0	0	0.2
Total	4	5	5	.500	83	4	1	0	2	137	132	8.7	14	66	4.3	108	7.1	5.26	76	.258	.341	-22	-19	104	84	0.3	-0	-0	-1.7
■ **JEFF HAMILTON** Hamilton, Jeffrey Robert b: 3/19/64, Flint, Mich. BR/TR, 6'3", 190 lbs. Deb: 6/28/86																													
1989	LA-N	0	1	.000	1	0	0	0	0	2	2	9.0	0	1	4.5	2	9.0	4.50	72	.286	.375	-0	-0	93	96	-0.4	0	0	0.0
■ **ATLEE HAMMAKER** Hammaker, Charlton Atlee b: 1/24/58, Carmel, Cal. BB/TL, 6'3", 200 lbs. Deb: 8/13/81																													
1981	KC-A	1	3	.250	10	6	0	0	0	39	44	10.2	2	12	2.8	11	2.5	5.54	65	.286	.331	-8	-8	99	72	-0.9	0	-1	-0.8
1982	SF-N	12	8	.600	29	27	4	1	0	175	189	9.7	16	28	1.4	102	5.2	4.11	82	.278	.302	-10	-14	94	91	1.5	-4	1	-1.6
1983	SF-N	10	9	.526	23	23	8	3	0	172	147	7.7	9	32	**1.7**	127	6.6	**2.25**	**163**	.228	**.262**	27	27	101	96	0.8	-1	1	2.9
1984	SF-N	2	0	1.000	6	6	0	0	0	33	32	8.7	2	9	2.5	24	6.5	2.18	161	.256	.295	5	5	98	148	1.0	1	0	0.6
1985	SF-N	5	12	.294	29	29	1	1	0	171	161	8.5	17	47	2.5	100	5.3	3.74	91	.247	.292	-3	-6	95	88	-2.0	-2	1	-0.8
1987	SF-N	10	10	.500	31	27	2	0	0	168	159	8.5	22	57	3.1	107	5.7	3.59	108	.248	.310	9	5	95	107	-1.0	-1	-1	0.3
1988	SF-N	9	9	.500	43	17	3	1	5	145	136	8.4	11	41	2.5	65	4.0	3.72	87	.248	.297	-4	-8	93	89	-0.1	-0	2	-0.6
1989	SF-N	6	6	.500	28	9	0	0	0	77	78	9.1	5	23	2.7	30	3.5	3.74	90	.271	.317	-2	-3	96	104	-0.7	2	-1	-0.1
Total	8	55	57	.491	199	144	18	6	5	980	946	8.7	84	249	2.3	566	5.2	3.54	99	.253	.296	14	-3	96	96	-1.4	-6	2	-0.1
■ **ERIK HANSON** Hanson, Erik Brian b: 5/18/65, Kinnelon, N.J. BR/TR, 6'6", 210 lbs. Deb: 9/05/88																													
1988	Sea-A	2	3	.400	6	6	0	0	0	42	35	7.5	4	12	2.6	36	7.7	3.21	134	.230	.286	4	5	108	96	0.0	0	-0	0.5
1989	Sea-A	9	5	.643	17	17	1	0	0	113	103	8.2	7	32	2.5	75	6.0	3.19	126	.243	.301	9	11	104	98	2.6	0	0	1.1
Total	2	11	8	.579	23	23	1	0	0	155	138	8.0	11	44	2.6	111	6.4	3.19	128	.240	.297	12	16	105	97	2.6	0	-0	1.6
■ **JACK HARDY** Hardy, John Graydon b: 10/8/59, St.Petersburg, Fla. BR/TR, 6'2", 175 lbs. Deb: 5/23/89																													
1989	Chi-A	0	0	—	5	0	0	0	0	12	14	10.5	1	5	3.8	4	3.0	6.75	54	.286	.357	-4	-4	93	71	0.0	0	1	-0.2
■ **PETE HARNISCH** Harnisch, Peter Thomas b: 9/23/66, Commack, N.Y. BB/TR, 6'1", 195 lbs. Deb: 9/13/88																													
1988	Bal-A	0	2	.000	2	2	0	0	0	13	13	9.0	1	9	6.2	10	6.9	5.54	70	.260	.361	-2	-2	97	85	-0.9	0	0	-0.1
1989	Bal-A	5	9	.357	18	17	2	0	0	103	97	8.5	10	64	5.6	70	6.1	4.63	83	.249	.355	-8	-9	99	96	-2.4	0	-1	-0.9
Total	2	5	11	.313	20	19	2	0	0	116	110	8.5	11	73	5.7	80	6.2	4.73	81	.250	.355	-11	-12	98	95	-3.3	0	-1	-1.0
■ **GREG HARRIS** Harris, Greg Allen b: 11/2/55, Lynwood, Cal. BB/TR, 6', 165 lbs. Deb: 5/20/81																													
1981	NY-N	3	5	.375	16	14	0	0	1	69	65	8.5	8	28	3.7	54	7.0	4.43	81	.245	.317	-7	-7	103	85	-0.2	0	-0	-0.6
1982	Cin-N	2	6	.250	34	10	1	0	1	91	96	9.5	12	37	3.7	67	6.6	4.85	77	.274	.339	-13	-11	104	96	-1.3	-0	0	-1.0
1983	Cin-N	0	0	—	1	0	0	0	0	1	2	18.0	0	3	27.0	1	9.0	27.00	14	.500	.667	-3	-3	104	74	0.0	-0	0	-0.1
1984	Mon-N	0	1	.000	15	0	0	0	2	18	10	5.0	0	7	3.5	15	7.5	2.00	164	.172	.279	3	3	91	86	-0.4	-0	0	0.3
	SD-N	2	1	.667	19	1	0	0	1	37	28	6.8	3	18	4.4	30	7.3	2.68	131	.209	.304	4	3	98	112	0.3	1	-0	0.5
	Yr	2	2	.500	34	1	0	0	3	55	38	6.2	3	25	4.1	45	7.4	2.45	140	.196	.288	7	6	96	112	-0.1	-0	-0	0.8
1985	Tex-A	5	4	.556	58	0	0	0	11	113	74	5.9	7	43	3.4	111	8.8	2.47	185	.186	.271	21	**26**	110	85	1.3	0	1	2.8
1986	Tex-A	10	8	.556	73	0	0	0	20	111	103	8.4	12	42	3.4	95	7.7	2.84	140	.251	.316	17	14	95	137	0.4	0	1	1.5
1987	Tex-A	5	10	.333	42	19	0	0	0	141	157	10.0	18	56	3.6	106	6.8	4.85	96	.281	.345	-6	-3	104	101	-2.1	0	0	-0.2
1988	Phi-N	4	6	.400	66	1	0	0	1	107	80	6.7	7	52	4.4	71	6.0	2.36	151	.209	.305	13	14	103	125	0.0	1	-0	1.7
1989	Phi-N	2	2	.500	44	0	0	0	1	75	64	7.7	7	43	5.2	51	6.1	3.60	100	.234	.336	-1	-0	102	110	0.3	1	1	0.1
	Bos-A	2	2	.500	15	0	0	0	0	28	21	6.8	1	15	4.8	25	8.0	2.57	158	.208	.305	4	5	104	103	0.0	0	0	0.5
Total	9	35	45	.438	383	45	1	0	38	791	700	8.0	75	344	3.9	626	7.1	3.52	113	.239	.318	33	42	103	106	-1.7	3	3	5.5
■ **GREG HARRIS** Harris, Gregory Wade b: 12/1/63, Greensboro, N.C. BR/TR, 6'3", 190 lbs. Deb: 9/14/88																													
1988	SD-N	2	0	1.000	3	1	1	0	0	18	13	6.5	0	3	1.5	15	7.5	1.50	224	.200	.235	4	4	97	79	1.0	-1	0	0.3
1989	SD-N	8	9	.471	56	8	0	0	6	135	106	7.1	8	52	3.5	106	7.1	2.60	135	.215	.289	14	14	101	102	-1.2	-1	1	1.5
Total	2	10	9	.526	59	9	1	0	6	153	119	7.0	8	55	3.2	121	7.1	2.47	142	.213	.283	17	18	100	99	-0.2	-2	1	1.8
■ **GENE HARRIS** Harris, Tyrone Eugene b: 12/5/64, Sebring, Fla. BR/TR, 5'11", 190 lbs. Deb: 4/05/89																													
1989	Mon-N	1	1	.500	11	0	0	0	0	20	16	7.2	1	10	4.5	11	4.9	4.95	72	.242	.310	-3	-3	102	75	0.0	-0	2	-0.1
	Sea-A	1	4	.200	10	6	0	0	1	33	47	12.8	3	15	4.1	14	3.8	6.55	62	.353	.414	-10	-9	104	104	-1.3	0	-1	-0.9
■ **MIKE HARTLEY** Hartley, Michael Edward b: 8/31/61, Hawthorne, Cal. BR/TR, 6'1", 192 lbs. Deb: 9/10/89																													
1989	LA-N	0	1	.000	5	0	0	0	0	6	2	3.0	0	0	0.0	4	6.0	1.50	216	.100	.100	1	1	93	96	-0.4	-0	0	0.1
■ **BRYAN HARVEY** Harvey, Bryan Stanley b: 6/2/63, Chattanooga, Tenn. BR/TR, 6'3", 205 lbs. Deb: 5/16/87																													
1987	Cal-A	0	0	—	3	0	0	0	0	5	6	10.8	0	2	3.6	3	5.4	0.00	—	.300	.364	2	2	100	0	0.0	0	-0	0.2
1988	Cal-A	7	5	.583	50	0	0	0	17	76	59	7.0	4	20	2.4	67	7.9	2.13	177	.214	.264	16	14	95	105	1.4	0	-1	1.3
1989	Cal-A	3	3	.500	51	0	0	0	25	55	36	5.9	6	41	6.7	78	12.8	3.44	111	.183	.314	3	2	98	92	-0.2	0	0	0.2
Total	3	10	8	.556	104	0	0	0	42	136	101	6.7	10	63	4.2	148	9.8	2.58	147	.205	.289	21	18	96	96	1.2	0	-1	1.7
■ **MICKEY HATCHER** Hatcher, Michael Vaughn b: 3/15/55, Cleveland, Ohio BR/TR, 6'2", 200 lbs. Deb: 8/03/79																													
1989	LA-N	0	0	—	1	0	0	0	0	1	0	0.0	0	3	27.0	0	0.0	9.00	36	.000	.667	-1	-1	93	114	0.0	0	0	0.0
■ **BRAD HAVENS** Havens, Bradley David b: 11/17/59, Highland Park, Mich BL/TL, 6'1", 180 lbs. Deb: 6/05/81																													
1981	Min-A	3	6	.333	14	12	1	1	0	78	76	8.8	6	24	2.8	43	5.0	3.58	109	.257	.313	1	3	107	98	-0.5	0	-0	0.2
1982	Min-A	10	14	.417	33	32	4	1	0	209	201	8.7	32	80	3.4	129	5.6	4.31	96	.250	.315	-5	-4	102	95	1.0	0	-3	-0.6
1983	Min-A	5	8	.385	16	14	1	0	0	80	110	12.4	11	38	4.3	40	4.5	8.21	53	.333	.392	-37	-34	106	80	-0.7	0	-2	-3.2
1985	Bal-A	0	1	.000	8	1	0	0	0	14	20	12.9	4	10	6.4	19	12.2	9.00	45	.333	.429	-8	-8	98	94	-0.4	0	0	-0.6
1986	Bal-A	3	3	.500	46	0	0	0	1	71	64	8.1	7	29	3.7	57	7.2	4.56	91	.248	.316	-3	-3	99	84	0.3	0	1	-0.2

YEAR	TM/L	W	L	PCT	G	GS	CG	SHO	SV	IP	H	H/G	HR	BB	BB/G	SO	SO/G	ERA	/A	OAVG	OOBP	PR	/A	PF	CPI	WAT	PB	PD	TPI
1987	LA-N	0	0	—	31	1	0	0	1	35	30	7.7	2	23	5.9	23	5.9	4.37	86	.227	.344	-1	-2	92	82	0.0	-0	-1	-0.2
1988	LA-N	0	0	—	9	0	0	0	0	10	15	13.5	1	4	3.6	8	7.2	4.50	81	.357	.404	-1	-1	105	152	0.0	-0	1	0.0
	Cle-A	2	3	.400	28	0	0	0	1	57	62	9.8	7	17	2.7	30	4.7	3.16	129	.273	.319	5	6	102	135	-0.3	0	-0	0.5
1989	Cle-A	0	0	—	7	0	0	0	0	13	18	12.5	3	7	4.8	6	4.2	4.15	98	.353	.417	-0	-0	104	193	0.0	0	1	0.1
	Det-A	1	2	.333	13	1	0	0	0	23	28	11.0	3	14	5.5	15	5.9	5.48	70	.308	.409	-4	-4	99	119	0.0	0	0	-0.3
	Yr	1	2	.333	20	1	0	0	0	36	46	11.5	6	21	5.3	21	5.3	5.00	79	.319	.412	-4	-4	101	119	0.0	0	1	-0.2
Total	8	24	37	.393	205	61	6	2	3	590	624	9.5	76	246	3.8	370	5.6	4.82	85	.272	.339	-53	-48	102	99	-0.6	-0	-4	-4.3

■ ANDY HAWKINS Hawkins, Melton Andrew b: 1/21/60, Waco, Tex. BR/TR, 6'4", 200 lbs. Deb: 7/17/82

YEAR	TM/L	W	L	PCT	G	GS	CG	SHO	SV	IP	H	H/G	HR	BB	BB/G	SO	SO/G	ERA	/A	OAVG	OOBP	PR	/A	PF	CPI	WAT	PB	PD	TPI
1982	SD-N	2	5	.286	15	10	1	0	0	64	66	9.3	4	27	3.8	25	3.5	4.08	81	.274	.338	-3	-6	92	103	-1.4	-2	-1	-0.7
1983	SD-N	5	7	.417	21	19	4	1	0	120	106	8.0	8	48	3.6	59	4.4	2.93	123	.244	.317	9	9	99	118	-1.0	-1	1	0.9
1984	SD-N	8	9	.471	36	22	2	1	0	146	143	8.8	13	72	4.4	77	4.7	4.68	75	.254	.334	-18	-19	98	86	-1.5	1	-1	-1.9
1985	SD-N	18	8	.692	33	33	5	2	0	229	229	9.0	18	65	2.6	69	2.7	3.14	116	.267	.313	12	13	101	119	5.3	-4	-1	0.8
1986	SD-N	10	8	.556	37	35	3	1	0	209	218	9.4	24	75	3.2	117	5.0	4.31	83	.268	.329	-14	-17	96	99	1.8	-0	-2	-1.9
1987	SD-N	3	10	.231	24	20	0	0	0	118	131	10.0	16	49	3.7	51	3.9	5.03	79	.287	.353	-12	-14	98	102	-2.8	-0	0	-1.3
1988	SD-N	14	11	.560	33	33	4	2	0	218	196	8.1	16	76	3.1	91	3.8	3.34	100	.244	.307	3	0	97	102	1.3	-2	-3	-0.3
1989	NY-A	15	15	.500	34	34	5	2	0	208	238	10.3	23	76	3.3	98	4.2	4.80	85	.290	.352	-21	-16	105	102	1.4	0	-3	-1.8
Total	8	75	73	.507	233	206	24	9	0	1312	1327	9.1	122	488	3.3	587	4.0	3.99	91	.266	.329	-44	-50	99	104	3.1	-8	-10	-6.2

■ NEAL HEATON Heaton, Neal b: 3/3/60, Holtsville, N.Y. BL/TL, 6'1", 197 lbs. Deb: 9/03/82

YEAR	TM/L	W	L	PCT	G	GS	CG	SHO	SV	IP	H	H/G	HR	BB	BB/G	SO	SO/G	ERA	/A	OAVG	OOBP	PR	/A	PF	CPI	WAT	PB	PD	TPI
1982	Cle-A	0	2	.000	8	4	0	0	0	31	32	9.3	1	16	4.6	14	4.1	5.23	79	.260	.338	-4	-4	101	71	-0.9	0	-0	-0.3
1983	Cle-A	11	7	.611	39	16	4	3	7	149	157	9.5	11	44	2.7	75	4.5	4.17	104	.269	.317	-2	3	106	91	3.1	0	-2	0.1
1984	Cle-A	12	15	.444	38	34	4	1	0	199	231	10.4	21	75	3.4	75	3.4	5.20	81	.293	.348	-27	-21	106	93	-0.5	0	-3	-2.2
1985	Cle-A	9	17	.346	36	33	5	1	0	208	244	10.6	19	80	3.5	82	3.5	4.89	81	.298	.359	-17	-22	95	105	-0.9	0	-3	-2.2
1986	Cle-A	3	6	.333	12	12	2	0	0	74	73	8.9	8	34	4.1	24	2.9	4.26	96	.254	.333	-1	-1	98	96	-1.6	0	-0	-0.1
	Min-A	4	9	.308	21	17	3	0	1	124	128	9.3	18	47	3.4	66	4.8	3.99	115	.273	.335	3	8	109	118	-2.0	0	-1	0.7
	Yr	7	15	.318	33	29	5	0	1	198	201	9.1	26	81	3.7	90	4.1	4.09	107	.266	.333	2	7	105	118	-3.6	0	-1	0.6
1987	Mon-N	13	10	.565	32	32	3	1	0	193	207	9.7	25	37	1.7	105	4.9	4.52	96	.273	.306	-9	-4	106	90	0.1	2	-1	-0.3
1988	Mon-N	3	10	.231	32	11	0	0	2	97	98	9.1	14	43	4.0	43	4.0	5.01	72	.271	.347	-17	-15	105	99	-3.5	-0	-0	-1.5
1989	Pit-N	6	7	.462	42	18	1	0	0	147	127	7.8	12	55	3.4	67	4.1	3.06	108	.233	.303	7	4	94	108	0.1	1	1	0.5
Total	8	61	83	.424	260	177	22	6	10	1222	1297	9.6	129	431	3.2	551	4.1	4.46	91	.274	.332	-66	-53	102	99	-6.1	2	-9	-5.3

■ DON HEINKEL Heinkel, Donald Elliott b: 10/20/59, Racine, Wis. BL/TR, 6', 185 lbs. Deb: 4/07/88

YEAR	TM/L	W	L	PCT	G	GS	CG	SHO	SV	IP	H	H/G	HR	BB	BB/G	SO	SO/G	ERA	/A	OAVG	OOBP	PR	/A	PF	CPI	WAT	PB	PD	TPI
1988	Det-A	0	0	—	21	0	0	0	1	36	30	7.5	4	12	3.0	30	7.5	4.00	93	.219	.285	-0	-1	94	73	0.0	0	0	0.0
1989	StL-N	1	1	.500	7	5	0	0	0	26	40	13.8	2	7	2.4	16	5.5	5.88	60	.348	.376	-7	-7	100	104	0.0	-0	0	-0.6
Total	2	1	1	.500	28	5	0	0	1	62	70	10.2	6	19	2.8	46	6.7	4.79	76	.278	.326	-7	-8	97	86	0.0	-0	0	-0.6

■ TOM HENKE Henke, Thomas Anthony b: 12/21/57, Kansas City, Mo. BR/TR, 6'5", 215 lbs. Deb: 9/10/82

YEAR	TM/L	W	L	PCT	G	GS	CG	SHO	SV	IP	H	H/G	HR	BB	BB/G	SO	SO/G	ERA	/A	OAVG	OOBP	PR	/A	PF	CPI	WAT	PB	PD	TPI
1982	Tex-A	1	0	1.000	8	0	0	0	0	16	14	7.9	0	8	4.5	9	5.1	1.13	342	.246	.343	5	5	94	306	0.5	0	0	0.5
1983	Tex-A	1	0	1.000	8	0	0	0	1	16	16	9.0	1	4	2.3	17	9.6	3.38	122	.262	.308	1	1	101	101	0.5	0	0	0.1
1984	Tex-A	1	1	.500	25	0	0	0	2	28	36	11.6	0	20	6.4	25	8.0	6.43	63	.313	.404	-8	-7	101	88	0.1	0	-0	-0.7
1985	Tor-A	3	3	.500	28	0	0	0	13	40	29	6.5	4	8	1.8	42	9.4	2.02	203	.206	.242	9	9	99	112	-0.5	0	-0	0.9
1986	Tor-A	9	5	.643	63	0	0	0	27	91	63	6.2	6	32	3.2	118	11.7	3.36	130	.191	.259	8	10	104	58	1.8	0	-1	0.8
1987	Tor-A	0	6	.000	72	0	0	0	**34**	94	62	5.9	10	25	2.4	128	12.3	2.49	178	.188	.240	**21**	20	99	82	-2.9	0	1	2.1
1988	Tor-A	4	4	.500	52	0	0	0	25	68	60	7.9	6	24	3.2	66	8.7	2.91	135	.237	.302	8	8	99	115	-0.2	0	0	0.8
1989	Tor-A	8	3	.727	64	0	0	0	20	89	66	6.7	5	25	2.5	116	11.7	1.92	189	.205	.261	19	17	93	107	2.3	0	0	1.7
Total	8	27	22	.551	320	0	0	0	122	442	346	7.0	32	146	3.0	521	10.6	2.81	146	.215	.277	65	63	99	99	1.6	0	-0	6.2

■ MIKE HENNEMAN Henneman, Michael Alan b: 12/11/61, St.Charles, Mo. BR/TR, 6'4", 205 lbs. Deb: 5/11/87

YEAR	TM/L	W	L	PCT	G	GS	CG	SHO	SV	IP	H	H/G	HR	BB	BB/G	SO	SO/G	ERA	/A	OAVG	OOBP	PR	/A	PF	CPI	WAT	PB	PD	TPI
1987	Det-A	11	3	.786	55	0	0	0	7	97	86	8.0	8	30	2.8	75	7.0	2.97	144	.238	.298	16	14	96	107	3.4	0	0	1.3
1988	Det-A	9	6	.600	65	0	0	0	22	91	72	7.1	7	24	2.4	58	5.7	1.88	199	.218	.269	**21**	**19**	94	135	1.0	0	-1	1.8
1989	Det-A	11	4	.733	60	0	0	0	8	90	84	8.4	4	51	5.1	69	6.9	3.70	104	.251	.349	2	2	99	108	4.5	0	0	0.2
Total	3	31	13	.705	180	0	0	0	37	278	242	7.8	19	105	3.4	202	6.5	2.85	139	.235	.307	39	34	96	117	8.9	0	-1	3.3

■ DWAYNE HENRY Henry, Dwayne Allen b: 2/16/62, Elkton, Md. BR/TR, 6'3", 205 lbs. Deb: 9/07/84

YEAR	TM/L	W	L	PCT	G	GS	CG	SHO	SV	IP	H	H/G	HR	BB	BB/G	SO	SO/G	ERA	/A	OAVG	OOBP	PR	/A	PF	CPI	WAT	PB	PD	TPI
1984	Tex-A	0	1	.000	3	0	0	0	0	4	5	11.3	0	7	15.8	2	4.5	9.00	45	.294	.480	-2	-2	101	87	-0.4	0	0	-0.1
1985	Tex-A	2	2	.500	16	0	0	0	3	21	16	6.9	0	7	3.0	20	8.6	2.57	177	.211	.267	4	5	110	74	0.4	0	0	0.5
1986	Tex-A	1	0	1.000	19	0	0	0	0	19	14	6.6	1	22	10.4	17	8.1	4.74	84	.209	.398	-1	-2	95	100	0.5	0	0	0.0
1987	Tex-A	0	0	—	5	0	0	0	0	10	12	10.8	2	9	8.1	7	6.3	9.00	52	.293	.420	-5	-5	104	78	0.0	0	0	-0.3
1988	Tex-A	0	1	.000	11	0	0	0	1	10	15	13.5	1	9	8.1	10	9.0	9.00	45	.326	.458	-6	-5	102	91	-0.4	0	-0	-0.5
1989	Atl-N	0	2	.000	12	0	0	0	1	13	12	8.3	2	5	3.5	16	11.1	4.15	87	.250	.309	-1	-1	104	102	-0.9	0	-0	0.0
Total	6	3	6	.333	66	0	0	0	5	77	74	8.6	6	59	6.9	72	8.4	5.38	78	.251	.372	-11	-10	103	89	-0.8	0	0	-0.4

■ XAVIER HERNANDEZ Hernandez, Francis Xavier b: 8/16/65, Port Arthur, Tex. BL/TR, 6'2", 185 lbs. Deb: 6/04/89

YEAR	TM/L	W	L	PCT	G	GS	CG	SHO	SV	IP	H	H/G	HR	BB	BB/G	SO	SO/G	ERA	/A	OAVG	OOBP	PR	/A	PF	CPI	WAT	PB	PD	TPI
1989	Tor-A	1	0	1.000	7	0	0	0	0	23	25	9.8	2	8	3.1	7	2.7	4.70	77	.278	.337	-2	-3	93	93	0.5	0	-0	-0.2

■ GUILLERMO HERNANDEZ Hernandez, Guillermo (Villanueva) "Willie" b: 11/14/54, Aguada, P.R. BL/TL, 6'3", 180 lbs. Deb: 4/09/77

YEAR	TM/L	W	L	PCT	G	GS	CG	SHO	SV	IP	H	H/G	HR	BB	BB/G	SO	SO/G	ERA	/A	OAVG	OOBP	PR	/A	PF	CPI	WAT	PB	PD	TPI
1977	Chi-N	8	7	.533	67	1	0	0	4	110	94	7.7	11	28	2.3	78	6.4	3.03	148	.234	.281	11	18	115	97	0.5	-2	3	2.0
1978	Chi-N	8	2	.800	54	0	0	0	3	60	57	8.6	6	35	5.3	38	5.7	3.75	106	.263	.352	-1	2	111	125	3.1	-0	1	0.2
1979	Chi-N	4	4	.500	51	2	0	0	0	79	85	9.7	8	39	4.4	53	6.0	5.01	84	.281	.357	-11	-7	112	97	0.1	0	0	-0.6
1980	Chi-N	1	9	.100	53	7	0	0	0	108	115	9.6	8	45	3.8	75	6.3	4.42	88	.276	.342	-10	-6	108	97	-3.7	0	2	-0.4
1981	Chi-N	0	0	—	12	0	0	0	2	14	14	9.0	0	8	5.1	13	8.4	3.86	96	.280	.355	-1	-0	106	111	0.0	0	0	0.0
1982	Chi-N	4	6	.400	75	0	0	0	10	75	74	8.9	3	24	2.9	54	6.5	3.00	125	.268	.317	5	6	104	119	-0.5	-0	2	0.9
1983	Chi-N	1	0	1.000	11	1	0	0	1	20	16	7.2	0	6	2.7	18	8.1	3.15	117	.222	.275	1	1	101	63	0.5	0	0	0.2
	Phi-N	8	4	.667	63	0	0	0	7	96	93	8.7	9	26	2.4	75	7.0	3.28	111	.254	.302	4	4	100	103	1.6	1	-0	0.5
	Yr	9	4	.692	74	1	0	0	8	116	109	8.5	9	32	2.5	93	7.2	3.26	112	.249	.297	5	5	100	103	2.1	0	0	0.7
1984	Det-A	9	3	.750	**80**	0	0	0	32	140	96	6.2	6	36	2.3	112	7.2	1.93	195	.194	.248	**32**	**29**	94	86	1.9	0	-1	2.8
1985	Det-A	8	10	.444	74	0	0	0	31	107	82	6.9	13	14	1.2	76	6.4	2.69	163	.210	.234	17	20	106	84	-1.4	0	-1	1.9
1986	Det-A	8	7	.533	64	0	0	0	24	89	87	8.8	13	21	2.1	77	7.8	3.54	112	.251	.301	6	4	95	107	0.0	0	1	0.5
1987	Det-A	3	4	.429	45	0	0	0	8	49	53	9.7	8	20	3.7	30	5.5	3.67	116	.276	.336	4	3	96	136	-1.0	0	-1	0.2
1988	Det-A	6	5	.545	63	0	0	0	10	68	50	6.6	8	31	4.1	59	7.8	3.04	123	.208	.299	7	5	94	110	0.0	0	1	0.7
1989	Det-A	2	2	.500	32	0	0	0	15	31	36	10.5	4	16	4.6	30	8.7	5.81	66	.293	.376	-7	-7	99	95	0.4	0	0	-0.6
Total	13	70	63	.526	744	11	0	0	147	1046	952	8.2	97	349	3.0	788	6.8	3.37	118	.245	.304	59	72	103	101	1.5	1	7	8.3

■ MANNY HERNANDEZ Hernandez, Manuel Antonio (Montas) b: 5/7/61, La Romana, D.R. BR/TR, 6', 150 lbs. Deb: 6/05/86

YEAR	TM/L	W	L	PCT	G	GS	CG	SHO	SV	IP	H	H/G	HR	BB	BB/G	SO	SO/G	ERA	/A	OAVG	OOBP	PR	/A	PF	CPI	WAT	PB	PD	TPI
1986	Hou-N	2	3	.400	9	4	0	0	0	28	33	10.6	2	12	3.9	9	2.9	3.86	98	.306	.360	-0	-0	102	132	-0.7	-1	0	0.0
1987	Hou-N	0	4	.000	6	3	0	0	0	22	25	10.2	1	5	2.0	12	4.9	5.32	71	.301	.326	-3	-4	93	83	-1.9	-0	0	-0.3
1989	NY-N	0	0	—	1	0	0	0	0	1	0	0.0	0	0	0.0	1	9.0	0.00	—	.000	.000	0	0	95	0	0.0	0	0	0.0
Total	3	2	7	.222	16	7	0	0	0	51	58	10.2	3	17	3.0	22	3.9	4.41	86	.299	.341	-3	-4	98	108	-2.6	-1	0	-0.3

■ OREL HERSHISER Hershiser, Orel Leonard b: 9/16/58, Buffalo, N.Y. BR/TR, 6'3", 190 lbs. Deb: 9/01/83

YEAR	TM/L	W	L	PCT	G	GS	CG	SHO	SV	IP	H	H/G	HR	BB	BB/G	SO	SO/G	ERA	/A	OAVG	OOBP	PR	/A	PF	CPI	WAT	PB	PD	TPI
1983	LA-N	0	0	—	8	0	0	0	1	8	7	7.9	1	6	6.8	5	5.6	3.38	107	.233	.351	0	0	100	130	0.0	0	0	0.0
1984	LA-N	11	8	.579	45	20	8	**4**	2	190	160	7.6	9	50	2.4	150	7.1	2.65	141	.225	.278	20	23	104	89	1.9	1	1	2.7
1985	LA-N	19	3	**.864**	36	34	9	5	0	240	179	6.7	8	68	2.6	157	5.9	2.03	163	.206	.265	42	34	92	93	7.7	3	2	4.4
1986	LA-N	14	14	.500	35	35	8	1	0	231	213	8.3	13	86	3.4	153	6.0	3.86	91	.243	.308	-3	-9	95	83	1.5	4	1	-0.4
1987	LA-N	16	16	.500	37	35	10	1	1	**265**	247	8.4	17	74	2.5	190	6.5	3.06	123	.247	.302	30	21	92	104	1.8	5	1	2.6
1988	LA-N	**23**	8	.742	35	34	**15**	**8**	1	**267**	208	7.0	18	73	2.5	178	6.0	2.26	161	.213	.267	**35**	**41**	105	104	6.7	-1	6	**5.4**
1989	LA-N	15	15	.500	35	33	8	4	0	**257**	226	7.9	9	77	2.7	178	6.2	2.31	140	.240	.292	**34**	**27**	93	124	0.7	4	4	**3.8**
Total	7	98	64	.605	231	191	58	23	5	1458	1240	7.7	75	434	2.7	1011	6.2	2.69	132	.229	.286	158	137	96	100	20.3	16	15	18.5

YEAR TM/L	W	L	PCT	G	GS	CG	SHO	SV	IP	H	H/G	HR	BB	BB/G	SO	SO/G	ERA	/A	OAVG	OOBP	PR	/A	PF	CPI	WAT	PB	PD	TPI
■ **JOE HESKETH**	Hesketh, Joseph Thomas b: 2/15/59, Lackawanna, N.Y. BR/TL, 6'2", 170 lbs. Deb: 8/07/84																											
1984 Mon-N	2	2	.500	11	5	1	1	1	45	38	7.6	2	15	3.0	32	6.4	1.80	182	.233	.291	9	7	91	153	0.1	0	0	0.8
1985 Mon-N	10	5	.667	25	25	2	1	0	155	125	7.3	10	45	2.6	113	6.6	2.50	135	.222	.275	19	15	94	99	2.4	-1	-1	1.4
1986 Mon-N	6	5	.545	15	15	0	0	0	83	92	10.0	11	31	3.4	67	7.3	4.99	73	.283	.345	-12	-12	98	97	0.7	-2	-1	-1.4
1987 Mon-N	0	0	—	18	0	0	0	1	29	23	7.1	2	15	4.7	31	9.6	3.10	139	.211	.313	3	4	106	96	0.0	-0	-1	0.3
1988 Mon-N	4	3	.571	60	0	0	0	9	73	63	7.8	1	35	4.3	64	7.9	2.84	128	.242	.322	5	6	105	115	0.5	0	1	0.9
1989 Mon-N	6	4	.600	43	0	0	0	3	48	54	10.1	5	26	4.9	44	8.3	5.81	62	.292	.365	-12	-12	102	92	1.1	0	1	-1.0
Total 6	28	19	.596	172	45	3	2	14	433	395	8.2	31	167	3.5	351	7.3	3.37	105	.246	.312	12	9	98	106	4.8	-2	-0	1.0
■ **ERIC HETZEL**	Hetzel, Eric Paul b: 9/25/63, Crowley, La. BR/TR, 6'3", 175 lbs. Deb: 7/01/89																											
1989 Bos-A	2	3	.400	12	11	0	0	0	50	61	11.0	7	28	5.0	33	5.9	6.30	64	.296	.381	-13	-12	104	92	-0.5	0	-1	-1.2
■ **GREG HIBBARD**	Hibbard, James Gregory b: 9/13/64, New Orleans, La. BL/TL, 6', 180 lbs. Deb: 5/31/89																											
1989 Chi-A	6	7	.462	23	23	2	0	0	137	142	9.3	5	41	2.7	55	3.6	3.22	113	.268	.318	10	6	93	109	0.4	0	1	0.8
■ **KEVIN HICKEY**	Hickey, Kevin John b: 2/25/57, Chicago, Ill. BL/TL, 6'1", 170 lbs. Deb: 4/14/81																											
1981 Chi-A	0	2	.000	41	0	0	0	3	44	38	7.8	3	18	3.7	17	3.5	3.68	98	.232	.303	-0	-0	99	84	-0.9	0	1	0.0
1982 Chi-A	4	4	.500	60	0	0	0	6	78	73	8.4	4	30	3.5	38	4.4	3.00	132	.256	.321	9	8	97	121	-0.2	0	2	1.0
1983 Chi-A	1	2	.333	23	0	0	0	5	21	23	9.9	5	11	4.7	8	3.4	5.14	81	.264	.347	-2	-2	102	105	-0.6	0	0	-0.1
1989 Bal-A	2	3	.400	51	0	0	0	2	49	38	7.0	3	23	4.2	28	5.1	2.94	130	.220	.312	5	5	99	105	-0.6	0	-0	0.5
Total 4	7	11	.389	175	0	0	0	16	192	172	8.1	15	82	3.8	91	4.3	3.38	115	.243	.318	12	10	98	107	-2.3	0	3	1.4
■ **TEDDY HIGUERA**	Higuera, Teodoro Valenzuela (Valenzuela) b: 11/9/58, Los Mochis, Mexico BB/TL, 5'10", 178 lbs. Deb: 4/23/85																											
1985 Mil-A	15	8	.652	32	30	7	2	0	212	186	7.9	22	63	2.7	127	5.4	3.91	112	.235	.288	6	11	106	82	4.8	0	-3	0.9
1986 Mil-A	20	11	.645	34	34	15	4	0	248	226	8.2	26	74	2.7	207	7.5	2.79	154	.241	.294	38	42	103	119	5.7	0	-1	4.2
1987 Mil-A	18	10	.643	35	35	14	3	0	262	236	8.1	24	87	3.0	240	8.2	3.85	119	.241	.300	18	21	102	87	3.0	0	-2	1.8
1988 Mil-A	16	9	.640	31	31	8	1	0	227	168	6.7	15	59	2.3	192	7.6	2.46	166	.207	**.260**	**38**	41	103	90	3.2	0	1	4.6
1989 Mil-A	9	6	.600	22	22	2	1	0	135	125	8.3	9	48	3.2	91	6.1	3.47	108	.248	.312	6	4	96	99	1.6	0	-2	0.2
Total 5	78	44	.639	154	152	46	11	0	1084	941	7.8	96	331	2.7	857	7.1	3.28	130	.234	.290	107	119	102	95	18.3	0	-7	11.7
■ **KEN HILL**	Hill, Kenneth Wade b: 12/14/65, Lynn, Mass. BR/TR, 6'4", 200 lbs. Deb: 9/03/88																											
1988 StL-N	0	1	.000	4	1	0	0	0	14	16	10.3	0	6	3.9	6	3.9	5.14	70	.286	.355	-3	-2	105	79	-0.4	-0	0	-0.2
1989 StL-N	7	15	.318	33	33	2	1	0	197	186	8.5	9	99	4.5	112	5.1	3.79	93	.252	.336	-6	-6	100	101	-4.7	-0	0	-0.5
Total 2	7	16	.304	37	34	2	1	0	211	202	8.6	9	105	4.5	118	5.0	3.88	91	.254	.338	-9	-8	101	99	-5.1	-1	0	-0.7
■ **SHAWN HILLEGAS**	Hillegas, Shawn Patrick b: 8/21/64, Dos Palos, Cal. BR/TR, 6'3", 205 lbs. Deb: 8/09/87																											
1987 LA-N	4	3	.571	12	10	0	0	0	58	52	8.1	5	31	4.8	51	7.9	3.57	105	.241	.329	3	1	92	107	0.8	-1	-1	0.0
1988 LA-N	3	4	.429	11	10	0	0	0	57	54	8.5	5	17	2.7	30	4.7	4.11	88	.250	.310	-4	-3	105	87	-0.9	-0	-1	-0.3
Chi-A	3	2	.600	6	6	0	0	0	40	30	6.7	4	18	4.0	26	5.8	3.15	124	.207	.295	4	3	99	94	0.7	0	-0	0.3
1989 Chi-A	7	11	.389	50	13	0	0	3	120	132	9.9	12	51	3.8	76	5.7	4.72	77	.279	.349	-11	-15	93	98	-0.8	0	-1	-1.5
Total 3	17	20	.459	79	39	0	0	3	275	268	8.8	26	117	3.8	183	6.0	4.12	90	.255	.329	-8	-13	96	97	-0.2	-1	-3	-1.5
■ **BRIAN HOLMAN**	Holman, Brian Scott b: 1/25/65, Denver, Colo. BR/TR, 6'4", 185 lbs. Deb: 6/25/88																											
1988 Mon-N	4	8	.333	18	16	1	1	0	100	101	9.1	3	34	3.1	58	5.2	3.24	112	.264	.320	2	4	105	107	-2.0	-1	-1	0.2
1989 Mon-N	1	2	.333	10	3	0	0	0	32	34	9.6	2	15	4.2	23	6.5	4.78	75	.270	.345	-5	-4	102	90	-0.4	-0	-0	-0.4
Sea-A	8	10	.444	23	22	6	2	0	160	160	9.0	9	62	3.5	82	4.6	3.43	117	.261	.331	8	11	104	110	0.0	0	1	1.2
Total 2	13	20	.394	51	41	7	3	0	292	295	9.1	14	111	3.4	163	5.0	3.51	109	.263	.329	6	11	104	107	-2.4	-1	-1	1.0
■ **SHAWN HOLMAN**	Holman, Shawn Leroy b: 11/10/64, Sewickley, Pa. BR/TR, 6'2", 185 lbs. Deb: 9/05/89																											
1989 Det-A	0	0	—	5	0	0	0	0	10	8	7.2	0	11	9.9	9	8.1	1.80	214	.211	.380	2	2	99	214	0.0	0	0	0.2
■ **BRIAN HOLTON**	Holton, Brian John b: 11/29/59, Mc Keesport, Pa. BR/TR, 6'2", 190 lbs. Deb: 9/09/85																											
1985 LA-N	1	1	.500	3	0	0	0	0	4	9	20.3	0	1	2.3	1	2.3	9.00	37	.450	.476	-2	-3	92	102	0.0	0	0	-0.2
1986 LA-N	2	3	.400	12	3	0	0	0	24	28	10.5	1	6	2.3	24	9.0	4.50	78	.292	.330	-2	-3	95	91	-0.2	-0	0	-0.2
1987 LA-N	3	2	.600	53	1	0	0	2	83	87	9.4	11	32	3.5	58	6.3	3.90	96	.269	.331	2	-1	92	114	0.7	0	1	0.0
1988 LA-N	7	3	.700	45	0	0	0	1	85	69	7.3	1	26	2.8	49	5.2	1.69	214	.228	.283	17	18	105	145	1.5	-1	-0	1.9
1989 Bal-A	5	7	.417	39	12	0	0	0	116	140	10.9	11	39	3.0	51	4.0	4.03	95	.300	.350	-2	-3	99	121	-1.3	0	-0	-0.2
Total 5	18	16	.529	152	16	0	0	3	312	333	9.6	24	104	3.0	183	5.3	3.46	108	.276	.328	12	10	98	123	0.7	-1	1	1.3
■ **RICK HONEYCUTT**	Honeycutt, Frederick Wayne b: 6/29/52, Chattanooga, Tenn. BL/TL, 6'1", 185 lbs. Deb: 8/24/77																											
1977 Sea-A	0	1	.000	10	3	0	0	0	29	26	8.1	7	11	3.4	17	5.3	4.34	92	.239	.320	-1	-1	98	108	-0.4	0	-1	-0.1
1978 Sea-A	5	11	.313	26	24	4	1	0	134	150	10.1	12	49	3.3	50	3.4	4.90	80	.285	.340	-17	-14	104	91	-0.8	0	1	-1.2
1979 Sea-A	11	12	.478	33	28	8	1	0	194	201	9.3	22	67	3.1	83	3.9	4.04	106	.268	.327	4	5	101	105	1.5	0	-1	0.3
1980 Sea-A	10	17	.370	30	30	9	1	0	203	221	9.8	22	60	2.7	79	3.5	3.95	108	.280	.326	2	7	105	108	0.2	0	-0	0.6
1981 Tex-A	11	6	.647	20	20	8	2	0	128	120	8.4	12	17	**1.2**	40	2.8	3.30	100	.246	.269	5	-0	90	85	2.2	0	1	0.1
1982 Tex-A	5	17	.227	30	26	4	1	0	164	201	11.0	20	54	3.0	64	3.5	5.27	73	.305	.354	-22	-26	94	100	-5.0	0	1	-2.3
1983 Tex-A	14	8	.636	25	25	5	2	0	175	168	8.6	9	37	1.9	56	2.9	**2.42**	**170**	.262	.304	**32**	33	101	**140**	3.7	0	3	3.9
LA-N	2	3	.400	9	7	1	0	0	39	46	10.6	6	13	3.0	18	4.2	5.77	63	.297	.355	-9	-9	100	92	-0.6	-1	2	-0.7
1984 LA-N	10	9	.526	29	28	6	2	0	184	180	8.8	11	51	2.5	75	3.7	2.84	132	.258	.306	15	18	104	117	0.8	-1	2	2.2
1985 LA-N	8	12	.400	31	25	1	0	1	142	141	8.9	9	49	3.1	67	4.2	3.42	96	.261	.318	3	-2	92	105	-3.4	0	3	0.1
1986 LA-N	11	9	.550	32	28	0	0	0	171	164	8.6	9	45	2.4	100	5.3	3.32	106	.249	.297	8	4	95	90	2.0	0	2	0.6
1987 LA-N	2	12	.143	27	20	1	1	0	116	133	10.3	10	45	3.5	92	7.1	4.58	82	.278	.343	-6	-10	92	95	-4.8	2	-0	-0.8
Oak-A	1	4	.200	7	4	0	0	0	24	25	9.4	3	9	3.4	10	3.8	5.25	77	.275	.340	-2	-3	91	92	-1.4	0	-0	-0.2
1988 Oak-A	3	2	.600	55	0	0	0	7	80	74	8.3	6	25	2.8	47	5.3	3.49	106	.253	.309	4	2	93	104	-0.1	0	1	0.3
1989 Oak-A	2	2	.500	64	0	0	0	12	77	56	6.5	5	26	3.0	52	6.1	2.34	170	.207	.272	13	14	102	102	-0.3	0	1	1.5
Total 13	95	125	.432	428	268	47	11	20	1860	1906	9.2	163	558	2.7	850	4.1	3.76	102	.267	.318	30	16	98	104	-6.4	1	14	4.3
■ **RICKY HORTON**	Horton, Ricky Neal b: 7/30/59, Poughkeepsie, N.Y. BL/TL, 6'2", 195 lbs. Deb: 4/07/84																											
1984 StL-N	9	4	.692	37	18	1	1	1	126	140	10.0	14	39	2.8	76	5.4	3.43	103	.285	.335	2	2	99	132	2.5	-2	3	0.3
1985 StL-N	3	2	.600	49	3	0	0	1	90	84	8.4	5	34	3.4	59	5.9	2.90	116	.251	.317	7	5	93	120	0.0	-0	2	0.6
1986 StL-N	4	3	.571	42	9	1	0	3	100	77	6.9	7	26	2.3	49	4.4	2.25	171	.218	.269	16	18	103	108	0.6	0	2	2.1
1987 StL-N	8	3	.727	67	6	0	0	7	125	127	9.1	15	42	3.0	55	4.0	3.82	104	.263	.317	4	2	97	107	2.0	1	3	0.5
1988 Chi-A	6	10	.375	52	9	1	0	2	109	120	9.9	6	36	3.0	28	2.3	4.87	80	.291	.342	-11	-12	99	93	-1.2	0	1	-1.0
LA-N	1	1	.500	12	0	0	0	0	9	11	11.0	2	2	2.0	8	8.0	5.00	73	.306	.317	-2	-1	105	115	0.0	0	1	0.0
1989 LA-N	0	0	—	23	0	0	0	0	27	35	11.7	1	11	3.7	12	4.0	5.00	65	.343	.392	-4	-5	93	119	0.0	-0	0	-0.5
StL-N	0	3	.000	11	8	0	0	0	46	50	9.8	2	10	2.0	14	2.7	4.70	75	.282	.325	-6	-6	100	84	-1.4	1	0	-0.4
Yr	0	3	.000	34	8	0	0	0	73	85	10.5	3	21	2.6	26	3.2	4.81	71	.301	.347	-11	-11	97	84	-1.4	-0	0	-0.9
Total 6	31	26	.544	293	53	3	1	14	632	644	9.2	52	200	2.8	301	4.3	3.67	101	.270	.322	6	2	98	110	2.5	-0	11	1.6
■ **CHARLIE HOUGH**	Hough, Charles Oliver b: 1/5/48, Honolulu, Hawaii BR/TR, 6'2", 190 lbs. Deb: 8/12/70																											
1970 LA-N	0	0	—	8	0	0	0	2	17	18	9.5	7	11	5.8	8	4.2	5.29	68	.265	.367	-2	-3	89	136	0.0	0	0	-0.2
1971 LA-N	0	0	—	4	0	0	0	0	4	3	6.8	1	3	6.8	4	9.0	4.50	75	.200	.316	-0	-0	98	100	0.0	0	0	0.0
1972 LA-N	0	0	—	2	0	0	0	0	3	2	6.0	0	2	6.0	4	12.0	3.00	107	.200	.385	0	0	93	120	0.0	0	0	0.0
1973 LA-N	4	2	.667	37	0	0	0	5	72	52	6.5	3	45	5.6	70	8.8	2.75	132	.207	.333	7	7	99	114	0.6	0	0	0.8
1974 LA-N	9	4	.692	49	0	0	0	1	96	65	6.1	12	40	3.8	63	5.9	3.75	87	.196	.280	-1	-5	90	76	1.2	-1	-0	-0.6
1975 LA-N	3	7	.300	38	0	0	0	4	61	43	6.3	3	34	5.0	34	5.0	2.95	115	.195	.320	5	3	93	91	-2.2	1	-1	0.3
1976 LA-N	12	8	.600	77	0	0	0	18	143	102	6.4	6	77	4.8	81	5.1	2.20	157	.200	.312	**21**	**20**	99	120	0.8	2	-0	2.3
1977 LA-N	6	12	.333	70	1	0	0	22	127	98	6.9	10	70	5.0	105	7.4	3.33	115	.213	.318	8	7	98	96	-4.2	1	-0	0.7
1978 LA-N	5	5	.500	55	0	0	0	7	93	69	6.7	6	48	4.6	66	6.4	3.29	106	.205	.313	3	2	97	85	-0.7	1	-0	0.3
1979 LA-N	7	5	.583	42	14	0	0	0	151	152	9.1	16	66	3.9	76	4.5	4.77	78	.264	.341	-17	-18	99	91	1.2	-0	0	-1.7

YEAR	TM/L	W	L	PCT	G	GS	CG	SHO	SV	IP	H	H/G	HR	BB	BB/G	SO	SO/G	ERA	/A	OAVG	OOBP	PR	/A	PF	CPI	WAT	PB	PD	TPI
1980	LA-N	1	3	.250	19	1	0	0	1	32	37	10.4	4	21	5.9	25	7.0	5.63	61	.291	.385	-7	-8	96	104	-1.0	0	-0	-0.7
	Tex-A	2	2	.500	16	2	2	1	0	61	54	8.0	2	37	5.5	47	6.9	3.98	102	.240	.348	0	0	100	92	0.1	0	-0	0.0
1981	Tex-A	4	1	.800	21	5	2	0	1	82	61	6.7	4	31	3.4	69	7.6	2.96	111	.207	.288	6	3	90	80	1.4	0	-1	0.2
1982	Tex-A	16	13	.552	34	34	12	2	0	228	217	8.6	21	72	2.8	128	5.1	3.95	98	.251	.310	3	-2	94	90	4.3	0	1	-0.1
1983	Tex-A	15	13	.536	34	33	11	3	0	252	219	7.8	22	95	3.4	152	5.4	3.18	129	.238	.308	25	26	101	107	1.9	0	4	3.1
1984	Tex-A	16	14	.533	36	36	**17**	1	0	266	260	8.8	26	94	3.2	164	5.5	3.76	107	.255	.320	7	8	101	101	3.2	0	3	1.1
1985	Tex-A	14	16	.467	34	34	14	1	0	250	198	7.1	23	83	3.0	141	5.1	3.31	138	.215	.283	23	35	110	84	2.4	0	1	3.7
1986	Tex-A	17	10	.630	33	33	7	2	0	230	188	7.4	32	89	3.5	146	5.7	3.80	105	.221	.299	10	5	95	90	3.1	0	1	0.5
1987	Tex-A	18	13	.581	40	40	13	0	0	**285**	238	7.5	36	124	3.9	223	7.0	3.79	122	.223	.310	22	27	104	94	4.0	0	3	2.9
1988	Tex-A	15	16	.484	34	34	10	0	0	252	202	7.2	20	126	4.5	174	6.2	3.32	122	.221	.319	18	21	102	102	1.6	0	4	2.6
1989	Tex-A	10	13	.435	30	30	5	1	0	182	168	8.3	28	95	4.7	94	4.6	4.35	92	.245	.338	-9	-7	103	103	-1.9	0	-1	-0.8
Total	20	174	157	.526	713	297	93	11	61	2887	2446	7.6	282	1263	3.9	1874	5.8	3.60	110	.229	.314	122	118	100	96	15.8	4	12	14.4

■ JAY HOWELL Howell, Jay Canfield b: 11/26/55, Miami, Fla. BR/TR, 6'3", 200 lbs. Deb: 8/10/80

YEAR	TM/L	W	L	PCT	G	GS	CG	SHO	SV	IP	H	H/G	HR	BB	BB/G	SO	SO/G	ERA	/A	OAVG	OOBP	PR	/A	PF	CPI	WAT	PB	PD	TPI
1980	Cin-N	0	0	—	5	0	0	0	0	3	8	24.0	0	0	0.0	1	3.0	15.00	24	.471	.474	-4	-4	101	72	0.0	0	0	-0.3
1981	Chi-N	2	0	1.000	10	2	0	0	0	22	23	9.4	3	10	4.1	10	4.1	4.91	76	.277	.361	-3	-3	106	105	1.0	0	1	-0.1
1982	NY-A	2	3	.400	6	6	0	0	0	28	42	13.5	1	13	4.2	21	6.8	7.71	51	.341	.399	-11	-12	97	78	-0.4	0	-0	-1.0
1983	NY-A	1	5	.167	19	12	2	0	0	82	89	9.8	7	35	3.8	61	6.7	5.38	74	.275	.345	-12	-13	98	83	-2.0	0	0	-1.1
1984	NY-A	9	4	.692	61	1	0	0	7	104	86	7.4	5	34	2.9	109	9.4	2.68	139	.223	.282	15	12	93	91	2.3	0	2	1.4
1985	Oak-A	9	8	.529	63	0	0	0	29	98	98	9.0	5	31	2.8	68	6.2	2.85	136	.261	.314	14	11	93	124	1.0	0	0	1.1
1986	Oak-A	3	6	.333	38	0	0	0	16	53	53	9.0	3	23	3.9	42	7.1	3.40	116	.262	.335	5	3	94	115	-1.3	0	-0	0.3
1987	Oak-A	3	4	.429	36	0	0	0	16	44	48	9.8	6	21	4.3	35	7.2	5.93	69	.277	.350	-7	-9	91	85	-0.4	0	-0	-0.8
1988	LA-N	5	3	.625	50	0	0	0	21	65	44	6.1	1	21	2.9	70	9.7	2.08	175	.188	.252	10	11	105	72	0.4	-0	0	1.2
1989	LA-N	5	3	.625	56	0	0	0	28	80	60	6.7	3	22	2.5	55	6.2	1.57	206	.211	.263	17	15	93	134	1.1	-0	0	1.6
Total	10	39	36	.520	344	21	2	0	117	579	551	8.6	34	210	3.3	472	7.3	3.58	105	.250	.313	24	13	96	101	1.7	-0	2	2.3

■ KEN HOWELL Howell, Kenneth b: 11/28/60, Detroit, Mich. BR/TR, 6'3", 200 lbs. Deb: 6/25/84

YEAR	TM/L	W	L	PCT	G	GS	CG	SHO	SV	IP	H	H/G	HR	BB	BB/G	SO	SO/G	ERA	/A	OAVG	OOBP	PR	/A	PF	CPI	WAT	PB	PD	TPI
1984	LA-N	5	5	.500	32	1	0	0	6	51	51	9.0	1	9	1.6	54	9.5	3.35	111	.267	.295	1	2	104	90	0.1	-1	0	0.2
1985	LA-N	4	7	.364	56	0	0	0	12	86	66	6.9	8	35	3.7	85	8.9	3.77	88	.208	.284	-2	-4	92	70	-2.1	-0	0	-0.4
1986	LA-N	6	12	.333	62	0	0	0	12	98	86	7.9	7	63	5.8	104	9.6	3.86	91	.239	.348	-1	-4	95	105	-2.5	-0	-1	-0.5
1987	LA-N	3	4	.429	40	2	0	0	1	55	54	8.8	7	29	4.7	60	9.8	4.91	77	.265	.347	-5	-7	92	97	-0.1	0	0	-0.6
1988	LA-N	0	1	.000	4	1	0	0	0	13	16	11.1	0	4	2.8	12	8.3	6.23	58	.320	.364	-4	-4	105	75	-0.4	-0	-0	-0.3
1989	Phi-N	12	12	.500	33	32	1	1	0	204	155	6.8	11	86	3.8	164	7.2	3.44	104	.215	.294	1	3	102	80	2.0	-2	-1	0.0
Total	6	30	41	.423	227	36	1	1	31	507	428	7.6	34	226	4.0	479	8.5	3.80	94	.232	.311	-9	-13	98	86	-3.0	-3	-2	-1.6

■ CHARLES HUDSON Hudson, Charles Lynn b: 3/16/58, Ennis, Tex. BB/TR, 6'3", 185 lbs. Deb: 5/31/83

YEAR	TM/L	W	L	PCT	G	GS	CG	SHO	SV	IP	H	H/G	HR	BB	BB/G	SO	SO/G	ERA	/A	OAVG	OOBP	PR	/A	PF	CPI	WAT	PB	PD	TPI
1983	Phi-N	8	8	.500	26	26	3	0	0	169	158	8.4	13	53	2.8	101	5.4	3.36	109	.248	.301	5	5	100	95	-0.8	-2	-1	0.3
1984	Phi-N	9	11	.450	30	30	1	1	0	174	181	9.4	12	52	2.7	94	4.9	4.03	90	.265	.314	-9	-8	101	90	-1.0	-2	-2	-1.1
1985	Phi-N	8	13	.381	38	26	3	0	0	193	188	8.8	23	74	3.5	122	5.7	3.78	97	.252	.316	-4	-2	102	102	-2.0	-1	-2	-0.4
1986	Phi-N	7	10	.412	33	23	0	0	0	144	165	10.3	20	58	3.6	82	5.1	4.94	78	.291	.350	-19	-17	104	104	-2.0	-3	-0	-2.0
1987	NY-A	11	7	.611	35	16	6	2	0	155	137	8.0	19	57	3.3	100	5.8	3.60	121	.239	.307	15	13	97	103	1.4	0	-1	1.1
1988	NY-A	6	6	.500	28	12	1	0	2	106	93	7.9	9	36	3.1	58	4.9	4.50	84	.235	.298	-6	-8	96	73	-0.2	0	-0	-0.8
1989	Det-A	1	5	.167	18	7	0	0	0	67	75	10.1	14	31	4.2	23	3.1	6.31	61	.288	.364	-18	-18	99	93	-1.6	0	-1	-1.7
Total	7	50	60	.455	208	140	14	3	2	1008	997	8.9	110	361	3.2	580	5.2	4.13	93	.258	.318	-36	-34	100	95	-6.2	-9	-7	-4.6

■ MARK HUISMANN Huismann, Mark Lawrence b: 5/11/58, Littleton, Colo. BR/TR, 6'3", 195 lbs. Deb: 8/16/83

YEAR	TM/L	W	L	PCT	G	GS	CG	SHO	SV	IP	H	H/G	HR	BB	BB/G	SO	SO/G	ERA	/A	OAVG	OOBP	PR	/A	PF	CPI	WAT	PB	PD	TPI
1983	KC-A	2	1	.667	13	0	0	0	0	31	29	8.4	1	17	4.9	20	5.8	5.52	75	.250	.341	-5	-5	102	67	0.5	0	-0	-0.4
1984	KC-A	3	3	.500	38	0	0	0	3	75	84	10.1	7	21	2.5	54	6.5	4.20	95	.286	.327	-2	-2	99	103	0.0	0	0	-0.1
1985	KC-A	1	0	1.000	9	0	0	0	0	19	14	6.6	1	3	1.4	9	4.3	1.89	222	.219	.243	5	5	101	119	0.5	0	0	0.5
1986	KC-A	0	1	.000	10	0	0	0	1	17	18	9.5	1	6	3.2	13	6.9	4.24	99	.269	.324	-0	-0	100	89	-0.4	0	0	0.0
	Sea-A	3	3	.500	36	1	0	0	4	80	80	9.0	18	19	2.1	59	6.6	3.71	120	.256	.299	4	7	106	119	0.5	0	0	0.6
	Yr	3	4	.429	46	1	0	0	5	97	98	9.1	19	25	2.3	72	6.7	3.80	116	.258	.304	4	6	105	119	0.1	0	0	0.6
1987	Sea-A	0	0	—	6	0	0	0	0	15	10	6.0	1	4	2.4	15	9.0	4.80	96	.196	.262	-1	-0	103	51	0.0	0	0	0.0
	Cle-A	2	3	.400	20	0	0	0	2	35	38	9.8	6	8	2.1	23	5.9	5.14	91	.271	.305	-3	-2	105	85	0.1	0	-0	-0.1
	Yr	2	3	.400	26	0	0	0	2	50	48	8.6	7	12	2.2	38	6.8	5.04	92	.247	.283	-3	-2	104	85	0.1	0	0	-0.1
1988	Det-A	1	0	1.000	5	0	0	0	0	5	6	10.8	0	2	3.6	6	10.8	5.40	69	.286	.348	-1	-1	94	72	0.5	0	0	0.0
1989	Bal-A	0	0	—	8	0	0	0	1	11	13	10.6	0	0	0.0	13	10.6	6.55	59	.277	.271	-3	-3	99	37	0.0	0	1	-0.2
Total	7	12	11	.522	145	1	0	0	11	288	292	9.1	35	80	2.5	212	6.6	4.31	99	.263	.308	-5	-2	102	96	1.7	0	1	0.3

■ BRUCE HURST Hurst, Bruce Vee b: 3/24/58, St.George, Utah BL/TL, 6'4", 200 lbs. Deb: 4/12/80

YEAR	TM/L	W	L	PCT	G	GS	CG	SHO	SV	IP	H	H/G	HR	BB	BB/G	SO	SO/G	ERA	/A	OAVG	OOBP	PR	/A	PF	CPI	WAT	PB	PD	TPI
1980	Bos-A	2	2	.500	12	7	0	0	0	31	39	11.3	4	16	4.6	16	4.6	9.00	46	.307	.388	-17	-17	102	66	0.0	0	-0	-1.5
1981	Bos-A	2	0	1.000	5	5	0	0	0	23	23	9.0	1	12	4.7	11	4.3	4.30	90	.258	.346	-2	-1	106	91	1.0	0	-0	-0.1
1982	Bos-A	3	7	.300	28	19	0	0	0	117	161	12.4	16	40	3.1	53	4.1	5.77	78	.333	.381	-22	-17	110	108	-2.2	0	1	-1.4
1983	Bos-A	12	12	.500	33	32	6	2	0	211	241	10.3	22	62	2.6	115	4.9	4.09	101	.290	.339	-0	1	102	113	0.5	0	1	0.2
1984	Bos-A	12	12	.500	33	33	9	2	0	218	232	9.6	25	88	3.6	136	5.6	3.92	112	.271	.340	2	11	110	113	-0.7	0	0	1.2
1985	Bos-A	11	13	.458	35	31	6	1	0	229	243	9.6	31	70	2.8	189	7.4	4.52	93	.273	.325	-9	-8	102	99	-1.1	0	0	-0.7
1986	Bos-A	13	8	.619	25	25	11	4	0	174	169	8.7	18	50	2.6	167	8.6	3.00	138	.256	.308	23	22	99	**123**	0.8	0	-1	2.1
1987	Bos-A	15	13	.536	33	33	15	3	0	239	239	9.0	35	76	2.9	190	7.2	4.41	100	.262	.316	2	0	99	97	1.7	0	0	0.0
1988	Bos-A	18	6	.750	33	32	7	1	0	217	222	9.2	21	65	2.7	166	6.9	3.65	117	.264	.313	8	15	108	106	5.8	0	0	1.6
1989	SD-N	15	11	.577	33	33	**10**	2	0	245	214	7.9	16	66	2.4	179	6.6	2.68	131	.237	.283	22	23	101	108	0.9	-2	1	2.5
Total	10	103	84	.551	270	250	64	15	0	1704	1783	9.4	189	545	2.9	1222	6.5	4.01	104	.270	.324	6	31	103	107	6.7	-2	3	3.9

■ JEFF INNIS Innis, Jeffrey David b: 7/5/62, Decatur, Ill. BR/TR, 6'1", 170 lbs. Deb: 5/16/87

YEAR	TM/L	W	L	PCT	G	GS	CG	SHO	SV	IP	H	H/G	HR	BB	BB/G	SO	SO/G	ERA	/A	OAVG	OOBP	PR	/A	PF	CPI	WAT	PB	PD	TPI
1987	NY-N	0	1	.000	17	1	0	0	0	26	29	10.0	5	4	1.4	28	9.7	3.12	127	.279	.312	3	2	97	148	-0.4	-0	0	0.2
1988	NY-N	1	1	.500	12	0	0	0	0	19	19	9.0	0	2	0.9	14	6.6	1.89	160	.250	.262	3	2	88	113	-0.1	0	-1	0.2
1989	NY-N	0	1	.000	29	0	0	0	0	40	38	8.5	2	8	1.8	16	3.6	3.15	106	.255	.294	2	1	95	99	-0.4	-0	1	0.1
Total	3	1	3	.250	58	1	0	0	0	85	86	9.1	7	14	1.5	58	6.1	2.86	121	.261	.292	8	6	94	117	-0.9	-1	0	0.5

■ DANNY JACKSON Jackson, Danny Lynn b: 1/5/62, San Antonio, Tex. BR/TL, 6', 205 lbs. Deb: 9/11/83

YEAR	TM/L	W	L	PCT	G	GS	CG	SHO	SV	IP	H	H/G	HR	BB	BB/G	SO	SO/G	ERA	/A	OAVG	OOBP	PR	/A	PF	CPI	WAT	PB	PD	TPI
1983	KC-A	1	1	.500	4	3	0	0	0	19	26	12.3	1	6	2.8	9	4.3	5.21	80	.325	.368	-2	-2	102	101	0.0	0	0	-0.1
1984	KC-A	2	6	.250	15	11	1	0	0	76	84	9.9	4	35	4.1	40	4.7	4.26	93	.285	.367	-2	-2	99	109	-2.0	0	-0	-0.2
1985	KC-A	14	12	.538	32	32	4	3	0	208	209	9.0	7	76	3.3	114	4.9	3.42	123	.261	.326	17	18	101	104	-0.5	0	-1	1.7
1986	KC-A	11	12	.478	32	27	4	1	1	186	177	8.6	13	79	3.8	115	5.6	3.19	131	.256	.330	21	21	100	121	0.2	0	-1	2.0
1987	KC-A	9	18	.333	36	34	11	2	0	224	219	8.8	11	109	4.4	152	6.1	4.02	116	.258	.341	11	16	104	98	-5.2	0	-2	1.3
1988	Cin-N	**23**	8	.742	35	35	**15**	6	0	261	206	7.1	13	71	2.4	161	5.6	2.72	133	.218	.270	21	26	105	87	7.6	-0	2	3.1
1989	Cin-N	6	11	.353	20	20	1	0	0	116	122	9.5	10	57	4.4	70	5.4	5.59	65	.271	.347	-27	-25	104	81	-2.1	1	-1	-2.4
Total	7	66	68	.493	174	162	36	12	1	1090	1043	8.6	59	433	3.6	661	5.5	3.66	111	.254	.323	38	51	103	99	-2.0	1	-3	5.4

■ MICHAEL JACKSON Jackson, Michael Ray b: 12/22/64, Houston, Tex. BR/TR, 6'1", 185 lbs. Deb: 8/11/86

YEAR	TM/L	W	L	PCT	G	GS	CG	SHO	SV	IP	H	H/G	HR	BB	BB/G	SO	SO/G	ERA	/A	OAVG	OOBP	PR	/A	PF	CPI	WAT	PB	PD	TPI
1986	Phi-N	0	0	—	9	0	0	0	0	13	12	8.3	2	4	2.8	3	2.1	3.46	112	.250	.333	0	1	104	126	0.0	0	-0	0.0
1987	Phi-N	3	10	.231	55	7	0	0	1	109	88	7.3	16	56	4.6	93	7.7	4.21	101	.219	.314	-2	1	105	88	-3.5	-0	-1	0.0
1988	Sea-A	6	5	.545	62	0	0	0	4	99	74	6.7	10	43	3.9	76	6.9	2.64	163	.209	.289	15	18	108	115	1.2	0	-0	1.8
1989	Sea-A	4	6	.400	65	0	0	0	7	99	81	7.4	8	54	4.9	94	8.5	3.18	127	.223	.327	8	9	104	111	-0.5	0	-1	0.9
Total	4	13	21	.382	191	7	0	0	12	320	255	7.2	36	157	4.4	266	7.5	3.37	124	.219	.311	21	29	105	105	-2.8	-0	-2	2.7

■ MIKE JEFFCOAT Jeffcoat, James Michael b: 8/3/59, Pine Bluff, Ark. BL/TL, 6'2", 187 lbs. Deb: 8/21/83

YEAR	TM/L	W	L	PCT	G	GS	CG	SHO	SV	IP	H	H/G	HR	BB	BB/G	SO	SO/G	ERA	/A	OAVG	OOBP	PR	/A	PF	CPI	WAT	PB	PD	TPI
1983	Cle-A	1	3	.250	11	2	0	0	0	33	32	8.7	1	13	3.5	9	2.5	3.27	132	.256	.329	3	4	106	106	-0.8	0	-0	0.4
1984	Cle-A	5	2	.714	63	1	0	0	1	75	82	9.8	7	24	2.9	41	4.9	3.00	141	.281	.327	8	10	106	144	1.7	0	1	1.1
1985	Cle-A	0	0	—	9	0	0	0	0	10	8	7.2	1	6	5.4	4	3.6	2.70	146	.235	.318	2	1	95	157	0.0	0	1	0.2

YEAR	TM/L	W	L	PCT	G	GS	CG	SHO	SV	IP	H	H/G	HR	BB	BB/G	SO	SO/G	ERA	/A	OAVG	OOBP	PR	/A	PF	CPI	WAT	PB	PD	TPI
	SF-N	0	2	.000	19	1	0	0	0	22	27	11.0	4	6	2.5	10	4.1	5.32	64	.307	.354	-4	-5	95	109	-0.9	0	1	-0.3
1987	Tex-A	0	1	.000	2	2	0	0	0	7	11	14.1	4	4	5.1	1	1.3	12.86	36	.355	.429	-7	-6	104	85	-0.4	0	-0	-0.5
1988	Tex-A	0	2	.000	5	2	0	0	0	10	19	17.1	1	5	4.5	5	4.5	11.70	35	.432	.500	-9	-8	102	87	-0.9	0	0	-0.7
1989	Tex-A	9	6	.600	22	22	2	2	0	131	139	9.5	7	33	2.3	64	4.4	3.57	112	.270	.315	5	6	103	100	1.5	0	0	0.6
Total	6	15	16	.484	131	30	2	2	1	288	318	9.9	25	91	2.8	134	4.2	4.00	102	.282	.334	-2	2	103	114	0.2	0	2	0.8

■ **TOMMY JOHN** John, Thomas Edward b: 5/22/43, Terre Haute, Ind. BR/TL, 6'3", 180 lbs. Deb: 9/06/63

YEAR	TM/L	W	L	PCT	G	GS	CG	SHO	SV	IP	H	H/G	HR	BB	BB/G	SO	SO/G	ERA	/A	OAVG	OOBP	PR	/A	PF	CPI	WAT	PB	PD	TPI
1963	Cle-A	0	2	.000	6	3	0	0	0	20	23	10.3	1	6	2.7	9	4.0	2.25	158	.284	.319	3	3	98	176	-0.9	-1	0	0.2
1964	Cle-A	2	9	.182	25	14	2	1	0	94	97	9.3	10	35	3.4	65	6.2	3.93	95	.262	.320	-3	-2	103	100	-3.4	0	1	-0.1
1965	Chi-A	14	7	.667	39	27	6	1	3	184	162	7.9	12	58	2.8	126	6.2	3.08	102	.237	.295	8	1	91	95	2.3	2	3	0.6
1966	Chi-A	14	11	.560	34	33	10	**5**	0	223	195	7.9	13	57	2.3	138	5.6	2.62	122	.235	.287	20	14	93	108	1.4	2	1	1.9
1967	Chi-A	10	13	.435	31	29	9	**6**	0	178	143	7.2	12	47	2.4	110	5.6	2.48	121	.219	.273	15	10	93	101	-2.6	-0	6	1.8
1968	Chi-A	10	5	.667	25	25	5	1	0	177	135	6.9	10	49	2.5	117	5.9	1.98	153	.212	.278	20	21	102	119	3.4	2	6	3.6
1969	Chi-A	9	11	.450	33	33	6	2	0	232	230	8.9	16	90	3.5	128	5.0	3.26	122	.261	.326	10	19	110	114	0.6	-2	7	2.6
1970	Chi-A	12	17	.414	37	37	10	3	0	269	253	8.5	19	101	3.4	138	4.6	3.28	122	.251	.320	13	22	108	107	1.8	1	4	3.0
1971	Chi-A	13	16	.448	38	35	10	3	0	229	244	9.6	17	58	2.3	131	5.1	3.62	93	.274	.315	-4	-6	97	102	-1.3	-1	-1	-0.8
1972	LA-N	11	5	.688	29	29	4	1	0	187	172	8.3	14	40	1.9	117	5.6	2.89	111	.244	.281	12	7	93	99	2.7	-1	4	1.0
1973	LA-N	16	7	**.696**	36	31	4	2	0	218	202	8.3	16	50	2.1	116	4.8	3.10	117	.246	.288	14	13	99	95	3.3	2	7	2.3
1974	LA-N	13	3	.813	22	22	5	3	0	153	133	7.8	4	42	2.5	78	4.6	2.59	126	.235	.286	18	11	90	92	4.2	-1	2	1.2
1976	LA-N	10	10	.500	31	31	6	2	0	207	207	9.0	7	61	2.7	91	4.0	3.09	112	.261	.309	10	9	99	104	-1.2	-2	-1	0.6
1977	LA-N	20	7	.741	31	31	11	3	0	220	225	9.2	12	50	2.0	123	5.0	2.78	138	.267	.307	28	26	98	120	5.2	1	2	3.1
1978	LA-N	17	10	.630	33	30	7	0	1	213	230	9.7	11	53	2.2	124	5.2	3.30	105	.271	.316	7	4	97	106	1.7	-1	2	0.5
1979	NY-A	21	9	.700	37	36	17	3	0	276	268	8.7	9	65	2.1	111	3.6	2.97	135	.260	.302	**39**	32	95	104	5.6	0	2	3.4
1980	NY-A	22	9	.710	36	36	16	**6**	0	265	270	9.2	13	56	1.9	78	2.6	3.43	115	.268	.305	18	15	98	96	3.7	0	1	1.6
1981	NY-A	9	8	.529	20	20	7	0	0	140	135	8.7	10	39	2.5	50	3.2	2.64	137	.256	.305	16	15	99	128	-0.3	0	1	1.8
1982	NY-A	10	10	.500	30	26	9	2	0	187	190	9.1	11	34	1.6	54	2.6	3.66	108	.266	.296	9	6	97	90	0.3	0	2	0.7
	Cal-A	4	2	.667	7	7	1	0	0	35	49	12.6	4	5	1.3	14	3.6	3.86	104	.336	.355	1	1	99	143	0.7	0	1	0.1
	Yr	14	12	.538	37	33	10	2	0	222	239	9.7	15	39	**1.6**	68	2.8	3.69	107	.274	.303	10	7	97	143	1.0	0	2	0.8
1983	Cal-A	11	13	.458	34	34	9	0	0	235	287	11.0	20	49	1.9	65	2.5	4.33	91	.304	.335	-7	-11	96	107	0.6	0	1	-0.9
1984	Cal-A	7	13	.350	32	29	4	1	0	181	223	11.1	15	56	2.8	47	2.3	4.52	90	.306	.355	-11	-9	101	109	-3.2	0	0	-0.8
1985	Cal-A	2	4	.333	12	6	0	0	0	38	51	12.1	3	15	3.6	17	4.0	4.74	88	.329	.381	-2	-2	101	125	-1.1	0	1	0.0
	Oak-A	2	6	.250	11	11	0	0	0	48	66	12.4	6	13	2.4	8	1.5	6.19	62	.332	.362	-11	-12	93	97	-1.8	0	1	-1.0
	Yr	4	10	.286	23	17	0	0	0	86	117	12.2	9	28	2.9	25	2.6	5.55	72	.328	.368	-13	-15	96	97	-2.9	0	2	-1.0
1986	NY-A	5	3	.625	13	10	1	0	0	71	73	9.3	8	15	1.9	28	3.5	2.92	147	.275	.310	10	11	103	142	0.7	0	1	1.2
1987	NY-A	13	6	.684	33	33	3	1	0	188	212	10.1	12	47	2.3	63	3.0	4.02	108	.288	.330	9	7	97	105	3.1	0	-1	0.5
1988	NY-A	9	8	.529	35	32	0	0	0	176	221	11.3	11	46	2.4	81	4.1	4.50	84	.308	.352	-10	-14	96	107	0.0	0	2	-1.1
1989	NY-A	2	7	.222	10	10	0	0	0	64	87	12.2	6	22	3.1	18	2.5	5.77	71	.336	.386	-13	-12	105	105	-2.3	0	2	-0.9
Total	26	288	231	.555	760	700	162	46	4	4708	4783	9.1	302	1259	2.4	2245	4.3	3.34	110	.265	.312	216	178	98	106	23.2	1	56	26.1

■ **DAVE JOHNSON** Johnson, David Wayne b: 10/24/59, Baltimore, Md. BR/TR, 5'10", 180 lbs. Deb: 5/29/87

YEAR	TM/L	W	L	PCT	G	GS	CG	SHO	SV	IP	H	H/G	HR	BB	BB/G	SO	SO/G	ERA	/A	OAVG	OOBP	PR	/A	PF	CPI	WAT	PB	PD	TPI
1987	Pit-N	0	0	—	5	0	0	0	0	6	13	19.5	1	2	3.0	4	6.0	10.50	41	.448	.484	-4	-4	105	100	0.0	0	0	-0.3
1989	Bal-A	4	7	.364	14	14	4	0	0	89	90	9.1	11	28	2.8	26	2.6	4.25	90	.265	.323	-4	-4	99	99	-1.8	0	-2	-0.5
Total	2	4	7	.364	19	14	4	0	0	95	103	9.8	12	30	2.8	30	2.8	4.64	83	.279	.335	-8	-8	99	99	-1.8	0	-2	-0.8

■ **RANDY JOHNSON** Johnson, Randall David b: 9/10/63, Walnut Creek, Cal. BL/TR, 6'10", 225 lbs. Deb: 9/15/88

YEAR	TM/L	W	L	PCT	G	GS	CG	SHO	SV	IP	H	H/G	HR	BB	BB/G	SO	SO/G	ERA	/A	OAVG	OOBP	PR	/A	PF	CPI	WAT	PB	PD	TPI
1988	Mon-N	3	0	1.000	4	4	1	0	0	26	23	8.0	3	7	2.4	25	8.7	2.42	150	.225	.275	3	3	105	117	1.5	-0	-1	0.2
1989	Mon-N	0	4	.000	7	6	0	0	0	30	29	8.7	2	26	7.8	26	7.8	6.60	54	.264	.385	-10	-10	102	80	-1.9	-0	0	-0.9
	Sea-A	7	9	.438	22	22	2	0	0	131	118	8.1	11	70	4.8	104	7.1	4.40	92	.244	.334	-7	-5	104	90	-0.2	0	0	-0.4
Total	2	10	13	.435	33	32	3	0	0	187	170	8.2	16	103	5.0	155	7.5	4.48	87	.245	.335	-15	-12	104	92	-0.6	-1	-1	-1.1

■ **BARRY JONES** Jones, Barry Louis b: 2/15/63, Centerville, Ind. BR/TR, 6'2", 215 lbs. Deb: 7/18/86

YEAR	TM/L	W	L	PCT	G	GS	CG	SHO	SV	IP	H	H/G	HR	BB	BB/G	SO	SO/G	ERA	/A	OAVG	OOBP	PR	/A	PF	CPI	WAT	PB	PD	TPI
1986	Pit-N	3	4	.429	26	0	0	0	3	37	29	7.1	3	21	5.1	29	7.1	2.92	128	.215	.314	3	3	101	109	0.2	0	1	0.4
1987	Pit-N	2	4	.333	32	0	0	0	1	43	55	11.5	6	23	4.8	28	5.9	5.65	76	.314	.384	-7	-7	105	110	-0.9	-0	0	-0.5
1988	Pit-N	1	1	.500	42	0	0	0	2	56	57	9.2	3	21	3.4	31	5.0	3.05	110	.271	.328	2	2	97	132	0.0	-0	0	0.1
	Chi-A	2	2	.500	17	0	0	0	1	26	15	5.2	3	17	5.9	17	5.9	2.42	162	.170	.302	4	4	99	120	0.2	0	0	0.5
1989	Chi-A	3	2	.600	22	0	0	0	1	30	22	6.6	2	8	2.4	17	5.1	2.40	151	.208	.256	5	4	93	95	0.8	0	1	0.5
Total	4	11	13	.458	139	0	0	0	8	192	178	8.3	17	90	4.2	122	5.7	3.42	110	.249	.325	8	7	99	115	0.3	-0	2	1.0

■ **DOUG JONES** Jones, Douglas Reid b: 6/24/57, Lebanon, Ind. BR/TR, 6'3", 195 lbs. Deb: 4/09/82

YEAR	TM/L	W	L	PCT	G	GS	CG	SHO	SV	IP	H	H/G	HR	BB	BB/G	SO	SO/G	ERA	/A	OAVG	OOBP	PR	/A	PF	CPI	WAT	PB	PD	TPI
1982	Mil-A	0	0	—	4	0	0	0	0	3	5	15.0	1	1	3.0	1	3.0	9.00	42	.385	.429	-2	-2	92	103	0.0	0	0	-0.1
1986	Cle-A	1	0	1.000	11	0	0	0	1	18	18	9.0	0	6	3.0	12	6.0	2.50	164	.257	.316	3	3	98	124	0.5	0	0	0.4
1987	Cle-A	6	5	.545	49	0	0	0	8	91	101	10.0	4	24	2.4	87	8.6	3.16	148	.281	.327	13	15	105	125	1.6	0	1	1.5
1988	Cle-A	3	4	.429	51	0	0	0	37	83	69	7.5	1	16	1.7	72	7.8	2.28	178	.218	.257	16	16	102	75	-0.3	0	0	1.7
1989	Cle-A	7	10	.412	59	0	0	0	32	81	76	8.4	4	13	1.4	65	7.2	2.33	174	.251	.272	14	15	104	119	-0.7	0	1	1.7
Total	5	17	19	.472	174	0	0	0	78	276	269	8.8	10	60	2.0	237	7.7	2.67	159	.253	.292	45	49	103	108	1.1	0	2	5.2

■ **JIMMY JONES** Jones, James Condia b: 4/20/64, Dallas, Tex. BR/TR, 6'2", 175 lbs. Deb: 9/21/86

YEAR	TM/L	W	L	PCT	G	GS	CG	SHO	SV	IP	H	H/G	HR	BB	BB/G	SO	SO/G	ERA	/A	OAVG	OOBP	PR	/A	PF	CPI	WAT	PB	PD	TPI
1986	SD-N	2	0	1.000	3	3	1	1	0	18	10	5.0	1	3	1.5	15	7.5	2.50	143	.164	.200	2	2	96	33	1.0	-0	0	0.2
1987	SD-N	9	7	.563	30	22	2	1	0	146	154	9.5	14	54	3.3	51	3.1	4.13	97	.270	.333	-1	-2	98	103	2.3	1	1	0.0
1988	SD-N	9	14	.391	29	29	3	0	0	179	192	9.7	14	44	2.2	82	4.1	4.12	81	.277	.314	-13	-15	97	96	-3.0	2	1	-1.2
1989	NY-A	2	1	.667	11	6	0	0	0	48	56	10.5	7	16	3.0	25	4.7	5.25	78	.293	.351	-7	-6	105	99	0.6	0	1	-0.4
Total	4	22	22	.500	73	60	6	2	0	391	412	9.5	36	117	2.7	173	4.0	4.19	88	.272	.322	-19	-22	98	96	0.9	3	4	-1.4

■ **JEFF KAISER** Kaiser, Jeffrey Patrick b: 7/24/60, Wyandotte, Mich. BR/TL, 6'3", 195 lbs. Deb: 4/11/85

YEAR	TM/L	W	L	PCT	G	GS	CG	SHO	SV	IP	H	H/G	HR	BB	BB/G	SO	SO/G	ERA	/A	OAVG	OOBP	PR	/A	PF	CPI	WAT	PB	PD	TPI
1985	Oak-A	0	0	—	15	0	0	0	0	17	25	13.2	6	20	10.6	10	5.3	14.29	27	.342	.474	-19	-20	93	75	0.0	0	1	-1.7
1987	Cle-A	0	0	—	2	0	0	0	0	3	4	12.0	1	3	9.0	2	6.0	18.00	26	.286	.444	-5	-4	105	49	0.0	0	0	-0.3
1988	Cle-A	0	0	—	3	0	0	0	0	3	2	6.0	0	1	3.0	0	0.0	0.00	—	.286	.273	1	1	102	0	0.0	0	0	0.2
1989	Cle-A	0	1	.000	6	0	0	0	0	4	5	11.3	1	5	11.3	4	9.0	6.75	60	.313	.455	-1	-1	104	133	-0.4	0	0	0.0
Total	4	0	1	.000	26	0	0	0	0	27	36	12.0	8	29	9.7	16	5.3	12.00	33	.327	.453	-24	-24	97	72	-0.4	0	1	-1.8

■ **JIMMY KEY** Key, James Edward b: 4/22/61, Huntsville, Ala. BR/TL, 6'1", 185 lbs. Deb: 4/06/84

YEAR	TM/L	W	L	PCT	G	GS	CG	SHO	SV	IP	H	H/G	HR	BB	BB/G	SO	SO/G	ERA	/A	OAVG	OOBP	PR	/A	PF	CPI	WAT	PB	PD	TPI
1984	Tor-A	4	5	.444	63	0	0	0	10	62	70	10.2	8	32	4.6	44	6.4	4.65	87	.286	.361	-4	-4	101	113	-0.8	0	1	-0.2
1985	Tor-A	14	6	.700	35	32	3	0	0	213	188	7.9	22	50	2.1	85	3.6	3.00	137	.237	.280	27	26	99	103	2.4	0	4	3.2
1986	Tor-A	14	11	.560	36	35	4	2	0	232	222	8.6	24	74	2.9	141	5.5	3.57	122	.256	.312	16	21	104	107	0.9	0	3	2.4
1987	Tor-A	17	8	.680	36	36	8	1	0	261	210	**7.2**	24	66	2.3	161	5.6	**2.76**	**161**	**.221**	**.269**	**50**	**49**	99	96	3.1	0	2	**5.1**
1988	Tor-A	12	5	.706	21	21	2	2	0	131	127	8.7	13	30	2.1	65	4.5	3.30	119	.250	.294	10	9	99	102	3.3	0	0	0.9
1989	Tor-A	13	14	.481	33	33	5	1	0	216	226	9.4	18	27	**1.1**	118	4.9	3.88	94	.270	.289	0	-6	93	88	-1.9	0	2	-0.3
Total	6	74	49	.602	224	157	22	6	10	1115	1043	8.4	109	279	2.3	614	5.0	3.36	123	.248	.293	99	94	99	100	7.0	0	12	11.1

■ **PAUL KILGUS** Kilgus, Paul Nelson b: 2/2/62, Bowling Green, Ky. BL/TL, 6'1", 175 lbs. Deb: 6/07/87

YEAR	TM/L	W	L	PCT	G	GS	CG	SHO	SV	IP	H	H/G	HR	BB	BB/G	SO	SO/G	ERA	/A	OAVG	OOBP	PR	/A	PF	CPI	WAT	PB	PD	TPI
1987	Tex-A	2	7	.222	25	12	0	0	0	89	95	9.6	14	31	3.1	42	4.2	4.15	112	.271	.332	3	5	104	113	-2.3	0	-1	0.4
1988	Tex-A	12	15	.444	32	32	5	3	0	203	190	8.4	18	71	3.1	88	3.9	4.17	98	.243	.311	-4	-2	102	84	0.3	0	1	-0.1
1989	Chi-N	6	10	.375	35	23	0	0	2	146	164	10.1	9	49	3.0	61	3.8	4.38	86	.283	.340	-14	-10	107	98	-2.9	-3	0	-1.2
Total	3	20	32	.385	92	67	5	3	2	438	449	9.2	41	151	3.1	191	3.9	4.23	97	.262	.325	-15	-7	104	95	-4.9	-3	0	-0.9

■ **ERIC KING** King, Eric Steven b: 4/10/64, Oxnard, Cal. BR/TR, 6'2", 180 lbs. Deb: 5/15/86

YEAR	TM/L	W	L	PCT	G	GS	CG	SHO	SV	IP	H	H/G	HR	BB	BB/G	SO	SO/G	ERA	/A	OAVG	OOBP	PR	/A	PF	CPI	WAT	PB	PD	TPI
1986	Det-A	11	4	.733	33	16	3	1	3	138	108	7.0	11	63	4.1	79	5.2	3.52	112	.216	.309	10	7	95	88	3.4	0	0	0.7
1987	Det-A	6	9	.400	55	4	0	0	9	116	111	8.6	15	60	4.7	89	6.9	4.89	87	.251	.341	-5	-8	96	91	-2.6	0	2	-0.4
1988	Det-A	4	1	.800	23	5	0	0	3	69	60	7.8	5	34	4.4	45	5.9	3.39	110	.233	.327	4	3	94	108	1.4	0	-0	0.2

YEAR	TM/L	W	L	PCT	G	GS	CG	SHO	SV	IP	H	H/G	HR	BB	BB/G	SO	SO/G	ERA	/A	OAVG	OOBP	PR	/A	PF	CPI	WAT	PB	PD	TPI
1989	Chi-A	9	10	.474	25	25	1	1	0	159	144	8.2	13	64	3.6	72	4.1	3.40	107	.244	.318	9	4	93	105	0.8	0	-1	0.4
Total	4	30	24	.556	136	50	4	2	15	482	423	7.9	44	221	4.1	285	5.3	3.79	103	.236	.323	18	6	94	97	3.0	0	1	0.9
■ MATT KINZER	Kinzer, Matthew Roy b: 6/17/63, Indianapolis, Ind. BR/TR, 6'2", 210 lbs. Deb: 5/18/89																												
1989	StL-N	0	2	.000	8	1	0	0	0	13	25	17.3	3	4	2.8	8	5.5	13.15	27	.403	.433	-14	-14	100	71	-0.9	-0	-0	-1.3
■ BOB KIPPER	Kipper, Robert Wayne b: 7/8/64, Aurora, Ill. BR/TL, 6'2", 200 lbs. Deb: 4/12/85																												
1985	Cal-A	0	1	.000	2	1	0	0	0	3	7	21.0	1	3	9.0	0	0.0	24.00	17	.467	.500	-7	-7	101	61	-0.4	0	0	-0.5
	Pit-N	1	2	.333	5	4	0	0	0	25	21	7.6	4	7	2.5	13	4.7	5.04	75	.221	.269	-4	-4	104	60	0.0	0	0	-0.2
1986	Pit-N	6	8	.429	20	19	0	0	0	114	123	9.7	17	34	2.7	81	6.4	4.03	93	.271	.321	-4	-4	101	109	0.4	-3	-1	-0.6
1987	Pit-N	5	9	.357	24	20	1	1	0	111	117	9.5	25	52	4.2	83	6.7	5.92	72	.271	.347	-23	-20	105	93	-2.0	2	-0	-1.7
1988	Pit-N	2	6	.250	50	0	0	0	0	65	54	7.5	7	26	3.6	39	5.4	3.74	90	.234	.307	-2	-3	97	98	-2.1	-0	1	-0.1
1989	Pit-N	3	4	.429	52	0	0	0	4	83	55	6.0	5	33	3.6	58	6.3	2.93	113	.188	.263	5	3	94	70	-0.1	-0	-1	0.3
Total	5	17	30	.362	153	44	1	1	4	401	377	8.5	59	155	3.5	274	6.1	4.49	83	.248	.314	-34	-34	100	91	-4.2	-1	-0	-2.8
■ BOB KNEPPER	Knepper, Robert Wesley b: 5/25/54, Akron, Ohio BL/TL, 6'3", 195 lbs. Deb: 9/10/76																												
1976	SF-N	1	2	.333	4	4	0	0	0	25	26	9.4	0	7	2.5	11	4.0	3.24	113	.277	.317	1	1	104	102	-0.3	-0	0	0.1
1977	SF-N	11	9	.550	27	27	6	2	0	166	151	8.2	14	72	3.9	100	5.4	3.36	122	.242	.318	10	14	105	104	1.8	1	-1	1.4
1978	SF-N	17	11	.607	36	35	16	**6**	0	260	218	7.5	10	85	2.9	147	5.1	2.63	124	.229	.289	**27**	18	91	98	2.1	-3	-2	1.3
1979	SF-N	9	12	.429	34	34	6	2	0	207	241	10.5	30	77	3.3	123	5.3	4.65	75	.289	.347	-21	-27	93	107	-0.2	3	-1	-2.5
1980	SF-N	9	16	.360	35	33	8	1	0	215	242	10.1	15	61	2.6	103	4.3	4.10	85	.281	.330	-12	-15	96	99	-3.1	-0	2	-1.3
1981	Hou-N	9	5	.643	22	22	6	5	0	157	128	7.3	5	38	2.2	75	4.3	2.18	139	.226	.276	23	15	87	105	1.5	1	-0	1.7
1982	Hou-N	5	15	.250	33	29	4	0	1	180	193	9.6	14	60	3.0	108	5.4	4.45	81	.278	.332	-17	-17	100	93	-5.0	-3	1	-1.8
1983	Hou-N	6	13	.316	35	29	4	3	0	203	202	9.0	12	71	3.1	125	5.5	3.19	103	.261	.319	10	2	90	111	-4.0	3	1	0.6
1984	Hou-N	15	10	.600	35	34	11	3	0	234	223	8.6	26	55	2.1	140	5.4	3.19	103	.251	.292	10	3	92	107	3.0	4	-1	0.5
1985	Hou-N	15	13	.536	37	37	4	0	0	241	253	9.4	21	54	2.0	131	4.9	3.55	97	.271	.305	1	-3	96	104	0.8	0	-3	-0.5
1986	Hou-N	17	12	.586	40	38	8	**5**	0	258	232	8.1	19	62	2.2	143	5.0	3.14	121	.242	.283	17	18	102	94	-0.1	-3	2	1.8
1987	Hou-N	8	17	.320	33	31	1	0	0	178	226	11.4	26	54	2.7	76	3.8	5.26	72	.313	.359	-23	-29	93	107	-4.3	-1	1	-2.7
1988	Hou-N	14	5	.737	27	27	3	2	0	175	156	8.0	13	67	3.4	103	5.3	3.14	103	.243	.310	6	2	93	111	4.7	-0	2	0.3
1989	Hou-N	4	10	.286	22	20	0	0	0	113	135	10.8	12	60	4.8	45	3.6	5.89	61	.303	.379	-30	-29	103	97	-3.3	5	1	-2.2
	SF-N	3	2	.600	13	6	1	1	0	52	55	9.5	4	15	2.6	19	3.3	3.46	97	.270	.314	0	-1	96	112	0.2	1	-1	0.0
	Yr	7	12	.368	35	26	1	1	0	165	190	10.4	16	75	4.1	64	3.5	5.13	69	.290	.357	-30	-29	100	112	-3.1	5	0	-2.2
Total	14	143	152	.485	433	406	78	30	1	2664	2681	9.1	221	838	2.8	1449	4.9	3.64	96	.263	.316	3	-48	95	103	-6.2	7	1	-3.3
■ MARK KNUDSON	Knudson, Mark Richard b: 10/28/60, Denver, Colo. BR/TR, 6'5", 215 lbs. Deb: 7/08/85																												
1985	Hou-N	0	2	.000	2	2	0	0	0	11	21	17.2	0	3	2.5	4	3.3	9.00	38	.429	.453	-7	-7	96	89	-0.9	0	0	-0.5
1986	Hou-N	1	5	.167	9	7	0	0	0	43	48	10.0	5	15	3.1	20	4.2	4.19	90	.279	.335	-2	-2	102	108	-2.1	-1	-1	-0.3
	Mil-A	0	1	.000	4	1	0	0	0	18	22	11.0	7	5	2.5	9	4.5	7.50	57	.286	.329	-7	-6	103	86	-0.4	0	0	-0.5
1987	Mil-A	4	4	.500	15	8	1	0	0	62	88	12.8	7	14	2.0	26	3.8	5.37	85	.331	.354	-6	-6	102	106	-0.4	0	-1	-0.5
1988	Mil-A	0	0	—	5	0	0	0	0	16	17	9.6	1	2	1.1	7	3.9	1.13	363	.279	.302	5	5	103	314	0.0	0	0	0.6
1989	Mil-A	8	5	.615	40	7	1	0	0	124	110	8.0	15	29	2.1	47	3.4	3.34	112	.237	.285	8	6	96	96	1.6	0	-1	0.4
Total	5	13	17	.433	75	25	2	0	0	274	306	10.1	35	68	2.2	113	3.7	4.30	92	.281	.321	-9	-10	99	112	-2.2	-1	-3	-0.8
■ JOE KRAEMER	Kraemer, Joseph Wayne b: 9/10/64, Olympia, Wash. BL/TL, 6'2", 185 lbs. Deb: 8/22/89																												
1989	Chi-N	0	1	.000	1	1	0	0	0	4	7	15.8	0	2	4.5	5	11.3	4.50	84	.368	.429	-0	-0	107	154	-0.4	-0	0	0.0
■ RANDY KRAMER	Kramer, Randall John b: 9/20/60, Palo Alto, Cal. BR/TR, 6'2", 170 lbs. Deb: 9/11/88																												
1988	Pit-N	1	2	.333	5	1	0	0	0	10	12	10.8	1	1	0.9	7	6.3	5.40	62	.316	.333	-2	-2	97	93	-0.5	-0	-0	-0.2
1989	Pit-N	5	9	.357	35	15	1	1	2	111	90	7.3	10	61	4.9	52	4.2	3.97	83	.224	.328	-6	-8	94	94	-1.5	-0	-1	-0.9
Total	2	6	11	.353	40	16	1	1	2	121	102	7.6	11	62	4.6	59	4.4	4.09	81	.232	.328	-8	-10	95	94	-2.0	-0	-1	-1.1
■ RAY KRAWCZYK	Krawczyk, Raymond Allen b: 10/9/59, Pittsburgh, Pa. BR/TR, 6'1", 184 lbs. Deb: 6/29/84																												
1984	Pit-N	0	0	—	4	0	0	0	0	5	7	12.6	0	4	7.2	3	5.4	3.60	94	.350	.440	-0	-0	94	190	0.0	0	-0	0.0
1985	Pit-N	0	2	.000	8	0	0	0	0	8	20	22.5	1	6	6.8	9	10.1	14.63	26	.455	.529	-10	-10	104	86	-0.9	0	0	-0.8
1986	Pit-N	0	1	.000	12	0	0	0	0	12	17	12.8	3	10	7.5	7	5.3	7.50	50	.321	.415	-5	-5	101	107	-0.4	0	-0	-0.4
1988	Cal-A	0	1	.000	14	1	0	0	1	24	29	10.9	2	8	3.0	17	6.4	4.88	77	.299	.361	-2	-3	95	103	-0.4	0	1	-0.1
1989	Mil-A	0	0	—	1	0	0	0	0	2	4	18.0	0	1	4.5	6	27.0	13.50	28	.400	.455	-2	-2	96	60	0.0	0	0	-0.1
Total	5	0	4	.000	39	1	0	0	1	51	77	13.6	6	29	5.1	42	7.4	7.24	51	.344	.419	-19	-20	98	108	-1.7	0	0	-1.4
■ BILL KRUEGER	Krueger, William Culp b: 4/24/58, Waukegan, Ill. BL/TL, 6'5", 205 lbs. Deb: 4/10/83																												
1983	Oak-A	7	6	.538	17	16	2	0	0	110	104	8.5	7	53	4.3	58	4.7	3.60	109	.252	.336	6	4	96	107	1.0	0	-2	0.2
1984	Oak-A	10	10	.500	26	24	1	0	0	142	156	9.9	9	85	5.4	61	3.9	4.75	77	.285	.376	-12	-17	92	105	0.5	0	-2	-1.7
1985	Oak-A	9	10	.474	32	23	2	0	0	151	165	9.8	13	69	4.1	56	3.3	4.53	85	.276	.350	-6	-11	93	101	0.0	0	-1	-1.1
1986	Oak-A	1	2	.333	11	3	0	0	1	34	40	10.6	4	13	3.4	10	2.6	6.09	64	.301	.356	-7	-8	94	86	-0.3	0	1	-0.6
1987	Oak-A	0	3	.000	9	0	0	0	0	6	9	13.5	0	8	12.0	2	3.0	9.00	45	.360	.515	-3	-3	91	98	-1.4	0	-0	-0.2
	LA-N	0	0	—	2	0	0	0	0	2	3	13.5	0	1	4.5	2	9.0	0.00	—	.250	.308	1	1	92	0	0.0	0	0	0.1
1988	LA-N	0	0	—	1	1	0	0	0	2	4	18.0	0	2	9.0	1	4.5	13.50	27	.364	.500	-2	-2	105	73	0.0	0	0	-0.1
1989	Mil-A	3	2	.600	34	5	0	0	3	94	96	9.2	9	33	3.2	72	6.9	3.83	98	.264	.320	1	-1	96	103	0.5	0	-0	0.0
Total	7	30	33	.476	132	72	5	0	4	541	577	9.6	42	264	4.4	262	4.4	4.44	86	.274	.352	-23	-38	94	102	0.3	0	-4	-3.4
■ MIKE KRUKOW	Krukow, Michael Edward b: 1/21/52, Long Beach, Cal. BR/TR, 6'5", 205 lbs. Deb: 9/06/76																												
1976	Chi-N	0	0	—	2	0	0	0	0	4	6	13.5	0	2	4.5	1	2.3	9.00	43	.333	.400	-2	-2	111	62	0.0	-0	-0	-0.2
1977	Chi-N	8	14	.364	34	33	1	1	0	172	195	10.2	16	61	3.2	106	5.5	4.40	102	.281	.338	-9	2	115	98	-3.2	-1	1	0.3
1978	Chi-N	9	3	.750	27	20	3	1	0	138	125	8.2	11	53	3.5	81	5.3	3.91	102	.243	.314	-5	1	111	88	3.2	3	-0	0.4
1979	Chi-N	9	9	.500	28	28	0	0	0	165	172	9.4	13	81	4.4	119	6.5	4.20	100	.275	.355	-8	0	112	107	0.1	5	-1	0.4
1980	Chi-N	10	15	.400	34	34	3	0	0	205	200	8.8	13	80	3.5	130	5.7	4.39	88	.258	.326	-18	-12	108	85	0.1	3	-3	-1.1
1981	Chi-N	9	9	.500	25	25	2	1	0	144	146	9.1	11	55	3.4	101	6.3	3.69	101	.264	.326	-3	0	106	106	2.2	-0	0	0.1
1982	Phi-N	13	11	.542	33	33	7	2	0	208	211	9.1	8	82	3.5	138	6.0	3.12	108	.268	.331	11	6	94	120	-0.1	0	2	0.7
1983	SF-N	11	11	.500	31	31	2	1	0	184	189	9.2	17	76	3.7	136	6.7	3.96	93	.261	.328	-7	-6	101	99	0.3	5	-2	-0.3
1984	SF-N	11	12	.478	35	33	3	1	1	199	234	10.6	22	78	3.5	141	6.4	4.57	77	.290	.351	-22	-23	98	107	1.6	-1	-1	-2.6
1985	SF-N	8	11	.421	28	28	6	1	0	195	176	8.1	19	49	2.3	150	6.9	3.37	101	.238	.284	5	1	95	89	0.7	4	-0	0.4
1986	SF-N	20	9	.690	34	34	10	2	0	245	204	7.5	24	55	2.0	178	6.5	2.94	120	.223	.266	21	16	95	88	6.0	0	-1	1.6
1987	SF-N	5	6	.455	30	28	3	0	0	163	182	10.0	24	46	2.5	104	5.7	4.80	81	.288	.329	-13	-17	95	101	-1.0	1	1	-1.3
1988	SF-N	7	4	.636	20	20	1	0	0	125	111	8.0	13	31	2.2	75	5.4	3.53	91	.236	.284	-1	-4	93	90	1.5	-0	-0	-0.4
1989	SF-N	4	3	.571	8	8	0	0	0	43	37	7.7	5	18	3.8	18	3.8	3.98	84	.236	.316	-2	-3	96	94	0.0	-1	0	-0.3
Total	14	124	117	.515	369	355	41	10	1	2190	2188	9.0	196	767	3.2	1478	6.1	3.89	96	.260	.320	-53	-42	101	98	11.4	18	-4	-2.3
■ JEFF KUNKEL	Kunkel, Jeffrey William b: 3/25/62, W.Palm Beach, Fla. BR/TR, 6'2", 180 lbs. Deb: 7/23/84																												
1988	Tex-A	0	0	—	1	0	0	0	0	1	0	0.0	0	0	0.0	1	9.0	0.00	—	.000	.000	0	0	102	0	0.0	1	0	0.0
1989	Tex-A	0	0	—	1	0	0	0	0	2	4	18.0	1	3	13.5	0	0.0	18.00	22	.444	.583	-3	-3	103	88	0.0	1	0	-0.2
Total	2	0	0	—	2	0	0	0	0	3	4	12.0	1	3	9.0	1	3.0	12.00	33	.333	.467	-3	-3	103	59	0.0	2	0	-0.2
■ MIKE LaCOSS	LaCoss, Michael James b: 5/30/56, Glendale, Cal. BR/TR, 6'5", 185 lbs. Deb: 7/18/78																												
1978	Cin-N	4	8	.333	16	15	2	1	0	96	104	9.8	5	46	4.3	31	2.9	4.50	81	.288	.360	-10	-9	102	103	-2.5	-2	-0	-1.0
1979	Cin-N	14	8	.636	35	32	6	1	0	206	202	8.8	13	79	3.5	73	3.2	3.50	103	.263	.326	6	2	96	106	2.2	-1	1	0.2
1980	Cin-N	10	12	.455	34	29	4	2	0	169	207	11.0	9	68	3.6	59	3.1	4.63	79	.303	.362	-19	-18	101	103	-2.0	-3	1	-2.0
1981	Cin-N	4	7	.364	20	13	1	1	1	78	102	11.8	7	30	3.5	22	2.5	6.12	57	.325	.376	-23	-23	101	93	-2.3	-2	0	-2.4
1982	Hou-N	6	6	.500	41	8	0	0	0	115	107	8.4	3	54	4.2	51	4.0	2.90	124	.252	.338	9	9	100	121	0.3	1	-1	1.0
1983	Hou-N	5	7	.417	38	17	2	0	1	138	142	9.3	10	56	3.7	53	3.5	4.43	74	.273	.339	-12	-18	90	93	-1.2	-1	1	-1.8
1984	Hou-N	7	5	.583	39	18	2	1	3	132	132	9.0	3	55	3.8	86	5.9	4.02	82	.261	.331	-6	-11	92	86	1.1	-0	0	-1.1

YEAR	TM/L	W	L	PCT	G	GS	CG	SHO	SV	IP	H	H/G	HR	BB	BB/G	SO	SO/G	ERA	/A	OAVG	OOBP	PR	/A	PF	CPI	WAT	PB	PD	TPI
1985	KC-A	1	1	.500	21	0	0	0	1	41	49	10.8	2	29	6.4	26	5.7	5.05	83	.304	.404	-4	-4	101	114	0.0	0	0	-0.2
1986	SF-N	10	13	.435	37	31	4	1	0	204	179	7.9	14	70	3.1	86	3.8	3.57	99	.240	.303	3	-1	95	90	-1.9	5	1	0.5
1987	SF-N	13	10	.565	39	26	2	1	0	171	184	9.7	16	63	3.3	79	4.2	3.68	105	.283	.342	8	4	95	**124**	0.3	-2	4	0.4
1988	SF-N	7	7	.500	19	19	1	1	0	114	99	7.8	5	47	3.7	70	5.5	3.63	89	.234	.308	-2	-5	93	84	-0.1	2	3	0.0
1989	SF-N	10	10	.500	45	18	1	0	6	150	143	8.6	3	65	3.9	78	4.7	3.18	106	.255	.332	5	3	96	113	-1.2	-1	-1	0.2
Total	12	91	94	.492	384	226	25	9	12	1614	1650	9.2	90	662	3.7	714	4.0	3.93	90	.270	.337	-45	-71	96	102	-7.3	-3	9	-6.2

■ **DENNIS LAMP** Lamp, Dennis Patrick b: 9/23/52, Los Angeles, Cal. BR/TR, 6'4", 200 lbs. Deb: 8/21/77

YEAR	TM/L	W	L	PCT	G	GS	CG	SHO	SV	IP	H	H/G	HR	BB	BB/G	SO	SO/G	ERA	/A	OAVG	OOBP	PR	/A	PF	CPI	WAT	PB	PD	TPI
1977	Chi-N	0	2	.000	11	3	0	0	0	30	43	12.9	3	8	2.4	12	3.6	6.30	71	.344	.387	-8	-6	115	98	-0.9	1	0	-0.4
1978	Chi-N	7	15	.318	37	36	6	3	0	224	221	8.9	16	56	2.3	73	2.9	3.29	121	.258	.303	7	17	111	101	-4.1	0	3	2.3
1979	Chi-N	11	10	.524	38	32	6	1	0	200	223	10.0	14	46	2.1	86	3.9	3.51	120	.287	.325	5	15	112	114	0.7	-1	3	1.9
1980	Chi-N	10	14	.417	41	37	2	1	0	203	259	11.5	16	82	3.6	83	3.7	5.19	75	.317	.371	-36	-29	108	104	0.5	-3	3	-2.9
1981	Chi-A	7	6	.538	27	10	3	0	0	127	103	7.3	4	43	3.0	71	5.0	2.41	150	.222	.286	18	17	99	98	0.4	0	1	1.9
1982	Chi-A	11	8	.579	44	27	3	2	5	190	206	9.8	9	59	2.8	78	3.7	3.98	99	.279	.332	2	-1	97	99	1.0	0	2	0.1
1983	Chi-A	7	7	.500	49	5	1	0	15	116	123	9.5	6	29	2.3	44	3.4	3.72	111	.275	.323	5	5	102	101	-1.3	0	0	0.5
1984	Tor-A	8	8	.500	56	4	0	0	9	85	97	10.3	9	38	4.0	45	4.8	4.55	89	.285	.351	-5	-5	101	106	-0.7	0	1	-0.3
1985	Tor-A	11	0	1.000	53	1	0	0	2	106	96	8.2	7	27	2.3	68	5.8	3.31	124	.247	.289	10	9	99	95	5.5	0	2	1.2
1986	Tor-A	2	6	.250	40	2	0	0	2	73	93	11.5	5	23	2.8	30	3.7	5.05	86	.309	.353	-7	-6	104	96	-2.1	0	0	-0.4
1987	Oak-A	1	3	.250	36	5	0	0	0	57	76	12.0	5	22	3.5	36	5.7	5.05	80	.326	.378	-4	-6	91	116	-0.9	0	0	-0.5
1988	Bos-A	7	6	.538	46	0	0	0	0	83	92	10.0	3	19	2.1	49	5.3	3.47	124	.284	.323	5	8	108	110	0.0	0	1	0.9
1989	Bos-A	4	2	.667	42	0	0	0	2	112	96	7.7	4	27	2.2	61	4.9	2.33	174	.235	.276	19	21	104	108	1.0	0	2	2.4
Total	13	86	87	.497	520	162	21	7	35	1606	1728	9.7	101	479	2.7	736	4.1	3.81	106	.278	.327	11	42	105	104	-0.9	-3	18	6.7

■ **LES LANCASTER** Lancaster, Lester Wayne b: 4/21/62, Dallas, Tex. BR/TR, 6'2", 205 lbs. Deb: 4/07/87

YEAR	TM/L	W	L	PCT	G	GS	CG	SHO	SV	IP	H	H/G	HR	BB	BB/G	SO	SO/G	ERA	/A	OAVG	OOBP	PR	/A	PF	CPI	WAT	PB	PD	TPI
1987	Chi-N	8	3	.727	27	18	0	0	0	132	138	9.4	14	51	3.5	78	5.3	4.91	85	.268	.329	-12	-11	102	86	2.8	-2	-1	-1.3
1988	Chi-N	4	6	.400	44	3	1	0	5	86	89	9.3	4	34	3.6	36	3.8	3.77	96	.273	.334	-3	-1	105	107	-0.7	-1	1	-0.2
1989	Chi-N	4	2	.667	42	0	0	0	8	73	60	7.4	2	15	1.8	56	6.9	1.36	277	.226	.260	17	20	107	158	0.7	0	-0	2.1
Total	3	16	11	.593	113	21	1	0	13	291	287	8.9	20	100	3.1	170	5.3	3.68	106	.259	.314	2	7	104	110	2.8	-4	-1	0.6

■ **BILL LANDRUM** Landrum, Thomas William b: 8/17/57, Columbia, S.C. BR/TR, 6'2", 185 lbs. Deb: 8/31/86

YEAR	TM/L	W	L	PCT	G	GS	CG	SHO	SV	IP	H	H/G	HR	BB	BB/G	SO	SO/G	ERA	/A	OAVG	OOBP	PR	/A	PF	CPI	WAT	PB	PD	TPI
1986	Cin-N	0	0	—	10	0	0	0	0	13	23	15.9	0	4	2.8	14	9.7	6.92	56	.390	.415	-5	-4	104	100	0.0	-0	-0	-0.4
1987	Cin-N	3	2	.600	44	2	0	0	2	65	68	9.4	3	34	4.7	42	5.8	4.71	89	.292	.370	-4	-4	103	104	0.4	0	1	-0.2
1988	Chi-N	1	0	1.000	7	0	0	0	0	12	19	14.3	1	3	2.3	6	4.5	6.00	60	.365	.400	-3	-3	105	110	0.5	-0	-0	-0.3
1989	Pit-N	2	3	.400	56	0	0	0	26	81	60	6.7	2	28	3.1	51	5.7	1.67	198	.205	.271	17	15	94	121	-0.2	-0	0	1.6
Total	4	6	5	.545	117	2	0	0	28	171	170	8.9	6	69	3.6	113	5.9	3.53	105	.267	.331	4	3	99	112	0.7	-1	0	0.7

■ **MARK LANGSTON** Langston, Mark Edward b: 8/20/60, San Diego, Cal. BR/TL, 6'2", 177 lbs. Deb: 4/07/84

YEAR	TM/L	W	L	PCT	G	GS	CG	SHO	SV	IP	H	H/G	HR	BB	BB/G	SO	SO/G	ERA	/A	OAVG	OOBP	PR	/A	PF	CPI	WAT	PB	PD	TPI
1984	Sea-A	17	10	.630	35	33	5	2	0	225	188	7.5	16	118	4.7	**204**	**8.2**	3.40	121	.230	.325	15	18	103	103	4.8	0	1	2.0
1985	Sea-A	7	14	.333	24	24	2	0	0	127	122	8.6	22	91	6.4	72	5.1	5.46	73	.255	.373	-18	-21	95	100	-3.0	0	2	-1.7
1986	Sea-A	12	14	.462	37	36	9	0	0	239	234	8.8	30	123	4.6	**245**	**9.2**	4.86	92	.255	.342	-18	-11	106	91	1.2	0	-1	-1.1
1987	Sea-A	19	13	.594	35	35	14	3	0	272	242	8.0	30	114	3.8	**262**	**8.7**	3.84	120	.238	.313	19	23	103	96	4.1	0	1	2.3
1988	Sea-A	15	11	.577	35	35	9	3	0	261	222	7.7	32	110	3.8	235	8.1	3.34	129	.233	.311	18	28	108	110	3.9	0	3	3.2
1989	Sea-A	4	5	.444	10	10	2	1	0	73	60	7.4	3	19	2.3	60	7.4	3.58	113	.221	.279	3	4	104	65	0.0	0	-0	0.3
	Mon-N	12	9	.571	24	24	6	4	0	177	138	7.0	13	93	4.7	175	**8.9**	2.39	**150**	.218	.312	22	23	102	**135**	1.7	-0	-0	2.6
Total	6	86	76	.531	200	197	47	13	0	1374	1206	7.9	146	668	4.4	1253	8.2	3.80	111	.237	.324	40	64	104	103	12.7	-0	6	7.6

■ **DAVE LaPOINT** LaPoint, David Jeffrey b: 7/29/59, Glens Falls, N.Y. BL/TL, 6'3", 205 lbs. Deb: 9/10/80

YEAR	TM/L	W	L	PCT	G	GS	CG	SHO	SV	IP	H	H/G	HR	BB	BB/G	SO	SO/G	ERA	/A	OAVG	OOBP	PR	/A	PF	CPI	WAT	PB	PD	TPI
1980	Mil-A	1	0	1.000	5	3	0	0	1	15	17	10.2	2	13	7.8	5	3.0	6.00	63	.293	.400	-3	-4	93	107	0.5	0	-1	-0.3
1981	StL-N	1	0	1.000	3	2	0	0	0	11	12	9.8	1	2	1.6	4	3.3	4.09	86	.293	.333	-1	-1	101	109	0.5	-1	0	0.0
1982	StL-N	9	3	.750	42	21	0	0	0	153	170	10.0	8	52	3.1	81	4.8	3.41	108	.290	.343	3	5	102	126	2.6	-3	-3	0.0
1983	StL-N	12	9	.571	37	29	1	0	0	191	191	9.0	12	84	4.0	113	5.3	3.96	90	.267	.335	-7	-8	98	102	1.9	1	-1	-0.8
1984	StL-N	12	10	.545	33	33	2	1	0	193	205	9.6	9	77	3.6	130	6.1	3.96	89	.278	.342	-8	-9	99	103	0.7	-3	-2	-1.4
1985	SF-N	7	17	.292	31	31	2	1	0	207	215	9.3	18	74	3.2	122	5.3	3.57	96	.269	.326	1	-4	95	112	-3.1	2	-2	-0.4
1986	Det-A	3	6	.333	16	8	0	0	0	68	85	11.3	11	32	4.2	36	4.8	5.69	70	.307	.373	-11	-13	95	105	-1.7	0	-0	-1.2
	SD-N	1	4	.200	24	4	0	0	0	61	67	9.9	8	24	3.5	41	6.0	4.28	83	.276	.336	-4	-5	96	108	-1.3	-1	-0	-0.5
1987	StL-N	1	1	.500	6	2	0	0	0	16	26	14.6	4	5	2.8	8	4.5	6.75	59	.351	.392	-5	-5	97	113	0.0	-0	0	-0.4
	Chi-A	6	3	.667	14	12	2	1	0	83	69	7.5	7	31	3.4	43	4.7	2.93	166	.224	.296	14	18	109	102	1.7	0	2	2.0
1988	Chi-A	10	11	.476	25	25	1	1	0	161	151	8.4	10	47	2.6	79	4.4	3.41	115	.245	.295	10	9	99	90	0.8	0	-2	0.7
	Pit-N	4	2	.667	8	8	1	0	0	52	54	9.3	4	10	1.7	19	3.3	2.77	121	.271	.298	4	3	97	131	0.9	-1	0	0.3
1989	NY-A	6	9	.400	20	20	0	0	0	114	146	11.5	12	45	3.6	51	4.0	5.61	73	.310	.368	-22	-19	105	97	-1.0	0	-2	-1.9
Total	10	73	75	.493	264	198	9	4	1	1325	1408	9.6	106	496	3.4	732	5.0	3.96	94	.275	.334	-28	-33	99	106	2.5	-6	-11	-3.9

■ **TERRY LEACH** Leach, Terry Hester b: 3/13/54, Selma, Ala. BR/TR, 6', 215 lbs. Deb: 8/12/81

YEAR	TM/L	W	L	PCT	G	GS	CG	SHO	SV	IP	H	H/G	HR	BB	BB/G	SO	SO/G	ERA	/A	OAVG	OOBP	PR	/A	PF	CPI	WAT	PB	PD	TPI
1981	NY-N	1	1	.500	21	1	0	0	0	35	26	6.7	2	12	3.1	16	4.1	2.57	139	.205	.273	4	4	103	82	0.2	0	0	0.5
1982	NY-N	2	1	.667	21	1	1	1	3	45	46	9.2	2	18	3.6	30	6.0	4.20	86	.271	.330	-3	-3	100	91	0.7	-0	0	-0.3
1985	NY-N	3	4	.429	22	4	1	1	1	56	48	7.7	3	14	2.3	30	4.8	2.89	119	.235	.279	4	3	95	92	-1.0	1	1	0.5
1986	NY-N	0	0	—	6	0	0	0	0	7	6	7.7	0	3	3.9	4	5.1	2.57	135	.222	.300	1	1	93	87	0.0	0	0	0.1
1987	NY-N	11	1	.917	44	12	1	1	0	131	132	9.1	14	29	2.0	61	4.2	3.23	123	.262	.299	12	11	97	113	4.9	-2	1	1.0
1988	NY-N	7	2	.778	52	0	0	0	3	92	95	9.3	5	24	2.3	51	5.0	2.54	119	.268	.311	9	5	88	143	1.9	0	2	0.8
1989	NY-N	0	0	—	10	0	0	0	0	21	19	8.1	1	4	1.7	2	0.9	4.29	78	.244	.282	-2	-2	95	66	0.0	-0	1	-0.1
	KC-A	5	6	.455	30	3	0	0	0	74	78	9.5	4	36	4.4	34	4.1	4.14	90	.278	.351	-2	-4	95	107	-1.1	0	1	-0.2
Total	7	29	15	.659	206	21	3	3	7	461	450	8.8	31	140	2.7	228	4.5	3.28	109	.258	.308	24	15	95	109	5.6	-1	6	2.3

■ **TIM LEARY** Leary, Timothy James b: 12/23/58, Santa Monica, Cal. BR/TR, 6'3", 205 lbs. Deb: 4/12/81

YEAR	TM/L	W	L	PCT	G	GS	CG	SHO	SV	IP	H	H/G	HR	BB	BB/G	SO	SO/G	ERA	/A	OAVG	OOBP	PR	/A	PF	CPI	WAT	PB	PD	TPI
1981	NY-N	0	0	—	1	1	0	0	0	2	0	0.0	0	1	4.5	3	13.5	0.00	—	.000	.143	1	1	103	0	0.0	-0	0	0.1
1983	NY-N	1	1	.500	2	2	1	0	0	11	15	12.3	0	4	3.3	9	7.4	3.27	111	.319	.358	0	0	100	143	0.1	0	0	0.1
1984	NY-N	3	3	.500	20	7	0	0	0	54	61	10.2	2	18	3.0	29	4.8	4.00	90	.285	.342	-2	-2	100	102	-0.2	2	-1	-0.1
1985	Mil-A	1	4	.200	5	5	0	0	0	33	40	10.9	5	8	2.2	29	7.9	4.09	107	.296	.336	0	1	106	124	-1.3	0	1	0.2
1986	Mil-A	12	12	.500	33	30	3	2	0	188	216	10.3	20	53	2.5	110	5.3	4.21	102	.289	.338	-1	2	103	110	0.6	0	1	0.3
1987	LA-N	3	11	.214	39	12	0	0	1	108	121	10.1	15	36	3.0	61	5.1	4.75	79	.285	.339	-8	-12	92	102	-3.7	2	1	-0.8
1988	LA-N	17	11	.607	35	34	9	6	0	229	201	7.9	13	56	2.2	180	7.1	2.91	125	.234	.282	14	18	105	93	0.9	5	2	2.7
1989	LA-N	6	7	.462	19	17	2	0	0	117	107	8.2	9	37	2.8	59	4.5	3.38	96	.247	.304	2	-2	93	100	-0.2	-2	1	-0.3
	Cin-N	2	7	.222	14	14	0	0	0	90	98	9.8	8	31	3.1	64	6.4	3.70	98	.278	.336	-2	-1	104	119	-2.3	2	0	0.2
	Yr	8	14	.364	33	31	2	0	0	207	205	8.9	17	68	3.0	123	5.3	3.52	97	.259	.316	-0	-2	97	119	-2.5	-2	1	-0.1
Total	8	45	56	.446	168	122	15	8	1	832	859	9.3	72	244	2.6	544	5.9	3.71	102	.267	.319	-4	6	101	104	-6.1	8	4	2.4

■ **CRAIG LEFFERTS** Lefferts, Craig Lindsey b: 9/29/57, Munich, W.Germany BL/TL, 6'1", 180 lbs. Deb: 4/07/83

YEAR	TM/L	W	L	PCT	G	GS	CG	SHO	SV	IP	H	H/G	HR	BB	BB/G	SO	SO/G	ERA	/A	OAVG	OOBP	PR	/A	PF	CPI	WAT	PB	PD	TPI
1983	Chi-N	3	4	.429	56	5	0	0	1	89	80	8.1	13	29	2.9	60	6.1	3.13	117	.243	.302	5	5	101	119	0.0	-1	0	0.5
1984	SD-N	3	4	.429	62	0	0	0	10	106	88	7.5	4	24	2.0	56	4.8	2.12	166	.229	.269	17	16	98	109	-0.8	1	-1	1.7
1985	SD-N	7	6	.538	60	0	0	0	2	83	75	8.1	7	30	3.3	48	5.2	3.36	109	.244	.304	2	3	101	101	0.4	0	-0	0.2
1986	SD-N	9	8	.529	**83**	0	0	0	4	108	98	8.2	7	44	3.7	72	6.0	3.08	116	.253	.321	8	6	96	120	1.3	1	2	0.8
1987	SD-N	2	2	.500	33	0	0	0	2	51	56	9.9	9	15	2.6	39	6.9	4.41	90	.272	.324	-2	-2	98	106	0.3	0	-1	-0.2
	SF-N	3	3	.500	44	0	0	0	4	47	36	6.9	4	18	3.4	18	3.4	3.26	119	.216	.283	4	3	95	87	-0.2	0	-0	0.3
	Yr	5	5	.500	77	0	0	0	6	98	92	8.4	13	33	3.0	57	5.2	3.86	102	.245	.300	2	1	96	87	0.1	0	-1	0.1
1988	SF-N	3	8	.273	64	0	0	0	11	92	74	7.2	7	23	2.3	58	5.7	2.93	110	.225	.271	5	3	93	92	-2.6	-1	-1	0.1
1989	SF-N	2	4	.333	70	0	0	0	20	107	93	7.8	11	22	1.9	71	6.0	2.69	125	.233	.270	10	8	96	108	-1.2	-1	-1	0.6
Total	7	32	39	.451	472	5	0	0	54	683	600	7.9	62	205	2.7	422	5.6	3.00	118	.239	.292	50	42	97	107	-2.8	1	-3	4.0

YEAR	TM/L	W	L	PCT	G	GS	CG	SHO	SV	IP	H	H/G	HR	BB	BB/G	SO	SO/G	ERA	/A	OAVG	OOBP	PR	/A	PF	CPI	WAT	PB	PD	TPI
■ CHARLIE LEIBRANDT	Leibrandt, Charles Louis b: 10/4/56, Chicago, Ill. BR/TL, 6'3", 195 lbs. Deb: 9/17/79																												
1979	Cin-N	0	0	—	3	0	0	0	0	4	2	4.5	0	2	4.5	1	2.3	0.00	—	.154	.250	2	2	96	0	0.0	0	0	0.2
1980	Cin-N	10	9	.526	36	27	5	2	0	174	200	10.3	15	54	2.8	62	3.2	4.24	86	.292	.340	-12	-11	101	106	-0.3	1	1	-0.8
1981	Cin-N	1	1	.500	7	4	1	1	0	30	28	8.4	0	15	4.5	9	2.7	3.60	97	.262	.336	-0	-0	101	101	-0.1	-0	0	0.0
1982	Cin-N	5	7	.417	36	11	0	0	2	108	130	10.8	4	48	4.0	34	2.8	5.08	74	.308	.372	-18	-16	104	97	0.4	-1	-0	-1.7
1984	KC-A	11	7	.611	23	23	0	0	0	144	158	9.9	11	38	2.4	53	3.3	3.63	110	.277	.320	6	6	99	108	1.9	0	-1	0.4
1985	KC-A	17	9	.654	33	33	8	3	0	238	223	8.4	17	68	2.6	108	4.1	2.68	157	.248	.298	39	40	101	**121**	3.1	0	4	4.7
1986	KC-A	14	11	.560	35	34	8	1	0	231	238	9.3	18	63	2.5	108	4.2	4.09	103	.268	.313	2	3	100	92	2.5	0	2	0.4
1987	KC-A	16	11	.593	35	35	8	3	0	240	235	8.8	23	74	2.8	151	5.7	3.41	136	.253	.305	28	33	104	104	2.6	0	4	3.7
1988	KC-A	13	12	.520	35	35	7	2	0	243	244	9.0	20	62	2.3	125	4.6	3.19	128	.264	.309	21	24	103	116	0.0	0	2	2.7
1989	KC-A	5	11	.313	33	27	3	1	0	161	196	11.0	13	54	3.0	73	4.1	5.14	72	.304	.354	-22	-26	95	96	-3.7	0	-0	-2.5
Total	10	92	78	.541	276	229	40	13	2	1573	1654	9.5	121	478	2.7	724	4.1	3.76	108	.272	.322	46	53	101	106	6.4	-0	11	7.1
■ DAVE LEIPER	Leiper, David Paul b: 6/18/62, Whittier, Cal. BL/TL, 6'1", 160 lbs. Deb: 9/02/84																												
1984	Oak-A	1	0	1.000	8	0	0	0	0	7	12	15.4	2	5	6.4	3	3.9	9.00	41	.353	.436	-4	-4	92	101	0.5	0	0	-0.3
1986	Oak-A	2	2	.500	33	0	0	0	1	32	28	7.9	3	18	5.1	15	4.2	4.78	82	.252	.353	-2	-3	94	96	0.1	0	0	-0.2
1987	Oak-A	2	1	.667	45	0	0	0	1	52	49	8.5	6	18	3.1	33	5.7	3.81	107	.246	.304	4	1	91	97	0.5	0	1	0.2
	SD-N	1	0	1.000	12	0	0	0	1	16	16	9.0	2	5	2.8	10	5.6	4.50	89	.267	.313	-1	-1	98	93	0.5	0	-0	0.0
1988	SD-N	3	0	1.000	35	0	0	0	1	54	45	7.5	1	14	2.3	33	5.5	2.17	155	.231	.272	8	7	97	110	1.5	0	0	0.8
1989	SD-N	0	1	.000	22	0	0	0	0	29	40	12.4	2	20	6.2	7	2.2	4.97	71	.333	.434	-5	-5	101	139	-0.4	-0	1	-0.4
Total	5	9	4	.692	155	0	0	0	4	190	190	9.0	16	80	3.8	101	4.8	3.93	95	.264	.333	0	-4	95	107	2.7	0	2	0.1
■ AL LEITER	Leiter, Alois Terry b: 10/23/65, Toms River, N.J. BL/TL, 6'2", 200 lbs. Deb: 9/15/87																												
1987	NY-A	2	2	.500	4	4	0	0	0	23	24	9.4	2	15	5.9	28	11.0	6.26	69	.273	.375	-5	-5	97	80	-0.1	0	-0	-0.4
1988	NY-A	4	4	.500	14	14	0	0	0	57	49	7.7	7	33	5.2	60	9.5	3.95	96	.231	.347	0	-1	96	108	-0.1	0	1	0.0
1989	NY-A	1	2	.333	4	4	0	0	0	27	23	7.7	1	21	7.0	22	7.3	6.00	68	.235	.374	-6	-6	105	70	-0.3	0	-0	-0.5
	Tor-A	0	0	—	1	1	0	0	0	7	9	11.6	1	2	2.6	4	5.1	3.86	94	.310	.355	0	-0	93	140	0.0	0	-0	0.0
	Yr	1	2	.333	5	5	0	0	0	34	32	8.5	2	23	6.1	26	6.9	5.56	72	.246	.357	-6	-6	103	140	-0.3	0	-1	-0.5
Total	3	7	8	.467	23	23	0	0	0	114	105	8.3	11	71	5.6	114	9.0	4.89	81	.246	.360	-11	-12	98	95	-0.5	0	-0	-0.9
■ DEREK LILLIQUIST	Lilliquist, Derek Jansen b: 2/20/66, Winter Park, Fla. BL/TL, 6', 200 lbs. Deb: 4/13/89																												
1989	Atl-N	8	10	.444	32	30	0	0	0	166	202	11.0	16	34	1.8	79	4.3	3.96	92	.301	.331	-8	-6	104	117	0.8	0	-1	-0.7
■ BILL LONG	Long, William Douglas b: 2/29/60, Cincinnati, Ohio BR/TR, 6', 185 lbs. Deb: 7/21/85																												
1985	Chi-A	0	1	.000	4	3	0	0	0	14	25	16.1	4	5	3.2	13	8.4	10.29	40	.391	.423	-10	-10	100	91	-0.4	0	0	-0.7
1987	Chi-A	8	8	.500	29	23	5	2	1	169	179	9.5	20	28	**1.5**	72	3.8	4.37	111	.272	.300	2	9	109	89	0.4	0	0	0.8
1988	Chi-A	8	11	.421	47	18	3	0	2	174	187	9.7	21	43	2.2	77	4.0	4.03	97	.280	.320	-1	-2	99	109	-0.4	0	-0	-0.2
1989	Chi-A	5	5	.500	30	8	0	0	1	99	101	9.2	8	37	3.4	51	4.6	3.91	93	.265	.329	-0	-3	93	103	0.7	0	0	-0.2
Total	4	21	25	.457	110	52	8	2	4	456	492	9.7	53	113	2.2	213	4.2	4.32	97	.277	.319	-9	-7	101	100	0.3	0	0	-0.3
■ VANCE LOVELACE	Lovelace, Vance Odell b: 8/9/63, Tampa, Fla. BL/TL, 6'5", 205 lbs. Deb: 9/10/88																												
1988	Cal-A	0	0	—	3	0	0	0	0	1	2	18.0	1	3	27.0	0	0.0	18.00	21	.400	.625	-2	-2	95	127	0.0	0	0	-0.1
1989	Cal-A	0	0	—	1	0	0	0	0	1	0	0.0	0	1	9.0	1	9.0	0.00	—	.000	.250	0	0	98	0	0.0	0	0	0.0
Total	2	0	0	—	4	0	0	0	0	2	2	9.0	1	4	18.0	1	4.5	9.00	42	.250	.500	-1	-1	96	63	0.0	0	0	-0.1
■ RICK LUECKEN	Luecken, Richard Fred b: 11/15/60, McAllen, Tex. BR/TR, 6'6", 210 lbs. Deb: 6/06/89																												
1989	KC-A	2	1	.667	19	0	0	0	1	24	23	8.6	3	13	4.9	16	6.0	3.38	110	.258	.346	1	1	95	137	0.3	0	-0	0.1
■ RAFAEL LUGO	Lugo, Rafael Urbano (Colina) b: 8/12/62, Punto Fijo, Venez. BR/TR, 6', 185 lbs. Deb: 4/28/85																												
1985	Cal-A	3	4	.429	20	10	1	0	0	83	86	9.3	10	29	3.1	42	4.6	3.69	113	.274	.339	4	4	101	126	-0.7	0	0	0.5
1986	Cal-A	1	1	.500	6	3	0	0	0	21	21	9.0	4	6	2.6	9	3.9	3.86	103	.266	.314	1	0	95	119	0.0	0	-0	0.0
1987	Cal-A	0	2	.000	7	5	0	0	0	28	42	13.5	8	18	5.8	24	7.7	9.32	48	.339	.420	-15	-15	100	90	-0.9	0	-0	-1.2
1988	Cal-A	0	0	—	1	0	0	0	0	2	2	9.0	1	1	4.5	1	4.5	9.00	42	.250	.333	-1	-1	95	78	0.0	0	0	0.0
1989	Mon-N	0	0	—	3	0	0	0	0	4	4	9.0	1	0	0.0	3	6.8	6.75	53	.250	.250	-1	-1	102	56	0.0	0	0	0.0
Total	5	4	7	.364	37	18	1	0	0	138	155	10.1	24	54	3.5	79	5.2	5.02	83	.287	.352	-13	-13	99	115	-1.6	0	-0	-0.7
■ JULIO MACHADO	Machado, Julio S. b: 12/1/65, Zulia, Venezuela BR/TR, 6', 175 lbs. Deb: 9/07/89																												
1989	NY-N	0	1	.000	10	0	0	0	0	11	9	7.4	0	3	2.5	14	11.5	3.27	102	.214	.267	0	0	95	52	-0.4	0	0	0.0
■ MORRIS MADDEN	Madden, Morris DeWayne b: 8/31/60, Laurens, S.C. BL/TL, 6' ", 155 lbs. Deb: 6/11/87																												
1987	Det-A	0	0	—	2	0	0	0	0	2	4	18.0	0	3	13.5	0	0.0	13.50	32	.444	.583	-2	-2	96	90	0.0	0	0	-0.1
1988	Pit-N	0	0	—	5	0	0	0	0	6	5	7.5	0	7	10.5	3	4.5	0.00	—	.294	.480	2	2	97	0	0.0	0	0	0.3
1989	Pit-N	2	2	.500	9	3	0	0	0	14	17	10.9	0	13	8.4	6	3.9	7.07	47	.327	.448	-6	-6	94	93	0.2	-0	-1	-0.6
Total	3	2	2	.500	16	3	0	0	0	22	26	10.6	0	23	9.4	9	3.7	5.73	60	.333	.471	-5	-6	95	67	0.2	-0	-0	-0.4
■ GREG MADDUX	Maddux, Gregory Alan b: 4/14/66, San Angelo, Tex. BR/TR, 6', 150 lbs. Deb: 9/03/86																												
1986	Chi-N	2	4	.333	6	5	1	0	0	31	44	12.8	3	11	3.2	20	5.8	5.52	73	.336	.389	-6	-5	108	110	-0.6	1	0	-0.3
1987	Chi-N	6	14	.300	30	27	1	1	0	156	181	10.4	17	74	4.3	101	5.8	5.60	74	.294	.369	-26	-25	102	95	-3.9	-2	6	-1.9
1988	Chi-N	18	8	.692	34	34	9	3	0	249	230	8.3	13	81	2.9	140	5.1	3.18	114	.244	.306	8	12	105	100	5.9	2	2	1.9
1989	Chi-N	19	12	.613	35	35	7	1	0	238	222	8.4	13	82	3.1	135	5.1	2.95	128	.249	.309	15	21	107	115	1.7	2	3	3.1
Total	4	45	38	.542	105	101	18	5	0	674	677	9.0	46	248	3.3	396	5.3	3.77	101	.262	.327	-10	4	105	104	3.1	3	12	2.8
■ MIKE MADDUX	Maddux, Michael Ausley b: 8/27/61, Dayton, Ohio BL/TR, 6'2", 180 lbs. Deb: 6/03/86																												
1986	Phi-N	3	7	.300	16	16	0	0	0	78	88	10.2	6	34	3.9	44	5.1	5.42	71	.286	.356	-15	-13	104	87	-2.2	-2	-1	-1.4
1987	Phi-N	2	0	1.000	7	2	0	0	0	17	17	9.0	0	5	2.6	15	7.9	2.65	161	.254	.306	3	3	105	103	1.0	-0	-0	0.2
1988	Phi-N	4	3	.571	25	11	0	0	0	89	91	9.2	6	34	3.4	59	6.0	3.74	95	.275	.342	-3	-2	103	116	1.0	-0	1	0.0
1989	Phi-N	1	3	.250	16	4	2	1	1	44	52	10.6	3	14	2.9	26	5.3	5.11	70	.304	.356	-8	-7	102	96	-0.7	-1	2	-0.6
Total	4	10	13	.435	64	33	2	1	1	228	248	9.8	15	87	3.4	144	5.7	4.50	83	.283	.347	-23	-20	103	101	-0.9	-3	2	-1.8
■ ALEX MADRID	Madrid, Alexander b: 4/18/63, Springerville, Ariz BR/TR, 6'3", 200 lbs. Deb: 7/20/87																												
1987	Mil-A	0	0	—	3	0	0	0	0	5	11	19.8	1	1	1.8	1	1.8	16.20	28	.440	.429	-7	-6	102	64	0.0	0	-0	-0.5
1988	Phi-N	1	1	.500	5	2	1	0	0	16	15	8.4	0	6	3.4	2	1.1	2.81	126	.246	.300	1	1	103	102	0.2	-0	-0	0.1
1989	Phi-N	1	2	.333	6	3	0	0	0	25	32	11.5	3	14	5.0	13	4.7	5.40	66	.314	.398	-5	-5	102	116	-0.2	-0	-0	-0.5
Total	3	2	3	.400	14	5	1	0	0	46	58	11.3	4	21	4.1	16	3.1	5.67	65	.309	.370	-11	-10	103	105	0.0	-1	-1	-0.9
■ JOE MAGRANE	Magrane, Joseph David b: 7/2/64, Des Moines, Iowa BR/TL, 6'6", 225 lbs. Deb: 4/25/87																												
1987	StL-N	9	7	.563	27	26	4	2	0	170	157	8.3	9	60	3.2	101	5.3	3.55	112	.245	.314	10	8	97	94	-0.3	2	0	0.9
1988	StL-N	5	9	.357	24	24	4	3	0	165	133	7.3	6	51	2.8	100	5.5	**2.18**	**166**	.217	.275	23	26	105	105	-1.7	1	2	3.5
1989	StL-N	18	9	.667	34	33	9	3	0	235	219	8.4	5	72	2.8	127	4.9	2.91	121	.251	.306	15	16	100	106	4.4	1	-1	1.7
Total	3	32	25	.561	85	83	17	8	0	570	509	8.0	20	183	2.9	328	5.2	2.89	128	.240	.300	49	51	101	102	2.4	4	1	6.1
■ RICKY MAHLER	Mahler, Richard Keith b: 8/5/53, Austin, Tex. BR/TR, 6'1", 195 lbs. Deb: 4/20/79																												
1979	Atl-N	0	0	—	15	0	0	0	0	22	28	11.5	4	11	4.5	12	4.9	6.14	67	.311	.386	-6	-5	110	101	0.0	0	-0	-0.4
1980	Atl-N	0	0	—	2	0	0	0	0	4	2	4.5	0	0	0.0	1	2.3	2.25	163	.154	.154	1	1	101	8	0.0	0	0	0.1
1981	Atl-N	8	6	.571	34	14	1	0	2	112	109	8.8	5	43	3.5	54	4.3	2.81	124	.258	.320	8	8	100	124	1.5	-0	1	0.9
1982	Atl-N	9	10	.474	39	33	5	2	0	205	213	9.4	18	62	2.7	105	4.6	4.21	91	.272	.322	-14	-8	107	94	-1.4	2	2	-0.4
1983	Atl-N	0	0	—	10	0	0	0	0	14	16	10.3	0	9	5.8	7	4.5	5.14	74	.296	.379	-2	-2	104	94	0.0	-0	-0	-0.2
1984	Atl-N	13	10	.565	38	29	9	1	0	222	209	8.5	13	62	2.5	106	4.3	3.12	126	.251	.298	12	20	110	101	1.8	5	2	**3.1**
1985	Atl-N	17	15	.531	39	39	6	1	0	267	272	9.2	24	79	2.7	107	3.6	3.47	112	.268	.318	4	13	108	111	4.0	-1	1	1.4
1986	Atl-N	14	18	.438	39	39	7	1	0	238	283	10.7	25	95	3.6	137	5.2	4.88	79	.301	.361	-31	-27	103	106	-0.3	2	1	-2.3
1987	Atl-N	8	13	.381	39	28	3	1	0	197	212	9.7	24	85	3.9	95	4.3	4.98	90	.283	.352	-20	-11	109	99	-1.2	1	2	-0.7

YEAR	TM/L	W	L	PCT	G	GS	CG	SHO	SV	IP	H	H/G	HR	BB	BB/G	SO	SO/G	ERA	/A	OAVG	OOBP	PR	/A	PF	CPI	WAT	PB	PD	TPI
1988	Atl-N	9	16	.360	39	34	5	0	0	249	279	10.1	17	42	1.5	131	4.7	3.69	100	.282	.310	-6	0	107	104	0.5	-2	1	0.0
1989	Cin-N	9	13	.409	40	31	5	2	0	221	242	9.9	15	51	2.1	102	4.2	3.83	95	.282	.322	-8	-5	104	106	-1.4	2	-0	-0.3
Total	11	87	101	.463	334	247	41	8	2	1751	1865	9.6	145	539	2.8	857	4.4	3.95	98	.276	.327	-62	-17	106	105	3.5	8	10	1.2

■ DENNIS MARTINEZ Martinez, Jose Dennis (Emilia) b: 5/14/55, Granada, Nicaragua BR/TR, 6'1", 160 lbs. Deb: 9/14/76

YEAR	TM/L	W	L	PCT	G	GS	CG	SHO	SV	IP	H	H/G	HR	BB	BB/G	SO	SO/G	ERA	/A	OAVG	OOBP	PR	/A	PF	CPI	WAT	PB	PD	TPI
1976	Bal-A	1	2	.333	4	2	1	0	0	28	23	7.4	1	8	2.6	18	5.8	2.57	133	.237	.292	3	3	97	106	-0.5	0	0	0.3
1977	Bal-A	14	7	.667	42	13	5	0	4	167	157	8.5	10	64	3.4	107	5.8	4.10	92	.253	.323	-0	-6	92	87	1.9	0	0	-0.5
1978	Bal-A	16	11	.593	40	38	15	2	0	276	257	8.4	20	93	3.0	142	4.6	3.52	97	.250	.310	8	-3	91	94	1.2	0	4	0.0
1979	Bal-A	15	16	.484	40	39	**18**	3	0	**292**	279	8.6	28	78	2.4	132	4.1	3.67	110	.253	.297	18	12	96	93	-4.4	0	3	1.5
1980	Bal-A	6	4	.600	25	12	2	0	1	100	103	9.3	12	44	4.0	42	3.8	3.96	101	.272	.348	1	1	99	116	0.0	0	0	0.1
1981	Bal-A	**14**	5	.737	25	24	9	2	0	179	173	8.7	10	62	3.1	88	4.4	3.32	109	.254	.315	7	6	99	101	4.3	0	4	1.1
1982	Bal-A	16	12	.571	40	39	10	2	0	252	262	9.4	30	87	3.1	111	4.0	4.21	96	.267	.326	-4	-5	99	101	-0.2	0	0	-0.4
1983	Bal-A	7	16	.304	32	25	4	0	0	153	209	12.3	21	45	2.6	71	4.2	5.53	73	.330	.372	-25	-26	99	109	-6.1	0	5	-1.9
1984	Bal-A	6	9	.400	34	20	2	0	0	142	145	9.2	26	37	2.3	77	4.9	5.01	75	.263	.312	-16	-20	94	87	-1.8	0	1	-1.7
1985	Bal-A	13	11	.542	33	31	3	1	0	180	203	10.1	29	63	3.2	68	3.4	5.15	79	.288	.349	-20	-22	98	103	0.8	0	0	-1.9
1986	Bal-A	0	0	—	4	0	0	0	0	7	11	14.1	0	2	2.6	2	2.6	6.43	65	.367	.394	-2	-2	99	94	0.0	0	0	0.0
	Mon-N	3	6	.333	19	15	1	1	0	98	103	9.5	11	28	2.6	63	5.8	4.59	80	.274	.322	-9	-10	98	92	-1.4	-0	1	-0.9
1987	Mon-N	11	4	.733	22	22	2	1	0	145	133	8.3	9	40	2.5	84	5.2	3.29	131	.244	.299	13	17	106	93	3.1	-2	0	1.5
1988	Mon-N	15	13	.536	34	34	9	2	0	235	215	8.2	21	55	2.1	120	4.6	2.72	133	.239	.285	19	24	105	112	1.2	2	0	2.9
1989	Mon-N	16	7	.696	34	33	5	2	0	232	227	8.8	21	49	1.9	142	5.5	3.18	113	.257	.298	8	10	102	109	4.9	-1	3	1.4
Total	14	153	123	.554	428	347	86	16	5	2486	2500	9.1	249	755	2.7	1267	4.6	3.90	98	.263	.317	1	-19	98	100	3.0	-2	23	1.5

■ RAMON MARTINEZ Martinez, Ramon Jaime (born Ramon Jaime (Martinez) b: 3/22/68, Santo Domingo, D.R. BR/TR, 6'416", 508 lbs. Deb: /13/1988

YEAR	TM/L	W	L	PCT	G	GS	CG	SHO	SV	IP	H	H/G	HR	BB	BB/G	SO	SO/G	ERA	/A	OAVG	OOBP	PR	/A	PF	CPI	WAT	PB	PD	TPI
1988	LA-N	1	3	.250	9	6	0	0	0	36	27	6.8	0	22	5.5	23	5.8	3.75	97	.216	.325	-1	-0	105	78	-1.1	-1	-0	-0.1
1989	LA-N	6	4	.600	15	15	2	2	0	99	79	7.2	11	41	3.7	89	8.1	3.18	102	.219	.305	4	1	93	105	1.2	0	1	0.2
Total	2	7	7	.500	24	21	2	2	0	135	106	7.1	11	63	4.2	112	7.5	3.33	100	.219	.310	2	0	96	98	0.1	-0	1	0.1

■ ROGER MASON Mason, Roger Le Roy b: 9/18/58, Bellaire, Mich. BR/TR, 6'6", 215 lbs. Deb: 9/04/84

YEAR	TM/L	W	L	PCT	G	GS	CG	SHO	SV	IP	H	H/G	HR	BB	BB/G	SO	SO/G	ERA	/A	OAVG	OOBP	PR	/A	PF	CPI	WAT	PB	PD	TPI
1984	Det-A	1	1	.500	5	2	0	0	1	22	23	9.4	1	10	4.1	15	6.1	4.50	84	.271	.340	-1	-2	94	89	-0.1	0	0	-0.1
1985	SF-N	1	3	.250	5	5	1	1	0	30	28	8.4	1	11	3.3	26	7.8	2.10	162	.243	.305	5	4	95	139	-0.6	-0	-0	0.4
1986	SF-N	3	4	.429	11	11	1	0	0	60	56	8.4	5	30	4.5	43	6.5	4.80	73	.250	.340	-7	-8	95	84	-0.5	-2	-1	-1.0
1987	SF-N	1	1	.500	5	5	0	0	0	26	30	10.4	4	10	3.5	18	6.2	4.50	86	.303	.364	-1	-2	95	125	0.0	0	0	-0.1
1989	Hou-N	0	0	—	2	0	0	0	0	1	2	18.0	0	2	18.0	3	27.0	27.00	13	.333	.500	-3	-3	103	38	0.0	0	0	-0.1
Total	5	6	9	.400	28	23	2	1	1	139	139	9.0	11	63	4.1	105	6.8	4.27	84	.263	.339	-7	-10	95	104	-1.2	-2	-1	-0.9

■ RANDY McCAMENT McCament, Larry Randall b: 7/29/62, Albuquerque, N.Mex BR/TR, 6'3", 195 lbs. Deb: 6/28/89

YEAR	TM/L	W	L	PCT	G	GS	CG	SHO	SV	IP	H	H/G	HR	BB	BB/G	SO	SO/G	ERA	/A	OAVG	OOBP	PR	/A	PF	CPI	WAT	PB	PD	TPI
1989	SF-N	1	1	.500	25	0	0	0	0	37	32	7.8	4	23	5.6	12	2.9	3.89	86	.241	.352	-2	-2	96	113	0.0	0	0	-0.1

■ TOM McCARTHY McCarthy, Thomas Michael b: 6/18/61, Lundstahl, W.Ger. BR/TR, 6', 180 lbs. Deb: 7/05/85

YEAR	TM/L	W	L	PCT	G	GS	CG	SHO	SV	IP	H	H/G	HR	BB	BB/G	SO	SO/G	ERA	/A	OAVG	OOBP	PR	/A	PF	CPI	WAT	PB	PD	TPI
1985	Bos-A	0	0	—	3	0	0	0	0	5	7	12.6	1	4	7.2	2	3.6	10.80	39	.350	.440	-4	-4	102	79	0.0	0	0	-0.2
1988	Chi-A	2	0	1.000	6	0	0	0	1	13	9	6.2	0	2	1.4	5	3.5	1.38	283	.191	.255	4	4	99	97	1.0	0	0	0.4
1989	Chi-A	1	2	.333	31	0	0	0	0	67	72	9.7	8	20	2.7	27	3.6	3.49	104	.280	.330	3	1	93	129	-0.2	0	1	0.2
Total	3	3	2	.600	40	0	0	0	1	85	88	9.3	9	26	2.8	34	3.6	3.60	103	.272	.327	3	1	95	121	0.8	0	1	0.4

■ KIRK McCASKILL McCaskill, Kirk Edward b: 4/9/61, Kapuskasing, Ont., Can BR/TR, 6'1", 185 lbs. Deb: 5/01/85

YEAR	TM/L	W	L	PCT	G	GS	CG	SHO	SV	IP	H	H/G	HR	BB	BB/G	SO	SO/G	ERA	/A	OAVG	OOBP	PR	/A	PF	CPI	WAT	PB	PD	TPI
1985	Cal-A	12	12	.500	30	29	6	1	0	190	189	9.0	23	64	3.0	102	4.8	4.69	89	.258	.318	-11	-11	101	87	-1.3	0	-0	-1.0
1986	Cal-A	17	10	.630	34	33	10	2	0	246	207	7.6	19	92	3.4	202	7.4	3.37	119	.229	.300	22	17	95	91	2.2	0	0	1.7
1987	Cal-A	4	6	.400	14	13	1	1	0	75	84	10.1	14	34	4.1	56	6.7	5.64	79	.286	.359	-10	-10	100	100	-0.6	0	1	-0.8
1988	Cal-A	8	6	.571	23	23	4	2	0	146	155	9.6	9	61	3.8	98	6.0	4.32	87	.274	.342	-6	-9	95	98	1.5	0	0	-0.8
1989	Cal-A	15	10	.600	32	32	6	4	0	212	202	8.6	16	59	2.5	107	4.5	2.93	130	.254	.306	23	20	98	116	1.3	0	2	2.4
Total	5	56	44	.560	133	130	27	10	0	869	837	8.7	81	310	3.2	565	5.9	3.90	102	.254	.318	18	8	97	98	3.1	0	3	1.5

■ BOB McCLURE McClure, Robert Craig b: 4/29/52, Oakland, Cal. BR/TL, 5'11", 170 lbs. Deb: 8/13/75

YEAR	TM/L	W	L	PCT	G	GS	CG	SHO	SV	IP	H	H/G	HR	BB	BB/G	SO	SO/G	ERA	/A	OAVG	OOBP	PR	/A	PF	CPI	WAT	PB	PD	TPI
1975	KC-A	1	0	1.000	12	0	0	0	1	15	4	2.4	0	14	8.4	15	9.0	0.00	—	.077	.273	6	6	101	0	0.5	0	-0	0.6
1976	KC-A	0	0	—	8	0	0	0	0	4	3	6.8	0	8	18.0	3	6.8	9.00	39	.214	.500	-2	-2	99	74	0.0	0	0	-0.2
1977	Mil-A	2	1	.667	68	0	0	0	6	71	64	8.1	2	34	4.3	57	7.2	2.54	155	.249	.328	12	11	97	136	0.7	0	2	1.3
1978	Mil-A	2	6	.250	44	0	0	0	9	65	53	7.3	8	30	4.2	47	6.5	3.74	105	.223	.314	0	1	104	96	-2.2	0	-0	0.1
1979	Mil-A	5	2	.714	36	0	0	0	5	51	53	9.4	6	24	4.2	37	6.5	3.88	108	.269	.349	2	2	99	121	1.1	0	-0	0.1
1980	Mil-A	5	8	.385	52	5	2	1	10	91	83	8.2	6	37	3.7	47	4.6	3.07	123	.241	.313	10	7	93	105	-1.8	0	-1	0.6
1981	Mil-A	0	0	—	4	0	0	0	0	8	7	7.9	1	4	4.5	6	6.8	3.38	103	.233	.324	0	0	95	112	0.0	0	-0	0.0
1982	Mil-A	12	7	.632	34	26	5	0	0	173	160	8.3	21	74	3.8	99	5.2	4.21	89	.248	.324	-3	-9	92	95	1.2	0	-1	-0.8
1983	Mil-A	9	9	.500	24	23	4	0	0	142	152	9.6	11	68	4.3	68	4.3	4.50	82	.277	.360	-7	-12	91	104	-0.6	0	-1	-1.2
1984	Mil-A	4	8	.333	39	18	1	0	1	140	154	9.9	9	52	3.3	68	4.4	4.37	85	.282	.338	-6	-10	93	97	-1.2	0	-0	-1.0
1985	Mil-A	4	1	.800	38	1	0	0	3	86	91	9.5	10	30	3.1	57	6.0	4.29	102	.274	.335	-1	1	106	106	1.6	0	0	0.1
1986	Mil-A	2	1	.667	13	0	0	0	0	16	18	10.1	2	10	5.6	11	6.2	3.94	110	.286	.373	0	1	103	140	0.5	0	-0	0.0
	Mon-N	2	5	.286	52	0	0	0	6	63	53	7.6	2	23	3.3	42	6.0	3.00	122	.232	.300	5	5	98	93	-1.4	0	0	0.5
1987	Mon-N	6	1	.857	52	0	0	0	5	52	47	8.1	8	20	3.5	33	5.7	3.46	125	.241	.302	4	5	106	113	2.4	-0	0	0.5
1988	Mon-N	1	3	.250	19	0	0	0	2	19	23	10.9	3	6	2.8	12	5.7	6.16	59	.307	.345	-6	-5	105	92	-0.9	-0	0	-0.5
	NY-N	1	0	1.000	14	0	0	0	1	11	12	9.8	1	2	1.6	7	5.7	4.09	74	.279	.326	-1	-1	88	101	0.5	0	-0	-0.1
	Yr	2	3	.400	33	0	0	0	3	30	35	10.5	4	8	2.4	19	5.7	5.40	63	.289	.331	-6	-7	99	101	-0.4	-0	0	-0.6
1989	Cal-A	6	1	.857	48	0	0	0	3	52	39	6.8	2	15	2.6	36	6.2	1.56	244	.212	.268	13	13	98	140	2.4	0	-1	1.3
Total	15	62	53	.539	557	73	12	1	52	1059	1016	8.6	92	451	3.8	645	5.5	3.76	103	.254	.328	28	11	96	105	2.8	-0	-3	1.3

■ LANCE McCULLERS McCullers, Lance Graye b: 3/8/64, Tampa, Fla. BB/TR, 6'1", 185 lbs. Deb: 8/12/85

YEAR	TM/L	W	L	PCT	G	GS	CG	SHO	SV	IP	H	H/G	HR	BB	BB/G	SO	SO/G	ERA	/A	OAVG	OOBP	PR	/A	PF	CPI	WAT	PB	PD	TPI
1985	SD-N	0	2	.000	21	0	0	0	5	35	23	5.9	3	16	4.1	27	6.9	2.31	158	.195	.282	5	5	101	117	-0.9	-0	0	0.5
1986	SD-N	10	10	.500	70	7	0	0	5	136	103	6.8	12	58	3.8	92	6.1	2.78	128	.216	.300	14	12	96	111	0.9	1	-1	1.2
1987	SD-N	8	10	.444	78	0	0	0	16	123	115	8.4	11	59	4.3	126	9.2	3.73	107	.244	.326	5	4	98	101	0.7	-1	0	0.3
1988	SD-N	3	6	.333	60	0	0	0	10	98	70	6.4	8	55	5.1	81	7.4	2.48	135	.205	.307	11	10	97	126	-1.6	1	0	1.1
1989	NY-A	4	3	.571	52	1	0	0	3	85	83	8.8	9	37	3.9	82	8.7	4.55	90	.255	.330	-6	-4	105	91	0.8	0	-0	-0.4
Total	5	25	31	.446	281	8	0	0	39	477	394	7.4	43	225	4.2	408	7.7	3.25	115	.227	.313	28	26	99	108	-0.1	0	-1	2.7

■ BEN McDONALD McDonald, Larry Benard b: 11/14/67, Baton Rouge, La. BR/TR, 6'7", 212 lbs. Deb: 9/06/89

YEAR	TM/L	W	L	PCT	G	GS	CG	SHO	SV	IP	H	H/G	HR	BB	BB/G	SO	SO/G	ERA	/A	OAVG	OOBP	PR	/A	PF	CPI	WAT	PB	PD	TPI
1989	Bal-A	1	0	1.000	6	0	0	0	0	7	8	10.3	2	4	5.1	3	3.9	9.00	43	.286	.364	-4	-4	99	73	0.5	0	0	-0.3

■ ROGER McDOWELL McDowell, Roger Alan b: 12/21/60, Cincinnati, Ohio BR/TR, 6'1", 175 lbs. Deb: 4/11/85

YEAR	TM/L	W	L	PCT	G	GS	CG	SHO	SV	IP	H	H/G	HR	BB	BB/G	SO	SO/G	ERA	/A	OAVG	OOBP	PR	/A	PF	CPI	WAT	PB	PD	TPI
1985	NY-N	6	5	.545	62	2	0	0	17	127	108	7.7	9	37	2.6	70	5.0	2.83	121	.230	.283	11	8	95	96	-0.5	0	2	1.2
1986	NY-N	14	9	.609	75	0	0	0	22	128	107	7.5	4	42	3.0	65	4.6	3.02	115	.228	.290	10	6	93	84	-1.0	1	3	1.1
1987	NY-N	7	5	.583	56	0	0	0	25	89	95	9.6	7	28	2.8	32	3.2	4.15	96	.276	.326	-1	-2	97	99	0.2	1	1	0.0
1988	NY-N	5	5	.500	62	0	0	0	16	89	80	8.1	1	31	3.1	46	4.7	2.63	115	.238	.302	8	4	88	105	-1.0	2	2	0.8
1989	NY-N	1	5	.167	25	0	0	0	4	35	34	8.7	1	16	4.1	15	3.9	3.34	100	.254	.333	1	-0	95	110	-2.0	0	2	0.3
	Phi-N	3	3	.500	44	0	0	0	19	57	45	7.1	2	22	3.5	32	5.1	1.11	324	.220	.294	15	16	102	238	0.5	-0	1	1.8
	Yr	4	8	.333	69	0	0	0	23	92	79	7.7	3	38	3.7	47	4.6	1.96	178	.231	.305	16	16	100	238	-1.5	0	3	2.1
Total	5	36	32	.529	324	2	0	0	103	525	469	8.0	24	176	3.0	260	4.5	2.91	119	.240	.300	44	32	95	112	-3.8	5	11	5.2

■ CHUCK McELROY McElroy, Charles Dwayne b: 10/1/67, Galveston, Tex. BL/TL, 6', 160 lbs. Deb: 9/04/89

YEAR	TM/L	W	L	PCT	G	GS	CG	SHO	SV	IP	H	H/G	HR	BB	BB/G	SO	SO/G	ERA	/A	OAVG	OOBP	PR	/A	PF	CPI	WAT	PB	PD	TPI
1989	Phi-N	0	0	—	11	0	0	0	0	10	12	10.8	1	4	3.6	8	7.2	1.80	199	.286	.348	2	2	102	262	0.0	0	-0	0.2

■ ANDY McGAFFIGAN McGaffigan, Andrew Joseph b: 10/25/56, W.Palm Beach, Fla. BR/TR, 6'3", 185 lbs. Deb: 9/22/81

YEAR	TM/L	W	L	PCT	G	GS	CG	SHO	SV	IP	H	H/G	HR	BB	BB/G	SO	SO/G	ERA	/A	OAVG	OOBP	PR	/A	PF	CPI	WAT	PB	PD	TPI
1981	NY-A	0	0	—	2	0	0	0	0	7	5	6.4	1	3	3.9	2	2.6	2.57	141	.200	.258	1	1	99	115	0.0	0	-0	0.1
1982	SF-N	1	0	1.000	4	0	0	0	0	8	5	5.6	0	1	1.1	4	4.5	0.00	—	.179	.233	3	3	94	0	0.5	-0	-0	0.3

YEAR	TM/L	W	L	PCT	G	GS	CG	SHO	SV	IP	H	H/G	HR	BB	BB/G	SO	SO/G	ERA	/A	OAVG	OOBP	PR	/A	PF	CPI	WAT	PB	PD	TPI
1983	SF-N	3	9	.250	43	16	0	0	2	134	131	8.8	17	39	2.6	93	6.2	4.30	85	.255	.305	-10	-9	101	86	-2.9	-1	-3	-1.4
1984	Mon-N	3	4	.429	21	3	0	0	1	46	37	7.2	2	15	2.9	39	7.6	2.54	129	.220	.283	5	4	91	94	-0.3	-1	0	0.3
	Cin-N	0	2	.000	9	3	0	0	0	23	23	9.0	2	8	3.1	18	7.0	5.48	70	.261	.316	-5	-4	107	69	-0.9	-0	-1	-0.4
	Yr	3	6	.333	30	6	0	0	1	69	60	7.8	4	23	3.0	57	7.4	3.52	99	.233	.294	1	-0	97	69	-1.2	-1	-1	-0.1
1985	Cin-N	3	3	.500	15	15	2	0	0	94	88	8.4	4	30	2.9	83	7.9	3.73	101	.247	.306	-1	0	105	81	-0.2	-2	0	0.0
1986	Mon-N	10	5	.667	48	14	1	1	2	143	114	7.2	9	55	3.5	104	6.5	2.64	138	.223	.293	17	16	98	108	2.8	-2	-1	1.3
1987	Mon-N	5	2	.714	69	0	0	0	12	120	105	7.9	5	42	3.2	100	7.5	2.40	180	.235	.300	22	26	106	119	1.3	-1	-0	2.4
1988	Mon-N	6	0	1.000	63	0	0	0	4	91	81	8.0	4	37	3.7	71	7.0	2.77	131	.233	.306	7	9	105	109	3.0	-0	-1	0.8
1989	Mon-N	3	5	.375	57	0	0	0	2	75	85	10.2	3	30	3.6	40	4.8	4.68	76	.293	.354	-10	-9	102	99	-0.9	0	-1	-0.9
Total	9	34	30	.531	331	51	3	1	23	741	674	8.2	47	260	3.2	554	6.7	3.32	113	.243	.306	30	36	102	98	2.4	-7	-7	2.5
■ **CRAIG McMURTRY**	McMurtry, Joe Craig b: 11/5/59, Troy, Tex. BR/TR, 6'5", 195 lbs. Deb: 4/10/83																												
1983	Atl-N	15	9	.625	36	35	6	3	0	225	204	8.2	13	88	3.5	105	4.2	3.08	123	.243	.311	14	18	104	103	2.4	-4	3	1.9
1984	Atl-N	9	17	.346	37	30	0	0	0	183	184	9.0	16	102	5.0	99	4.9	4.33	91	.268	.354	-15	-8	110	106	-4.3	-2	4	-0.4
1985	Atl-N	0	3	.000	17	6	0	0	1	45	56	11.2	6	27	5.4	28	5.6	6.60	59	.306	.382	-15	-14	108	92	-1.4	-1	1	-1.3
1986	Atl-N	1	6	.143	37	5	0	0	0	80	82	9.2	7	43	4.8	50	5.6	4.72	81	.265	.357	-9	-8	103	95	-2.3	-0	0	-0.7
1988	Tex-A	3	3	.500	32	0	0	0	3	60	37	5.6	5	24	3.6	35	5.3	2.25	181	.180	.263	11	12	102	98	0.4	0	1	1.3
1989	Tex-A	0	0	—	19	0	0	0	0	23	29	11.3	3	13	5.1	14	5.5	7.43	54	.312	.396	-9	-9	103	86	0.0	0	0	-0.8
Total	6	28	38	.424	178	76	6	3	4	616	592	8.6	50	297	4.3	331	4.8	4.00	97	.256	.335	-22	-8	106	101	-5.2	-6	9	0.0
■ **LARRY McWILLIAMS**	McWilliams, Larry Dean b: 2/10/54, Wichita, Kan. BL/TL, 6'5", 180 lbs. Deb: 7/17/78																												
1978	Atl-N	9	3	.750	15	15	3	1	0	99	84	7.6	11	35	3.2	42	3.8	2.82	145	.224	.290	8	14	114	107	3.5	-2	1	1.5
1979	Atl-N	3	2	.600	13	13	1	0	0	66	69	9.4	4	22	3.0	32	4.4	5.59	74	.272	.331	-14	-11	110	70	0.8	1	1	-0.7
1980	Atl-N	9	14	.391	30	30	4	1	0	164	188	10.3	27	39	2.1	77	4.2	4.94	74	.285	.327	-24	-23	101	97	-2.8	0	-0	-2.3
1981	Atl-N	2	1	.667	6	5	2	1	0	38	31	7.3	2	8	1.9	23	5.4	3.08	113	.230	.265	2	2	100	78	0.6	-0	1	0.3
1982	Atl-N	2	3	.400	27	2	0	0	0	38	52	12.3	3	20	4.7	24	5.7	6.16	62	.327	.400	-11	-10	107	100	-0.6	0	2	-0.7
	Pit-N	6	5	.545	19	18	2	2	1	122	106	7.8	9	24	1.8	94	6.9	3.10	128	.232	.272	7	12	110	83	0.3	-0	2	1.5
	Yr	8	8	.500	46	20	2	2	1	160	158	8.9	12	44	2.5	118	6.6	3.82	103	.255	.304	-4	2	109	83	-0.3	0	4	0.8
1983	Pit-N	15	8	.652	35	35	8	4	0	238	205	7.8	19	87	3.3	199	7.5	3.25	115	.230	.294	10	13	103	90	3.6	-3	1	1.1
1984	Pit-N	12	11	.522	34	32	7	2	1	227	226	9.0	18	78	3.1	149	5.9	2.93	115	.263	.320	17	11	94	**129**	1.4	-2	0	0.8
1985	Pit-N	7	9	.438	30	19	2	0	0	126	139	9.9	9	62	4.4	52	3.7	4.71	80	.283	.366	-16	-13	104	101	1.1	-1	-0	-1.4
1986	Pit-N	3	11	.214	49	15	0	0	0	122	129	9.5	16	49	3.6	80	5.9	5.16	72	.268	.339	-20	-19	101	89	-3.3	0	-0	-1.9
1987	Atl-N	0	1	.000	9	2	0	0	0	20	25	11.2	2	7	3.1	13	5.8	5.85	76	.301	.358	-4	-3	109	90	-0.4	0	-0	-0.2
1988	StL-N	6	9	.400	42	17	2	1	1	136	130	8.6	10	45	3.0	70	4.6	3.90	93	.253	.308	-7	-4	105	92	-1.1	1	-0	-0.3
1989	Phi-N	2	11	.154	40	16	2	1	0	121	123	9.1	3	49	3.6	54	4.0	4.09	88	.265	.331	-8	-7	102	91	-4.1	-1	0	-0.6
	KC-A	2	2	.500	8	5	1	0	0	33	31	8.5	2	8	2.2	24	6.5	4.09	90	.254	.309	-1	-1	95	84	-0.1	0	-0	-0.1
Total	12	78	90	.464	357	224	34	13	3	1550	1538	8.9	135	533	3.1	933	5.4	3.95	94	.259	.319	-59	-41	103	97	-1.1	-8	8	-3.0
■ **SCOTT MEDVIN**	Medvin, Scott Howard b: 9/16/61, North Olmstead, Ohio BR/TR, 6'1", 195 lbs. Deb: 5/11/88																												
1988	Pit-N	3	0	1.000	17	0	0	0	0	28	23	7.4	1	9	2.9	16	5.1	4.82	70	.230	.295	-4	-5	97	58	1.5	-0	0	-0.4
1989	Pit-N	0	1	.000	6	0	0	0	0	6	6	9.0	0	5	7.5	4	6.0	6.00	55	.240	.367	-2	-2	94	63	-0.4	0	0	-0.1
Total	2	3	1	.750	23	0	0	0	0	34	29	7.7	1	14	3.7	20	5.3	5.03	67	.232	.310	-6	-6	97	59	1.1	-0	0	-0.5
■ **KENT MERCKER**	Mercker, Kent Franklin b: 2/1/68, Dublin, Ohio BL/TL, 6'1", 175 lbs. Deb: 9/22/89																												
1989	Atl-N	0	0	—	2	1	0	0	0	4	8	18.0	0	6	13.5	4	9.0	13.50	27	.400	.538	-4	-4	104	81	0.0	-0	0	-0.3
■ **BRIAN MEYER**	Meyer, Brian Scott b: 1/29/63, Camden, N.J. BR/TR, 6', 190 lbs. Deb: 9/03/88																												
1988	Hou-N	0	0	—	8	0	0	0	0	12	9	6.8	2	4	3.0	10	7.5	1.50	215	.225	.283	3	2	93	249	0.0	0	1	0.3
1989	Hou-N	0	1	.000	12	0	0	0	1	18	16	8.0	0	13	6.5	13	6.5	4.50	80	.239	.366	-2	-2	103	85	-0.4	0	0	-0.1
Total	2	0	1	.000	20	0	0	0	1	30	25	7.5	2	17	5.1	23	6.9	3.30	104	.234	.336	1	0	99	151	-0.4	0	1	0.2
■ **GARY MIELKE**	Mielke, Gary Roger b: 1/28/63, St. James, Minn. BR/TR, 6'3", 185 lbs. Deb: 8/19/87																												
1987	Tex-A	0	0	—	3	0	0	0	0	3	3	9.0	2	1	3.0	3	9.0	6.00	77	.250	.286	-1	-0	104	130	0.0	0	0	0.0
1989	Tex-A	1	0	1.000	43	0	0	0	1	50	52	9.4	4	25	4.5	26	4.7	3.24	123	.280	.364	4	4	103	149	0.5	0	-0	0.4
Total	2	1	0	1.000	46	0	0	0	1	53	55	9.3	6	26	4.4	29	4.9	3.40	119	.278	.359	3	4	103	148	0.5	0	-0	0.4
■ **BOB MILACKI**	Milacki, Robert b: 7/28/64, Trenton, N.J. BR/TR, 6'4", 220 lbs. Deb: 9/18/88																												
1988	Bal-A	2	0	1.000	3	3	1	1	0	25	9	3.2	1	9	3.2	18	6.5	0.72	538	.110	.198	9	9	97	24	1.0	0	0	1.1
1989	Bal-A	14	12	.538	37	36	3	2	0	243	233	8.6	21	88	3.3	113	4.2	3.74	102	.254	.316	4	3	99	98	0.0	0	-0	0.2
Total	2	16	12	.571	40	39	4	3	0	268	242	8.1	22	97	3.3	131	4.4	3.46	111	.242	.306	13	11	98	91	1.0	0	-0	1.3
■ **GREG MINTON**	Minton, Gregory Brian b: 7/29/51, Lubbock, Tex. BB/TR, 6'2", 180 lbs. Deb: 9/07/75																												
1975	SF-N	1	1	.500	4	2	0	0	0	17	19	10.1	1	11	5.8	6	3.2	6.88	54	.288	.392	-6	-6	102	75	0.0	-1	0	-0.5
1976	SF-N	0	3	.000	10	2	0	0	0	26	32	11.1	0	12	4.2	7	2.4	4.85	75	.317	.385	-4	-3	104	103	-1.4	-0	0	-0.3
1977	SF-N	1	1	.500	2	2	0	0	0	14	14	9.0	0	4	2.6	5	3.2	4.50	91	.264	.316	-1	-1	105	66	0.1	1	1	0.0
1978	SF-N	0	1	.000	11	0	0	0	0	16	22	12.4	3	8	4.5	6	3.4	7.88	41	.338	.408	-8	-8	91	92	-0.4	-0	0	-0.7
1979	SF-N	4	3	.571	46	0	0	0	4	80	59	6.6	0	27	3.0	33	3.7	1.80	194	.215	.280	17	15	93	115	0.9	-0	2	1.8
1980	SF-N	4	6	.400	68	0	0	0	19	91	81	8.0	0	34	3.4	42	4.2	2.47	141	.243	.305	11	10	96	110	-0.6	-0	2	1.2
1981	SF-N	4	5	.444	55	0	0	0	21	84	84	9.0	0	36	3.9	29	3.1	2.89	127	.267	.334	6	7	105	121	-0.5	-1	3	0.9
1982	SF-N	10	4	.714	78	0	0	0	30	123	108	7.9	5	42	3.1	58	4.2	1.83	185	.244	.306	**24**	21	94	168	2.8	0	1	2.3
1983	SF-N	7	11	.389	73	0	0	0	22	107	117	9.8	6	47	4.0	38	3.2	3.53	104	.283	.345	1	2	101	122	-1.9	4	-0	0.6
1984	SF-N	4	9	.308	74	1	0	0	19	124	130	9.4	6	57	4.1	48	3.5	3.77	93	.267	.336	-2	-4	98	104	-1.6	-1	2	-0.2
1985	SF-N	5	4	.556	68	0	0	0	4	97	98	9.1	6	54	5.0	37	3.4	3.53	97	.272	.358	1	-1	95	127	1.3	-0	2	0.0
1986	SF-N	4	4	.500	48	0	0	0	5	69	63	8.2	4	34	4.4	34	4.4	3.91	90	.251	.331	-1	-3	95	97	0.0	2	2	0.0
1987	SF-N	1	0	1.000	15	0	0	0	1	23	30	11.7	2	10	3.9	9	3.5	3.52	110	.323	.390	1	1	95	167	0.5	-0	0	0.1
	Cal-A	5	4	.556	41	0	0	0	10	76	71	8.4	4	29	3.4	35	4.1	3.08	145	.257	.323	12	12	100	121	0.8	0	2	1.3
1988	Cal-A	4	5	.444	44	0	0	0	7	79	67	7.6	1	34	3.9	46	5.2	2.85	132	.233	.314	10	8	95	103	-0.1	0	2	1.0
1989	Cal-A	4	3	.571	62	0	0	0	8	90	76	7.6	4	37	3.7	42	4.2	2.20	173	.230	.308	17	16	98	134	0.1	0	1	1.8
Total	15	58	64	.475	699	7	0	0	150	1116	1071	8.6	42	476	3.8	475	3.8	3.10	117	.258	.329	78	66	97	121	0.0	2	19	9.3
■ **PAUL MIRABELLA**	Mirabella, Paul Thomas b: 3/20/54, Belleville, N.J. BL/TL, 6'1", 190 lbs. Deb: 7/28/78																												
1978	Tex-A	3	2	.600	10	4	0	0	1	28	30	9.6	2	17	5.5	23	7.4	5.79	62	.286	.376	-6	-7	96	86	0.3	0	-0	-0.6
1979	NY-A	0	4	.000	10	1	0	0	0	14	16	10.3	3	10	6.4	4	2.6	9.00	45	.276	.380	-7	-8	95	69	-1.9	0	-0	-0.6
1980	Tor-A	5	12	.294	33	22	3	1	0	131	151	10.4	11	66	4.5	53	3.6	4.33	95	.294	.369	-4	-3	101	118	-2.6	0	0	-0.2
1981	Tor-A	0	0	—	8	1	0	0	0	15	20	12.0	2	7	4.2	9	5.4	7.20	57	.313	.384	-6	-5	113	84	0.0	0	-0	-0.5
1982	Tex-A	1	1	.500	40	0	0	0	3	51	46	8.1	4	22	3.9	29	5.1	4.76	81	.241	.323	-4	-5	94	74	0.2	0	-0	-0.4
1983	Bal-A	0	0	—	3	2	0	0	0	10	9	8.1	1	7	6.3	4	3.6	5.40	75	.243	.356	-1	-2	99	83	0.0	0	-0	-0.1
1984	Sea-A	2	5	.286	52	1	0	0	3	68	74	9.8	6	32	4.2	41	5.4	4.37	94	.282	.353	-3	-2	103	109	-1.2	0	1	0.0
1985	Sea-A	0	0	—	10	0	0	0	0	14	9	5.8	0	4	2.6	8	5.1	1.29	308	.188	.263	4	4	95	137	0.0	0	-0	0.4
1986	Sea-A	0	0	—	8	0	0	0	0	6	13	19.5	1	3	4.5	6	9.0	9.00	49	.419	.471	-3	-3	106	113	0.0	0	0	-0.2
1987	Mil-A	2	1	.667	29	0	0	0	2	29	30	9.3	0	16	5.0	14	4.3	4.97	92	.268	.346	-2	-1	102	79	0.4	0	1	0.0
1988	Mil-A	2	2	.500	38	0	0	0	4	60	44	6.6	3	21	3.2	33	5.0	1.65	247	.204	.270	15	16	103	132	0.0	0	1	1.7
1989	Mil-A	0	0	—	13	0	0	0	0	15	18	10.8	1	7	4.2	6	3.6	7.80	48	.290	.351	-7	-7	96	63	0.0	0	0	-0.5
Total	12	15	27	.357	254	31	3	1	13	441	460	9.4	34	212	4.3	230	4.7	4.51	90	.271	.347	-23	-22	100	104	-4.8	0	1	-1.0
■ **JOHN MITCHELL**	Mitchell, John Kyle b: 8/11/65, Dickson, Tenn. BR/TR, 6'2", 165 lbs. Deb: 9/08/86																												
1986	NY-N	0	1	.000	4	1	0	0	0	10	10	9.0	1	4	3.6	2	1.8	3.60	96	.278	.350	0	-0	93	126	-0.4	-0	0	0.0
1987	NY-N	3	6	.333	20	19	1	0	0	112	124	10.0	6	36	2.9	57	4.6	4.10	97	.279	.329	-0	-2	97	97	-1.8	-1	1	-0.1
1988	NY-N	0	0	—	1	0	0	0	0	1	2	18.0	0	1	9.0	1	9.0	0.00	—	.500	.600	0	0	88	0	0.0	-0	0	0.0

YEAR	TM/L	W	L	PCT	G	GS	CG	SHO	SV	IP	H	H/G	HR	BB	BB/G	SO	SO/G	ERA	/A	OAVG	OOBP	PR	/A	PF	CPI	WAT	PB	PD	TPI
1989	NY-N	0	1	.000	2	0	0	0	0	3	3	9.0	0	4	12.0	4	12.0	6.00	56	.231	.412	-1	-1	95	81	-0.4	0	0	0.0
Total	4	3	8	.273	27	20	1	0	0	126	139	9.9	7	45	3.2	64	4.6	4.07	96	.280	.335	-0	-2	97	98	-2.6	-1	1	-0.1
■ **KEVIN MMAHAT**	Mmahat, Kevin Paul b: 11/9/64, Memphis, Tenn. BL/TL, 6'5", 220 lbs. Deb: 9/09/89																												
1989	NY-A	0	2	.000	4	2	0	0	0	8	13	14.6	2	8	9.0	3	3.4	12.38	33	.406	.500	-8	-7	105	92	-0.9	0	-0	-0.6
■ **DALE MOHORCIC**	Mohorcic, Dale Robert b: 1/25/56, Cleveland, Ohio BL/TL, 6'3", 220 lbs. Deb: 5/31/86																												
1986	Tex-A	2	4	.333	58	0	0	0	7	79	86	9.8	5	15	1.7	29	3.3	2.51	159	.279	.314	15	13	95	148	-1.1	0	0	1.3
1987	Tex-A	7	6	.538	74	0	0	0	16	99	88	8.0	11	19	1.7	48	4.4	3.00	155	.244	.279	16	18	104	110	1.0	0	2	1.9
1988	Tex-A	2	6	.250	43	0	0	0	5	52	62	10.7	6	20	3.5	25	4.3	4.85	84	.295	.363	-5	-5	102	110	-1.7	0	0	-0.3
	NY-A	2	2	.500	13	0	0	0	1	23	21	8.2	1	9	3.5	19	7.4	2.74	139	.239	.324	3	3	96	123	0.0	0	-0	0.2
	Yr	4	8	.333	56	0	0	0	6	75	83	10.0	7	29	3.5	44	5.3	4.20	95	.269	.336	-2	-2	100	123	-1.7	0	0	-0.1
1989	NY-A	2	1	.667	32	0	0	0	2	58	65	10.1	8	18	2.8	24	3.7	4.97	82	.286	.350	-7	-6	105	102	0.6	0	1	-0.4
Total	4	15	19	.441	220	0	0	0	31	311	322	9.3	31	81	2.3	145	4.2	3.53	119	.270	.320	22	24	101	119	-1.2	0	3	2.7
■ **RICH MONTELEONE**	Monteleone, Richard b: 3/22/63, Tampa, Fla. BR/TR, 6'2", 205 lbs. Deb: 4/15/87																												
1987	Sea-A	0	0	—	3	0	0	0	0	7	10	12.9	2	4	5.1	2	2.6	6.43	72	.345	.441	-2	-1	103	137	0.0	0	0	0.0
1988	Cal-A	0	0	—	3	0	0	0	0	4	4	9.0	0	1	2.3	3	6.8	0.00	—	.222	.300	2	2	95	0	0.0	0	0	0.2
1989	Cal-A	2	2	.500	24	0	0	0	0	40	39	8.8	3	13	2.9	27	6.1	3.15	121	.255	.312	3	3	98	112	-0.1	0	0	0.3
Total	3	2	2	.500	30	0	0	0	0	51	53	9.4	5	18	3.2	32	5.6	3.35	116	.265	.330	4	3	98	107	-0.1	0	1	0.5
■ **JEFF MONTGOMERY**	Montgomery, Jeffrey Thomas b: 1/7/62, Wellston, Ohio BR/TR, 5'11", 170 lbs. Deb: 8/01/87																												
1987	Cin-N	2	2	.500	14	1	0	0	0	19	25	11.8	2	9	4.3	13	6.2	6.63	64	.313	.382	-5	-5	103	86	0.0	-0	0	-0.4
1988	KC-A	7	2	.778	45	0	0	0	1	63	54	7.7	6	30	4.3	47	6.7	3.43	119	.231	.317	4	5	103	105	2.5	0	0	0.5
1989	KC-A	7	3	.700	63	0	0	0	18	92	66	6.5	3	25	2.4	94	9.2	1.37	270	.198	.256	**26**	**24**	95	121	1.6	0	-0	2.4
Total	3	16	7	.696	122	1	0	0	19	174	145	7.5	11	64	3.3	154	8.0	2.69	145	.224	.295	24	23	99	111	4.1	-0	-0	2.5
■ **MIKE MOORE**	Moore, Michael Wayne b: 11/26/59, Eakly, Okla. BR/TR, 6'4", 205 lbs. Deb: 4/11/82																												
1982	Sea-A	7	14	.333	28	27	1	1	0	144	159	9.9	21	79	4.9	73	4.6	5.38	83	.285	.369	-21	-14	110	102	-3.2	0	1	-1.2
1983	Sea-A	6	8	.429	22	21	3	2	0	128	130	9.1	10	60	4.2	108	7.6	4.71	88	.267	.347	-9	-8	101	92	0.7	0	2	-0.6
1984	Sea-A	7	17	.292	34	33	6	0	0	212	236	10.0	16	85	3.6	158	6.7	4.97	83	.282	.348	-23	-20	103	90	-4.7	0	3	-1.6
1985	Sea-A	17	10	.630	35	34	14	2	0	247	230	8.4	18	70	2.6	155	5.6	3.46	114	.247	.299	19	14	95	94	4.8	0	2	1.6
1986	Sea-A	11	13	.458	38	37	11	1	1	266	279	9.4	28	94	3.2	146	4.9	4.30	104	.273	.336	-3	5	106	103	1.1	0	-1	0.3
1987	Sea-A	9	19	.321	33	33	12	0	0	231	268	10.4	29	84	3.3	115	4.5	4.71	98	.292	.345	-6	-3	103	106	-5.2	0	1	-0.1
1988	Sea-A	9	15	.375	37	32	9	3	1	229	196	7.7	24	63	2.5	182	7.2	3.77	114	.232	.285	5	14	108	82	-1.5	0	1	1.4
1989	Oak-A	19	11	.633	35	35	6	3	0	242	193	7.2	14	83	3.1	172	6.4	2.60	152	.219	.285	35	37	102	99	1.0	0	2	4.2
Total	8	85	107	.443	262	252	62	12	2	1699	1691	9.0	160	618	3.3	1109	5.9	4.13	103	.261	.324	-3	23	103	96	-7.0	0	11	4.0
■ **MIKE MORGAN**	Morgan, Michael Thomas b: 10/8/59, Tulare, Cal. BR/TR, 6'3", 195 lbs. Deb: 6/11/78																												
1978	Oak-A	0	3	.000	3	3	1	0	0	12	19	14.3	1	8	6.0	0	0.0	7.50	52	.373	.450	-5	-5	103	104	-1.4	0	1	-0.3
1979	Oak-A	2	10	.167	13	13	2	0	0	77	102	11.9	7	50	5.8	17	2.0	5.96	65	.332	.421	-15	-18	91	113	-3.0	0	1	-1.5
1982	NY-A	7	11	.389	30	23	2	0	0	150	167	10.0	15	67	4.0	71	4.3	4.38	90	.285	.357	-5	-7	97	111	-1.9	0	1	-0.6
1983	Tor-A	0	3	.000	16	4	0	0	0	45	48	9.6	6	21	4.2	22	4.4	5.20	84	.273	.348	-6	-4	108	92	-1.4	0	1	-0.3
1985	Sea-A	1	1	.500	2	2	0	0	0	6	11	16.5	2	5	7.5	2	3.0	12.00	33	.393	.485	-5	-5	95	93	0.1	0	0	-0.4
1986	Sea-A	11	17	.393	37	33	9	1	1	216	243	10.1	24	86	3.6	116	4.8	4.54	98	.286	.350	-9	-2	106	106	-0.7	0	-0	-0.2
1987	Sea-A	12	17	.414	34	31	8	2	0	207	245	10.7	25	53	2.3	85	3.7	4.65	99	.296	.337	-4	-1	103	105	-2.3	0	1	0.0
1988	Bal-A	1	6	.143	22	10	2	0	1	71	70	8.9	6	23	2.9	29	3.7	5.45	71	.255	.314	-12	-12	97	67	-1.9	0	0	-1.1
1989	LA-N	8	11	.421	40	19	0	0	0	153	130	7.6	6	33	1.9	72	4.2	2.53	128	.234	.273	17	12	93	100	-1.2	-2	5	1.6
Total	9	42	79	.347	197	138	24	3	2	937	1035	9.9	92	346	3.3	414	4.0	4.51	91	.283	.343	-43	-44	100	102	-13.7	-2	8	-2.8
■ **JACK MORRIS**	Morris, John Scott b: 5/16/55, St.Paul, Minn. BR/TR, 6'3", 195 lbs. Deb: 7/26/77																												
1977	Det-A	1	1	.500	7	6	1	0	0	46	38	7.4	4	23	4.5	28	5.5	3.72	115	.235	.323	2	3	105	97	0.1	0	0	0.3
1978	Det-A	3	5	.375	28	7	0	0	0	106	107	9.1	8	49	4.2	48	4.1	4.33	93	.268	.339	-6	-3	107	97	-1.1	0	-0	-0.3
1979	Det-A	17	7	.708	27	27	9	1	0	198	179	8.1	19	59	2.7	113	5.1	3.27	124	.244	.300	21	17	96	102	5.1	0	-1	1.6
1980	Det-A	16	15	.516	36	36	11	2	0	250	252	9.1	20	87	3.1	112	4.0	4.18	101	.262	.319	-4	2	105	89	0.0	0	3	0.4
1981	Det-A	**14**	7	.667	25	25	15	1	0	198	153	7.0	14	78	3.5	97	4.4	3.05	126	.218	.292	14	17	105	93	3.2	0	-0	1.9
1982	Det-A	17	16	.515	37	37	17	3	0	266	247	8.4	37	96	3.2	135	4.6	4.06	100	.247	.310	1	1	100	95	0.1	0	-0	0.0
1983	Det-A	20	13	.606	37	37	20	1	0	**294**	257	7.9	30	83	2.5	**232**	7.1	3.34	115	.233	.285	24	17	95	92	1.8	0	-1	1.6
1984	Det-A	19	11	.633	35	35	9	1	0	240	221	8.3	20	87	3.3	148	5.6	3.60	105	.241	.305	11	4	94	90	-0.1	0	2	0.6
1985	Det-A	16	11	.593	35	35	13	4	0	257	212	7.4	21	110	3.9	191	6.7	3.33	132	.225	.304	23	30	106	96	2.3	0	-1	3.1
1986	Det-A	21	8	.724	35	35	15	**6**	0	267	229	7.7	40	82	2.8	223	7.5	3.27	121	.229	.285	27	20	95	102	6.6	0	0	2.1
1987	Det-A	18	11	.621	34	34	13	0	0	266	227	7.7	39	93	3.1	208	7.0	3.38	126	.228	.292	32	26	96	102	0.7	0	-2	2.4
1988	Det-A	15	13	.536	34	34	10	2	0	235	225	8.6	20	83	3.2	168	6.4	3.94	95	.251	.313	1	-6	94	92	-0.1	0	0	-0.5
1989	Det-A	6	14	.300	24	24	10	0	0	170	189	10.0	23	59	3.1	115	6.1	4.87	79	.283	.336	-18	-19	99	98	-1.9	0	1	-1.7
Total	13	183	132	.581	394	372	143	21	0	2793	2536	8.2	295	989	3.2	1818	5.9	3.66	110	.242	.305	127	112	99	95	16.7	0	0	11.5
■ **JOHN MOSES**	Moses, John William b: 8/9/57, Los Angeles, Cal. BB/TL, 5'10", 165 lbs. Deb: 8/23/82																												
1989	Min-A	0	0	—	1	0	0	0	0	1	0	0.0	0	1	9.0	0	0.0	0.00	—	.000	.333	0	0	106	0	0.0	1	0	0.0
■ **JAMIE MOYER**	Moyer, Jamie b: 11/18/62, Sellersville, Pa. BL/TL, 6', 170 lbs. Deb: 6/16/86																												
1986	Chi-N	7	4	.636	16	16	1	1	0	87	107	11.1	10	42	4.3	45	4.7	5.07	79	.311	.385	-13	-10	108	115	2.0	-0	1	-0.8
1987	Chi-N	12	15	.444	35	33	1	0	0	201	210	9.4	28	97	4.3	147	6.6	5.10	81	.271	.347	-23	-21	102	96	-0.8	4	2	-1.4
1988	Chi-N	9	15	.375	34	30	3	1	0	202	212	9.4	20	55	2.5	121	5.4	3.48	104	.272	.317	-0	3	105	118	-2.8	-2	3	0.4
1989	Tex-A	4	9	.308	15	15	1	0	0	76	84	9.9	10	33	3.9	44	5.2	4.86	82	.283	.353	-8	-7	103	104	-2.6	0	1	-0.6
Total	4	32	43	.427	100	94	6	2	0	566	613	9.7	68	227	3.6	357	5.7	4.48	88	.279	.344	-44	-35	104	108	-4.2	1	6	-2.4
■ **TERRY MULHOLLAND**	Mulholland, Terence John b: 3/9/63, Uniontown, Pa. BR/TL, 6'3", 200 lbs. Deb: 6/08/86																												
1986	SF-N	1	7	.125	15	10	0	0	0	55	51	8.3	3	35	5.7	27	4.4	4.91	72	.251	.355	-7	-8	95	85	-3.0	-1	-1	-0.9
1988	SF-N	2	1	.667	9	6	2	1	0	46	50	9.8	3	7	1.4	18	3.5	3.72	87	.281	.304	-1	-3	93	100	0.5	-1	0	-0.2
1989	SF-N	0	0	—	5	1	0	0	0	11	15	12.3	0	4	3.3	6	4.9	4.09	82	.319	.373	-1	-1	96	119	0.0	-0	0	0.0
	Phi-N	4	7	.364	20	17	2	1	0	104	122	10.6	8	32	2.8	60	5.2	5.02	71	.292	.342	-18	-17	102	91	-0.6	-2	1	-1.8
	Yr	4	7	.364	25	18	2	1	0	115	137	10.7	8	36	2.8	66	5.2	4.93	72	.295	.345	-18	-17	102	91	-0.6	-0	1	-1.8
Total	3	7	15	.318	49	34	4	2	0	216	238	9.9	14	78	3.3	111	4.6	4.67	75	.281	.339	-27	-28	98	93	-3.1	-4	1	-2.9
■ **MIKE MUNOZ**	Munoz, Michael Anthony b: 7/12/65, Baldwin Park, Cal. BL/TL, 6'2", 190 lbs. Deb: 9/06/89																												
1989	LA-N	0	0	—	3	0	0	0	0	3	5	15.0	1	2	6.0	3	9.0	15.00	22	.417	.500	-4	-4	93	73	0.0	0	0	-0.3
■ **DAN MURPHY**	Murphy, Daniel Lee b: 9/18/64, Artesia, Cal. BR/TR, 6'2", 195 lbs. Deb: 8/10/89																												
1989	SD-N	0	0	—	7	0	0	0	0	6	6	9.0	1	4	6.0	1	1.5	6.00	59	.231	.333	-2	-2	101	71	0.0	0	0	-0.1
■ **ROB MURPHY**	Murphy, Robert Albert b: 5/26/60, Miami, Fla. BL/TL, 6'2", 200 lbs. Deb: 9/13/85																												
1985	Cin-N	0	0	—	2	0	0	0	0	3	2	6.0	1	2	6.0	1	3.0	6.00	63	.200	.333	-1	-1	105	88	0.0	0	0	0.0
1986	Cin-N	6	0	1.000	34	0	0	0	1	50	26	4.7	0	21	3.8	36	6.5	0.72	538	.155	.241	17	18	104	128	3.0	-0	0	1.9
1987	Cin-N	8	5	.615	87	0	0	0	3	101	91	8.1	7	32	2.9	99	8.8	3.03	139	.239	.296	12	13	103	100	1.4	0	0	1.4
1988	Cin-N	0	6	.000	**76**	0	0	0	3	85	69	7.3	3	38	4.0	74	7.8	3.07	118	.229	.309	4	5	105	100	-2.9	0	1	0.6
1989	Bos-A	5	7	.417	74	0	0	0	9	105	97	8.3	7	41	3.5	107	9.2	2.74	148	.251	.317	13	15	104	131	-1.1	0	1	1.6
Total	5	19	18	.514	273	0	0	0	16	344	285	7.5	18	134	3.5	317	8.3	2.64	150	.229	.299	45	51	104	113	0.4	-0	2	5.5
■ **JEFF MUSSELMAN**	Musselman, Jeffrey Joseph b: 6/21/63, Doylestown, Pa. BL/TL, 6', 180 lbs. Deb: 9/02/86																												
1986	Tor-A	0	0	—	6	0	0	0	0	5	8	14.4	1	5	9.0	4	7.2	10.80	40	.333	.448	-4	-4	104	79	0.0	0	0	-0.2
1987	Tor-A	12	5	.706	68	1	0	0	3	89	75	7.6	7	54	5.5	54	5.5	4.15	107	.237	.346	3	3	99	100	2.6	0	1	0.4

YEAR	TM/L	W	L	PCT	G	GS	CG	SHO	SV	IP	H	H/G	HR	BB	BB/G	SO	SO/G	ERA	/A	OAVG	OOBP	PR	/A	PF	CPI	WAT	PB	PD	TPI
1988	Tor-A	8	5	.615	15	15	0	0	0	85	80	8.5	4	30	3.2	39	4.1	3.18	124	.252	.319	8	7	99	108	1.2	0	-1	0.6
1989	Tor-A	0	1	.000	5	3	0	0	0	11	19	15.5	2	9	7.4	3	2.5	10.64	34	.404	.483	-8	-9	93	95	-0.4	0	0	-0.7
	NY-N	3	2	.600	20	0	0	0	0	26	27	9.3	1	14	4.8	11	3.8	3.12	107	.267	.345	1	1	95	134	0.3	0	2	0.3
Total	4	23	13	.639	114	19	0	0	3	216	209	8.7	15	112	4.7	111	4.6	4.13	98	.259	.348	-0	-2	98	106	3.7	0	2	0.4
■ RANDY MYERS		Myers, Randall Kirk b: 9/19/62, Vancouver, Wash. BL/TL, 6'1", 190 lbs. Deb: 10/06/85																											
1985	NY-N	0	0	—	1	0	0	0	0	2	0	0.0	0	1	4.5	2	9.0	0.00	—	.000	.143	1	1	95	0	0.0	0	0	0.1
1986	NY-N	0	0	—	10	0	0	0	0	11	11	9.0	1	9	7.4	13	10.6	4.09	85	.256	.396	-0	-1	93	127	0.0	0	0	0.0
1987	NY-N	3	6	.333	54	0	0	0	6	75	61	7.3	6	30	3.6	92	11.0	3.96	100	.225	.290	1	0	97	77	-1.8	0	0	0.1
1988	NY-N	7	3	.700	55	0	0	0	26	68	45	6.0	5	17	2.3	69	9.1	1.72	176	.190	.245	13	10	88	111	1.1	1	-1	1.0
1989	NY-N	7	4	.636	65	0	0	0	24	84	62	6.6	4	40	4.3	88	9.4	2.36	142	.206	.292	11	9	95	110	1.2	-1	0	0.9
Total	5	17	13	.567	185	0	0	0	56	240	179	6.7	16	97	3.6	264	9.9	2.74	126	.209	.284	25	19	94	100	0.5	0	-0	2.1
■ JAIME NAVARRO		Navarro, Jaime (Cintron) b: 3/27/67, Bayamon, P.R. BR/TR, 6'4", 210 lbs. Deb: 6/20/89																											
1989	Mil-A	7	8	.467	19	17	1	0	0	110	119	9.7	6	32	2.6	56	4.6	3.11	120	.277	.323	10	8	96	123	-0.4	0	-0	0.8
■ GENE NELSON		Nelson, Wayland Eugene b: 12/3/60, Tampa, Fla. BR/TR, 6', 172 lbs. Deb: 5/04/81																											
1981	NY-A	3	1	.750	8	7	0	0	0	39	40	9.2	5	23	5.3	16	3.7	4.85	75	.261	.358	-5	-5	99	99	0.9	0	0	-0.5
1982	Sea-A	6	9	.400	22	19	2	1	0	123	133	9.7	16	60	4.4	71	5.2	4.61	97	.279	.358	-7	-2	110	109	-1.1	0	1	0.0
1983	Sea-A	0	3	.000	10	5	1	0	0	32	38	10.7	6	21	5.9	11	3.1	7.88	52	.295	.392	-14	-13	101	82	-1.4	0	0	-1.1
1984	Chi-A	3	5	.375	20	9	2	0	1	75	72	8.6	9	17	2.0	36	4.3	4.44	100	.254	.296	-4	0	111	80	-0.6	0	0	0.0
1985	Chi-A	10	10	.500	46	18	1	0	2	146	144	8.9	23	67	4.1	101	6.2	4.25	97	.258	.339	-2	-2	100	112	-0.4	0	0	-0.1
1986	Chi-A	6	6	.500	54	1	0	0	6	115	118	9.2	7	41	3.2	70	5.5	3.83	111	.271	.332	4	5	101	104	0.6	0	1	0.6
1987	Oak-A	6	5	.545	54	6	0	0	3	124	120	8.7	12	35	2.5	94	6.8	3.92	104	.249	.302	8	2	91	88	0.5	0	-1	0.1
1988	Oak-A	9	6	.600	54	1	0	0	3	112	93	7.5	9	38	3.1	67	5.4	3.05	121	.228	.294	11	8	93	100	-0.4	0	-1	0.7
1989	Oak-A	3	5	.375	50	0	0	0	3	80	60	6.7	5	30	3.4	70	7.9	3.26	122	.203	.275	6	6	102	69	-1.5	0	-1	0.5
Total	9	46	50	.479	318	66	6	1	18	846	818	8.7	92	332	3.5	536	5.7	4.13	100	.254	.323	-2	-0	101	97	-3.4	0	-0	0.2
■ ROD NICHOLS		Nichols, Rodney Lea b: 12/29/64, Burlington, Iowa BR/TR, 6'2", 190 lbs. Deb: 7/30/88																											
1988	Cle-A	1	7	.125	11	10	3	0	0	69	73	9.5	5	23	3.0	31	4.0	5.09	80	.272	.330	-9	-8	102	80	-2.9	0	-0	-0.7
1989	Cle-A	4	6	.400	15	11	0	0	0	72	81	10.1	9	24	3.0	42	5.3	4.38	93	.285	.340	-4	-3	104	109	-0.5	0	-0	-0.2
Total	2	5	13	.278	26	21	3	0	0	141	154	9.8	14	47	3.0	73	4.7	4.72	86	.279	.335	-12	-10	103	95	-3.4	0	-0	-0.9
■ TOM NIEDENFUER		Niedenfuer, Thomas Edward b: 8/13/59, St. Louis Park, Minn BR/TR, 6'5", 225 lbs. Deb: 8/15/81																											
1981	LA-N	3	1	.750	17	0	0	0	2	26	25	8.7	1	6	2.1	12	4.2	3.81	88	.258	.299	-1	-1	96	82	0.8	0	-0	-0.1
1982	LA-N	3	4	.429	55	0	0	0	9	70	71	9.1	3	25	3.2	60	7.7	2.70	125	.269	.328	7	5	94	139	-0.7	-0	-1	0.5
1983	LA-N	8	3	.727	66	0	0	0	11	95	55	5.2	6	29	2.7	66	6.3	1.89	191	.170	.232	18	18	100	72	2.2	-0	-1	1.8
1984	LA-N	2	5	.286	33	0	0	0	11	47	39	7.5	3	23	4.4	45	8.6	2.49	150	.227	.315	6	7	104	132	-1.4	-0	-0	0.6
1985	LA-N	7	9	.438	64	0	0	0	19	106	86	7.3	6	24	2.0	102	8.7	2.72	121	.223	.267	10	7	92	84	-2.1	-0	-1	0.6
1986	LA-N	6	6	.500	60	0	0	0	11	80	86	9.7	11	29	3.3	55	6.2	3.71	95	.280	.336	0	-2	95	128	0.6	1	0	0.0
1987	LA-N	1	0	1.000	15	0	0	0	1	16	13	7.3	1	9	5.1	10	5.6	2.81	134	.220	.329	2	2	92	119	0.5	0	0	0.2
	Bal-A	3	5	.375	45	0	0	0	13	52	55	9.5	11	22	3.8	37	6.4	5.02	88	.266	.335	-3	-3	99	102	-0.3	0	-1	-0.3
1988	Bal-A	3	4	.429	52	0	0	0	18	59	59	9.0	8	19	2.9	40	6.1	3.51	110	.259	.317	3	2	97	119	0.5	0	-1	0.2
1989	Sea-A	0	3	.000	25	0	0	0	0	36	46	11.5	7	15	3.8	15	3.8	6.75	60	.309	.363	-11	-11	104	92	-1.4	0	0	-1.0
Total	9	36	40	.474	432	0	0	0	95	587	535	8.2	57	201	3.1	442	6.8	3.28	111	.244	.304	32	23	97	105	-1.3	-0	-4	2.5
■ SCOTT NIELSEN		Nielsen, Jeffrey Scott b: 12/18/58, Salt Lake City, Ut. BR/TR, 6'1", 190 lbs. Deb: 7/07/86																											
1986	NY-A	4	4	.500	10	9	2	2	0	56	66	10.6	12	12	1.9	20	3.2	4.02	107	.299	.340	1	2	103	138	-0.3	0	-1	0.1
1987	Chi-A	3	5	.375	19	7	1	1	2	66	83	11.3	9	25	3.4	23	3.1	6.27	77	.307	.365	-13	-10	109	90	-0.8	0	-1	-0.9
1988	NY-A	1	2	.333	7	2	0	0	0	20	27	12.1	5	13	5.8	4	1.8	6.75	56	.333	.426	-6	-7	96	118	-0.5	0	0	-0.5
1989	NY-A	1	0	1.000	2	0	0	0	0	1	2	18.0	0	1	9.0	0	0.0	9.00	45	.500	.500	-1	-1	105	131	0.5	0	0	0.0
Total	4	9	11	.450	38	18	3	3	2	143	178	11.2	26	51	3.2	47	3.0	5.48	82	.309	.366	-19	-16	104	113	-1.1	0	-1	-1.3
■ ERIC NOLTE		Nolte, Eric Carl b: 4/28/64, Canoga Park, Cal. BL/TL, 6'3", 205 lbs. Deb: 8/01/87																											
1987	SD-N	2	6	.250	12	12	1	0	0	67	57	7.7	6	36	4.8	44	5.9	3.22	124	.226	.324	6	6	98	109	-1.5	-1	-0	0.4
1988	SD-N	0	0	—	2	0	0	0	0	3	3	9.0	1	2	6.0	1	3.0	6.00	56	.273	.357	-1	-1	97	117	0.0	0	0	0.0
1989	SD-N	0	0	—	3	1	0	0	0	9	15	15.0	1	7	7.0	8	8.0	11.00	32	.375	.449	-7	-7	101	79	0.0	-0	0	-0.6
Total	3	2	6	.250	17	13	1	0	0	79	75	8.5	8	45	5.1	53	6.0	4.22	93	.248	.343	-2	-3	98	105	-1.5	-1	-0	-0.2
■ RANDY NOSEK		Nosek, Randall William b: 1/8/67, Omaha, Neb. BR/TR, 6'4", 215 lbs. Deb: 5/27/89																											
1989	Det-A	0	2	.000	2	2	0	0	0	5	7	12.6	2	10	18.0	4	7.2	14.40	27	.333	.548	-6	-6	99	89	-0.9	0	-0	-0.4
■ ED NUNEZ		Nunez, Edwin (Martinez) b: 5/27/63, Humacao, P.R. BR/TR, 6'5", 235 lbs. Deb: 4/07/82																											
1982	Sea-A	1	2	.333	8	5	0	0	0	35	36	9.3	7	16	4.1	27	6.9	4.63	97	.269	.340	-2	-1	110	112	-0.3	0	0	0.0
1983	Sea-A	0	4	.000	14	5	0	0	0	37	40	9.7	3	22	5.4	35	8.5	4.38	94	.278	.382	-1	-1	101	117	-1.9	0	0	0.0
1984	Sea-A	2	2	.500	37	0	0	0	7	68	55	7.3	8	21	2.8	57	7.5	3.18	130	.218	.282	6	7	103	92	0.2	0	-0	0.7
1985	Sea-A	7	3	.700	70	0	0	0	16	90	79	7.9	13	34	3.4	58	5.8	3.10	128	.234	.299	10	9	95	119	2.3	0	0	0.9
1986	Sea-A	1	2	.333	14	1	0	0	0	22	25	10.2	5	5	2.0	17	7.0	5.73	78	.284	.323	-4	-3	106	90	-0.2	0	-0	-0.2
1987	Sea-A	3	4	.429	48	0	0	0	12	47	45	8.6	7	18	3.4	34	6.5	3.83	120	.262	.323	3	4	103	120	-0.3	0	-0	0.3
1988	Sea-A	1	4	.200	14	3	0	0	0	29	45	14.0	4	14	4.3	19	5.9	8.07	53	.366	.421	-13	-12	108	97	-1.2	0	1	-1.0
	NY-N	1	0	1.000	10	0	0	0	0	14	21	13.5	1	3	1.9	8	5.1	4.50	67	.339	.369	-2	-2	88	124	0.5	0	0	-0.2
1989	Det-A	3	4	.429	27	0	0	0	1	54	49	8.2	6	36	6.0	41	6.8	4.17	93	.254	.357	-2	-2	99	115	0.4	0	1	0.0
Total	8	19	25	.432	242	14	0	0	36	396	395	9.0	54	169	3.8	296	6.7	4.16	99	.262	.333	-4	-1	101	110	-0.5	0	1	0.5
■ JOSE NUNEZ		Nunez, Jose (Jimenez) b: 1/13/64, Jarabacoa, D.R. BR/TR, 6'3", 175 lbs. Deb: 4/09/87																											
1987	Tor-A	5	2	.714	37	9	0	0	0	97	91	8.4	12	58	5.4	99	9.2	5.01	89	.256	.349	-6	-6	99	95	1.1	0	-1	-0.6
1988	Tor-A	0	1	.000	13	2	0	0	0	29	28	8.7	3	17	5.3	18	5.6	3.10	127	.259	.362	3	3	99	153	-0.4	0	0	0.3
1989	Tor-A	0	0	—	6	1	0	0	0	11	8	6.5	0	2	1.6	14	11.5	2.45	148	.200	.238	2	1	93	47	0.0	0	-0	0.1
Total	3	5	3	.625	56	12	0	0	0	137	127	8.3	15	77	5.1	131	8.6	4.40	97	.252	.344	-1	-2	99	103	0.7	0	-1	-0.2
■ BOBBY OJEDA		Ojeda, Robert Michael b: 12/17/57, Los Angeles, Cal. BL/TL, 6'1", 185 lbs. Deb: 7/13/80																											
1980	Bos-A	1	1	.500	7	7	0	0	0	26	39	13.5	2	14	4.8	12	4.2	6.92	60	.361	.434	-8	-8	102	102	0.0	0	-0	-0.7
1981	Bos-A	6	2	.750	10	10	2	0	0	66	50	6.8	6	25	3.4	28	3.8	3.14	123	.212	.288	4	5	106	89	1.9	0	-0	0.5
1982	Bos-A	4	6	.400	22	14	0	0	0	78	95	11.0	13	29	3.3	52	6.0	5.65	79	.296	.355	-14	-10	110	96	-1.3	0	-1	-1.0
1983	Bos-A	12	7	.632	29	28	5	0	0	174	173	8.9	15	73	3.8	94	4.9	4.03	103	.265	.334	1	2	102	104	3.0	0	0	0.2
1984	Bos-A	12	12	.500	33	32	8	**5**	0	217	211	8.8	17	96	4.0	137	5.7	3.98	110	.259	.333	0	10	110	99	-0.7	0	1	1.0
1985	Bos-A	9	11	.450	39	22	5	0	1	158	166	9.5	11	48	2.7	102	5.8	3.99	106	.273	.322	3	4	102	100	-1.0	0	0	0.4
1986	NY-N	18	5	**.783**	32	30	7	2	0	217	185	7.7	15	52	2.2	148	6.1	2.57	135	.230	.274	28	22	93	101	4.4	-2	1	2.1
1987	NY-N	3	5	.375	10	7	0	0	0	46	45	8.8	5	10	2.0	21	4.1	3.91	101	.253	.286	1	0	97	86	-1.3	-0	0	0.0
1988	NY-N	10	13	.435	29	29	5	5	0	190	158	7.5	6	33	1.6	133	6.3	2.89	105	.225	.259	12	3	88	72	-3.8	1	2	0.6
1989	NY-N	13	11	.542	31	31	5	2	0	192	179	8.4	16	78	3.7	95	4.5	3.47	96	.245	.314	1	-3	95	104	0.1	-2	2	-0.2
Total	10	88	73	.547	242	210	37	14	1	1364	1301	8.6	106	458	3.0	822	5.4	3.65	104	.252	.310	27	23	99	96	1.3	-3	4	2.9
■ STEVE OLIN		Olin, Steven Robert b: 10/10/65, Portland, Ore. BR/TR, 6'3", 185 lbs. Deb: 7/29/89																											
1989	Cle-A	1	4	.200	25	0	0	0	1	36	35	8.8	1	14	3.5	24	6.0	3.75	108	.255	.322	1	1	104	88	-1.3	0	0	0.1
■ FRANCISCO OLIVERAS		Oliveras, Francisco Javier (Noa) b: 1/31/63, Santurce, P.R. BR/TR, 5'10", 170 lbs. Deb: 5/03/89																											
1989	Min-A	3	4	.429	12	8	1	0	0	56	64	10.3	8	15	2.4	24	3.9	4.50	92	.288	.335	-4	-2	106	106	-0.4	0	-1	-0.2
■ GREGG OLSON		Olson, Greggory William b: 10/11/66, Scribner, Neb. BR/TR, 6'4", 210 lbs. Deb: 9/02/88																											
1988	Bal-A	1	1	.500	10	0	0	0	0	11	10	8.2	1	10	8.2	9	7.4	3.27	118	.244	.392	1	1	97	154	0.2	0	0	0.1

YEAR TM/L	W	L	PCT	G	GS	CG	SHO	SV	IP	H	H/G	HR	BB	BB/G	SO	SO/G	ERA	/A	OAVG	OOBP	PR	/A	PF	CPI	WAT	PB	PD	TPI
1989 Bal-A	5	2	.714	64	0	0	0	27	85	57	6.0	1	46	4.9	90	9.5	1.69	226	.188	.292	21	20	99	118	1.4	0	0	2.1
Total 2	6	3	.667	74	0	0	0	27	96	67	6.3	2	56	5.3	99	9.3	1.88	205	.194	.305	22	21	98	122	1.6	0	1	2.2
■ **RANDY O'NEAL**	O'Neal, Randall Jeffrey b: 8/30/60, Ashland, Ky. BR/TR, 6'2", 195 lbs. Deb: 9/12/84																											
1984 Det-A	2	1	.667	4	3	0	0	0	19	16	7.6	0	6	2.8	12	5.7	3.32	114	.222	.282	1	1	94	59	0.1	0	-0	0.1
1985 Det-A	5	5	.500	28	12	1	0	1	94	82	7.9	8	36	3.4	52	5.0	3.26	135	.240	.309	9	12	106	108	-0.1	0	1	1.3
1986 Det-A	3	7	.300	37	11	1	0	2	123	121	8.9	13	44	3.2	68	5.0	4.32	92	.260	.322	-2	-5	95	93	-2.2	0	1	-0.3
1987 Atl-N	4	2	.667	16	10	0	0	0	61	79	11.7	12	24	3.5	33	4.9	5.61	80	.316	.376	-10	-8	109	114	1.3	-1	1	-0.6
StL-N	0	0	—	1	1	0	0	0	5	2	3.6	0	2	3.6	4	7.2	1.80	221	.111	.190	1	1	97	32	0.0	0	0	0.2
Yr	4	2	.667	17	11	0	0	0	66	81	11.0	12	26	3.5	37	5.0	5.32	83	.298	.357	-9	-7	108	32	1.3	-1	1	-0.4
1988 StL-N	2	3	.400	10	8	0	0	0	53	57	9.7	7	10	1.7	20	3.4	4.58	79	.274	.311	-7	-6	105	91	-0.3	-2	1	-0.6
1989 Phi-N	0	1	.000	20	1	0	0	0	39	46	10.6	5	9	2.1	29	6.7	6.23	57	.301	.329	-12	-11	102	79	-0.4	-1	1	-1.1
Total 6	16	19	.457	116	46	2	0	3	394	403	9.2	45	131	3.0	218	5.0	4.41	92	.267	.324	-19	-16	102	96	-1.6	-3	5	-1.0
■ **STEVE ONTIVEROS**	Ontiveros, Steven b: 3/5/61, Tularosa, N.Mex. BR/TR, 6', 180 lbs. Deb: 6/14/85																											
1985 Oak-A	1	3	.250	39	0	0	0	8	75	45	5.4	4	19	2.3	36	4.3	1.92	201	.174	.232	19	16	93	72	-0.9	0	1	1.7
1986 Oak-A	2	2	.500	46	0	0	0	10	73	72	8.9	10	25	3.1	54	6.7	4.68	84	.265	.321	-4	-6	94	93	0.1	0	0	-0.5
1987 Oak-A	10	8	.556	35	22	2	1	1	151	141	8.4	19	50	3.0	97	5.8	3.99	102	.242	.302	8	1	91	90	1.1	0	2	0.3
1988 Oak-A	3	4	.429	10	10	0	0	0	55	57	9.3	4	21	3.4	30	4.9	4.58	81	.265	.324	-4	-5	93	85	-1.1	0	1	-0.3
1989 Phi-N	2	1	.667	6	5	0	0	0	31	34	9.9	2	15	4.4	12	3.5	3.77	95	.288	.366	-1	-1	102	127	0.7	-0	1	0.0
Total 5	18	18	.500	136	37	2	1	19	385	349	8.2	39	130	3.0	229	5.4	3.79	103	.241	.302	18	6	93	89	-0.1	-0	5	1.2
■ **JESSE OROSCO**	Orosco, Jesse Russell b: 4/21/57, Santa Barbara, Cal. BR/TL, 6'2", 174 lbs. Deb: 4/05/79																											
1979 NY-N	1	2	.333	18	2	0	0	0	35	33	8.5	4	22	5.7	22	5.7	4.89	74	.260	.370	-4	-5	96	100	-0.1	-1	1	-0.4
1981 NY-N	0	1	.000	8	0	0	0	1	17	13	6.9	2	6	3.2	18	9.5	1.59	225	.213	.275	4	4	103	180	-0.4	-0	0	0.4
1982 NY-N	4	10	.286	54	2	0	0	4	109	92	7.6	7	40	3.3	89	7.3	2.72	132	.230	.297	11	11	100	107	-2.0	-0	0	1.1
1983 NY-N	13	7	.650	62	0	0	0	17	110	76	6.2	3	38	3.1	84	6.9	1.47	247	.197	.266	**26**	**26**	100	121	4.3	1	1	3.0
1984 NY-N	10	6	.625	60	0	0	0	31	87	58	6.0	7	34	3.5	85	8.8	2.59	139	.185	.265	10	10	100	79	1.4	1	-0	1.1
1985 NY-N	8	6	.571	54	0	0	0	17	79	66	7.5	6	34	3.9	68	7.7	2.73	126	.224	.302	8	6	95	107	-0.3	1	-1	0.7
1986 NY-N	8	6	.571	58	0	0	0	21	81	64	7.1	6	35	3.9	62	6.9	2.33	148	.217	.302	13	10	93	126	-1.0	0	-1	1.0
1987 NY-N	3	9	.250	58	0	0	0	16	77	78	9.1	5	31	3.6	78	9.1	4.44	89	.266	.331	-3	-4	97	90	-3.4	-1	0	-0.4
1988 LA-N	3	2	.600	55	0	0	0	9	53	41	7.0	4	30	5.1	43	7.3	2.72	133	.215	.319	4	5	105	124	0.1	-0	0	0.6
1989 Cle-A	3	4	.429	69	0	0	0	3	78	54	6.2	7	26	3.0	79	9.1	2.08	195	.198	.263	16	17	104	115	-0.1	0	1	1.9
Total 10	53	53	.500	496	4	0	0	119	726	575	7.1	51	296	3.7	628	7.8	2.67	137	.218	.295	83	80	99	110	-1.5	1	2	9.0
■ **DAVE OTTO**	Otto, David Alan b: 11/12/64, Chicago, Ill. BL/TL, 6'7", 210 lbs. Deb: 9/08/87																											
1987 Oak-A	0	0	—	3	0	0	0	0	6	7	10.5	1	1	1.5	3	4.5	9.00	45	.304	.333	-3	-3	91	58	0.0	0	0	-0.2
1988 Oak-A	0	0	—	3	2	0	0	0	10	9	8.1	0	6	5.4	7	6.3	1.80	206	.243	.349	2	2	93	193	0.0	0	0	0.2
1989 Oak-A	0	0	—	1	1	0	0	0	7	6	7.7	0	2	2.6	4	5.1	2.57	154	.261	.308	1	1	102	124	0.0	0	0	0.1
Total 3	0	0	—	7	3	0	0	0	23	22	8.6	1	9	3.5	14	5.5	3.91	99	.265	.333	0	-0	95	136	0.0	0	0	0.1
■ **DONN PALL**	Pall, Donn Steven b: 1/11/62, Chicaho, Ill. BR/TR, 6'2", 185 lbs. Deb: 8/01/88																											
1988 Chi-A	0	2	.000	17	0	0	0	0	29	39	12.1	1	8	2.5	16	5.0	3.41	115	.328	.362	2	2	99	150	-0.9	0	1	0.2
1989 Chi-A	4	5	.444	53	0	0	0	6	87	90	9.3	9	19	2.0	58	6.0	3.31	110	.270	.316	6	3	93	123	0.1	0	-1	0.2
Total 2	4	7	.364	70	0	0	0	6	116	129	10.0	10	27	2.1	74	5.7	3.34	111	.285	.328	7	5	95	130	-0.8	0	-1	0.4
■ **DAVID PALMER**	Palmer, David William b: 10/19/57, Glens Falls, N.Y. BR/TR, 6'1", 195 lbs. Deb: 9/09/78																											
1978 Mon-N	0	1	.000	5	1	0	0	0	10	9	8.1	1	2	1.8	7	6.3	2.70	127	.243	.282	1	1	96	111	-0.4	-0	1	0.1
1979 Mon-N	10	2	.833	36	11	2	1	2	123	110	8.0	10	30	2.2	72	5.3	2.63	143	.237	.283	15	16	101	105	3.7	-3	-0	1.3
1980 Mon-N	8	6	.571	24	19	3	1	0	130	124	8.6	11	30	2.1	73	5.1	2.98	119	.255	.295	9	8	98	110	0.3	1	1	1.1
1982 Mon-N	6	4	.600	13	13	1	0	0	74	60	7.3	3	36	4.4	46	5.6	3.16	119	.224	.314	4	5	104	94	0.8	-2	0	0.3
1984 Mon-N	7	3	.700	20	19	1	1	0	105	101	8.7	5	44	3.8	66	5.7	3.86	85	.256	.327	-3	-7	91	93	2.2	1	1	-0.5
1985 Mon-N	7	10	.412	24	23	0	0	0	136	128	8.5	5	67	4.4	106	7.0	3.71	91	.250	.337	-2	-5	94	97	-1.9	-1	2	-0.4
1986 Atl-N	11	10	.524	35	35	2	0	0	210	181	7.8	17	102	4.4	170	7.3	3.64	106	.234	.324	2	5	103	97	1.6	2	2	0.9
1987 Atl-N	8	11	.421	28	28	0	0	0	152	169	10.0	17	64	3.8	111	6.6	4.91	91	.281	.349	-14	-8	109	98	-0.1	-1	1	-0.6
1988 Phi-N	7	9	.438	22	22	1	1	0	129	129	9.0	8	48	3.3	85	5.9	4.47	80	.261	.321	-14	-13	103	84	0.5	5	-1	-0.8
1989 Det-A	0	3	.000	5	5	0	0	0	17	25	13.2	1	11	5.8	12	6.4	7.94	49	.342	.424	-8	-8	99	85	-1.4	0	-0	-0.6
Total 10	64	59	.520	212	176	10	4	2	1086	1036	8.6	78	434	3.6	748	6.2	3.78	99	.252	.322	-10	-7	101	97	5.3	2	5	0.8
■ **CLAY PARKER**	Parker, James Clayton b: 12/19/62, Columbia, La. BR/TR, 6'1", 185 lbs. Deb: 9/14/87																											
1987 Sea-A	0	0	—	3	1	0	0	0	8	15	16.9	2	4	4.5	8	9.0	10.13	45	.405	.465	-5	-5	103	103	0.0	0	0	-0.3
1989 NY-A	4	5	.444	22	17	2	0	0	120	123	9.2	12	31	2.3	53	4.0	3.68	111	.264	.308	3	6	105	102	-0.1	0	0	0.6
Total 2	4	5	.444	25	18	2	0	0	128	138	9.7	14	35	2.5	61	4.3	4.08	101	.274	.320	-2	1	105	102	-0.1	0	0	0.3
■ **JEFF PARRETT**	Parrett, Jeffrey Dale b: 8/26/61, Indianapolis, Ind. BR/TR, 6'4", 185 lbs. Deb: 4/11/86																											
1986 Mon-N	0	1	.000	12	0	0	0	0	20	19	8.5	3	13	5.8	21	9.4	4.95	74	.247	.352	-3	-3	98	95	-0.4	0	0	-0.2
1987 Mon-N	7	6	.538	45	0	0	0	6	62	53	7.7	8	30	4.4	56	8.1	4.21	103	.229	.311	-1	1	106	88	-0.2	-1	0	0.0
1988 Mon-N	12	4	.750	61	0	0	0	6	92	66	6.5	8	45	4.4	62	6.1	2.64	137	.214	.304	8	10	105	126	4.2	0	-1	1.0
1989 Phi-N	12	6	.667	72	0	0	0	6	106	90	7.6	6	44	3.7	98	8.3	2.97	121	.232	.302	6	7	102	105	4.1	-1	-1	0.6
Total 4	31	17	.646	190	0	0	0	18	280	228	7.3	25	132	4.2	237	7.6	3.28	115	.227	.308	11	15	104	107	7.7	-0	-2	1.4
■ **KEN PATTERSON**	Patterson, Kenneth Brian b: 7/8/64, Costa Mesa, Cal. BL/TL, 6'4", 210 lbs. Deb: 7/09/88																											
1988 Chi-A	0	2	.000	9	2	0	0	1	21	25	10.7	2	7	3.0	8	3.4	4.71	83	.294	.348	-2	-2	99	101	-0.9	0	-0	-0.1
1989 Chi-A	6	1	.857	50	1	0	0	0	66	64	8.7	11	28	3.8	43	5.9	4.50	81	.257	.331	-4	-6	93	103	2.7	0	-1	-0.7
Total 2	6	3	.667	59	3	0	0	1	87	89	9.2	13	35	3.6	51	5.3	4.55	81	.266	.335	-6	-8	95	102	1.8	0	-1	-0.8
■ **BOB PATTERSON**	Patterson, Robert Chandler b: 5/16/59, Jacksonville, Fla. BR/TR, 6'2", 185 lbs. Deb: 9/02/85																											
1985 SD-N	0	0	—	3	0	0	0	0	4	13	29.3	2	3	6.8	1	2.3	24.75	15	.565	.615	-9	-9	101	80	0.0	0	-0	-0.8
1986 Pit-N	2	3	.400	11	5	0	0	0	36	49	12.3	0	5	1.3	20	5.0	5.00	75	.322	.340	-5	-5	101	85	0.0	-0	1	-0.4
1987 Pit-N	1	4	.200	15	7	0	0	0	43	49	10.3	5	22	4.6	27	5.7	6.70	64	.290	.358	-12	-12	105	80	-1.4	-1	-0	-1.1
1989 Pit-N	4	3	.571	12	3	0	0	1	27	23	7.7	3	8	2.7	20	6.7	4.00	83	.232	.284	-1	-2	94	80	0.8	0	-0	-0.2
Total 4	7	10	.412	41	15	0	0	1	110	134	11.0	10	38	3.1	68	5.6	6.14	62	.302	.349	-28	-28	101	81	-0.6	-1	0	-2.5
■ **ALEJANDRO PENA**	Pena, Alejandro (Vasquez) b: 6/25/59, Cambiaso, D.R. BR/TR, 5'11", 165 lbs. Deb: 9/14/81																											
1981 LA-N	1	1	.500	14	0	0	0	2	25	18	6.5	2	11	4.0	14	5.0	2.88	116	.194	.279	2	1	96	76	0.0	-1	0	0.1
1982 LA-N	0	2	.000	29	0	0	0	0	36	37	9.3	2	21	5.3	20	5.0	4.75	71	.272	.369	-5	-6	94	96	-0.9	0	1	-0.4
1983 LA-N	12	9	.571	34	26	4	3	1	177	152	7.7	7	51	2.6	120	6.1	2.75	132	.229	.279	18	17	100	85	0.3	-2	2	1.8
1984 LA-N	12	6	.667	28	28	8	**4**	0	199	186	8.4	7	46	2.1	135	6.1	**2.49**	**150**	.246	.289	**24**	**28**	104	108	3.4	-1	-1	2.8
1985 LA-N	0	1	.000	2	1	0	0	0	4	7	15.8	1	3	6.8	2	4.5	9.00	37	.350	.435	-2	-3	92	99	-0.4	-0	0	-0.2
1986 LA-N	1	2	.333	24	10	0	0	1	70	74	9.5	6	30	3.9	46	5.9	4.89	72	.270	.340	-9	-11	95	87	-0.3	0	-1	-1.1
1987 LA-N	2	7	.222	37	7	0	0	11	87	82	8.5	9	37	3.8	76	7.9	3.52	107	.251	.321	5	2	92	113	-2.2	-1	-2	0.0
1988 LA-N	6	7	.462	60	0	0	0	12	94	75	7.2	4	27	2.6	83	7.9	1.91	189	.218	.272	16	18	105	121	-1.4	-1	-0	1.9
1989 LA-N	4	3	.571	53	0	0	0	5	76	62	7.3	6	18	2.1	75	8.9	2.13	152	.220	.268	12	9	93	118	0.6	0	-1	0.9
Total 9	38	38	.500	281	72	12	7	32	768	693	8.1	44	244	2.9	571	6.7	2.93	123	.239	.296	61	58	99	102	-0.9	-5	-3	5.8
■ **RAMON PENA**	Pena, Ramon Arturo (Padilla) b: 5/5/62, Santiago, D.R. BR/TR, 5'10", 155 lbs. Deb: 4/27/89																											
1989 Det-A	0	0	—	8	0	0	0	0	18	26	13.0	0	8	4.0	12	6.0	6.00	64	.338	.409	-4	-4	99	98	0.0	0	1	-0.3
■ **MELIDO PEREZ**	Perez, Melido Turpen Gross (born Melido Turpen Gross (Perez)) b: 2/15/66, San Cristobal, D.R. BR/TR, 6'4", 180 lbs. Deb: 9/04/87																											
1987 KC-A	1	1	.500	3	3	0	0	0	10	18	16.2	2	5	4.5	5	4.5	8.10	57	.375	.434	-4	-4	104	107	0.0	0	-0	-0.3
1988 Chi-A	12	10	.545	32	32	3	1	0	197	186	8.5	26	72	3.3	138	6.3	3.79	103	.248	.311	4	3	99	104	2.3	0	-2	0.1

YEAR	TM/L	W	L	PCT	G	GS	CG	SHO	SV	IP	H	H/G	HR	BB	BB/G	SO	SO/G	ERA	/A	OAVG	OOBP	PR	/A	PF	CPI	WAT	PB	PD	TPI
1989	Chi-A	11	14	.440	31	31	2	0	0	183	187	9.2	23	90	4.4	141	6.9	5.02	72	.264	.346	-23	-28	93	92	0.3	0	-1	-2.7
Total	3	24	25	.490	66	66	5	1	0	390	391	9.0	51	167	3.9	284	6.6	4.48	85	.260	.331	-23	-29	96	98	2.6	0	-3	-2.9

■ **PASCUAL PEREZ** Perez, Pascual Gross (born Pascual Gross (Perez)) b: 5/17/57, San Cristobal, D.R. BR/TR, 6'2", 162 lbs. Deb: 5/07/80

YEAR	TM/L	W	L	PCT	G	GS	CG	SHO	SV	IP	H	H/G	HR	BB	BB/G	SO	SO/G	ERA	/A	OAVG	OOBP	PR	/A	PF	CPI	WAT	PB	PD	TPI
1980	Pit-N	0	1	.000	2	2	0	0	0	12	15	11.3	0	2	1.5	7	5.3	3.75	99	.341	.373	-0	-0	103	138	-0.4	0	0	0.0
1981	Pit-N	2	7	.222	17	13	2	0	0	86	92	9.6	5	34	3.6	46	4.8	3.98	84	.273	.339	-5	-6	96	102	-2.3	-0	0	-0.5
1982	Atl-N	4	4	.500	16	11	0	0	0	79	85	9.7	4	17	1.9	29	3.3	3.08	125	.276	.306	5	7	107	113	-0.3	1	0	0.9
1983	Atl-N	15	8	.652	33	33	7	1	0	215	213	8.9	20	51	2.1	144	6.0	3.43	111	.260	.301	5	9	104	102	3.1	-1	1	1.0
1984	Atl-N	14	8	.636	30	30	4	1	0	212	208	8.8	26	51	2.2	145	6.2	3.74	106	.260	.303	-3	5	110	101	3.4	-2	3	0.7
1985	Atl-N	1	13	.071	22	22	0	0	0	95	115	10.9	10	57	5.4	57	5.4	6.16	63	.297	.382	-27	-24	108	91	-5.8	-0	-1	-2.4
1987	Mon-N	7	0	1.000	10	10	2	0	0	70	52	6.7	5	16	2.1	58	7.5	2.31	187	.206	.253	14	16	106	89	3.5	-2	1	1.6
1988	Mon-N	12	8	.600	27	27	4	2	0	188	133	6.4	15	44	2.1	131	6.3	2.44	149	.196	**.248**	21	25	105	82	2.2	-3	2	2.7
1989	Mon-N	9	13	.409	33	28	2	0	0	198	178	8.1	15	45	2.0	152	6.9	3.32	108	.237	.280	4	6	102	86	-2.2	2	0	0.9
Total	9	64	62	.508	190	176	21	4	0	1155	1091	8.5	100	317	2.5	769	6.0	3.48	108	.249	.299	13	36	105	95	1.2	-5	7	4.9

■ **PAT PERRY** Perry, William Patrick b: 2/4/59, Taylorsville, Ill. BL/TL, 6'1", 170 lbs. Deb: 9/12/85

YEAR	TM/L	W	L	PCT	G	GS	CG	SHO	SV	IP	H	H/G	HR	BB	BB/G	SO	SO/G	ERA	/A	OAVG	OOBP	PR	/A	PF	CPI	WAT	PB	PD	TPI
1985	StL-N	1	0	1.000	6	0	0	0	0	12	3	2.3	0	3	2.3	6	4.5	0.00	—	.077	.143	5	4	93	0	0.5	0	-0	0.5
1986	StL-N	2	3	.400	46	0	0	0	2	69	59	7.7	5	34	4.4	29	3.8	3.78	102	.239	.323	-0	0	103	95	-0.4	-1	1	0.0
1987	StL-N	4	2	.667	45	0	0	0	1	66	54	7.4	7	21	2.9	33	4.5	4.36	91	.222	.286	-2	-3	97	68	0.6	-0	0	-0.2
	Cin-N	1	0	1.000	12	0	0	0	1	15	6	3.6	0	4	2.4	6	3.6	0.00	—	.122	.200	7	7	103	0	0.5	0	0	0.7
	Yr	5	2	.714	57	0	0	0	2	81	60	6.7	7	25	2.8	39	4.3	3.56	113	.203	.265	5	4	98	0	1.1	-0	1	0.5
1988	Cin-N	2	2	.500	12	0	0	0	0	21	21	9.0	4	9	3.9	11	4.7	5.57	65	.262	.323	-5	-5	105	88	-0.1	-0	-0	-0.4
	Chi-N	2	2	.500	35	0	0	0	1	38	40	9.5	5	7	1.7	24	5.7	3.32	109	.270	.304	1	1	105	122	0.1	1	-0	0.3
	Yr	4	4	.500	47	0	0	0	1	59	61	9.3	9	16	2.4	35	5.3	4.12	88	.264	.311	-4	-3	105	122	0.0	-0	-0	-0.1
1989	Chi-N	0	1	.000	19	0	0	0	1	36	23	5.8	2	16	4.0	20	5.0	1.75	215	.187	.277	7	8	107	127	-0.4	-0	-1	0.8
Total	5	12	10	.545	175	0	0	0	6	257	206	7.2	23	94	3.3	129	4.5	3.33	115	.222	.291	12	14	102	86	0.8	0	0	1.7

■ **JEFF PETEREK** Peterek, Jeffrey Allen b: 9/22/63, Michigan City, Ind. BR/TR, 6'2", 195 lbs. Deb: 8/14/89

YEAR	TM/L	W	L	PCT	G	GS	CG	SHO	SV	IP	H	H/G	HR	BB	BB/G	SO	SO/G	ERA	/A	OAVG	OOBP	PR	/A	PF	CPI	WAT	PB	PD	TPI
1989	Mil-A	0	2	.000	7	4	0	0	0	31	31	9.0	3	14	4.1	16	4.6	4.06	92	.252	.328	-1	-1	96	94	-0.9	0	0	0.0

■ **ADAM PETERSON** Peterson, Adam Charles b: 12/11/65, Long Beach, Cal. BR/TR, 6'3", 190 lbs. Deb: 9/19/87

YEAR	TM/L	W	L	PCT	G	GS	CG	SHO	SV	IP	H	H/G	HR	BB	BB/G	SO	SO/G	ERA	/A	OAVG	OOBP	PR	/A	PF	CPI	WAT	PB	PD	TPI
1987	Chi-A	0	0	—	1	1	0	0	0	4	8	18.0	1	3	6.8	1	2.3	13.50	36	.444	.500	-4	-4	109	89	0.0	0	0	-0.2
1988	Chi-A	0	1	.000	2	2	0	0	0	6	6	9.0	0	6	9.0	5	7.5	13.50	29	.240	.387	-6	-6	99	31	-0.4	0	-0	-0.5
1989	Chi-A	0	1	.000	3	2	0	0	0	5	13	23.4	1	2	3.6	3	5.4	16.20	22	.464	.484	-7	-7	93	75	-0.4	0	-0	-0.5
Total	3	0	2	.000	6	5	0	0	0	15	27	16.2	2	11	6.6	9	5.4	14.40	28	.380	.452	-17	-17	99	61	-0.8	0	-0	-1.2

■ **DAN PETRY** Petry, Daniel Joseph b: 11/13/58, Palo Alto, Cal. BR/TR, 6'4", 185 lbs. Deb: 7/08/79

YEAR	TM/L	W	L	PCT	G	GS	CG	SHO	SV	IP	H	H/G	HR	BB	BB/G	SO	SO/G	ERA	/A	OAVG	OOBP	PR	/A	PF	CPI	WAT	PB	PD	TPI
1979	Det-A	6	5	.545	15	15	2	0	0	98	90	8.3	11	33	3.0	43	3.9	3.95	103	.254	.317	3	1	96	100	0.2	0	-1	0.0
1980	Det-A	10	9	.526	27	25	4	3	0	165	156	8.5	9	83	4.5	88	4.8	3.93	108	.253	.335	2	6	105	95	0.2	0	2	0.7
1981	Det-A	10	9	.526	23	22	7	2	0	141	115	7.3	10	57	3.6	79	5.0	3.00	128	.224	.297	10	13	105	97	-0.4	0	2	1.6
1982	Det-A	15	9	.625	35	35	8	1	0	246	220	8.0	15	100	3.7	132	4.8	3.22	127	.241	.314	24	23	100	103	3.1	0	4	2.9
1983	Det-A	19	11	.633	38	38	9	2	0	266	256	8.7	37	99	3.3	122	4.1	3.92	98	.256	.324	4	-2	95	108	2.7	0	3	0.1
1984	Det-A	18	8	.692	35	35	7	2	0	233	231	8.9	21	66	2.5	144	5.6	3.24	116	.259	.310	20	14	94	111	2.1	0	3	1.7
1985	Det-A	15	13	.536	34	34	8	0	0	239	190	7.2	24	81	3.1	109	4.1	3.35	131	.217	.285	21	28	106	85	0.5	0	1	2.9
1986	Det-A	5	10	.333	20	20	2	0	0	116	122	9.5	15	53	4.1	56	4.3	4.66	85	.268	.346	-6	-9	95	101	-2.9	0	1	-0.7
1987	Det-A	9	7	.563	30	21	0	0	0	135	148	9.9	22	76	5.1	93	6.2	5.60	76	.279	.373	-17	-20	96	102	-0.5	0	1	-1.7
1988	Cal-A	3	9	.250	22	22	4	1	0	140	139	8.9	18	59	3.8	64	4.1	4.37	86	.263	.338	-6	-9	95	105	-2.8	0	2	-0.6
1989	Cal-A	3	2	.600	19	4	0	0	0	51	53	9.4	8	23	4.1	21	3.7	5.47	69	.275	.345	-9	-9	98	93	0.2	0	0	-0.8
Total	11	113	92	.551	298	271	51	11	0	1830	1720	8.5	190	730	3.6	951	4.7	3.85	104	.250	.322	46	35	99	101	2.4	0	19	6.1

■ **JEFF PICO** Pico, Jeffrey Mark b: 2/12/66, Antioch, Cal. BR/TR, 6'1", 190 lbs. Deb: 5/31/88

YEAR	TM/L	W	L	PCT	G	GS	CG	SHO	SV	IP	H	H/G	HR	BB	BB/G	SO	SO/G	ERA	/A	OAVG	OOBP	PR	/A	PF	CPI	WAT	PB	PD	TPI
1988	Chi-N	6	7	.462	29	13	3	2	1	113	108	8.6	6	37	2.9	57	4.5	4.14	87	.252	.307	-9	-7	105	80	-0.1	-0	0	-0.6
1989	Chi-N	3	1	.750	53	5	0	0	2	91	99	9.8	8	31	3.1	38	3.8	3.76	100	.278	.330	-3	0	107	114	0.8	-1	1	0.1
Total	2	9	8	.529	82	18	3	2	3	204	207	9.1	14	68	3.0	95	4.2	3.97	93	.264	.318	-11	-7	106	95	0.7	-1	2	-0.5

■ **DAN PLESAC** Plesac, Daniel Thomas b: 2/4/62, Gary, Ind. BL/TL, 6'5", 205 lbs. Deb: 4/11/86

YEAR	TM/L	W	L	PCT	G	GS	CG	SHO	SV	IP	H	H/G	HR	BB	BB/G	SO	SO/G	ERA	/A	OAVG	OOBP	PR	/A	PF	CPI	WAT	PB	PD	TPI
1986	Mil-A	10	7	.588	51	0	0	0	14	91	81	8.0	5	29	2.9	75	7.4	2.97	145	.240	.292	12	14	103	100	2.0	0	-0	1.3
1987	Mil-A	5	6	.455	57	0	0	0	23	79	63	7.2	8	23	2.6	89	10.1	2.62	174	.213	.274	16	17	102	99	-1.0	0	0	1.6
1988	Mil-A	1	2	.333	50	0	0	0	30	52	46	8.0	2	12	2.1	52	9.0	2.42	168	.234	.275	9	10	103	99	-0.5	0	-0	1.0
1989	Mil-A	3	4	.429	52	0	0	0	33	61	47	6.9	6	17	2.5	52	7.7	2.36	159	.213	.264	10	9	96	107	-0.4	0	0	0.9
Total	4	19	19	.500	210	0	0	0	100	283	237	7.5	21	81	2.6	268	8.5	2.64	160	.225	.278	48	49	101	101	0.1	0	-0	4.8

■ **ERIC PLUNK** Plunk, Eric Vaughn b: 9/3/63, Wilmington, Cal. BR/TR, 6'5", 210 lbs. Deb: 5/12/86

YEAR	TM/L	W	L	PCT	G	GS	CG	SHO	SV	IP	H	H/G	HR	BB	BB/G	SO	SO/G	ERA	/A	OAVG	OOBP	PR	/A	PF	CPI	WAT	PB	PD	TPI
1986	Oak-A	4	7	.364	26	15	0	0	0	120	91	6.8	14	102	7.7	98	7.4	5.33	74	.214	.369	-15	-19	94	84	-1.2	0	-2	-1.9
1987	Oak-A	4	6	.400	32	11	0	0	2	95	91	8.6	8	62	5.9	90	8.5	4.74	86	.253	.359	-3	-7	91	95	-1.0	0	-1	-0.7
1988	Oak-A	7	2	.778	49	0	0	0	5	78	62	7.2	6	39	4.5	79	9.1	3.00	123	.217	.308	8	6	93	104	1.8	0	-1	0.5
1989	Oak-A	1	1	.500	23	0	0	0	1	29	17	5.3	1	12	3.7	24	7.4	2.17	183	.172	.265	6	6	102	76	-0.1	0	-0	0.6
	NY-A	7	5	.583	27	7	0	0	0	76	65	7.7	9	52	6.2	61	7.2	3.67	112	.237	.352	2	4	105	121	1.5	0	-2	0.2
	Yr	8	6	.571	50	7	0	0	1	105	82	7.0	10	64	5.5	85	7.3	3.26	125	.219	.328	7	9	104	121	1.4	0	-2	0.8
Total	4	23	21	.523	157	33	0	0	8	398	326	7.4	38	267	6.0	352	8.0	4.18	95	.226	.345	-2	-10	96	97	1.0	0	-6	-1.3

■ **MARK PORTUGAL** Portugal, Mark Steven b: 10/30/62, Los Angeles, Cal. BR/TR, 6', 170 lbs. Deb: 8/14/85

YEAR	TM/L	W	L	PCT	G	GS	CG	SHO	SV	IP	H	H/G	HR	BB	BB/G	SO	SO/G	ERA	/A	OAVG	OOBP	PR	/A	PF	CPI	WAT	PB	PD	TPI
1985	Min-A	1	3	.250	6	4	0	0	0	24	24	9.0	3	14	5.3	12	4.5	5.63	77	.270	.362	-4	-3	104	91	-0.9	0	1	-0.1
1986	Min-A	6	10	.375	27	15	3	0	1	113	112	8.9	10	50	4.0	67	5.3	4.30	106	.265	.339	-1	3	109	99	-1.2	0	-0	0.3
1987	Min-A	1	3	.250	13	7	0	0	0	44	58	11.9	13	24	4.9	28	5.7	7.77	55	.326	.407	-16	-17	96	101	-1.0	0	0	-1.4
1988	Min-A	3	3	.500	26	0	0	0	3	58	60	9.3	11	17	2.6	31	4.8	4.50	93	.274	.322	-3	-2	105	109	-0.2	0	-2	-0.3
1989	Hou-N	7	1	.875	20	15	2	1	0	108	91	7.6	7	37	3.1	86	7.2	2.75	131	.232	.295	9	10	103	111	3.0	2	0	1.4
Total	5	18	20	.474	92	41	5	1	4	347	345	8.9	44	142	3.7	224	5.8	4.38	95	.265	.334	-16	-9	105	104	-0.3	2	-1	-0.1

■ **DENNIS POWELL** Powell, Dennis Clay b: 8/13/63, Moultrie, Ga. BR/TL, 6'3", 175 lbs. Deb: 7/07/85

YEAR	TM/L	W	L	PCT	G	GS	CG	SHO	SV	IP	H	H/G	HR	BB	BB/G	SO	SO/G	ERA	/A	OAVG	OOBP	PR	/A	PF	CPI	WAT	PB	PD	TPI
1985	LA-N	1	1	.500	16	2	0	0	1	29	30	9.3	7	13	4.0	19	5.9	5.28	63	.263	.331	-5	-6	92	101	0.0	-0	0	-0.6
1986	LA-N	2	7	.222	27	6	0	0	0	65	65	9.0	5	25	3.5	31	4.3	4.29	82	.272	.335	-4	-6	95	98	-2.2	1	-1	-0.4
1987	Sea-A	1	3	.250	16	3	0	0	0	34	32	8.5	3	15	4.0	17	4.5	3.18	145	.250	.320	5	5	103	121	-0.9	0	0	0.5
1988	Sea-A	1	3	.250	12	2	0	0	0	19	29	13.7	2	11	5.2	15	7.1	8.53	50	.363	.442	-10	-9	108	92	-0.7	0	0	-0.8
1989	Sea-A	2	2	.500	43	1	0	0	2	45	49	9.8	6	21	4.2	27	5.4	5.00	81	.285	.358	-6	-5	104	105	0.2	0	1	-0.3
Total	5	7	16	.304	114	14	0	0	3	192	205	9.6	23	85	4.0	109	5.1	4.83	80	.280	.349	-20	-21	99	104	-3.6	1	1	-1.6

■ **TED POWER** Power, Ted Henry b: 1/31/55, Guthrie, Okla. BR/TR, 6'4", 215 lbs. Deb: 9/09/81

YEAR	TM/L	W	L	PCT	G	GS	CG	SHO	SV	IP	H	H/G	HR	BB	BB/G	SO	SO/G	ERA	/A	OAVG	OOBP	PR	/A	PF	CPI	WAT	PB	PD	TPI
1981	LA-N	1	3	.250	5	2	0	0	0	14	16	10.3	0	7	4.5	7	4.5	3.21	104	.286	.364	0	0	96	135	-1.0	-0	-0	0.0
1982	LA-N	1	1	.500	12	4	0	0	0	34	38	10.1	4	23	6.1	15	4.0	6.62	51	.288	.381	-11	-12	94	85	0.0	-1	0	-1.2
1983	Cin-N	5	6	.455	49	6	1	0	2	111	120	9.7	10	49	4.0	57	4.6	4.54	83	.286	.354	-11	-9	104	104	0.0	-1	-2	-1.2
1984	Cin-N	9	7	.563	**78**	0	0	0	11	109	93	7.7	4	46	3.8	81	6.7	2.81	137	.237	.305	10	13	107	109	2.0	-0	0	1.3
1985	Cin-N	8	6	.571	64	0	0	0	27	80	65	7.3	2	45	5.1	42	4.7	2.70	140	.227	.325	8	10	105	116	0.3	0	-2	0.8
1986	Cin-N	10	6	.625	56	10	0	0	1	129	115	8.0	13	52	3.6	95	6.6	3.70	105	.245	.313	0	3	104	101	1.7	0	-0	0.3
1987	Cin-N	10	13	.435	34	34	2	1	0	204	213	9.4	28	71	3.1	133	5.9	4.50	94	.267	.324	-9	-7	103	97	-2.0	0	-3	-0.8
1988	KC-A	5	6	.455	22	12	2	2	0	80	98	11.0	7	30	3.4	44	4.9	5.96	68	.305	.364	-18	-17	103	88	-0.7	0	-0	-1.6
	Det-A	1	1	.500	4	2	0	0	0	19	23	10.9	1	8	3.8	13	6.2	5.68	66	.307	.373	-4	-4	94	89	0.0	0	0	-0.3
	Yr	6	7	.462	26	14	2	2	0	99	121	11.0	8	38	3.5	57	5.2	5.91	68	.300	.359	-21	-21	101	89	-0.7	0	-0	-1.9
1989	StL-N	7	7	.500	23	15	0	0	0	97	96	8.9	7	21	1.9	43	4.0	3.71	95	.255	.290	-2	-2	100	86	-0.3	-2	-2	-0.5
Total	9	57	56	.504	347	85	5	3	41	877	877	9.0	76	352	3.6	530	5.4	4.15	94	.264	.328	-37	-26	103	99	0.0	-4	-9	-3.2

YEAR	TM/L	W	L	PCT	G	GS	CG	SHO	SV	IP	H	H/G	HR	BB	BB/G	SO	SO/G	ERA	/A	OAVG	OOBP	PR	/A	PF	CPI	WAT	PB	PD	TPI
■ JOE PRICE	Price, Joseph Walter b: 11/29/56, Inglewood, Cal. BR/TL, 6'4", 220 lbs. Deb: 6/14/80																												
1980	Cin-N	7	3	.700	24	13	2	0	0	111	95	7.7	10	37	3.0	44	3.6	3.57	102	.236	.297	1	1	101	89	1.7	-2	-1	-0.1
1981	Cin-N	6	1	.857	41	0	0	0	4	54	42	7.0	3	18	3.0	41	6.8	2.50	140	.222	.278	6	6	101	105	2.3	-0	1	0.7
1982	Cin-N	3	4	.429	59	1	0	0	3	73	73	9.0	7	32	3.9	71	8.8	2.84	132	.263	.343	6	7	104	150	0.3	0	-1	0.7
1983	Cin-N	10	6	.625	21	21	5	0	0	144	118	7.4	12	46	2.9	83	5.2	2.88	131	.225	.282	12	14	104	95	2.7	-1	-0	1.4
1984	Cin-N	7	13	.350	30	30	3	1	0	172	176	9.2	19	61	3.2	129	6.8	4.19	92	.261	.320	-11	-6	107	95	-2.0	-1	-3	-0.9
1985	Cin-N	2	2	.500	26	8	0	0	1	65	59	8.2	10	23	3.2	52	7.2	3.88	97	.242	.299	-2	-1	105	98	-0.1	-1	-1	-0.2
1986	Cin-N	1	2	.333	25	2	0	0	0	42	49	10.5	5	22	4.7	30	6.4	5.36	72	.293	.366	-8	-7	104	100	-0.5	0	-1	-0.7
1987	SF-N	2	2	.500	20	0	0	0	1	35	19	4.9	5	13	3.3	42	10.8	2.57	150	.154	.241	6	5	95	69	-0.1	-0	-0	0.5
1988	SF-N	1	6	.143	38	3	0	0	4	62	59	8.6	5	27	3.9	49	7.1	3.92	82	.249	.323	-3	-5	93	96	-2.5	-0	-0	-0.5
1989	SF-N	1	1	.500	7	1	0	0	0	14	16	10.3	3	4	2.6	10	6.4	5.79	58	.314	.339	-4	-4	96	105	0.0	0	0	-0.3
	Bos-A	2	5	.286	31	5	0	0	0	70	71	9.1	8	30	3.9	52	6.7	4.37	93	.262	.331	-4	-2	104	97	-1.5	0	-1	-0.3
Total	10	42	45	.483	322	84	10	1	13	842	777	8.3	87	313	3.3	603	6.4	3.64	103	.246	.310	-1	9	103	99	0.3	-5	-7	0.3
■ CHARLIE PULEO	Puleo, Charles Michael b: 2/7/55, Glen Ridge, N.J. BR/TR, 6'2", 190 lbs. Deb: 9/16/81																												
1981	NY-N	0	0	—	4	1	0	0	0	13	8	5.5	0	8	5.5	8	5.5	0.00	—	.182	.302	5	5	103	0	0.0	-0	0	0.6
1982	NY-N	9	9	.500	36	24	1	1	1	171	179	9.4	13	90	4.7	98	5.2	4.47	81	.275	.357	-16	-16	100	102	1.6	-1	3	-1.4
1983	Cin-N	6	12	.333	27	24	0	0	0	144	145	9.1	18	91	5.7	71	4.4	4.88	77	.269	.371	-20	-18	104	105	-2.5	-2	-2	-2.0
1984	Cin-N	1	2	.333	5	4	0	0	0	22	27	11.0	2	15	6.1	6	2.5	5.73	67	.297	.393	-5	-5	107	99	-0.2	0	-1	-0.4
1986	Atl-N	1	2	.333	5	3	1	0	0	24	13	4.9	4	12	4.5	18	6.8	3.00	128	.160	.268	2	2	103	89	-0.3	0	-0	0.3
1987	Atl-N	6	8	.429	35	16	1	0	0	123	122	8.9	11	40	2.9	99	7.2	4.24	105	.262	.315	-2	3	109	92	0.0	1	-2	0.2
1988	Atl-N	5	5	.500	53	3	0	0	1	106	101	8.6	9	47	4.0	70	5.9	3.48	106	.251	.327	-0	2	107	112	1.3	0	-0	0.2
1989	Atl-N	1	1	.500	15	1	0	0	0	29	26	8.1	2	16	5.0	17	5.3	4.66	78	.245	.328	-4	-3	104	84	0.2	-0	-1	-0.3
Total	8	29	39	.426	180	76	3	1	2	632	621	8.8	59	319	4.5	387	5.5	4.26	90	.261	.343	-41	-29	104	99	0.1	-1	-1	-2.8
■ DAN QUISENBERRY	Quisenberry, Daniel Raymond b: 2/7/53, Santa Monica, Cal. BR/TR, 6'2", 170 lbs. Deb: 7/08/79																												
1979	KC-A	3	2	.600	32	0	0	0	5	40	42	9.4	5	7	1.6	13	2.9	3.15	141	.278	.301	5	6	105	129	0.4	0	1	0.6
1980	KC-A	12	7	.632	**75**	0	0	0	**33**	128	129	9.1	5	27	1.9	37	2.6	3.09	127	.265	.297	14	12	97	100	0.9	0	3	1.5
1981	KC-A	1	4	.200	40	0	0	0	18	62	59	8.6	1	15	2.2	20	2.9	1.74	208	.258	.295	13	13	99	168	-1.4	0	3	1.7
1982	KC-A	9	7	.563	72	0	0	0	**35**	137	126	8.3	12	12	0.8	46	3.0	2.56	159	.252	.261	23	23	100	114	0.1	0	6	2.9
1983	KC-A	5	3	.625	**69**	0	0	0	**45**	139	118	7.6	6	11	0.7	48	3.1	1.94	214	.229	.241	**33**	**34**	102	99	1.1	0	2	3.7
1984	KC-A	6	3	.667	72	0	0	0	**44**	129	121	8.4	10	12	0.8	41	2.9	2.65	150	.247	.263	19	19	99	99	1.4	0	3	2.2
1985	KC-A	8	9	.471	**84**	0	0	0	**37**	129	142	9.9	8	16	1.1	54	3.8	2.37	177	.280	.299	25	26	101	150	-1.4	0	1	2.7
1986	KC-A	3	7	.300	62	0	0	0	12	81	92	10.2	2	24	2.7	36	4.0	2.78	151	.291	.338	13	13	100	148	-1.8	0	2	1.5
1987	KC-A	4	1	.800	47	0	0	0	8	49	58	10.7	3	10	1.8	17	3.1	2.76	168	.287	.321	9	10	104	143	1.5	0	2	1.1
1988	KC-A	0	1	.000	20	0	0	0	1	25	32	11.5	0	5	1.8	9	3.2	3.60	113	.305	.336	1	1	103	109	-0.4	0	1	0.2
	StL-N	2	0	1.000	33	0	0	0	0	38	54	12.8	4	6	1.4	19	4.5	6.16	59	.344	.357	-11	-11	105	94	1.0	0	0	-1.0
1989	StL-N	3	1	.750	63	0	0	0	6	78	78	9.0	2	14	1.6	37	4.3	2.65	132	.261	.290	7	7	100	110	0.9	0	2	1.1
Total	11	56	45	.554	669	0	0	0	244	1035	1051	9.1	58	159	1.4	377	3.3	2.70	150	.266	.289	151	154	101	119	2.3	0	24	18.2
■ DENNIS RASMUSSEN	Rasmussen, Dennis Lee b: 4/18/59, Los Angles, Cal. BL/TL, 6'7", 230 lbs. Deb: 9/16/83																												
1983	SD-N	0	0	—	4	1	0	0	0	14	10	6.4	1	8	5.1	13	8.4	1.93	187	.200	.310	3	3	99	142	0.0	-0	1	0.3
1984	NY-A	9	6	.600	24	24	1	0	0	148	127	7.7	16	60	3.6	110	6.7	4.56	82	.234	.310	-9	-14	93	77	1.1	0	-1	-1.4
1985	NY-A	3	5	.375	22	16	2	0	0	102	97	8.6	10	42	3.7	63	5.6	3.97	98	.255	.326	2	-1	94	102	-1.5	0	0	0.0
1986	NY-A	18	6	.750	31	31	3	1	0	202	160	7.1	28	74	3.3	131	5.8	3.88	111	.217	.288	7	9	103	82	5.7	0	-1	0.8
1987	NY-A	9	7	.563	26	25	2	0	0	146	145	8.9	31	55	3.4	89	5.5	4.75	92	.260	.325	-4	-6	97	104	0.3	0	-0	-0.5
	Cin-N	4	1	.800	7	7	0	0	0	45	39	7.8	5	12	2.4	39	7.8	4.00	105	.229	.278	0	1	103	74	1.5	-1	0	0.0
1988	Cin-N	2	6	.250	11	11	1	1	0	56	68	10.9	8	22	3.5	27	4.3	5.79	63	.300	.361	-15	-13	105	96	-2.1	1	0	-1.2
	SD-N	14	4	.778	20	20	6	0	0	148	131	8.0	9	36	2.2	85	5.2	2.55	131	.238	.282	15	13	97	110	5.1	2	2	1.9
	Yr	16	10	.615	31	31	7	1	0	204	199	8.8	17	58	2.6	112	4.9	3.44	100	.254	.303	0	-0	99	110	3.0	1	2	0.7
1989	SD-N	10	10	.500	33	33	1	0	0	184	190	9.3	18	72	3.5	87	4.3	4.26	83	.270	.332	-15	-15	101	102	-0.9	1	-1	-1.5
Total	7	69	45	.605	178	168	16	2	0	1045	967	8.3	126	381	3.3	644	5.5	4.07	95	.247	.311	-17	-23	99	95	9.2	3	-0	-1.6
■ SHANE RAWLEY	Rawley, Shane William b: 7/27/55, Racine, Wis. BR/TL, 6', 170 lbs. Deb: 4/06/78																												
1978	Sea-A	4	9	.308	52	2	0	0	4	111	114	9.2	7	51	4.1	66	5.4	4.14	95	.275	.352	-4	-2	104	105	-0.7	0	1	-0.1
1979	Sea-A	5	9	.357	48	3	0	0	11	84	88	9.4	2	40	4.3	48	5.1	3.86	111	.278	.354	3	4	101	108	-0.9	0	1	0.4
1980	Sea-A	7	7	.500	59	0	0	0	13	114	103	8.1	3	63	5.0	68	5.4	3.32	128	.257	.349	9	12	105	119	1.6	0	2	1.4
1981	Sea-A	4	6	.400	46	0	0	0	8	68	64	8.5	1	38	5.0	35	4.6	3.97	93	.257	.349	-2	-2	101	95	0.0	0	0	-0.1
1982	NY-A	11	10	.524	47	17	3	0	3	164	165	9.1	10	54	3.0	111	6.1	4.06	97	.267	.316	0	-2	97	93	0.8	0	1	0.0
1983	NY-A	14	14	.500	34	33	13	2	1	238	246	9.3	19	79	3.0	124	4.7	3.78	106	.269	.325	8	6	98	105	-1.7	0	0	0.5
1984	NY-A	2	3	.400	11	10	0	0	0	42	46	9.9	0	27	5.8	24	5.1	6.21	60	.272	.369	-10	-12	93	67	-0.6	0	-0	-1.0
	Phi-N	10	6	.625	18	18	3	0	0	120	117	8.8	13	27	2.0	58	4.3	3.83	95	.257	.295	-3	-2	101	92	2.2	-2	-1	-0.4
1985	Phi-N	13	8	.619	36	31	6	2	0	199	188	8.5	16	81	3.7	106	4.8	3.30	111	.249	.319	7	8	102	109	3.4	0	1	1.0
1986	Phi-N	11	7	.611	23	23	7	1	0	158	166	9.5	13	50	2.8	73	4.2	3.53	110	.270	.322	3	6	104	110	1.6	0	-0	0.6
1987	Phi-N	17	11	.607	36	36	4	1	0	230	250	9.8	23	86	3.4	123	4.8	4.38	98	.279	.339	-8	-3	105	103	3.6	-0	-1	-0.3
1988	Phi-N	8	16	.333	32	32	4	1	0	198	220	10.0	27	78	3.5	87	4.0	4.18	85	.286	.346	-16	-14	103	122	-2.3	-1	-0	-1.5
1989	Min-A	5	12	.294	27	25	1	0	0	145	167	10.4	19	60	3.7	68	4.2	5.21	79	.293	.356	-21	-17	106	100	-3.6	0	-1	-1.7
Total	12	111	118	.485	469	230	41	7	40	1871	1934	9.3	153	734	3.5	991	4.8	4.02	98	.271	.334	-34	-19	102	105	3.4	-3	2	-1.2
■ JEFF REARDON	Reardon, Jeffrey James b: 10/1/55, Dalton, Mass. BR/TR, 6', 190 lbs. Deb: 8/25/79																												
1979	NY-N	1	2	.333	18	0	0	0	2	21	12	5.1	2	9	3.9	10	4.3	1.71	210	.174	.259	5	4	96	125	-0.1	0	-0	0.4
1980	NY-N	8	7	.533	61	0	0	0	6	110	96	7.9	10	47	3.8	101	8.3	2.62	134	.231	.301	12	11	97	122	1.7	-1	-2	0.8
1981	NY-N	1	0	1.000	18	0	0	0	2	29	27	8.4	2	12	3.7	28	8.7	3.41	105	.245	.323	0	1	103	102	0.5	-0	-0	0.0
	Mon-N	2	0	1.000	25	0	0	0	6	42	21	4.5	3	9	1.9	21	4.5	1.29	266	.148	.200	10	10	98	59	1.0	-0	-1	0.9
	Yr	3	0	1.000	43	0	0	0	8	71	48	6.1	5	21	2.7	49	6.2	2.15	162	.189	.251	11	10	100	59	1.5	-0	-1	0.9
1982	Mon-N	7	4	.636	75	0	0	0	26	109	87	7.2	6	36	3.0	86	7.1	2.06	182	.221	.282	19	21	104	123	1.3	-0	-1	2.0
1983	Mon-N	7	9	.438	66	0	0	0	21	92	87	8.5	7	44	4.3	78	7.6	3.03	121	.250	.328	6	7	101	123	-1.1	-0	-2	0.4
1984	Mon-N	7	7	.500	68	0	0	0	23	87	70	7.2	5	37	3.8	79	8.2	2.90	113	.220	.303	7	4	91	99	0.2	-1	-2	0.1
1985	Mon-N	2	8	.200	63	0	0	0	**41**	88	68	7.0	7	26	2.7	67	6.9	3.17	106	.209	.267	4	2	94	71	-3.1	0	-0	0.2
1986	Mon-N	7	9	.438	62	0	0	0	35	89	83	8.4	12	26	2.6	67	6.8	3.94	93	.251	.299	-2	-3	98	96	-0.8	-0	-0	-0.2
1987	Min-A	8	8	.500	63	0	0	0	31	80	70	7.9	14	28	3.1	83	9.3	4.50	95	.232	.300	-0	-2	96	85	-0.3	0	-1	-0.2
1988	Min-A	2	4	.333	63	0	0	0	42	73	68	8.4	6	15	1.8	56	6.9	2.47	170	.245	.284	12	14	105	125	-1.1	0	-2	1.2
1989	Min-A	5	4	.556	65	0	0	0	31	73	68	8.4	8	12	1.5	46	5.7	4.07	102	.246	.279	-1	1	106	78	0.6	0	-2	0.0
Total	11	57	62	.479	647	0	0	0	266	893	757	7.6	82	301	3.0	722	7.3	3.02	123	.229	.291	72	68	99	102	-1.2	-2	-13	5.6
■ JERRY REED	Reed, Jerry Maxwell b: 10/8/55, Bryson City, N.C. BR/TR, 6'1", 190 lbs. Deb: 9/11/81																												
1981	Phi-N	0	1	.000	4	0	0	0	0	5	7	12.6	0	6	10.8	5	9.0	7.20	54	.333	.481	-2	-2	112	104	-0.4	0	0	-0.1
1982	Phi-N	1	0	1.000	7	0	0	0	0	9	11	11.0	0	3	3.0	1	1.0	5.00	67	.324	.395	-1	-2	94	101	0.5	0	-0	-0.1
	Cle-A	1	1	.500	6	1	0	0	0	16	15	8.4	1	3	1.7	10	5.6	3.38	122	.250	.286	1	1	101	85	0.0	0	0	0.1
1983	Cle-A	0	0	—	7	0	0	0	0	21	26	11.1	4	9	3.9	11	4.7	7.29	59	.310	.368	-7	-7	106	85	0.0	0	1	-0.5
1985	Cle-A	3	5	.375	33	5	0	0	8	72	67	8.4	12	19	2.4	37	4.6	4.13	96	.245	.296	0	-1	95	95	0.0	0	1	0.0
1986	Sea-A	4	0	1.000	11	4	0	0	0	35	38	9.8	3	13	3.3	16	4.1	3.09	144	.273	.336	4	5	106	134	2.0	0	-0	0.5
1987	Sea-A	1	2	.333	39	1	0	0	7	82	79	8.7	7	24	2.6	51	5.6	3.40	135	.255	.312	10	11	103	107	-0.4	0	-0	1.0
1988	Sea-A	1	1	.500	46	0	0	0	1	86	82	8.6	8	33	3.5	48	5.0	3.98	108	.256	.322	-0	3	108	100	0.1	0	1	0.4
1989	Sea-A	7	7	.500	52	1	0	0	0	102	89	7.9	10	43	3.8	50	4.4	3.18	127	.235	.308	8	10	104	109	0.7	0	-0	1.0
Total	8	18	17	.514	205	12	0	0	16	428	414	8.7	45	153	3.2	229	4.8	3.83	110	.256	.319	13	19	103	104	2.5	0	2	2.3

YEAR	TM/L	W	L	PCT	G	GS	CG	SHO	SV	IP	H	H/G	HR	BB	BB/G	SO	SO/G	ERA	/A	OAVG	OOBP	PR	/A	PF	CPI	WAT	PB	PD	TPI
■ **RICHARD REED**	Reed, Richard Allen b: 8/16/64, Huntington, W.Va. BR/TR, 6', 195 lbs. Deb: 8/08/88																												
1988	Pit-N	1	0	1.000	2	2	0	0	0	12	10	7.5	1	2	1.5	6	4.5	3.00	112	.233	.255	1	0	97	89	0.5	-0	0	0.0
1989	Pit-N	1	4	.200	15	7	0	0	0	55	62	10.1	5	11	1.8	34	5.5	5.56	59	.290	.323	-13	-14	94	78	-1.3	-0	-0	-1.4
Total	2	2	4	.333	17	9	0	0	0	67	72	9.7	6	13	1.7	40	5.4	5.10	65	.280	.312	-12	-13	95	80	-0.8	-0	0	-1.4
■ **RICK REUSCHEL**	Reuschel, Rickey Eugene b: 5/16/49, Quincy, Ill. BR/TR, 6'3", 215 lbs. Deb: 6/19/72																												
1972	Chi-N	10	8	.556	21	18	5	4	0	129	127	8.9	3	29	2.0	87	6.1	2.93	132	.259	.300	8	14	112	99	0.2	-1	-0	1.4
1973	Chi-N	14	15	.483	36	36	7	3	0	237	244	9.3	15	62	2.4	168	6.4	3.00	133	.263	.310	18	26	109	111	0.2	-3	4	2.9
1974	Chi-N	13	12	.520	41	38	8	2	0	241	262	9.8	18	83	3.1	160	6.0	4.29	86	.276	.331	-18	-16	102	94	2.7	2	5	-0.9
1975	Chi-N	11	17	.393	38	37	6	0	1	234	244	9.4	17	67	2.6	155	6.0	3.73	103	.268	.316	-3	2	105	98	-2.4	2	3	0.8
1976	Chi-N	14	12	.538	38	37	9	2	1	260	260	9.0	17	64	2.2	146	5.1	3.46	112	.265	.308	1	12	111	101	2.1	4	3	2.3
1977	Chi-N	20	10	.667	39	37	8	4	1	252	233	8.3	13	74	2.6	166	5.9	2.79	161	.247	.303	32	**47**	115	108	5.7	2	3	**5.9**
1978	Chi-N	14	15	.483	35	35	9	1	0	243	235	8.7	16	54	2.0	115	4.3	3.41	117	.254	.292	5	15	111	92	-0.1	-1	2	1.9
1979	Chi-N	18	12	.600	36	36	5	1	0	239	251	9.5	16	75	2.8	125	4.7	3.62	116	.274	.329	3	16	112	108	3.7	1	5	2.3
1980	Chi-N	11	13	.458	38	38	6	0	0	257	281	9.8	13	76	2.7	140	4.9	3.40	114	.286	.330	6	14	108	**119**	1.4	-1	5	2.0
1981	Chi-N	4	7	.364	13	13	1	0	0	86	87	9.1	4	23	2.4	53	5.5	3.45	108	.267	.318	0	3	106	102	0.0	-2	2	0.3
	NY-A	4	4	.500	12	11	3	0	0	71	75	9.5	4	10	1.3	22	2.8	2.66	136	.280	.305	8	8	99	132	-0.3	0	1	0.9
1983	Chi-N	1	1	.500	4	4	0	0	0	21	18	7.7	1	10	4.3	9	3.9	3.86	95	.234	.318	-1	-0	101	80	0.1	-0	1	0.0
1984	Chi-N	5	5	.500	19	14	1	0	0	92	123	12.0	7	23	2.3	43	4.2	5.18	75	.339	.368	-16	-13	109	109	-0.8	2	1	-0.9
1985	Pit-N	14	8	.636	31	26	9	1	1	194	153	7.1	7	52	2.4	138	6.4	2.27	165	.215	.269	29	32	104	90	5.2	2	4	4.3
1986	Pit-N	9	16	.360	35	34	4	2	0	216	232	9.7	20	57	2.4	125	5.2	3.96	95	.274	.319	-6	-5	101	102	-1.2	0	3	-0.1
1987	Pit-N	8	6	.571	25	25	9	3	0	177	163	8.3	12	35	1.8	80	4.1	2.75	156	.246	.285	26	30	105	108	1.2	1	1	3.5
	SF-N	5	3	.625	9	8	3	1	0	50	44	7.9	1	7	1.3	27	4.9	4.32	90	.230	.259	-1	-3	95	45	0.7	-0	0	-0.1
	Yr	13	9	.591	34	33	**12**	**4**	0	227	207	8.2	13	42	**1.7**	107	4.2	3.09	135	.239	.273	25	**27**	102	45	1.9	1	1	3.4
1988	SF-N	19	11	.633	36	36	7	2	0	245	242	8.9	11	42	1.5	92	3.4	3.12	103	.260	.290	9	3	93	99	4.3	-1	-2	-0.1
1989	SF-N	17	8	.680	32	32	2	0	0	208	195	8.4	18	54	2.3	111	4.8	2.94	114	.247	.292	13	10	96	111	3.7	1	-0	1.1
Total	17	211	183	.536	538	515	102	26	4	3452	3469	9.0	213	897	2.3	1962	5.1	3.36	115	.263	.308	113	193	106	103	26.4	9	38	27.5
■ **JERRY REUSS**	Reuss, Jerry b: 6/19/49, St.Louis, Mo. BL/TL, 6'5", 200 lbs. Deb: 9/27/69																												
1969	StL-N	1	0	1.000	1	1	0	0	0	7	2	2.6	0	3	3.9	3	3.9	0.00	—	.091	.259	3	3	99	0	0.5	0	0	0.4
1970	StL-N	7	8	.467	20	20	5	2	0	127	132	9.4	9	49	3.5	74	5.2	4.11	105	.271	.332	-1	3	106	100	0.0	-3	-0	0.0
1971	StL-N	14	14	.500	36	35	7	2	0	211	228	9.7	15	109	4.6	131	5.6	4.78	73	.279	.361	-31	-31	100	96	-1.6	1	-2	-3.2
1972	Hou-N	9	13	.409	33	30	4	1	1	192	177	8.3	14	83	3.9	174	8.2	4.17	87	.246	.325	-15	-11	105	87	-3.0	-2	-1	-1.3
1973	Hou-N	16	13	.552	41	40	12	3	0	279	271	8.7	17	117	3.8	177	5.7	3.74	93	.256	.326	-2	-8	95	96	1.6	-1	-2	-1.1
1974	Pit-N	16	11	.593	35	35	14	1	0	260	259	9.0	20	101	3.5	105	3.6	3.50	100	.261	.321	4	0	97	106	1.7	-0	-2	-0.2
1975	Pit-N	18	11	.621	32	32	15	6	0	237	224	8.5	10	78	3.0	131	5.0	2.54	139	.253	.307	29	26	98	**122**	2.0	2	2	3.3
1976	Pit-N	14	9	.609	31	29	11	3	2	209	209	9.0	16	51	2.2	108	4.7	3.53	99	.256	.298	-1	-1	99	92	1.2	6	-1	0.3
1977	Pit-N	10	13	.435	33	33	8	2	0	208	225	9.7	11	71	3.1	116	5.0	4.11	97	.280	.336	-5	-3	102	97	-3.3	1	1	0.0
1978	Pit-N	3	2	.600	23	12	3	1	0	83	97	10.5	5	23	2.5	42	4.6	4.88	77	.297	.341	-12	-10	105	90	0.3	0	-0	-1.0
1979	LA-N	7	14	.333	39	21	4	1	3	160	178	10.0	4	60	3.4	83	4.7	3.54	105	.282	.338	4	3	99	109	-3.5	1	1	0.5
1980	LA-N	18	6	.750	37	29	10	**6**	3	229	193	7.6	12	40	1.6	111	4.4	2.52	137	.227	.257	28	24	96	84	5.6	-1	1	2.6
1981	LA-N	10	4	.714	22	22	8	2	0	153	138	8.1	6	27	1.6	51	3.0	2.29	146	.243	.278	20	18	96	111	2.5	0	3	2.4
1982	LA-N	18	11	.621	39	37	8	4	0	255	232	8.2	11	50	1.8	138	4.9	3.11	109	.240	.274	14	8	94	78	2.9	3	2	1.3
1983	LA-N	12	11	.522	32	31	7	0	0	223	233	9.4	12	50	2.0	143	5.8	2.95	123	.271	.305	17	17	100	116	-0.8	5	4	2.8
1984	LA-N	5	7	.417	30	15	2	0	1	99	102	9.3	4	31	2.8	44	4.0	3.82	98	.266	.311	-2	-1	104	90	-0.8	1	-0	0.0
1985	LA-N	14	10	.583	34	33	5	3	0	213	210	8.9	13	58	2.5	84	3.5	2.92	113	.260	.307	16	9	92	116	0.0	-1	-2	0.6
1986	LA-N	2	6	.250	19	13	0	0	1	74	96	11.7	13	17	2.1	29	3.5	5.84	60	.313	.347	-17	-19	95	96	-1.7	2	1	-1.6
1987	LA-N	0	0	—	1	0	0	0	0	2	2	9.0	0	0	0.0	2	9.0	4.50	84	.333	.250	-0	-0	92	93	0.0	0	0	0.0
	Cin-N	0	5	.000	7	7	0	0	0	35	52	13.4	2	12	3.1	10	2.6	7.71	55	.351	.399	-14	-14	103	81	-2.4	0	-1	-1.2
	Yr	0	5	.000	8	7	0	0	0	37	54	13.1	2	12	2.9	12	2.9	7.54	56	.348	.392	-14	-14	103	81	-2.4	0	-1	-1.2
	Cal-A	4	5	.444	17	16	1	1	0	82	112	12.3	16	17	1.9	37	4.1	5.27	84	.327	.356	-7	-7	100	118	-0.1	0	1	-0.5
1988	Chi-A	13	9	.591	32	29	2	0	0	183	183	9.0	15	43	2.1	73	3.6	3.44	114	.263	.305	11	10	99	105	3.3	0	0	1.0
1989	Chi-A	8	5	.615	23	19	1	1	0	107	135	11.4	12	21	1.8	27	2.3	5.05	72	.308	.338	-14	-17	93	97	2.2	0	-2	-1.7
	Mil-A	1	4	.200	7	7	0	0	0	34	36	9.5	7	13	3.4	13	3.4	5.29	71	.273	.340	-5	-6	96	98	-1.4	0	-0	-0.5
	Yr	9	9	.500	30	26	1	1	0	141	171	10.9	19	34	2.2	40	2.6	5.11	72	.295	.334	-19	-23	94	98	0.8	0	-2	-2.2
Total	21	220	191	.535	624	546	127	39	11	3662	3726	9.2	244	1124	2.8	1906	4.7	3.64	99	.265	.316	19	-9	98	100	5.2	15	4	2.9
■ **CRAIG REYNOLDS**	Reynolds, Gordon Craig b: 12/27/52, Houston, Tex. BL/TR, 6'1", 175 lbs. Deb: 8/01/75																												
1986	Hou-N	0	0	—	1	0	0	0	0	1	3	27.0	0	2	18.0	1	9.0	27.00	14	.500	.625	-3	-3	102	64	0.0	0	0	-0.1
1989	Hou-N	0	0	—	1	0	0	0	0	1	3	27.0	0	1	9.0	0	0.0	27.00	13	.500	.556	-3	-3	103	64	0.0	0	0	-0.1
Total	2	0	0	—	2	0	0	0	0	2	6	27.0	0	3	13.5	1	4.5	27.00	14	.500	.588	-5	-5	102	64	0.0	0	0	-0.2
■ **RICK RHODEN**	Rhoden, Richard Alan b: 5/16/53, Boynton Beach, Fla. BR/TR, 6'3", 195 lbs. Deb: 7/05/74																												
1974	LA-N	1	0	1.000	4	0	0	0	0	9	5	5.0	1	4	4.0	7	7.0	2.00	163	.161	.257	2	1	90	92	0.5	0	0	0.2
1975	LA-N	3	3	.500	26	11	1	0	0	99	94	8.5	8	32	2.9	40	3.6	3.09	110	.253	.306	6	3	93	109	-0.1	-2	0	0.1
1976	LA-N	12	3	.800	27	26	10	3	0	181	165	8.2	17	53	2.6	77	3.8	2.98	116	.242	.294	11	10	99	107	4.2	7	-2	1.5
1977	LA-N	16	10	.615	31	31	4	1	0	216	223	9.3	20	63	2.6	122	5.1	3.75	102	.270	.318	4	2	98	103	0.4	5	-2	0.4
1978	LA-N	10	8	.556	30	23	6	3	0	165	160	8.7	13	51	2.8	79	4.3	3.65	95	.255	.307	-1	-3	97	95	-0.4	-0	-1	-0.4
1979	Pit-N	0	1	.000	1	1	0	0	0	5	5	9.0	0	2	3.6	2	3.6	7.20	54	.263	.333	-2	-2	104	45	-0.4	0	0	0.0
1980	Pit-N	7	5	.583	20	19	2	0	0	127	133	9.4	9	40	2.8	70	5.0	3.83	97	.273	.328	-3	-2	103	102	0.9	6	0	0.5
1981	Pit-N	9	4	.692	21	21	4	2	0	136	147	9.7	6	53	3.5	76	5.0	3.90	86	.283	.344	-6	-8	96	107	3.1	1	1	-0.6
1982	Pit-N	11	14	.440	35	35	6	1	0	230	239	9.4	14	70	2.7	128	5.0	4.15	96	.267	.316	-14	-5	110	86	-2.1	8	2	0.7
1983	Pit-N	13	13	.500	36	35	7	2	1	244	256	9.4	13	68	2.5	153	5.6	3.10	121	.276	.322	15	17	103	**119**	-0.4	-2	1	1.7
1984	Pit-N	14	9	.609	33	33	6	3	0	238	216	8.2	13	62	2.3	136	5.1	2.72	124	.243	.290	23	17	94	105	3.5	10	2	3.1
1985	Pit-N	10	15	.400	35	35	2	0	0	213	254	10.7	18	69	2.9	128	5.4	4.48	84	.296	.349	-21	-17	104	104	1.0	1	-0	-1.5
1986	Pit-N	15	12	.556	34	34	12	1	0	254	211	7.5	17	76	2.7	159	5.6	2.83	132	.228	.285	25	26	101	96	4.1	10	1	3.9
1987	NY-A	16	10	.615	30	29	4	0	0	182	184	9.1	22	61	3.0	107	5.3	3.86	113	.268	.325	12	10	97	113	2.2	0	0	0.9
1988	NY-A	12	12	.500	30	30	5	1	0	197	206	9.4	20	56	2.6	94	4.3	4.29	88	.269	.319	-7	-11	96	97	-0.6	0	-0	-0.9
1989	Hou-N	2	6	.250	20	17	0	0	0	97	108	10.0	7	41	3.8	41	3.8	4.27	84	.289	.352	-8	-7	103	112	-2.1	1	1	-0.5
Total	16	151	125	.547	413	380	69	17	1	2593	2606	9.0	198	801	2.8	1419	4.9	3.60	103	.264	.316	35	32	100	103	13.8	46	2	9.1
■ **RUSTY RICHARDS**	Richards, Russell Earl b: 1/27/65, Houston, Tex. BL/TR, 6'4", 200 lbs. Deb: 9/20/89																												
1989	Atl-N	0	0	—	2	2	0	0	0	9	10	10.0	2	6	6.0	4	4.0	5.00	73	.278	.395	-1	-1	104	130	0.0	-0	0	0.0
■ **DAVE RIGHETTI**	Righetti, David Allan b: 11/28/58, San Jose, Cal. BL/TL, 6'2", 170 lbs. Deb: 9/16/79																												
1979	NY-A	0	1	.000	3	3	0	0	0	17	10	5.3	2	10	5.3	13	6.9	3.71	108	.182	.299	1	1	95	83	-0.4	0	0	0.1
1981	NY-A	8	4	.667	15	15	2	0	0	105	75	6.4	1	38	3.3	89	7.6	2.06	176	.196	.268	19	18	99	77	1.7	0	-1	1.9
1982	NY-A	11	10	.524	33	27	4	0	1	183	155	7.6	11	108	5.3	163	**8.0**	3.79	104	.229	.335	6	3	97	94	0.8	0	-1	0.1
1983	NY-A	14	8	.636	31	31	7	2	0	217	194	8.0	12	67	2.8	169	7.0	3.44	116	.237	.292	15	13	98	84	2.1	0	-1	1.2
1984	NY-A	5	6	.455	64	0	0	0	31	96	79	7.4	5	37	3.5	90	8.4	2.34	159	.223	.290	18	15	93	112	-0.8	0	0	1.5
1985	NY-A	12	7	.632	74	0	0	0	29	107	96	8.1	5	45	3.8	92	7.7	2.78	141	.241	.312	16	13	94	118	0.8	0	-1	1.3
1986	NY-A	8	8	.500	74	0	0	0	**46**	107	88	7.4	4	35	2.9	83	7.0	2.44	176	.226	.287	21	22	103	106	-0.8	0	-1	2.1
1987	NY-A	8	6	.571	60	0	0	0	31	95	95	9.0	9	44	4.2	77	7.3	3.51	124	.262	.337	10	9	97	124	0.4	0	-0	0.8
1988	NY-A	5	4	.556	60	0	0	0	25	87	86	8.9	5	37	3.8	70	7.2	3.52	108	.257	.329	4	3	96	106	0.3	0	-1	0.2
1989	NY-A	2	6	.250	55	0	0	0	25	69	73	9.5	3	26	3.4	51	6.7	3.00	136	.277	.333	7	8	105	134	-1.8	0	-0	0.8
Total	10	73	60	.549	469	76	13	2	188	1083	951	7.9	57	447	3.7	897	7.5	3.09	128	.236	.309	117	105	98	101	2.3	0	-7	10.0

YEAR	TM/L	W	L	PCT	G	GS	CG	SHO	SV	IP	H	H/G	HR	BB	BB/G	SO	SO/G	ERA	/A	OAVG	OOBP	PR	/A	PF	CPI	WAT	PB	PD	TPI
■ **JOSE RIJO**	Rijo, Jose Antonio (Abreu) b: 5/13/65, San Cristobal, D.R. BR/TR, 6'1", 200 lbs. Deb: 4/05/84																												
1984	NY-A	2	8	.200	24	5	0	0	2	62	74	10.7	5	33	4.8	47	6.8	4.79	78	.298	.374	-5	-7	93	110	-3.1	0	1	-0.6
1985	Oak-A	6	4	.600	12	9	0	0	0	64	57	8.0	6	28	3.9	65	9.1	3.52	110	.239	.316	5	2	93	104	1.2	0	-1	0.2
1986	Oak-A	9	11	.450	39	26	4	0	1	194	172	8.0	24	108	5.0	176	8.2	4.64	85	.237	.332	-10	-15	94	89	-0.4	0	-1	-1.5
1987	Oak-A	2	7	.222	21	14	1	0	0	82	106	11.6	10	41	4.5	67	7.4	5.93	69	.305	.378	-13	-17	91	97	-2.5	0	0	-1.4
1988	Cin-N	13	8	.619	49	19	0	0	0	162	120	6.7	7	63	3.5	160	8.9	2.39	152	.209	.285	19	22	105	104	2.0	-2	0	2.3
1989	Cin-N	7	6	.538	19	19	1	1	0	111	101	8.2	6	48	3.9	86	7.0	2.84	128	.249	.325	8	10	104	129	1.0	1	-0	1.2
Total	6	39	44	.470	164	92	6	1	3	675	630	8.4	58	321	4.3	601	8.0	3.87	99	.248	.329	3	-4	98	103	-1.8	-1	-1	0.2
■ **KEVIN RITZ**	Ritz, Kevin D. b: 6/8/65, Eatontown, N.J. BR/TR, 6'4", 195 lbs. Deb: 7/15/89																												
1989	Det-A	4	6	.400	12	12	1	0	0	74	75	9.1	2	44	5.4	56	6.8	4.38	88	.265	.359	-4	-4	99	95	0.3	0	0	-0.3
■ **DON ROBINSON**	Robinson, Don Allen b: 6/8/57, Ashland, Ky. BR/TR, 6'4", 225 lbs. Deb: 4/10/78																												
1978	Pit-N	14	6	.700	35	32	9	1	1	228	203	8.0	20	57	2.3	135	5.3	3.47	108	.236	.281	3	7	105	82	3.7	2	-1	0.9
1979	Pit-N	8	8	.500	29	25	4	0	0	161	171	9.6	12	52	2.9	96	5.4	3.86	101	.277	.332	-2	1	104	105	-1.4	1	-3	0.0
1980	Pit-N	7	10	.412	29	24	3	2	1	160	157	8.8	14	45	2.5	103	5.8	3.99	93	.257	.308	-7	-5	103	89	-1.7	6	0	0.1
1981	Pit-N	0	3	.000	16	2	0	0	2	38	47	11.1	4	23	5.4	17	4.0	5.92	57	.313	.385	-10	-11	96	102	-1.4	1	1	-0.9
1982	Pit-N	15	13	.536	38	30	6	0	0	227	213	8.4	26	103	4.1	165	6.5	4.28	93	.250	.327	-17	-8	110	94	0.6	8	-2	0.0
1983	Pit-N	2	2	.500	9	6	0	0	0	36	43	10.8	5	21	5.3	28	7.0	4.50	83	.297	.381	-3	-3	103	127	0.0	1	0	-0.1
1984	Pit-N	5	6	.455	51	1	0	0	10	122	99	7.3	6	49	3.6	110	8.1	3.02	111	.226	.296	8	5	94	93	0.0	4	1	1.0
1985	Pit-N	5	11	.313	44	6	0	0	3	95	95	9.0	6	42	4.0	65	6.2	3.88	97	.255	.333	-3	-1	104	95	-0.9	2	-0	0.1
1986	Pit-N	3	4	.429	50	0	0	0	14	69	61	8.0	5	27	3.5	53	6.9	3.39	110	.237	.305	3	3	101	96	0.2	2	0	0.5
1987	Pit-N	6	6	.500	42	0	0	0	12	65	66	9.1	6	22	3.0	53	7.3	3.88	110	.267	.319	2	3	105	103	0.1	0	0	0.3
	SF-N	5	1	.833	25	0	0	0	7	43	39	8.2	1	18	3.8	26	5.4	2.72	142	.239	.310	7	5	95	107	1.9	2	-1	0.7
	Yr	11	7	.611	67	0	0	0	19	108	105	8.8	7	40	3.3	79	6.6	3.42	120	.255	.315	8	8	101	107	2.0	0	-1	1.0
1988	SF-N	10	5	.667	51	19	3	2	6	177	152	7.7	11	49	2.5	122	6.2	2.44	132	.231	.281	20	15	93	113	2.5	3	-2	1.7
1989	SF-N	12	11	.522	34	32	5	1	0	197	184	8.4	22	37	**1.7**	96	4.4	3.43	98	.248	.281	2	-1	96	96	-1.0	4	-4	-0.2
Total	12	92	86	.517	453	177	30	6	56	1618	1530	8.5	138	545	3.0	1069	5.9	3.62	101	.250	.308	-0	9	101	97	2.6	36	-10	4.1
■ **JEFF ROBINSON**	Robinson, Jeffrey Daniel b: 12/13/60, Santa Ana, Cal. BR/TR, 6'4", 195 lbs. Deb: 4/07/84																												
1984	SF-N	7	15	.318	34	33	1	1	0	172	195	10.2	12	52	2.7	102	5.3	4.55	77	.288	.339	-18	-20	98	95	-2.6	-2	0	-2.1
1985	SF-N	0	0	—	8	0	0	0	0	12	16	12.0	2	10	7.5	8	6.0	5.25	65	.333	.441	-2	-2	95	147	0.0	0	-0	-0.2
1986	SF-N	6	3	.667	64	1	0	0	8	104	92	8.0	8	32	2.8	90	7.8	3.38	104	.234	.290	4	2	95	85	1.5	-1	-0	0.0
1987	SF-N	6	8	.429	63	0	0	0	10	97	69	6.4	10	48	4.5	82	7.6	2.78	139	.207	.299	14	12	95	115	-1.6	-1	1	1.2
	Pit-N	2	1	.667	18	0	0	0	4	27	20	6.7	1	6	2.0	19	6.3	3.00	142	.215	.260	3	4	105	70	0.5	1	0	0.5
	Yr	8	9	.471	81	0	0	0	14	124	89	6.5	11	54	3.9	101	7.3	2.83	140	.206	.289	17	16	97	70	-1.1	-1	1	1.7
1988	Pit-N	11	5	.688	75	0	0	0	9	125	113	8.1	6	39	2.8	87	6.3	3.02	111	.244	.302	6	5	97	103	2.9	0	0	0.6
1989	Pit-N	7	13	.350	50	19	0	0	4	141	161	10.3	14	59	3.8	95	6.1	4.60	72	.283	.344	-17	-20	94	103	-2.5	2	1	-1.7
Total	6	39	45	.464	312	53	1	1	35	678	666	8.8	53	246	3.3	483	6.4	3.80	93	.258	.320	-10	-21	96	99	-1.8	0	2	-1.7
■ **JEFF ROBINSON**	Robinson, Jeffrey Mark b: 12/14/61, Ventura, Cal. BR/TR, 6'6", 210 lbs. Deb: 4/12/87																												
1987	Det-A	9	6	.600	29	21	2	1	0	127	132	9.4	16	54	3.8	98	6.9	5.39	79	.262	.339	-13	-16	96	83	0.0	0	-1	-1.5
1988	Det-A	13	6	.684	24	23	6	2	0	172	121	**6.3**	19	72	3.8	114	6.0	2.98	125	**.197**	.281	19	14	94	91	3.2	0	0	1.5
1989	Det-A	4	5	.444	16	16	1	1	0	78	76	8.8	10	46	5.3	40	4.6	4.73	82	.259	.354	-7	-8	99	101	0.6	0	-1	-0.8
Total	3	26	17	.605	69	60	9	4	0	377	329	7.9	45	172	4.1	252	6.0	4.15	95	.233	.317	-1	-9	96	90	3.8	0	-2	-0.8
■ **RON ROBINSON**	Robinson, Ronald Dean b: 3/24/62, Exeter, Cal. BR/TR, 6'4", 235 lbs. Deb: 8/14/84																												
1984	Cin-N	1	2	.333	12	5	1	0	0	40	35	7.9	3	13	2.9	24	5.4	2.70	143	.232	.289	4	5	107	105	-0.2	-1	0	0.5
1985	Cin-N	7	7	.500	33	12	0	0	1	108	107	8.9	11	32	2.7	76	6.3	4.00	94	.259	.309	-5	-3	105	92	-0.6	-1	1	-0.2
1986	Cin-N	10	3	.769	70	0	0	0	14	117	110	8.5	10	43	3.3	117	9.0	3.23	120	.253	.318	6	8	104	114	3.4	-1	1	0.9
1987	Cin-N	7	5	.583	48	18	0	0	4	154	148	8.6	14	43	2.5	99	5.8	3.68	114	.256	.301	7	9	103	96	0.9	0	-2	0.7
1988	Cin-N	3	7	.300	17	16	0	0	0	79	88	10.0	5	26	3.0	38	4.3	4.10	88	.285	.334	-6	-4	105	105	-2.2	1	-0	-0.3
1989	Cin-N	5	3	.625	15	15	0	0	0	83	80	8.7	8	28	3.0	36	3.9	3.36	108	.252	.312	1	3	104	111	1.2	1	-0	0.4
Total	6	33	27	.550	195	66	1	0	19	581	568	8.8	51	185	2.9	390	6.0	3.59	108	.258	.311	8	18	104	103	2.5	-2	0	2.0
■ **MIKE ROCHFORD**	Rochford, Michael Joseph b: 3/14/63, Methuen, Mass. BL/TL, 6'4", 205 lbs. Deb: 9/03/88																												
1988	Bos-A	0	0	—	2	0	0	0	0	2	4	18.0	0	1	4.5	1	4.5	0.00	—	.364	.417	1	1	108	0	0.0	0	0	0.1
1989	Bos-A	0	0	—	4	0	0	0	0	4	4	9.0	1	4	9.0	1	2.3	6.75	60	.267	.400	-1	-1	104	105	0.0	0	-0	0.0
Total	2	0	0	—	6	0	0	0	0	6	8	12.0	1	5	7.5	2	3.0	4.50	92	.308	.406	-0	-0	105	70	0.0	0	0	0.1
■ **ROSARIO RODRIGUEZ**	Rodriguez, Rosario Isabel (Echavarria) b: 7/8/69, Los Mochis, Mexico BR/TL, 6', 185 lbs. Deb: 9/01/89																												
1989	Cin-N	1	1	.500	7	0	0	0	0	4	3	6.8	0	3	6.8	0	0.0	4.50	81	.188	.316	-0	-0	104	48	0.1	0	0	0.0
■ **MIKE ROESLER**	Roesler, Michael Joseph b: 9/12/63, Fort Wayne, Ind. BR/TR, 6'5", 195 lbs. Deb: 8/09/89																												
1989	Cin-N	0	1	.000	17	0	0	0	0	25	22	7.9	4	9	3.2	14	5.0	3.96	92	.239	.304	-1	-1	104	99	-0.4	0	-1	-0.1
■ **KEN ROGERS**	Rogers, Kenneth Scott b: 11/10/64, Savannah, Ga. BL/TL, 6'1", 200 lbs. Deb: 4/06/89																												
1989	Tex-A	3	4	.429	73	0	0	0	2	74	60	7.3	2	42	5.1	63	7.7	2.92	137	.232	.338	8	9	103	120	-0.5	0	2	1.1
■ **STEVE ROSENBERG**	Rosenberg, Steven Allen b: 10/31/64, Brooklyn, N.Y. BL/TL, 6', 186 lbs. Deb: 6/04/88																												
1988	Chi-A	0	1	.000	33	0	0	0	1	46	53	10.4	5	19	3.7	28	5.5	4.30	91	.298	.355	-2	-2	99	121	-0.4	0	-0	-0.1
1989	Chi-A	4	13	.235	38	21	2	0	0	142	148	9.4	14	58	3.7	77	4.9	4.94	74	.273	.335	-17	-21	93	89	-4.0	0	0	-2.0
Total	2	4	14	.222	71	21	2	0	1	188	201	9.6	19	77	3.7	105	5.0	4.79	77	.279	.340	-18	-23	95	97	-4.4	0	-0	-2.1
■ **BRUCE RUFFIN**	Ruffin, Bruce Wayne b: 10/4/63, Lubbock, Tex BR/TL, 6'2", 205 lbs. Deb: 6/28/86																												
1986	Phi-N	9	4	.692	21	21	6	0	0	146	138	8.5	6	44	2.7	70	4.3	2.47	157	.251	.305	20	23	104	125	2.3	-3	-1	2.0
1987	Phi-N	11	14	.440	35	35	3	1	0	205	236	10.4	17	73	3.2	93	4.1	4.35	98	.298	.352	-6	-2	105	112	-1.5	-5	-1	-0.6
1988	Phi-N	6	10	.375	55	15	3	0	3	144	151	9.4	7	80	5.0	82	5.1	4.44	80	.275	.362	-16	-14	103	103	-0.5	-0	1	-1.3
1989	Phi-N	6	10	.375	24	23	1	0	0	126	152	10.9	10	62	4.4	70	5.0	4.43	81	.301	.372	-13	-12	102	119	-0.7	2	2	-0.7
Total	4	32	38	.457	135	94	13	1	3	621	677	9.8	40	259	3.8	315	4.6	3.94	98	.283	.348	-14	-5	104	114	-0.4	-6	1	-0.6
■ **JEFF RUSSELL**	Russell, Jeffrey Lee b: 9/2/61, Cincinnati, Ohio BR/TR, 6'4", 200 lbs. Deb: 8/13/83																												
1983	Cin-N	4	5	.444	10	10	2	0	0	68	58	7.7	7	22	2.9	40	5.3	3.04	124	.233	.284	4	6	104	101	0.0	1	-0	0.7
1984	Cin-N	6	18	.250	33	30	4	2	0	182	186	9.2	15	65	3.2	101	5.0	4.25	91	.263	.324	-13	-8	107	91	-5.4	-0	1	-0.6
1985	Tex-A	3	6	.333	13	13	0	0	0	62	85	12.3	10	27	3.9	44	6.4	7.55	60	.324	.386	-23	-21	110	87	-0.5	0	1	-1.7
1986	Tex-A	5	2	.714	37	0	0	0	2	82	74	8.1	11	31	3.4	54	5.9	3.40	117	.244	.314	7	5	95	114	1.4	0	2	0.7
1987	Tex-A	5	4	.556	52	2	0	0	3	97	109	10.1	9	52	4.8	56	5.2	4.45	104	.285	.369	0	2	104	114	0.8	0	1	0.3
1988	Tex-A	10	9	.526	34	24	5	0	0	189	183	8.7	15	66	3.1	88	4.2	3.81	107	.257	.323	3	5	102	100	1.7	0	2	0.7
1989	Tex-A	6	4	.600	71	0	0	0	**38**	73	45	5.5	4	24	3.0	77	9.5	1.97	202	.182	.259	16	16	103	95	0.9	0	2	1.9
Total	7	39	48	.448	250	79	11	2	43	753	740	8.8	71	287	3.4	460	5.5	4.02	102	.258	.325	-6	6	104	100	-1.1	1	8	2.0
■ **JOHN RUSSELL**	Russell, John William b: 1/5/61, Oklahoma City, Okla. BR/TR, 6', 200 lbs. Deb: 6/22/84																												
1989	Atl-N	0	0	—	1	0	0	0	0	0	0	—	0	0	—	0	—	—	—	.000	.000	0	0	104	0	0.0	0	0	0.0
■ **NOLAN RYAN**	Ryan, Lynn Nolan b: 1/31/47, Refugio, Tex. BR/TR, 6'2", 170 lbs. Deb: 9/11/66																												
1966	NY-N	0	1	.000	2	1	0	0	0	3	5	15.0	1	3	9.0	6	18.0	15.00	23	.357	.471	-4	-4	97	69	-0.4	0	0	-0.3
1968	NY-N	6	9	.400	21	18	3	0	0	134	93	6.2	12	75	5.0	133	8.9	3.09	99	.200	.308	-2	-0	103	99	-0.8	-1	-2	-0.3
1969	NY-N	6	3	.667	25	10	2	0	1	89	60	6.1	3	53	5.4	92	9.3	3.54	101	.189	.304	1	0	99	66	0.6	-1	-2	-0.2
1970	NY-N	7	11	.389	27	19	5	2	1	132	86	5.9	10	97	6.6	125	8.5	3.41	123	.188	.328	9	11	103	96	-2.3	-1	-1	1.0
1971	NY-N	10	14	.417	30	26	3	0	0	152	125	7.4	8	116	6.9	137	8.1	3.97	84	.219	.363	-8	-11	96	95	-2.4	-0	-1	-1.2
1972	Cal-A	19	16	.543	39	39	20	**9**	0	284	166	**5.3**	14	157	5.0	**329**	**10.4**	2.28	120	**.171**	.289	25	15	90	88	2.5	1	-2	1.4

YEAR	TM/L	W	L	PCT	G	GS	CG	SHO	SV	IP	H	H/G	HR	BB	BB/G	SO	SO/G	ERA	/A	OAVG	OOBP	PR	/A	PF	CPI	WAT	PB	PD	TPI
1973	Cal-A	21	16	.568	41	39	26	4	1	326	238	6.6	18	162	4.5	**383**	**10.6**	2.87	128	.203	.300	34	29	96	88	3.6	0	-2	2.9
1974	Cal-A	22	16	.579	42	41	26	3	0	**333**	221	**6.0**	18	202	5.5	**367**	**9.9**	2.89	116	**.190**	.310	27	17	93	89	6.3	0	1	2.0
1975	Cal-A	14	12	.538	28	28	10	5	0	198	152	6.9	13	132	6.0	186	8.5	3.45	105	.213	.337	7	4	96	98	2.5	0	-1	0.2
1976	Cal-A	17	18	.486	39	39	21	**7**	0	284	193	**6.1**	13	183	5.8	**327**	**10.4**	3.36	98	**.195**	.319	5	-3	93	83	0.7	0	0	-0.2
1977	Cal-A	19	16	.543	37	37	**22**	4	0	299	198	**6.0**	12	204	6.1	**341**	**10.3**	2.77	139	**.193**	.323	**43**	36	95	103	3.4	0	0	3.8
1978	Cal-A	10	13	.435	31	31	14	3	0	235	183	7.0	12	148	5.7	**260**	**10.0**	3.71	103	.220	.331	2	3	101	89	-2.4	0	1	0.4
1979	Cal-A	16	14	.533	34	34	17	**5**	0	223	169	**6.8**	15	114	4.6	**223**	**9.0**	3.59	108	**.212**	.308	16	7	92	82	-0.2	0	-0	0.6
1980	Hou-N	11	10	.524	35	35	4	2	0	234	205	7.9	10	98	3.8	200	7.7	3.35	105	.236	.312	7	4	97	90	-0.9	-1	-1	0.0
1981	Hou-N	11	5	.688	21	21	5	3	0	149	99	**6.0**	2	68	4.1	140	8.5	**1.69**	**179**	**.188**	.278	**30**	22	87	104	2.7	3	-1	2.8
1982	Hou-N	16	12	.571	35	35	10	3	0	250	196	7.1	20	109	3.9	245	8.8	3.17	113	**.213**	.298	12	12	100	89	3.0	-2	-0	1.0
1983	Hou-N	14	9	.609	29	29	5	2	0	196	134	**6.2**	9	101	4.6	183	8.4	2.98	110	**.195**	.297	14	6	90	80	2.3	-3	-0	0.2
1984	Hou-N	12	11	.522	30	30	5	2	0	184	143	7.0	12	69	3.4	197	9.6	3.03	109	.211	.284	11	5	92	82	0.7	-1	-3	0.1
1985	Hou-N	10	12	.455	35	35	4	0	0	232	205	8.0	12	95	3.7	209	8.1	3.80	91	.239	.314	-5	-9	96	86	-1.3	-1	-3	-1.3
1986	Hou-N	12	8	.600	30	30	1	0	0	178	119	6.0	14	82	4.1	194	9.8	3.34	113	.188	.281	8	9	102	69	0.2	-3	-1	0.5
1987	Hou-N	8	16	.333	34	34	0	0	0	212	154	**6.5**	14	87	3.7	**270**	**11.5**	**2.76**	138	**.199**	.281	**31**	25	93	84	-3.8	-3	-1	2.1
1988	Hou-N	12	11	.522	33	33	4	1	0	220	186	7.6	18	87	3.6	**228**	**9.3**	3.52	92	.227	.301	-2	-7	93	91	0.4	-3	-3	-1.3
1989	Tex-A	16	10	.615	32	32	6	2	0	239	162	**6.1**	17	98	3.7	**301**	**11.3**	3.20	125	**.187**	.272	18	21	103	66	3.1	0	-1	2.0
Total	23	289	263	.524	710	676	213	57	3	4786	3492	6.6	277	2540	4.8	5076	9.5	3.15	111	.204	.307	281	192	95	87	17.5	-16	-23	16.2

BRET SABERHAGEN Saberhagen, Bret William b: 4/11/64, Chicago Heights, Ill. BR/TR, 6'1", 160 lbs. Deb: 4/04/84

YEAR	TM/L	W	L	PCT	G	GS	CG	SHO	SV	IP	H	H/G	HR	BB	BB/G	SO	SO/G	ERA	/A	OAVG	OOBP	PR	/A	PF	CPI	WAT	PB	PD	TPI
1984	KC-A	10	11	.476	38	18	2	1	1	158	138	7.9	13	36	2.1	73	4.2	3.47	114	.237	.278	9	9	99	82	-0.9	0	0	0.9
1985	KC-A	20	6	.769	32	32	10	1	0	235	211	8.1	19	38	1.5	158	6.1	2.87	146	.241	**.269**	33	35	101	98	6.7	0	2	3.9
1986	KC-A	7	12	.368	30	25	4	2	0	156	165	9.5	15	29	1.7	112	6.5	4.15	101	.268	.301	1	1	100	87	-2.1	0	1	0.2
1987	KC-A	18	10	.643	33	33	15	4	0	257	246	8.6	27	53	1.9	163	5.7	3.36	138	.252	.291	32	37	104	102	4.3	0	0	3.7
1988	KC-A	14	16	.467	35	35	9	0	0	261	271	9.3	18	59	2.0	171	5.9	3.79	107	.269	.307	5	8	103	95	-1.8	0	0	0.8
1989	KC-A	**23**	6	**.793**	36	35	**12**	4	0	**262**	209	7.2	13	43	1.5	193	6.6	**2.16**	**171**	.217	**.249**	**50**	**45**	95	90	**8.3**	0	0	**4.9**
Total	6	92	61	.601	204	178	52	12	1	1329	1240	8.4	105	258	1.7	870	5.9	3.23	128	.247	.282	130	133	100	93	14.5	0	5	14.4

RANDY ST.CLAIRE St.Claire, Randy Anthony b: 8/23/60, Glens Falls, N.Y. BR/TR, 6'3", 180 lbs. Deb: 9/11/84

YEAR	TM/L	W	L	PCT	G	GS	CG	SHO	SV	IP	H	H/G	HR	BB	BB/G	SO	SO/G	ERA	/A	OAVG	OOBP	PR	/A	PF	CPI	WAT	PB	PD	TPI
1984	Mon-N	0	0	—	4	0	0	0	0	8	11	12.4	0	2	2.3	4	4.5	4.50	73	.344	.368	-1	-1	91	122	0.0	0	0	0.0
1985	Mon-N	5	3	.625	42	0	0	0	0	69	69	9.0	3	26	3.4	25	3.3	3.91	86	.265	.327	-2	-4	94	94	0.9	1	0	-0.2
1986	Mon-N	2	0	1.000	11	0	0	0	1	19	13	6.2	2	6	2.8	21	9.9	2.37	155	.186	.250	3	3	98	79	1.0	-0	1	0.3
1987	Mon-N	3	3	.500	44	0	0	0	7	67	64	8.6	9	20	2.7	43	5.8	4.03	107	.249	.301	0	2	106	92	-0.2	0	-0	0.2
1988	Mon-N	0	0	—	6	0	0	0	0	7	11	14.1	2	5	6.4	6	7.7	6.43	56	.344	.421	-2	-2	105	138	0.0	0	0	-0.1
	Cin-N	1	0	1.000	10	0	0	0	0	14	13	8.4	3	5	3.2	8	5.1	2.57	141	.241	.300	1	2	105	167	0.5	-0	0	0.2
	Yr	1	0	1.000	16	0	0	0	0	21	24	10.3	5	10	4.3	14	6.0	3.86	94	.276	.347	-1	-1	105	167	0.5	0	0	0.1
1989	Min-A	1	0	1.000	14	0	0	0	1	22	19	7.8	4	10	4.1	14	5.7	5.32	78	.226	.316	-3	-3	106	77	0.5	0	0	-0.2
Total	6	12	6	.667	131	0	0	0	9	206	200	8.7	23	74	3.2	121	5.3	3.98	96	.253	.315	-4	-4	100	98	2.7	1	1	0.2

ROGER SAMUELS Samuels, Roger Howard b: 1/5/61, San Jose, Cal. BL/TL, 6'5", 210 lbs. Deb: 7/20/88

YEAR	TM/L	W	L	PCT	G	GS	CG	SHO	SV	IP	H	H/G	HR	BB	BB/G	SO	SO/G	ERA	/A	OAVG	OOBP	PR	/A	PF	CPI	WAT	PB	PD	TPI
1988	SF-N	1	2	.333	15	0	0	0	0	23	17	6.7	4	7	2.7	22	8.6	3.52	92	.202	.272	-0	-1	93	87	-0.4	-0	0	0.0
1989	Pit-N	0	0	—	5	0	0	0	0	4	9	20.3	1	4	9.0	2	4.5	9.00	37	.474	.565	-2	-3	94	153	0.0	0	0	-0.2
Total	2	1	2	.333	20	0	0	0	0	27	26	8.7	5	11	3.7	24	8.0	4.33	75	.252	.330	-3	-3	93	97	-0.4	-0	0	-0.2

ALEX SANCHEZ Sanchez, Alex Anthony b: 4/8/66, Concord, Cal. BR/TR, 6'2", 185 lbs. Deb: 5/23/89

YEAR	TM/L	W	L	PCT	G	GS	CG	SHO	SV	IP	H	H/G	HR	BB	BB/G	SO	SO/G	ERA	/A	OAVG	OOBP	PR	/A	PF	CPI	WAT	PB	PD	TPI
1989	Tor-A	0	1	.000	4	3	0	0	0	12	16	12.0	1	14	10.5	4	3.0	9.75	37	.356	.492	-8	-8	93	89	-0.4	0	1	-0.6

SCOTT SANDERSON Sanderson, Scott Douglas b: 7/22/56, Dearborn, Mich. BR/TR, 6'5", 195 lbs. Deb: 8/06/78

YEAR	TM/L	W	L	PCT	G	GS	CG	SHO	SV	IP	H	H/G	HR	BB	BB/G	SO	SO/G	ERA	/A	OAVG	OOBP	PR	/A	PF	CPI	WAT	PB	PD	TPI
1978	Mon-N	4	2	.667	10	9	1	1	0	61	52	7.7	3	21	3.1	50	7.4	2.51	136	.232	.295	7	6	96	111	1.1	-1	-1	0.5
1979	Mon-N	9	8	.529	34	24	5	3	1	168	148	7.9	16	54	2.9	138	7.4	3.43	110	.236	.295	6	6	101	90	-0.9	-0	-2	0.4
1980	Mon-N	16	11	.593	33	33	7	3	0	211	206	8.8	18	56	2.4	125	5.3	3.11	114	.257	.303	12	10	98	111	1.3	-3	-2	0.5
1981	Mon-N	9	7	.563	22	22	4	1	0	137	122	8.0	10	31	2.0	77	5.1	2.96	116	.236	.275	8	7	98	90	0.1	2	-2	0.8
1982	Mon-N	12	12	.500	32	32	7	0	0	224	212	8.5	24	58	2.3	158	6.3	3.46	109	.251	.296	4	8	104	99	-0.7	1	-3	0.5
1983	Mon-N	6	7	.462	18	16	0	0	1	81	98	10.9	12	20	2.2	55	6.1	4.67	79	.303	.341	-9	-9	101	108	-0.5	-0	-1	-1.0
1984	Chi-N	8	5	.615	24	24	3	0	0	141	140	8.9	5	24	1.5	76	4.9	3.13	125	.264	.291	7	12	109	96	0.3	-1	1	1.3
1985	Chi-N	5	6	.455	19	19	2	0	0	121	100	7.4	13	27	2.0	80	6.0	3.12	134	.228	.265	6	14	117	89	-0.2	-2	1	1.5
1986	Chi-N	9	11	.450	37	28	1	1	1	170	165	8.7	21	37	2.0	124	6.6	4.18	96	.255	.293	-9	-3	108	85	0.3	-3	-1	-0.7
1987	Chi-N	8	9	.471	32	22	0	0	2	145	156	9.7	23	50	3.1	106	6.6	4.28	97	.274	.331	-3	-2	102	110	0.0	-1	-1	-0.3
1988	Chi-N	1	2	.333	11	0	0	0	0	15	13	7.8	1	3	1.8	6	3.6	5.40	67	.232	.258	-3	-3	105	47	-0.4	0	-0	-0.3
1989	Chi-N	11	9	.550	37	23	2	0	0	146	155	9.6	16	31	1.9	86	5.3	3.95	95	.273	.308	-7	-3	107	102	-0.4	-2	-2	-0.6
Total	12	98	89	.524	309	252	32	9	5	1620	1567	8.7	162	412	2.3	1081	6.0	3.55	107	.255	.298	19	44	104	98	0.0	-11	-13	2.6

DAN SCHATZEDER Schatzeder, Daniel Ernest b: 12/1/54, Elmhurst, Ill. BL/TL, 6', 185 lbs. Deb: 9/04/77

YEAR	TM/L	W	L	PCT	G	GS	CG	SHO	SV	IP	H	H/G	HR	BB	BB/G	SO	SO/G	ERA	/A	OAVG	OOBP	PR	/A	PF	CPI	WAT	PB	PD	TPI
1977	Mon-N	2	1	.667	6	3	1	1	0	22	16	6.5	0	13	5.3	14	5.7	2.45	158	.203	.312	4	3	99	94	0.6	0	0	0.4
1978	Mon-N	7	7	.500	29	18	2	0	0	144	108	6.8	10	68	4.3	69	4.3	3.06	112	.213	.304	8	6	96	95	0.4	3	-2	0.8
1979	Mon-N	10	5	.667	32	21	3	0	1	162	136	7.6	17	59	3.3	106	5.9	2.83	**133**	.225	.290	16	17	101	105	1.5	4	-3	1.9
1980	Det-A	11	13	.458	32	26	9	2	0	193	178	8.3	23	58	2.7	94	4.4	4.01	106	.246	.301	1	5	105	87	-1.5	0	-2	0.3
1981	Det-A	6	8	.429	17	14	1	0	0	71	74	9.4	13	29	3.7	20	2.5	6.08	63	.265	.330	-19	-18	105	79	-1.6	0	-0	-1.7
1982	SF-N	1	4	.200	13	3	0	0	0	33	47	12.8	3	12	3.3	18	4.9	7.36	46	.333	.381	-14	-15	94	79	-1.5	-0	0	-1.3
	Mon-N	0	2	.000	26	1	0	0	0	36	37	9.3	1	12	3.0	15	3.8	3.50	107	.276	.336	0	1	104	110	-0.9	1	-0	0.2
	Yr	1	6	.143	39	4	0	0	0	69	84	11.0	4	24	3.1	33	4.3	5.35	67	.304	.358	-13	-14	99	110	-2.4	-0	0	-1.1
1983	Mon-N	5	2	.714	58	2	0	0	2	87	88	9.1	3	25	2.6	48	5.0	3.21	115	.265	.320	4	5	101	106	1.5	0	-1	0.4
1984	Mon-N	7	7	.500	36	14	1	1	1	136	112	7.4	13	36	2.4	89	5.9	2.71	121	.224	.274	13	9	91	100	0.2	5	-3	1.1
1985	Mon-N	3	5	.375	24	15	1	0	0	104	101	8.7	13	31	2.7	64	5.5	3.81	89	.259	.306	-2	-5	94	102	-1.1	3	0	-0.1
1986	Mon-N	3	2	.600	30	1	0	0	1	59	53	8.1	6	19	2.9	33	5.0	3.20	114	.240	.295	3	3	98	102	0.6	6	-1	0.9
	Phi-N	3	3	.500	25	0	0	0	1	29	28	8.7	3	16	5.0	14	4.3	3.41	113	.252	.336	1	1	104	124	-0.1	0	-0	0.2
	Yr	6	5	.545	55	1	0	0	2	88	81	8.3	9	35	3.6	47	4.8	3.27	114	.243	.309	4	4	100	124	0.5	6	-1	1.1
1987	Phi-N	3	1	.750	26	0	0	0	0	38	40	9.5	4	14	3.3	28	6.6	4.03	106	.278	.329	0	1	105	111	1.0	0	-1	0.0
	Min-A	3	1	.750	30	1	0	0	0	44	64	13.1	8	18	3.7	30	6.1	6.34	68	.342	.399	-9	-10	96	113	1.0	0	-0	-0.9
1988	Cle-A	0	2	.000	15	0	0	0	3	16	26	14.6	6	2	1.1	10	5.6	9.56	42	.351	.377	-10	-10	102	87	-0.9	0	-0	-0.9
	Min-A	0	1	.000	10	0	0	0	0	10	8	7.2	1	5	4.5	7	6.3	1.80	233	.216	.318	2	3	105	195	-0.4	0	0	0.3
	Yr	0	3	.000	25	0	0	0	3	26	34	11.8	7	7	2.4	17	5.9	6.58	62	.304	.347	-8	-7	103	195	-1.3	0	-0	-0.6
1989	Hou-N	4	1	.800	36	0	0	0	1	57	64	10.1	2	28	4.4	46	7.3	4.42	81	.287	.367	-6	-5	103	106	1.5	-1	0	-0.6
Total	13	68	65	.511	445	119	18	4	10	1241	1180	8.6	126	445	3.2	705	5.1	3.80	98	.252	.314	-6	-10	99	99	0.3	22	-12	1.0

CURT SCHILLING Schilling, Curtis Montague b: 11/14/66, Anchorage, Alaska BR/TR, 6'5", 205 lbs. Deb: 9/07/88

YEAR	TM/L	W	L	PCT	G	GS	CG	SHO	SV	IP	H	H/G	HR	BB	BB/G	SO	SO/G	ERA	/A	OAVG	OOBP	PR	/A	PF	CPI	WAT	PB	PD	TPI
1988	Bal-A	0	3	.000	4	4	0	0	0	15	22	13.2	3	10	6.0	4	2.4	9.60	40	.355	.434	-9	-10	97	88	-1.4	0	-1	-0.8
1989	Bal-A	0	1	.000	5	1	0	0	0	9	10	10.0	2	3	3.0	6	6.0	6.00	64	.286	.342	-2	-2	99	91	-0.4	0	-0	-0.1
Total	2	0	4	.000	9	5	0	0	0	24	32	12.0	5	13	4.9	10	3.8	8.25	47	.330	.404	-11	-12	98	89	-1.8	0	-1	-0.9

CALVIN SCHIRALDI Schiraldi, Calvin Drew b: 6/16/62, Houston, Tex. BR/TR, 6'4", 200 lbs. Deb: 9/01/84

YEAR	TM/L	W	L	PCT	G	GS	CG	SHO	SV	IP	H	H/G	HR	BB	BB/G	SO	SO/G	ERA	/A	OAVG	OOBP	PR	/A	PF	CPI	WAT	PB	PD	TPI
1984	NY-N	0	2	.000	5	3	0	0	0	17	20	10.6	3	10	5.3	16	8.5	5.82	62	.286	.375	-4	-4	100	99	-0.9	-0	0	-0.3
1985	NY-N	2	1	.667	10	4	0	0	0	26	43	14.9	4	11	3.8	21	7.3	9.00	38	.368	.435	-16	-16	95	89	0.2	-0	0	-1.5
1986	Bos-A	4	2	.667	25	0	0	0	9	51	36	6.4	5	15	2.6	55	9.7	1.41	292	.201	.263	16	15	99	171	0.6	0	-1	1.5
1987	Bos-A	8	5	.615	62	1	0	0	6	84	75	8.0	15	40	4.3	93	10.0	4.39	101	.240	.321	1	0	99	100	1.8	0	0	0.0
1988	Chi-N	9	13	.409	29	27	2	1	1	166	166	9.0	13	63	3.4	140	7.6	4.39	82	.257	.322	-17	-14	105	86	-1.6	-2	-2	-1.8
1989	Chi-N	3	6	.333	54	0	0	0	4	79	60	6.8	7	50	5.7	54	6.2	3.76	100	.209	.325	-2	0	107	91	-1.9	-1	-1	-0.1
	SD-N	3	1	.750	5	4	0	0	0	21	12	5.1	1	13	5.6	17	7.3	2.57	137	.162	.287	2	2	101	75	0.9	1	-0	0.3

YEAR TM/L	W	L	PCT	G	GS	CG	SHO	SV	IP	H	H/G	HR	BB	BB/G	SO	SO/G	ERA	/A	OAVG	OOBP	PR	/A	PF	CPI	WAT	PB	PD	TPI
Yr	6	7	.462	59	4	0	0	4	100	72	6.5	8	63	5.7	71	6.4	3.51	106	.198	.315	-0	2	106	75	-1.0	-1	-1	0.2
Total 6	29	30	.492	190	39	2	1	20	444	412	8.4	48	202	4.1	396	8.0	4.18	92	.244	.325	-21	-16	103	99	-0.9	-3	-4	-1.9
■ DAVE SCHMIDT	Schmidt, David Joseph b: 4/22/57, Niles, Mich. BR/TR, 6'1", 185 lbs. Deb: 5/01/81																											
1981 Tex-A	0	1	.000	14	1	0	0	1	32	31	8.7	1	11	3.1	13	3.7	3.09	106	.258	.326	2	1	90	109	-0.4	0	0	0.1
1982 Tex-A	4	6	.400	33	8	0	0	6	110	118	9.7	5	25	2.0	69	5.6	3.19	121	.279	.320	11	8	94	118	0.0	0	-0	0.8
1983 Tex-A	3	3	.500	31	0	0	0	2	46	42	8.2	3	14	2.7	29	5.7	3.91	105	.241	.298	1	1	101	78	0.1	0	0	0.1
1984 Tex-A	6	6	.500	43	0	0	0	12	70	69	8.9	3	20	2.6	46	5.9	2.57	157	.262	.304	11	11	101	129	0.8	0	1	1.3
1985 Tex-A	7	6	.538	51	4	1	1	5	86	81	8.5	6	22	2.3	46	4.8	3.14	145	.246	.289	10	14	110	97	1.7	0	1	1.5
1986 Chi-A	3	6	.333	49	1	0	0	8	92	94	9.2	10	27	2.6	67	6.6	3.33	128	.264	.320	9	9	101	121	-1.1	0	-1	0.8
1987 Bal-A	10	5	.667	35	14	2	2	1	124	128	9.3	13	26	1.9	70	5.1	3.77	118	.263	.301	10	9	99	96	3.4	0	-1	0.8
1988 Bal-A	8	5	.615	41	9	0	0	2	130	129	8.9	14	38	2.6	67	4.6	3.39	114	.262	.314	8	7	97	117	2.9	0	2	0.8
1989 Bal-A	10	13	.435	38	26	2	0	0	157	196	11.2	24	36	2.1	46	2.6	5.68	68	.310	.341	-31	-32	99	94	-2.4	0	1	-2.9
Total 9	51	51	.500	335	63	5	3	37	847	888	9.4	79	219	2.3	453	4.8	3.76	108	.271	.315	30	28	99	107	5.0	0	3	3.3
■ MIKE SCHOOLER	Schooler, Michael Ralph b: 8/10/62, Anaheim, Cal. BR/TR, 6'3", 220 lbs. Deb: 6/10/88																											
1988 Sea-A	5	8	.385	40	0	0	0	15	48	45	8.4	4	24	4.5	54	10.1	3.56	121	.245	.327	2	4	108	108	-0.5	0	-0	0.4
1989 Sea-A	1	7	.125	67	0	0	0	33	77	81	9.5	2	19	2.2	69	8.1	2.81	144	.266	.310	9	10	104	115	-2.8	0	1	1.2
Total 2	6	15	.286	107	0	0	0	48	125	126	9.1	6	43	3.1	123	8.9	3.10	133	.258	.317	11	14	105	112	-3.3	0	1	1.6
■ DON SCHULZE	Schulze, Donald Arthur b: 9/27/62, Roselle, Ill. BR/TR, 6'3", 215 lbs. Deb: 9/13/83																											
1983 Chi-N	0	1	.000	4	3	0	0	0	14	19	12.2	1	7	4.5	8	5.1	7.07	52	.322	.403	-5	-5	101	83	-0.4	0	0	-0.4
1984 Chi-N	0	0	—	1	1	0	0	0	3	8	24.0	0	1	3.0	2	6.0	12.00	33	.571	.563	-3	-3	109	109	0.0	0	0	-0.1
Cle-A	3	6	.333	19	14	2	0	0	86	105	11.0	9	27	2.8	39	4.1	4.81	88	.302	.347	-8	-6	106	102	-1.2	0	-0	-0.5
1985 Cle-A	4	10	.286	19	18	1	0	0	94	128	12.3	10	19	1.8	37	3.5	6.03	66	.322	.352	-20	-22	95	90	-1.6	0	1	-1.9
1986 Cle-A	4	4	.500	19	13	1	0	0	85	88	9.3	9	34	3.6	33	3.5	4.98	82	.266	.342	-7	-8	98	88	-0.1	0	-1	-0.8
1987 NY-N	1	2	.333	5	4	0	0	0	22	24	9.8	4	6	2.5	5	2.0	6.14	65	.296	.341	-5	-5	97	89	-0.5	0	1	-0.3
1989 NY-A	1	1	.500	2	2	0	0	0	11	12	9.8	1	5	4.1	5	4.1	4.09	100	.300	.367	-0	0	105	134	0.1	0	0	0.0
SD-N	2	1	.667	7	4	0	0	0	24	38	14.3	6	6	2.3	15	5.6	5.63	63	.352	.373	-6	-6	101	134	0.4	-0	1	-0.5
Total 6	15	25	.375	76	59	4	0	0	339	422	11.2	40	105	2.8	144	3.8	5.47	74	.306	.354	-54	-54	100	97	-3.3	0	1	-4.5
■ MIKE SCHWABE	Schwabe, Michael Scott b: 7/12/64, Ft. Dodge, Iowa BR/TR, 6'4", 200 lbs. Deb: 5/27/89																											
1989 Det-A	2	4	.333	13	4	0	0	0	45	58	11.6	6	16	3.2	13	2.6	6.00	64	.307	.359	-11	-11	99	91	-0.2	0	1	-0.9
■ MIKE SCOTT	Scott, Michael Warren b: 4/26/55, Santa Monica, Cal. BR/TR, 6'2", 210 lbs. Deb: 4/18/79																											
1979 NY-N	1	3	.250	18	9	0	0	0	52	59	10.2	4	20	3.5	21	3.6	5.37	67	.289	.345	-9	-10	96	83	-0.6	-1	-0	-1.1
1980 NY-N	1	1	.500	6	6	1	1	0	29	40	12.4	1	8	2.5	13	4.0	4.34	81	.331	.364	-2	-3	97	117	0.1	0	0	-0.2
1981 NY-N	5	10	.333	23	23	1	0	0	136	130	8.6	11	34	2.3	54	3.6	3.90	92	.261	.299	-6	-5	103	90	-1.3	-2	3	-0.3
1982 NY-N	7	13	.350	37	22	1	0	3	147	185	11.3	13	60	3.7	63	3.9	5.14	70	.321	.369	-25	-25	100	109	-1.3	1	3	-2.1
1983 Hou-N	10	6	.625	24	24	2	2	0	145	143	8.9	8	46	2.9	73	4.5	3.72	88	.258	.317	-1	-7	90	91	1.8	1	0	-0.6
1984 Hou-N	5	11	.313	31	29	0	0	0	154	179	10.5	7	43	2.5	83	4.9	4.68	70	.293	.333	-19	-24	92	89	-3.0	0	0	-2.3
1985 Hou-N	18	8	.692	36	35	4	2	0	222	194	7.9	20	80	3.2	137	5.6	3.28	105	.235	.300	8	4	96	97	5.3	2	-2	0.5
1986 Hou-N	18	10	.643	37	37	7	**5**	0	**275**	182	**6.0**	17	72	2.4	**306**	**10.0**	**2.23**	**170**	**.186**	**.240**	**46**	**48**	102	70	2.0	-2	2	**5.4**
1987 Hou-N	16	13	.552	36	36	8	3	0	248	199	7.2	21	79	2.9	233	8.5	3.23	118	.217	**.279**	24	16	93	81	2.7	-1	0	1.4
1988 Hou-N	14	8	.636	32	32	8	5	0	219	162	6.7	19	53	2.2	190	7.8	2.92	111	.204	.255	13	8	93	78	3.2	-2	-1	0.4
1989 Hou-N	**20**	10	.667	33	32	9	2	0	229	180	7.1	23	62	2.4	172	6.8	3.10	116	.212	.265	10	12	103	82	**5.0**	-1	-1	1.0
Total 11	115	93	.553	313	285	41	20	3	1856	1653	8.0	144	557	2.7	1345	6.5	3.47	102	.239	.292	37	14	97	86	13.9	-6	5	2.1
■ SCOTT SCUDDER	Scudder, William Scott b: 2/14/68, Paris, Tex. BR/TR, 6'2", 180 lbs. Deb: 6/06/89																											
1989 Cin-N	4	9	.308	23	17	0	0	0	100	91	8.2	14	61	5.5	66	5.9	4.50	81	.239	.339	-11	-10	104	99	-2.2	1	-1	-0.9
■ RUDY SEANZ	Seanz, Rudy Caballero b: 10/20/68, Brawley, Cal. BR/TR, 6', 70 lbs. Deb: 90/7 /89																											
1989 Cle-A	0	0	—	5	0	0	0	0	5	1	1.8	0	4	7.2	7	12.6	3.60	113	.071	.250	0	0	104	28	0.0	0	0	0.0
■ RAY SEARAGE	Searage, Raymond Mark b: 5/1/55, Freeport, N.Y. BL/TL, 6'1", 180 lbs. Deb: 6/11/81																											
1981 NY-N	1	0	1.000	26	0	0	0	1	37	34	8.3	2	17	4.1	16	3.9	3.65	98	.252	.327	-1	-0	103	100	0.5	0	-0	0.0
1984 Mil-A	2	1	.667	21	0	0	0	6	38	20	4.7	0	16	3.8	29	6.9	0.71	521	.155	.248	14	13	93	135	0.7	0	-0	1.3
1985 Mil-A	1	4	.200	33	0	0	0	1	38	54	12.8	2	24	5.7	36	8.5	5.92	74	.338	.413	-7	-6	106	111	-1.3	0	-1	-0.6
1986 Mil-A	0	1	.000	17	0	0	0	1	22	29	11.9	6	9	3.7	10	4.1	6.95	62	.315	.379	-7	-6	103	101	-0.4	0	0	-0.5
Chi-A	1	0	1.000	29	0	0	0	0	29	15	4.7	1	19	5.9	26	8.1	0.62	684	.156	.291	11	12	101	318	0.5	0	0	1.2
Yr	1	1	.500	46	0	0	0	1	51	44	7.8	7	28	4.9	36	6.4	3.35	127	.233	.327	5	5	102	318	0.1	0	0	0.7
1987 Chi-A	2	3	.400	58	0	0	0	2	56	56	9.0	9	24	3.9	33	5.3	4.18	116	.264	.338	2	4	109	115	-0.3	0	0	0.4
1989 LA-N	3	4	.429	41	0	0	0	0	36	29	7.3	1	18	4.5	24	6.0	3.50	93	.225	.309	0	-1	93	85	-0.3	0	1	0.0
Total 6	10	13	.435	225	0	0	0	11	256	237	8.3	21	127	4.5	174	6.1	3.59	114	.249	.332	12	14	101	133	-0.6	0	0	1.8
■ STEVE SEARCY	Searcy, William Steven b: 6/4/64, Knoxville, Tenn. BL/TL, 6'1", 190 lbs. Deb: 8/29/88																											
1988 Det-A	0	2	.000	2	2	0	0	0	8	8	9.0	3	4	4.5	5	5.6	5.63	66	.242	.324	-1	-2	94	103	-0.9	0	0	-0.1
1989 Det-A	1	1	.500	8	2	0	0	0	22	27	11.0	3	12	4.9	11	4.5	6.14	63	.307	.390	-5	-6	99	97	0.2	0	-0	-0.5
Total 2	1	3	.250	10	4	0	0	0	30	35	10.5	6	16	4.8	16	4.8	6.00	64	.289	.372	-7	-7	98	99	-0.7	0	-0	-0.6
■ BOB SEBRA	Sebra, Robert Bush b: 12/11/61, Ridgewood, N.J. BR/TR, 6'2", 200 lbs. Deb: 6/26/85																											
1985 Tex-A	0	2	.000	7	4	0	0	0	20	26	11.7	4	14	6.3	13	5.8	7.65	60	.306	.402	-8	-7	110	92	-0.9	0	-0	-0.6
1986 Mon-N	5	5	.500	17	13	3	1	0	91	82	8.1	9	25	2.5	66	6.5	3.56	103	.239	.292	2	1	98	89	0.2	1	-1	0.1
1987 Mon-N	6	15	.286	36	27	4	1	0	177	184	9.4	15	67	3.4	156	7.9	4.42	98	.272	.332	-7	-2	106	96	-5.4	-0	-1	-0.2
1988 Phi-N	1	2	.333	3	3	0	0	0	11	15	12.3	0	10	8.2	7	5.7	8.18	43	.333	.417	-6	-6	103	83	-0.2	-1	-0	-0.5
1989 Phi-N	2	3	.400	6	5	0	0	0	34	41	10.9	6	10	2.6	21	5.6	4.50	80	.295	.350	-4	-3	102	125	0.0	-0	-0	-0.3
Cin-N	0	0	—	15	0	0	0	1	21	24	10.3	2	18	7.7	14	6.0	6.43	57	.296	.425	-7	-7	104	104	0.0	-0	-0	-0.6
Yr	2	3	.400	21	5	0	0	1	55	65	10.6	8	28	4.6	35	5.7	5.24	69	.289	.365	-11	-10	103	104	0.0	-0	-0	-0.9
Total 5	14	27	.341	84	52	7	2	1	354	372	9.5	36	144	3.7	277	7.0	4.63	87	.272	.338	-29	-24	104	97	-6.3	-0	-2	-2.1
■ JOSE SEGURA	Segura, Jose Altagracia (Mota) b: 1/26/63, Fundacion, D.R. BR/TR, 5'11", 180 lbs. Deb: 4/10/88																											
1988 Chi-A	0	0	—	4	0	0	0	0	9	19	19.0	1	8	8.0	2	2.0	13.00	30	.432	.519	-9	-9	99	86	0.0	0	0	-0.7
1989 Chi-A	0	1	.000	7	0	0	0	0	6	13	19.5	2	3	4.5	4	6.0	15.00	24	.464	.471	-7	-8	93	84	-0.4	0	0	-0.6
Total 2	0	1	.000	11	0	0	0	0	15	32	19.2	3	11	6.6	6	3.6	13.80	28	.444	.500	-16	-17	96	85	-0.4	0	1	-1.3
■ STEVE SHIELDS	Shields, Stephen Mack b: 11/30/58, Gasden, Ala. BR/TR, 6'5", 220 lbs. Deb: 6/01/85																											
1985 Atl-N	1	2	.333	23	6	0	0	0	68	86	11.4	9	32	4.2	29	3.8	5.16	75	.320	.383	-12	-10	108	118	-0.2	-1	-1	-1.0
1986 Atl-N	0	0	—	6	0	0	0	0	13	13	9.0	4	7	4.8	6	4.2	6.92	56	.271	.364	-5	-4	103	91	0.0	-0	-0	-0.4
KC-A	0	0	—	3	0	0	0	0	9	3	3.0	1	4	4.0	2	2.0	2.00	210	.111	.212	2	2	100	69	0.0	0	0	0.2
1987 Sea-A	2	0	1.000	20	0	0	0	3	30	43	12.9	7	12	3.6	22	6.6	6.60	70	.333	.382	-7	-7	103	108	1.0	0	0	-0.5
1988 NY-A	5	5	.500	39	0	0	0	0	82	96	10.5	8	30	3.3	55	6.0	4.39	86	.298	.354	-4	-5	96	115	-0.2	0	0	-0.5
1989 Min-A	0	1	.000	11	0	0	0	0	17	28	14.8	3	6	3.2	12	6.4	7.94	52	.354	.395	-8	-7	106	91	-0.4	0	0	-0.6
Total 5	8	8	.500	102	6	0	0	3	219	269	11.1	32	91	3.7	126	5.2	5.26	76	.308	.366	-33	-31	102	110	0.2	-1	-1	-2.8
■ ERIC SHOW	Show, Eric Vaughn b: 5/19/56, Riverside, Cal. BR/TR, 6'1", 185 lbs. Deb: 9/02/81																											
1981 SD-N	1	3	.250	15	0	0	0	3	23	17	6.7	2	9	3.5	22	8.6	3.13	106	.213	.293	1	0	95	93	-0.6	0	0	0.0
1982 SD-N	10	6	.625	47	14	2	2	3	150	117	7.0	10	48	2.9	88	5.3	2.64	125	.217	.278	16	11	92	97	2.2	-1	2	1.2
1983 SD-N	15	12	.556	35	33	4	2	0	201	201	9.0	25	74	3.3	120	5.4	4.16	87	.263	.328	-12	-13	99	101	1.8	0	-2	-1.3
1984 SD-N	15	9	.625	32	32	3	1	0	207	175	7.6	18	88	3.8	104	4.5	3.39	104	.234	.310	5	3	98	101	1.8	7	-1	0.9
1985 SD-N	12	11	.522	35	35	5	2	0	233	212	8.2	27	87	3.4	141	5.4	3.09	118	.243	.311	13	14	101	119	0.3	-2	-2	1.1
1986 SD-N	9	5	.643	24	22	2	0	0	136	109	7.2	11	69	4.6	94	6.2	2.98	120	.225	.320	11	9	96	115	2.5	1	-1	0.8

YEAR TM/L	W	L	PCT	G	GS	CG	SHO	SV	IP	H	H/G	HR	BB	BB/G	SO	SO/G	ERA	/A	OAVG	OOBP	PR	/A	PF	CPI	WAT	PB	PD	TPI
1987 SD-N	8	16	.333	34	34	5	3	0	206	188	8.2	26	85	3.7	117	5.1	3.84	104	.241	.318	6	3	98	101	-2.2	-4	-1	-0.1
1988 SD-N	16	11	.593	32	32	13	1	0	235	201	7.7	22	53	2.0	144	5.5	3.26	103	.231	.278	5	3	97	89	2.5	-0	-4	-0.1
1989 SD-N	8	6	.571	16	16	1	0	0	106	113	9.6	9	39	3.3	66	5.6	4.25	83	.274	.332	-9	-9	101	101	0.4	2	-1	-0.8
Total 9	94	79	.543	270	218	35	11	6	1497	1333	8.0	150	552	3.3	896	5.4	3.43	104	.240	.308	36	23	98	103	8.7	3	-11	1.7

■ JOE SKALSKI Skalski, Joseph Douglas b: 9/26/64, Chicago, Ill. BR/TR, 6'3", 190 lbs. Deb: 4/10/89

YEAR TM/L	W	L	PCT	G	GS	CG	SHO	SV	IP	H	H/G	HR	BB	BB/G	SO	SO/G	ERA	/A	OAVG	OOBP	PR	/A	PF	CPI	WAT	PB	PD	TPI
1989 Cle-A	0	2	.000	2	1	0	0	0	7	7	9.0	0	4	5.1	3	3.9	6.43	63	.259	.394	-2	-2	104	70	-0.9	0	0	-0.1

■ JOHN SMILEY Smiley, John Patrick b: 3/17/65, Phoenixville, Pa. BL/TL, 6'4", 180 lbs. Deb: 9/01/86

YEAR TM/L	W	L	PCT	G	GS	CG	SHO	SV	IP	H	H/G	HR	BB	BB/G	SO	SO/G	ERA	/A	OAVG	OOBP	PR	/A	PF	CPI	WAT	PB	PD	TPI
1986 Pit-N	1	0	1.000	12	0	0	0	0	12	4	3.0	2	4	3.0	9	6.8	3.75	100	.105	.190	-0	-0	101	28	0.5	0	0	0.0
1987 Pit-N	5	5	.500	63	0	0	0	4	75	69	8.3	7	50	6.0	58	7.0	5.76	74	.244	.354	-14	-12	105	74	0.1	0	0	-1.1
1988 Pit-N	13	11	.542	34	32	5	1	0	205	185	8.1	15	46	2.0	129	5.7	3.25	103	.241	.280	5	2	97	91	0.3	-2	-0	0.0
1989 Pit-N	12	8	.600	28	28	8	1	0	205	174	7.6	22	49	2.2	123	5.4	2.81	118	.226	.272	16	11	94	102	2.9	1	-2	1.0
Total 4	31	24	.564	137	60	13	2	4	497	432	7.8	46	149	2.7	319	5.8	3.46	101	.233	.287	6	1	97	91	3.8	-1	-2	-0.1

■ BRYN SMITH Smith, Bryn Nelson b: 8/11/55, Marietta, Ga. BR/TR, 6'2", 200 lbs. Deb: 9/08/81

YEAR TM/L	W	L	PCT	G	GS	CG	SHO	SV	IP	H	H/G	HR	BB	BB/G	SO	SO/G	ERA	/A	OAVG	OOBP	PR	/A	PF	CPI	WAT	PB	PD	TPI
1981 Mon-N	1	0	1.000	7	0	0	0	0	13	14	9.7	1	3	2.1	9	6.2	2.77	123	.280	.321	1	1	98	140	0.5	-0	-0	0.0
1982 Mon-N	2	4	.333	47	1	0	0	3	79	81	9.2	5	23	2.6	50	5.7	4.22	89	.264	.310	-5	-4	104	82	-1.0	-0	0	-0.3
1983 Mon-N	6	11	.353	49	12	5	3	3	155	142	8.2	13	43	2.5	101	5.9	2.50	147	.248	.299	20	20	101	132	-2.7	0	0	2.2
1984 Mon-N	12	13	.480	28	28	4	2	0	179	178	8.9	15	51	2.6	101	5.1	3.32	99	.259	.309	5	-1	91	107	0.0	1	2	0.1
1985 Mon-N	18	5	.783	32	32	4	2	0	222	193	7.8	12	41	1.7	127	5.1	2.92	116	.232	.264	17	11	94	80	6.7	3	-1	1.4
1986 Mon-N	10	8	.556	30	30	1	0	0	187	182	8.8	15	63	3.0	105	5.1	3.95	93	.251	.311	-5	-6	98	88	1.4	1	3	-0.1
1987 Mon-N	10	9	.526	26	26	2	0	0	150	164	9.8	16	31	1.9	94	5.6	4.38	99	.274	.306	-5	-1	106	89	-0.6	-0	-0	0.0
1988 Mon-N	12	10	.545	32	32	1	0	0	198	179	8.1	15	32	**1.5**	122	5.5	3.00	121	.243	.279	10	14	105	99	1.1	-1	-1	1.2
1989 Mon-N	10	11	.476	33	32	3	1	0	216	177	7.4	16	54	2.3	129	5.4	2.83	126	.223	.272	16	18	102	91	-0.5	-2	2	2.0
Total 9	81	71	.533	284	193	20	8	6	1399	1310	8.4	108	341	2.2	838	5.4	3.29	110	.247	.292	54	52	100	96	4.9	2	5	6.5

■ DAVE SMITH Smith, David Stanley b: 1/21/55, Richmond, Cal. BR/TR, 6'1", 195 lbs. Deb: 4/11/80

YEAR TM/L	W	L	PCT	G	GS	CG	SHO	SV	IP	H	H/G	HR	BB	BB/G	SO	SO/G	ERA	/A	OAVG	OOBP	PR	/A	PF	CPI	WAT	PB	PD	TPI
1980 Hou-N	7	5	.583	57	0	0	0	10	103	90	7.9	1	32	2.8	85	7.4	1.92	182	.237	.299	19	18	97	134	0.2	-1	-1	1.7
1981 Hou-N	5	3	.625	42	0	0	0	8	75	54	6.5	2	23	2.8	52	6.2	2.76	110	.198	.259	6	2	87	61	0.7	0	-0	0.2
1982 Hou-N	5	4	.556	49	1	0	0	11	63	69	9.9	4	31	4.4	28	4.0	3.86	93	.285	.350	-2	-2	100	120	0.7	-0	-1	-0.2
1983 Hou-N	3	1	.750	42	0	0	0	6	73	72	8.9	2	36	4.4	41	5.1	3.08	106	.258	.334	5	2	90	116	1.0	-0	-2	0.0
1984 Hou-N	5	4	.556	53	0	0	0	5	77	60	7.0	5	20	2.3	45	5.3	2.22	148	.214	.266	12	9	92	101	0.6	-0	-0	0.9
1985 Hou-N	9	5	.643	64	0	0	0	27	79	69	7.9	3	17	1.9	40	4.6	2.28	151	.235	.276	12	10	96	106	2.0	0	-1	0.9
1986 Hou-N	4	7	.364	54	0	0	0	33	56	39	6.3	5	22	3.5	46	7.4	2.73	138	.200	.278	6	7	102	94	-2.1	-0	0	0.7
1987 Hou-N	2	3	.400	50	0	0	0	24	60	39	5.8	0	21	3.2	73	10.9	1.65	230	.182	.254	16	14	93	76	-0.3	1	-0	1.5
1988 Hou-N	4	5	.444	51	0	0	0	27	57	60	9.5	1	19	3.0	38	6.0	2.68	120	.268	.321	5	3	93	130	-0.5	-0	-0	0.3
1989 Hou-N	3	4	.429	52	0	0	0	25	58	49	7.6	1	19	2.9	31	4.8	2.64	136	.233	.289	6	6	103	101	-0.6	-0	1	0.7
Total 10	47	41	.534	514	1	0	0	176	701	601	7.7	24	240	3.1	479	6.1	2.54	135	.232	.294	84	70	95	105	1.7	-2	-5	6.7

■ LEE SMITH Smith, Lee Arthur b: 12/4/57, Shreveport, La. BR/TR, 6'5", 220 lbs. Deb: 9/01/80

YEAR TM/L	W	L	PCT	G	GS	CG	SHO	SV	IP	H	H/G	HR	BB	BB/G	SO	SO/G	ERA	/A	OAVG	OOBP	PR	/A	PF	CPI	WAT	PB	PD	TPI
1980 Chi-N	2	0	1.000	18	0	0	0	0	22	21	8.6	0	14	5.7	17	7.0	2.86	135	.259	.361	2	2	108	135	1.0	0	0	0.2
1981 Chi-N	3	6	.333	40	1	0	0	1	67	57	7.7	2	31	4.2	50	6.7	3.49	106	.239	.318	-0	2	106	92	-0.4	-1	-0	0.0
1982 Chi-N	2	5	.286	72	5	0	0	17	117	105	8.1	5	37	2.8	99	7.6	2.69	139	.245	.302	12	14	104	112	-1.2	-0	-1	1.3
1983 Chi-N	4	10	.286	66	0	0	0	**29**	103	70	6.1	5	41	3.6	91	8.0	1.66	221	.194	.271	23	23	101	123	-2.5	-0	-1	2.4
1984 Chi-N	9	7	.563	69	0	0	0	33	101	98	8.7	6	35	3.1	86	7.7	3.65	107	.255	.311	-1	3	109	93	-0.4	-1	0	0.2
1985 Chi-N	7	4	.636	65	0	0	0	33	98	87	8.0	9	32	2.9	112	10.3	3.03	139	.242	.302	6	13	117	109	1.7	-0	-1	1.2
1986 Chi-N	9	9	.500	66	0	0	0	31	90	69	6.9	7	42	4.2	93	9.3	3.10	130	.215	.298	6	9	108	95	1.1	-1	0	0.9
1987 Chi-N	4	10	.286	62	0	0	0	36	84	84	9.0	4	32	3.4	96	10.3	3.11	134	.259	.322	9	10	102	114	-2.8	-0	-0	0.9
1988 Bos-A	4	5	.444	64	0	0	0	29	84	72	7.7	7	37	4.0	96	10.3	2.79	154	.225	.303	11	14	108	112	-0.8	0	-1	1.3
1989 Bos-A	6	1	.857	64	0	0	0	25	71	53	6.7	6	33	4.2	96	12.2	3.55	114	.209	.297	3	4	104	82	2.5	0	-1	0.3
Total 10	50	57	.467	586	6	0	0	234	837	716	7.7	51	334	3.6	836	9.0	2.96	134	.233	.304	71	94	107	106	-1.8	-3	-4	8.7

■ ROY SMITH Smith, Le Roy Purdy b: 9/6/61, Mt.Vernon, N.Y. BR/TR, 6'3", 200 lbs. Deb: 6/23/84

YEAR TM/L	W	L	PCT	G	GS	CG	SHO	SV	IP	H	H/G	HR	BB	BB/G	SO	SO/G	ERA	/A	OAVG	OOBP	PR	/A	PF	CPI	WAT	PB	PD	TPI
1984 Cle-A	5	5	.500	22	14	0	0	0	86	91	9.5	14	40	4.2	55	5.8	4.60	92	.270	.346	-6	-4	106	107	0.4	0	-1	-0.4
1985 Cle-A	1	4	.200	12	11	1	0	0	62	84	12.2	8	17	2.5	28	4.1	5.37	74	.321	.358	-8	-10	95	106	-1.1	0	-1	-0.9
1986 Min-A	0	2	.000	5	0	0	0	0	10	13	11.7	1	5	4.5	8	7.2	7.20	64	.295	.380	-3	-3	109	75	-0.9	0	0	-0.2
1987 Min-A	1	0	1.000	7	1	0	0	0	16	20	11.3	3	6	3.4	8	4.5	5.06	85	.290	.359	-1	-1	96	112	0.5	0	-0	0.0
1988 Min-A	3	0	1.000	9	4	0	0	0	37	29	7.1	3	12	2.9	17	4.1	2.68	157	.210	.276	5	6	105	93	1.5	0	-1	0.6
1989 Min-A	10	6	.625	32	26	2	0	1	172	180	9.4	22	51	2.7	92	4.8	3.92	106	.269	.322	-1	4	106	108	2.2	0	-3	0.1
Total 6	20	17	.541	87	56	3	0	1	383	417	9.8	51	131	3.1	208	4.9	4.32	96	.275	.333	-14	-7	104	105	2.6	0	-5	-0.8

■ MIKE SMITH Smith, Michael Anthony b: 2/23/61, Hinds, Miss. BB/TR, 6', 175 lbs. Deb: 4/06/84

YEAR TM/L	W	L	PCT	G	GS	CG	SHO	SV	IP	H	H/G	HR	BB	BB/G	SO	SO/G	ERA	/A	OAVG	OOBP	PR	/A	PF	CPI	WAT	PB	PD	TPI
1984 Cin-N	1	0	1.000	8	0	0	0	0	10	12	10.8	1	5	4.5	7	6.3	5.40	71	.286	.362	-2	-2	107	91	0.5	0	-0	-0.1
1985 Cin-N	0	0	—	2	0	0	0	0	3	2	6.0	2	1	3.0	2	6.0	6.00	63	.167	.231	-1	-1	105	90	0.0	0	0	0.0
1986 Cin-N	0	0	—	2	1	0	0	0	3	7	21.0	0	1	3.0	1	3.0	15.00	26	.412	.444	-4	-4	104	56	0.0	0	0	-0.3
1988 Mon-N	0	0	—	5	0	0	0	1	9	6	6.0	0	5	5.0	4	4.0	3.00	121	.207	.314	0	1	105	91	0.0	-0	-0	0.0
1989 Pit-N	0	1	.000	16	0	0	0	0	24	28	10.5	1	10	3.8	12	4.5	3.75	88	.301	.355	-1	-1	94	128	-0.4	-0	1	0.0
Total 5	1	1	.500	33	1	0	0	1	49	55	10.1	4	22	4.0	26	4.8	4.78	74	.285	.350	-7	-7	100	107	0.1	-1	1	-0.4

■ MIKE SMITH Smith, Michael Anthony b: 10/31/63, San Antonio, Tex. BR/TR, 6'3", 180 lbs. Deb: 6/30/89

YEAR TM/L	W	L	PCT	G	GS	CG	SHO	SV	IP	H	H/G	HR	BB	BB/G	SO	SO/G	ERA	/A	OAVG	OOBP	PR	/A	PF	CPI	WAT	PB	PD	TPI
1989 Bal-A	2	0	1.000	13	1	0	0	0	20	25	11.2	3	14	6.3	12	5.4	7.65	50	.313	.402	-8	-8	99	87	1.0	0	0	-0.7

■ PETE SMITH Smith, Peter John b: 2/27/66, Abington, Mass. BR/TR, 6'2", 185 lbs. Deb: 9/08/87

YEAR TM/L	W	L	PCT	G	GS	CG	SHO	SV	IP	H	H/G	HR	BB	BB/G	SO	SO/G	ERA	/A	OAVG	OOBP	PR	/A	PF	CPI	WAT	PB	PD	TPI
1987 Atl-N	1	2	.333	6	6	0	0	0	32	39	11.0	3	14	3.9	11	3.1	4.78	93	.307	.371	-2	-1	109	113	-0.2	-1	-1	-0.2
1988 Atl-N	7	15	.318	32	32	5	3	0	195	183	8.4	15	88	4.1	124	5.7	3.69	100	.250	.325	-5	0	107	103	-0.6	-2	-2	-0.3
1989 Atl-N	5	14	.263	28	27	1	0	0	142	144	9.1	13	57	3.6	115	7.3	4.75	76	.263	.328	-20	-18	104	86	-3.3	-0	-1	-1.9
Total 3	13	31	.295	66	65	6	3	0	369	366	8.9	31	159	3.9	250	6.1	4.20	89	.260	.330	-27	-19	106	97	-4.1	-3	-4	-2.4

■ ZANE SMITH Smith, Zane William b: 12/28/60, Madison, Wis. BL/TL, 6'2", 185 lbs. Deb: 9/10/84

YEAR TM/L	W	L	PCT	G	GS	CG	SHO	SV	IP	H	H/G	HR	BB	BB/G	SO	SO/G	ERA	/A	OAVG	OOBP	PR	/A	PF	CPI	WAT	PB	PD	TPI
1984 Atl-N	1	0	1.000	3	3	0	0	0	20	16	7.2	1	13	5.8	16	7.2	2.25	175	.219	.333	3	4	110	147	0.5	2	0	0.7
1985 Atl-N	9	10	.474	42	18	2	2	0	147	135	8.3	4	80	4.9	85	5.2	3.80	103	.254	.345	-3	2	108	100	1.2	-1	2	0.4
1986 Atl-N	8	16	.333	38	32	3	1	1	205	209	9.2	8	105	4.6	139	6.1	4.04	95	.275	.359	-7	-4	103	108	-3.3	-3	3	-0.4
1987 Atl-N	15	10	.600	36	36	9	3	0	242	245	9.1	19	91	3.4	130	4.8	4.09	109	.266	.329	-0	10	109	98	4.2	-1	1	1.2
1988 Atl-N	5	10	.333	23	22	3	0	0	140	159	10.2	8	44	2.8	59	3.8	4.31	86	.292	.338	-13	-10	107	102	0.0	0	3	-0.5
1989 Atl-N	1	12	.077	17	17	0	0	0	99	102	9.3	5	33	3.0	58	5.3	4.45	81	.267	.317	-10	-9	104	84	-5.2	-0	2	-0.7
Mon-N	0	1	.000	31	0	0	0	2	48	39	7.3	2	19	3.6	35	6.6	1.50	239	.220	.292	11	11	102	179	-0.4	0	1	1.4
Yr	1	13	.071	48	17	0	0	2	147	141	8.6	7	52	3.2	93	5.7	3.49	104	.249	.306	0	2	103	179	-5.6	-0	3	0.7
Total 6	39	59	.398	190	128	17	6	3	901	905	9.0	47	385	3.8	522	5.2	3.93	101	.267	.337	-21	3	106	105	-3.0	-2	12	2.1

■ MIKE SMITHSON Smithson, Billy Mike b: 1/21/55, Centerville, Tenn. BL/TR, 6'8", 215 lbs. Deb: 8/27/82

YEAR TM/L	W	L	PCT	G	GS	CG	SHO	SV	IP	H	H/G	HR	BB	BB/G	SO	SO/G	ERA	/A	OAVG	OOBP	PR	/A	PF	CPI	WAT	PB	PD	TPI
1982 Tex-A	3	4	.429	8	8	3	0	0	47	51	9.8	5	13	2.5	24	4.6	4.98	77	.282	.337	-5	-6	94	90	0.2	0	-1	-0.5
1983 Tex-A	10	14	.417	33	33	10	0	0	223	233	9.4	14	71	2.9	135	5.4	3.91	105	.269	.325	4	5	101	98	-1.6	0	1	0.6
1984 Min-A	15	13	.536	36	36	10	1	0	252	246	8.8	35	54	1.9	144	5.1	3.68	115	.252	.294	9	15	106	98	1.2	0	-1	1.5
1985 Min-A	15	14	.517	37	37	8	3	0	257	264	9.2	25	78	2.7	127	4.4	4.34	99	.270	.328	-6	-1	104	98	1.4	0	-2	-0.2
1986 Min-A	13	14	.481	34	33	8	1	0	198	234	10.6	26	57	2.6	114	5.2	4.77	96	.294	.347	-13	-4	109	106	1.2	0	1	-0.3
1987 Min-A	4	7	.364	21	20	0	0	0	109	126	10.4	17	38	3.1	53	4.4	5.94	72	.286	.350	-18	-20	96	88	-1.7	0	-1	-1.8
1988 Bos-A	9	6	.600	31	18	1	0	0	127	149	10.6	25	37	2.6	73	5.2	5.95	72	.292	.342	-28	-23	108	92	0.9	0	-1	-2.3
1989 Bos-A	7	14	.333	40	19	1	1	2	144	170	10.6	21	35	2.2	61	3.8	4.94	82	.297	.340	-17	-14	104	103	-3.9	0	-1	-1.4
Total 8	76	86	.469	240	204	41	6	2	1357	1473	9.8	168	383	2.5	731	4.8	4.58	93	.277	.329	-73	-48	104	98	-2.3	0	-4	-4.4

YEAR	TM/L	W	L	PCT	G	GS	CG	SHO	SV	IP	H	H/G	HR	BB	BB/G	SO	SO/G	ERA	/A	OAVG	OOBP	PR	/A	PF	CPI	WAT	PB	PD	TPI
■ JOHN SMOLTZ		Smoltz, John Andrew b: 5/15/67, Detroit, Mich. BR/TR, 6'3", 210 lbs. Deb: 7/23/88																											
1988	Atl-N	2	7	.222	12	12	0	0	0	64	74	10.4	10	33	4.6	37	5.2	5.48	67	.285	.367	-14	-13	107	101	-1.5	-0	-1	-1.3
1989	Atl-N	12	11	.522	29	29	5	0	0	208	160	6.9	15	72	3.1	168	7.3	2.94	123	.212	.276	13	16	104	87	2.7	1	2	2.0
Total	2	14	18	.438	41	41	5	0	0	272	234	7.7	25	105	3.5	205	6.8	3.54	103	.230	.300	-2	3	104	90	1.2	1	1	0.7
■ BRIAN SNYDER		Snyder, Brian Robert b: 2/20/58, Flemington, N.J. BL/TL, 6'3", 185 lbs. Deb: 5/25/85																											
1985	Sea-A	1	2	.333	15	6	0	0	1	35	44	11.3	2	19	4.9	23	5.9	6.43	62	.306	.386	-9	-10	95	85	-0.3	0	1	-0.8
1989	Oak-A	0	0	—	2	0	0	0	0	1	2	18.0	1	2	18.0	1	9.0	18.00	22	.500	.667	-2	-2	102	124	0.0	0	0	-0.1
Total	2	1	2	.333	17	6	0	0	1	36	46	11.5	3	21	5.3	24	6.0	6.75	59	.311	.395	-10	-11	96	86	-0.3	0	1	-0.9
■ JULIO SOLANO		Solano, Julio Cesar b: 1/8/60, Aqua Blanca, D.R. BR/TR, 6'1", 160 lbs. Deb: 4/05/83																											
1983	Hou-N	0	2	.000	4	0	0	0	0	6	5	7.5	1	4	6.0	3	4.5	6.00	55	.217	.333	-2	-2	90	67	-0.9	0	0	-0.1
1984	Hou-N	1	3	.250	31	0	0	0	0	51	31	5.5	3	18	3.2	33	5.8	1.94	170	.179	.249	9	8	92	90	-0.9	0	-1	0.7
1985	Hou-N	2	2	.500	20	0	0	0	0	34	34	9.0	5	13	3.4	17	4.5	3.44	100	.262	.326	1	0	96	126	0.0	-0	-1	0.0
1986	Hou-N	3	1	.750	16	1	0	0	0	32	39	11.0	5	22	6.2	21	5.9	7.59	50	.310	.413	-14	-14	102	90	0.8	-1	-0	-1.3
1987	Hou-N	0	0	—	11	0	0	0	0	20	25	11.2	5	9	4.0	12	5.4	7.65	50	.298	.362	-8	-9	93	82	0.0	-0	0	-0.7
1988	Sea-A	0	0	—	17	0	0	0	3	22	22	9.0	3	12	4.9	10	4.1	4.09	105	.268	.347	-0	1	108	123	0.0	0	0	0.1
1989	Sea-A	0	0	—	7	0	0	0	0	10	6	5.4	1	4	3.6	6	5.4	5.40	75	.176	.282	-2	-2	104	45	0.0	0	0	0.0
Total	7	6	8	.429	106	1	0	0	3	175	162	8.3	23	82	4.2	102	5.2	4.53	80	.248	.329	-15	-17	97	97	-1.0	-1	-1	-1.3
■ BOB STANLEY		Stanley, Robert William b: 11/10/54, Portland, Maine BR/TR, 6'4", 210 lbs. Deb: 4/16/77																											
1977	Bos-A	8	7	.533	41	13	3	1	3	151	176	10.5	10	43	2.6	44	2.6	3.99	118	.294	.341	1	12	116	108	-0.8	0	3	1.6
1978	Bos-A	15	2	.882	52	3	0	0	10	142	142	9.0	5	34	2.2	38	2.4	2.60	154	.266	.306	19	22	106	122	6.1	0	2	2.6
1979	Bos-A	16	12	.571	40	30	9	4	1	217	250	10.4	14	44	1.8	56	2.3	3.98	113	.294	.326	6	12	106	104	0.1	0	2	1.3
1980	Bos-A	10	8	.556	52	17	5	1	14	175	186	9.6	11	52	2.7	71	3.7	3.39	121	.278	.332	13	14	102	117	0.8	0	3	1.8
1981	Bos-A	10	8	.556	35	1	0	0	0	99	110	10.0	3	38	3.5	28	2.5	3.82	101	.294	.358	-2	1	106	118	0.2	0	3	0.4
1982	Bos-A	12	7	.632	48	0	0	0	14	168	161	8.6	11	50	2.7	83	4.4	3.11	**144**	.255	.310	18	**26**	110	110	1.9	0	4	3.1
1983	Bos-A	8	10	.444	64	0	0	0	33	145	145	9.0	7	38	2.4	65	4.0	2.86	145	.266	.309	20	21	102	123	-0.7	0	-1	2.0
1984	Bos-A	9	10	.474	57	0	0	0	22	107	113	9.5	9	23	1.9	52	4.4	3.53	124	.267	.303	6	10	110	100	-1.0	0	2	1.3
1985	Bos-A	6	6	.500	48	0	0	0	10	88	76	7.8	7	30	3.1	46	4.7	2.86	147	.237	.300	13	13	102	115	0.0	0	0	1.3
1986	Bos-A	6	6	.500	66	1	0	0	16	82	109	12.0	9	22	2.4	54	5.9	4.39	94	.322	.358	-2	-2	99	125	-0.9	0	1	-0.1
1987	Bos-A	4	15	.211	34	20	4	1	0	153	198	11.6	17	42	2.5	67	3.9	5.00	88	.321	.357	-9	-10	99	111	-5.5	0	1	-0.8
1988	Bos-A	6	4	.600	57	0	0	0	5	102	90	7.9	6	29	2.6	57	5.0	3.18	135	.242	.301	9	13	108	102	0.6	0	-0	1.2
1989	Bos-A	5	2	.714	43	0	0	0	4	79	102	11.6	4	26	3.0	32	3.6	4.90	83	.321	.362	-9	-7	104	105	1.5	0	1	-0.6
Total	13	115	97	.542	637	85	21	7	132	1708	1858	9.8	113	471	2.5	693	3.7	3.64	118	.282	.327	82	125	106	112	2.3	0	22	15.1
■ MIKE STANTON		Stanton, William Michael b: 6/2/67, Galena Park, Tex. BL/TL, 6'1", 190 lbs. Deb: 8/24/89																											
1989	Atl-N	0	1	.000	20	0	0	0	7	24	17	6.4	0	8	3.0	27	10.1	1.50	242	.207	.266	5	6	104	132	-0.4	0	-0	0.6
■ DAVE STEWART		Stewart, David Keith b: 2/19/57, Oakland, Cal. BR/TR, 6'2", 200 lbs. Deb: 9/22/78																											
1978	LA-N	0	0	—	1	0	0	0	0	2	1	4.5	0	0	0.0	1	4.5	0.00	—	.167	.167	1	1	97	0	0.0	0	0	0.1
1981	LA-N	4	3	.571	32	0	0	0	6	43	40	8.4	3	14	2.9	29	6.1	2.51	133	.250	.293	5	4	96	132	0.0	2	0	0.6
1982	LA-N	9	8	.529	45	14	0	0	1	146	137	8.4	14	49	3.0	80	4.9	3.82	88	.249	.305	-3	-7	94	92	-0.1	1	-1	-0.7
1983	LA-N	5	2	.714	46	1	0	0	8	76	67	7.9	4	33	3.9	54	6.4	2.96	122	.237	.311	6	6	100	106	1.3	-0	-0	0.5
	Tex-A	5	2	.714	8	8	2	0	0	59	50	7.6	2	17	2.6	24	3.7	2.14	193	.233	.291	13	13	101	125	1.6	0	0	1.4
1984	Tex-A	7	14	.333	32	27	3	0	0	192	193	9.0	26	87	4.1	119	5.6	4.73	85	.258	.335	-16	-15	101	93	-2.5	0	-1	-1.5
1985	Tex-A	0	6	.000	42	5	0	0	4	81	86	9.6	13	37	4.1	64	7.1	5.44	84	.273	.346	-12	-8	110	94	-2.9	0	0	-0.7
	Phi-N	0	0	—	4	0	0	0	0	4	5	11.3	0	4	9.0	2	4.5	6.75	54	.278	.409	-1	-1	102	77	0.0	0	-0	-0.1
1986	Phi-N	0	0	—	8	0	0	0	0	12	15	11.3	1	4	3.0	9	6.8	6.75	57	.306	.339	-4	-4	104	73	0.0	0	-0	-0.3
	Oak-A	9	5	.643	29	17	4	1	0	149	137	8.3	15	65	3.9	102	6.2	3.74	105	.241	.318	7	3	94	98	2.4	0	-0	0.3
1987	Oak-A	**20**	13	.606	37	37	8	1	0	261	224	7.7	24	105	3.6	205	7.1	3.69	110	.229	.304	23	11	91	88	4.2	0	-3	0.7
1988	Oak-A	21	12	.636	37	37	**14**	2	0	**276**	240	7.8	14	110	3.6	192	6.3	3.23	115	.234	.305	23	14	93	95	-0.1	0	-3	1.1
1989	Oak-A	21	9	.700	36	36	8	0	0	258	260	9.1	23	69	2.4	155	5.4	3.31	120	.263	.310	17	19	102	112	4.0	0	-1	1.8
Total	10	101	74	.577	357	182	39	4	19	1559	1455	8.4	139	594	3.4	1036	6.0	3.68	106	.246	.313	57	36	97	99	7.9	2	-10	3.2
■ DAVE STIEB		Stieb, David Andrew b: 7/22/57, Santa Ana, Cal. BR/TR, 6', 185 lbs. Deb: 6/29/79																											
1979	Tor-A	8	8	.500	18	18	7	1	0	129	139	9.7	11	48	3.3	52	3.6	4.33	103	.276	.339	-1	2	106	99	2.2	0	3	0.4
1980	Tor-A	12	15	.444	34	32	14	4	0	243	232	8.6	12	83	3.1	108	4.0	3.70	110	.260	.320	9	10	101	95	0.8	0	6	1.6
1981	Tor-A	11	10	.524	25	25	11	2	0	184	148	7.2	10	61	3.0	89	4.4	3.18	130	.223	.294	10	20	113	86	3.3	0	2	2.4
1982	Tor-A	17	14	.548	38	38	**19**	**5**	0	**288**	271	8.5	27	75	2.3	141	4.4	3.25	137	.248	.296	27	**38**	109	101	2.4	0	4	**4.5**
1983	Tor-A	17	12	.586	36	36	14	4	0	278	223	7.2	21	93	3.0	187	6.1	3.04	144	.219	.289	32	**42**	108	91	1.4	0	0	**4.4**
1984	Tor-A	16	8	.667	35	35	11	2	0	**267**	215	**7.2**	19	88	3.0	198	6.7	2.83	143	**.221**	.289	35	36	101	97	3.5	0	1	3.9
1985	Tor-A	14	13	.519	36	36	8	2	0	265	206	**7.0**	22	96	3.3	167	5.7	**2.48**	**166**	**.213**	.286	**49**	**48**	99	112	-2.4	0	5	**5.7**
1986	Tor-A	7	12	.368	37	34	1	1	1	205	239	10.5	29	87	3.8	127	5.6	4.74	92	.297	.371	-13	-8	104	119	-3.1	0	2	-0.6
1987	Tor-A	13	9	.591	33	31	3	1	0	185	164	8.0	16	87	4.2	115	5.6	4.09	109	.239	.327	8	7	99	92	0.0	0	1	0.8
1988	Tor-A	16	8	.667	32	31	8	4	0	207	157	6.8	15	79	3.4	147	6.4	3.04	129	.210	.295	21	20	99	91	3.8	0	1	2.2
1989	Tor-A	17	8	.680	33	33	3	2	0	207	164	7.1	12	76	3.3	101	4.4	3.35	108	.219	.298	13	6	93	84	4.1	0	0	0.6
Total	11	148	117	.558	357	349	99	28	1	2458	2158	7.9	194	873	3.2	1432	5.2	3.37	124	.237	.307	189	222	103	97	16.0	0	23	25.9
■ TIM STODDARD		Stoddard, Timothy Paul b: 1/24/53, E.Chicago, Ind. BR/TR, 6'7", 230 lbs. Deb: 9/07/75																											
1975	Chi-A	0	0	—	1	0	0	0	0	1	2	18.0	1	0	0.0	0	0.0	9.00	44	.400	.400	-1	-1	104	158	0.0	0	0	0.0
1978	Bal-A	0	1	.000	8	0	0	0	0	18	22	11.0	3	8	4.0	14	7.0	6.00	57	.301	.381	-4	-5	91	99	-0.4	0	0	-0.4
1979	Bal-A	3	1	.750	29	0	0	0	3	58	44	6.8	3	19	2.9	47	7.3	1.71	237	.212	.276	16	15	96	131	0.6	0	0	1.5
1980	Bal-A	5	3	.625	64	0	0	0	26	86	72	7.5	2	38	4.0	64	6.7	2.51	160	.233	.315	15	14	99	115	0.1	0	-1	1.4
1981	Bal-A	4	2	.667	31	0	0	0	7	37	38	9.2	6	18	4.4	32	7.8	3.89	93	.268	.358	-1	-1	99	130	0.8	0	0	0.0
1982	Bal-A	3	4	.429	50	0	0	0	12	56	53	8.5	4	29	4.7	42	6.8	4.02	101	.249	.333	0	0	99	96	-0.8	0	-0	0.0
1983	Bal-A	4	3	.571	47	0	0	0	9	58	65	10.1	10	29	4.5	50	7.8	6.05	67	.293	.365	-13	-13	99	97	-0.1	0	0	-1.2
1984	Chi-N	10	6	.625	58	0	0	0	7	92	77	7.5	9	57	5.6	87	8.5	3.82	102	.236	.339	-2	1	109	108	0.6	-1	-1	0.0
1985	SD-N	1	6	.143	44	0	0	0	1	60	63	9.4	3	37	5.6	42	6.3	4.65	78	.269	.358	-7	-7	101	95	-2.5	-1	-1	-0.7
1986	SD-N	1	3	.250	30	0	0	0	0	45	33	6.6	6	34	6.8	47	9.4	3.80	94	.200	.330	-0	-1	96	98	-0.8	1	0	0.0
	NY-A	4	1	.800	24	0	0	0	0	49	41	7.5	6	23	4.2	34	6.2	3.86	111	.232	.308	2	2	103	97	1.4	0	0	0.2
1987	NY-A	4	3	.571	57	0	0	0	8	93	83	8.0	13	30	2.9	78	7.5	3.48	125	.235	.293	10	9	97	99	0.2	0	-1	0.8
1988	NY-A	2	2	.500	28	0	0	0	3	55	62	10.1	5	27	4.4	33	5.4	6.38	59	.286	.360	-15	-16	96	79	0.0	0	0	-1.4
1989	Cle-A	0	0	—	14	0	0	0	0	21	25	10.7	1	7	3.0	12	5.1	3.00	135	.313	.352	2	2	104	163	0.0	0	0	0.3
Total	13	41	35	.539	485	0	0	0	76	729	680	8.4	72	356	4.4	582	7.2	3.95	100	.250	.331	2	1	100	106	-0.9	-0	-2	0.5
■ TODD STOTTLEMYRE		Stottlemyre, Todd Vernon b: 5/20/65, Sunnyside, Wash. BL/TR, 6'3", 195 lbs. Deb: 4/06/88																											
1988	Tor-A	4	8	.333	28	16	0	0	0	98	109	10.0	15	46	4.2	67	6.2	5.69	69	.283	.359	-19	-19	99	95	-2.3	0	-0	-1.8
1989	Tor-A	7	7	.500	27	18	0	0	0	128	137	9.6	11	44	3.1	63	4.4	3.87	94	.282	.341	0	-3	93	116	-0.6	0	-1	-0.4
Total	2	11	15	.423	55	34	0	0	0	226	246	9.8	26	90	3.6	130	5.2	4.66	81	.282	.349	-18	-23	96	107	-2.9	0	-1	-2.2
■ RICK SUTCLIFFE		Sutcliffe, Richard Lee b: 6/21/56, Independence, Mo. BL/TR, 6'7", 215 lbs. Deb: 9/29/76																											
1976	LA-N	0	0	—	1	1	0	0	0	5	2	3.6	0	1	1.8	3	5.4	0.00	—	.125	.176	2	2	99	0	0.0	-0	-0	0.2
1978	LA-N	0	0	—	2	0	0	0	0	2	2	9.0	0	1	4.5	0	0.0	0.00	—	.286	.444	1	1	97	0	0.0	0	0	0.1
1979	LA-N	17	10	.630	39	30	5	1	0	242	217	8.1	16	97	3.6	117	4.4	3.46	108	.243	.311	8	7	99	95	4.3	5	-2	1.0
1980	LA-N	3	9	.250	42	10	1	1	5	110	122	10.0	10	55	4.5	59	4.8	5.56	62	.285	.363	-24	-26	96	87	-3.4	-0	-1	-2.6
1981	LA-N	2	2	.500	14	6	0	0	0	47	41	7.9	5	20	3.8	16	3.1	4.02	83	.238	.320	-3	-3	96	92	-0.2	1	0	-0.2
1982	Cle-A	14	8	.636	34	27	6	1	1	216	174	**7.3**	16	98	4.1	142	5.9	**2.96**	139	**.226**	.311	**27**	28	101	110	3.6	0	1	3.0
1983	Cle-A	17	11	.607	36	35	10	2	0	243	251	9.3	23	102	3.8	160	5.9	4.30	101	.268	.338	-6	1	106	101	4.9	0	2	0.2

YEAR	TM/L	W	L	PCT	G	GS	CG	SHO	SV	IP	H	H/G	HR	BB	BB/G	SO	SO/G	ERA	/A	OAVG	OOBP	PR	/A	PF	CPI	WAT	PB	PD	TPI
1984	Cle-A	4	5	.444	15	15	2	0	0	94	111	10.6	7	46	4.4	58	5.6	5.17	82	.298	.371	-12	-10	106	99	-0.1	0	-0	-0.9
	Chi-N	16	1	**.941**	20	20	7	3	0	150	123	7.4	9	39	2.3	155	9.3	2.70	145	.220	.271	15	20	109	84	**7.4**	3	2	2.9
1985	Chi-N	8	8	.500	20	20	6	3	0	130	119	8.2	12	44	3.0	102	7.1	3.18	132	.240	.302	6	15	117	103	0.4	2	1	2.1
1986	Chi-N	5	14	.263	28	27	4	1	0	177	166	8.4	18	96	4.9	122	6.2	4.63	87	.252	.344	-18	-12	108	92	-4.0	3	1	-0.7
1987	Chi-N	**18**	10	.643	34	34	6	1	0	237	223	8.5	24	106	4.0	174	6.6	3.68	113	.252	.329	11	12	102	110	**5.1**	3	4	1.9
1988	Chi-N	13	14	.481	32	32	12	2	0	226	232	9.2	18	70	2.8	144	5.7	3.86	94	.269	.317	-10	-6	105	102	0.2	3	1	-0.1
1989	Chi-N	16	11	.593	35	34	5	1	0	229	202	7.9	18	69	2.7	153	6.0	3.66	103	.240	.291	-4	3	107	87	0.7	1	1	0.6
Total	13	133	103	.564	352	291	64	16	6	2108	1985	8.5	176	844	3.6	1405	6.0	3.81	104	.251	.320	-8	32	104	98	18.9	20	9	7.5
■ **RUSS SWAN**	Swan, Russell Howard b: 1/3/64, Fremont, Cal. BL/TL, 6'4", 210 lbs. Deb: 8/03/89																												
1989	SF-N	0	2	.000	2	2	0	0	0	7	11	14.1	4	4	5.1	2	2.6	10.29	33	.393	.441	-5	-5	96	116	-0.9	-0	0	-0.4
■ **BILL SWIFT**	Swift, William Charles b: 10/27/61, Portland, Maine BR/TR, 6', 170 lbs. Deb: 6/07/85																												
1985	Sea-A	6	10	.375	23	21	0	0	0	121	131	9.7	8	48	3.6	55	4.1	4.76	83	.279	.346	-8	-11	95	93	-1.5	0	0	-0.9
1986	Sea-A	2	9	.182	29	17	1	0	0	115	148	11.6	5	55	4.3	55	4.3	5.48	81	.319	.393	-17	-13	106	102	-3.1	0	1	-1.0
1988	Sea-A	8	12	.400	38	24	6	1	0	175	199	10.2	10	65	3.3	47	2.4	4.58	94	.294	.359	-12	-5	108	103	-0.5	0	2	-0.3
1989	Sea-A	7	3	.700	37	16	0	0	1	130	140	9.7	7	38	2.6	45	3.1	4.43	91	.278	.327	-8	-6	104	87	2.3	0	5	0.0
Total	4	23	34	.404	127	78	7	1	1	541	618	10.3	30	206	3.4	202	3.4	4.77	88	.292	.356	-44	-35	104	97	-2.8	0	8	-2.2
■ **GREG SWINDELL**	Swindell, Forrest Gregory b: 1/2/65, Houston, Tex. BR/TL, 6'2", 225 lbs. Deb: 8/21/86																												
1986	Cle-A	5	2	.714	9	9	1	0	0	62	57	8.3	9	15	2.2	46	6.7	4.21	97	.243	.286	-0	-1	98	83	1.5	0	1	0.0
1987	Cle-A	3	8	.273	16	15	4	1	0	102	112	9.9	18	37	3.3	97	8.6	5.12	91	.283	.340	-7	-5	105	102	-1.5	0	-0	-0.4
1988	Cle-A	18	14	.563	33	33	12	4	0	242	234	8.7	18	45	1.7	180	6.7	3.20	127	.252	.283	21	23	102	96	3.0	0	-1	2.3
1989	Cle-A	13	6	.684	28	28	5	2	0	184	170	8.3	16	51	2.5	129	6.3	3.38	120	.246	.295	11	14	104	96	4.3	0	-0	1.4
Total	4	39	30	.565	86	85	22	7	0	590	573	8.7	61	148	2.3	452	6.9	3.69	113	.255	.298	24	31	103	96	7.3	0	-1	3.3
■ **FRANK TANANA**	Tanana, Frank Daryl b: 7/3/53, Detroit, Mich. BL/TL, 6'2", 180 lbs. Deb: 9/09/73																												
1973	Cal-A	2	2	.500	4	4	2	1	0	26	20	6.9	2	8	2.8	22	7.6	3.12	118	.200	.259	2	2	96	57	0.0	0	0	0.2
1974	Cal-A	14	19	.424	39	35	12	4	0	269	262	8.8	27	77	2.6	180	6.0	3.11	108	.255	.308	15	8	93	113	0.2	0	0	0.8
1975	Cal-A	16	9	.640	34	33	16	5	0	257	211	7.4	21	73	2.6	**269**	**9.4**	2.63	138	.226	.283	33	29	96	104	4.8	0	3	3.4
1976	Cal-A	19	10	.655	34	34	23	2	0	288	212	6.6	24	73	2.3	261	8.2	2.44	134	.203	**.257**	35	27	93	87	5.7	0	2	3.2
1977	Cal-A	15	9	.625	31	31	20	**7**	0	241	201	7.5	19	61	2.3	205	7.7	**2.54**	152	.227	.282	41	35	95	106	4.1	0	1	3.9
1978	Cal-A	18	12	.600	33	33	10	4	0	239	239	9.0	26	60	2.3	137	5.2	3.65	105	.258	.304	3	5	101	98	2.4	0	-2	0.2
1979	Cal-A	7	5	.583	18	17	2	1	0	90	93	9.3	9	25	2.5	46	4.6	3.90	99	.264	.314	3	-0	92	96	0.6	0	-1	0.0
1980	Cal-A	11	12	.478	32	31	7	0	0	204	223	9.8	18	45	2.0	113	5.0	4.15	94	.277	.317	-2	-5	97	93	1.6	0	-1	-0.5
1981	Bos-A	4	10	.286	24	23	5	2	0	141	142	9.1	17	43	2.7	78	5.0	4.02	96	.265	.317	-6	-2	106	102	-3.5	0	1	-0.1
1982	Tex-A	7	18	.280	30	30	7	0	0	194	199	9.2	16	55	2.6	87	4.0	4.22	91	.264	.314	-3	-8	94	89	-4.0	0	-0	-0.7
1983	Tex-A	7	9	.438	29	22	3	0	0	159	144	8.2	14	49	2.8	108	6.1	3.17	130	.240	.300	16	17	101	103	-0.6	0	3	2.0
1984	Tex-A	15	15	.500	35	35	9	1	0	246	234	8.6	30	81	3.0	141	5.2	3.26	124	.245	.305	20	21	101	110	2.2	0	1	2.3
1985	Tex-A	2	7	.222	13	13	0	0	0	78	89	10.3	15	23	2.7	52	6.0	5.88	78	.287	.332	-15	-11	110	89	-1.9	0	0	-1.0
	Det-A	10	7	.588	20	20	4	0	0	137	131	8.6	13	34	2.2	107	7.0	3.35	131	.250	.295	12	16	106	101	1.3	0	1	1.7
	Yr	12	14	.462	33	33	4	0	0	215	220	9.2	28	57	2.4	159	6.7	4.27	104	.262	.308	-3	4	107	101	-0.6	0	1	0.7
1986	Det-A	12	9	.571	32	31	3	1	0	188	196	9.4	23	65	3.1	119	5.7	4.16	95	.268	.325	0	-4	95	103	0.9	0	1	-0.2
1987	Det-A	15	10	.600	34	34	5	3	0	219	216	8.9	27	56	2.3	146	6.0	3.90	110	.256	.300	14	9	96	97	0.0	0	1	0.9
1988	Det-A	14	11	.560	32	32	2	0	0	203	213	9.4	25	64	2.8	127	5.6	4.21	89	.267	.321	-5	-11	94	100	0.5	0	1	-0.9
1989	Det-A	10	14	.417	33	33	6	1	0	224	227	9.1	21	74	3.0	147	5.9	3.58	108	.265	.324	8	7	99	112	1.1	0	2	0.9
Total	17	198	188	.513	507	491	136	32	0	3403	3252	8.6	347	966	2.6	2345	6.2	3.49	110	.251	.303	172	132	97	100	15.4	0	13	16.1
■ **KEVIN TAPANI**	Tapani, Kevin Ray b: 2/18/64, Des Moines, Iowa BR/TR, 6', 180 lbs. Deb: 7/04/89																												
1989	NY-N	0	0	—	3	0	0	0	0	7	5	6.4	1	4	5.1	2	2.6	3.86	87	.192	.290	-0	-0	95	81	0.0	-0	0	0.0
	Min-A	2	2	.500	5	5	0	0	0	33	34	9.3	2	8	2.2	21	5.7	3.82	108	.266	.304	0	1	106	89	0.0	0	0	0.1
■ **STU TATE**	Tate, Stuart Douglas b: 6/17/62, Huntsville, Ala. BR/TR, 6'3", 205 lbs. Deb: 9/20/89																												
1989	SF-N	0	0	—	2	0	0	0	0	3	3	9.0	0	0	0.0	4	12.0	3.00	112	.250	.250	0	0	96	62	0.0	0	0	0.0
■ **DORN TAYLOR**	Taylor, Donald Clyde b: 8/11/58, Abington, Pa. BR/TR, 6'2", 180 lbs. Deb: 4/30/87																												
1987	Pit-N	2	3	.400	14	8	0	0	0	53	48	8.2	10	28	4.8	37	6.3	5.77	74	.247	.341	-10	-9	105	84	-0.4	-0	-0	-0.8
1989	Pit-N	1	1	.500	9	0	0	0	0	11	14	11.5	0	5	4.1	3	2.5	4.91	67	.333	.404	-2	-2	94	111	0.1	-0	-0	-0.1
Total	2	3	4	.429	23	8	0	0	0	64	62	8.7	10	33	4.6	40	5.6	5.63	73	.263	.352	-12	-11	103	89	-0.3	-0	-1	-0.9
■ **KENT TEKULVE**	Tekulve, Kenton Charles b: 3/5/47, Cincinnati, Ohio BR/TR, 6'4", 180 lbs. Deb: 5/20/74																												
1974	Pit-N	1	1	.500	8	0	0	0	0	9	12	12.0	1	5	5.0	6	6.0	6.00	58	.343	.409	-2	-2	97	117	0.0	0	1	-0.1
1975	Pit-N	1	2	.333	34	0	0	0	5	56	43	6.9	2	23	3.7	28	4.5	2.25	157	.215	.289	9	8	98	108	-0.5	-0	2	1.0
1976	Pit-N	5	3	.625	64	0	0	0	9	103	91	8.0	3	25	2.2	68	5.9	2.45	142	.241	.284	12	12	99	103	0.6	-1	2	1.4
1977	Pit-N	10	1	.909	72	0	0	0	7	103	89	7.8	5	33	2.9	59	5.2	3.06	130	.236	.291	10	11	102	91	4.3	0	4	1.5
1978	Pit-N	8	7	.533	**91**	0	0	0	31	135	115	7.7	5	55	3.7	77	5.1	2.33	161	.228	.300	**19**	21	105	116	-0.1	-1	3	2.5
1979	Pit-N	10	8	.556	**94**	0	0	0	31	134	109	7.3	5	49	3.3	75	5.0	2.75	141	.222	.291	15	17	104	89	-0.7	-0	2	1.9
1980	Pit-N	8	12	.400	78	0	0	0	21	93	96	9.3	6	40	3.9	47	4.5	3.39	110	.267	.337	2	3	103	117	-2.3	-1	1	0.3
1981	Pit-N	5	5	.500	45	0	0	0	3	65	61	8.4	1	17	2.4	34	4.7	2.49	135	.250	.295	7	6	96	110	0.5	-0	1	0.8
1982	Pit-N	12	8	.600	**85**	0	0	0	20	129	113	7.9	7	46	3.2	66	4.6	2.86	139	.237	.299	11	16	110	105	1.9	-1	2	1.7
1983	Pit-N	7	5	.583	76	0	0	0	18	99	78	7.1	1	36	3.3	52	4.7	1.64	228	.223	.286	22	23	103	142	0.9	-1	1	2.4
1984	Pit-N	3	9	.250	72	0	0	0	13	88	86	8.8	4	33	3.4	36	3.7	2.66	127	.262	.324	9	7	94	136	-2.8	-1	3	0.9
1985	Pit-N	0	0	—	3	0	0	0	0	3	7	21.0	1	5	15.0	4	12.0	18.00	21	.467	.571	-5	-5	104	90	0.0	0	0	-0.3
	Phi-N	4	10	.286	58	0	0	0	14	72	67	8.4	4	25	3.1	36	4.5	3.00	123	.246	.307	5	5	102	107	-2.7	-0	0	0.6
	Yr	4	10	.286	61	0	0	0	14	75	74	8.9	5	30	3.6	40	4.8	3.60	102	.258	.324	-0	1	102	107	-2.7	0	0	0.3
1986	Phi-N	11	5	.688	73	0	0	0	4	110	99	8.1	2	25	2.0	57	4.7	2.54	153	.240	.278	15	16	104	93	2.8	-0	0	1.7
1987	Phi-N	6	4	.600	**90**	0	0	0	3	105	96	8.2	8	29	2.5	60	5.1	3.09	139	.243	.289	12	14	105	99	1.1	0	1	1.5
1988	Phi-N	3	7	.300	70	0	0	0	4	80	87	9.8	3	22	2.5	43	4.8	3.60	99	.276	.320	-1	-0	103	104	-1.2	-0	1	0.0
1989	Cin-N	0	3	.000	37	0	0	0	1	52	56	9.7	5	23	4.0	31	5.4	5.02	72	.272	.336	-9	-8	104	89	-1.4	0	0	-0.7
Total	16	94	90	.511	1050	0	0	0	184	1436	1305	8.2	63	491	3.1	779	4.9	2.85	132	.244	.302	129	144	103	107	0.4	-6	22	17.1
■ **WALT TERRELL**	Terrell, Charles Walter b: 5/11/58, Jeffersonville, Ind BL/TR, 6'2", 205 lbs. Deb: 9/08/82																												
1982	NY-N	0	3	.000	3	3	0	0	0	21	22	9.4	2	14	6.0	8	3.4	3.43	105	.268	.371	0	0	100	142	-1.4	1	-0	0.1
1983	NY-N	8	8	.500	21	20	4	2	0	134	123	8.3	7	55	3.7	59	4.0	3.56	102	.251	.321	1	1	100	97	1.2	3	-0	0.4
1984	NY-N	11	12	.478	33	33	3	1	0	215	232	9.7	16	80	3.3	114	4.8	3.52	102	.282	.341	2	2	100	124	-1.7	-4	0	-0.1
1985	Det-A	15	10	.600	34	34	5	3	0	229	221	8.7	9	95	3.7	130	5.1	3.85	114	.255	.326	8	14	106	93	2.4	0	3	1.7
1986	Det-A	15	12	.556	34	33	9	2	0	217	199	8.3	30	98	4.1	93	3.9	4.56	87	.245	.327	-9	-15	95	91	0.6	0	2	-1.2
1987	Det-A	17	10	.630	35	35	10	1	0	245	254	9.3	30	94	3.5	143	5.3	4.04	106	.268	.332	12	6	96	110	1.0	0	-1	0.5
1988	Det-A	7	16	.304	29	29	11	1	0	206	199	8.7	20	78	3.4	84	3.7	3.98	94	.258	.321	-0	-6	94	101	-5.4	0	1	-0.4
1989	SD-N	5	13	.278	19	19	4	1	0	123	134	9.8	14	26	1.9	63	4.6	4.02	87	.277	.308	-7	-7	101	102	-4.6	-0	3	-0.4
	NY-A	6	5	.545	13	13	1	1	0	83	102	11.1	9	24	2.6	30	3.3	5.20	79	.307	.354	-12	-10	105	98	0.9	0	-0	-0.9
Total	8	84	89	.486	221	219	47	12	0	1473	1486	9.1	137	564	3.4	724	4.4	4.01	98	.265	.329	-6	-13	99	103	-7.0	-0	8	-0.3
■ **SCOTT TERRY**	Terry, Scott Ray b: 11/11/59, Hobbs, N.Mex. BR/TR, 5'11", 195 lbs. Deb: 4/09/86																												
1986	Cin-N	1	2	.333	28	3	0	0	0	56	66	10.6	8	32	5.1	32	5.1	6.11	63	.300	.380	-15	-14	104	96	-0.5	0	0	-1.3
1987	StL-N	0	0	—	11	0	0	0	0	13	13	9.0	0	8	5.5	9	6.2	3.46	115	.260	.356	1	1	97	111	0.0	-0	0	0.1
1988	StL-N	9	6	.600	51	11	1	0	3	129	119	8.3	5	34	2.4	65	4.5	2.93	124	.247	.292	8	10	105	100	2.0	2	0	1.3
1989	StL-N	8	10	.444	31	24	1	0	2	149	142	8.6	14	43	2.6	69	4.2	3.56	99	.253	.304	-1	-1	100	101	-1.5	2	2	0.3
Total	4	18	18	.500	121	38	2	0	5	347	340	8.8	27	117	3.0	175	4.5	3.73	97	.259	.315	-7	-4	102	100	0.0	4	2	0.4

YEAR	TM/L	W	L	PCT	G	GS	CG	SHO	SV	IP	H	H/G	HR	BB	BB/G	SO	SO/G	ERA	/A	OAVG	OOBP	PR	/A	PF	CPI	WAT	PB	PD	TPI
■ **BOB TEWKSBURY**	Tewksbury, Robert Alan b: 11/30/60, Concord, N.H. BR/TR, 6'4", 200 lbs. Deb: 4/11/86																												
1986	NY-A	9	5	.643	23	20	2	0	0	130	144	10.0	8	31	2.1	49	3.4	3.32	129	.282	.323	12	14	103	119	1.5	0	2	1.6
1987	NY-A	1	4	.200	8	6	0	0	0	33	47	12.8	5	7	1.9	12	3.3	6.82	64	.338	.369	-9	-9	97	92	-1.5	0	0	-0.7
	Chi-N	0	4	.000	7	3	0	0	0	18	32	16.0	1	13	6.5	10	5.0	6.50	64	.421	.484	-5	-5	102	144	-1.9	-1	-1	-0.5
1988	Chi-N	0	0	—	1	1	0	0	0	3	6	18.0	1	2	6.0	1	3.0	9.00	40	.400	.444	-2	-2	105	124	0.0	-0	0	-0.1
1989	StL-N	1	0	1.000	7	4	1	1	0	30	25	7.5	2	10	3.0	17	5.1	3.30	106	.225	.296	1	1	100	89	0.5	-0	-0	0.0
Total	4	11	13	.458	46	34	3	1	0	214	254	10.7	17	63	2.6	89	3.7	4.21	99	.298	.345	-2	-1	101	113	-1.4	-1	1	0.3
■ **BOBBY THIGPEN**	Thigpen, Robert Thomas b: 7/17/63, Tallahassee, Fla. BR/TR, 6'3", 195 lbs. Deb: 8/06/86																												
1986	Chi-A	2	0	1.000	20	0	0	0	7	36	26	6.5	1	12	3.0	20	5.0	1.75	243	.205	.275	10	10	101	119	1.0	0	0	1.0
1987	Chi-A	7	5	.583	51	0	0	0	16	89	86	8.7	10	24	2.4	52	5.3	2.73	178	.256	.306	17	**21**	109	139	1.3	0	0	2.1
1988	Chi-A	5	8	.385	68	0	0	0	34	90	96	9.6	6	33	3.3	62	6.2	3.30	119	.273	.334	7	6	99	126	-0.8	0	0	0.6
1989	Chi-A	2	6	.250	61	0	0	0	34	79	62	7.1	10	40	4.6	47	5.4	3.76	97	.218	.307	1	-1	93	94	-1.6	0	-1	-0.1
Total	4	16	19	.457	200	0	0	0	91	294	270	8.3	27	109	3.3	181	5.5	3.06	136	.245	.312	35	36	101	121	-0.1	0	-0	3.6
■ **RICH THOMPSON**	Thompson, Richard Neil b: 11/1/58, New York, N.Y. BB/TR, 6'3", 225 lbs. Deb: 4/28/85																												
1985	Cle-A	3	8	.273	57	0	0	0	5	80	95	10.7	8	48	5.4	30	3.4	6.30	63	.303	.393	-19	-21	95	96	-1.4	0	-2	-2.1
1989	Mon-N	0	2	.000	19	1	0	0	0	33	27	7.4	2	11	3.0	15	4.1	2.18	164	.241	.310	5	5	102	158	-0.9	0	-0	0.5
Total	2	3	10	.231	76	1	0	0	5	113	122	9.7	10	59	4.7	45	3.6	5.10	76	.286	.372	-14	-16	97	114	-2.3	0	-2	-1.6
■ **MARK THURMOND**	Thurmond, Mark Anthony b: 9/12/56, Houston, Tex. BL/TL, 6', 180 lbs. Deb: 5/14/83																												
1983	SD-N	7	3	.700	21	18	2	0	0	115	104	8.1	7	33	2.6	49	3.8	2.66	135	.248	.298	12	12	99	117	2.1	-2	1	1.2
1984	SD-N	14	8	.636	32	29	1	1	0	179	174	8.7	12	55	2.8	57	2.9	2.97	118	.256	.305	12	11	98	113	2.0	1	2	1.5
1985	SD-N	7	11	.389	36	23	1	1	2	138	154	10.0	9	44	2.9	57	3.7	3.98	92	.291	.340	-6	-5	101	110	-2.3	-2	1	-0.5
1986	SD-N	3	7	.300	17	15	2	1	0	71	96	12.2	7	27	3.4	32	4.1	6.46	55	.325	.375	-22	-23	96	89	-1.7	1	0	-2.0
	Det-A	4	1	.800	25	4	0	0	3	52	44	7.6	7	17	2.9	17	2.9	1.90	208	.234	.292	13	12	95	184	1.4	0	-1	1.1
1987	Det-A	0	1	.000	48	0	0	0	5	62	83	12.0	5	24	3.5	21	3.0	4.21	102	.331	.382	2	0	96	140	-0.4	0	-0	0.0
1988	Bal-A	1	8	.111	43	6	0	0	3	75	80	9.6	10	27	3.2	29	3.5	4.56	85	.277	.339	-5	-6	97	104	-3.0	0	-1	-0.6
1989	Bal-A	2	4	.333	49	2	0	0	4	90	102	10.2	6	17	1.7	34	3.4	3.90	98	.288	.320	-0	-1	99	101	-1.1	0	-1	-0.1
Total	7	38	43	.469	271	97	6	3	17	782	837	9.6	63	244	2.8	296	3.4	3.71	100	.278	.328	8	1	98	116	-3.0	-1	1	0.6
■ **JAY TIBBS**	Tibbs, Jay Lindsey b: 1/4/62, Birmingham, Ala. BR/TR, 6'3", 185 lbs. Deb: 7/15/84																												
1984	Cin-N	6	2	.750	14	14	3	1	0	101	87	7.8	4	33	2.9	40	3.6	2.85	135	.238	.298	8	11	107	100	2.3	-1	-1	1.0
1985	Cin-N	10	16	.385	35	34	5	2	0	218	216	8.9	14	83	3.4	98	4.0	3.92	96	.262	.322	-8	-3	105	94	-4.4	-3	1	-0.5
1986	Mon-N	7	9	.438	35	31	3	2	0	190	181	8.6	12	70	3.3	117	5.5	3.98	92	.256	.319	-5	-7	98	91	-0.8	0	-1	-0.7
1987	Mon-N	4	5	.444	19	12	0	0	0	83	95	10.3	10	34	3.7	54	5.9	4.99	87	.289	.352	-8	-6	106	100	-0.9	0	-1	-0.5
1988	Bal-A	4	15	.211	30	24	1	0	0	159	184	10.4	18	63	3.6	82	4.6	5.38	72	.293	.353	-25	-27	97	95	-3.7	0	0	-2.5
1989	Bal-A	5	0	1.000	10	8	1	0	0	54	62	10.3	2	20	3.3	30	5.0	2.83	135	.287	.345	6	6	99	146	2.5	0	-0	0.6
Total	6	36	47	.434	143	123	13	5	0	805	825	9.2	60	303	3.4	421	4.7	4.13	93	.269	.330	-32	-25	102	98	-5.0	-4	-2	-2.6
■ **FREDDIE TOLIVER**	Toliver, Freddie Lee b: 2/3/61, Natchez, Miss. BR/TR, 6'1", 165 lbs. Deb: 9/15/84																												
1984	Cin-N	0	0	—	3	1	0	0	0	10	7	6.3	0	7	6.3	4	3.6	0.90	428	.206	.333	3	3	107	323	0.0	-0	-0	0.3
1985	Phi-N	0	4	.000	11	3	0	0	1	25	27	9.7	2	17	6.1	23	8.3	4.68	79	.273	.376	-3	-3	102	105	-1.9	1	0	-0.1
1986	Phi-N	0	2	.000	5	5	0	0	0	26	28	9.7	0	11	3.8	20	6.9	3.46	112	.286	.348	1	1	104	116	-0.9	-0	0	0.2
1987	Phi-N	1	1	.500	10	4	0	0	0	30	34	10.2	2	17	5.1	25	7.5	5.70	75	.291	.374	-5	-5	105	91	0.0	-1	0	-0.4
1988	Min-A	7	6	.538	21	19	0	0	0	115	116	9.1	8	52	4.1	69	5.4	4.23	99	.270	.344	-3	-0	105	102	-0.2	0	0	0.0
1989	Min-A	1	3	.250	7	5	0	0	0	29	39	12.1	2	15	4.7	11	3.4	7.76	53	.317	.393	-12	-12	106	74	-0.9	0	1	-0.9
	SD-N	0	0	—	9	0	0	0	0	14	17	10.9	5	9	5.8	14	9.0	7.07	50	.321	.415	-6	-6	101	121	0.0	0	0	-0.5
Total	6	9	16	.360	66	37	0	0	1	249	268	9.7	19	128	4.6	166	6.0	4.81	84	.281	.362	-26	-21	105	109	-3.9	0	2	-1.4
■ **STEVE TROUT**	Trout, Steven Russell b: 7/30/57, Detroit, Mich. BL/TL, 6'4", 195 lbs. Deb: 7/01/78																												
1978	Chi-A	3	0	1.000	4	3	1	0	0	22	19	7.8	0	11	4.5	11	4.5	4.09	94	.229	.309	-1	-1	102	63	1.5	0	0	0.0
1979	Chi-A	11	8	.579	34	18	6	2	4	155	165	9.6	10	59	3.4	76	4.4	3.89	111	.273	.338	6	8	103	105	2.4	0	1	0.9
1980	Chi-A	9	16	.360	32	30	7	2	0	200	229	10.3	14	49	2.2	89	4.0	3.69	107	.290	.331	8	6	98	113	-2.4	0	2	0.8
1981	Chi-A	8	7	.533	20	18	3	0	0	125	122	8.8	7	38	2.7	54	3.9	3.46	105	.261	.317	3	2	99	102	0.4	0	0	0.3
1982	Chi-A	6	9	.400	25	19	2	0	0	120	130	9.8	9	50	3.8	62	4.7	4.28	92	.273	.339	-3	-4	97	98	-2.0	0	0	-0.3
1983	Chi-N	10	14	.417	34	32	1	0	0	180	217	10.9	13	59	3.0	80	4.0	4.65	79	.305	.352	-20	-19	101	103	-0.6	1	2	-1.6
1984	Chi-N	13	7	.650	32	31	6	2	0	190	205	9.7	7	59	2.8	81	3.8	3.41	115	.285	.334	4	11	109	117	1.5	-1	4	1.4
1985	Chi-N	9	7	.563	24	24	3	1	0	141	142	9.1	8	63	4.0	44	2.8	3.38	124	.270	.343	3	13	117	122	1.4	-2	2	1.5
1986	Chi-N	5	7	.417	37	25	0	0	0	161	184	10.3	6	78	4.4	69	3.9	4.75	85	.298	.370	-18	-13	108	101	-0.2	1	1	-1.1
1987	Chi-N	6	3	.667	11	11	3	2	0	75	72	8.6	3	27	3.2	32	3.8	3.00	138	.260	.325	9	10	102	118	1.7	-0	0	1.0
	NY-A	0	4	.000	14	9	0	0	0	46	51	10.0	4	37	7.2	27	5.3	6.65	65	.274	.397	-11	-12	97	82	-1.9	0	0	-1.0
1988	Sea-A	4	7	.364	15	13	0	0	0	56	86	13.8	6	31	5.0	14	2.3	7.88	55	.361	.439	-24	-22	108	98	-0.7	0	0	-2.0
1989	Sea-A	4	3	.571	19	3	0	0	0	30	43	12.9	3	17	5.1	17	5.1	6.60	61	.333	.405	-9	-9	104	99	0.8	0	0	-0.7
Total	12	88	92	.489	301	236	32	9	4	1501	1665	10.0	90	578	3.5	656	3.9	4.18	96	.286	.347	-54	-30	104	107	1.9	-2	13	-0.8
■ **MIKE TRUJILLO**	Trujillo, Michael Andrew b: 1/12/60, Denver, Colo. BR/TR, 6'1", 180 lbs. Deb: 4/14/85																												
1985	Bos-A	4	4	.500	27	7	1	0	1	84	112	12.0	7	23	2.5	19	2.0	4.82	87	.320	.364	-6	-6	102	111	0.0	0	2	-0.3
1986	Bos-A	0	0	—	3	0	0	0	0	6	7	10.5	0	6	9.0	4	6.0	9.00	46	.304	.433	-3	-3	99	69	0.0	0	1	-0.2
	Sea-A	3	2	.600	11	4	1	1	1	41	32	7.0	5	15	3.3	19	4.2	2.41	184	.215	.281	8	9	106	123	0.8	0	0	0.9
	Yr	3	2	.600	14	4	1	1	1	47	39	7.5	5	21	4.0	23	4.4	3.26	135	.227	.305	5	6	105	123	0.8	0	1	0.7
1987	Sea-A	4	4	.500	28	7	0	0	1	66	70	9.5	12	26	3.5	36	4.9	6.14	75	.277	.345	-12	-11	103	85	0.2	0	-1	-1.1
1988	Det-A	0	0	—	6	0	0	0	0	12	11	8.3	2	5	3.8	5	3.8	5.25	71	.234	.308	-2	-2	94	73	0.0	0	0	-0.1
1989	Det-A	1	2	.333	8	4	1	0	0	26	35	12.1	3	13	4.5	13	4.5	5.88	66	.333	.393	-6	-6	99	110	0.0	0	0	-0.5
Total	5	12	12	.500	83	22	3	1	3	235	267	10.2	29	88	3.4	96	3.7	5.02	86	.288	.348	-21	-19	102	103	1.0	0	2	-1.3
■ **JOHN TUDOR**	Tudor, John Thomas b: 2/2/54, Schenectady, N.Y. BL/TL, 6', 185 lbs. Deb: 8/16/79																												
1979	Bos-A	1	2	.333	6	6	1	0	0	28	39	12.5	2	9	2.9	11	3.5	6.43	70	.345	.375	-7	-6	106	93	-0.5	0	1	-0.4
1980	Bos-A	8	5	.615	16	13	5	0	0	92	81	7.9	4	31	3.0	45	4.4	3.03	136	.238	.301	10	11	102	94	1.4	0	2	1.4
1981	Bos-A	4	3	.571	18	11	2	0	1	79	74	8.4	11	28	3.2	44	5.0	4.56	85	.252	.317	-8	-6	106	89	0.2	0	1	-0.5
1982	Bos-A	13	10	.565	32	30	6	1	0	196	215	9.9	20	59	2.7	146	6.7	3.63	124	.280	.333	10	19	110	121	0.5	0	2	2.2
1983	Bos-A	13	12	.520	34	34	7	2	0	242	236	8.8	32	81	3.0	136	5.1	4.09	101	.255	.314	-0	1	102	98	1.1	0	-1	0.0
1984	Pit-N	12	11	.522	32	32	6	1	0	212	200	8.5	19	56	2.4	117	5.0	3.27	103	.248	.292	8	2	94	98	1.4	3	-0	0.5
1985	StL-N	21	8	.724	36	36	14	**10**	0	275	209	6.8	14	49	1.6	169	5.5	1.93	174	.209	**.248**	51	44	93	91	4.5	2	1	5.1
1986	StL-N	13	7	.650	30	30	3	0	0	219	197	8.1	22	53	2.2	107	4.4	2.92	132	.244	.286	20	23	103	109	3.4	-1	1	2.4
1987	StL-N	10	2	.833	16	16	0	0	0	96	100	9.4	11	32	3.0	54	5.1	3.84	103	.272	.328	3	1	97	113	3.7	1	1	0.3
1988	StL-N	6	5	.545	21	21	4	1	0	145	131	8.1	5	31	1.9	55	3.4	2.30	158	.247	.282	19	21	105	121	0.8	-1	1	2.5
	LA-N	4	3	.571	9	9	1	0	0	52	58	10.0	5	10	1.7	32	5.5	2.42	150	.284	.315	6	7	105	169	0.0	-1	0	0.7
	Yr	10	8	.556	30	30	5	1	0	197	189	8.6	10	41	1.9	87	4.0	2.33	155	.255	.290	25	28	105	**169**	0.8	-1	1	3.2
1989	LA-N	0	0	—	6	3	0	0	0	14	17	10.9	1	6	3.9	9	5.8	3.21	101	.309	.371	0	0	93	164	0.0	-0	0	0.0
Total	11	105	68	.607	256	241	49	15	1	1650	1557	8.5	146	445	2.4	925	5.0	3.19	120	.250	.299	111	116	101	106	16.5	3	8	14.2
■ **LEE TUNNELL**	Tunnell, Byron Lee b: 10/30/60, Tyler, Tex. BR/TR, 6'1", 180 lbs. Deb: 9/04/82																												
1982	Pit-N	1	1	.500	5	3	0	0	0	18	17	8.5	1	5	2.5	4	2.0	4.00	99	.254	.320	-1	-0	110	86	0.0	-0	0	0.0
1983	Pit-N	11	6	.647	35	25	5	3	0	178	167	8.4	15	58	2.9	95	4.8	3.64	103	.252	.311	-0	2	103	95	2.5	-1	2	0.3
1984	Pit-N	1	7	.125	26	6	0	0	1	68	81	10.7	6	40	5.3	51	6.8	5.29	64	.298	.382	-13	-15	94	103	-2.9	-1	1	-1.3
1985	Pit-N	4	10	.286	24	23	0	0	0	132	126	8.6	11	57	3.9	74	5.0	4.02	93	.251	.326	-6	-4	104	92	-1.4	-2	1	-0.5
1987	StL-N	4	4	.500	32	9	0	0	0	74	90	10.9	5	34	4.1	49	6.0	4.86	82	.307	.373	-6	-7	97	109	-0.5	1	0	-0.5
1989	Min-A	1	0	1.000	10	0	0	0	0	12	18	13.5	1	6	4.5	7	5.3	6.00	69	.340	.407	-3	-2	106	107	0.5	0	-0	-0.2

YEAR	TM/L	W	L	PCT	G	GS	CG	SHO	SV	IP	H	H/G	HR	BB	BB/G	SO	SO/G	ERA	/A	OAVG	OOBP	PR	/A	PF	CPI	WAT	PB	PD	TPI
Total	6	22	28	.440	132	66	5	3	1	482	499	9.3	39	200	3.7	280	5.2	4.24	88	.270	.339	-29	-26	101	97	-1.8	-4	4	-2.2
■ SERGIO VALDEZ	Valdez, Sergio Sanchez (born Sergio Sanchez (Valdez)) b: 9/7/64, Elias Pina, D.R. BR/TR, 6', 165 lbs. Deb: 9/10/86																												
1986	Mon-N	0	4	.000	5	5	0	0	0	25	39	14.0	2	11	4.0	20	7.2	6.84	54	.361	.425	-9	-9	98	102	-1.9	-0	-0	-0.8
1989	Atl-N	1	2	.333	19	1	0	0	0	33	31	8.5	5	17	4.6	26	7.1	6.00	60	.246	.331	-9	-9	104	74	-0.1	0	-0	-0.8
Total	2	1	6	.143	24	6	0	0	0	58	70	10.9	7	28	4.3	46	7.1	6.36	57	.299	.374	-18	-18	101	86	-2.0	0	-1	-1.6
■ FERNANDO VALENZUELA	Valenzuela, Fernando (Anguamea) b: 11/1/60, Navoja, Mexico BL/TL, 5'11", 180 lbs. Deb: 9/15/80																												
1980	LA-N	2	0	1.000	10	0	0	0	1	18	8	4.0	0	5	2.5	16	8.0	0.00	—	.136	.197	7	7	96	0	1.0	-0	0	0.8
1981	LA-N	13	7	.650	25	25	**11**	**8**	0	**192**	140	6.6	11	61	2.9	**180**	8.4	2.48	135	.205	.266	21	19	96	85	2.1	3	2	2.6
1982	LA-N	19	13	.594	37	37	18	4	0	285	247	7.8	13	83	2.6	199	6.3	2.87	117	.236	.287	23	16	94	94	2.1	1	5	2.3
1983	LA-N	15	10	.600	35	35	9	4	0	257	245	8.6	16	99	3.5	189	6.6	3.75	97	.255	.317	-3	-4	100	94	1.3	2	4	0.2
1984	LA-N	12	17	.414	34	34	12	2	0	**261**	218	7.5	14	106	3.7	240	8.3	3.03	123	.229	.302	16	20	104	97	-2.5	4	4	3.1
1985	LA-N	17	10	.630	35	35	14	5	0	272	211	7.0	14	101	3.3	208	6.9	2.45	135	.214	.282	35	26	92	99	1.7	4	2	3.3
1986	LA-N	**21**	11	.656	34	34	**20**	3	0	269	226	7.6	18	85	2.8	242	8.1	3.14	112	.226	.283	17	11	95	85	**6.8**	4	4	2.0
1987	LA-N	14	14	.500	34	34	**12**	1	0	251	254	9.1	25	124	4.4	190	6.8	3.98	95	.262	.342	3	-6	92	110	1.5	0	3	-0.3
1988	LA-N	5	8	.385	23	22	3	0	1	142	142	9.0	11	76	4.8	64	4.1	4.25	85	.268	.348	-13	-10	105	106	-2.2	1	3	-0.5
1989	LA-N	10	13	.435	31	31	3	0	0	197	185	8.5	11	98	4.5	116	5.3	3.43	95	.251	.335	2	-4	93	111	-1.2	1	2	-0.1
Total	10	128	103	.554	298	287	102	27	2	2144	1876	7.9	133	838	3.5	1644	6.9	3.19	110	.237	.305	109	76	96	96	10.6	20	28	13.4
■ RANDY VERES	Veres, Randolf Ruhland b: 11/25/65, Sacramento, Cal. BR/TR, 6'3", 190 lbs. Deb: 7/01/89																												
1989	Mil-A	0	1	.000	3	1	0	0	0	8	9	10.1	0	4	4.5	8	9.0	4.50	83	.290	.361	-1	-1	96	97	-0.4	0	0	0.0
■ FRANK VIOLA	Viola, Frank John b: 4/19/60, Hempstead, N.Y. BL/TL, 6'4", 200 lbs. Deb: 6/06/82																												
1982	Min-A	4	10	.286	22	22	3	1	0	126	152	10.9	22	38	2.7	84	6.0	5.21	80	.302	.350	-16	-15	102	104	-1.6	0	-1	-1.5
1983	Min-A	7	15	.318	35	34	4	0	0	210	242	10.4	34	92	3.9	127	5.4	5.49	79	.287	.360	-33	-27	106	99	-3.1	0	-1	-2.7
1984	Min-A	18	12	.600	35	35	10	4	0	258	225	7.8	28	73	2.5	149	5.2	3.21	132	.233	.288	23	29	106	96	3.5	0	-3	2.7
1985	Min-A	18	14	.563	36	36	9	0	0	251	262	9.4	26	68	2.4	135	4.8	4.09	106	.268	.314	2	6	104	97	3.2	0	-2	0.4
1986	Min-A	16	13	.552	37	37	7	1	0	246	257	9.4	37	83	3.0	191	7.0	4.50	102	.268	.326	-9	2	109	99	3.4	0	-3	0.0
1987	Min-A	17	10	.630	36	36	7	1	0	252	230	8.2	29	66	2.4	197	7.0	2.89	148	.241	.291	44	39	96	**115**	3.4	0	-1	3.8
1988	Min-A	**24**	7	**.774**	35	35	7	2	0	255	236	8.3	20	54	1.9	193	6.8	2.65	158	.245	.284	38	**44**	105	115	**8.3**	0	-1	4.6
1989	Min-A	8	12	.400	24	24	7	1	0	176	171	8.7	17	47	2.4	138	7.1	3.78	109	.256	.302	2	7	106	94	-2.0	0	0	0.7
	NY-N	5	5	.500	12	12	2	1	0	85	75	7.9	5	27	2.9	73	7.7	3.39	98	.236	.293	1	-0	95	87	-0.3	-0	-0	-0.1
Total	8	117	98	.544	272	271	56	11	0	1859	1850	9.0	218	548	2.7	1287	6.2	3.83	111	.259	.311	52	86	104	102	14.8	-0	-13	7.9
■ BOB WALK	Walk, Robert Vernon b: 11/26/56, Van Nuys, Cal. BR/TR, 6'3", 185 lbs. Deb: 5/26/80																												
1980	Phi-N	11	7	.611	27	27	2	0	0	152	163	9.7	8	71	4.2	94	5.6	4.56	84	.276	.351	-16	-12	106	93	1.1	-0	-1	-1.2
1981	Atl-N	1	4	.200	12	8	0	0	0	43	41	8.6	6	23	4.8	16	3.3	4.60	76	.250	.339	-5	-5	100	95	-1.4	-0	-1	-0.5
1982	Atl-N	11	9	.550	32	27	3	1	0	164	179	9.8	19	59	3.2	84	4.6	4.88	79	.280	.340	-23	-19	107	94	0.0	2	-2	-1.9
1983	Atl-N	0	0	—	1	1	0	0	0	4	7	15.8	0	2	4.5	4	9.0	6.75	56	.412	.450	-1	-1	104	117	0.0	-0	0	0.0
1984	Pit-N	1	1	.500	2	2	0	0	0	10	8	7.2	1	4	3.6	10	9.0	2.70	125	.200	.273	1	1	94	82	0.1	-0	-0	0.0
1985	Pit-N	2	3	.400	9	9	1	1	0	59	60	9.2	3	18	2.7	40	6.1	3.66	103	.265	.315	-0	1	104	95	0.2	-2	-1	-0.1
1986	Pit-N	7	8	.467	44	15	1	1	2	142	129	8.2	14	64	4.1	78	4.9	3.74	100	.251	.331	-0	0	101	108	1.0	1	2	0.2
1987	Pit-N	8	2	.800	39	12	1	1	0	117	107	8.2	11	51	3.9	78	6.0	3.31	129	.245	.323	10	13	105	115	3.1	1	1	1.4
1988	Pit-N	12	10	.545	32	32	1	1	0	213	183	7.7	6	65	2.7	81	3.4	2.70	124	.230	.284	18	15	97	93	0.4	-2	0	1.5
1989	Pit-N	13	10	.565	33	31	2	0	0	196	208	9.6	15	65	3.0	83	3.8	4.41	75	.271	.329	-20	-24	94	92	2.6	3	1	-2.1
Total	10	66	54	.550	231	164	11	5	2	1100	1085	8.9	83	422	3.5	568	4.6	3.93	93	.259	.325	-38	-33	101	97	7.1	1	1	-2.7
■ TIM WALLACH	Wallach, Timothy Charles b: 9/14/57, Huntington Park, Cal. BR/TR, 6'3", 220 lbs. Deb: 9/06/80																												
1987	Mon-N	0	0	—	1	0	0	0	0	1	1	9.0	0	0	0.0	0	0.0	0.00	—	.333	.333	0	0	106	0	0.0	1	0	0.0
1989	Mon-N	0	0	—	1	0	0	0	0	1	2	18.0	0	0	0.0	0	0.0	9.00	40	.500	.500	-1	-1	102	100	0.0	0	0	0.0
Total	2	0	0	—	2	0	0	0	0	2	3	13.5	0	0	0.0	0	0.0	4.50	88	.429	.429	-0	-0	104	50	0.0	1	0	0.0
■ DUANE WARD	Ward, Roy Duane b: 5/28/64, Park View, N.Mex. BR/TR, 6'4", 185 lbs. Deb: 4/12/86																												
1986	Atl-N	0	1	.000	10	0	0	0	0	16	22	12.4	2	8	4.5	8	4.5	7.31	53	.349	.411	-6	-6	103	95	-0.4	-0	1	-0.5
	Tor-A	0	1	.000	2	1	0	0	0	2	3	13.5	0	4	18.0	1	4.5	13.50	32	.300	.533	-2	-2	104	74	-0.4	0	0	-0.1
1987	Tor-A	1	0	1.000	12	1	0	0	0	12	14	10.5	0	12	9.0	10	7.5	6.75	66	.326	.456	-3	-3	99	102	0.5	0	0	-0.2
1988	Tor-A	9	3	.750	64	0	0	0	15	112	101	8.1	5	60	4.8	91	7.3	3.29	119	.245	.341	8	8	99	115	2.9	0	-0	0.7
1989	Tor-A	4	10	.286	66	0	0	0	15	115	94	7.4	4	58	4.5	122	9.5	3.76	97	.230	.318	2	-2	93	88	-3.4	0	2	0.0
Total	4	14	15	.483	154	2	0	0	30	257	234	8.2	11	142	5.0	232	8.1	3.99	96	.250	.344	-1	-5	97	101	-0.8	-0	2	-0.1
■ GARY WAYNE	Wayne, Gary Anthony b: 11/30/62, Dearborn, Mich. BL/TL, 6'3", 185 lbs. Deb: 4/07/89																												
1989	Min-A	3	4	.429	60	0	0	0	1	71	55	7.0	4	36	4.6	41	5.2	3.30	126	.212	.305	5	7	106	86	-0.4	0	0	0.7
■ BILL WEGMAN	Wegman, William Edward b: 12/19/62, Cincinnati, Ohio BR/TR, 6'5", 200 lbs. Deb: 9/14/85																												
1985	Mil-A	2	0	1.000	3	3	0	0	0	18	17	8.5	3	3	1.5	6	3.0	3.50	125	.246	.274	1	2	106	101	1.0	0	-0	0.1
1986	Mil-A	5	12	.294	35	32	2	0	0	198	217	9.9	32	43	2.0	82	3.7	5.14	84	.279	.319	-21	-18	103	89	-3.4	0	-1	-1.8
1987	Mil-A	12	11	.522	34	33	7	0	0	225	229	9.2	31	53	2.1	102	4.1	4.24	108	.265	.308	6	8	102	97	-0.8	0	0	0.7
1988	Mil-A	13	13	.500	32	31	4	1	0	199	207	9.4	24	50	2.3	84	3.8	4.12	99	.265	.308	-3	-1	103	97	-1.0	0	-1	-0.1
1989	Mil-A	2	6	.250	11	8	0	0	0	51	69	12.2	6	21	3.7	27	4.8	6.71	56	.321	.375	-16	-17	96	87	-2.0	0	1	-1.4
Total	5	34	42	.447	115	107	13	1	0	691	739	9.6	96	170	2.2	301	3.9	4.62	93	.273	.316	-33	-26	102	94	-6.2	0	-2	-2.5
■ BOB WELCH	Welch, Robert Lynn b: 11/3/56, Detroit, Mich. BR/TR, 6'3", 190 lbs. Deb: 6/20/78																												
1978	LA-N	7	4	.636	23	13	4	3	3	111	92	7.5	6	26	2.1	66	5.4	2.03	171	.229	.271	19	18	97	120	0.7	0	-1	1.8
1979	LA-N	5	6	.455	25	12	1	0	5	81	82	9.1	7	32	3.6	64	7.1	4.00	93	.265	.335	-2	-3	99	101	-0.3	-0	-1	-0.3
1980	LA-N	14	9	.609	32	32	3	2	0	214	190	8.0	15	79	3.3	141	5.9	3.28	105	.242	.306	8	4	96	100	1.3	3	-1	0.7
1981	LA-N	9	5	.643	23	23	2	1	0	141	141	9.0	11	41	2.6	88	5.6	3.45	97	.259	.308	1	-1	96	102	1.3	2	-1	0.0
1982	LA-N	16	11	.593	36	36	9	3	0	236	199	7.6	19	81	3.1	176	6.7	3.36	101	.229	.295	7	0	94	88	1.7	-1	-1	-0.1
1983	LA-N	15	12	.556	31	31	4	3	0	204	164	7.2	13	72	3.2	156	6.9	2.65	137	.222	.289	22	22	100	100	-0.1	-2	-0	2.1
1984	LA-N	13	13	.500	31	29	3	1	0	179	191	9.6	11	58	2.9	126	6.3	3.77	99	.273	.326	-4	-1	104	102	0.4	-3	2	-0.1
1985	LA-N	14	4	.778	23	23	8	3	0	167	141	7.6	16	35	1.9	96	5.2	2.32	142	.225	.270	24	18	92	113	4.4	2	1	2.2
1986	LA-N	7	13	.350	33	33	7	3	0	236	227	8.7	14	55	2.1	183	7.0	3.28	107	.251	.295	12	6	95	93	-2.4	-0	-1	0.5
1987	LA-N	15	9	.625	35	35	6	**4**	0	252	204	7.3	21	86	3.1	196	7.0	3.21	117	.221	.286	24	15	92	88	4.2	2	2	1.8
1988	Oak-A	17	9	.654	36	36	4	2	0	245	237	8.7	22	81	3.0	158	5.8	3.64	102	.257	.317	9	2	93	106	0.5	0	0	0.2
1989	Oak-A	17	8	.680	33	33	1	0	0	210	191	8.2	13	78	3.3	137	5.9	3.00	132	.241	.311	21	23	102	107	2.5	0	-1	2.3
Total	12	149	103	.591	361	336	52	25	8	2276	2059	8.1	168	724	2.9	1587	6.3	3.18	113	.242	.300	141	105	96	100	14.2	3	-1	11.1
■ DAVID WELLS	Wells, David Lee b: 5/20/63, Torrance, Cal. BL/TL, 6'3", 187 lbs. Deb: 6/30/87																												
1987	Tor-A	4	3	.571	18	2	0	0	1	29	37	11.5	0	12	3.7	32	9.9	4.03	110	.311	.371	1	1	99	117	0.0	0	0	0.1
1988	Tor-A	3	5	.375	41	0	0	0	4	64	65	9.1	12	31	4.4	56	7.9	4.64	85	.269	.351	-5	-5	99	115	-1.2	0	-0	-0.4
1989	Tor-A	7	4	.636	54	0	0	0	2	86	66	6.9	5	28	2.9	78	8.2	2.41	151	.207	.267	14	12	93	88	1.1	0	0	1.2
Total	3	14	12	.538	113	2	0	0	7	179	168	8.4	17	71	3.6	166	8.3	3.47	111	.247	.316	11	8	96	102	-0.1	0	1	0.9
■ DAVID WEST	West, David Lee b: 9/1/64, Memphis, Tenn. BL/TL, 6'6", 205 lbs. Deb: 9/24/88																												
1988	NY-N	1	0	1.000	2	1	0	0	0	6	6	9.0	0	3	4.5	3	4.5	3.00	101	.273	.360	0	0	88	132	0.5	1	0	0.1
1989	NY-N	0	2	.000	11	2	0	0	0	24	25	9.4	4	14	5.3	19	7.1	7.50	44	.260	.357	-11	-11	95	69	-0.9	0	-1	-1.1
	Min-A	3	2	.600	10	5	0	0	0	39	48	11.1	5	19	4.4	31	7.2	6.46	64	.306	.379	-11	-10	106	91	0.5	0	-1	-1.0
Total	2	4	4	.500	23	8	0	0	0	69	79	10.3	9	36	4.7	53	6.9	6.52	58	.287	.370	-21	-21	101	87	0.1	1	-1	-2.0
■ MICKEY WESTON	Weston, Michael Lee b: 3/26/61, Flint, Mich. BR/TR, 6'1", 180 lbs. Deb: 6/18/89																												
1989	Bal-A	1	0	1.000	7	0	0	0	1	13	18	12.5	1	2	1.4	7	4.8	5.54	69	.346	.382	-2	-2	99	104	0.5	0	-0	-0.2

YEAR	TM/L	W	L	PCT	G	GS	CG	SHO	SV	IP	H	H/G	HR	BB	BB/G	SO	SO/G	ERA	/A	OAVG	OOBP	PR	/A	PF	CPI	WAT	PB	PD	TPI
■ **JOHN WETTELAND**	Wetteland, John Karl b: 8/21/66, San Mateo, Cal. BR/TR, 6'2", 195 lbs. Deb: 5/31/89																												
1989	LA-N	5	8	.385	31	12	0	0	1	103	81	7.1	8	34	3.0	96	8.4	3.76	86	.218	.280	-3	-6	93	72	-1.3	-0	-1	-0.7
■ **WALLY WHITEHURST**	Whitehurst, Walter Richard b: 4/11/64, Shreveport, La. BR/TR, 6'3", 180 lbs. Deb: 7/17/89																												
1989	NY-N	0	1	.000	9	1	0	0	0	14	17	10.9	2	5	3.2	9	5.8	4.50	74	.293	.344	-2	-2	95	114	-0.4	0	-0	-0.1
■ **EDDIE WHITSON**	Whitson, Eddie Lee b: 5/19/55, Johnson City, Tenn. BR/TR, 6'3", 195 lbs. Deb: 9/04/77																												
1977	Pit-N	1	0	1.000	5	2	0	0	0	16	11	6.2	0	9	5.1	10	5.6	3.38	118	.204	.303	1	1	102	72	0.5	-1	-0	0.0
1978	Pit-N	5	6	.455	43	0	0	0	4	74	66	8.0	5	37	4.5	64	7.8	3.28	114	.243	.330	2	4	105	112	-0.9	-0	-1	0.3
1979	Pit-N	2	3	.400	19	7	0	0	1	58	53	8.2	6	36	5.6	31	4.8	4.34	90	.238	.342	-4	-3	104	91	-0.8	-1	-0	-0.4
	SF-N	5	8	.385	18	17	2	0	0	100	98	8.8	5	39	3.5	62	5.6	3.96	88	.254	.321	-2	-5	93	86	-0.8	-0	-0	-0.5
	Yr	7	11	.389	37	24	2	0	1	158	151	8.6	11	75	4.3	93	5.3	4.10	89	.248	.328	-6	-8	97	86	-1.6	-1	-1	-0.9
1980	SF-N	11	13	.458	34	34	6	2	0	212	222	9.4	7	56	2.4	90	3.8	3.10	112	.271	.314	12	9	96	110	-0.1	-4	-2	0.3
1981	SF-N	6	9	.400	22	22	2	1	0	123	130	9.5	10	47	3.4	65	4.8	4.02	91	.273	.335	-7	-5	105	103	-1.6	-1	-2	-0.7
1982	Cle-A	4	2	.667	40	9	1	1	2	108	91	7.6	6	58	4.8	61	5.1	3.25	127	.231	.319	10	10	101	103	1.1	0	-2	0.9
1983	SD-N	5	7	.417	31	21	2	0	1	144	143	8.9	23	50	3.1	81	5.1	4.31	84	.256	.314	-11	-11	99	95	-1.0	1	-4	-1.4
1984	SD-N	14	8	.636	31	31	1	0	0	189	181	8.6	16	42	2.0	103	4.9	3.24	109	.255	.292	7	6	98	102	2.0	-4	1	0.3
1985	NY-A	10	8	.556	30	30	2	2	0	159	201	11.4	19	43	2.4	89	5.0	4.87	80	.309	.349	-13	-17	94	108	-0.7	0	-1	-1.7
1986	NY-A	5	2	.714	14	4	0	0	0	37	54	13.1	5	23	5.6	27	6.6	7.54	57	.335	.407	-14	-13	103	93	1.3	0	0	-1.2
	SD-N	1	7	.125	17	12	0	0	0	76	85	10.1	8	37	4.4	46	5.4	5.57	64	.287	.362	-16	-17	96	90	-2.8	-0	0	-1.6
1987	SD-N	10	13	.435	36	34	3	1	0	206	197	8.6	36	64	2.8	135	5.9	4.72	85	.251	.308	-14	-17	98	88	0.7	-1	-2	-1.9
1988	SD-N	13	11	.542	34	33	3	1	0	205	202	8.9	17	45	2.0	118	5.2	3.78	89	.259	.293	-7	-10	97	91	0.8	1	-1	-0.9
1989	SD-N	16	11	.593	33	33	5	1	0	227	198	7.9	22	48	1.9	117	4.6	2.66	132	.235	.275	21	22	101	112	1.5	1	-2	2.2
Total	13	108	108	.500	407	289	27	9	8	1934	1932	9.0	185	634	3.0	1099	5.1	3.88	95	.261	.315	-34	-46	99	100	-0.8	-11	-15	-6.3
■ **KEVIN WICKANDER**	Wickander, Kevin Dean b: 1/5/65, Fort Dodge, Iowa BL/TL, 6'2", 202 lbs. Deb: 8/10/89																												
1989	Cle-A	0	0	—	2	0	0	0	0	3	6	18.0	0	2	6.0	0	0.0	3.00	135	.462	.533	0	0	104	335	0.0	0	0	0.0
■ **DEAN WILKINS**	Wilkins, Dean Allan b: 8/24/66, Blue Island, Ill. BR/TR, 6'1", 170 lbs. Deb: 8/21/89																												
1989	Chi-N	1	0	1.000	11	0	0	0	0	16	13	7.3	2	9	5.1	14	7.9	4.50	84	.228	.328	-2	-1	107	89	0.5	-0	0	0.0
■ **FRANK WILLIAMS**	Williams, Frank Lee b: 2/13/58, Seattle, Wash. BR/TR, 6'1", 180 lbs. Deb: 4/05/84																												
1984	SF-N	9	4	.692	61	1	1	1	3	106	88	7.5	2	51	4.3	91	7.7	3.57	98	.226	.313	0	-1	98	80	3.3	1	4	0.5
1985	SF-N	2	4	.333	49	0	0	0	0	73	65	8.0	5	35	4.3	54	6.7	4.19	81	.242	.333	-5	-6	95	90	-0.3	-0	0	-0.6
1986	SF-N	3	1	.750	36	0	0	0	1	52	35	6.1	0	21	3.6	33	5.7	1.21	291	.212	.309	15	13	95	217	1.0	0	1	1.5
1987	Cin-N	4	0	1.000	85	0	0	0	2	106	101	8.6	5	39	3.3	60	5.1	2.29	184	.254	.318	21	23	103	151	2.0	-1	1	2.3
1988	Cin-N	3	2	.600	60	0	0	0	1	63	59	8.4	6	35	5.0	43	6.1	2.57	141	.252	.348	6	7	105	171	0.3	-0	0	0.8
1989	Det-A	3	3	.500	42	0	0	0	1	72	70	8.8	5	46	5.8	33	4.1	3.63	107	.254	.361	2	2	99	121	0.7	0	-0	0.1
Total	6	24	14	.632	333	1	1	1	8	472	418	8.0	23	227	4.3	314	6.0	2.99	124	.242	.330	39	38	99	131	7.0	1	5	4.6
■ **MITCH WILLIAMS**	Williams, Mitchell Steven b: 11/17/64, Santa Ana, Cal. BL/TL, 6'3", 180 lbs. Deb: 4/09/86																												
1986	Tex-A	8	6	.571	**80**	0	0	0	8	98	69	6.3	8	79	7.3	90	8.3	3.58	111	.202	.366	7	4	95	112	0.6	0	-1	0.3
1987	Tex-A	8	6	.571	85	1	0	0	6	109	63	5.2	9	94	7.8	129	10.7	3.22	144	.175	.350	15	17	104	111	1.5	0	1	1.7
1988	Tex-A	2	7	.222	67	0	0	0	18	68	48	6.4	4	47	6.2	61	8.1	4.63	88	.203	.341	-5	-4	102	77	-2.2	0	0	-0.3
1989	Chi-N	4	4	.500	**76**	0	0	0	36	82	71	7.8	6	52	5.7	67	7.4	2.74	137	.238	.359	7	9	107	157	-0.4	1	-1	1.0
Total	4	22	23	.489	308	1	0	0	68	357	251	6.3	27	272	6.9	347	8.7	3.48	119	.203	.355	24	27	102	115	-0.5	1	-1	2.7
■ **MARK WILLIAMSON**	Williamson, Mark Alan b: 7/21/59, Corpus Christi, Tex. BR/TR, 6' ", 155 lbs. Deb: 4/08/87																												
1987	Bal-A	8	9	.471	61	2	0	0	3	125	122	8.8	12	41	3.0	73	5.3	4.03	110	.261	.319	6	6	99	98	0.9	0	1	0.6
1988	Bal-A	5	8	.385	37	10	2	0	2	118	125	9.5	14	40	3.1	69	5.3	4.88	79	.272	.329	-12	-13	97	90	0.5	0	-0	-1.3
1989	Bal-A	10	5	.667	65	0	0	0	9	107	105	8.8	4	30	2.5	55	4.6	2.94	130	.261	.308	11	11	99	112	2.3	0	-1	1.0
Total	3	23	22	.511	163	12	2	0	14	350	352	9.1	30	111	2.9	197	5.1	3.99	102	.265	.319	5	3	98	100	3.7	0	-0	0.3
■ **FRANK WILLS**	Wills, Frank Lee b: 10/26/58, New Orleans, La. BR/TR, 6'2", 200 lbs. Deb: 7/31/83																												
1983	KC-A	2	1	.667	6	4	0	0	0	35	35	9.0	2	15	3.9	23	5.9	4.11	101	.259	.329	-0	0	102	91	0.5	0	-0	0.0
1984	KC-A	2	3	.400	10	5	0	0	0	37	39	9.5	3	13	3.2	21	5.1	5.11	78	.271	.323	-5	-5	99	78	-0.5	0	-1	-0.4
1985	Sea-A	5	11	.313	24	18	1	0	1	123	122	8.9	18	68	5.0	67	4.9	6.00	66	.266	.357	-25	-28	95	86	-2.6	0	0	-2.5
1986	Cle-A	4	4	.500	26	0	0	0	4	40	43	9.7	6	16	3.6	32	7.2	4.95	83	.272	.324	-3	-4	98	95	-0.1	0	0	-0.3
1987	Cle-A	0	1	.000	6	0	0	0	1	5	3	5.4	0	7	12.6	4	7.2	5.40	87	.176	.385	-1	-0	105	78	-0.4	0	0	0.0
1988	Tor-A	0	0	—	10	0	0	0	0	21	22	9.4	2	6	2.6	19	8.1	5.14	76	.272	.315	-3	-3	99	78	0.0	0	1	-0.1
1989	Tor-A	3	1	.750	24	4	0	0	0	71	65	8.2	4	30	3.8	41	5.2	3.68	99	.242	.318	2	-0	93	90	0.9	0	0	0.0
Total	7	16	21	.432	106	31	1	0	6	332	329	8.9	35	155	4.2	207	5.6	5.02	78	.261	.336	-35	-40	97	87	-2.2	0	0	-3.3
■ **PAUL WILMET**	Wilmet, Paul Richard b: 11/8/58, Green Bay, Wis. BR/TR, 5'11", 170 lbs. Deb: 7/25/89																												
1989	Tex-A	0	0	—	3	0	0	0	0	2	5	22.5	0	2	9.0	1	4.5	18.00	22	.417	.500	-3	-3	103	59	0.0	0	0	-0.2
■ **STEVE WILSON**	Wilson, Stephen Douglas b: 12/13/64, Victoria, B.C., Can. BL/TL, 6'4", 205 lbs. Deb: 9/16/88																												
1988	Tex-A	0	0	—	3	0	0	0	0	8	7	7.9	1	4	4.5	1	1.1	5.63	72	.259	.355	-1	-1	102	84	0.0	0	-0	-0.1
1989	Chi-N	6	4	.600	53	8	0	0	2	86	83	8.7	6	31	3.2	65	6.8	4.19	90	.257	.316	-7	-4	107	89	0.3	-1	0	-0.4
Total	2	6	4	.600	56	8	0	0	2	94	90	8.6	7	35	3.4	66	6.3	4.31	88	.257	.319	-8	-5	107	88	0.3	-1	0	-0.5
■ **TREVOR WILSON**	Wilson, Trevor Kirk b: 6/7/66, Torrance, Cal. BL/TL, 6', 190 lbs. Deb: 9/05/88																												
1988	SF-N	0	2	.000	4	4	0	0	0	22	25	10.2	1	8	3.3	15	6.1	4.09	79	.298	.344	-2	-2	93	112	-0.9	0	-0	-0.1
1989	SF-N	2	3	.400	14	4	0	0	0	39	28	6.5	2	24	5.5	22	5.1	4.38	77	.207	.335	-4	-4	96	78	-0.7	1	0	-0.3
Total	2	2	5	.286	18	8	0	0	0	61	53	7.8	3	32	4.7	37	5.5	4.28	77	.242	.338	-5	-7	95	90	-1.6	1	-0	-0.4
■ **MIKE WITT**	Witt, Michael Atwater b: 7/20/60, Fullerton, Cal. BR/TR, 6'7", 185 lbs. Deb: 4/11/81																												
1981	Cal-A	8	9	.471	22	21	7	1	0	129	123	8.6	9	47	3.3	75	5.2	3.28	116	.251	.326	6	7	104	111	0.1	0	-1	0.7
1982	Cal-A	8	6	.571	33	26	5	1	0	180	177	8.9	8	47	2.3	85	4.3	3.50	115	.260	.309	12	11	99	95	0.0	0	-0	1.0
1983	Cal-A	7	14	.333	43	19	2	0	5	154	173	10.1	14	75	4.4	77	4.5	4.91	80	.293	.372	-14	-17	96	107	-2.6	0	0	-1.6
1984	Cal-A	15	11	.577	34	34	9	2	0	247	227	8.3	17	84	3.1	196	7.1	3.46	117	.244	.306	15	16	101	94	2.3	0	-1	1.6
1985	Cal-A	15	9	.625	35	35	6	1	0	250	228	8.2	22	98	3.5	180	6.5	3.56	117	.243	.315	16	17	101	100	2.1	0	0	1.7
1986	Cal-A	18	10	.643	34	34	14	3	0	269	218	7.3	22	73	2.4	208	7.0	2.84	140	.221	.275	40	34	95	91	2.8	0	2	3.7
1987	Cal-A	16	14	.533	36	36	10	0	0	247	252	9.2	34	84	3.1	192	7.0	4.01	111	.261	.319	13	12	100	105	2.3	0	-0	1.1
1988	Cal-A	13	16	.448	34	34	12	2	0	250	263	9.5	14	87	3.1	133	4.8	4.14	91	.272	.329	-5	-10	95	96	-0.5	0	-0	-1.0
1989	Cal-A	9	15	.375	33	33	5	0	0	220	252	10.3	26	48	2.0	123	5.0	4.54	84	.292	.322	-16	-18	98	100	-4.3	0	4	-1.4
Total	9	109	104	.512	304	272	70	10	5	1946	1913	8.8	166	643	3.0	1269	5.9	3.77	106	.258	.317	66	52	98	99	2.2	0	4	5.8
■ **BOBBY WITT**	Witt, Robert Andrew b: 5/11/64, Arlington, Mass. BR/TR, 6'2", 190 lbs. Deb: 4/10/86																												
1986	Tex-A	11	9	.550	31	31	0	0	0	158	130	7.4	18	143	8.1	174	9.9	5.47	73	.223	.372	-23	-26	95	85	0.3	0	0	-2.3
1987	Tex-A	8	10	.444	26	25	1	0	0	143	114	7.2	10	140	8.8	160	10.1	4.91	95	.219	.382	-7	-4	104	92	-0.3	0	0	-0.3
1988	Tex-A	8	10	.444	22	22	13	2	0	174	134	6.9	13	101	5.2	148	7.7	3.93	103	.216	.321	1	3	102	86	0.2	0	-1	0.2
1989	Tex-A	12	13	.480	31	31	5	1	0	194	182	8.4	14	114	5.3	166	7.7	5.15	78	.248	.343	-27	-25	103	79	-0.8	0	-0	-2.4
Total	4	39	42	.481	110	109	19	3	0	669	560	7.5	55	498	6.7	648	8.7	4.86	85	.228	.353	-56	-53	101	85	-0.6	0	-0	-4.8
■ **ED WOJNA**	Wojna, Edward David b: 8/20/60, Bridgeport, Conn. BR/TR, 6'1", 185 lbs. Deb: 6/16/85																												
1985	SD-N	2	4	.333	15	7	0	0	0	42	53	11.4	6	19	4.1	18	3.9	5.79	63	.312	.379	-10	-10	101	105	-1.0	-0	0	-0.9
1986	SD-N	2	2	.500	7	7	1	0	0	39	42	9.7	2	16	3.7	19	4.4	3.23	111	.268	.335	2	1	96	119	0.2	-0	-1	0.1
1987	SD-N	0	3	.000	5	3	0	0	0	18	25	12.5	2	6	3.0	13	6.5	6.00	67	.333	.381	-4	-4	98	103	-1.4	-1	1	-0.3
1989	Cle-A	0	1	.000	9	3	0	0	0	33	31	8.5	0	14	3.8	10	2.7	4.09	99	.254	.324	-1	-0	104	79	-0.4	0	1	0.0
Total	4	4	10	.286	36	20	1	0	0	132	151	10.3	10	55	3.8	60	4.1	4.64	81	.288	.353	-13	-13	100	102	-2.6	-1	1	-1.1

YEAR	TM/L	W	L	PCT	G	GS	CG	SHO	SV	IP	H	H/G	HR	BB	BB/G	SO	SO/G	ERA	/A	OAVG	OOBP	PR	/A	PF	CPI	WAT	PB	PD	TPI
■ TODD WORRELL							Worrell, Todd Roland		b: 9/28/59, Arcadia, Cal.		BR/TR, 6'5", 215 lbs.		Deb: 8/28/85																
1985	StL-N	3	0	1.000	17	0	0	0	5	22	17	7.0	2	7	2.9	17	7.0	2.86	117	.215	.273	2	1	93	91	1.5	-0	-0	0.1
1986	StL-N	9	10	.474	74	0	0	0	36	104	86	7.4	9	41	3.5	73	6.3	2.08	185	.229	.298	19	20	103	154	-0.3	0	-2	2.0
1987	StL-N	8	6	.571	75	0	0	0	33	95	86	8.1	8	34	3.2	92	8.7	2.65	150	.242	.304	15	14	97	126	-0.1	-0	0	1.4
1988	StL-N	5	9	.357	68	0	0	0	32	90	69	6.9	7	34	3.4	78	7.8	3.00	121	.214	.284	5	6	105	92	-1.7	-0	-0	0.6
1989	StL-N	3	5	.375	47	0	0	0	20	52	42	7.3	4	26	4.5	41	7.1	2.94	119	.222	.311	3	3	100	111	-1.1	-0	1	0.4
Total	5	28	30	.483	281	0	0	0	126	363	300	7.4	30	142	3.5	301	7.5	2.63	143	.227	.296	44	45	101	121	-1.7	-1	-1	4.5
■ RICH YETT							Yett, Richard Martin		b: 10/6/62, Pomona, Cal.		BR/TR, 6'2", 187 lbs.		Deb: 4/13/85																
1985	Min-A	0	0	—	1	1	0	0	0	0	1	—	0	2	—	0	—	∞	—	.333	.600	-1	-1	104	63	0.0	0	0	0.0
1986	Cle-A	5	3	.625	39	3	1	1	1	79	84	9.6	10	37	4.2	50	5.7	5.13	80	.275	.349	-8	-9	98	94	0.9	0	-1	-0.9
1987	Cle-A	3	9	.250	37	11	2	0	1	98	96	8.8	21	49	4.5	59	5.4	5.23	89	.257	.343	-8	-6	105	100	-2.0	0	-1	-0.6
1988	Cle-A	9	6	.600	23	22	0	0	0	134	146	9.8	11	55	3.7	71	4.8	4.63	88	.275	.342	-10	-9	102	94	1.8	0	-2	-0.9
1989	Cle-A	5	6	.455	32	12	1	0	0	99	111	10.1	10	47	4.3	47	4.3	5.00	81	.283	.359	-12	-10	104	98	0.0	0	-1	-1.1
Total	5	22	24	.478	132	49	4	1	2	410	438	9.6	52	190	4.2	227	5.0	4.98	85	.273	.348	-40	-35	102	96	0.7	0	-5	-3.5
■ FLOYD YOUMANS							Youmans, Floyd Everett		b: 5/11/64, Tampa, Fla.		BR/TR, 6'2", 180 lbs.		Deb: 7/01/85																
1985	Mon-N	4	3	.571	14	12	0	0	0	77	57	6.7	3	49	5.7	54	6.3	2.45	137	.206	.323	10	8	94	118	0.4	-0	-2	0.6
1986	Mon-N	13	12	.520	33	32	6	2	0	219	145	6.0	14	118	4.8	202	8.3	3.53	104	.188	.295	5	3	98	70	1.0	2	-3	0.1
1987	Mon-N	9	8	.529	23	23	3	3	0	116	112	8.7	13	47	3.6	94	7.3	4.66	93	.251	.317	-7	-4	106	84	-0.4	1	-0	-0.3
1988	Mon-N	3	6	.333	14	13	1	1	0	84	64	6.9	8	41	4.4	54	5.8	3.21	113	.213	.305	2	4	105	100	-1.5	-0	-0	0.4
1989	Phi-N	1	5	.167	10	10	0	0	0	43	50	10.5	7	25	5.2	20	4.2	5.65	63	.299	.385	-10	-10	102	111	-1.7	-1	0	-1.0
Total	5	30	34	.469	94	90	10	6	0	539	428	7.1	45	280	4.7	424	7.1	3.74	100	.218	.313	-1	0	101	88	-2.2	1	-5	-0.2
■ CURT YOUNG							Young, Curtis Allen		b: 4/16/60, Saginaw, Mich.		BR/TL, 6'1", 175 lbs.		Deb: 6/24/83																
1983	Oak-A	0	1	.000	8	2	0	0	0	17	17.0		1	5	5.0	5	5.0	16.00	25	.386	.460	-12	-12	96	55	-0.4	0	-0	-1.0
1984	Oak-A	9	4	.692	20	17	2	1	0	109	118	9.7	9	31	2.6	41	3.4	4.05	91	.274	.331	-1	-4	92	101	2.8	0	-1	-0.4
1985	Oak-A	0	4	.000	19	7	0	0	0	46	57	11.2	15	22	4.3	19	3.7	7.24	53	.300	.374	-16	-17	93	99	-1.9	0	-0	-1.6
1986	Oak-A	13	9	.591	29	27	5	2	0	198	176	8.0	19	57	2.6	116	5.3	3.45	114	.236	.291	16	10	94	91	2.8	0	0	1.0
1987	Oak-A	13	7	.650	31	31	6	0	0	203	194	8.6	38	44	2.0	124	· 5.5	4.08	100	.252	.291	9	-0	91	99	3.3	0	0	0.0
1988	Oak-A	11	8	.579	26	26	1	0	0	156	162	9.3	23	50	2.9	69	4.0	4.15	89	.275	.332	-3	-8	93	114	-0.9	0	-1	-0.8
1989	Oak-A	5	9	.357	25	20	1	0	0	111	117	9.5	10	47	3.8	55	4.5	3.73	106	.264	.337	2	3	102	110	-3.0	0	-1	0.2
Total	7	51	42	.548	158	130	15	3	0	832	841	9.1	115	256	2.8	429	4.6	4.20	93	.262	.318	-4	-28	94	101	2.7	0	-3	-2.6
■ MATT YOUNG							Young, Matthew John		b: 8/9/58, Pasadena, Cal.		BL/TL, 6'3", 205 lbs.		Deb: 4/06/83																
1983	Sea-A	11	15	.423	33	32	5	2	0	204	178	7.9	17	79	3.5	130	5.7	3.26	126	.236	.310	18	20	101	104	1.3	0	2	2.2
1984	Sea-A	6	8	.429	22	22	1	0	0	113	141	11.2	11	57	4.5	73	5.8	5.73	72	.307	.380	-22	-20	103	97	-0.4	0	1	-1.8
1985	Sea-A	12	19	.387	37	35	5	2	1	218	242	10.0	23	76	3.1	136	5.6	4.91	81	.282	.342	-19	-23	95	95	-2.7	0	-2	-2.3
1986	Sea-A	8	6	.571	65	5	1	0	13	104	108	9.3	9	46	4.0	82	7.1	3.81	117	.272	.354	4	7	106	121	2.0	0	-1	0.6
1987	LA-N	5	8	.385	47	0	0	0	11	54	62	10.3	8	17	2.8	42	7.0	4.50	84	.288	.338	-2	-4	92	93	-0.9	-0	-2	-0.5
1989	Oak-A	1	4	.200	26	4	0	0	0	37	42	10.2	2	31	7.5	27	6.6	6.81	58	.286	.399	-12	-12	102	81	-1.6	0	0	-1.0
Total	6	43	60	.417	230	98	12	4	25	730	773	9.5	65	306	3.8	490	6.0	4.49	91	.273	.344	-32	-32	100	101	-2.3	-0	-2	-2.8
■ CLINT ZAVARAS							Zavaras, Clinton Wayne		b: 1/4/67, Denver, Colo.		BR/TR, 6'1", 175 lbs.		Deb: 6/03/89																
1989	Sea-A	1	6	.143	10	10	0	0	0	52	49	8.5	4	30	5.2	31	5.4	5.19	78	.253	.351	-8	-7	104	82	-2.3	0	-0	-0.6

The All-Time Leaders

This section is divided into two parts: lifetime leaders and single season leaders. What follows are the all-time great achievements in 95 categories, both the traditional statistics and the new. For most of these we will give not the top 10 or 20 but the top 100, because some categories would otherwise be dominated by players of a certain era (for example, slugging average by batters of the 1920s and 1930s, earned run average by pitchers of 1900–1919). And for many stats we will offer a second kind of ranking, broken out into the five distinct eras of baseball, with the top 10 or 15 leaders in each.*

Let's set some ground rules, define some terms that may still be unfamiliar after you've browsed through the Annual Record and Player and Pitcher registers, and get on with the show. Note that National Association totals (1871–1875) are not incorporated with records from other leagues and NA single-season marks are likewise excluded.

To be eligible for a lifetime pitching category that is stated as an average, a man must have pitched 1,500 or more innings, or 750 or more innings in a relief pitching category, in the major leagues; for a counting statistic, he must simply have attained the necessary quantity to crack the list. For a single season category expressed as an average, he must have pitched one inning per league scheduled game or have attained the necessary quantity (wins, strikeouts, saves) to head a counted list.

To be eligible for a lifetime batting category that is stated as an average, a man must have played in 1,000 or more games; for counting stats such as stolen bases, a Vince Coleman can take his place on the list despite his distance from 1,000 games played. And to reach the single-season batting lists, a man must have 3.1 plate appearances per scheduled game.

We provide tables of the top fielding performances, too, sorted by position as you would expect. But we go one step further and rank several *batting* categories by position, thus recognizing and illustrating the greater demands for fielding skill at such positions as shortstop, catcher and second base, and the comparatively plentiful supply of batting talent in the outfield and at first base.

For the three principal categories—Total Player Rating, Total Pitcher Index, and Total Baseball Ranking—we have introduced several variations. For example, TPR and TBR are shown 500 deep for lifetime leaders—sorted first by highest value; then alphabetically so that the reader may find a particular player without scanning 500 names; and last by the above-named eras, the top 25 in each. Total Pitcher Index is also sorted this way, but because far fewer pitchers than position players meet the longevity criteria, the lifetime groupings go 300 and 200 deep rather than 500 and 300. Ties are calculated to as many decimal places as needed to break them, but averages are shown to only three places. When two or more players

are tied in an averaged category with a narrow base of data, such as a season's won-lost percentage, the reader can presume a numerical dead heat (and obviously this goes for counting stats, too—one man's 39 doubles are as good as another's). But where there is a tie for batting average, earned run average, or any of the sabermetric measures, the reader may assume that the man listed above the other(s) has the minutely higher average.

Here are the few stats carried in this section that are not carried in the Annual Record or Registers, with definitions where the terms are not self-explanatory (see page 188 for formulas):

Batting, Baserunning, Fielding

Runs (scored) Per Game
Home Run Percentage   Home runs per 100 at bats
Bases on Balls Percentage   Walks (most) per 100 at bats
At Bats Per Strikeout
Relative Batting Average   Normalized to league average
Isolated Power   Slugging average minus batting average
Extra Base Hits
Pinch Hits
Pinch Hit Batting Average   Pinch Hit Home Runs
Total Chances Per Game   Broken out by position
Chances Accepted Per Game   Broken out by position
Putouts   Broken out by position
Putouts Per Game   Broken out by position
Assists   Broken out by position
Assists Per Game   Broken out by position
Double Plays   Broken out by position

Pitching

Hit Batsmen
Wins Above League   A pitcher's won-lost record restated by adding his Pitching Wins above the league average to the record that a league-average pitcher would have had with the same number of decisions (for example, Tom Seaver goes 20–10 with 7 Pitching Wins; applying the 7 wins to a 15–15 mark in the same 30 decisions results in a WAL of 22–8).
Percentage of Team Wins
Relief Games
Pitchers' Batting Runs
Pitchers' Fielding Runs
Relief Wins
Relief Losses
Relief Innings Pitched
Relief Points   Relief wins plus saves minus losses.

---

* Attentive readers of *Total Baseball* will notice some differences between its Leaders section and the one presented here. We have included some additional raw data for such formerly incomplete areas as: nineteenth-century fielding records; zero-stat games in the American League of 1912 and 1914; pinch-hit records; pitching records of some stars whose primary play was at other positions; and adjustments to league-average figures for the NL of 1902 and the AL of 1908.

We have also worked out some computer-program bugs that resulted in: Batter Park factor being applied to Pitchers' Adjusted ERAs (this did not affect the Pitcher Register of *Total Baseball*, only the All-Time Leaders); the omission of some career RBI leaders who were active in 1890–1891; the absence from Stolen Base category leaders of men who stole 100 or more bases in a single season; the use of last-season GIDP figures rather than lifetime GIDP figures in calculating career Total Average; the assigning of some star pitchers to the wrong chronological era in the subdivided

Pitcher Totals, such as Grover Alexander being ranked with hurlers of the period 1920–1945 in *Total Baseball* rather than 1893–1919; a major error in estimating at bats against those pitchers before 1908 (failing to factor in pitcher batting) which skewed OAVG and OOBP to the high direction by about 10 percent; and the absence from Save leaders of some significant relievers who had pitched in the former qualifying criterion (there should not have been one).

Also, our rectification of a transcription error in Tommy Burns's 1884 RBI count in *Total Baseball* (was 94, now 44) altered his Clutch Hitting Index significantly. For Total Player Rating, we have changed our minimum number of games from 800 to 700, as TPR is a counting stat; this added several pre-1900 players. Finally, our corrections of fielding stats for 1903 NL outfielders and stolen base totals for the NL in 1916 also affected some Total Baseball Rankings by fractional Wins.

Games

1	Pete Rose	3562
2	Carl Yastrzemski	3308
3	Hank Aaron	3298
4	Ty Cobb	3035
5	Stan Musial	3026
6	Willie Mays	2992
7	Rusty Staub	2951
8	Brooks Robinson	2896
9	Al Kaline	2834
10	Eddie Collins	2826
11	Reggie Jackson	2820
12	Frank Robinson	2808
13	Honus Wagner	2792
14	Tris Speaker	2789
15	Tony Perez	2777
16	Mel Ott	2730
17	Graig Nettles	2700
18	Darrell Evans	2687
19	Rabbit Maranville	2670
20	Joe Morgan	2649
21	Lou Brock	2616
22	Luis Aparicio	2599
23	Willie McCovey	2588
24	Paul Waner	2549
25	Ernie Banks	2528
26	Sam Crawford	2517
27	Babe Ruth	2503
28	Bill Buckner	2495
29	Dave Concepcion	2488
	Billy Williams	2488
31	Nap Lajoie	2480
32	Max Carey	2476
33	Rod Carew	2469
	Vada Pinson	2469
35	Ted Simmons	2456
36	Bill Dahlen	2443
37	Ron Fairly	2442
38	Harmon Killebrew	2435
39	Roberto Clemente	2433
40	Willie Davis	2429
41	Luke Appling	2422
42	Zach Wheat	2410
43	Mickey Vernon	2409
44	Buddy Bell	2405
45	Sam Rice	2404
	Mike Schmidt	2404
47	Mickey Mantle	2401
48	Eddie Mathews	2391
49	Jake Beckley	2386
50	Bobby Wallace	2383
51	Dwight Evans	2382
52	Enos Slaughter	2380
53	George Davis	2368
	Al Oliver	2368
55	Nellie Fox	2367
56	Willie Stargell	2360
57	Jose Cruz	2353
58	Steve Garvey	2332
59	Bert Campaneris	2328
60	Charlie Gehringer	2323
61	Jimmie Foxx	2317
62	Frankie Frisch	2311
63	Harry Hooper	2309
64	Don Baylor	2292
	Ted Williams	2292
66	Robin Yount	2291
67	Goose Goslin	2287
68	Jimmy Dykes	2282
69	Cap Anson	2276
70	Lave Cross	2274
71	Dave Winfield	2269
72	Chris Speier	2260
73	Rogers Hornsby	2259
74	Larry Bowa	2247
75	Ron Santo	2243
76	Fred Clarke	2242
	Frank White	2242
78	Doc Cramer	2239
79	Bob Boone	2224
80	Red Schoendienst	2216
81	Al Simmons	2215
82	Joe Torre	2209
83	Tommy Corcoran	2200
84	Tony Taylor	2195
85	Richie Ashburn	2189
86	Bill Russell	2181
87	Dave Parker	2177
88	Chris Chambliss	2175
89	Joe Judge	2171
90	Charlie Grimm	2166
	Pee Wee Reese	2166
92	Lou Gehrig	2164
93	Bill Mazeroski	2163
94	Johnny Bench	2158
95	Tommy Leach	2156
96	Toby Harrah	2155
97	Harry Heilmann	2148
98	Duke Snider	2143
99	Carlton Fisk	2141
100	George Brett	2137

At Bats

1	Pete Rose	14053
2	Hank Aaron	12364
3	Carl Yastrzemski	11988
4	Ty Cobb	11434
5	Stan Musial	10972
6	Willie Mays	10881
7	Brooks Robinson	10654
8	Honus Wagner	10430
9	Lou Brock	10332
10	Luis Aparicio	10230
11	Tris Speaker	10207
12	Al Kaline	10116
13	Rabbit Maranville	10078
14	Frank Robinson	10006
15	Eddie Collins	9948
16	Reggie Jackson	9864
17	Tony Perez	9778
18	Rusty Staub	9720
19	Vada Pinson	9645
20	Nap Lajoie	9589
21	Sam Crawford	9570
22	Jake Beckley	9526
23	Paul Waner	9459
24	Mel Ott	9456
25	Roberto Clemente	9454
26	Ernie Banks	9421
27	Max Carey	9363
28	Bill Buckner	9354
29	Billy Williams	9350
30	Rod Carew	9315
31	Joe Morgan	9277
32	Sam Rice	9269
33	Nellie Fox	9232
34	Willie Davis	9174
35	Doc Cramer	9140
36	Frankie Frisch	9112
37	Zach Wheat	9106
38	Cap Anson	9101
39	Lave Cross	9068
40	Al Oliver	9049
41	Bill Dahlen	9031
	George Davis	9031
43	Buddy Bell	8995
44	Graig Nettles	8986
45	Darrell Evans	8973
46	Robin Yount	8907
47	Charlie Gehringer	8860
48	Luke Appling	8856
49	Steve Garvey	8835
50	Tommy Corcoran	8804
51	Harry Hooper	8785
52	Al Simmons	8759
53	Mickey Vernon	8731
54	Dave Concepcion	8723
55	Bert Campaneris	8684
56	Ted Simmons	8680
57	Goose Goslin	8656
58	Bobby Wallace	8618
59	Willie Keeler	8591
60	Fred Clarke	8568
61	Eddie Mathews	8537
62	Red Schoendienst	8479
63	Jesse Burkett	8421
	Dave Winfield	8421
65	Larry Bowa	8418
66	Babe Ruth	8399
67	Richie Ashburn	8365
68	Mike Schmidt	8352
69	Bid McPhee	8291
70	Dwight Evans	8281
71	George Sisler	8267
72	Dave Parker	8246
73	Jim Rice	8225
74	Don Baylor	8198
75	Willie McCovey	8197
76	Rogers Hornsby	8173
77	Jimmy Ryan	8164
78	George Brett	8148
79	Harmon Killebrew	8147
80	Ron Santo	8143
81	Jimmie Foxx	8134
82	Mickey Mantle	8102
83	Pee Wee Reese	8058
84	Jimmy Dykes	8046
85	George VanHaltren	8021
86	Lou Gehrig	8001
87	Joe Kuhel	7984
88	Tommy Leach	7959
89	Enos Slaughter	7946
90	Orlando Cepeda	7927
	Willie Stargell	7927
92	Jose Cruz	7917
	Charlie Grimm	7917
94	Joe Judge	7898
95	Joe Torre	7874
96	Stuffy McInnis	7822
97	Roger Connor	7794
98	Harry Heilmann	7787
99	Lloyd Waner	7772
100	Bill Mazeroski	7755

Runs

1	Ty Cobb	2245
2	Hank Aaron	2174
	Babe Ruth	2174
4	Pete Rose	2165
5	Willie Mays	2062
6	Stan Musial	1949
7	Lou Gehrig	1888
8	Tris Speaker	1881
9	Mel Ott	1859
10	Frank Robinson	1829
11	Eddie Collins	1819
12	Carl Yastrzemski	1816
13	Ted Williams	1798
14	Charlie Gehringer	1774
15	Jimmie Foxx	1751
16	Honus Wagner	1736
17	Jesse Burkett	1720
18	Cap Anson	1719
	Willie Keeler	1719
20	Billy Hamilton	1690
21	Bid McPhee	1678
22	Mickey Mantle	1677
23	Joe Morgan	1650
24	Jimmy Ryan	1642
25	George VanHaltren	1639
26	Paul Waner	1626
27	Al Kaline	1622
28	Roger Connor	1620
29	Fred Clarke	1619
30	Lou Brock	1610
31	Jake Beckley	1600
32	Ed Delahanty	1599
33	Bill Dahlen	1586
34	Rogers Hornsby	1579
35	Hugh Duffy	1553
36	Reggie Jackson	1551
37	Max Carey	1545
38	George Davis	1539
39	Frankie Frisch	1532
40	Dan Brouthers	1523
41	Tom Brown	1521
42	Sam Rice	1514
43	Eddie Mathews	1509
44	Al Simmons	1507
45	Mike Schmidt	1506
46	Nap Lajoie	1502
47	Harry Stovey	1492
48	Goose Goslin	1483
49	Arlie Latham	1478
50	Herman Long	1456
51	Jim O'Rourke	1446
52	Harry Hooper	1429
53	Dummy Hoy	1426
54	Rod Carew	1424
55	Joe Kelley	1421
56	Roberto Clemente	1416
57	Billy Williams	1410
58	Monte Ward	1408
59	Mike Griffin	1405
60	Sam Crawford	1391
61	Joe DiMaggio	1390
62	Dwight Evans	1369
63	Vada Pinson	1366
64	Doc Cramer	1357
	King Kelly	1357
66	Tommy Leach	1355
67	Darrell Evans	1344
68	Pee Wee Reese	1338
69	Luis Aparicio	1335
	Robin Yount	1335
71	Lave Cross	1332
72	George Gore	1327
73	Richie Ashburn	1322
74	Luke Appling	1319
75	Patsy Donovan	1318
76	Dave Winfield	1314
77	Mike Tiernan	1313
78	Ernie Banks	1305
79	George Brett	1300
80	Jimmy Sheckard	1296
81	Kiki Cuyler	1295
82	Harry Heilmann	1291
83	Heinie Manush	1287
84	George Sisler	1284
85	Harmon Killebrew	1283
86	Donie Bush	1280
87	Nellie Fox	1279
88	Fred Tenney	1278
89	Tony Perez	1272
90	Duke Snider	1259
91	Bobby Bonds	1258
92	Sam Thompson	1256
93	Rabbit Maranville	1255
94	Jim Rice	1249
95	Enos Slaughter	1247
96	Stan Hack	1239
	Bob Johnson	1239
98	Don Baylor	1236
	Joe Kuhel	1236

Runs per Game

1	Billy Hamilton	1.06
2	George Gore	1.01
3	Harry Stovey	1.00
4	King Kelly	.93
5	John McGraw	.93
6	Mike Griffin	.93
7	Dan Brouthers	.91
8	Arlie Latham	.91
9	Hugh Duffy	.89
10	Sam Thompson	.89
11	Mike Tiernan	.89
12	Lou Gehrig	.87
13	Ed Delahanty	.87
14	Babe Ruth	.87
15	Buck Ewing	.86
16	Tom Brown	.85
17	Hardy Richardson	.84
18	Tommy McCarthy	.84
19	Tip O'Neill	.83
20	Cupid Childs	.83
21	Jesse Burkett	.83
22	Denny Lyons	.83
23	Curt Welch	.83
24	George VanHaltren	.83
25	Jimmy Ryan	.82
26	Earle Combs	.82
27	Jim O'Rourke	.82
28	Roger Connor	.81
29	Willie Keeler	.81
30	Pete Browning	.81
31	Red Rolfe	.80
32	Joe DiMaggio	.80
33	Rickey Henderson	.80
34	Dummy Hoy	.79
35	John Reilly	.79
36	Bid McPhee	.79
37	Ted Williams	.78
38	Henry Larkin	.78
39	Herman Long	.78
40	Hughie Jennings	.77
41	Monte Ward	.77
42	Joe Kelley	.77
43	Charlie Gehringer	.76
44	Jimmie Foxx	.76
45	Cap Anson	.76
46	Hank Greenberg	.75
47	George Wood	.75
48	George Pinkney	.75
49	Dom DiMaggio	.75
50	Ed McKean	.74
51	Ty Cobb	.74
52	Mike Smith	.74
53	Ned Hanlon	.73
54	Earl Averill	.73
55	Oyster Burns	.73
56	Jack Rowe	.73
57	Paul Hines	.73
58	Patsy Donovan	.72
59	Fred Clarke	.72
60	Max Bishop	.72
61	Ezra Sutton	.72
62	Charlie Comiskey	.72
63	Lu Blue	.71
64	Sam Wise	.71
65	Mickey Cochrane	.70
66	Tommy Henrich	.70
67	Mike Hornung	.70
68	Blondie Purcell	.70
69	Rogers Hornsby	.70
70	Mickey Mantle	.70
71	Billy Shindle	.70
72	Wade Boggs	.70
73	Paul Radford	.70
74	Billy Nash	.69
75	Dave Foutz	.69
76	Kiki Cuyler	.69
77	Willie Mays	.69
78	Paul Molitor	.69
79	Roy Thomas	.69
80	Jackie Robinson	.69
81	Tommy Dowd	.68
82	Johnny Pesky	.68
83	Tim Raines	.68
84	Mel Ott	.68
85	Bobby Bonds	.68
86	Al Simmons	.68
87	Harlond Clift	.68
88	Billy Werber	.68
89	Tris Speaker	.67
90	Ned Williamson	.67
91	Jake Beckley	.67
92	Ross Youngs	.67
93	Jack Glasscock	.67
94	Chuck Klein	.67
95	Ben Chapman	.67
96	Ron LeFlore	.67
97	Bob Johnson	.67
98	Frankie Frisch	.66
99	Kip Selbach	.66
100	Cub Stricker	.66

Hits

#	Player	Total
1	Pete Rose	4256
2	Ty Cobb	4190
3	Hank Aaron	3771
4	Stan Musial	3630
5	Tris Speaker	3514
6	Carl Yastrzemski	3419
7	Honus Wagner	3415
8	Eddie Collins	3310
9	Willie Mays	3283
10	Nap Lajoie	3242
11	Paul Waner	3152
12	Rod Carew	3053
13	Lou Brock	3023
14	Al Kaline	3007
15	Roberto Clemente	3000
16	Cap Anson	2995
17	Sam Rice	2987
18	Sam Crawford	2961
19	Frank Robinson	2943
20	Willie Keeler	2932
21	Jake Beckley	2930
	Rogers Hornsby	2930
23	Al Simmons	2927
24	Zach Wheat	2884
25	Frankie Frisch	2880
26	Mel Ott	2876
27	Babe Ruth	2873
28	Jesse Burkett	2850
29	Brooks Robinson	2848
30	Charlie Gehringer	2839
31	George Sisler	2812
32	Vada Pinson	2757
33	Luke Appling	2749
34	Al Oliver	2743
35	Goose Goslin	2735
36	Tony Perez	2732
37	Lou Gehrig	2721
38	Rusty Staub	2716
39	Billy Williams	2711
40	Bill Buckner	2707
41	Doc Cramer	2705
42	Luis Aparicio	2677
43	Fred Clarke	2672
44	Max Carey	2665
45	Nellie Fox	2663
46	George Davis	2660
	Harry Heilmann	2660
48	Ted Williams	2654
49	Jimmie Foxx	2646
50	Lave Cross	2644
51	Rabbit Maranville	2605
52	Robin Yount	2602
53	Steve Garvey	2599
54	Ed Delahanty	2597
55	Reggie Jackson	2584
56	Ernie Banks	2583
57	Richie Ashburn	2574
58	Willie Davis	2561
59	George VanHaltren	2532
60	George Brett	2528
61	Heinie Manush	2524
62	Joe Morgan	2517
63	Buddy Bell	2514
64	Jimmy Ryan	2502
65	Mickey Vernon	2495
66	Ted Simmons	2472
67	Joe Medwick	2471
68	Roger Connor	2467
69	Harry Hooper	2466
70	Lloyd Waner	2459
71	Bill Dahlen	2457
72	Jim Rice	2452
73	Red Schoendienst	2449
74	Dave Winfield	2421
75	Dave Parker	2416
	Pie Traynor	2416
77	Mickey Mantle	2415
78	Stuffy McInnis	2405
79	Enos Slaughter	2383
80	Edd Roush	2376
81	Joe Judge	2352
82	Orlando Cepeda	2351
83	Billy Herman	2345
84	Joe Torre	2342
85	Dave Concepcion	2326
	Jake Daubert	2326
87	Eddie Mathews	2315
88	Jim Bottomley	2313
89	Bobby Wallace	2309
90	Jim O'Rourke	2304
91	Kiki Cuyler	2299
	Charlie Grimm	2299
93	Dan Brouthers	2296
94	Joe Cronin	2285
95	Hugh Duffy	2282
96	Dwight Evans	2262
97	Jimmy Dykes	2256
98	Ron Santo	2254
99	Patsy Donovan	2253
100	Tommy Corcoran	2252

Doubles

#	Player	Total
1	Tris Speaker	793
2	Pete Rose	746
3	Stan Musial	725
4	Ty Cobb	724
5	Nap Lajoie	657
6	Carl Yastrzemski	646
7	Honus Wagner	640
8	Hank Aaron	624
9	Paul Waner	603
10	Charlie Gehringer	574
11	Harry Heilmann	542
12	Rogers Hornsby	541
13	Joe Medwick	540
14	Al Simmons	539
15	Lou Gehrig	534
16	Al Oliver	529
17	Cap Anson	528
	Frank Robinson	528
19	Ted Williams	525
20	Willie Mays	523
21	Ed Delahanty	522
22	Joe Cronin	515
23	George Brett	514
24	Babe Ruth	506
25	Tony Perez	505
26	Goose Goslin	500
27	Rusty Staub	499
28	Bill Buckner	498
	Al Kaline	498
	Sam Rice	498
31	Heinie Manush	491
32	Mickey Vernon	490
33	Mel Ott	488
34	Lou Brock	486
	Billy Herman	486
36	Vada Pinson	485
37	Hal McRae	484
38	Ted Simmons	483
39	Brooks Robinson	482
40	Robin Yount	481
41	Zach Wheat	476
42	Jake Beckley	473
43	Dave Parker	470
44	Frankie Frisch	466
45	Jim Bottomley	465
46	Reggie Jackson	463
47	Dan Brouthers	460
48	Sam Crawford	458
	Jimmie Foxx	458
50	Dwight Evans	456
51	Jimmy Dykes	453
52	Jimmy Ryan	451
53	George Davis	450
54	Joe Morgan	449
55	Rod Carew	445
56	George Burns	444
57	Dick Bartell	442
58	Roger Connor	441
59	Luke Appling	440
	Roberto Clemente	440
	Steve Garvey	440
62	Eddie Collins	437
63	Cesar Cedeno	436
	Joe Sewell	436
65	Wally Moses	435
66	Billy Williams	434
67	Joe Judge	433
68	Red Schoendienst	427
69	Buddy Bell	425
	Sherry Magee	425
	George Sisler	425
72	Keith Hernandez	424
73	Willie Stargell	423
74	Max Carey	419
75	Orlando Cepeda	417
76	Cecil Cooper	415
77	Jim O'Rourke	414
78	Bill Dahlen	413
	Enos Slaughter	413
80	Joe Kuhel	412
	Dave Winfield	412
82	Lave Cross	411
83	Mike Schmidt	408
84	Ernie Banks	407
	Ben Chapman	407
86	Earl Averill	401
	Marty McManus	401
88	Babe Herman	399
	Gee Walker	399
90	Chuck Klein	398
91	Doc Cramer	396
	Gabby Hartnett	396
	Bob Johnson	396
94	Willie Davis	395
95	Luis Aparicio	394
	Kiki Cuyler	394
	Charlie Grimm	394
98	Bobby Veach	393
	Frank White	393
100	2 players tied	392

Triples

#	Player	Total
1	Sam Crawford	309
2	Ty Cobb	294
3	Honus Wagner	252
4	Jake Beckley	243
5	Roger Connor	233
6	Tris Speaker	223
7	Fred Clarke	220
8	Dan Brouthers	205
9	Joe Kelley	194
10	Paul Waner	190
11	Bid McPhee	188
12	Eddie Collins	186
13	Ed Delahanty	185
14	Sam Rice	184
15	Edd Roush	183
16	Jesse Burkett	182
17	Ed Konetchy	181
18	Buck Ewing	178
19	Rabbit Maranville	177
	Stan Musial	177
21	Harry Stovey	175
22	Goose Goslin	173
23	Tommy Leach	172
	Zach Wheat	172
25	Rogers Hornsby	169
26	Joe Jackson	168
27	Roberto Clemente	166
	Sherry Magee	166
29	Jake Daubert	165
	George Davis	165
31	Elmer Flick	164
	George Sisler	164
	Pie Traynor	164
34	Bill Dahlen	163
	Lou Gehrig	163
	Nap Lajoie	163
37	Mike Tiernan	162
38	George VanHaltren	161
39	Harry Hooper	160
	Heinie Manush	160
	Sam Thompson	160
42	Max Carey	159
	Joe Judge	159
44	Ed McKean	158
45	Kiki Cuyler	157
	Jimmy Ryan	157
47	Tommy Corcoran	155
48	Earle Combs	154
49	Jim Bottomley	151
	Harry Heilmann	151
51	Kip Selbach	149
	Al Simmons	149
53	Wally Pipp	148
	Enos Slaughter	148
55	Bobby Veach	147
56	Harry Davis	146
	Charlie Gehringer	146
58	Willie Keeler	145
59	Bobby Wallace	143
60	Lou Brock	141
61	Willie Mays	140
62	John Reilly	139
63	Tom Brown	138
	Willie Davis	138
	Frankie Frisch	138
	Jimmy Williams	138
67	Babe Ruth	136
	Jimmy Sheckard	136
	Mike Smith	136
70	Lave Cross	135
	Pete Rose	135
72	Shano Collins	133
73	Jim O'Rourke	132
	George Wood	132
75	Joe DiMaggio	131
	Buck Freeman	131
77	Buddy Myer	130
	Willie Wilson	130
79	Oyster Burns	129
	Larry Gardner	129
81	Earl Averill	128
	Arky Vaughan	128
83	Vada Pinson	127
84	Hardy Richardson	126
85	Jimmie Foxx	125
86	John Anderson	124
	Cap Anson	124
	Hal Chase	124
	Frank Schulte	124
90	Larry Doyle	123
	Duke Farrell	123
92	Dummy Hoy	121
93	George Brett	120
	Mickey Vernon	120
95	Fred Pfeffer	119
96	Joe Cronin	118
	Hugh Duffy	118
	Lloyd Waner	118
99	4 players tied	117

Triples (by era)

1876-1892

#	Player	Total
1	Roger Connor	233
2	Dan Brouthers	205
3	Bid McPhee	188
4	Buck Ewing	178
5	Harry Stovey	175
6	Sam Thompson	160
7	John Reilly	139
8	Tom Brown	138
9	Jim O'Rourke	132
	George Wood	132
11	Oyster Burns	129
12	Hardy Richardson	126
13	Cap Anson	124
14	Fred Pfeffer	119
15	Bill Kuehne	115

1893-1919

#	Player	Total
1	Sam Crawford	309
2	Ty Cobb	294
3	Honus Wagner	252
4	Jake Beckley	243
5	Tris Speaker	223
6	Fred Clarke	220
7	Joe Kelley	194
8	Eddie Collins	186
9	Ed Delahanty	185
10	Jesse Burkett	182
11	Ed Konetchy	181
12	Tommy Leach	172
	Zach Wheat	172
14	Joe Jackson	168
15	Sherry Magee	166

1920-1941

#	Player	Total
1	Paul Waner	190
2	Sam Rice	184
3	Edd Roush	183
4	Rabbit Maranville	177
5	Goose Goslin	173
6	Rogers Hornsby	169
7	George Sisler	164
	Pie Traynor	164
9	Lou Gehrig	163
10	Heinie Manush	160
11	Max Carey	159
	Joe Judge	159
13	Kiki Cuyler	157
14	Earle Combs	154
15	2 players tied	151

1942-1960

#	Player	Total
1	Stan Musial	177
2	Enos Slaughter	148
3	Joe DiMaggio	131
4	Mickey Vernon	120
5	Nellie Fox	112
6	Wally Moses	110
7	Richie Ashburn	109
8	Bill Bruton	102
	Jeff Heath	102
10	Phil Cavarretta	99
11	Dixie Walker	96
12	Bob Elliott	94
13	Bobby Doerr	89
14	Duke Snider	85
15	2 players tied	83

1961-1989

#	Player	Total
1	Roberto Clemente	166
2	Lou Brock	141
3	Willie Mays	140
4	Willie Davis	138
5	Pete Rose	135
6	Willie Wilson	130
7	Vada Pinson	127
8	George Brett	120
9	Rod Carew	112
10	Robin Yount	111
11	Garry Templeton	101
12	Larry Bowa	99
13	Hank Aaron	98
14	Joe Morgan	96
15	Jose Cruz	94

Home Runs

#	Player	HR
1	Hank Aaron	755
2	Babe Ruth	714
3	Willie Mays	660
4	Frank Robinson	586
5	Harmon Killebrew	573
6	Reggie Jackson	563
7	Mike Schmidt	548
8	Mickey Mantle	536
9	Jimmie Foxx	534
10	Willie McCovey	521
	Ted Williams	521
12	Ernie Banks	512
	Eddie Mathews	512
14	Mel Ott	511
15	Lou Gehrig	493
16	Stan Musial	475
	Willie Stargell	475
18	Carl Yastrzemski	452
19	Dave Kingman	442
20	Billy Williams	426
21	Darrell Evans	414
22	Duke Snider	407
23	Al Kaline	399
24	Graig Nettles	390
25	Johnny Bench	389
26	Frank Howard	382
	Jim Rice	382
28	Orlando Cepeda	379
	Tony Perez	379
30	Norm Cash	377
31	Rocky Colavito	374
32	Gil Hodges	370
33	Ralph Kiner	369
34	Dwight Evans	366
35	Joe DiMaggio	361
36	Johnny Mize	359
37	Yogi Berra	358
38	Dave Winfield	357
39	Lee May	354
	Dale Murphy	354
41	Eddie Murray	353
42	Dick Allen	351
43	George Foster	348
44	Ron Santo	342
45	Boog Powell	339
46	Don Baylor	338
47	Joe Adcock	336
	Carlton Fisk	336
49	Bobby Bonds	332
50	Hank Greenberg	331
51	Willie Horton	325
52	Andre Dawson	319
53	Roy Sievers	318
54	Ron Cey	316
55	Reggie Smith	314
56	Greg Luzinski	307
	Dave Parker	307
	Al Simmons	307
59	Gary Carter	304
60	Rogers Hornsby	301
61	Chuck Klein	300
	Fred Lynn	300
63	Rusty Staub	292
64	Jim Wynn	291
65	Del Ennis	288
	Bob Johnson	288
	Hank Sauer	288
68	Frank Thomas	286
69	Ken Boyer	282
	Jack Clark	282
71	Ted Kluszewski	279
72	Rudy York	277
73	Roger Maris	275
74	Steve Garvey	272
75	George Scott	271
76	Joe Morgan	268
	Brooks Robinson	268
	Gorman Thomas	268
79	George Brett	267
	George Hendrick	267
81	Vic Wertz	266
82	Bobby Thomson	264
83	Lance Parrish	261
84	Bob Allison	256
	Larry Parrish	256
	Vada Pinson	256
87	John Mayberry	255
88	Larry Doby	253
	Joe Gordon	253
	Andy Thornton	253
91	Bobby Murcer	252
	Joe Torre	252
93	Tony Armas	251
	Cy Williams	251
95	Goose Goslin	248
	Ted Simmons	248
97	Vern Stephens	247
98	Ken Singleton	246
99	Deron Johnson	245
100	Hack Wilson	244

Home Runs (by era)

1876-1892
#	Player	HR
1	Roger Connor	137
2	Sam Thompson	127
3	Harry Stovey	121
4	Dan Brouthers	106
5	Cap Anson	97
6	Fred Pfeffer	94
7	Jack Clements	77
8	Jerry Denny	74
9	Buck Ewing	71
10	King Kelly	69
11	Hardy Richardson	68
	George Wood	68
13	John Reilly	67
14	Oyster Burns	65
	Bug Holliday	65

1893-1919
#	Player	HR
1	Zach Wheat	132
2	Gavvy Cravath	119
3	Ty Cobb	118
	Jimmy Ryan	118
	Tilly Walker	118
6	Tris Speaker	117
7	Hugh Duffy	105
	Mike Tiernan	105
9	Ed Delahanty	101
	Honus Wagner	101
11	Sam Crawford	98
12	Frank Baker	96
13	Frank Schulte	93
14	Herman Long	91
15	Jake Beckley	87

1920-1941
#	Player	HR
1	Babe Ruth	714
2	Jimmie Foxx	534
3	Mel Ott	511
4	Lou Gehrig	493
5	Hank Greenberg	331
6	Al Simmons	307
7	Rogers Hornsby	301
8	Chuck Klein	300
9	Bob Johnson	288
10	Cy Williams	251
11	Goose Goslin	248
12	Hack Wilson	244
13	Wally Berger	242
14	Dolph Camilli	239
15	Earl Averill	238

1942-1960
#	Player	HR
1	Mickey Mantle	536
2	Ted Williams	521
3	Eddie Mathews	512
4	Stan Musial	475
5	Duke Snider	407
6	Gil Hodges	370
7	Ralph Kiner	369
8	Joe DiMaggio	361
9	Johnny Mize	359
10	Yogi Berra	358
11	Joe Adcock	336
12	Roy Sievers	318
13	Del Ennis	288
	Hank Sauer	288
15	Frank Thomas	286

1961-1989
#	Player	HR
1	Hank Aaron	755
2	Willie Mays	660
3	Frank Robinson	586
4	Harmon Killebrew	573
5	Reggie Jackson	563
6	Mike Schmidt	548
7	Willie McCovey	521
8	Ernie Banks	512
9	Willie Stargell	475
10	Carl Yastrzemski	452
11	Dave Kingman	442
12	Billy Williams	426
13	Darrell Evans	414
14	Al Kaline	399
15	Graig Nettles	390

Home Run Percentage

#	Player	Pct
1	Babe Ruth	8.50
2	Ralph Kiner	7.09
3	Harmon Killebrew	7.03
4	Ted Williams	6.76
5	Dave Kingman	6.62
6	Mickey Mantle	6.62
7	Jimmie Foxx	6.57
8	Mike Schmidt	6.56
9	Hank Greenberg	6.37
10	Willie McCovey	6.36
11	Lou Gehrig	6.16
12	Hank Aaron	6.11
13	Willie Mays	6.07
14	Hank Sauer	6.01
15	Eddie Mathews	6.00
16	Willie Stargell	5.99
17	Frank Howard	5.89
18	Frank Robinson	5.86
19	Bob Horner	5.77
20	Roy Campanella	5.76
21	Rocky Colavito	5.75
22	Gus Zernial	5.74
23	Gorman Thomas	5.73
24	Reggie Jackson	5.71
25	Dick Stuart	5.70
26	Duke Snider	5.68
27	Norm Cash	5.62
28	Johnny Mize	5.57
29	Dick Allen	5.54
30	Ernie Banks	5.43
31	Mel Ott	5.40
32	Roger Maris	5.39
33	Joe DiMaggio	5.29
34	Gil Hodges	5.26
35	Dale Murphy	5.25
36	Wally Post	5.24
37	Al Rosen	5.15
38	Hack Wilson	5.13
39	Bob Allison	5.09
40	Joe Adcock	5.09
41	Johnny Bench	5.08
42	Boog Powell	5.07
43	Nate Colbert	5.06
44	Jesse Barfield	5.05
45	Charlie Keller	4.99
46	Roy Sievers	4.98
47	Cliff Johnson	4.97
48	Don Mincher	4.97
49	George Foster	4.96
50	Jack Clark	4.88
51	Tony Armas	4.86
52	Kent Hrbek	4.81
53	Andy Thornton	4.78
54	Orlando Cepeda	4.78
55	Leon Wagner	4.77
56	Jim Lemon	4.76
57	Eddie Murray	4.75
58	Yogi Berra	4.74
59	Don Demeter	4.73
60	Larry Doby	4.73
61	Greg Luzinski	4.72
62	Bobby Bonds	4.71
63	Ted Kluszewski	4.71
64	Rudy York	4.70
65	Tom Brunansky	4.70
66	Wally Berger	4.69
67	John Mayberry	4.68
68	Lance Parrish	4.66
69	Lee May	4.65
70	Jim Rice	4.64
71	Chuck Klein	4.63
72	Darrell Evans	4.61
73	Kirk Gibson	4.59
74	Gene Tenace	4.58
75	George Bell	4.56
76	Charlie Maxwell	4.56
77	Billy Williams	4.56
78	Frank Thomas	4.55
79	Jim Ray Hart	4.49
80	Gary Roenicke	4.47
81	Pedro Guerrero	4.47
82	Dolph Camilli	4.46
83	Reggie Smith	4.46
84	Fred Lynn	4.46
85	Woodie Held	4.45
86	Willie Horton	4.45
87	Oscar Gamble	4.44
88	Joe Gordon	4.43
89	Dwight Evans	4.42
90	Carlton Fisk	4.42
91	Hal Trosky	4.42
92	Ron Cey	4.41
93	Wes Covington	4.40
94	Andre Dawson	4.40
95	Jim Wynn	4.37
96	Dale Long	4.37
97	Vic Wertz	4.36
98	Graig Nettles	4.34
99	Jeff Burroughs	4.34
100	Jason Thompson	4.33

Home Run Pctg. (by era)

1876-1892
#	Player	Pct
1	Sam Thompson	2.12
2	Harry Stovey	1.97
3	Jack Clements	1.80
4	Roger Connor	1.76
5	Dan Brouthers	1.58
6	Jerry Denny	1.50
7	Denny Lyons	1.44
8	Charlie Bennett	1.44
9	Fred Pfeffer	1.43
10	John Reilly	1.43
11	Oyster Burns	1.40
12	Ned Williamson	1.38
13	Buck Ewing	1.32
14	George Wood	1.27
15	Tip O'Neill	1.22

1893-1919
#	Player	Pct
1	Gavvy Cravath	3.01
2	Tilly Walker	2.33
3	Buck Freeman	1.95
4	Mike Tiernan	1.78
5	Fred Luderus	1.73
6	Frank Baker	1.60
7	Hugh Duffy	1.49
8	Charlie Hickman	1.48
9	Zach Wheat	1.45
10	Jimmy Ryan	1.45
11	Frank Schulte	1.42
12	Casey Stengel	1.40
13	Ed Delahanty	1.35
14	Mike Donlin	1.32
15	Chief Wilson	1.28

1920-1941
#	Player	Pct
1	Babe Ruth	8.50
2	Jimmie Foxx	6.57
3	Hank Greenberg	6.37
4	Lou Gehrig	6.16
5	Mel Ott	5.40
6	Hack Wilson	5.13
7	Wally Berger	4.69
8	Chuck Klein	4.63
9	Dolph Camilli	4.46
10	Hal Trosky	4.42
11	Bob Johnson	4.16
12	Ken Williams	4.03
13	Earl Averill	3.75
14	Cy Williams	3.70
15	Rogers Hornsby	3.68

1942-1960
#	Player	Pct
1	Ralph Kiner	7.09
2	Ted Williams	6.76
3	Mickey Mantle	6.62
4	Hank Sauer	6.01
5	Eddie Mathews	6.00
6	Roy Campanella	5.76
7	Gus Zernial	5.74
8	Duke Snider	5.68
9	Johnny Mize	5.57
10	Joe DiMaggio	5.29
11	Gil Hodges	5.26
12	Wally Post	5.24
13	Al Rosen	5.15
14	Joe Adcock	5.09
15	Charlie Keller	4.99

1961-1989
#	Player	Pct
1	Harmon Killebrew	7.03
2	Dave Kingman	6.62
3	Mike Schmidt	6.56
4	Willie McCovey	6.36
5	Hank Aaron	6.11
6	Willie Mays	6.07
7	Willie Stargell	5.99
8	Frank Howard	5.89
9	Frank Robinson	5.86
10	Bob Horner	5.77
11	Rocky Colavito	5.75
12	Gorman Thomas	5.73
13	Reggie Jackson	5.71
14	Dick Stuart	5.70
15	Norm Cash	5.62

Total Bases

1	Hank Aaron	6856
2	Stan Musial	6134
3	Willie Mays	6066
4	Ty Cobb	5856
5	Babe Ruth	5793
6	Pete Rose	5752
7	Carl Yastrzemski	5539
8	Frank Robinson	5373
9	Tris Speaker	5104
10	Lou Gehrig	5060
11	Mel Ott	5041
12	Jimmie Foxx	4956
13	Ted Williams	4884
14	Honus Wagner	4862
15	Al Kaline	4852
16	Reggie Jackson	4834
17	Rogers Hornsby	4712
18	Ernie Banks	4706
19	Al Simmons	4685
20	Billy Williams	4599
21	Tony Perez	4532
22	Mickey Mantle	4511
23	Roberto Clemente	4492
24	Nap Lajoie	4474
	Paul Waner	4474
26	Mike Schmidt	4404
27	Eddie Mathews	4349
28	Sam Crawford	4331
29	Goose Goslin	4325
30	Brooks Robinson	4270
31	Vada Pinson	4264
32	Eddie Collins	4260
33	Charlie Gehringer	4257
34	Lou Brock	4238
35	Willie McCovey	4219
36	Willie Stargell	4190
37	Rusty Staub	4185
38	Jake Beckley	4150
39	Harmon Killebrew	4143
40	Jim Rice	4129
41	Zach Wheat	4100
42	George Brett	4083
	Al Oliver	4083
44	Cap Anson	4062
45	Harry Heilmann	4053
46	Dave Winfield	4052
47	Rod Carew	3998
48	Joe Morgan	3962
49	Orlando Cepeda	3959
50	Sam Rice	3955
51	Dwight Evans	3954
52	Joe DiMaggio	3948
53	Dave Parker	3947
54	Steve Garvey	3941
55	Frankie Frisch	3937
56	Robin Yount	3929
57	George Sisler	3868
58	Darrell Evans	3866
59	Duke Snider	3865
60	Joe Medwick	3852
61	Bill Buckner	3822
62	Ted Simmons	3793
63	Ed Delahanty	3792
64	Roger Connor	3785
65	Graig Nettles	3779
	Ron Santo	3779
67	Willie Davis	3778
68	Jesse Burkett	3759
69	Mickey Vernon	3741
70	Jim Bottomley	3737
71	Fred Clarke	3674
72	Heinie Manush	3665
73	George Davis	3659
	Eddie Murray	3659
75	Buddy Bell	3654
76	Johnny Bench	3644
77	Yogi Berra	3643
78	Johnny Mize	3621
	Jimmy Ryan	3621
80	Max Carey	3609
81	Enos Slaughter	3599
82	Don Baylor	3571
83	Willie Keeler	3566
84	Joe Torre	3560
85	Joe Cronin	3546
86	Carlton Fisk	3534
87	Luke Appling	3528
	Andre Dawson	3528
89	Chuck Klein	3522
90	Luis Aparicio	3504
91	Bob Johnson	3501
92	Lee May	3495
93	Dan Brouthers	3484
94	Lave Cross	3466
95	Bill Dahlen	3448
96	Ken Boyer	3443
97	Reggie Smith	3439
98	Doc Cramer	3430
99	Cecil Cooper	3424
100	2 players tied	3423

Runs Batted In

1	Hank Aaron	2297
2	Babe Ruth	2209
3	Lou Gehrig	1990
4	Stan Musial	1951
5	Ty Cobb	1933
6	Jimmie Foxx	1922
7	Willie Mays	1903
8	Cap Anson	1879
9	Mel Ott	1860
10	Carl Yastrzemski	1844
11	Ted Williams	1839
12	Al Simmons	1827
13	Frank Robinson	1812
14	Honus Wagner	1732
15	Reggie Jackson	1702
16	Tony Perez	1652
17	Ernie Banks	1636
18	Goose Goslin	1609
19	Nap Lajoie	1599
20	Mike Schmidt	1595
21	Rogers Hornsby	1584
	Harmon Killebrew	1584
23	Al Kaline	1583
24	Jake Beckley	1575
25	Willie McCovey	1555
26	Willie Stargell	1540
27	Harry Heilmann	1538
28	Joe DiMaggio	1537
29	Tris Speaker	1528
30	Sam Crawford	1525
31	Mickey Mantle	1509
32	Billy Williams	1475
33	Rusty Staub	1466
34	Ed Delahanty	1464
35	Eddie Mathews	1453
36	Jim Rice	1451
37	Dave Winfield	1438
38	George Davis	1435
39	Yogi Berra	1430
40	Charlie Gehringer	1427
41	Joe Cronin	1424
42	Jim Bottomley	1422
43	Ted Simmons	1389
44	Joe Medwick	1383
45	Johnny Bench	1376
46	Orlando Cepeda	1365
47	Brooks Robinson	1357
48	Darrell Evans	1354
49	Dave Parker	1342
50	Johnny Mize	1337
51	Duke Snider	1333
52	Ron Santo	1331
53	Al Oliver	1326
54	Roger Connor	1322
55	Graig Nettles	1314
	Pete Rose	1314
57	George Brett	1311
	Mickey Vernon	1311
59	Paul Waner	1309
60	Steve Garvey	1308
61	Roberto Clemente	1305
62	Enos Slaughter	1304
63	Eddie Collins	1299
	Hugh Duffy	1299
	Sam Thompson	1299
66	Dan Brouthers	1295
67	Del Ennis	1284
68	Dwight Evans	1283
	Bob Johnson	1283
70	Eddie Murray	1278
71	Don Baylor	1276
	Hank Greenberg	1276
73	Gil Hodges	1274
74	Pie Traynor	1273
75	Zach Wheat	1248
76	Bobby Doerr	1247
77	Frankie Frisch	1244
	Lee May	1244
79	George Foster	1239
80	Bill Dahlen	1233
81	Bill Dickey	1210
	Dave Kingman	1210
83	Bill Buckner	1205
84	Chuck Klein	1201
85	Bob Elliott	1195
86	Joe Kelley	1194
87	Tony Lazzeri	1191
88	Boog Powell	1187
89	Joe Torre	1185
90	Heinie Manush	1183
91	Gabby Hartnett	1179
92	Vic Wertz	1178
93	Sherry Magee	1176
94	George Sisler	1175
95	Vern Stephens	1174
96	Vada Pinson	1170
97	Carlton Fisk	1166
	Bobby Veach	1166
99	Earl Averill	1164
100	Willie Horton	1163

Runs Batted In (by era)

1876-1892

1	Cap Anson	1879
2	Roger Connor	1322
3	Sam Thompson	1299
4	Dan Brouthers	1295
5	Fred Pfeffer	1019
6	Jim O'Rourke	1010
7	King Kelly	950
8	Buck Ewing	883
9	Monte Ward	867
10	Hardy Richardson	818
11	Deacon White	756
12	Paul Hines	751
13	Tom Burns	683
14	Sam Wise	672
15	2 players tied	667

1893-1919

1	Ty Cobb	1933
2	Honus Wagner	1732
3	Nap Lajoie	1599
4	Jake Beckley	1575
5	Tris Speaker	1528
6	Sam Crawford	1525
7	Ed Delahanty	1464
8	George Davis	1435
9	Eddie Collins	1299
	Hugh Duffy	1299
11	Zach Wheat	1248
12	Bill Dahlen	1233
13	Joe Kelley	1194
14	Sherry Magee	1176
15	Bobby Veach	1166

1920-1941

1	Babe Ruth	2209
2	Lou Gehrig	1990
3	Jimmie Foxx	1922
4	Mel Ott	1860
5	Al Simmons	1827
6	Goose Goslin	1609
7	Rogers Hornsby	1584
8	Harry Heilmann	1538
9	Charlie Gehringer	1427
10	Joe Cronin	1424
11	Jim Bottomley	1422
12	Joe Medwick	1383
13	Paul Waner	1309
14	Bob Johnson	1283
15	Hank Greenberg	1276

1942-1960

1	Stan Musial	1951
2	Ted Williams	1839
3	Joe DiMaggio	1537
4	Mickey Mantle	1509
5	Eddie Mathews	1453
6	Yogi Berra	1430
7	Johnny Mize	1337
8	Duke Snider	1333
9	Mickey Vernon	1311
10	Enos Slaughter	1304
11	Del Ennis	1284
12	Gil Hodges	1274
13	Bobby Doerr	1247
14	Bob Elliott	1195
15	Vic Wertz	1178

1961-1989

1	Hank Aaron	2297
2	Willie Mays	1903
3	Carl Yastrzemski	1844
4	Frank Robinson	1812
5	Reggie Jackson	1702
6	Tony Perez	1652
7	Ernie Banks	1636
8	Mike Schmidt	1595
9	Harmon Killebrew	1584
10	Al Kaline	1583
11	Willie McCovey	1555
12	Willie Stargell	1540
13	Billy Williams	1475
14	Rusty Staub	1466
15	Jim Rice	1451

Runs Batted In per Game

1	Sam Thompson	.92
2	Lou Gehrig	.92
3	Hank Greenberg	.92
4	Joe DiMaggio	.89
5	Babe Ruth	.88
6	Jimmie Foxx	.83
7	Cap Anson	.83
8	Al Simmons	.82
9	Ted Williams	.80
10	Ed Delahanty	.80
11	Hack Wilson	.79
12	Dan Brouthers	.77
13	Bob Meusel	.76
14	Hal Trosky	.75
15	Hugh Duffy	.75
16	Rudy York	.72
17	Harry Heilmann	.72
18	Jim Bottomley	.71
19	Johnny Mize	.71
20	Don Mattingly	.71
21	Roy Campanella	.70
22	Goose Goslin	.70
23	Rogers Hornsby	.70
24	Earl Averill	.70
25	Joe Medwick	.70
26	Hank Aaron	.70
27	Jim Rice	.69
28	Ralph Kiner	.69
29	Bob Johnson	.69
30	Al Rosen	.69
31	Chuck Klein	.69
32	Tony Lazzeri	.68
33	Vern Stephens	.68
34	Mel Ott	.68
35	Bill Dickey	.68
36	Del Ennis	.67
37	Yogi Berra	.67
38	Bob Horner	.67
39	Buck Ewing	.67
40	Joe Cronin	.67
41	Bobby Doerr	.67
42	Dick Stuart	.67
43	Wally Berger	.67
44	Mike Schmidt	.66
45	Roger Connor	.66
46	Jake Beckley	.66
47	Pie Traynor	.66
48	Hughie Jennings	.65
49	Ken Williams	.65
50	King Kelly	.65
51	Willie Stargell	.65
52	Harmon Killebrew	.65
53	Charlie Keller	.65
54	Chick Hafey	.65
55	Ernie Banks	.65
56	Glenn Wright	.65
57	Jackie Jensen	.65
58	Eddie Murray	.65
59	Frank Robinson	.65
60	Nap Lajoie	.64
61	Stan Musial	.64
62	Joe Kelley	.64
63	Orlando Cepeda	.64
64	Babe Herman	.64
65	Jeff Heath	.64
66	Bobby Veach	.64
67	Dick Allen	.64
68	Johnny Bench	.64
69	Dolph Camilli	.64
70	Ty Cobb	.64
71	Willie Mays	.64
72	Irish Meusel	.64
73	Dave Winfield	.63
74	Buck Freeman	.63
75	Larry Doby	.63
76	Vic Wertz	.63
77	Patsy Tebeau	.63
78	Rocky Colavito	.63
79	George Bell	.63
80	George Kelly	.63
81	Gus Zernial	.63
82	Mickey Mantle	.63
83	George Foster	.63
84	Frank Baker	.63
85	Bill Terry	.63
86	Steve Brodie	.63
87	Kent Hrbek	.63
88	Hank Sauer	.63
89	Dave Kingman	.62
90	Joe Gordon	.62
91	Duke Snider	.62
92	Honus Wagner	.62
93	Frank McCormick	.62
94	Greg Luzinski	.62
95	Tommy Henrich	.62
96	Joe Vosmik	.62
97	Jack Rowe	.62
98	Dave Parker	.62
99	Gil Hodges	.62
100	Hardy Richardson	.61

Walks

1	Babe Ruth	2056
2	Ted Williams	2019
3	Joe Morgan	1865
4	Carl Yastrzemski	1845
5	Mickey Mantle	1734
6	Mel Ott	1708
7	Eddie Yost	1614
8	Darrell Evans	1605
9	Stan Musial	1599
10	Pete Rose	1566
11	Harmon Killebrew	1559
12	Lou Gehrig	1508
13	Mike Schmidt	1507
14	Eddie Collins	1499
15	Willie Mays	1464
16	Jimmie Foxx	1452
17	Eddie Mathews	1444
18	Frank Robinson	1420
19	Hank Aaron	1402
20	Tris Speaker	1381
21	Reggie Jackson	1375
22	Willie McCovey	1345
23	Luke Appling	1302
24	Al Kaline	1277
25	Dwight Evans	1270
26	Ken Singleton	1263
27	Rusty Staub	1255
28	Ty Cobb	1249
29	Jim Wynn	1224
30	Pee Wee Reese	1210
31	Richie Ashburn	1198
32	Billy Hamilton	1187
33	Charlie Gehringer	1186
34	Donie Bush	1158
35	Max Bishop	1153
	Toby Harrah	1153
37	Harry Hooper	1136
38	Jimmy Sheckard	1135
39	Ron Santo	1108
40	Lu Blue	1092
	Stan Hack	1092
42	Paul Waner	1091
43	Graig Nettles	1088
44	Bobby Grich	1087
45	Willie Randolph	1083
46	Bob Johnson	1075
47	Harlond Clift	1070
48	Bill Dahlen	1064
49	Joe Cronin	1059
50	Keith Hernandez	1056
51	Ron Fairly	1052
52	Billy Williams	1045
53	Norm Cash	1043
	Eddie Joost	1043
55	Roy Thomas	1042
56	Max Carey	1040
57	Rogers Hornsby	1038
58	Jim Gilliam	1036
59	Sal Bando	1031
60	Jesse Burkett	1029
61	Brian Downing	1027
62	Rod Carew	1018
	Enos Slaughter	1018
64	Ron Cey	1012
65	Ralph Kiner	1011
66	Jack Clark	1006
67	Dummy Hoy	1004
68	Miller Huggins	1003
69	Roger Connor	1002
70	Boog Powell	1001
71	Rickey Henderson	996
	Eddie Stanky	996
73	Cupid Childs	990
74	Gene Tenace	984
75	Bid McPhee	981
76	Joe Kuhel	980
	Earl Torgeson	980
78	Augie Galan	979
79	Duke Snider	971
80	Bob Elliott	967
81	Mike Hargrove	965
	Joe Judge	965
	Buddy Myer	965
84	Honus Wagner	963
85	Jimmy Dykes	958
86	Mickey Vernon	955
87	Cap Anson	952
88	Rocky Colavito	951
89	Goose Goslin	948
90	Dolph Camilli	947
91	Eddie Murray	944
92	Gil Hodges	943
93	Elmer Valo	942
94	Gary Matthews	940
95	Willie Stargell	937
	Arky Vaughan	937
97	Dave Winfield	936
98	Roy White	934
99	Rick Ferrell	931
100	Tony Perez	925

Walks Ratio

1	Ted Williams	20.76
2	Max Bishop	20.42
3	Babe Ruth	19.67
4	Eddie Stanky	18.80
5	Ferris Fain	18.70
6	Gene Tenace	18.31
7	Roy Cullenbine	18.03
8	Eddie Yost	18.01
9	Mickey Mantle	17.63
10	John McGraw	17.56
11	Charlie Keller	17.14
12	Joe Morgan	16.74
13	Earl Torgeson	16.47
14	Bernie Carbo	16.45
15	Roy Thomas	16.44
16	Ralph Kiner	16.26
17	Harmon Killebrew	16.06
18	Billy Hamilton	15.92
19	Lou Gehrig	15.86
20	Elmer Valo	15.78
21	Joe Ferguson	15.77
22	Harlond Clift	15.74
23	Eddie Joost	15.69
24	Lu Blue	15.61
25	Jim Wynn	15.54
26	Mel Ott	15.30
27	Miller Huggins	15.29
28	Mike Schmidt	15.29
29	Rickey Henderson	15.28
30	Darrell Evans	15.17
31	Jimmie Foxx	15.15
32	Joe Cunningham	15.12
33	Dolph Camilli	15.03
34	Cupid Childs	14.98
35	Ken Singleton	14.94
36	Elbie Fletcher	14.85
37	Jack Clark	14.84
38	Merv Rettenmund	14.83
39	Mike Hargrove	14.78
40	Topsy Hartsel	14.74
41	Dwayne Murphy	14.66
42	Wayne Garrett	14.59
43	Jason Thompson	14.52
44	Eddie Mathews	14.47
45	Wade Boggs	14.26
46	Mickey Cochrane	14.22
47	Andy Thornton	14.20
48	Augie Galan	14.16
49	Gene Woodling	14.15
50	Willie McCovey	14.10
51	Hank Greenberg	14.09
52	Darrell Porter	14.04
53	Larry Doby	14.01
54	John Mayberry	13.92
55	John Briggs	13.87
56	Bill North	13.85
57	Donie Bush	13.85
58	Wally Schang	13.79
59	Roger Bresnahan	13.74
60	Paul Radford	13.71
61	Steve Braun	13.69
62	Norm Siebern	13.64
63	Bob Allison	13.64
64	Bobby Grich	13.63
65	Al Rosen	13.61
66	Willie Randolph	13.54
67	Toby Harrah	13.48
68	Lee Mazzilli	13.47
69	Norm Cash	13.46
70	Mike Jorgensen	13.46
71	Bob Johnson	13.45
72	Tommy Henrich	13.40
73	Rick Ferrell	13.38
74	Wayne Gross	13.36
75	Carl Yastrzemski	13.34
76	Grady Hatton	13.31
77	Dwight Evans	13.30
78	Jim Lary	13.28
79	Ed Bailey	13.21
80	Jackie Robinson	13.17
81	Jack Graney	13.14
82	Brian Downing	13.13
83	Eddie Collins	13.10
84	Rick Monday	13.09
85	Don Mincher	13.08
86	Pee Wee Reese	13.06
87	Jeff Burroughs	13.05
88	Stan Hack	13.05
89	Gary Roenicke	13.04
90	Boog Powell	13.03
91	Jimmy Sheckard	12.99
92	Charlie Maxwell	12.98
93	Gorman Thomas	12.97
94	Andy Seminick	12.92
95	Don Buford	12.86
96	Luke Appling	12.82
97	John Milner	12.79
98	Ron Fairly	12.77
99	Sid Gordon	12.77
100	Snuffy Stirnweiss	12.77

Strikeouts

1	Reggie Jackson	2597
2	Willie Stargell	1936
3	Mike Schmidt	1883
4	Tony Perez	1867
5	Dave Kingman	1816
6	Bobby Bonds	1757
7	Lou Brock	1730
8	Mickey Mantle	1710
9	Harmon Killebrew	1699
10	Dwight Evans	1570
	Lee May	1570
12	Dick Allen	1556
13	Willie McCovey	1550
14	Frank Robinson	1532
15	Willie Mays	1526
16	Rick Monday	1513
17	Dale Murphy	1497
18	Greg Luzinski	1495
19	Eddie Mathews	1487
20	Frank Howard	1460
21	Jim Wynn	1427
22	Jim Rice	1423
23	George Foster	1419
24	George Scott	1418
25	Darrell Evans	1410
26	Carl Yastrzemski	1393
27	Hank Aaron	1383
28	Larry Parrish	1359
29	Ron Santo	1343
30	Gorman Thomas	1339
31	Dave Parker	1337
32	Babe Ruth	1330
33	Deron Johnson	1318
34	Willie Horton	1313
35	Jimmie Foxx	1311
36	Johnny Bench	1278
	Bobby Grich	1278
38	Ken Singleton	1246
39	Claudell Washington	1241
40	Duke Snider	1237
41	Ernie Banks	1236
42	Ron Cey	1235
43	Roberto Clemente	1230
44	Boog Powell	1226
45	Dave Winfield	1224
46	Graig Nettles	1209
47	Tony Armas	1201
48	Vada Pinson	1196
49	Dave Concepcion	1186
50	Carlton Fisk	1178
51	Orlando Cepeda	1170
52	Lance Parrish	1148
53	Pete Rose	1143
54	Bert Campaneris	1142
55	Donn Clendenon	1140
56	Gil Hodges	1137
57	Jeff Burroughs	1135
	Leo Cardenas	1135
59	Andre Dawson	1134
60	Jack Clark	1130
61	Bob Bailey	1126
62	Gary Matthews	1125
63	Jim Fregosi	1097
64	Joe Torre	1094
65	Norm Cash	1091
66	Tony Taylor	1083
67	Tommy Harper	1080
68	Fred Lynn	1072
69	Don Baylor	1069
70	Johnny Callison	1064
71	Joe Adcock	1059
72	Doug Rader	1055
73	Billy Williams	1046
74	Bob Allison	1033
75	Jose Cruz	1031
76	Reggie Smith	1030
77	Rod Carew	1028
78	Darrell Porter	1025
79	Al Kaline	1020
80	Ken Boyer	1017
81	George Hendrick	1015
	Lloyd Moseby	1015
83	George Hendrick	1013
84	Eddie Murray	1012
85	Larry Doby	1011
86	Amos Otis	1008
	Robin Yount	1008
88	Steve Garvey	1003
	Frank White	1003
90	Gene Tenace	998
91	Keith Hernandez	995
	Garry Templeton	995
93	Brooks Robinson	990
94	Chris Speier	988
95	Jesse Barfield	977
	Willie Davis	977
97	Dick McAuliffe	974
98	Chet Lemon	963
	Jim Sundberg	963
100	Dolph Camilli	961

At Bats per Strikeout

1	Joe Sewell	62.6
2	Lloyd Waner	44.9
3	Nellie Fox	42.7
4	Tommy Holmes	40.9
5	Andy High	33.8
6	Sam Rice	33.7
7	Frankie Frisch	33.5
8	Dale Mitchell	33.5
9	Johnny Cooney	31.5
10	Frank McCormick	30.3
11	Don Mueller	29.9
12	Billy Southworth	29.5
13	Rip Radcliff	28.9
14	Edd Roush	28.3
15	Pie Traynor	27.2
16	Doc Cramer	26.5
17	Carson Bigbee	26.0
18	Hank Severeid	25.5
19	George Sisler	25.3
20	Paul Waner	25.2
21	Sparky Adams	24.9
22	Lou Finney	24.9
23	Deacon White	24.8
24	Jack Rowe	24.8
25	Irish Meusel	24.6
26	Ezra Sutton	24.6
27	Red Schoendienst	24.5
28	Vic Power	24.5
29	Arky Vaughan	24.0
30	Felix Millan	23.9
31	Mickey Cochrane	23.8
32	Charlie Gehringer	23.8
33	Monte Ward	23.5
34	George Kell	23.4
35	George Cutshaw	23.2
36	Jack Tobin	23.1
37	Taffy Wright	23.1
38	Hughie Critz	23.1
39	Mark Koenig	22.5
40	Ernie Lombardi	22.3
41	Heinie Manush	22.2
42	Bobby Richardson	22.2
43	Jo-Jo Moore	22.0
44	Earl Sheely	21.8
45	Bill Dickey	21.8
46	Johnny Pesky	21.8
47	Rick Ferrell	21.8
48	Glenn Beckert	21.4
49	Dick Siebert	21.2
50	Eddie Waitkus	20.9
51	Max Flack	20.8
52	Bill Buckner	20.7
53	Dixie Walker	20.7
54	Everett Scott	20.7
55	Earle Combs	20.7
56	Paul Hines	20.6
57	Freddy Lindstrom	20.3
58	Mickey Owen	20.2
59	Joe Vosmik	20.1
60	Lou Boudreau	19.5
61	Milt Stock	19.5
62	Willard Marshall	19.3
63	Debs Garms	19.3
64	Charlie Grimm	19.3
65	Harry Rice	19.3
66	Skeeter Newsome	19.2
67	Curt Walker	19.1
68	Peanuts Lowrey	19.1
69	Charlie Jamieson	19.0
70	Muddy Ruel	19.0
71	Tommy Griffith	18.9
72	Tommy Thevenow	18.8
73	Joe Stripp	18.6
74	Joe DiMaggio	18.5
75	Bob Fothergill	18.5
76	Bing Miller	18.3
77	Riggs Stephenson	18.3
78	Yogi Berra	18.2
79	Billy Herman	18.0
80	Lee Magee	18.0
81	Dave Cash	18.0
82	Elmer Valo	17.7
83	Heinie Groh	17.6
84	Luke Sewell	17.5
85	Tony Gwynn	17.5
86	Rich Dauer	17.5
87	Buddy Lewis	17.4
88	Billy Goodman	17.2
89	Jim Gilliam	17.1
90	Harvey Kuenn	17.1
91	Gus Mancuso	17.1
92	Jimmy Wilson	17.1
93	Billy Cox	17.0
94	Ken Williams	16.9
95	Don Mattingly	16.9
96	George Case	16.9
97	Cecil Travis	16.9
98	Johnny Ray	16.8
99	Luke Appling	16.8
100	Jackie Hayes	16.8

Batting Average

1	Ty Cobb	.366
2	Rogers Hornsby	.358
3	Joe Jackson	.356
4	Wade Boggs	.352
5	Ed Delahanty	.346
6	Ted Williams	.344
7	Billy Hamilton	.344
8	Tris Speaker	.344
9	Dan Brouthers	.342
10	Babe Ruth	.342
11	Harry Heilmann	.342
12	Pete Browning	.341
13	Willie Keeler	.341
14	Bill Terry	.341
15	George Sisler	.340
16	Lou Gehrig	.340
17	Jesse Burkett	.338
18	Nap Lajoie	.338
19	Riggs Stephenson	.336
20	Al Simmons	.334
21	John McGraw	.334
22	Paul Waner	.333
23	Eddie Collins	.333
24	Mike Donlin	.333
25	Tony Gwynn	.332
26	Stan Musial	.331
27	Sam Thompson	.331
28	Heinie Manush	.330
29	Cap Anson	.329
30	Rod Carew	.328
31	Honus Wagner	.327
32	Tip O'Neill	.326
33	Bob Fothergill	.325
34	Jimmie Foxx	.325
35	Earle Combs	.325
36	Joe DiMaggio	.325
37	Babe Herman	.324
38	Hugh Duffy	.324
39	Joe Medwick	.324
40	Don Mattingly	.323
41	Edd Roush	.323
42	Sam Rice	.322
43	Ross Youngs	.322
44	Kiki Cuyler	.321
45	Charlie Gehringer	.320
46	Chuck Klein	.320
47	Pie Traynor	.320
48	Mickey Cochrane	.320
49	Ken Williams	.319
50	Earl Averill	.318
51	Arky Vaughan	.318
52	Roberto Clemente	.317
53	Chick Hafey	.317
54	Joe Kelley	.317
55	Zach Wheat	.317
56	Roger Connor	.317
57	Lloyd Waner	.316
58	Frankie Frisch	.316
59	Goose Goslin	.316
60	George VanHaltren	.316
61	Bibb Falk	.314
62	Cecil Travis	.314
63	Hank Greenberg	.313
64	Jack Fournier	.313
65	Elmer Flick	.313
66	Bill Dickey	.313
67	Dale Mitchell	.312
68	Johnny Mize	.312
69	Joe Sewell	.312
70	Fred Clarke	.312
71	Barney McCosky	.312
72	Bing Miller	.312
73	Hughie Jennings	.311
74	Freddy Lindstrom	.311
75	Jackie Robinson	.311
76	Baby Doll Jacobson	.311
77	Taffy Wright	.311
78	Rip Radcliff	.311
79	Ginger Beaumont	.311
80	Mike Tiernan	.311
81	Denny Lyons	.310
82	Luke Appling	.310
83	Irish Meusel	.310
84	Mike Smith	.310
85	George Brett	.310
86	Bobby Veach	.310
87	Jim O'Rourke	.310
88	John Stone	.310
89	Jim Bottomley	.310
90	Sam Crawford	.309
91	Bob Meusel	.309
92	Jack Tobin	.309
93	Spud Davis	.308
94	Pedro Guerrero	.308
95	Richie Ashburn	.308
96	King Kelly	.308
97	Jake Beckley	.308
98	Stuffy McInnis	.307
99	Joe Vosmik	.307
100	Frank Baker	.307

Batting Average (by era)

1876-1892

1	Dan Brouthers	.342
2	Pete Browning	.341
3	Sam Thompson	.331
4	Cap Anson	.329
5	Tip O'Neill	.326
6	Roger Connor	.317
7	Denny Lyons	.310
8	Jim O'Rourke	.310
9	King Kelly	.308
10	Deacon White	.303
11	Henry Larkin	.303
12	Buck Ewing	.303
13	George Gore	.301
14	Paul Hines	.301
15	Oyster Burns	.300

1893-1919

1	Ty Cobb	.366
2	Joe Jackson	.356
3	Ed Delahanty	.346
4	Billy Hamilton	.344
5	Tris Speaker	.344
6	Willie Keeler	.341
7	Jesse Burkett	.338
8	Nap Lajoie	.338
9	John McGraw	.334
10	Eddie Collins	.333
11	Mike Donlin	.333
12	Honus Wagner	.327
13	Hugh Duffy	.324
14	Joe Kelley	.317
15	Zach Wheat	.317

1920-1941

1	Rogers Hornsby	.358
2	Babe Ruth	.342
3	Harry Heilmann	.342
4	Bill Terry	.341
5	George Sisler	.340
6	Lou Gehrig	.340
7	Riggs Stephenson	.336
8	Al Simmons	.334
9	Paul Waner	.333
10	Heinie Manush	.330
11	Bob Fothergill	.325
12	Jimmie Foxx	.325
13	Earle Combs	.325
14	Babe Herman	.324
15	Joe Medwick	.324

1942-1960

1	Ted Williams	.344
2	Stan Musial	.331
3	Joe DiMaggio	.325
4	Dale Mitchell	.312
5	Johnny Mize	.312
6	Barney McCosky	.312
7	Jackie Robinson	.311
8	Taffy Wright	.311
9	Richie Ashburn	.308
10	Johnny Pesky	.307
11	George Kell	.306
12	Dixie Walker	.306
13	Harvey Kuenn	.303
14	Tommy Holmes	.302
15	Enos Slaughter	.300

1961-1989

1	Wade Boggs	.352
2	Tony Gwynn	.332
3	Rod Carew	.328
4	Don Mattingly	.323
5	Roberto Clemente	.317
6	George Brett	.310
7	Pedro Guerrero	.308
8	Matty Alou	.307
9	Ralph Garr	.306
10	Hank Aaron	.305
11	Bill Madlock	.305
12	Tony Oliva	.304
13	Manny Mota	.304
14	Al Oliver	.303
15	Pete Rose	.303

Batting Average (by position)

First Base

1	Dan Brouthers	.342
2	Bill Terry	.341
3	George Sisler	.340
4	Lou Gehrig	.340
5	Cap Anson	.329
6	Rod Carew	.328
7	Jimmie Foxx	.325
8	Roger Connor	.317
9	Hank Greenberg	.313
10	Jack Fournier	.313

Second Base

1	Rogers Hornsby	.358
2	Nap Lajoie	.338
3	Eddie Collins	.333
4	Charlie Gehringer	.320
5	Frankie Frisch	.316
6	Cupid Childs	.306
7	Billy Herman	.304
8	Buddy Myer	.303
9	Del Pratt	.292
10	Tony Lazzeri	.292

Shortstop

1	Honus Wagner	.327
2	Arky Vaughan	.318
3	Joe Sewell	.312
4	Luke Appling	.310
5	Ed McKean	.303
6	Joe Cronin	.301
7	Lou Boudreau	.295
8	George Davis	.295
9	Glenn Wright	.294
10	Robin Yount	.292

Third Base

1	Wade Boggs	.352
2	Pie Traynor	.320
3	Denny Lyons	.310
4	George Brett	.310
5	Frank Baker	.307
6	George Kell	.306
7	Bill Madlock	.305
8	Stan Hack	.301
9	Pinky Whitney	.295
10	Carney Lansford	.294

Outfield

1	Ty Cobb	.366
2	Joe Jackson	.356
3	Ed Delahanty	.346
4	Ted Williams	.344
5	Billy Hamilton	.344
6	Tris Speaker	.344
7	Babe Ruth	.342
8	Harry Heilmann	.342
9	Willie Keeler	.341
10	Jesse Burkett	.338

Catcher

1	Mickey Cochrane	.320
2	Bill Dickey	.313
3	Spud Davis	.308
4	Ernie Lombardi	.306
5	Gabby Hartnett	.297
6	Manny Sanguillen	.296
7	Smoky Burgess	.295
8	Thurman Munson	.292
9	Hank Severeid	.289
10	Jack Clements	.286

Relative Batting Average

1	Ty Cobb	134.8
2	Wade Boggs	134.2
3	Joe Jackson	133.1
4	Pete Browning	131.5
5	Ted Williams	128.1
6	Dan Brouthers	127.8
7	Nap Lajoie	127.3
8	Tony Gwynn	127.1
9	Rod Carew	127.0
10	Rogers Hornsby	126.2
11	Tris Speaker	125.2
12	Tip O'Neill	125.2
13	Willie Keeler	124.6
14	Stan Musial	123.9
15	Mike Donlin	123.6
16	Don Mattingly	123.3
17	Honus Wagner	123.1
18	Billy Hamilton	122.7
19	Ed Delahanty	122.7
20	Cap Anson	122.7
21	Jesse Burkett	121.7
22	Eddie Collins	121.6
23	Sam Thompson	121.1
24	Roberto Clemente	120.7
25	Tony Oliva	120.4
26	Harry Heilmann	119.4
27	Babe Ruth	119.2
28	George Sisler	118.9
29	Sam Crawford	118.9
30	George Brett	118.4
31	King Kelly	118.2
32	Jim O'Rourke	118.1
33	Matty Alou	117.9
34	Joe Medwick	117.8
35	Paul Waner	117.8
36	Elmer Flick	117.4
37	Roger Connor	117.4
38	Pedro Guerrero	117.3
39	Bill Terry	117.3
40	Lou Gehrig	117.2
41	Joe DiMaggio	117.1
42	Ginger Beaumont	117.0
43	Ralph Garr	116.7
44	Manny Mota	116.4
45	Dale Mitchell	116.3
46	John McGraw	116.2
47	Henry Larkin	116.2
48	Deacon White	116.0
49	Hank Aaron	116.0
50	Paul Hines	115.8
51	George Gore	115.7
52	Jackie Robinson	115.7
53	Pete Rose	115.6
54	Tim Raines	115.5
55	Edd Roush	115.5
56	Al Simmons	115.4
57	Frank Baker	115.4
58	Al Kaline	115.4
59	Bill Madlock	115.2
60	Arky Vaughan	115.1
61	Al Oliver	115.1
62	Riggs Stephenson	115.0
63	Mickey Mantle	115.0
64	Johnny Mize	114.9
65	Zach Wheat	114.9
66	Hugh Duffy	114.8
67	George Kell	114.8
68	Barney McCosky	114.7
69	Richie Ashburn	114.6
70	Hardy Richardson	114.6
71	Johnny Pesky	114.5
72	Harvey Kuenn	114.5
73	Rico Carty	114.4
74	Willie Mays	114.3
75	Paul Molitor	114.1
76	Fred Clarke	114.0
77	Heinie Manush	114.0
78	Cy Seymour	113.9
79	Jimmie Foxx	113.8
80	Joe Torre	113.8
81	Cecil Cooper	113.5
82	Jim Rice	113.5
83	Julio Franco	113.5
84	Frank Robinson	113.4
85	Taffy Wright	113.4
86	Tommy Davis	113.4
87	Minnie Minoso	113.1
88	Tommy Holmes	113.0
89	Joe Kelley	112.9
90	Orlando Cepeda	112.9
91	Denny Lyons	112.9
92	Mickey Rivers	112.9
93	Keith Hernandez	112.8
94	Bake McBride	112.8
95	Manny Sanguillen	112.8
96	Thurman Munson	112.8
97	Hal Chase	112.7
98	Heinie Zimmerman	112.7
99	Ross Youngs	112.7
100	John Reilly	112.6

On Base Percentage

1	Ted Williams	.483
2	Babe Ruth	.474
3	John McGraw	.460
4	Billy Hamilton	.455
5	Lou Gehrig	.447
6	Wade Boggs	.446
7	Rogers Hornsby	.434
8	Ty Cobb	.432
9	Jimmie Foxx	.428
10	Tris Speaker	.427
11	Ferris Fain	.425
12	Eddie Collins	.424
13	Max Bishop	.423
	Dan Brouthers	.423
	Joe Jackson	.423
	Mickey Mantle	.423
17	Mickey Cochrane	.419
18	Stan Musial	.418
19	Cupid Childs	.414
	Mel Ott	.414
21	Jesse Burkett	.413
22	Hank Greenberg	.412
23	Ed Delahanty	.410
	Harry Heilmann	.410
	Charlie Keller	.410
	Jackie Robinson	.410
	Eddie Stanky	.410
28	Roy Cullenbine	.408
	Roy Thomas	.408
30	Denny Lyons	.407
	Riggs Stephenson	.407
32	Joe Cunningham	.406
	Arky Vaughan	.406
34	Charlie Gehringer	.404
	Paul Waner	.404
36	Pete Browning	.403
37	Lu Blue	.402
	Rickey Henderson	.402
39	Mike Hargrove	.400
40	Luke Appling	.399
	Joe Kelley	.399
	Elmer Valo	.399
	Ross Youngs	.399
44	Joe DiMaggio	.398
	Ralph Kiner	.398
46	Richie Ashburn	.397
	Earle Combs	.397
	Roger Connor	.397
	Johnny Mize	.397
	Mike Smith	.397
51	Cap Anson	.395
	Earl Averill	.395
	Rod Carew	.395
	Joe Morgan	.395
	Hack Wilson	.395
	Eddie Yost	.395
57	Stan Hack	.394
	Johnny Pesky	.394
	Tim Raines	.394
60	Bob Johnson	.393
	Wally Schang	.393
	Bill Terry	.393
	Ken Williams	.393
64	Jack Fournier	.392
	George Grantham	.392
	Tip O'Neill	.392
	Frank Robinson	.392
	Mike Tiernan	.392
69	Tony Gwynn	.391
	Minnie Minoso	.391
	Joe Sewell	.391
	Ken Singleton	.391
	Gene Tenace	.391
74	Harlond Clift	.390
	Joe Cronin	.390
	Augie Galan	.390
77	Bernie Carbo	.389
	Keith Hernandez	.389
	Buddy Myer	.389
80	Dolph Camilli	.388
	Mike Griffin	.388
	Gene Woodling	.388
83	Larry Doby	.387
	Goose Goslin	.387
	Willie Mays	.387
	Earl Torgeson	.387
	Honus Wagner	.387
88	Kiki Cuyler	.386
	George Gore	.386
	Pedro Guerrero	.386
	Barney McCosky	.386
	Al Rosen	.386
93	George VanHaltren	.385
94	Hugh Duffy	.384
	Elbie Fletcher	.384
	Dummy Hoy	.384
	Hughie Jennings	.384
	Willie Keeler	.384
	Mike Schmidt	.384
	Sam Thompson	.384

Slugging Average

1	Babe Ruth	.690
2	Ted Williams	.634
3	Lou Gehrig	.632
4	Jimmie Foxx	.609
5	Hank Greenberg	.605
6	Joe DiMaggio	.579
7	Rogers Hornsby	.577
8	Johnny Mize	.562
9	Stan Musial	.559
10	Willie Mays	.557
11	Mickey Mantle	.557
12	Hank Aaron	.555
13	Ralph Kiner	.548
14	Hack Wilson	.545
15	Chuck Klein	.543
16	Duke Snider	.540
17	Frank Robinson	.537
18	Al Simmons	.535
19	Dick Allen	.534
20	Earl Averill	.534
21	Mel Ott	.533
22	Babe Herman	.532
23	Ken Williams	.530
24	Willie Stargell	.529
25	Mike Schmidt	.527
26	Chick Hafey	.526
27	Hal Trosky	.522
28	Wally Berger	.522
29	Don Mattingly	.521
30	Harry Heilmann	.520
31	Dan Brouthers	.519
32	Charlie Keller	.518
33	Joe Jackson	.517
34	Willie McCovey	.515
35	Ty Cobb	.512
36	Eddie Mathews	.509
37	Jeff Heath	.509
38	Harmon Killebrew	.509
39	Bob Johnson	.506
40	Bill Terry	.506
41	Ed Delahanty	.505
42	Sam Thompson	.505
43	Joe Medwick	.505
44	Pedro Guerrero	.504
45	Jim Rice	.502
46	George Brett	.501
47	Jim Bottomley	.500
48	Tris Speaker	.500
49	Goose Goslin	.500
50	Roy Campanella	.500
51	Ernie Banks	.500
52	Orlando Cepeda	.499
53	Bob Horner	.499
54	Frank Howard	.499
55	Ted Kluszewski	.498
56	Bob Meusel	.497
57	Hank Sauer	.496
58	Kent Hrbek	.496
59	George Bell	.495
60	Al Rosen	.495
61	Billy Williams	.492
62	Eddie Murray	.492
63	Ripper Collins	.492
64	Dolph Camilli	.492
65	Tommy Henrich	.491
66	Larry Doby	.490
67	Reggie Jackson	.490
68	Dick Stuart	.489
69	Reggie Smith	.489
70	Gabby Hartnett	.489
71	Rocky Colavito	.489
72	Norm Cash	.488
73	Fred Lynn	.488
74	Gil Hodges	.487
75	Andre Dawson	.486
76	Bill Dickey	.486
77	Gus Zernial	.486
78	Roger Connor	.486
79	Joe Adcock	.485
80	Wally Post	.485
81	Jack Fournier	.483
82	Rudy York	.483
83	Yogi Berra	.482
84	Dale Murphy	.481
85	Dave Winfield	.481
86	Charlie Gehringer	.480
87	Jack Clark	.480
88	George Foster	.480
89	Wade Boggs	.480
90	Al Kaline	.480
91	Heinie Manush	.479
92	Dave Parker	.479
93	Gavvy Cravath	.478
94	Dave Kingman	.478
95	Mickey Cochrane	.478
96	Greg Luzinski	.478
97	Dwight Evans	.477
98	Tony Oliva	.476
99	Roger Maris	.476
100	Johnny Bench	.476

Production

1	Babe Ruth	1.163
2	Ted Williams	1.116
3	Lou Gehrig	1.080
4	Jimmie Foxx	1.038
5	Hank Greenberg	1.017
6	Rogers Hornsby	1.010
7	Mickey Mantle	.979
8	Joe DiMaggio	.977
	Stan Musial	.977
10	Johnny Mize	.959
11	Mel Ott	.947
12	Ralph Kiner	.946
13	Ty Cobb	.945
14	Willie Mays	.944
15	Dan Brouthers	.942
16	Joe Jackson	.940
	Hack Wilson	.940
18	Hank Aaron	.932
19	Harry Heilmann	.930
20	Frank Robinson	.929
21	Earl Averill	.928
	Charlie Keller	.928
23	Tris Speaker	.927
24	Wade Boggs	.926
25	Ken Williams	.924
26	Chuck Klein	.922
27	Duke Snider	.921
28	Ed Delahanty	.915
	Babe Herman	.915
	Al Simmons	.915
31	Dick Allen	.914
32	Mike Schmidt	.912
33	Bob Johnson	.899
	Bill Terry	.899
35	Chick Hafey	.898
36	Mickey Cochrane	.897
37	Don Mattingly	.894
38	Willie McCovey	.892
	Willie Stargell	.892
	Hal Trosky	.892
41	Pedro Guerrero	.890
42	Eddie Mathews	.888
	Sam Thompson	.888
44	Goose Goslin	.887
	Billy Hamilton	.887
	Harmon Killebrew	.887
47	Charlie Gehringer	.884
48	Roger Connor	.883
	Jackie Robinson	.883
50	George Brett	.882
	Al Rosen	.882
52	Wally Berger	.881
53	Dolph Camilli	.880
	Riggs Stephenson	.880
55	Jeff Heath	.879
56	Larry Doby	.877
	Paul Waner	.877
58	Jack Fournier	.875
59	Tommy Henrich	.873
60	John McGraw	.871
61	Pete Browning	.870
62	Jim Bottomley	.869
63	Bill Dickey	.868
64	Kent Hrbek	.867
	Joe Medwick	.867
66	Norm Cash	.865
67	Eddie Murray	.864
68	Roy Campanella	.861
	Jack Clark	.861
70	Jesse Burkett	.860
	Kiki Cuyler	.860
72	Earle Combs	.859
	Al Kaline	.859
	Reggie Smith	.859
	Arky Vaughan	.859
76	Gabby Hartnett	.858
	Jim Rice	.858
78	Gavvy Cravath	.857
	Joe Cronin	.857
80	Heinie Manush	.856
	Billy Williams	.856
82	George Grantham	.854
	Mike Tiernan	.854
84	Frank Howard	.853
	Fred Lynn	.853
	Honus Wagner	.853
87	Orlando Cepeda	.852
	Eddie Collins	.852
	Ripper Collins	.852
	Ted Kluszewski	.852
	Bob Meusel	.852
92	Rocky Colavito	.851
	Mike Donlin	.851
	Minnie Minoso	.851
95	Dwight Evans	.850
	Joe Kelley	.850
	Denny Lyons	.850
	Tip O'Neill	.850
99	Bob Nieman	.849
100	2 players tied	.848

Adjusted Production

1	Babe Ruth	209
2	Ted Williams	186
3	Lou Gehrig	181
4	Rogers Hornsby	176
5	Mickey Mantle	173
6	Dan Brouthers	171
7	Ty Cobb	168
	Joe Jackson	168
9	Pete Browning	166
10	Jimmie Foxx	162
11	Johnny Mize	157
	Stan Musial	157
13	Hank Aaron	156
	Joe DiMaggio	156
	Willie Mays	156
	Tris Speaker	156
17	Dick Allen	155
	Ed Delahanty	155
	Hank Greenberg	155
	Mel Ott	155
21	Roger Connor	154
	Charlie Keller	154
	Frank Robinson	154
24	Nap Lajoie	151
25	Elmer Flick	150
	Honus Wagner	150
27	Wade Boggs	149
	Gavvy Cravath	149
	Pedro Guerrero	149
	Harry Heilmann	149
31	Ralph Kiner	148
	Willie McCovey	148
	Willie Stargell	148
	Sam Thompson	148
35	Mike Schmidt	147
36	Eddie Mathews	145
	Don Mattingly	145
	Hack Wilson	145
39	Sam Crawford	144
	Mike Donlin	144
	Harry Stovey	144
42	Frank Howard	143
	Henry Larkin	143
44	Jesse Burkett	142
	Eddie Collins	142
	Jack Fournier	142
	Harmon Killebrew	142
48	George Brett	141
	Jack Clark	141
	Billy Hamilton	141
	Babe Herman	141
	Denny Lyons	141
	Eddie Murray	141
	Tip O'Neill	141
55	Jeff Heath	140
	Reggie Jackson	140
	Bob Johnson	140
	Mike Tiernan	140
59	Cap Anson	139
	Wally Berger	139
	Duke Snider	139
62	Norm Cash	138
	Al Rosen	138
64	Oyster Burns	137
	Sherry Magee	137
	Gene Tenace	137
	Bill Terry	137
68	Larry Doby	136
	King Kelly	136
	John McGraw	136
	Reggie Smith	136
	Arky Vaughan	136
	Dave Winfield	136
74	Frank Baker	135
	Dolph Camilli	135
	Chuck Klein	135
	Ken Williams	135
78	Orlando Cepeda	134
	George Gore	134
	Rickey Henderson	134
	Al Kaline	134
	Jim O'Rourke	134
	Boog Powell	134
84	Frank Chance	133
	Fred Clarke	133
	Rocky Colavito	133
	Tony Gwynn	133
	Chick Hafey	133
	Charlie Hickman	133
	Paul Hines	133
	Joe Morgan	133
	Bob Nieman	133
	Paul Waner	133
94	Earl Averill	132
	Tommy Henrich	132
	Joe Kelley	132
	Joe Medwick	132
	Bill Nicholson	132
	Tim Raines	132
	Ken Singleton	132

Batting Runs

1	Babe Ruth	1322
2	Ted Williams	1166
3	Ty Cobb	1033
4	Stan Musial	983
5	Lou Gehrig	918
6	Hank Aaron	878
7	Rogers Hornsby	843
8	Tris Speaker	841
9	Willie Mays	827
10	Jimmie Foxx	803
	Mickey Mantle	803
12	Frank Robinson	773
13	Mel Ott	767
14	Honus Wagner	663
15	Dan Brouthers	648
16	Carl Yastrzemski	617
17	Eddie Collins	604
18	Mike Schmidt	592
19	Cap Anson	564
20	Roger Connor	563
21	Nap Lajoie	555
22	Ed Delahanty	544
23	Harmon Killebrew	532
24	Willie McCovey	524
25	Jesse Burkett	522
26	Johnny Mize	520
27	Harry Heilmann	517
28	Al Kaline	513
29	Joe DiMaggio	507
30	Sam Crawford	504
31	Billy Hamilton	491
32	Paul Waner	490
33	Willie Stargell	483
34	Eddie Mathews	480
35	George Brett	474
36	Dick Allen	469
37	Hank Greenberg	468
	Reggie Jackson	468
39	Billy Williams	463
40	Joe Jackson	452
41	Duke Snider	441
42	Joe Morgan	438
43	Rod Carew	431
44	Pete Rose	416
45	Dwight Evans	406
46	Al Simmons	399
47	Ralph Kiner	391
48	Norm Cash	390
49	Joe Kelley	388
50	Wade Boggs	383
	Fred Clarke	383
52	Reggie Smith	379
53	Charlie Gehringer	376
	Sam Thompson	376
55	Chuck Klein	375
56	Eddie Murray	372
57	Pete Browning	369
	Jim Rice	369
59	Bob Johnson	366
60	Arky Vaughan	361
61	Harry Stovey	360
62	Roberto Clemente	353
	Joe Medwick	353
64	Willie Keeler	350
65	Ron Santo	345
66	Goose Goslin	340
67	Orlando Cepeda	337
	Dave Winfield	337
69	Elmer Flick	335
70	Earl Averill	334
	Zach Wheat	334
72	Ken Singleton	332
73	Sherry Magee	330
74	Frank Howard	324
75	King Kelly	321
76	Dolph Camilli	319
77	Keith Hernandez	318
	Rusty Staub	318
	Bill Terry	318
80	Fred Lynn	314
81	Jimmy Ryan	311
82	Jack Clark	310
83	Mike Tiernan	309
84	Enos Slaughter	306
85	Boog Powell	305
	Hack Wilson	305
87	Babe Herman	304
88	Jim O'Rourke	303
89	Minnie Minoso	299
90	Joe Torre	298
91	George Gore	297
92	Rocky Colavito	296
93	Jake Beckley	292
	Tony Perez	292
95	Greg Luzinski	291
96	Ernie Banks	288
97	Hugh Duffy	286
	Charlie Keller	286
99	Jack Fournier	285
100	John McGraw	282

Adjusted Batting Runs

1	Babe Ruth	1357
2	Ted Williams	1089
3	Ty Cobb	1025
4	Lou Gehrig	963
5	Stan Musial	927
6	Hank Aaron	901
7	Rogers Hornsby	858
8	Mickey Mantle	838
9	Willie Mays	837
10	Tris Speaker	809
11	Mel Ott	772
12	Jimmie Foxx	768
13	Frank Robinson	754
14	Honus Wagner	646
15	Dan Brouthers	634
16	Eddie Collins	620
17	Ed Delahanty	562
	Nap Lajoie	562
19	Mike Schmidt	561
20	Roger Connor	552
21	Willie McCovey	538
22	Eddie Mathews	535
23	Harry Heilmann	534
24	Joe DiMaggio	522
25	Carl Yastrzemski	513
26	Reggie Jackson	507
27	Johnny Mize	505
28	Jesse Burkett	500
29	Harmon Killebrew	498
30	Willie Stargell	486
31	Sam Crawford	485
32	Al Kaline	484
33	Joe Morgan	476
34	Paul Waner	473
35	Cap Anson	466
36	Dick Allen	463
37	George Brett	460
38	Joe Jackson	442
39	Joe Jackson	439
40	Hank Greenberg	434
41	Rod Carew	419
42	Duke Snider	407
43	Eddie Murray	404
44	Billy Williams	401
45	Bob Johnson	389
46	Pete Browning	387
47	Dave Winfield	386
48	Pete Rose	382
49	Fred Clarke	379
50	Ralph Kiner	373
51	Norm Cash	369
52	Al Simmons	367
53	Sam Thompson	364
54	Roberto Clemente	362
55	Goose Goslin	359
56	Wade Boggs	357
	Arky Vaughan	357
58	Ken Singleton	350
59	Reggie Smith	349
60	Elmer Flick	345
	Frank Howard	345
62	Charlie Gehringer	342
63	Zach Wheat	341
64	Dwight Evans	340
65	Orlando Cepeda	339
66	Joe Kelley	338
67	Bill Terry	332
68	Rusty Staub	331
69	Jack Clark	328
70	Sherry Magee	327
71	Keith Hernandez	326
72	Chuck Klein	324
	Mike Tiernan	324
74	Harry Stovey	323
75	Babe Herman	318
76	Joe Medwick	317
77	Jake Beckley	313
78	Hack Wilson	311
79	Willie Keeler	310
80	Boog Powell	309
81	Joe Torre	304
82	Earl Averill	303
83	Jack Fournier	301
84	Jim O'Rourke	300
85	Jim Rice	299
86	Minnie Minoso	298
87	Charlie Keller	296
88	Rickey Henderson	292
89	Rocky Colavito	291
90	Fred Lynn	284
91	Jim Wynn	283
92	Pedro Guerrero	282
	Ron Santo	282
94	Dolph Camilli	281
95	Larry Doby	276
96	Bobby Bonds	274
97	George VanHaltren	273
98	George Davis	272
	Tony Perez	272
100	Darrell Evans	270

Batting Wins

1	Babe Ruth	127.5
2	Ted Williams	115.9
3	Ty Cobb	106.6
4	Stan Musial	99.7
5	Hank Aaron	91.1
6	Tris Speaker	85.9
7	Willie Mays	85.5
8	Lou Gehrig	85.4
9	Rogers Hornsby	84.8
10	Mickey Mantle	82.9
11	Frank Robinson	80.7
12	Mel Ott	76.2
13	Jimmie Foxx	75.3
14	Honus Wagner	68.5
15	Carl Yastrzemski	64.3
16	Eddie Collins	62.0
17	Mike Schmidt	61.8
18	Nap Lajoie	57.0
19	Dan Brouthers	56.7
20	Harmon Killebrew	55.8
21	Willie McCovey	54.9
22	Sam Crawford	53.6
23	Al Kaline	53.4
24	Johnny Mize	52.2
25	Willie Stargell	51.0
26	Harry Heilmann	50.8
27	Cap Anson	49.9
28	Dick Allen	49.8
29	Roger Connor	49.3
30	Eddie Mathews	49.2
31	Joe DiMaggio	48.6
32	Billy Williams	48.6
33	Paul Waner	48.5
34	Reggie Jackson	48.1
35	Ed Delahanty	48.0
36	Jesse Burkett	47.9
37	George Brett	47.8
38	Joe Jackson	47.4
39	Joe Morgan	45.9
40	Rod Carew	44.7
41	Hank Greenberg	44.5
42	Duke Snider	44.4
43	Pete Rose	43.9
44	Billy Hamilton	42.8
45	Norm Cash	41.1
46	Dwight Evans	40.9
47	Reggie Smith	40.3
48	Ralph Kiner	39.1
49	Wade Boggs	38.1
50	Fred Clarke	37.4
51	Al Simmons	37.4
52	Eddie Murray	37.3
53	Jim Rice	37.1
54	Roberto Clemente	36.7
55	Chuck Klein	36.7
56	Arky Vaughan	36.4
57	Ron Santo	36.3
58	Sherry Magee	35.7
59	Joe Kelley	35.7
60	Joe Medwick	35.7
61	Bob Johnson	35.2
62	Charlie Gehringer	35.1
63	Orlando Cepeda	35.1
64	Frank Howard	34.4
65	Zach Wheat	34.4
66	Dave Winfield	34.3
67	Elmer Flick	34.1
68	Ken Singleton	34.0
69	Willie Keeler	33.8
70	Rusty Staub	33.3
71	Keith Hernandez	33.2
72	Sam Thompson	32.6
73	Boog Powell	32.4
74	Jack Clark	32.3
75	Dolph Camilli	32.2
76	Pete Browning	32.1
77	Goose Goslin	31.8
78	Harry Stovey	31.6
79	Fred Lynn	31.6
80	Joe Torre	31.4
81	Enos Slaughter	30.9
82	Earl Averill	30.8
83	Bill Terry	30.8
84	Rocky Colavito	30.7
85	Tony Perez	30.6
86	Minnie Minoso	30.3
87	Greg Luzinski	30.1
88	Ernie Banks	29.8
89	Gavvy Cravath	29.6
90	Hack Wilson	29.5
91	Babe Herman	29.5
92	Dale Murphy	29.1
93	Tony Oliva	28.9
94	King Kelly	28.8
95	Jack Fournier	28.8
96	Charlie Keller	28.5
97	Bobby Bonds	28.4
98	Pedro Guerrero	28.4
99	Cy Williams	28.4
100	Darrell Evans	27.9

Adjusted Batting Wins

1	Babe Ruth	130.9
2	Ted Williams	108.2
3	Ty Cobb	105.7
4	Stan Musial	94.0
5	Hank Aaron	93.4
6	Lou Gehrig	89.6
7	Willie Mays	86.5
8	Mickey Mantle	86.5
9	Rogers Hornsby	86.3
10	Tris Speaker	82.6
11	Frank Robinson	78.7
12	Mel Ott	76.7
13	Jimmie Foxx	72.0
14	Honus Wagner	66.7
15	Eddie Collins	63.6
16	Mike Schmidt	58.6
17	Nap Lajoie	57.7
18	Willie McCovey	56.4
19	Dan Brouthers	55.5
20	Eddie Mathews	54.8
21	Carl Yastrzemski	53.4
22	Harry Heilmann	52.4
23	Harmon Killebrew	52.2
24	Reggie Jackson	52.1
25	Sam Crawford	51.6
26	Willie Stargell	51.3
27	Johnny Mize	50.7
28	Al Kaline	50.4
29	Joe DiMaggio	50.1
30	Joe Morgan	49.9
31	Ed Delahanty	49.6
32	Dick Allen	49.2
33	Roger Connor	48.3
34	Paul Waner	46.8
35	George Brett	46.4
36	Joe Jackson	46.0
37	Jesse Burkett	45.9
38	Rod Carew	43.5
39	Billy Williams	42.1
40	Cap Anson	41.3
41	Hank Greenberg	41.3
42	Duke Snider	41.0
43	Eddie Murray	40.5
44	Pete Rose	40.3
45	Dave Winfield	39.3
46	Norm Cash	38.9
47	Billy Hamilton	38.6
48	Roberto Clemente	37.7
49	Bob Johnson	37.4
50	Ralph Kiner	37.3
51	Reggie Smith	37.1
52	Fred Clarke	37.0
53	Frank Howard	36.7
54	Arky Vaughan	36.0
55	Ken Singleton	35.8
56	Wade Boggs	35.5
57	Sherry Magee	35.4
58	Orlando Cepeda	35.3
59	Elmer Flick	35.2
60	Zach Wheat	35.1
61	Rusty Staub	34.7
62	Al Simmons	34.4
63	Dwight Evans	34.3
64	Jack Clark	34.1
65	Keith Hernandez	34.1
66	Goose Goslin	33.6
67	Pete Browning	33.6
68	Boog Powell	32.8
69	Bill Terry	32.1
70	Joe Medwick	32.1
71	Joe Torre	32.0
72	Charlie Gehringer	31.9
73	Chuck Klein	31.7
74	Sam Thompson	31.6
75	Joe Kelley	31.1
76	Babe Herman	30.9
77	Jack Fournier	30.4
78	Rocky Colavito	30.2
79	Minnie Minoso	30.2
80	Hack Wilson	30.1
81	Jim Rice	30.1
82	Willie Keeler	30.0
83	Jim Wynn	29.9
84	Ron Santo	29.6
85	Pedro Guerrero	29.6
86	Charlie Keller	29.5
87	Rickey Henderson	29.2
88	Jake Beckley	28.6
89	Fred Lynn	28.5
90	Tony Perez	28.5
91	Bobby Bonds	28.4
92	Harry Stovey	28.4
93	Dolph Camilli	28.4
94	Mike Tiernan	28.1
95	Earl Averill	28.0
96	Darrell Evans	27.9
97	Greg Luzinski	27.9
98	Larry Doby	27.5
99	Gavvy Cravath	27.5
100	Johnny Bench	27.4

Runs Created

1	Babe Ruth	2841
2	Ty Cobb	2801
3	Stan Musial	2625
4	Hank Aaron	2550
5	Ted Williams	2538
6	Willie Mays	2372
7	Tris Speaker	2320
8	Lou Gehrig	2317
9	Mel Ott	2235
10	Pete Rose	2220
11	Honus Wagner	2203
12	Jimmie Foxx	2190
13	Carl Yastrzemski	2147
14	Frank Robinson	2126
15	Rogers Hornsby	2074
16	Mickey Mantle	2070
17	Eddie Collins	2050
18	Nap Lajoie	1875
19	Paul Waner	1851
20	Al Kaline	1846
21	Ed Delahanty	1821
22	Joe Morgan	1804
23	Jesse Burkett	1785
	Charlie Gehringer	1785
25	Reggie Jackson	1772
26	Al Simmons	1771
27	Mike Schmidt	1757
28	Cap Anson	1751
29	Eddie Mathews	1738
30	Goose Goslin	1702
31	Sam Crawford	1700
32	Billy Hamilton	1698
33	Harry Heilmann	1693
34	Billy Williams	1671
35	Jake Beckley	1654
36	Roger Connor	1645
37	Fred Clarke	1639
38	Willie McCovey	1638
39	Willie Keeler	1633
40	Dan Brouthers	1622
41	Harmon Killebrew	1609
42	Joe DiMaggio	1606
43	George Davis	1605
44	Rod Carew	1595
45	Red Rolfe	1579
46	George Brett	1563
47	Roberto Clemente	1557
	George VanHaltren	1557
49	Jimmy Ryan	1549
50	Zach Wheat	1539
51	Rusty Staub	1534
52	Willie Stargell	1531
53	Tony Perez	1523
54	Ernie Banks	1513
55	Lou Brock	1512
56	Joe Kelley	1510
57	Dwight Evans	1508
58	Johnny Mize	1502
59	Darrell Evans	1499
60	Sam Rice	1497
61	Hugh Duffy	1495
62	Luke Appling	1493
63	George Sisler	1492
64	Duke Snider	1487
65	Bill Dahlen	1473
66	Max Carey	1471
67	Frankie Frisch	1465
68	Enos Slaughter	1432
69	Joe Cronin	1426
70	Dave Winfield	1424
71	Bob Johnson	1418
72	Vada Pinson	1394
73	Heinie Manush	1387
	Mickey Vernon	1387
75	Richie Ashburn	1386
76	Jim Bottomley	1384
77	Jim Rice	1382
78	Robin Yount	1381
79	Ron Santo	1379
80	Chuck Klein	1378
81	Joe Medwick	1372
82	Eddie Murray	1363
83	Earl Averill	1358
	Brooks Robinson	1358
85	Harry Hooper	1349
86	Al Oliver	1348
87	Orlando Cepeda	1338
88	Kiki Cuyler	1336
89	Bid McPhee	1334
90	Hank Greenberg	1331
91	Arky Vaughan	1323
92	Dave Parker	1314
93	Sherry Magee	1311
94	Joe Judge	1306
95	Sam Thompson	1296
96	Dick Allen	1290
97	Yogi Berra	1284
	Lave Cross	1284
	Ted Simmons	1284
100	2 players tied	1278

Total Average

1	Babe Ruth	1.421
2	Ted Williams	1.323
3	Lou Gehrig	1.249
4	Billy Hamilton	1.190
5	Jimmie Foxx	1.156
6	John McGraw	1.135
7	Rogers Hornsby	1.117
8	Hank Greenberg	1.112
9	Mickey Mantle	1.098
10	Ty Cobb	1.091
11	Dan Brouthers	1.061
12	Mel Ott	1.036
13	Stan Musial	1.033
14	Ed Delahanty	1.031
15	Tris Speaker	1.030
16	Joe Jackson	1.027
17	Rickey Henderson	1.016
18	Joe DiMaggio	1.014
19	Charlie Keller	1.008
20	Ralph Kiner	1.007
21	Johnny Mize	1.006
	Hack Wilson	1.006
23	Willie Mays	.995
24	Harry Heilmann	.976
	Ken Williams	.976
26	Tim Raines	.975
27	Frank Robinson	.971
28	Earl Averill	.970
29	Mike Tiernan	.969
30	Mike Schmidt	.968
31	Eddie Collins	.966
32	Mickey Cochrane	.961
33	Wade Boggs	.960
34	Denny Lyons	.954
35	Joe Kelley	.953
36	Roger Connor	.952
37	Hank Aaron	.948
	Jackie Robinson	.948
39	Pete Browning	.946
40	Chuck Klein	.944
41	Babe Herman	.942
	Duke Snider	.942
43	Dick Allen	.941
44	Sam Thompson	.939
	Honus Wagner	.939
46	Jesse Burkett	.937
47	Bob Johnson	.933
	Joe Morgan	.933
49	Hugh Duffy	.929
50	Dolph Camilli	.928
51	Charlie Gehringer	.926
52	Eddie Mathews	.922
	Harry Stovey	.922
54	Goose Goslin	.917
55	Willie McCovey	.915
	Al Simmons	.915
57	Harmon Killebrew	.913
58	Chick Hafey	.910
59	Jack Fournier	.909
	Mike Smith	.909
61	Gavvy Cravath	.907
	Kiki Cuyler	.907
	Mike Donlin	.907
64	Mike Griffin	.905
65	Riggs Stephenson	.903
66	Larry Doby	.902
67	Pedro Guerrero	.901
	Bill Terry	.901
69	Tommy Henrich	.899
70	George Grantham	.897
	Tip O'Neill	.897
72	Cupid Childs	.896
73	Hal Trosky	.895
74	Elmer Flick	.894
	Arky Vaughan	.894
76	Willie Stargell	.892
77	Roy Cullenbine	.888
78	Al Rosen	.887
	Paul Waner	.887
80	George Brett	.885
81	Frank Chance	.884
82	Jeff Heath	.882
83	Norm Cash	.880
	George VanHaltren	.880
85	Jack Clark	.878
	Tony Lazzeri	.878
87	Kirk Gibson	.875
88	Bobby Bonds	.873
	Oyster Burns	.873
	Fred Clarke	.873
91	Earle Combs	.872
	Joe Cronin	.872
93	Wally Berger	.870
94	Harlond Clift	.868
	Gene Tenace	.868
96	Cap Anson	.867
97	Jimmy Ryan	.866
98	Max Bishop	.865
	Jim Bottomley	.865
	Hughie Jennings	.865

Runs Produced

1	Ty Cobb	4060
2	Hank Aaron	3716
3	Babe Ruth	3669
4	Cap Anson	3501
5	Stan Musial	3425
6	Lou Gehrig	3385
7	Honus Wagner	3367
8	Pete Rose	3319
9	Willie Mays	3305
10	Tris Speaker	3292
11	Mel Ott	3208
	Carl Yastrzemski	3208
13	Jimmie Foxx	3139
14	Ted Williams	3116
15	Jake Beckley	3088
16	Eddie Collins	3071
17	Frank Robinson	3055
18	Al Simmons	3027
19	Nap Lajoie	3018
20	Charlie Gehringer	3017
21	Ed Delahanty	2962
22	George Davis	2901
23	Rogers Hornsby	2862
24	Goose Goslin	2844
25	Paul Waner	2822
26	Sam Crawford	2818
27	Al Kaline	2806
28	Roger Connor	2805
29	Hugh Duffy	2747
30	Bill Dahlen	2735
31	Dan Brouthers	2712
32	Reggie Jackson	2690
33	Frankie Frisch	2671
34	Mickey Mantle	2650
35	Harry Heilmann	2646
36	Jimmy Ryan	2617
37	Jesse Burkett	2597
38	George VanHaltren	2584
39	Fred Clarke	2567
40	Joe DiMaggio	2566
41	Sam Rice	2558
42	Mike Schmidt	2553
43	Joe Kelley	2550
44	Tony Perez	2545
45	Joe Morgan	2515
46	Willie Keeler	2495
47	Joe Cronin	2487
48	Roberto Clemente	2481
49	Billy Williams	2459
50	Eddie Mathews	2450
51	Ernie Banks	2429
52	Sam Thompson	2428
53	Herman Long	2417
54	Jim O'Rourke	2406
55	Zach Wheat	2405
56	Pie Traynor	2398
57	Dave Winfield	2395
58	Luke Appling	2390
59	Billy Hamilton	2386
60	Enos Slaughter	2382
61	Jim Bottomley	2380
62	Joe Medwick	2376
63	Rusty Staub	2363
64	Lou Brock	2361
65	Heinie Manush	2360
66	George Sisler	2358
67	Rod Carew	2347
68	George Brett	2344
69	Mickey Vernon	2335
70	Brooks Robinson	2321
71	Jim Rice	2318
72	Al Oliver	2296
73	Harmon Killebrew	2294
74	Dwight Evans	2286
75	Tommy Corcoran	2285
76	Darrell Evans	2284
77	Vada Pinson	2280
78	Max Carey	2276
79	Willie McCovey	2263
80	Willie Stargell	2260
81	Robin Yount	2251
82	Monte Ward	2249
83	Yogi Berra	2247
84	King Kelly	2238
85	Bob Johnson	2234
86	Kiki Cuyler	2232
87	Ted Simmons	2215
88	Sherry Magee	2205
89	Dave Parker	2189
90	Duke Snider	2185
91	Steve Garvey	2179
92	Don Baylor	2174
93	Harry Hooper	2171
94	Doc Cramer	2162
95	Joe Kuhel	2154
96	Earl Averill	2150
97	Joe Judge	2147
98	Joe Sewell	2145
99	Bobby Wallace	2144
100	Ron Santo	2127

Clutch Hitting Index

1	Cap Anson	139
2	Duffy Lewis	136
	Earl Sheely	136
	Pie Traynor	136
5	Bobby Veach	135
6	Kitty Bransfield	132
7	Tommy Thevenow	131
8	Tommy Davis	130
	Chick Gandil	130
	Sherry Magee	130
	Sam Mertes	130
	Possum Whitted	130
13	Larry Gardner	129
	Stuffy McInnis	129
	Pinky Whitney	129
	Heinie Zimmerman	129
17	Red Smith	128
18	Frank Chance	127
	Bob Elliott	127
	Ted Simmons	127
	Patsy Tebeau	127
22	Rube Bressler	126
	Harry Steinfeldt	126
	Glenn Wright	126
25	Frank McCormick	125
	Fred Pfeffer	125
	Enos Slaughter	125
	Gus Suhr	125
29	Gavvy Cravath	124
	Joe Cronin	124
	George Cutshaw	124
	Bob Fothergill	124
	Hughie Jennings	124
	Frank LaPorte	124
	Cookie Lavagetto	124
	Dots Miller	124
	Red Murray	124
	Billy Nash	124
	Lee Tannehill	124
	Ned Williamson	124
	Taffy Wright	124
42	Frank Baker	123
	Tom Burns	123
	Ferris Fain	123
	Jackie Jensen	123
	Keith Moreland	123
	Luke Sewell	123
	Billy Sullivan	123
	Bobby Wallace	123
	Vic Wertz	123
	Deacon White	123
52	Frank Bowerman	122
	Roy Campanella	122
	Tony Cuccinello	122
	Art Devlin	122
	Del Ennis	122
	Art Fletcher	122
	Harry Heilmann	122
	Solly Hofman	122
	Willie Kamm	122
	Sam Mele	122
	Willie Montanez	122
	Muddy Ruel	122
	Ray Schalk	122
65	Lou Criger	121
	Ron Fairly	121
	Steve Kemp	121
	Dan McGann	121
	Tony Perez	121
	Boog Powell	121
	Joe Sewell	121
	Riggs Stephenson	121
	Joe Tinker	121
74	Steve Brodie	120
	Tommy Corcoran	120
	Walt Dropo	120
	Kid Elberfeld	120
	Bibb Falk	120
	Carl Furillo	120
	Keith Hernandez	120
	Mike Higgins	120
	George Kelly	120
	Tony Lazzeri	120
	Irish Meusel	120
	Mike Mowrey	120
	Del Pratt	120
	Elmer Smith	120
	Dick Stuart	120
	Honus Wagner	120
	Bob Watson	120
91	Sal Bando	119
	Duke Farrell	119
	Hank Majeski	119
	Frank Malzone	119
	Joe Medwick	119
	Jimmy Wilson	119
	Hack Wilson	119
	Rudy York	119
99	20 players tied	117

Isolated Power

1	Babe Ruth	.348
2	Lou Gehrig	.292
3	Hank Greenberg	.292
4	Ted Williams	.289
5	Jimmie Foxx	.284
6	Ralph Kiner	.269
7	Mike Schmidt	.260
8	Mickey Mantle	.259
9	Willie Mays	.256
10	Joe DiMaggio	.254
11	Harmon Killebrew	.252
12	Johnny Mize	.250
13	Hank Aaron	.250
14	Willie Stargell	.247
15	Willie McCovey	.245
16	Duke Snider	.244
17	Frank Robinson	.243
18	Dave Kingman	.242
19	Dick Allen	.242
20	Eddie Mathews	.238
21	Hack Wilson	.238
22	Charlie Keller	.231
23	Hank Sauer	.230
24	Mel Ott	.229
25	Stan Musial	.228
26	Reggie Jackson	.228
27	Dick Stuart	.225
28	Ernie Banks	.225
29	Frank Howard	.225
30	Roy Campanella	.224
31	Chuck Klein	.223
32	Gorman Thomas	.223
33	Rocky Colavito	.223
34	Bob Horner	.222
35	Wally Berger	.221
36	Gus Zernial	.221
37	Wally Post	.220
38	Hal Trosky	.219
39	Rogers Hornsby	.218
40	Norm Cash	.217
41	Bob Allison	.217
42	Roger Maris	.216
43	Earl Averill	.216
44	Jeff Heath	.216
45	Dolph Camilli	.215
46	Gil Hodges	.214
47	Jesse Barfield	.212
48	Dale Murphy	.212
49	Ken Williams	.211
50	Jack Clark	.210
51	Al Rosen	.210
52	Bob Johnson	.210
53	Tommy Henrich	.209
54	Chick Hafey	.209
55	Johnny Bench	.208
56	Roy Sievers	.208
57	Rudy York	.208
58	Joe Adcock	.208
59	Nate Colbert	.207
60	Babe Herman	.207
61	Larry Doby	.207
62	George Bell	.207
63	George Foster	.206
64	Kent Hrbek	.206
65	Andre Dawson	.205
66	Dwight Evans	.204
67	Jim Rice	.204
68	Fred Lynn	.203
69	Bobby Bonds	.203
70	Orlando Cepeda	.203
71	Billy Williams	.202
72	Greg Luzinski	.202
73	Cliff Johnson	.202
74	Reggie Smith	.202
75	Kirk Gibson	.201
76	Al Simmons	.201
77	Don Mincher	.201
78	Eddie Murray	.200
79	Tony Armas	.200
80	Ted Kluszewski	.200
81	Leon Durham	.199
82	Jim Lemon	.198
83	Andy Thornton	.198
84	Bill Nicholson	.198
85	Dale Long	.198
86	Yogi Berra	.198
87	Joe Gordon	.197
88	Don Mattingly	.197
89	Pedro Guerrero	.196
90	Tom Brunansky	.196
91	Boog Powell	.196
92	Ripper Collins	.196
93	Don Demeter	.195
94	Lance Parrish	.194
95	Dave Winfield	.194
96	Carlton Fisk	.193
97	Lee May	.192
98	Vic Wertz	.192
99	Mack Jones	.192
100	Gabby Hartnett	.192

Extra Base Hits

1	Hank Aaron	1477
2	Stan Musial	1377
3	Babe Ruth	1356
4	Willie Mays	1323
5	Lou Gehrig	1190
6	Frank Robinson	1186
7	Carl Yastrzemski	1157
8	Ty Cobb	1136
9	Tris Speaker	1133
10	Jimmie Foxx	1117
	Ted Williams	1117
12	Reggie Jackson	1075
13	Mel Ott	1071
14	Pete Rose	1041
15	Mike Schmidt	1015
16	Rogers Hornsby	1011
17	Ernie Banks	1009
18	Al Simmons	995
19	Honus Wagner	993
20	Al Kaline	972
21	Tony Perez	963
22	Willie Stargell	953
23	Mickey Mantle	952
24	Billy Williams	948
25	Eddie Mathews	938
26	Goose Goslin	921
27	Willie McCovey	920
28	Paul Waner	906
29	Charlie Gehringer	904
30	Nap Lajoie	903
31	George Brett	901
32	Dwight Evans	891
33	Harmon Killebrew	887
34	Joe DiMaggio	881
35	Harry Heilmann	876
36	Vada Pinson	868
37	Sam Crawford	865
38	Joe Medwick	858
39	Duke Snider	850
40	Dave Parker	847
41	Roberto Clemente	846
42	Dave Winfield	843
43	Rusty Staub	838
44	Jim Bottomley	835
45	Jim Rice	834
46	Al Oliver	825
47	Orlando Cepeda	823
48	Brooks Robinson	818
49	Joe Morgan	813
50	Roger Connor	811
51	Johnny Mize	809
52	Ed Delahanty	808
53	Jake Beckley	803
	Joe Cronin	803
55	Robin Yount	800
56	Johnny Bench	794
57	Mickey Vernon	782
58	Hank Greenberg	781
59	Zach Wheat	780
60	Darrell Evans	779
	Bob Johnson	779
62	Ted Simmons	778
63	Lou Brock	776
64	Ron Santo	774
65	Chuck Klein	772
66	Dan Brouthers	771
67	Andre Dawson	770
68	Earl Averill	767
69	Heinie Manush	761
70	Eddie Murray	759
71	Steve Garvey	755
72	Carlton Fisk	753
73	Dick Allen	750
74	Cap Anson	749
75	Graig Nettles	746
76	Hal McRae	741
77	Reggie Smith	734
78	Don Baylor	732
79	Enos Slaughter	730
80	Yogi Berra	728
81	Fred Lynn	727
82	Jimmy Ryan	726
83	Lee May	725
84	Bill Buckner	720
85	Sam Rice	716
86	Willie Davis	715
	Del Ennis	715
88	Gil Hodges	713
89	Frankie Frisch	709
90	Dave Kingman	707
91	Cecil Cooper	703
92	George Foster	702
93	Bobby Bonds	700
94	Gabby Hartnett	696
95	Cesar Cedeno	695
96	Bobby Doerr	693
97	Babe Herman	690
	George Sisler	690
99	George Davis	688
100	Dale Murphy	683

Pinch Hits

1	Manny Mota	150
2	Smoky Burgess	145
3	Greg Gross	143
4	Jose Morales	123
5	Jerry Lynch	116
6	Red Lucas	114
7	Steve Braun	113
8	Terry Crowley	108
9	Gates Brown	107
10	Mike Lum	103
11	Rusty Staub	100
12	Jim Dwyer	96
13	Larry Biittner	95
	Vic Davalillo	95
15	Jerry Hairston	94
16	Dave Philley	93
	Denny Walling	93
	Joel Youngblood	93
19	Jay Johnstone	92
20	Ed Kranepool	90
	Elmer Valo	90
22	Jesus Alou	82
	Kurt Bevacqua	82
	Tim McCarver	82
25	Dave Collins	79
	Tom Hutton	79

Pinch Hit Average

1	Tommy Davis	.320
2	Frenchy Bordagaray	.312
3	Frankie Baumholtz	.307
4	Red Schoendienst	.303
5	Bob Fothergill	.300
6	Dave Philley	.299
7	Manny Mota	.297
8	Ted Easterly	.296
9	Rance Mulliniks	.296
10	Harvey Hendrick	.295
11	Larry Herndon	.294
12	Manny Sanguillen	.288
13	Thad Bosley	.286
14	Smoky Burgess	.286
15	Rick Miller	.286
16	Ken Griffey	.284
17	Johnny Mize	.283
18	Terry Puhl	.282
19	Bubba Morton	.281
20	Steve Braun	.281
21	Don Mueller	.280
22	Rusty Staub	.279
23	Mickey Vernon	.279
24	Wallace Johnson	.278
25	Gene Woodling	.278

Pinch Hit Home Runs

1	Cliff Johnson	20
2	Jerry Lynch	18
3	Gates Brown	16
	Smoky Burgess	16
	Willie McCovey	16
6	George Crowe	14
7	Joe Adcock	12
	Bob Cerv	12
	Jose Morales	12
	Graig Nettles	12
11	Jeff Burroughs	11
	Jay Johnstone	11
	Fred Whitfield	11
	Cy Williams	11
15	Jim Dwyer	10
	Mike Lum	10
	Ken McMullen	10
	Don Mincher	10
	Wally Post	10
	Champ Summers	10
	Jerry Turner	10
	Gus Zernial	10

Stolen Bases

1	Lou Brock	938
2	Billy Hamilton	912
3	Ty Cobb	892
4	Rickey Henderson	871
5	Eddie Collins	743
6	Arlie Latham	739
7	Max Carey	738
8	Honus Wagner	722
9	Joe Morgan	689
10	Tom Brown	657
11	Bert Campaneris	649
12	George Davis	616
13	Dummy Hoy	594
14	Willie Wilson	588
15	Maury Wills	586
16	Tim Raines	585
17	George VanHaltren	583
18	Hugh Duffy	574
19	Bid McPhee	568
20	Davey Lopes	557
21	Cesar Cedeno	550
22	Bill Dahlen	547
23	Monte Ward	540
24	Herman Long	534
25	Patsy Donovan	518
26	Jack Doyle	515
27	Harry Stovey	509
28	Luis Aparicio	506
	Fred Clarke	506
30	Willie Keeler	495
31	Clyde Milan	494
32	Omar Moreno	487
33	Mike Griffin	473
34	Vince Coleman	472
35	Tommy McCarthy	468
36	Jimmy Sheckard	465
37	Bobby Bonds	461
38	Ed Delahanty	455
	Ron LeFlore	455
40	Curt Welch	453
41	Joe Kelley	443
42	Sherry Magee	441
43	John McGraw	436
44	Tris Speaker	433
45	Ozzie Smith	432
46	Bob Bescher	428
	Mike Tiernan	428
48	Charlie Comiskey	419
	Frankie Frisch	419
50	Jimmy Ryan	418
51	Tommy Harper	408
52	Donie Bush	405
53	Frank Chance	401
54	Bill Lange	399
55	Willie Davis	398
56	Sam Mertes	396
57	Bill North	395
58	Jesse Burkett	389
59	Dave Collins	388
60	Tommy Corcoran	387
61	Tom Daly	385
	Freddie Patek	385
63	George Burns	383
	Hugh Nicol	383
65	Fred Pfeffer	382
66	Nap Lajoie	381
	Walt Wilmot	381
68	Harry Hooper	375
	George Sisler	375
70	Jack Glasscock	372
71	King Kelly	368
72	Sam Crawford	366
	Tommy Dowd	366
74	Hal Chase	363
75	Tommy Leach	361
76	Hughie Jennings	359
	Fielder Jones	359
78	Buck Ewing	354
79	Rod Carew	353
80	Tommy Tucker	352
81	Sam Rice	351
82	George Case	349
83	Paul Radford	346
84	Paul Molitor	344
85	Julio Cruz	343
86	Amos Otis	341
87	John Anderson	338
	Willie Mays	338
89	Lonnie Smith	337
90	Joe Tinker	336
91	Kip Selbach	334
92	Steve Sax	333
93	Elmer Flick	330
94	Jose Cardenal	329
	Ned Hanlon	329
96	Monte Cross	328
	Kiki Cuyler	328
	Kid Gleason	328
99	Jim Fogarty	325
100	2 players tied	324

Stolen Base Average

1	Tim Raines	86.7
2	Willie Wilson	83.9
3	Davey Lopes	83.0
4	Vince Coleman	82.8
5	Julio Cruz	81.5
6	Rickey Henderson	81.3
7	Joe Morgan	81.0
8	Gary Redus	80.6
9	Ozzie Smith	80.4
10	Mickey Mantle	80.1
11	Andy VanSlyke	79.7
12	Enzo Hernandez	79.6
13	Joe Carter	79.4
14	Gary Pettis	79.1
15	Luis Aparicio	78.8
16	Amos Otis	78.6
17	Ryne Sandberg	78.4
18	Kirk Gibson	78.3
19	Tommy Harper	77.9
20	Paul Molitor	77.8
21	Rudy Law	77.8
22	Bob Dernier	77.6
23	Miguel Dilone	77.4
24	Hank Aaron	76.7
25	Willie Mays	76.6
26	Bert Campaneris	76.5
27	Mookie Wilson	76.3
28	Juan Samuel	76.3
29	Ron LeFlore	76.2
30	George Case	76.2
31	Howard Johnson	76.0
32	Willie McGee	75.9
33	Dick Howser	75.5
34	Cesar Cedeno	75.4
35	Lou Brock	75.3
36	Willie Davis	75.2
37	Larry Bowa	75.2
38	Bump Wills	75.1
39	Mickey Rivers	74.8
40	Lloyd Moseby	74.8
41	Dave Concepcion	74.7
42	Willie Randolph	74.6
43	Freddie Patek	74.6
44	Andre Dawson	74.5
45	Alan Bannister	74.5
46	Johnny Temple	74.5
	John Wathan	74.5
48	Bake McBride	74.4
49	Sandy Alomar	73.9
50	Frank Taveras	73.9

Stolen Base Runs

1	Rickey Henderson	141
2	Tim Raines	122
3	Joe Morgan	110
4	Willie Wilson	109
5	Davey Lopes	99
6	Lou Brock	97
7	Vince Coleman	83
8	Bert Campaneris	75
9	Luis Aparicio	70
10	Ozzie Smith	67
11	Cesar Cedeno	58
12	Julio Cruz	56
13	Tommy Harper	53
14	Ron LeFlore	51
	Maury Wills	51
16	Amos Otis	47
17	Paul Molitor	44
	Gary Redus	44
19	Willie Davis	41
20	Willie Mays	40
21	George Case	39
	Gary Pettis	39
23	Bobby Bonds	37
	Omar Moreno	37
	Freddie Patek	37
26	Dave Collins	34
	Ryne Sandberg	34
28	Miguel Dilone	33
	Mookie Wilson	33
30	Larry Bowa	32
	Juan Samuel	32
32	Dave Concepcion	31
33	Rudy Law	29
	Lonnie Smith	29
35	Hank Aaron	28
	Bob Dernier	28
	Kirk Gibson	28
38	Andre Dawson	27
	Willie McGee	27
	Andy VanSlyke	27
41	Mickey Rivers	26
	Frank Taveras	26
43	Lloyd Moseby	25
	Willie Randolph	25
45	Mickey Mantle	23
46	Al Bumbry	21
	Bill North	21
	Gene Richards	21
49	Sandy Alomar	20
	Bump Wills	20

Stolen Base Wins

1	Rickey Henderson	14.1
2	Tim Raines	12.8
3	Joe Morgan	11.5
4	Willie Wilson	10.9
5	Davey Lopes	10.2
6	Lou Brock	10.2
7	Vince Coleman	8.7
8	Bert Campaneris	7.9
9	Luis Aparicio	7.3
10	Ozzie Smith	7.0
11	Cesar Cedeno	6.1
12	Tommy Harper	5.6
13	Julio Cruz	5.6
14	Maury Wills	5.3
15	Ron LeFlore	5.2
16	Amos Otis	4.9
17	Gary Redus	4.5
18	Paul Molitor	4.4
19	Willie Davis	4.3
20	Willie Mays	4.1
21	George Case	3.9
22	Gary Pettis	3.9
23	Freddie Patek	3.8
24	Omar Moreno	3.8
25	Bobby Bonds	3.8
26	Ryne Sandberg	3.6
27	Dave Collins	3.5
28	Mookie Wilson	3.5
29	Miguel Dilone	3.4
30	Larry Bowa	3.3
31	Juan Samuel	3.3
32	Dave Concepcion	3.2
33	Lonnie Smith	3.0
34	Bob Dernier	2.9
35	Rudy Law	2.9
36	Hank Aaron	2.9
37	Kirk Gibson	2.8
38	Andre Dawson	2.8
39	Andy VanSlyke	2.8
40	Willie McGee	2.8
41	Frank Taveras	2.7
42	Mickey Rivers	2.7
43	Willie Randolph	2.5
44	Lloyd Moseby	2.5
45	Mickey Mantle	2.4
46	Gene Richards	2.2
47	Bill North	2.2
48	Al Bumbry	2.1
49	Sandy Alomar	2.1
50	Bump Wills	2.0

Games

First Base
1	Jake Beckley	2377
2	Mickey Vernon	2237
3	Lou Gehrig	2137
4	Charlie Grimm	2131
5	Joe Judge	2084
6	Ed Konetchy	2073
7	Steve Garvey	2059
8	Cap Anson	2058
9	Joe Kuhel	2057
10	Willie McCovey	2045

Second Base
1	Eddie Collins	2650
2	Joe Morgan	2527
3	Nellie Fox	2295
4	Charlie Gehringer	2206
5	Bid McPhee	2125
6	Bill Mazeroski	2094
7	Frank White	2071
8	Nap Lajoie	2035
9	Bobby Doerr	1852
10	Willie Randolph	1842

Shortstop
1	Luis Aparicio	2581
2	Larry Bowa	2222
3	Luke Appling	2218
4	Dave Concepcion	2176
5	Rabbit Maranville	2153
6	Bill Dahlen	2132
7	Bert Campaneris	2097
8	Tommy Corcoran	2073
9	Roy McMillan	2028
10	Pee Wee Reese	2014

Third Base
1	Brooks Robinson	2870
2	Graig Nettles	2412
3	Mike Schmidt	2209
4	Buddy Bell	2181
	Eddie Mathews	2181
6	Ron Santo	2130
7	Eddie Yost	2008
8	Ron Cey	1989
9	Aurelio Rodriguez	1983
10	Sal Bando	1896

Outfield
1	Ty Cobb	2935
2	Willie Mays	2843
3	Hank Aaron	2760
4	Tris Speaker	2698
5	Lou Brock	2507
6	Al Kaline	2488
7	Max Carey	2421
8	Vada Pinson	2403
9	Roberto Clemente	2370
10	Zach Wheat	2337

Catcher
1	Bob Boone	2185
2	Carlton Fisk	1928
3	Jim Sundberg	1927
4	Al Lopez	1918
5	Gary Carter	1823
6	Rick Ferrell	1806
7	Gabby Hartnett	1793
8	Ted Simmons	1772
9	Johnny Bench	1744
10	Ray Schalk	1727

Pitcher
1	Hoyt Wilhelm	1070
2	Kent Tekulve	1050
3	Lindy McDaniel	987
4	Rollie Fingers	944
5	Gene Garber	931
6	Sparky Lyle	899
7	Jim Kaat	898
8	Cy Young	889
9	Don McMahon	874
10	Phil Niekro	864

Fielding Average

First Base
1	Steve Garvey	.996
2	Wes Parker	.996
3	Dan Driessen	.995
4	Jim Spencer	.995
5	Frank McCormick	.995
6	Keith Hernandez	.994
7	Vic Power	.994
8	Joe Adcock	.994
9	Mike Jorgensen	.994
10	Ernie Banks	.994

Second Base
1	Ryne Sandberg	.989
2	Tom Herr	.989
3	Jim Gantner	.985
4	Frank White	.984
5	Bobby Grich	.984
6	Jerry Lumpe	.984
7	Cookie Rojas	.984
8	Dave Cash	.984
9	Nellie Fox	.984
10	Tommy Helms	.983

Shortstop
1	Larry Bowa	.980
2	Ozzie Smith	.978
3	Mark Belanger	.977
4	Alan Trammell	.976
5	Bucky Dent	.976
6	Roger Metzger	.976
7	Cal Ripken	.975
8	Tim Foli	.973
9	Dal Maxvill	.973
10	Lou Boudreau	.973

Third Base
1	Brooks Robinson	.971
2	Ken Reitz	.970
3	George Kell	.969
4	Don Money	.968
5	Don Wert	.968
6	Willie Kamm	.967
7	Heinie Groh	.967
8	Ken Oberkfell	.966
9	Gary Gaetti	.966
10	Carney Lansford	.966

Outfield
1	Terry Puhl	.993
2	Pete Rose	.991
3	Brett Butler	.991
4	Amos Otis	.991
5	Joe Rudi	.991
6	Mickey Stanley	.991
7	Jim Piersall	.990
8	Jim Landis	.989
9	Ken Berry	.989
10	Tommy Holmes	.989

Catcher
1	Bill Freehan	.993
2	Elston Howard	.993
3	Jim Sundberg	.993
4	Sherm Lollar	.992
5	Johnny Edwards	.992
6	Tom Haller	.992
7	Jerry Grote	.991
8	Ernie Whitt	.991
9	Gary Carter	.991
10	Lance Parrish	.991

Pitcher
1	Don Mossi	.990
2	Gary Nolan	.990
3	Rick Rhoden	.989
4	Lon Warneke	.988
5	Jim Wilson	.988
6	Woodie Fryman	.988
7	Larry Gura	.986
8	Pete Alexander	.985
9	General Crowder	.984
10	Bill Monbouquette	.984

Total Chances per Game

First Base
1	Tom Jones	11.38
2	George Stovall	11.30
3	George Kelly	11.09
4	Candy LaChance	11.05
5	Wally Pipp	11.05
6	Ed Konetchy	11.04
7	George Burns	10.92
8	Bill Terry	10.91
9	Cap Anson	10.84
10	Walter Holke	10.83
11	Bill Phillips	10.83
12	Fred Tenney	10.83

Second Base
1	Fred Pfeffer	6.95
2	Bid McPhee	6.71
3	Cub Stricker	6.53
4	Lou Bierbauer	6.42
5	Cupid Childs	6.32
6	Ski Melillo	6.16
7	Hughie Critz	6.07
8	Frankie Frisch	6.05
9	Bobby Lowe	6.01
10	Bucky Harris	6.00
11	Nap Lajoie	6.00

Shortstop
1	Dave Bancroft	6.33
2	Herman Long	6.32
3	Bill Dahlen	6.26
4	George Davis	6.22
5	Rabbit Maranville	6.10
6	Bobby Wallace	6.10
7	Tommy Corcoran	6.09
8	Monte Cross	6.06
9	Bones Ely	6.06
10	Honus Wagner	5.99

Third Base
1	Jerry Denny	4.22
2	Billy Shindle	4.15
3	Billy Nash	4.09
4	Arlie Latham	4.04
5	Denny Lyons	3.98
6	Jimmy Collins	3.89
7	Hick Carpenter	3.81
8	Jimmy Austin	3.74
9	Lave Cross	3.73
10	Frank Baker	3.64

Outfield
1	Taylor Douthit	3.16
2	Richie Ashburn	3.04
3	Dom DiMaggio	2.99
4	Mike Kreevich	2.95
5	Dwayne Murphy	2.92
6	Sam Chapman	2.91
7	Sam West	2.88
8	Max Carey	2.87
9	Fred Schulte	2.84
10	Lloyd Waner	2.81

Catcher
1	Johnny Edwards	6.98
2	John Roseboro	6.83
3	Bill Freehan	6.79
4	Mike Scioscia	6.56
5	Jerry Grote	6.53
6	Gary Carter	6.48
7	Tony Pena	6.43
8	Tim McCarver	6.41
9	Tom Haller	6.33
10	Bill Killefer	6.27

Pitcher
1	Nick Altrock	3.72
2	Harry Howell	3.61
3	Addie Joss	3.60
4	Ed Walsh	3.48
5	Nixey Callahan	3.47
6	Willie Sudhoff	3.31
7	George Mullin	3.21
8	Barney Pelty	3.20
9	Chick Fraser	3.12
10	Bill Hart	3.01

Chances Accepted per Game

First Base
1	Tom Jones	11.21
2	George Stovall	11.15
3	George Kelly	11.00
4	Wally Pipp	10.96
5	Ed Konetchy	10.93
6	Candy LaChance	10.87
7	Bill Terry	10.82
8	George Burns	10.77
9	Walter Holke	10.75
10	Stuffy McInnis	10.71

Second Base
1	Fred Pfeffer	6.39
2	Bid McPhee	6.33
3	Lou Bierbauer	6.00
4	Ski Melillo	6.00
5	Cub Stricker	5.92
6	Hughie Critz	5.91
7	Frankie Frisch	5.89
8	Cupid Childs	5.88
9	Bucky Harris	5.79
10	Nap Lajoie	5.78

Shortstop
1	Dave Bancroft	5.98
2	George Davis	5.85
3	Rabbit Maranville	5.81
4	Bill Dahlen	5.80
5	Herman Long	5.78
6	Bobby Wallace	5.73
7	Travis Jackson	5.67
8	Dick Bartell	5.64
9	Tommy Corcoran	5.63
10	Honus Wagner	5.63

Third Base
1	Jerry Denny	3.73
2	Billy Shindle	3.70
3	Billy Nash	3.67
4	Jimmy Collins	3.61
5	Arlie Latham	3.52
6	Denny Lyons	3.51
7	Lave Cross	3.50
8	Jimmy Austin	3.49
9	Frank Baker	3.43
10	Bill Bradley	3.37

Outfield
1	Taylor Douthit	3.07
2	Richie Ashburn	2.98
3	Dom DiMaggio	2.92
4	Mike Kreevich	2.89
5	Dwayne Murphy	2.88
6	Sam Chapman	2.83
7	Sam West	2.83
8	Max Carey	2.77
9	Fred Schulte	2.77
10	Lloyd Waner	2.76

Catcher
1	Johnny Edwards	6.92
2	John Roseboro	6.76
3	Bill Freehan	6.75
4	Mike Scioscia	6.48
5	Jerry Grote	6.47
6	Gary Carter	6.42
7	Tony Pena	6.36
8	Tim McCarver	6.35
9	Tom Haller	6.28
10	Earl Battey	6.15

Pitcher
1	Nick Altrock	3.59
2	Addie Joss	3.47
3	Harry Howell	3.46
4	Ed Walsh	3.35
5	Nixey Callahan	3.25
6	Willie Sudhoff	3.11
7	George Mullin	3.04
8	Barney Pelty	3.00
9	Chick Fraser	2.90
10	Bill Hart	2.84

Putouts

First Base

1	Jake Beckley	23709
2	Ed Konetchy	21361
3	Cap Anson	20759
4	Charlie Grimm	20711
5	Stuffy McInnis	20119
6	Mickey Vernon	19808
7	Jake Daubert	19634
8	Lou Gehrig	19510
9	Joe Kuhel	19386
10	Joe Judge	19264

Second Base

1	Bid McPhee	6545
2	Eddie Collins	6526
3	Nellie Fox	6090
4	Joe Morgan	5742
5	Nap Lajoie	5496
6	Charlie Gehringer	5369
7	Bill Mazeroski	4974
8	Bobby Doerr	4928
9	Billy Herman	4780
10	Fred Pfeffer	4714

Shortstop

1	Rabbit Maranville	5139
2	Bill Dahlen	4850
3	Dave Bancroft	4623
4	Honus Wagner	4576
5	Tommy Corcoran	4550
6	Luis Aparicio	4548
7	Luke Appling	4398
8	Herman Long	4228
9	Bobby Wallace	4142
10	Pee Wee Reese	4040

Third Base

1	Brooks Robinson	2697
2	Jimmy Collins	2372
3	Eddie Yost	2356
4	Lave Cross	2304
5	Pie Traynor	2289
6	Billy Nash	2201
7	Frank Baker	2154
8	Willie Kamm	2151
9	Eddie Mathews	2049
10	Puddin' Head Jones	2045

Outfield

1	Willie Mays	7095
2	Tris Speaker	6787
3	Max Carey	6363
4	Ty Cobb	6361
5	Richie Ashburn	6089
6	Hank Aaron	5539
7	Willie Davis	5449
8	Doc Cramer	5412
9	Vada Pinson	5097
10	Al Kaline	5035

Catcher

1	Bob Boone	11017
2	Gary Carter	10626
3	Bill Freehan	9941
4	Carlton Fisk	9847
5	Jim Sundberg	9767
6	John Roseboro	9291
7	Johnny Bench	9260
8	Johnny Edwards	8925
9	Ted Simmons	8906
10	Yogi Berra	8729

Pitcher

1	Phil Niekro	386
2	Ferguson Jenkins	363
3	Gaylord Perry	349
4	Don Sutton	334
5	Tony Mullane	329
6	Tom Seaver	328
7	Rick Reuschel	327
8	Jim Galvin	324
9	Robin Roberts	316
10	Chick Fraser	315

Putouts per Game

First Base

1	Tom Jones	10.53
2	Candy LaChance	10.48
3	George Stovall	10.45
4	George Kelly	10.37
5	Wally Pipp	10.33
6	Ed Konetchy	10.31
7	Bill Phillips	10.22
8	Walter Holke	10.20
9	Charlie Comiskey	10.15
10	John Reilly	10.12
11	Bill Terry	10.12

Second Base

1	Bid McPhee	3.09
2	Fred Pfeffer	3.07
3	Cub Stricker	2.99
4	Jerry Priddy	2.74
5	Bucky Harris	2.73
6	Nap Lajoie	2.71
7	Bobby Doerr	2.67
8	Lou Bierbauer	2.66
9	Cupid Childs	2.66
10	Nellie Fox	2.66

Shortstop

1	Dave Bancroft	2.47
2	Honus Wagner	2.43
3	Rabbit Maranville	2.39
4	Monte Cross	2.37
5	George Davis	2.36
6	Herman Long	2.36
7	Dick Bartell	2.31
8	Bill Dahlen	2.28
9	Ivy Olson	2.27
10	Bobby Wallace	2.27

Third Base

1	Jerry Denny	1.61
2	Denny Lyons	1.55
3	Billy Nash	1.53
4	Jimmy Austin	1.43
5	Billy Shindle	1.43
6	Jimmy Collins	1.41
7	Frank Baker	1.40
8	Hick Carpenter	1.37
9	Lave Cross	1.34
10	Hans Lobert	1.30

Outfield

1	Taylor Douthit	3.01
2	Richie Ashburn	2.90
3	Dom DiMaggio	2.82
4	Dwayne Murphy	2.82
5	Mike Kreevich	2.81
6	Sam Chapman	2.74
7	Sam West	2.74
8	Fred Schulte	2.70
9	Lloyd Waner	2.68
10	Bill North	2.65

Catcher

1	Johnny Edwards	6.42
2	John Roseboro	6.30
3	Bill Freehan	6.29
4	Jerry Grote	6.00
5	Mike Scioscia	5.94
6	Tim McCarver	5.92
7	Tom Haller	5.85
8	Gary Carter	5.83
9	Tony Pena	5.75
10	Earl Battey	5.69

Pitcher

1	Mike Boddicker	0.79
2	Nick Altrock	0.78
3	Dave Foutz	0.78
4	Dan Petry	0.76
5	Chick Fraser	0.73
6	Jack Morris	0.72
7	Carl Morton	0.72
8	Mel Stottlemyre	0.68
9	Nixey Callahan	0.66
10	Larry Corcoran	0.66

Assists

First Base

1	Keith Hernandez	1662
2	George Sisler	1529
3	Mickey Vernon	1448
4	Eddie Murray	1380
5	Fred Tenney	1363
6	Chris Chambliss	1351
7	Bill Buckner	1345
8	Norm Cash	1317
9	Jake Beckley	1315
10	Joe Judge	1301

Second Base

1	Eddie Collins	7630
2	Charlie Gehringer	7068
3	Joe Morgan	6967
4	Bid McPhee	6905
5	Bill Mazeroski	6685
6	Nellie Fox	6373
7	Nap Lajoie	6262
8	Frank White	6033
9	Frankie Frisch	6026
10	Bobby Doerr	5710

Shortstop

1	Luis Aparicio	8016
2	Bill Dahlen	7500
3	Rabbit Maranville	7354
4	Luke Appling	7218
5	Tommy Corcoran	7106
6	Larry Bowa	6857
7	Dave Concepcion	6594
8	Dave Bancroft	6561
9	Roger Peckinpaugh	6337
10	Bobby Wallace	6303

Third Base

1	Brooks Robinson	6205
2	Graig Nettles	5279
3	Mike Schmidt	5046
4	Buddy Bell	4925
5	Ron Santo	4581
6	Eddie Mathews	4322
7	Aurelio Rodriguez	4150
8	Ron Cey	4018
9	Sal Bando	3720
10	Jimmy Collins	3701
	Lave Cross	3701

Outfield

1	Tris Speaker	448
2	Ty Cobb	392
3	Jimmy Ryan	375
4	George VanHaltren	351
5	Tom Brown	348
6	Harry Hooper	344
7	Max Carey	339
8	Jimmy Sheckard	307
9	Clyde Milan	294
10	Sam Thompson	283

Catcher

1	Deacon McGuire	1859
2	Ray Schalk	1811
3	Steve O'Neill	1698
4	Red Dooin	1590
5	Chief Zimmer	1580
6	Johnny Kling	1552
7	Ivey Wingo	1487
8	Wilbert Robinson	1452
9	Wally Schang	1420
10	Duke Farrell	1417

Pitcher

1	Cy Young	1987
2	Christy Mathewson	1503
3	Pete Alexander	1419
4	Jim Galvin	1390
5	Walter Johnson	1351
6	Burleigh Grimes	1252
7	Jack Quinn	1243
8	George Mullin	1237
9	Ed Walsh	1207
10	Eppa Rixey	1195

Assists per Game

First Base

1	Bill Buckner	0.88
2	Keith Hernandez	0.85
3	Ferris Fain	0.84
4	Vic Power	0.83
5	Pete O'Brien	0.80
6	Eddie Murray	0.79
7	George Sisler	0.78
8	Rudy York	0.77
9	Fred Tenney	0.76
10	Mike Hargrove	0.75
11	Dick Stuart	0.75

Second Base

1	Hughie Critz	3.54
2	Frankie Frisch	3.42
3	Ski Melillo	3.38
4	Lou Bierbauer	3.34
5	Glenn Hubbard	3.34
6	Fred Pfeffer	3.33
7	Rogers Hornsby	3.31
8	Ryne Sandberg	3.31
9	Bid McPhee	3.25
10	Tony Cuccinello	3.23

Shortstop

1	Germany Smith	3.70
2	Art Fletcher	3.56
3	Bill Dahlen	3.52
4	Dave Bancroft	3.51
5	Bones Ely	3.50
6	Travis Jackson	3.50
7	George Davis	3.49
8	Ozzie Smith	3.49
9	Jack Glasscock	3.46
10	Bobby Wallace	3.46

Third Base

1	Mike Schmidt	2.29
2	Billy Shindle	2.27
3	Buddy Bell	2.26
4	Arlie Latham	2.26
5	Clete Boyer	2.24
6	Jimmy Collins	2.20
7	Graig Nettles	2.19
8	George Brett	2.18
9	Darrell Evans	2.17
10	Brooks Robinson	2.17

Outfield

1	Tommy McCarthy	0.23
2	Pop Corkhill	0.22
3	Chicken Wolf	0.22
4	Sam Thompson	0.21
5	Tom Brown	0.20
6	Jimmy Ryan	0.20
7	George VanHaltren	0.20
8	Curt Welch	0.20
9	Ed Delahanty	0.19
10	George Gore	0.19

Catcher

1	Duke Farrell	1.42
2	Red Dooin	1.34
3	Johnny Kling	1.33
4	Bill Killefer	1.32
5	Oscar Stanage	1.29
6	Chief Zimmer	1.28
7	John Warner	1.27
8	Ivey Wingo	1.21
9	Billy Sullivan	1.18
10	George Gibson	1.17

Pitcher

1	Addie Joss	2.96
2	Harry Howell	2.84
3	Nick Altrock	2.81
4	Ed Walsh	2.81
5	Willie Sudhoff	2.73
6	Nixey Callahan	2.60
7	George Mullin	2.57
8	Ed Willett	2.55
9	Barney Pelty	2.51
10	Red Donahue	2.46

Double Plays

First Base

1	Mickey Vernon	2044
2	Joe Kuhel	1769
3	Charlie Grimm	1733
4	Chris Chambliss	1687
5	Keith Hernandez	1626
6	Gil Hodges	1614
7	Eddie Murray	1585
8	Jim Bottomley	1582
9	Lou Gehrig	1574
10	Jimmie Foxx	1528

Second Base

1	Bill Mazeroski	1706
2	Nellie Fox	1619
3	Bobby Doerr	1507
4	Joe Morgan	1505
5	Charlie Gehringer	1444
6	Red Schoendienst	1368
7	Frank White	1331
8	Willie Randolph	1326
9	Bobby Grich	1302
10	Eddie Collins	1215

Shortstop

1	Luis Aparicio	1553
2	Luke Appling	1424
3	Roy McMillan	1304
4	Dave Concepcion	1290
5	Larry Bowa	1265
6	Pee Wee Reese	1246
7	Dick Groat	1237
8	Phil Rizzuto	1217
9	Bert Campaneris	1186
10	Rabbit Maranville	1183

Third Base

1	Brooks Robinson	618
2	Graig Nettles	470
3	Mike Schmidt	450
4	Buddy Bell	430
5	Aurelio Rodriguez	408
6	Ron Santo	395
7	Eddie Mathews	369
8	Ken Boyer	355
9	Sal Bando	345
	Eddie Yost	345

Outfield

1	Tris Speaker	139
2	Ty Cobb	107
3	Max Carey	86
4	Tom Brown	85
5	Harry Hooper	81
6	Jimmy Sheckard	80
7	Mike Griffin	74
8	Dummy Hoy	72
	Jimmy Ryan	72
10	Fielder Jones	70

Catcher

1	Ray Schalk	226
2	Yogi Berra	175
	Steve O'Neill	175
4	Gabby Hartnett	163
5	Bob Boone	154
6	Jimmy Wilson	153
7	Wally Schang	149
8	Jim Sundberg	145
9	Gary Carter	142
	Deacon McGuire	142

Pitcher

1	Phil Niekro	83
2	Warren Spahn	82
3	Freddie Fitzsimmons	79
4	Bob Lemon	78
5	Bucky Walters	76
6	Burleigh Grimes	74
7	Walter Johnson	72
8	Tommy John	69
9	Jim Kaat	65
10	Dizzy Trout	63

Fielding Runs

1	Bill Mazeroski	351
2	Nap Lajoie	300
3	Bill Dahlen	278
4	Bid McPhee	276
5	Ozzie Smith	267
6	Mike Schmidt	242
7	Fred Pfeffer	234
8	George Davis	208
9	Glenn Hubbard	188
10	Jack Glasscock	187
11	Buddy Bell	180
12	Clete Boyer	178
13	Tris Speaker	177
14	Dave Bancroft	176
15	Max Carey	170
	Bobby Wallace	170
17	Bobby Doerr	168
	Joe Tinker	168
19	Richie Ashburn	167
20	Dick Bartell	163
21	Art Fletcher	155
22	Manny Trillo	151
23	Frankie Frisch	150
24	Gary Carter	149
25	Graig Nettles	143
26	Hughie Jennings	142
27	Aurelio Rodriguez	140
28	Bobby Grich	139
29	Lee Tannehill	138
30	Pop Snyder	136
31	Bobby Knoop	135
32	George McBride	134
	Brooks Robinson	134
34	Jimmy Collins	131
35	Darrell Evans	130
36	Ron Santo	129
37	Keith Hernandez	127
38	Fred Dunlap	125
39	Red Schoendienst	123
40	Lou Bierbauer	122
	Mickey Doolan	122
42	Lou Boudreau	121
43	Bill Freehan	120
	Joe Gerhardt	120
45	Ski Melillo	119
46	Danny Richardson	118
47	Mark Belanger	116
48	Gene Alley	115
49	Terry Pendleton	114
	Phil Rizzuto	114
	Roy Smalley	114
52	Roberto Clemente	113
53	Jim Sundberg	110
54	Germany Smith	107
55	Thurman Munson	106
56	Luis Aparicio	105
57	Ryne Sandberg	103
58	Rick Burleson	102
	Fred Tenney	102
60	Lave Cross	101
	Julio Cruz	101
	Johnny Logan	101
	Gil McDougald	101
64	Buck Ewing	100
65	Hobe Ferris	99
66	Luke Appling	98
67	Hughie Critz	97
	Rabbit Maranville	97
69	Willie Mays	96
70	Jim Fogarty	95
71	Del Crandall	94
	Davy Force	94
	Ozzie Guillen	94
	Billy Jurges	94
75	Bill Buckner	93
	Carlton Fisk	93
	Monte Ward	93
78	Ron Hansen	92
	Rickey Henderson	92
	Tony Pena	92
81	Del Pratt	90
82	Billy Herman	89
83	Jerry Denny	88
84	Duke Farrell	87
	Bump Wills	87
86	Dick Groat	86
	Ted Simmons	86
	Curt Welch	86
89	Billy Shindle	85
	George Sisler	85
	Burgess Whitehead	85
92	Tim Foli	84
	Babe Pinelli	84
94	Bill Bergen	83
	Travis Jackson	83
96	Bob Johnson	81
	Vic Power	81
	Hardy Richardson	81
99	Joe Sewell	80
100	6 players tied	78

Fielding Wins

1	Bill Mazeroski	36.5
2	Nap Lajoie	30.8
3	Ozzie Smith	28.0
4	Bill Dahlen	26.5
5	Mike Schmidt	25.3
6	Bid McPhee	24.0
7	Fred Pfeffer	20.4
8	George Davis	19.6
9	Glenn Hubbard	19.5
10	Clete Boyer	18.5
11	Buddy Bell	18.4
12	Tris Speaker	18.1
13	Dave Bancroft	17.9
14	Joe Tinker	17.8
15	Max Carey	17.4
16	Bobby Wallace	17.2
17	Richie Ashburn	16.7
18	Jack Glasscock	16.6
19	Art Fletcher	16.5
20	Bobby Doerr	16.5
21	Dick Bartell	16.0
22	Manny Trillo	15.7
23	Gary Carter	15.6
24	Lee Tannehill	15.0
25	Graig Nettles	14.8
26	Frankie Frisch	14.7
27	Aurelio Rodriguez	14.6
28	Bobby Knoop	14.6
29	George McBride	14.4
30	Bobby Grich	14.2
31	Brooks Robinson	14.1
32	Deacon McGuire	13.7
33	Ron Santo	13.6
34	Darrell Evans	13.4
35	Keith Hernandez	13.3
36	Mickey Doolan	13.1
37	Bill Freehan	12.8
38	Jimmy Collins	12.7
39	Hughie Jennings	12.5
40	Red Schoendienst	12.3
41	Gene Alley	12.2
42	Lou Boudreau	12.1
43	Mark Belanger	12.1
44	Pop Snyder	12.1
45	Terry Pendleton	11.9
46	Roberto Clemente	11.8
47	Roy Smalley	11.4
48	Phil Rizzuto	11.4
49	Fred Dunlap	11.3
50	Jim Sundberg	11.1
51	Ski Melillo	11.1
52	Thurman Munson	11.0
53	Luis Aparicio	11.0
54	Ryne Sandberg	10.8
55	Joe Gerhardt	10.6
56	Hobe Ferris	10.5
57	Rick Burleson	10.3
58	Lou Bierbauer	10.3
59	Danny Richardson	10.3
60	Gil McDougald	10.2
61	Johnny Logan	10.2
62	Julio Cruz	10.1
63	Fred Tenney	10.1
64	Willie Mays	9.9
65	Rabbit Maranville	9.8
66	Ron Hansen	9.7
67	Tony Pena	9.7
68	Bill Buckner	9.6
69	Billy Jurges	9.5
70	Del Crandall	9.5
71	Carlton Fisk	9.4
72	Luke Appling	9.4
73	Hughie Critz	9.4
74	Ozzie Guillen	9.3
75	Lave Cross	9.3
76	Del Pratt	9.3
77	Germany Smith	9.2
78	Rickey Henderson	9.2
79	Billy Herman	9.0
80	Ted Simmons	8.9
81	Dick Groat	8.8
82	Bump Wills	8.8
83	Bill Bergen	8.8
84	Tim Foli	8.7
85	Buck Ewing	8.7
86	Davy Force	8.6
87	Burgess Whitehead	8.5
88	Jim Fogarty	8.4
89	George Sisler	8.4
90	Vic Power	8.3
91	Jim Wynn	8.2
92	Monte Ward	8.2
93	Babe Pinelli	8.1
94	Travis Jackson	8.0
95	Everett Scott	7.9
96	Roy McMillan	7.9
97	Roger Peckinpaugh	7.9
98	Nellie Fox	7.9
99	Maury Wills	7.9
100	Jerry Denny	7.8

Fielding Wins (by position)

First Base

1	Keith Hernandez	13.3
2	Fred Tenney	10.1
3	Bill Buckner	9.6
4	George Sisler	8.4
5	Vic Power	8.3
6	Bill Terry	6.3
7	Ed Konetchy	6.0
8	Eddie Murray	5.3
9	Cap Anson	4.8
10	Fred Luderus	4.7

Second Base

1	Bill Mazeroski	36.5
2	Nap Lajoie	30.8
3	Bid McPhee	24.0
4	Fred Pfeffer	20.4
5	Glenn Hubbard	19.5
6	Bobby Doerr	16.5
7	Manny Trillo	15.7
8	Frankie Frisch	14.7
9	Bobby Knoop	14.6
10	Bobby Grich	14.2

Shortstop

1	Ozzie Smith	28.0
2	Bill Dahlen	26.5
3	George Davis	19.6
4	Dave Bancroft	17.9
5	Joe Tinker	17.8
6	Bobby Wallace	17.2
7	Jack Glasscock	16.6
8	Art Fletcher	16.5
9	Dick Bartell	16.0
10	George McBride	14.4

Third Base

1	Mike Schmidt	25.3
2	Clete Boyer	18.5
3	Buddy Bell	18.4
4	Graig Nettles	14.8
5	Aurelio Rodriguez	14.6
6	Brooks Robinson	14.1
7	Ron Santo	13.6
8	Darrell Evans	13.4
9	Jimmy Collins	12.7
10	Lave Cross	9.3

Outfield

1	Tris Speaker	18.1
2	Max Carey	17.4
3	Richie Ashburn	16.7
4	Roberto Clemente	11.8
5	Willie Mays	9.9
6	Rickey Henderson	9.2
7	Jim Wynn	8.2
8	Bob Johnson	7.8
9	Curt Welch	7.4
10	Tommy Leach	7.3

Catcher

1	Gary Carter	15.6
2	Deacon McGuire	13.7
3	Bill Freehan	12.8
4	Jim Sundberg	11.1
5	Thurman Munson	11.0
6	Tony Pena	9.7
7	Del Crandall	9.5
8	Carlton Fisk	9.4
9	Ted Simmons	8.9
10	Duke Farrell	7.7

Total Player Rating

1	Babe Ruth	105.1
2	Ty Cobb	91.2
3	Hank Aaron	90.1
4	Ted Williams	89.8
5	Willie Mays	86.2
6	Nap Lajoie	85.2
7	Tris Speaker	79.3
8	Mike Schmidt	77.8
9	Rogers Hornsby	77.3
10	Honus Wagner	75.6
11	Frank Robinson	71.2
12	Eddie Collins	70.5
13	Stan Musial	70.1
14	Mickey Mantle	69.8
15	Joe Morgan	63.9
16	Lou Gehrig	60.8
17	Mel Ott	60.1
18	Jimmie Foxx	53.2
19	George Davis	48.4
	Eddie Mathews	48.4
21	Rickey Henderson	48.2
22	Bobby Grich	47.4
23	Ed Delahanty	46.1
	Carl Yastrzemski	46.1
25	Al Kaline	45.9
26	George Brett	45.3
27	Reggie Jackson	44.0
28	Joe DiMaggio	43.6
29	Charlie Gehringer	43.5
30	Bill Dahlen	43.3
31	Rod Carew	41.0
32	Dan Brouthers	40.4
33	Arky Vaughan	40.3
34	Ozzie Smith	40.0
35	Roberto Clemente	39.6
36	Paul Waner	38.9
37	Roger Connor	38.8
38	Luke Appling	38.5
39	Joe Cronin	38.2
40	Willie McCovey	38.1
	Ron Santo	38.1
42	Bob Johnson	37.8
43	Bid McPhee	37.5
44	Frankie Frisch	37.2
45	Wade Boggs	36.9
46	Keith Hernandez	36.6
	Dave Winfield	36.6
48	Johnny Mize	36.5
49	Carlton Fisk	36.4
50	Gary Carter	36.3
51	Joe Jackson	36.0
52	Robin Yount	35.9
53	Gabby Hartnett	35.7
54	Dick Allen	35.6
	Bobby Doerr	35.6
	Eddie Murray	35.6
57	Yogi Berra	34.8
58	Frank Baker	34.6
59	Bill Mazeroski	34.4
	Ted Simmons	34.4
61	Lou Boudreau	34.3
62	Billy Herman	34.0
	Bobby Wallace	34.0
64	Reggie Smith	33.4
65	Jackie Robinson	33.3
66	Jack Glasscock	33.2
67	Joe Sewell	33.1
68	Tim Raines	33.0
69	Harmon Killebrew	32.8
70	Darrell Evans	31.8
71	Willie Stargell	31.6
72	Cap Anson	31.3
	Bobby Bonds	31.3
74	Jim Wynn	31.1
75	Bill Dickey	30.6
76	Johnny Bench	30.2
	Jesse Burkett	30.2
	Billy Williams	30.2
79	Joe Torre	29.8
80	Dave Bancroft	29.7
81	Norm Cash	29.6
	Cupid Childs	29.6
83	Rusty Staub	29.4
	Sam Thompson	29.4
85	Bill Freehan	28.9
	Hank Greenberg	28.9
87	Cal Ripken	28.7
88	Jack Clark	28.5
	Elmer Flick	28.5
	Sherry Magee	28.5
91	Dwight Evans	28.4
92	Fred Dunlap	28.0
93	Bill Terry	27.8
94	Buck Ewing	27.6
	Joe Gordon	27.6
96	Fred Clarke	27.5
	Mickey Cochrane	27.5
98	Richie Ashburn	27.0
	Pete Browning	27.0
	Ralph Kiner	27.0

Total Player Rating

101	Max Carey	26.9
	Willie Randolph	26.9
103	Hughie Jennings	26.5
104	Tony Oliva	26.1
105	Hardy Richardson	25.9
106	Stan Hack	25.8
	Jim Rice	25.8
108	Joe Medwick	25.7
109	Heinie Groh	25.6
110	Harry Heilmann	25.3
111	Dick Bartell	25.2
	Pedro Guerrero	25.2
	Wally Schang	25.2
114	Thurman Munson	25.1
115	Buddy Bell	25.0
	Rocky Colavito	25.0
	Andre Dawson	25.0
	Billy Hamilton	25.0
119	Ernie Banks	24.9
	George Sisler	24.9
121	Pete Rose	24.7
122	Chuck Klein	24.3
	Duke Snider	24.3
124	Jake Beckley	24.2
	King Kelly	24.2
	Al Simmons	24.2
127	Graig Nettles	24.1
128	Sam Crawford	24.0
129	Cesar Cedeno	23.8
	Jimmy Collins	23.8
131	Jack Fournier	23.7
132	Minnie Minoso	23.6
	Harry Stovey	23.6
134	Ed Konetchy	23.5
135	Charlie Keller	23.4
	Ernie Lombardi	23.4
137	Brooks Robinson	23.3
138	Ryne Sandberg	23.1
139	Goose Goslin	22.9
	Joe Kelley	22.9
141	Harlond Clift	22.7
	Paul Molitor	22.7
	Roy Smalley	22.7
144	Lou Whitaker	22.5
145	Tony Gwynn	22.4
	Dave Parker	22.4
	Roy Thomas	22.4
148	Roy Campanella	22.2
149	George Foster	22.1
150	Ron Cey	21.9
151	Eddie Stanky	21.6
152	Gil McDougald	21.5
153	Del Pratt	21.4
154	Zach Wheat	21.1
155	Art Fletcher	21.0
	Jim Fregosi	21.0
	Travis Jackson	21.0
	Charley Jones	21.0
	Fred Lynn	21.0
160	Darryl Strawberry	20.9
161	Fred Pfeffer	20.3
	Ken Singleton	20.3
163	Joe Tinker	20.2
164	Denny Lyons	20.1
165	Frank Howard	20.0
166	Mike Griffin	19.7
167	Ken Williams	19.6
168	Orlando Cepeda	19.5
169	Kiki Cuyler	19.4
170	Gavvy Cravath	19.3
	Darrell Porter	19.3
172	Roy White	19.2
173	Bill Joyce	19.1
174	Miller Huggins	19.0
	Pee Wee Reese	19.0
176	Ken Boyer	18.9
	Jose Cruz	18.9
	Fred Tenney	18.9
179	Jimmy Sheckard	18.7
180	Dale Murphy	18.6
181	Bob Elliott	18.5
	Alan Trammell	18.5
183	Earl Averill	18.4
	Roger Bresnahan	18.4
	Pie Traynor	18.4
186	Gene Alley	18.3
	Wally Berger	18.3
	Babe Herman	18.3
189	Ferris Fain	18.1
190	Brian Downing	17.9
191	Larry Doby	17.7
	Paul Hines	17.7
	Lance Parrish	17.7
194	Rico Carty	17.3
	Roy Cullenbine	17.3
	John McGraw	17.3
197	Dolph Camilli	17.2
	Ray Chapman	17.2
	Hal McRae	17.2
	Amos Otis	17.2

Total Player Rating

201	Art Devlin	16.9
202	Charlie Bennett	16.8
	Hack Wilson	16.8
204	Johnny Evers	16.6
	Toby Harrah	16.6
	Jocko Milligan	16.6
207	Chet Lemon	16.4
208	Benny Kauff	16.3
209	Duke Farrell	16.2
	Lonny Frey	16.2
211	Frank Chance	16.1
	Deacon McGuire	16.1
	Rudy York	16.1
214	George Gore	16.0
	Bill Nicholson	16.0
	Dave Orr	16.0
	Edd Roush	16.0
	Andy Thornton	16.0
219	Ed Bailey	15.9
	Don Buford	15.9
221	Jimmy Ryan	15.8
222	Doug DeCinces	15.7
	Jeff Heath	15.7
	Tommy Leach	15.7
	Boog Powell	15.7
226	Smoky Burgess	15.6
	Jim O'Rourke	15.6
228	Mike Hargrove	15.5
229	Phil Rizzuto	15.4
	Vern Stephens	15.4
	Maury Wills	15.4
232	Don Baylor	15.2
	Ben Chapman	15.2
	Billy Nash	15.2
235	Dave Concepcion	15.1
236	Rick Ferrell	15.0
	Tony Lazzeri	15.0
	Red Schoendienst	15.0
239	Henry Larkin	14.8
	George VanHaltren	14.8
241	Sid Gordon	14.7
	Glenn Hubbard	14.7
243	Tommy Henrich	14.6
244	Kirby Puckett	14.5
245	Harry Davis	14.4
	Kirk Gibson	14.4
	Mike Tiernan	14.4
248	Enos Slaughter	14.3
249	Andy Seminick	14.2
250	Walker Cooper	14.1
	Gil Hodges	14.1
252	Mike Donlin	14.0
	Johnny Logan	14.0
	Roger Peckinpaugh	14.0
255	Kip Selbach	13.9
	Richie Zisk	13.9
257	Tony Perez	13.8
258	Fred Carroll	13.7
	Elston Howard	13.7
260	Tony Cuccinello	13.6
261	Bobby Murcer	13.5
	Johnny Pesky	13.5
263	Don Mattingly	13.3
	Dwayne Murphy	13.3
265	Bob Allison	13.0
	Luis Aparicio	13.0
	Bill Bradley	13.0
	Augie Galan	13.0
269	Roy Sievers	12.9
	Bump Wills	12.9
	Heinie Zimmerman	12.9
272	Jesse Barfield	12.8
	Willie Kamm	12.8
	Ken Keltner	12.8
	Sixto Lezcano	12.8
276	Jack Clements	12.7
	Lave Cross	12.7
	Buddy Myer	12.7
279	Solly Hemus	12.6
	Larry Hisle	12.6
	Cliff Johnson	12.6
	George Stone	12.6
283	Nellie Fox	12.5
	Chief Zimmer	12.5
285	Bobby Knoop	12.4
286	Tim McCarver	12.3
287	Ron Hunt	12.2
	John Romano	12.2
289	Charlie Hickman	12.1
	Ed McFarland	12.1
	Al Oliver	12.1
	John Titus	12.1
	Bob Watson	12.1
	Jimmy Williams	12.1
295	Tony Fernandez	12.0
	Ross Youngs	12.0
297	Orator Shaffer	11.9
298	Ron Hansen	11.8
299	Davey Lopes	11.7
	Kevin McReynolds	11.7

Total Player Rating

301	Dave Johnson	11.6
302	Donie Bush	11.5
	Ed Swartwood	11.5
304	Del Crandall	11.4
305	Jim Gentile	11.3
	Greg Luzinski	11.3
	Tip O'Neill	11.3
	Cy Seymour	11.3
	Mike Smith	11.3
	Dickie Thon	11.3
	Dixie Walker	11.3
312	Oyster Burns	11.2
	Jake Daubert	11.2
	Stan Spence	11.2
	Sam Wise	11.2
316	George Griffey	10.9
317	Roger Maris	10.8
	Bill Melton	10.8
	Manny Sanguillen	10.8
	Red Smith	10.8
321	Sal Bando	10.7
	Tommy Holmes	10.7
	Jackie Jensen	10.7
	Whitey Kurowski	10.7
	Al Rosen	10.7
	Chicken Wolf	10.7
327	Johnny Kling	10.6
328	Rick Burleson	10.5
	Harry Danning	10.5
	Larry Doyle	10.5
	Topsy Hartsel	10.5
332	Cecil Cooper	10.4
	Tom Daly	10.4
	Tony Pena	10.4
	Jim Sundberg	10.4
	Gene Tenace	10.4
337	Kid Elberfeld	10.3
	Bill Madlock	10.3
339	Johnny Callison	10.2
	Jerry Denny	10.2
	Chick Hafey	10.2
	Stan Lopata	10.2
	Jerry Priddy	10.2
344	Oscar Gamble	10.1
	Cecil Travis	10.1
346	Bobby Avila	10.0
	Monte Irvin	10.0
	Riggs Stephenson	10.0
349	Ray Boone	9.9
	Dick Groat	9.9
	George Kell	9.9
	George Wood	9.9
353	Dave Cash	9.8
	Spud Davis	9.8
	Curt Welch	9.8
	Vic Wertz	9.8
357	Frank Fennelly	9.7
	Willie Keeler	9.7
	Ben Oglivie	9.7
	Andy VanSlyke	9.7
361	Bill Lange	9.6
	Mickey Vernon	9.6
	Ned Williamson	9.6
364	Joe Adcock	9.5
	Earl Torgeson	9.5
366	Frankie Hayes	9.4
	Freddie Patek	9.4
	John Stearns	9.4
	Cy Williams	9.4
370	Earle Combs	9.3
	Tom Haller	9.3
	Hank Sauer	9.3
	Gene Woodling	9.3
374	Tony Bernazard	9.2
	Lefty O'Doul	9.2
	Bob O'Farrell	9.2
	Claude Ritchey	9.2
	Snuffy Stirnweiss	9.2
379	Jack Crooks	9.1
	Marty McManus	9.1
381	Jimmy Barrett	9.0
382	Johnny Bates	8.9
	Max Bishop	8.9
	Bert Campaneris	8.9
	Phil Cavarretta	8.9
	Freddy Lindstrom	8.9
	Ken Phelps	8.9
	Lonnie Smith	8.9
389	Hugh Duffy	8.7
	Woody English	8.7
	Von Hayes	8.7
	Bob Horner	8.7
393	Hank Gowdy	8.6
	Garry Templeton	8.6
	Butch Wynegar	8.6
396	Clete Boyer	8.5
	Phil Bradley	8.5
	Joe Ferguson	8.5
	Ken McMullen	8.5
	Mike Mitchell	8.5

Total Player Rating

401	Alvin Davis	8.4
	Fred Luderus	8.4
	Doug Rader	8.4
	Ezra Sutton	8.4
	Hank Thompson	8.4
406	Willie Horton	8.3
	Don Mincher	8.3
	Rico Petrocelli	8.3
409	Elbie Fletcher	8.2
	Jim Fogarty	8.2
	Don Money	8.2
412	Ripper Collins	8.1
	Dom DiMaggio	8.1
	Joe Harris	8.1
	Kent Hrbek	8.1
416	Bernie Carbo	7.9
	George Grantham	7.9
	Sherm Lollar	7.9
	Bill Sweeney	7.9
	Billy Werber	7.9
421	Johnny Ray	7.8
422	George Selkirk	7.7
423	Dan McGann	7.6
	Pete Runnels	7.6
	Lee Tannehill	7.6
	Pinky Whitney	7.6
427	Brett Butler	7.5
	Buck Herzog	7.5
429	Larry Gardner	7.4
	Ossee Schreckengost	7.4
	Deacon White	7.4
432	Marty Marion	7.3
	Pete Reiser	7.3
	Jake Stenzel	7.3
	Tim Wallach	7.3
436	Mike Grady	7.2
	Heinie Manush	7.2
	Denis Menke	7.2
	Pop Snyder	7.2
	Tom Tresh	7.2
441	Mark Belanger	7.1
	Del Ennis	7.1
	Bill Skowron	7.1
	Bobby Veach	7.1
445	Harold Baines	7.0
446	Julio Cruz	6.9
	Bubbles Hargrave	6.9
	Billy Jurges	6.9
	Sammy Strang	6.9
450	Ival Goodman	6.8
	Jason Thompson	6.8
452	Ginger Beaumont	6.7
	John Mayberry	6.7
	Duke Sims	6.7
	John Stone	6.7
456	Julio Franco	6.6
	Socks Seybold	6.6
	Ozzie Virgil	6.6
459	Abner Dalrymple	6.5
	George Hendrick	6.5
461	Bob Caruthers	6.4
	Howard Johnson	6.4
	Eddie Joost	6.4
	Lyn Lary	6.4
	Buddy Lewis	6.4
466	Heinie Peitz	6.3
	Eric Soderholm	6.3
468	George Bell	6.2
	Chili Davis	6.2
	Glenn Davis	6.2
	Gary Gaetti	6.2
	Bake McBride	6.2
	Matty McIntyre	6.2
	Babe Phelps	6.2
	Art Wilson	6.2
476	Al Bridwell	6.1
	John Briggs	6.1
	Tommy Clarke	6.1
	Lou Criger	6.1
	Happy Felsch	6.1
	Dick McAuliffe	6.1
	Jim McTamany	6.1
	Danny Murphy	6.1
	Terry Pendleton	6.1
485	Bob Nieman	6.0
486	Odell Hale	5.9
	Gary Redus	5.9
	Harry Steinfeldt	5.9
	Glenn Wright	5.9
490	Merv Rettenmund	5.8
	Danny Richardson	5.8
	Mickey Rivers	5.8
493	Hal Chase	5.7
	Mike Epstein	5.7
	Steve Kemp	5.7
	Pepper Martin	5.7
	Gary Matthews	5.7
	Emmett Seery	5.7
	Pete Ward	5.7
500	5 players tied	5.6

Total Player Rating (alpha.)

Hank Aaron	90.1
Joe Adcock	9.5
Dick Allen	35.6
Gene Alley	18.3
Bob Allison	13.0
Cap Anson	31.3
Luis Aparicio	13.0
Luke Appling	38.5
Richie Ashburn	27.0
Earl Averill	18.4
Bobby Avila	10.0
Ed Bailey	15.9
Harold Baines	7.0
Frank Baker	34.6
Dave Bancroft	29.7
Sal Bando	10.7
Ernie Banks	24.9
Jesse Barfield	12.8
Jimmy Barrett	9.0
Dick Bartell	25.2
Johnny Bates	8.9
Don Baylor	15.2
Ginger Beaumont	6.7
Jake Beckley	24.2
Mark Belanger	7.1
Buddy Bell	25.0
George Bell	6.2
Johnny Bench	30.2
Charlie Bennett	16.8
Wally Berger	18.3
Tony Bernazard	9.2
Yogi Berra	34.8
Max Bishop	8.9
Wade Boggs	36.9
Bobby Bonds	31.3
Ray Boone	9.9
Lou Boudreau	34.3
Clete Boyer	8.5
Ken Boyer	18.9
Phil Bradley	8.5
Bill Bradley	13.0
Roger Bresnahan	18.4
George Brett	45.3
Al Bridwell	6.1
John Briggs	6.1
Dan Brouthers	40.4
Pete Browning	27.0
Don Buford	15.9
Smoky Burgess	15.6
Jesse Burkett	30.2
Rick Burleson	10.5
Oyster Burns	11.2
Donie Bush	11.5
Brett Butler	7.5
Johnny Callison	10.2
Dolph Camilli	17.2
Roy Campanella	22.2
Bert Campaneris	8.9
Bernie Carbo	7.9
Rod Carew	41.0
Max Carey	26.9
Fred Carroll	13.7
Gary Carter	36.3
Rico Carty	17.3
Bob Caruthers	6.4
Dave Cash	9.8
Norm Cash	29.6
Phil Cavarretta	8.9
Cesar Cedeno	23.8
Orlando Cepeda	19.5
Ron Cey	21.9
Frank Chance	16.1
Ray Chapman	17.2
Ben Chapman	15.2
Hal Chase	5.7
Cupid Childs	29.6
Jack Clark	28.5
Fred Clarke	27.5
Tommy Clarke	6.1
Roberto Clemente	39.6
Jack Clements	12.7
Harlond Clift	22.7
Ty Cobb	91.2
Mickey Cochrane	27.5
Rocky Colavito	25.0
Eddie Collins	70.5
Ripper Collins	8.1
Jimmy Collins	23.8
Earle Combs	9.3
Dave Concepcion	15.1
Roger Connor	38.8
Cecil Cooper	10.4
Walker Cooper	14.1
Del Crandall	11.4
Gavvy Cravath	19.3
Sam Crawford	24.0
Lou Criger	6.1
Joe Cronin	38.2
Jack Crooks	9.1
Lave Cross	12.7

Total Player Rating (alpha.)

Jose Cruz	18.9
Julio Cruz	6.9
Tony Cuccinello	13.6
Roy Cullenbine	17.3
Kiki Cuyler	19.4
Bill Dahlen	43.3
Abner Dalrymple	6.5
Tom Daly	10.4
Harry Danning	10.5
Jake Daubert	11.2
Alvin Davis	8.4
Chili Davis	6.2
George Davis	48.4
Glenn Davis	6.2
Harry Davis	14.4
Spud Davis	9.8
Andre Dawson	25.0
Ed Delahanty	46.1
Jerry Denny	10.2
Art Devlin	16.9
Bill Dickey	30.6
Larry Doby	17.7
Bobby Doerr	35.6
Mike Donlin	14.0
Brian Downing	17.9
Larry Doyle	10.5
Hugh Duffy	8.7
Fred Dunlap	28.0
Doug DeCinces	15.7
Dom DiMaggio	8.1
Joe DiMaggio	43.6
Kid Elberfeld	10.3
Bob Elliott	18.5
Woody English	8.7
Del Ennis	7.1
Mike Epstein	5.7
Darrell Evans	31.8
Dwight Evans	28.4
Johnny Evers	16.6
Buck Ewing	27.6
Ferris Fain	18.1
Duke Farrell	16.2
Happy Felsch	6.1
Frank Fennelly	9.7
Joe Ferguson	8.5
Tony Fernandez	12.0
Rick Ferrell	15.0
Carlton Fisk	36.4
Art Fletcher	21.0
Elbie Fletcher	8.2
Elmer Flick	28.5
Jim Fogarty	8.2
George Foster	22.1
Jack Fournier	23.7
Nellie Fox	12.5
Jimmie Foxx	53.2
Julio Franco	6.6
Bill Freehan	28.9
Jim Fregosi	21.0
Lonny Frey	16.2
Frankie Frisch	37.2
Gary Gaetti	6.2
Augie Galan	13.0
Oscar Gamble	10.1
Larry Gardner	7.4
Lou Gehrig	60.8
Charlie Gehringer	43.5
Jim Gentile	11.3
Kirk Gibson	14.4
Jack Glasscock	33.2
Ival Goodman	6.8
Joe Gordon	27.6
Sid Gordon	14.7
George Gore	16.0
Goose Goslin	22.9
Hank Gowdy	8.6
Mike Grady	7.2
George Grantham	7.9
Hank Greenberg	28.9
Bobby Grich	47.4
George Griffey	10.9
Mike Griffin	19.7
Dick Groat	9.9
Heinie Groh	25.6
Pedro Guerrero	25.2
Tony Gwynn	22.4
Stan Hack	25.8
Chick Hafey	10.2
Odell Hale	5.9
Tom Haller	9.3
Billy Hamilton	25.0
Ron Hansen	11.8
Bubbles Hargrave	6.9
Mike Hargrove	15.5
Toby Harrah	16.6
Joe Harris	8.1
Gabby Hartnett	35.7
Topsy Hartsel	10.5
Frankie Hayes	9.4
Von Hayes	8.7

Total Player Rating (alpha.)

Jeff Heath	15.7
Harry Heilmann	25.3
Solly Hemus	12.6
Rickey Henderson	48.2
George Hendrick	6.5
Tommy Henrich	14.6
Babe Herman	18.3
Billy Herman	34.0
Keith Hernandez	36.6
Buck Herzog	7.5
Charlie Hickman	12.1
Paul Hines	17.7
Larry Hisle	12.6
Gil Hodges	14.1
Tommy Holmes	10.7
Bob Horner	8.7
Rogers Hornsby	77.3
Willie Horton	8.3
Elston Howard	13.7
Frank Howard	20.0
Kent Hrbek	8.1
Glenn Hubbard	14.7
Miller Huggins	19.0
Ron Hunt	12.2
Monte Irvin	10.0
Joe Jackson	36.0
Reggie Jackson	44.0
Travis Jackson	21.0
Hughie Jennings	26.5
Jackie Jensen	10.7
Cliff Johnson	12.6
Dave Johnson	11.6
Howard Johnson	6.4
Bob Johnson	37.8
Charley Jones	21.0
Eddie Joost	6.4
Bill Joyce	19.1
Billy Jurges	6.9
Al Kaline	45.9
Willie Kamm	12.8
Benny Kauff	16.3
Willie Keeler	9.7
George Kell	9.9
Charlie Keller	23.4
Joe Kelley	22.9
King Kelly	24.2
Ken Keltner	12.8
Steve Kemp	5.7
Harmon Killebrew	32.8
Ralph Kiner	27.0
Chuck Klein	24.3
Johnny Kling	10.6
Bobby Knoop	12.4
Ed Konetchy	23.5
Whitey Kurowski	10.7
Nap Lajoie	85.2
Bill Lange	9.6
Henry Larkin	14.8
Lyn Lary	6.4
Tony Lazzeri	15.0
Tommy Leach	15.7
Chet Lemon	16.4
Buddy Lewis	6.4
Sixto Lezcano	12.8
Freddy Lindstrom	8.9
Johnny Logan	14.0
Sherm Lollar	7.9
Ernie Lombardi	23.4
Stan Lopata	10.2
Davey Lopes	11.7
Fred Luderus	8.4
Greg Luzinski	11.3
Fred Lynn	21.0
Denny Lyons	20.1
Bill Madlock	10.3
Sherry Magee	28.5
Mickey Mantle	69.8
Heinie Manush	7.2
Roger Maris	10.8
Pepper Martin	5.7
Eddie Mathews	48.4
Gary Matthews	5.7
Don Mattingly	13.3
John Mayberry	6.7
Willie Mays	86.2
Bill Mazeroski	34.4
Joe Medwick	25.7
Bill Melton	10.8
Denis Menke	7.2
Jocko Milligan	16.6
Don Mincher	8.3
Minnie Minoso	23.6
Mike Mitchell	8.5
Johnny Mize	36.5
Paul Molitor	22.7
Don Money	8.2
Joe Morgan	63.9
Thurman Munson	25.1
Bobby Murcer	13.5

Total Player Rating (alpha.)

Dale Murphy	18.6
Danny Murphy	6.1
Dwayne Murphy	13.3
Eddie Murray	35.6
Stan Musial	70.1
Buddy Myer	12.7
Dick McAuliffe	6.1
Bake McBride	6.2
Tim McCarver	12.3
Willie McCovey	38.1
Gil McDougald	21.5
Ed McFarland	12.1
Dan McGann	7.6
John McGraw	17.3
Deacon McGuire	16.1
Matty McIntyre	6.2
Marty McManus	9.1
Ken McMullen	8.5
Bid McPhee	37.5
Hal McRae	17.2
Kevin McReynolds	11.7
Jim McTamany	6.1
Billy Nash	15.2
Graig Nettles	24.1
Bill Nicholson	16.0
Bob Nieman	6.0
Lefty O'Doul	9.2
Bob O'Farrell	9.2
Tip O'Neill	11.3
Jim O'Rourke	15.6
Ben Oglivie	9.7
Tony Oliva	26.1
Al Oliver	12.1
Dave Orr	16.0
Amos Otis	17.2
Mel Ott	60.1
Dave Parker	22.4
Lance Parrish	17.7
Freddie Patek	9.4
Roger Peckinpaugh	14.0
Heinie Peitz	6.3
Tony Pena	10.4
Terry Pendleton	6.1
Tony Perez	13.8
Johnny Pesky	13.5
Rico Petrocelli	8.3
Fred Pfeffer	20.3
Babe Phelps	6.2
Ken Phelps	8.9
Darrell Porter	19.3
Boog Powell	15.7
Del Pratt	21.4
Jerry Priddy	10.2
Kirby Puckett	14.5
Doug Rader	8.4
Tim Raines	33.0
Willie Randolph	26.9
Johnny Ray	7.8
Gary Redus	5.9
Pete Reiser	7.3
Merv Rettenmund	5.8
Jim Rice	25.8
Hardy Richardson	25.9
Danny Richardson	5.8
Cal Ripken	28.7
Claude Ritchey	9.2
Mickey Rivers	5.8
Phil Rizzuto	15.4
Brooks Robinson	23.3
Frank Robinson	71.2
Jackie Robinson	33.3
John Romano	12.2
Pete Rose	24.7
Al Rosen	10.7
Edd Roush	16.0
Pete Runnels	7.6
Babe Ruth	105.1
Jimmy Ryan	15.8
Ryne Sandberg	23.1
Manny Sanguillen	10.8
Ron Santo	38.1
Hank Sauer	9.3
Wally Schang	25.2
Mike Schmidt	77.8
Red Schoendienst	15.0
Ossee Schreckengost	7.4
Emmett Seery	5.7
Kip Selbach	13.9
George Selkirk	7.7
Andy Seminick	14.2
Joe Sewell	33.1
Socks Seybold	6.6
Cy Seymour	11.3
Orator Shaffer	11.9
Jimmy Sheckard	18.7
Roy Sievers	12.9
Al Simmons	24.2
Ted Simmons	34.4
Duke Sims	6.7
Ken Singleton	20.3

Total Player Rating (alpha.)

George Sisler	24.9
Bill Skowron	7.1
Enos Slaughter	14.3
Roy Smalley	22.7
Reggie Smith	33.4
Mike Smith	11.3
Red Smith	10.8
Lonnie Smith	8.9
Ozzie Smith	40.0
Duke Snider	24.3
Pop Snyder	7.2
Eric Soderholm	6.3
Tris Speaker	79.3
Stan Spence	11.2
Eddie Stanky	21.6
Willie Stargell	31.6
Rusty Staub	29.4
John Stearns	9.4
Harry Steinfeldt	5.9
Jake Stenzel	7.3
Vern Stephens	15.4
Riggs Stephenson	10.0
Snuffy Stirnweiss	9.2
George Stone	12.6
John Stone	6.7
Harry Stovey	23.6
Sammy Strang	6.9
Darryl Strawberry	20.9
Jim Sundberg	10.4
Ezra Sutton	8.4
Ed Swartwood	11.5
Bill Sweeney	7.9
Lee Tannehill	7.6
Garry Templeton	8.6
Gene Tenace	10.4
Fred Tenney	18.9
Bill Terry	27.8
Roy Thomas	22.4
Hank Thompson	8.4
Jason Thompson	6.8
Sam Thompson	29.4
Dickie Thon	11.3
Andy Thornton	16.0
Mike Tiernan	14.4
Joe Tinker	20.2
John Titus	12.1
Earl Torgeson	9.5
Joe Torre	29.8
Alan Trammell	18.5
Cecil Travis	10.1
Pie Traynor	18.4
Tom Tresh	7.2
Arky Vaughan	40.3
Bobby Veach	7.1
Mickey Vernon	9.6
Ozzie Virgil	6.6
George VanHaltren	14.8
Andy VanSlyke	9.7
Honus Wagner	75.6
Dixie Walker	11.3
Bobby Wallace	34.0
Tim Wallach	7.3
Paul Waner	38.9
Pete Ward	5.7
Bob Watson	12.1
Pee Wee Reese	19.0
Curt Welch	9.8
Billy Werber	7.9
Vic Wertz	9.8
Zach Wheat	21.1
Lou Whitaker	22.5
Deacon White	7.4
Roy White	19.2
Pinky Whitney	7.6
Billy Williams	30.2
Cy Williams	9.4
Jimmy Williams	12.1
Ken Williams	19.6
Ted Williams	89.8
Ned Williamson	9.6
Bump Wills	12.9
Maury Wills	15.4
Art Wilson	6.2
Hack Wilson	16.8
Dave Winfield	36.6
Sam Wise	11.2
Chicken Wolf	10.7
George Wood	9.9
Gene Woodling	9.3
Glenn Wright	5.9
Butch Wynegar	8.6
Jim Wynn	31.1
Carl Yastrzemski	46.1
Rudy York	16.1
Ross Youngs	12.0
Robin Yount	35.9
Chief Zimmer	12.5
Heinie Zimmerman	12.9
Richie Zisk	13.9

Total Player Rating (by era)

1876-1892

1	Dan Brouthers	40.4
2	Roger Connor	38.8
3	Bid McPhee	37.5
4	Jack Glasscock	33.2
5	Cap Anson	31.3
6	Sam Thompson	29.4
7	Fred Dunlap	28.0
8	Buck Ewing	27.6
9	Pete Browning	27.0
10	Hardy Richardson	25.9
11	King Kelly	24.2
12	Harry Stovey	23.6
13	Charley Jones	21.0
14	Fred Pfeffer	20.3
15	Denny Lyons	20.1
16	Mike Griffin	19.7
17	Paul Hines	17.7
18	Charlie Bennett	16.8
19	Jocko Milligan	16.6
20	George Gore	16.0
	Dave Orr	16.0
22	Jim O'Rourke	15.6
23	Billy Nash	15.2
24	Henry Larkin	14.8
25	Fred Carroll	13.7

1893-1919

1	Ty Cobb	91.2
2	Nap Lajoie	85.2
3	Tris Speaker	79.3
4	Honus Wagner	75.6
5	Eddie Collins	70.5
6	George Davis	48.4
7	Ed Delahanty	46.1
8	Bill Dahlen	43.3
9	Joe Jackson	36.0
10	Frank Baker	34.6
11	Bobby Wallace	34.0
12	Jesse Burkett	30.2
13	Cupid Childs	29.6
14	Elmer Flick	28.5
	Sherry Magee	28.5
16	Fred Clarke	27.5
17	Hughie Jennings	26.5
18	Heinie Groh	25.6
19	Billy Hamilton	25.0
20	Jake Beckley	24.2
21	Sam Crawford	24.0
22	Jimmy Collins	23.8
23	Ed Konetchy	23.5
24	Joe Kelley	22.9
25	Roy Thomas	22.4

1920-1941

1	Babe Ruth	105.1
2	Rogers Hornsby	77.3
3	Lou Gehrig	60.8
4	Mel Ott	60.1
5	Jimmie Foxx	53.2
6	Charlie Gehringer	43.5
7	Arky Vaughan	40.3
8	Paul Waner	38.9
9	Luke Appling	38.5
10	Joe Cronin	38.2
11	Bob Johnson	37.8
12	Frankie Frisch	37.2
13	Gabby Hartnett	35.7
14	Billy Herman	34.0
15	Joe Sewell	33.1
16	Bill Dickey	30.6
17	Dave Bancroft	29.7
18	Hank Greenberg	28.9
19	Bill Terry	27.8
20	Mickey Cochrane	27.5
21	Max Carey	26.9
22	Stan Hack	25.8
23	Joe Medwick	25.7
24	Harry Heilmann	25.3
25	2 players tied	25.2

Total Player Rating (by era)

1942-1960

1	Ted Williams	89.8
2	Stan Musial	70.1
3	Mickey Mantle	69.8
4	Eddie Mathews	48.4
5	Joe DiMaggio	43.6
6	Johnny Mize	36.5
7	Bobby Doerr	35.6
8	Yogi Berra	34.8
9	Lou Boudreau	34.3
10	Jackie Robinson	33.3
11	Joe Gordon	27.6
12	Richie Ashburn	27.0
	Ralph Kiner	27.0
14	Duke Snider	24.3
15	Minnie Minoso	23.6
16	Charlie Keller	23.4
17	Roy Campanella	22.2
18	Eddie Stanky	21.6
19	Gil McDougald	21.5
20	Pee Wee Reese	19.0
21	Bob Elliott	18.5
22	Ferris Fain	18.1
23	Larry Doby	17.7
24	Roy Cullenbine	17.3
25	Rudy York	16.1

1961-1989

1	Hank Aaron	90.1
2	Willie Mays	86.2
3	Mike Schmidt	77.8
4	Frank Robinson	71.2
5	Joe Morgan	63.9
6	Rickey Henderson	48.2
7	Bobby Grich	47.4
8	Carl Yastrzemski	46.1
9	Al Kaline	45.9
10	George Brett	45.3
11	Reggie Jackson	44.0
12	Rod Carew	41.0
13	Ozzie Smith	40.0
14	Roberto Clemente	39.6
15	Willie McCovey	38.1
	Ron Santo	38.1
17	Wade Boggs	36.9
18	Keith Hernandez	36.6
	Dave Winfield	36.6
20	Carlton Fisk	36.4
21	Gary Carter	36.3
22	Robin Yount	35.9
23	Dick Allen	35.6
	Eddie Murray	35.6
25	2 players tied	34.4

Wins

Rank	Player	Wins
1	Cy Young	511
2	Walter Johnson	417
3	Pete Alexander	373
4	Christy Mathewson	372
5	Warren Spahn	363
6	Kid Nichols	362
7	Jim Galvin	361
8	Tim Keefe	342
9	Steve Carlton	329
10	John Clarkson	327
11	Eddie Plank	326
12	Don Sutton	324
13	Phil Niekro	318
14	Gaylord Perry	314
15	Tom Seaver	311
16	Charley Radbourn	310
17	Mickey Welch	307
18	Lefty Grove	300
	Early Wynn	300
20	Nolan Ryan	289
21	Tommy John	288
22	Robin Roberts	286
23	Tony Mullane	285
24	Ferguson Jenkins	284
25	Jim Kaat	283
26	Red Ruffing	273
27	Bert Blyleven	271
28	Burleigh Grimes	270
29	Jim Palmer	268
30	Bob Feller	266
	Eppa Rixey	266
32	Jim McCormick	265
33	Gus Weyhing	264
34	Ted Lyons	260
35	Red Faber	254
36	Carl Hubbell	253
37	Bob Gibson	251
38	Jack Quinn	247
	Vic Willis	247
40	Joe McGinnity	246
41	Jack Powell	245
	Amos Rusie	245
43	Juan Marichal	243
44	Herb Pennock	240
45	Mordecai Brown	239
46	Clark Griffith	237
	Waite Hoyt	237
48	Whitey Ford	236
49	Charlie Buffinton	232
50	Sam Jones	229
	Luis Tiant	229
	Will White	229
53	George Mullin	228
54	Jim Bunning	224
	Jim Hunter	224
56	Paul Derringer	223
	Mel Harder	223
58	Hooks Dauss	222
	Jerry Koosman	222
60	Joe Niekro	221
61	Jerry Reuss	220
62	Bob Caruthers	218
	Earl Whitehill	218
64	Freddie Fitzsimmons	217
	Mickey Lolich	217
66	Wilbur Cooper	216
67	Stan Coveleski	215
	Jim Perry	215
69	Chief Bender	212
70	Bobo Newsom	211
	Billy Pierce	211
	Rick Reuschel	211
73	Jesse Haines	210
74	Vida Blue	209
	Don Drysdale	209
	Milt Pappas	209
77	Eddie Cicotte	208
78	Bob Lemon	207
	Carl Mays	207
	Hal Newhouser	207
81	Silver King	204
	Al Orth	204
83	Lew Burdette	203
84	Jack Stivetts	202
85	Rube Marquard	201
	Charlie Root	201
87	George Uhle	200
88	Jack Chesbro	198
	Frank Tanana	198
	Bucky Walters	198
91	Larry French	197
	Bob Friend	197
	Jesse Tannehill	197
	Adonis Terry	197
	Dazzy Vance	197
96	Claude Osteen	196
	Bob Shawkey	196
98	Joe Bush	195
	Sam Leever	195
	Ed Walsh	195

Losses

Rank	Player	Losses
1	Cy Young	315
2	Jim Galvin	307
3	Walter Johnson	279
4	Phil Niekro	274
5	Gaylord Perry	265
6	Nolan Ryan	263
7	Don Sutton	256
8	Jack Powell	253
9	Eppa Rixey	251
10	Robin Roberts	245
	Warren Spahn	245
12	Steve Carlton	244
	Early Wynn	244
14	Jim Kaat	237
15	Gus Weyhing	232
16	Bert Blyleven	231
	Tommy John	231
18	Bob Friend	230
	Ted Lyons	230
20	Ferguson Jenkins	226
21	Tim Keefe	225
	Red Ruffing	225
23	Bobo Newsom	222
24	Tony Mullane	220
25	Jack Quinn	218
26	Sam Jones	217
27	Jim McCormick	214
28	Red Faber	213
29	Paul Derringer	212
	Chick Fraser	212
	Burleigh Grimes	212
32	Jerry Koosman	209
	Mickey Welch	209
34	Pete Alexander	208
35	Kid Nichols	207
36	Tom Seaver	205
37	Joe Niekro	204
	Jim Whitney	204
	Vic Willis	204
40	George Mullin	196
41	Claude Osteen	195
	Charley Radbourn	195
	Adonis Terry	195
44	Eddie Plank	193
45	Mickey Lolich	191
	Jerry Reuss	191
	Tom Zachary	191
48	Al Orth	189
49	Frank Tanana	188
50	Christy Mathewson	187
51	Mel Harder	186
52	Earl Whitehill	185
53	Jim Bunning	184
54	Joe Bush	183
	Larry Jackson	183
	Rick Reuschel	183
	Curt Simmons	183
58	Hooks Dauss	182
	Waite Hoyt	182
60	Murry Dickson	181
	Dutch Leonard	181
	Rick Wise	181
63	Lee Meadows	180
64	Bill Dinneen	179
	Pink Hawley	179
	Dolf Luque	179
67	John Clarkson	178
	Wilbur Cooper	178
69	Rube Marquard	177
70	Red Donahue	175
	Tom Hughes	175
72	Doyle Alexander	174
	Bob Gibson	174
	Jim Perry	174
	Amos Rusie	174
76	Luis Tiant	172
77	Larry French	171
78	Ted Breitenstein	170
	Camilo Pascual	170
80	Billy Pierce	169
81	Red Ames	167
	Bert Cunningham	167
	Red Ehret	167
84	Don Drysdale	166
	Howard Ehmke	166
	Jim Hunter	166
	George Uhle	166
	Will White	166
89	Mark Baldwin	165
	Bump Hadley	165
	Si Johnson	165
92	Milt Gaston	164
	Win Mercer	164
	Milt Pappas	164
95	Bob Feller	162
	Bill Hutchinson	162
	Herb Pennock	162
98	Vida Blue	161
	Dizzy Trout	161
100	4 players tied	160

Winning Percentage

Rank	Player	Pct
1	Dave Foutz	.690
2	Whitey Ford	.690
3	Bob Caruthers	.688
4	Lefty Grove	.680
5	Vic Raschi	.667
6	Christy Mathewson	.665
7	Larry Corcoran	.665
8	Sam Leever	.661
9	Sal Maglie	.657
10	Sandy Koufax	.655
11	Johnny Allen	.654
12	Ron Guidry	.651
13	Lefty Gomez	.649
14	Mordecai Brown	.648
15	John Clarkson	.648
16	Dizzy Dean	.644
17	Pete Alexander	.642
18	Jim Palmer	.638
19	Kid Nichols	.636
20	Joe McGinnity	.634
21	Deacon Phillippe	.633
22	Ed Reulbach	.632
23	Juan Marichal	.631
24	Mort Cooper	.631
25	Allie Reynolds	.630
26	Jesse Tannehill	.629
27	Eddie Plank	.628
28	Ray Kremer	.627
29	Firpo Marberry	.627
30	Tommy Bond	.627
31	Chief Bender	.624
32	Don Newcombe	.623
33	Nig Cuppy	.623
34	Addie Joss	.623
35	Fred Goldsmith	.622
36	Doc Crandall	.622
37	Carl Hubbell	.622
	Carl Mays	.622
39	Bob Feller	.621
40	Mel Parnell	.621
41	Clark Griffith	.619
42	Cy Young	.619
43	Bob Lemon	.618
44	Monte Ward	.617
45	Urban Shocker	.615
46	Jeff Tesreau	.615
47	Jim Maloney	.615
48	Charley Radbourn	.614
49	Lon Warneke	.613
50	Gary Nolan	.611
51	Schoolboy Rowe	.610
52	Carl Erskine	.610
53	John Candelaria	.609
54	Ed Walsh	.607
55	Charlie Ferguson	.607
56	Dave McNally	.607
57	Hooks Wiltse	.607
58	John Tudor	.607
59	Art Nehf	.605
60	Jack Stivetts	.605
61	Charlie Buffinton	.604
62	Orval Overall	.603
63	Tim Keefe	.603
64	Tom Seaver	.603
65	Stan Coveleski	.602
66	Preacher Roe	.602
67	Wes Ferrell	.601
68	J.R. Richard	.601
69	Jack Chesbro	.600
70	Walter Johnson	.599
71	Freddie Fitzsimmons	.598
72	Eddie Lopat	.597
73	Warren Spahn	.597
74	Herb Pennock	.597
75	Rip Sewell	.596
76	Mickey Welch	.595
77	Mike Garcia	.594
78	Pat Malone	.593
79	General Crowder	.592
80	Bob Welch	.591
81	Harry Brecheen	.591
82	Jim Bagby	.591
83	Bob Gibson	.591
84	Dutch Ruether	.591
85	Denny McLain	.590
86	Eddie Rommel	.590
87	Jack Coombs	.590
88	Tiny Bonham	.589
89	Mike Cuellar	.587
90	Bill Bernhard	.586
91	Jeff Pfeffer	.585
92	Ed Stein	.585
93	Lew Burdette	.585
94	Amos Rusie	.585
95	Dazzy Vance	.585
96	Tommy Bridges	.584
97	Ed Morris	.584
98	Noodles Hahn	.583
99	Eddie Cicotte	.583
100	Jack Morris	.581

Games

Rank	Player	Games
1	Hoyt Wilhelm	1070
2	Kent Tekulve	1050
3	Lindy McDaniel	987
4	Rollie Fingers	944
5	Gene Garber	931
6	Cy Young	906
7	Sparky Lyle	899
8	Jim Kaat	898
9	Don McMahon	874
10	Phil Niekro	864
11	Rich Gossage	853
12	Roy Face	848
13	Tug McGraw	824
14	Walter Johnson	802
15	Gaylord Perry	777
16	Don Sutton	774
17	Darold Knowles	765
18	Tommy John	760
19	Jack Quinn	756
20	Ron Reed	751
21	Warren Spahn	750
22	Tom Burgmeier	745
	Gary Lavelle	745
24	Willie Hernandez	744
25	Steve Carlton	741
26	Ron Perranoski	737
27	Ron Kline	736
28	Clay Carroll	731
29	Mike Marshall	723
30	Charlie Hough	713
31	Johnny Klippstein	711
32	Nolan Ryan	710
33	Stu Miller	704
34	Joe Niekro	702
35	Bill Campbell	700
36	Greg Minton	699
37	Jim Galvin	697
38	Pete Alexander	696
39	Bob Miller	694
40	Grant Jackson	692
	Eppa Rixey	692
42	Early Wynn	691
43	Eddie Fisher	690
44	Ted Abernathy	681
45	Robin Roberts	676
46	Waite Hoyt	674
47	Red Faber	669
	Dan Quisenberry	669
49	Dave Giusti	668
50	Ferguson Jenkins	664
51	Bruce Sutter	661
52	Tom Seaver	656
53	Paul Lindblad	655
54	Wilbur Wood	651
55	Sam Jones	647
	Dave LaRoche	647
	Jeff Reardon	647
58	Bert Blyleven	644
59	Dutch Leonard	640
	Gerry Staley	640
61	Diego Segui	639
62	Bob Stanley	637
63	Christy Mathewson	634
64	Charlie Root	632
65	Jim Perry	630
66	Lew Burdette	626
67	Murry Dickson	625
	Woodie Fryman	625
69	Jerry Reuss	624
	Red Ruffing	624
71	Eddie Plank	622
72	Kid Nichols	621
73	Dick Tidrow	620
74	Herb Pennock	617
75	Burleigh Grimes	616
	Lefty Grove	616
77	Terry Forster	614
78	Jerry Koosman	612
79	Bob Friend	602
	Al Worthington	602
81	Elias Sosa	601
82	Tim Keefe	600
	Bobo Newsom	600
84	Ted Lyons	594
85	Pedro Borbon	593
86	Jim Bunning	591
87	Turk Farrell	590
88	Moe Drabowsky	589
89	Mickey Lolich	586
	Lee Smith	586
91	Billy Pierce	585
92	Jim Brewer	584
93	Mel Harder	582
	Pedro Ramos	582
95	Paul Derringer	579
96	Jack Powell	578
97	Bob Locker	576
98	Stan Bahnsen	574
99	Luis Tiant	573
100	Jim Grant	571

Games Started

1	Cy Young	815
2	Don Sutton	756
3	Phil Niekro	716
4	Steve Carlton	709
5	Tommy John	700
6	Gaylord Perry	690
7	Jim Galvin	682
8	Nolan Ryan	676
9	Walter Johnson	665
	Warren Spahn	665
11	Tom Seaver	647
12	Bert Blyleven	638
13	Jim Kaat	625
14	Early Wynn	612
15	Robin Roberts	609
16	Pete Alexander	598
17	Ferguson Jenkins	594
	Tim Keefe	594
19	Kid Nichols	562
20	Eppa Rixey	552
21	Christy Mathewson	551
22	Mickey Welch	549
23	Jerry Reuss	546
24	Red Ruffing	536
25	Eddie Plank	529
26	Jerry Koosman	527
27	Jim Palmer	521
28	Jim Bunning	519
29	John Clarkson	518
30	Jack Powell	516
31	Rick Reuschel	515
32	Tony Mullane	505
33	Charley Radbourn	503
	Gus Weyhing	503
35	Joe Niekro	500
36	Bob Friend	497
37	Mickey Lolich	496
38	Burleigh Grimes	495
39	Frank Tanana	491
40	Claude Osteen	488
41	Sam Jones	487
42	Jim McCormick	485
43	Bob Feller	484
	Ted Lyons	484
	Luis Tiant	484
46	Red Faber	483
	Bobo Newsom	483
48	Bob Gibson	482
49	Jim Hunter	476
50	Vida Blue	473
	Earl Whitehill	473
52	Vic Willis	471
53	Don Drysdale	465
	Milt Pappas	465
55	Doyle Alexander	464
56	Curt Simmons	461
57	Mike Torrez	458
58	Lefty Grove	457
	Juan Marichal	457
60	Rick Wise	455
61	Jim Perry	447
62	Paul Derringer	445
63	Jack Quinn	444
64	Whitey Ford	438
65	Mel Harder	433
66	Billy Pierce	432
67	Carl Hubbell	431
68	Larry Jackson	429
69	George Mullin	428
70	Amos Rusie	427
71	Freddie Fitzsimmons	426
72	Waite Hoyt	423
73	Bob Forsch	422
74	Herb Pennock	420
75	Ken Holtzman	410
76	Tom Zachary	409
77	Wilbur Cooper	408
78	Adonis Terry	407
79	Bob Knepper	406
80	Lee Meadows	404
	Camilo Pascual	404
82	Rube Marquard	403
83	Will White	401
84	Mike Flanagan	398
	Bucky Walters	398
86	Charlie Buffinton	396
	Dave McNally	396
	Jim Whitney	396
89	Al Orth	394
90	Steve Rogers	393
91	Paul Splittorff	392
92	Chick Fraser	389
93	Hooks Dauss	388
	Jesse Haines	388
95	Stan Coveleski	385
96	Larry French	384
97	Joe McGinnity	381
98	Rick Rhoden	380
99	Mike Cuellar	379
100	Bill Lee	378

Games Started (by era)

1876-1892

1	Jim Galvin	682
2	Tim Keefe	594
3	Mickey Welch	549
4	John Clarkson	518
5	Tony Mullane	505
6	Charley Radbourn	503
	Gus Weyhing	503
8	Jim McCormick	485
9	Adonis Terry	407
10	Will White	401
11	Charlie Buffinton	396
	Jim Whitney	396
13	Silver King	371
14	Bill Hutchinson	345
15	Jack Stivetts	332

1893-1919

1	Cy Young	815
2	Walter Johnson	665
3	Pete Alexander	598
4	Kid Nichols	562
5	Christy Mathewson	551
6	Eddie Plank	529
7	Jack Powell	516
8	Vic Willis	471
9	George Mullin	428
10	Amos Rusie	427
11	Rube Marquard	403
12	Al Orth	394
13	Chick Fraser	389
14	Hooks Dauss	388
15	Joe McGinnity	381

1920-1941

1	Eppa Rixey	552
2	Red Ruffing	536
3	Burleigh Grimes	495
4	Sam Jones	487
5	Ted Lyons	484
6	Red Faber	483
	Bobo Newsom	483
8	Earl Whitehill	473
9	Lefty Grove	457
10	Paul Derringer	445
11	Jack Quinn	444
12	Mel Harder	433
13	Carl Hubbell	431
14	Freddie Fitzsimmons	426
15	Waite Hoyt	423

1942-1960

1	Warren Spahn	665
2	Early Wynn	612
3	Robin Roberts	609
4	Bob Friend	497
5	Bob Feller	484
6	Curt Simmons	461
7	Whitey Ford	438
8	Billy Pierce	432
9	Dutch Leonard	375
10	Hal Newhouser	374
11	Lew Burdette	373
12	Bob Buhl	369
13	Vern Law	364
14	Bob Lemon	350

1961-1989

1	Don Sutton	756
2	Phil Niekro	716
3	Steve Carlton	709
4	Tommy John	700
5	Gaylord Perry	690
6	Nolan Ryan	676
7	Tom Seaver	647
8	Bert Blyleven	638
9	Jim Kaat	625
10	Ferguson Jenkins	594
11	Jerry Reuss	546
12	Jerry Koosman	527
13	Jim Palmer	521
14	Jim Bunning	519
15	Rick Reuschel	515

Complete Games

1	Cy Young	749
2	Jim Galvin	639
3	Tim Keefe	557
4	Kid Nichols	533
5	Walter Johnson	531
6	Mickey Welch	525
7	Charley Radbourn	489
8	John Clarkson	485
9	Tony Mullane	469
10	Jim McCormick	466
11	Gus Weyhing	448
12	Pete Alexander	438
13	Christy Mathewson	434
14	Jack Powell	422
15	Eddie Plank	410
16	Will White	394
17	Amos Rusie	392
18	Vic Willis	388
19	Warren Spahn	382
20	Jim Whitney	377
21	Adonis Terry	368
22	Ted Lyons	356
23	George Mullin	353
24	Charlie Buffinton	351
25	Chick Fraser	342
26	Clark Griffith	337
27	Red Ruffing	335
28	Silver King	329
29	Al Orth	324
30	Bill Hutchinson	319
31	Burleigh Grimes	314
	Joe McGinnity	314
33	Red Donahue	313
34	Guy Hecker	310
35	Bill Dinneen	306
36	Robin Roberts	305
37	Gaylord Perry	303
38	Ted Breitenstein	300
39	Bob Caruthers	298
	Lefty Grove	298
41	Pink Hawley	297
	Ed Morris	297
43	Mark Baldwin	296
44	Tommy Bond	295
45	Brickyard Kennedy	293
46	Eppa Rixey	290
	Early Wynn	290
48	Bill Donovan	289
	Bobby Mathews	289
50	Bert Cunningham	286
51	Wilbur Cooper	279
	Bob Feller	279
	Sadie McMahon	279
54	Jack Stivetts	278
	Jack Taylor	278
56	Charlie Getzien	277
57	Red Faber	273
58	Mordecai Brown	271
59	Jouett Meekin	270
	Frank Dwyer	270
61	Ferguson Jenkins	267
62	Icebox Chamberlin	264
	Matt Kilroy	264
64	Jesse Tannehill	263
65	Doc White	262
66	Jack Chesbro	261
	Rube Waddell	261
68	Red Ehret	260
	Carl Hubbell	260
70	Larry Corcoran	256
71	Chief Bender	255
	Bob Gibson	255
73	Steve Carlton	254
74	Frank Killen	253
75	Win Mercer	252
76	Paul Derringer	251
77	Sam Jones	250
	Ed Walsh	250
79	Eddie Cicotte	249
	Stump Weidman	249
81	Herb Pennock	247
82	Bobo Newsom	246
83	George Bradley	245
	Hooks Dauss	245
	Phil Niekro	245
86	Harry Howell	244
	Juan Marichal	244
	Monte Ward	244
89	Jack Quinn	243
90	Deacon Phillippe	242
	Bucky Walters	242
92	Sam Leever	241
93	Kid Gleason	240
94	Bert Blyleven	239
95	Addie Joss	234
96	George Uhle	232
97	Carl Mays	231
	Tom Seaver	231
	Harry Staley	231
100	Earl Moore	230

Complete Games (by era)

1876-1892

1	Jim Galvin	639
2	Tim Keefe	557
3	Mickey Welch	525
4	Charley Radbourn	489
5	John Clarkson	485
6	Tony Mullane	469
7	Jim McCormick	466
8	Gus Weyhing	448
9	Will White	394
10	Jim Whitney	377
11	Adonis Terry	368
12	Charlie Buffinton	351
13	Silver King	329
14	Bill Hutchinson	319
15	Guy Hecker	310

1893-1919

1	Cy Young	749
2	Kid Nichols	533
3	Walter Johnson	531
4	Pete Alexander	438
5	Christy Mathewson	434
6	Jack Powell	422
7	Eddie Plank	410
8	Amos Rusie	392
9	Vic Willis	388
10	George Mullin	353
11	Chick Fraser	342
12	Clark Griffith	337
13	Al Orth	324
14	Joe McGinnity	314
15	Red Donahue	313

1920-1941

1	Ted Lyons	356
2	Red Ruffing	335
3	Burleigh Grimes	314
4	Lefty Grove	298
5	Eppa Rixey	290
6	Wilbur Cooper	279
7	Red Faber	273
8	Carl Hubbell	260
9	Paul Derringer	251
10	Sam Jones	250
11	Herb Pennock	247
12	Bobo Newsom	246
13	Jack Quinn	243
14	Bucky Walters	242
15	George Uhle	232

1942-1960

1	Warren Spahn	382
2	Robin Roberts	305
3	Early Wynn	290
4	Bob Feller	279
5	Hal Newhouser	212
6	Billy Pierce	193
7	Dutch Leonard	192
8	Bob Lemon	188
9	Eddie Lopat	164
10	Bob Friend	163
	Curt Simmons	163
12	Lew Burdette	158
	Dizzy Trout	158
14	Whitey Ford	156
	Jim Tobin	156

1961-1989

1	Gaylord Perry	303
2	Ferguson Jenkins	267
3	Bob Gibson	255
4	Steve Carlton	254
5	Phil Niekro	245
6	Juan Marichal	244
7	Bert Blyleven	239
8	Tom Seaver	231
9	Nolan Ryan	213
10	Jim Palmer	211
11	Mickey Lolich	195
12	Luis Tiant	187
13	Jim Hunter	181
14	Jim Kaat	180
15	Don Sutton	178

Shutouts

1	Walter Johnson	110
2	Pete Alexander	90
3	Christy Mathewson	79
4	Cy Young	76
5	Eddie Plank	69
6	Warren Spahn	63
7	Tom Seaver	61
8	Bert Blyleven	60
9	Don Sutton	58
10	Nolan Ryan	57
	Ed Walsh	57
12	Jim Galvin	56
	Bob Gibson	56
14	Mordecai Brown	55
	Steve Carlton	55
16	Jim Palmer	53
	Gaylord Perry	53
18	Juan Marichal	52
19	Rube Waddell	50
	Vic Willis	50
21	Don Drysdale	49
	Ferguson Jenkins	49
	Luis Tiant	49
	Early Wynn	49
25	Kid Nichols	48
26	Tommy John	46
	Jack Powell	46
28	Whitey Ford	45
	Addie Joss	45
	Phil Niekro	45
	Robin Roberts	45
	Red Ruffing	45
	Doc White	45
34	Babe Adams	44
	Bob Feller	44
36	Milt Pappas	43
37	Jim Hunter	42
	Bucky Walters	42
39	Mickey Lolich	41
	Hippo Vaughn	41
	Mickey Welch	41
42	Chief Bender	40
	Jim Bunning	40
	Larry French	40
	Sandy Koufax	40
	Claude Osteen	40
	Ed Reulbach	40
	Mel Stottlemyre	40
49	Tim Keefe	39
	Sam Leever	39
	Jerry Reuss	39
52	Stan Coveleski	38
	Billy Pierce	38
	Nap Rucker	38
55	Vida Blue	37
	John Clarkson	37
	Larry Jackson	37
	Eppa Rixey	37
	Steve Rogers	37
60	Tommy Bond	36
	Mike Cuellar	36
	Bob Friend	36
	Carl Hubbell	36
	Sam Jones	36
	Camilo Pascual	36
	Allie Reynolds	36
	Curt Simmons	36
	Will White	36
69	Joe Bush	35
	Jack Chesbro	35
	Eddie Cicotte	35
	Jack Coombs	35
	Wilbur Cooper	35
	Bill Doak	35
	Bill Donovan	35
	Burleigh Grimes	35
	Lefty Grove	35
	George Mullin	35
	Herb Pennock	35
	Charley Radbourn	35
81	Earl Moore	34
	Jesse Tannehill	34
83	Tommy Bridges	33
	Lew Burdette	33
	Dean Chance	33
	Mort Cooper	33
	Jerry Koosman	33
	Lefty Leifield	33
	Dutch Leonard	33
	Jim McCormick	33
	Dave McNally	33
	Hal Newhouser	33
	Bob Shawkey	33
	Virgil Trucks	33
95	Paul Derringer	32
	Joe McGinnity	32
	Jim Perry	32
	Frank Tanana	32
99	7 players tied	31

Saves

1	Rollie Fingers	341
2	Rich Gossage	307
3	Bruce Sutter	300
4	Jeff Reardon	266
5	Dan Quisenberry	244
6	Sparky Lyle	238
7	Lee Smith	234
8	Hoyt Wilhelm	227
9	Gene Garber	218
10	Roy Face	193
11	Mike Marshall	188
	Dave Righetti	188
13	Kent Tekulve	184
14	Tug McGraw	180
15	Ron Perranoski	179
16	Dave Smith	176
17	Lindy McDaniel	172
18	Steve Bedrosian	161
19	Stu Miller	154
20	Don McMahon	153
21	Greg Minton	150
22	Ted Abernathy	148
	Johnny Franco	148
24	Willie Hernandez	147
25	Dave Giusti	145
26	Clay Carroll	143
	Darold Knowles	143
28	Gary Lavelle	136
29	Jim Brewer	132
	Bob Stanley	132
31	Ron Davis	130
32	Terry Forster	127
33	Bill Campbell	126
	Dave LaRoche	126
	Todd Worrell	126
36	John Hiller	125
37	Jack Aker	123
38	Tom Henke	122
	Dick Radatz	122
40	Jesse Orosco	119
41	Jay Howell	117
42	Tippy Martinez	115
43	Frank Linzy	111
44	Al Worthington	110
45	Fred Gladding	109
46	Wayne Granger	108
	Ron Kline	108
48	Johnny Murphy	107
49	Bill Caudill	106
50	Roger McDowell	103
	Ron Reed	103
	John Wyatt	103
53	Tom Burgmeier	102
	Ellis Kinder	102
55	Firpo Marberry	101
56	Dan Plesac	100
57	Joe Hoerner	99
58	Dennis Eckersley	97
	Al Hrabosky	97
60	Clem Labine	96
	Randy Moffitt	96
62	Bob Locker	95
	Tom Niedenfuer	95
64	Aurelio Lopez	93
65	Tom Hume	92
	Phil Regan	92
67	Bobby Thigpen	91
68	Bill Henry	90
69	Donnie Moore	89
70	Jim Kern	88
71	Ken Sanders	86
	Cecil Upshaw	86
73	Mark Davis	85
74	Joe Sambito	84
75	Mark Clear	83
	Turk Farrell	83
	Claude Raymond	83
	Elias Sosa	83
79	Larry Sherry	82
80	Doug Bair	81
	Eddie Fisher	81
82	Pedro Borbon	80
	Eddie Watt	80
84	Don Aase	79
	Grant Jackson	79
86	Al Holland	78
	Doug Jones	78
88	Tim Burke	76
	Joe Page	76
	Tim Stoddard	76
91	Neil Allen	75
	Ed Farmer	75
93	Jim Konstanty	74
94	Bob James	73
	Turk Lown	73
96	Ron Taylor	72
97	Diego Segui	71
98	4 players tied	68

Innings Pitched

1	Cy Young	7357
2	Jim Galvin	5941
3	Walter Johnson	5925
4	Phil Niekro	5404
5	Gaylord Perry	5352
6	Don Sutton	5282
7	Warren Spahn	5246
8	Steve Carlton	5217
9	Pete Alexander	5189
10	Tim Keefe	5061
	Kid Nichols	5061
12	Mickey Welch	4801
13	Nolan Ryan	4786
14	Tom Seaver	4782
15	Christy Mathewson	4778
16	Tommy John	4708
17	Bert Blyleven	4702
18	Robin Roberts	4689
19	Early Wynn	4566
20	Tony Mullane	4540
21	John Clarkson	4537
22	Charley Radbourn	4535
23	Jim Kaat	4529
24	Ferguson Jenkins	4498
25	Eddie Plank	4497
26	Eppa Rixey	4494
27	Jack Powell	4388
28	Red Ruffing	4342
29	Gus Weyhing	4324
30	Jim McCormick	4276
31	Burleigh Grimes	4181
32	Ted Lyons	4162
33	Red Faber	4086
34	Vic Willis	3997
35	Jim Palmer	3948
36	Lefty Grove	3940
37	Jack Quinn	3920
38	Bob Gibson	3885
39	Sam Jones	3884
40	Jerry Koosman	3839
41	Bob Feller	3828
42	Amos Rusie	3769
43	Waite Hoyt	3763
44	Bobo Newsom	3762
45	Jim Bunning	3759
46	George Mullin	3686
47	Jerry Reuss	3662
48	Paul Derringer	3646
49	Mickey Lolich	3640
50	Bob Friend	3612
51	Carl Hubbell	3591
52	Joe Niekro	3585
53	Herb Pennock	3571
54	Earl Whitehill	3562
55	Will White	3542
56	Adonis Terry	3522
57	Juan Marichal	3506
58	Jim Whitney	3496
59	Luis Tiant	3486
60	Wilbur Cooper	3482
61	Claude Osteen	3459
62	Rick Reuschel	3452
63	Jim Hunter	3449
64	Joe McGinnity	3441
65	Don Drysdale	3432
66	Mel Harder	3426
67	Charlie Buffinton	3403
	Frank Tanana	3403
69	Hooks Dauss	3391
70	Clark Griffith	3387
71	Doyle Alexander	3367
72	Al Orth	3356
73	Chick Fraser	3355
74	Curt Simmons	3348
75	Vida Blue	3344
76	Rube Marquard	3309
77	Billy Pierce	3305
78	Jim Perry	3287
79	Larry Jackson	3262
80	Freddie Fitzsimmons	3225
81	Eddie Cicotte	3223
82	Dolf Luque	3221
83	Dutch Leonard	3220
84	Jesse Haines	3208
85	Red Ames	3197
	Charlie Root	3197
87	Silver King	3190
88	Milt Pappas	3187
89	Mordecai Brown	3171
	Whitey Ford	3171
91	Lee Meadows	3160
92	Larry French	3152
93	Tom Zachary	3128
94	Rick Wise	3125
95	George Uhle	3120
96	Bucky Walters	3104
97	Joe Bush	3088
98	Stan Coveleski	3081
99	Bill Dinneen	3075
100	Lew Burdette	3067

Innings Pitched (by era)

1876-1892

1	Jim Galvin	5941
2	Tim Keefe	5061
3	Mickey Welch	4801
4	Tony Mullane	4540
5	John Clarkson	4537
6	Charley Radbourn	4535
7	Gus Weyhing	4324
8	Jim McCormick	4276
9	Will White	3542
10	Adonis Terry	3522
11	Jim Whitney	3496
12	Charlie Buffinton	3403
13	Silver King	3190
14	Bill Hutchinson	3066
15	Guy Hecker	2906

1893-1919

1	Cy Young	7357
2	Walter Johnson	5925
3	Pete Alexander	5189
4	Kid Nichols	5061
5	Christy Mathewson	4778
6	Eddie Plank	4497
7	Jack Powell	4388
8	Vic Willis	3997
9	Amos Rusie	3769
10	George Mullin	3686
11	Joe McGinnity	3441
12	Hooks Dauss	3391
13	Clark Griffith	3387
14	Al Orth	3356
15	Chick Fraser	3355

1920-1941

1	Eppa Rixey	4494
2	Red Ruffing	4342
3	Burleigh Grimes	4181
4	Ted Lyons	4162
5	Red Faber	4086
6	Lefty Grove	3940
7	Jack Quinn	3920
8	Sam Jones	3884
9	Waite Hoyt	3763
10	Bobo Newsom	3762
11	Paul Derringer	3646
12	Carl Hubbell	3591
13	Herb Pennock	3571
14	Earl Whitehill	3562
15	Wilbur Cooper	3482

1942-1960

1	Warren Spahn	5246
2	Robin Roberts	4689
3	Early Wynn	4566
4	Bob Feller	3828
5	Bob Friend	3612
6	Curt Simmons	3348
7	Billy Pierce	3305
8	Dutch Leonard	3220
9	Whitey Ford	3171
10	Lew Burdette	3067
11	Murry Dickson	3053
12	Hal Newhouser	2993
13	Bob Lemon	2849
14	Dizzy Trout	2726
15	Virgil Trucks	2684

1961-1989

1	Phil Niekro	5404
2	Gaylord Perry	5352
3	Don Sutton	5282
4	Steve Carlton	5217
5	Nolan Ryan	4786
6	Tom Seaver	4782
7	Tommy John	4708
8	Bert Blyleven	4702
9	Jim Kaat	4529
10	Ferguson Jenkins	4498
11	Jim Palmer	3948
12	Bob Gibson	3885
13	Jerry Koosman	3839
14	Jim Bunning	3759
15	Jerry Reuss	3662

Hits per Game

1	Nolan Ryan	6.57
2	Sandy Koufax	6.79
3	J.R. Richard	6.88
4	Andy Messersmith	6.94
5	Hoyt Wilhelm	7.02
6	Sam McDowell	7.04
7	Ed Walsh	7.12
8	Bob Turley	7.19
9	Orval Overall	7.23
10	Jeff Tesreau	7.24
11	Ed Reulbach	7.24
12	Mario Soto	7.25
13	Addie Joss	7.30
14	Rich Gossage	7.37
15	Jim Maloney	7.39
16	Rube Waddell	7.47
17	Tom Seaver	7.47
18	Walter Johnson	7.48
19	Bob Gibson	7.60
20	Don Wilson	7.61
21	Charlie Hough	7.63
22	Jim Palmer	7.63
23	Sam Jones	7.68
24	Larry Cheney	7.68
25	Mordecai Brown	7.69
26	Bob Feller	7.69
27	Johnny Vander Meer	7.70
28	Jim Hunter	7.72
29	Al Downing	7.72
30	Jim Scott	7.73
31	Bobby Bolin	7.79
32	Stan Williams	7.80
33	Rollie Fingers	7.80
34	Frank Smith	7.80
35	Dean Chance	7.81
36	Tug McGraw	7.82
37	Barney Pelty	7.84
38	Whitey Ford	7.85
39	Denny McLain	7.86
40	Bob Veale	7.87
41	Fernando Valenzuela	7.88
42	Jack Coombs	7.89
43	George McQuillan	7.89
44	Chief Bender	7.89
45	Dave Stieb	7.90
46	Moe Drabowsky	7.91
47	Vida Blue	7.91
48	Nap Rucker	7.92
49	Tim Keefe	7.92
50	Eddie Plank	7.92
51	Allie Reynolds	7.92
52	Luis Tiant	7.94
53	Christy Mathewson	7.94
54	Rudy May	7.95
55	Ray Culp	7.96
56	Bill Donovan	7.98
57	Juan Pizarro	7.99
58	Howie Camnitz	7.99
59	Don Sutton	7.99
60	Gary Bell	8.01
61	Mike Scott	8.02
62	Earl Moore	8.02
63	Sonny Siebert	8.03
64	Lefty Tyler	8.04
65	Hal Newhouser	8.04
66	Claude Hendrix	8.06
67	Steve Carlton	8.06
68	Hooks Wiltse	8.07
69	Willie Mitchell	8.07
70	Larry Corcoran	8.07
71	Amos Rusie	8.08
72	Bill Singer	8.08
73	Bob Lemon	8.08
74	Stu Miller	8.09
75	Gary Nolan	8.09
76	Don Drysdale	8.09
77	Eddie Cicotte	8.09
78	Juan Marichal	8.09
79	Virgil Trucks	8.10
80	Hippo Vaughn	8.11
81	Doc White	8.12
82	Kirby Higbe	8.12
83	Blue Moon Odom	8.13
84	Mort Cooper	8.14
85	Mike Cuellar	8.14
86	Jim Shaw	8.14
87	Billy Pierce	8.14
88	Bob Welch	8.14
89	Red Ames	8.15
90	Vic Willis	8.15
91	Eddie Fisher	8.17
92	Earl Wilson	8.17
93	Jack Morris	8.17
94	Harry Brecheen	8.18
95	Jim Bibby	8.18
96	Steve Barber	8.18
97	Dave Davenport	8.19
98	Lefty Leifield	8.19
99	Gary Peters	8.19
100	Bob Ewing	8.20

Home Runs Allowed

1	Robin Roberts	505
2	Ferguson Jenkins	484
3	Phil Niekro	482
4	Don Sutton	472
5	Warren Spahn	434
6	Steve Carlton	414
7	Gaylord Perry	399
8	Bert Blyleven	398
9	Jim Kaat	395
10	Tom Seaver	380
11	Jim Hunter	374
12	Jim Bunning	372
13	Mickey Lolich	347
	Frank Tanana	347
15	Luis Tiant	346
16	Early Wynn	338
17	Doyle Alexander	324
18	Juan Marichal	320
19	Pedro Ramos	315
20	Jim Perry	308
21	Jim Palmer	303
22	Murry Dickson	302
	Tommy John	302
24	Milt Pappas	298
25	Jack Morris	295
26	Jim Grant	292
27	Jerry Koosman	290
28	Lew Burdette	289
	Dennis Eckersley	289
30	Bob Friend	286
31	Billy Pierce	284
32	Floyd Bannister	283
33	Charlie Hough	282
34	Don Drysdale	280
35	Nolan Ryan	277
	Jim Slaton	277
37	Joe Niekro	276
38	Vern Law	268
39	Vida Blue	263
40	Rick Wise	261
41	Larry Jackson	259
42	Bob Gibson	257
43	Camilo Pascual	256
44	Mike McCormick	255
	Curt Simmons	255
46	Red Ruffing	254
47	Don Newcombe	252
48	Ken Holtzman	249
	Dennis Martinez	249
	Claude Osteen	249
51	Steve Renko	248
52	Jerry Reuss	244
53	Denny McLain	242
	Johnny Podres	242
55	Harvey Haddix	240
	Ray Sadecki	240
57	Mike Flanagan	239
58	Bob Buhl	238
59	Earl Wilson	236
60	Scott McGregor	235
61	Joe Coleman	234
62	Jim Lonborg	233
63	Jim Clancy	232
64	Dave McNally	230
65	John Candelaria	228
	Whitey Ford	228
67	Carl Hubbell	227
68	Ron Guidry	226
69	Don Cardwell	225
70	Bob Feller	224
71	Stan Bahnsen	223
	Ted Lyons	223
	Mike Torrez	223
74	Mike Cuellar	222
75	Ray Burris	221
	Bob Knepper	221
77	Mike Caldwell	218
	Ron Kline	218
	Frank Viola	218
80	Bob Forsch	216
	Ralph Terry	216
82	Ned Garver	213
	Rick Reuschel	213
84	Bill Monbouquette	211
85	Herm Wehmeier	210
86	Joe Nuxhall	209
	Marty Pattin	209
	Wilbur Wood	209
89	Gary Bell	206
	Bobo Newsom	206
91	Larry Gura	204
	Sandy Koufax	204
	Milt Wilcox	204
94	Johnny Klippstein	203
95	Ross Grimsley	202
	Dennis Leonard	202
97	Juan Pizarro	201
98	Carl Erskine	199
	Rudy May	199
	Preacher Roe	199

Home Runs Allowed (by era)

1876-1892

1	John Clarkson	161
2	Jack Stivetts	131
3	Jim Galvin	122
4	Gus Weyhing	121
5	Charley Radbourn	117
6	Mickey Welch	106
7	Bill Hutchinson	104
8	Tony Mullane	96
9	Charlie Getzien	95
10	Harry Staley	93
11	Charlie Buffinton	87
12	Jim McCormick	85
13	Mark Baldwin	81
	Ad Gumbert	81
15	Jim Whitney	78

1893-1919

1	Pete Alexander	164
2	Kid Nichols	156
3	Cy Young	139
4	Jack Powell	110
5	Frank Dwyer	109
6	Rube Marquard	107
7	Walter Johnson	97
8	Christy Mathewson	92
9	Brickyard Kennedy	91
10	Hooks Dauss	87
11	Kid Carsey	81
12	Ted Breitenstein	79
13	Bill Dinneen	78
14	Amos Rusie	76
15	2 players tied	75

1920-1941

1	Red Ruffing	254
2	Carl Hubbell	227
3	Ted Lyons	223
4	Bobo Newsom	206
5	Earl Whitehill	192
6	Charlie Root	187
7	Freddie Fitzsimmons	186
8	Tommy Bridges	181
9	Lon Warneke	175
10	George Blaeholder	173
	Syl Johnson	173
12	Bump Hadley	167
13	Jesse Haines	165
14	Larry French	164
15	Rube Walberg	163

1942-1960

1	Robin Roberts	505
2	Warren Spahn	434
3	Early Wynn	338
4	Pedro Ramos	315
5	Murry Dickson	302
6	Lew Burdette	289
7	Bob Friend	286
8	Billy Pierce	284
9	Vern Law	268
10	Curt Simmons	255
11	Don Newcombe	252
12	Johnny Podres	242
13	Harvey Haddix	240
14	Bob Buhl	238
15	Whitey Ford	228

1961-1989

1	Ferguson Jenkins	484
2	Phil Niekro	482
3	Don Sutton	472
4	Steve Carlton	414
5	Gaylord Perry	399
6	Bert Blyleven	398
7	Jim Kaat	395
8	Tom Seaver	380
9	Jim Hunter	374
10	Jim Bunning	372
11	Mickey Lolich	347
	Frank Tanana	347
13	Luis Tiant	346
14	Doyle Alexander	324
15	Juan Marichal	320

Walks

1	Nolan Ryan	2540
2	Steve Carlton	1833
3	Phil Niekro	1809
4	Early Wynn	1775
5	Bob Feller	1764
6	Bobo Newsom	1732
7	Amos Rusie	1704
8	Gus Weyhing	1566
9	Red Ruffing	1541
10	Bump Hadley	1442
11	Warren Spahn	1434
12	Earl Whitehill	1431
13	Tony Mullane	1409
14	Sam Jones	1396
15	Tom Seaver	1390
16	Gaylord Perry	1379
17	Mike Torrez	1371
18	Walter Johnson	1359
19	Don Sutton	1343
20	Bob Gibson	1336
21	Chick Fraser	1332
22	Sam McDowell	1312
23	Jim Palmer	1311
24	Mark Baldwin	1307
25	Adonis Terry	1301
26	Mickey Welch	1297
27	Burleigh Grimes	1295
28	Bert Blyleven	1268
	Kid Nichols	1268
30	Joe Bush	1263
	Charlie Hough	1263
32	Joe Niekro	1262
33	Allie Reynolds	1261
34	Tommy John	1259
35	Bob Lemon	1251
36	Hal Newhouser	1249
37	George Mullin	1238
38	Tim Keefe	1224
39	Cy Young	1217
40	Red Faber	1213
41	Vic Willis	1212
42	Ted Breitenstein	1203
43	Brickyard Kennedy	1201
44	Jerry Koosman	1198
45	Tommy Bridges	1192
46	John Clarkson	1191
47	Lefty Grove	1187
48	Vida Blue	1185
49	Billy Pierce	1178
50	Jack Stivetts	1155
51	Johnny Vander Meer	1132
52	Bill Hutchinson	1128
53	Jerry Reuss	1124
54	Ted Lyons	1121
	Bucky Walters	1121
56	Mel Harder	1118
57	Earl Moore	1108
58	Bob Buhl	1105
59	Luis Tiant	1104
60	Mickey Lolich	1099
61	Lefty Gomez	1095
62	Virgil Trucks	1088
63	Whitey Ford	1086
64	Jim Kaat	1083
65	Eppa Rixey	1082
66	Eddie Plank	1072
67	Camilo Pascual	1069
68	Bob Turley	1068
69	Hooks Dauss	1067
70	Icebox Chamberlin	1065
71	Bert Cunningham	1064
72	Curt Simmons	1063
73	Bill Donovan	1059
74	Murry Dickson	1058
	Jouett Meekin	1058
76	Vern Kennedy	1049
77	Dizzy Trout	1046
78	Howard Ehmke	1042
79	Wes Ferrell	1040
80	Tommy Byrne	1037
81	Red Ames	1034
82	Rube Walberg	1031
83	Jack Powell	1021
84	Bob Shawkey	1018
85	Steve Renko	1010
86	Jim Slaton	1004
87	Joe Coleman	1003
	Waite Hoyt	1003
89	Jim Bunning	1000
90	Jim Perry	998
91	Ferguson Jenkins	997
92	Jack Morris	989
93	Kirby Higbe	979
94	Doyle Alexander	978
	Johnny Klippstein	978
96	Pink Hawley	974
97	Silver King	970
98	Frank Tanana	966
	George Uhle	966
100	Rudy May	958

Fewest Walks per Game

1	Tommy Bond	0.58
2	George Bradley	0.67
3	Terry Larkin	0.71
4	Monte Ward	0.92
5	Fred Goldsmith	0.96
6	Jim Whitney	1.06
7	Bobby Mathews	1.11
8	Jim Galvin	1.13
9	Deacon Phillippe	1.25
10	Will White	1.26
11	Babe Adams	1.29
12	Jack Lynch	1.39
13	Addie Joss	1.41
14	Cy Young	1.49
15	Guy Hecker	1.51
16	Lee Richmond	1.53
17	Jesse Tannehill	1.56
18	Jim McCormick	1.58
19	Christy Mathewson	1.58
20	Red Lucas	1.61
21	Nick Altrock	1.62
22	Pete Alexander	1.65
23	Jumbo McGinnis	1.65
24	Tiny Bonham	1.66
25	Ed Morris	1.67
26	Noodles Hahn	1.69
27	Charlie Ferguson	1.72
28	Fritz Peterson	1.73
29	Robin Roberts	1.73
30	Charley Radbourn	1.74
31	Dick Rudolph	1.77
32	Al Orth	1.77
33	Stump Weidman	1.78
34	Pete Donohue	1.80
35	Jess Barnes	1.80
36	Carl Hubbell	1.82
37	Juan Marichal	1.82
38	Slim Sallee	1.83
39	Bill Bernhard	1.83
40	Lew Burdette	1.84
41	Curt Davis	1.85
42	Ed Siever	1.86
43	Larry Corcoran	1.87
44	Ed Walsh	1.87
45	Ken Raffensberger	1.88
46	Paul Derringer	1.88
47	Bob Caruthers	1.90
48	Mordecai Brown	1.91
49	Sherry Smith	1.93
50	Bill Swift	1.93
51	George Suggs	1.93
52	Watty Clark	1.97
53	Jack Quinn	1.97
54	Frank Kitson	1.98
55	Doc White	1.98
56	Sam Leever	1.99
57	Henry Boyle	1.99
58	Ferguson Jenkins	1.99
59	Jack Taylor	2.00
60	Vern Law	2.01
61	Dupee Shaw	2.02
62	Syl Johnson	2.03
63	Jim Barr	2.04
64	Don Newcombe	2.05
65	John Candelaria	2.05
66	Clark Griffith	2.06
67	George Winter	2.06
68	Dutch Leonard	2.06
69	Walter Johnson	2.06
70	Scott Stratton	2.07
71	Hal Brown	2.08
72	Lary Sorensen	2.08
73	Red Donahue	2.09
74	Larry Jansen	2.09
75	Jack Powell	2.09
76	Dizzy Dean	2.10
77	Bill Monbouquette	2.12
78	Hooks Wiltse	2.12
79	Joe McGinnity	2.12
80	Chief Bender	2.12
81	Art Nehf	2.13
82	Charlie Getzien	2.13
83	Ken Johnson	2.14
84	Jack Chesbro	2.14
85	Eddie Plank	2.15
86	Dennis Eckersley	2.15
87	Jim Kaat	2.15
88	Sloppy Thurston	2.15
89	Phil Douglas	2.16
90	Eppa Rixey	2.17
91	Ralph Terry	2.17
92	Bob Purkey	2.17
93	Tim Keefe	2.18
94	Scott McGregor	2.18
95	Bill Gullickson	2.18
96	Carl Mays	2.19
97	Bill Sherdel	2.20
98	Bill Duggleby	2.20
99	Doc Crandall	2.20
100	Wilbur Cooper	2.20

Strikeouts

1	Nolan Ryan	5076
2	Steve Carlton	4136
3	Tom Seaver	3640
4	Don Sutton	3574
5	Bert Blyleven	3562
6	Gaylord Perry	3534
7	Walter Johnson	3506
8	Phil Niekro	3342
9	Ferguson Jenkins	3192
10	Bob Gibson	3117
11	Jim Bunning	2855
12	Mickey Lolich	2832
13	Cy Young	2803
14	Warren Spahn	2583
15	Bob Feller	2581
16	Jerry Koosman	2556
17	Tim Keefe	2527
18	Christy Mathewson	2502
19	Don Drysdale	2486
20	Jim Kaat	2461
21	Sam McDowell	2453
22	Luis Tiant	2416
23	Sandy Koufax	2396
24	Robin Roberts	2357
25	Frank Tanana	2345
26	Early Wynn	2334
27	Rube Waddell	2316
28	Juan Marichal	2303
29	Lefty Grove	2266
30	Eddie Plank	2246
31	Tommy John	2245
32	Jim Palmer	2212
33	Pete Alexander	2198
34	Vida Blue	2175
35	Camilo Pascual	2167
36	Bobo Newsom	2082
37	Dazzy Vance	2045
38	Jim Hunter	2012
39	Billy Pierce	1999
40	Red Ruffing	1987
41	John Clarkson	1978
42	Rick Reuschel	1962
43	Whitey Ford	1956
44	Amos Rusie	1934
45	Jerry Reuss	1906
46	Charlie Hough	1874
47	Kid Nichols	1868
48	Dennis Eckersley	1865
49	Mickey Welch	1850
50	Charley Radbourn	1830
51	Jack Morris	1818
52	Tony Mullane	1807
53	Jim Galvin	1799
54	Hal Newhouser	1796
55	Ron Guidry	1778
56	Rudy May	1760
57	Joe Niekro	1747
58	Ed Walsh	1736
59	Bob Friend	1734
60	Joe Coleman	1728
	Milt Pappas	1728
62	Chief Bender	1711
63	Larry Jackson	1709
64	Jim McCormick	1704
65	Bob Veale	1703
66	Red Ames	1702
67	Charlie Buffinton	1700
68	Curt Simmons	1697
69	Floyd Bannister	1677
	Carl Hubbell	1677
71	Tommy Bridges	1674
72	Gus Weyhing	1665
73	Vic Willis	1651
74	Rick Wise	1647
75	Fernando Valenzuela	1644
76	Al Downing	1639
77	Mike Cuellar	1632
78	Chris Short	1629
79	Andy Messersmith	1625
80	Jack Powell	1621
	Steve Rogers	1621
82	Ray Sadecki	1614
83	Claude Osteen	1612
84	Hoyt Wilhelm	1610
85	Jim Maloney	1605
86	Ken Holtzman	1601
87	Rube Marquard	1593
88	Woodie Fryman	1587
	Bob Welch	1587
90	Jim Perry	1576
91	Harvey Haddix	1575
92	Jim Whitney	1571
93	Adonis Terry	1555
94	Bill Donovan	1552
95	Dean Chance	1534
	Virgil Trucks	1534
97	John Candelaria	1532
98	Doyle Alexander	1528
99	Juan Pizarro	1522
100	Jon Matlack	1516

Strikeouts per Game

1	Nolan Ryan	9.55
2	Sandy Koufax	9.27
3	Sam McDowell	8.86
4	J.R. Richard	8.37
5	Bob Veale	7.96
6	Jim Maloney	7.81
7	Rich Gossage	7.59
8	Mario Soto	7.53
9	Sam Jones	7.53
10	Bob Gibson	7.22
11	Steve Carlton	7.14
12	Rube Waddell	7.03
13	Mickey Lolich	7.00
14	Fernando Valenzuela	6.90
15	Rollie Fingers	6.87
16	Tom Seaver	6.85
17	Jim Bunning	6.84
18	Bert Blyleven	6.82
19	Juan Pizarro	6.73
20	Bobby Bolin	6.71
21	Ray Culp	6.69
22	Ron Guidry	6.69
23	Stan Williams	6.66
24	Bob Turley	6.66
25	Camilo Pascual	6.66
26	Don Wilson	6.61
27	Tug McGraw	6.58
28	Denny Lemaster	6.57
29	Andy Messersmith	6.56
30	Mike Scott	6.52
31	Don Drysdale	6.52
32	Al Downing	6.50
33	Floyd Bannister	6.49
34	Toad Ramsey	6.49
35	Diego Segui	6.46
36	Bruce Hurst	6.45
37	Hoyt Wilhelm	6.43
38	Dean Chance	6.43
39	Ferguson Jenkins	6.39
40	Moe Drabowsky	6.38
41	Earl Wilson	6.37
42	Harvey Haddix	6.34
43	Sonny Siebert	6.32
44	Chris Short	6.31
45	Bob Welch	6.28
46	Bill Singer	6.27
47	Luis Tiant	6.24
48	Frank Viola	6.23
49	Turk Farrell	6.22
50	Dazzy Vance	6.20
51	Frank Tanana	6.20
52	Stu Miller	6.18
53	Clay Kirby	6.16
54	Gary Bell	6.15
55	Gary Peters	6.14
56	Dennis Eckersley	6.12
57	Denny McLain	6.12
58	Don Sutton	6.09
59	Mike Krukow	6.07
60	Bob Feller	6.07
61	Fred Norman	6.05
62	Joe Coleman	6.05
63	Rudy May	6.04
64	Scott Sanderson	6.01
65	Rick Sutcliffe	6.00
66	Jerry Koosman	5.99
67	Dave Stewart	5.98
68	Don Robinson	5.95
69	Gaylord Perry	5.94
70	Danny Darwin	5.94
71	Mike Boddicker	5.93
72	Woodie Fryman	5.92
73	Juan Marichal	5.91
74	John Montefusco	5.90
75	Steve Barber	5.89
76	Mike Moore	5.87
77	Mike Witt	5.87
78	Jack Morris	5.86
79	Vida Blue	5.85
80	Charlie Hough	5.84
81	John Candelaria	5.82
82	Joey Jay	5.81
83	Ray Sadecki	5.81
84	Jim O'Toole	5.79
85	Dave Giusti	5.78
86	Jon Matlack	5.77
87	Larry Dierker	5.75
88	Lindy McDaniel	5.72
89	Tony Cloninger	5.70
90	Johnny Podres	5.70
91	Jim Bibby	5.64
92	Billy O'Dell	5.62
93	Gene Garber	5.61
94	Gary Nolan	5.58
95	Phil Niekro	5.57
96	Billy Hoeft	5.55
97	Whitey Ford	5.55
98	Johnny Vander Meer	5.54
99	Pat Dobson	5.53
100	Orval Overall	5.48

Earned Run Average

1	Ed Walsh	1.82
2	Addie Joss	1.89
3	Mordecai Brown	2.06
4	Monte Ward	2.10
5	Christy Mathewson	2.13
6	Rube Waddell	2.16
7	Walter Johnson	2.17
8	Orval Overall	2.24
9	Tommy Bond	2.25
10	Ed Reulbach	2.28
	Will White	2.28
12	Jim Scott	2.30
13	Larry Corcoran	2.35
	Eddie Plank	2.35
15	Eddie Cicotte	2.38
	Ed Killian	2.38
	George McQuillan	2.38
18	Doc White	2.39
19	Nap Rucker	2.42
20	Jim McCormick	2.43
	Jeff Tesreau	2.43
22	Terry Larkin	2.44
23	Chief Bender	2.46
24	Sam Leever	2.47
	Lefty Leifield	2.47
	Hooks Wiltse	2.47
27	Hippo Vaughn	2.48
28	Bob Ewing	2.49
29	George Bradley	2.50
30	Hoyt Wilhelm	2.52
31	Noodles Hahn	2.55
32	Pete Alexander	2.56
	Slim Sallee	2.56
34	Deacon Phillippe	2.58
	Frank Smith	2.58
36	Ed Siever	2.60
37	Bob Rhoads	2.61
38	Tim Keefe	2.62
39	Red Ames	2.63
	Barney Pelty	2.63
	Vic Willis	2.63
	Cy Young	2.63
43	Claude Hendrix	2.65
44	Joe McGinnity	2.66
	Dick Rudolph	2.66
46	Nick Altrock	2.67
	Charlie Ferguson	2.67
	Jack Taylor	2.67
	Carl Weilman	2.67
50	Jack Chesbro	2.68
	Cy Falkenberg	2.68
	Charley Radbourn	2.68
53	Bill Donovan	2.69
	Fred Toney	2.69
55	Larry Cheney	2.70
56	Mickey Welch	2.71
57	Fred Goldsmith	2.73
58	Whitey Ford	2.74
	Harry Howell	2.74
60	Howie Camnitz	2.75
	Dummy Taylor	2.75
62	Babe Adams	2.76
	Sandy Koufax	2.76
	Dutch Leonard	2.76
65	Jeff Pfeffer	2.77
66	Jack Coombs	2.78
	Earl Moore	2.78
68	Tully Sparks	2.79
	Jesse Tannehill	2.79
70	Phil Douglas	2.80
71	John Clarkson	2.81
72	Ray Fisher	2.82
	Ed Morris	2.82
	George Mullin	2.82
75	Bob Caruthers	2.84
	Dave Foutz	2.84
77	Andy Messersmith	2.86
	Jim Palmer	2.86
	Tom Seaver	2.86
80	Jim Galvin	2.87
	George Winter	2.87
82	Willie Mitchell	2.88
83	Wilbur Cooper	2.89
	Stan Coveleski	2.89
	Juan Marichal	2.89
86	Rollie Fingers	2.90
87	Bob Gibson	2.91
88	Harry Brecheen	2.92
	Dean Chance	2.92
	Doc Crandall	2.92
	Rich Gossage	2.92
	Guy Hecker	2.92
	Carl Mays	2.92
	Jumbo McGinnis	2.92
95	Dave Davenport	2.93
96	Don Drysdale	2.95
	Kid Nichols	2.95
	Lefty Tyler	2.95
99	Charlie Buffinton	2.96
	Mort Cooper	2.96

Earned Run Average (by era)

1876-1892

1	Monte Ward	2.10
2	Tommy Bond	2.25
3	Will White	2.28
4	Larry Corcoran	2.35
5	Jim McCormick	2.43
6	Terry Larkin	2.44
7	George Bradley	2.50
8	Tim Keefe	2.62
9	Charlie Ferguson	2.67
10	Charley Radbourn	2.68
11	Mickey Welch	2.71
12	Fred Goldsmith	2.73
13	John Clarkson	2.81
14	Ed Morris	2.82
15	2 players tied	2.84

1893-1919

1	Ed Walsh	1.82
2	Addie Joss	1.89
3	Mordecai Brown	2.06
4	Christy Mathewson	2.13
5	Rube Waddell	2.16
6	Walter Johnson	2.17
7	Orval Overall	2.24
8	Ed Reulbach	2.28
9	Jim Scott	2.30
10	Eddie Plank	2.35
11	Eddie Cicotte	2.38
	Ed Killian	2.38
	George McQuillan	2.38
14	Doc White	2.39
15	Nap Rucker	2.42

1920-1941

1	Wilbur Cooper	2.89
	Stan Coveleski	2.89
3	Carl Mays	2.92
4	Carl Hubbell	2.98
5	Dizzy Dean	3.04
6	Lefty Grove	3.06
7	Bob Shawkey	3.09
8	Red Faber	3.15
	Eppa Rixey	3.15
10	Urban Shocker	3.17
11	Lon Warneke	3.18
12	Art Nehf	3.20
13	Jess Barnes	3.21
14	George Mogridge	3.23
15	2 players tied	3.24

1942-1960

1	Hoyt Wilhelm	2.52
2	Whitey Ford	2.74
3	Harry Brecheen	2.92
4	Mort Cooper	2.96
5	Max Lanier	3.01
6	Tiny Bonham	3.06
	Hal Newhouser	3.06
8	Warren Spahn	3.08
9	Sal Maglie	3.15
10	Eddie Lopat	3.21
11	Bob Lemon	3.23
	Dizzy Trout	3.23
13	Stu Miller	3.24
14	Bob Feller	3.25
	Dutch Leonard	3.25

1961-1989

1	Sandy Koufax	2.76
2	Andy Messersmith	2.86
	Jim Palmer	2.86
	Tom Seaver	2.86
5	Juan Marichal	2.89
6	Rollie Fingers	2.90
7	Bob Gibson	2.91
8	Dean Chance	2.92
	Rich Gossage	2.92
10	Don Drysdale	2.95
11	Mel Stottlemyre	2.97
12	Bob Veale	3.07
13	Gary Nolan	3.08
14	Joe Horlen	3.10
	Gaylord Perry	3.10

Adjusted Earned Run Average

1	Lefty Grove	148
2	Walter Johnson	147
3	Ed Walsh	146
	Hoyt Wilhelm	146
5	Addie Joss	142
6	Mordecai Brown	140
	Kid Nichols	140
8	Cy Young	138
9	Rube Waddell	136
10	Pete Alexander	135
	Christy Mathewson	135
12	John Clarkson	134
13	Harry Brecheen	133
	Whitey Ford	133
	Noodles Hahn	133
16	Sandy Koufax	131
17	Carl Hubbell	130
	Hal Newhouser	130
19	Dizzy Dean	129
	Amos Rusie	129
21	Rich Gossage	128
22	Stan Coveleski	127
	Nig Cuppy	127
	Bob Gibson	127
	Tom Seaver	127
26	Tommy Bridges	126
	Tim Keefe	126
	Max Lanier	126
	Sal Maglie	126
30	Lefty Gomez	125
	Jim Palmer	125
32	Dave Foutz	124
	Mel Parnell	124
	Urban Shocker	124
	Dave Stieb	124
	Dizzy Trout	124
	Dazzy Vance	124
38	Mort Cooper	123
	Silver King	123
	Sam Leever	123
	Ed Reulbach	123
42	Eddie Cicotte	122
	Larry Corcoran	122
	Bob Feller	122
	Juan Marichal	122
	Andy Messersmith	122
	Eddie Plank	122
	Eddie Rommel	122
49	Bert Blyleven	121
	Bob Caruthers	121
	Don Drysdale	121
	Clark Griffith	121
	Joe McGinnity	121
	Orval Overall	121
	Deacon Phillippe	121
	Jack Stivetts	121
	Hippo Vaughn	121
	Will White	121
59	Tiny Bonham	120
	Jim Scott	120
	John Tudor	120
	Lon Warneke	120
63	Dean Chance	119
	Red Faber	119
	Rollie Fingers	119
	Ron Guidry	119
	Bob Lemon	119
	Dutch Leonard	119
	Carl Mays	119
	Billy Pierce	119
	Charley Radbourn	119
	Toad Ramsey	119
	Nap Rucker	119
	Bobby Shantz	119
	Monte Ward	119
76	Charlie Ferguson	118
	Thornton Lee	118
	Dolf Luque	118
	Ted Lyons	118
	Jim McCormick	118
	Sadie McMahon	118
	Warren Spahn	118
	Bob Stanley	118
84	Babe Adams	117
	Wes Ferrell	117
	Gene Garber	117
	Mike Garcia	117
	Firpo Marberry	117
	Tony Mullane	117
	Gary Nolan	117
	Gaylord Perry	117
	Ed Siever	117
	Virgil Trucks	117
94	12 players tied	116

Adjusted ERA (by era)

1876-1892

1	John Clarkson	134
2	Tim Keefe	126
3	Dave Foutz	124
4	Silver King	123
5	Larry Corcoran	122
6	Bob Caruthers	121
	Jack Stivetts	121
	Will White	121
9	Charley Radbourn	119
	Toad Ramsey	119
	Monte Ward	119
12	Charlie Ferguson	118
	Jim McCormick	118
	Sadie McMahon	118
15	Tony Mullane	117

1893-1919

1	Walter Johnson	147
2	Ed Walsh	146
3	Addie Joss	142
4	Mordecai Brown	140
	Kid Nichols	140
6	Cy Young	138
7	Rube Waddell	136
8	Pete Alexander	135
	Christy Mathewson	135
10	Noodles Hahn	133
11	Amos Rusie	129
12	Nig Cuppy	127
13	Sam Leever	123
	Ed Reulbach	123
15	2 players tied	122

1920-1941

1	Lefty Grove	148
2	Carl Hubbell	130
3	Dizzy Dean	129
4	Stan Coveleski	127
5	Tommy Bridges	126
6	Lefty Gomez	125
7	Urban Shocker	124
	Dazzy Vance	124
9	Eddie Rommel	122
10	Lon Warneke	120
11	Red Faber	119
	Carl Mays	119
13	Thornton Lee	118
	Dolf Luque	118
	Ted Lyons	118

1942-1960

1	Hoyt Wilhelm	146
2	Harry Brecheen	133
	Whitey Ford	133
4	Hal Newhouser	130
5	Max Lanier	126
	Sal Maglie	126
7	Mel Parnell	124
	Dizzy Trout	124
9	Mort Cooper	123
10	Bob Feller	122
11	Tiny Bonham	120
12	Bob Lemon	119
	Dutch Leonard	119
	Billy Pierce	119
	Bobby Shantz	119

1961-1989

1	Sandy Koufax	131
2	Rich Gossage	128
3	Bob Gibson	127
	Tom Seaver	127
5	Jim Palmer	125
6	Dave Stieb	124
7	Juan Marichal	122
	Andy Messersmith	122
9	Bert Blyleven	121
	Don Drysdale	121
11	John Tudor	120
12	Dean Chance	119
	Rollie Fingers	119
	Ron Guidry	119
15	Bob Stanley	118

Pitching Runs

1	Cy Young	755
2	Walter Johnson	706
3	Lefty Grove	595
4	Kid Nichols	533
5	Pete Alexander	484
6	Warren Spahn	471
7	Tom Seaver	422
8	Christy Mathewson	417
	Amos Rusie	417
10	Tim Keefe	402
11	Carl Hubbell	394
12	Whitey Ford	387
13	Bob Feller	385
14	Jim Palmer	378
15	John Clarkson	369
16	Lefty Gomez	322
17	Gaylord Perry	315
18	Ted Lyons	314
19	Ed Walsh	312
20	Hoyt Wilhelm	310
21	Bert Blyleven	307
22	Charley Radbourn	299
23	Red Faber	294
24	Mordecai Brown	293
25	Bob Gibson	291
26	Nolan Ryan	281
	Dazzy Vance	281
28	Red Ruffing	271
29	Dutch Leonard	267
	Eddie Plank	267
31	Don Drysdale	266
32	Robin Roberts	264
33	Don Sutton	263
34	Juan Marichal	262
35	Tommy Bridges	257
	Stan Coveleski	257
37	Hal Newhouser	256
38	Bob Lemon	250
	Eppa Rixey	250
40	Billy Pierce	249
41	Tony Mullane	247
42	Dolf Luque	245
43	Sandy Koufax	244
44	Steve Carlton	240
	Rube Waddell	240
46	Clark Griffith	233
47	Carl Mays	217
48	Tommy John	216
49	Addie Joss	215
50	Bob Caruthers	213
	Jim McCormick	213
	Mickey Welch	213
53	Waite Hoyt	210
	Urban Shocker	210
55	Silver King	207
56	Ron Guidry	204
57	Nig Cuppy	201
58	Eddie Cicotte	200
59	Will White	198
60	Phil Niekro	196
61	Harry Brecheen	193
62	Mel Harder	190
63	Dave Stieb	189
64	Lon Warneke	187
65	Eddie Lopat	185
66	Dizzy Dean	184
67	Joe McGinnity	183
68	Eddie Rommel	180
69	Jim Bunning	179
70	Larry French	178
71	Ed Morris	177
	Dizzy Trout	177
73	Spud Chandler	176
74	Mike Garcia	175
75	Freddie Fitzsimmons	174
	Andy Messersmith	174
77	Sam Leever	173
	Sadie McMahon	173
79	Frank Tanana	172
80	Early Wynn	171
81	Vic Willis	170
82	Wilbur Cooper	169
	Thornton Lee	169
84	Ed Reulbach	167
85	Jack Quinn	162
86	Babe Adams	161
87	Charlie Buffinton	160
	Ferguson Jenkins	160
89	Noodles Hahn	158
	Orel Hershiser	158
91	Jim Galvin	157
92	Vida Blue	155
	Sal Maglie	155
	Firpo Marberry	155
95	Guy Hecker	153
96	Deacon Phillippe	152
	Joe Wood	152
98	4 players tied	151

Adjusted Pitching Runs

1	Cy Young	811
2	Kid Nichols	667
3	Walter Johnson	666
4	Lefty Grove	644
5	Pete Alexander	523
6	John Clarkson	485
7	Tom Seaver	415
8	Christy Mathewson	395
9	Tim Keefe	382
10	Amos Rusie	372
11	Bert Blyleven	361
12	Carl Hubbell	354
13	Bob Gibson	338
14	Warren Spahn	331
15	Gaylord Perry	320
16	Whitey Ford	318
	Jim Palmer	318
18	Hal Newhouser	305
19	Ted Lyons	304
20	Phil Niekro	302
21	Bob Feller	299
22	Tommy Bridges	293
23	Hoyt Wilhelm	289
24	Mordecai Brown	288
25	Ed Walsh	273
26	Steve Carlton	271
27	Stan Coveleski	270
28	Red Faber	266
29	Eddie Plank	261
	Dazzy Vance	261
31	Clark Griffith	258
	Tony Mullane	258
33	Charley Radbourn	256
34	Ferguson Jenkins	255
	Jack Stivetts	255
36	Silver King	253
	Rube Waddell	253
38	Eppa Rixey	248
39	Juan Marichal	246
40	Nig Cuppy	242
41	Robin Roberts	239
42	Don Drysdale	232
	Dizzy Trout	232
44	Urban Shocker	230
45	Lefty Gomez	229
46	Billy Pierce	228
47	Sandy Koufax	223
48	Dave Stieb	222
49	Dutch Leonard	221
50	Eddie Rommel	217
51	Joe McGinnity	213
52	Jim McCormick	208
53	Harry Brecheen	206
54	Addie Joss	205
	Dolf Luque	205
56	Jack Quinn	204
57	Jim Bunning	200
58	Wes Ferrell	198
59	Dizzy Dean	194
60	Rick Reuschel	193
61	Nolan Ryan	192
	Lon Warneke	192
63	Bob Caruthers	190
	Bob Lemon	190
65	Noodles Hahn	189
	Mickey Welch	189
67	Carl Mays	187
	Sadie McMahon	187
	Vic Willis	187
70	Eddie Cicotte	186
71	Will White	184
72	Mel Harder	182
73	Wilbur Cooper	180
74	Waite Hoyt	179
75	Tommy John	178
76	Virgil Trucks	175
77	Red Ruffing	173
78	Frank Dwyer	172
79	Roger Clemens	170
80	Ron Guidry	169
	Bucky Walters	169
82	Thornton Lee	168
	Sam Leever	168
84	Larry French	167
85	Luis Tiant	164
86	Mel Parnell	163
87	Steve Rogers	159
88	Sal Maglie	158
89	Babe Adams	157
	Deacon Phillippe	157
91	Larry Jackson	156
	Hippo Vaughn	156
93	Jim Galvin	154
	Dan Quisenberry	154
	Joe Wood	154
96	Andy Messersmith	153
	Ed Reulbach	153
98	4 players tied	151

Pitching Wins

1	Walter Johnson	73.2
2	Cy Young	71.0
3	Lefty Grove	55.5
4	Pete Alexander	49.7
5	Warren Spahn	47.5
6	Kid Nichols	47.3
7	Tom Seaver	44.1
8	Christy Mathewson	43.9
9	Whitey Ford	39.4
10	Jim Palmer	39.2
11	Carl Hubbell	38.8
12	Bob Feller	37.5
13	Tim Keefe	36.0
14	Amos Rusie	35.9
15	Ed Walsh	33.6
16	Gaylord Perry	33.0
17	John Clarkson	32.9
18	Hoyt Wilhelm	31.9
19	Bert Blyleven	31.6
20	Mordecai Brown	31.3
21	Bob Gibson	30.6
22	Lefty Gomez	29.9
23	Ted Lyons	29.5
24	Nolan Ryan	29.3
25	Red Faber	28.9
26	Eddie Plank	28.3
27	Don Drysdale	27.7
28	Juan Marichal	27.6
29	Don Sutton	27.3
30	Dazzy Vance	27.0
31	Robin Roberts	26.6
32	Charley Radbourn	26.6
33	Dutch Leonard	26.4
34	Hal Newhouser	25.9
35	Stan Coveleski	25.7
36	Red Ruffing	25.5
37	Rube Waddell	25.3
38	Sandy Koufax	25.2
39	Steve Carlton	25.2
40	Eppa Rixey	25.1
41	Billy Pierce	25.0
42	Bob Lemon	24.9
43	Tommy Bridges	24.2
44	Dolf Luque	23.9
45	Addie Joss	23.3
46	Tommy John	22.3
47	Carl Mays	22.0
48	Tony Mullane	21.6
49	Eddie Cicotte	21.4
50	Clark Griffith	20.8
51	Urban Shocker	20.5
52	Phil Niekro	20.4
53	Ron Guidry	20.4
54	Waite Hoyt	20.2
55	Harry Brecheen	19.5
56	Jim McCormick	19.5
57	Mickey Welch	19.4
58	Dave Stieb	18.9
59	Lon Warneke	18.8
60	Bob Caruthers	18.7
61	Eddie Lopat	18.7
62	Jim Bunning	18.6
63	Andy Messersmith	18.4
64	Joe McGinnity	18.3
65	Dizzy Dean	18.3
66	Will White	18.1
67	Mel Harder	18.1
68	Ed Reulbach	18.0
69	Dizzy Trout	17.9
70	Silver King	17.9
71	Sam Leever	17.6
72	Spud Chandler	17.6
73	Larry French	17.6
74	Wilbur Cooper	17.6
75	Mike Garcia	17.5
76	Vic Willis	17.5
77	Frank Tanana	17.4
78	Early Wynn	17.3
79	Nig Cuppy	17.1
80	Eddie Rommel	17.1
81	Freddie Fitzsimmons	17.1
82	Babe Adams	16.7
83	Ferguson Jenkins	16.7
84	Orel Hershiser	16.5
85	Thornton Lee	16.3
86	Jack Quinn	16.2
87	Vida Blue	16.2
88	Joe Wood	15.9
89	Ed Morris	15.8
90	Steve Rogers	15.6
91	Sal Maglie	15.5
92	Rich Gossage	15.5
93	Noodles Hahn	15.5
94	Jerry Koosman	15.4
95	Deacon Phillippe	15.3
96	Bucky Walters	15.3
97	Jon Matlack	15.3
98	Bob Shawkey	15.2
99	Rollie Fingers	15.2
100	Dwight Gooden	15.2

Adjusted Pitching Wins

1	Cy Young	76.2
2	Walter Johnson	69.0
3	Lefty Grove	60.0
4	Kid Nichols	59.2
5	Pete Alexander	53.7
6	Tom Seaver	43.4
7	John Clarkson	43.3
8	Christy Mathewson	41.6
9	Bert Blyleven	37.1
10	Bob Gibson	35.5
11	Carl Hubbell	34.9
12	Tim Keefe	34.2
13	Gaylord Perry	33.5
14	Warren Spahn	33.4
15	Jim Palmer	33.0
16	Whitey Ford	32.4
17	Amos Rusie	32.0
18	Phil Niekro	31.5
19	Hal Newhouser	30.9
20	Mordecai Brown	30.8
21	Hoyt Wilhelm	29.7
22	Ed Walsh	29.4
23	Bob Feller	29.1
24	Ted Lyons	28.6
25	Steve Carlton	28.4
26	Eddie Plank	27.7
27	Tommy Bridges	27.6
28	Stan Coveleski	27.0
29	Ferguson Jenkins	26.6
30	Rube Waddell	26.6
31	Red Faber	26.2
32	Juan Marichal	25.9
33	Dazzy Vance	25.1
34	Eppa Rixey	24.9
35	Don Drysdale	24.2
36	Robin Roberts	24.1
37	Dizzy Trout	23.5
38	Clark Griffith	23.1
39	Sandy Koufax	23.1
40	Billy Pierce	22.9
41	Charley Radbourn	22.8
42	Tony Mullane	22.5
43	Urban Shocker	22.5
44	Addie Joss	22.2
45	Dave Stieb	22.2
46	Dutch Leonard	21.9
47	Silver King	21.8
48	Jack Stivetts	21.3
49	Joe McGinnity	21.3
50	Lefty Gomez	21.3
51	Harry Brecheen	20.8
52	Jim Bunning	20.8
53	Nig Cuppy	20.6
54	Eddie Rommel	20.6
55	Jack Quinn	20.4
56	Rick Reuschel	20.2
57	Dolf Luque	20.0
58	Nolan Ryan	20.0
59	Eddie Cicotte	19.9
60	Lon Warneke	19.3
61	Dizzy Dean	19.3
62	Vic Willis	19.2
63	Jim McCormick	19.0
64	Bob Lemon	18.9
65	Carl Mays	18.9
66	Wilbur Cooper	18.7
67	Noodles Hahn	18.5
68	Tommy John	18.4
69	Wes Ferrell	18.2
70	Virgil Trucks	17.7
71	Mel Harder	17.3
72	Luis Tiant	17.2
73	Mickey Welch	17.2
74	Waite Hoyt	17.2
75	Bucky Walters	17.2
76	Sam Leever	17.1
77	Hippo Vaughn	17.0
78	Ron Guidry	16.9
79	Roger Clemens	16.9
80	Will White	16.8
81	Bob Caruthers	16.7
82	Steve Rogers	16.6
83	Larry French	16.5
84	Ed Reulbach	16.5
85	Babe Adams	16.3
86	Red Ruffing	16.3
87	Larry Jackson	16.2
88	Thornton Lee	16.2
89	Andy Messersmith	16.2
90	Joe Wood	16.1
91	Mel Parnell	16.1
92	Deacon Phillippe	15.8
93	Sal Maglie	15.8
94	Don Sutton	15.7
95	Jerry Koosman	15.7
96	Sadie McMahon	15.6
97	Rich Gossage	15.5
98	Dan Quisenberry	15.5
99	Dennis Eckersley	15.3
100	Kent Tekulve	15.1

Opponents' Batting Average

1	Nolan Ryan	.204
2	Sandy Koufax	.205
3	Andy Messersmith	.212
	J.R. Richard	.212
5	Sam McDowell	.215
6	Hoyt Wilhelm	.216
7	Ed Walsh	.218
8	Mario Soto	.220
	Bob Turley	.220
10	Addie Joss	.223
	Jeff Tesreau	.223
12	Jim Maloney	.224
	Orval Overall	.224
14	Ed Reulbach	.225
15	Tim Keefe	.226
	Tom Seaver	.226
17	Larry Corcoran	.227
	Rich Gossage	.227
	Walter Johnson	.227
20	Bob Gibson	.228
	Rube Waddell	.228
	Don Wilson	.228
23	Charlie Hough	.229
24	Sam Jones	.230
	Jim Palmer	.230
26	Bobby Bolin	.231
	Bob Feller	.231
	Jim Hunter	.231
29	Al Downing	.232
	Johnny Vander Meer	.232
	Stan Williams	.232
32	Larry Cheney	.233
33	Dean Chance	.234
	Denny McLain	.234
	Amos Rusie	.234
36	Mordecai Brown	.235
	Ray Culp	.235
	Charlie Ferguson	.235
	Rollie Fingers	.235
	Whitey Ford	.235
	Dave Foutz	.235
	Ed Morris	.235
	Tony Mullane	.235
	Monte Ward	.235
45	Moe Drabowsky	.236
	Toad Ramsey	.236
	Frank Smith	.236
	Don Sutton	.236
	Luis Tiant	.236
	Bob Veale	.236
51	Vida Blue	.237
	Juan Marichal	.237
	Tug McGraw	.237
	Juan Pizarro	.237
	Dave Stieb	.237
	Fernando Valenzuela	.237
57	Rudy May	.238
	Allie Reynolds	.238
	Jim Scott	.238
	Sonny Siebert	.238
61	Gary Bell	.239
	Chief Bender	.239
	Bill Donovan	.239
	Don Drysdale	.239
	Christy Mathewson	.239
	Jim McCormick	.239
	Hal Newhouser	.239
	Gary Nolan	.239
	Barney Pelty	.239
	Eddie Plank	.239
	Mike Scott	.239
72	Steve Carlton	.240
	Mort Cooper	.240
	Billy Pierce	.240
	Charley Radbourn	.240
	Bill Singer	.240
	Virgil Trucks	.240
	Will White	.240
79	Bob Caruthers	.241
	John Clarkson	.241
	Jack Coombs	.241
	Kirby Higbe	.241
	Bob Lemon	.241
	Earl Moore	.241
	Mickey Welch	.241
86	Harry Brecheen	.242
	Jim Bunning	.242
	Jumbo McGinnis	.242
	George McQuillan	.242
	Stu Miller	.242
	Jack Morris	.242
	Nap Rucker	.242
	Dupee Shaw	.242
	Bob Welch	.242
	Earl Wilson	.242
96	13 players tied	.243

Opponents' On Base Pctg.

1	Monte Ward	.254
2	Addie Joss	.256
3	Tommy Bond	.262
4	George Bradley	.263
	Ed Walsh	.263
6	Larry Corcoran	.266
	Will White	.266
8	Terry Larkin	.267
9	Ed Morris	.269
10	Charlie Ferguson	.270
11	Tim Keefe	.271
	Jim McCormick	.271
13	Fred Goldsmith	.274
14	Christy Mathewson	.275
	Jumbo McGinnis	.275
	Charley Radbourn	.275
	Jim Whitney	.275
18	Sandy Koufax	.276
19	Guy Hecker	.278
	Juan Marichal	.278
21	Bob Caruthers	.279
	Walter Johnson	.279
23	Mordecai Brown	.280
24	Dave Foutz	.282
	Dupee Shaw	.282
26	Babe Adams	.283
	Jim Galvin	.283
	Rube Waddell	.283
	Cy Young	.283
30	Bobby Mathews	.285
	Deacon Phillippe	.285
	Tom Seaver	.285
33	Jack Lynch	.286
34	Pete Alexander	.287
	Jim Hunter	.287
	Gary Nolan	.287
	Don Sutton	.287
38	Chief Bender	.288
	John Clarkson	.288
	Noodles Hahn	.288
	Eddie Plank	.288
42	Nick Altrock	.289
	Tiny Bonham	.289
	Ferguson Jenkins	.289
	Andy Messersmith	.289
	Mickey Welch	.289
47	Doc White	.290
	Hoyt Wilhelm	.290
49	Charlie Buffinton	.291
	Carl Hubbell	.291
	Tony Mullane	.291
52	Henry Boyle	.292
	Jack Chesbro	.292
	Denny McLain	.292
	Hooks Wiltse	.292
56	Robin Roberts	.293
57	Don Drysdale	.294
	Ron Guidry	.294
	Sam Leever	.294
	Toad Ramsey	.294
	Frank Smith	.294
	Jeff Tesreau	.294
	George Winter	.294
64	Rollie Fingers	.295
	George McQuillan	.295
66	John Candelaria	.296
	Dennis Eckersley	.296
	Jim Palmer	.296
	Barney Pelty	.296
	Mario Soto	.296
	Ralph Terry	.296
72	Kid Nichols	.297
	Gaylord Perry	.297
	Lee Richmond	.297
	Warren Spahn	.297
	Jesse Tannehill	.297
77	Harry Brecheen	.298
	Eddie Cicotte	.298
	Dizzy Dean	.298
	Dick Rudolph	.298
	Slim Sallee	.298
	Mike Scott	.298
	Luis Tiant	.298
84	Jim Bunning	.299
	Mike Cuellar	.299
	Eddie Fisher	.299
	Bob Gibson	.299
	Don Mossi	.299
	Don Newcombe	.299
	Ed Reulbach	.299
	Jack Taylor	.299
92	Mort Cooper	.300
	Hardie Henderson	.300
	Joe Horlen	.300
	Orval Overall	.300
	Fritz Peterson	.300
97	7 players tied	.301

Wins Above Team

1	Cy Young	100.3
2	Walter Johnson	90.3
3	Pete Alexander	81.9
4	Christy Mathewson	66.0
5	Lefty Grove	63.2
6	Tom Seaver	59.4
7	Jim McCormick	56.6
8	Jim Galvin	55.8
9	Charley Radbourn	51.5
10	Warren Spahn	46.3
11	Clark Griffith	46.1
12	Whitey Ford	44.7
13	Will White	44.0
14	Juan Marichal	39.1
15	Mickey Welch	37.7
16	Bob Feller	37.5
17	Tony Mullane	37.3
18	Phil Niekro	36.9
19	Eddie Plank	36.8
20	Ted Lyons	36.5
21	Amos Rusie	36.2
22	Kid Nichols	36.0
23	Jesse Tannehill	35.9
24	Wes Ferrell	35.4
25	Steve Carlton	34.9
26	Carl Hubbell	34.7
27	Charlie Buffinton	34.5
28	Dazzy Vance	33.9
29	Joe McGinnity	32.7
30	Jim Devlin	32.5
31	Ed Walsh	32.0
32	Bob Gibson	31.5
33	Eddie Rommel	31.1
34	Ed Morris	31.0
35	Sandy Koufax	30.9
	Jim Palmer	30.9
37	Robin Roberts	30.6
38	Bob Caruthers	30.5
39	Urban Shocker	30.3
40	Guy Hecker	29.8
	Ferguson Jenkins	29.8
	Sadie McMahon	29.8
43	Ron Guidry	29.7
44	Mordecai Brown	29.5
45	Addie Joss	28.7
46	Dizzy Dean	27.7
47	Bobby Mathews	27.1
48	Schoolboy Rowe	27.0
49	Rick Reuschel	26.4
50	Sam Leever	26.3
51	John Candelaria	26.1
52	Rip Sewell	25.7
53	Jack Chesbro	25.3
54	Frank Killen	25.0
55	Roger Clemens	24.9
56	Red Lucas	24.7
	Herb Pennock	24.7
	Nap Rucker	24.7
59	Russ Ford	24.4
60	Gaylord Perry	24.2
61	Red Faber	24.1
62	Johnny Allen	23.9
63	Charlie Ferguson	23.6
	Noodles Hahn	23.6
65	Chief Bender	23.2
	Tommy John	23.2
	Tim Keefe	23.2
	Firpo Marberry	23.2
	Joe Wood	23.2
70	Sal Maglie	23.1
71	Gus Weyhing	23.0
72	John Clarkson	22.9
	Dwight Gooden	22.9
74	Burleigh Grimes	22.3
75	Carl Mays	22.2
76	Dutch Leonard	21.8
	Hippo Vaughn	21.8
78	Bert Blyleven	21.6
	Claude Passeau	21.6
	George Uhle	21.6
81	Spud Chandler	21.4
	Jim Maloney	21.4
	Bucky Walters	21.4
84	Hal Newhouser	21.2
	J.R. Richard	21.2
	Slim Sallee	21.2
87	Freddie Fitzsimmons	21.1
88	Vida Blue	21.0
89	Babe Adams	20.9
90	Art Nehf	20.7
91	Allie Reynolds	20.6
	Luis Tiant	20.6
93	Lon Warneke	20.5
94	Ted Breitenstein	20.4
95	Stan Coveleski	20.3
	Orel Hershiser	20.3
97	Jim Hunter	20.2
98	Ray Kremer	20.1
99	Don Newcombe	20.0
100	2 players tied	19.8

Wins Above League

1	Cy Young	413.0
2	Walter Johnson	348.0
3	Jim Galvin	334.0
4	Warren Spahn	304.0
5	Phil Niekro	296.0
6	Pete Alexander	290.5
7	Don Sutton	290.0
8	Gaylord Perry	289.5
9	Steve Carlton	286.5
10	Kid Nichols	284.5
11	Tim Keefe	283.5
12	Christy Mathewson	279.5
13	Nolan Ryan	276.0
14	Early Wynn	272.0
15	Robin Roberts	265.5
16	Jim Kaat	260.0
17	Tommy John	259.5
	Eddie Plank	259.5
19	Eppa Rixey	258.5
20	Tom Seaver	258.0
	Mickey Welch	258.0
22	Ferguson Jenkins	255.0
23	John Clarkson	252.5
	Tony Mullane	252.5
	Charley Radbourn	252.5
26	Bert Blyleven	251.0
27	Jack Powell	249.0
	Red Ruffing	249.0
29	Gus Weyhing	248.0
30	Ted Lyons	245.0
31	Burleigh Grimes	241.0
32	Jim McCormick	239.5
33	Red Faber	233.5
34	Jack Quinn	232.5
35	Vic Willis	225.5
36	Sam Jones	223.0
37	Lefty Grove	220.5
38	Paul Derringer	217.5
39	Bobo Newsom	216.5
40	Jerry Koosman	215.5
41	Bob Feller	214.0
42	Bob Friend	213.5
43	Bob Gibson	212.5
	Joe Niekro	212.5
45	George Mullin	212.0
46	Jim Palmer	210.0
47	Waite Hoyt	209.5
	Amos Rusie	209.5
49	Jerry Reuss	205.5
50	Mel Harder	204.5
51	Jim Bunning	204.0
	Mickey Lolich	204.0
53	Carl Hubbell	203.5
54	Hooks Dauss	202.0
55	Earl Whitehill	201.5
56	Herb Pennock	201.0
57	Luis Tiant	200.5
58	Will White	197.5
	Jim Whitney	197.5
60	Wilbur Cooper	197.0
	Rick Reuschel	197.0
62	Al Orth	196.5
63	Adonis Terry	196.0
64	Claude Osteen	195.5
65	Jim Hunter	195.0
66	Jim Perry	194.5
67	Joe McGinnity	194.0
68	Chick Fraser	193.5
69	Frank Tanana	193.0
70	Juan Marichal	192.5
71	Charlie Buffinton	192.0
72	Clark Griffith	191.5
73	Billy Pierce	190.0
74	Joe Bush	189.0
	Rube Marquard	189.0
76	Larry Jackson	188.5
	Tom Zachary	188.5
78	Curt Simmons	188.0
79	Don Drysdale	187.5
80	Dolf Luque	186.5
	Milt Pappas	186.5
82	Dutch Leonard	186.0
83	Vida Blue	185.0
84	Mordecai Brown	184.5
	Rick Wise	184.5
86	Doyle Alexander	184.0
	Larry French	184.0
	Jesse Haines	184.0
	Lee Meadows	184.0
90	George Uhle	183.0
91	Freddie Fitzsimmons	181.5
92	Charlie Root	180.5
93	Bucky Walters	179.0
94	Eddie Cicotte	178.5
	Stan Coveleski	178.5
	Silver King	178.5
	Hal Newhouser	178.5
98	Murry Dickson	176.5
99	Red Ames	175.0
	Bill Dinneen	175.0

Relief Games

1	Kent Tekulve	1050
2	Hoyt Wilhelm	1018
3	Gene Garber	922
4	Lindy McDaniel	913
5	Rollie Fingers	907
6	Sparky Lyle	899
7	Don McMahon	872
8	Roy Face	821
9	Rich Gossage	816
10	Tug McGraw	785
11	Darold Knowles	757
12	Tom Burgmeier	742
	Gary Lavelle	742
14	Ron Perranoski	736
15	Willie Hernandez	733
16	Clay Carroll	703
17	Mike Marshall	699
18	Greg Minton	692
19	Bill Campbell	691
20	Dan Quisenberry	669
21	Bruce Sutter	661
22	Ted Abernathy	647
	Jeff Reardon	647
24	Dave LaRoche	632
25	Eddie Fisher	627
26	Paul Lindblad	623
27	Stu Miller	611
28	Grant Jackson	609
29	Elias Sosa	598
30	Bob Miller	595
31	Pedro Borbon	589
32	Lee Smith	580
33	Bob Locker	576
34	Terry Forster	575
35	Doug Bair	557
36	Bob Stanley	552
37	Jim Brewer	549
	Johnny Klippstein	549
39	Al Hrabosky	544
	Tippy Martinez	544
41	Dave Giusti	535
42	Ron Kline	533
	Randy Moffitt	533
	Al Worthington	533
45	Dale Murray	517
46	Frank Linzy	514
47	Dave Smith	513
48	John Hiller	502
49	Jack Aker	495
50	Joe Hoerner	493

Relief Wins

1	Hoyt Wilhelm	143
2	Lindy McDaniel	141
3	Bob Stanley	115
4	Rollie Fingers	114
	Ron Kline	114
6	Rich Gossage	113
7	Turk Farrell	106
8	Stu Miller	105
9	Roy Face	104
10	Johnny Klippstein	101
11	Dave Giusti	100
	Dick Tidrow	100
13	Sparky Lyle	99
14	Mike Marshall	97
15	Clay Carroll	96
	Gene Garber	96
	Tug McGraw	96
	Phil Regan	96
19	Kent Tekulve	94
20	Dick Hall	93
	Johnny Murphy	93
22	Diego Segui	92
23	Don McMahon	90
24	Moe Drabowsky	88
25	John Hiller	87
26	Grant Jackson	86
27	Eddie Fisher	85
28	Bill Campbell	83
29	Gary Lavelle	80
	Pete Richert	80
31	Tom Burgmeier	79
	Ron Perranoski	79
33	Clem Labine	77
34	Mace Brown	76
	Joe Heving	76
36	Hugh Casey	75
	Dan Spillner	75
	Al Worthington	75
39	Doug Bird	73
	Dave Righetti	73
	Clyde Shoun	73
42	Mark Clear	71
43	Willie Hernandez	70
44	Pedro Borbon	69
	Jim Brewer	69
	Bob Miller	69
47	Paul Lindblad	68
	Dan Schatzeder	68
	Bruce Sutter	68
50	2 players tied	67

Relief Losses

1	Ron Kline	144
2	Hoyt Wilhelm	122
3	Lindy McDaniel	119
4	Rollie Fingers	118
	Johnny Klippstein	118
6	Gene Garber	113
7	Mike Marshall	112
8	Turk Farrell	111
	Diego Segui	111
10	Moe Drabowsky	105
11	Stu Miller	103
12	Rich Gossage	98
13	Skip Lockwood	97
	Bob Stanley	97
15	Roy Face	95
16	Dick Tidrow	94
17	Dave Giusti	93
18	Tug McGraw	92
19	Kent Tekulve	90
20	Dan Spillner	89
21	Al Worthington	82
22	Bob Miller	81
	Phil Regan	81
24	Gary Lavelle	77
	Orlando Pena	77
26	John Hiller	76
	Sparky Lyle	76
28	Dick Hall	75
	Grant Jackson	75
30	Darold Knowles	74
	Ron Perranoski	74
32	Clay Carroll	73
	Pete Richert	73
34	Andy Hassler	71
	Tom Hume	71
	Bruce Sutter	71
37	Neil Allen	70
	Eddie Fisher	70
39	Ted Abernathy	69
40	Bill Campbell	68
	Don McMahon	68
42	Jim Brewer	65
	Mark Davis	65
	Terry Forster	65
	Joe Gibbon	65
	Dan Schatzeder	65
47	Mike Fornieles	64
	Greg Minton	64
49	Willie Hernandez	63
	Paul Lindblad	63

Relief Innings Pitched

1	Hoyt Wilhelm	2253
2	Lindy McDaniel	2140
3	Ron Kline	2078
4	Johnny Klippstein	1970
5	Diego Segui	1808
6	Dick Tidrow	1748
7	Dave Giusti	1718
8	Bob Stanley	1708
9	Turk Farrell	1704
10	Rollie Fingers	1701
11	Stu Miller	1694
12	Moe Drabowsky	1640
13	Rich Gossage	1636
14	Bob Miller	1552
15	Eddie Fisher	1540
16	Tug McGraw	1516
17	Gene Garber	1509
18	Dan Spillner	1493
19	Kent Tekulve	1436
20	Sparky Lyle	1391
21	Mike Marshall	1387
22	Roy Face	1375
23	Phil Regan	1373
24	Grant Jackson	1359
25	Clay Carroll	1353
26	Don McMahon	1313
27	Clyde Shoun	1286
28	Dick Hall	1259
29	Tom Burgmeier	1258
30	Al Worthington	1245
31	John Hiller	1241
	Dan Schatzeder	1241
33	Skip Lockwood	1236
34	Bill Campbell	1229
35	Paul Lindblad	1214
36	Doug Bird	1213
37	Orlando Pena	1202
38	Ron Perranoski	1176
39	Pete Richert	1164
40	Mike Fornieles	1156
41	Ted Abernathy	1146
42	Andy Hassler	1122
43	Joe Gibbon	1118
44	Greg Minton	1116
45	Terry Forster	1105
46	Darold Knowles	1091
47	Tom Hume	1086
	Gary Lavelle	1086
49	Dave Righetti	1083
50	Clem Labine	1079

Relief Points

1	Rollie Fingers	792
2	Rich Gossage	742
3	Bruce Sutter	665
4	Hoyt Wilhelm	618
5	Sparky Lyle	598
6	Jeff Reardon	584
7	Dan Quisenberry	555
8	Gene Garber	515
9	Lee Smith	511
10	Lindy McDaniel	507
11	Roy Face	499
12	Kent Tekulve	466
13	Dave Righetti	462
14	Tug McGraw	460
15	Mike Marshall	458
16	Ron Perranoski	442
17	Don McMahon	418
18	Stu Miller	415
19	Clay Carroll	405
	Dave Smith	405
21	Dave Giusti	397
	Bob Stanley	397
23	Steve Bedrosian	373
24	Willie Hernandez	371
25	Gary Lavelle	355
26	Ted Abernathy	353
27	Greg Minton	352
28	Bill Campbell	350
	Johnny Franco	350
30	John Hiller	348
31	Johnny Murphy	347
32	Darold Knowles	344
33	Jim Brewer	337
34	Dave LaRoche	324
35	Tom Burgmeier	307
36	Dick Radatz	305
37	Ron Davis	301
38	Ron Kline	300
39	Tippy Martinez	298
40	Terry Forster	297
41	Jack Aker	295
	Phil Regan	295
43	Jesse Orosco	291
44	Clem Labine	290
45	Frank Linzy	289
46	Al Worthington	288
47	Al Hrabosky	287
48	Fred Gladding	280
49	Todd Worrell	278
50	2 players tied	276

Relief Ranking

1	Hoyt Wilhelm	371.4
2	Rich Gossage	237.4
3	Bruce Sutter	218.5
4	Dan Quisenberry	216.9
5	Kent Tekulve	207.6
6	John Hiller	186.0
7	Sparky Lyle	185.1
8	Rollie Fingers	177.9
9	Lee Smith	167.3
10	Bob Stanley	161.4
11	Dave Righetti	157.1
12	Gene Garber	147.7
13	Johnny Franco	146.8
14	Mike Marshall	141.2
15	Gary Lavelle	139.3
16	Jesse Orosco	134.6
17	Jeff Reardon	127.1
18	Clay Carroll	121.2
19	Ron Perranoski	121.1
20	Tug McGraw	120.3
21	Dave Smith	118.6
22	Stu Miller	115.2
23	Don McMahon	110.3
24	Willie Hernandez	105.2
25	Johnny Murphy	102.8
26	Tom Henke	102.0
27	Todd Worrell	99.9
28	Dan Plesac	98.2
29	Steve Bedrosian	94.8
30	Tom Burgmeier	94.7
31	Frank Linzy	93.8
32	Lindy McDaniel	91.7
33	Tim Burke	90.2
34	Doug Jones	88.7
35	Greg Minton	84.9
36	Dick Radatz	84.6
37	Al Hrabosky	81.5
38	Roy Face	80.9
39	Bill Henry	75.8
40	Bob Locker	71.2
41	Darold Knowles	69.6
42	Terry Forster	68.8
43	Jim Kern	67.4
44	Dick Hall	66.1
45	Joe Beggs	65.6
46	Clem Labine	64.2
47	Al Worthington	64.0
48	Bobby Thigpen	63.6
49	Bill Campbell	61.5
50	Rick Camp	60.4

Relievers' Runs

1	Hoyt Wilhelm	310
2	Dan Quisenberry	151
3	Rich Gossage	150
4	Rollie Fingers	146
5	Kent Tekulve	129
6	Sparky Lyle	122
7	Dave Righetti	117
8	John Hiller	112
9	Stu Miller	107
10	Ron Perranoski	100
11	Johnny Murphy	98
12	Don McMahon	97
13	Clay Carroll	94
14	Gary Lavelle	93
15	Bruce Sutter	91
16	Mike Marshall	85
17	Dave Smith	84
18	Tug McGraw	83
	Jesse Orosco	83
20	Bob Stanley	82
21	Greg Minton	78
22	Tom Burgmeier	73
23	Jeff Reardon	72
24	Lee Smith	71
25	Johnny Franco	69
26	Tom Henke	65
27	Tim Burke	64
	Bob Locker	64
29	Alejandro Pena	61
30	Gene Garber	60
31	Jim Brewer	59
	Willie Hernandez	59
33	Frank Linzy	58
34	Lindy McDaniel	56
35	Joe Beggs	55
	Scott Garrelts	55
	Dick Hall	55
	Jim Konstanty	55
	Ted Wilks	55
40	Darold Knowles	53
	Gary Lucas	53
42	Bill Henry	52
43	Craig Lefferts	50
	Joe Sambito	50
	Sammy Stewart	50
46	Terry Forster	49
	Al Holland	49
	Al Hrabosky	49
	Jim Kern	49
50	3 players tied	48

Adjusted Relievers' Runs

1	Hoyt Wilhelm	289
2	Dan Quisenberry	154
3	Rich Gossage	150
4	Kent Tekulve	144
5	John Hiller	132
6	Bob Stanley	125
7	Sparky Lyle	122
8	Bruce Sutter	118
9	Rollie Fingers	106
10	Dave Righetti	105
11	Gene Garber	94
	Lee Smith	94
13	Clay Carroll	89
14	Gary Lavelle	88
	Stu Miller	88
16	Tug McGraw	87
17	Mike Marshall	85
18	Tom Burgmeier	83
19	Don McMahon	82
20	Jesse Orosco	80
	Ron Perranoski	80
22	Johnny Franco	79
23	Willie Hernandez	72
	Lindy McDaniel	72
25	Dave Smith	70
26	Johnny Murphy	69
27	Jeff Reardon	68
28	Greg Minton	66
29	Bill Henry	65
30	Tim Burke	64
31	Tom Henke	63
32	Steve Bedrosian	61
33	Ted Wilks	59
34	Frank Linzy	58
	Bob Locker	58
	Alejandro Pena	58
37	Joe Beggs	56
	Terry Forster	56
39	Rick Camp	53
	Al Hrabosky	53
41	Steve Mingori	52
	Dick Radatz	52
43	Doug Corbett	50
	Roy Face	50
	Dick Hall	50
46	Marv Grissom	49
	Doug Jones	49
	Clem Labine	49
	Dan Plesac	49
50	4 players tied	48

Clutch Pitching Index

1	Bob Rhoads	117
	Ed Siever	117
3	Ed Killian	114
	Will White	114
5	Ron Kline	113
	Bill Lee	113
	Dummy Taylor	113
8	Al Benton	112
	Lefty Leifield	112
	Eddie Lopat	112
	Win Mercer	112
	Bob Stanley	112
	Tom Zachary	112
14	Whitey Ford	111
	Preacher Roe	111
16	Steve Blass	110
	Bob Miller	110
	Bill Wight	110
19	Bob Buhl	109
	Max Butcher	109
	Max Lanier	109
	Sal Maglie	109
	Mel Parnell	109
	Bob Shaw	109
	Gerry Staley	109
	Geoff Zahn	109
27	Steve Barber	108
	Sheriff Blake	108
	Dan Casey	108
	Bill Duggleby	108
	Frank Dwyer	108
	Lefty Gomez	108
	Lefty Grove	108
	Mel Harder	108
	Carl Morton	108
	George Mullin	108
	Togie Pittinger	108
	Dizzy Trout	108
	Bob Veale	108
40	Nelson Briles	107
	Lloyd Brown	107
	Larry French	107
	Bruce Hurst	107
	Claude Osteen	107
	Eddie Rommel	107
	Dutch Ruether	107
	Eddie Smith	107
	Steve Trout	107
49	Jim Bagby	106
	Roger Craig	106
	Red Faber	106
	Freddie Fitzsimmons	106
	Joe Haynes	106
	Tommy John	106
	Charlie Leibrandt	106
	Bobby Mathews	106
	Cal McLish	106
	Jeff Pfeffer	106
	Howie Pollet	106
	Sherry Smith	106
	Sloppy Thurston	106
	John Tudor	106
	Rube Waddell	106
	Bucky Walters	106
65	Nixey Callahan	105
	Nig Cuppy	105
	Jack Curtis	105
	Murry Dickson	105
	Red Donahue	105
	Dick Ellsworth	105
	Wes Ferrell	105
	Fred Frankhouse	105
	Gene Garber	105
	Mike Garcia	105
	Guy Hecker	105
	Ken Heintzelman	105
	Johnny Klippstein	105
	Thornton Lee	105
	Dutch Leonard	105
	Ted Lyons	105
	Ricky Mahler	105
	Tug McGraw	105
	Stu Miller	105
	Clarence Mitchell	105
	Shane Rawley	105
	Allie Reynolds	105
	Johnny Sain	105
	Jim Scott	105
	Jim Slaton	105
	Al Smith	105
	Jack Taylor	105
	Hippo Vaughn	105
	Lon Warneke	105
	Wilbur Wood	105
95	38 players tied	104

Pitcher Batting Runs

1	Red Ruffing	135
2	Bob Caruthers	112
3	Wes Ferrell	104
4	Walter Johnson	98
5	Red Lucas	97
6	George Uhle	93
7	George Mullin	90
8	Jim Whitney	88
9	Guy Hecker	87
10	Bob Lemon	86
11	Warren Spahn	82
12	Don Newcombe	81
13	Schoolboy Rowe	77
14	Babe Ruth	75
15	Jack Stivetts	71
16	Early Wynn	69
17	Bob Gibson	67
18	Al Orth	65
19	Carl Mays	62
20	Earl Wilson	60
21	Don Drysdale	59
22	Doc Crandall	58
	Bucky Walters	58
24	Gary Peters	57
25	Christy Mathewson	56
26	Jesse Tannehill	55
27	Jim Tobin	54
28	Claude Hendrix	53
29	Charlie Ferguson	52
	Ad Gumbert	52
31	Steve Carlton	51
	Burleigh Grimes	51
33	Tony Mullane	50
34	Joe Bush	48
	Bob Forsch	48
36	Dave Foutz	46
	Rick Rhoden	46
	Adonis Terry	46
39	Vern Law	45
	Dutch Ruether	45
	Scott Stratton	45
42	Don Larsen	43
	Jack Scott	43
44	Jim Kaat	42
45	Tommy Byrne	40
	Wilbur Cooper	40
	Fred Hutchinson	40
	Frank Killen	40
49	Charley Radbourn	39
	Johnny Sain	39
51	Sloppy Thurston	38
52	Clark Griffith	36
	Mickey McDermott	36
	Claude Osteen	36
	Don Robinson	36
	Doc White	36
57	Ken Brett	35
	Jack Coombs	35
	Harvey Haddix	35
	Dolf Luque	35
	Jack Taylor	35
62	Chief Bender	34
	Frank Smith	34
	Rick Wise	34
65	Win Mercer	33
	Art Nehf	33
	Robin Roberts	33
	Ben Sanders	33
69	Ray Caldwell	32
	Hooks Dauss	32
	Al Maul	32
	Jouett Meekin	32
	Dizzy Trout	32
74	Jim Hunter	31
	Ted Lyons	31
	Joe Wood	31
77	Lefty Tyler	30
78	Charlie Buffinton	29
	Lew Burdette	29
	Jack Harshman	29
	Brickyard Kennedy	29
	Joe Nuxhall	29
	Camilo Pascual	29
	Urban Shocker	29
	Monte Ward	29
86	Ed Brandt	28
	Eddie Lopat	28
	Jim Maloney	28
	Clarence Mitchell	28
	Juan Pizarro	28
	Tom Seaver	28
92	Frank Kitson	27
	Bill Sherdel	27
	Lon Warneke	27
95	Ned Garver	26
	Johnny Lush	26
	Joe Shaute	26
	Mike Smith	26
99	9 players tied	25

Pitcher Fielding Runs

1	Ed Walsh	83
2	Carl Mays	73
3	Christy Mathewson	65
4	Freddie Fitzsimmons	59
	Bob Lemon	59
6	Burleigh Grimes	58
7	Tommy John	56
8	Harry Gumbert	50
9	Harry Howell	47
10	Jack Quinn	45
11	Bill Doak	42
12	John Clarkson	41
	Eddie Rommel	41
14	Willis Hudlin	40
15	Jim Galvin	39
	Bobby Shantz	39
17	Rick Reuschel	38
	Dizzy Trout	38
19	Hooks Dauss	37
20	Amos Rusie	35
	Jack Russell	35
	Mel Stottlemyre	35
23	Charlie Buffinton	34
	Johnny Schmitz	34
25	Nick Altrock	32
	Howard Ehmke	32
27	John Denny	31
	Murry Dickson	31
	Randy Jones	31
30	Pete Alexander	30
	Red Ames	30
	Tommy Bond	30
	Curt Davis	30
	Hal Schumacher	30
35	Addie Joss	29
	Ed Willett	29
37	Ben Cantwell	28
	George Mullin	28
	Gerry Staley	28
	Fernando Valenzuela	28
41	Ted Abernathy	27
	Tom Burgmeier	27
	Spud Chandler	27
	Tony Mullane	27
	Phil Niekro	27
	Frank Smith	27
	Bucky Walters	27
	Monte Ward	27
	Vic Willis	27
	Cy Young	27
51	Don Drysdale	26
	Whitey Ford	26
	Sid Hudson	26
	Sherry Smith	26
55	Nixey Callahan	25
	Willie Sudhoff	25
57	Mike Boddicker	24
	Mike Caldwell	24
	Larry Jackson	24
	Matt Kilroy	24
	Dan Quisenberry	24
	Jack Taylor	24
63	Jean Dubuc	23
	Joe Horlen	23
	Dutch Leonard	23
	Dennis Martinez	23
	Gene Packard	23
	Gaylord Perry	23
	Ed Reulbach	23
	Dave Stieb	23
	Doc White	23
72	Tom Brewer	22
	Frank Corridon	22
	Ned Garvin	22
	Carl Hubbell	22
	Brickyard Kennedy	22
	Lindy McDaniel	22
	Stu Miller	22
	Hal Newhouser	22
	Cy Seymour	22
	Bob Stanley	22
	Kent Tekulve	22
	Lefty Tyler	22
84	Ted Breitenstein	21
	Claude Hendrix	21
	Frank Owen	21
87	Eldon Auker	20
	Jess Barnes	20
	Joe Bush	20
	Harry Coveleski	20
	Red Donahue	20
	Benny Frey	20
	Gene Garber	20
	Darold Knowles	20
	Frank Linzy	20
	Mike Marshall	20
	Wilcy Moore	20
	Claude Osteen	20
	Bob Purkey	20
100	11 players tied	19

Total Pitcher Index

1	Walter Johnson	81.5
2	Cy Young	81.0
3	Kid Nichols	65.3
4	Pete Alexander	64.8
5	Lefty Grove	59.9
6	Christy Mathewson	54.6
7	John Clarkson	52.6
8	Tom Seaver	51.2
9	Bob Gibson	46.3
10	Warren Spahn	43.1
11	Ed Walsh	41.6
12	Tim Keefe	38.8
13	Whitey Ford	38.6
	Carl Hubbell	38.6
15	Hal Newhouser	38.5
16	Phil Niekro	38.0
17	Bert Blyleven	37.8
18	Amos Rusie	37.7
19	Gaylord Perry	36.8
20	Jim Palmer	36.4
21	Steve Carlton	35.6
22	Ted Lyons	35.4
23	Bob Lemon	35.2
	Tony Mullane	35.2
25	Mordecai Brown	35.0
26	Carl Mays	34.8
27	Don Drysdale	34.7
28	Jack Stivetts	34.1
29	Dizzy Trout	33.7
30	Ferguson Jenkins	32.1
31	Wes Ferrell	30.9
32	Juan Marichal	30.8
33	Clark Griffith	29.4
	Charley Radbourn	29.4
35	Bob Caruthers	29.2
	Bucky Walters	29.2
	Hoyt Wilhelm	29.2
38	Tommy Bridges	28.5
39	Rube Waddell	28.4
40	Rick Reuschel	27.5
41	Bob Feller	26.9
	Addie Joss	26.9
43	Burleigh Grimes	26.7
44	Red Ruffing	26.5
45	Tommy John	26.1
	Silver King	26.1
47	Stan Coveleski	26.0
48	Robin Roberts	25.9
	Dave Stieb	25.9
50	Dolf Luque	25.8
51	Eddie Plank	25.5
52	Dazzy Vance	25.4
53	Red Faber	25.3
54	Eppa Rixey	25.1
55	Jack Quinn	25.0
56	Eddie Rommel	24.9
57	Urban Shocker	24.8
58	Nig Cuppy	24.3
59	Harry Brecheen	23.9
60	Lon Warneke	23.4
61	Guy Hecker	23.2
62	Eddie Cicotte	23.0
63	Freddie Fitzsimmons	22.7
	Dutch Leonard	22.7
65	Billy Pierce	22.4
66	Jim McCormick	21.9
67	Joe Wood	21.8
68	Vic Willis	21.7
69	Spud Chandler	21.3
70	Jim Kaat	21.2
71	Joe McGinnity	21.0
72	Wilbur Cooper	20.8
73	Charlie Buffinton	20.7
74	Jesse Tannehill	20.6
75	Bobby Shantz	20.4
76	Larry Jackson	20.1
77	Sandy Koufax	20.0
78	Dizzy Dean	19.9
79	Murry Dickson	19.8
	Hippo Vaughn	19.8
81	Ed Reulbach	19.4
82	Curt Davis	19.3
83	Don Newcombe	19.1
84	Andy Messersmith	19.0
85	Steve Rogers	18.8
86	Jim Bunning	18.7
	Doc White	18.7
88	Orel Hershiser	18.5
89	Jim Whitney	18.4
90	Dave Foutz	18.3
	Lefty Gomez	18.3
92	Dan Quisenberry	18.2
	Early Wynn	18.2
94	Mel Harder	18.0
95	Noodles Hahn	17.9
96	Mel Stottlemyre	17.8
	Luis Tiant	17.8
98	Ned Garver	17.7
	Ron Guidry	17.7
100	Babe Adams	17.5

Total Pitcher Index

	Eddie Lopat	17.5
	Mel Parnell	17.5
103	Claude Hendrix	17.3
104	Roger Clemens	17.1
	Thornton Lee	17.1
	Claude Passeau	17.1
	Kent Tekulve	17.1
108	Larry French	16.8
109	Waite Hoyt	16.4
	George Mullin	16.4
	Hal Schumacher	16.4
	Virgil Trucks	16.4
113	Jim Devlin	16.3
	Frank Dwyer	16.3
115	Nolan Ryan	16.2
116	Frank Tanana	16.1
117	Sadie McMahon	15.9
	Mickey Welch	15.9
119	Harry Howell	15.8
120	Max Lanier	15.7
	Sam Leever	15.7
122	John Candelaria	15.5
	Charlie Ferguson	15.5
124	Larry Corcoran	15.4
125	Dennis Eckersley	15.2
	Dwight Gooden	15.2
	Bill Hutchinson	15.2
128	Schoolboy Rowe	15.1
	Bob Stanley	15.1
	Wilbur Wood	15.1
131	Frank Killen	15.0
	George Uhle	15.0
133	Sal Maglie	14.9
134	Mort Cooper	14.6
	Rich Gossage	14.6
	Deacon Phillippe	14.6
137	Mike Garcia	14.5
	Howie Pollet	14.5
139	Charlie Hough	14.4
	Bret Saberhagen	14.4
	Bob Shawkey	14.4
142	Babe Ruth	14.2
	John Tudor	14.2
144	Johnny Antonelli	14.1
	Milt Pappas	14.1
146	Jerry Koosman	13.9
	Jim Maloney	13.9
	Curt Simmons	13.9
149	Fred Hutchinson	13.8
	Nap Rucker	13.8
	Jack Taylor	13.8
152	Don Sutton	13.7
153	Will White	13.6
154	Jim Galvin	13.4
	Fernando Valenzuela	13.4
156	Russ Ford	13.3
	Monte Ward	13.3
158	John Hiller	13.2
	Jim Tobin	13.2
160	Sparky Lyle	13.0
161	Gary Peters	12.9
162	Ted Breitenstein	12.8
	Bruce Sutter	12.8
164	Chief Bender	12.6
	Rollie Fingers	12.6
	Gene Garber	12.6
	Claude Osteen	12.6
168	Tom Burgmeier	12.5
	Jon Matlack	12.5
170	Harvey Haddix	12.4
	Sam McDowell	12.4
	Ben Sanders	12.4
173	Stu Miller	12.3
174	Ewell Blackwell	12.2
	Frank Lary	12.2
	Mike Marshall	12.2
177	Sonny Siebert	12.1
178	Dean Chance	11.9
179	Camilo Pascual	11.8
180	Teddy Higuera	11.7
	Tex Hughson	11.7
182	Firpo Marberry	11.6
183	Jack Morris	11.5
	Sherry Smith	11.5
185	Clay Carroll	11.4
	Icebox Chamberlin	11.4
	Ned Garvin	11.4
188	Frank Sullivan	11.3
189	Jimmy Key	11.1
	Bob Welch	11.1
191	Lindy McDaniel	11.0
	Fritz Ostermueller	11.0
	Bob Rush	11.0
194	Tommy Bond	10.9
	Jack Chesbro	10.9
	Mark Gubicza	10.9
	Van Mungo	10.9
	Jake Weimer	10.9
199	Jim Perry	10.8
	Tom Zachary	10.8

Total Pitcher Index

201	Red Ames	10.7
	Al Orth	10.7
203	Al Brazle	10.6
	Ellis Kinder	10.6
	Tug McGraw	10.6
	Toad Ramsey	10.6
207	Mark Baldwin	10.5
	Pink Hawley	10.5
209	Jeff Pfeffer	10.4
210	Bill Hands	10.3
	Red Lucas	10.3
	Charlie Root	10.3
213	Joe Dobson	10.1
	Art Nehf	10.1
215	Harry Coveleski	10.0
	Dave Righetti	10.0
217	Ed Morris	9.9
218	Lefty Leifield	9.8
	Gary Nolan	9.8
	Monte Pearson	9.8
221	Johnny Allen	9.7
	Mike Cuellar	9.7
	Hooks Dauss	9.7
	Don Mossi	9.7
	Gerry Staley	9.7
226	Nixey Callahan	9.6
	Orval Overall	9.6
228	Mike Boddicker	9.5
	Joe Horlen	9.5
	Rip Sewell	9.5
231	Vida Blue	9.4
	Clint Brown	9.4
	Gary Lavelle	9.4
	Billy Rhines	9.4
235	Terry Forster	9.3
	Greg Minton	9.3
	Johnny Rigney	9.3
	Jim Scott	9.3
239	Bill Lee	9.2
	Slim Sallee	9.2
241	Matt Kilroy	9.1
	Rick Rhoden	9.1
243	Joe Benz	9.0
	Larry Jansen	9.0
	Jesse Orosco	9.0
246	Howard Ehmke	8.9
	Frank Linzy	8.9
248	Watty Clark	8.8
	Johnny Franco	8.8
	Sam Jones	8.8
	Don McMahon	8.8
	Preacher Roe	8.8
253	John Denny	8.7
	Burt Hooton	8.7
	Johnny Sain	8.7
	Lee Smith	8.7
257	Bob Ewing	8.6
	Jeff Tesreau	8.6
259	Bill Lee	8.5
	Bob Locker	8.5
261	Dave Rozema	8.4
262	Willie Hernandez	8.3
	Ray Kremer	8.3
264	Lady Baldwin	8.2
	Bill Dinneen	8.2
	Vern Law	8.2
	Ron Perranoski	8.2
	Johnny Schmitz	8.2
269	Joe Bush	8.1
	George Mogridge	8.1
	Hooks Wiltse	8.1
272	Jess Barnes	8.0
	Adonis Terry	8.0
	Whit Wyatt	8.0
275	Win Mercer	7.9
	Lefty Tyler	7.9
	Frank Viola	7.9
278	Al Benton	7.8
	Tiny Bonham	7.8
	Paul Derringer	7.8
	Bill Doak	7.8
	Harry Gumbert	7.8
	Jack Harshman	7.8
	Willis Hudlin	7.8
285	Bob Friend	7.7
	Darold Knowles	7.7
	Herb Pennock	7.7
	Jack Pfiester	7.7
289	Mark Langston	7.6
	Dave McNally	7.6
	Dutch Ruether	7.6
292	Bump Hadley	7.5
	Rick Sutcliffe	7.5
294	Paul Minner	7.4
	Johnny Murphy	7.4
	Lefty Stewart	7.4
	Bob Veale	7.4
298	Scott Stratton	7.3
299	3 players tied	7.2

Total Pitcher Index (alpha.)

Babe Adams	17.5
Pete Alexander	64.8
Johnny Allen	9.7
Red Ames	10.7
Johnny Antonelli	14.1
Lady Baldwin	8.2
Mark Baldwin	10.5
Jess Barnes	8.0
Chief Bender	12.6
Al Benton	7.8
Joe Benz	9.0
Ewell Blackwell	12.2
Vida Blue	9.4
Bert Blyleven	37.8
Mike Boddicker	9.5
Tommy Bond	10.9
Tiny Bonham	7.8
Al Brazle	10.6
Harry Brecheen	23.9
Ted Breitenstein	12.8
Tommy Bridges	28.5
Clint Brown	9.4
Mordecai Brown	35.0
Charlie Buffinton	20.7
Jim Bunning	18.7
Tom Burgmeier	12.5
Joe Bush	8.1
Nixey Callahan	9.6
John Candelaria	15.5
Steve Carlton	35.6
Clay Carroll	11.4
Bob Caruthers	29.2
Icebox Chamberlin	11.4
Dean Chance	11.9
Spud Chandler	21.3
Jack Chesbro	10.9
Eddie Cicotte	23.0
Watty Clark	8.8
John Clarkson	52.6
Roger Clemens	17.1
Wilbur Cooper	20.8
Mort Cooper	14.6
Larry Corcoran	15.4
Harry Coveleski	10.0
Stan Coveleski	26.0
Mike Cuellar	9.7
Nig Cuppy	24.3
Hooks Dauss	9.7
Curt Davis	19.3
Dizzy Dean	19.9
John Denny	8.7
Paul Derringer	7.8
Jim Devlin	16.3
Murry Dickson	19.8
Bill Dinneen	8.2
Bill Doak	7.8
Joe Dobson	10.1
Don Drysdale	34.7
Frank Dwyer	16.3
Dennis Eckersley	15.2
Howard Ehmke	8.9
Bob Ewing	8.6
Red Faber	25.3
Bob Feller	26.9
Charlie Ferguson	15.5
Wes Ferrell	30.9
Rollie Fingers	12.6
Freddie Fitzsimmons	22.7
Whitey Ford	38.6
Russ Ford	13.3
Terry Forster	9.3
Dave Foutz	18.3
Johnny Franco	8.8
Larry French	16.8
Bob Friend	7.7
Jim Galvin	13.4
Gene Garber	12.6
Mike Garcia	14.5
Ned Garver	17.7
Ned Garvin	11.4
Bob Gibson	46.3
Lefty Gomez	18.3
Dwight Gooden	15.2
Rich Gossage	14.6
Clark Griffith	29.4
Burleigh Grimes	26.7
Lefty Grove	59.9
Mark Gubicza	10.9
Ron Guidry	17.7
Harry Gumbert	7.8
Harvey Haddix	12.4
Bump Hadley	7.5
Noodles Hahn	17.9
Bill Hands	10.3
Mel Harder	18.0
Jack Harshman	7.8
Pink Hawley	10.5
Guy Hecker	23.2
Claude Hendrix	17.3
Willie Hernandez	8.3

Total Pitcher Index (alpha.)

Orel Hershiser	18.5
Teddy Higuera	11.7
John Hiller	13.2
Burt Hooton	8.7
Joe Horlen	9.5
Charlie Hough	14.4
Harry Howell	15.8
Waite Hoyt	16.4
Carl Hubbell	38.6
Willis Hudlin	7.8
Tex Hughson	11.7
Fred Hutchinson	13.8
Bill Hutchinson	15.2
Larry Jackson	20.1
Larry Jansen	9.0
Ferguson Jenkins	32.1
Tommy John	26.1
Walter Johnson	81.5
Sam Jones	8.8
Addie Joss	26.9
Jim Kaat	21.2
Tim Keefe	38.8
Jimmy Key	11.1
Frank Killen	15.0
Matt Kilroy	9.1
Ellis Kinder	10.6
Silver King	26.1
Darold Knowles	7.7
Jerry Koosman	13.9
Sandy Koufax	20.0
Ray Kremer	8.3
Mark Langston	7.6
Max Lanier	15.7
Frank Lary	12.2
Gary Lavelle	9.4
Vern Law	8.2
Thornton Lee	17.1
Bill Lee	8.5
Bill Lee	9.2
Sam Leever	15.7
Lefty Leifield	9.8
Bob Lemon	35.2
Dutch Leonard	22.7
Frank Linzy	8.9
Bob Locker	8.5
Eddie Lopat	17.5
Red Lucas	10.3
Dolf Luque	25.8
Sparky Lyle	13.0
Ted Lyons	35.4
Sal Maglie	14.9
Jim Maloney	13.9
Firpo Marberry	11.6
Juan Marichal	30.8
Mike Marshall	12.2
Christy Mathewson	54.6
Jon Matlack	12.5
Carl Mays	34.8
Win Mercer	7.9
Andy Messersmith	19.0
Stu Miller	12.3
Paul Minner	7.4
Greg Minton	9.3
George Mogridge	8.1
Ed Morris	9.9
Jack Morris	11.5
Don Mossi	9.7
Tony Mullane	35.2
George Mullin	16.4
Van Mungo	10.9
Johnny Murphy	7.4
Jim McCormick	21.9
Lindy McDaniel	11.0
Sam McDowell	12.4
Joe McGinnity	21.0
Tug McGraw	10.6
Don McMahon	8.8
Sadie McMahon	15.9
Dave McNally	7.6
Art Nehf	10.1
Don Newcombe	19.1
Hal Newhouser	38.5
Kid Nichols	65.3
Phil Niekro	38.0
Gary Nolan	9.8
Jesse Orosco	9.0
Al Orth	10.7
Claude Osteen	12.6
Fritz Ostermueller	11.0
Orval Overall	9.6
Jim Palmer	36.4
Milt Pappas	14.1
Mel Parnell	17.5
Camilo Pascual	11.8
Claude Passeau	17.1
Monte Pearson	9.8
Herb Pennock	7.7
Ron Perranoski	8.2
Gaylord Perry	36.8
Jim Perry	10.8

Total Pitcher Index (alpha.)

Gary Peters	12.9
Jeff Pfeffer	10.4
Jack Pfiester	7.7
Deacon Phillippe	14.6
Billy Pierce	22.4
Eddie Plank	25.5
Howie Pollet	14.5
Jack Quinn	25.0
Dan Quisenberry	18.2
Charley Radbourn	29.4
Toad Ramsey	10.6
Ed Reulbach	19.4
Rick Reuschel	27.5
Billy Rhines	9.4
Rick Rhoden	9.1
Dave Righetti	10.0
Johnny Rigney	9.3
Eppa Rixey	25.1
Robin Roberts	25.9
Preacher Roe	8.8
Steve Rogers	18.8
Eddie Rommel	24.9
Charlie Root	10.3
Schoolboy Rowe	15.1
Dave Rozema	8.4
Nap Rucker	13.8
Dutch Ruether	7.6
Red Ruffing	26.5
Bob Rush	11.0
Amos Rusie	37.7
Babe Ruth	14.2
Nolan Ryan	16.2
Bret Saberhagen	14.4
Johnny Sain	8.7
Slim Sallee	9.2
Ben Sanders	12.4
Johnny Schmitz	8.2
Hal Schumacher	16.4
Jim Scott	9.3
Tom Seaver	51.2
Rip Sewell	9.5
Bobby Shantz	20.4
Bob Shawkey	14.4
Urban Shocker	24.8
Sonny Siebert	12.1
Curt Simmons	13.9
Lee Smith	8.7
Sherry Smith	11.5
Warren Spahn	43.1
Gerry Staley	9.7
Bob Stanley	15.1
Lefty Stewart	7.4
Dave Stieb	25.9
Jack Stivetts	34.1
Mel Stottlemyre	17.8
Scott Stratton	7.3
Frank Sullivan	11.3
Rick Sutcliffe	7.5
Bruce Sutter	12.8
Don Sutton	13.7
Frank Tanana	16.1
Jesse Tannehill	20.6
Jack Taylor	13.8
Kent Tekulve	17.1
Adonis Terry	8.0
Jeff Tesreau	8.6
Luis Tiant	17.8
Jim Tobin	13.2
Dizzy Trout	33.7
Virgil Trucks	16.4
John Tudor	14.2
Lefty Tyler	7.9
George Uhle	15.0
Fernando Valenzuela	13.4
Dazzy Vance	25.4
Hippo Vaughn	19.8
Bob Veale	7.4
Frank Viola	7.9
Rube Waddell	28.4
Ed Walsh	41.6
Bucky Walters	29.2
Monte Ward	13.3
Lon Warneke	23.4
Jake Weimer	10.9
Mickey Welch	15.9
Bob Welch	11.1
Doc White	18.7
Will White	13.6
Jim Whitney	18.4
Hoyt Wilhelm	29.2
Vic Willis	21.7
Hooks Wiltse	8.1
Joe Wood	21.8
Wilbur Wood	15.1
Whit Wyatt	8.0
Early Wynn	18.2
Cy Young	81.0
Tom Zachary	10.8

Total Pitcher Index (by era)

1876-1892

1	John Clarkson	52.6
2	Tim Keefe	38.8
3	Tony Mullane	35.2
4	Jack Stivetts	34.1
5	Charley Radbourn	29.4
6	Bob Caruthers	29.2
7	Silver King	26.1
8	Guy Hecker	23.2
9	Jim McCormick	21.9
10	Charlie Buffinton	20.7
11	Jim Whitney	18.4
12	Dave Foutz	18.3
13	Jim Devlin	16.3
14	Sadie McMahon	15.9
	Mickey Welch	15.9
16	Charlie Ferguson	15.5
17	Larry Corcoran	15.4
18	Bill Hutchinson	15.2
19	Will White	13.6
20	Jim Galvin	13.4
21	Monte Ward	13.3
22	Ben Sanders	12.4
23	Icebox Chamberlin	11.4
24	Tommy Bond	10.9
25	Toad Ramsey	10.6

1893-1919

1	Walter Johnson	81.5
2	Cy Young	81.0
3	Kid Nichols	65.3
4	Pete Alexander	64.8
5	Christy Mathewson	54.6
6	Ed Walsh	41.6
7	Amos Rusie	37.7
8	Mordecai Brown	35.0
9	Clark Griffith	29.4
10	Rube Waddell	28.4
11	Addie Joss	26.9
12	Eddie Plank	25.5
13	Nig Cuppy	24.3
14	Eddie Cicotte	23.0
15	Joe Wood	21.8
16	Vic Willis	21.7
17	Joe McGinnity	21.0
18	Jesse Tannehill	20.6
19	Hippo Vaughn	19.8
20	Ed Reulbach	19.4
21	Doc White	18.7
22	Noodles Hahn	17.9
23	Babe Adams	17.5
24	Claude Hendrix	17.3
25	George Mullin	16.4

1920-1941

1	Lefty Grove	59.9
2	Carl Hubbell	38.6
3	Ted Lyons	35.4
4	Carl Mays	34.8
5	Wes Ferrell	30.9
6	Bucky Walters	29.2
7	Tommy Bridges	28.5
8	Burleigh Grimes	26.7
9	Red Ruffing	26.5
10	Stan Coveleski	26.0
11	Dolf Luque	25.8
12	Dazzy Vance	25.4
13	Red Faber	25.3
14	Eppa Rixey	25.1
15	Jack Quinn	25.0
16	Eddie Rommel	24.9
17	Urban Shocker	24.8
18	Lon Warneke	23.4
19	Freddie Fitzsimmons	22.7
20	Wilbur Cooper	20.8
21	Dizzy Dean	19.9
22	Curt Davis	19.3
23	Lefty Gomez	18.3
24	Mel Harder	18.0
25	2 players tied	17.1

1942-1960

1	Warren Spahn	43.1
2	Whitey Ford	38.6
3	Hal Newhouser	38.5
4	Bob Lemon	35.2
5	Dizzy Trout	33.7
6	Hoyt Wilhelm	29.2
7	Bob Feller	26.9
8	Robin Roberts	25.9
9	Harry Brecheen	23.9
10	Dutch Leonard	22.7
11	Billy Pierce	22.4
12	Spud Chandler	21.3
13	Bobby Shantz	20.4
14	Murry Dickson	19.8
15	Don Newcombe	19.1
16	Early Wynn	18.2
17	Ned Garver	17.7
18	Eddie Lopat	17.5
	Mel Parnell	17.5
20	Virgil Trucks	16.4
21	Max Lanier	15.7
22	Sal Maglie	14.9
23	Mort Cooper	14.6
24	Mike Garcia	14.5
	Howie Pollet	14.5

1961-1989

1	Tom Seaver	51.2
2	Bob Gibson	46.3
3	Phil Niekro	38.0
4	Bert Blyleven	37.8
5	Gaylord Perry	36.8
6	Jim Palmer	36.4
7	Steve Carlton	35.6
8	Don Drysdale	34.7
9	Ferguson Jenkins	32.1
10	Juan Marichal	30.8
11	Rick Reuschel	27.5
12	Tommy John	26.1
13	Dave Stieb	25.9
14	Jim Kaat	21.2
15	Larry Jackson	20.1
16	Sandy Koufax	20.0
17	Andy Messersmith	19.0
18	Steve Rogers	18.8
19	Jim Bunning	18.7
20	Orel Hershiser	18.5
21	Dan Quisenberry	18.2
22	Mel Stottlemyre	17.8
	Luis Tiant	17.8
24	Ron Guidry	17.7
25	2 players tied	17.1

Total Baseball Ranking

1	Babe Ruth	119.3
2	Ty Cobb	91.2
3	Hank Aaron	90.1
4	Ted Williams	89.8
5	Willie Mays	86.2
6	Nap Lajoie	85.2
7	Walter Johnson	81.5
8	Cy Young	81.0
9	Tris Speaker	79.3
10	Mike Schmidt	77.8
11	Rogers Hornsby	77.3
12	Honus Wagner	75.9
13	Frank Robinson	71.2
14	Eddie Collins	70.5
15	Stan Musial	70.1
16	Mickey Mantle	69.8
17	Kid Nichols	65.3
18	Pete Alexander	64.8
19	Joe Morgan	63.9
20	Lou Gehrig	60.8
21	Mel Ott	60.1
22	Lefty Grove	59.9
23	Christy Mathewson	54.6
24	Jimmie Foxx	53.9
25	John Clarkson	52.6
26	Tom Seaver	51.2
27	Eddie Mathews	48.4
28	Rickey Henderson	48.2
29	George Davis	48.1
30	Bobby Grich	47.4
31	Bob Gibson	46.3
32	Ed Delahanty	46.1
	Carl Yastrzemski	46.1
34	Al Kaline	45.9
35	George Brett	45.3
36	Reggie Jackson	44.0
37	Joe DiMaggio	43.6
38	Charlie Gehringer	43.5
39	Bill Dahlen	43.3
40	Warren Spahn	43.1
41	Ed Walsh	41.6
42	Rod Carew	41.0
43	Arky Vaughan	40.3
44	Ozzie Smith	40.0
45	Dan Brouthers	39.6
46	Roberto Clemente	39.6
47	Paul Waner	38.9
48	Roger Connor	38.8
	Tim Keefe	38.8
50	Whitey Ford	38.6
	Carl Hubbell	38.6
52	Luke Appling	38.5
	Hal Newhouser	38.5
54	Joe Cronin	38.2
55	Willie McCovey	38.1
	Ron Santo	38.1
57	Phil Niekro	38.0
58	Bob Johnson	37.8
	Bert Blyleven	37.8
60	Amos Rusie	37.7
61	Bid McPhee	37.5
62	Frankie Frisch	37.2
63	Wade Boggs	36.9
64	Bobby Wallace	36.8
	Gaylord Perry	36.8
66	Keith Hernandez	36.6
	Dave Winfield	36.6
68	Johnny Mize	36.5
69	Carlton Fisk	36.4
	Jim Palmer	36.4
71	Gary Carter	36.3
72	Joe Jackson	36.0
73	Robin Yount	35.9
74	Gabby Hartnett	35.7
75	Bob Caruthers	35.6
	Tony Mullane	35.6
	Dick Allen	35.6
	Bobby Doerr	35.6
	Eddie Murray	35.6
	Steve Carlton	35.6
81	Ted Lyons	35.4
82	Bob Lemon	35.2
83	Mordecai Brown	35.0
	Jack Stivetts	35.0
85	Yogi Berra	34.8
	Carl Mays	34.8
87	Don Drysdale	34.7
88	Frank Baker	34.6
89	Bill Mazeroski	34.4
	Ted Simmons	34.4
91	Lou Boudreau	34.3
92	Billy Herman	34.0
93	Dizzy Trout	33.7
94	Reggie Smith	33.4
95	Jackie Robinson	33.3
96	Jack Glasscock	33.1
	Joe Sewell	33.1
98	Tim Raines	33.0
99	Harmon Killebrew	32.8
100	Ferguson Jenkins	32.1

Total Baseball Ranking

101	Darrell Evans	31.8
102	Willie Stargell	31.6
103	Cap Anson	31.4
104	Bobby Bonds	31.3
105	Jim Wynn	31.1
106	Wes Ferrell	30.9
107	Juan Marichal	30.8
108	Bill Dickey	30.6
109	Johnny Bench	30.2
	Billy Williams	30.2
111	Joe Torre	29.8
112	Dave Bancroft	29.7
113	Norm Cash	29.6
	Cupid Childs	29.6
115	Rusty Staub	29.4
	Sam Thompson	29.4
	Clark Griffith	29.4
118	Charley Radbourn	29.3
119	Hoyt Wilhelm	29.2
120	Bill Freehan	28.9
	Hank Greenberg	28.9
122	Cal Ripken	28.7
123	Jack Clark	28.5
	Elmer Flick	28.5
	Sherry Magee	28.5
	Tommy Bridges	28.5
127	Dwight Evans	28.4
	Rube Waddell	28.4
129	Fred Dunlap	28.0
130	Jesse Burkett	27.9
131	Bill Terry	27.8
132	Buck Ewing	27.7
133	Joe Gordon	27.6
134	Fred Clarke	27.5
	Mickey Cochrane	27.5
	Rick Reuschel	27.5
137	Bucky Walters	27.4
138	Richie Ashburn	27.0
	Ralph Kiner	27.0
140	Pete Browning	26.9
	Max Carey	26.9
	Willie Randolph	26.9
	Bob Feller	26.9
	Addie Joss	26.9
145	Burleigh Grimes	26.7
146	Hughie Jennings	26.5
	Red Ruffing	26.5
148	Tony Oliva	26.1
	Tommy John	26.1
	Silver King	26.1
151	Stan Coveleski	26.0
152	Hardy Richardson	25.9
	Robin Roberts	25.9
	Dave Stieb	25.9
155	Stan Hack	25.8
	Jim Rice	25.8
	Dolf Luque	25.8
158	Joe Medwick	25.7
	George Sisler	25.7
160	Heinie Groh	25.6
161	Eddie Plank	25.5
162	Dazzy Vance	25.4
163	Harry Heilmann	25.3
	Red Faber	25.3
165	Dick Bartell	25.2
	Rocky Colavito	25.2
	Pedro Guerrero	25.2
	Wally Schang	25.2
169	Thurman Munson	25.1
	Eppa Rixey	25.1
171	Buddy Bell	25.0
	Andre Dawson	25.0
	Billy Hamilton	25.0
	Jack Quinn	25.0
175	Ernie Banks	24.9
	Eddie Rommel	24.9
177	Urban Shocker	24.8
178	Pete Rose	24.7
179	Chuck Klein	24.3
	Duke Snider	24.3
	Nig Cuppy	24.3
182	Al Simmons	24.2
183	Jake Beckley	24.1
	Graig Nettles	24.1
185	Sam Crawford	24.0
	Guy Hecker	24.0
187	Harry Brecheen	23.9
188	Cesar Cedeno	23.8
	Jimmy Collins	23.8
190	Jack Fournier	23.7
	King Kelly	23.7
192	Minnie Minoso	23.6
193	Ed Konetchy	23.5
	Harry Stovey	23.5
195	Charlie Keller	23.4
	Ernie Lombardi	23.4
	Lon Warneke	23.4
198	Brooks Robinson	23.3
199	Ryne Sandberg	23.1
200	Eddie Cicotte	23.0

Total Baseball Ranking

201	Goose Goslin	22.9
	Joe Kelley	22.9
203	Harlond Clift	22.7
	Paul Molitor	22.7
	Roy Smalley	22.7
	Freddie Fitzsimmons	22.7
	Dutch Leonard	22.7
208	Lou Whitaker	22.5
209	Tony Gwynn	22.4
	Dave Parker	22.4
	Roy Thomas	22.4
	Billy Pierce	22.4
213	Roy Campanella	22.2
214	George Foster	22.1
215	Ron Cey	21.9
	Jim McCormick	21.9
217	Vic Willis	21.7
218	Eddie Stanky	21.6
219	Gil McDougald	21.5
220	Del Pratt	21.4
221	Spud Chandler	21.3
222	Jim Kaat	21.2
223	Zach Wheat	21.1
224	Art Fletcher	21.0
	Jim Fregosi	21.0
	Travis Jackson	21.0
	Charley Jones	21.0
	Fred Lynn	21.0
	Joe McGinnity	21.0
230	Darryl Strawberry	20.9
231	Wilbur Cooper	20.8
232	Fred Pfeffer	20.7
233	Jesse Tannehill	20.6
234	Bobby Shantz	20.4
235	Ken Singleton	20.3
236	Joe Tinker	20.2
237	Denny Lyons	20.1
	Larry Jackson	20.1
239	Frank Howard	20.0
	Sandy Koufax	20.0
241	Dizzy Dean	19.9
242	Murry Dickson	19.8
	Hippo Vaughn	19.8
244	Mike Griffin	19.7
245	Ken Williams	19.6
246	Orlando Cepeda	19.5
247	Kiki Cuyler	19.4
	Ed Reulbach	19.4
249	Charlie Buffinton	19.3
	Gavvy Cravath	19.3
	Darrell Porter	19.3
	Curt Davis	19.3
	Joe Wood	19.3
254	Roy White	19.2
255	Bill Joyce	19.1
	Don Newcombe	19.1
257	Miller Huggins	19.0
	Pee Wee Reese	19.0
	Andy Messersmith	19.0
260	Ken Boyer	18.9
	Jose Cruz	18.9
	Fred Tenney	18.9
263	Doc White	18.8
	Roger Bresnahan	18.8
	Steve Rogers	18.8
266	Jimmy Sheckard	18.7
	Jim Bunning	18.7
268	Dale Murphy	18.6
269	Bob Elliott	18.5
	Alan Trammell	18.5
	Orel Hershiser	18.5
272	Earl Averill	18.4
	Pie Traynor	18.4
	Monte Ward	18.4
	Jim Whitney	18.4
276	Gene Alley	18.3
	Wally Berger	18.3
	Babe Herman	18.3
	Lefty Gomez	18.3
280	Dan Quisenberry	18.2
	Early Wynn	18.2
282	Ferris Fain	18.1
283	Mel Harder	18.0
284	Brian Downing	17.9
	Noodles Hahn	17.9
286	Mel Stottlemyre	17.8
	Luis Tiant	17.8
288	Larry Doby	17.7
	Paul Hines	17.7
	Lance Parrish	17.7
	Mike Smith	17.7
	Ned Garver	17.7
	Ron Guidry	17.7
294	Babe Adams	17.5
	Eddie Lopat	17.5
	Mel Parnell	17.5
297	Rico Carty	17.3
	Roy Cullenbine	17.3
	John McGraw	17.3
	Claude Hendrix	17.3

Total Baseball Ranking

301	Dolph Camilli	17.2
	Ray Chapman	17.2
	Hal McRae	17.2
	Amos Otis	17.2
305	Roger Clemens	17.1
	Thornton Lee	17.1
	Claude Passeau	17.1
	Kent Tekulve	17.1
309	Art Devlin	16.9
310	Charlie Bennett	16.8
	Hack Wilson	16.8
	Larry French	16.8
313	Johnny Evers	16.6
	Toby Harrah	16.6
	Jocko Milligan	16.6
316	Cy Seymour	16.5
317	Chet Lemon	16.4
	Dave Foutz	16.4
	Waite Hoyt	16.4
	George Mullin	16.4
	Hal Schumacher	16.4
	Virgil Trucks	16.4
323	Benny Kauff	16.3
	Jim Devlin	16.3
	Frank Dwyer	16.3
326	Duke Farrell	16.2
	Lonny Frey	16.2
	Jimmy Ryan	16.2
	Nolan Ryan	16.2
330	Frank Chance	16.1
	Deacon McGuire	16.1
	Rudy York	16.1
	Frank Tanana	16.1
334	George Gore	16.0
	Bill Nicholson	16.0
	Edd Roush	16.0
	Andy Thornton	16.0
338	Ed Bailey	15.9
	Don Buford	15.9
	Sadie McMahon	15.9
	Mickey Welch	15.9
342	Harry Howell	15.8
343	Doug DeCinces	15.7
	Jeff Heath	15.7
	Tommy Leach	15.7
	Dave Orr	15.7
	Boog Powell	15.7
	Max Lanier	15.7
	Sam Leever	15.7
350	Smoky Burgess	15.6
351	Mike Hargrove	15.5
	Jim O'Rourke	15.5
	John Candelaria	15.5
	Charlie Ferguson	15.5
355	Phil Rizzuto	15.4
	Vern Stephens	15.4
	Maury Wills	15.4
	Larry Corcoran	15.4
359	Don Baylor	15.2
	Billy Nash	15.2
	Dennis Eckersley	15.2
	Dwight Gooden	15.2
	Bill Hutchinson	15.2
364	Dave Concepcion	15.1
	Schoolboy Rowe	15.1
	Bob Stanley	15.1
	Wilbur Wood	15.1
368	Rick Ferrell	15.0
	Tony Lazzeri	15.0
	Red Schoendienst	15.0
	Frank Killen	15.0
	George Uhle	15.0
373	Sal Maglie	14.9
374	Henry Larkin	14.8
375	Ben Chapman	14.7
	Sid Gordon	14.7
	Glenn Hubbard	14.7
378	Tommy Henrich	14.6
	Mort Cooper	14.6
	Rich Gossage	14.6
	Deacon Phillippe	14.6
382	Kirby Puckett	14.5
	Mike Garcia	14.5
	Howie Pollet	14.5
385	Harry Davis	14.4
	Kirk Gibson	14.4
	Charlie Hough	14.4
	Bret Saberhagen	14.4
	Bob Shawkey	14.4
390	Enos Slaughter	14.3
391	Andy Seminick	14.2
	John Tudor	14.2
393	Walker Cooper	14.1
	Gil Hodges	14.1
	Johnny Antonelli	14.1
	Milt Pappas	14.1
397	Johnny Logan	14.0
	Roger Peckinpaugh	14.0
399	George VanHaltren	13.9
	Kip Selbach	13.9

Total Baseball Ranking

	Richie Zisk	13.9
	Jerry Koosman	13.9
	Jim Maloney	13.9
	Curt Simmons	13.9
405	Tony Perez	13.8
	Fred Hutchinson	13.8
	Nap Rucker	13.8
	Jack Taylor	13.8
409	Fred Carroll	13.7
	Elston Howard	13.7
	Mike Tiernan	13.7
	Don Sutton	13.7
413	Tony Cuccinello	13.6
	Mike Donlin	13.6
	Will White	13.6
416	Bobby Murcer	13.5
	Johnny Pesky	13.5
418	Jim Galvin	13.4
	Fernando Valenzuela	13.4
420	Don Mattingly	13.3
	Dwayne Murphy	13.3
	Russ Ford	13.3
423	John Hiller	13.2
	Jim Tobin	13.2
425	Bob Allison	13.0
	Luis Aparicio	13.0
	Bill Bradley	13.0
	Augie Galan	13.0
	Sparky Lyle	13.0
430	Roy Sievers	12.9
	Bump Wills	12.9
	Heinie Zimmerman	12.9
	Gary Peters	12.9
434	Jesse Barfield	12.8
	Willie Kamm	12.8
	Ken Keltner	12.8
	Sixto Lezcano	12.8
	Ted Breitenstein	12.8
	Bruce Sutter	12.8
440	Jack Clements	12.7
	Lave Cross	12.7
	Buddy Myer	12.7
443	Solly Hemus	12.6
	Larry Hisle	12.6
	Cliff Johnson	12.6
	George Stone	12.6
	Chief Bender	12.6
	Rollie Fingers	12.6
	Gene Garber	12.6
	Claude Osteen	12.6
451	Nellie Fox	12.5
	Chief Zimmer	12.5
	Tom Burgmeier	12.5
	Jon Matlack	12.5
455	Bobby Knoop	12.4
	Harvey Haddix	12.4
	Sam McDowell	12.4
	Ben Sanders	12.4
459	Tim McCarver	12.3
	Stu Miller	12.3
461	Ron Hunt	12.2
	John Romano	12.2
	Ewell Blackwell	12.2
	Frank Lary	12.2
	Mike Marshall	12.2
466	Charlie Hickman	12.1
	Ed McFarland	12.1
	Al Oliver	12.1
	John Titus	12.1
	Bob Watson	12.1
	Jimmy Williams	12.1
	Sonny Siebert	12.1
473	Tony Fernandez	12.0
	Ross Youngs	12.0
475	Orator Shaffer	11.9
	Dean Chance	11.9
477	Ron Hansen	11.8
	Camilo Pascual	11.8
479	Davey Lopes	11.7
	Kevin McReynolds	11.7
	Teddy Higuera	11.7
	Tex Hughson	11.7
483	Dave Johnson	11.6
	Firpo Marberry	11.6
485	Donie Bush	11.5
	Ed Swartwood	11.5
	Jack Morris	11.5
	Sherry Smith	11.5
489	Del Crandall	11.4
	Clay Carroll	11.4
	Icebox Chamberlin	11.4
	Ned Garvin	11.4
493	Jim Gentile	11.3
	Greg Luzinski	11.3
	Dickie Thon	11.3
	Dixie Walker	11.3
	Frank Sullivan	11.3
498	4 players tied	11.2

Total Baseball Rank (alpha.)

Hank Aaron	90.1
Babe Adams	17.5
Pete Alexander	64.8
Dick Allen	35.6
Gene Alley	18.3
Bob Allison	13.0
Cap Anson	31.4
Johnny Antonelli	14.1
Luis Aparicio	13.0
Luke Appling	38.5
Richie Ashburn	27.0
Earl Averill	18.4
Ed Bailey	15.9
Frank Baker	34.6
Dave Bancroft	29.7
Ernie Banks	24.9
Jesse Barfield	12.8
Dick Bartell	25.2
Don Baylor	15.2
Jake Beckley	24.1
Buddy Bell	25.0
Johnny Bench	30.2
Chief Bender	12.6
Charlie Bennett	16.8
Wally Berger	18.3
Yogi Berra	34.8
Ewell Blackwell	12.2
Bert Blyleven	37.8
Wade Boggs	36.9
Bobby Bonds	31.3
Lou Boudreau	34.3
Ken Boyer	18.9
Bill Bradley	13.0
Harry Brecheen	23.9
Ted Breitenstein	12.8
Roger Bresnahan	18.8
George Brett	45.3
Tommy Bridges	28.5
Dan Brouthers	39.6
Mordecai Brown	35.0
Pete Browning	26.9
Charlie Buffinton	19.3
Don Buford	15.9
Jim Bunning	18.7
Smoky Burgess	15.6
Tom Burgmeier	12.5
Jesse Burkett	27.9
Donie Bush	11.5
Dolph Camilli	17.2
Roy Campanella	22.2
John Candelaria	15.5
Rod Carew	41.0
Max Carey	26.9
Steve Carlton	35.6
Fred Carroll	13.7
Clay Carroll	11.4
Gary Carter	36.3
Rico Carty	17.3
Bob Caruthers	35.6
Norm Cash	29.6
Cesar Cedeno	23.8
Orlando Cepeda	19.5
Ron Cey	21.9
Icebox Chamberlin	11.4
Frank Chance	16.1
Dean Chance	11.9
Spud Chandler	21.3
Ray Chapman	17.2
Ben Chapman	14.7
Cupid Childs	29.6
Eddie Cicotte	23.0
Jack Clark	28.5
Fred Clarke	27.5
John Clarkson	52.6
Roger Clemens	17.1
Roberto Clemente	39.6
Jack Clements	12.7
Harlond Clift	22.7
Ty Cobb	91.2
Mickey Cochrane	27.5
Rocky Colavito	25.2
Eddie Collins	70.5
Jimmy Collins	23.8
Dave Concepcion	15.1
Roger Connor	38.8
Walker Cooper	14.1
Wilbur Cooper	20.8
Mort Cooper	14.6
Larry Corcoran	15.4
Stan Coveleski	26.0
Del Crandall	11.4
Gavvy Cravath	19.3
Sam Crawford	24.0
Joe Cronin	38.2
Lave Cross	12.7
Jose Cruz	18.9
Tony Cuccinello	13.6
Roy Cullenbine	17.3
Nig Cuppy	24.3
Kiki Cuyler	19.4

Total Baseball Rank (alpha.)

Bill Dahlen	43.3
George Davis	48.1
Harry Davis	14.4
Curt Davis	19.3
Andre Dawson	25.0
Dizzy Dean	19.9
Ed Delahanty	46.1
Art Devlin	16.9
Jim Devlin	16.3
Bill Dickey	30.6
Murry Dickson	19.8
Larry Doby	17.7
Bobby Doerr	35.6
Mike Donlin	13.6
Brian Downing	17.9
Don Drysdale	34.7
Fred Dunlap	28.0
Frank Dwyer	16.3
Doug DeCinces	15.7
Joe DiMaggio	43.6
Dennis Eckersley	15.2
Bob Elliott	18.5
Darrell Evans	31.8
Dwight Evans	28.4
Johnny Evers	16.6
Buck Ewing	27.7
Red Faber	25.3
Ferris Fain	18.1
Duke Farrell	16.2
Bob Feller	26.9
Charlie Ferguson	15.5
Tony Fernandez	12.0
Rick Ferrell	15.0
Wes Ferrell	30.9
Rollie Fingers	12.6
Carlton Fisk	36.4
Freddie Fitzsimmons	22.7
Art Fletcher	21.0
Elmer Flick	28.5
Whitey Ford	38.6
Russ Ford	13.3
George Foster	22.2
Jack Fournier	23.7
Dave Foutz	16.4
Nellie Fox	12.5
Jimmie Foxx	53.9
Bill Freehan	28.9
Jim Fregosi	21.0
Larry French	16.8
Lonny Frey	16.2
Frankie Frisch	37.2
Augie Galan	13.0
Jim Galvin	13.4
Gene Garber	12.6
Mike Garcia	14.5
Ned Garver	17.7
Ned Garvin	11.4
Lou Gehrig	60.8
Charlie Gehringer	43.5
Jim Gentile	11.3
Kirk Gibson	14.4
Bob Gibson	46.3
Jack Glasscock	33.1
Lefty Gomez	18.3
Dwight Gooden	15.2
Joe Gordon	27.6
Sid Gordon	14.7
George Gore	16.0
Goose Goslin	22.9
Rich Gossage	14.6
Hank Greenberg	28.9
Bobby Grich	47.4
Mike Griffin	19.7
Clark Griffith	29.4
Burleigh Grimes	26.7
Heinie Groh	25.6
Lefty Grove	59.9
Pedro Guerrero	25.2
Ron Guidry	17.7
Tony Gwynn	22.4
Stan Hack	25.8
Harvey Haddix	12.4
Noodles Hahn	17.9
Billy Hamilton	25.0
Ron Hansen	11.8
Mel Harder	18.0
Mike Hargrove	15.5
Toby Harrah	16.6
Gabby Hartnett	35.7
Jeff Heath	15.7
Guy Hecker	24.0
Harry Heilmann	25.3
Solly Hemus	12.6
Rickey Henderson	48.2
Claude Hendrix	17.3
Tommy Henrich	14.6
Babe Herman	18.3
Billy Herman	34.0
Keith Hernandez	36.6
Orel Hershiser	18.5

Total Baseball Rank (alpha.)

Charlie Hickman	12.1
Teddy Higuera	11.7
John Hiller	13.2
Paul Hines	17.7
Larry Hisle	12.6
Gil Hodges	14.1
Rogers Hornsby	77.3
Charlie Hough	14.4
Elston Howard	13.7
Frank Howard	20.0
Harry Howell	15.8
Waite Hoyt	16.4
Glenn Hubbard	14.7
Carl Hubbell	38.6
Miller Huggins	19.0
Tex Hughson	11.7
Ron Hunt	12.2
Fred Hutchinson	13.8
Bill Hutchinson	15.2
Joe Jackson	36.0
Reggie Jackson	44.0
Travis Jackson	21.0
Larry Jackson	20.1
Ferguson Jenkins	32.1
Hughie Jennings	26.5
Tommy John	26.1
Cliff Johnson	12.6
Dave Johnson	11.6
Bob Johnson	37.8
Walter Johnson	81.5
Charley Jones	21.0
Addie Joss	26.9
Bill Joyce	19.1
Jim Kaat	21.2
Al Kaline	45.9
Willie Kamm	12.8
Benny Kauff	16.3
Tim Keefe	38.8
Charlie Keller	23.4
Joe Kelley	22.9
King Kelly	23.7
Ken Keltner	12.8
Harmon Killebrew	32.8
Frank Killen	15.0
Ralph Kiner	27.0
Silver King	26.1
Chuck Klein	24.3
Bobby Knoop	12.4
Ed Konetchy	23.5
Jerry Koosman	13.9
Sandy Koufax	20.0
Nap Lajoie	85.2
Max Lanier	15.7
Henry Larkin	14.8
Frank Lary	12.2
Tony Lazzeri	15.0
Tommy Leach	15.7
Thornton Lee	17.1
Sam Leever	15.7
Chet Lemon	16.4
Bob Lemon	35.2
Dutch Leonard	22.7
Sixto Lezcano	12.8
Johnny Logan	14.0
Ernie Lombardi	23.4
Eddie Lopat	17.5
Davey Lopes	11.7
Dolf Luque	25.8
Greg Luzinski	11.3
Sparky Lyle	13.0
Fred Lynn	21.0
Denny Lyons	20.1
Ted Lyons	35.4
Sherry Magee	28.5
Sal Maglie	14.9
Jim Maloney	13.9
Mickey Mantle	69.8
Firpo Marberry	11.6
Juan Marichal	30.8
Mike Marshall	12.2
Eddie Mathews	48.4
Christy Mathewson	54.6
Jon Matlack	12.5
Don Mattingly	13.3
Willie Mays	86.2
Carl Mays	34.8
Bill Mazeroski	34.4
Joe Medwick	25.7
Andy Messersmith	19.0
Stu Miller	12.3
Jocko Milligan	16.6
Minnie Minoso	23.6
Johnny Mize	36.5
Paul Molitor	22.7
Joe Morgan	63.9
Jack Morris	11.5
Tony Mullane	35.6
George Mullin	16.4
Thurman Munson	25.1
Bobby Murcer	13.5

Total Baseball Rank (alpha.)

Dale Murphy	18.6
Dwayne Murphy	13.3
Eddie Murray	35.6
Stan Musial	70.1
Buddy Myer	12.7
Tim McCarver	12.3
Jim McCormick	21.9
Willie McCovey	38.1
Gil McDougald	21.5
Sam McDowell	12.4
Ed McFarland	12.1
Joe McGinnity	21.0
John McGraw	17.3
Deacon McGuire	16.1
Sadie McMahon	15.9
Bid McPhee	37.5
Hal McRae	17.2
Kevin McReynolds	11.7
Billy Nash	15.2
Graig Nettles	24.1
Don Newcombe	19.1
Hal Newhouser	38.5
Kid Nichols	65.3
Bill Nicholson	16.0
Phil Niekro	38.0
Jim O'Rourke	15.5
Tony Oliva	26.1
Al Oliver	12.1
Dave Orr	15.7
Claude Osteen	12.6
Amos Otis	17.2
Mel Ott	60.1
Jim Palmer	36.4
Milt Pappas	14.1
Dave Parker	22.4
Mel Parnell	17.5
Lance Parrish	17.7
Camilo Pascual	11.8
Claude Passeau	17.1
Roger Peckinpaugh	14.0
Tony Perez	13.8
Gaylord Perry	36.8
Johnny Pesky	13.5
Gary Peters	12.9
Fred Pfeffer	20.7
Deacon Phillippe	14.6
Billy Pierce	22.4
Eddie Plank	25.5
Howie Pollet	14.5
Darrell Porter	19.3
Boog Powell	15.7
Del Pratt	21.4
Kirby Puckett	14.5
Jack Quinn	25.0
Dan Quisenberry	18.2
Charley Radbourn	29.3
Tim Raines	33.0
Willie Randolph	26.9
Ed Reulbach	19.4
Rick Reuschel	27.5
Jim Rice	25.8
Hardy Richardson	25.9
Cal Ripken	28.7
Eppa Rixey	25.1
Phil Rizzuto	15.4
Robin Roberts	25.9
Brooks Robinson	23.3
Frank Robinson	71.2
Jackie Robinson	33.3
Steve Rogers	18.8
John Romano	12.2
Eddie Rommel	24.9
Pete Rose	24.7
Edd Roush	16.0
Schoolboy Rowe	15.1
Nap Rucker	13.8
Red Ruffing	26.5
Amos Rusie	37.7
Babe Ruth	119.3
Jimmy Ryan	16.2
Nolan Ryan	16.2
Bret Saberhagen	14.4
Ryne Sandberg	23.1
Ben Sanders	12.4
Ron Santo	38.1
Wally Schang	25.2
Mike Schmidt	77.8
Red Schoendienst	15.0
Hal Schumacher	16.4
Tom Seaver	51.2
Kip Selbach	13.9
Andy Seminick	14.2
Joe Sewell	33.1
Cy Seymour	16.5
Orator Shaffer	11.9
Bobby Shantz	20.4
Bob Shawkey	14.4
Jimmy Sheckard	18.7
Urban Shocker	24.8
Sonny Siebert	12.1

Total Baseball Rank (alpha.)

Roy Sievers	12.9
Al Simmons	24.2
Ted Simmons	34.4
Curt Simmons	13.9
Ken Singleton	20.3
George Sisler	25.7
Enos Slaughter	14.3
Roy Smalley	22.7
Reggie Smith	33.4
Mike Smith	17.7
Ozzie Smith	40.0
Sherry Smith	11.5
Duke Snider	24.3
Warren Spahn	43.1
Tris Speaker	79.3
Eddie Stanky	21.6
Bob Stanley	15.1
Willie Stargell	31.6
Rusty Staub	29.4
Vern Stephens	15.4
Dave Stieb	25.9
Jack Stivetts	35.0
George Stone	12.6
Mel Stottlemyre	17.8
Harry Stovey	23.5
Darryl Strawberry	20.9
Frank Sullivan	11.3
Bruce Sutter	12.8
Don Sutton	13.7
Ed Swartwood	11.5
Frank Tanana	16.1
Jesse Tannehill	20.6
Jack Taylor	13.8
Kent Tekulve	17.1
Fred Tenney	18.9
Bill Terry	27.8
Roy Thomas	22.4
Sam Thompson	29.4
Dickie Thon	11.3
Andy Thornton	16.0
Luis Tiant	17.8
Mike Tiernan	13.7
Joe Tinker	20.2
John Titus	12.1
Jim Tobin	13.2
Joe Torre	29.8
Alan Trammell	18.5
Pie Traynor	18.4
Dizzy Trout	33.7
Virgil Trucks	16.4
John Tudor	14.2
George Uhle	15.0
Fernando Valenzuela	13.4
Dazzy Vance	25.4
Arky Vaughan	40.3
Hippo Vaughn	19.8
George VanHaltren	13.9
Rube Waddell	28.4
Honus Wagner	75.9
Dixie Walker	11.3
Bobby Wallace	36.8
Ed Walsh	41.6
Bucky Walters	27.4
Paul Waner	38.9
Monte Ward	18.4
Lon Warneke	23.4
Bob Watson	12.1
Pee Wee Reese	19.0
Mickey Welch	15.9
Zach Wheat	21.1
Lou Whitaker	22.5
Roy White	19.2
Doc White	18.8
Will White	13.6
Jim Whitney	18.4
Hoyt Wilhelm	29.2
Billy Williams	30.2
Jimmy Williams	12.1
Ken Williams	19.6
Ted Williams	89.8
Vic Willis	21.7
Bump Wills	12.9
Maury Wills	15.4
Hack Wilson	16.8
Dave Winfield	36.6
Joe Wood	19.3
Wilbur Wood	15.1
Jim Wynn	31.1
Early Wynn	18.2
Carl Yastrzemski	46.1
Rudy York	16.1
Cy Young	81.0
Ross Youngs	12.0
Robin Yount	35.9
Chief Zimmer	12.5
Heinie Zimmerman	12.9
Richie Zisk	13.9

Total Baseball Rank (by era)

1876-1892

1	John Clarkson	52.6
2	Dan Brouthers	39.6
3	Roger Connor	38.8
	Tim Keefe	38.8
5	Bid McPhee	37.5
6	Bob Caruthers	35.6
	Tony Mullane	35.6
8	Jack Stivetts	35.0
9	Jack Glasscock	33.1
10	Cap Anson	31.4
11	Sam Thompson	29.4
12	Charley Radbourn	29.3
13	Fred Dunlap	28.0
14	Buck Ewing	27.7
15	Pete Browning	26.9
16	Silver King	26.1
17	Hardy Richardson	25.9
18	Guy Hecker	24.0
19	King Kelly	23.7
20	Harry Stovey	23.5
21	Jim McCormick	21.9
22	Charley Jones	21.0
23	Fred Pfeffer	20.7
24	Denny Lyons	20.1
25	Mike Griffin	19.7

1893-1919

1	Ty Cobb	91.2
2	Nap Lajoie	85.2
3	Walter Johnson	81.5
4	Cy Young	81.0
5	Tris Speaker	79.3
6	Honus Wagner	75.9
7	Eddie Collins	70.5
8	Kid Nichols	65.3
9	Pete Alexander	64.8
10	Christy Mathewson	54.6
11	George Davis	48.2
12	Ed Delahanty	46.1
13	Bill Dahlen	43.3
14	Ed Walsh	41.6
15	Amos Rusie	37.7
16	Bobby Wallace	36.8
17	Joe Jackson	36.0
18	Mordecai Brown	35.0
19	Frank Baker	34.6
20	Cupid Childs	29.6
21	Clark Griffith	29.4
22	Elmer Flick	28.5
	Sherry Magee	28.5
24	Rube Waddell	28.4
25	Jesse Burkett	27.9

1920-1941

1	Babe Ruth	119.3
2	Rogers Hornsby	77.3
3	Lou Gehrig	60.8
4	Mel Ott	60.1
5	Lefty Grove	59.9
6	Jimmie Foxx	53.9
7	Charlie Gehringer	43.5
8	Arky Vaughan	40.3
9	Paul Waner	38.9
10	Carl Hubbell	38.6
11	Luke Appling	38.5
12	Joe Cronin	38.2
13	Bob Johnson	37.8
14	Frankie Frisch	37.2
15	Gabby Hartnett	35.7
16	Ted Lyons	35.4
17	Carl Mays	34.8
18	Billy Herman	34.0
19	Joe Sewell	33.1
20	Wes Ferrell	30.9
21	Bill Dickey	30.6
22	Dave Bancroft	29.7
23	Hank Greenberg	28.9
24	Tommy Bridges	28.5
25	Bill Terry	27.8

1942-1960

1	Ted Williams	89.8
2	Stan Musial	70.1
3	Mickey Mantle	69.8
4	Eddie Mathews	48.4
5	Joe DiMaggio	43.6
6	Warren Spahn	43.1
7	Whitey Ford	38.6
8	Hal Newhouser	38.5
9	Johnny Mize	36.5
10	Bobby Doerr	35.6
11	Bob Lemon	35.2
12	Yogi Berra	34.8
13	Lou Boudreau	34.3
14	Dizzy Trout	33.7
15	Jackie Robinson	33.3
16	Hoyt Wilhelm	29.2
17	Joe Gordon	27.6
18	Richie Ashburn	27.0
	Ralph Kiner	27.0
20	Bob Feller	26.9
21	Robin Roberts	25.9
22	Duke Snider	24.3
23	Harry Brecheen	23.9
24	Minnie Minoso	23.6
25	Charlie Keller	23.4

1961-1989

1	Hank Aaron	90.1
2	Willie Mays	86.2
3	Mike Schmidt	77.8
4	Frank Robinson	71.2
5	Joe Morgan	63.9
6	Tom Seaver	51.2
7	Rickey Henderson	48.2
8	Bobby Grich	47.4
9	Bob Gibson	46.3
10	Carl Yastrzemski	46.1
11	Al Kaline	45.9
12	George Brett	45.3
13	Reggie Jackson	44.0
14	Rod Carew	41.0
15	Ozzie Smith	40.0
16	Roberto Clemente	39.6
17	Willie McCovey	38.1
	Ron Santo	38.1
19	Phil Niekro	38.0
20	Bert Blyleven	37.8
21	Wade Boggs	36.9
22	Gaylord Perry	36.8
23	Keith Hernandez	36.6
	Dave Winfield	36.6
25	2 players tied	36.4

At Bats

1	Willie Wilson, 1980	705
2	Juan Samuel, 1984	701
3	Dave Cash, 1975	699
4	Matty Alou, 1969	698
5	Woody Jensen, 1936	696
6	Maury Wills, 1962	695
	Omar Moreno, 1979	695
8	Bobby Richardson, 1962	692
9	Kirby Puckett, 1985	691
10	Lou Brock, 1967	689
	Sandy Alomar, 1971	689
12	Dave Cash, 1974	687
	Tony Fernandez, 1986	687
14	Horace Clarke, 1970	686
15	Lloyd Waner, 1931	681
	Jo-Jo Moore, 1935	681
17	Pete Rose, 1973	680
	Frank Taveras, 1979	680
	Kirby Puckett, 1986	680
20	Harvey Kuenn, 1953	679
	Curt Flood, 1964	679
	Bobby Richardson, 1964	679
23	Dick Groat, 1962	678
24	Matty Alou, 1970	677
	Jim Rice, 1978	677
	Don Mattingly, 1986	677
27	Felix Millan, 1975	676
	Omar Moreno, 1980	676
29	Rennie Stennett, 1974	673
	Bill Buckner, 1985	673
31	Rabbit Maranville, 1922	672
	Tony Oliva, 1964	672
	Sandy Alomar, 1970	672
	Garry Templeton, 1979	672
35	Jack Tobin, 1921	671
36	Al Simmons, 1932	670
	Pete Rose, 1965	670
	Buddy Bell, 1979	670
39	Vada Pinson, 1965	669
	Larry Bowa, 1974	669
41	Buddy Lewis, 1937	668
	Brooks Robinson, 1961	668
	Ralph Garr, 1973	668
44	Carl Furillo, 1951	667
45	Billy Herman, 1935	666
	Zoilo Versalles, 1965	666
	Felipe Alou, 1966	666
	Dave Cash, 1976	666
	Ron LeFlore, 1978	666
	Paul Molitor, 1982	666
51	Tommy Davis, 1962	665
	Pete Rose, 1976	665
53	Taylor Douthit, 1930	664
	Bobby Richardson, 1965	664
	Don Kessinger, 1969	664
	Lou Brock, 1970	664
57	Jake Wood, 1961	663
	Bill Virdon, 1962	663
	Bobby Bonds, 1970	663
	Rick Burleson, 1977	663
	Cal Ripken, 1983	663
	Juan Samuel, 1985	663
	Joe Carter, 1986	663
64	Lloyd Waner, 1929	662
	Hughie Critz, 1930	662
	Richie Ashburn, 1949	662
	Granny Hamner, 1949	662
	Bobby Richardson, 1961	662
	Curt Flood, 1963	662
	Felipe Alou, 1968	662
	Pete Rose, 1975	662
72	Doc Cramer, 1933	661
	Doc Cramer, 1940	661
	Ken Hubbs, 1962	661
	Cecil Cooper, 1983	661
76	Tom Brown, 1892	660
	Doc Cramer, 1941	660
	Lou Brock, 1968	660
	Enos Cabell, 1978	660
80	Lloyd Waner, 1928	659
	Hughie Critz, 1932	659
	Red Schoendienst, 1947	659
	Billy Moran, 1962	659
	Zoilo Versalles, 1964	659
	Luis Aparicio, 1966	659
	Steve Garvey, 1975	659
	Warren Cromartie, 1979	659
88	Heinie Manush, 1933	658
	Doc Cramer, 1938	658
	Bill White, 1963	658
	Dave Cash, 1978	658
	Steve Garvey, 1980	658
	Julio Franco, 1984	658
94	Cesar Tovar, 1971	657
	Bill Buckner, 1982	657
	Jim Rice, 1984	657
	Kirby Puckett, 1988	657
98	9 players tied	656

Runs

1	Billy Hamilton, 1894	192
2	Tom Brown, 1891	177
	Babe Ruth, 1921	177
4	Tip O'Neill, 1887	167
	Lou Gehrig, 1936	167
6	Billy Hamilton, 1895	166
7	Willie Keeler, 1894	165
	Joe Kelley, 1894	165
9	Arlie Latham, 1887	163
	Babe Ruth, 1928	163
	Lou Gehrig, 1931	163
12	Willie Keeler, 1895	162
13	Hugh Duffy, 1890	161
	Hugh Duffy, 1894	161
15	Fred Dunlap, 1884	160
	Jesse Burkett, 1896	160
17	Hughie Jennings, 1895	159
18	Bobby Lowe, 1894	158
	Babe Ruth, 1920	158
	Babe Ruth, 1927	158
	Chuck Klein, 1930	158
22	John McGraw, 1894	156
	Rogers Hornsby, 1929	156
24	King Kelly, 1886	155
	Kiki Cuyler, 1930	155
26	Dan Brouthers, 1887	153
	Jesse Burkett, 1895	153
	Willie Keeler, 1896	153
29	Arlie Latham, 1886	152
	Mike Griffin, 1889	152
	Harry Stovey, 1889	152
	Billy Hamilton, 1896	152
	Billy Hamilton, 1897	152
	Lefty O'Doul, 1929	152
	Woody English, 1930	152
	Al Simmons, 1930	152
	Chuck Klein, 1932	152
38	Babe Ruth, 1923	151
	Jimmie Foxx, 1932	151
	Joe DiMaggio, 1937	151
41	George Gore, 1886	150
	Babe Ruth, 1930	150
	Ted Williams, 1949	150
44	Herman Long, 1893	149
	Bill Dahlen, 1894	149
	Ed Delahanty, 1895	149
	Lou Gehrig, 1927	149
	Babe Ruth, 1931	149
49	Hub Collins, 1890	148
	Jake Stenzel, 1894	148
	Joe Kelley, 1895	148
	Joe Kelley, 1896	148
53	Mike Tiernan, 1889	147
	Hugh Duffy, 1893	147
	Ed Delahanty, 1894	147
	Ty Cobb, 1911	147
57	Darby O'Brien, 1889	146
	Tom Brown, 1890	146
	Hack Wilson, 1930	146
	Rickey Henderson, 1985	146
61	Jesse Burkett, 1893	145
	Cupid Childs, 1893	145
	Ed Delahanty, 1893	145
	Patsy Donovan, 1894	145
	Willie Keeler, 1897	145
	Nap Lajoie, 1901	145
	Harlond Clift, 1936	145
68	Hugh Duffy, 1889	144
	Billy Hamilton, 1889	144
	Ty Cobb, 1915	144
	Kiki Cuyler, 1925	144
	Charlie Gehringer, 1930	144
	Al Simmons, 1932	144
	Charlie Gehringer, 1936	144
	Hank Greenberg, 1938	144
76	Cupid Childs, 1894	143
	John McGraw, 1898	143
	Babe Ruth, 1924	143
	Babe Herman, 1930	143
	Lou Gehrig, 1930	143
	Earle Combs, 1932	143
	Red Rolfe, 1937	143
83	Mike Griffin, 1887	142
	Harry Stovey, 1890	142
	Jesse Burkett, 1901	142
	Paul Waner, 1928	142
	Ted Williams, 1946	142
88	Billy Hamilton, 1891	141
	Rogers Hornsby, 1922	141
	Ted Williams, 1942	141
91	Tom Poorman, 1887	140
	Jimmy Ryan, 1889	140
	Jim McTamany, 1890	140
	Mike Griffin, 1895	140
	Willie Keeler, 1899	140
	John McGraw, 1899	140
	Max Carey, 1922	140
	Earl Averill, 1931	140
99	9 players tied	139

Runs per Game

1	Ross Barnes, 1876	1.91
2	Fred Dunlap, 1884	1.58
3	Billy Hamilton, 1894	1.49
4	George Gore, 1890	1.42
5	Billy Hamilton, 1895	1.35
6	Tip O'Neill, 1887	1.35
7	Billy Hamilton, 1893	1.34
8	Herman Long, 1894	1.32
9	King Kelly, 1886	1.31
10	Tom Brown, 1891	1.29
11	Ed Delahanty, 1894	1.29
12	Hugh Duffy, 1894	1.29
13	Ed Delahanty, 1895	1.28
14	Willie Keeler, 1894	1.28
	Joe Kelley, 1894	1.28
16	George Gore, 1886	1.27
17	John McGraw, 1894	1.26
18	Dan Brouthers, 1887	1.24
19	Willie Keeler, 1895	1.24
20	Bill Dahlen, 1894	1.23
21	Orator Shaffer, 1884	1.23
22	Jimmy Ryan, 1894	1.22
23	Willie Keeler, 1896	1.21
24	Hughie Jennings, 1895	1.21
25	Cupid Childs, 1894	1.21
26	Mike Tiernan, 1889	1.20
27	Harry Stovey, 1890	1.20
28	Jesse Burkett, 1896	1.20
29	Arlie Latham, 1887	1.20
30	Billy Hamilton, 1897	1.20
31	John McGraw, 1899	1.20
32	Harry Stovey, 1884	1.19
33	Bobby Lowe, 1894	1.19
34	George Gore, 1882	1.18
35	George Gore, 1881	1.18
36	Harry Stovey, 1883	1.17
37	Cupid Childs, 1893	1.17
38	Jesse Burkett, 1895	1.17
39	Hugh Duffy, 1890	1.17
40	Babe Ruth, 1921	1.16
41	Herman Long, 1893	1.16
42	Harry Stovey, 1885	1.16
43	Billy Hamilton, 1896	1.16
44	Jesse Burkett, 1893	1.16
45	King Kelly, 1885	1.16
46	Dan Brouthers, 1886	1.15
47	Hub Collins, 1890	1.15
48	John McGraw, 1895	1.15
49	Abner Dalrymple, 1882	1.14
50	George Gore, 1883	1.14
51	Tom Brown, 1890	1.14
52	Mike Griffin, 1894	1.14
53	Hughie Jennings, 1897	1.14
54	Arlie Latham, 1886	1.13
55	Ed Swartwood, 1882	1.13
56	Pete Browning, 1883	1.13
57	Jake Stenzel, 1894	1.13
	Joe Kelley, 1895	1.13
	Joe Kelley, 1896	1.13
60	Willie Keeler, 1897	1.12
61	Hugh Duffy, 1893	1.12
62	Jim McTamany, 1890	1.12
63	Jim O'Rourke, 1877	1.11
64	Dan Brouthers, 1894	1.11
65	Babe Ruth, 1920	1.11
66	Charlie Comiskey, 1887	1.11
67	King Kelly, 1884	1.11
68	Mike Griffin, 1889	1.11
	Harry Stovey, 1889	1.11
70	Nap Lajoie, 1901	1.11
71	Mike Griffin, 1890	1.10
72	Jesse Burkett, 1894	1.10
73	Jim O'Rourke, 1884	1.10
74	Al Simmons, 1930	1.10
75	Sam Thompson, 1895	1.10
76	George Gore, 1889	1.10
77	Ed Delahanty, 1893	1.10
	Patsy Donovan, 1894	1.10
79	Tom Daly, 1894	1.10
80	Bill Dahlen, 1896	1.10
81	Mike Hornung, 1883	1.09
82	Hardy Richardson, 1887	1.09
83	Sam Thompson, 1894	1.09
84	Jack Rowe, 1887	1.09
85	John Reilly, 1884	1.09
86	Jim O'Rourke, 1883	1.09
87	Emmett Seery, 1884	1.08
88	Billy Hamilton, 1890	1.08
	Roger Connor, 1890	1.08
90	Lou Gehrig, 1936	1.08
91	Ezra Sutton, 1883	1.07
92	Darby O'Brien, 1889	1.07
93	Curt Welch, 1889	1.07
94	Harry Stovey, 1882	1.07
95	Mike Griffin, 1895	1.07
96	Ed Delahanty, 1896	1.07
97	Dick Burns, 1884	1.06
98	Jim O'Rourke, 1885	1.06
99	Bid McPhee, 1887	1.06
100	2 players tied	1.06

Hits

1	George Sisler, 1920	257
2	Lefty O'Doul, 1929	254
	Bill Terry, 1930	254
4	Al Simmons, 1925	253
5	Rogers Hornsby, 1922	250
	Chuck Klein, 1930	250
7	Ty Cobb, 1911	248
8	George Sisler, 1922	246
9	Heinie Manush, 1928	241
	Babe Herman, 1930	241
11	Jesse Burkett, 1896	240
	Wade Boggs, 1985	240
13	Willie Keeler, 1897	239
	Rod Carew, 1977	239
15	Ed Delahanty, 1899	238
	Don Mattingly, 1986	238
17	Hugh Duffy, 1894	237
	Harry Heilmann, 1921	237
	Paul Waner, 1927	237
	Joe Medwick, 1937	237
21	Jack Tobin, 1921	236
22	Rogers Hornsby, 1921	235
23	Lloyd Waner, 1929	234
	Kirby Puckett, 1988	234
25	Joe Jackson, 1911	233
26	Nap Lajoie, 1901	232
	Earl Averill, 1936	232
28	Earle Combs, 1927	231
	Freddy Lindstrom, 1928	231
	Freddy Lindstrom, 1930	231
	Matty Alou, 1969	231
32	Stan Musial, 1948	230
	Tommy Davis, 1962	230
	Joe Torre, 1971	230
	Pete Rose, 1973	230
	Willie Wilson, 1980	230
37	Rogers Hornsby, 1929	229
38	Kiki Cuyler, 1930	228
	Stan Musial, 1946	228
40	Nap Lajoie, 1910	227
	Ty Cobb, 1912	227
	Rogers Hornsby, 1924	227
	Jim Bottomley, 1925	227
	Sam Rice, 1925	227
	Billy Herman, 1935	227
	Charlie Gehringer, 1936	227
47	Jesse Burkett, 1901	226
	Joe Jackson, 1912	226
	Bill Terry, 1929	226
	Chuck Klein, 1932	226
51	Tip O'Neill, 1887	225
	Jesse Burkett, 1895	225
	Ty Cobb, 1917	225
	Harry Heilmann, 1925	225
	Johnny Hodapp, 1930	225
	Bill Terry, 1932	225
57	George Sisler, 1925	224
	Joe Medwick, 1935	224
	Tommy Holmes, 1945	224
60	Frankie Frisch, 1923	223
	Lloyd Waner, 1927	223
	Paul Waner, 1928	223
	Chuck Klein, 1933	223
	Joe Medwick, 1936	223
	Hank Aaron, 1959	223
	Kirby Puckett, 1986	223
67	Sam Thompson, 1893	222
	Tris Speaker, 1912	222
	Eddie Collins, 1920	222
	Charlie Jamieson, 1923	222
71	Jesse Burkett, 1899	221
	Zach Wheat, 1925	221
	Lloyd Waner, 1928	221
	Heinie Manush, 1933	221
	Richie Ashburn, 1951	221
76	Pete Browning, 1887	220
	Billy Hamilton, 1894	220
	Kiki Cuyler, 1925	220
	Lou Gehrig, 1930	220
	Stan Musial, 1943	220
81	Ed Delahanty, 1893	219
	Willie Keeler, 1894	219
	Jimmy Williams, 1899	219
	Cy Seymour, 1905	219
	Chuck Klein, 1929	219
	Lefty O'Doul, 1932	219
	Paul Waner, 1937	219
	Ralph Garr, 1971	219
	Cecil Cooper, 1980	219
90	12 players tied	218

Doubles

1	Earl Webb, 1931	67
2	George Burns, 1926	64
	Joe Medwick, 1936	64
4	Hank Greenberg, 1934	63
5	Paul Waner, 1932	62
6	Charlie Gehringer, 1936	60
7	Tris Speaker, 1923	59
	Chuck Klein, 1930	59
9	Billy Herman, 1935	57
	Billy Herman, 1936	57
11	Joe Medwick, 1937	56
	George Kell, 1950	56
13	Ed Delahanty, 1899	55
	Gee Walker, 1936	55
15	Hal McRae, 1977	54
16	Tris Speaker, 1912	53
	Al Simmons, 1926	53
	Paul Waner, 1936	53
	Stan Musial, 1953	53
	Don Mattingly, 1986	53
21	Tip O'Neill, 1887	52
	Tris Speaker, 1921	52
	Tris Speaker, 1926	52
	Lou Gehrig, 1927	52
	Johnny Frederick, 1929	52
	Enos Slaughter, 1939	52
27	Hugh Duffy, 1894	51
	Nap Lajoie, 1910	51
	Baby Doll Jacobson, 1926	51
	George Burns, 1927	51
	Johnny Hodapp, 1930	51
	Beau Bell, 1937	51
	Joe Cronin, 1938	51
	Stan Musial, 1944	51
	Mickey Vernon, 1946	51
	Frank Robinson, 1962	51
	Pete Rose, 1978	51
	Wade Boggs, 1989	51
39	Tris Speaker, 1920	50
	Harry Heilmann, 1927	50
	Paul Waner, 1928	50
	Kiki Cuyler, 1930	50
	Chuck Klein, 1932	50
	Charlie Gehringer, 1934	50
	Odell Hale, 1936	50
	Ben Chapman, 1936	50
	Hank Greenberg, 1940	50
	Stan Musial, 1946	50
	Stan Spence, 1946	50
50	Ned Williamson, 1883	49
	Ed Delahanty, 1895	49
	Nap Lajoie, 1904	49
	George Sisler, 1920	49
	Heinie Manush, 1930	49
	Riggs Stephenson, 1932	49
	Hank Greenberg, 1937	49
	Robin Yount, 1980	49
58	Joe Kelley, 1894	48
	Nap Lajoie, 1901	48
	Nap Lajoie, 1906	48
	Tris Speaker, 1922	48
	Joe Sewell, 1927	48
	Babe Herman, 1930	48
	Dick Bartell, 1932	48
	Earl Averill, 1934	48
	Wally Moses, 1937	48
	Joe Medwick, 1939	48
	Stan Musial, 1943	48
	Keith Hernandez, 1979	48
	Don Mattingly, 1985	48
71	Harry Davis, 1905	47
	Ty Cobb, 1911	47
	George Burns, 1923	47
	Lou Gehrig, 1926	47
	Bob Meusel, 1927	47
	Lou Gehrig, 1928	47
	Heinie Manush, 1928	47
	Rogers Hornsby, 1929	47
	Chick Hafey, 1929	47
	Adam Comorosky, 1930	47
	Ed Morgan, 1930	47
	Charlie Gehringer, 1930	47
	Dale Alexander, 1931	47
	Eric McNair, 1932	47
	Joe Vosmik, 1935	47
	Joe Vosmik, 1937	47
	Joe Medwick, 1938	47
	Tommy Holmes, 1945	47
	Vada Pinson, 1959	47
	Wes Parker, 1970	47
	Pete Rose, 1975	47
	Fred Lynn, 1975	47
	Cal Ripken, 1983	47
	Wade Boggs, 1986	47
95	24 players tied	46

Triples

1	Chief Wilson, 1912	36
2	Dave Orr, 1886	31
	Heinie Reitz, 1894	31
4	Perry Werden, 1893	29
5	Harry Davis, 1897	28
6	George Davis, 1893	27
	Sam Thompson, 1894	27
	Jimmy Williams, 1899	27
9	John Reilly, 1890	26
	George Treadway, 1894	26
	Joe Jackson, 1912	26
	Sam Crawford, 1914	26
	Kiki Cuyler, 1925	26
14	Roger Connor, 1894	25
	Buck Freeman, 1899	25
	Sam Crawford, 1903	25
	Larry Doyle, 1911	25
	Tom Long, 1915	25
19	Ed McKean, 1893	24
	Ty Cobb, 1911	24
21	Harry Stovey, 1884	23
	Sam Thompson, 1887	23
	Mike Smith, 1893	23
	Dan Brouthers, 1894	23
	Nap Lajoie, 1897	23
	Ty Cobb, 1912	23
	Sam Crawford, 1913	23
	Ty Cobb, 1917	23
	Earle Combs, 1927	23
	Adam Comorosky, 1930	23
	Dale Mitchell, 1949	23
32	Roger Connor, 1887	22
	Bid McPhee, 1890	22
	Jake Beckley, 1890	22
	Joe Visner, 1890	22
	Willie Keeler, 1894	22
	Kip Selbach, 1895	22
	John Anderson, 1898	22
	Honus Wagner, 1900	22
	Tommy Leach, 1902	22
	Sam Crawford, 1902	22
	Bill Bradley, 1903	22
	Elmer Flick, 1906	22
	Mike Mitchell, 1911	22
	Birdie Cree, 1911	22
	Tris Speaker, 1913	22
	Hi Myers, 1920	22
	Jake Daubert, 1922	22
	Paul Waner, 1926	22
	Earle Combs, 1930	22
	Snuffy Stirnweiss, 1945	22
52	Dave Orr, 1885	21
	Mike Tiernan, 1890	21
	Billy Shindle, 1890	21
	Tom Brown, 1891	21
	Ed Delahanty, 1892	21
	Sam Thompson, 1895	21
	Mike Tiernan, 1895	21
	Tom McCreery, 1896	21
	George VanHaltren, 1896	21
	Bobby Wallace, 1897	21
	Jimmy Williams, 1901	21
	Bill Keister, 1901	21
	Jimmy Williams, 1902	21
	Cy Seymour, 1905	21
	Frank Schulte, 1911	21
	Frank Baker, 1912	21
	Sam Crawford, 1912	21
	Vic Saier, 1913	21
	Joe Jackson, 1916	21
	Edd Roush, 1924	21
	Earle Combs, 1928	21
	Willie Wilson, 1985	21
74	36 players tied	20

Triples (by era)

1876-1892

1	Dave Orr, 1886	31
2	John Reilly, 1890	26
3	Harry Stovey, 1884	23
	Sam Thompson, 1887	23
5	Roger Connor, 1887	22
	Bid McPhee, 1890	22
	Jake Beckley, 1890	22
	Joe Visner, 1890	22
9	Dave Orr, 1885	21
	Mike Tiernan, 1890	21
	Billy Shindle, 1890	21
	Tom Brown, 1891	21
	Ed Delahanty, 1892	21
14	10 players tied	20

1893-1919

1	Chief Wilson, 1912	36
2	Heinie Reitz, 1894	31
3	Perry Werden, 1893	29
4	Harry Davis, 1897	28
5	George Davis, 1893	27
	Sam Thompson, 1894	27
	Jimmy Williams, 1899	27
8	George Treadway, 1894	26
	Joe Jackson, 1912	26
	Sam Crawford, 1914	26
11	Roger Connor, 1894	25
	Buck Freeman, 1899	25
	Sam Crawford, 1903	25
	Larry Doyle, 1911	25
	Tom Long, 1915	25

1920-1941

1	Kiki Cuyler, 1925	26
2	Earle Combs, 1927	23
	Adam Comorosky, 1930	23
4	Hi Myers, 1920	22
	Jake Daubert, 1922	22
	Paul Waner, 1926	22
	Earle Combs, 1930	22
8	Edd Roush, 1924	21
	Earle Combs, 1928	21
10	12 players tied	20

1942-1960

1	Dale Mitchell, 1949	23
2	Snuffy Stirnweiss, 1945	22
3	Stan Musial, 1943	20
	Stan Musial, 1946	20
	Willie Mays, 1957	20
6	Johnny Barrett, 1944	19
7	Stan Musial, 1948	18
	Minnie Minoso, 1954	18
9	Enos Slaughter, 1942	17
	Jim Gilliam, 1953	17
11	6 players tied	16

1961-1989

1	Willie Wilson, 1985	21
2	George Brett, 1979	20
3	Garry Templeton, 1979	19
	Juan Samuel, 1984	19
	Ryne Sandberg, 1984	19
6	Garry Templeton, 1977	18
	Willie McGee, 1985	18
8	Ralph Garr, 1974	17
9	Johnny Callison, 1965	16
	Willie Davis, 1970	16
	Rod Carew, 1977	16
	Paul Molitor, 1979	16
13	11 players tied	15

Home Runs

1	Roger Maris, 1961	61
2	Babe Ruth, 1927	60
3	Babe Ruth, 1921	59
4	Jimmie Foxx, 1932	58
	Hank Greenberg, 1938	58
6	Hack Wilson, 1930	56
7	Babe Ruth, 1920	54
	Babe Ruth, 1928	54
	Ralph Kiner, 1949	54
	Mickey Mantle, 1961	54
11	Mickey Mantle, 1956	52
	Willie Mays, 1965	52
	George Foster, 1977	52
14	Ralph Kiner, 1947	51
	Johnny Mize, 1947	51
	Willie Mays, 1955	51
17	Jimmie Foxx, 1938	50
18	Babe Ruth, 1930	49
	Lou Gehrig, 1934	49
	Lou Gehrig, 1936	49
	Ted Kluszewski, 1954	49
	Willie Mays, 1962	49
	Harmon Killebrew, 1964	49
	Frank Robinson, 1966	49
	Harmon Killebrew, 1969	49
	Andre Dawson, 1987	49
	Mark McGwire, 1987	49
28	Jimmie Foxx, 1933	48
	Harmon Killebrew, 1962	48
	Frank Howard, 1969	48
	Willie Stargell, 1971	48
	Dave Kingman, 1979	48
	Mike Schmidt, 1980	48
34	Babe Ruth, 1926	47
	Lou Gehrig, 1927	47
	Ralph Kiner, 1950	47
	Eddie Mathews, 1953	47
	Ted Kluszewski, 1955	47
	Ernie Banks, 1958	47
	Willie Mays, 1964	47
	Reggie Jackson, 1969	47
	Hank Aaron, 1971	47
	George Bell, 1987	47
	Kevin Mitchell, 1989	47
45	Babe Ruth, 1924	46
	Babe Ruth, 1929	46
	Babe Ruth, 1931	46
	Lou Gehrig, 1931	46
	Joe DiMaggio, 1937	46
	Eddie Mathews, 1959	46
	Orlando Cepeda, 1961	46
	Jim Gentile, 1961	46
	Harmon Killebrew, 1961	46
	Jim Rice, 1978	46
55	Ernie Banks, 1959	45
	Rocky Colavito, 1961	45
	Hank Aaron, 1962	45
	Harmon Killebrew, 1963	45
	Willie McCovey, 1969	45
	Johnny Bench, 1970	45
	Mike Schmidt, 1979	45
	Gorman Thomas, 1979	45
63	Jimmie Foxx, 1934	44
	Hank Greenberg, 1946	44
	Ernie Banks, 1955	44
	Hank Aaron, 1957	44
	Hank Aaron, 1963	44
	Willie McCovey, 1963	44
	Hank Aaron, 1966	44
	Harmon Killebrew, 1967	44
	Carl Yastrzemski, 1967	44
	Frank Howard, 1968	44
	Hank Aaron, 1969	44
	Frank Howard, 1970	44
	Willie Stargell, 1973	44
	Dale Murphy, 1987	44
77	Chuck Klein, 1929	43
	Johnny Mize, 1940	43
	Ted Williams, 1949	43
	Al Rosen, 1953	43
	Duke Snider, 1956	43
	Ernie Banks, 1957	43
	Dave Johnson, 1973	43
	Tony Armas, 1984	43
85	Rogers Hornsby, 1922	42
	Mel Ott, 1929	42
	Hal Trosky, 1936	42
	Ralph Kiner, 1951	42
	Duke Snider, 1953	42
	Gus Zernial, 1953	42
	Gil Hodges, 1954	42
	Duke Snider, 1955	42
	Roy Sievers, 1957	42
	Mickey Mantle, 1958	42
	Rocky Colavito, 1959	42
	Harmon Killebrew, 1959	42
	Dick Stuart, 1963	42
	Billy Williams, 1970	42
	Jose Canseco, 1988	42
100	18 players tied	41

Home Runs (by era)

1876-1892

1	Ned Williamson, 1884	27
2	Fred Pfeffer, 1884	25
3	Abner Dalrymple, 1884	22
4	Cap Anson, 1884	21
5	Sam Thompson, 1889	20
6	Billy O'Brien, 1887	19
	Bug Holliday, 1889	19
	Harry Stovey, 1889	19
9	Jerry Denny, 1889	18
10	Roger Connor, 1887	17
	Jimmy Ryan, 1889	17
12	Fred Pfeffer, 1887	16
	Jimmy Ryan, 1888	16
	Harry Stovey, 1891	16
	Mike Tiernan, 1891	16

1893-1919

1	Babe Ruth, 1919	29
2	Buck Freeman, 1899	25
3	Gavvy Cravath, 1915	24
4	Frank Schulte, 1911	21
5	Ed Delahanty, 1893	19
	Gavvy Cravath, 1913	19
	Gavvy Cravath, 1914	19
8	Hugh Duffy, 1894	18
	Sam Thompson, 1895	18
	Fred Luderus, 1913	18
	Vic Saier, 1914	18
12	5 players tied	17

1920-1941

1	Babe Ruth, 1927	60
2	Babe Ruth, 1921	59
3	Jimmie Foxx, 1932	58
	Hank Greenberg, 1938	58
5	Hack Wilson, 1930	56
6	Babe Ruth, 1920	54
	Babe Ruth, 1928	54
8	Jimmie Foxx, 1938	50
9	Babe Ruth, 1930	49
	Lou Gehrig, 1934	49
	Lou Gehrig, 1936	49
12	Jimmie Foxx, 1933	48
13	Babe Ruth, 1926	47
	Lou Gehrig, 1927	47
15	5 players tied	46

1942-1960

1	Ralph Kiner, 1949	54
2	Mickey Mantle, 1956	52
3	Ralph Kiner, 1947	51
	Johnny Mize, 1947	51
	Willie Mays, 1955	51
6	Ted Kluszewski, 1954	49
7	Ralph Kiner, 1950	47
	Eddie Mathews, 1953	47
	Ted Kluszewski, 1955	47
	Ernie Banks, 1958	47
11	Eddie Mathews, 1959	46
12	Ernie Banks, 1959	45
13	Hank Greenberg, 1946	44
	Ernie Banks, 1955	44
	Hank Aaron, 1957	44

1961-1989

1	Roger Maris, 1961	61
2	Mickey Mantle, 1961	54
3	Willie Mays, 1965	52
	George Foster, 1977	52
5	Willie Mays, 1962	49
	Harmon Killebrew, 1964	49
	Frank Robinson, 1966	49
	Harmon Killebrew, 1969	49
	Andre Dawson, 1987	49
	Mark McGwire, 1987	49
11	Harmon Killebrew, 1962	48
	Frank Howard, 1969	48
	Willie Stargell, 1971	48
	Dave Kingman, 1979	48
	Mike Schmidt, 1980	48

Home Run Percentage

1	Babe Ruth, 1920	11.79
2	Babe Ruth, 1927	11.11
3	Babe Ruth, 1921	10.93
4	Mickey Mantle, 1961	10.51
5	Hank Greenberg, 1938	10.43
6	Roger Maris, 1961	10.34
7	Babe Ruth, 1928	10.07
8	Jimmie Foxx, 1932	9.91
9	Ralph Kiner, 1949	9.84
10	Mickey Mantle, 1956	9.76
11	Hack Wilson, 1930	9.57
12	Babe Ruth, 1926	9.49
	Hank Aaron, 1971	9.49
14	Jim Gentile, 1961	9.47
15	Babe Ruth, 1930	9.46
16	Willie Stargell, 1971	9.39
17	Willie Mays, 1965	9.32
18	Babe Ruth, 1929	9.22
19	Boog Powell, 1964	9.20
20	Willie McCovey, 1969	9.16
21	Ted Williams, 1957	9.05
22	Ralph Kiner, 1947	9.03
23	Dave Kingman, 1979	9.02
24	Babe Ruth, 1932	8.97
25	Jimmie Foxx, 1938	8.85
26	Harmon Killebrew, 1969	8.83
27	Mark McGwire, 1987	8.80
28	Willie Mays, 1955	8.79
29	Mike Schmidt, 1980	8.76
30	Mike Schmidt, 1981	8.76
31	Harmon Killebrew, 1963	8.74
32	Johnny Mize, 1947	8.70
33	Babe Ruth, 1924	8.70
	Harmon Killebrew, 1962	8.70
35	Kevin Mitchell, 1989	8.66
36	Babe Ruth, 1922	8.62
37	Babe Ruth, 1931	8.61
38	Ralph Kiner, 1950	8.59
39	Reggie Jackson, 1969	8.56
40	Ted Kluszewski, 1954	8.55
41	Frank Robinson, 1966	8.51
42	Harmon Killebrew, 1961	8.50
43	Harmon Killebrew, 1964	8.49
44	Lou Gehrig, 1934	8.46
	Lou Gehrig, 1936	8.46
46	George Foster, 1977	8.46
47	Willie Stargell, 1973	8.43
48	Hank Greenberg, 1946	8.41
49	Eddie Mathews, 1954	8.40
50	Rocky Colavito, 1958	8.38
51	Jimmie Foxx, 1933	8.38
52	Joe Adcock, 1956	8.37
53	Jack Clark, 1987	8.35
54	Mike Schmidt, 1979	8.32
55	Eddie Mathews, 1955	8.22
56	Jimmie Foxx, 1934	8.16
57	Willie Mays, 1964	8.13
58	Eddie Mathews, 1953	8.12
59	Ted Williams, 1941	8.11
60	Frank Howard, 1969	8.11
61	Mickey Mantle, 1958	8.09
62	Gorman Thomas, 1979	8.08
63	Lou Gehrig, 1927	8.05
64	Harmon Killebrew, 1967	8.04
	Hank Aaron, 1969	8.04
66	Reggie Jackson, 1980	7.98
67	Mickey Mantle, 1962	7.96
68	Duke Snider, 1956	7.93
69	Darrell Evans, 1985	7.92
70	Ralph Kiner, 1951	7.91
71	Roy Campanella, 1953	7.90
72	Willie Mays, 1962	7.89
	Andre Dawson, 1987	7.89
74	Hank Sauer, 1954	7.88
75	Willie McCovey, 1970	7.88
76	Duke Snider, 1957	7.87
77	Orlando Cepeda, 1961	7.86
78	Babe Ruth, 1923	7.85
79	Roger Maris, 1960	7.82
80	Duke Snider, 1955	7.81
81	Dave Kingman, 1976	7.81
	Eric Davis, 1987	7.81
83	Willie McCovey, 1963	7.80
84	Harmon Killebrew, 1970	7.78
85	Frank Howard, 1970	7.77
	Dale Murphy, 1987	7.77
87	Eddie Mathews, 1959	7.74
88	Rogers Hornsby, 1925	7.74
89	Rocky Colavito, 1961	7.72
90	Mel Ott, 1929	7.71
91	George Bell, 1987	7.70
92	Harmon Killebrew, 1959	7.69
	Norm Cash, 1962	7.69
	Dave Johnson, 1973	7.69
95	Ted Kluszewski, 1955	7.68
96	Cy Williams, 1923	7.66
	Norm Cash, 1961	7.66
98	Ernie Banks, 1959	7.64
99	Dick Allen, 1966	7.63
100	Ernie Banks, 1958	7.62

Home Run Pctg. (by era)

1876-1892

1	Ned Williamson, 1884	6.47
2	Fred Pfeffer, 1884	5.35
3	Cap Anson, 1884	4.42
4	Abner Dalrymple, 1884	4.22
5	Billy O'Brien, 1887	4.19
6	Sam Thompson, 1889	3.75
7	Roger Connor, 1887	3.61
8	Dan Brouthers, 1884	3.52
9	Harry Stovey, 1889	3.42
10	Bug Holliday, 1889	3.37
11	Fred Pfeffer, 1887	3.34
12	Harry Stovey, 1883	3.33
13	Jerry Denny, 1889	3.11
14	Dan Brouthers, 1881	2.96
15	Mike Tiernan, 1891	2.95

1893-1919

1	Babe Ruth, 1919	6.71
2	Bill Joyce, 1894	4.79
3	Gavvy Cravath, 1915	4.60
4	Jack Clements, 1893	4.52
5	Buck Freeman, 1899	4.25
6	Gavvy Cravath, 1914	3.81
7	Jim Canavan, 1894	3.65
8	Frank Schulte, 1911	3.64
9	Gavvy Cravath, 1913	3.62
10	Bill Joyce, 1895	3.59
11	Sherry Magee, 1911	3.37
12	Vic Saier, 1914	3.35
13	Sam Thompson, 1895	3.35
14	Hugh Duffy, 1894	3.34
15	Ed Delahanty, 1893	3.19

1920-1941

1	Babe Ruth, 1920	11.79
2	Babe Ruth, 1927	11.11
3	Babe Ruth, 1921	10.93
4	Hank Greenberg, 1938	10.43
5	Babe Ruth, 1928	10.07
6	Jimmie Foxx, 1932	9.91
7	Hack Wilson, 1930	9.57
8	Babe Ruth, 1926	9.49
9	Babe Ruth, 1930	9.46
10	Babe Ruth, 1929	9.22
11	Babe Ruth, 1932	8.97
12	Jimmie Foxx, 1938	8.85
13	Babe Ruth, 1924	8.70
14	Babe Ruth, 1922	8.62
15	Babe Ruth, 1931	8.61

1942-1960

1	Ralph Kiner, 1949	9.84
2	Mickey Mantle, 1956	9.76
3	Ted Williams, 1957	9.05
4	Ralph Kiner, 1947	9.03
5	Willie Mays, 1955	8.79
6	Johnny Mize, 1947	8.70
7	Ralph Kiner, 1950	8.59
8	Ted Kluszewski, 1954	8.55
9	Hank Greenberg, 1946	8.41
10	Eddie Mathews, 1954	8.40
11	Rocky Colavito, 1958	8.38
12	Joe Adcock, 1956	8.37
13	Eddie Mathews, 1955	8.22
14	Eddie Mathews, 1953	8.12
15	Mickey Mantle, 1958	8.09

1961-1989

1	Mickey Mantle, 1961	10.51
2	Roger Maris, 1961	10.34
3	Hank Aaron, 1971	9.49
4	Jim Gentile, 1961	9.47
5	Willie Stargell, 1971	9.39
6	Willie Mays, 1965	9.32
7	Boog Powell, 1964	9.20
8	Willie McCovey, 1969	9.16
9	Dave Kingman, 1979	9.02
10	Harmon Killebrew, 1969	8.83
11	Mark McGwire, 1987	8.80
12	Mike Schmidt, 1980	8.76
13	Mike Schmidt, 1981	8.76
14	Harmon Killebrew, 1963	8.74
15	Harmon Killebrew, 1962	8.70

Total Bases

1	Babe Ruth, 1921	457
2	Rogers Hornsby, 1922	450
3	Lou Gehrig, 1927	447
4	Chuck Klein, 1930	445
5	Jimmie Foxx, 1932	438
6	Stan Musial, 1948	429
7	Hack Wilson, 1930	423
8	Chuck Klein, 1932	420
9	Lou Gehrig, 1930	419
10	Joe DiMaggio, 1937	418
11	Babe Ruth, 1927	417
12	Babe Herman, 1930	416
13	Lou Gehrig, 1931	410
14	Rogers Hornsby, 1929	409
	Lou Gehrig, 1934	409
16	Joe Medwick, 1937	406
	Jim Rice, 1978	406
18	Chuck Klein, 1929	405
	Hal Trosky, 1936	405
20	Jimmie Foxx, 1933	403
	Lou Gehrig, 1936	403
22	Hank Aaron, 1959	400
23	George Sisler, 1920	399
	Babe Ruth, 1923	399
25	Jimmie Foxx, 1938	398
26	Lefty O'Doul, 1929	397
	Hank Greenberg, 1937	397
28	Al Simmons, 1925	392
	Bill Terry, 1930	392
	Al Simmons, 1930	392
31	Babe Ruth, 1924	391
32	Hank Greenberg, 1935	389
33	Babe Ruth, 1920	388
	George Foster, 1977	388
	Don Mattingly, 1986	388
36	Earl Averill, 1936	385
37	Hank Greenberg, 1940	384
38	Stan Musial, 1949	382
	Willie Mays, 1955	382
	Willie Mays, 1962	382
	Jim Rice, 1977	382
42	Rogers Hornsby, 1925	381
43	Babe Ruth, 1928	380
	Hank Greenberg, 1938	380
	Frank Robinson, 1962	380
46	Babe Ruth, 1930	379
	Ernie Banks, 1958	379
48	Rogers Hornsby, 1921	378
	Duke Snider, 1954	378
50	Willie Mays, 1954	377
51	Mickey Mantle, 1956	376
52	Babe Ruth, 1931	374
	Hal Trosky, 1934	374
	Tony Oliva, 1964	374
55	Rogers Hornsby, 1924	373
	Al Simmons, 1929	373
	Bill Terry, 1932	373
	Billy Williams, 1970	373
59	Hugh Duffy, 1894	372
60	Lou Gehrig, 1932	370
	Duke Snider, 1953	370
	Hank Aaron, 1963	370
	Don Mattingly, 1985	370
64	Kiki Cuyler, 1925	369
	Ripper Collins, 1934	369
	Jimmie Foxx, 1936	369
	Hank Aaron, 1957	369
	Jim Rice, 1979	369
	George Bell, 1987	369
70	Johnny Mize, 1940	368
	Ted Williams, 1949	368
	Ted Kluszewski, 1954	368
73	Ty Cobb, 1911	367
	Ken Williams, 1922	367
	Heinie Manush, 1928	367
	Al Simmons, 1932	367
	Joe Medwick, 1936	367
	Joe DiMaggio, 1936	367
	Tommy Holmes, 1945	367
	Al Rosen, 1953	367
	Frank Robinson, 1966	367
	Robin Yount, 1982	367
83	Lou Gehrig, 1937	366
	Stan Musial, 1946	366
	Willie Mays, 1957	366
	Roger Maris, 1961	366
	Hank Aaron, 1962	366
88	Harry Heilmann, 1921	365
	Babe Ruth, 1926	365
	Chuck Klein, 1933	365
	Joe Medwick, 1935	365
	Kirby Puckett, 1986	365
93	Lou Gehrig, 1928	364
94	Dale Alexander, 1929	363
	Eddie Mathews, 1953	363
	George Brett, 1979	363
97	Jim Bottomley, 1928	362
98	4 players tied	361

Runs Batted In

1	Hack Wilson, 1930	190
2	Lou Gehrig, 1931	184
3	Hank Greenberg, 1937	183
4	Lou Gehrig, 1927	175
	Jimmie Foxx, 1938	175
6	Lou Gehrig, 1930	174
7	Babe Ruth, 1921	171
8	Chuck Klein, 1930	170
	Hank Greenberg, 1935	170
10	Jimmie Foxx, 1932	169
11	Joe DiMaggio, 1937	167
12	Sam Thompson, 1887	166
13	Sam Thompson, 1895	165
	Al Simmons, 1930	165
	Lou Gehrig, 1934	165
16	Babe Ruth, 1927	164
17	Babe Ruth, 1931	163
	Jimmie Foxx, 1933	163
19	Hal Trosky, 1936	162
20	Hack Wilson, 1929	159
	Lou Gehrig, 1937	159
	Ted Williams, 1949	159
	Vern Stephens, 1949	159
24	Al Simmons, 1929	157
25	Jimmie Foxx, 1930	156
26	Ken Williams, 1922	155
	Joe DiMaggio, 1948	155
28	Babe Ruth, 1929	154
	Joe Medwick, 1937	154
30	Babe Ruth, 1930	153
	Tommy Davis, 1962	153
32	Rogers Hornsby, 1922	152
	Lou Gehrig, 1936	152
34	Mel Ott, 1929	151
	Lou Gehrig, 1932	151
	Al Simmons, 1932	151
37	Hank Greenberg, 1940	150
38	Rogers Hornsby, 1929	149
	George Foster, 1977	149
40	Johnny Bench, 1970	148
41	Cap Anson, 1886	147
42	Ed Delahanty, 1893	146
	Babe Ruth, 1926	146
	Hank Greenberg, 1938	146
45	Hugh Duffy, 1894	145
	Chuck Klein, 1929	145
	Ted Williams, 1939	145
	Al Rosen, 1953	145
	Don Mattingly, 1985	145
50	Walt Dropo, 1950	144
	Vern Stephens, 1950	144
52	Hardy Richardson, 1890	143
	Rogers Hornsby, 1925	143
	Earl Averill, 1931	143
	Don Hurst, 1932	143
	Jimmie Foxx, 1936	143
	Ernie Banks, 1959	143
58	Lou Gehrig, 1928	142
	Babe Ruth, 1928	142
	Hal Trosky, 1934	142
	Roy Campanella, 1953	142
	Orlando Cepeda, 1961	142
	Roger Maris, 1961	142
64	Sam Thompson, 1894	141
	Ted Kluszewski, 1954	141
	Jim Gentile, 1961	141
	Willie Mays, 1962	141
68	Joe DiMaggio, 1938	140
	Rocky Colavito, 1961	140
	Harmon Killebrew, 1969	140
71	Harry Heilmann, 1921	139
	Lou Gehrig, 1933	139
	Hank Greenberg, 1934	139
	Jim Rice, 1978	139
	Don Baylor, 1979	139
76	Bob Meusel, 1925	138
	Goose Goslin, 1930	138
	Joe Medwick, 1936	138
	Zeke Bonura, 1936	138
	Johnny Mize, 1947	138
81	Ed Delahanty, 1899	137
	Babe Ruth, 1920	137
	Jim Bottomley, 1929	137
	Dale Alexander, 1929	137
	Chuck Klein, 1932	137
	Babe Ruth, 1932	137
	Johnny Mize, 1940	137
	Ted Williams, 1942	137
	Vern Stephens, 1948	137
	Joe Torre, 1971	137
	Andre Dawson, 1987	137
92	George Kelly, 1924	136
	Jim Bottomley, 1928	136
	Ed Morgan, 1930	136
	Duke Snider, 1955	136
	Frank Robinson, 1962	136
97	5 players tied	135

Runs Batted In per Game

1	Sam Thompson, 1894	1.42
2	Sam Thompson, 1895	1.39
3	Sam Thompson, 1887	1.31
4	Hack Wilson, 1930	1.23
5	Al Simmons, 1930	1.20
6	Hank Greenberg, 1937	1.19
7	Lou Gehrig, 1931	1.19
8	Cap Anson, 1886	1.18
9	Jimmie Foxx, 1938	1.17
10	Hugh Duffy, 1894	1.16
11	Dave Orr, 1890	1.16
12	Ed Delahanty, 1894	1.15
13	Babe Ruth, 1929	1.14
14	Lou Gehrig, 1930	1.13
15	Lou Gehrig, 1927	1.13
16	Babe Ruth, 1921	1.13
17	Babe Ruth, 1931	1.12
18	Hank Greenberg, 1935	1.12
19	Ed Delahanty, 1893	1.11
20	Joe DiMaggio, 1937	1.11
21	Hardy Richardson, 1890	1.10
22	Al Simmons, 1929	1.10
23	Jimmie Foxx, 1932	1.10
24	Jimmie Foxx, 1933	1.09
25	Chuck Klein, 1930	1.09
26	Babe Ruth, 1927	1.09
27	Oyster Burns, 1890	1.08
28	Hal Trosky, 1936	1.07
29	Lou Gehrig, 1934	1.07
30	Ed McKean, 1893	1.06
31	Hack Wilson, 1929	1.06
32	Walt Dropo, 1950	1.06
33	Babe Ruth, 1930	1.06
34	Buck Ewing, 1893	1.05
35	Lave Cross, 1894	1.05
36	Joe DiMaggio, 1939	1.05
37	Dan Brouthers, 1894	1.04
38	Rogers Hornsby, 1925	1.04
39	Jim O'Rourke, 1890	1.04
40	George Davis, 1897	1.03
41	Babe Ruth, 1932	1.03
42	Ted Williams, 1949	1.03
	Vern Stephens, 1949	1.03
44	Ed Delahanty, 1896	1.02
45	Steve Brodie, 1895	1.02
	Joe Kelley, 1895	1.02
47	Jimmie Foxx, 1930	1.02
48	Hank Greenberg, 1940	1.01
49	Ken Williams, 1922	1.01
	Joe DiMaggio, 1948	1.01
51	Lou Gehrig, 1937	1.01
52	Cap Anson, 1882	1.01
53	George Decker, 1894	1.01
54	George Brett, 1980	1.01
55	Joe DiMaggio, 1940	1.01
56	Mel Ott, 1929	1.01
57	Nap Lajoie, 1897	1.00
	Al Simmons, 1931	1.00
59	Roger Connor, 1889	.99
60	Tommy McCarthy, 1894	.99
61	Jake Beckley, 1890	.99
62	Dan Brouthers, 1883	.99
63	Joe Medwick, 1937	.99
64	Rogers Hornsby, 1922	.99
65	Roy Campanella, 1953	.99
66	Jimmy Collins, 1897	.99
67	Ed McKean, 1894	.98
68	Bug Holliday, 1894	.98
69	Lou Gehrig, 1936	.98
70	Al Simmons, 1932	.98
71	Walt Wilmot, 1894	.98
72	Cap Anson, 1881	.98
73	Chuck Klein, 1929	.97
	Ted Williams, 1939	.97
75	Heinie Reitz, 1894	.97
76	Lou Gehrig, 1932	.97
77	Vern Stephens, 1950	.97
78	Joe DiMaggio, 1938	.97
79	Babe Ruth, 1920	.96
80	Cap Anson, 1885	.96
81	Hugh Duffy, 1897	.96
82	Sam Thompson, 1893	.96
83	Billy Nash, 1893	.96
84	Babe Ruth, 1926	.96
85	Harry Heilmann, 1929	.96
86	Tommy McCarthy, 1893	.96
87	Rogers Hornsby, 1929	.96
88	Hughie Jennings, 1895	.95
	Nap Lajoie, 1901	.95
90	Don Hurst, 1932	.95
91	Jim Gentile, 1961	.95
92	Jack Doyle, 1894	.95
93	Bill Dickey, 1937	.95
94	Ted Kluszewski, 1954	.95
95	George Kelly, 1924	.94
96	George Foster, 1977	.94
97	Hank Greenberg, 1938	.94
98	Rudy York, 1938	.94
99	Tommy Davis, 1962	.94
100	2 players tied	.94

Walks

1	Babe Ruth, 1923	170
2	Ted Williams, 1947	162
	Ted Williams, 1949	162
4	Ted Williams, 1946	156
5	Eddie Yost, 1956	151
6	Eddie Joost, 1949	149
7	Babe Ruth, 1920	148
	Eddie Stanky, 1945	148
	Jim Wynn, 1969	148
10	Jimmy Sheckard, 1911	147
11	Mickey Mantle, 1957	146
12	Ted Williams, 1941	145
	Ted Williams, 1942	145
	Harmon Killebrew, 1969	145
15	Babe Ruth, 1921	144
	Babe Ruth, 1926	144
	Eddie Stanky, 1950	144
	Ted Williams, 1951	144
19	Babe Ruth, 1924	142
20	Eddie Yost, 1950	141
21	Babe Ruth, 1927	138
22	Eddie Stanky, 1946	137
	Roy Cullenbine, 1947	137
	Ralph Kiner, 1951	137
	Willie McCovey, 1970	137
26	Jack Crooks, 1892	136
	Babe Ruth, 1930	136
	Ferris Fain, 1949	136
	Ted Williams, 1954	136
	Jack Clark, 1987	136
31	Babe Ruth, 1928	135
	Eddie Yost, 1959	135
33	Ferris Fain, 1950	133
34	Lou Gehrig, 1935	132
	Frank Howard, 1970	132
	Joe Morgan, 1975	132
	Jack Clark, 1989	132
38	Bob Elliott, 1948	131
	Eddie Yost, 1954	131
	Harmon Killebrew, 1967	131
41	Babe Ruth, 1932	130
	Lou Gehrig, 1936	130
43	Eddie Yost, 1952	129
	Mickey Mantle, 1958	129
45	Max Bishop, 1929	128
	Max Bishop, 1930	128
	Babe Ruth, 1931	128
	Harmon Killebrew, 1970	128
	Carl Yastrzemski, 1970	128
	Mike Schmidt, 1983	128
51	Lu Blue, 1931	127
	Lou Gehrig, 1937	127
	Eddie Stanky, 1951	127
	Jim Wynn, 1976	127
55	Billy Hamilton, 1894	126
	Lu Blue, 1929	126
	Ted Williams, 1948	126
	Eddie Yost, 1951	126
	Mickey Mantle, 1961	126
	Darrell Evans, 1974	126
	Rickey Henderson, 1989	126
62	Richie Ashburn, 1954	125
	Eddie Yost, 1960	125
	Gene Tenace, 1977	125
	Wade Boggs, 1988	125
66	John McGraw, 1899	124
	Norm Cash, 1961	124
	Eddie Mathews, 1963	124
	Darrell Evans, 1973	124
70	Bill Joyce, 1890	123
	Eddie Yost, 1953	123
	Ken Singleton, 1973	123
73	Jimmy Sheckard, 1912	122
	Lou Gehrig, 1929	122
	Luke Appling, 1935	122
	Ralph Kiner, 1950	122
	Eddie Joost, 1952	122
	Mickey Mantle, 1962	122
	John Mayberry, 1973	122
80	Jack Crooks, 1893	121
	Topsy Hartsel, 1905	121
	Roy Cullenbine, 1941	121
	Luke Appling, 1949	121
	Willie McCovey, 1969	121
	Darrell Porter, 1979	121
	Von Hayes, 1987	121
87	Cupid Childs, 1893	120
	Eddie Lake, 1947	120
	Joe Morgan, 1974	120
	Mike Schmidt, 1979	120
91	14 players tied	119

Strikeouts

1	Bobby Bonds, 1970	189
2	Bobby Bonds, 1969	187
3	Rob Deer, 1987	186
4	Pete Incaviglia, 1986	185
5	Mike Schmidt, 1975	180
6	Rob Deer, 1986	179
7	Dave Nicholson, 1963	175
	Gorman Thomas, 1979	175
	Jose Canseco, 1986	175
10	Jim Presley, 1986	172
	Bo Jackson, 1989	172
12	Reggie Jackson, 1968	171
13	Gorman Thomas, 1980	170
14	Juan Samuel, 1984	168
	Pete Incaviglia, 1987	168
16	Gary Alexander, 1978	166
	Steve Balboni, 1985	166
	Cory Snyder, 1987	166
19	Donn Clendenon, 1968	163
20	Butch Hobson, 1977	162
	Juan Samuel, 1987	162
22	Dick Allen, 1968	161
	Reggie Jackson, 1971	161
24	Bo Jackson, 1987	158
	Andres Galarraga, 1989	158
	Rob Deer, 1989	158
27	Dan Tartabull, 1986	157
	Jose Canseco, 1987	157
	Jim Presley, 1987	157
30	Tommie Agee, 1970	156
	Dave Kingman, 1982	156
	Reggie Jackson, 1982	156
	Tony Armas, 1984	156
34	Frank Howard, 1967	155
	Jeff Burroughs, 1975	155
36	Willie Stargell, 1971	154
	Larry Parrish, 1987	154
38	Dave Kingman, 1975	153
	Andres Galarraga, 1988	153
	Rob Deer, 1988	153
	Pete Incaviglia, 1988	153
42	George Scott, 1966	152
	Larry Hisle, 1969	152
44	Don Lock, 1963	151
	Greg Luzinski, 1975	151
	Juan Samuel, 1988	151
47	Dick Allen, 1965	150
	Nate Colbert, 1970	150
	Ron Kittle, 1983	150
	Jesse Barfield, 1989	150
51	Billy Grabarkewitz, 1970	149
	Mike Schmidt, 1976	149
	Fred McGriff, 1988	149
54	Bobby Bonds, 1973	148
	Mike Schmidt, 1983	148
	Gorman Thomas, 1983	148
57	Deron Johnson, 1971	146
	Nate Colbert, 1973	146
	Steve Balboni, 1986	146
	Jesse Barfield, 1986	146
	Bo Jackson, 1988	146
62	Lee May, 1972	145
	Bobby Darwin, 1972	145
	Dale Murphy, 1978	145
	Jack Clark, 1989	145
66	Dick Stuart, 1963	144
	Bobby Knoop, 1966	144
	Dick Allen, 1969	144
69	Nelson Mathews, 1964	143
	Byron Browne, 1966	143
	Rick Monday, 1968	143
	Gorman Thomas, 1982	143
	Jesse Barfield, 1985	143
74	Harmon Killebrew, 1962	142
	Donn Clendenon, 1966	142
	Lee May, 1969	142
	Jim Wynn, 1969	142
	Reggie Jackson, 1969	142
	Cito Gaston, 1970	142
	Juan Samuel, 1986	142
	Dale Murphy, 1989	142
82	Jake Wood, 1961	141
	Frank Howard, 1968	141
	Bobby Bonds, 1977	141
	Reggie Jackson, 1984	141
	Dale Murphy, 1985	141
	Juan Samuel, 1985	141
	Dale Murphy, 1986	141
	Darryl Strawberry, 1986	141
	Jesse Barfield, 1987	141
	Jack Clark, 1988	141
92	Dave Kingman, 1972	140
	Greg Luzinski, 1977	140
	Reggie Jackson, 1983	140
95	Larry Hisle, 1970	139
	Ron LeFlore, 1975	139
	Steve Balboni, 1984	139
	Jack Clark, 1987	139
99	6 players tied	138

At Bats per Strikeout

1	Mike McGeary, 1876	276.0
2	Cap Anson, 1878	261.0
3	Joe Sewell, 1932	167.7
4	John Peters, 1876	158.0
5	Joe Sewell, 1925	152.0
6	John Clapp, 1876	149.0
7	Joe Sewell, 1929	144.5
8	Jack Doyle, 1894	140.7
9	Joe Start, 1877	135.5
10	Joe Start, 1876	132.0
11	Joe Sewell, 1933	131.0
12	Levi Meyerle, 1876	128.0
13	Jim Holdsworth, 1876	120.5
14	Lon Knight, 1876	120.0
15	Charlie Hollocher, 1922	118.4
16	Ezra Sutton, 1876	118.0
17	Monte Ward, 1893	117.6
18	Bobby Mathews, 1876	109.0
19	Stuffy McInnis, 1922	107.4
20	Paul Hines, 1876	101.7
21	Deacon White, 1876	101.0
22	Willie Keeler, 1894	98.3
23	Al Spalding, 1876	97.3
24	Stuffy McInnis, 1924	96.8
25	Joe Sewell, 1926	96.3
26	Davy Force, 1876	95.7
27	Joe Start, 1878	95.0
28	Joe Quinn, 1895	90.5
29	Monte Ward, 1894	90.0
30	Deacon White, 1877	88.7
31	Cap Anson, 1881	85.8
32	Cap Anson, 1877	85.0
33	Everett Mills, 1876	84.7
34	John Cassidy, 1877	83.7
35	Joe Sewell, 1927	81.3
36	Dan Brouthers, 1889	80.8
37	Joe Start, 1879	79.3
38	Joe Quinn, 1893	78.1
39	Pie Traynor, 1929	77.1
40	Cal McVey, 1876	77.0
41	Lave Cross, 1894	75.6
42	Tom Carey, 1876	72.3
43	Steve Brodie, 1894	71.6
44	Ned Cuthbert, 1876	70.8
45	Tommy Holmes, 1945	70.7
46	Jack Glasscock, 1893	69.7
47	Wes Fisler, 1876	69.5
48	Sam Rice, 1929	68.4
49	Monte Ward, 1889	68.4
50	Emil Verban, 1947	67.5
51	George Hall, 1876	67.0
52	Lave Cross, 1895	66.9
53	Tom York, 1876	65.8
54	Tris Speaker, 1927	65.4
55	Joe Sewell, 1928	65.3
56	Sam Rice, 1925	64.9
57	Stuffy McInnis, 1921	64.9
58	Homer Summa, 1926	64.6
59	Mickey Cochrane, 1929	64.3
60	Jack Glasscock, 1890	64.0
61	Mike Dorgan, 1881	63.5
62	Ed McKean, 1896	63.4
63	Eddie Collins, 1923	63.1
64	Dummy Hoy, 1893	62.7
65	Lloyd Waner, 1933	62.5
66	Patsy Donovan, 1893	62.4
67	Lou Boudreau, 1948	62.2
68	Farmer Vaughn, 1896	61.9
69	Mickey Cochrane, 1927	61.7
70	Frankie Frisch, 1927	61.7
71	Joe Sewell, 1931	60.5
72	Willie Keeler, 1896	60.4
73	Jack Glasscock, 1887	60.4
74	Jimmy Hallinan, 1876	60.0
75	Lave Cross, 1893	59.3
76	Joe Gerhardt, 1876	58.4
77	Lou Bierbauer, 1894	58.3
	Dan Brouthers, 1894	58.3
79	Lou Bierbauer, 1895	58.3
80	Jack Glasscock, 1889	58.2
81	Dale Mitchell, 1949	58.2
82	Sam Dungan, 1893	58.1
83	Jim McCormick, 1880	57.8
84	Jack Manning, 1876	57.6
85	Tommy Holmes, 1944	57.4
86	Freddy Leach, 1931	57.2
87	Eddie Booth, 1876	57.0
88	Pie Traynor, 1928	56.9
89	Roger Connor, 1885	56.9
90	Dale Mitchell, 1952	56.8
91	Nellie Fox, 1958	56.6
92	Jack Farrell, 1880	56.5
93	Lloyd Waner, 1938	56.3
94	Sam Rice, 1921	56.1
95	Tommy Holmes, 1942	55.8
96	George Pinkney, 1893	55.8
97	John Morrill, 1876	55.6
98	Dan Brouthers, 1887	55.6
99	Ivy Olson, 1922	55.1
100	Jimmy Brown, 1942	55.1

Strikeouts per At Bat

1	Rob Deer, 1987	39.24
2	Dave Nicholson, 1963	38.98
3	Rob Deer, 1986	38.41
4	Pete Incaviglia, 1986	34.26
5	Rob Deer, 1989	33.91
6	Bo Jackson, 1989	33.40
7	Gary Alexander, 1978	33.33
8	Jack Clark, 1987	33.17
9	Pete Incaviglia, 1987	33.01
10	Dick Allen, 1969	32.88
11	Mike Schmidt, 1975	32.03
12	Jack Clark, 1989	31.87
13	Reggie Jackson, 1970	31.69
14	Larry Hisle, 1969	31.54
15	Gorman Thomas, 1979	31.42
16	Rob Deer, 1988	31.10
17	Reggie Jackson, 1968	30.92
18	Dick Allen, 1968	30.90
19	Dan Tartabull, 1986	30.72
20	Dave Kingman, 1975	30.48
21	Willie Stargell, 1971	30.14
22	Bobby Bonds, 1969	30.06
23	Reggie Jackson, 1985	30.00
24	Frank Howard, 1967	29.87
25	Dave Kingman, 1981	29.75
26	Darryl Strawberry, 1986	29.68
27	Rick Monday, 1968	29.67
28	Dave Kingman, 1972	29.66
29	Willie Mays, 1971	29.50
30	Reggie Jackson, 1982	29.43
31	Gorman Thomas, 1978	29.42
32	Ron Kittle, 1984	29.40
33	Jose Canseco, 1986	29.17
34	Dave Kingman, 1982	29.16
35	Ron Kittle, 1983	28.85
36	Jesse Barfield, 1989	28.79
37	Cory Snyder, 1987	28.77
38	Jim Wynn, 1969	28.69
39	Steve Balboni, 1986	28.52
40	Bobby Bonds, 1970	28.51
41	Dave Kingman, 1976	28.48
42	Don Lock, 1963	28.44
43	Jack Clark, 1988	28.43
44	Reggie Jackson, 1971	28.40
45	Eric Davis, 1987	28.27
46	Bobby Darwin, 1972	28.27
47	Gary Pettis, 1985	28.22
48	Billy Grabarkewitz, 1970	28.17
49	Jim Presley, 1986	27.92
50	Donn Clendenon, 1968	27.91
51	Dan Tartabull, 1989	27.89
52	Fred McGriff, 1988	27.80
53	Jim Gentile, 1964	27.79
54	Mike Schmidt, 1983	27.72
55	Steve Balboni, 1985	27.67
56	Gorman Thomas, 1983	27.66
57	Larry Parrish, 1987	27.65
58	Andres Galarraga, 1989	27.62
59	Nate Colbert, 1973	27.60
60	Reggie Jackson, 1986	27.45
61	Cory Snyder, 1989	27.40
62	Dale Murphy, 1978	27.36
63	Butch Hobson, 1977	27.32
64	Mike Marshall, 1983	27.31
65	Jim Presley, 1987	27.30
66	Gene Tenace, 1977	27.23
67	Mike Epstein, 1970	27.21
68	Gorman Thomas, 1980	27.07
69	Reggie Jackson, 1984	26.86
70	Don Lock, 1964	26.76
71	Bobby Knoop, 1967	26.61
72	Jerry Martin, 1982	26.59
73	Pancho Herrera, 1960	26.56
74	Jesse Barfield, 1985	26.53
75	Jeff Burroughs, 1975	26.50
76	Mike Marshall, 1985	26.45
77	Jack Howell, 1989	26.37
78	Jack Howell, 1987	26.28
79	Eric Davis, 1988	26.27
80	Nate Colbert, 1970	26.22
81	Tony Armas, 1981	26.14
82	Frank Meinke, 1884	26.10
83	Willie Stargell, 1972	26.06
84	Gorman Thomas, 1985	26.03
85	Bob Allison, 1965	26.03
	Reggie Jackson, 1978	26.03
87	Jack Howell, 1988	26.00
88	Dick Allen, 1966	25.95
89	Bobby Knoop, 1968	25.91
	John Shelby, 1988	25.91
91	Bobby Bonds, 1975	25.90
92	Reggie Jackson, 1969	25.87
93	Billy Cowan, 1964	25.75
94	Harmon Killebrew, 1962	25.72
95	Dick Allen, 1970	25.71
96	Mickey Mantle, 1967	25.68
97	Jim Lemon, 1956	25.65
98	Mike Schmidt, 1976	25.51
99	Gene Tenace, 1975	25.50
100	Mike Schmidt, 1982	25.49

Batting Average

1	Hugh Duffy, 1894	.440
2	Tip O'Neill, 1887	.435
3	Ross Barnes, 1876	.429
4	Nap Lajoie, 1901	.426
5	Willie Keeler, 1897	.424
6	Rogers Hornsby, 1924	.424
7	George Sisler, 1922	.420
8	Ty Cobb, 1911	.420
9	Fred Dunlap, 1884	.412
10	Ty Cobb, 1912	.410
11	Ed Delahanty, 1899	.410
12	Jesse Burkett, 1896	.410
13	Jesse Burkett, 1895	.409
14	Joe Jackson, 1911	.408
15	Sam Thompson, 1894	.407
16	George Sisler, 1920	.407
17	Ed Delahanty, 1894	.407
18	Ted Williams, 1941	.406
19	Billy Hamilton, 1894	.404
20	Ed Delahanty, 1895	.404
21	Rogers Hornsby, 1925	.403
22	Harry Heilmann, 1923	.403
23	Pete Browning, 1887	.402
24	Rogers Hornsby, 1922	.401
25	Bill Terry, 1930	.401
26	Hughie Jennings, 1896	.401
27	Ty Cobb, 1922	.401
28	Cap Anson, 1881	.399
29	Lefty O'Doul, 1929	.398
30	Harry Heilmann, 1927	.398
31	Rogers Hornsby, 1921	.397
32	Ed Delahanty, 1896	.397
33	Jesse Burkett, 1899	.396
34	Joe Jackson, 1912	.395
35	Harry Heilmann, 1921	.394
36	Babe Ruth, 1923	.393
37	Harry Heilmann, 1925	.393
38	Babe Herman, 1930	.393
39	Joe Kelley, 1894	.393
40	Sam Thompson, 1895	.392
41	John McGraw, 1899	.391
42	Ty Cobb, 1913	.390
43	Fred Clarke, 1897	.390
44	Al Simmons, 1931	.390
45	George Brett, 1980	.390
46	Tris Speaker, 1925	.389
47	Bill Lange, 1895	.389
48	Billy Hamilton, 1895	.389
49	Ty Cobb, 1921	.389
50	Ted Williams, 1957	.388
51	King Kelly, 1886	.388
52	Rod Carew, 1977	.388
53	Luke Appling, 1936	.388
54	Tris Speaker, 1920	.388
55	Deacon White, 1877	.387
56	Al Simmons, 1925	.387
57	Rogers Hornsby, 1928	.387
58	Tris Speaker, 1916	.386
59	Willie Keeler, 1896	.386
60	Chuck Klein, 1930	.386
61	Lave Cross, 1894	.386
	Hughie Jennings, 1895	.386
63	Willie Keeler, 1898	.385
64	Arky Vaughan, 1935	.385
65	Rogers Hornsby, 1923	.384
66	Ty Cobb, 1919	.384
67	Nap Lajoie, 1910	.384
68	Ty Cobb, 1910	.383
69	Jesse Burkett, 1897	.383
70	Tris Speaker, 1912	.383
71	Ty Cobb, 1917	.383
72	Lefty O'Doul, 1930	.383
73	Joe Jackson, 1920	.382
74	Ty Cobb, 1918	.382
75	Honus Wagner, 1900	.381
76	Babe Herman, 1929	.381
77	Joe DiMaggio, 1939	.381
78	Al Simmons, 1930	.381
79	Paul Waner, 1927	.380
80	Rogers Hornsby, 1929	.380
81	Billy Hamilton, 1893	.380
82	Tris Speaker, 1923	.380
83	Goose Goslin, 1928	.379
84	Freddy Lindstrom, 1930	.379
85	Willie Keeler, 1899	.379
86	Lou Gehrig, 1930	.379
87	John Cassidy, 1877	.378
88	Pete Browning, 1882	.378
89	Ty Cobb, 1925	.378
90	Babe Ruth, 1924	.378
91	Sam Crawford, 1911	.378
92	Tris Speaker, 1922	.378
93	Earl Averill, 1936	.378
94	Babe Ruth, 1921	.378
95	Heinie Manush, 1928	.378
96	Heinie Manush, 1926	.378
97	Ed Delahanty, 1897	.377
98	Willie Keeler, 1895	.377
99	Ty Cobb, 1909	.377
100	Cy Seymour, 1905	.377

Batting Average (by era)

1876-1892

1	Tip O'Neill, 1887	.435
2	Ross Barnes, 1876	.429
3	Fred Dunlap, 1884	.412
4	Pete Browning, 1887	.402
5	Cap Anson, 1881	.399
6	King Kelly, 1886	.388
7	Deacon White, 1877	.387
8	John Cassidy, 1877	.378
9	Pete Browning, 1882	.378
10	Dan Brouthers, 1883	.374
11	Pete Browning, 1890	.373
12	Dan Brouthers, 1889	.373
13	Dave Orr, 1890	.373
14	Sam Thompson, 1887	.372
15	Tommy Tucker, 1889	.372

1893-1919

1	Hugh Duffy, 1894	.440
2	Nap Lajoie, 1901	.426
3	Willie Keeler, 1897	.424
4	Ty Cobb, 1911	.420
5	Ty Cobb, 1912	.410
6	Ed Delahanty, 1899	.410
7	Jesse Burkett, 1896	.410
8	Jesse Burkett, 1895	.409
9	Joe Jackson, 1911	.408
10	Sam Thompson, 1894	.407
11	Ed Delahanty, 1894	.407
12	Billy Hamilton, 1894	.404
13	Ed Delahanty, 1895	.404
14	Hughie Jennings, 1896	.401
15	Ed Delahanty, 1896	.397

1920-1941

1	Rogers Hornsby, 1924	.424
2	George Sisler, 1922	.420
3	George Sisler, 1920	.407
4	Ted Williams, 1941	.406
5	Rogers Hornsby, 1925	.403
6	Harry Heilmann, 1923	.403
7	Rogers Hornsby, 1922	.401
8	Bill Terry, 1930	.401
9	Ty Cobb, 1922	.401
10	Lefty O'Doul, 1929	.398
11	Harry Heilmann, 1927	.398
12	Rogers Hornsby, 1921	.397
13	Harry Heilmann, 1921	.394
14	Babe Ruth, 1923	.393
15	Harry Heilmann, 1925	.393

1942-1960

1	Ted Williams, 1957	.388
2	Stan Musial, 1948	.376
3	Ted Williams, 1948	.369
4	Stan Musial, 1946	.365
5	Mickey Mantle, 1957	.365
6	Harry Walker, 1947	.363
7	Dixie Walker, 1944	.357
8	Stan Musial, 1943	.357
9	Ted Williams, 1942	.356
10	Phil Cavarretta, 1945	.355
11	Lou Boudreau, 1948	.355
12	Stan Musial, 1951	.355
13	Hank Aaron, 1959	.355
14	Billy Goodman, 1950	.354
15	Harvey Kuenn, 1959	.353

1961-1989

1	George Brett, 1980	.390
2	Rod Carew, 1977	.388
3	Tony Gwynn, 1987	.370
4	Wade Boggs, 1985	.368
5	Wade Boggs, 1988	.366
6	Rico Carty, 1970	.366
7	Rod Carew, 1974	.364
8	Wade Boggs, 1987	.363
9	Joe Torre, 1971	.363
10	Wade Boggs, 1983	.361
11	Norm Cash, 1961	.361
12	Rod Carew, 1975	.359
13	Roberto Clemente, 1967	.357
14	Wade Boggs, 1986	.357
15	Kirby Puckett, 1988	.356

Batting Average (by position)

First Base
1	George Sisler, 1922	.420
2	George Sisler, 1920	.407
3	Bill Terry, 1930	.401
4	Cap Anson, 1881	.399
5	Rod Carew, 1977	.388
6	Lou Gehrig, 1930	.379
7	Dan Brouthers, 1883	.374
8	Lou Gehrig, 1928	.374
9	Lou Gehrig, 1927	.373
10	Dan Brouthers, 1889	.373

Second Base
1	Ross Barnes, 1876	.429
2	Nap Lajoie, 1901	.426
3	Rogers Hornsby, 1924	.424
4	Fred Dunlap, 1884	.412
5	Rogers Hornsby, 1925	.403
6	Rogers Hornsby, 1922	.401
7	Rogers Hornsby, 1921	.397
8	Rogers Hornsby, 1928	.387
9	Nap Lajoie, 1910	.384
10	Rogers Hornsby, 1929	.380

Shortstop
1	Hughie Jennings, 1896	.401
2	Luke Appling, 1936	.388
3	Hughie Jennings, 1895	.386
4	Arky Vaughan, 1935	.385
5	Honus Wagner, 1905	.363
6	Hughie Jennings, 1897	.355
7	Honus Wagner, 1903	.355
8	Honus Wagner, 1908	.354
9	Honus Wagner, 1907	.350
10	Honus Wagner, 1904	.349

Third Base
1	John McGraw, 1899	.391
2	George Brett, 1980	.390
3	Lave Cross, 1894	.386
4	Freddy Lindstrom, 1930	.379
5	Heinie Zimmerman, 1912	.372
6	John McGraw, 1895	.369
7	Wade Boggs, 1985	.368
8	Denny Lyons, 1887	.367
9	Wade Boggs, 1988	.366
10	Pie Traynor, 1930	.366

Outfield
1	Hugh Duffy, 1894	.440
2	Tip O'Neill, 1887	.435
3	Willie Keeler, 1897	.424
4	Ty Cobb, 1911	.420
5	Ty Cobb, 1912	.410
6	Ed Delahanty, 1899	.410
7	Jesse Burkett, 1896	.410
8	Jesse Burkett, 1895	.409
9	Joe Jackson, 1911	.408
10	Sam Thompson, 1894	.407

Catcher
1	Cal McVey, 1877	.368
2	Mickey Cochrane, 1930	.357
3	Wilbert Robinson, 1894	.353
4	Spud Davis, 1933	.349
5	Mickey Cochrane, 1931	.349
6	Ernie Lombardi, 1938	.342
7	Gabby Hartnett, 1930	.339
8	Mickey Cochrane, 1932	.338
9	Ted Simmons, 1975	.332
10	Bill Dickey, 1937	.332

Relative Batting Average

1	Fred Dunlap, 1884	1.667
2	Ross Barnes, 1876	1.608
3	Tip O'Neill, 1887	1.564
4	Nap Lajoie, 1910	1.537
5	Ty Cobb, 1910	1.534
6	Pete Browning, 1882	1.526
7	Cap Anson, 1881	1.512
8	King Kelly, 1886	1.508
9	Ty Cobb, 1912	1.507
10	Roger Connor, 1885	1.507
11	Tris Speaker, 1916	1.506
12	Ty Cobb, 1917	1.501
13	Nap Lajoie, 1904	1.500
14	Nap Lajoie, 1901	1.500
15	Ty Cobb, 1911	1.494
16	Ty Cobb, 1909	1.492
17	Ted Williams, 1957	1.476
18	Ty Cobb, 1913	1.475
19	Ted Williams, 1941	1.472
20	Ty Cobb, 1918	1.469
21	George Gore, 1880	1.461
22	Rogers Hornsby, 1924	1.461
23	Rod Carew, 1977	1.458
24	Orator Shaffer, 1884	1.455
25	Dan Brouthers, 1885	1.455
26	Joe Jackson, 1911	1.453
27	Joe Jackson, 1912	1.451
28	Dan Brouthers, 1882	1.449
29	Dave Orr, 1884	1.448
30	George Brett, 1980	1.448
31	Ty Cobb, 1915	1.448
32	Pete Browning, 1887	1.446
33	Ty Cobb, 1916	1.445
34	Cap Anson, 1886	1.442
35	Pete Browning, 1885	1.439
36	Dan Brouthers, 1886	1.439
37	Honus Wagner, 1908	1.434
38	George Sisler, 1922	1.433
39	Cap Anson, 1882	1.428
40	Cy Seymour, 1905	1.425
41	Willie Keeler, 1897	1.422
42	Ed Delahanty, 1899	1.414
43	Wade Boggs, 1988	1.413
44	King Kelly, 1884	1.411
45	Joe Jackson, 1913	1.410
46	Rod Carew, 1974	1.408
47	Wade Boggs, 1985	1.407
48	Tris Speaker, 1912	1.406
49	Deacon White, 1877	1.405
50	Dan Brouthers, 1883	1.401
51	Chicken Wolf, 1890	1.401
52	Stan Musial, 1948	1.400
53	George Stone, 1906	1.400
54	Cap Anson, 1888	1.399
55	George Sisler, 1920	1.398
56	Joe Torre, 1971	1.397
57	Hugh Duffy, 1894	1.395
58	Stan Musial, 1946	1.392
59	Ty Cobb, 1919	1.392
60	Rod Carew, 1975	1.391
61	Tommy Tucker, 1889	1.390
62	Nap Lajoie, 1906	1.390
63	John Reilly, 1884	1.389
64	Ed Swartwood, 1883	1.389
65	Harry Heilmann, 1923	1.389
66	Mickey Mantle, 1957	1.388
67	Willie Keeler, 1898	1.387
68	Honus Wagner, 1907	1.387
69	Roberto Clemente, 1967	1.385
70	George Sisler, 1917	1.383
71	Jim O'Rourke, 1884	1.383
72	Pete Browning, 1886	1.382
73	Tris Speaker, 1917	1.380
74	Ezra Sutton, 1884	1.380
75	Ty Cobb, 1907	1.379
76	Hick Carpenter, 1882	1.379
77	Roger Connor, 1886	1.378
78	Jesse Burkett, 1896	1.378
79	Paul Hines, 1879	1.377
80	Tony Gwynn, 1987	1.375
81	Pete Browning, 1884	1.374
82	Tris Speaker, 1913	1.374
83	Kirby Puckett, 1988	1.374
84	John Cassidy, 1877	1.373
85	Honus Wagner, 1905	1.372
86	Dave Orr, 1886	1.372
87	Rico Carty, 1970	1.372
88	George Hall, 1876	1.372
89	Tip O'Neill, 1888	1.371
90	Eddie Collins, 1909	1.370
91	Wade Boggs, 1987	1.370
92	Dan Brouthers, 1889	1.370
93	Ty Cobb, 1922	1.369
94	Norm Cash, 1961	1.368
95	Cap Anson, 1880	1.367
96	Jesse Burkett, 1899	1.367
97	Willie Keeler, 1904	1.366
98	Jesse Burkett, 1901	1.365
99	Hardy Richardson, 1886	1.365
100	Wade Boggs, 1986	1.365

On Base Percentage

1	Ted Williams, 1941	.551
2	John McGraw, 1899	.547
3	Babe Ruth, 1923	.545
4	Babe Ruth, 1920	.530
5	Ted Williams, 1957	.528
6	Billy Hamilton, 1894	.523
7	Ted Williams, 1954	.516
8	Babe Ruth, 1926	.516
9	Mickey Mantle, 1957	.515
10	Babe Ruth, 1924	.513
11	Babe Ruth, 1921	.512
12	Rogers Hornsby, 1924	.507
13	Joe Kelley, 1894	.502
14	Hugh Duffy, 1894	.502
15	Ed Delahanty, 1895	.500
16	Ted Williams, 1942	.499
17	Ted Williams, 1947	.499
18	Rogers Hornsby, 1928	.498
19	Ted Williams, 1946	.497
20	Ted Williams, 1948	.497
21	Bill Joyce, 1894	.496
22	Babe Ruth, 1931	.495
23	Babe Ruth, 1930	.493
24	Arky Vaughan, 1935	.491
25	Ted Williams, 1949	.490
26	Billy Hamilton, 1895	.490
27	Billy Hamilton, 1893	.490
28	Tip O'Neill, 1887	.490
29	Rogers Hornsby, 1925	.489
	Babe Ruth, 1932	.489
31	Norm Cash, 1961	.488
32	Mickey Mantle, 1962	.488
33	Babe Ruth, 1927	.487
34	Ty Cobb, 1915	.486
35	Jesse Burkett, 1895	.486
36	Tris Speaker, 1920	.483
37	King Kelly, 1886	.483
38	Harry Heilmann, 1923	.481
39	Wade Boggs, 1988	.480
40	Billy Hamilton, 1898	.480
41	Tris Speaker, 1925	.479
	Ted Williams, 1956	.479
43	Ed Delahanty, 1894	.478
44	Lou Gehrig, 1936	.478
45	Billy Hamilton, 1896	.477
46	Cupid Childs, 1894	.475
47	Harry Heilmann, 1927	.475
48	John McGraw, 1898	.474
49	Tris Speaker, 1922	.474
50	Lou Gehrig, 1927	.474
51	Luke Appling, 1936	.474
52	Lou Gehrig, 1930	.473
53	Lou Gehrig, 1937	.473
54	Hughie Jennings, 1896	.472
55	Ed Delahanty, 1896	.472
56	John McGraw, 1897	.471
57	Joe Morgan, 1975	.471
58	Dan Brouthers, 1891	.471
59	Tris Speaker, 1916	.470
60	Bill Joyce, 1896	.470
61	Joe Kelley, 1896	.469
62	Tris Speaker, 1923	.469
63	Jimmie Foxx, 1932	.469
64	Jesse Burkett, 1897	.468
65	Ty Cobb, 1925	.468
66	Joe Jackson, 1911	.468
67	Lou Gehrig, 1928	.467
68	Ty Cobb, 1913	.467
69	George Sisler, 1922	.467
70	Mike Griffin, 1894	.467
71	Cupid Childs, 1896	.467
72	Mickey Mantle, 1956	.467
73	Wade Boggs, 1987	.467
74	Ty Cobb, 1911	.467
75	Dan Brouthers, 1890	.466
76	Lou Gehrig, 1935	.466
77	Lou Gehrig, 1934	.465
78	Lefty O'Doul, 1929	.465
79	Jimmie Foxx, 1939	.464
80	Tris Speaker, 1912	.464
81	Pete Browning, 1887	.464
82	Ted Williams, 1951	.464
83	Willie Keeler, 1897	.464
84	Bob Caruthers, 1887	.463
85	Ed Delahanty, 1899	.463
86	Cupid Childs, 1893	.463
87	Jimmie Foxx, 1929	.463
88	Hughie Jennings, 1897	.463
89	Jesse Burkett, 1899	.463
90	Ross Barnes, 1876	.462
	Jimmie Foxx, 1938	.462
	Ted Williams, 1958	.462
93	Dan Brouthers, 1889	.462
94	Ty Cobb, 1922	.462
95	Babe Ruth, 1928	.461
96	Jack Clark, 1987	.461
97	Eddie Collins, 1925	.461
98	Billy Hamilton, 1897	.461
99	Jesse Burkett, 1896	.461
100	Fred Clarke, 1897	.461

Slugging Average

1	Babe Ruth, 1920	.847
2	Babe Ruth, 1921	.846
3	Babe Ruth, 1927	.772
4	Lou Gehrig, 1927	.765
5	Babe Ruth, 1923	.764
6	Rogers Hornsby, 1925	.756
7	Jimmie Foxx, 1932	.749
8	Babe Ruth, 1924	.739
9	Babe Ruth, 1926	.737
10	Ted Williams, 1941	.735
11	Babe Ruth, 1930	.732
12	Ted Williams, 1957	.731
13	Hack Wilson, 1930	.723
14	Rogers Hornsby, 1922	.722
15	Lou Gehrig, 1930	.721
16	Babe Ruth, 1928	.709
17	Al Simmons, 1930	.708
18	Lou Gehrig, 1934	.706
19	Mickey Mantle, 1956	.705
20	Jimmie Foxx, 1938	.704
21	Jimmie Foxx, 1933	.703
22	Stan Musial, 1948	.702
23	Babe Ruth, 1931	.700
24	Babe Ruth, 1929	.697
25	Lou Gehrig, 1936	.696
26	Rogers Hornsby, 1924	.696
27	Jimmie Foxx, 1939	.694
28	Tip O'Neill, 1887	.691
29	Hugh Duffy, 1894	.690
30	Mickey Mantle, 1961	.687
31	Chuck Klein, 1930	.687
32	Sam Thompson, 1894	.686
33	Hank Greenberg, 1938	.683
34	Rogers Hornsby, 1929	.679
35	Babe Herman, 1930	.678
36	Joe DiMaggio, 1937	.673
37	Babe Ruth, 1922	.672
38	Joe DiMaggio, 1939	.671
39	Hank Greenberg, 1940	.670
40	Hank Aaron, 1971	.669
41	Hank Greenberg, 1937	.668
42	Ted Williams, 1946	.667
43	Willie Mays, 1954	.667
44	Mickey Mantle, 1957	.665
45	George Brett, 1980	.664
46	Lou Gehrig, 1931	.662
47	Norm Cash, 1961	.662
48	Babe Ruth, 1932	.661
49	Willie Mays, 1955	.659
50	Ralph Kiner, 1949	.658
51	Chuck Klein, 1929	.657
52	Babe Ruth, 1919	.657
53	Willie McCovey, 1969	.656
54	Sam Thompson, 1895	.654
55	Jimmie Foxx, 1934	.653
56	Chick Hafey, 1930	.652
57	Ted Williams, 1949	.650
58	Bill Joyce, 1894	.648
59	Lou Gehrig, 1928	.648
60	Ted Williams, 1942	.648
61	Duke Snider, 1954	.647
62	Chuck Klein, 1932	.646
63	Jim Gentile, 1961	.646
64	Willie Stargell, 1973	.646
65	Willie Mays, 1965	.645
66	Mike Schmidt, 1981	.644
67	Hal Trosky, 1936	.644
68	Nap Lajoie, 1901	.643
69	Joe DiMaggio, 1941	.643
70	Lou Gehrig, 1937	.643
71	Ted Kluszewski, 1954	.642
72	Al Simmons, 1929	.642
73	Joe Medwick, 1937	.641
74	Al Simmons, 1931	.641
75	Ralph Kiner, 1947	.639
76	Rogers Hornsby, 1921	.639
77	Frank Robinson, 1966	.637
78	Jimmie Foxx, 1930	.637
79	Fred Lynn, 1979	.637
80	Hank Aaron, 1959	.636
81	Johnny Mize, 1940	.636
82	Jimmie Foxx, 1935	.636
83	Kevin Mitchell, 1989	.635
84	Mel Ott, 1929	.635
85	Ted Williams, 1954	.635
86	Ted Williams, 1947	.634
87	Chick Hafey, 1929	.632
88	George Sisler, 1920	.632
89	Rogers Hornsby, 1928	.632
90	Harry Heilmann, 1923	.632
	Dick Allen, 1966	.632
92	Ed Delahanty, 1896	.631
93	George Foster, 1977	.631
94	Jimmie Foxx, 1936	.631
95	Gabby Hartnett, 1930	.630
96	Jim Bottomley, 1928	.628
97	Hank Greenberg, 1935	.628
98	Duke Snider, 1955	.628
99	Willie Stargell, 1971	.628
100	Rogers Hornsby, 1923	.627

Production

1	Babe Ruth, 1920	1.378
2	Babe Ruth, 1921	1.358
3	Babe Ruth, 1923	1.309
4	Ted Williams, 1941	1.286
5	Babe Ruth, 1927	1.259
6	Ted Williams, 1957	1.259
7	Babe Ruth, 1926	1.253
8	Babe Ruth, 1924	1.252
9	Rogers Hornsby, 1925	1.245
10	Lou Gehrig, 1927	1.240
11	Babe Ruth, 1930	1.225
12	Jimmie Foxx, 1932	1.218
13	Rogers Hornsby, 1924	1.203
14	Babe Ruth, 1931	1.195
15	Lou Gehrig, 1930	1.194
16	Hugh Duffy, 1894	1.192
17	Rogers Hornsby, 1922	1.181
18	Tip O'Neill, 1887	1.180
19	Mickey Mantle, 1957	1.179
20	Hack Wilson, 1930	1.177
21	Lou Gehrig, 1936	1.174
22	Mickey Mantle, 1956	1.172
23	Lou Gehrig, 1934	1.172
24	Babe Ruth, 1928	1.170
25	Jimmie Foxx, 1938	1.166
26	Ted Williams, 1946	1.164
27	Jimmie Foxx, 1939	1.158
28	Jimmie Foxx, 1933	1.153
29	Stan Musial, 1948	1.152
30	Ted Williams, 1954	1.151
31	Babe Ruth, 1932	1.150
32	Norm Cash, 1961	1.150
33	Ted Williams, 1942	1.147
34	Sam Thompson, 1894	1.145
35	Bill Joyce, 1894	1.143
36	Ted Williams, 1949	1.141
37	Rogers Hornsby, 1929	1.139
38	Mickey Mantle, 1961	1.138
39	Ted Williams, 1947	1.133
40	Babe Herman, 1930	1.132
41	Al Simmons, 1930	1.130
42	Rogers Hornsby, 1928	1.130
43	Babe Ruth, 1929	1.128
44	George Brett, 1980	1.124
45	Chuck Klein, 1930	1.123
46	Hank Greenberg, 1938	1.122
47	Joe DiMaggio, 1939	1.119
48	Ed Delahanty, 1895	1.117
49	Lou Gehrig, 1937	1.116
50	Lou Gehrig, 1928	1.115
51	Babe Ruth, 1919	1.114
52	Willie McCovey, 1969	1.114
53	Harry Heilmann, 1923	1.113
54	Ted Williams, 1948	1.112
55	Lou Gehrig, 1931	1.108
56	Babe Ruth, 1922	1.106
57	Hank Greenberg, 1937	1.105
58	Joe Kelley, 1894	1.104
59	Hank Greenberg, 1940	1.103
60	Ed Delahanty, 1896	1.103
61	Jimmie Foxx, 1934	1.102
62	Arky Vaughan, 1935	1.098
63	Rogers Hornsby, 1921	1.097
64	Jimmie Foxx, 1935	1.096
65	Nap Lajoie, 1901	1.094
66	Mickey Mantle, 1962	1.093
67	Harry Heilmann, 1927	1.091
68	Ralph Kiner, 1949	1.089
69	Jimmie Foxx, 1929	1.088
70	Ty Cobb, 1911	1.088
71	Lefty O'Doul, 1929	1.087
72	Rogers Hornsby, 1923	1.086
73	Al Simmons, 1931	1.085
74	Joe DiMaggio, 1937	1.085
75	Sam Thompson, 1895	1.085
76	Ted Williams, 1956	1.084
77	Mel Ott, 1929	1.084
78	Joe DiMaggio, 1941	1.083
79	Willie Mays, 1954	1.083
80	Mike Schmidt, 1981	1.083
81	Hank Aaron, 1971	1.082
82	George Sisler, 1920	1.082
83	Tris Speaker, 1922	1.080
84	Ralph Kiner, 1951	1.079
85	Tris Speaker, 1923	1.079
86	Jim Gentile, 1961	1.074
87	Duke Snider, 1954	1.074
88	Lou Gehrig, 1932	1.072
89	Bill Terry, 1930	1.071
90	Jimmie Foxx, 1936	1.071
91	Johnny Mize, 1939	1.070
92	Fred Dunlap, 1884	1.069
93	Jimmie Foxx, 1930	1.066
94	Ty Cobb, 1925	1.066
95	Earl Averill, 1936	1.065
96	Chuck Klein, 1929	1.065
97	Ed Delahanty, 1894	1.063
98	Stan Musial, 1951	1.063
99	Willie Mays, 1955	1.063
100	Fred Lynn, 1979	1.063

Adjusted Production

1	Babe Ruth, 1920	255
2	Fred Dunlap, 1884	249
3	Babe Ruth, 1921	235
4	Mickey Mantle, 1957	234
5	Babe Ruth, 1923	232
6	Babe Ruth, 1919	231
7	Pete Browning, 1882	231
8	Ted Williams, 1941	231
9	Babe Ruth, 1930	230
10	Babe Ruth, 1926	226
11	Babe Ruth, 1927	223
12	Babe Ruth, 1924	222
13	Babe Ruth, 1928	221
14	Lou Gehrig, 1930	221
15	Dave Orr, 1885	220
16	Jimmie Foxx, 1933	219
17	Ted Williams, 1957	219
18	Lou Gehrig, 1927	218
19	Honus Wagner, 1908	217
20	Babe Ruth, 1931	215
21	Ty Cobb, 1917	215
22	Rogers Hornsby, 1924	214
23	Ted Williams, 1954	213
24	Ted Williams, 1942	213
25	Norm Cash, 1961	213
26	Ty Cobb, 1910	211
27	Tip O'Neill, 1887	210
28	Roger Connor, 1886	209
29	Rogers Hornsby, 1925	209
30	Ty Cobb, 1912	209
31	Mickey Mantle, 1956	209
32	George Hall, 1876	208
33	Lou Gehrig, 1934	208
34	George Brett, 1980	207
35	Dan Brouthers, 1885	207
36	Mickey Mantle, 1961	207
37	Lou Gehrig, 1928	207
38	Stan Musial, 1948	207
39	Willie McCovey, 1969	206
40	Mickey Mantle, 1962	205
41	Babe Ruth, 1932	204
42	Rogers Hornsby, 1923	204
43	Nap Lajoie, 1901	203
44	Nap Lajoie, 1904	201
45	Nap Lajoie, 1910	201
46	Willie Stargell, 1973	200
47	Joe DiMaggio, 1939	199
48	Rogers Hornsby, 1928	199
49	Frank Robinson, 1967	199
50	Ted Williams, 1947	198
51	Ross Barnes, 1876	198
52	Harry Lumley, 1906	198
53	Rogers Hornsby, 1922	198
54	Harry Heilmann, 1923	198
55	Rogers Hornsby, 1921	197
56	Reggie Jackson, 1969	197
57	Lou Gehrig, 1936	197
58	Ed Swartwood, 1882	196
59	Orator Shaffer, 1878	196
60	Frank Robinson, 1966	196
61	Orator Shaffer, 1884	195
62	Ty Cobb, 1913	195
63	Ed Delahanty, 1899	195
64	Ted Williams, 1946	195
65	Kevin Mitchell, 1989	195
66	Ty Cobb, 1918	195
67	Ted Williams, 1948	194
68	Joe Jackson, 1912	193
69	Honus Wagner, 1904	193
70	Dave Orr, 1884	193
71	Dan Brouthers, 1882	193
72	Dan Brouthers, 1886	193
73	Pete Browning, 1884	193
74	Roger Connor, 1888	193
75	Tris Speaker, 1916	192
76	Lip Pike, 1876	192
77	Ed Delahanty, 1895	192
78	George Stone, 1906	191
79	Lou Gehrig, 1931	191
80	Ed Delahanty, 1902	191
81	Cupid Childs, 1890	191
82	Pedro Guerrero, 1985	191
83	Dick Allen, 1972	191
84	Cy Seymour, 1905	190
85	Dan Brouthers, 1883	190
86	Ed Swartwood, 1883	190
87	Willie Stargell, 1971	189
88	Joe Jackson, 1911	189
89	Rocky Colavito, 1958	189
90	King Kelly, 1879	189
91	Pete Browning, 1885	189
92	Willie McCovey, 1970	188
93	Ed Delahanty, 1896	188
94	Babe Ruth, 1929	188
95	John Reilly, 1884	188
96	Dan Brouthers, 1891	188
97	Roger Connor, 1882	188
98	Jim Gentile, 1961	188
99	Ty Cobb, 1911	187
100	Ted Williams, 1949	187

Batting Runs

1	Babe Ruth, 1921	119
2	Babe Ruth, 1923	119
3	Babe Ruth, 1920	113
4	Ted Williams, 1941	102
5	Lou Gehrig, 1927	101
6	Babe Ruth, 1924	101
7	Babe Ruth, 1927	101
8	Babe Ruth, 1926	97
9	Jimmie Foxx, 1932	97
10	Ted Williams, 1946	94
11	Rogers Hornsby, 1924	94
12	Ted Williams, 1942	93
13	Babe Ruth, 1931	92
14	Ted Williams, 1947	91
15	Stan Musial, 1948	90
16	Rogers Hornsby, 1922	90
17	Ted Williams, 1957	90
18	Babe Ruth, 1930	90
19	Mickey Mantle, 1957	89
20	Ted Williams, 1949	89
21	Lou Gehrig, 1930	88
22	Tip O'Neill, 1887	88
23	Rogers Hornsby, 1925	87
24	Norm Cash, 1961	86
25	Lou Gehrig, 1934	86
26	Babe Ruth, 1928	84
27	Mickey Mantle, 1956	83
28	Jimmie Foxx, 1933	83
29	Lou Gehrig, 1936	82
30	Lou Gehrig, 1931	80
31	Ty Cobb, 1911	78
32	Jimmie Foxx, 1938	78
33	Hugh Duffy, 1894	77
34	Carl Yastrzemski, 1967	76
35	Mickey Mantle, 1961	76
36	Willie McCovey, 1969	76
37	Lou Gehrig, 1928	76
38	Ted Williams, 1948	76
39	Hack Wilson, 1930	75
40	Ty Cobb, 1917	75
41	Rogers Hornsby, 1921	74
42	Rogers Hornsby, 1929	74
43	Frank Robinson, 1966	74
44	Lou Gehrig, 1937	73
45	George Sisler, 1920	73
46	Tris Speaker, 1912	73
47	Fred Dunlap, 1884	72
48	Rogers Hornsby, 1928	72
49	Stan Musial, 1949	72
50	Arky Vaughan, 1935	72
51	Joe Jackson, 1911	72
52	Carl Yastrzemski, 1970	72
53	Ty Cobb, 1915	72
54	Nap Lajoie, 1901	72
55	Babe Ruth, 1932	71
56	Ted Williams, 1954	71
57	Tris Speaker, 1923	71
58	Stan Musial, 1946	71
59	Ralph Kiner, 1951	71
60	Harry Heilmann, 1923	71
61	Joe Jackson, 1912	70
62	Stan Musial, 1951	70
63	Ralph Kiner, 1949	70
64	Ed Delahanty, 1899	70
65	Chuck Klein, 1933	69
66	Joe Medwick, 1937	69
67	Hank Greenberg, 1940	69
68	Johnny Mize, 1939	69
69	Babe Herman, 1930	69
70	Lou Gehrig, 1932	69
71	Lefty O'Doul, 1929	68
72	Nap Lajoie, 1910	68
73	Chuck Klein, 1932	68
74	Ed Delahanty, 1895	68
75	Ty Cobb, 1910	68
76	Ty Cobb, 1912	68
77	Wade Boggs, 1987	68
78	Chuck Klein, 1930	67
79	Jimmie Foxx, 1935	67
80	Hank Greenberg, 1937	67
81	Rod Carew, 1977	67
82	Frank Robinson, 1962	67
83	Babe Ruth, 1919	66
84	Jimmie Foxx, 1934	66
85	Ed Delahanty, 1896	66
86	Dick Allen, 1972	66
87	Jimmie Foxx, 1939	66
88	Hank Greenberg, 1938	66
89	Dan Brouthers, 1886	66
90	Cy Seymour, 1905	66
91	Wade Boggs, 1988	66
92	Tris Speaker, 1920	66
93	Harmon Killebrew, 1969	66
94	Joe Jackson, 1913	66
95	Stan Musial, 1943	65
96	Hank Aaron, 1971	65
97	Honus Wagner, 1908	65
98	George Brett, 1980	65
99	Willie Mays, 1965	65
100	Tris Speaker, 1916	65

Adjusted Batting Runs

1	Babe Ruth, 1921	117
2	Babe Ruth, 1923	115
3	Babe Ruth, 1920	111
4	Babe Ruth, 1924	102
5	Lou Gehrig, 1927	101
6	Babe Ruth, 1927	101
7	Ted Williams, 1941	100
8	Babe Ruth, 1930	99
9	Lou Gehrig, 1930	99
10	Babe Ruth, 1926	98
11	Mickey Mantle, 1957	93
12	Babe Ruth, 1931	93
13	Rogers Hornsby, 1924	92
14	Babe Ruth, 1928	91
15	Ted Williams, 1942	90
16	Jimmie Foxx, 1933	90
17	Stan Musial, 1948	90
18	Lou Gehrig, 1934	90
19	Norm Cash, 1961	89
20	Rogers Hornsby, 1922	89
21	Lou Gehrig, 1936	88
22	Rogers Hornsby, 1925	86
23	Ted Williams, 1947	85
24	Mickey Mantle, 1956	84
25	Ted Williams, 1957	84
26	Ted Williams, 1946	84
27	Jimmie Foxx, 1932	84
28	Lou Gehrig, 1928	83
29	Ted Williams, 1949	83
30	Lou Gehrig, 1931	82
31	Mickey Mantle, 1961	79
32	Rogers Hornsby, 1921	79
33	Tip O'Neill, 1887	79
34	Ty Cobb, 1917	76
35	Jimmie Foxx, 1938	76
36	Ted Williams, 1948	75
37	Willie McCovey, 1969	75
38	Babe Ruth, 1932	75
39	Rogers Hornsby, 1928	75
40	Harry Heilmann, 1923	73
41	Lou Gehrig, 1932	73
42	Frank Robinson, 1966	73
43	Rogers Hornsby, 1929	73
44	Ed Delahanty, 1899	72
45	Ty Cobb, 1911	72
46	Ty Cobb, 1912	72
47	Babe Ruth, 1919	72
48	Lou Gehrig, 1937	72
49	Nap Lajoie, 1901	71
50	Ted Williams, 1954	71
51	Hack Wilson, 1930	70
52	Tris Speaker, 1923	70
53	Fred Dunlap, 1884	70
54	Joe Jackson, 1911	69
55	Joe Jackson, 1912	69
56	Stan Musial, 1951	69
57	Ralph Kiner, 1949	69
58	Ed Delahanty, 1895	69
59	Jimmie Foxx, 1934	69
60	Nap Lajoie, 1910	69
61	Joe Medwick, 1937	68
62	Wade Boggs, 1987	68
63	Honus Wagner, 1908	68
64	Babe Herman, 1930	68
65	Reggie Jackson, 1969	68
66	Lou Gehrig, 1935	68
67	Billy Hamilton, 1894	68
68	Lou Gehrig, 1933	68
69	Jimmie Foxx, 1935	67
70	Tris Speaker, 1912	67
71	Al Rosen, 1953	67
72	Hank Aaron, 1959	67
73	Ty Cobb, 1910	67
74	Arky Vaughan, 1935	67
75	Carl Yastrzemski, 1967	66
76	Stan Musial, 1946	66
77	Joe DiMaggio, 1941	66
78	Hank Greenberg, 1938	66
79	George Brett, 1980	66
80	Ralph Kiner, 1951	66
81	Ty Cobb, 1915	65
82	Willie McCovey, 1970	65
83	Frank Robinson, 1962	65
84	Tris Speaker, 1916	65
85	Al Simmons, 1930	65
86	Johnny Mize, 1939	65
87	Ed Delahanty, 1896	65
88	Rod Carew, 1977	65
89	Rogers Hornsby, 1920	64
90	Kevin Mitchell, 1989	64
91	Harmon Killebrew, 1969	64
92	Duke Snider, 1954	64
93	Cy Seymour, 1905	64
94	Willie Mays, 1955	64
95	Carl Yastrzemski, 1970	64
96	Stan Musial, 1949	63
97	George Sisler, 1920	63
98	Willie Stargell, 1973	63
99	Babe Ruth, 1929	63
100	Rogers Hornsby, 1927	63

Batting Wins

1	Babe Ruth, 1923	11.5
2	Babe Ruth, 1921	11.2
3	Babe Ruth, 1920	11.0
4	Ted Williams, 1941	9.9
5	Ted Williams, 1946	9.9
6	Lou Gehrig, 1927	9.6
7	Babe Ruth, 1927	9.6
8	Babe Ruth, 1924	9.5
9	Ted Williams, 1942	9.5
10	Ted Williams, 1947	9.4
11	Babe Ruth, 1926	9.4
12	Rogers Hornsby, 1924	9.3
13	Ted Williams, 1957	9.3
14	Mickey Mantle, 1957	9.2
15	Stan Musial, 1948	9.0
16	Jimmie Foxx, 1932	8.9
17	Ted Williams, 1949	8.6
18	Norm Cash, 1961	8.5
19	Babe Ruth, 1931	8.5
20	Rogers Hornsby, 1922	8.5
21	Carl Yastrzemski, 1967	8.4
22	Ty Cobb, 1917	8.3
23	Rogers Hornsby, 1925	8.2
24	Mickey Mantle, 1956	8.1
25	Babe Ruth, 1928	8.1
26	Babe Ruth, 1930	8.1
27	Lou Gehrig, 1930	8.0
28	Willie McCovey, 1969	8.0
29	Lou Gehrig, 1934	8.0
30	Frank Robinson, 1966	7.9
31	Jimmie Foxx, 1933	7.8
32	Ty Cobb, 1911	7.7
33	Ty Cobb, 1915	7.6
34	Nap Lajoie, 1910	7.6
35	Honus Wagner, 1908	7.6
36	Mickey Mantle, 1961	7.6
37	Ty Cobb, 1910	7.5
38	Stan Musial, 1946	7.5
39	Dick Allen, 1972	7.5
40	Lou Gehrig, 1931	7.4
41	Carl Yastrzemski, 1970	7.4
42	Rogers Hornsby, 1921	7.3
43	Lou Gehrig, 1928	7.3
44	Ted Williams, 1948	7.3
45	Ted Williams, 1954	7.3
46	Chuck Klein, 1933	7.3
47	Lou Gehrig, 1936	7.3
48	Tris Speaker, 1912	7.3
49	Ty Cobb, 1909	7.2
50	Stan Musial, 1949	7.2
51	Tris Speaker, 1916	7.2
52	Tip O'Neill, 1887	7.1
53	Ralph Kiner, 1951	7.1
54	George Sisler, 1920	7.1
55	Rogers Hornsby, 1928	7.1
56	Jimmie Foxx, 1938	7.1
57	Joe Jackson, 1911	7.1
58	Stan Musial, 1951	7.0
59	Joe Jackson, 1912	7.0
60	Hank Aaron, 1971	7.0
61	Stan Musial, 1943	7.0
62	Arky Vaughan, 1935	7.0
63	Joe Jackson, 1913	7.0
64	Babe Ruth, 1919	7.0
65	Ralph Kiner, 1949	6.9
66	Harmon Killebrew, 1967	6.9
67	Nap Lajoie, 1904	6.9
68	Harmon Killebrew, 1969	6.9
69	Johnny Mize, 1939	6.9
70	Tris Speaker, 1923	6.9
71	Cy Seymour, 1905	6.8
72	Willie Mays, 1965	6.8
73	Harry Heilmann, 1923	6.8
74	Hank Aaron, 1963	6.8
75	Joe Medwick, 1937	6.8
76	Ty Cobb, 1912	6.8
77	Chuck Klein, 1932	6.7
78	Rogers Hornsby, 1929	6.7
79	Lou Gehrig, 1937	6.7
80	Rogers Hornsby, 1920	6.7
81	Joe Torre, 1971	6.7
82	Hack Wilson, 1930	6.7
83	Rod Carew, 1977	6.7
84	Wade Boggs, 1988	6.7
85	Kevin Mitchell, 1989	6.7
86	Frank Robinson, 1962	6.6
87	Mickey Mantle, 1958	6.6
88	Carl Yastrzemski, 1968	6.6
89	Babe Ruth, 1932	6.6
90	Billy Williams, 1972	6.6
91	Joe Morgan, 1976	6.5
92	Reggie Jackson, 1969	6.5
93	Hank Greenberg, 1940	6.5
94	Johnny Mize, 1940	6.5
95	George Brett, 1980	6.5
96	Nap Lajoie, 1901	6.5
97	Wade Boggs, 1987	6.4
98	Duke Snider, 1954	6.4
99	Ty Cobb, 1916	6.4
100	Tris Speaker, 1920	6.4

Adjusted Batting Wins

1	Babe Ruth, 1923	11.2
2	Babe Ruth, 1921	10.9
3	Babe Ruth, 1920	10.8
4	Ted Williams, 1941	9.7
5	Mickey Mantle, 1957	9.6
6	Lou Gehrig, 1927	9.6
7	Babe Ruth, 1924	9.6
8	Babe Ruth, 1927	9.6
9	Babe Ruth, 1926	9.5
10	Ted Williams, 1942	9.2
11	Rogers Hornsby, 1924	9.1
12	Babe Ruth, 1930	9.0
13	Stan Musial, 1948	9.0
14	Lou Gehrig, 1930	8.9
15	Norm Cash, 1961	8.9
16	Ted Williams, 1947	8.8
17	Ted Williams, 1946	8.8
18	Babe Ruth, 1928	8.8
19	Babe Ruth, 1931	8.7
20	Ted Williams, 1957	8.7
21	Jimmie Foxx, 1933	8.5
22	Ty Cobb, 1917	8.5
23	Rogers Hornsby, 1922	8.4
24	Lou Gehrig, 1934	8.3
25	Mickey Mantle, 1956	8.3
26	Ted Williams, 1949	8.0
27	Rogers Hornsby, 1925	8.0
28	Lou Gehrig, 1928	8.0
29	Honus Wagner, 1908	7.9
30	Willie McCovey, 1969	7.9
31	Mickey Mantle, 1961	7.8
32	Frank Robinson, 1966	7.8
33	Rogers Hornsby, 1921	7.8
34	Lou Gehrig, 1936	7.7
35	Jimmie Foxx, 1932	7.7
36	Lou Gehrig, 1931	7.6
37	Nap Lajoie, 1910	7.6
38	Babe Ruth, 1919	7.5
39	Ty Cobb, 1910	7.4
40	Carl Yastrzemski, 1967	7.3
41	Ted Williams, 1948	7.3
42	Ted Williams, 1954	7.3
43	Rogers Hornsby, 1928	7.3
44	Tris Speaker, 1916	7.2
45	Ty Cobb, 1912	7.2
46	Dick Allen, 1972	7.1
47	Reggie Jackson, 1969	7.1
48	Harry Heilmann, 1923	7.1
49	Ty Cobb, 1911	7.1
50	Stan Musial, 1946	7.0
51	Stan Musial, 1951	7.0
52	Ty Cobb, 1915	6.9
53	Babe Ruth, 1932	6.9
54	Joe Jackson, 1912	6.9
55	Rogers Hornsby, 1920	6.9
56	Ralph Kiner, 1949	6.9
57	Jimmie Foxx, 1938	6.9
58	Kevin Mitchell, 1989	6.9
59	Joe Jackson, 1911	6.8
60	Joe Medwick, 1937	6.8
61	Nap Lajoie, 1904	6.8
62	Tris Speaker, 1923	6.8
63	Hank Aaron, 1963	6.8
64	Lou Gehrig, 1932	6.8
65	Hank Aaron, 1959	6.7
66	Al Rosen, 1953	6.7
67	Harmon Killebrew, 1969	6.7
68	Tris Speaker, 1912	6.7
69	Joe Torre, 1971	6.6
70	Rogers Hornsby, 1929	6.6
71	Stan Musial, 1943	6.6
72	Cy Seymour, 1905	6.6
73	Carl Yastrzemski, 1970	6.6
74	Willie Stargell, 1973	6.6
75	Lou Gehrig, 1937	6.6
76	Ralph Kiner, 1951	6.6
77	Ed Delahanty, 1899	6.6
78	George Brett, 1980	6.6
79	Carl Yastrzemski, 1968	6.6
80	Joe Jackson, 1913	6.6
81	Wade Boggs, 1987	6.5
82	Frank Robinson, 1962	6.5
83	Willie McCovey, 1970	6.5
84	Ty Cobb, 1909	6.5
85	Arky Vaughan, 1935	6.5
86	Johnny Mize, 1939	6.5
87	Nap Lajoie, 1901	6.4
88	George Stone, 1906	6.4
89	Mickey Mantle, 1958	6.4
90	Rod Carew, 1977	6.4
91	Jimmie Foxx, 1934	6.4
92	Lou Gehrig, 1933	6.4
93	Willie Mays, 1963	6.4
94	Joe DiMaggio, 1941	6.4
95	Tip O'Neill, 1887	6.4
96	Hank Aaron, 1971	6.4
97	Harmon Killebrew, 1967	6.4
98	Willie Stargell, 1971	6.4
99	Lou Gehrig, 1935	6.3
100	Joe Morgan, 1976	6.3

Runs Created

1	Babe Ruth, 1921	238
2	Babe Ruth, 1923	223
3	Hugh Duffy, 1894	216
4	Babe Ruth, 1920	211
5	Lou Gehrig, 1927	208
6	Jimmie Foxx, 1932	207
7	Ty Cobb, 1911	207
8	Billy Hamilton, 1894	206
9	Babe Ruth, 1924	205
10	Babe Ruth, 1927	204
11	Ted Williams, 1941	202
12	Rogers Hornsby, 1922	200
13	Lou Gehrig, 1936	199
14	Babe Ruth, 1926	196
15	Lou Gehrig, 1930	195
16	Lou Gehrig, 1934	195
17	Tip O'Neill, 1887	194
18	Ted Williams, 1949	193
19	Babe Ruth, 1931	192
20	Babe Ruth, 1930	191
21	Pete Browning, 1887	191
22	Stan Musial, 1948	191
23	Hack Wilson, 1930	189
24	Jimmie Foxx, 1938	189
25	Ted Williams, 1946	188
26	Mickey Mantle, 1956	188
27	Rogers Hornsby, 1925	187
28	Ted Williams, 1947	186
29	Rogers Hornsby, 1924	186
30	Chuck Klein, 1930	186
31	Lou Gehrig, 1931	185
32	Ted Williams, 1942	185
33	Jimmie Foxx, 1933	184
34	Rogers Hornsby, 1929	183
35	Babe Herman, 1930	183
36	Babe Ruth, 1928	182
37	Lou Gehrig, 1937	181
38	Joe Kelley, 1894	181
39	Lefty O'Doul, 1929	180
40	Mickey Mantle, 1957	178
41	Norm Cash, 1961	178
42	Hank Greenberg, 1937	178
43	Joe Kelley, 1896	178
44	Billy Hamilton, 1895	177
45	Willie Keeler, 1897	176
46	George Sisler, 1920	176
47	Ed Delahanty, 1895	175
48	Tris Speaker, 1912	175
49	Ed Delahanty, 1899	175
50	Joe Jackson, 1911	175
51	Nap Lajoie, 1901	174
52	Mickey Mantle, 1961	174
53	Ty Cobb, 1912	174
54	Stan Musial, 1949	173
55	Joe DiMaggio, 1937	173
56	Benny Kauff, 1914	172
57	Hank Greenberg, 1938	172
58	Ted Williams, 1948	172
59	Chuck Klein, 1932	171
60	Hank Greenberg, 1940	171
61	Ed Delahanty, 1896	170
62	Joe Medwick, 1937	170
63	Bill Terry, 1930	170
64	Stan Musial, 1951	169
65	Lou Gehrig, 1928	169
66	Rogers Hornsby, 1921	169
67	Earl Averill, 1936	168
68	Jimmie Foxx, 1936	168
69	Lou Gehrig, 1932	168
70	Sam Thompson, 1895	167
71	Ted Williams, 1957	167
72	Ed Delahanty, 1893	167
73	Stan Musial, 1953	166
74	Joe Jackson, 1912	166
75	Tris Speaker, 1923	166
76	Jesse Burkett, 1896	166
77	Jimmie Foxx, 1934	165
78	Ralph Kiner, 1951	165
79	Ty Cobb, 1917	165
80	Jake Stenzel, 1894	165
81	Jesse Burkett, 1895	164
82	Stan Musial, 1946	164
83	Ralph Kiner, 1949	163
84	Arky Vaughan, 1935	163
85	Jimmie Foxx, 1935	163
86	Al Simmons, 1930	163
87	Johnny Mize, 1939	162
88	Chuck Klein, 1933	162
89	George Sisler, 1922	162
90	Joe DiMaggio, 1941	162
91	Duke Snider, 1954	161
92	Hank Greenberg, 1935	161
93	Duke Snider, 1953	161
94	Rod Carew, 1977	160
95	Bill Lange, 1895	160
96	Denny Lyons, 1887	160
97	Frank Robinson, 1962	160
98	Harry Heilmann, 1923	159
99	Billy Hamilton, 1896	159
100	Harry Heilmann, 1921	159

Total Average

1	Babe Ruth, 1920	1.843
2	Babe Ruth, 1921	1.782
3	Babe Ruth, 1923	1.746
4	Ted Williams, 1941	1.702
5	Babe Ruth, 1926	1.634
6	Babe Ruth, 1927	1.615
7	Hugh Duffy, 1894	1.613
8	Billy Hamilton, 1894	1.605
9	Ted Williams, 1957	1.602
10	John McGraw, 1899	1.601
11	Babe Ruth, 1924	1.596
12	Lou Gehrig, 1927	1.555
13	Rogers Hornsby, 1925	1.549
14	Mickey Mantle, 1957	1.544
15	Babe Ruth, 1930	1.538
16	Bill Joyce, 1894	1.528
17	Ed Delahanty, 1895	1.517
18	Tip O'Neill, 1887	1.514
19	Joe Kelley, 1894	1.503
20	Babe Ruth, 1931	1.499
21	Jimmie Foxx, 1932	1.470
22	Ty Cobb, 1911	1.464
23	Rogers Hornsby, 1924	1.461
24	Ted Williams, 1954	1.452
25	Billy Hamilton, 1895	1.443
26	Babe Ruth, 1932	1.439
27	Lou Gehrig, 1936	1.437
28	Ted Williams, 1946	1.431
29	Joe Kelley, 1896	1.430
30	Mickey Mantle, 1956	1.429
31	Lou Gehrig, 1930	1.427
32	Pete Browning, 1887	1.422
33	Babe Ruth, 1928	1.418
34	Lou Gehrig, 1934	1.414
35	Hack Wilson, 1930	1.411
36	Rogers Hornsby, 1928	1.409
37	Sam Thompson, 1894	1.409
38	Ed Delahanty, 1896	1.405
39	Jimmie Foxx, 1938	1.403
40	Ted Williams, 1942	1.400
41	Ted Williams, 1947	1.394
42	Mickey Mantle, 1961	1.387
43	Billy Hamilton, 1893	1.386
44	Mickey Mantle, 1962	1.385
45	Rogers Hornsby, 1922	1.384
46	Bill Lange, 1895	1.373
47	Norm Cash, 1961	1.372
48	Bob Caruthers, 1887	1.368
49	King Kelly, 1886	1.366
50	Babe Ruth, 1919	1.358
51	Jimmie Foxx, 1933	1.353
52	Babe Herman, 1930	1.351
53	Ted Williams, 1949	1.349
54	Ted Williams, 1948	1.347
55	Lou Gehrig, 1937	1.347
56	Joe Morgan, 1976	1.346
57	Rogers Hornsby, 1929	1.338
58	Ty Cobb, 1912	1.328
59	Ty Cobb, 1910	1.321
60	Jake Stenzel, 1894	1.320
61	Hank Greenberg, 1938	1.319
62	Arky Vaughan, 1935	1.317
63	Billy Hamilton, 1896	1.316
64	Jimmie Foxx, 1934	1.316
65	Bill Joyce, 1896	1.315
66	Ty Cobb, 1913	1.314
67	Jimmie Foxx, 1939	1.313
68	Tris Speaker, 1912	1.310
69	Joe Jackson, 1911	1.308
70	Joe Morgan, 1975	1.307
71	Harry Heilmann, 1923	1.306
72	Harry Heilmann, 1927	1.303
73	Jimmie Foxx, 1935	1.299
74	Stan Musial, 1948	1.298
75	Babe Ruth, 1929	1.297
76	Willie McCovey, 1969	1.296
77	Lou Gehrig, 1931	1.295
78	Ed Delahanty, 1894	1.290
79	Joe Kelley, 1895	1.289
80	Mel Ott, 1929	1.287
81	Lou Gehrig, 1928	1.287
82	Nap Lajoie, 1901	1.285
83	Hank Greenberg, 1937	1.285
84	Tris Speaker, 1922	1.284
85	Jimmie Foxx, 1929	1.282
86	George Brett, 1980	1.278
87	Al Simmons, 1930	1.278
88	Chuck Klein, 1930	1.274
89	Willie Keeler, 1897	1.271
90	Billy Hamilton, 1891	1.270
91	Sam Thompson, 1895	1.269
92	Fred Clarke, 1897	1.269
93	Babe Ruth, 1922	1.268
94	Ty Cobb, 1915	1.267
95	Jack Clark, 1987	1.265
96	Jesse Burkett, 1895	1.265
97	Hughie Jennings, 1896	1.263
98	Billy Hamilton, 1898	1.262
99	George Sisler, 1922	1.256
100	Ty Cobb, 1917	1.256

Runs Produced

1	Lou Gehrig, 1931	301
2	Babe Ruth, 1921	289
3	Hugh Duffy, 1894	288
	Chuck Klein, 1930	288
5	Al Simmons, 1930	281
6	Hughie Jennings, 1895	280
	Hack Wilson, 1930	280
	Hank Greenberg, 1937	280
9	Sam Thompson, 1895	278
10	Lou Gehrig, 1927	277
11	Kiki Cuyler, 1930	276
	Lou Gehrig, 1930	276
13	Billy Hamilton, 1894	275
14	Ed Delahanty, 1894	274
15	Sam Thompson, 1887	273
16	Ed Delahanty, 1893	272
	Joe Kelley, 1895	272
	Joe DiMaggio, 1937	272
19	Joe Kelley, 1894	270
	Lou Gehrig, 1936	270
21	Ty Cobb, 1911	266
	Rogers Hornsby, 1929	266
	Babe Ruth, 1931	266
	Ted Williams, 1949	266
25	Jimmie Foxx, 1938	264
26	Ed Delahanty, 1899	263
27	Babe Ruth, 1927	262
	Jimmie Foxx, 1932	262
29	Al Simmons, 1932	260
	Lou Gehrig, 1937	260
31	Hugh Duffy, 1893	259
	Walt Wilmot, 1894	259
33	Hardy Richardson, 1890	258
34	Dan Brouthers, 1894	256
	Bobby Lowe, 1894	256
	Jake Stenzel, 1894	256
	Nap Lajoie, 1901	256
38	Hack Wilson, 1929	255
	Lou Gehrig, 1932	255
	Hank Greenberg, 1935	255
41	Cap Anson, 1886	254
	Willie Keeler, 1894	254
	Lou Gehrig, 1928	254
	Babe Ruth, 1930	254
45	Harry Stovey, 1889	252
46	Rogers Hornsby, 1922	251
	Babe Ruth, 1928	251
	Earl Averill, 1931	251
	Chuck Klein, 1932	251
50	Charlie Gehringer, 1934	250
51	Hugh Duffy, 1897	248
52	John McGraw, 1894	247
	Mel Ott, 1929	247
54	Hughie Jennings, 1896	246
	Tris Speaker, 1923	246
	Jimmie Foxx, 1930	246
	Zeke Bonura, 1936	246
	Tommy Davis, 1962	246
59	Sam Thompson, 1893	245
	Bill Terry, 1930	245
	Lou Gehrig, 1933	245
	Charlie Gehringer, 1936	245
	Ted Williams, 1939	245
64	Steve Brodie, 1894	244
	Ed Delahanty, 1895	244
	Ed Delahanty, 1896	244
	Ken Williams, 1922	244
	Lou Gehrig, 1934	244
	Hal Trosky, 1936	244
70	Tom Brown, 1891	243
71	Dan Brouthers, 1887	242
	Ed McKean, 1895	242
	Lefty O'Doul, 1929	242
	Ted Williams, 1942	242
75	Lave Cross, 1894	241
	Bill Dahlen, 1894	241
	Babe Ruth, 1920	241
78	Dan Brouthers, 1892	240
	Joe Kelley, 1896	240
	Ty Cobb, 1915	240
	George Sisler, 1920	240
	Babe Ruth, 1923	240
	Joe Cronin, 1930	240
	Jimmie Foxx, 1933	240
85	Hughie Jennings, 1894	239
	Vern Stephens, 1950	239
87	Babe Ruth, 1926	238
	Babe Herman, 1930	238
	Hank Greenberg, 1940	238
90	Rogers Hornsby, 1925	237
	Al Simmons, 1929	237
	Joe DiMaggio, 1938	237
93	Hugh Duffy, 1890	236
	Ed McKean, 1894	236
	Sam Thompson, 1894	236
	Willie Keeler, 1895	236
	George Davis, 1897	236
	Frank Baker, 1912	236
	Tris Speaker, 1920	236
	Rogers Hornsby, 1921	236

Clutch Hitting Index

1	Tom Herr, 1987	200
2	Ed Abbaticchio, 1907	194
3	Bill McClellan, 1878	193
4	George Davis, 1906	179
5	Sam Crawford, 1910	178
6	Frank LaPorte, 1914	176
7	Possum Whitted, 1920	176
8	Jack Barry, 1913	176
9	Heinie Reitz, 1896	176
10	George Stovall, 1911	176
11	Stuffy McInnis, 1914	176
12	John Sullivan, 1943	175
13	Cy Seymour, 1908	175
14	Cookie Lavagetto, 1941	173
15	Cap Anson, 1893	172
16	Farmer Vaughn, 1893	172
17	Pie Traynor, 1928	172
18	Larry Kopf, 1920	172
19	Larry Gardner, 1920	171
20	Cap Anson, 1880	171
21	Heinie Zimmerman, 1917	171
22	Bill Dahlen, 1904	170
	Sherry Magee, 1918	170
24	Ned Williamson, 1885	170
25	Clyde Barnhart, 1925	170
26	Cap Anson, 1881	169
27	Cap Anson, 1885	169
28	Joe Kelley, 1898	169
29	John Gochnauer, 1903	168
30	Cap Anson, 1882	167
31	Jim O'Rourke, 1887	167
32	Maurice VanRobays, 1940	167
33	Monte Ward, 1881	167
34	Mike Higgins, 1938	167
35	Frank LaPorte, 1910	166
36	Bill Hague, 1878	166
37	Ross Youngs, 1921	166
38	Bob Ferguson, 1877	165
39	Deacon White, 1876	165
40	Johnny Berardino, 1941	165
41	Cap Anson, 1896	165
42	King Kelly, 1880	165
43	Larry Gardner, 1921	164
44	Bernie Friberg, 1924	164
45	Fred Pfeffer, 1886	164
46	Russ McKelvy, 1878	164
47	Steve Brodie, 1895	163
48	Tom Burns, 1888	163
49	Harmon Killebrew, 1971	163
50	Earl Sheely, 1931	163
51	Kid Gleason, 1897	163
52	John Ganzel, 1901	162
53	Joe Gerhardt, 1879	162
	Mike Dorgan, 1886	162
	Sam Mertes, 1905	162
56	Art Croft, 1877	162
	Sherry Magee, 1910	162
58	Dixie Walker, 1946	161
59	Joe Tinker, 1906	161
60	Enos Slaughter, 1952	161
61	Ed Konetchy, 1918	160
	Wally Pipp, 1923	160
63	Harry Swacina, 1914	160
64	Amos Otis, 1982	160
65	John Mayberry, 1976	160
66	Bill Brubaker, 1936	160
67	Tommy Corcoran, 1904	159
68	George Davis, 1902	159
69	Fred Pfeffer, 1885	159
	Milt Stock, 1923	159
71	Stuffy McInnis, 1918	159
72	Fred Pfeffer, 1882	159
73	Ed McKean, 1892	159
74	Tommy Corcoran, 1903	158
75	Enos Slaughter, 1950	158
76	Charlie Dexter, 1901	158
77	Jack Burdock, 1883	158
	Rudy York, 1946	158
79	Billy Nash, 1892	158
	Steve Evans, 1910	158
	Bobby Veach, 1915	158
	Irish Meusel, 1924	158
	Roy Schalk, 1945	158
84	Fred Hartman, 1898	158
85	Dixie Walker, 1945	157
86	Del Pratt, 1916	157
87	Glenn Wright, 1927	157
	Bob Elliott, 1945	157
89	Mike Mowrey, 1916	157
	Red Smith, 1918	157
91	Clyde Engle, 1909	157
	Bill Johnson, 1943	157
93	Denis Menke, 1969	157
94	Jim Nealon, 1906	156
95	Bid McPhee, 1896	156
	Gus Bell, 1959	156
	Tommy Davis, 1973	156
98	Art Fletcher, 1915	156
99	Ray Bates, 1917	156
100	2 players tied	155

Isolated Power

1	Babe Ruth, 1920	.472
2	Babe Ruth, 1921	.469
3	Babe Ruth, 1927	.417
4	Lou Gehrig, 1927	.392
5	Babe Ruth, 1928	.386
6	Jimmie Foxx, 1932	.385
7	Babe Ruth, 1930	.373
8	Babe Ruth, 1923	.372
9	Mickey Mantle, 1961	.370
10	Hank Greenberg, 1938	.369
11	Hack Wilson, 1930	.368
12	Babe Ruth, 1926	.366
13	Babe Ruth, 1924	.361
14	Babe Ruth, 1922	.357
15	Jimmie Foxx, 1938	.356
16	Rogers Hornsby, 1925	.353
17	Mickey Mantle, 1956	.353
18	Babe Ruth, 1929	.353
19	Roger Maris, 1961	.351
20	Ralph Kiner, 1949	.348
21	Jimmie Foxx, 1933	.347
22	Willie Stargell, 1973	.347
23	Kevin Mitchell, 1989	.344
24	Lou Gehrig, 1934	.344
25	Jim Gentile, 1961	.344
26	Ted Williams, 1957	.343
27	Lou Gehrig, 1930	.343
28	Lou Gehrig, 1936	.342
29	Hank Aaron, 1971	.341
30	Willie Mays, 1955	.340
31	Mike Schmidt, 1980	.338
32	Willie McCovey, 1969	.336
33	Babe Ruth, 1919	.336
34	Jimmie Foxx, 1939	.334
35	Reggie Jackson, 1969	.333
36	Willie Stargell, 1971	.333
37	Hank Greenberg, 1937	.332
38	Hank Greenberg, 1940	.330
39	Ted Williams, 1941	.329
40	Mark McGwire, 1987	.329
41	Willie Mays, 1965	.328
42	Babe Ruth, 1931	.328
43	Mike Schmidt, 1981	.328
44	Hank Greenberg, 1946	.327
45	Joe DiMaggio, 1937	.327
46	Al Simmons, 1930	.327
47	Stan Musial, 1948	.326
48	Ralph Kiner, 1947	.326
49	Dave Kingman, 1979	.325
50	Ted Williams, 1946	.325
51	Eddie Mathews, 1953	.325
52	Willie McCovey, 1970	.323
53	Willie Mays, 1954	.322
54	Lou Gehrig, 1931	.321
55	Johnny Mize, 1940	.321
56	Frank Robinson, 1966	.321
57	Rogers Hornsby, 1922	.321
58	Duke Snider, 1955	.320
59	Babe Ruth, 1932	.319
60	Jimmie Foxx, 1934	.319
61	Ralph Kiner, 1951	.318
62	Ralph Kiner, 1950	.318
63	Harmon Killebrew, 1961	.318
64	Rocky Colavito, 1958	.317
65	Chick Hafey, 1930	.316
66	Boog Powell, 1964	.316
67	Ted Kluszewski, 1954	.316
68	Dick Allen, 1966	.315
69	Eddie Mathews, 1954	.313
70	Duke Snider, 1957	.313
71	Eddie Mathews, 1955	.313
72	Johnny Mize, 1947	.312
73	Willie Mays, 1964	.311
74	Willie Mays, 1962	.311
75	George Foster, 1977	.311
76	Mike Schmidt, 1979	.311
77	Jack Clark, 1987	.310
78	Hank Greenberg, 1939	.310
79	Harmon Killebrew, 1969	.308
80	Ted Williams, 1949	.307
81	Hank Aaron, 1969	.307
82	Duke Snider, 1954	.307
83	Mel Ott, 1929	.306
84	Duke Snider, 1956	.306
85	Joe Adcock, 1956	.306
86	Mickey Mantle, 1955	.306
87	Wally Berger, 1930	.305
88	Jim Bottomley, 1928	.304
89	Fred Lynn, 1979	.303
90	Harmon Killebrew, 1962	.303
91	Jimmie Foxx, 1930	.302
92	Chuck Klein, 1929	.302
93	Ernie Banks, 1958	.301
94	Norm Cash, 1961	.301
95	Chuck Klein, 1930	.301
96	Hank Greenberg, 1935	.300
97	Hal Trosky, 1936	.300
98	Ernie Banks, 1955	.300
99	Mike Schmidt, 1977	.300
100	2 players tied	.300

Extra Base Hits

1	Babe Ruth, 1921	119
2	Lou Gehrig, 1927	117
3	Chuck Klein, 1930	107
4	Chuck Klein, 1932	103
	Hank Greenberg, 1937	103
	Stan Musial, 1948	103
7	Rogers Hornsby, 1922	102
8	Lou Gehrig, 1930	100
	Jimmie Foxx, 1932	100
10	Babe Ruth, 1920	99
	Babe Ruth, 1923	99
	Hank Greenberg, 1940	99
13	Hank Greenberg, 1935	98
14	Babe Ruth, 1927	97
	Hack Wilson, 1930	97
	Joe Medwick, 1937	97
17	Hank Greenberg, 1934	96
	Hal Trosky, 1936	96
	Joe DiMaggio, 1937	96
20	Lou Gehrig, 1934	95
	Joe Medwick, 1936	95
22	Rogers Hornsby, 1929	94
	Chuck Klein, 1929	94
	Babe Herman, 1930	94
	Jimmie Foxx, 1933	94
26	Jim Bottomley, 1928	93
	Al Simmons, 1930	93
	Lou Gehrig, 1936	93
29	Babe Ruth, 1924	92
	Lou Gehrig, 1931	92
	Jimmie Foxx, 1938	92
	Stan Musial, 1953	92
	Hank Aaron, 1959	92
	Frank Robinson, 1962	92
35	Babe Ruth, 1928	91
36	Rogers Hornsby, 1925	90
	Stan Musial, 1949	90
	Willie Mays, 1962	90
	Willie Stargell, 1973	90
40	Hal Trosky, 1934	89
	Duke Snider, 1954	89
42	Joe DiMaggio, 1936	88
43	Tris Speaker, 1923	87
	Kiki Cuyler, 1925	87
	Lou Gehrig, 1928	87
	Ripper Collins, 1934	87
	Charlie Gehringer, 1936	87
	Johnny Mize, 1940	87
	Willie Mays, 1954	87
	Robin Yount, 1982	87
	Kevin Mitchell, 1989	87
52	George Sisler, 1920	86
	Babe Ruth, 1930	86
	Wally Moses, 1937	86
	Johnny Mize, 1939	86
	Ted Williams, 1939	86
	Stan Musial, 1946	86
	Eddie Mathews, 1953	86
	Reggie Jackson, 1969	86
	Hal McRae, 1977	86
	Jim Rice, 1978	86
	Don Mattingly, 1985	86
	Don Mattingly, 1986	86
64	Tip O'Neill, 1887	85
	Chick Hafey, 1929	85
	Goose Goslin, 1930	85
	Lou Gehrig, 1932	85
	Lou Gehrig, 1933	85
	Earl Averill, 1934	85
	Hank Greenberg, 1938	85
	Rudy York, 1940	85
	Ted Williams, 1949	85
	Stan Musial, 1954	85
	Frank Robinson, 1966	85
	George Foster, 1977	85
	George Brett, 1979	85
77	Hugh Duffy, 1894	84
	Sam Thompson, 1895	84
	Ken Williams, 1922	84
	Al Simmons, 1929	84
	Ed Morgan, 1930	84
	Earl Webb, 1931	84
	Joe DiMaggio, 1941	84
	Duke Snider, 1953	84
	Tony Oliva, 1964	84
	Johnny Bench, 1970	84
	Jim Rice, 1979	84
88	Rogers Hornsby, 1921	83
	Lou Gehrig, 1926	83
	Dale Alexander, 1929	83
	Jimmie Foxx, 1930	83
	Earl Averill, 1932	83
	Lou Gehrig, 1937	83
	Ted Williams, 1946	83
	Ernie Banks, 1957	83
	Hank Aaron, 1961	83
	Jim Rice, 1977	83
	George Bell, 1987	83
99	14 players tied	82

Pinch Hits

1	Jose Morales, 1976	25
2	Dave Philley, 1961	24
	Vic Bavalillo, 1970	24
	Rusty Staub, 1983	24
5	Sam Leslie, 1932	22
	Red Schoendienst, 1962	22
	Wallace Johnson, 1988	22
9	Doc Miller, 1913	21
	Peanuts Lowrey, 1953	21
	Smoky Burgess, 1966	21
	Merv Rettenmund, 1977	21
13	Ed Coleman, 1936	20
	Frenchy Bordagaray, 1938	20
	Joe Frazier, 1954	20
	Smoky Burgess, 1965	20
	Ken Boswell, 1976	20
	Jerry Turner, 1978	20
	Thad Bosley, 1985	20
	Chris Chambliss, 1986	20
21	many players tied	19

Pinch Hit Average

1	Ed Kranepool, 1974	.486
2	Smead Jolley, 1931	.467
3	Frenchy Bordagaray, 1938	.465
4	Rick Miller, 1983	.457
5	Jose Pagan, 1969	.452
6	Elmer Valo, 1955	.452
7	Gates Brown, 1968	.450
8	Ted Easterly, 1912	.433
	Milt Thompson, 1985	.433
	Randy Bush, 1986	.433
11	Joe Cronin, 1943	.429
	Don Dillard, 1961	.429
13	Candy Maldonado, 1986	.425
14	Richie Ashburn, 1962	.419
	Dick Williams, 1962	.419
16	Merritt Ranew, 1963	.415
	Carl Taylor, 1969	.415
18	Kurt Bevacqua, 1983	.412
19	Jerry Turner, 1978	.408
20	Bob Bowman, 1958	.406
	Harry Spilman, 1986	.406
22	Frankie Baumholtz, 1955	.405
23	6 players tied	.400

Pinch Hit Home Runs

1	Johnny Frederick, 1932	6
2	Joe Cronin, 1943	5
	Butch Nieman, 1945	5
	Gene Freese, 1959	5
	Jerry Lynch, 1961	5
	Cliff Johnson, 1974	5
	Lee Lacy, 1978	5
	Jerry Turner, 1978	5
9	Ernie Lombardi, 1946	4
	Del Wilber, 1953	4
	Bill Taylor, 1955	4
	Bob Thurman, 1957	4
	Rip Repulski, 1958	4
	George Crowe, 1959	4
	George Crowe, 1960	4
	Johnny Blanchard, 1961	4
	Carl Sawatski, 1961	4
	Jerry Lynch, 1963	4
	Don Mincher, 1964	4
	Hal Breeden, 1973	4
	Mike Ivie, 1978	4
	Del Unser, 1979	4
	Jeff Burroughs, 1982	4
	Danny Heep, 1983	4
	Candy Maldonado, 1986	4
	Mark Carreon, 1989	4

Stolen Bases

1	Hugh Nicol, 1887	138
2	Rickey Henderson, 1982	130
3	Arlie Latham, 1887	129
4	Lou Brock, 1974	118
5	Charlie Comiskey, 1887	117
6	Monte Ward, 1887	111
	Billy Hamilton, 1889	111
	Billy Hamilton, 1891	111
9	Vince Coleman, 1985	110
10	Arlie Latham, 1888	109
	Vince Coleman, 1987	109
12	Rickey Henderson, 1983	108
13	Vince Coleman, 1986	107
14	Tom Brown, 1891	106
15	Maury Wills, 1962	104
16	Pete Browning, 1887	103
	Hugh Nicol, 1888	103
18	Jim Fogarty, 1887	102
	Billy Hamilton, 1890	102
20	Rickey Henderson, 1980	100
21	Jim Fogarty, 1889	99
22	Billy Hamilton, 1894	98
23	Harry Stovey, 1890	97
	Billy Hamilton, 1895	97
	Ron LeFlore, 1980	97
26	Ty Cobb, 1915	96
	Omar Moreno, 1980	96
28	Bid McPhee, 1887	95
	Curt Welch, 1888	95
30	Mike Griffin, 1887	94
	Maury Wills, 1965	94
32	Tommy McCarthy, 1888	93
	Rickey Henderson, 1988	93
34	Darby O'Brien, 1889	91
35	Tim Raines, 1983	90
36	Curt Welch, 1887	89
	Herman Long, 1889	89
38	Tom Poorman, 1887	88
	Blondie Purcell, 1887	88
	Monte Ward, 1892	88
	Clyde Milan, 1912	88
42	Harry Stovey, 1888	87
	Arlie Latham, 1891	87
	Joe Kelley, 1896	87
	Rickey Henderson, 1986	87
46	Cub Stricker, 1887	86
47	Tommy Tucker, 1887	85
	Hub Collins, 1890	85
	Hugh Duffy, 1891	85
50	King Kelly, 1887	84
	Chippy McGarr, 1887	84
	Billy Sunday, 1890	84
	Bill Lange, 1896	84
54	Tommy McCarthy, 1890	83
	Billy Hamilton, 1896	83
	Ty Cobb, 1911	83
	Willie Wilson, 1979	83
58	Dummy Hoy, 1888	82
	John Reilly, 1888	82
60	Eddie Collins, 1910	81
	Bob Bescher, 1911	81
	Vince Coleman, 1988	81
63	Emmett Seery, 1888	80
	Hugh Nicol, 1889	80
	Rickey Henderson, 1985	80
	Eric Davis, 1986	80
67	Tom Brown, 1890	79
	Dave Collins, 1980	79
	Willie Wilson, 1980	79
70	Hugh Duffy, 1890	78
	Tom Brown, 1892	78
	John McGraw, 1894	78
	Ron LeFlore, 1979	78
	Tim Raines, 1982	78
75	Ted Scheffler, 1890	77
	Jimmy Sheckard, 1899	77
	Davey Lopes, 1975	77
	Omar Moreno, 1979	77
	Rudy Law, 1983	77
	Rickey Henderson, 1989	77
81	Ed McKean, 1887	76
	Walt Wilmot, 1890	76
	Dusty Miller, 1896	76
	Ty Cobb, 1909	76
85	Yank Robinson, 1887	75
	George VanHaltren, 1891	75
	Benny Kauff, 1914	75
	Bill North, 1976	75
	Tim Raines, 1984	75
90	Frank Fennelly, 1887	74
	Harry Stovey, 1887	74
	Walt Wilmot, 1894	74
	Clyde Milan, 1913	74
	Fritz Maisel, 1914	74
	Lou Brock, 1966	74
96	7 players tied	73

Stolen Base Average

1	Kevin McReynolds, 1988	100.0
2	Max Carey, 1922	96.2
3	Ken Griffey, 1980	95.8
4	Stan Javier, 1988	95.2
5	Amos Otis, 1970	94.3
6	Jack Perconte, 1985	93.9
7	Miguel Dilone, 1984	93.1
	Bob Dernier, 1986	93.1
9	Don Baylor, 1972	92.3
	Oddibe McDowell, 1987	92.3
11	Davey Lopes, 1985	92.2
12	Eric Davis, 1988	92.1
13	Bobby Bonds, 1969	91.8
	Davey Lopes, 1978	91.8
15	Davey Lopes, 1979	91.7
16	Jim Wynn, 1965	91.5
17	Larry Bowa, 1977	91.4
18	Ryne Sandberg, 1987	91.3
	Alan Trammell, 1987	91.3
20	Jerry Mumphrey, 1980	91.2
21	Tom Herr, 1985	91.2
22	Jack Smith, 1925	90.9
	Davey Lopes, 1981	90.9
	Tim Raines, 1987	90.9
25	Willie Wilson, 1984	90.4
26	Bake McBride, 1978	90.3
27	Henry Cotto, 1988	90.0
28	Mitchell Page, 1977	89.4
29	Tommy Harper, 1971	89.3
	Rick Manning, 1981	89.3
	Eric Davis, 1987	89.3
32	Maury Wills, 1962	88.9
	Jake Wood, 1962	88.9
	Tommy Harper, 1964	88.9
	Enzo Hernandez, 1972	88.9
	Dusty Baker, 1973	88.9
	Leon Lacy, 1981	88.9
	Rickey Henderson, 1985	88.9
39	Willie Wilson, 1980	88.8
40	Tim Raines, 1985	88.6
	Tim Raines, 1986	88.6
42	Bert Campaneris, 1969	88.6
	Kirk Gibson, 1988	88.6
44	Willie Mays, 1971	88.5
45	Vince Coleman, 1986	88.4
46	Dale Murphy, 1983	88.2
	Tim Raines, 1984	88.2
	Kirk Gibson, 1985	88.2
49	Willie Wilson, 1983	88.1
50	4 players tied	88.0

Stolen Base Runs

1	Vince Coleman, 1986	24
2	Maury Wills, 1962	23
3	Rickey Henderson, 1983	21
4	Rickey Henderson, 1988	20
5	Vince Coleman, 1987	20
6	Tim Raines, 1983	19
7	Vince Coleman, 1985	18
	Rickey Henderson, 1985	18
9	Willie Wilson, 1979	18
	Ron LeFlore, 1980	18
	Willie Wilson, 1980	18
12	Eric Davis, 1986	17
13	Tim Raines, 1984	17
14	Davey Lopes, 1975	16
	Rudy Law, 1983	16
16	Lou Brock, 1974	16
	Tim Raines, 1985	16
	Tim Raines, 1986	16
19	Rickey Henderson, 1986	15
20	Ron LeFlore, 1979	15
21	Tim Raines, 1981	15
	Rickey Henderson, 1989	15
23	Rickey Henderson, 1980	14
24	Max Carey, 1922	14
	Joe Morgan, 1975	14
26	Bert Campaneris, 1969	14
	Tim Raines, 1982	14
	Rickey Henderson, 1982	14
29	Vince Coleman, 1989	14
30	Davey Lopes, 1976	13
	Willie Wilson, 1983	13
32	Mickey Rivers, 1975	13
	Joe Morgan, 1976	13
	Jerry Mumphrey, 1980	13
	Juan Samuel, 1984	13
36	Fritz Maisel, 1914	12
	Al Wiggins, 1983	12
	Tim Raines, 1987	12
39	Julio Cruz, 1978	12
	Davey Lopes, 1985	12
	Ozzie Smith, 1988	12
42	Lou Brock, 1966	11
	Lou Brock, 1968	11
	Gary Pettis, 1985	11
	Eric Davis, 1987	11
46	8 players tied	11

Stolen Base Wins

1	Vince Coleman, 1986	2.5
2	Maury Wills, 1962	2.3
3	Rickey Henderson, 1983	2.1
4	Rickey Henderson, 1988	2.0
5	Tim Raines, 1983	1.9
6	Vince Coleman, 1987	1.9
7	Vince Coleman, 1985	1.9
8	Ron LeFlore, 1980	1.9
9	Eric Davis, 1986	1.8
10	Rickey Henderson, 1985	1.8
11	Willie Wilson, 1980	1.8
12	Tim Raines, 1984	1.7
13	Willie Wilson, 1979	1.7
14	Davey Lopes, 1975	1.7
15	Tim Raines, 1985	1.6
16	Lou Brock, 1974	1.6
17	Tim Raines, 1986	1.6
18	Rudy Law, 1983	1.6
19	Tim Raines, 1981	1.6
20	Rickey Henderson, 1986	1.5
21	Rickey Henderson, 1989	1.5
22	Joe Morgan, 1975	1.5
23	Ron LeFlore, 1979	1.5
24	Tim Raines, 1982	1.4
25	Bert Campaneris, 1969	1.4
26	Vince Coleman, 1989	1.4
27	Rickey Henderson, 1980	1.4
28	Rickey Henderson, 1982	1.4
29	Davey Lopes, 1976	1.4
30	Joe Morgan, 1976	1.3
31	Jerry Mumphrey, 1980	1.3
32	Max Carey, 1922	1.3
33	Fritz Maisel, 1914	1.3
34	Juan Samuel, 1984	1.3
35	Lou Brock, 1968	1.3
36	Willie Wilson, 1983	1.3
37	Mickey Rivers, 1975	1.3
38	Ozzie Smith, 1988	1.3
39	Al Wiggins, 1983	1.3
40	Davey Lopes, 1985	1.2
41	Julio Cruz, 1978	1.2
42	Lou Brock, 1966	1.2
43	Tim Raines, 1987	1.2
44	Davey Lopes, 1978	1.2
45	Dave Collins, 1980	1.2
	Rod Scott, 1980	1.2
47	Bobby Bonds, 1969	1.2
48	Tommy Harper, 1969	1.2
49	Amos Otis, 1971	1.2
50	Joe Morgan, 1973	1.2

Fielding Average

First Base

1	Steve Garvey, 1984	1.000
2	Stuffy McInnis, 1921	.999
3	Frank McCormick, 1946	.999
4	Steve Garvey, 1981	.999
5	Jim Spencer, 1973	.999
6	Wes Parker, 1968	.999
7	Eddie Murray, 1981	.999
8	Jim Spencer, 1976	.998
9	Jim Spencer, 1981	.998
10	Joe Judge, 1930	.998

Second Base

1	Bobby Grich, 1985	.997
2	Rob Wilfong, 1980	.995
3	Bobby Grich, 1973	.995
4	Frank White, 1988	.994
5	Jose Oquendo, 1989	.994
6	Jerry Adair, 1964	.994
7	Ryne Sandberg, 1986	.994
8	Tim Cullen, 1970	.994
9	Manny Trillo, 1982	.994
10	Johnny Ray, 1986	.993

Shortstop

1	Tony Fernandez, 1989	.992
2	Larry Bowa, 1979	.991
3	Ed Brinkman, 1972	.990
4	Cal Ripken, 1989	.990
5	Larry Bowa, 1972	.987
6	Ozzie Smith, 1987	.987
7	Larry Bowa, 1971	.987
8	Larry Bowa, 1978	.986
9	Frank Duffy, 1973	.986
10	Roger Metzger, 1976	.986

Third Base

1	Don Money, 1974	.989
2	Hank Majeski, 1947	.988
3	Aurelio Rodriguez, 1978	.987
4	Willie Kamm, 1933	.984
5	George Kell, 1946	.983
6	Heinie Groh, 1924	.983
7	Carney Lansford, 1979	.983
8	George Kell, 1950	.982
9	Pinky Whitney, 1937	.982
10	Buddy Bell, 1980	.981

Outfield

1	Danny Litwhiler, 1942	1.000
	Willard Marshall, 1951	1.000
	Sam Mele, 1952	1.000
	Tony Gonzalez, 1962	1.000
	Don Demeter, 1963	1.000
	Rocky Colavito, 1965	1.000
	Curt Flood, 1966	1.000
	Johnny Callison, 1968	1.000
	Mickey Stanley, 1968	1.000
	Ken Harrelson, 1968	1.000
	Ken Berry, 1969	1.000
	Mickey Stanley, 1970	1.000
	Roy White, 1971	1.000
	Al Kaline, 1971	1.000
	Ken Berry, 1972	1.000
	Carl Yastrzemski, 1977	1.000
	Terry Puhl, 1979	1.000
	Gary Roenicke, 1980	1.000
	Ken Landreaux, 1981	1.000
	Terry Puhl, 1981	1.000
	Ken Singleton, 1981	1.000
	Brian Downing, 1982	1.000
	John Lowenstein, 1982	1.000
	Brian Downing, 1984	1.000

Catcher

1	Spud Davis, 1939	1.000
	Buddy Rosar, 1946	1.000
	Lou Berberet, 1957	1.000
	Pete Daley, 1957	1.000
	Yogi Berra, 1958	1.000
	Rick Cerone, 1988	1.000
7	Joe Azcue, 1967	.999
8	Wes Westrum, 1950	.999
9	Thurman Munson, 1971	.998
10	Rick Cerone, 1987	.998

Pitcher

1	Kid Nichols, 1896	1.000
	Frank Owen, 1904	1.000
	Mordecai Brown, 1908	1.000
	Pete Alexander, 1913	1.000
	Walter Johnson, 1913	1.000
	Eppa Rixey, 1917	1.000
	Walter Johnson, 1917	1.000
	Hal Schumacher, 1935	1.000
	Larry Jackson, 1964	1.000
	Randy Jones, 1976	1.000

Total Chances per Game

First Base

1	Joe Gerhardt, 1876	13.28
2	Jiggs Donahue, 1907	12.73
3	Oscar Walker, 1879	12.60
4	Joe Start, 1878	12.54
5	Tim Murnane, 1878	12.52
6	Joe Start, 1879	12.49
7	Jake Goodman, 1878	12.45
8	Herman Dehlman, 1876	12.36
9	Phil Todt, 1926	12.36
10	Joe Start, 1877	12.35

Second Base

1	Thorny Hawkes, 1879	8.44
2	Chick Fulmer, 1879	8.34
3	Jack Burdock, 1878	8.30
4	Ed Somerville, 1876	8.28
5	Joe Gerhardt, 1877	8.12
6	Fred Pfeffer, 1884	8.08
7	Jack Burdock, 1879	7.88
8	Joe Quest, 1878	7.81
9	Pop Smith, 1885	7.74
10	Joe Quest, 1879	7.73

Shortstop

1	Herman Long, 1889	7.27
2	Hughie Jennings, 1895	7.16
3	Dave Bancroft, 1918	7.14
4	George Davis, 1899	7.08
5	Hughie Jennings, 1896	7.07
6	Hughie Jennings, 1897	7.01
7	Bobby Wallace, 1901	6.97
8	Monte Cross, 1897	6.97
9	Bill Dahlen, 1895	6.93
10	Gene DeMontreville, 1897	6.91

Third Base

1	Al Nichols, 1876	5.81
2	Bob Ferguson, 1877	5.61
3	Jumbo Davis, 1888	5.13
4	Cap Anson, 1876	5.03
5	Billy Shindle, 1892	4.93
6	Jack Gleason, 1882	4.90
7	Bill Bradley, 1900	4.87
8	George Bradley, 1880	4.84
9	Will Foley, 1877	4.79
10	Levi Meyerle, 1876	4.78

Outfield

1	Fred Treacey, 1876	4.39
2	Redleg Snyder, 1876	3.84
3	Taylor Douthit, 1928	3.68
4	Mike Mansell, 1879	3.64
5	Richie Ashburn, 1951	3.64
6	Chet Lemon, 1977	3.60
7	Thurman Tucker, 1944	3.58
8	Kirby Puckett, 1984	3.57
9	Irv Noren, 1951	3.53
10	Richie Ashburn, 1949	3.49

Catcher

1	Bill Holbert, 1883	10.63
2	Sam Trott, 1884	10.35
3	Bill Holbert, 1884	9.66
4	Jocko Milligan, 1884	9.40
5	Mert Hackett, 1884	9.35
6	Barney Gilligan, 1884	9.30
7	Mike Hines, 1883	9.27
8	George Baker, 1884	8.99
9	Jocko Milligan, 1885	8.82
10	Lew Brown, 1877	8.65

Pitcher

1	Harry Howell, 1905	5.42
2	Harry Howell, 1904	5.12
3	Will White, 1882	4.76
4	Ed Walsh, 1907	4.75
5	George Mullin, 1904	4.53
6	Tony Mullane, 1882	4.38
7	Red Donahue, 1902	4.37
8	Nick Altrock, 1905	4.37
9	Harry Howell, 1906	4.34
10	Nick Altrock, 1904	4.26

Chances Accepted per Game

First Base
1 Jiggs Donahue, 1907 . . . . . . 12.65
2 Joe Gerhardt, 1876 . . . . 12.54
3 Phil Todt, 1926 . . . . 12.21
4 Joe Start, 1879 . . . . 12.15
5 George Burns, 1914 . . . . 12.10
6 Stuffy McInnis, 1918 . . . . . . 12.10
7 George Stovall, 1908 . . . . . . 12.08
8 George Kelly, 1920 . . . . 12.01
9 Joe Start, 1878 . . . . 12.00
10 Oscar Walker, 1879 . . . . 11.92

Second Base
1 Jack Burdock, 1878 . . . . 7.62
2 Thorny Hawkes, 1879 . . . . . . 7.56
3 Chick Fulmer, 1879 . . . . 7.55
4 Fred Pfeffer, 1884 . . . . 7.29
5 Joe Gerhardt, 1877 . . . . 7.21
6 Ed Somerville, 1876 . . . . 7.20
7 Jack Burdock, 1879 . . . . 7.18
8 Joe Quest, 1879 . . . . 7.16
9 Joe Gerhardt, 1890 . . . . 7.14
10 Pop Smith, 1885 . . . . 7.13

Shortstop
1 Hughie Jennings, 1895 . . . . . 6.73
2 George Davis, 1899 . . . . 6.69
3 Dave Bancroft, 1918 . . . . . . 6.62
4 Hughie Jennings, 1896 . . . . . 6.56
5 Hughie Jennings, 1897 . . . . . 6.53
6 Rabbit Maranville, 1919 . . . . 6.48
7 Bobby Wallace, 1901 . . . . . . 6.48
8 Monte Cross, 1897 . . . . 6.41
9 Dave Bancroft, 1920 . . . . . . 6.40
10 George Davis, 1900 . . . . 6.39

Third Base
1 Bob Ferguson, 1877 . . . . 4.71
2 Al Nichols, 1876 . . . . 4.53
3 Billy Shindle, 1892 . . . . 4.34
4 Jumbo Davis, 1888 . . . . 4.33
5 Bill Bradley, 1900 . . . . 4.29
6 Cap Anson, 1876 . . . . 4.27
7 Lave Cross, 1899 . . . . 4.21
8 Joe Battin, 1883 . . . . 4.17
9 Bill Hague, 1878 . . . . 4.16
10 George Bradley, 1880 . . . . . . 4.14

Outfield
1 Fred Treacey, 1876 . . . . 3.70
2 Taylor Douthit, 1928 . . . . 3.62
3 Richie Ashburn, 1951 . . . . . . 3.59
4 Thurman Tucker, 1944 . . . . . 3.55
5 Kirby Puckett, 1984 . . . . 3.55
6 Chet Lemon, 1977 . . . . 3.52
7 Irv Noren, 1951 . . . . 3.45
8 Richie Ashburn, 1949 . . . . . . 3.42
9 Carden Gillenwater, 1945 . . . 3.39
10 Jim Busby, 1952 . . . . 3.39

Catcher
1 Bill Holbert, 1883 . . . . 9.78
2 Sam Trott, 1884 . . . . 9.63
3 Jocko Milligan, 1884 . . . . . . 8.83
4 Bill Holbert, 1884 . . . . 8.75
5 Mert Hackett, 1884 . . . . 8.68
6 Barney Gilligan, 1884 . . . . . . 8.63
7 Duffy Dyer, 1972 . . . . 8.25
8 Jocko Milligan, 1885 . . . . . . 8.25
9 Mike Hines, 1883 . . . . 8.22
10 George Baker, 1884 . . . . 8.06

Pitcher
1 Harry Howell, 1905 . . . . 5.24
2 Harry Howell, 1904 . . . . 4.97
3 Ed Walsh, 1907 . . . . 4.68
4 Will White, 1882 . . . . 4.56
5 Nick Altrock, 1905 . . . . 4.32
6 George Mullin, 1904 . . . . 4.24
7 Tony Mullane, 1882 . . . . 4.20
8 Willie Sudhoff, 1904 . . . . 4.19
9 Red Donahue, 1902 . . . . 4.14
10 Nick Altrock, 1904 . . . . 4.13

Putouts

First Base
1 Jiggs Donahue, 1907 1846
2 George Kelly, 1920 1759
3 Phil Todt, 1926 1755
4 Wally Pipp, 1926 1710
5 Jiggs Donahue, 1906 1697
6 Candy LaChance, 1904 1691
7 Tom Jones, 1907 1687
8 Ernie Banks, 1965 1682
9 Wally Pipp, 1922 1667
10 Lou Gehrig, 1927 1662

Second Base
1 Bid McPhee, 1886 529
2 Bobby Grich, 1974 484
3 Bucky Harris, 1922 483
4 Nellie Fox, 1956 478
5 Lou Bierbauer, 1889 472
6 Billy Herman, 1933 466
7 Bill Wambsganss, 1924 463
8 Cub Stricker, 1887 461
9 Buddy Myer, 1935 460
10 Bill Sweeney, 1912 459

Shortstop
1 Hughie Jennings, 1895 425
  Donie Bush, 1914 425
3 Joe Cassidy, 1905 408
4 Rabbit Maranville, 1914 407
5 Dave Bancroft, 1922 405
  Eddie Miller, 1940 405
7 Monte Cross, 1898 404
8 Dave Bancroft, 1921 396
9 Mickey Doolan, 1906 395
10 Buck Weaver, 1913 392

Third Base
1 Denny Lyons, 1887 255
2 Jimmy Williams, 1899 251
  Jimmy Collins, 1900 251
4 Jimmy Collins, 1898 243
  Willie Kamm, 1928 243
6 Willie Kamm, 1927 236
7 Frank Baker, 1913 233
8 Bill Coughlin, 1901 232
9 Ernie Courtney, 1905 229
10 Jimmy Austin, 1911 228

Outfield
1 Taylor Douthit, 1928 547
2 Richie Ashburn, 1951 538
3 Richie Ashburn, 1949 514
4 Chet Lemon, 1977 512
5 Dwayne Murphy, 1980 507
6 Dom DiMaggio, 1948 503
  Richie Ashburn, 1956 503
8 Richie Ashburn, 1957 502
9 Richie Ashburn, 1953 496
10 Richie Ashburn, 1958 495

Catcher
1 Johnny Edwards, 1969 1135
2 Johnny Edwards, 1963 1008
3 Randy Hundley, 1969 978
4 Tony Pena, 1983 976
5 Bill Freehan, 1968 971
6 Gary Carter, 1985 956
7 Gary Carter, 1982 954
8 Bill Freehan, 1967 950
9 Johnny Bench, 1968 942
10 Elston Howard, 1964 939

Pitcher
1 Dave Foutz, 1886 57
2 Tony Mullane, 1882 54
3 George Bradley, 1876 50
  Guy Hecker, 1884 50
5 Mike Boddicker, 1984 49
6 Larry Corcoran, 1884 47
7 Al Spalding, 1876 45
  Ted Breitenstein, 1895 45
9 Jim Devlin, 1876 44
  Dave Foutz, 1887 44
  Bill Hutchinson, 1890 44

Putouts per Game

First Base
1 Joe Gerhardt, 1876 . . . . 12.30
2 Joe Start, 1879 . . . . 11.98
3 Joe Start, 1878 . . . . 11.79
4 Jiggs Donahue, 1907 . . . . . . 11.76
5 Joe Start, 1877 . . . . 11.73
6 Herman Dehlman, 1876 . . . . . 11.72
7 Joe Start, 1880 . . . . 11.63
8 Jake Goodman, 1878 . . . . . . 11.55
9 George Burns, 1914 . . . . 11.53
10 Oscar Walker, 1879 . . . . 11.50

Second Base
1 Jack Burdock, 1878 . . . . 4.08
2 Jack Burdock, 1880 . . . . 3.81
3 Bid McPhee, 1886 . . . . 3.78
4 Bid McPhee, 1884 . . . . 3.71
5 Joe Quest, 1878 . . . . 3.68
6 Cub Stricker, 1887 . . . . 3.66
7 Lou Bierbauer, 1889 . . . . 3.63
8 Joe Gerhardt, 1890 . . . . 3.63
9 Jack Burdock, 1879 . . . . 3.61
10 Chick Fulmer, 1879 . . . . 3.59

Shortstop
1 Hughie Jennings, 1895 . . . . . 3.24
2 Dave Bancroft, 1918 . . . . . . 2.97
3 Hughie Jennings, 1896 . . . . . 2.90
4 George Davis, 1898 . . . . 2.88
5 George Davis, 1899 . . . . 2.88
6 Hughie Jennings, 1897 . . . . . 2.87
7 Rabbit Maranville, 1919 . . . . 2.76
8 Honus Wagner, 1913 . . . . . . 2.75
9 Kid Elberfeld, 1901 . . . . 2.74
10 Buck Weaver, 1914 . . . . 2.74

Third Base
1 Al Nichols, 1876 . . . . 2.16
2 Cap Anson, 1876 . . . . 2.05
3 Hick Carpenter, 1880 . . . . . . 2.03
4 Bob Ferguson, 1877 . . . . 1.95
5 Denny Lyons, 1887 . . . . 1.86
6 Patsy Tebeau, 1890 . . . . 1.85
7 Cap Anson, 1877 . . . . 1.85
8 Joe Battin, 1876 . . . . 1.83
9 Jerry Denny, 1883 . . . . 1.82
10 Frank Hankinson, 1881 . . . . . 1.80

Outfield
1 Taylor Douthit, 1928 . . . . 3.55
2 Fred Treacey, 1876 . . . . 3.54
3 Richie Ashburn, 1951 . . . . . . 3.49
4 Thurman Tucker, 1944 . . . . . 3.45
5 Chet Lemon, 1977 . . . . 3.44
6 Kirby Puckett, 1984 . . . . 3.42
7 Jim Busby, 1952 . . . . 3.36
8 Richie Ashburn, 1949 . . . . . . 3.34
9 Irv Noren, 1951 . . . . 3.33
10 Sam West, 1935 . . . . 3.33

Catcher
1 Sam Trott, 1884 . . . . 8.18
2 Bill Holbert, 1883 . . . . 7.75
3 Duffy Dyer, 1972 . . . . 7.58
4 Johnny Edwards, 1969 . . . . . 7.52
5 Barney Gilligan, 1884 . . . . . . 7.47
6 John Romano, 1964 . . . . 7.44
7 Johnny Edwards, 1964 . . . . . 7.42
8 Joe Azcue, 1967 . . . . 7.40
9 John Roseboro, 1960 . . . . . . 7.36
10 Jerry Grote, 1971 . . . . 7.31

Pitcher
1 Mike Boddicker, 1984 . . . . . . 1.44
2 Oil Can Boyd, 1985 . . . . 1.20
3 Nick Altrock, 1904 . . . . 1.13
4 Snake Wiltse, 1902 . . . . 1.11
5 Rube Waddell, 1901 . . . . 1.10
6 Dave Foutz, 1887 . . . . 1.10
7 Dwight Gooden, 1986 . . . . . . 1.09
8 Dan Petry, 1984 . . . . 1.09
9 Nat Hudson, 1888 . . . . 1.08
  Al Nipper, 1986 . . . . 1.08

Assists

First Base
1 Bill Buckner, 1985 184
2 Sid Bream, 1986 166
3 Bill Buckner, 1983 161
4 Bill Buckner, 1982 159
5 Bill Buckner, 1986 157
6 Mickey Vernon, 1949 155
7 Fred Tenney, 1905 152
  Eddie Murray, 1985 152
9 Ferris Fain, 1952 150
10 Rudy York, 1943 149
  Keith Hernandez, 1986 149
  Keith Hernandez, 1987 149

Second Base
1 Frankie Frisch, 1927 641
2 Hughie Critz, 1926 588
3 Rogers Hornsby, 1927 582
4 Ski Melillo, 1930 572
5 Ryne Sandberg, 1983 571
6 Rabbit Maranville, 1924 568
7 Frank Parkinson, 1922 562
8 Tony Cuccinello, 1936 559
9 Johnny Hodapp, 1930 557
10 Lou Bierbauer, 1892 555

Shortstop
1 Ozzie Smith, 1980 621
2 Glenn Wright, 1924 601
3 Dave Bancroft, 1920 598
4 Tommy Thevenow, 1926 597
5 Ivan DeJesus, 1977 595
6 Cal Ripken, 1984 583
7 Whitey Wietelmann, 1943 . . . 581
8 Dave Bancroft, 1922 579
9 Rabbit Maranville, 1914 574
10 Don Kessinger, 1968 573

Third Base
1 Graig Nettles, 1971 412
2 Graig Nettles, 1973 410
  Brooks Robinson, 1974 410
4 Harlond Clift, 1937 405
  Brooks Robinson, 1967 405
6 Mike Schmidt, 1974 404
7 Doug DeCinces, 1982 399
8 Clete Boyer, 1962 396
  Mike Schmidt, 1977 396
  Buddy Bell, 1982 396

Outfield
1 Orator Shaffer, 1879 50
2 Hugh Nicol, 1884 48
3 Hardy Richardson, 1881 45
4 Tommy McCarthy, 1888 44
  Jimmy Bannon, 1894 44
  Chuck Klein, 1930 44
7 Charlie Duffee, 1889 43
8 Jim Fogarty, 1889 42
9 Orator Shaffer, 1883 41
  Jim Lillie, 1884 41

Catcher
1 Bill Rariden, 1915 238
2 Bill Rariden, 1914 215
3 Pat Moran, 1903 214
4 Oscar Stanage, 1911 212
  Art Wilson, 1914 212
6 Gabby Street, 1909 210
7 Frank Snyder, 1915 204
8 George Gibson, 1910 203
9 Bill Bergen, 1909 202
  Claude Berry, 1914 202

Pitcher
1 Ed Walsh, 1907 227
2 Will White, 1882 223
3 Ed Walsh, 1908 190
4 Harry Howell, 1905 178
5 Tony Mullane, 1882 177
6 John Clarkson, 1885 174
7 John Clarkson, 1889 172
8 Matt Kilroy, 1887 167
9 Jack Chesbro, 1904 166
10 George Mullin, 1904 163

Assists per Game

First Base
1	Bill Buckner, 1986	1.14
2	Bill Buckner, 1985	1.14
3	Bill Buckner, 1983	1.12
4	Sid Bream, 1986	1.08
5	Ferris Fain, 1951	1.05
6	Ferris Fain, 1952	1.04
7	Fred Tenney, 1905	1.03
8	Keith Hernandez, 1983	1.02
9	Bob Robertson, 1971	1.02
10	Sid Bream, 1988	1.01

Second Base
1	Joe Gerhardt, 1877	4.28
2	Frankie Frisch, 1927	4.19
3	Thorny Hawkes, 1879	4.13
4	Hughie Critz, 1933	4.07
5	Frank Parkinson, 1922	4.04
6	Joe Quest, 1879	3.99
7	Chick Fulmer, 1879	3.96
8	Ed Somerville, 1876	3.92
9	Ski Melillo, 1930	3.86
10	Glenn Hubbard, 1985	3.85

Shortstop
1	Germany Smith, 1885	4.21
2	Arthur Irwin, 1880	4.13
3	Art Fletcher, 1919	4.10
4	Bill Dahlen, 1895	4.09
5	Bobby Wallace, 1901	4.04
6	Jack Glasscock, 1887	4.04
7	Germany Smith, 1892	4.04
8	Henry Easterday, 1888	3.99
9	Dave Bancroft, 1920	3.99
10	Rogers Hornsby, 1918	3.98

Third Base
1	Jumbo Davis, 1888	2.96
2	Buddy Bell, 1981	2.93
3	George Bradley, 1880	2.89
4	Bill Hague, 1878	2.85
5	Billy Shindle, 1892	2.85
6	Bob Ferguson, 1877	2.77
7	Ned Williamson, 1879	2.76
8	Arlie Latham, 1884	2.75
9	Bill Bradley, 1900	2.75
10	Arlie Latham, 1891	2.74

Outfield
1	Orator Shaffer, 1879	0.69
2	Hardy Richardson, 1881	0.57
3	Hugh Nicol, 1884	0.55
4	King Kelly, 1878	0.51
5	John Cassidy, 1878	0.50
	King Kelly, 1880	0.50
7	King Kelly, 1883	0.46
8	Jake Evans, 1882	0.46
9	Orator Shaffer, 1878	0.44
10	Dick Higham, 1878	0.44

Catcher
1	Bill Holbert, 1884	2.41
2	Tom Daly, 1887	2.31
3	Bill Holbert, 1882	2.14
4	Pop Snyder, 1884	2.08
5	Bill Holbert, 1883	2.03
6	Buck Ewing, 1881	2.02
7	Pat Moran, 1903	2.00
8	Charlie Reipschlager, 1885	1.98
9	Connie Mack, 1888	1.92
10	King Kelly, 1888	1.92

Pitcher
1	Harry Howell, 1905	4.68
2	Harry Howell, 1904	4.21
3	Will White, 1882	4.13
4	Ed Walsh, 1907	4.05
5	Willie Sudhoff, 1904	3.85
6	Red Donahue, 1902	3.71
7	George Mullin, 1904	3.62
8	Frank Owen, 1904	3.51
9	Carl Mays, 1918	3.49
10	Nick Altrock, 1905	3.47

Double Plays

First Base
1	Ferris Fain, 1949	194
2	Ferris Fain, 1950	192
3	Donn Clendenon, 1966	182
4	Ron Jackson, 1979	175
5	Gil Hodges, 1951	171
6	Mickey Vernon, 1949	168
7	Ted Kluszewski, 1954	166
8	Rudy York, 1944	163
9	Donn Clendenon, 1965	161
	Rod Carew, 1977	161

Second Base
1	Bill Mazeroski, 1966	161
2	Jerry Priddy, 1950	150
3	Bill Mazeroski, 1961	144
4	Nellie Fox, 1957	141
	Dave Cash, 1974	141
6	Buddy Myer, 1935	138
	Bill Mazeroski, 1962	138
8	Jerry Coleman, 1950	137
	Jackie Robinson, 1951	137
	Red Schoendienst, 1954	137

Shortstop
1	Rick Burleson, 1980	147
2	Roy Smalley, 1979	144
3	Bobby Wine, 1970	137
4	Lou Boudreau, 1944	134
5	Spike Owen, 1986	133
6	Rafael Ramirez, 1982	130
7	Roy McMillan, 1954	129
8	Hod Ford, 1928	128
	Vern Stephens, 1949	128
	Gene Alley, 1966	128

Third Base
1	Graig Nettles, 1971	54
2	Harlond Clift, 1937	50
3	Johnny Pesky, 1949	48
	Paul Molitor, 1982	48
5	Sammy Hale, 1927	46
	Clete Boyer, 1965	46
	Gary Gaetti, 1983	46
8	Eddie Yost, 1950	45
	Frank Malzone, 1961	45
	Darrell Evans, 1974	45

Outfield
1	Happy Felsch, 1919	15
2	Jimmy Sheckard, 1899	14
3	Tom Brown, 1893	13
4	Tom Brown, 1886	12
	Tommy McCarthy, 1888	12
	Jimmy Bannon, 1894	12
	Mike Griffin, 1895	12
	Danny Green, 1899	12
	Cy Seymour, 1905	12
	Ginger Beaumont, 1907	12
	Ty Cobb, 1907	12
	Tris Speaker, 1909	12
	Jimmy Sheckard, 1911	12
	Tris Speaker, 1914	12
	Mel Ott, 1929	12

Catcher
1	Steve O'Neill, 1916	36
2	Frankie Hayes, 1945	29
3	Ray Schalk, 1916	25
	Yogi Berra, 1951	25
5	Jack Lapp, 1915	23
	Muddy Ruel, 1924	23
	Frankie Hayes, 1945	23
	Tom Haller, 1968	23
9	Steve O'Neill, 1914	22
	Bob O'Farrell, 1922	22

Pitcher
1	Bob Lemon, 1953	15
2	Eddie Rommel, 1924	12
	Curt Davis, 1934	12
	Randy Jones, 1976	12
5	Scott Perry, 1919	11
	Tom Rogers, 1919	11
	Art Nehf, 1920	11
	Burleigh Grimes, 1925	11
	Gene Bearden, 1948	11
10	Nick Altrock, 1905	10
	Carl Mays, 1926	10
	Willis Hudlin, 1931	10
	Freddie Fitzsimmons, 1932	10
	Freddie Fitzsimmons, 1934	10
	Bucky Walters, 1939	10
	Dave Ferriss, 1945	10
	Bob Hooper, 1950	10
	Don Drysdale, 1958	10
	Dan Petry, 1983	10

Fielding Runs

1	Glenn Hubbard, 1985	56.8
2	Rabbit Maranville, 1914	49.5
3	Danny Richardson, 1892	49.4
4	Frankie Frisch, 1927	48.8
5	Freddie Maguire, 1928	48.2
6	Nap Lajoie, 1908	46.7
7	Bill Mazeroski, 1963	46.6
8	Herman Long, 1889	45.1
9	Danny Richardson, 1891	43.6
10	Dick Bartell, 1936	43.4
11	George Davis, 1899	43.3
12	Ozzie Smith, 1980	42.8
	Ozzie Guillen, 1988	42.8
14	Dave Shean, 1910	42.2
15	Cupid Childs, 1896	41.9
16	Bill Mazeroski, 1966	40.9
17	Bill Mazeroski, 1962	40.7
18	Ryne Sandberg, 1983	40.5
19	Fred Pfeffer, 1884	40.4
	Hughie Critz, 1933	40.4
21	Harlond Clift, 1937	40.1
22	Graig Nettles, 1971	39.6
23	Nap Lajoie, 1907	39.3
24	Cal Ripken, 1984	38.8
25	Bid McPhee, 1889	38.3
26	John Kerins, 1886	37.7
	Everett Scott, 1921	37.7
28	Fred Pfeffer, 1888	37.4
29	Buddy Bell, 1982	37.0
30	Tim Wallach, 1985	36.8
31	Bill Holbert, 1883	36.7
	Germany Smith, 1885	36.7
	Nap Lajoie, 1903	36.7
	Dick Bartell, 1937	36.7
35	Bobby Knoop, 1964	36.6
36	Arlie Latham, 1884	36.5
37	Buck Weaver, 1913	36.4
38	Lou Bierbauer, 1889	36.2
39	Miller Huggins, 1905	36.1
	Ivan DeJesus, 1977	36.1
41	Billy Shindle, 1888	35.9
	Billy Shindle, 1892	35.9
	Manny Trillo, 1977	35.9
44	Joe Cassidy, 1905	35.7
45	Clete Boyer, 1962	35.5
46	Marty Barrett, 1987	35.2
47	Jack Glasscock, 1887	34.6
48	Freddie Patek, 1973	34.5
49	Ollie Beard, 1889	34.4
50	Zoilo Versalles, 1962	34.1
51	Bobby Wallace, 1899	34.0
52	Joe Gerhardt, 1890	33.9
	Manny Trillo, 1978	33.9
	Ozzie Smith, 1982	33.9
55	Glenn Hubbard, 1986	33.8
56	Ski Melillo, 1931	33.7
57	Bill Mazeroski, 1964	33.5
58	Donie Bush, 1914	33.1
59	Harry Steinfeldt, 1900	33.0
	Eddie Collins, 1910	33.0
	Art Fletcher, 1915	33.0
	Chuck Klein, 1930	33.0
	Tony Pena, 1985	33.0
64	Bob Allen, 1890	32.9
	George Davis, 1898	32.9
	Roy Smalley, 1979	32.9
67	Ozzie Smith, 1978	32.7
68	Jerry Priddy, 1950	32.6
69	Bid McPhee, 1893	32.5
70	Bill Dahlen, 1894	32.2
	Tommy Leach, 1904	32.2
	Joe Tinker, 1908	32.2
	Pep Young, 1938	32.2
74	Mike Mowrey, 1913	31.8
75	Germany Smith, 1887	31.6
76	Bid McPhee, 1886	31.5
	Hughie Jennings, 1894	31.5
	George McBride, 1908	31.5
	Bill Mazeroski, 1961	31.5
	Clete Boyer, 1961	31.5
	Ed Brinkman, 1970	31.5
82	Arthur Irwin, 1880	31.4
83	Luis Aparicio, 1960	31.3
84	Pop Smith, 1885	31.2
	Leo Cardenas, 1969	31.2
	Garry Templeton, 1980	31.2
87	Johnny Evers, 1904	31.1
	Ron Santo, 1967	31.1
89	Bid McPhee, 1888	31.0
	Rick Burleson, 1980	31.0
91	Buck Herzog, 1915	30.9
	Bucky Dent, 1979	30.9
	Ozzie Smith, 1984	30.9
94	Tommy McCarthy, 1888	30.7
	Mark Belanger, 1977	30.7
96	Jack Glasscock, 1889	30.6
	Bill Mazeroski, 1965	30.6
98	Buck Herzog, 1914	30.5
99	Hughie Jennings, 1895	30.4
100	2 players tied	30.3

Fielding Runs

First Base
1	Bill Buckner, 1985	25.0
2	Chick Gandil, 1914	21.4
3	Jiggs Donahue, 1907	20.8
4	Vic Power, 1960	20.7
5	Fred Tenney, 1905	20.3
6	Jake Beckley, 1892	19.7
7	Mickey Vernon, 1949	18.5
8	Rudy York, 1943	18.3
9	Jack Burns, 1931	17.9
10	Keith Hernandez, 1979	17.8

Second Base
1	Glenn Hubbard, 1985	56.8
2	Frankie Frisch, 1927	48.8
3	Freddie Maguire, 1928	48.2
4	Nap Lajoie, 1908	46.7
5	Bill Mazeroski, 1963	46.6
6	Danny Richardson, 1891	43.6
7	Dave Shean, 1910	42.2
8	Cupid Childs, 1896	41.9
9	Bill Mazeroski, 1966	40.9
10	Bill Mazeroski, 1962	40.7

Shortstop
1	Rabbit Maranville, 1914	49.5
2	Herman Long, 1889	45.1
3	Dick Bartell, 1936	43.4
4	George Davis, 1899	43.3
5	Ozzie Smith, 1980	42.8
6	Ozzie Guillen, 1988	42.8
7	Cal Ripken, 1984	38.8
8	Everett Scott, 1921	37.7
9	Germany Smith, 1885	36.7
10	Dick Bartell, 1937	36.7

Third Base
1	Harlond Clift, 1937	40.1
2	Graig Nettles, 1971	39.6
3	Buddy Bell, 1982	37.0
4	Tim Wallach, 1985	36.8
5	Arlie Latham, 1884	36.5
6	Billy Shindle, 1888	35.9
7	Billy Shindle, 1892	35.9
8	Clete Boyer, 1962	35.5
9	Tommy Leach, 1904	32.2
10	Mike Mowrey, 1913	31.8

Outfield
1	Chuck Klein, 1930	33.0
2	Tommy McCarthy, 1888	30.7
3	Dave Parker, 1977	30.0
4	Jim Fogarty, 1887	28.6
5	Richie Ashburn, 1957	27.3
6	Tom Brown, 1893	26.9
7	Ed Delahanty, 1893	26.7
8	Chet Lemon, 1977	26.5
9	Johnny Callison, 1962	25.8
10	Richie Ashburn, 1951	25.5

Catcher
1	Bill Holbert, 1883	36.7
2	Tony Pena, 1985	33.0
3	Gary Carter, 1983	28.7
4	Gary Carter, 1978	25.0
5	Pop Snyder, 1884	24.8
6	Del Crandall, 1959	24.8
7	Johnny Edwards, 1962	24.7
8	John Stearns, 1978	23.9
9	Gary Carter, 1980	23.7
10	Bill Rariden, 1915	23.5

Fielding Wins

1	Glenn Hubbard, 1985	6.0
2	Rabbit Maranville, 1914	5.3
3	Nap Lajoie, 1908	5.3
4	Bill Mazeroski, 1963	5.1
5	Frankie Frisch, 1927	4.8
6	Freddie Maguire, 1928	4.7
7	Danny Richardson, 1892	4.6
8	Ozzie Smith, 1980	4.5
9	Dave Shean, 1910	4.4
10	Nap Lajoie, 1907	4.3
11	Ozzie Guillen, 1988	4.3
12	Bill Mazeroski, 1966	4.3
13	Hughie Critz, 1933	4.3
14	Graig Nettles, 1971	4.3
15	Ryne Sandberg, 1983	4.2
16	Dick Bartell, 1936	4.2
17	Bill Mazeroski, 1962	4.1
18	George Davis, 1899	3.9
19	Joe Cassidy, 1905	3.9
20	Cal Ripken, 1984	3.9
21	Danny Richardson, 1891	3.9
22	Buck Weaver, 1913	3.9
23	Tim Wallach, 1985	3.9
24	Bobby Knoop, 1964	3.8
25	Herman Long, 1889	3.8
26	Nap Lajoie, 1903	3.8
27	Miller Huggins, 1905	3.8
28	Joe Tinker, 1908	3.7
29	Buddy Bell, 1982	3.7
30	Harlond Clift, 1937	3.7
31	Fred Pfeffer, 1888	3.7
32	Eddie Collins, 1910	3.7
33	Art Fletcher, 1915	3.7
34	Donie Bush, 1914	3.7
35	Ivan DeJesus, 1977	3.7
36	Dick Bartell, 1937	3.6
37	Manny Trillo, 1977	3.6
38	Fred Pfeffer, 1884	3.6
39	George McBride, 1908	3.6
40	Manny Trillo, 1978	3.6
41	Clete Boyer, 1962	3.6
42	Ozzie Smith, 1982	3.6
43	Cupid Childs, 1896	3.6
44	Bill Mazeroski, 1964	3.5
45	Freddie Patek, 1973	3.5
46	Everett Scott, 1921	3.5
47	Glenn Hubbard, 1986	3.5
48	Horace Clarke, 1968	3.5
49	Tony Pena, 1985	3.5
50	Ozzie Smith, 1978	3.5
51	Buck Herzog, 1915	3.4
52	Zoilo Versalles, 1962	3.4
53	Tommy Leach, 1904	3.4
54	Ron Santo, 1967	3.4
55	Heinie Wagner, 1908	3.4
56	Marty Barrett, 1987	3.4
57	Arlie Latham, 1884	3.3
58	Billy Shindle, 1892	3.3
59	Billy Shindle, 1888	3.3
60	Brooks Robinson, 1967	3.3
61	John Kerins, 1886	3.3
62	Mike Mowrey, 1913	3.3
63	Germany Smith, 1885	3.3
64	Garry Templeton, 1980	3.3
65	Johnny Evers, 1904	3.3
66	Buck Herzog, 1914	3.3
67	Leo Cardenas, 1969	3.3
68	Ed Brinkman, 1970	3.3
69	Al Burch, 1908	3.3
70	Ozzie Smith, 1984	3.2
71	Bid McPhee, 1889	3.2
72	Pep Young, 1938	3.2
73	Bill Mazeroski, 1965	3.2
74	Bill Holbert, 1883	3.2
75	Luis Aparicio, 1968	3.2
76	Rabbit Maranville, 1919	3.2
77	Roy Smalley, 1979	3.2
78	Johnny Evers, 1907	3.2
79	Luis Aparicio, 1969	3.2
80	Luis Aparicio, 1960	3.2
81	Ski Melillo, 1931	3.1
82	Freddie Patek, 1972	3.1
83	Bill Mazeroski, 1961	3.1
84	Clete Boyer, 1961	3.1
85	Dave Cash, 1974	3.1
86	Billy Herman, 1933	3.1
87	Rick Burleson, 1980	3.1
88	Dave Bancroft, 1920	3.1
89	Dave Bancroft, 1917	3.1
90	Bobby Wallace, 1899	3.1
91	George Davis, 1898	3.1
92	Art Devlin, 1906	3.1
93	Lou Bierbauer, 1889	3.1
94	Arthur Irwin, 1880	3.1
95	Jerry Priddy, 1950	3.1
96	Mark Belanger, 1977	3.0
97	Dave Parker, 1977	3.0
98	Roy McMillan, 1956	3.0
99	Harry Steinfeldt, 1900	3.0
100	Bucky Dent, 1979	3.0

Total Player Rating

1	Babe Ruth, 1921	9.9
2	Babe Ruth, 1923	9.0
	Cal Ripken, 1984	9.0
4	Nap Lajoie, 1910	8.9
5	Babe Ruth, 1920	8.8
6	Babe Ruth, 1927	8.5
7	Babe Ruth, 1924	8.3
	Ted Williams, 1942	8.3
9	Lou Gehrig, 1927	8.2
10	Ted Williams, 1947	8.1
	Stan Musial, 1948	8.1
	Mickey Mantle, 1957	8.1
13	Rogers Hornsby, 1920	8.0
	Ted Williams, 1941	8.0
	Joe Morgan, 1975	8.0
16	Nap Lajoie, 1903	7.9
	Ty Cobb, 1917	7.9
18	Babe Ruth, 1926	7.8
	Willie Mays, 1955	7.8
20	George Sisler, 1920	7.7
	Babe Ruth, 1930	7.7
	Ted Williams, 1946	7.7
23	Fred Dunlap, 1884	7.6
	Jimmie Foxx, 1933	7.6
	Mickey Mantle, 1956	7.6
	Norm Cash, 1961	7.6
	Ron Santo, 1966	7.6
28	Ted Williams, 1949	7.5
	Jackie Robinson, 1951	7.5
30	Nap Lajoie, 1901	7.4
	Mike Schmidt, 1980	7.4
	Rickey Henderson, 1985	7.4
33	Nap Lajoie, 1904	7.3
	Tris Speaker, 1912	7.3
35	Rogers Hornsby, 1921	7.2
	Rogers Hornsby, 1922	7.2
	Chuck Klein, 1930	7.2
	Carl Yastrzemski, 1967	7.2
	Mike Schmidt, 1977	7.2
40	Tris Speaker, 1913	7.1
	Babe Ruth, 1919	7.1
	Harlond Clift, 1937	7.1
	Rod Carew, 1974	7.1
44	Honus Wagner, 1905	7.0
	Tris Speaker, 1914	7.0
	Babe Ruth, 1928	7.0
	Rogers Hornsby, 1929	7.0
	Stan Musial, 1951	7.0
	Mickey Mantle, 1961	7.0
	Ron Santo, 1967	7.0
	Carl Yastrzemski, 1968	7.0
	Mike Schmidt, 1974	7.0
	George Brett, 1985	7.0
54	Ty Cobb, 1909	6.9
	Joe Jackson, 1912	6.9
	Reggie Jackson, 1969	6.9
57	Nap Lajoie, 1906	6.8
	Honus Wagner, 1908	6.8
	Nap Lajoie, 1908	6.8
	Rogers Hornsby, 1924	6.8
	Lou Gehrig, 1930	6.8
	Lou Boudreau, 1944	6.8
	Mike Schmidt, 1982	6.8
64	Ted Williams, 1957	6.7
	George Brett, 1980	6.7
66	Honus Wagner, 1906	6.6
	Ty Cobb, 1916	6.6
	Snuffy Stirnweiss, 1944	6.6
	Ted Williams, 1948	6.6
	Mike Schmidt, 1981	6.6
	Robin Yount, 1982	6.6
72	Nap Lajoie, 1907	6.5
	Ty Cobb, 1911	6.5
	Joe Jackson, 1911	6.5
	Joe Cronin, 1930	6.5
	Eddie Lake, 1945	6.5
	Frank Robinson, 1966	6.5
	Ryne Sandberg, 1984	6.5
79	Babe Ruth, 1931	6.4
	Charlie Gehringer, 1936	6.4
	Arky Vaughan, 1938	6.4
	Snuffy Stirnweiss, 1945	6.4
	Willie Mays, 1958	6.4
	Willie Mays, 1964	6.4
	Pedro Guerrero, 1985	6.4
86	Ty Cobb, 1910	6.3
	Honus Wagner, 1912	6.3
	Duke Kenworthy, 1914	6.3
	Eddie Collins, 1915	6.3
	Benny Kauff, 1915	6.3
	Frankie Frisch, 1927	6.3
	Hank Aaron, 1959	6.3
	Frank Robinson, 1962	6.3
	Willie Mays, 1965	6.3
	Eric Davis, 1987	6.3
	Kevin Mitchell, 1989	6.3
97	15 players tied	6.2

Total Player Rating (alpha.)

Hank Aaron, 1959	6.3
Lou Boudreau, 1944	6.8
George Brett, 1980	6.7
George Brett, 1985	7.0
Rod Carew, 1974	7.1
Norm Cash, 1961	7.6
Harlond Clift, 1937	7.1
Ty Cobb, 1909	6.9
Ty Cobb, 1910	6.3
Ty Cobb, 1911	6.5
Ty Cobb, 1916	6.6
Ty Cobb, 1917	7.9
Eddie Collins, 1915	6.3
Joe Cronin, 1930	6.5
Eric Davis, 1987	6.3
Fred Dunlap, 1884	7.6
Jimmie Foxx, 1933	7.6
Frankie Frisch, 1927	6.3
Lou Gehrig, 1927	8.2
Lou Gehrig, 1930	6.8
Charlie Gehringer, 1936	6.4
Pedro Guerrero, 1985	6.4
Rickey Henderson, 1985	7.4
Rogers Hornsby, 1920	8.0
Rogers Hornsby, 1921	7.2
Rogers Hornsby, 1922	7.2
Rogers Hornsby, 1924	6.8
Rogers Hornsby, 1929	7.0
Joe Jackson, 1911	6.5
Joe Jackson, 1912	6.9
Reggie Jackson, 1969	6.9
Benny Kauff, 1915	6.3
Duke Kenworthy, 1914	6.3
Chuck Klein, 1930	7.2
Nap Lajoie, 1901	7.4
Nap Lajoie, 1903	7.9
Nap Lajoie, 1904	7.3
Nap Lajoie, 1906	6.8
Nap Lajoie, 1907	6.5
Nap Lajoie, 1908	6.8
Nap Lajoie, 1910	8.9
Eddie Lake, 1945	6.5
Mickey Mantle, 1956	7.6
Mickey Mantle, 1957	8.1
Mickey Mantle, 1961	7.0
Willie Mays, 1955	7.8
Willie Mays, 1958	6.4
Willie Mays, 1964	6.4
Willie Mays, 1965	6.3
Kevin Mitchell, 1989	6.3
Joe Morgan, 1975	8.0
Stan Musial, 1948	8.1
Stan Musial, 1951	7.0
Cal Ripken, 1984	9.0
Jackie Robinson, 1951	7.5
Frank Robinson, 1962	6.3
Frank Robinson, 1966	6.5
Babe Ruth, 1919	7.1
Babe Ruth, 1920	8.8
Babe Ruth, 1921	9.9
Babe Ruth, 1923	9.0
Babe Ruth, 1924	8.3
Babe Ruth, 1926	7.8
Babe Ruth, 1927	8.5
Babe Ruth, 1928	7.0
Babe Ruth, 1930	7.7
Babe Ruth, 1931	6.4
Ryne Sandberg, 1984	6.5
Ron Santo, 1966	7.6
Ron Santo, 1967	7.0
Mike Schmidt, 1974	7.0
Mike Schmidt, 1977	7.2
Mike Schmidt, 1980	7.4
Mike Schmidt, 1981	6.6
Mike Schmidt, 1982	6.8
George Sisler, 1920	7.7
Tris Speaker, 1912	7.3
Tris Speaker, 1913	7.1
Tris Speaker, 1914	7.0
Snuffy Stirnweiss, 1944	6.6
Snuffy Stirnweiss, 1945	6.4
Arky Vaughan, 1938	6.4
Honus Wagner, 1905	7.0
Honus Wagner, 1906	6.6
Honus Wagner, 1908	6.8
Honus Wagner, 1912	6.3
Ted Williams, 1941	8.0
Ted Williams, 1942	8.3
Ted Williams, 1946	7.7
Ted Williams, 1947	8.1
Ted Williams, 1948	6.6
Ted Williams, 1949	7.5
Ted Williams, 1957	6.7
Carl Yastrzemski, 1967	7.2
Carl Yastrzemski, 1968	7.0
Robin Yount, 1982	6.6

Total Player Rating (by era)

1876-1892

1	Fred Dunlap, 1884	7.6
2	Cupid Childs, 1890	6.1
3	Fred Pfeffer, 1884	5.8
4	Bill Dahlen, 1892	5.5
5	Tip O'Neill, 1887	5.2
6	Dan Brouthers, 1892	5.1
7	Jack Glasscock, 1889	4.9
	Harry Stovey, 1889	4.9
9	Hub Collins, 1888	4.8
10	King Kelly, 1886	4.7
	Bid McPhee, 1886	4.7
	Herman Long, 1889	4.7
13	Sam Barkley, 1884	4.6
14	6 players tied	4.5

1893-1919

1	Nap Lajoie, 1910	8.9
2	Nap Lajoie, 1903	7.9
	Ty Cobb, 1917	7.9
4	Nap Lajoie, 1901	7.4
5	Nap Lajoie, 1904	7.3
	Tris Speaker, 1912	7.3
7	Tris Speaker, 1913	7.1
	Babe Ruth, 1919	7.1
9	Honus Wagner, 1905	7.0
	Tris Speaker, 1914	7.0
11	Ty Cobb, 1909	6.9
	Joe Jackson, 1912	6.9
13	Nap Lajoie, 1906	6.8
	Honus Wagner, 1908	6.8
	Nap Lajoie, 1908	6.8

1920-1941

1	Babe Ruth, 1921	9.9
2	Babe Ruth, 1923	9.0
3	Babe Ruth, 1920	8.8
4	Babe Ruth, 1927	8.5
5	Babe Ruth, 1924	8.3
6	Lou Gehrig, 1927	8.2
7	Rogers Hornsby, 1920	8.0
	Ted Williams, 1941	8.0
9	Babe Ruth, 1926	7.8
10	George Sisler, 1920	7.7
	Babe Ruth, 1930	7.7
12	Jimmie Foxx, 1933	7.6
13	Rogers Hornsby, 1921	7.2
	Rogers Hornsby, 1922	7.2
	Chuck Klein, 1930	7.2

1942-1960

1	Ted Williams, 1942	8.3
2	Ted Williams, 1947	8.1
	Stan Musial, 1948	8.1
	Mickey Mantle, 1957	8.1
5	Willie Mays, 1955	7.8
6	Ted Williams, 1946	7.7
7	Mickey Mantle, 1956	7.6
8	Ted Williams, 1949	7.5
	Jackie Robinson, 1951	7.5
10	Stan Musial, 1951	7.0
11	Lou Boudreau, 1944	6.8
12	Ted Williams, 1957	6.7
13	Snuffy Stirnweiss, 1944	6.6
	Ted Williams, 1948	6.6
15	Eddie Lake, 1945	6.5

1961-1989

1	Cal Ripken, 1984	9.0
2	Joe Morgan, 1975	8.0
3	Norm Cash, 1961	7.6
	Ron Santo, 1966	7.6
5	Mike Schmidt, 1980	7.4
	Rickey Henderson, 1985	7.4
7	Carl Yastrzemski, 1967	7.2
	Mike Schmidt, 1977	7.2
9	Rod Carew, 1974	7.1
10	Mickey Mantle, 1961	7.0
	Ron Santo, 1967	7.0
	Carl Yastrzemski, 1968	7.0
	Mike Schmidt, 1974	7.0
	George Brett, 1985	7.0
15	Reggie Jackson, 1969	6.9

Wins

1	Charley Radbourn, 1884	60
2	John Clarkson, 1885	53
3	Guy Hecker, 1884	52
4	John Clarkson, 1889	49
5	Charley Radbourn, 1883	48
	Charlie Buffinton, 1884	48
7	Al Spalding, 1876	47
	Monte Ward, 1879	47
9	Jim Galvin, 1883	46
	Jim Galvin, 1884	46
	Matt Kilroy, 1887	46
12	George Bradley, 1876	45
	Jim McCormick, 1880	45
	Silver King, 1888	45
15	Mickey Welch, 1885	44
	Bill Hutchinson, 1891	44
17	Tommy Bond, 1879	43
	Will White, 1879	43
	Larry Corcoran, 1880	43
	Will White, 1883	43
21	Lady Baldwin, 1886	42
	Tim Keefe, 1886	42
	Bill Hutchinson, 1890	42
24	Tim Keefe, 1883	41
	Dave Foutz, 1886	41
	Ed Morris, 1886	41
	Jack Chesbro, 1904	41
28	Tommy Bond, 1877	40
	Tommy Bond, 1878	40
	Will White, 1882	40
	Bill Sweeney, 1884	40
	Bob Caruthers, 1885	40
	Bob Caruthers, 1889	40
	Ed Walsh, 1908	40
35	Monte Ward, 1880	39
	Mickey Welch, 1884	39
	Ed Morris, 1885	39
38	Toad Ramsey, 1886	38
	John Clarkson, 1887	38
	Kid Gleason, 1890	38
41	Jim Galvin, 1879	37
	Jim Whitney, 1883	37
	Tim Keefe, 1884	37
	Jack Lynch, 1884	37
	Tony Mullane, 1884	37
	Toad Ramsey, 1887	37
	Bill Hutchinson, 1892	37
	Christy Mathewson, 1908	37
49	Jim McCormick, 1882	36
	John Clarkson, 1886	36
	Sadie McMahon, 1890	36
	Cy Young, 1892	36
	Amos Rusie, 1894	36
	Walter Johnson, 1913	36
55	Jim Devlin, 1877	35
	Tony Mullane, 1883	35
	Larry Corcoran, 1884	35
	Tim Keefe, 1887	35
	Tim Keefe, 1888	35
	Ed Seward, 1888	35
	Silver King, 1889	35
	Kid Nichols, 1892	35
	Jack Stivetts, 1892	35
	Cy Young, 1895	35
	Joe McGinnity, 1904	35
66	Mickey Welch, 1880	34
	Larry Corcoran, 1883	34
	Ed Morris, 1884	34
	Will White, 1884	34
	Mike Smith, 1887	34
	Scott Stratton, 1890	34
	Mark Baldwin, 1890	34
	George Haddock, 1891	34
	Sadie McMahon, 1891	34
	Frank Killen, 1893	34
	Kid Nichols, 1893	34
	Cy Young, 1893	34
	Joe Wood, 1912	34
79	Charley Radbourn, 1882	33
	Dave Foutz, 1885	33
	Henry Porter, 1885	33
	Mickey Welch, 1886	33
	Tony Mullane, 1886	33
	John Clarkson, 1888	33
	John Clarkson, 1891	33
	Amos Rusie, 1891	33
	Jack Stivetts, 1891	33
	Amos Rusie, 1893	33
	Jouett Meekin, 1894	33
	Cy Young, 1901	33
	Christy Mathewson, 1904	33
	Walter Johnson, 1912	33
	Pete Alexander, 1916	33
94	9 players tied	32

Wins (by era)

1876-1892

1	Charley Radbourn, 1884	60
2	John Clarkson, 1885	53
3	Guy Hecker, 1884	52
4	John Clarkson, 1889	49
5	Charley Radbourn, 1883	48
	Charlie Buffinton, 1884	48
7	Al Spalding, 1876	47
	Monte Ward, 1879	47
9	Jim Galvin, 1883	46
	Jim Galvin, 1884	46
	Matt Kilroy, 1887	46
12	George Bradley, 1876	45
	Jim McCormick, 1880	45
	Silver King, 1888	45
15	2 players tied	44

1893-1919

1	Jack Chesbro, 1904	41
2	Ed Walsh, 1908	40
3	Christy Mathewson, 1908	37
4	Amos Rusie, 1894	36
	Walter Johnson, 1913	36
6	Cy Young, 1895	35
	Joe McGinnity, 1904	35
8	Frank Killen, 1893	34
	Kid Nichols, 1893	34
	Cy Young, 1893	34
	Joe Wood, 1912	34
12	6 players tied	33

1920-1941

1	Jim Bagby, 1920	31
	Lefty Grove, 1931	31
3	Dizzy Dean, 1934	30
4	Dazzy Vance, 1924	28
	Lefty Grove, 1930	28
	Dizzy Dean, 1935	28
7	Pete Alexander, 1920	27
	Carl Mays, 1921	27
	Urban Shocker, 1921	27
	Eddie Rommel, 1922	27
	Dolf Luque, 1923	27
	George Uhle, 1926	27
	Bucky Walters, 1939	27
	Bob Feller, 1940	27
15	7 players tied	26

1942-1960

1	Hal Newhouser, 1944	29
2	Robin Roberts, 1952	28
3	Dizzy Trout, 1944	27
	Don Newcombe, 1956	27
5	Hal Newhouser, 1946	26
	Bob Feller, 1946	26
7	Hal Newhouser, 1945	25
	Dave Ferriss, 1946	25
	Mel Parnell, 1949	25
10	Johnny Sain, 1948	24
	Bobby Shantz, 1952	24
12	13 players tied	23

1961-1989

1	Denny McLain, 1968	31
2	Sandy Koufax, 1966	27
	Steve Carlton, 1972	27
4	Sandy Koufax, 1965	26
	Juan Marichal, 1968	26
6	12 players tied	25

Losses

1	John Coleman, 1883	48
2	Will White, 1880	42
3	Larry McKeon, 1884	41
4	George Bradley, 1879	40
	Jim McCormick, 1879	40
6	Henry Porter, 1888	37
	Kid Carsey, 1891	37
	George Cobb, 1892	37
9	Stump Weidman, 1886	36
	Bill Hutchinson, 1892	36
11	Jim Devlin, 1876	35
	Jim Galvin, 1880	35
	Fleury Sullivan, 1884	35
	Adonis Terry, 1884	35
	Hardie Henderson, 1885	35
	Red Donahue, 1897	35
17	Bobby Mathews, 1876	34
	Bob Barr, 1884	34
	Matt Kilroy, 1886	34
	Al Mays, 1887	34
	Mark Baldwin, 1889	34
	Amos Rusie, 1890	34
23	Harry McCormick, 1879	33
	Jim Whitney, 1881	33
	Lee Richmond, 1882	33
	Frank Mountain, 1883	33
	Jersey Bakely, 1888	33
28	Lee Richmond, 1880	32
	Hardie Henderson, 1883	32
	John Harkins, 1884	32
	Jim Whitney, 1885	32
	Jim Whitney, 1886	32
33	Sam Weaver, 1878	31
	Will White, 1879	31
	Charley Radbourn, 1886	31
	Dupee Shaw, 1886	31
	Billy Crowell, 1887	31
	Ed Beatin, 1890	31
	Amos Rusie, 1892	31
40	Mickey Welch, 1880	30
	Jim McCormick, 1881	30
	Jim McCormick, 1882	30
	Jack Lynch, 1886	30
	Phenomenal Smith, 1887	30
	Toad Ramsey, 1888	30
	John Ewing, 1889	30
	Ted Breitenstein, 1895	30
	Jim Hughey, 1899	30
49	Tommy Bond, 1880	29
	Jim Galvin, 1883	29
	Egyptian Healy, 1887	29
	Hank O'Day, 1888	29
	Bert Cunningham, 1888	29
	Red Ehret, 1889	29
	Silver King, 1891	29
	Bill Hart, 1896	29
	Jack Taylor, 1898	29
	Vic Willis, 1905	29
59	Jim McCormick, 1880	28
	Doc Landis, 1882	28
	Hank O'Day, 1884	28
	Hugh Daily, 1884	28
	Al Mays, 1886	28
	Gus Weyhing, 1887	28
	Mark Baldwin, 1891	28
	Duke Esper, 1893	28
	Bill Hill, 1896	28
68	Jim Galvin, 1879	27
	Tim Keefe, 1881	27
	Tim Keefe, 1883	27
	Jersey Bakely, 1884	27
	Charlie Buffinton, 1885	27
	Tony Mullane, 1886	27
	Toad Ramsey, 1886	27
	Toad Ramsey, 1887	27
	Park Swartzel, 1889	27
	Phil Knell, 1891	27
	Mark Baldwin, 1892	27
	Pink Hawley, 1894	27
	Chick Fraser, 1896	27
	Bill Hart, 1897	27
	Willie Sudhoff, 1898	27
	Bill Carrick, 1899	27
	Dummy Taylor, 1901	27
	George Bell, 1910	27
	Paul Derringer, 1933	27
87	18 players tied	26

Winning Percentage

1	Roy Face, 1959	.947
2	Rick Sutcliffe, 1984	.941
3	Ron Guidry, 1978	.893
4	Freddie Fitzsimmons, 1940	.889
5	Lefty Grove, 1931	.886
6	Preacher Roe, 1951	.880
7	Fred Goldsmith, 1880	.875
	Jim McCormick, 1884	.875
9	Joe Wood, 1912	.872
10	David Cone, 1988	.870
11	Orel Hershiser, 1985	.864
12	Billy Taylor, 1884	.862
	Bill Donovan, 1907	.862
	Whitey Ford, 1961	.862
15	Dwight Gooden, 1985	.857
	Roger Clemens, 1986	.857
17	Chief Bender, 1914	.850
18	Lefty Grove, 1930	.848
19	Tom Hughes, 1916	.842
	Emil Yde, 1924	.842
	Schoolboy Rowe, 1940	.842
	Sandy Consuegra, 1954	.842
	Ralph Terry, 1961	.842
	Ron Perranoski, 1963	.842
25	Lefty Gomez, 1934	.839
26	Bill Hoffer, 1895	.838
	Denny McLain, 1968	.838
28	Walter Johnson, 1913	.837
29	Charley Radbourn, 1884	.833
	King Cole, 1910	.833
	Spud Chandler, 1943	.833
	Sandy Koufax, 1963	.833
33	Ed Reulbach, 1906	.826
	Elmer Riddle, 1941	.826
35	Jim Hughes, 1899	.824
	Jack Chesbro, 1902	.824
	Dazzy Vance, 1924	.824
38	Chief Bender, 1910	.821
	Bob Purkey, 1962	.821
40	Sal Maglie, 1950	.818
41	Joe McGinnity, 1904	.814
42	Mordecai Brown, 1906	.813
	Russ Ford, 1910	.813
	Eddie Plank, 1912	.813
	Carl Hubbell, 1936	.813
46	Dizzy Dean, 1934	.811
47	Ed Reulbach, 1907	.810
	Doc Crandall, 1910	.810
	Johnny Allen, 1932	.810
	Ted Wilks, 1944	.810
	Phil Niekro, 1982	.810
52	General Crowder, 1928	.808
	Bobo Newsom, 1940	.808
	Tiny Bonham, 1942	.808
	Larry Jansen, 1947	.808
	Dave McNally, 1971	.808
	Jim Hunter, 1973	.808
58	Christy Mathewson, 1909	.806
	Howie Camnitz, 1909	.806
	Dave Ferriss, 1946	.806
	Juan Marichal, 1966	.806
62	Eddie Cicotte, 1919	.806
63	Mickey Welch, 1885	.800
	Ed Doheny, 1902	.800
	Sam Leever, 1905	.800
	Bert Humphries, 1913	.800
	Stan Coveleski, 1925	.800
	Firpo Marberry, 1931	.800
	Robin Roberts, 1952	.800
	Eddie Lopat, 1953	.800
	Don Newcombe, 1955	.800
	Jim Palmer, 1969	.800
	John Candelaria, 1977	.800
	Larry Gura, 1978	.800
75	Al Spalding, 1876	.797
76	Christy Mathewson, 1905	.795
77	Don Newcombe, 1956	.794
78	Jocko Flynn, 1886	.793
	Ellis Kinder, 1949	.793
	Sal Maglie, 1951	.793
	Bret Saberhagen, 1989	.793
82	Dutch Leonard, 1914	.792
	Sandy Koufax, 1964	.792
	Wally Bunker, 1964	.792
85	Fred Klobedanz, 1897	.788
	Bill James, 1914	.788
	Joe Bush, 1922	.788
88	Jouett Meekin, 1894	.786
	Lon Warneke, 1932	.786
	Tex Hughson, 1942	.786
	Ron Guidry, 1985	.786
92	Bob Caruthers, 1889	.784
93	George Mullin, 1909	.784
94	8 players tied	.783

Winning Percentage (by era)

1876-1892
1	Fred Goldsmith, 1880	.875
	Jim McCormick, 1884	.875
3	Billy Taylor, 1884	.862
4	Charley Radbourn, 1884	.833
5	Mickey Welch, 1885	.800
6	Al Spalding, 1876	.797
7	Jocko Flynn, 1886	.793
8	Bob Caruthers, 1889	.784
9	Manning, 1876	.783
10	Charlie Sweeney, 1884	.774
11	Will White, 1882	.769
	Charlie Ferguson, 1886	.769
13	John Clarkson, 1885	.768
14	Lady Baldwin, 1886	.764
15	2 players tied	.763

1893-1919
1	Joe Wood, 1912	.872
2	Bill Donovan, 1907	.862
3	Chief Bender, 1914	.850
4	Tom Hughes, 1916	.842
5	Bill Hoffer, 1895	.838
6	Walter Johnson, 1913	.837
7	King Cole, 1910	.833
8	Ed Reulbach, 1906	.826
9	Jim Hughes, 1899	.824
	Jack Chesbro, 1902	.824
11	Chief Bender, 1910	.821
12	Joe McGinnity, 1904	.814
13	Mordecai Brown, 1906	.813
	Russ Ford, 1910	.813
	Eddie Plank, 1912	.813

1920-1941
1	Freddie Fitzsimmons, 1940	.889
2	Lefty Grove, 1931	.886
3	Lefty Grove, 1930	.848
4	Emil Yde, 1924	.842
	Schoolboy Rowe, 1940	.842
6	Lefty Gomez, 1934	.839
7	Elmer Riddle, 1941	.826
8	Dazzy Vance, 1924	.824
9	Carl Hubbell, 1936	.813
10	Dizzy Dean, 1934	.811
11	Johnny Allen, 1932	.810
12	General Crowder, 1928	.808
	Bobo Newsom, 1940	.808
14	Stan Coveleski, 1925	.800
	Firpo Marberry, 1931	.800

1942-1960
1	Roy Face, 1959	.947
2	Preacher Roe, 1951	.880
3	Sandy Consuegra, 1954	.842
4	Spud Chandler, 1943	.833
5	Sal Maglie, 1950	.818
6	Ted Wilks, 1944	.810
7	Tiny Bonham, 1942	.808
	Larry Jansen, 1947	.808
9	Dave Ferriss, 1946	.806
10	Robin Roberts, 1952	.800
	Eddie Lopat, 1953	.800
	Don Newcombe, 1955	.800
13	Don Newcombe, 1956	.794
14	Ellis Kinder, 1949	.793
	Sal Maglie, 1951	.793

1961-1989
1	Rick Sutcliffe, 1984	.941
2	Ron Guidry, 1978	.893
3	David Cone, 1988	.870
4	Orel Hershiser, 1985	.864
5	Whitey Ford, 1961	.862
6	Dwight Gooden, 1985	.857
	Roger Clemens, 1986	.857
8	Ralph Terry, 1961	.842
	Ron Perranoski, 1963	.842
10	Denny McLain, 1968	.838
11	Sandy Koufax, 1963	.833
12	Bob Purkey, 1962	.821
13	Phil Niekro, 1982	.810
14	Dave McNally, 1971	.808
	Jim Hunter, 1973	.808

Games

1	Mike Marshall, 1974	106
2	Kent Tekulve, 1979	94
3	Mike Marshall, 1973	92
4	Kent Tekulve, 1978	91
5	Wayne Granger, 1969	90
	Mike Marshall, 1979	90
	Kent Tekulve, 1987	90
8	Mark Eichhorn, 1987	89
9	Wilbur Wood, 1968	88
10	Rob Murphy, 1987	87
11	Kent Tekulve, 1982	85
	Frank Williams, 1987	85
	Mitch Williams, 1987	85
14	Ted Abernathy, 1965	84
	Enrique Romo, 1979	84
	Dick Tidrow, 1980	84
	Dan Quisenberry, 1985	84
18	Ken Sanders, 1971	83
	Craig Lefferts, 1986	83
20	Eddie Fisher, 1965	82
	Bill Campbell, 1983	82
22	John Wyatt, 1964	81
	Dale Murray, 1976	81
	Jeff Robinson, 1987	81
25	Pedro Borbon, 1973	80
	Willie Hernandez, 1984	80
	Mitch Williams, 1986	80
28	Dick Radatz, 1964	79
29	Hal Woodeshick, 1965	78
	Ted Abernathy, 1968	78
	Bill Campbell, 1976	78
	Rollie Fingers, 1977	78
	Tom Hume, 1980	78
	Kent Tekulve, 1980	78
	Greg Minton, 1982	78
	Ed Vande Berg, 1982	78
	Ted Power, 1984	78
	Tim Burke, 1985	78
	Lance McCullers, 1987	78
40	Bob Locker, 1967	77
	Wilbur Wood, 1970	77
	Charlie Hough, 1976	77
	Butch Metzger, 1976	77
	Rick Camp, 1980	77
	Gary Lavelle, 1984	77
	Mark Davis, 1985	77
	Craig Lefferts, 1987	77
48	Will White, 1879	76
	Jim Galvin, 1883	76
	Charley Radbourn, 1883	76
	Wilbur Wood, 1969	76
	Ron Herbel, 1970	76
	Larry Hardy, 1974	76
	Rollie Fingers, 1974	76
	Dan Spillner, 1977	76
	Dave Tomlin, 1977	76
	Sid Monge, 1979	76
	Rod Scurry, 1982	76
	Tippy Martinez, 1982	76
	Kent Tekulve, 1983	76
	Ed Vande Berg, 1985	76
	Rob Murphy, 1988	76
	Mitch Williams, 1989	76
	Chuck Crim, 1989	76
65	Charley Radbourn, 1884	75
	Guy Hecker, 1884	75
	Bill Hutchinson, 1892	75
	Ron Perranoski, 1969	75
	Rollie Fingers, 1975	75
	Butch Metzger, 1977	75
	Dan Quisenberry, 1980	75
	Willie Hernandez, 1982	75
	Jeff Reardon, 1982	75
	Roger McDowell, 1986	75
	Todd Worrell, 1987	75
	Juan Agosto, 1988	75
	Jeff Robinson, 1988	75
78	Jim McCormick, 1880	74
	Lee Richmond, 1880	74
	Jim Konstanty, 1950	74
	Bob Miller, 1964	74
	Ron Kline, 1965	74
	Dan McGinn, 1969	74
	Bob Lacey, 1978	74
	Enrique Romo, 1980	74
	Willie Hernandez, 1983	74
	Greg Minton, 1984	74
	Scott Garrelts, 1985	74
	Willie Hernandez, 1985	74
	Dave Righetti, 1985	74
	Johnny Franco, 1986	74
	Todd Worrell, 1986	74
	Dave Righetti, 1986	74
	Dale Mohorcic, 1987	74
	Rob Dibble, 1989	74
	Rob Murphy, 1989	74
97	14 players tied	73

Games (by era)

1876-1892
1	Will White, 1879	76
	Jim Galvin, 1883	76
	Charley Radbourn, 1883	76
4	Charley Radbourn, 1884	75
	Guy Hecker, 1884	75
	Bill Hutchinson, 1892	75
7	Jim McCormick, 1880	74
	Lee Richmond, 1880	74
9	John Clarkson, 1889	73
10	Jim Galvin, 1884	72
11	Bill Hutchinson, 1890	71
12	Monte Ward, 1879	70
	Monte Ward, 1880	70
	John Clarkson, 1885	70
15	Matt Kilroy, 1887	69

1893-1919
1	Ed Walsh, 1908	66
2	Ed Walsh, 1912	62
3	Dave Davenport, 1916	59
4	Amos Rusie, 1893	56
	Ted Breitenstein, 1894	56
	Pink Hawley, 1895	56
	Ed Walsh, 1907	56
	Christy Mathewson, 1908	56
	Ed Walsh, 1911	56
	Reb Russell, 1916	56
11	Frank Killen, 1893	55
	Joe McGinnity, 1903	55
	Jack Chesbro, 1904	55
	Dave Davenport, 1915	55
15	3 players tied	54

1920-1941
1	Firpo Marberry, 1926	64
2	Clint Brown, 1939	61
3	Garland Braxton, 1927	58
	Russ VanAtta, 1935	58
5	Eddie Rommel, 1923	56
	Firpo Marberry, 1927	56
	Hugh Mulcahy, 1937	56
8	Firpo Marberry, 1925	55
	Bump Hadley, 1931	55
	Jim Walkup, 1935	55
11	George Uhle, 1923	54
	Firpo Marberry, 1932	54
	Jack Russell, 1934	54
	Chubby Dean, 1939	54
	Clyde Shoun, 1940	54

1942-1960
1	Jim Konstanty, 1950	74
2	Hoyt Wilhelm, 1952	71
3	Ace Adams, 1943	70
	Mike Fornieles, 1960	70
5	Ellis Kinder, 1953	69
	Don Elston, 1958	69
7	Hoyt Wilhelm, 1953	68
	Roy Face, 1956	68
	Roy Face, 1960	68
10	Andy Karl, 1945	67
	Turk Lown, 1957	67
	Gerry Staley, 1959	67
13	6 players tied	65

1961-1989
1	Mike Marshall, 1974	106
2	Kent Tekulve, 1979	94
3	Mike Marshall, 1973	92
4	Kent Tekulve, 1978	91
5	Wayne Granger, 1969	90
	Mike Marshall, 1979	90
	Kent Tekulve, 1987	90
8	Mark Eichhorn, 1987	89
9	Wilbur Wood, 1968	88
10	Rob Murphy, 1987	87
11	Kent Tekulve, 1982	85
	Frank Williams, 1987	85
	Mitch Williams, 1987	85
14	4 players tied	84

Games Started

1	Will White, 1879	75
	Jim Galvin, 1883	75
3	Jim McCormick, 1880	74
4	Charley Radbourn, 1884	73
	Guy Hecker, 1884	73
6	Jim Galvin, 1884	72
	John Clarkson, 1889	72
8	Bill Hutchinson, 1892	71
9	John Clarkson, 1885	70
10	Matt Kilroy, 1887	69
11	Jim Devlin, 1876	68
	Charley Radbourn, 1883	68
	Tim Keefe, 1883	68
	Matt Kilroy, 1886	68
15	Monte Ward, 1880	67
	Jim McCormick, 1882	67
	Charlie Buffinton, 1884	67
	Toad Ramsey, 1886	67
19	Jim Galvin, 1879	66
	Lee Richmond, 1880	66
	Tony Mullane, 1884	66
	Bill Hutchinson, 1890	66
23	Mickey Welch, 1884	65
	Silver King, 1888	65
25	George Bradley, 1876	64
	Tommy Bond, 1879	64
	Mickey Welch, 1880	64
	Will White, 1883	64
	Tim Keefe, 1886	64
	Toad Ramsey, 1887	64
31	Jim Whitney, 1881	63
	Ed Morris, 1885	63
	Ed Morris, 1886	63
	Amos Rusie, 1890	63
35	Will White, 1880	62
36	Jim Devlin, 1877	61
	John Coleman, 1883	61
	Hardie Henderson, 1885	61
	Jersey Bakely, 1888	61
	Amos Rusie, 1892	61
41	Al Spalding, 1876	60
	Jim McCormick, 1879	60
	Monte Ward, 1879	60
	Larry Corcoran, 1880	60
	Larry McKeon, 1884	60
	Bill Sweeney, 1884	60
47	Tommy Bond, 1878	59
	Frank Mountain, 1883	59
	Larry Corcoran, 1884	59
	Mickey Welch, 1886	59
	John Clarkson, 1887	59
	Mark Baldwin, 1889	59
53	Tommy Bond, 1877	58
	Terry Larkin, 1879	58
	Jim McCormick, 1881	58
	Tim Keefe, 1884	58
	Hugh Daily, 1884	58
	Charley Radbourn, 1886	58
	Bill Hutchinson, 1891	58
	Sadie McMahon, 1891	58
61	Tommy Bond, 1880	57
	Dave Foutz, 1886	57
	Ed Seward, 1888	57
	Sadie McMahon, 1890	57
	Mark Baldwin, 1890	57
	Amos Rusie, 1891	57
67	Bobby Mathews, 1876	56
	Terry Larkin, 1877	56
	Terry Larkin, 1878	56
	Jim Whitney, 1883	56
	Adonis Terry, 1884	56
	Lady Baldwin, 1886	56
	Tony Mullane, 1886	56
	Tim Keefe, 1887	56
	Matt Kilroy, 1889	56
	Silver King, 1890	56
	Jack Stivetts, 1891	56
78	George Derby, 1881	55
	Tony Mullane, 1882	55
	Mickey Welch, 1885	55
	John Clarkson, 1886	55
	Phenomenal Smith, 1887	55
	Gus Weyhing, 1887	55
	Ed Morris, 1888	55
	Kid Gleason, 1890	55
86	George Bradley, 1879	54
	Harry McCormick, 1879	54
	Jim Galvin, 1880	54
	Will White, 1882	54
	John Clarkson, 1888	54
	Henry Porter, 1885	54
	Henry Porter, 1888	54
	Ed Beatin, 1890	54
	Bob Barr, 1890	54
95	9 players tied	53

Games Started (by era)

1876-1892

1	Will White, 1879	75
	Jim Galvin, 1883	75
3	Jim McCormick, 1880	74
4	Charley Radbourn, 1884	73
	Guy Hecker, 1884	73
6	Jim Galvin, 1884	72
	John Clarkson, 1889	72
8	Bill Hutchinson, 1892	71
9	John Clarkson, 1885	70
10	Matt Kilroy, 1887	69
11	Jim Devlin, 1876	68
	Charley Radbourn, 1883	68
	Tim Keefe, 1883	68
	Matt Kilroy, 1886	68
15	4 players tied	67

1893-1919

1	Amos Rusie, 1893	52
2	Jack Chesbro, 1904	51
3	Ted Breitenstein, 1894	50
	Amos Rusie, 1894	50
	Ted Breitenstein, 1895	50
	Pink Hawley, 1895	50
	Frank Killen, 1896	50
8	Ed Walsh, 1908	49
9	Frank Killen, 1893	48
	Jouett Meekin, 1894	48
	Joe McGinnity, 1903	48
12	Cy Young, 1894	47
	Amos Rusie, 1895	47
	Jack Taylor, 1898	47
15	8 players tied	46

1920-1941

1	George Uhle, 1923	44
2	Pete Alexander, 1920	40
	Stan Coveleski, 1921	40
	George Uhle, 1922	40
	George Caster, 1938	40
	Bobo Newsom, 1938	40
	Bob Feller, 1941	40
8	Red Faber, 1920	39
	Red Faber, 1921	39
	Hooks Dauss, 1923	39
	Howard Ehmke, 1923	39
	George Earnshaw, 1930	39
	General Crowder, 1932	39
	Kirby Higbe, 1941	39
15	24 players tied	38

1942-1960

1	Bob Feller, 1946	42
	Bob Friend, 1956	42
3	Bill Voiselle, 1944	41
	Robin Roberts, 1953	41
5	Dizzy Trout, 1944	40
6	Johnny Sain, 1948	39
	Robin Roberts, 1950	39
	Warren Spahn, 1950	39
	Vern Bickford, 1950	39
	Robin Roberts, 1951	39
	Ron Kline, 1956	39
	Lew Burdette, 1959	39
13	10 players tied	38

1961-1989

1	Wilbur Wood, 1972	49
2	Wilbur Wood, 1973	48
3	Mickey Lolich, 1971	45
4	Phil Niekro, 1979	44
5	Wilbur Wood, 1975	43
	Phil Niekro, 1977	43
7	10 players tied	42

Complete Games

1	Will White, 1879	75
2	Charley Radbourn, 1884	73
3	Jim McCormick, 1880	72
	Jim Galvin, 1883	72
	Guy Hecker, 1884	72
6	Jim Galvin, 1884	71
7	Tim Keefe, 1883	68
	John Clarkson, 1885	68
	John Clarkson, 1889	68
10	Bill Hutchinson, 1892	67
11	Jim Devlin, 1876	66
	Charley Radbourn, 1883	66
	Matt Kilroy, 1886	66
	Toad Ramsey, 1886	66
	Matt Kilroy, 1887	66
16	Jim Galvin, 1879	65
	Jim McCormick, 1882	65
	Tony Mullane, 1884	65
	Bill Hutchinson, 1890	65
20	Mickey Welch, 1880	64
	Will White, 1883	64
	Silver King, 1888	64
23	George Bradley, 1876	63
	Charlie Buffinton, 1884	63
	Ed Morris, 1885	63
	Ed Morris, 1886	63
27	Mickey Welch, 1884	62
	Tim Keefe, 1886	62
29	Jim Devlin, 1877	61
	Toad Ramsey, 1887	61
31	Tommy Bond, 1879	60
	Jersey Bakely, 1888	60
33	Jim McCormick, 1879	59
	Monte Ward, 1880	59
	John Coleman, 1883	59
	Larry McKeon, 1884	59
	Hardie Henderson, 1885	59
38	Tommy Bond, 1877	58
	Monte Ward, 1879	58
	Will White, 1880	58
	Bill Sweeney, 1884	58
	Amos Rusie, 1892	58
43	Tommy Bond, 1878	57
	Terry Larkin, 1879	57
	Larry Corcoran, 1880	57
	Lee Richmond, 1880	57
	Jim McCormick, 1881	57
	Jim Whitney, 1881	57
	Frank Mountain, 1883	57
	Larry Corcoran, 1884	57
	Tim Keefe, 1884	57
	Charley Radbourn, 1886	57
	Ed Seward, 1888	57
54	Terry Larkin, 1878	56
	Hugh Daily, 1884	56
	Mickey Welch, 1886	56
	John Clarkson, 1887	56
	Amos Rusie, 1890	56
	Bill Hutchinson, 1891	56
60	Bobby Mathews, 1876	55
	Terry Larkin, 1877	55
	George Derby, 1881	55
	Adonis Terry, 1884	55
	Mickey Welch, 1885	55
	Lady Baldwin, 1886	55
	Dave Foutz, 1886	55
	Tony Mullane, 1886	55
	Matt Kilroy, 1889	55
	Sadie McMahon, 1890	55
70	Al Spalding, 1876	54
	Jim Whitney, 1883	54
	Tim Keefe, 1887	54
	Phenomenal Smith, 1887	54
	Ed Morris, 1888	54
	Mark Baldwin, 1889	54
	Kid Gleason, 1890	54
	Mark Baldwin, 1890	54
78	George Bradley, 1879	53
	Jack Lynch, 1884	53
	Bob Caruthers, 1885	53
	Henry Porter, 1885	53
	Gus Weyhing, 1887	53
	John Clarkson, 1888	53
	Henry Porter, 1888	53
	Ed Beatin, 1890	53
	Sadie McMahon, 1891	53
87	Will White, 1878	52
	Will White, 1882	52
	Will White, 1884	52
	Ed Seward, 1887	52
	Bob Barr, 1890	52
	Amos Rusie, 1891	52
93	Charley Radbourn, 1882	51
	Tony Mullane, 1882	51
	Larry Corcoran, 1883	51
	Fleury Sullivan, 1884	51
	Guy Hecker, 1885	51
	Tim Keefe, 1888	51
	Gus Weyhing, 1891	51
100	11 players tied	50

Complete Games (by era)

1876-1892

1	Will White, 1879	75
2	Charley Radbourn, 1884	73
3	Jim McCormick, 1880	72
	Jim Galvin, 1883	72
	Guy Hecker, 1884	72
6	Jim Galvin, 1884	71
7	Tim Keefe, 1883	68
	John Clarkson, 1885	68
	John Clarkson, 1889	68
10	Bill Hutchinson, 1892	67
11	Jim Devlin, 1876	66
	Charley Radbourn, 1883	66
	Matt Kilroy, 1886	66
	Toad Ramsey, 1886	66
	Matt Kilroy, 1887	66

1893-1919

1	Amos Rusie, 1893	50
2	Jack Chesbro, 1904	48
3	Ted Breitenstein, 1894	46
	Ted Breitenstein, 1895	46
5	Amos Rusie, 1894	45
	Vic Willis, 1902	45
7	Kid Nichols, 1893	44
	Cy Young, 1894	44
	Pink Hawley, 1895	44
	Frank Killen, 1896	44
	Joe McGinnity, 1903	44
12	7 players tied	42

1920-1941

1	Pete Alexander, 1920	33
	Burleigh Grimes, 1923	33
3	Red Faber, 1921	32
	George Uhle, 1926	32
5	Red Faber, 1922	31
	Wes Ferrell, 1935	31
	Bobo Newsom, 1938	31
	Bucky Walters, 1939	31
	Bob Feller, 1940	31
10	8 players tied	30

1942-1960

1	Bob Feller, 1946	36
2	Dizzy Trout, 1944	33
	Robin Roberts, 1953	33
4	Robin Roberts, 1952	30
5	Hal Newhouser, 1945	29
	Hal Newhouser, 1946	29
	Robin Roberts, 1954	29
8	Jim Tobin, 1942	28
	Jim Tobin, 1944	28
	Johnny Sain, 1948	28
	Bob Lemon, 1952	28
12	Bucky Walters, 1944	27
	Mel Parnell, 1949	27
	Vern Bickford, 1950	27
	Bobby Shantz, 1952	27

1961-1989

1	Juan Marichal, 1968	30
	Ferguson Jenkins, 1971	30
	Steve Carlton, 1972	30
	Jim Hunter, 1975	30
5	Mickey Lolich, 1971	29
	Gaylord Perry, 1972	29
	Gaylord Perry, 1973	29
	Ferguson Jenkins, 1974	29
9	Bob Gibson, 1968	28
	Denny McLain, 1968	28
	Bob Gibson, 1969	28
	Gaylord Perry, 1974	28
	Rick Langford, 1980	28
14	4 players tied	27

Shutouts

1	George Bradley, 1876	16
	Pete Alexander, 1916	16
3	Jack Coombs, 1910	13
	Bob Gibson, 1968	13
5	Tommy Bond, 1879	12
	Jim Galvin, 1884	12
	Ed Morris, 1886	12
	Pete Alexander, 1915	12
9	Charley Radbourn, 1884	11
	Dave Foutz, 1886	11
	Christy Mathewson, 1908	11
	Ed Walsh, 1908	11
	Walter Johnson, 1913	11
	Sandy Koufax, 1963	11
	Dean Chance, 1964	11
16	John Clarkson, 1885	10
	Cy Young, 1904	10
	Ed Walsh, 1906	10
	Joe Wood, 1912	10
	Dave Davenport, 1915	10
	Carl Hubbell, 1933	10
	Mort Cooper, 1942	10
	Bob Feller, 1946	10
	Bob Lemon, 1948	10
	Juan Marichal, 1965	10
	Jim Palmer, 1975	10
	John Tudor, 1985	10
28	Al Spalding, 1876	9
	Tommy Bond, 1878	9
	George Derby, 1881	9
	Cy Young, 1892	9
	Joe McGinnity, 1904	9
	Mordecai Brown, 1906	9
	Addie Joss, 1906	9
	Mordecai Brown, 1908	9
	Addie Joss, 1908	9
	Orval Overall, 1909	9
	Pete Alexander, 1913	9
	Walter Johnson, 1914	9
	Cy Falkenberg, 1914	9
	Babe Ruth, 1916	9
	Stan Coveleski, 1917	9
	Pete Alexander, 1919	9
	Bill Lee, 1938	9
	Bob Porterfield, 1953	9
	Luis Tiant, 1968	9
	Denny McLain, 1969	9
	Don Sutton, 1972	9
	Nolan Ryan, 1972	9
	Bert Blyleven, 1973	9
	Ron Guidry, 1978	9
52	Monte Ward, 1880	8
	Will White, 1882	8
	Charlie Buffinton, 1884	8
	Tony Mullane, 1884	8
	Tim Keefe, 1888	8
	Ben Sanders, 1888	8
	John Clarkson, 1889	8
	Christy Mathewson, 1902	8
	Jack Chesbro, 1902	8
	Rube Waddell, 1904	8
	Christy Mathewson, 1905	8
	Ed Killian, 1905	8
	Lefty Leifield, 1906	8
	Rube Waddell, 1906	8
	Orval Overall, 1907	8
	Christy Mathewson, 1907	8
	Eddie Plank, 1907	8
	Mordecai Brown, 1909	8
	Christy Mathewson, 1909	8
	Ed Walsh, 1909	8
	Russ Ford, 1910	8
	Walter Johnson, 1910	8
	Reb Russell, 1913	8
	Jeff Tesreau, 1914	8
	Al Mamaux, 1915	8
	Jeff Tesreau, 1915	8
	Joe Bush, 1916	8
	Pete Alexander, 1917	8
	Jim Bagby, 1917	8
	Walter Johnson, 1917	8
	Hippo Vaughn, 1918	8
	Walter Johnson, 1918	8
	Carl Mays, 1918	8
	Babe Adams, 1920	8
	Hal Newhouser, 1945	8
	Steve Barber, 1961	8
	Camilo Pascual, 1961	8
	Whitey Ford, 1964	8
	Sandy Koufax, 1965	8
	Don Drysdale, 1968	8
	Juan Marichal, 1969	8
	Vida Blue, 1971	8
	Steve Carlton, 1972	8
	Wilbur Wood, 1972	8
	Fernando Valenzuela, 1981	8
	Dwight Gooden, 1985	8
	Orel Hershiser, 1988	8
	Roger Clemens, 1988	8
	Tim Belcher, 1989	8

Saves

1	Dave Righetti, 1986	46
2	Dan Quisenberry, 1983	45
	Bruce Sutter, 1984	45
	Dennis Eckersley, 1988	45
5	Dan Quisenberry, 1984	44
	Mark Davis, 1989	44
7	Jeff Reardon, 1988	42
8	Jeff Reardon, 1985	41
9	Steve Bedrosian, 1987	40
10	Johnny Franco, 1988	39
11	John Hiller, 1973	38
	Jeff Russell, 1989	38
13	Clay Carroll, 1972	37
	Rollie Fingers, 1978	37
	Bruce Sutter, 1979	37
	Dan Quisenberry, 1985	37
	Doug Jones, 1988	37
18	Bruce Sutter, 1982	36
	Bill Caudill, 1984	36
	Todd Worrell, 1986	36
	Lee Smith, 1987	36
	Mitch Williams, 1989	36
23	Wayne Granger, 1970	35
	Sparky Lyle, 1972	35
	Rollie Fingers, 1977	35
	Dan Quisenberry, 1982	35
	Jeff Reardon, 1986	35
28	Ron Perranoski, 1970	34
	Don Aase, 1986	34
	Tom Henke, 1987	34
	Jim Gott, 1988	34
	Bobby Thigpen, 1988	34
	Bobby Thigpen, 1989	34
34	Rich Gossage, 1980	33
	Dan Quisenberry, 1980	33
	Bob Stanley, 1983	33
	Lee Smith, 1984	33
	Lee Smith, 1985	33
	Dave Smith, 1986	33
	Todd Worrell, 1987	33
	Dennis Eckersley, 1989	33
	Dan Plesac, 1989	33
	Mike Schooler, 1989	33
44	Jack Aker, 1966	32
	Mike Marshall, 1979	32
	Willie Hernandez, 1984	32
	Bob James, 1985	32
	Johnny Franco, 1987	32
	Todd Worrell, 1988	32
	Johnny Franco, 1989	32
	Doug Jones, 1989	32
52	Ted Abernathy, 1965	31
	Ron Perranoski, 1969	31
	Ken Sanders, 1971	31
	Mike Marshall, 1973	31
	Bruce Sutter, 1977	31
	Bill Campbell, 1977	31
	Kent Tekulve, 1978	31
	Kent Tekulve, 1979	31
	Jesse Orosco, 1984	31
	Dave Righetti, 1984	31
	Willie Hernandez, 1985	31
	Donnie Moore, 1985	31
	Lee Smith, 1986	31
	Jeff Reardon, 1987	31
	Dave Righetti, 1987	31
	Jeff Reardon, 1989	31
68	Dave Giusti, 1971	30
	Ed Farmer, 1980	30
	Gene Garber, 1982	30
	Greg Minton, 1982	30
	Rich Gossage, 1982	30
	Ron Davis, 1983	30
	Dan Plesac, 1988	30
75	Luis Arroyo, 1961	29
	Dick Radatz, 1964	29
	Ron Kline, 1965	29
	Fred Gladding, 1969	29
	Lindy McDaniel, 1970	29
	Terry Forster, 1972	29
	Jim Kern, 1979	29
	Rollie Fingers, 1982	29
	Lee Smith, 1983	29
	Al Holland, 1984	29
	Ron Davis, 1984	29
	Jay Howell, 1985	29
	Dave Righetti, 1985	29
	Steve Bedrosian, 1986	29
	Johnny Franco, 1986	29
	Lee Smith, 1988	29
91	Roy Face, 1962	28
	Ted Abernathy, 1967	28
	Doug Bair, 1978	28
	Bruce Sutter, 1980	28
	Rollie Fingers, 1981	28
	Steve Bedrosian, 1988	28
	Mark Davis, 1988	28
	Tim Burke, 1989	28
	Jay Howell, 1989	28
100	18 players tied	27

Innings Pitched

1	Will White, 1879	680
2	Charley Radbourn, 1884	679
3	Guy Hecker, 1884	671
4	Jim McCormick, 1880	658
5	Jim Galvin, 1883	656
6	Jim Galvin, 1884	636
7	Charley Radbourn, 1883	632
8	Bill Hutchinson, 1892	627
9	John Clarkson, 1885	623
10	Jim Devlin, 1876	622
11	John Clarkson, 1889	620
12	Tim Keefe, 1883	619
13	Bill Hutchinson, 1890	603
14	Jim McCormick, 1882	596
15	Monte Ward, 1880	595
16	Jim Galvin, 1879	593
17	Lee Richmond, 1880	591
18	Toad Ramsey, 1886	589
	Matt Kilroy, 1887	589
20	Monte Ward, 1879	587
	Charlie Buffinton, 1884	587
22	Silver King, 1888	586
23	Matt Kilroy, 1886	583
24	Ed Morris, 1885	581
25	Will White, 1883	577
26	Tony Mullane, 1884	576
27	Mickey Welch, 1880	574
28	George Bradley, 1876	573
29	Toad Ramsey, 1887	561
	Bill Hutchinson, 1891	561
31	Jim Devlin, 1877	559
32	Mickey Welch, 1884	557
33	Tommy Bond, 1879	555
	Ed Morris, 1886	555
35	Jim Whitney, 1881	552
36	Amos Rusie, 1890	549
37	Jim McCormick, 1879	546
38	Tim Keefe, 1886	540
39	Hardie Henderson, 1885	539
40	John Coleman, 1883	538
	Bill Sweeney, 1884	538
42	Larry Corcoran, 1880	536
43	Tommy Bond, 1878	533
	Jersey Bakely, 1888	533
45	Amos Rusie, 1892	532
46	Tony Mullane, 1886	530
47	Al Spalding, 1876	529
48	Jim McCormick, 1881	526
49	John Clarkson, 1887	523
50	Tommy Bond, 1877	521
51	Ed Seward, 1888	519
52	Will White, 1880	517
	Larry Corcoran, 1884	517
54	Bobby Mathews, 1876	516
55	Jim Whitney, 1883	514
	Mark Baldwin, 1889	514
57	Terry Larkin, 1879	513
58	Larry McKeon, 1884	512
59	Charley Radbourn, 1886	509
	Sadie McMahon, 1890	509
61	Terry Larkin, 1878	506
	Kid Gleason, 1890	506
63	Dave Foutz, 1886	504
64	Frank Mountain, 1883	503
	Sadie McMahon, 1891	503
66	Terry Larkin, 1877	501
	Hugh Daily, 1884	501
	Mark Baldwin, 1890	501
69	Mickey Welch, 1886	500
	Amos Rusie, 1891	500
71	George Derby, 1881	495
72	Tommy Bond, 1880	493
	Bob Barr, 1890	493
74	Tim Keefe, 1884	492
	Mickey Welch, 1885	492
76	Phenomenal Smith, 1887	491
77	George Bradley, 1879	487
	Jack Lynch, 1884	487
	Lady Baldwin, 1886	487
80	Adonis Terry, 1884	485
81	John Clarkson, 1888	483
82	Bob Caruthers, 1885	482
	Henry Porter, 1885	482
	Amos Rusie, 1893	482
85	Matt Kilroy, 1889	481
86	Will White, 1882	480
	Guy Hecker, 1885	480
	Ed Morris, 1888	480
89	Tim Keefe, 1887	479
90	Jim Galvin, 1881	474
	Charley Radbourn, 1882	474
	Larry Corcoran, 1883	474
	Henry Porter, 1888	474
	Ed Beatin, 1890	474
95	Ed Seward, 1887	471
96	Gus Weyhing, 1892	470
97	Will White, 1878	468
98	John Clarkson, 1886	467
99	Gus Weyhing, 1887	466
100	Ed Walsh, 1908	464

Innings Pitched (by era)

1876-1892

1	Will White, 1879	680
2	Charley Radbourn, 1884	679
3	Guy Hecker, 1884	671
4	Jim McCormick, 1880	658
5	Jim Galvin, 1883	656
6	Jim Galvin, 1884	636
7	Charley Radbourn, 1883	632
8	Bill Hutchinson, 1892	627
9	John Clarkson, 1885	623
10	Jim Devlin, 1876	622
11	John Clarkson, 1889	620
12	Tim Keefe, 1883	619
13	Bill Hutchinson, 1890	603
14	Jim McCormick, 1882	596
15	Monte Ward, 1880	595

1893-1919

1	Amos Rusie, 1893	482
2	Ed Walsh, 1908	464
3	Jack Chesbro, 1904	455
4	Ted Breitenstein, 1894	447
5	Amos Rusie, 1894	444
	Pink Hawley, 1895	444
7	Joe McGinnity, 1903	434
8	Frank Killen, 1896	432
9	Ted Breitenstein, 1895	430
10	Kid Nichols, 1893	425
11	Cy Young, 1893	423
12	Ed Walsh, 1907	422
13	Frank Killen, 1893	415
14	Cy Young, 1896	414
15	Vic Willis, 1902	410

1920-1941

1	Pete Alexander, 1920	363
2	George Uhle, 1923	358
3	Red Faber, 1922	352
4	Urban Shocker, 1922	348
5	Bob Feller, 1941	343
6	Jim Bagby, 1920	340
7	Carl Mays, 1921	337
8	Red Faber, 1921	331
	Burleigh Grimes, 1928	331
10	Bobo Newsom, 1938	330
11	Wilbur Cooper, 1920	327
	Wilbur Cooper, 1921	327
	Urban Shocker, 1921	327
	Burleigh Grimes, 1923	327
	General Crowder, 1932	327

1942-1960

1	Bob Feller, 1946	371
2	Dizzy Trout, 1944	352
3	Robin Roberts, 1953	347
4	Robin Roberts, 1954	337
5	Robin Roberts, 1952	330
6	Johnny Sain, 1948	315
	Robin Roberts, 1951	315
8	Bob Friend, 1956	314
9	Bill Voiselle, 1944	313
	Hal Newhouser, 1945	313
11	Hal Newhouser, 1944	312
	Vern Bickford, 1950	312
13	Warren Spahn, 1951	311
14	Bob Lemon, 1952	310
15	Robin Roberts, 1955	305

1961-1989

1	Wilbur Wood, 1972	377
2	Mickey Lolich, 1971	376
3	Wilbur Wood, 1973	359
4	Steve Carlton, 1972	346
5	Gaylord Perry, 1973	344
6	Gaylord Perry, 1972	343
7	Phil Niekro, 1979	342
8	Sandy Koufax, 1965	336
	Denny McLain, 1968	336
10	Wilbur Wood, 1971	334
	Phil Niekro, 1978	334
12	Nolan Ryan, 1974	333
13	Phil Niekro, 1977	330
14	Gaylord Perry, 1970	329
15	2 players tied	328

Hits per Game

1	Nolan Ryan, 1972	5.26
2	Luis Tiant, 1968	5.30
3	Ed Reulbach, 1906	5.33
4	Dutch Leonard, 1914	5.56
5	Carl Lundgren, 1907	5.65
6	Sid Fernandez, 1985	5.72
7	Tommy Byrne, 1949	5.74
8	Dave McNally, 1968	5.77
9	Sandy Koufax, 1965	5.79
10	Russ Ford, 1910	5.82
11	Al Downing, 1963	5.83
12	Bob Gibson, 1968	5.84
13	Herb Score, 1956	5.86
14	Sam McDowell, 1965	5.87
15	Ed Walsh, 1910	5.89
16	Mike Scott, 1986	5.96
17	Floyd Youmans, 1986	5.96
18	Nolan Ryan, 1977	5.96
19	Mario Soto, 1980	5.97
20	Nolan Ryan, 1974	5.97
21	Nolan Ryan, 1981	5.98
22	Nolan Ryan, 1986	6.02
23	Vida Blue, 1971	6.03
24	Sam McDowell, 1966	6.03
25	Walter Johnson, 1913	6.03
26	Jim Bibby, 1973	6.05
27	Sam McDowell, 1968	6.06
28	Pete Alexander, 1915	6.06
29	Joe Horlen, 1964	6.06
30	Andy Messersmith, 1969	6.08
31	Tim Keefe, 1880	6.09
32	Nolan Ryan, 1989	6.10
33	Stan Coveleski, 1917	6.10
34	Jim Hunter, 1972	6.10
35	Sid Fernandez, 1988	6.11
36	Nolan Ryan, 1976	6.12
37	Bob Turley, 1955	6.12
38	Don Sutton, 1972	6.13
39	Bob Turley, 1957	6.14
40	Ron Guidry, 1978	6.14
41	Nolan Ryan, 1983	6.15
42	Mordecai Brown, 1908	6.17
43	Sandy Koufax, 1963	6.19
44	Sandy Koufax, 1964	6.22
45	Charlie Sweeney, 1884	6.23
46	Roger Nelson, 1972	6.24
47	Cy Morgan, 1909	6.24
48	Herb Score, 1955	6.26
49	Dean Chance, 1964	6.28
50	Christy Mathewson, 1909	6.28
	J.R. Richard, 1978	6.28
52	Art Fromme, 1909	6.29
53	Vean Gregg, 1911	6.32
54	Rube Waddell, 1905	6.32
55	Jack Coombs, 1910	6.32
56	Jeff Robinson, 1988	6.33
57	Allie Reynolds, 1943	6.33
58	Larry Cheney, 1916	6.33
59	Walter Johnson, 1912	6.33
60	Sonny Siebert, 1968	6.33
61	Roger Clemens, 1986	6.34
62	Willie Mitchell, 1913	6.35
63	Jose DeLeon, 1989	6.36
64	Pascual Perez, 1988	6.37
65	Harry Krause, 1909	6.38
66	Eddie Cicotte, 1917	6.38
67	Spec Shea, 1947	6.39
68	Babe Ruth, 1916	6.39
69	Dave Boswell, 1966	6.39
70	Wayne Simpson, 1970	6.39
71	Dutch Leonard, 1915	6.39
72	Ed Reulbach, 1905	6.41
73	Addie Joss, 1908	6.42
74	Gaylord Perry, 1974	6.43
75	Frank Smith, 1908	6.43
76	Mordecai Brown, 1906	6.43
	Dwight Gooden, 1985	6.43
78	Jack Pfiester, 1906	6.43
79	Luis Tiant, 1972	6.44
80	Eddie Fisher, 1965	6.44
81	Orval Overall, 1909	6.44
82	Sid Fernandez, 1989	6.45
83	Mordecai Brown, 1909	6.45
84	Denny McLain, 1968	6.46
85	Fred Toney, 1915	6.46
86	Ray Caldwell, 1914	6.46
87	Dupee Shaw, 1884	6.47
88	Jim McCormick, 1884	6.47
89	Gary Peters, 1967	6.47
90	Walter Johnson, 1910	6.47
91	Frank Smith, 1910	6.48
92	Bob Turley, 1954	6.49
93	Guy Hecker, 1882	6.49
94	Ed Walsh, 1909	6.50
95	Al Mamaux, 1915	6.50
96	Tom Seaver, 1981	6.51
97	Sam Jones, 1955	6.51
98	Bobby Bolin, 1968	6.51
99	Claude Hendrix, 1914	6.51
	Jim Palmer, 1969	6.51

Hits per Game (by era)

1876-1892
1 Tim Keefe, 1880 .... 6.09
2 Charlie Sweeney, 1884 ..... 6.23
3 Dupee Shaw, 1884 ...... 6.47
4 Jim McCormick, 1884 ...... 6.47
5 Guy Hecker, 1882 ...... 6.49
6 Tim Keefe, 1888 .... 6.55
7 Adonis Terry, 1888 ...... 6.69
8 Silver King, 1888 ...... 6.71
9 Tim Keefe, 1885 ...... 6.72
10 Frank Knauss, 1890 ...... 6.72
11 Ed Seward, 1888 ...... 6.73
12 Tony Mullane, 1892 ...... 6.77
13 Larry Corcoran, 1880 ...... 6.78
14 Mickey Welch, 1885 .... 6.80
15 Cannonball Titcomb, 1888 .. 6.81

1893-1919
1 Ed Reulbach, 1906 ...... 5.33
2 Dutch Leonard, 1914 ...... 5.56
3 Carl Lundgren, 1907 ...... 5.65
4 Russ Ford, 1910 ...... 5.82
5 Ed Walsh, 1910 .... 5.89
6 Walter Johnson, 1913 ...... 6.03
7 Pete Alexander, 1915 ...... 6.06
8 Stan Coveleski, 1917 ...... 6.10
9 Mordecai Brown, 1908 ..... 6.17
10 Cy Morgan, 1909 ...... 6.24
11 Christy Mathewson, 1909... 6.28
12 Art Fromme, 1909 ...... 6.29
13 Vean Gregg, 1911 .... 6.32
14 Rube Waddell, 1905 ...... 6.32
15 Jack Coombs, 1910 ...... 6.32

1920-1941
1 Johnny Vander Meer, 1941 .. 6.85
2 Bob Feller, 1939 .... 6.88
3 Bob Feller, 1940 ...... 6.89
4 Hal Schumacher, 1933 ..... 6.92
5 Dazzy Vance, 1924 ...... 6.93
6 Whit Wyatt, 1941 ...... 6.97
7 Bucky Walters, 1939 ...... 7.05
8 Johnny Vander Meer, 1938.. 7.08
9 Bucky Walters, 1940 ...... 7.11
10 Lefty Gomez, 1934 ...... 7.12
11 Ernie White, 1941 ...... 7.24
12 Bump Hadley, 1931 ...... 7.25
13 Dazzy Vance, 1928 ...... 7.26
14 Dolf Luque, 1920 ...... 7.27
15 Bob Feller, 1938 ...... 7.28

1942-1960
1 Tommy Byrne, 1949 ...... 5.74
2 Herb Score, 1956 .... 5.86
3 Bob Turley, 1955 .... 6.12
4 Bob Turley, 1957 ...... 6.14
5 Herb Score, 1955 ...... 6.26
6 Allie Reynolds, 1943 ...... 6.33
7 Spec Shea, 1947 .... 6.39
8 Bob Turley, 1954 ...... 6.49
9 Sam Jones, 1955 ...... 6.51
10 Bob Turley, 1958 ...... 6.54
11 Hal Newhouser, 1946 ...... 6.60
12 Don Larsen, 1956 ...... 6.65
13 Whitey Ford, 1955 .... 6.66
14 Johnny Niggeling, 1943 .... 6.67
15 Mort Cooper, 1942 ...... 6.68

1961-1989
1 Nolan Ryan, 1972 .... 5.26
2 Luis Tiant, 1968 .... 5.30
3 Sid Fernandez, 1985 ...... 5.72
4 Dave McNally, 1968 ...... 5.77
5 Sandy Koufax, 1965 ...... 5.79
6 Al Downing, 1963 .... 5.83
7 Bob Gibson, 1968 .... 5.84
8 Sam McDowell, 1965 ...... 5.87
9 Mike Scott, 1986 ...... 5.96
10 Floyd Youmans, 1986 ...... 5.96
11 Nolan Ryan, 1977 ...... 5.96
12 Mario Soto, 1980 ...... 5.97
13 Nolan Ryan, 1974 ...... 5.97
14 Nolan Ryan, 1981 ...... 5.98
15 Nolan Ryan, 1986 .... 6.02

Home Runs Allowed

1 Bert Blyleven, 1986 50
2 Robin Roberts, 1956 46
　Bert Blyleven, 1987 46
4 Pedro Ramos, 1957 43
5 Denny McLain, 1966 42
6 Robin Roberts, 1955 41
　Phil Niekro, 1979 41
8 Robin Roberts, 1957 40
　Ralph Terry, 1962 40
　Orlando Pena, 1964 40
　Phil Niekro, 1970 40
　Ferguson Jenkins, 1979 40
　Jack Morris, 1986 40
14 Murry Dickson, 1948 39
　Pedro Ramos, 1961 39
　Jim Perry, 1971 39
　Jim Hunter, 1973 39
　Jack Morris, 1987 39
19 Warren Hacker, 1955 38
　Pedro Ramos, 1958 38
　Lew Burdette, 1959 38
　Jim Bunning, 1963 38
　Don Sutton, 1970 38
　Mickey Lolich, 1974 38
　Matt Keough, 1982 38
　Floyd Bannister, 1987 .. 38
　Don Sutton, 1987 38
　Curt Young, 1987 38
29 Jim Bunning, 1959 37
　Earl Wilson, 1964 37
　Luis Tiant, 1969 37
　Ferguson Jenkins, 1975 37
　Jack Morris, 1982 37
　Dan Petry, 1983 37
　Frank Viola, 1986 37
36 Larry Jansen, 1949 36
　Art Mahaffey, 1962 36
　Pete Richert, 1966 36
　Mickey Lolich, 1971 36
　Eddie Whitson, 1987 36
　Charlie Hough, 1987 36
　Tom Browning, 1988 36
43 Larry Corcoran, 1884 35
　Warren Hacker, 1953 35
　Robin Roberts, 1954 35
　Don Newcombe, 1955 35
　Jim Perry, 1960 35
　Roger Craig, 1962 35
　Robin Roberts, 1963 35
　Sammy Ellis, 1966 35
　Denny McLain, 1967 35
　Ferguson Jenkins, 1973 35
　Mickey Lolich, 1973 35
　Mike Caldwell, 1983 35
　Mike Smithson, 1984 35
　Scott McGregor, 1986 35
　Scott Bankhead, 1987 35
　Bruce Hurst, 1987 35
59 Preacher Roe, 1950 34
　Johnny Sain, 1950 34
　Ken Raffensberger, 1950 ... 34
　Robin Roberts, 1959 34
　Paul Foytack, 1959 34
　Juan Marichal, 1962 34
　Dick Ellsworth, 1964 34
　Bill Monbouquette, 1964 ... 34
　Bob Gibson, 1965 34
　Jim Grant, 1965 34
　Earl Wilson, 1967 34
　Jim Hunter, 1969 34
　Mike Cuellar, 1970 34
　Gaylord Perry, 1973 34
　Rick Wise, 1975 34
　Frank Viola, 1983 34
　Danny Darwin, 1985 34
　Scott McGregor, 1985...... 34
　Ken Schrom, 1986 34
　Don Carman, 1987 34
　Mike Witt, 1987 34
80 Don Newcombe, 1956 33
　Camilo Pascual, 1956 33
　Jim Bunning, 1957 33
　Billy Pierce, 1958 33
　Mike McCormick, 1961 33
　Gene Conley, 1961 33
　Phil Regan, 1963 33
　Phil Ortega, 1965 33
　Jim Merritt, 1969 33
　Lew Krausse, 1970 33
　Jerry Garvin, 1977 33
　Dennis Leonard, 1979 33
　Bill Travers, 1979 33
　Rick Langford, 1982 33
　Ken Dixon, 1986 33
　Bill Gullickson, 1987 33
　Willie Fraser, 1988 33
97 26 players tied 32

Home Runs Allowed (by era)

1876-1892
1 Larry Corcoran, 1884 35
2 Charlie Getzien, 1889 27
3 Bill Hutchinson, 1891 26
4 Charlie Getzien, 1887 24
　Egyptian Healy, 1887 24
6 Jim Galvin, 1884 23
　Mark Baldwin, 1887 23
　Lev Shreve, 1888 23
9 Billy Serad, 1884 21
　John Clarkson, 1885 21
　Park Swartzel, 1889 21
　George Cobb, 1892 21
13 8 players tied 20

1893-1919
1 Frank Dwyer, 1894 27
　Jack Stivetts, 1894 27
3 Kid Nichols, 1894 23
4 Harry Staley, 1893 22
　Kid Carsey, 1894 22
6 Ted Breitenstein, 1894 21
7 Jack Stivetts, 1896 20
8 Tom Parrott, 1894 19
　Cy Young, 1894 19
10 Kid Gleason, 1893 18
　Al Orth, 1902 18
12 5 players tied 17

1920-1941
1 Lon Warneke, 1937 32
2 Phil Collins, 1934 30
　Bobo Newsom, 1938 30
4 Ray Kremer, 1930 29
　Lynn Nelson, 1934 29
6 George Earnshaw, 1932 ... 28
　George Earnshaw, 1934 28
8 Roy Mahaffey, 1932 27
　Carl Hubbell, 1935 27
　Luke Hamlin, 1939 27
　Lynn Nelson, 1939 27
　Johnny Marcum, 1939 27
13 Freddie Fitzsimmons, 1930 . 26
　Gordon Rhodes, 1936 26
　Nels Potter, 1939.......... 26

1942-1960
1 Robin Roberts, 1956 46
2 Pedro Ramos, 1957 43
3 Robin Roberts, 1955 41
4 Robin Roberts, 1957 40
5 Murry Dickson, 1948 39
6 Warren Hacker, 1955 38
　Pedro Ramos, 1958 38
　Lew Burdette, 1959 38
9 Jim Bunning, 1959 37
10 Larry Jansen, 1949 36
11 Warren Hacker, 1953 35
　Robin Roberts, 1954 35
　Don Newcombe, 1955 35
　Jim Perry, 1960 35
15 5 players tied 34

1961-1989
1 Bert Blyleven, 1986 50
2 Bert Blyleven, 1987 46
3 Denny McLain, 1966 42
4 Phil Niekro, 1979 41
5 Ralph Terry, 1962 40
　Orlando Pena, 1964 40
　Phil Niekro, 1970 40
　Ferguson Jenkins, 1979 40
　Jack Morris, 1986 40
10 Pedro Ramos, 1961 39
　Jim Perry, 1971 39
　Jim Hunter, 1973 39
　Jack Morris, 1987 39
14 7 players tied 38

Walks

1 Amos Rusie, 1890.......... 289
2 Mark Baldwin, 1889 274
3 Amos Rusie, 1892 267
4 Amos Rusie, 1891 262
5 Mark Baldwin, 1890 249
6 Jack Stivetts, 1891 232
7 Mark Baldwin, 1891 227
8 Phil Knell, 1891 226
9 Bob Barr, 1890 219
10 Amos Rusie, 1893 218
11 Cy Seymour, 1898.......... 213
12 Gus Weyhing, 1889 212
13 Ed Crane, 1890 210
14 Bob Feller, 1938 208
15 Toad Ramsey, 1886 207
16 Iceberg Chamberlin, 1891 .. 206
17 Mike Morrison, 1887 205
18 Henry Gruber, 1890 204
　Nolan Ryan, 1977 204
20 John Clarkson, 1889...... 203
21 Nolan Ryan, 1974 202
22 Bert Cunningham, 1890 201
23 Amos Rusie, 1894 200
24 Bill Hutchinson, 1890 199
25 Mark Baldwin, 1892 194
　Bob Feller, 1941 194
27 Bobo Newsom, 1938 192
28 Ted Breitenstein, 1894 191
29 Ed Crane, 1892 189
　Tony Mullane, 1893 189
31 Tony Mullane, 1891 187
　Bill Hutchinson, 1892 187
　Kid Gleason, 1893 187
34 Ed Beatin, 1890 186
35 Sam Jones, 1955 185
36 Tom Vickery, 1890 184
37 Nolan Ryan, 1976 183
38 Matt Kilroy, 1887 182
　Frank Killen, 1892 182
40 Willie Mains, 1893 181
　Bob Harmon, 1911 181
　Bob Turley, 1954 181
43 Jack Stivetts, 1890 179
　Gus Weyhing, 1890 179
　Tommy Byrne, 1949 179
46 Bill Hutchinson, 1891 178
　Ted Breitenstein, 1895 178
48 Bob Turley, 1955 177
49 Phenomenal Smith, 1887 ... 176
　George Hemming, 1893 176
51 Silver King, 1892 174
52 Jack Stivetts, 1892 171
　Jouett Meekin, 1894 171
　Ed Stein, 1894 171
　Bump Hadley, 1932 171
56 Iceberg Chamberlin, 1892 .. 170
　Cy Seymour, 1899.......... 170
58 Willie McGill, 1891 168
　Gus Weyhing, 1892 168
　Brickyard Kennedy, 1893 ... 168
　Elmer Myers, 1916 168
62 Toad Ramsey, 1887 167
　Gus Weyhing, 1887 167
　Darby O'Brien, 1889 167
　Kid Gleason, 1890 167
　Bill Daley, 1890 167
　Bobo Newsom, 1937 167
68 Tony Mullane, 1886 166
　Sadie McMahon, 1890 166
　Phil Knell, 1890 166
　Chick Fraser, 1896 166
72 Iceberg Chamberlin, 1889 .. 165
　Dan Casey, 1890 165
　Kid Gleason, 1891 165
　John Wyckoff, 1915 165
76 Cy Seymour, 1897.......... 164
　Earl Moore, 1911 164
　Phil Niekro, 1977 164
79 Mickey Welch, 1886 163
　Silver King, 1890 163
　Hank O'Day, 1890 163
　George Haddock, 1892..... 163
83 Johnny Vander Meer, 1943 . 162
　Nolan Ryan, 1973 162
85 John Sowders, 1890 161
　Kid Carsey, 1891 161
　Gus Weyhing, 1891 161
88 Tommy Byrne, 1950 160
89 George Hemming, 1894 159
　Amos Rusie, 1895.......... 159
　Marty O'Toole, 1912 159
92 Joe Coleman, 1974 158
93 Matt Kilroy, 1887 157
　Bert Cunningham, 1888 157
　Pink Hawley, 1896.......... 157
　Grover Lowdermilk, 1915 ... 157
　Nolan Ryan, 1972 157
98 5 players tied 156

Fewest Walks per Game

1	George Zettlein, 1876	0.23
2	Cherokee Fisher, 1876	0.24
3	George Bradley, 1880	0.28
4	Tommy Bond, 1876	0.29
5	Tommy Bond, 1879	0.39
6	Bobby Mathews, 1876	0.42
7	Charlie Sweeney, 1884	0.43
8	Guy Hecker, 1882	0.43
9	Dale Williams, 1876	0.43
10	Al Spalding, 1876	0.44
11	Jim Galvin, 1879	0.47
12	George Bradley, 1879	0.48
13	Sam Weaver, 1878	0.49
14	Terry Larkin, 1879	0.53
15	Jim Devlin, 1876	0.54
16	Denny Driscoll, 1882	0.54
17	Terry Larkin, 1878	0.55
18	Monte Ward, 1879	0.55
19	Tommy Bond, 1878	0.56
20	Candy Cummings, 1876	0.58
21	George Bradley, 1876	0.60
22	Henry Boyle, 1884	0.60
	Jim McCormick, 1884	0.60
24	George Bradley, 1884	0.61
25	Harry McCormick, 1879	0.61
26	Jim Whitney, 1883	0.61
27	Babe Adams, 1920	0.62
28	Christy Mathewson, 1913	0.62
29	John Murphy, 1884	0.62
30	Tommy Bond, 1877	0.62
31	Jim Galvin, 1880	0.63
32	Jim Devlin, 1877	0.66
33	Christy Mathewson, 1914	0.66
34	Tommy Bond, 1884	0.67
35	Monte Ward, 1880	0.68
36	Jim Galvin, 1883	0.69
37	Cy Young, 1904	0.69
38	Bobby Mathews, 1882	0.69
39	Stump Weidman, 1880	0.71
40	Jim Whitney, 1884	0.72
41	Sam Weaver, 1884	0.73
42	Bobby Mathews, 1883	0.73
43	Tricky Nichols, 1878	0.73
44	Red Lucas, 1933	0.74
45	Candy Cummings, 1877	0.75
46	Guy Hecker, 1884	0.75
47	Jim Whitney, 1885	0.76
48	Fred Goldsmith, 1880	0.77
49	Jack Lynch, 1884	0.78
50	Cy Young, 1906	0.78
51	Babe Adams, 1919	0.79
52	Slim Sallee, 1919	0.79
	Babe Adams, 1922	0.79
54	Charley Radbourn, 1883	0.80
55	John Coleman, 1883	0.80
56	Jim Galvin, 1882	0.81
57	Ed Dugan, 1884	0.81
58	Sam Weaver, 1883	0.82
59	Slim Sallee, 1918	0.82
60	Dory Dean, 1876	0.82
61	Tommy Bond, 1880	0.82
62	Addie Joss, 1908	0.83
63	Foghorn Bradley, 1876	0.83
64	Curry Foley, 1879	0.83
65	Cy Young, 1905	0.84
66	Fred Goldsmith, 1882	0.84
67	Sam Weaver, 1882	0.85
68	Stump Weidman, 1882	0.85
69	Lamarr Hoyt, 1985	0.86
70	Deacon Phillippe, 1902	0.86
71	Will White, 1878	0.87
72	Walter Burke, 1884	0.87
73	Jim Galvin, 1881	0.87
74	Jim Whitney, 1882	0.88
75	Jack Lynch, 1883	0.88
76	Pete Alexander, 1923	0.89
77	Jumbo McGinnis, 1884	0.89
78	George Bradley, 1877	0.89
79	Jim Galvin, 1884	0.89
80	Cy Young, 1901	0.90
81	Will White, 1879	0.90
82	Deacon Phillippe, 1903	0.90
83	Monte Ward, 1878	0.92
84	Fred Goldsmith, 1883	0.92
85	George Bradley, 1883	0.93
86	Jim Whitney, 1887	0.93
87	Stump Weidman, 1881	0.94
88	Terry Larkin, 1877	0.95
89	Blondie Purcell, 1879	0.95
90	Tiny Bonham, 1942	0.96
91	Christy Mathewson, 1908	0.97
92	Christy Mathewson, 1915	0.97
93	Charley Radbourn, 1882	0.97
94	Fred Corey, 1880	0.97
95	Cy Young, 1903	0.97
96	Jesse Tannehill, 1902	0.97
97	Will White, 1880	0.97
98	Cy Young, 1898	0.98
99	Bill Burns, 1908	0.98
100	Christy Mathewson, 1912	0.99

Fewest Walks/Game (by era)

1876-1892

1	George Zettlein, 1876	0.23
2	Cherokee Fisher, 1876	0.24
3	George Bradley, 1880	0.28
4	Tommy Bond, 1876	0.29
5	Tommy Bond, 1879	0.39
6	Bobby Mathews, 1876	0.42
7	Charlie Sweeney, 1884	0.43
8	Guy Hecker, 1882	0.43
9	Dale Williams, 1876	0.43
10	Al Spalding, 1876	0.44
11	Jim Galvin, 1879	0.47
12	George Bradley, 1879	0.48
13	Sam Weaver, 1878	0.49
14	Terry Larkin, 1879	0.53
15	Jim Devlin, 1876	0.54

1893-1919

1	Christy Mathewson, 1913	0.62
2	Christy Mathewson, 1914	0.66
3	Cy Young, 1904	0.69
4	Cy Young, 1906	0.78
5	Babe Adams, 1919	0.79
6	Slim Sallee, 1919	0.79
7	Slim Sallee, 1918	0.82
8	Addie Joss, 1908	0.83
9	Cy Young, 1905	0.84
10	Deacon Phillippe, 1902	0.86
11	Cy Young, 1901	0.90
12	Deacon Phillippe, 1903	0.90
13	Christy Mathewson, 1908	0.97
14	Christy Mathewson, 1915	0.97
15	Cy Young, 1903	0.97

1920-1941

1	Babe Adams, 1920	0.62
2	Red Lucas, 1933	0.74
3	Babe Adams, 1922	0.79
4	Pete Alexander, 1923	0.89
5	Babe Adams, 1921	1.01
6	Paul Derringer, 1939	1.05
7	Carl Hubbell, 1934	1.06
8	Bill Swift, 1932	1.09
9	Pete Alexander, 1925	1.11
10	Herb Pennock, 1930	1.15
11	Red Lucas, 1932	1.17
12	Pete Alexander, 1921	1.18
13	Watty Clark, 1935	1.22
14	Pete Donohue, 1926	1.23
15	Pete Alexander, 1922	1.24

1942-1960

1	Tiny Bonham, 1942	0.96
2	Tiny Bonham, 1945	1.09
3	Don Newcombe, 1959	1.09
4	Lew Burdette, 1960	1.14
5	Lew Burdette, 1959	1.18
6	Robin Roberts, 1956	1.21
7	Robin Roberts, 1959	1.23
8	Robin Roberts, 1952	1.23
9	Hal Brown, 1960	1.25
10	Ray Prim, 1945	1.25
11	Robin Roberts, 1960	1.29
12	Fred Hutchinson, 1951	1.29
13	Ted Lyons, 1942	1.30
14	Schoolboy Rowe, 1943	1.31
15	Vern Law, 1960	1.32

1961-1989

1	Lamarr Hoyt, 1985	0.86
2	Dennis Eckersley, 1985	1.01
3	Gary Nolan, 1976	1.02
4	Ferguson Jenkins, 1971	1.02
5	Juan Marichal, 1966	1.06
6	Lamarr Hoyt, 1983	1.07
7	Lew Burdette, 1961	1.09
8	Jimmy Key, 1989	1.13
9	Scott McGregor, 1979	1.18
10	Jim Merritt, 1967	1.18
11	Rick Honeycutt, 1981	1.20
12	Vern Law, 1966	1.21
13	Dick Donovan, 1963	1.22
14	Fritz Peterson, 1968	1.23
15	Ferguson Jenkins, 1974	1.23

Strikeouts

1	Matt Kilroy, 1886	513
2	Toad Ramsey, 1886	499
3	Hugh Daily, 1884	483
4	Charley Radbourn, 1884	441
5	Charlie Buffinton, 1884	417
6	Guy Hecker, 1884	385
7	Nolan Ryan, 1973	383
8	Sandy Koufax, 1965	382
9	Bill Sweeney, 1884	374
10	Jim Galvin, 1884	369
11	Mark Baldwin, 1889	368
12	Nolan Ryan, 1974	367
13	Tim Keefe, 1883	361
14	Toad Ramsey, 1887	355
15	Rube Waddell, 1904	349
16	Bob Feller, 1946	348
17	Hardie Henderson, 1884	346
18	Jim Whitney, 1883	345
	Mickey Welch, 1884	345
20	Amos Rusie, 1890	341
	Nolan Ryan, 1977	341
22	Amos Rusie, 1891	337
23	Tim Keefe, 1888	333
24	Tony Mullane, 1884	329
	Nolan Ryan, 1972	329
26	Nolan Ryan, 1976	327
27	Ed Morris, 1886	326
28	Sam McDowell, 1965	325
29	Tim Keefe, 1884	323
	Lady Baldwin, 1886	323
31	Sandy Koufax, 1966	317
32	Bill Hutchinson, 1892	316
33	Charley Radbourn, 1883	315
34	John Clarkson, 1886	313
	Walter Johnson, 1910	313
	J.R. Richard, 1979	313
37	Steve Carlton, 1972	310
38	Dupee Shaw, 1884	309
39	Larry McKeon, 1884	308
	John Clarkson, 1885	308
	Mickey Lolich, 1971	308
42	Sandy Koufax, 1963	306
	Mike Scott, 1986	306
44	Sam McDowell, 1970	304
45	Walter Johnson, 1912	303
	J.R. Richard, 1978	303
47	Ed Morris, 1884	302
	Rube Waddell, 1903	302
49	Vida Blue, 1971	301
	Nolan Ryan, 1989	301
51	Ed Morris, 1885	298
52	Tim Keefe, 1886	291
	Sadie McMahon, 1890	291
	Roger Clemens, 1988	291
55	Bill Hutchinson, 1890	289
	Jack Stivetts, 1890	289
	Tom Seaver, 1971	289
58	Amos Rusie, 1892	288
59	Rube Waddell, 1905	287
60	Jack Lynch, 1884	286
	Bobby Mathews, 1884	286
	Bobby Mathews, 1885	286
	Steve Carlton, 1980	286
	Steve Carlton, 1982	286
65	John Clarkson, 1889	284
66	Dave Foutz, 1886	283
	Sam McDowell, 1968	283
	Tom Seaver, 1970	283
69	Denny McLain, 1968	280
70	Jim Galvin, 1883	279
	Sam McDowell, 1969	279
72	Bob Veale, 1965	276
	Dwight Gooden, 1984	276
74	Hal Newhouser, 1946	275
	Steve Carlton, 1983	275
76	Bob Gibson, 1970	274
	Ferguson Jenkins, 1970	274
	Mario Soto, 1982	274
79	Ferguson Jenkins, 1969	273
80	Larry Corcoran, 1884	272
	Mickey Welch, 1886	272
	Ed Seward, 1888	272
83	Mickey Lolich, 1969	271
84	Jim Whitney, 1884	270
	Bob Gibson, 1965	270
	Nolan Ryan, 1987	270
87	Ed Walsh, 1908	269
	Sandy Koufax, 1961	269
	Bob Gibson, 1969	269
	Frank Tanana, 1975	269
91	Larry Corcoran, 1880	268
	Bill Wise, 1884	268
	Jim Bunning, 1965	268
	Bob Gibson, 1968	268
	Dwight Gooden, 1985	268
96	Christy Mathewson, 1903	267
97	Jim Maloney, 1963	265
98	Bob Emslie, 1884	264
	Luis Tiant, 1968	264
100	3 players tied	263

Strikeouts (by era)

1876-1892

1	Matt Kilroy, 1886	513
2	Toad Ramsey, 1886	499
3	Hugh Daily, 1884	483
4	Charley Radbourn, 1884	441
5	Charlie Buffinton, 1884	417
6	Guy Hecker, 1884	385
7	Bill Sweeney, 1884	374
8	Jim Galvin, 1884	369
9	Mark Baldwin, 1889	368
10	Tim Keefe, 1883	361
11	Toad Ramsey, 1887	355
12	Hardie Henderson, 1884	346
13	Jim Whitney, 1883	345
	Mickey Welch, 1884	345
15	Amos Rusie, 1890	341

1893-1919

1	Rube Waddell, 1904	349
2	Walter Johnson, 1910	313
3	Walter Johnson, 1912	303
4	Rube Waddell, 1903	302
5	Rube Waddell, 1905	287
6	Ed Walsh, 1908	269
7	Christy Mathewson, 1903	267
8	Christy Mathewson, 1908	259
9	Ed Walsh, 1910	258
	Joe Wood, 1912	258
11	Ed Walsh, 1911	255
12	Ed Walsh, 1912	254
13	Walter Johnson, 1913	243
14	Pete Alexander, 1915	241

1920-1941

1	Dazzy Vance, 1924	262
2	Bob Feller, 1940	261
3	Bob Feller, 1941	260
4	Bob Feller, 1939	246
5	Bob Feller, 1938	240
6	Van Mungo, 1936	238
7	Bobo Newsom, 1938	226
8	Dazzy Vance, 1925	221
9	Lefty Grove, 1930	209
10	Johnny Vander Meer, 1941	202
11	Dazzy Vance, 1928	200
12	Dizzy Dean, 1933	199
13	Dazzy Vance, 1923	197
14	Dizzy Dean, 1934	195
	Dizzy Dean, 1936	195

1942-1960

1	Bob Feller, 1946	348
2	Hal Newhouser, 1946	275
3	Herb Score, 1956	263
4	Don Drysdale, 1960	246
5	Herb Score, 1955	245
6	Don Drysdale, 1959	242
7	Sam Jones, 1958	225
8	Hal Newhouser, 1945	212
9	Bob Turley, 1955	210
10	Sam Jones, 1959	209
11	Jim Bunning, 1959	201
	Jim Bunning, 1960	201
13	Robin Roberts, 1953	198
	Sam Jones, 1955	198
15	Sandy Koufax, 1960	197

1961-1989

1	Nolan Ryan, 1973	383
2	Sandy Koufax, 1965	382
3	Nolan Ryan, 1974	367
4	Nolan Ryan, 1977	341
5	Nolan Ryan, 1972	329
6	Nolan Ryan, 1976	327
7	Sam McDowell, 1965	325
8	Sandy Koufax, 1966	317
9	J.R. Richard, 1979	313
10	Steve Carlton, 1972	310
11	Mickey Lolich, 1971	308
12	Sandy Koufax, 1963	306
	Mike Scott, 1986	306
14	Sam McDowell, 1970	304
15	J.R. Richard, 1978	303

Strikeouts per Game

1	Nolan Ryan, 1987	11.46
2	Dwight Gooden, 1984	11.39
3	Nolan Ryan, 1989	11.33
4	Sam McDowell, 1965	10.71
5	Nolan Ryan, 1973	10.57
6	Sandy Koufax, 1962	10.57
7	Sam McDowell, 1966	10.44
8	Nolan Ryan, 1972	10.43
9	Nolan Ryan, 1976	10.36
10	Nolan Ryan, 1977	10.26
11	Sandy Koufax, 1965	10.23
12	Sandy Koufax, 1960	10.13
13	Mike Scott, 1986	10.01
14	Nolan Ryan, 1978	9.96
15	Roger Clemens, 1988	9.92
16	Nolan Ryan, 1974	9.92
17	J.R. Richard, 1978	9.92
18	Nolan Ryan, 1986	9.81
19	Herb Score, 1955	9.71
20	J.R. Richard, 1979	9.65
21	Nolan Ryan, 1984	9.64
22	Tom Griffin, 1969	9.57
23	Mario Soto, 1982	9.56
24	Jim Maloney, 1963	9.54
25	Sid Fernandez, 1985	9.53
26	Herb Score, 1956	9.51
27	Sam McDowell, 1968	9.47
28	Sandy Koufax, 1961	9.46
29	Frank Tanana, 1975	9.42
30	Don Wilson, 1969	9.40
31	Bob Veale, 1965	9.34
32	Nolan Ryan, 1988	9.33
33	Mark Langston, 1986	9.23
34	Dave Boswell, 1966	9.21
35	Luis Tiant, 1967	9.21
36	Luis Tiant, 1968	9.21
37	Sam McDowell, 1964	9.21
38	Sid Fernandez, 1988	9.10
39	Sonny Siebert, 1965	9.10
40	Tom Seaver, 1971	9.09
41	Dennis Eckersley, 1976	9.05
42	Sandy Koufax, 1964	9.00
	Sam McDowell, 1967	9.00
	Nolan Ryan, 1979	9.00
45	Sam McDowell, 1970	8.97
46	Jim Maloney, 1964	8.92
47	Mark Langston, 1989	8.90
48	Jose Rijo, 1988	8.89
49	Sandy Koufax, 1963	8.86
50	Sandy Koufax, 1966	8.83
51	Sid Fernandez, 1986	8.82
52	Nolan Ryan, 1982	8.82
53	Sam McDowell, 1969	8.81
54	Dupee Shaw, 1884	8.80
55	Tom Seaver, 1970	8.75
56	Al Downing, 1963	8.74
57	Bob Moose, 1969	8.74
58	Steve Carlton, 1983	8.71
59	Dwight Gooden, 1985	8.71
60	Steve Carlton, 1982	8.70
61	Vida Blue, 1971	8.68
62	Mickey Lolich, 1969	8.68
63	Juan Pizarro, 1961	8.68
64	Hugh Daily, 1884	8.68
65	Mark Langston, 1987	8.67
66	Bob Johnson, 1970	8.66
67	Jim Maloney, 1966	8.64
68	Bruce Hurst, 1986	8.64
69	Mario Soto, 1980	8.62
70	Jim Maloney, 1965	8.61
71	Tom Seaver, 1972	8.55
72	Dick Selma, 1969	8.53
73	Bob Veale, 1969	8.48
74	Steve Carlton, 1981	8.48
75	Steve Carlton, 1980	8.47
76	Nolan Ryan, 1981	8.46
77	Mike Scott, 1987	8.46
78	Nolan Ryan, 1975	8.45
79	Tom Gordon, 1989	8.45
80	Hal Newhouser, 1946	8.45
81	Floyd Bannister, 1985	8.45
82	Bob Feller, 1946	8.44
83	Fernando Valenzuela, 1981	8.44
84	Roger Clemens, 1986	8.43
85	Ed Correa, 1986	8.42
86	Nolan Ryan, 1983	8.40
87	Rube Waddell, 1903	8.39
88	Bob Gibson, 1970	8.39
89	Sam Jones, 1956	8.38
90	Mickey Lolich, 1965	8.34
91	Don Sutton, 1966	8.32
92	Jose DeLeon, 1988	8.32
93	Floyd Youmans, 1986	8.30
94	David Cone, 1988	8.30
95	Jim Bunning, 1965	8.29
96	Fernando Valenzuela, 1984	8.28
97	Teddy Higuera, 1987	8.24
98	Dave Boswell, 1967	8.23
99	Don Drysdale, 1960	8.23
100	Jose DeLeon, 1985	8.23

Strikeouts per Game (by era)

1876-1892

1	Dupee Shaw, 1884	8.80
2	Hugh Daily, 1884	8.68
3	Charlie Geggus, 1884	7.93
4	Matt Kilroy, 1886	7.92
5	John Clarkson, 1884	7.78
6	Toad Ramsey, 1886	7.62
7	Jim Whitney, 1884	7.23
8	Mike Dorgan, 1884	7.17
9	Walter Burke, 1884	7.13
10	Hardie Henderson, 1884	7.09
11	Tim Keefe, 1888	6.91
12	Jim McCormick, 1884	6.90
13	Bob Black, 1884	6.80
14	Lady Baldwin, 1885	6.79
15	Jack Stivetts, 1889	6.70

1893-1919

1	Rube Waddell, 1903	8.39
2	Rube Waddell, 1904	8.20
3	Rube Waddell, 1905	7.85
4	Rube Marquard, 1911	7.67
5	Joe Wood, 1911	7.53
6	Walter Johnson, 1910	7.53
7	Walter Johnson, 1912	7.41
8	Rube Waddell, 1907	7.33
9	Rube Waddell, 1908	7.30
10	Dutch Leonard, 1914	7.04
11	Red Ames, 1906	6.92
12	Rube Waddell, 1902	6.85
13	Red Ames, 1905	6.78
14	Joe Wood, 1912	6.75
15	Orval Overall, 1908	6.68

1920-1941

1	Johnny Vander Meer, 1941	8.04
2	Bob Feller, 1938	7.77
3	Dazzy Vance, 1924	7.63
4	Dazzy Vance, 1925	7.51
5	Dazzy Vance, 1926	7.46
6	Bob Feller, 1939	7.45
7	Bob Feller, 1940	7.34
8	Van Mungo, 1936	6.87
9	Bob Feller, 1941	6.82
10	Van Mungo, 1937	6.82
11	Lefty Grove, 1926	6.77
12	Bill Hallahan, 1930	6.72
13	George Earnshaw, 1928	6.66
14	Red Ruffing, 1932	6.60
15	Lefty Grove, 1930	6.46

1942-1960

1	Sandy Koufax, 1960	10.13
2	Herb Score, 1955	9.71
3	Herb Score, 1956	9.51
4	Hal Newhouser, 1946	8.45
5	Bob Feller, 1946	8.44
6	Sam Jones, 1956	8.38
7	Don Drysdale, 1960	8.23
8	Herb Score, 1959	8.22
9	Sam Jones, 1958	8.10
10	Don Drysdale, 1959	8.04
11	Bob Turley, 1957	7.77
12	Camilo Pascual, 1956	7.71
13	Bob Turley, 1955	7.65
14	Stan Williams, 1960	7.61
15	Sam Jones, 1957	7.57

1961-1989

1	Nolan Ryan, 1987	11.46
2	Dwight Gooden, 1984	11.39
3	Nolan Ryan, 1989	11.33
4	Sam McDowell, 1965	10.71
5	Nolan Ryan, 1973	10.57
6	Sandy Koufax, 1962	10.57
7	Sam McDowell, 1966	10.44
8	Nolan Ryan, 1972	10.43
9	Nolan Ryan, 1976	10.36
10	Nolan Ryan, 1977	10.26
11	Sandy Koufax, 1965	10.23
12	Mike Scott, 1986	10.01
13	Nolan Ryan, 1978	9.96
14	Roger Clemens, 1988	9.92
15	Nolan Ryan, 1974	9.92

Earned Run Average

1	Tim Keefe, 1880	0.86
2	Dutch Leonard, 1914	0.96
3	Mordecai Brown, 1906	1.04
4	Bob Gibson, 1968	1.12
5	Walter Johnson, 1913	1.14
6	Christy Mathewson, 1909	1.15
7	Jack Pfiester, 1907	1.15
8	Addie Joss, 1908	1.16
9	Carl Lundgren, 1907	1.17
10	Denny Driscoll, 1882	1.21
11	Pete Alexander, 1915	1.22
12	George Bradley, 1876	1.23
13	Cy Young, 1908	1.26
14	Ed Walsh, 1910	1.26
15	Walter Johnson, 1918	1.27
16	Christy Mathewson, 1905	1.27
17	Guy Hecker, 1882	1.30
18	Jack Coombs, 1910	1.30
19	Mordecai Brown, 1909	1.31
20	Jack Taylor, 1902	1.33
21	Walter Johnson, 1910	1.35
22	George Bradley, 1880	1.38
23	Charley Radbourn, 1884	1.38
24	Mordecai Brown, 1907	1.39
25	Walter Johnson, 1912	1.39
26	Harry Krause, 1909	1.39
27	Ed Walsh, 1909	1.41
28	Ed Walsh, 1908	1.42
29	Ed Reulbach, 1905	1.42
30	Orval Overall, 1909	1.42
31	Christy Mathewson, 1908	1.43
32	Fred Anderson, 1917	1.44
33	Mordecai Brown, 1908	1.47
34	Rube Waddell, 1905	1.48
35	Walter Johnson, 1919	1.49
36	Joe Wood, 1915	1.49
37	Monte Ward, 1878	1.51
38	Harry McCormick, 1882	1.51
39	Doc White, 1906	1.52
40	George McQuillan, 1908	1.52
41	Dwight Gooden, 1985	1.53
42	Eddie Cicotte, 1917	1.53
43	Will White, 1882	1.54
44	Jim McCormick, 1884	1.54
45	Cy Morgan, 1910	1.55
46	Charlie Sweeney, 1884	1.55
47	Walter Johnson, 1915	1.55
48	Pete Alexander, 1916	1.55
49	Howie Camnitz, 1908	1.56
50	Jack Pfiester, 1906	1.56
51	Jim Devlin, 1876	1.56
52	Fred Toney, 1915	1.57
53	Eddie Cicotte, 1913	1.58
54	Rube Marquard, 1916	1.58
55	Tim Keefe, 1885	1.58
56	Chief Bender, 1910	1.58
57	Barney Pelty, 1906	1.59
58	Addie Joss, 1904	1.59
59	Ed Walsh, 1907	1.60
60	Luis Tiant, 1968	1.60
61	Joe McGinnity, 1904	1.61
62	Ray Collins, 1910	1.62
63	Rube Waddell, 1904	1.62
64	Howie Camnitz, 1909	1.62
65	Cy Young, 1901	1.63
66	Spud Chandler, 1943	1.64
67	Ernie Shore, 1915	1.64
68	Silver King, 1888	1.64
69	Ed Summers, 1908	1.64
70	Walter Johnson, 1908	1.65
71	Russ Ford, 1910	1.65
72	Dean Chance, 1964	1.65
73	Ed Reulbach, 1906	1.65
74	Chief Bender, 1909	1.66
75	Sam Leever, 1907	1.66
76	Carl Hubbell, 1933	1.66
77	Mickey Welch, 1885	1.66
78	Candy Cummings, 1876	1.67
79	Joe Wood, 1910	1.67
80	Tommy Bond, 1876	1.68
81	Billy Taylor, 1884	1.68
82	Ned Garvin, 1904	1.68
83	Ed Reulbach, 1907	1.69
84	Claude Hendrix, 1914	1.69
85	Bill Burns, 1908	1.69
86	Nolan Ryan, 1981	1.69
87	Jim McCormick, 1878	1.69
88	Orval Overall, 1907	1.70
	Rube Foster, 1914	1.70
90	Addie Joss, 1909	1.70
91	Ed Killian, 1909	1.72
92	Walter Johnson, 1914	1.72
93	Doc White, 1909	1.72
94	Bill Doak, 1914	1.72
95	Addie Joss, 1906	1.72
	Pete Alexander, 1919	1.72
97	Sandy Koufax, 1966	1.73
98	Bob Ewing, 1907	1.73
99	Vic Willis, 1906	1.73
100	Charlie Chech, 1908	1.73

Earned Run Average (by era)

1876-1892

1	Tim Keefe, 1880	0.86
2	Denny Driscoll, 1882	1.21
3	George Bradley, 1876	1.23
4	Guy Hecker, 1882	1.30
5	George Bradley, 1880	1.38
6	Charley Radbourn, 1884	1.38
7	Monte Ward, 1878	1.51
8	Harry McCormick, 1882	1.51
9	Will White, 1882	1.54
10	Jim McCormick, 1884	1.54
11	Charlie Sweeney, 1884	1.55
12	Jim Devlin, 1876	1.56
13	Tim Keefe, 1885	1.58
14	Silver King, 1888	1.64
15	Mickey Welch, 1885	1.66

1893-1919

1	Dutch Leonard, 1914	0.96
2	Mordecai Brown, 1906	1.04
3	Walter Johnson, 1913	1.14
4	Christy Mathewson, 1909	1.15
5	Jack Pfiester, 1907	1.15
6	Addie Joss, 1908	1.16
7	Carl Lundgren, 1907	1.17
8	Pete Alexander, 1915	1.22
9	Cy Young, 1908	1.26
10	Ed Walsh, 1910	1.26
11	Walter Johnson, 1918	1.27
12	Christy Mathewson, 1905	1.27
13	Jack Coombs, 1910	1.30
14	Mordecai Brown, 1909	1.31
15	Jack Taylor, 1902	1.33

1920-1941

1	Carl Hubbell, 1933	1.66
2	Pete Alexander, 1920	1.91
3	Dolf Luque, 1923	1.93
4	Lon Warneke, 1933	2.01
5	Lefty Grove, 1931	2.06
6	Dazzy Vance, 1928	2.09
7	Hal Schumacher, 1933	2.15
8	Dazzy Vance, 1924	2.16
9	Babe Adams, 1920	2.16
10	Burleigh Grimes, 1920	2.22
11	Elmer Riddle, 1941	2.24
12	Bill Walker, 1931	2.26
13	Wilcy Moore, 1927	2.28
14	Bucky Walters, 1939	2.29
15	Carl Hubbell, 1934	2.30

1942-1960

1	Spud Chandler, 1943	1.64
2	Mort Cooper, 1942	1.77
3	Hal Newhouser, 1945	1.81
4	Max Lanier, 1943	1.90
5	Hal Newhouser, 1946	1.94
6	Billy Pierce, 1955	1.97
7	Whitey Ford, 1958	2.01
8	Al Benton, 1945	2.02
9	Allie Reynolds, 1952	2.07
10	Howie Pollet, 1946	2.10
	Warren Spahn, 1953	2.10
12	Ted Lyons, 1942	2.10
13	Spud Chandler, 1946	2.10
14	Dizzy Trout, 1944	2.12
15	Roger Wolff, 1945	2.12

1961-1989

1	Bob Gibson, 1968	1.12
2	Dwight Gooden, 1985	1.53
3	Luis Tiant, 1968	1.60
4	Dean Chance, 1964	1.65
5	Nolan Ryan, 1981	1.69
6	Sandy Koufax, 1966	1.73
7	Sandy Koufax, 1964	1.74
8	Ron Guidry, 1978	1.74
9	Tom Seaver, 1971	1.76
10	Sam McDowell, 1968	1.81
11	Vida Blue, 1971	1.82
12	Phil Niekro, 1967	1.87
13	Joe Horlen, 1964	1.88
14	Sandy Koufax, 1963	1.88
15	Luis Tiant, 1972	1.91

Adjusted Earned Run Average

1	Tim Keefe, 1880	309
2	Dutch Leonard, 1914	274
3	Walter Johnson, 1913	268
4	Mordecai Brown, 1906	251
5	Bob Gibson, 1968	248
6	Pete Alexander, 1915	235
7	Christy Mathewson, 1909	234
8	Walter Johnson, 1912	233
9	Christy Mathewson, 1905	225
10	Dwight Gooden, 1985	225
11	Walter Johnson, 1918	224
12	Jack Pfiester, 1907	218
13	Lefty Grove, 1931	215
14	Denny Driscoll, 1882	215
15	Walter Johnson, 1919	214
16	Carl Lundgren, 1907	214
17	Addie Joss, 1908	213
18	Cy Young, 1901	212
19	Ed Reulbach, 1905	211
20	Ron Guidry, 1978	211
21	Charley Radbourn, 1884	207
22	Al Maul, 1895	206
23	Jim McCormick, 1884	205
24	Dolf Luque, 1923	200
25	Jack Taylor, 1902	199
26	Sandy Koufax, 1966	199
27	Hank Aguirre, 1962	198
28	Silver King, 1888	198
29	Billy Pierce, 1955	197
30	Monty Stratton, 1937	196
31	Clark Griffith, 1898	195
32	Dean Chance, 1964	195
33	Hal Newhouser, 1945	194
34	Lefty Grove, 1939	194
35	Billy Rhines, 1890	194
36	Carl Hubbell, 1933	193
37	Lefty Gomez, 1937	193
38	Vean Gregg, 1911	192
39	Mort Cooper, 1942	191
40	Walter Johnson, 1910	191
41	Hal Newhouser, 1946	191
42	Rube Waddell, 1905	191
43	Ed Walsh, 1910	190
44	Lefty Grove, 1936	190
45	Joe Wood, 1915	189
46	Walter Johnson, 1915	189
47	Phil Niekro, 1967	189
48	Tom Seaver, 1971	189
49	Jack Coombs, 1910	189
50	Amos Rusie, 1894	189
51	Spud Chandler, 1943	189
52	Vida Blue, 1971	189
53	Mordecai Brown, 1909	188
54	Dazzy Vance, 1928	188
55	Dazzy Vance, 1930	188
56	Ed Siever, 1902	187
57	Warren Spahn, 1953	187
58	Luis Tiant, 1968	187
59	Sandy Koufax, 1964	186
60	Guy Hecker, 1882	186
61	Whitey Ford, 1958	186
62	Jack Stivetts, 1889	186
63	Lefty Grove, 1926	185
64	Rube Waddell, 1902	185
65	Cy Young, 1908	184
66	Charlie Sweeney, 1884	184
67	Billy Rhines, 1896	184
68	Russ Ford, 1914	183
69	Fred Toney, 1915	182
70	Tim Keefe, 1885	182
71	Juan Marichal, 1965	181
72	Eddie Cicotte, 1919	181
73	Mordecai Brown, 1907	181
74	Johnny Antonelli, 1954	181
75	Joe Horlen, 1964	180
76	Nolan Ryan, 1981	179
77	Lefty Gomez, 1934	179
78	Joe Wood, 1912	179
79	Lefty Grove, 1935	179
80	Max Lanier, 1943	178
81	Ted Lyons, 1939	178
82	Harry McCormick, 1882	177
83	Tom Seaver, 1973	177
84	Lefty Grove, 1930	177
85	Jim McCormick, 1883	177
86	Red Faber, 1921	177
87	Eddie Cicotte, 1913	177
88	Wilbur Wood, 1971	176
89	Dazzy Vance, 1924	176
90	Billy Taylor, 1884	176
91	Johnny Allen, 1937	175
92	Walter Johnson, 1911	175
93	Al Benton, 1945	175
94	Fred Anderson, 1917	175
95	Lefty Grove, 1932	175
96	Harry Brecheen, 1948	175
97	Ted Lyons, 1942	174
98	Will White, 1882	174
99	John Tudor, 1985	174
100	Orval Overall, 1909	174

Adjusted ERA (by era)

1876-1892

1	Tim Keefe, 1880	309
2	Denny Driscoll, 1882	215
3	Charley Radbourn, 1884	207
4	Jim McCormick, 1884	205
5	Silver King, 1888	198
6	Billy Rhines, 1890	194
7	Guy Hecker, 1882	186
8	Jack Stivetts, 1889	186
9	Charlie Sweeney, 1884	184
10	Tim Keefe, 1885	182
11	Harry McCormick, 1882	177
12	Jim McCormick, 1883	177
13	Billy Taylor, 1884	176
14	Will White, 1882	174
15	Kid Nichols, 1890	174

1893-1919

1	Dutch Leonard, 1914	274
2	Walter Johnson, 1913	268
3	Mordecai Brown, 1906	251
4	Pete Alexander, 1915	235
5	Christy Mathewson, 1909	234
6	Walter Johnson, 1912	233
7	Christy Mathewson, 1905	225
8	Walter Johnson, 1918	224
9	Jack Pfiester, 1907	218
10	Walter Johnson, 1919	214
11	Carl Lundgren, 1907	214
12	Addie Joss, 1908	213
13	Cy Young, 1901	212
14	Ed Reulbach, 1905	211
15	Al Maul, 1895	206

1920-1941

1	Lefty Grove, 1931	215
2	Dolf Luque, 1923	200
3	Monty Stratton, 1937	196
4	Lefty Grove, 1939	194
5	Carl Hubbell, 1933	193
6	Lefty Gomez, 1937	193
7	Lefty Grove, 1936	190
8	Dazzy Vance, 1928	188
9	Dazzy Vance, 1930	188
10	Lefty Grove, 1926	185
11	Lefty Gomez, 1934	179
12	Lefty Grove, 1935	179
13	Ted Lyons, 1939	178
14	Lefty Grove, 1930	177
15	Red Faber, 1921	177

1942-1960

1	Billy Pierce, 1955	197
2	Hal Newhouser, 1945	194
3	Mort Cooper, 1942	191
4	Hal Newhouser, 1946	191
5	Spud Chandler, 1943	189
6	Warren Spahn, 1953	187
7	Whitey Ford, 1958	186
8	Johnny Antonelli, 1954	181
9	Max Lanier, 1943	178
10	Al Benton, 1945	175
11	Harry Brecheen, 1948	175
12	Ted Lyons, 1942	174
13	Hoyt Wilhelm, 1959	173
14	Mike Garcia, 1949	171

1961-1989

1	Bob Gibson, 1968	248
2	Dwight Gooden, 1985	225
3	Ron Guidry, 1978	211
4	Sandy Koufax, 1966	199
5	Hank Aguirre, 1962	198
6	Dean Chance, 1964	195
7	Phil Niekro, 1967	189
8	Tom Seaver, 1971	189
9	Vida Blue, 1971	189
10	Luis Tiant, 1968	187
11	Sandy Koufax, 1964	186
12	Juan Marichal, 1965	181
13	Joe Horlen, 1964	180
14	Nolan Ryan, 1981	179
15	Tom Seaver, 1973	177

Pitching Runs

1	Amos Rusie, 1894	126.1
2	Charley Radbourn, 1884	120.6
3	Guy Hecker, 1884	107.9
4	Silver King, 1888	92.3
5	John Clarkson, 1889	89.5
6	Cy Young, 1901	84.0
7	Matt Kilroy, 1887	80.3
8	Walter Johnson, 1912	79.9
9	Pink Hawley, 1895	79.3
10	Silver King, 1890	78.8
11	Will White, 1883	77.6
12	Amos Rusie, 1893	77.5
13	Charley Radbourn, 1883	76.4
14	Dave Foutz, 1886	75.2
15	Lefty Grove, 1931	74.7
16	Jouett Meekin, 1894	74.4
17	Dolf Luque, 1923	74.2
18	Scott Stratton, 1890	72.2
19	Billy Rhines, 1890	71.8
20	Lefty Gomez, 1937	70.7
21	Jim Galvin, 1884	69.4
22	George Bradley, 1876	69.1
23	Walter Johnson, 1913	68.6
24	Cy Young, 1892	68.5
25	Lefty Grove, 1930	68.5
26	Kid Nichols, 1897	68.5
27	Dazzy Vance, 1930	68.1
28	Lefty Gomez, 1934	67.9
29	Mike Smith, 1887	67.5
30	Sandy Koufax, 1966	67.5
31	John Clarkson, 1885	67.1
32	Red Faber, 1921	66.5
33	Toad Ramsey, 1886	64.8
34	Warren Spahn, 1953	64.7
35	Christy Mathewson, 1905	64.7
36	Kid Nichols, 1890	64.0
37	Pete Alexander, 1915	64.0
38	Cy Young, 1895	63.9
39	Dwight Gooden, 1985	63.8
40	Kid Nichols, 1896	63.5
41	Kid Nichols, 1898	63.5
42	Amos Rusie, 1897	63.4
43	Cy Young, 1894	63.4
44	Bob Gibson, 1968	63.2
45	Mickey Welch, 1885	63.1
46	Ted Breitenstein, 1893	63.1
47	Bob Caruthers, 1885	62.9
48	Bob Feller, 1940	62.8
49	Clark Griffith, 1898	62.6
50	Lefty Grove, 1936	62.6
51	Ron Guidry, 1978	62.0
52	Cy Young, 1893	61.9
53	Ed Morris, 1886	61.8
54	Will White, 1882	61.4
55	Amos Rusie, 1890	61.3
56	Carl Hubbell, 1934	61.3
57	Tim Keefe, 1883	61.0
58	Jim Palmer, 1975	61.0
59	Dean Chance, 1964	61.0
60	Claude Hendrix, 1914	60.9
61	Cy Young, 1902	60.7
62	Hugh Daily, 1884	60.6
63	Ed Seward, 1888	60.5
64	Robin Roberts, 1953	59.2
65	Thornton Lee, 1941	59.2
66	Dazzy Vance, 1928	59.0
67	Dazzy Vance, 1924	58.8
68	Bob Feller, 1939	58.5
69	Charlie Ferguson, 1886	58.3
70	Win Mercer, 1894	58.3
71	Kid Nichols, 1895	58.2
72	Bucky Walters, 1939	57.8
73	Carl Hubbell, 1936	57.8
74	Lady Baldwin, 1886	57.7
75	Bill Hutchinson, 1890	57.7
76	Wilbur Wood, 1971	57.7
77	Ed Morris, 1885	57.7
78	Carl Hubbell, 1933	57.6
79	Jesse Duryea, 1889	57.4
80	Guy Hecker, 1885	57.2
81	Vida Blue, 1971	57.2
82	Tony Mullane, 1883	57.1
83	Steve Carlton, 1972	56.9
84	John Clarkson, 1887	56.5
85	Sandy Koufax, 1965	56.1
86	Warren Spahn, 1947	56.1
87	Walter Johnson, 1919	55.9
88	Bill Hoffer, 1895	55.1
89	Joe Wood, 1912	54.9
90	Kid Nichols, 1893	54.9
91	Tim Keefe, 1885	54.7
92	Bob Feller, 1946	54.4
93	Tom Seaver, 1971	54.3
94	Charlie Buffinton, 1884	54.2
95	Hal Newhouser, 1945	54.0
96	Toad Ramsey, 1887	54.0
97	Walter Johnson, 1918	53.9
98	Mel Harder, 1934	53.4
99	Lefty Grove, 1932	53.3
100	Red Ehret, 1890	53.3

Adjusted Pitching Runs

1	Amos Rusie, 1894	121.6
2	Charley Radbourn, 1884	110.9
3	Silver King, 1888	104.9
4	John Clarkson, 1887	92.3
5	Cy Young, 1894	89.0
6	Dave Foutz, 1886	86.6
7	Jim Devlin, 1877	86.4
8	John Clarkson, 1889	85.0
9	Amos Rusie, 1893	84.5
10	Silver King, 1890	84.5
11	Toad Ramsey, 1886	82.2
12	Billy Rhines, 1890	81.4
13	Mike Smith, 1887	81.2
14	Jim Galvin, 1884	80.5
15	Scott Stratton, 1890	79.4
16	John Clarkson, 1885	77.9
17	Kid Nichols, 1890	77.2
18	Lefty Grove, 1931	76.2
19	Guy Hecker, 1884	75.9
20	Walter Johnson, 1912	75.9
21	Kid Nichols, 1896	75.8
22	Cy Young, 1901	75.4
23	Kid Nichols, 1897	74.5
24	Walter Johnson, 1913	74.1
25	Bill Hutchinson, 1890	73.7
26	Will White, 1883	73.4
27	Tim Keefe, 1883	73.3
28	Ed Morris, 1885	71.3
29	Lefty Grove, 1936	70.8
30	Pink Hawley, 1895	70.3
31	Jouett Meekin, 1894	70.2
32	Cy Young, 1892	69.8
33	Red Faber, 1921	69.8
34	Toad Ramsey, 1887	69.2
35	Pete Alexander, 1915	69.0
36	Dolf Luque, 1923	69.0
37	Lefty Grove, 1932	68.6
38	Charley Radbourn, 1883	68.1
39	Cy Young, 1893	67.8
40	Cy Young, 1896	67.3
41	Lefty Gomez, 1937	66.7
42	Mickey Welch, 1885	66.2
43	Kid Gleason, 1890	66.1
44	Dazzy Vance, 1930	65.9
45	Tony Mullane, 1883	65.4
46	Kid Nichols, 1898	65.0
47	Clark Griffith, 1898	64.8
48	Lefty Grove, 1935	64.5
49	Dizzy Dean, 1934	64.5
50	Matt Kilroy, 1887	64.3
51	Lady Baldwin, 1886	63.4
52	John Clarkson, 1886	63.2
53	Nig Cuppy, 1896	63.1
54	Jesse Duryea, 1889	63.1
55	Guy Hecker, 1885	62.9
56	Cy Young, 1899	62.9
57	Lefty Grove, 1930	62.9
58	Ted Breitenstein, 1893	62.9
59	Jack Stivetts, 1891	62.8
60	Tim Keefe, 1887	62.5
61	Kid Nichols, 1895	62.5
62	Tony Mullane, 1887	61.4
63	Bill Hoffer, 1895	61.3
64	Jim Devlin, 1876	61.2
65	Lefty Grove, 1926	61.1
66	Sandy Koufax, 1966	61.1
67	Will White, 1882	60.9
68	Hugh Daily, 1884	60.6
69	Christy Mathewson, 1905	59.9
70	Kid Nichols, 1891	59.7
71	Hal Newhouser, 1945	59.4
72	Red Ehret, 1890	59.3
73	Tony Mullane, 1884	59.2
74	Ron Guidry, 1978	58.7
75	Dwight Gooden, 1985	58.7
76	Cy Young, 1902	57.9
77	Amos Rusie, 1897	57.9
78	Mark Baldwin, 1890	57.8
79	Win Mercer, 1894	57.7
80	Bucky Walters, 1939	57.7
81	Frank Killen, 1893	57.6
82	Lefty Gomez, 1934	57.6
83	Joe Wood, 1912	57.6
84	Joe McGinnity, 1899	57.6
85	Charlie Buffinton, 1888	57.6
86	Hal Newhouser, 1946	57.3
87	Dazzy Vance, 1928	57.2
88	Tim Keefe, 1885	57.2
89	Bob Caruthers, 1886	57.1
90	Walter Johnson, 1918	56.9
91	Iceberg Chamberlin, 1889	56.7
92	Juan Marichal, 1965	56.7
93	Bobo Newsom, 1940	56.6
94	Kid Nichols, 1893	56.5
95	Dazzy Vance, 1924	56.4
96	Bob Gibson, 1968	56.3
97	Frank Sullivan, 1955	56.0
98	Dizzy Trout, 1944	55.8
99	Vic Willis, 1899	55.8
100	Vida Blue, 1971	55.8

Pitching Wins

1	Charley Radbourn, 1884	10.8
2	Guy Hecker, 1884	9.9
3	Amos Rusie, 1894	9.7
4	Silver King, 1888	8.5
5	Walter Johnson, 1912	8.0
6	John Clarkson, 1889	7.8
7	Cy Young, 1901	7.6
8	Walter Johnson, 1913	7.3
9	Bob Gibson, 1968	7.2
10	Dolf Luque, 1923	7.1
11	Pete Alexander, 1915	7.1
12	Sandy Koufax, 1966	7.1
13	Lefty Grove, 1931	7.0
14	Will White, 1883	6.8
15	Christy Mathewson, 1905	6.7
16	Dwight Gooden, 1985	6.7
17	Charley Radbourn, 1883	6.7
18	Dave Foutz, 1886	6.6
19	Matt Kilroy, 1887	6.5
20	Lefty Gomez, 1937	6.5
21	Pink Hawley, 1895	6.4
22	Dean Chance, 1964	6.4
23	Ron Guidry, 1978	6.4
24	Billy Rhines, 1890	6.4
25	Amos Rusie, 1893	6.4
26	Scott Stratton, 1890	6.4
27	Cy Young, 1892	6.3
28	Claude Hendrix, 1914	6.3
29	John Clarkson, 1885	6.3
30	Lefty Gomez, 1934	6.3
31	Silver King, 1890	6.3
32	Warren Spahn, 1953	6.2
33	Jim Palmer, 1975	6.2
34	Red Faber, 1921	6.2
35	Wilbur Wood, 1971	6.2
36	Jim Galvin, 1884	6.2
37	Lefty Grove, 1930	6.2
38	Vida Blue, 1971	6.2
39	Steve Carlton, 1972	6.1
40	Carl Hubbell, 1933	6.1
41	George Bradley, 1876	6.1
42	Walter Johnson, 1918	6.0
43	Dazzy Vance, 1930	6.0
44	Carl Hubbell, 1934	6.0
45	Mickey Welch, 1885	5.9
46	Bob Feller, 1940	5.9
47	Kid Nichols, 1898	5.9
48	Sandy Koufax, 1965	5.9
49	Kid Nichols, 1897	5.9
50	Clark Griffith, 1898	5.9
51	Walter Johnson, 1919	5.8
52	Dazzy Vance, 1924	5.8
53	Tom Seaver, 1971	5.8
54	Hal Newhouser, 1945	5.8
55	Bucky Walters, 1939	5.8
56	Dazzy Vance, 1928	5.8
57	Ed Walsh, 1910	5.8
58	Cy Young, 1902	5.8
59	Ed Walsh, 1908	5.8
60	Thornton Lee, 1941	5.7
61	Robin Roberts, 1953	5.7
62	Jouett Meekin, 1894	5.7
63	Bob Feller, 1946	5.7
64	Kid Nichols, 1890	5.7
65	Toad Ramsey, 1886	5.7
66	Bob Caruthers, 1885	5.7
67	Will White, 1882	5.6
68	Carl Hubbell, 1936	5.6
69	Ed Seward, 1888	5.6
70	Walter Johnson, 1915	5.6
71	Lefty Grove, 1936	5.5
72	Warren Spahn, 1947	5.5
73	Jack Taylor, 1902	5.5
74	Joe Wood, 1912	5.5
75	Mike Smith, 1887	5.5
76	Amos Rusie, 1890	5.5
77	Walter Johnson, 1910	5.4
78	Mordecai Brown, 1906	5.4
79	Mordecai Brown, 1909	5.4
80	Amos Rusie, 1897	5.4
81	Ed Morris, 1886	5.4
82	Kid Nichols, 1896	5.4
83	Bob Feller, 1939	5.4
84	Dizzy Trout, 1944	5.4
85	Tim Keefe, 1883	5.4
86	Joe McGinnity, 1904	5.4
87	John Tudor, 1985	5.4
88	Hal Newhouser, 1946	5.3
89	Jack Coombs, 1910	5.3
90	Tom Seaver, 1973	5.3
91	Hugh Daily, 1884	5.3
92	Ed Reulbach, 1905	5.3
93	Pete Alexander, 1920	5.3
94	Pete Alexander, 1916	5.3
95	Charlie Ferguson, 1886	5.3
96	Sandy Koufax, 1963	5.3
97	Juan Marichal, 1969	5.2
98	Lady Baldwin, 1886	5.2
99	Ed Walsh, 1912	5.2
100	Bob Gibson, 1969	5.2

Adjusted Pitching Wins

1	Charley Radbourn, 1884	9.9
2	Silver King, 1888	9.7
3	Amos Rusie, 1894	9.3
4	Walter Johnson, 1913	7.9
5	John Clarkson, 1887	7.8
6	Jim Devlin, 1877	7.7
7	Pete Alexander, 1915	7.7
8	Dave Foutz, 1886	7.6
9	Walter Johnson, 1912	7.6
10	John Clarkson, 1889	7.4
11	John Clarkson, 1885	7.3
12	Billy Rhines, 1890	7.2
13	Toad Ramsey, 1886	7.2
14	Jim Galvin, 1884	7.2
15	Lefty Grove, 1931	7.1
16	Scott Stratton, 1890	7.0
17	Guy Hecker, 1884	6.9
18	Amos Rusie, 1893	6.9
19	Kid Nichols, 1890	6.9
20	Cy Young, 1894	6.8
21	Cy Young, 1901	6.8
22	Silver King, 1890	6.7
23	Dolf Luque, 1923	6.6
24	Mike Smith, 1887	6.6
25	Bill Hutchinson, 1890	6.6
26	Red Faber, 1921	6.5
27	Cy Young, 1892	6.5
28	Will White, 1883	6.5
29	Bob Gibson, 1968	6.5
30	Tim Keefe, 1883	6.5
31	Kid Nichols, 1896	6.4
32	Ed Morris, 1885	6.4
33	Sandy Koufax, 1966	6.4
34	Kid Nichols, 1897	6.4
35	Hal Newhouser, 1945	6.4
36	Walter Johnson, 1918	6.3
37	Lefty Grove, 1932	6.3
38	Dizzy Dean, 1934	6.3
39	Lefty Grove, 1936	6.3
40	Christy Mathewson, 1905	6.2
41	Mickey Welch, 1885	6.2
42	Dwight Gooden, 1985	6.2
43	Lefty Gomez, 1937	6.1
44	Kid Nichols, 1898	6.1
45	Clark Griffith, 1898	6.1
46	Gaylord Perry, 1972	6.1
47	Ron Guidry, 1978	6.0
48	Lefty Grove, 1935	6.0
49	Hal Newhouser, 1946	6.0
50	Vida Blue, 1971	6.0
51	Juan Marichal, 1965	6.0
52	Jack Chesbro, 1904	6.0
53	Charley Radbourn, 1883	5.9
54	Steve Carlton, 1972	5.9
55	Lefty Grove, 1926	5.9
56	Kid Gleason, 1890	5.9
57	Dizzy Trout, 1944	5.9
58	Wilbur Wood, 1971	5.8
59	Dazzy Vance, 1930	5.8
60	Bucky Walters, 1939	5.8
61	Tony Mullane, 1883	5.8
62	Joe Wood, 1912	5.7
63	Lady Baldwin, 1886	5.7
64	Walter Johnson, 1919	5.7
65	John Clarkson, 1886	5.7
66	Cy Young, 1896	5.7
67	Cy Young, 1899	5.7
68	Pink Hawley, 1895	5.7
69	Lefty Grove, 1930	5.7
70	Guy Hecker, 1885	5.7
71	Charlie Buffinton, 1888	5.7
72	Walter Johnson, 1910	5.7
73	Carl Hubbell, 1933	5.6
74	Frank Sullivan, 1955	5.6
75	Toad Ramsey, 1887	5.6
76	Dazzy Vance, 1924	5.6
77	Will White, 1882	5.6
78	Dazzy Vance, 1928	5.6
79	Cy Young, 1893	5.6
80	Cy Young, 1902	5.5
81	Walter Johnson, 1915	5.5
82	Jim Palmer, 1973	5.4
83	Cy Falkenberg, 1914	5.4
84	Jack Stivetts, 1891	5.4
85	Tony Mullane, 1884	5.4
86	Carl Hubbell, 1936	5.4
87	Addie Joss, 1908	5.4
88	Mort Cooper, 1942	5.4
89	Jouett Meekin, 1894	5.4
90	Jim Devlin, 1876	5.4
91	Rube Waddell, 1905	5.4
92	Tim Keefe, 1885	5.4
93	Robin Roberts, 1953	5.4
94	Tom Seaver, 1973	5.4
95	Lefty Gomez, 1934	5.4
96	Mordecai Brown, 1906	5.4
97	Nig Cuppy, 1896	5.4
98	Bobo Newsom, 1940	5.3
99	Steve Carlton, 1980	5.3
100	Jesse Duryea, 1889	5.3

Opponents' Batting Average

1	Luis Tiant, 1968	.168
2	Nolan Ryan, 1972	.171
3	Ed Reulbach, 1906	.179
4	Sandy Koufax, 1965	.179
5	Dutch Leonard, 1914	.180
6	Sid Fernandez, 1985	.181
7	Tim Keefe, 1880	.182
8	Dave McNally, 1968	.182
9	Tommy Byrne, 1949	.183
10	Al Downing, 1963	.184
11	Bob Gibson, 1968	.184
12	Charlie Sweeney, 1884	.185
13	Sam McDowell, 1965	.185
14	Herb Score, 1956	.186
15	Mike Scott, 1986	.186
16	Carl Lundgren, 1907	.186
17	Nolan Ryan, 1989	.187
18	Ed Walsh, 1910	.187
19	Mario Soto, 1980	.187
20	Walter Johnson, 1913	.187
21	Nolan Ryan, 1981	.188
22	Russ Ford, 1910	.188
23	Nolan Ryan, 1986	.188
24	Dupee Shaw, 1884	.188
25	Jim McCormick, 1884	.188
26	Floyd Youmans, 1986	.188
27	Sam McDowell, 1966	.188
28	Guy Hecker, 1882	.188
29	Sandy Koufax, 1963	.189
30	Sam McDowell, 1968	.189
31	Don Sutton, 1972	.189
32	Jim Hunter, 1972	.189
33	Vida Blue, 1971	.189
34	Nolan Ryan, 1974	.190
35	Andy Messersmith, 1969	.190
36	Joe Horlen, 1964	.190
37	Sid Fernandez, 1988	.191
38	Pete Alexander, 1915	.191
39	Sandy Koufax, 1964	.191
40	Jim Bibby, 1973	.192
41	Bob Turley, 1955	.193
42	Nolan Ryan, 1977	.193
43	Ron Guidry, 1978	.193
44	Stan Coveleski, 1917	.194
45	Bob Turley, 1957	.194
46	Herb Score, 1955	.194
47	Nolan Ryan, 1976	.195
48	Nolan Ryan, 1983	.195
49	Dean Chance, 1964	.195
50	Roger Clemens, 1986	.195
51	Walter Johnson, 1912	.196
52	Roger Nelson, 1972	.196
53	J.R. Richard, 1978	.196
54	Tim Keefe, 1888	.196
55	Pascual Perez, 1988	.196
56	Jeff Robinson, 1988	.197
57	Jose DeLeon, 1989	.197
58	Dave Boswell, 1966	.197
59	Sandy Koufax, 1962	.197
60	Addie Joss, 1908	.197
61	Charlie Sweeney, 1884	.197
62	Sonny Siebert, 1968	.198
63	Sid Fernandez, 1989	.198
64	Tim Keefe, 1885	.198
65	Larry Cheney, 1916	.198
66	Wayne Simpson, 1970	.198
67	Orval Overall, 1909	.198
68	Gary Peters, 1967	.199
69	Larry Corcoran, 1880	.199
70	Jeff Tesreau, 1912	.199
71	Willie Mitchell, 1913	.199
72	Nolan Ryan, 1987	.199
73	Christy Mathewson, 1909	.200
74	Adonis Terry, 1888	.200
75	Denny McLain, 1968	.200
76	Mickey Welch, 1885	.200
77	Bobby Bolin, 1968	.200
	Jim Palmer, 1969	.200
79	Silver King, 1888	.200
80	Rube Waddell, 1905	.200
81	Spec Shea, 1947	.200
82	Ed Seward, 1888	.201
83	Art Fromme, 1909	.201
84	Babe Ruth, 1916	.201
85	Tony Mullane, 1892	.201
86	Toad Ramsey, 1886	.201
87	Dwight Gooden, 1985	.201
88	Hal Newhouser, 1946	.201
89	Jack Coombs, 1910	.201
90	Dwight Gooden, 1984	.202
91	Frank Knauss, 1890	.202
92	Jim Maloney, 1963	.202
93	Cy Morgan, 1909	.202
94	Mordecai Brown, 1909	.202
95	Mordecai Brown, 1908	.202
96	Lady Baldwin, 1885	.202
97	Allie Reynolds, 1943	.202
98	Tim Keefe, 1883	.202
99	Henry Boyle, 1884	.202
100	Juan Marichal, 1966	.202

Opponents' On Base Pctg.

1	Guy Hecker, 1882	.198
2	Jim McCormick, 1884	.202
3	Charlie Sweeney, 1884	.207
4	Dupee Shaw, 1884	.212
5	Charlie Sweeney, 1884	.212
6	Henry Boyle, 1884	.216
7	George Bradley, 1880	.216
8	Tim Keefe, 1880	.216
9	Walter Johnson, 1913	.217
10	Denny Driscoll, 1882	.218
11	Addie Joss, 1908	.218
12	Guy Hecker, 1884	.221
13	George Bradley, 1876	.221
14	Tommy Bond, 1876	.224
15	Jim Whitney, 1884	.225
16	Ed Walsh, 1910	.226
17	Silver King, 1888	.227
18	Ed Morris, 1884	.227
19	Sandy Koufax, 1965	.228
20	Christy Mathewson, 1909	.228
21	Sandy Koufax, 1963	.230
22	Juan Marichal, 1966	.230
23	Charley Radbourn, 1884	.232
24	Monte Ward, 1880	.232
25	Ed Walsh, 1908	.232
26	Jack Lynch, 1884	.233
27	Luis Tiant, 1968	.233
28	Tim Keefe, 1883	.233
29	Bob Gibson, 1968	.233
30	Lady Baldwin, 1885	.233
31	Pete Alexander, 1915	.234
32	Dave McNally, 1968	.234
33	Tim Keefe, 1884	.236
34	Perry Werden, 1884	.236
35	Larry Corcoran, 1880	.236
36	Cy Young, 1905	.236
37	Roger Nelson, 1972	.236
38	Christy Mathewson, 1908	.237
39	Jim Devlin, 1876	.237
40	Tony Mullane, 1883	.238
41	Mordecai Brown, 1909	.239
42	Tim Keefe, 1888	.239
43	Larry Corcoran, 1882	.239
44	John Clarkson, 1885	.240
45	Juan Marichal, 1965	.240
46	Cy Young, 1908	.240
47	Mordecai Brown, 1908	.240
48	Don Sutton, 1972	.240
49	Babe Adams, 1919	.241
50	Sandy Koufax, 1964	.241
51	Charlie Getzien, 1884	.241
52	Charley Radbourn, 1883	.241
53	Pete Conway, 1888	.242
54	Jim Hunter, 1972	.242
55	Ed Morris, 1885	.243
56	Harry McCormick, 1882	.243
57	Billy Taylor, 1884	.243
58	Charlie Buffinton, 1888	.243
59	Dave Foutz, 1884	.243
60	Denny McLain, 1968	.243
61	Mike Scott, 1986	.244
62	Lady Baldwin, 1886	.244
63	Will White, 1883	.244
64	Doc White, 1906	.244
65	Will White, 1882	.244
66	Jim Galvin, 1884	.244
67	Russ Ford, 1910	.245
68	Fred Goldsmith, 1880	.245
69	Charlie Buffinton, 1884	.245
70	Pete Alexander, 1919	.245
71	Charlie Ferguson, 1886	.245
72	Dutch Leonard, 1914	.246
73	Corey,F, 1880	.246
74	Tony Mullane, 1884	.246
75	Warren Hacker, 1952	.247
76	Charlie Geggus, 1884	.248
77	Tommy Bond, 1879	.248
78	Eddie Cicotte, 1917	.248
79	Jim McCormick, 1880	.248
80	John Clarkson, 1884	.248
81	Charley Radbourn, 1882	.248
82	Walter Johnson, 1912	.248
83	Henry Gruber, 1888	.249
84	Jack Chesbro, 1904	.249
85	Cy Young, 1904	.249
86	Cannonball Titcomb, 1888	.249
87	Jumbo McGinnis, 1883	.249
88	Tim Keefe, 1885	.249
89	John Tudor, 1985	.249
90	Ron Guidry, 1978	.250
91	Addie Joss, 1903	.250
92	Ben Sanders, 1888	.250
93	Joe Horlen, 1964	.250
94	Bill Bernhard, 1902	.250
95	Frank Mountain, 1884	.250
96	Hugh Daily, 1884	.250
97	Ed Seward, 1888	.250
98	Jim Whitney, 1883	.250
99	Addie Joss, 1906	.250
100	Monte Ward, 1879	.250

Wins Above Team

1	George Bradley, 1876	22.5
2	Will White, 1879	21.5
3	Charley Radbourn, 1884	21.0
4	Jim McCormick, 1880	19.4
5	Guy Hecker, 1884	18.0
6	Jim Galvin, 1883	17.6
7	Jim Devlin, 1877	17.5
8	Charley Radbourn, 1883	15.7
9	Matt Kilroy, 1887	15.4
10	Jim Galvin, 1884	15.1
11	Jim Devlin, 1876	15.0
12	Charlie Buffinton, 1884	14.9
13	Tony Mullane, 1884	14.8
14	Walter Johnson, 1913	14.7
15	Jack Chesbro, 1904	14.0
16	Sadie McMahon, 1890	13.6
17	Will White, 1882	13.1
18	Ed Morris, 1885	12.9
19	Joe Wood, 1912	12.8
20	Bill Sweeney, 1884	12.7
	Ed Walsh, 1908	12.7
22	John Clarkson, 1889	12.1
23	Tommy Bond, 1879	12.0
24	Lefty Grove, 1931	11.8
25	Steve Carlton, 1972	11.7
26	Cy Young, 1901	11.6
27	Bill Hutchinson, 1891	11.4
	Denny McLain, 1968	11.4
29	Terry Larkin, 1878	11.2
	Mickey Welch, 1884	11.2
	Bob Caruthers, 1889	11.2
32	Henry Porter, 1885	11.0
	Bill Hoffer, 1895	11.0
	Christy Mathewson, 1908	11.0
35	Cy Young, 1902	10.9
36	Cy Young, 1895	10.7
37	Dazzy Vance, 1924	10.6
	Robin Roberts, 1952	10.6
	Ron Guidry, 1978	10.6
40	Bobby Mathews, 1876	10.5
	Dizzy Dean, 1934	10.5
42	Toad Ramsey, 1886	10.2
	Cy Young, 1892	10.2
	Joe McGinnity, 1904	10.2
	Eddie Rommel, 1922	10.2
46	Lefty Grove, 1930	10.1
47	Ed Morris, 1886	10.0
	Bill Donovan, 1907	10.0
49	Frank Mountain, 1883	9.9
	Eddie Cicotte, 1919	9.9
	Lefty Gomez, 1934	9.9
52	Kid Gleason, 1890	9.8
	Pete Alexander, 1915	9.8
	Hal Newhouser, 1944	9.8
55	Bobby Mathews, 1885	9.7
	Russ Ford, 1910	9.7
	Roger Clemens, 1986	9.7
58	Charlie Ferguson, 1886	9.6
	Pete Conway, 1888	9.6
	Eddie Plank, 1912	9.6
61	Pete Alexander, 1916	9.5
	Carl Hubbell, 1936	9.5
	Dwight Gooden, 1985	9.5
64	Jouett Meekin, 1894	9.4
	Walter Johnson, 1912	9.4
	Claude Hendrix, 1914	9.4
67	Joe McGinnity, 1900	9.3
	Sandy Koufax, 1963	9.3
69	Bert Cunningham, 1898	9.2
	Walter Johnson, 1911	9.2
	Bobby Shantz, 1952	9.2
	Don Newcombe, 1956	9.2
	Juan Marichal, 1966	9.2
	Bob Gibson, 1970	9.2
75	Tim Keefe, 1888	9.1
	Whitey Ford, 1961	9.1
77	Jim McCormick, 1882	9.0
	Cy Young, 1893	9.0
	Preacher Roe, 1951	9.0
80	Frank Killen, 1892	8.9
	Red Faber, 1921	8.9
82	Tim Keefe, 1883	8.8
	Tim Keefe, 1887	8.8
	Christy Mathewson, 1909	8.8
	Dolf Luque, 1923	8.8
86	Lee Richmond, 1881	8.7
	Jim Hughes, 1899	8.7
	Juan Marichal, 1963	8.7
	Juan Marichal, 1968	8.7
90	Jumbo McGinnis, 1882	8.6
	Jim McCormick, 1883	8.6
	Lefty Grove, 1933	8.6
	Bob Feller, 1946	8.6
	Roy Face, 1959	8.6
95	7 players tied	8.5

Wins Above League

1	Charley Radbourn, 1884	45.9
2	Guy Hecker, 1884	42.9
3	Silver King, 1888	42.7
4	Charley Radbourn, 1883	42.4
5	John Clarkson, 1885	41.8
6	John Clarkson, 1889	41.4
7	Jim Galvin, 1884	41.2
8	Tim Keefe, 1883	40.5
9	Bill Hutchinson, 1890	40.1
10	Jim Galvin, 1883	40.0
11	Jim McCormick, 1880	39.8
12	Toad Ramsey, 1886	39.7
13	Will White, 1879	39.5
14	Will White, 1883	39.0
15	Bill Hutchinson, 1892	38.6
16	Ed Morris, 1885	37.9
17	Jim Devlin, 1876	37.9
18	Matt Kilroy, 1887	37.7
19	Jim Devlin, 1877	37.7
20	Toad Ramsey, 1887	37.6
21	John Clarkson, 1887	37.3
22	Tony Mullane, 1884	36.9
23	Dave Foutz, 1886	36.1
24	Amos Rusie, 1890	35.9
25	Charlie Buffinton, 1884	35.7
26	George Bradley, 1876	35.7
27	Bill Hutchinson, 1891	35.4
28	Jim Galvin, 1879	35.4
29	Lee Richmond, 1880	35.2
30	Monte Ward, 1880	34.4
31	Jim McCormick, 1882	34.3
32	Monte Ward, 1879	34.3
33	Bill Sweeney, 1884	34.2
34	Tommy Bond, 1879	34.2
35	Ed Morris, 1886	34.0
36	Al Spalding, 1876	34.0
37	Amos Rusie, 1893	33.9
38	Amos Rusie, 1894	33.8
39	Jim Whitney, 1883	33.7
40	Mickey Welch, 1885	33.7
41	Mark Baldwin, 1890	33.6
42	Sadie McMahon, 1891	33.5
43	Kid Gleason, 1890	33.4
44	Hugh Daily, 1884	33.3
45	Lady Baldwin, 1886	33.2
46	Amos Rusie, 1892	32.9
47	Jack Stivetts, 1891	32.9
48	Silver King, 1890	32.7
49	Mickey Welch, 1880	32.7
50	Larry Corcoran, 1884	32.6
51	Jim Whitney, 1881	32.6
52	Tim Keefe, 1886	32.6
53	Jack Chesbro, 1904	32.5
54	Tommy Bond, 1877	32.3
55	Tim Keefe, 1887	32.3
56	John Clarkson, 1886	32.2
57	Ed Walsh, 1908	32.2
58	Pink Hawley, 1895	32.2
59	Guy Hecker, 1885	32.2
60	Ed Seward, 1888	32.1
61	Mike Smith, 1887	32.1
62	Mickey Welch, 1884	32.0
63	Hardie Henderson, 1885	31.9
64	Will White, 1880	31.9
65	Will White, 1882	31.6
66	Sadie McMahon, 1890	31.5
67	Tommy Bond, 1878	31.4
68	George Derby, 1881	31.4
69	Matt Kilroy, 1889	31.3
70	Tim Keefe, 1884	31.1
71	Scott Stratton, 1890	31.0
72	Larry Corcoran, 1883	30.9
73	Jim McCormick, 1879	30.9
74	Jesse Duryea, 1889	30.8
75	Matt Kilroy, 1886	30.8
76	Tony Mullane, 1883	30.8
77	Larry Corcoran, 1880	30.7
78	Charley Radbourn, 1882	30.7
79	Cy Young, 1893	30.6
80	Cy Young, 1892	30.5
81	Bob Caruthers, 1885	30.4
82	Cy Young, 1894	30.3
83	Mark Baldwin, 1889	30.2
84	Walter Johnson, 1912	30.1
85	Charley Radbourn, 1886	30.0
86	Henry Porter, 1885	30.0
87	Gus Weyhing, 1892	30.0
88	Silver King, 1889	29.9
89	John Clarkson, 1891	29.9
90	Kid Nichols, 1890	29.9
91	Joe McGinnity, 1903	29.9
92	Billy Rhines, 1890	29.7
93	Jersey Bakely, 1888	29.6
94	Tony Mullane, 1882	29.5
95	Walter Johnson, 1913	29.4
96	Phil Knell, 1891	29.4
97	Kid Nichols, 1892	29.3
98	Jim McCormick, 1881	29.3
99	Amos Rusie, 1891	29.2
100	Tony Mullane, 1887	29.0

Relief Games

1	Mike Marshall, 1974	106
2	Kent Tekulve, 1979	94
3	Mike Marshall, 1973	92
4	Kent Tekulve, 1978	91
5	Wayne Granger, 1969	90
	Kent Tekulve, 1987	90
7	Mike Marshall, 1979	89
	Mark Eichhorn, 1987	89
9	Rob Murphy, 1987	87
10	Wilbur Wood, 1968	86
11	Kent Tekulve, 1982	85
	Frank Williams, 1987	85
13	Ted Abernathy, 1965	84
	Enrique Romo, 1979	84
	Dick Tidrow, 1980	84
	Dan Quisenberry, 1985	84
	Mitch Williams, 1987	84
18	Ken Sanders, 1971	83
	Craig Lefferts, 1986	83
20	Eddie Fisher, 1965	82
	Bill Campbell, 1983	82
22	John Wyatt, 1964	81
	Dale Murray, 1976	81
	Jeff Robinson, 1987	81
25	Pedro Borbon, 1973	80
	Willie Hernandez, 1984	80
	Mitch Williams, 1986	80
28	Dick Radatz, 1964	79
29	Hal Woodeshick, 1965	78
	Ted Abernathy, 1968	78
	Bill Campbell, 1976	78
	Rollie Fingers, 1977	78
	Tom Hume, 1980	78
	Kent Tekulve, 1980	78
	Greg Minton, 1982	78
	Ed Vande Berg, 1982	78
	Ted Power, 1984	78
	Tim Burke, 1985	78
	Lance McCullers, 1987	78
40	Bob Locker, 1967	77
	Wilbur Wood, 1970	77
	Charlie Hough, 1976	77
	Butch Metzger, 1976	77
	Rick Camp, 1980	77
	Gary Lavelle, 1984	77
	Craig Lefferts, 1987	77
47	13 players tied	76

Relief Wins

1	Roy Face, 1959	18
2	John Hiller, 1974	17
	Bill Campbell, 1976	17
4	Jim Konstanty, 1950	16
	Ron Perranoski, 1963	16
	Dick Radatz, 1964	16
	Tom Johnson, 1977	16
8	Mace Brown, 1938	15
	Hoyt Wilhelm, 1952	15
	Luis Arroyo, 1961	15
	Dick Radatz, 1963	15
	Eddie Fisher, 1965	15
	Mike Marshall, 1974	15
	Dale Murray, 1975	15
15	Joe Page, 1947	14
	Joe Black, 1952	14
	Hersh Freeman, 1956	14
	Stu Miller, 1961	14
	Stu Miller, 1965	14
	Phil Regan, 1966	14
	Frank Linzy, 1969	14
	Mike Marshall, 1972	14
	Mike Marshall, 1973	14
	Ron Davis, 1979	14
	Mark Clear, 1982	14
	Jim Slaton, 1983	14
	Roger McDowell, 1986	14
	Mark Eichhorn, 1986	14
29	Earl Caldwell, 1946	13
	Joe Page, 1949	13
	Clyde King, 1951	13
	Lindy McDaniel, 1959	13
	Larry Sherry, 1960	13
	Gerry Staley, 1960	13
	Lindy McDaniel, 1963	13
	Al Hrabosky, 1975	13
	Rollie Fingers, 1976	13
	Bill Campbell, 1977	13
	Sparky Lyle, 1977	13
	Gary Lavelle, 1978	13
	Bob Stanley, 1978	13
	Ron Reed, 1979	13
	Jim Kern, 1979	13
	Aurelio Lopez, 1980	13
	Jesse Orosco, 1983	13
	Rich Gossage, 1983	13
47	28 players tied	12

Relief Losses

1	Gene Garber, 1979	16
2	Darold Knowles, 1970	14
	John Hiller, 1974	14
	Mike Marshall, 1975	14
	Mike Marshall, 1979	14
6	Wilbur Wood, 1970	13
	Rollie Fingers, 1978	13
	Skip Lockwood, 1978	13
9	Roy Face, 1956	12
	Roy Face, 1961	12
	Ken Sanders, 1971	12
	Mike Marshall, 1974	12
	Gene Garber, 1975	12
	Jim Willoughby, 1976	12
	Charlie Hough, 1977	12
	Mike Marshall, 1978	12
	Kent Tekulve, 1980	12
	Ken Howell, 1986	12
19	Nels Potter, 1949	11
	Frank Funk, 1961	11
	Dick Radatz, 1965	11
	Frank Linzy, 1966	11
	Wilbur Wood, 1968	11
	Wilbur Wood, 1969	11
	Mike Marshall, 1973	11
	Rollie Fingers, 1976	11
	Rich Gossage, 1978	11
	Dave Heaverlo, 1979	11
	Mark Clear, 1980	11
	Greg Minton, 1983	11
	Ron Davis, 1984	11
	Mark Davis, 1985	11
	Joe Boever, 1989	11
34	43 players tied	10

Relief Innings Pitched

1	Mike Marshall, 1974	208
2	Mike Marshall, 1973	179
3	Bill Campbell, 1976	168
	Bob Stanley, 1982	168
5	Andy Karl, 1945	167
6	Eddie Fisher, 1965	165
7	Hoyt Wilhelm, 1952	159
8	Dick Radatz, 1964	157
	Mark Eichhorn, 1986	157
10	Jim Konstanty, 1950	152
11	John Hiller, 1974	150
12	Tom Johnson, 1977	147
13	Garland Braxton, 1927	146
14	Allan Russell, 1923	145
	Hoyt Wilhelm, 1953	145
	Wilbur Wood, 1968	145
	Wayne Granger, 1969	145
	Bob Stanley, 1983	145
19	Hoyt Wilhelm, 1965	144
	Steve Foucault, 1974	144
21	Charlie Hough, 1976	143
	Jim Kern, 1979	143
23	Rich Gossage, 1975	142
24	Jack Lamabe, 1963	140
	Bill Campbell, 1977	140
	Mike Marshall, 1979	140
	Sammy Stewart, 1983	140
	Willie Hernandez, 1984	140
29	Pedro Borbon, 1974	139
	Dan Quisenberry, 1983	139
31	Lindy McDaniel, 1973	138
	Aurelio Lopez, 1984	138
	Clay Carroll, 1966	137
	Sparky Lyle, 1977	137
	Tom Hume, 1980	137
	Dan Quisenberry, 1982	137
37	Ted Abernathy, 1965	136
	Ken Sanders, 1971	136
	Doug Corbett, 1980	136
40	Joe Page, 1949	135
	Ted Abernathy, 1968	135
	Clay Carroll, 1968	135
	Phil Regan, 1968	135
	Rollie Fingers, 1976	135
	Kent Tekulve, 1978	135
46	Joe Page, 1947	134
	Bill Henry, 1959	134
	Dick Selma, 1970	134
	Rich Gossage, 1978	134
	Kent Tekulve, 1979	134
	John Montague, 1979	134
	Dan Spillner, 1982	134

Relief Points

1	Dave Righetti, 1986	100
2	Dan Quisenberry, 1983	97
	Dan Quisenberry, 1984	97
4	Dennis Eckersley, 1988	96
5	Bruce Sutter, 1984	93
	Mark Davis, 1989	93
7	John Hiller, 1973	91
8	Steve Bedrosian, 1987	87
9	Johnny Franco, 1988	84
	Jeff Reardon, 1988	84
	Jeff Russell, 1989	84
12	Luis Arroyo, 1961	83
	Sparky Lyle, 1972	83
	Dan Quisenberry, 1980	83
	Bill Caudill, 1984	83
16	Clay Carroll, 1972	82
	Bruce Sutter, 1982	82
18	Dick Radatz, 1964	81
	Dan Quisenberry, 1982	81
	Dan Quisenberry, 1985	81
21	Bruce Sutter, 1979	80
	Todd Worrell, 1986	80
23	Mike Marshall, 1973	79
	Bill Campbell, 1977	79
	Jim Kern, 1979	79
	Willie Hernandez, 1984	79
27	Jeff Reardon, 1985	78
28	Wayne Granger, 1970	77
	Rollie Fingers, 1977	77
	Lee Smith, 1984	77
31	Jack Aker, 1966	76
	Rich Gossage, 1980	76
	Greg Minton, 1982	76
	Jesse Orosco, 1984	76
	Lee Smith, 1985	76
	Todd Worrell, 1987	76
	Doug Jones, 1988	76
	Mitch Williams, 1989	76
39	Dave Righetti, 1985	75
	Jeff Reardon, 1986	75
	Johnny Franco, 1987	75
42	Lindy McDaniel, 1960	74
	Dick Radatz, 1963	74
	Ron Perranoski, 1970	74
	Kent Tekulve, 1979	74
	Jim Gott, 1988	74
	Dennis Eckersley, 1989	74
48	5 players tied	73

Relief Ranking

1	Jim Kern, 1979	66.4
2	Mike Marshall, 1979	62.6
3	Rich Gossage, 1977	62.6
4	Mark Eichhorn, 1986	59.6
5	John Hiller, 1973	59.6
6	Bill Caudill, 1982	58.9
7	Lindy McDaniel, 1960	56.5
8	Ellis Kinder, 1953	56.2
9	Sid Monge, 1979	55.9
10	Bruce Sutter, 1977	55.7
11	Donnie Moore, 1985	53.4
12	Bill Campbell, 1977	52.6
13	Jesse Orosco, 1983	52.4
14	Dick Radatz, 1963	51.5
15	Dave Righetti, 1986	50.9
16	Todd Worrell, 1986	49.5
17	Rich Gossage, 1975	49.3
18	Doug Corbett, 1980	48.1
19	Dan Quisenberry, 1985	48.1
20	Mike Marshall, 1972	47.7
21	Dick Radatz, 1964	46.9
22	Bruce Sutter, 1984	46.6
23	Roy Face, 1962	46.4
24	Bob James, 1985	46.3
25	Rich Gossage, 1978	45.9
26	Tom Murphy, 1974	45.4
27	Ken Sanders, 1971	45.2
28	Al Hrabosky, 1975	44.9
29	Johnny Franco, 1988	44.6
30	Dan Spillner, 1982	44.4
31	Willie Hernandez, 1985	43.8
32	Sparky Lyle, 1977	43.4
33	John Hiller, 1974	43.3
34	Doug Jones, 1989	43.1
35	Lee Smith, 1983	42.9
36	Dan Quisenberry, 1983	42.7
37	Luis Arroyo, 1961	42.5
38	Frank Linzy, 1965	42.1
39	Bruce Sutter, 1979	41.9
40	Stu Miller, 1965	41.3
41	Joe Page, 1949	41.0
42	Ron Perranoski, 1969	40.8
43	Rich Gossage, 1983	40.3
44	Jeff Russell, 1989	39.4
45	Mark Clear, 1982	39.4
46	Rollie Fingers, 1981	39.2
47	Dick Radatz, 1962	38.9
48	Gary Lavelle, 1977	38.8
49	Hoyt Wilhelm, 1964	38.5
50	Mike Marshall, 1973	38.3

Relievers' Runs

1. Mark Eichhorn, 1986 ...... 43.0
2. Jim Kern, 1979 .... 42.2
3. Rich Gossage, 1977 .... 33.8
4. John Hiller, 1973 .... 33.1
5. Dan Quisenberry, 1983 ..... 33.0
6. Willie Hernandez, 1984 .... 32.2
7. Doug Corbett, 1980 .... 31.1
8. Rich Gossage, 1975 .... 30.8
9. Bruce Sutter, 1977 .... 30.5
10. Tim Burke, 1987 .... 29.3
11. Sparky Lyle, 1977 .... 29.0
12. Lindy McDaniel, 1960 ..... 28.5
13. Bob Lee, 1964 .... 28.3
14. Garland Braxton, 1927 .... 28.2
15. Bruce Sutter, 1984 .... 28.1
16. Mike Marshall, 1974 .... 27.9
17. Sid Monge, 1979 .... 26.6
18. Jesse Orosco, 1983 .... 26.5
19. Hoyt Wilhelm, 1965 .... 26.3
20. Rich Gossage, 1978 .... 26.3
21. Phil Regan, 1966 .... 25.9
22. Jim Grant, 1970 .... 25.8
23. Jeff Montgomery, 1989 ..... 25.8
24. Aurelio Lopez, 1979 .... 25.7
25. Ellis Kinder, 1953 .... 25.5
26. Donnie Moore, 1985 .... 25.5
27. Dan Quisenberry, 1985 ..... 25.5
28. Mike Marshall, 1979 .... 25.3
29. Ellis Kinder, 1951 .... 25.2
30. Jim Konstanty, 1950 .... 25.0
31. Sparky Lyle, 1974 .... 24.9
32. Ted Abernathy, 1967 .... 24.8
33. Bob James, 1985 .... 24.7
34. Rollie Fingers, 1973 .... 24.5
35. Greg Minton, 1982 .... 24.3
36. Gary Lavelle, 1977 .... 24.3
37. Dick Radatz, 1963 .... 24.2
38. Hoyt Wilhelm, 1954 .... 24.2
39. Luis Arroyo, 1961 .... 24.2
40. Dick Radatz, 1962 .... 24.1
41. Joe Black, 1952 .... 24.1
42. Joe Page, 1949 .... 24.0
43. Dan Spillner, 1982 .... 23.8
44. Hoyt Wilhelm, 1964 .... 23.8
45. Tom Murphy, 1974 .... 23.5
46. Ken Sanders, 1971 .... 23.4
47. Dick Radatz, 1964 .... 23.2
48. Dan Quisenberry, 1982 ..... 23.1
49. Dick Hyde, 1958 .... 23.1
50. Ron Perranoski, 1963 ...... 23.1

Adjusted Relievers' Runs

1. Mark Eichhorn, 1986 ...... 46.2
2. Jim Kern, 1979 .... 41.8
3. Bruce Sutter, 1977 .... 37.3
4. Doug Corbett, 1980 .... 36.8
5. Rich Gossage, 1977 .... 34.9
6. Dan Quisenberry, 1983 ..... 34.3
7. John Hiller, 1973 .... 33.8
8. Rich Gossage, 1975 .... 33.1
9. Lindy McDaniel, 1960 ...... 31.9
10. Tim Burke, 1987 .... 31.7
11. Mike Marshall, 1979 .... 30.7
12. Sid Monge, 1979 .... 30.4
13. Ellis Kinder, 1953 .... 29.4
14. Willie Hernandez, 1984 .... 28.6
15. Ellis Kinder, 1951 .... 28.5
16. Ted Abernathy, 1967 .... 28.1
17. Dick Radatz, 1963 .... 27.7
18. Bill Campbell, 1977 .... 27.5
19. Bruce Sutter, 1984 .... 27.4
20. Sparky Lyle, 1977 .... 27.0
21. Gary Lavelle, 1977 .... 26.8
22. Jesse Orosco, 1983 .... 26.4
23. Greg Harris, 1985 .... 26.3
24. Dan Quisenberry, 1985 ..... 26.2
25. Rod Scurry, 1982 .... 25.8
26. Bob Stanley, 1982 .... 25.7
27. Dick Radatz, 1962 .... 25.7
28. Donnie Moore, 1985 .... 25.7
29. Andy McGaffigan, 1987 .... 25.6
30. Ken Sanders, 1971 .... 25.6
31. Garland Braxton, 1927 ..... 25.5
32. Dick Radatz, 1964 .... 25.4
33. Bob Reynolds, 1973 .... 25.3
34. Hoyt Wilhelm, 1954 .... 25.1
35. Tom Burgmeier, 1982 ...... 24.8
36. Tom Murphy, 1974 .... 24.8
37. Rich Gossage, 1978 .... 24.6
38. Bob James, 1985 .... 24.6
39. Dan Spillner, 1982 .... 24.3
40. Joe Heving, 1933 .... 24.2
41. Tug McGraw, 1980 .... 24.2
42. Jeff Montgomery, 1989 ..... 23.8
43. Joe Pate, 1926 .... 23.8
44. Phil Regan, 1966 .... 23.6
45. Jim Grant, 1970 .... 23.6
46. Hoyt Wilhelm, 1952 .... 23.4
47. Aurelio Lopez, 1979 .... 23.4
48. Tom Burgmeier, 1980 ...... 23.4
49. Bob Lee, 1964 .... 23.3
50. Dick Hyde, 1958 .... 23.3

Percent of Team Wins (by era)

1876-1892

1. Will White, 1879 .... 100.0
   Bobby Mathews, 1876 ..... 100.0
   Jim Devlin, 1877 .... 100.0
   Jim Devlin, 1876 .... 100.0
   George Bradley, 1876 ..... 100.0
6. Tommy Bond, 1878 .... 97.6
7. Terry Larkin, 1878 .... 96.7
8. Jim McCormick, 1880 ...... 95.7
9. Tommy Bond, 1877 .... 95.2
10. Terry Larkin, 1877 .... 93.5
11. Al Spalding, 1876 .... 90.4
    Jim Galvin, 1883 .... 88.5
13. Will White, 1880 .... 85.7
    Jim McCormick, 1882 ...... 85.7
15. Mickey Welch, 1880 .... 82.9

1893-1919

1. Ted Breitenstein, 1895 ..... 48.7
2. Amos Rusie, 1893 .... 48.5
3. Ted Breitenstein, 1894 ..... 48.2
4. Cy Young, 1893 .... 46.6
5. Ed Walsh, 1908 .... 45.5
   Frank Killen, 1896 .... 45.5
7. Ted Breitenstein, 1896 ..... 45.0
8. Jack Chesbro, 1904 .... 44.6
9. Pink Hawley, 1895 .... 43.7
10. Win Mercer, 1896 .... 43.1
11. Noodles Hahn, 1901 .... 42.3
12. Frank Killen, 1893 .... 42.0
13. Cy Young, 1901 .... 41.8
14. Cy Young, 1895 .... 41.6
15. Cy Young, 1902 .... 41.6

1920-1941

1. Eddie Rommel, 1922 ...... 41.5
2. Red Faber, 1921 .... 40.3
3. Buck Newsom, 1938 .... 36.4
4. Jimmy Ring, 1923 .... 36.0
   Pete Alexander, 1920 ...... 36.0
6. Ted Lyons, 1930 .... 35.5
7. Curt Davis, 1934 .... 33.9
8. Urban Shocker, 1921 ...... 33.3
   Bob Feller, 1941 .... 33.3
   Ed Morris, 1928 .... 33.3
11. Howard Ehmke, 1923 ...... 32.8
12. Dazzy Vance, 1925 .... 32.4
    Paul Derringer, 1935 ...... 32.4
14. Wes Ferrell, 1935 .... 32.1
15. George Uhle, 1923 .... 31.7

1942-1960

1. Ned Garver, 1951 .... 38.5
2. Bob Feller, 1946 .... 38.2
3. Murry Dickson, 1952 ...... 33.3
4. Robin Roberts, 1952 ...... 32.2
5. Bill Voiselle, 1944 .... 31.3
6. Murry Dickson, 1951 ...... 31.3
7. Phil Marchildon, 1942 ..... 30.9
8. Dizzy Trout, 1944 .... 30.7
9. Robin Roberts, 1954 ...... 30.7
10. Bobby Shantz, 1952 .... 30.4
11. Ewell Blackwell, 1947 ..... 30.1
12. Robin Roberts, 1955 ...... 29.9
13. Johnny Antonelli, 1956 .... 29.9
14. Dave Ferriss, 1945 .... 29.6
15. 2 players tied 29.0

1961-1989

1. Steve Carlton, 1972 .... 45.8
2. Gaylord Perry, 1972 .... 33.3
3. Nolan Ryan, 1974 .... 32.4
4. Phil Niekro, 1979 .... 31.8
5. Larry Jackson, 1964 .... 31.6
6. Wilbur Wood, 1973 .... 31.2
7. Bob Gibson, 1970 .... 30.3
8. Randy Jones, 1976 .... 30.1
9. Denny McLain, 1968 .... 30.1
10. Fergie Jenkins, 1974 ...... 29.8
11. Dave Stieb, 1981 .... 29.7
12. Juan Marichal, 1968 .... 29.5
13. Sam McDowell, 1969 ...... 29.0
14. Fergie Jenkins, 1971 ...... 28.9
15. Fernando Valenzuela, 1986 . 28.8

Clutch Pitching Index

1. Henry Boyle, 1886 .... 171.4
2. Freddie Fitzsimmons, 1933 . 153.6
3. Ned Garvin, 1904 .... 152.8
4. Mordecai Brown, 1903 .... 152.1
5. Doc White, 1904 .... 151.8
6. Max Lanier, 1943 .... 150.7
7. Carl Lundgren, 1902 ...... 149.8
8. Jim McCormick, 1878 ...... 148.3
9. Ed Summers, 1908 .... 147.9
10. Mike O'Neill, 1904 .... 145.9
11. Pete Schneider, 1917 ...... 145.3
12. Sammy Stewart, 1981 ...... 144.3
13. Joe McGinnity, 1908 .... 144.2
14. Andy Coakley, 1905 .... 144.0
15. Ed Willett, 1908 .... 143.4
16. Ed Killian, 1907 .... 142.5
17. Bob Rhoads, 1908 .... 141.9
18. Cy Morgan, 1910 .... 141.6
19. Ben Tincup, 1914 .... 141.5
    Dick Rudolph, 1919 .... 141.5
21. Lefty Gomez, 1931 .... 141.4
22. Sherry Smith, 1919 .... 141.3
23. Vic Willis, 1906 .... 141.1
24. Fred Olmstead, 1910 ...... 140.9
25. Fred Blanding, 1913 .... 140.8
26. Bert Humphries, 1915 ..... 139.6
    Rick Honeycutt, 1983 ..... 139.6
28. Sloppy Thurston, 1923 ..... 139.3
29. Doug Rau, 1976 .... 139.2
30. Mal Eason, 1902 .... 139.1
31. Al Benton, 1945 .... 139.0
32. Mordecai Brown, 1906 .... 138.8
33. Al Brazle, 1947 .... 138.7
34. Charlie Hodnett, 1884 ..... 138.6
35. Andy Coakley, 1908 .... 138.0
36. Allan Anderson, 1988 ..... 137.5
37. Ed Poole, 1902 .... 137.0
38. Spud Chandler, 1942 ...... 136.4
39. King Cole, 1910 .... 136.2
40. Red Faber, 1917 .... 136.1
41. Ed Siever, 1904 .... 135.9
42. Jack Pfiester, 1907 .... 135.3
43. Bob Buhl, 1957 .... 135.1
44. Mark Langston, 1989 ...... 134.9
45. Al Maul, 1895 .... 134.8
46. Stu Miller, 1959 .... 134.6
47. Dutch Leonard, 1948 ...... 134.5
    Doug Rau, 1978 .... 134.5
49. Ken Chase, 1940 .... 134.4
50. John Tudor, 1988 .... 134.3
51. Harry Salisbury, 1879 ..... 134.0
52. Charlie Chech, 1905 ...... 133.9
53. Mike Marshall, 1973 ...... 133.7
54. Eddie Plank, 1911 .... 133.4
55. Bill Burns, 1909 .... 133.3
    Joe Horlen, 1968 .... 133.3
57. Lon Knight, 1876 .... 133.1
58. Bill Bernhard, 1904 .... 133.0
59. Art Nehf, 1928 .... 132.9
60. Win Mercer, 1894 .... 132.6
61. Walt Dickson, 1914 .... 132.5
    Gene Bearden, 1948 ...... 132.5
63. Howie Camnitz, 1908 ...... 132.4
64. Harry Moran, 1915 .... 132.3
    Hoyt Wilhelm, 1959 .... 132.3
66. Stan Baumgartner, 1924 .... 132.1
67. Hugh Daily, 1887 .... 132.0
68. Bump Hadley, 1939 .... 131.9
69. Chick Fraser, 1900 .... 131.8
70. Mike Sullivan, 1892 .... 131.7
71. Steve Blass, 1972 .... 131.5
72. Don Schwall, 1961 .... 131.4
73. Jim Pastorius, 1907 .... 131.2
74. Andy Coakley, 1907 .... 131.0
75. Bobby Shantz, 1957 .... 130.9
76. Pete Vuckovich, 1982 ..... 130.8
77. George Mullin, 1914 ...... 130.7
78. Ted Lyons, 1942 .... 130.6
79. Bill Lee, 1978 .... 130.5
80. Lon Warneke, 1933 .... 130.4
81. Hal McKain, 1929 .... 130.3
82. Larry Pape, 1911 .... 130.2
    Vean Gregg, 1913 .... 130.2
84. Hi Bithorn, 1942 .... 130.1
85. John Cerutti, 1989 .... 130.0
86. Johnny Lush, 1906 .... 129.9
87. Will White, 1880 .... 129.8
    George Kaiserling, 1915 .... 129.8
    Rollie Naylor, 1920 .... 129.8
    Ruben Gomez, 1954 ...... 129.8
91. Earl Moore, 1911 .... 129.6
    Lefty Weinert, 1922 .... 129.6
93. Tom Hughes, 1912 .... 129.4
    Bill Walker, 1929 .... 129.4
    Larry McWilliams, 1984 .... 129.4
96. Clint Rogge, 1915 .... 129.3
    Ned Garver, 1948 .... 129.3
98. Carl Lundgren, 1907 ...... 129.2
    Clarence Mitchell, 1929 .... 129.2
    Atley Donald, 1944 .... 129.2

Pitcher Batting Runs

1	Guy Hecker, 1884	28.9
2	Bob Caruthers, 1886	22.5
3	Jim Whitney, 1882	21.3
4	Wes Ferrell, 1935	21.2
5	Don Drysdale, 1965	20.4
6	Bob Caruthers, 1887	19.9
7	Don Newcombe, 1955	19.9
8	Guy Hecker, 1886	18.3
9	Wes Ferrell, 1931	17.7
10	Billy Taylor, 1884	17.3
11	Tony Mullane, 1884	17.1
12	Schoolboy Rowe, 1943	17.1
13	Bob Caruthers, 1889	17.1
14	Red Ruffing, 1930	16.5
15	Jim Whitney, 1883	16.4
16	Warren Spahn, 1958	16.3
17	Charlie Ferguson, 1887	16.2
18	George Uhle, 1923	16.1
19	Walter Johnson, 1925	16.0
20	Red Lucas, 1930	15.6
21	Bob Lemon, 1950	15.3
22	Charlie Ferguson, 1885	15.2
23	Babe Ruth, 1917	15.1
24	Don Newcombe, 1959	15.0
25	Bob Lemon, 1949	14.8
26	Jack Stivetts, 1890	14.8
27	Dave Foutz, 1887	14.6
28	Claude Hendrix, 1912	14.6
29	Doc Crandall, 1915	14.5
30	Jack Bentley, 1923	14.5
31	Jim Tobin, 1942	14.3
32	Babe Ruth, 1915	14.3
33	Red Ruffing, 1936	14.2
34	Babe Ruth, 1916	14.0
35	Jack Stivetts, 1892	14.0
36	Jack Coombs, 1911	13.9
37	Red Lucas, 1932	13.8
38	Scott Stratton, 1888	13.7
39	Pete Conway, 1888	13.4
40	Monte Ward, 1879	13.4
41	Scott Stratton, 1890	13.2
42	Joe Bush, 1924	13.1
43	Terry Larkin, 1878	13.1
44	Elam Vangilder, 1922	13.1
45	Robin Roberts, 1955	13.0
46	Adonis Terry, 1890	12.9
47	Charley Radbourn, 1883	12.9
48	Clark Griffith, 1901	12.7
49	Adonis Terry, 1889	12.6
50	Red Lucas, 1933	12.5
51	Schoolboy Rowe, 1935	12.5
52	Bob Lemon, 1948	12.4
53	Curt Davis, 1939	12.4
54	Red Ruffing, 1935	12.4
55	Red Ruffing, 1932	12.4
56	Bucky Walters, 1939	12.4
57	Ferguson Jenkins, 1971	12.3
58	Jim Whitney, 1881	12.2
59	Red Ruffing, 1928	12.2
60	Pink Hawley, 1895	12.1
61	Dave Ferriss, 1945	11.9
62	Charlie Ferguson, 1886	11.9
63	Dizzy Trout, 1944	11.9
64	Al Maul, 1893	11.9
65	Johnny Sain, 1947	11.8
66	Wes Ferrell, 1936	11.8
67	Ad Gumbert, 1889	11.8
68	Jim Hunter, 1971	11.8
69	Amos Rusie, 1890	11.8
70	Babe Ruth, 1918	11.7
71	Charley Radbourn, 1885	11.7
72	Joe Bowman, 1939	11.6
73	Schoolboy Rowe, 1934	11.6
74	Bob Gibson, 1970	11.6
75	Frank Killen, 1893	11.5
76	George Mullin, 1904	11.5
77	Charlie Buffinton, 1884	11.4
78	Dutch Ruether, 1921	11.4
79	Cy Young, 1903	11.4
80	Bob Caruthers, 1891	11.4
81	Jouett Meekin, 1896	11.4
82	Erv Brame, 1929	11.4
83	George VanHaltren, 1888	11.4
84	Erv Brame, 1930	11.3
85	Claude Hendrix, 1915	11.1
86	Matt Kilroy, 1889	11.1
87	Jack Stivetts, 1896	11.1
88	Fred Hutchinson, 1950	11.0
89	Red Ruffing, 1941	10.8
90	Carl Mays, 1921	10.8
91	Jim Whitney, 1887	10.8
92	Blue Moon Odom, 1969	10.8
93	Red Lucas, 1931	10.7
94	Fred Hutchinson, 1947	10.5
95	Jack Scott, 1921	10.5
96	Dick Burns, 1884	10.5
97	Walter Johnson, 1917	10.4
98	Ad Gumbert, 1891	10.4
99	Lon Warneke, 1933	10.4
100	Jack Powell, 1900	10.3

Pitcher Fielding Runs

1	Ed Walsh, 1907	21.5
2	Harry Howell, 1905	17.5
3	Ed Walsh, 1911	14.7
4	Ed Walsh, 1908	13.7
5	Will White, 1882	12.5
6	Park Swartzel, 1889	12.3
7	John Clarkson, 1889	11.0
8	Tommy Bond, 1880	10.2
9	Frank Smith, 1909	10.1
	Gene Packard, 1914	10.1
11	Carl Mays, 1926	10.0
12	Matt Kilroy, 1887	9.9
13	Ed Walsh, 1910	9.8
14	Sadie McMahon, 1890	9.6
	Ed Scott, 1900	9.6
	Gene Packard, 1915	9.6
17	Tony Mullane, 1882	9.5
	Mike Morrison, 1887	9.5
	Christy Mathewson, 1908	9.5
20	Harry Howell, 1904	9.4
21	Nick Cullop, 1915	9.3
22	Al Mays, 1887	9.2
23	Carl Mays, 1916	9.1
24	Charlie Buffinton, 1888	9.0
	Amos Rusie, 1894	9.0
	Hooks Dauss, 1915	9.0
27	Cy Young, 1895	8.9
	Carl Mays, 1918	8.9
29	Curt Davis, 1934	8.7
30	Matt Kilroy, 1889	8.6
	Jack Taylor, 1898	8.6
32	Cy Seymour, 1897	8.5
	Cy Seymour, 1898	8.5
	Nick Altrock, 1905	8.5
	Elmer Stricklett, 1906	8.5
	Claude Hendrix, 1914	8.5
	Bob Lemon, 1948	8.5
38	Tony Mullane, 1884	8.4
	Cy Young, 1896	8.4
	Elmer Stricklett, 1905	8.4
41	Silver King, 1890	8.3
	Cy Young, 1892	8.3
	Gene Krapp, 1915	8.3
	Hooks Dauss, 1920	8.3
	Wilcy Moore, 1927	8.3
	Bucky Walters, 1936	8.3
47	John Clarkson, 1887	8.2
	Addie Joss, 1907	8.2
49	Carl Mays, 1924	8.1
	Randy Jones, 1976	8.1
51	Harry Howell, 1907	8.0
	Burleigh Grimes, 1925	8.0
53	Carl Mays, 1917	7.9
	Fred Newman, 1965	7.9
55	Jack Stivetts, 1892	7.8
	Cy Young, 1894	7.8
	Eddie Rommel, 1924	7.8
	Mel Stottlemyre, 1969	7.8
59	Freddie Fitzsimmons, 1931	7.7
	Mel Harder, 1933	7.7
	Harry Gumbert, 1938	7.7
	Bob Lemon, 1953	7.7
63	Tommy Bond, 1879	7.6
	John Clarkson, 1885	7.6
	Willie Sudhoff, 1898	7.6
	Harry Gumbert, 1937	7.6
	Russ Christopher, 1943	7.6
	John Denny, 1978	7.6
69	George Mullin, 1904	7.5
	Ed Walsh, 1906	7.5
	Joe Wood, 1912	7.5
	Carl Hubbell, 1933	7.5
73	Larry Corcoran, 1884	7.4
	Jim Galvin, 1884	7.4
	George Suggs, 1914	7.4
76	Jean Dubuc, 1913	7.3
	Gene Krapp, 1914	7.3
78	Jim McCormick, 1883	7.2
	Scott Stratton, 1890	7.2
	Mark Baldwin, 1890	7.2
	Red Ames, 1909	7.2
	Christy Mathewson, 1911	7.2
	Russ Christopher, 1945	7.2
84	Monte Ward, 1880	7.1
	Jim Galvin, 1887	7.1
	Harry Howell, 1906	7.1
	Bill Doak, 1915	7.1
88	Larry Corcoran, 1880	7.0
	Jim Galvin, 1881	7.0
	Christy Mathewson, 1901	7.0
	Ned Garvin, 1903	7.0
	Doc White, 1908	7.0
	Ed Walsh, 1912	7.0
	Harry Coveleski, 1914	7.0
	George McConnell, 1915	7.0
	Hal Schumacher, 1935	7.0
97	Guy Hecker, 1884	6.9
	Eddie Cicotte, 1913	6.9
99	6 players tied	6.8

Total Pitcher Index

1	Silver King, 1888	11.9
2	Amos Rusie, 1894	11.1
3	Charley Radbourn, 1884	10.7
	Guy Hecker, 1884	10.7
5	Bob Caruthers, 1886	10.5
6	Dave Foutz, 1886	10.3
7	Scott Stratton, 1890	10.1
8	John Clarkson, 1887	9.8
9	Walter Johnson, 1912	9.5
10	Pete Alexander, 1915	9.3
11	Jim Devlin, 1877	9.2
	Tony Mullane, 1884	9.2
13	John Clarkson, 1885	9.1
14	John Clarkson, 1889	9.0
15	Walter Johnson, 1913	8.8
	Dizzy Trout, 1944	8.8
17	Joe Wood, 1912	8.5
18	Bucky Walters, 1939	8.4
19	Walter Johnson, 1918	8.3
20	Charley Radbourn, 1883	8.2
21	Amos Rusie, 1893	8.1
	Ed Walsh, 1907	8.1
	Hal Newhouser, 1945	8.1
24	Jack Stivetts, 1891	7.9
	Dwight Gooden, 1985	7.9
26	Will White, 1882	7.8
	Jim Whitney, 1883	7.8
	Guy Hecker, 1885	7.8
29	Kid Nichols, 1890	7.7
	Cy Young, 1896	7.7
31	Tim Keefe, 1883	7.6
	Christy Mathewson, 1905	7.6
33	Billy Rhines, 1890	7.5
	Cy Young, 1901	7.5
	Bob Gibson, 1968	7.5
36	Silver King, 1890	7.4
	Dolf Luque, 1923	7.4
	Lefty Grove, 1931	7.4
	Wes Ferrell, 1935	7.4
40	Guy Hecker, 1886	7.3
	Toad Ramsey, 1886	7.3
	Cy Young, 1894	7.3
	Pink Hawley, 1895	7.3
	Kid Nichols, 1897	7.3
45	Charlie Ferguson, 1886	7.2
	Ed Walsh, 1910	7.2
	Gaylord Perry, 1972	7.2
48	Jim Devlin, 1876	7.1
	Jim Galvin, 1884	7.1
	Charlie Buffinton, 1888	7.1
	Bill Hutchinson, 1890	7.1
	Cy Young, 1892	7.1
	Carl Hubbell, 1933	7.1
54	Jack Chesbro, 1904	7.0
	Dizzy Dean, 1934	7.0
56	Matt Kilroy, 1887	6.9
	Mike Smith, 1887	6.9
	Walter Johnson, 1915	6.9
	Ron Guidry, 1978	6.9
60	John Clarkson, 1886	6.8
	Nig Cuppy, 1896	6.8
	Kid Nichols, 1896	6.8
	Red Faber, 1921	6.8
	Hal Newhouser, 1946	6.8
	Steve Carlton, 1972	6.8
66	Will White, 1883	6.7
	Lady Baldwin, 1886	6.7
	Clark Griffith, 1898	6.7
	Kid Nichols, 1898	6.7
	Cy Young, 1899	6.7
	Claude Hendrix, 1914	6.7
	Lefty Grove, 1936	6.7
	Juan Marichal, 1965	6.7
74	Tony Mullane, 1883	6.6
	Ed Walsh, 1908	6.6
	Walter Johnson, 1919	6.6
	Lefty Grove, 1932	6.6
78	Matt Kilroy, 1889	6.5
	Jack Stivetts, 1890	6.5
	Christy Mathewson, 1909	6.5
	Tom Seaver, 1971	6.5
82	Frank Killen, 1893	6.4
	Rube Waddell, 1902	6.4
	Dazzy Vance, 1928	6.4
85	Al Spalding, 1876	6.3
	Jesse Duryea, 1889	6.3
	Walter Johnson, 1914	6.3
	Pete Alexander, 1917	6.3
	Pete Alexander, 1920	6.3
	Burleigh Grimes, 1928	6.3
	Lefty Grove, 1935	6.3
	Lefty Gomez, 1937	6.3
	Bob Lemon, 1948	6.3
	Bobby Shantz, 1952	6.3
	Warren Spahn, 1953	6.3
	Bob Gibson, 1969	6.3
97	7 players tied	6.2

Total Pitcher Index (alpha.)

Pete Alexander, 1915	9.3
Pete Alexander, 1917	6.3
Pete Alexander, 1920	6.3
Lady Baldwin, 1886	6.7
Charlie Buffinton, 1888	7.1
Steve Carlton, 1972	6.8
Bob Caruthers, 1886	10.5
Jack Chesbro, 1904	7.0
John Clarkson, 1885	9.1
John Clarkson, 1886	6.8
John Clarkson, 1887	9.8
John Clarkson, 1889	9.0
Nig Cuppy, 1896	6.8
Dizzy Dean, 1934	7.0
Jim Devlin, 1876	7.1
Jim Devlin, 1877	9.2
Jesse Duryea, 1889	6.3
Red Faber, 1921	6.8
Charlie Ferguson, 1886	7.2
Wes Ferrell, 1935	7.4
Dave Foutz, 1886	10.3
Jim Galvin, 1884	7.1
Bob Gibson, 1968	7.5
Bob Gibson, 1969	6.3
Lefty Gomez, 1937	6.3
Dwight Gooden, 1985	7.9
Clark Griffith, 1898	6.7
Burleigh Grimes, 1928	6.3
Lefty Grove, 1931	7.4
Lefty Grove, 1932	6.6
Lefty Grove, 1935	6.3
Lefty Grove, 1936	6.7
Ron Guidry, 1978	6.9
Pink Hawley, 1895	7.3
Guy Hecker, 1884	10.7
Guy Hecker, 1885	7.8
Guy Hecker, 1886	7.3
Claude Hendrix, 1914	6.7
Carl Hubbell, 1933	7.1
Bill Hutchinson, 1890	7.1
Walter Johnson, 1912	9.5
Walter Johnson, 1913	8.8
Walter Johnson, 1914	6.3
Walter Johnson, 1915	6.9
Walter Johnson, 1918	8.3
Walter Johnson, 1919	6.6
Tim Keefe, 1883	7.6
Frank Killen, 1893	6.4
Matt Kilroy, 1887	6.9
Matt Kilroy, 1889	6.5
Silver King, 1888	11.9
Silver King, 1890	7.4
Bob Lemon, 1948	6.3
Dolf Luque, 1923	7.4
Juan Marichal, 1965	6.7
Christy Mathewson, 1905	7.6
Christy Mathewson, 1909	6.5
Tony Mullane, 1883	6.6
Tony Mullane, 1884	9.2
Hal Newhouser, 1945	8.1
Hal Newhouser, 1946	6.8
Kid Nichols, 1890	7.7
Kid Nichols, 1896	6.8
Kid Nichols, 1897	7.3
Kid Nichols, 1898	6.7
Gaylord Perry, 1972	7.2
Charley Radbourn, 1883	8.2
Charley Radbourn, 1884	10.7
Toad Ramsey, 1886	7.3
Billy Rhines, 1890	7.5
Amos Rusie, 1893	8.1
Amos Rusie, 1894	11.1
Tom Seaver, 1971	6.5
Bobby Shantz, 1952	6.3
Mike Smith, 1887	6.9
Warren Spahn, 1953	6.3
Al Spalding, 1876	6.3
Jack Stivetts, 1890	6.5
Jack Stivetts, 1891	7.9
Scott Stratton, 1890	10.1
Dizzy Trout, 1944	8.8
Dazzy Vance, 1928	6.4
Rube Waddell, 1902	6.4
Ed Walsh, 1907	8.1
Ed Walsh, 1908	6.6
Ed Walsh, 1910	7.2
Bucky Walters, 1939	8.4
Will White, 1882	7.8
Will White, 1883	6.7
Jim Whitney, 1883	7.8
Joe Wood, 1912	8.5
Cy Young, 1892	7.1
Cy Young, 1894	7.3
Cy Young, 1896	7.7
Cy Young, 1899	6.7
Cy Young, 1901	7.5

Total Pitcher Index (by era)

1876-1892

1	Silver King, 1888	11.9
2	Charley Radbourn, 1884	10.7
	Guy Hecker, 1884	10.7
4	Bob Caruthers, 1886	10.5
5	Dave Foutz, 1886	10.3
6	Scott Stratton, 1890	10.1
7	John Clarkson, 1887	9.8
8	Jim Devlin, 1877	9.2
	Tony Mullane, 1884	9.2
10	John Clarkson, 1885	9.1
11	John Clarkson, 1889	9.0
12	Charley Radbourn, 1883	8.2
13	Jack Stivetts, 1891	7.9
14	3 players tied	7.8

1893-1919

1	Amos Rusie, 1894	11.1
2	Walter Johnson, 1912	9.5
3	Pete Alexander, 1915	9.3
4	Walter Johnson, 1913	8.8
5	Joe Wood, 1912	8.5
6	Walter Johnson, 1918	8.3
7	Amos Rusie, 1893	8.1
	Ed Walsh, 1907	8.1
9	Cy Young, 1896	7.7
10	Christy Mathewson, 1905	7.6
11	Cy Young, 1901	7.5
12	Cy Young, 1894	7.3
	Pink Hawley, 1895	7.3
	Kid Nichols, 1897	7.3
15	Ed Walsh, 1910	7.2

1920-1941

1	Bucky Walters, 1939	8.4
2	Dolf Luque, 1923	7.4
	Lefty Grove, 1931	7.4
	Wes Ferrell, 1935	7.4
5	Carl Hubbell, 1933	7.1
6	Dizzy Dean, 1934	7.0
7	Red Faber, 1921	6.8
8	Lefty Grove, 1936	6.7
9	Lefty Grove, 1932	6.6
10	Dazzy Vance, 1928	6.4
11	Pete Alexander, 1920	6.3
	Burleigh Grimes, 1928	6.3
	Lefty Grove, 1935	6.3
	Lefty Gomez, 1937	6.3
15	Burleigh Grimes, 1920	6.2

1942-1960

1	Dizzy Trout, 1944	8.8
2	Hal Newhouser, 1945	8.1
3	Hal Newhouser, 1946	6.8
4	Bob Lemon, 1948	6.3
	Bobby Shantz, 1952	6.3
	Warren Spahn, 1953	6.3
7	Spud Chandler, 1943	6.1
8	Hal Newhouser, 1944	5.9
	Johnny Antonelli, 1954	5.9
10	Ned Garver, 1950	5.8
	Robin Roberts, 1953	5.8
	Frank Sullivan, 1955	5.8
13	Dizzy Trout, 1946	5.6
	Mel Parnell, 1949	5.6
	Bob Lemon, 1949	5.6

1961-1989

1	Dwight Gooden, 1985	7.9
2	Bob Gibson, 1968	7.5
3	Gaylord Perry, 1972	7.2
4	Ron Guidry, 1978	6.9
5	Steve Carlton, 1972	6.8
6	Juan Marichal, 1965	6.7
7	Tom Seaver, 1971	6.5
8	Bob Gibson, 1969	6.3
9	Ferguson Jenkins, 1971	6.2
	Tom Seaver, 1973	6.2
11	Juan Marichal, 1969	6.1
12	Wilbur Wood, 1971	6.0
	Phil Niekro, 1978	6.0
14	Sandy Koufax, 1966	5.9
	Rick Reuschel, 1977	5.9

Total Baseball Ranking

1	Silver King, 1888	11.9
2	Amos Rusie, 1894	11.1
3	Charley Radbourn, 1884	10.7
	Guy Hecker, 1884	10.7
5	Bob Caruthers, 1886	10.5
6	Dave Foutz, 1886	10.3
7	Scott Stratton, 1890	10.1
8	Babe Ruth, 1921	9.9
9	John Clarkson, 1887	9.8
10	Walter Johnson, 1912	9.5
11	Pete Alexander, 1915	9.3
12	Jim Devlin, 1877	9.2
	Tony Mullane, 1884	9.2
14	John Clarkson, 1885	9.1
15	Babe Ruth, 1923	9.0
	Cal Ripken, 1984	9.0
	John Clarkson, 1889	9.0
18	Nap Lajoie, 1910	8.9
19	Babe Ruth, 1920	8.8
	Walter Johnson, 1913	8.8
	Dizzy Trout, 1944	8.8
22	Babe Ruth, 1927	8.5
	Joe Wood, 1912	8.5
24	Bucky Walters, 1939	8.4
25	Babe Ruth, 1924	8.3
	Ted Williams, 1942	8.3
	Walter Johnson, 1918	8.3
28	Lou Gehrig, 1927	8.2
	Charley Radbourn, 1883	8.2
30	Ted Williams, 1947	8.1
	Stan Musial, 1948	8.1
	Mickey Mantle, 1957	8.1
	Amos Rusie, 1893	8.1
	Ed Walsh, 1907	8.1
	Hal Newhouser, 1945	8.1
36	Rogers Hornsby, 1920	8.0
	Ted Williams, 1941	8.0
	Joe Morgan, 1975	8.0
39	Nap Lajoie, 1903	7.9
	Ty Cobb, 1917	7.9
	Jack Stivetts, 1891	7.9
	Dwight Gooden, 1985	7.9
43	Babe Ruth, 1926	7.8
	Willie Mays, 1955	7.8
	Will White, 1882	7.8
	Jim Whitney, 1883	7.8
	Guy Hecker, 1885	7.8
48	George Sisler, 1920	7.7
	Babe Ruth, 1930	7.7
	Ted Williams, 1946	7.7
	Kid Nichols, 1890	7.7
	Cy Young, 1896	7.7
53	Fred Dunlap, 1884	7.6
	Jimmie Foxx, 1933	7.6
	Mickey Mantle, 1956	7.6
	Norm Cash, 1961	7.6
	Ron Santo, 1966	7.6
	Tim Keefe, 1883	7.6
	Christy Mathewson, 1905	7.6
60	Ted Williams, 1949	7.5
	Jackie Robinson, 1951	7.5
	Billy Rhines, 1890	7.5
	Cy Young, 1901	7.5
	Bob Gibson, 1968	7.5
65	Nap Lajoie, 1901	7.4
	Mike Schmidt, 1980	7.4
	Rickey Henderson, 1985	7.4
	Silver King, 1890	7.4
	Dolf Luque, 1923	7.4
	Lefty Grove, 1931	7.4
	Wes Ferrell, 1935	7.4
72	Nap Lajoie, 1904	7.3
	Tris Speaker, 1912	7.3
	Guy Hecker, 1886	7.3
	Toad Ramsey, 1886	7.3
	Cy Young, 1894	7.3
	Pink Hawley, 1895	7.3
	Kid Nichols, 1897	7.3
79	Rogers Hornsby, 1921	7.2
	Rogers Hornsby, 1922	7.2
	Chuck Klein, 1930	7.2
	Carl Yastrzemski, 1967	7.2
	Mike Schmidt, 1977	7.2
	Charlie Ferguson, 1886	7.2
	Ed Walsh, 1910	7.2
	Gaylord Perry, 1972	7.2
87	Tris Speaker, 1913	7.1
	Babe Ruth, 1919	7.1
	Harlond Clift, 1937	7.1
	Rod Carew, 1974	7.1
	Jim Devlin, 1876	7.1
	Jim Galvin, 1884	7.1
	Charlie Buffinton, 1888	7.1
	Bill Hutchinson, 1890	7.1
	Cy Young, 1892	7.1
	Carl Hubbell, 1933	7.1
97	12 players tied	7.0

Total Baseball Rank (alpha.)

Pete Alexander, 1915	9.3
Charlie Buffinton, 1888	7.1
Rod Carew, 1974	7.1
Bob Caruthers, 1886	10.5
Norm Cash, 1961	7.6
John Clarkson, 1885	9.1
John Clarkson, 1887	9.8
John Clarkson, 1889	9.0
Harlond Clift, 1937	7.1
Ty Cobb, 1917	7.9
Jim Devlin, 1876	7.1
Jim Devlin, 1877	9.2
Fred Dunlap, 1884	7.6
Charlie Ferguson, 1886	7.2
Wes Ferrell, 1935	7.4
Dave Foutz, 1886	10.3
Jimmie Foxx, 1933	7.6
Jim Galvin, 1884	7.1
Lou Gehrig, 1927	8.2
Bob Gibson, 1968	7.5
Dwight Gooden, 1985	7.9
Lefty Grove, 1931	7.4
Pink Hawley, 1895	7.3
Guy Hecker, 1884	10.7
Guy Hecker, 1885	7.8
Guy Hecker, 1886	7.3
Rickey Henderson, 1985	7.4
Rogers Hornsby, 1920	8.0
Rogers Hornsby, 1921	7.2
Rogers Hornsby, 1922	7.2
Carl Hubbell, 1933	7.1
Bill Hutchinson, 1890	7.1
Walter Johnson, 1912	9.5
Walter Johnson, 1913	8.8
Walter Johnson, 1918	8.3
Tim Keefe, 1883	7.6
Silver King, 1888	11.9
Silver King, 1890	7.4
Chuck Klein, 1930	7.2
Nap Lajoie, 1901	7.4
Nap Lajoie, 1903	7.9
Nap Lajoie, 1904	7.3
Nap Lajoie, 1910	8.9
Dolf Luque, 1923	7.4
Mickey Mantle, 1956	7.6
Mickey Mantle, 1957	8.1
Christy Mathewson, 1905	7.6
Willie Mays, 1955	7.8
Joe Morgan, 1975	8.0
Tony Mullane, 1884	9.2
Stan Musial, 1948	8.1
Hal Newhouser, 1945	8.1
Kid Nichols, 1890	7.7
Kid Nichols, 1897	7.3
Gaylord Perry, 1972	7.2
Charley Radbourn, 1883	8.2
Charley Radbourn, 1884	10.7
Toad Ramsey, 1886	7.3
Billy Rhines, 1890	7.5
Cal Ripken, 1984	9.0
Jackie Robinson, 1951	7.5
Amos Rusie, 1893	8.1
Amos Rusie, 1894	11.1
Babe Ruth, 1919	7.1
Babe Ruth, 1920	8.8
Babe Ruth, 1921	9.9
Babe Ruth, 1923	9.0
Babe Ruth, 1924	8.3
Babe Ruth, 1926	7.8
Babe Ruth, 1927	8.5
Babe Ruth, 1930	7.7
Ron Santo, 1966	7.6
Mike Schmidt, 1977	7.2
Mike Schmidt, 1980	7.4
George Sisler, 1920	7.7
Tris Speaker, 1912	7.3
Tris Speaker, 1913	7.1
Jack Stivetts, 1891	7.9
Scott Stratton, 1890	10.1
Dizzy Trout, 1944	8.8
Ed Walsh, 1907	8.1
Ed Walsh, 1910	7.2
Bucky Walters, 1939	8.4
Will White, 1882	7.8
Jim Whitney, 1883	7.8
Ted Williams, 1941	8.0
Ted Williams, 1942	8.3
Ted Williams, 1946	7.7
Ted Williams, 1947	8.1
Ted Williams, 1949	7.5
Joe Wood, 1912	8.5
Carl Yastrzemski, 1967	7.2
Cy Young, 1892	7.1
Cy Young, 1894	7.3
Cy Young, 1896	7.7
Cy Young, 1901	7.5

Total Baseball Rank (by era)

1876-1892

1	Silver King, 1888	11.9
2	Charley Radbourn, 1884	10.7
	Guy Hecker, 1884	10.7
4	Bob Caruthers, 1886	10.5
5	Dave Foutz, 1886	10.3
6	Scott Stratton, 1890	10.1
7	John Clarkson, 1887	9.8
8	Jim Devlin, 1877	9.2
	Tony Mullane, 1884	9.2
10	John Clarkson, 1885	9.1
11	John Clarkson, 1889	9.0
12	Charley Radbourn, 1883	8.2
13	Jack Stivetts, 1891	7.9
14	3 players tied	7.8

1893-1919

1	Amos Rusie, 1894	11.1
2	Walter Johnson, 1912	9.5
3	Pete Alexander, 1915	9.3
4	Nap Lajoie, 1910	8.9
5	Walter Johnson, 1913	8.8
6	Joe Wood, 1912	8.5
7	Walter Johnson, 1918	8.3
8	Amos Rusie, 1893	8.1
	Ed Walsh, 1907	8.1
10	Nap Lajoie, 1903	7.9
	Ty Cobb, 1917	7.9
12	Cy Young, 1896	7.7
13	Christy Mathewson, 1905	7.6
14	Cy Young, 1901	7.5
15	Nap Lajoie, 1901	7.4

1920-1941

1	Babe Ruth, 1921	9.9
2	Babe Ruth, 1923	9.0
3	Babe Ruth, 1920	8.8
4	Babe Ruth, 1927	8.5
5	Bucky Walters, 1939	8.4
6	Babe Ruth, 1924	8.3
7	Lou Gehrig, 1927	8.2
8	Rogers Hornsby, 1920	8.0
	Ted Williams, 1941	8.0
10	Babe Ruth, 1926	7.8
11	George Sisler, 1920	7.7
	Babe Ruth, 1930	7.7
13	Jimmie Foxx, 1933	7.6
14	3 players tied	7.4

1942-1960

1	Dizzy Trout, 1944	8.8
2	Ted Williams, 1942	8.3
3	Ted Williams, 1947	8.1
	Stan Musial, 1948	8.1
	Mickey Mantle, 1957	8.1
	Hal Newhouser, 1945	8.1
7	Willie Mays, 1955	7.8
8	Ted Williams, 1946	7.7
9	Mickey Mantle, 1956	7.6
10	Ted Williams, 1949	7.5
	Jackie Robinson, 1951	7.5
12	Stan Musial, 1951	7.0
13	Lou Boudreau, 1944	6.8
	Hal Newhouser, 1946	6.8
15	Ted Williams, 1957	6.7

1961-1989

1	Cal Ripken, 1984	9.0
2	Joe Morgan, 1975	8.0
3	Dwight Gooden, 1985	7.9
4	Norm Cash, 1961	7.6
	Ron Santo, 1966	7.6
6	Bob Gibson, 1968	7.5
7	Mike Schmidt, 1980	7.4
	Rickey Henderson, 1985	7.4
9	Carl Yastrzemski, 1967	7.2
	Mike Schmidt, 1977	7.2
	Gaylord Perry, 1972	7.2
12	Rod Carew, 1974	7.1
13	5 players tied	7.0

The Rosters

Team Rosters

Atlanta

ATL 1989 N

M	R.Nixon
1B	G.Perry
2B	H.Treadway
SS	A.Thomas
3B	J.Blauser
OF	D.Murphy
OF	L.Smith
OF	O.McDowell
C	J.Davis
UT	D.Evans
UT	W.Gregg
P	J.Smoltz
P	T.Glavine
P	D.Lilliquist
P	P.Smith
P	M.Clary
RP	J.Acker
RP	J.Boever

Baltimore

BAL 1989 A

M	F.Robinson
1B	R.Milligan
2B	W.Ripken
SS	C.Ripken
3B	C.Worthington
OF	P.Bradley
OF	M.Devereaux
OF	J.Orsulak
C	M.Tettleton
DH	L.Sheets
P	R.Milacki
P	J.Ballard
P	D.Schmidt
P	P.Harnisch
RP	B.Holton
RP	M.Williamson

Boston

BOS 1989 A

M	J.Morgan
1B	N.Esasky
2B	M.Barrett
SS	L.Rivera
3B	W.Boggs
OF	M.Greenwell
OF	E.Burks
OF	K.Romine
C	R.Cerone
DH	D.Evans
UT	D.Heep
UT	J.Reed
P	W.Clemens
P	M.Boddicker
P	J.Dopson
P	B.Smithson
RP	D.Lamp
RP	R.Murphy

California

CAL 1989 A

M	D.Rader
1B	W.Joyner
2B	J.Ray
SS	R.Schofield
3B	J.Howell
OF	D.White
OF	C.Davis
OF	C.Washington
C	L.Parrish
DH	B.Downing
P	R.Blyleven
P	M.Witt
P	K.McCaskill
P	C.Finley

P	J.Abbott
RP	W.Fraser
RP	G.Minton

Chicago

CHI 1989 A

M	J.Torborg
1B	G.Walker
2B	S.Lyons
SS	O.Guillen
3B	C.Martinez
OF	D.Gallagher
OF	I.Calderon
OF	D.Boston
C	C.Fisk
DH	H.Baines
P	M.Perez
P	E.King
P	S.Rosenberg
P	J.Hibbard
P	J.Reuss
RP	S.Hillegas
RP	D.Pall

CHI 1989 N

M	D.Zimmer
1B	M.Grace
2B	R.Sandberg
SS	S.Dunston
3B	V.Law
OF	J.Walton
OF	A.Dawson
OF	D.Smith
C	D.Berryhill
UT	M.Webster
P	G.Maddux
P	R.Sutcliffe
P	M.Bielecki
P	S.Sanderson
P	P.Kilgus
RP	J.Pico
RP	S.Wilson

Cincinnati

CIN 1989 N

M	P.Rose
M	T.Helms
1B	T.Benzinger
2B	R.Oester
SS	B.Larkin
3B	C.Sabo
OF	E.Davis
OF	P.O'Neill
OF	R.Roomes
C	J.Reed
UT	G.Griffey
UT	L.Quinones
UT	H.Winningham
P	T.Browning
P	R.Mahler
P	D.Jackson
P	J.Rijo
P	W.Scudder
RP	R.Dibble
RP	N.Charlton

Cleveland

CLE 1989 A

M	H.Edwards
M	J.Hart
1B	P.O'Brien
2B	J.Browne
SS	F.Fermin
3B	B.Jacoby
OF	J.Carter
OF	J.Snyder
OF	B.Komminsk
C	A.Allanson

DH	D.Clark
P	H.Black
P	J.Farrell
P	T.Candiotti
P	F.Swindell
P	S.Bailes
RP	D.Jones
RP	J.Orosco

Detroit

DET 1989 A

M	G.Anderson
1B	D.Bergman
2B	L.Whitaker
SS	A.Trammell
3B	R.Schu
OF	G.Pettis
OF	C.Lemon
OF	K.Williams
C	M.Heath
DH	B.Moreland
UT	F.Lynn
UT	G.Ward
P	F.Tanana
P	D.Alexander
P	J.Morris
RP	P.Gibson
RP	M.Henneman

Houston

HOU 1989 N

M	A.Howe
1B	G.Davis
2B	W.Doran
SS	R.Ramirez
3B	K.Caminiti
OF	G.Young
OF	W.Hatcher
OF	T.Puhl
C	C.Biggio
UT	G.Reynolds
P	M.Scott
P	J.Deshaies
P	J.Clancy
P	R.Knepper
P	M.Portugal
RP	D.Darwin
RP	R.Forsch

Kansas City

KC 1989 A

M	J.Wathan
1B	G.Brett
2B	F.White
SS	K.Stillwell
3B	K.Seitzer
OF	J.Eisenreich
OF	V.Jackson
OF	W.Wilson
C	R.Boone
DH	D.Tartabull
UT	P.Tabler
UT	B.Wellman
P	B.Saberhagen
P	M.Gubicza
P	T.Gordon
P	C.Leibrandt
P	L.Aquino
RP	J.Montgomery
RP	T.Leach

Los Angeles

LA 1989 N

M	T.Lasorda

1B	E.Murray
2B	W.Randolph
SS	A.Griffin
3B	J.Hamilton
OF	M.Marshall
OF	J.Shelby
OF	J.Gonzalez
C	M.Scioscia
P	O.Hershiser
P	T.Belcher
P	F.Valenzuela
P	M.Morgan
P	T.Leary
RP	J.Howell
RP	A.Pena

Milwaukee

MIL 1989 A

M	T.Trebelhorn
1B	G.Brock
2B	J.Gantner
SS	W.Spiers
3B	P.Molitor
OF	R.Yount
OF	G.Braggs
OF	R.Deer
C	W.Surhoff
DH	T.Meyer
UT	M.Felder
P	C.Bosio
P	D.August
P	T.Higuera
P	M.Knudson
P	J.Navarro
RP	C.Crim
RP	W.Krueger

Minnesota

MIN 1989 A

M	J.Kelly
1B	K.Hrbek
2B	A.Newman
SS	G.Gagne
3B	G.Gaetti
OF	K.Puckett
OF	C.Gladden
OF	R.Bush
C	B.Harper
DH	J.Dwyer
UT	E.Larkin
UT	T.Laudner
UT	J.Moses
P	A.Anderson
P	F.Viola
P	L.Smith
P	S.Rawley
RP	J.Berenguer
RP	J.Reardon

Montreal

MON 1989 N

M	R.Rodgers
1B	A.Galarraga
2B	T.Foley
SS	S.Owen
3B	T.Wallach
OF	H.Brooks
OF	T.Raines
OF	D.Martinez
C	N.Santovenia
UT	M.Fitzgerald
UT	O.Nixon
P	J.Martinez
P	B.Smith
P	K.Gross
P	P.Perez
P	M.Langston
RP	T.Burke

RP	A.McGaffigan

New York

NY 1989 N

M	D.Johnson
1B	D.Magadan
2B	G.Jefferies
SS	K.Elster
3B	H.Johnson
OF	W.McReynolds
OF	D.Strawberry
OF	J.Samuel
C	B.Lyons
P	D.Cone
P	C.Fernandez
P	R.Darling
P	R.Ojeda
P	D.Gooden
RP	R.Myers
RP	R.Aguilera

NY 1989 A

M	G.Green
M	R.Dent
1B	D.Mattingly
2B	S.Sax
SS	A.Espinoza
3B	M.Pagliarulo
OF	R.Kelly
OF	J.Barfield
OF	M.Hall
C	D.Slaught
DH	S.Balboni
P	M.Hawkins
P	J.Parker
P	D.LaPoint
P	C.Cary
RP	A.Guetterman
RP	L.McCullers

Oakland

OAK 1989 A

M	A.LaRussa
1B	M.McGwire
2B	K.Phillips
SS	M.Gallego
3B	C.Lansford
OF	D.Henderson
OF	S.Javier
OF	R.Henderson
C	T.Steinbach
DH	D.Parker
UT	R.Hassey
UT	R.Roberts
P	D.Stewart
P	M.Moore
P	R.Welch
P	G.Davis
P	C.Young
RP	T.Burns
RP	W.Nelson

Philadelphia

PHI 1989 N

M	N.Leyva
1B	P.Jordan
2B	T.Herr
SS	R.Thon
3B	C.Hayes
OF	V.Hayes
OF	L.Dykstra
OF	R.Dernier
C	D.Daulton
UT	C.Ford
UT	L.Jeltz
P	K.Howell
P	D.Carman
P	B.Ruffin

P	L.McWilliams
P	D.Cook
RP	J.Parrett
RP	G.Harris

Pittsburgh

PIT 1989 N

M	J.Leyland
1B	G.Redus
2B	J.Lind
SS	J.Bell
3B	R.Bonilla
OF	B.Bonds
OF	A.Van Slyke
OF	R.Reynolds
C	A.Ortiz
UT	J.Cangelosi
UT	G.Wilson
P	D.Drabek
P	J.Smiley
P	R.Walk
P	N.Heaton
P	R.Kramer
RP	J.Robinson
RP	R.Kipper

St.Louis

STL 1989 N

M	D.Herzog
1B	P.Guerrero
2B	J.Oquendo
SS	O.Smith
3B	T.Pendleton
OF	T.Brunansky
OF	M.Thompson
OF	V.Coleman
C	A.Pena
P	J.DeLeon
P	J.Magrane
P	K.Hill
P	S.Terry
RP	F.DiPino
RP	D.Quisenberry

San Diego

SD 1989 N

M	J.McKeon
1B	J.Clark
2B	R.Alomar
SS	G.Templeton
3B	L.Salazar
OF	A.Gwynn
OF	M.Wynne
OF	D.James
C	B.Santiago
UT	C.Martinez
UT	L.Roberts
P	B.Hurst
P	E.Whitson
P	D.Rasmussen
P	C.Terrell
P	E.Show
RP	G.Harris
RP	M.Grant

San Francisco

SF 1989 N

M	R.Craig
1B	W.Clark
2B	R.Thompson
SS	J.Uribe
3B	E.Riles

OF	B.Butler
OF	K.Mitchell
OF	C.Maldonado
C	T.Kennedy
P	R.Reuschel
P	D.Robinson
P	S.Garrelts
P	M.LaCoss
RP	C.Lefferts
RP	J.Brantley

Seattle

SEA 1989 A

M	J.Lefebvre
1B	A.Davis
2B	H.Reynolds
SS	O.Vizquel
3B	J.Presley
OF	G.Griffey
OF	G.Briley
OF	H.Cotto
C	D.Valle
DH	J.Leonard
UT	S.Bradley
UT	D.Coles
P	M.Bankhead
P	B.Holman
P	R.Johnson
P	W.Swift
P	E.Hanson
RP	J.Reed
RP	M.Jackson

Texas

TEX 1989 A

M	R.Valentine
1B	R.Palmeiro
2B	J.Franco
SS	S.Fletcher
3B	S.Buechele
OF	R.Sierra
OF	C.Espy
OF	P.Incaviglia
C	C.Kreuter
DH	H.Baines
UT	J.Kunkel
UT	R.Leach
P	L.Ryan
P	R.Witt
P	J.Brown
P	C.Hough
P	J.Jeffcoat
RP	K.Rogers
RP	J.Russell

Toronto

TOR 1989 A

M	J.Williams
M	C.Gaston
1B	F.McGriff
2B	N.Liriano
SS	O.Fernandez
3B	K.Gruber
OF	J.Bell
OF	L.Moseby
OF	J.Felix
C	L.Whitt
DH	S.Mulliniks
UT	M.Lee
P	J.Key
P	D.Stieb
P	J.Cerutti
P	M.Flanagan
P	T.Stottlemyre
RP	R.Ward
RP	T.Henke

183

The Manager Roster

YEAR	TM/L	G	W	L	PCT	STANDING	M/Y
Anderson, George Lee "Sparky"							
1970	Cin-N	162	102	60	.630	♦1 W	
1971	Cin-N	162	79	83	.488	●4 W	
1972	Cin-N	154	95	59	.617	♦1 W	
1973	Cin-N	162	99	63	.611	1 W	
1974	Cin-N	163	98	64	.605	2 W	
1975	Cin-N	162	108	54	.667	★1 W	
1976	Cin-N	162	102	60	.630	★1 W	
1977	Cin-N	162	88	74	.543	2 W	
1978	Cin-N	161	92	69	.571	2 W	
1979	Det-A	106	56	50	.528	5 E 5 E	3/3
1980	Det-A	163	84	78	.519	5 E	
1981(1)	Det-A	57	31	26	.544	4 E	
(2)	Det-A	52	29	23	.558	●2 E	
1982	Det-A	162	83	79	.512	4 E	
1983	Det-A	162	92	70	.568	2 E	
1984	Det-A	162	104	58	.642	★1 E	
1985	Det-A	161	84	77	.522	3 E	
1986	Det-A	162	87	75	.537	3 E	
1987	Det-A	162	98	64	.605	1 E	
1988	Det-A	162	88	74	.543	2 E	
1989	Det-A	162	59	103	.364	7 E	
	20	3123	1758	1363	.563		
Craig, Roger Lee							
1978	SD-N	162	84	78	.519	4 W	
1979	SD-N	161	68	93	.422	5 W	
1985	SF-N	18	6	12	.333	6 W 6 W	2/2
1986	SF-N	162	83	79	.512	3 W	
1987	SF-N	162	90	72	.556	1 W	
1988	SF-N	162	83	79	.512	4 W	
1989	SF-N	162	92	70	.568	♦1 W	
	7	989	506	483	.512		
Dent, Russell Earl "Bucky"							
1989	NY-A	40	18	22	.450	6 E 5 E	2/2
Edwards, Howard Rodney "Doc"							
1987	Cle-A	75	30	45	.400	7 E 7 E	2/2
1988	Cle-A	162	78	84	.481	6 E	
1989	Cle-A	143	65	78	.455	6 E 6 E	1/2
	3	380	173	207	.455		
Gaston, Clarence Edwin "Cito"							
1989	Tor-A	126	77	49	.611	6 E 1 E	2/2
Green, George Dallas "Dallas"							
1979	Phi-N	30	19	11	.633	5 E 4 E	2/2
1980	Phi-N	162	91	71	.562	★1 E	
1981(1)	Phi-N	55	34	21	.618	1 E	
(2)	Phi-N	52	25	27	.481	3 E	
1989	NY-A	121	56	65	.463	6 E 5 E	1/2
	4	420	225	195	.536		
Hart, John Henry							
1989	Cle-A	19	8	11	.421	6 E 6 E	2/2
Helms, Tommy Vann							
1988	Cin-N	27	12	15	.444	4 W 4 W 2 W	2/3
1989	Cin-N	37	16	21	.432	●4 W 5 W	2/2
	2	64	28	36	.438		
Herzog, Dorrel Norman Elvert "Whitey"							
1973	Tex-A	138	47	91	.341	6 W 6 W	1/3
1974	Cal-A	4	2	2	.500	6 W 6 W 6 W	2/3
1975	KC-A	66	41	25	.621	2 W 2 W	2/2
1976	KC-A	162	90	72	.556	1 W	
1977	KC-A	162	102	60	.630	1 W	
1978	KC-A	162	92	70	.568	1 W	
1979	KC-A	162	85	77	.525	2 W	
1980	StL-N	73	38	35	.521	6 E 5 E 4 E	3/4
1981(1)	StL-N	51	30	20	.600	2 E	
(2)	StL-N	52	29	23	.558	2 E	
1982	StL-N	162	92	70	.568	★1 E	
1983	StL-N	162	79	83	.488	4 E	
1984	StL-N	162	84	78	.519	3 E	
1985	StL-N	162	101	61	.623	♦1 E	
1986	StL-N	161	79	82	.491	3 E	
1987	StL-N	162	95	67	.586	♦1 E	
1988	StL-N	162	76	86	.469	5 E	
1989	StL-N	164	86	76	.531	3 E	
	17	2329	1248	1078	.537		
Howe, Arthur Henry "Art"							
1989	Hou-N	162	86	76	.531	3 W	
Johnson, David Allen "Dave"							
1984	NY-N	162	90	72	.556	2 E	
1985	NY-N	162	98	64	.605	2 E	
1986	NY-N	162	108	54	.667	★1 E	
1987	NY-N	162	92	70	.568	2 E	
1988	NY-N	160	100	60	.625	1 E	
1989	NY-N	162	87	75	.537	2 E	

YEAR	TM/L	G	W	L	PCT	STANDING	M/Y
	6	970	575	395	.593		
Kelly, Jay Thomas "Tom"							
1986	Min-A	23	12	11	.522	7 W 6 W	2/2
1987	Min-A	162	85	77	.525	♦1 W	
1988	Min-A	162	91	71	.562	2 W	
1989	Min-A	162	80	82	.494	5 W	
	4	509	268	241	.527		
LaRussa, Anthony "Tony"							
1979	Chi-A	54	27	27	.500	5 W 5 W	2/2
1980	Chi-A	162	70	90	.438	5 W	
1981(1)	Chi-A	53	31	22	.585	3 W	
(2)	Chi-A	53	23	30	.434	6 W	
1982	Chi-A	162	87	75	.537	3 W	
1983	Chi-A	162	99	63	.611	1 W	
1984	Chi-A	162	74	88	.457	●5 W	
1985	Chi-A	163	85	77	.525	3 W	
1986	Chi-A	64	26	38	.406	6 W 5 W	1/3
	Oak-A	79	45	34	.570	7 W ●3 W	3/3
1987	Oak-A	162	81	81	.500	3 W	
1988	Oak-A	162	104	58	.642	♦1 W	
1989	Oak-A	162	99	63	.611	★1 W	
	11	1600	851	746	.533		
Lasorda, Thomas Charles "Tom"							
1976	LA-N	4	2	2	.500	2 W 2 W	2/2
1977	LA-N	162	98	64	.605	♦1 W	
1978	LA-N	162	95	67	.586	♦1 W	
1979	LA-N	162	79	83	.488	3 W	
1980	LA-N	163	92	71	.564	▲2 W	
1981(1)	LA-N	57	36	21	.632	★1 W	
(2)	LA-N	53	27	26	.509	4 W	
1982	LA-N	162	88	74	.543	2 W	
1983	LA-N	163	91	71	.562	1 W	
1984	LA-N	162	79	83	.488	4 W	
1985	LA-N	162	95	67	.586	1 W	
1986	LA-N	162	73	89	.451	5 W	
1987	LA-N	162	73	89	.451	4 W	
1988	LA-N	162	94	67	.584	★1 W	
1989	LA-N	160	77	83	.481	4 W	
	14	2058	1099	957	.535		
Lefebvre, James Kenneth "Jim"							
1989	Sea-A	162	73	89	.451	6 W	
Leyland, James Richard "Jim"							
1986	Pit-N	162	64	98	.395	6 E	
1987	Pit-N	162	80	82	.494	●4 E	
1988	Pit-N	160	85	75	.531	2 E	
1989	Pit-N	164	74	88	.457	5 E	
	4	648	303	343	.469		
Leyva, Nicolas Tomas "Nick"							
1989	Phi-N	163	67	95	.414	6 E	
McKeon, John Aloysius "Jack"							
1973	KC-A	162	88	74	.543	2 W	
1974	KC-A	162	77	85	.475	5 W	
1975	KC-A	96	50	46	.521	2 W 2 W	1/2
1977	Oak-A	53	26	27	.491	●5 W 7 W	1/2
1978	Oak-A	123	45	78	.366	1 W 6 W	2/2
1988	SD-N	115	67	48	.583	5 W 3 W	2/2
1989	SD-N	162	89	73	.549	2 W	
	7	873	442	431	.506		
Morgan, Joseph Michael "Joe"							
1988	Bos-A	77	46	31	.597	4 E 1 E	2/2
1989	Bos-A	162	83	79	.512	3 E	
	2	239	129	110	.540		
Nixon, Russell Eugene "Russ"							
1982	Cin-N	70	27	43	.386	6 W 6 W	2/2
1983	Cin-N	162	74	88	.457	6 W	
1988	Atl-N	121	42	79	.347	6 W 6 W	2/2
1989	Atl-N	161	63	97	.394	6 W	
	4	514	206	307	.402		
Rader, Douglas Lee "Doug"							
1983	Tex-A	163	77	85	.475	3 W	
1984	Tex-A	161	69	92	.429	7 W	
1985	Tex-A	32	9	23	.281	7 W 7 W	1/2
1986	Chi-A	2	1	1	.500	6 W 5 W 5 W	2/3
1989	Cal-A	162	91	71	.562	3 W	
	5	520	247	272	.476		
Robinson, Frank							
1975	Cle-A*	159	79	80	.497	4 E	
1976	Cle-A*	159	81	78	.509	4 E	
1977	Cle-A	57	26	31	.456	5 E 5 E	1/2
1981(1)	SF-N	59	27	32	.458	5 W	
(2)	SF-N	52	29	23	.558	3 W	
1982	SF-N	162	87	75	.537	3 W	

YEAR	TM/L	G	W	L	PCT	STANDING		M/Y
1983	SF-N	162	79	83	.488	5 W		
1984	SF-N	106	42	64	.396	6 W	6 W	1/2
1988	Bal-A	155	54	101	.348	7 W	7 E	2/2
1989	Bal-A	162	87	75	.537	2 E		
	9	1233	591	642	.479			

Rodgers, Robert Leroy "Bob"

YEAR	TM/L	G	W	L	PCT	STANDING		M/Y
1980	Mil-A	47	26	21	.553	2 E	3 E	1/3
	Mil-A	23	13	10	.565	4 E	3 E	3/3
1981(1)	Mil-A	56	31	25	.554	3 E		
(2)	Mil-A	53	31	22	.585	1 E		
1982	Mil-A	47	23	24	.489	5 E	◆1 E	1/2
1985	Mon-N	161	84	77	.522	3 E		
1986	Mon-N	161	78	83	.484	4 E		
1987	Mon-N	162	91	71	.562	3 E		
1988	Mon-N	163	81	81	.500	3 E		
1989	Mon-N	162	81	81	.500	4 E		
	8	1035	539	495	.521			

Rose, Peter Edward "Pete"

YEAR	TM/L	G	W	L	PCT	STANDING		M/Y
1984	Cin-N*	41	19	22	.463	5 W	5 W	2/2
1985	Cin-N*	162	89	72	.553	2 W		
1986	Cin-N*	162	86	76	.531	2 W		
1987	Cin-N	162	84	78	.519	2 W		
1988	Cin-N	23	11	12	.478	4 W	2 W	1/3
	Cin-N	111	64	47	.577	4 W	2 W	3/3
1989	Cin-N	125	59	66	.472	●4 W	5 W	1/2
	6	786	412	373	.525			

Torborg, Jeffrey Allen "Jeff"

YEAR	TM/L	G	W	L	PCT	STANDING		M/Y
1977	Cle-A	104	45	59	.433	5 E	5 E	2/2
1978	Cle-A	159	69	90	.434	6 E		
1979	Cle-A	95	43	52	.453	6 E	6 E	1/2
1989	Chi-A	161	69	92	.429	7 W		
	4	519	226	293	.435			

Trebelhorn, Thomas Lynn "Tom"

YEAR	TM/L	G	W	L	PCT	STANDING		M/Y
1986	Mil-A	9	6	3	.667	6 E	6 E	2/2
1987	Mil-A	162	91	71	.562	3 E		

YEAR	TM/L	G	W	L	PCT	STANDING		M/Y
1988	Mil-A	162	87	75	.537	●3 E		
1989	Mil-A	162	81	81	.500	4 E		
	4	495	265	230	.535			

Valentine, Robert John "Bobby"

YEAR	TM/L	G	W	L	PCT	STANDING		M/Y
1985	Tex-A	129	53	76	.411	7 W	7 W	2/2
1986	Tex-A	162	87	75	.537	2 W		
1987	Tex-A	162	75	87	.463	●6 W		
1988	Tex-A	161	70	91	.435	6 W		
1989	Tex-A	162	83	79	.512	4 W		
	5	776	368	408	.474			

Wathan, John David

YEAR	TM/L	G	W	L	PCT	STANDING		M/Y
1987	KC-A	36	21	15	.583	4 W	2 W	2/2
1988	KC-A	161	84	77	.522	3 W		
1989	KC-A	162	92	70	.568	2 W		
	3	359	197	162	.549			

Williams, James Francis "Jimy"

YEAR	TM/L	G	W	L	PCT	STANDING		M/Y
1986	Tor-A	163	86	76	.531	4 E		
1987	Tor-A	162	96	66	.593	2 E		
1988	Tor-A	162	87	75	.537	●3 E		
1989	Tor-A	36	12	24	.333	6 E	1 E	1/2
	4	523	281	241	.538			

Zimmer, Donald William "Don"

YEAR	TM/L	G	W	L	PCT	STANDING		M/Y
1972	SD-N	142	54	88	.380	4 W	6 W	2/2
1973	SD-N	162	60	102	.370	6 W		
1976	Bos-A	76	42	34	.553	5 E	3 E	2/2
1977	Bos-A	161	97	64	.602	●2 E		
1978	Bos-A	163	99	64	.607	▲2 E		
1979	Bos-A	160	91	69	.569	3 E		
1980	Bos-A	155	82	73	.529	3 E	4 E	1/2
1981(1)	Tex-A	55	33	22	.600	2 W		
(2)	Tex-A	50	24	26	.480	3 W		
1982	Tex-A	96	38	58	.396	6 W	6 W	1/2
1988	Chi-N	163	77	85	.475	4 E		
1989	Chi-N	162	93	69	.574	1 E		
	11	1545	790	754	.512			

The Coach Roster

Alomar, Santos C. "Sandy" SD-N 1986-89

Altobelli, Joseph S. "Joe" NY-A 1981-82, 1986, Chi-N 1988-89

Amalfitano, J. Joseph "Joey" Chi-N 1967-71, SF-N 1972-75, SD-N 1976-77, Chi-N 1978-80, Cin-N 1982, LA-N 1983-89

Baker, Johnnie B "Dusty" SF-N 1988-89

Bearnarth, Lawrence D. "Larry" Mon-N 1976, 1985-89

Berardino, Richard J. "Dick" Bos-A 1989

Berra, Lawrence P. "Yogi" NY-N 1965-71, NY-A 1976-83, Hou-N 1986-89

Bevington, Terry Paul Chi-A 1989

Bowa, Lawrence R. "Larry" Phi-N 1988-89

Breeden, H. Scott Cin-N 1986-89

Bristol, J. David "Dave" Cin-N 1966, Mon-N 1973-75, SF-N 1978-79, Phi-N 1982-85, 1988, Cin-N 1989

Bumbry, Alonza B. "Al" Bos-A 1988-89

Clark, Ronald B. "Ron" Chi-A 1988-89

Clines, Eugene A. "Gene" Chi-N 1979-81, Hou-N 1988, Sea-A 1989

Coleman, Joseph H. "Joe" Cal-A 1988-89

Connors, William J. "Billy" KC-A 1980-81, Chi-N 1982-86, Sea-A 1987-88, NY-A 1989

Consolo, William A. "Billy" Det-A 1979-89

Corrales, Patrick "Pat" Tex-A 1975-78, NY-A 1989

Cottier, Charles K. "Chuck" NY-N 1979-81, Sea-A 1982-84, Chi-N 1988-89

Cox, Larry E. Chi-N 1988-89

Cresse, Mark E. LA-N 1977-89

Dal Canton, J. Bruce Atl-N 1987-89

Davenport, James H. "Jim" SF-N 1970, SD-N 1974-75, SF-N 1976-82, 1984, Phi-N 1986-87, Cle-A 1989

Didier, Robert D. "Bob" Oak-A 1984-86, Sea-A 1989

Dobson, Patrick E. "Pat" Mil-A 1982-84, SD-N 1988-89

Donnelly, Richard F. "Rich" Tex-A 1980, 1983-85, Pit-N 1986-89

Duncan, David E. "Dave" Cle-A 1978-81, Sea-A 1982, Chi-A 1983-86, Oak-A 1986-89

Dyer, Don R. "Duffy" Chi-N 1983, Mil-A 1989

Egan, Richard W. "Dick" Tex-A 1988-89

Elia, Lee C. Phi-N 1980-81, 1985-87, NY-A 1989

Ellis, Samuel J. "Sammy" NY-A 1982, 1984, 1986, Chi-A 1989

Etchebarren, Andrew A. "Andy" Cal-A 1977, Mil-A 1984-89

Ezell, Glenn W. Tex-A 1983-85, KC-A 1989

Fahey, William R. "Bill" SF-N 1986-89

Ferguson, Joseph V. "Joe" Tex-A 1986-87, LA-N 1988-89

Ferraro, Michael D. "Mike" NY-A 1979-81, KC-A 1984-86, NY-A 1987-88, 1989

Fischer, William C. "Bill" Cin-N 1979-83, Bos-A 1985-89

Fox, Charles F. "Charlie" SF-N 1965-68, NY-A 1989

Funk, Franklin R. "Frank" SF-N 1976, Sea-A 1980-81, 1983-84, KC-A 1988-89

Galante, Matthew "Matt" Hou-N 1985-89

Garner, Philip M. "Phil" Hou-N 1989

Garrett, H. Adrian KC-A 1988-89

Gaston, Clarence E. Tor-A 1982-89

Grammas, Alexander P. "Alex" Pit-N 1965-69, Cin-N 1970-75, 1978, Atl-N 1979, Det-A 1980-89

Hacker, Richard W. "Rich" StL-N 1986-89

Haney, W. Larry Mil-A 1978-89

Hansen, Ronald L. "Ron" Mil-A 1980-83, Mon-N 1985-89

Harrah, Colbert D. "Toby" Tex-A 1989

Harrelson, Derrel M. "Bud" NY-N 1982, 1985-89

Hartenstein, Charles O. "Chuck" Cle-A 1979, Mil-A 1987-89

Hebner, Richard J. "Richie" Bos-A 1989

Helms, Tommy V. Tex-A 1981-82, Cin-N 1983-89

Hendricks, Elrod J. Bal-A 1978-89

Hines, Ben T. Sea-A 1984, LA-N 1988-89

House, Thomas R. "Tom" Tex-A 1985-89

Howard, Frank O. Mil-A 1977-80, NY-N 1982-83, 1984, Mil-A 1985-86, Sea-A 1987-88, NY-A 1989

Hriniak, Walter J. "Walt" Mon-N 1974-75, Bos-A 1977-88, Chi-A 1989

Isaac, Luis Cle-A 1988-89

Jackson, Alvin N. "Al" Bos-A 1977-79, Bal-A 1989

Johnson, Deron R. Cal-A 1979-80, NY-N 1981, Phi-N 1982-84, Sea-A 1985-86, Chi-A 1987, Cal-A 1989

Jones, Clarence W. Atl-N 1985, 1988-89

Kim, Wendell K. SF-N 1989

Kimm, Bruce E. Cin-N 1984-88, Pit-N 1989

Knoop, Robert F. "Bobby" Chi-A 1977-78, Cal-A 1979-89

Knowles, Darold D. StL-N 1983, Phi-N 1989

Kuntz, Russell J. "Rusty" Sea-A 1989

Kusnyer, Arthur W. "Art" Chi-A 1980-87, Oak-A 1989

Lachemann, Marcel E. Cal-A 1984-89

Lachemann, Rene G. Bos-A 1985-86, Oak-A 1987-89

Lamont, Gene W. Pit-N 1986-89

Landestoy, Rafael S. Mon-N 1989

LaRoche, David E. "Dave" Chi-A 1989

Lett, James C. "Jim" Cin-N 1988-89

Lewis, Johnny J. StL-N 1973-76, 1985-89

Lillis, Robert P. "Bob" Hou-N 1967, 1973-82, SF-N 1986-89

Lopes, David E. "Davey" Tex-A 1988-89

Lum, Michael K. "Mike" Chi-A 1985, KC-A 1988-89

Macha, Kenneth E. "Ken" Mon-N 1986-89

Majtyka, Roy Atl-N 1988-89

Manuel, Charles F. "Charlie" Cle-A 1988-89

Martinez, Jose KC-A 1980-87, Chi-N 1988-89

May, Lee A. KC-A 1984-86, Cin-N 1988-89

May, Milton S. "Milt" Pit-N 1987-89

Mayberry, John C. KC-A 1989

McCraw, Tommy L. Cle-A 1975, 1979-82, SF-N 1983-85, Bal-A 1989

McKay, David L. "Dave" Oak-A 1984-89

McLaren, John L. Tor-A 1986-89

Menke, Denis J. Tor-A 1980-81, Hou-N 1983-88, Phi-N 1989

Michael, Eugene R. "Gene" NY-A 1976-77, 1978, 1984-86, 1988, 1989

Miller, Raymond R. "Ray" Bal-A 1978-85, Pit-N 1987-89

Moore, Jackie S. Mil-A 1970-72, Tex-A 1973-74, 1975-76, Tor-A 1977-79, Tex-A 1980, Oak-A 1981-84, Mon-N 1987-89

Moss, J. Lester "Les" Chi-A 1967-68, 1970, Chi-N 1981, Hou-N 1982-84, 1985-89

Mota, Manuel R. "Manny" LA-N 1980-89

Muffett, Billy A.   StL-N 1967-70, Cal-A 1974-77,
   Det-A 1985-89
Muser, Anthony J. "Tony"   Mil-A 1985-89
Napoleon, Edward G. "Ed"   Cle-A 1983-85,
   KC-A 1987-88, Hou-N 1989
Oates, Johnny L.   Chi-N 1984-87, Bal-A 1989
Oliva, Pedro "Tony"   Min-A 1976-78, 1985-89
Oliver, David J. "Dave"   Tex-A 1987-89
Otis, Amos J.   SD-N 1988-89
Ott, N. Edward "Ed"   Hou-N 1989
Pattin, Martin W. "Marty"   Tor-A 1989
Paul, Michael G. "Mike"   Oak-A 1987-88,
   Sea-A 1989
Pavlick, Gregory M. "Greg"   NY-N 1985-86,
   1988-89
Perez, Atanacio R. "Tony"   Cin-N 1987-89
Perlozzo, Samuel B. "Sam"   NY-N 1987-89
Perranoski, Ronald P. "Ron"   LA-N 1981-89
Pinson, Vada E.   Sea-A 1977-80, Chi-A 1981,
   Sea-A 1982-83, Det-A 1985-89
Plummer, William F. "Bill"   Sea-A 1982-83, 1988-89
Pole, Richard H. "Dick"   Chi-N 1988-89
Reese, James H. "Jimmie"   Cal-A 1973-89
Renick, W. Richard "Rick"   KC-A 1981,
   Mon-N 1985-86, Min-A 1987-89
Rettenmund, Mervin W. "Merv"   Cal-A 1980-81,
   Tex-A 1983-85, Oak-A 1989

Reynolds, Tommie D   Oak-A 1989
Ricketts, David W. "Dave"   Pit-N 1971-73,
   StL-N 1974-75, 1978-89
Riddoch, Gregory L. "Greg"   SD-N 1987-89
Riggleman, James "Jim"   StL-N 1989
Ripken, Calvin E., Sr. "Cal"   Bal-A 1976-86, 1989
Roarke, Michael T. "Mike"   Det-A 1965-66,
   Cal-A 1967-69, Det-A 1970, Chi-N 1978-80,
   StL-N 1984-89
Robinson, William H. "Bill"   NY-N 1984-89
Robson, Thomas J. "Tom"   Tex-A 1986-89
Rosenbaum, Glen O.   Chi-A 1973-75, 1986-89
Russell, William E. "Bill"   LA-N 1987-89
Ryan, Michael J. "Mike"   Phi-N 1980-89
Sandt, Thomas J. "Tommy"   Pit-N 1987-89
Schaefer, Robert W. "Bob"   KC-A 1988-89
Schoendienst, Albert F. "Red"   StL-N 1963-64,
   Oak-A 1977-78, StL-N 1979-89
Sherry, Norman B. "Norm"   Cal-A 1970-71, 1976,
   Mon-N 1978-81, SD-N 1982-84, SF-N 1986-89
Slider, Rachel W. "Rac"   Bos-A 1987-89
Snitker, Brian G.   Atl-N 1985, 1988-89
Sommers, Dennis J. "Denny"   NY-N 1977-78,
   Cle-A 1980-85, SD-N 1988-89
Sparks, Joseph E. "Joe"   Chi-A 1979, Cin-N 1984,
   Mon-N 1989

Spencer, H. Thomas "Tom"   Cle-A 1988-89
Squires, Michael L. "Mike"   Tor-A 1989
Stearns, John H.   NY-A 1989
Stelmaszek, Richard F. "Rick"   Min-A 1981-89
Stottlemyre, Melvin L. "Mel"   NY-N 1984-89
Stubing, Lawrence G. "Moose"   Cal-A 1985-88,
   1989
Such, Richard S. "Dick"   Tex-A 1983-85,
   Min-A 1985-89
Sullivan, John P.   KC-A 1979, Atl-N 1980-81,
   Tor-A 1982-89
Summers, John J. "Champ"   NY-A 1989
Taylor, Antonio N. "Tony"   Phi-N 1977-79, 1988-89
Terwilliger, W. Wayne   Was-A 1969-71, Tex-A 1972,
   1981-85, Min-A 1986-89
Tracewski, Richard J. "Dick"   Det-A 1972-89
Vukovich, John C.   Chi-N 1982-87, Phi-N 1988,
   1989
Widmar, Albert J. "Al"   Phi-N 1962-64, 1968-69,
   Mil-A 1973-74, Tor-A 1980-88, 1989
Wiley, Mark E.   Bal-A 1987, Cle-A 1988-89
Wine, Robert P. "Bobby"   Phi-N 1972-83,
   Atl-N 1985, 1988-89

The Umpire Roster

National League (1989)

Bonin, Gregory, 1986-89
Brocklander, Fred W., 1979-89
Crawford, Gerald J., 1976-89
Darling, Gary, 1988-89
Davidson, Robert A., 1983-89
Davis, Gerald, 1985-89
DeMuth, Dana A., 1986-89
Engel, Robert A., 1965-89
Froemming, Bruce N., 1971-89
Gregg, Eric E., 1977-89
Hallion, Thomas F., 1986-89

Harvey, H. Douglas, 1962-77, 1979-88
Hirshbeck, Mark, 1988-89
Hohn, William, 1989
Kibler, John W., 1963-89
Layne, Jerry, 1989
Marsh, Randall G., 1983-89
McSherry, John P., 1971-89
Montague, Edward M., 1976-89
Pontino, Larry, 1986-89
Pulli, Frank V., 1972-89

Quick, James E., 1976-89
Reliford, Charles, 1989
Rennert, Laurence H. "Dutch", 1973-89
Rippley, T. Steven, 1985-89
Runge, Paul E., 1973-89
Tata, Terry A., 1973-89
Wendlestedt, Harry H., 1966-89
West, Joseph H., 1976, 1978-89
Williams, Charles H., 1978, 1983-89
Winters, Michael, 1989

American League (1989)

Barnett, Lawrence R., 1968-89
Brinkman, Joseph N., 1973-89
Cedarstrom, Gary, 1989
Clark, Alan M., 1976-89
Coble, G. Drew, 1983-89
Cooney, Terrance J., 1975-88
Cousins, Derryl, 1979-89
Craft, Terry, 1989
Denkinger, Donald A., 1968-89
Evans, James B., 1971-89
Ford, R. Dale 1975-89
Garcia, Richard R., 1975-89

Hendry, Eugene 'Ted', 1978-89
Hirshbeck, John F., 1984-89
Johnson, Mark S., 1984-89
Joyce, James, 1989
Kaiser, Kenneth J., 1977-89
Kosc, Gregory J., 1975-89
McClelland, Timothy R., 1984-89
McCoy, Larry S., 1970-89
McKean, James G., 1974-89
Meriwether, Julius "Chuck", 1989
Merrill, E. Durwood, 1977-89
Morrison, Daniel G., 1984-89

Palermo, Stephen M., 1977-89
Phillips, David R., 1971-89
Reed, Rick A., 1984-89
Reilly, Michael E., 1978-89
Roe, John 'Rocky', 1982-89
Scott, Dale A., 1986-89
Shulock, John R., 1979-89
Tschida, Timothy J., 1986-89
Voltaggio, Vito H. "Vic", 1977-89
Welke, Timothy J., 1985-89
Young, Larry E., 1985-89

Home-Road Statistics

Here are the abbreviations used below that have not been explained in the introductions to the Player and Pitcher Registers or the Annual Record.

OHR Opponents' Home Runs

RF Run Factor (A measure of the run scoring in a given park compared to other parks, with marks higher than 100 indicating favorable conditions for hitters.)

HRF Home Run Factor (A measure of the home runs hit in a given park, with figures as in RF above.)

HRB Home Run Batter Rating (A measure of a team's home-run ability, taking into account the HRF and the fact that its batters do not face its own pitchers; 100 represents the average and the highest figure is the best.)

HRP Home Run Pitcher Rating (A measure of a team's ability to prevent home runs, taking into account the HRF and the fact that its pitchers do not face its own batters; 100 represents the average and the lowest figure is the best.)

RB Run Rating for Batters (A measure of a team's run scoring ability, taking into account the HRF and the fact that its batters do not face its own pitchers; 100 represents the average and the highest figure is the best.)

RP Run Rating for Pitchers (A measure of a team's run prevention ability, taking into account the HRF and the fact that its pitchers do not face its own batters; 100 represents the average and the lowest figure is the best.)

BPF Batting Park Factor (Same as PF shown in the batters' section of the Annual Record and the Player Register.)

PPF Pitching Park Factor (Same as PF shown in the pitchers' section of the Annual Record and the Pitcher Register.)

H/R Home/Road Ratio of Production (Production, or On Base Plus Slugging, at home over Production away.)

TM	HOME G	W	L	T	R	OR	HR	OHR	ROAD G	W	L	T	R	OR	HR	OHR	ALL G	W	L	T	R	OR	HR	OHR	HRF	HRB	HRP	RF	RB	RP	BPF	PPF
1988 NATIONAL LEAGUE																																
ATL	79	33	46	0	309	334	55	61	82	30	51	1	275	346	73	53	161	63	97	1	584	680	128	114	95	116	105	106	90	104	102	104
CHI	81	48	33	0	381	334	61	64	81	45	36	0	321	289	63	42	162	93	69	0	702	623	124	106	118	100	85	116	101	91	108	107
CIN	81	38	43	0	312	377	59	71	81	37	44	0	320	314	69	54	162	75	87	0	632	691	128	125	105	111	108	107	96	104	103	104
HOU	82	47	35	0	340	344	42	50	80	39	41	0	307	325	55	55	162	86	76	0	647	669	97	105	83	92	100	105	99	102	102	103
LA	81	44	37	0	253	244	37	46	79	33	46	0	301	292	52	49	160	77	83	0	554	536	89	95	81	86	92	83	95	92	93	93
MON	81	44	37	0	336	309	55	60	81	37	44	0	296	321	45	60	162	81	81	0	632	630	100	120	109	84	100	104	97	97	102	102
NY	81	51	30	0	333	275	78	56	81	36	45	0	350	320	69	59	162	87	75	0	683	595	147	115	105	127	102	92	111	98	96	95
PHI	81	38	42	1	321	376	61	67	82	29	53	0	308	359	62	60	163	67	95	1	629	735	123	127	105	106	109	104	97	112	101	102
PIT	81	39	42	0	296	313	45	62	83	35	46	2	341	367	50	59	164	74	88	2	637	680	95	121	100	83	103	89	105	111	94	94
STL	83	46	35	2	319	308	27	36	81	40	41	0	313	300	46	48	164	86	76	2	632	608	73	84	68	73	85	100	97	94	101	100
SD	81	46	35	0	324	312	66	82	81	43	38	0	318	314	54	51	162	89	73	0	642	626	120	133	137	91	98	101	100	98	101	101
SF	81	53	28	0	368	255	63	61	81	39	42	0	331	345	78	59	162	92	70	0	699	600	141	120	92	130	113	93	113	98	97	96
1989 AMERICAN LEAGUE																																
BAL	81	47	34	0	347	338	61	65	81	40	41	0	361	348	68	69	162	87	75	0	708	686	129	134	93	110	114	97	103	100	99	98
BOS	81	46	35	0	419	374	52	70	81	37	44	0	355	361	56	61	162	83	79	0	774	735	108	131	104	87	103	110	106	102	105	104
CAL	81	52	29	0	317	285	73	75	81	39	42	0	352	293	72	38	162	91	71	0	669	578	145	113	132	103	78	94	98	85	99	98
CHI	80	35	45	0	301	365	36	58	81	34	47	0	392	385	58	86	161	69	92	0	693	750	94	144	67	93	139	87	108	117	93	93
CLE	81	41	40	0	319	332	56	51	81	32	49	0	285	322	71	56	162	73	89	0	604	654	127	107	85	111	95	106	84	90	104	104
DET	81	38	43	0	321	389	74	77	81	21	60	0	296	427	42	73	162	59	103	0	617	816	116	150	127	83	109	97	91	118	97	99
KC	81	55	26	0	335	288	38	26	81	37	44	0	355	347	63	60	162	92	70	0	690	635	101	86	54	106	87	90	104	96	96	95
MIL	81	45	36	0	344	321	69	54	81	36	45	0	363	358	57	75	162	81	81	0	707	679	126	129	94	107	108	93	105	101	97	96
MIN	81	45	36	0	387	404	59	69	81	35	46	0	353	334	58	70	162	80	82	0	740	738	117	139	100	96	113	114	100	99	106	106
NY	81	41	40	0	373	419	64	88	80	33	47	0	325	373	66	62	161	74	87	0	698	792	130	150	115	101	114	111	97	109	104	105
OAK	81	54	27	0	370	284	65	51	81	45	36	0	342	292	62	52	162	99	63	0	712	576	127	103	103	101	83	104	99	81	103	102
SEA	81	40	41	0	353	386	68	67	81	33	48	0	341	342	66	47	162	73	89	0	694	728	134	114	117	100	85	107	97	101	103	104
TEX	81	45	36	0	352	371	75	63	81	38	43	0	343	343	47	56	162	83	79	0	695	714	122	119	131	85	85	105	98	100	102	103
TOR	81	46	35	0	330	308	64	50	81	43	38	0	401	343	78	49	162	89	73	0	731	651	142	99	91	119	86	87	112	101	94	93

Park Factor Statistics

PARK	TM	LG	YEARS	RF	HRF	HOME W	L	T	R	OR	HR	OHR	ROAD W	L	T	R	OR	HR	OHR
AMERICAN LEAGUE																			
Memorial Stadium	BAL	A	1954–89	93	90	1614	1222	9	11613	10582	2336	2100	1445	1410	0	12309	11864	2656	2321
Fenway Park (II)	BOS	A	1934–89	114	112	2589	1793	16	23104	20340	3970	3522	2044	2342	12	19066	19267	3447	3243
Anaheim Stadium	CAL	A	1966–89	92	97	986	931	0	7552	7574	1392	1536	880	1028	2	7975	8394	1466	1538
Comiskey/White Sox Park	CHI	A	1910–89	97	86	3297	2886	32	26423	26060	2771	3409	2826	3379	34	26583	27505	3286	3939
Municipal/Cleveland Stadium	CLE	A	1947–89	98	112	1817	1569	7	14519	14352	3049	2913	1583	1803	9	14563	14775	2714	2617
Briggs/Tiger Park	DET	A	1938–89	105	128	2297	1800	16	19031	17720	3961	3838	1950	2126	18	17539	17384	3104	2959
Municipal Stadium (II)	KC	A	1969–72	100	65	159	159	1	1211	1227	137	175	136	185	0	1169	1277	216	268
Royals Stadium	KC	A	1973–89	103	76	798	545	1	6310	5504	843	834	653	698	0	5760	5826	1118	1121
County Stadium	MIL	A	1970–89	97	88	831	755	1	6809	6752	1264	1239	711	878	1	6889	7126	1409	1424
Humphrey Metrodome	MIN	A	1982–89	109	105	361	290	0	3145	3103	628	708	254	391	0	2625	3050	576	681
Yankee Stadium	NY	A	1976–89	95	97	672	428	0	5154	4398	1060	876	568	538	0	5248	4881	1090	927
Oakland Coliseum	OAK	A	1968–89	89	89	987	766	1	7206	6639	1456	1345	824	924	0	7764	7840	1588	1554
Kingdome	SEA	A	1977–89	105	139	467	565	0	4465	5064	1014	1148	393	625	2	3966	4911	683	839
Arlington Stadium	TEX	A	1972–89	99	93	727	698	0	6039	6176	1019	1120	607	813	4	5906	6405	1122	1158
Skydome	TOR	A	1989–89	86	90	46	35	0	330	308	64	50	43	38	0	401	343	78	49
NATIONAL LEAGUE																			
Atlanta/Fulton County Stadium	ATL	N	1966–89	113	140	947	952	4	8337	8726	1806	1823	826	1088	3	7173	7985	1375	1217
Wrigley Field	CHI	N	1916–89	106	116	3103	2669	30	26238	25564	4230	4075	2556	3165	32	23631	24890	3575	3527
Riverfront Stadium	CIN	N	1970–89	103	105	902	683	2	7104	6507	1321	1264	832	757	1	6852	6490	1290	1180
Astrodome	HOU	N	1965–89	89	61	1115	879	0	7683	7238	910	947	856	1139	2	8046	8724	1454	1579
Chavez Ravine/Dodger Stadium	LA	N	1962–89	88	86	1299	940	0	8598	7391	1468	1334	1143	1094	6	9481	8758	1742	1536
Olympic Stadium	MON	N	1977–89	99	86	564	461	0	4226	3933	665	702	493	529	2	4148	4131	818	772
Shea Stadium	NY	N	1964–89	94	99	1051	1020	5	7746	7830	1359	1498	931	1141	2	8029	8569	1384	1479
Veteran's Stadium	PHI	N	1971–89	106	110	841	668	3	6797	6283	1286	1124	681	825	1	5958	6375	1100	1077
Three Rivers Stadium	PIT	N	1970–89	100	95	892	692	1	6935	6193	1134	1075	756	828	3	6654	6502	1223	1120
Busch Stadium	STL	N	1966–89	100	79	1039	874	5	7908	7522	874	1085	954	952	1	7840	7522	1126	1349
Jack Murphy Stadium	SD	N	1969–89	90	92	809	864	1	6054	6615	988	1229	672	993	1	6363	7623	1076	1319
Candlestick Park	SF	N	1960–89	96	97	1341	1051	0	10132	9350	2013	1725	1128	1266	5	10124	10172	2062	1819

Formulas and Technical Information

Batting Runs = (.47)1B + (.78)2B + (1.09)3B + (1.40)HR + (.33)(BB + HB) − (.25)(AB − H) − (.50)(OOB)

Clutch Hitting Index Calculated for individuals, actual RBIs over expected RBIs, adjusted for league average and slot in batting order; 100 is a league-average performance. The spot in the batting order is figured as: 5 − (9 X BFPGP − BFPGT), where BFPGP is the batters facing pitcher per game for the player, or plate appearances divided by games, and BFPGT is the batters facing pitcher per game of the entire team. Expected RBIs are calculated as (.25 singles + .50 doubles + .75 triples + 1.75 homers) × LGAV × EXPSL where LGAV (league average) = league RBIs divided by (.25 singles + .50 doubles + .75 triples + 1.75 homers), and EXPSL (expected RBIs by slot number) = .88 for the leadoff batter, and for the remaining slots, descending to ninth, .90, .98, 1.08, 1.08, 1.04, 1.04, 1.04, and 1.02.

Calculated for teams, Clutch Hitting Index is actual runs scored over Batting Runs.

Clutch Pitching Index Expected runs allowed over actual runs allowed, with 100 being a league-average performance. Expected runs are figured on the basis of the pitcher's opposing at bats, hits, walks, and hit batsmen (doubles and triples are figured at league average).

Fielding Runs Calculated to take account of the particular demands of the different positions. (For a full explanation, see *Total Baseball*.)For second basemen, shortstops and third basemen, the formula begins by calculating the league average for each position as follows:

$$\text{League Average} = \left(\frac{.20\,(PO + 2\,A - E + DP)\ \text{league at position}}{PO\ \text{league total} - K\ \text{league total}} \right)$$

where PO = putouts, A = assists, E = errors, DP = double plays, and K = strikeouts. A rating is calculated for the team in question at that position:

Team Runs = .20 (PO + 2A − E + DP) team at position − Average pos.
per pos.   league × (team PO − team K)

For catchers, the equation is modified by removing strikeouts from their formula and subtracting not only errors but also passed balls divided by two. For pitchers, the equation is modified to subtract individual pitcher strikeouts from the total number of potential outs; also, pitchers' chances are weighted less than infielders' assists because a pitcher's style may produce fewer ground balls. Thus, the formula for pitchers is .10(PO + 2A − E + DP), whereas for second basemen, shortstops, and third basemen it is .20(PO + 2A − E + DP). For first basemen, the numerator is only .20(2A − E). For outfielders, the equation becomes .20(PO + 4A − E + 2DP).

Isolated Power Total bases minus hits, divided by at bats; or more simply, Slugging Average minus Batting Average.

On-Base Percentage The editors employ the version created by Allan Roth and Branch Rickey in the early 1950s: hits plus walks plus hit by pitch divided by at bats plus walks, without regard to sacrifice flies.

Park Factor Calculated separately for batters and pitchers and abbreviated PF. The computation of Park Factor is daunting and what follows is probably of interest to few readers but here's a taste; for the full explanation, consult the Glossary of *Total Baseball*.

Step 1: Find games, losses, and runs scored and allowed for each team at home and on the road. Take runs per game scored and allowed at home over runs per game scored and allowed on the road. This is the initial figure, but requires two corrections.

Step 2: The first correction is for innings pitched at home and on the road. First, find the team's home winning percentage (wins at home over games at home). Do the same for road games. Then calculate the Innings Pitched Corrector (IPC):

$$\text{IPC} = \frac{(18.5 - \text{Wins at home} / \text{Games at home})}{(18.5 - \text{Losses on road} / \text{Games on road})}$$

If the number is greater than 1, this means that the innings pitched on the road are higher because the other team is batting more often in the last of the ninth. The 18.5 figure is the average number of half innings per game if the home team always bats in the bottom of the ninth.

Step 3: Correct for the fact that the other road parks' total difference from the league average is offset by the park rating of the club being rated. Multiply this rating by the Other Parks Corrector (OPC):

$$\text{OPC} = \frac{\text{No. of teams}}{\text{No. of teams} - 1 + \text{Run Factor, team}}$$

Example: In 1982, Atlanta scored 388 runs allowed 387 runs at home in 81 games, and scored 351 and allowed 315 on the road in 81 games. The initial factor is (775/81) ÷ (666/81) = 1.164. The Braves's home record was 42–39, or .519, and their road record was 47–34, or .580. Thus the IPC = (18.5 − .519) ÷ (18.5 − .420) = .995. The team rating is now 1.164/.995 = 1.170. The OPC = (12) ÷ (12 − 1 + 1.170) = .986. The final runs-allowed rating is 1.170 × .986, or 1.154.

We warned you it wouldn't be easy! The succeeding rounds of refinement to the batter adjustment factor are, regrettably, even more complex.

Pitcher Runs = Innings Pitched × (League ERA/9) − Earned Runs Allowed. An alternative version is: Innings Pitched/9 × (Individual ERA − League ERA).

Production = On-Base Percentage plus Slugging Average. When PRO, as it is abbreviated, is adjusted, the calculation is modified slightly to create a baseline of 100 for league average performance. For PRO/A, the equation is:

$$\frac{\text{Player On Base Pct.}}{\text{League On Base Pct.}} + \frac{\text{Player Slugging Avg.}}{\text{League Slugging Avg.}} - 1$$

Relief Ranking = Relief Runs × ([Wins + Losses + Saves/4] / Innings Pitched)

Runs Created Bill James's formulation runs to fourteen separate versions; see the Glossary of *Total Baseball* for a full accounting. For 1963-1989, the years covered by the Player and Pitcher Registers, the formula is:

$$\frac{(H + BB + HBP - CS - GIDP)\,(TB + .26[BB - IBB + HBP] + .52[SH + SF + SB]}{AB + BB + HBP + SH + SF}$$

Runs per Win Calculated on a league-wide basis as the square root of (2 × runs per inning) multiplied by 10. The runs per inning is multiplied by two to account for the scoring of each team. Historically, the average number of runs per inning is one-half, or 4.5 runs per game per team, so the Runs per Win equation is generally the square root of a number very close to one times 10 or 10 runs per win. In a year with a lot of scoring, the Runs per Win figure will move closer to 11 and in low scoring years the figure will move closer to 9, but 10 is a good estimate for any season.

For individuals, the Runs per Win calculation has been improved by adjusting the runs per inning to reflect the contribution of the pitcher or batter. A pitcher who allows 45 runs less than average over the course of 25 games lowers the runs per game by 1.8, which is .2 runs per inning, so the new Runs per Win figure is 10 times the square root of average runs per inning for both teams minus the pitcher's rating. (A pitcher who allowed 45 more runs than average would have his runs per inning added to the league average.) If the league average was one run per inning, then the Runs per Win for that pitcher would become the square root of .8 runs per inning times 10, which is 8.9. Dividing his 45 pitching runs by 8.9 runs per wins gives him 5.1 linear weights wins. Similarly a batter who produces 45 runs more than average in 150 games contributes .3 runs per game or .03 per inning, which is added to the league average of one run per inning. His Runs per Win equation becomes 10 times the square root of 1.03, which is 10.1. Dividing his 45 batter runs over 10.1 runs per win gives him 4.4 linear weights wins. Although the batter and pitcher contribute the same number of linear weights runs to their team, the pitcher comes out with more linear weights wins, and is statistically more valuable to his team, because he contributes his runs over fewer games and because, as the number of runs scored decreases, each run becomes more valuable.

Slugging Average = Total Bases divided by At Bats.

Total Average = (Total Bases + Walks + Stolen Bases + HBP) / (At Bats − Hits + Caught Stealing + GIDP)

Wins Above Team For a pitcher with a winning percentage better than his team (a positive WAT):

Pitcher Decisions × ([Pitcher pct. − Team pct.] / [2 − 2 × Team pct.])

For a pitcher with a winning percentage lower than his team's winning percentage (a negative WAT), the equation is:

Pitcher Decisions × ([Pitcher pct. − Team pct.] / [2 × Team pct.])